PHYSICS OF SEMICONDUCTORS
AND THEIR HETEROSTRUCTURES

ELECTRONICS AND VLSI CIRCUITS

SENIOR CONSULTING EDITOR
Stephen W. Director, *Carnegie Mellon University*

Colclaser and Diehl-Nagle: *Materials and Devices for Electrical Engineers and Physicians*
Elliott: *Microlithography: Process Technology for IC Fabrication*
Fabricius: *Introduction to VLSI Design*
Ferendeci: *Physical Foundations of Solid State and Electron Devices*
Franco: *Design with Operational Amplifiers and Analog Integrated Circuits*
Geiger, Allen, and Strader: *VLSI Design Techniques for Analog and Digital Circuits*
Grinich and Jackson: *Introduction to Integrated Circuits*
Hamilton and Howard: *Basic Integrated Circuits Engineering*
Hodges and Jackson: *Analysis and Design of Digital Integrated Circuits*
Long and Butner: *Gallium Arsenide Digital Integrated Circuit Design*
Millman and Halkias: *Integrated Electronics: Analog, Digital Circuits, and Systems*
Millman and Grabel: *Microelectronics*
Millman and Taub: *Pulse, Digital, and Switching Waveforms*
Offen: *VLSI Image Processing*
Paul: *Analysis of Linear Circuits*
Roulston: *Bipolar Semiconductor Devices*
Ruska: *Microelectronic Processing: An Introduction to the Manufacture of Integrated Circuits*
Schilling and Belove: *Electronic Circuits: Discrete and Integrated*
Seraphim: *Principles of Electronic Packaging*
Singh: *Physics of Semiconductors and Their Heterostructures*
Smith: *Modern Communication Circuits*
Sze: *VLSI Technology*
Taub: *Digital Circuits and Microprocessors*
Taub and Schilling: *Digital Integrated Electronics*
Tsividis: *Operations and Modeling of the MOS Transistor*
Wait, Huelsman, and Korn: *Introduction to Operational and Amplifier Theory Applications*
Walsh: *Choosing and Using CMOS*
Yang: *Microelectronic Devices*
Zambuto: *Semiconductor Devices*

PHYSICS OF SEMICONDUCTORS AND THEIR HETEROSTRUCTURES

Jasprit Singh
University of Michigan

McGraw-Hill, Inc.

New York   St. Louis   San Francisco   Auckland   Bogotá   Caracas
Lisbon   London   Madrid   Mexico   Milan   Montreal   New Delhi
Paris   San Juan   Singapore   Sydney   Tokyo   Toronto

**PHYSICS OF SEMICONDUCTORS
AND THEIR HETEROSTRUCTURES**

1 2 3 4 5 6 7 8 9 0   DOC   DOC   9 0 9 8 7 6 5 4 3 2

ISBN 0-07-057607-6

The editor was Anne T. Brown;
the production supervisor was Denise L. Puryear.
R. R. Donnelley & Sons Company was printer and binder.

Library of Congress Cataloging-in-Publication Data

Singh, Jasprit.
    Physics of semiconductors and their heterostructures / Jasprit Singh.
    p.   cm. — (McGraw-Hill series in electrical and computer engineering)
    Includes index.
    ISBN 0-07-057607-6
    1. Semiconductors.   2. Energy-band theory of solids.
    3. Electronic structure.   I. Title.   II. Series.
    QC611.S584   1993
    537.6'22—dc20   92-30339

A Hundred Moons May Be Born / A Thousand Suns May Blaze
In This Intense Brilliance / Without My Teacher There Is Pitch Darkness
(Guru Angad Dev in the Granth Sahib)

To Teresa, Nirala, Gursharan, Gurcharn

CONTENTS

PREFACE   xvii

INTRODUCTION   xxi

1 THE FREE ELECTRON PICTURE   **1**
   1.1   Atoms in Solids   1
   1.2   The Drude Model   2
   1.3   Quantum Mechanics and Electrons   12
   1.4   The Density of States   16
   1.5   Filling of Electronic States   18
   1.6   For the Technologist in You   22
   1.7   Problems   25
   1.8   References   26

2 PERIODICITY: CRYSTAL STRUCTURES   **28**
   2.1   Periodicity of a Crystal   28
   2.2   Basic Lattice Types   32
   2.3   The Reciprocal Lattice   40
   2.4   Artificial Structures: Superlattices   47
   2.5   Surfaces: Ideal Versus Real   50
   2.6   Interfaces   53
   2.7   For the Technologist in You   55
   2.8   Problems   58
   2.9   References   60

3 WAVE DIFFRACTION IN PERIODIC STRUCTURES   **61**
   3.1   Bragg's Law   62
   3.2   Laue Conditions   64
   3.3   Diffraction from Random Scatterers   66
   3.4   Diffraction Methods   74
   3.5   Temperature Dependent Effects   78
   3.6   For the Technologist in You   84
   3.7   Problems   87
   3.8   References   89

4   ELECTRONS IN PERIODIC STRUCTURES   **91**
   4.1   Periodicity and Bloch's Theorem   92
   4.2   Significance of k: Crystal Momentum   97
   4.3   Electron States in a Weak Periodic Potential   100
   4.4   A Simple Description of Band Filling   115
   4.5   Holes in Semiconductors   117
   4.6   For the Technologist in You   120
   4.7   Problems   124
   4.8   References   125

5   SEMICONDUCTOR BANDSTRUCTURE   **126**
   5.1   The Tight Binding Method   127
   5.2   The Spin–Orbit Coupling   140
   5.3   Symmetry of Conduction Bandedge States   146
   5.4   Symmetry of Valence Bandedge States   147
   5.5   The Orthogonalized Plane Wave Method   149
   5.6   The Pseudopotential Method   150
   5.7   The $k \cdot p$ Method   151
   5.8   Selected Bandstructures   159
   5.9   Density of States in Semiconductors   169
   5.10 For the Technologist in You   171
   5.11 Problems   174
   5.12 References   176

6   BANDSTRUCTURE MODIFICATIONS: ALLOYS
AND HETEROSTRUCTURES   **178**
   6.1   Bandstructure of Semiconductor Alloys   179
   6.2   Bandstructure Modifications by Heterostructures   190
   6.3   Bandstructure in Quantum Wells   194
   6.4   Bandstructure in Superlattices   201
   6.5   For the Technologist in You   210
   6.6   Problems   213
   6.7   References   215

7   BANDSTRUCTURE MODIFICATIONS THROUGH
STRAIN   **218**
   7.1   Critical Thickness   218
   7.2   Elastic Strain   221
   7.3   The Elastic Constants   223
   7.4   Strain Tensor in Lattice Mismatched Epitaxy   226
   7.5   Deformation Potential Theory   228
   7.6   Bandgap Alteration   246
   7.7   Built-in Electric Fields in Strained Quantum Wells 246
   7.8   For the Technologist in You   248

| | 7.9 | Problems | 251 |
| | 7.10 | References | 252 |

8	**DOPING OF SEMICONDUCTORS**		**254**
	8.1	Intrinsic Carrier Concentration	254
	8.2	The Effective Mass Equation for Shallow Levels	258
	8.3	Extrinsic Carriers	266
	8.4	Population of Impurity Levels, Carrier Freeze-out	267
	8.5	Heavily Doped Semiconductors	270
	8.6	Modulation Doping	274
	8.7	Hydrogenic Impurities in Quantum Wells	276
	8.8	For the Technologist in You	280
	8.9	Problems	282
	8.10	References	283

9	**LATTICE VIBRATIONS: PHONONS**		**285**
	9.1	Considerations for Crystal Binding	286
	9.2	Crystal Vibrations for a Monatomic Basis	292
	9.3	Crystal Vibrations for a Diatomic Basis	296
	9.4	Phonons: Quantization of Lattice Vibrations	299
	9.5	Polar Optical Phonons	301
	9.6	Optical Phonon–Photon Interactions	304
	9.7	Phonon Statistics	309
	9.8	Models for Phonon Energy	312
	9.9	Phonon Dispersion Measurement Techniques	315
	9.10	Phonons in Heterostructures	318
	9.11	For the Technologist in You	320
	9.12	Problems	321
	9.13	References	322

10	**TRANSPORT: GENERAL FORMALISM**		**324**
	10.1	Relaxation Times	326
	10.2	The Boltzmann Transport Equation	327
	10.3	Averaging Procedures	336
	10.4	Mobility Measurement Techniques	338
	10.5	Hall Mobility	342
	10.6	Solution of the Boltzmann Transport Equation	346
	10.7	For the Technologist in You	353
	10.8	Problems	355
	10.9	References	356

11	**DEFECT AND CARRIER-CARRIER SCATTERING**		**357**
	11.1	Ionized Impurity Scattering	359
	11.2	Alloy Scattering	369
	11.3	Carrier-Carrier Scattering	374

11.4   Auger Processes and Impact Ionization   381
11.5   For the Technologist in You   391
11.6   Problems   393
11.7   References   394

12   PHONON SCATTERING   **397**
12.1   General Formalism   397
12.2   Limits on Phonon Wavevectors   403
12.3   Selection Rules for Phonon Scattering   410
12.4   Acoustic Phonon Scattering   411
12.5   Deformation Potential Optical Phonon Scattering   414
12.6   Polar Optical Phonon Scattering   417
12.7   Electron-Plasmon Scattering   424
12.8   Piezoelectric Scattering   425
12.9   Intervalley Scattering   427
12.10 The Polaron   429
12.11 For the Technologist in You   430
12.12 Problems   431
12.13 References   432

13   THE VELOCITY-FIELD RELATIONS   **433**
13.1   Low Field Transport   434
13.2   High Field Transport   437
13.3   Monte Carlo Simulation of Carrier Transport   439
13.4   Electron Transport Monte Carlo Calculations   459
13.5   High Field Electron Transport in Si   462
13.6   Hole Transport Monte Carlo Calculations   464
13.7   Balance Equation Approach to High Field Transport   471
13.8   Impact Ionization in Semiconductors   475
13.9   Zener-Bloch Oscillations   480
13.10 For the Technologist in You   484
13.11 Problems   491
13.12 References   492

14   TRANSPORT IN HETEROSTRUCTURES   **496**
14.1   Parallel Transport in Quantum Wells and MODFETs   498
14.2   Mobility in a MODFET Quantum Well   505
14.3   High Temperature / High Field Transport   511
14.4   Effect of Strain on Transport   511
14.5   Transport in Quantum Wires   517
14.6   Real Space Charge Transfer   518
14.7   Avalanche Processes in Quantum Well Structures   520
14.8   Quantum Transport   523
14.9   Resonant Tunneling   524

14.10 Tunneling in Heterostructures with Spatially Varying
       Central Cell Symmetry   530
14.11 Perpendicular Transport in Superlattices   539
14.12 Quantum Interference Effects   541
14.13 Density Matrix Formalism   544
14.14 For the Technoligist in You   549
14.15 References   554

**15 INTERACTIONS OF PHOTONS WITH
     SEMICONDUCTORS   557**
15.1 Maxwell Equations, Vector Potential, and Gauge
      Transformations   559
15.2 Drude-Zener Theory   564
15.3 Optical Modes in Ionic Crystals   567
15.4 Kramers-Kronig Relation   568
15.5 Electrons in an Electromagnetic Field   572
15.6 Selection Rules for Optical Processes   576
15.7 Interband Transitions   578
15.8 Optical Processes in Semiconductor Lasers   586
15.9 Indirect Interband Transitions   595
15.10 Intraband Transitions   599
15.11 For the Technologist in You   604
15.12 Problems   612
15.13 References   613

**16 OPTICAL PROPERTIES IN SEMICONDUCTORS:
     EXCITONIC TRANSITIONS   615**
16.1 Excitonic States in Semiconductors   617
16.2 Optical Properties with Inclusion of Excitonic Effects   622
16.3 Excitonic States in Quantum Wells   627
16.4 Excitonic Absorption in Quantum Wells   632
16.5 Exciton Broadening Effects   634
16.6 Modulation of Excitonic Transitions: Quantum Confined
      Stark Effect   637
16.7 Exciton Quenching   646
16.8 Refractive Index Modulation Due to Exciton Modulation   653
16.9 Strain Induced Electric Fields for Enhanced Optical
      Modulation   657
16.10 Radiative Recombination from Excitonic States   658
16.11 For the Technologist in You   660
16.12 Problems   665
16.13 References   665

17 SEMICONDUCTORS IN MAGNETIC FIELDS   **668**

17.1 Semiclassical Dynamics of Electrons in a Magnetic Field   670
17.2 Semiclassical Theory of Magnetotransport   675
17.3 Quantum Mechanical Approach to Electrons in a Magnetic Field   676
17.4 The Aharonov-Bohm Effect   683
17.5 The De Haas-Van Alphen Effect   686
17.6 The Shubnikov-De Haas Effect   691
17.7 The Quantum Hall Effect   695
17.8 Magneto-optics in Landau Levels   701
17.9 Excitons in Magnetic Field   703
17.10 Shallow Impurities in Magnetic Fields   707
17.11 Magnetic Semiconductors   709
17.12 For the Technologist in You   711
17.13 References   712

18 DEFECTS AND DISORDER IN SEMICONDUCTORS   **714**

18.1 Point Defects in Semiconductors   715
18.2 Trapping and Recombination   723
18.3 Dislocations and Lattice Mismatched Epitaxy   728
18.4 Disordered Semiconductors   738
18.5 Extended and Localized States   739
18.6 Mesoscopic Structures   751
18.7 For the Technologist in You   754
18.8 References   757

19 AND NOW SOMETHING OF REAL CONSEQUENCE: DEVICES   **759**

19.1 Some Recent Trends   759
19.2 Requirements for Successful Devices   760
19.3 A Summary of Some Important Devices   768
19.4 References   782

A THE WAVE PACKET PICTURE   **783**

A.1 Motion of a Wavepacket   784

B ELECTRON IN A QUANTUM WELL   **788**

C THE HARMONIC OSCILLATOR PROBLEM   **791**

D COMBINATION OF ANGULAR MOMENTUM STATES   **795**

E   STATIONARY PERTURBATION THEORY   797
        E.1   Nondegenerate Case   798
        E.2   Degenerate Case   799

F   EIGENVALUE METHOD TO SOLVE COUPLED
        EQUATIONS   801

G   THE ZEEMAN EFFECT   804

H   THE VARIATIONAL METHOD   807

I   TIME DEPENDENT PERTURBATION THEORY
        AND THE FERMI GOLDEN RULE   810
        I.1   Transition Probability   813

J   GAUSSIAN AND MKSA UNITS   815

K   NUMERICAL EVALUATION OF SOME PHYSICAL
        PARAMETERS   819
        K.1   Density of States   819
        K.2   Mobility   820
        K.3   Cyclotron Resonance Frequency   820
        K.4   Bohr Radius and Binding Energies of Dopants or Excitons   821
        K.5   Effective Density of States and Intrinsic Carrier
                Concentration   821
        K.6   Absorption Coefficient and Emission Rate   822
        K.7   Recombination Times   823

L   SELECTED PROPERTIES OF SEMICONDUCTORS   824
        L.1   Tabulated Values   824
        L.2   References   827

M   EVALUATION OF SCATTERING RATES FOR A
        MONTE CARLO PROGRAM   828
        M.1   Polar L-O Phonon Scattering   828
        M.2   Acoustic Phonon Scattering   830
        M.3   Equivalent Intervalley Scattering   831
        M.4   Non-equivalent Intervalley Scattering   832
        M.5   Ionized Impurity Scattering   833
        M.6   Alloy Scattering   835

N   WIDE BANDGAP SEMICONDUCTORS   836
        N.1   References   841

        INDEX   843

PREFACE

Solid state electronics is undergoing rapid changes driven by heteroepitaxy, lithography, and new device concepts. While ten years ago Si was the material of choice in solid state electronics, now GaAs, InGaAs, AlAs, InP, Ge, etc., have all become quite important. The advent of semiconductor lasers and integrated optoelectronic circuits have led to a flurry of activities in compound semiconductors. Additionally, the remarkable advances in thin film epitaxy have allowed active semiconductor devices with sub-3-dimensional properties and built in controlled biaxial strain due to lattice mismatch, providing a tremendous playground for the electrical engineer. Instead of working with a fixed set of material parameters, one now has a tailorable array of parameters which can be chosen for optimum device response.

In view of these rapid developments, many of which are even now being reported in journals, the electrical engineer needs an in-depth conceptual and quantitative knowledge of the physics of semiconductors (bulk and sub-3-dimensional, unstrained and strained). It is important to note that for the electrical engineer it is not sufficient to only understand simple concepts such as effective mass and bandgap, but to have a quantitative understanding of semiconductors. Many of the developments in solid state electronics are *evolutionary* and involve using materials which have improved but similar properties, the benefits being *quantitative* rather than *qualitative*.

Although a number of texts exist on solid state physics as well as semiconductor physics, they primarily address the need of physics students rather than electrical engineering students. While for the physics student it may be appropriate that a chapter on bandstructure simply introduces the concept of bandgaps and effective masses, for the the electrical engineering students a detailed discussion for various semiconductors is necessary. The student needs to be exposed to actual "numbers" since he or she may find himself needing such detailed information in the future. Unfortunately, there is a good reason why the traditional solid state physics books leave the student only with a conceptual knowledge. Only a handful of problems in quantum mechanics are solvable in analytical form. These handful include the square wells, the harmonic oscillator, the hydrogen atom, etc. Many real life problems are much more complex and only experts with great knowledge in numerical techniques have addressed these problems. Fortunately, along with advances in solid state electronics, another major advance has been in the area of access to computers. This tremendous asset should not be ignored in present day teaching. Calculations that until recently were unthinkable in a graduate class can now be done routinely due to the wide access to computer libraries, graphic packages, etc.

This text addresses three main areas of interest: i) electronic properties of semiconductors including the concept of effective masses, donors, acceptors, excitons etc; ii) modification of electronic properties by using heterostructure concepts, i.e., via reduced dimensionality, confinement and built in strain; iii) properties of electronic materials as reflected in electronic transport and optical properties. These areas will provide students an intimate knowledge of the material properties on which solid state electronic devices such as transistors, Gunn diodes, lasers, detectors, optical memories, etc., are based. Emphasis will be placed on not only conceptual understanding but quantitative understanding of a variety of semiconductors and their combinations via numerical calculations.

While this is not a text on semiconductor devices, I have attempted to maintain as much as possible a link between physics and real devices. This is done via the sections "For the technologist in you," in every chapter. Also a device chapter is presented (Chapter 19) where the focus is on how physics and devices relate to each other.

In the course of writing this book I was reminded again and again of the many teachers I had in my career—people who taught, inspired, and showed me how to do my best. Many were not officially my teachers, but were colleagues, especially experimentalists who would want a straight answer rather than a complex Hamiltonian to juggle around with. I have been especially mindful of these colleagues and their spirit in writing this book and I hope this reflects in the style and content of this book. This book is written for graduate students who have had a basic quantum mechanics course. A generous number of appendices have been included so that gaps that may appear in the student's knowledge can be overcome. The emphasis on actual numbers is also reflected in two appendices where explicit numbers are evaluated for various physical processes.

I would like to thank Prof. Morrel Cohen who introduced me to the field of semiconductors, Prof. Anupam Madhukar, Drs. K. K. Bajaj, D. Reynolds, C. Litton, G. McCoy, Prof. H. Morkoc, J. Arias, R. Zucca, S. Aranowitz, and my colleagues at the University of Michigan. Profs. G. I. Haddad, P. K. Bhattacharya, D. Pavlidis, and F. Terry deserve special thanks. Without my students (and teachers!) Drs. M. Jaffe, S. Hong, J. Hinckley, J. Loehr, and V. Sankaran this book would not have crystallized.

I would especially like to thank Dr. John Hinckley with whom I was able to sound off ideas and keep the book as error-free as possible. His help was quite central to the quality of the book. I would also like to thank Ms. Izena Goulding for her typing and illustrations. Thanks are also due to Ms. Anne Brown of McGraw-Hill for her support.

My wife Teresa was always there to absorb my stress and strain during the last two years of both writing and dealing with reviews, all while pursuing her own career and coping with a three-year old's random walk through life! She also contributed the cartoons for the book.

I sincerely hope this book will be of benefit to students of the exciting field of solid state electronics.

The following contributed artwork which was used in the book. I am greatly indebted to them:

Prof. Y. Arakawa (University of Tokyo), Figure 15.23.

Dr. S. Aronowitz (National Semiconductor), Figure 1.13.

Prof. P. K. Bhattacharya and Dr. K. Chang (University of Michigan), Figure 7.24.

Dr. J. M. Hinckley (University of Michigan), Figures 2.24, 4.18.

Dr. D. A. B. Miller (AT & T Bell Labs), Figure 16.31.

Prof. D. Pavlidis (University of Michigan), Figure 14.36.

Ms. T. Singh (Ann Arbor), Figure 19.6.

Dr. K. Vural (Rockwell International), Figure 6.23.

An instructor's manual is available to teachers who adopt the text for classroom use. The manual also has computer programs for a variety of applications including bandstructure calculations, Monte Carlo transport, and laser gain. Requests for the manual can be made on your departmental letterhead, addressed to:

McGraw-Hill
College Division
P. O. Box 445
Hightstown, New Jersey 08520

or by calling McGraw-Hill College Division Customer Service at:
1 (800) 338–3987.

INTRODUCTION

SOLID STATE ELECTRONICS IN TODAY'S LIFE

Consider the life of a typical teenager in an industrialized part of the world. She has saved some money from her daily allowance and wants to spend it. In the shopping mall she mulls over her choices: a portable CD player she could use when she is out with her mom and does not want to listen to a lecture; a remote control car with which she could scare her little sister by putting a scary mouse on it; a five-pound gadget which, it is claimed, holds an entire encyclopedia, the list is endless. As she pays for the CD player, a laser scanner reads off the price and remembers that a sale is going on. A card reader scans a credit card (her mom's), checks on the credit worthiness and approves the sale. The teenager happily heads into a record store to buy her favorite CD. As she reaches home, she sees that her parents have someone putting in a new home electronic system which will monitor their house's heating and cooling needs, turns lights on and off, and do a myriad of other things by itself.

From cable television to electronic banking, from cellular phones to factory robots, from sophisticated radars to laser-guided weapons, solid state electronics is changing our quality of life at a seemingly ever increasing pace. A tremendous positive feedback now exists between the material scientists, innovative device designers and systems and applications engineers. All this, coupled with new advances in software, are bringing into our lives products we never thought we needed and without which we cannot survive now.

The tremendous pace of recent developments which will only intensify in the future, puts a great burden on new and old students of solid state electronics. More than ever before, the electrical engineer has to open his mind to new ideas, even though this may often create great discomfort. From quantum mechanics to semiconductor bandstructure, the electrical engineer has to have a tremendous versatility to lead in the coming era of electronics and optoelectronics.

THE BUILDING BLOCKS OF SOLID STATE ELECTRONICS

What are the underlying driving forces for all the new technology which sits in the market today and which was the subject of science fiction a few years ago? One can identify at least four broad categories of such forces:

1. New material systems which have allowed the electrical engineer to play in a playground where Si is not the only ride (although it is still the most fun!). Materials like GaAs, InGaAs, AlGaAs, HgCdTe, etc., and their heterostructures, are driving new technologies.

2. Processing and manufacturing techniques allow devices and circuits to be made inexpensively.

3. The involvement of device physicists is resulting in new device concepts for transistors, lasers, detectors, modulators, etc.

4. New advances in software which couples electronic and optoelectronic systems efficiently are allowing systems to accomplish complex tasks.

For the student of solid state electronics, to contribute to this magical world, the tools required are rooted in a very broad-based education. This education must deal with the physical phenomena that occur in semiconductors and how these phenomena can be harnessed to produce solid state devices. The solid state devices are the building blocks of all electronic and optoelectronic systems. And these devices are, with rare exceptions, all made from semiconductors. What is so special about semiconductors? Why can't we make devices from metals or wood or plastics or hydrocarbons? What is so special about semiconductors that they provide us products which almost have a human touch? To answer these questions we need to know the properties of semiconductors and the variety of physical phenomenon that occur in them.

THE PHYSICAL PHENOMENA BEHIND DEVICES

The purpose of solid state devices is by and large to carry out some kind of information processing. This requires making use of some physical phenomenon to produce a response to an external stimulus as shown schematically in Figure I.1. The physical phenomenon may involve light absorption or emission (as in detectors, lasers, modulators) or transport of electrons (as in transistors). As explored further in Chapter 19, there must be some nonlinearity in the input–output response. This is essential to be able to distinguish information that is only "slightly" different. The "nonlinear" response allows one to "enhance" this difference. In addition to this very important property, a number of other guidelines have to be met if a useful device is to result as discussed in Chapter 19. The physical phenomena in semiconductors can satisfy all these requirements. Most other material systems cannot.

Once the physical phenomenon in a material is adequate for a device, one is always searching to improve things. This means looking for tunable phenomenon (e.g., a laser emitting at a chosen frequency, a microwave oscillator radiating in a special band), high speed phenomenon to produce faster devices, low power phenomenon, phenomena that survive to high temperatures, etc. All of this involves examining new semiconductors and their heterostructures. The advent of the heteroepitaxial techniques that can grow combinations of semiconductors with monolayer precision opens new vistas for the device physicist. It also means he has to learn about these structures where one literally can produce an infinite variety of responses. Figure I.2 describes some of the driving forces behind modern solid state electronics.

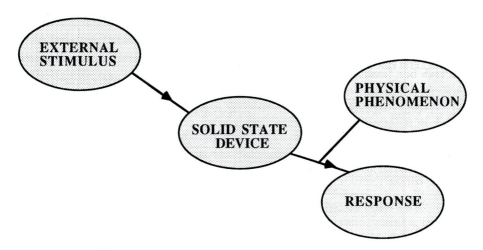

Figure I.1: A typical sequence of events in the information processing involving a device. The response to an external perturbation results in a particular response depending upon the physical phenomenon which could involve photon emission or absorption, electron transport, etc.

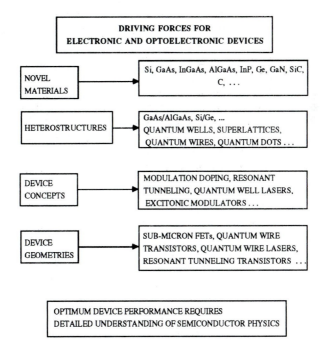

Figure I.2: Forces motivating modern solid state electronics.

THE ROLE OF THIS BOOK

As the variety of semiconductors that can now be tapped by the solid state electronics student increases, and the combinations of their alloys and heterostructures becomes limitless, the need to understand these structures grows. The purpose of this book is to provide an in-depth physical as well as quantitative knowledge of semiconductor phenomenon. It is our intent to take the student from a very basic level of understanding through several steps of increasing complexity. Thus, in a one semester course, only the basic physics could be covered and realistic results could be discussed without going through the rigorous derivations. For example, in the discussions on bandstructure, only Chapter 4 and the first part of Chapter 5 could be covered and the bandstructure of realistic semiconductors could be discussed without discussing the more complex formalism. In a more advanced course these details could also be covered.

This book has been written not only for students in universities, but also for professionals in industry. A great deal of "real-life" physical phenomenon is presented to make the book useful to scientists interested in "state of the art" and in the directions in which the field is evolving. Yet, the book only presumes a basic level understanding of quantum mechanics. Many-body theory problems are not dealt with except in a very qualitative manner. Fortunately, a great deal of exciting and important physics for devices can be appreciated without undue complexities.

In addition to the main book chapters, a series of appendices have been included. These have been written with two aims: to provide a brief overview of some important quantum mechanics and mathematical techniques which are useful for this book and to provide as much material parameter data and "real numbers" oriented information as possible.

The sequence of the chapters covered, and the sections within a chapter is chosen so that a logical progression occurs in our understanding of the physical phenomena important in modern solid state electronics. Chapter 19, however, can be studied by a student at any point since its role is to provide a link between the physics and devices.

CHAPTER 1

THE FREE ELECTRON PICTURE

1.1 ATOMS IN SOLIDS

This text is intended to provide an understanding of the physics behind semi-conductor devices. Semiconductor devices dominate our lives through computers, lasers, displays, etc. It is difficult to imagine life without semiconductors. Increasingly, functions previously carried out by nonsemiconductor devices are being taken over by semiconductors. The ultimate success of semiconductors will be the implementation of neural networks which are touted to think like the brain. The physics behind semiconductor devices can be based on extremely simple concepts such as a modified Newton's equation to very complex quantum phenomenon. Modern electronic devices rely on all ranges of such complexity. Very often experiments must be the judge of how complex the physics has to be to explain and understand the device. Semiconductor physics, perhaps more than any other branch of physics, relies on the art of approximations. The successful physicist is often one who has the intuition to make the correct approximations. Of course, to be able to do this he or she must possess a deep understanding of the relevant physical phenomenon. It is the purpose of this book to provide the reader with the basis to make good approximations.

Soon after the understanding of the atomic structure began to develop, theories were proposed to explain phenomenon such as Ohm's Law, Hall effect, etc., which were being observed in solid state materials. Many of these theories were extremely simple and, in some aspects, failed miserably. Nevertheless, they were important to the development of more rigorous theories and some of them are still used to form simple conceptual pictures of complex phenomenon.

In this chapter we will discuss the Drude and Sommerfeld formalism for charge transport. These formalisms were developed for metals, but under certain conditions are useful for semiconductors as well. These models had considerable successes and even their failures raised important conceptual issues which were resolved by later theories.

1.2   THE DRUDE MODEL

A great deal of early experimental work on current transport was carried out by A. M. Ampere, C. Coulomb, G. Ohm, and A. Volta. All this work was expressed in terms of simple mathematical relations with no microscopic understanding of concepts like resistance. However, with the discovery of the electron in 1897 by J. J. Thompson, microscopic models were constructed to explain the observations on transport. Using the newly developing understanding of the atomic structure, Drude constructed his model for electrical and thermal conduction.

For the purpose of explaining transport, Drude modeled the negatively charged electrons in a solid as an ideal gas which moves through the much heavier immobile nucleus. Drude did not at that time know the details of the heavier protons and neutrons making up the nucleus. He assumed that when atoms are brought together to form a solid, some of the electrons (which he assumed to be the valence electrons) somehow become detached from the atoms and are free to move through the materials. The ions, on the other hand, are assumed to be immobile and play the role of *scatterers* in Drude's theory. At this point there was no explanation of why the valence electrons get detached, or why the ions cause scattering. Drude was creating a model based on his physical intuition. This is an approach which is often followed in solid state physics. Very often the problems are so complex that one simply must take a headlong plunge and hope for something meaningful to emerge.

The basic ideas of the Drude model are schematically illustrated in Figure 1.1. In this figure we have shown the individual atoms, the atoms in a solid where they have given up their valence electrons and the conceptual picture for movement of the electrons.

It is useful to examine the number density of the electrons involved in a Drude model. An element contains 6.022×10^{23} atoms per mole (the Avagadro's number). If ρ is the density of the material, the number of moles per unit volume are ρ/A, where A is the atomic mass. Since each atom contributes Z_c electrons, the electron density is

$$n = 6.022 \times 10^{23} \frac{Z_c \rho}{A} \tag{1.1}$$

For most materials this number is $\approx 10^{23} \text{cm}^{-3}$! Thus there is a very large density of "free" electrons in the solid. Associated with this density we can define the average radius of the spherical volume per electron

$$\frac{4\pi r_s^3}{3} = \frac{1}{n} \tag{1.2}$$

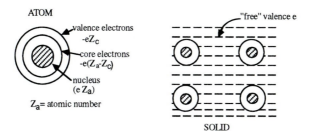

TRANSPORT OF

ELECTRONS

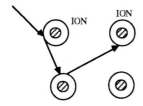

Figure 1.1: A conceptual picture of the atom with its valence and core electrons. The "free" valence electrons move through the rigid ions and collide with the ions in the Drude model.

or

$$r_s = \left(\frac{3}{4\pi n}\right)^{1/3} \tag{1.3}$$

This number is roughly 1 Å or ~ 2 Bohr radius for most materials.

The numbers described above are important because they suggest the magnitude of the problem. We are dealing with an enormously large number of electrons with very closed spacing. We certainly expect very strong interactions between the "free" electrons and the ions. However, all these expected complications are ignored in the Drude model which regards the "free" electrons as forming an ideal gas.

Before we describe the Drude model in detail, it is important to understand what we want to use the model for. The model must explain the "microscopic" details of macroscopic experiments such as current flow, heat flow, effects of magnetic field, etc. This is, of course, the usual purpose of such models which start from the microscopic description of the system. The assumptions made by Drude for his approach are the following:

1. As shown schematically in Figure 1.1, the valence or free electrons move in the solid, colliding with the background positively charged immobile

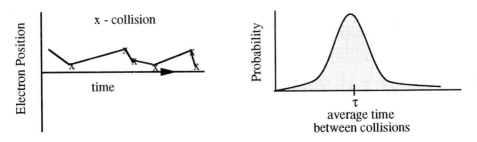

Figure 1.2: A schematic illustration of the concept of random scattering. As the electron moves in the solid, it suffers random collisions. The average time between collisions has a mean value of τ.

ions. It is assumed that between collisions, the electrons move as in free space, i.e., without any interaction with the ions or other electrons. In presence of external forces, the electron's motion between collisions is given by Newton's equations of motion. The approximation involved in ignoring electron-electron interaction is called the independent electron approximation. In view of our discussions on electron density and radius, it seems like this approximation is a very bad one. Nevertheless, detailed quantum mechanical theories show that the approximation is quite good for most materials. Neglecting the effect of the electron-ion interactions is called the free electron approximation. This certainly turns out to be a very poor approximation and most of the work on electronic bandstructure revolves around addressing this issue.

2. The collisions of the electrons occur with the background fixed ions. These collisions are *instantaneous* and are *randomizing* collisions, i.e., the velocity of the electron before and after the collisions are uncorrelated. It turns out that in most materials, there are essentially *no* collisions between the electrons and the fixed ions, even though this seems like a very plausible idea. Nevertheless, it was to Drude's credit that he introduced *some* source of electron scattering. The formulation of correct scattering mechanisms provides impetus to the still ongoing research in carrier transport.

3. Drude did not have any means to calculate the rate at which scattering was occurring. So he introduced a parameter τ which was the mean time between collisions. This microscopic parameter is an adjustable parameter whose value is then obtained by fitting experimental results. The assumption about the scattering time t does not mean than an electron will get scattered at times τ, 2τ, 3τ, etc. We are dealing with random scattering events and therefore we can only talk about the probability of scattering. This is an important concept which is schematically explained in Figure 1.2. If one follows an electron as it moves through the material and keeps track of the time between collisions, there is a distribution in this time. There will be cases where the time is very short and cases where the time is very

long. However, on the average the time will be τ. The probability that a collision occurs in a small time interval dt is:

$$\frac{dt}{\tau}. \tag{1.4}$$

4. The final assumption made by Drude also reflects the great intuition he possessed. The electrons are assumed to be in thermal equilibrium with the material. This equilibrium is established through collisions. The equilibrium is maintained in a simple manner: after each collision, the electron velocity is determined randomly by the thermodynamic equilibrium velocity distribution of the material. Any excess energy generated between collisions is lost to the ions due to the collisions.

It is important to reflect upon the assumptions Drude made for creating his model. The intellectual process he followed will be repeated throughout our studies. Drude took a seemingly insurmountable problem of dealing with 10^{23} electrons and simplified it, often, as it turned out later, by incorrect assumptions. His assumptions (some good, some bad) allowed a simple formulation which could be used to explain experiments. When experimental data appeared which could not be explained by his model, his approach provided a springboard for other theoretical models. Let us now apply his model to some important problems.

1.2.1 Electrical Transport

One of the earliest studies of current flow in metals resulted in the Ohm's law, according to which the current I flowing in a wire is proportional to the potential drop along the wire, i.e.

$$V = IR \tag{1.5}$$

where R is the resistance of the wire.

The resistance depends upon the dimensions of the wire, so that it is useful to rewrite Ohm's Law as

$$F = \rho j \tag{1.6}$$

where F is the electric field, j the current density, and ρ the resistivity. The relation between these quantities and the quantities in the earlier definition of the law are

$$
\begin{aligned}
V &= F \cdot L \\
R &= \rho L / A \\
I &= j \cdot A
\end{aligned}
\tag{1.7}
$$

where L and A are the length and the area of the wire as shown in Figure 1.3. The current density can also be written as:

$$j = -nev \tag{1.8}$$

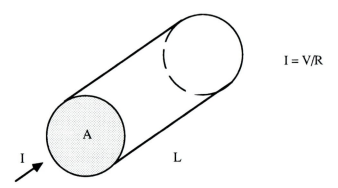

$$I = V/R$$

Figure 1.3: The resistance of a wire is a macroscopic quantity appearing in Ohm's Law. The Drude model attempts to relate it to microscopic properties of the solid.

where n is the mobile electron density, $-e$ is the electron's charge, and v is the average velocity along the applied electric field. In absence of a field, v is zero, even though the carriers are moving randomly with high velocities. This concept is illustrated in Figure 1.4. We will now calculate v using the Drude model.

According to our assumption for the Drude model, *immediately* after a collision, the electron emerges with a velocity representative of the thermodynamic equilibrium at the material temperature. Since the equilibrium velocity is zero, the average velocity immediately after a collision is zero. The electron gains velocity in the direction of the electric field *between collisions*.

This velocity change is simply given by Newton's equations of motion. Since the average time between collisions is τ, the average velocity in the field direction is

$$v_{avg} = -\frac{e\boldsymbol{F}\tau}{m} \tag{1.9}$$

leading to a current of density (from Equation 1.8) of

$$j = \frac{ne^2\tau}{m}F \tag{1.10}$$

or

$$j = \sigma F \tag{1.11}$$

where

$$\sigma = \frac{ne^2\tau}{m} \tag{1.12}$$

where σ $(= 1/\rho)$ is the conductivity of the material. This equation relates a macroscopic material property with the microscopic quantities such as the carrier density, scattering time, and electron mass. One finds that the conductivity increases as there are more "free" electrons to carry the current or if time between scatterings is large, i.e., there are fewer collisions. The basic form of the conductivity equation is retained to a large extent even when a more complete

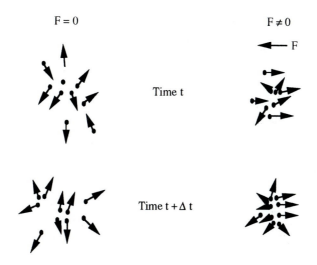

F = 0 F ≠ 0

Time t

Time t + Δt

Figure 1.4: This figure illustrates the concept of the random velocity and the average velocity used in Ohm's Law. At zero field, the individual electrons have large velocities (denoted by the arrows), but the electrons do not drift as an ensemble in any particular direction after a time interval. On the other hand, in presence of an electric field, the electrons are seen to drift in a direction opposite to the field.

analysis is carried out. However, a number of important conceptual changes occur. Drude's theory does not tell us what is the quantitative value of τ, and how it depends upon material parameters. We can, of course, estimate τ if we experimentally measure σ, since

$$
\begin{aligned}
\tau &= \frac{m\sigma}{ne^2} \\
&= \frac{m}{\rho ne^2}.
\end{aligned}
\tag{1.13}
$$

Most metals have room temperature resistivities of the order of microohm-centimeters or, about 10^{-18} statohm-cm. This yields a value of τ of about $10^{-14} - 10^{-15}$ sec.

Based on the value of τ we can define a mean free path, i.e., the average distance traveled between collisions. The mean free distance is

$$
l = u\tau
\tag{1.14}
$$

where u is the average speed of the electrons. Note that u is not the average drift velocity calculated earlier. This can be calculated in Drude's model which is based on the ideal gas model. Since the electron gas is in the thermodynamic equilibrium at temperature T,

$$
\frac{1}{2}mu^2 = \frac{3}{2}k_B T.
\tag{1.15}
$$

At room temperature this gives us

$$u \approx 10^7 \text{cm s}^{-1} \qquad (1.16)$$

or $l \approx 1 - 10$ Å.

This distance appears to be quite consistent with the Drude model since we expect the electrons to scatter off the ions in the material. However, it shall be shown later that if the ions are perfectly spaced, they cause no scattering. In this respect the Drude model is based on erroneous assumptions. However, we can continue to develop the Drude model as long as we do not consider what the source of scattering is. It is interesting to point out that the average speed at room temperature calculated above is comparable to the highest average drift velocity of electrons in very high speed devices.

1.2.2   Equation of Motion

One of the most amazing accomplishments of modern science are the spacecraft which are sending back pictures and data of the solar system after decades and after having traveled billions of miles. The extreme accuracy with which scientists were able to program the trajectories with respect to the planetary motion is a tribute to the power and accuracy of Newton's equations of motion. However, such a success is possible only for a few interacting particles. Even the most sophisticated computer cannot predict the equation of motion of a few hundred interacting particles. And in the solid we have 10^{23} electrons! Very clever approximations are needed to develop a useful description for such a large system of particles. Drude was the first to attempt this problem.

According to the Drude model, each electron obeys Newton's equation of motion between collisions. But how does the entire electron gas behave in presence of external forces? This obviously cannot be described by Newton's equations since there are complex collisions occurring. The Drude model allows us to write such an equation in terms of the scattering time τ.

Let us examine the average change in the momentum of electrons as they move from time t to time $t+\Delta t$. During the time interval Δt, there is a probability $\Delta t/\tau$ (Equation 1.4) that the electron will be scattered before the time interval is over. Immediately after the scattering the average momentum is zero and the electron gains additional momentum by moving in the force field for a time smaller than Δt. The electron has a probability $(1 - \Delta t/\tau)$ that there is no scattering and in this case the electron gains momentum according to Newton's laws. The net change in momentum is:

$$p(t + \Delta t) = \left(1 - \frac{\Delta t}{\tau}\right)\left(p(t) + f(t)\Delta t + 0(\Delta t)^2\right) + \frac{\Delta t}{\tau}(f(t)\Delta t) \qquad (1.17)$$

where the first term is the contribution from electrons which did not scatter and the second term is due to electrons which suffered scattering. Since Δt is infinitesimally small we ignore terms $0(\Delta t)^2$ and get

$$p(t + \Delta t) = -p(t)\frac{\Delta t}{\tau} + f(t)\Delta t + p(t) \tag{1.18}$$

Expanding the left-hand side in a binomial series

$$p(t) + \dot{p}(t)\Delta t = p(t) - p(t)\frac{\Delta t}{\tau} + f(t)\Delta t \tag{1.19}$$

or

$$\frac{dp(t)}{dt} = -\frac{p(t)}{\tau} + f(t) \tag{1.20}$$

This is the equation describing the flow of the electron gas in presence of external forces. It says that the effect of the collisions is to cause a "drag" term in Newton's equation. The vast complexity of the 10^{23} electrons is reduced to such a simple equation!

1.2.3 Hall Effect

We will now use the equation of motion determined for the electron gas in presence of collisions to understand the Hall effect. In 1879 E. H. Hall considered the following experiment: If we take a wire with a current flowing through it and apply a magnetic field, would the electrons feel the Lorentz force? He argued that the electrons would move to one side of the wire and thereby be forced to move through a narrower area of the wire and experience an increased resistance. However, in actual experiments, Hall didn't see a resistance increase, but instead saw a transverse voltage appearing which was later called the Hall voltage.

Hall effect was one of the key experiments which challenged the simplistic view of electron transport developed so far and was responsible for the concept of transport by positively charged particles or "holes." Hall's experiment is schematically shown in Figure 1.5. An electric field in the x-direction causes a current j_x in a slab of material. If a magnetic field is now applied in the z-direction, it causes the charged free particle to feel the Lorentz force causing the electrons to pile up along one face of the slab, leaving a positively charged region on the opposite face. This charge separation causes an electric field in the y-direction which continues to build up till the force on the electrons balances out the Lorentz force.

It is interesting to note that if the free carriers had a positive charge instead of a negative for the same current direction, the force on the particles will be in the *same* direction. In this case the *transverse* electric field will have an *opposite* direction. Thus the voltage sign allows one to determine whether the current flow is due to negative or positive carriers. Of course, so far we only know that electrons which are negatively charged carry current. However, we will eventually learn of situations where the charge flow is via "positive" charges.

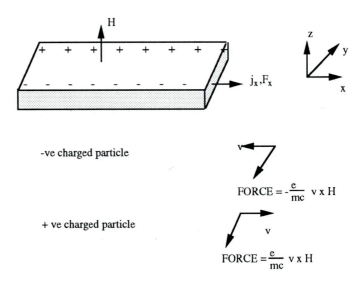

Figure 1.5: Configuration to carry out the Hall effect. The direction of the Lorentz force on a positive or negative charge carrying current in the same direction is the same.

In the Hall experiment we are interested in two physical quantities. The first is the magnetoresistance and is defined by

$$\rho(\boldsymbol{B}) = \frac{F_x}{j_x}. \tag{1.21}$$

The second is the Hall coefficient

$$R_H = \frac{F_y}{j_x \, |\boldsymbol{B}|}. \tag{1.22}$$

Naively, it may appear that since the electrons are pushed to one side of the material slab, they move through a smaller area and therefore the magnetoresistance should increase with field. However, this was not observed to be so by Hall. The simple Drude model explains this observation.

Using the equation of motion we derived earlier, we describe the effect of the electric field and magnetic field on the carrier momentum

$$\frac{d\boldsymbol{p}}{dt} = -e\left(\boldsymbol{F} + \frac{\boldsymbol{p}}{mc} \times \boldsymbol{B}\right) - \boldsymbol{p}/\tau \tag{1.23}$$

In steady state, the current and therefore momentum does not change. This gives us

$$\frac{dp_x}{dt} = -eF_x - \frac{e\,|\boldsymbol{B}|\,p_y}{mc} - \frac{p_x}{\tau} = 0$$

$$\frac{dp_y}{dt} = -eF_y + \frac{e\,|\boldsymbol{B}|\,p_x}{mc} - \frac{p_y}{\tau} = 0. \tag{1.24}$$

Denoting $e\,|\boldsymbol{B}|\,/\,(mc)$ by ω_c, the cyclotron frequency, we multiply these equations by $-ne\tau/m$, and using

$$\sigma_0 = \frac{ne^2\tau}{m}$$
$$j_x = \frac{-nep_x}{m}$$
$$j_y = \frac{-nep_y}{m}$$

we get

$$\sigma_0 F_x = \omega_c \tau j_y + j_x$$
$$\sigma_0 F_y = -\omega_c \tau j_x + j_y \tag{1.25}$$

where σ_0 is the Drude conductivity in absence of a magnetic field. Since there is no current in the y-direction (since this circuit is open),

$$F_y = -\frac{\omega_c \tau}{\sigma_0} j_x = -\frac{|\boldsymbol{B}|}{nec} j_x \tag{1.26}$$

This gives us a Hall factor of

$$R_H = -\frac{1}{nec} \tag{1.27}$$

Also one can immediately see that

$$\frac{j_x}{F_x} = \sigma_0 \tag{1.28}$$

i.e., the magnetoresistance is independent of the magnetic field. The result for the Hall factor is quite important. It says that the Hall factor is negative and depends only on the electron concentration n. The scattering times do not appear anywhere in these results. In several materials, positive Hall factors were observed. We know now that the Hall factor in semiconductors can be negative or positive depending upon whether we have n-type or p-type conduction. But these concepts will be developed later.

While the Drude model was a very important first step towards building a microscopic understanding of transport in solids, it was inadequate in many respects. We know now that the mean free path of electrons in high purity materials can be thousands of atomic spacings and not one or two spacings suggested by the Drude model. We also know that charge transport can occur by negative and positively charged particles. This, of course, was a big puzzle and was resolved only with a proper understanding of the bandstructure. We also know that when electrons are placed inside a solid they behave as if they have a different mass. We also know about energy gaps, etc. It seems like one has to go a long way from the Drude model to understand a real semiconductor. Of course, this provides us with an intellectual challenge that the remaining chapters of the text serve to address.

One of the first improvements on the Drude picture was by Sommerfeld who felt that electrons should be treated within quantum mechanics and they should obey quantum statistics. This is an important contribution and even though this does not resolve most of the problems discussed above, it does take us in the right direction.

1.3 QUANTUM MECHANICS AND ELECTRONS

In the previous discussions on the Drude model, we assumed that the average energy of an electron is $3k_BT/2$. This depends upon the assumption that the electrons are distributed in energy according to Boltzmann statistics. This, however, may not be true for electrons. We will briefly discuss the various statistics which describe physical systems. Before we do this we examine in Figure 1.6 the hierarchy of problems that need to be addressed to describe the response of a physical system to external perturbations.

Let us consider the first step, the energy versus momentum description, for a free electron gas. For this we need to solve the Schrödinger equation. In semiclassical quantum mechanics, the physical system of electrons is described by a wave function. The wave function gives a probabilistic description of the electron. Any physical observables (say, energy E, momentum p, position x, etc.) are represented by mathematical operators e.g.

$$E \;\; \rightarrow \;\; i\hbar\frac{\partial}{\partial t}$$
$$p_n \;\; \rightarrow \;\; -i\hbar\nabla_n. \tag{1.29}$$

In order to actually find the physical observable associated with a given state ψ, the operator corresponding to the observable must operate on the wave function. For example, the identity,

$$E\psi = E\psi \tag{1.30}$$

becomes

$$i\hbar\frac{\partial}{\partial t}\psi = E\psi \tag{1.31}$$

whose solutions give the set $\{E_n, \psi_n\}$ which represent the energies and the states of the electron. The above equation is the time dependent Schrödinger equation.

Similarly, the equation

$$E = \frac{p^2}{2m} + V = \text{kinetic energy} + \text{potential energy} \tag{1.32}$$

gives

$$\left[\frac{-\hbar^2}{2m}\left(\frac{\partial^2}{\partial x^2} + \frac{\partial^2}{\partial y^2} + \frac{\partial^2}{\partial z^2}\right) + V(r)\right]\psi(r) = E\psi(r) \tag{1.33}$$

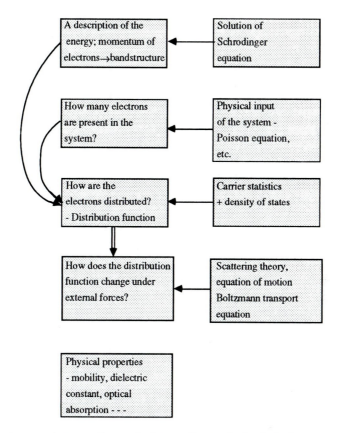

Figure 1.6: A general approach required to understand physical phenomenon in semi-conductors.

which is the time independent Schrödinger equation. We will now examine the time independent Schrödinger equation for free electrons, i.e., when $V = 0$.

$$\frac{-\hbar^2}{2m} \left(\frac{\partial^2}{\partial x^2} + \frac{\partial^2}{\partial y^2} + \frac{\partial^2}{\partial z^2} \right) \psi(\boldsymbol{r}) = E\psi(\boldsymbol{r}). \tag{1.34}$$

A general solution of this equation is

$$\psi(\boldsymbol{r}) = \frac{1}{\sqrt{V}} e^{i\mathbf{k}\cdot\mathbf{r}} \tag{1.35}$$

where the factor $1/\sqrt{V}$ applies because we wish to have one electron per volume V, or

$$\int_V d^3r \, |\psi(\boldsymbol{r})|^2 = 1. \tag{1.36}$$

We assume that the volume V is a cube, with sides of length L.

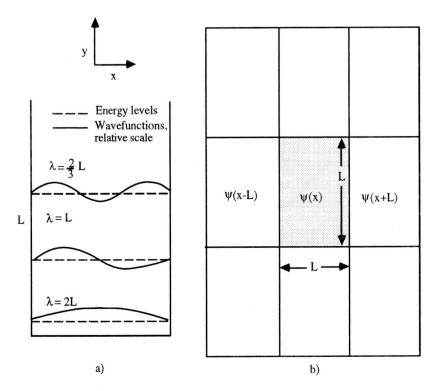

Figure 1.7: A schematic showing (a) the stationary boundary conditions leading to standing waves, and (b) the periodic boundary conditions leading to exponential solutions with the electron probability equal in all regions of space.

In classical mechanics the energy momentum relation for the free electron is $E = p^2/2m$, and p can be a continuous variable. The quantity $\hbar k$ appearing above seems to be replacing p, in quantum mechanics. Due to the wave nature of the electron, the quantity k is not continuous but discrete. To correlate with physical conditions that we may want to describe, there are two kinds of boundary conditions that are imposed on the wave function. In the first one the wave function is considered to go to zero at the boundaries of the volume. In this case, the wave solutions are sine or cosine functions and k values are restricted to the values

$$k = \frac{\pi}{L}, \frac{2\pi}{L}, \frac{3\pi}{L} \ldots \tag{1.37}$$

The standing wave solution is often used to describe stationary electrons confined in finite regions such as quantum wells to be discussed later. For describing moving electrons, the boundary condition used is known as a periodic boundary condition (Figure 1.7). Even though we focus our attention on a finite volume V, the wave can be considered to spread in all space as we conceive of

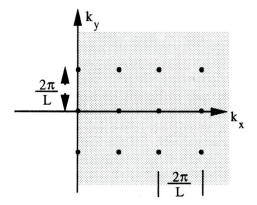

Figure 1.8: k-space volume of each electronic state. The separation between the various allowed values of the wave vector components, k_i, is $2\pi/L$.

the entire space as made up of identical cubes of sides L. Then,

$$
\begin{aligned}
\psi(x, y, z + L) &= \psi(x, y, z) \\
\psi(x, y + L, z) &= \psi(x, y, z) \\
\psi(x + L, y, z) &= \psi(x, y, z)
\end{aligned}
\tag{1.38}
$$

The boundary conditions impose certain restrictions in the k of the wave function which we will discuss shortly. The momentum of the electron is

$$
p = -i\hbar\nabla \Rightarrow \hbar k. \tag{1.39}
$$

The energy is

$$
E = \frac{p^2}{2m} \Rightarrow \frac{\hbar^2 k^2}{2m}. \tag{1.40}
$$

The velocity is

$$
v = \frac{p}{m} \Rightarrow \frac{\hbar k}{m} \tag{1.41}
$$

Because of the boundary conditions (Equation 1.38), the allowed values of k_x, k_y, and k_z, are:

$$
k_x = \frac{2\pi n_x}{L}; \ k_y = \frac{2\pi n_y}{L}; \ k_z = \frac{2\pi n_z}{L}. \tag{1.42}
$$

If L is large, the spacing between the allowed k_x, k_y, and k_z values is very small. It is useful to discuss the volume in k-space that each electronic state occupies. As can be seen from Figure 1.8, this volume is

$$
\left(\frac{2\pi}{L}\right)^3 = \frac{8\pi^3}{V} \tag{1.43}
$$

If Ω is a volume of k-space, the number of electronic states in this volume is

$$\frac{\Omega V}{8\pi^3} \tag{1.44}$$

We will now use this discussion to derive the extremely important concept of density of states. Although we will use the periodic boundary conditions to obtain the density of states, the stationary conditions lead to the same result.

1.4   THE DENSITY OF STATES

The concept of density of states is extremely powerful, and important physical properties such as optical absorption, transport, etc., are intimately dependent upon this concept. Density of states is the number of available electronic states *per unit volume per unit energy* around an energy E. If we denote the density of states by $N(E)$, the number of states in an energy interval dE around an energy E is $N(E)\,dE$. To calculate the density of states, we need to know the dimensionality of the system and the energy vs. wave vector relation that the electrons obey. For the free electron gas considered above, we have the parabolic relation

$$E = \frac{\hbar^2 k^2}{2m}. \tag{1.45}$$

1.4.1   Density of States for a Three-Dimensional System

In a three dimensional system, the k-space volume between vector $\mathbf{k}$ and $\mathbf{k} + d\mathbf{k}$ is (see Figure 1.9) $4\pi k^2 dk$. We had shown above that the k-space volume per electron state is $(2\pi/L)^3$. Therefore, the number of electron states in the region between $\mathbf{k}$ and $\mathbf{k} + d\mathbf{k}$ are

$$\frac{4\pi k^2 dk}{8\pi^3}V = \frac{k^2 dk}{2\pi^2}V. \tag{1.46}$$

Denoting the energy and energy interval corresponding to $\mathbf{k}$ and $d\mathbf{k}$ as E and dE, we see that the number of electron states between E and $E + dE$ per unit volume are

$$N(E)dE = \frac{k^2 dk}{2\pi^2} \tag{1.47}$$

and since $E = \hbar^2 k^2 / (2m)$, the numerator in Equation 1.47 is

$$k^2 dk = \frac{\sqrt{2}m^{3/2}E^{1/2}dE}{\hbar^3} \tag{1.48}$$

giving

$$N(E)dE = \frac{m^{3/2}E^{1/2}}{\sqrt{2}\pi^2\hbar^3}dE. \tag{1.49}$$

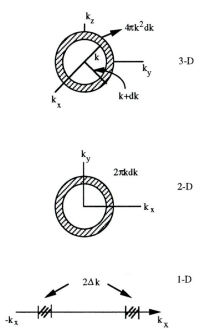

Figure 1.9: Geometry used to calculate density of states in three, two and one dimensions.

We must remember that the electron can have two states for a given k-value since it can have a spin state of $s = 1/2$ or $-1/2$. Accounting for spin, the density of the states is

$$N(E) = \frac{\sqrt{2}m^{3/2}E^{1/2}}{\pi^2\hbar^3}. \tag{1.50}$$

1.4.2 Density of States for Lower-Dimensional Systems

If we consider a 2-D system, a concept that has become a reality with use of quantum wells, similar arguments tell us that the density of states for a parabolic band is

$$N(E) = \frac{m}{\pi\hbar^2}. \tag{1.51}$$

Finally in a 1-D system, or "quantum wire," the density of states is

$$N(E) = \frac{\sqrt{2}m^{1/2}}{\pi\hbar}E^{-1/2}. \tag{1.52}$$

We notice that as the dimensionality of the system changes, the energy dependence of the density of states also changes. In three-dimensional systems we have a $E^{1/2}$ dependence as shown in Figure 1.10a. In two-dimensional systems there is no energy dependence (Figure 1.10b), while in one-dimensional systems,

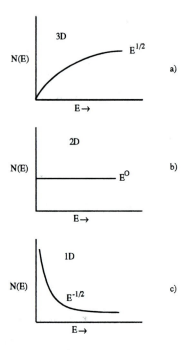

Figure 1.10: Variation in the energy dependence of the density of states in a) three-dimensional, b) two-dimensional, and, c) one-dimensional systems.

the density of states peaks at $E = 0$ (Figure 1.10c). The variations related to dimensionality are extremely important and are a key driving force to lower dimensional systems.

1.5 FILLING OF ELECTRONIC STATES

In the previous sections we derived how the electronic states are distributed in momentum and energy space. We will now address the question: If we have a density n of electrons available, how will they distribute themselves among the available states? To answer this question we must be able to define the distribution function for the electrons, i.e., be able to define the probability that a particular state with a given energy is occupied.

In a quantum mechanical treatment, particles fall in two categories: fermions and bosons. Particles such as electrons, protons, and neutrons are fermions. Particles like photons, mesons, and phonons are bosons. Fermions are characterized by an intrinsic angular momentum called spin which has a value $\hbar/2$, $3\hbar/2$, $5\hbar/2$, etc. Bosons, on the other hand, have spins of 0, $\hbar$, $2\hbar$, etc. This subtle difference forces a very important distinction on the occupation statistics. Only one fermion can occupy a quantum state, while any number of bosons can be placed in a particular state. When this fact is incorporated into distributing particles in an energy spectrum of quantum states, the distribution which minimizes the free energy of the system is, for fermions, the Fermi–Dirac distribution

$$f(E) = \frac{1}{\exp\left[(E-\mu)/(k_B T)\right]+1} \tag{1.53}$$

and for bosons, the Bose–Einstein distribution

$$f(E) = \frac{1}{\exp\left[E/(k_B T)\right]-1}. \tag{1.54}$$

The first expression shows that $f(E)$ is always less than unity. Here μ is called the chemical potential and it represents the energy where $f(\mu)$ becomes $1/2$. The chemical potential is determined once the density of states and the electron density are known. The distribution function for the bosons, which includes light particles (photons) and lattice vibrations (phonons), shows that $f(E)$ can be much larger than a unity, in principle. For finite mass bosons, one needs a μ as in the Fermi function. In addition to the quantum statistics discussed above, we also have the classical statistics of Boltzmann. In this case, the occupation probability is simply

$$\exp\left(-\frac{E}{k_B T}\right). \tag{1.55}$$

In order to determine the chemical potential, μ, of an electron gas having a density n, we note that

$$n = \int_0^\infty \frac{N(E)dE}{\exp\left[(E-\mu)/(k_B T)\right]+1} \tag{1.56}$$

where $N(E)$ is the density of states. This integral is particularly simple to evaluate at $T = 0$ K, since at this temperature

$$\frac{1}{\exp\left[(E-\mu)/(k_B T)\right]+1} = \begin{cases} 1 & \text{if } E \leq \mu \\ 0 & \text{otherwise.} \end{cases} \tag{1.57}$$

Denoting μ, at $T = 0$K, by E_F, which is known as the Fermi energy, we then have the electron concentration

$$n = \int_0^{E_F} N(E)dE \tag{1.58}$$

For the three–dimensional system we have

$$\begin{aligned} n &= \frac{\sqrt{2}m^{3/2}}{\pi^2 \hbar^3} \int_0^{E_F} E^{1/2}dE \\ &= \frac{2\sqrt{2}m^{3/2}}{3\pi^2 \hbar^3} E_F^{3/2} \end{aligned} \tag{1.59}$$

or

$$E_F = \frac{\hbar^2}{2m} \left(3\pi^2 n\right)^{2/3} \tag{1.60}$$

The quantity E_F is the highest occupied energy state at $T = 0$K. We can define a corresponding wave vector $\mathbf{k}_F$ called the Fermi wave vector

$$k_F = \left(3\pi^2 n\right)^{1/3} \tag{1.61}$$

and a Fermi velocity

$$v_F = \frac{\hbar}{m} \left(3\pi^2 n\right)^{1/3}. \tag{1.62}$$

It is important to note that even at $t = 0$K, the velocity of the highest occupied state is v_F and not zero as would be the case if we used Boltzmann statistics.

At finite temperatures, it is not so simple to invert the integral for n to obtain μ. One has to carry out the integration numerically or graphically to obtain the chemical potential. An approximation that is often useful and gives reasonable results is the Sommerfeld expansion [Ashcroft and Mermin, (1976), Appendix C]. The Sommerfeld expansion is applied to integrals of the form

$$I = \int_{-\infty}^{\infty} F(E) \, f(E) \, dE \tag{1.63}$$

where $f(E)$ is the Fermi–Dirac distribution function, and $F(E)$ vanishes as $E \to -\infty$ and diverges with E slower than an exponential. The integral can be shown to be given by

$$I = \int_{-\infty}^{\mu} F(E) \, dE + \sum_{n=1}^{\infty} a_n \left(k_B T\right)^{2n} \frac{d^{2n-1}}{dE^{2n-1}} F(E) \bigg|_{E=\mu} \tag{1.64}$$

with

$$
\begin{aligned}
a_1 &= 1.645 \\
a_2 &= 1.894 \\
a_3 &= 1.971
\end{aligned}
$$

If we now use the density of states expression for $F(E)$, we get

$$n = \frac{2\sqrt{2}m^{3/2}\mu^{3/2}}{3\pi^2\hbar^3} + \frac{1.163\left(k_B T\right)^2 m^{3/2}\mu^{-1/2}}{\pi^2\hbar^3} + \cdots. \tag{1.65}$$

Another useful approximation for the chemical potential is known as the Joyce–Dixon (1977) approximation. According to this,

$$\mu = k_B T \left[\ln\left(\frac{n}{n_c}\right) + \frac{1}{\sqrt{8}}\frac{n}{n_c}\right] \tag{1.66}$$

where n_c is the effective carrier density given by

$$n_c = 2 \left(\frac{m}{2\pi\hbar^2} \right)^{3/2} (k_B T)^{3/2} . \qquad (1.67)$$

One has to use these equations with care since they may not be valid over all ranges of temperature and concentration. Once the chemical potential is known, the total energy of the electron gas can be calculated by evaluating the integral

$$E_{tot} = \int_0^\infty E \, N(E) \, f(E) \, dE. \qquad (1.68)$$

It is interesting to note that in a two–dimensional system, where the density of states is constant, the chemical potential is analytically known once the carrier concentration is known. The carrier concentration is:

$$
\begin{aligned}
n &= \frac{m}{\pi\hbar^2} \int_0^\infty f(E) \, dE \\
&= \frac{m}{\pi\hbar^2} \int_0^\infty \frac{dE}{\exp(E - \mu)/(k_B T) + 1} \\
&= \frac{m k_B T}{\pi\hbar^2} \ln \left[1 + \exp \left(\frac{\mu}{k_B T} \right) \right]
\end{aligned}
\qquad (1.69)
$$

Note that at zero temperature, the chemical potential approaches the Fermi energy E_F, but as temperature increases the chemical potential departs. The temperature dependence of the chemical potential is very much dependent upon the dimensionality of the system since the density of states is very much dependent upon the dimensionality. In Figure 1.11 we show how the chemical potential varies with temperature, as the system dimensions are altered.

The two concepts introduced in this section, the density of states and distribution function, are extremely important and we will see them being invoked in the understanding of every physical phenomenon in semiconductors. The Fermi–Dirac distribution is a basic outcome of quantum mechanics and all fermions obey it regardless of the material they are in. The density of states, on the other hand, is an entity which is dependent upon the energy—momentum relation of the electron and this will depend upon the particular semiconductor. At this point it is difficult to see why the energy—momentum relation of an electron will depend upon which semiconductor the electron is in. But this is one of the conceptual breakthroughs needed to understand solid state electronics.

As this text progresses, we will find ourselves completely abandoning the basic assumption of Drude's model that requires electrons to scatter from the background ions. While an extremely attractive notion, we will see that if the background ions are arranged *periodically*, the electrons *do not scatter at all from the ions*. The effect of the ions is to alter the apparent energy–momentum relation of the electrons, change the mass, introduce bandgaps, and even make the electrons behave like positively charged particles!

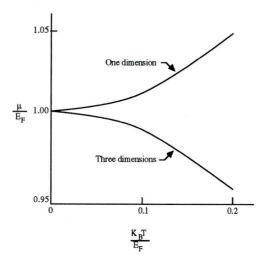

Figure 1.11: Variation of the chemical potential as a function of temperature for one–, two–, and three–dimensional systems.

To understand this immense transformation in the electron's behavior we need to understand what is special about periodic structures or crystalline materials. Semiconductor technology depends critically upon the crystalline nature of the solid state matter and our understanding of semiconductor physics depends to a great deal upon assuming that the background ions in Drude's model are arranged in a perfectly periodic arrangement.

1.6   FOR THE TECHNOLOGIST IN YOU

In this chapter we have seen some of the historical developments in the area of electronic properties of materials. In the early part of this century, the study of semiconductor materials was extremely frustrating to scientists. While metallic samples could be produced with reliability, semiconductors were considered impure since their conductivity varied widely from sample to sample. As we advance through this text, we will see why perfection in semiconductors is so much more important than for metals. As pure semiconductors started to become available, the richness of physical phenomena began to emerge and semiconductor physics became an active area of study. Of course, with the discovery of new physical phenomena, came new ideas in device physics and unprecedented positive feedback was created between basic physics and applied research. The observations of new physical phenomena have also resulted in modifications or in some cases complete abandonment of previous theories. The concepts developed in this chapter will be greatly modified as we go through this text.

In Figure 1.12, we show an overview of how various physical phenomena were discovered in semiconductors and their ramifications in the world of devices.

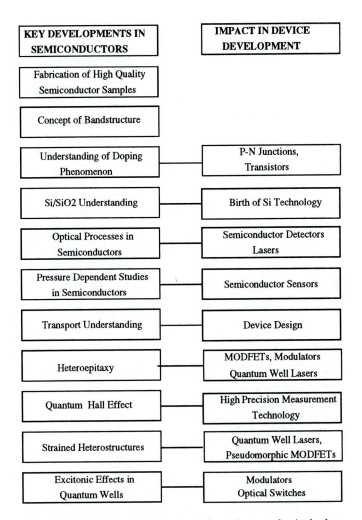

Figure 1.12: Some semiconductor devices and the primary physical phenomena upon which they depend.

A picture of the first monolithic integrated circuit is shown along with a modern high density integrated circuit, in Figure 1.13.

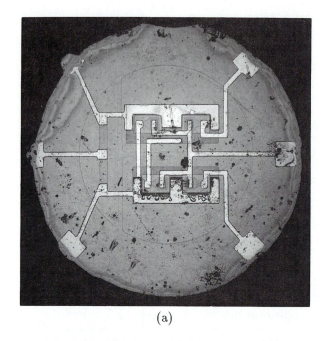

(a)

(b)

Figure 1.13: (a) The first monolithic integrated circuit (Fairchild F element flip-flop) and (b) a modern high density integrated circuit (National Semiconductor 32 bit "Swordfish" microprocessor). (*Courtesy of National Semiconductor Corp.*)

1.7 PROBLEMS

1.1. In the Drude model, as well as in the other scattering models to be studied later, the probability that one electron suffers a collision in a small time interval dt is dt/τ.

(a) Show that the probability that an electron picked at time 0, will on an average have no collision during the next time t is given by

$$P(T) = e^{-t/\tau}$$

(b) Show that the mean time between two successive collisions is τ.

(c) What is the mobility of electrons in a sample of GaAs where τ is calculated to be 1 ps according to the Drude model? Give your results in $\mathrm{cm^2V^{-1}s^{-1}}$.

(d) What is the length of a GaAs sample, using the value of τ from part (c), that an electron can transverse without scattering with a 90% probability. Assume that there is an electric field of 10 kV/cm and the electron is injected into the sample with zero velocity.

1.2. In the Drude model, the energy the electron gains between collisions from the electric field is lost to the background fixed ions since the electron gas remains at equilibrium with the material temperature. This energy loss is the heat generated during the electron motion.

(a) Show that the average energy lost to the ions in the second of two collisions separated by time t is $(eFt)^2/(2m)$ where F is the uniform electric field applied.

(b) Using results of Problem 1, show that the average energy loss per electron per collision is $(eF\tau)^2/m$. The average loss per unit volume per second is thus $(ne^2\tau F^2)/m = \sigma F^2$.

1.3. (a) Assume that the mass m used in the density of states expressions, has value $0.067m_0$ (m_0 = free electron mass). Plot the density of states in GaAs for the 3-D, 2-D and 1-D cases. Give your results in the units of $\mathrm{eV^{-1}cm^{-D}}$ where D is the dimensionality.

(b) In the example used above, what is the value of the Fermi level (at 0 K) if an electron concentration of $10^{18}\mathrm{cm^{-3}}$ (for the 3-D case), $10^{12}\mathrm{cm^{-2}}$ (for the 2-D case), and $10^6\mathrm{cm^{-1}}$(for the 1-D case) is present?

(c) What happens to the chemical potential if the temperature is raised to 300K?

(d) Plot the function $f(E)N(E)$ as a function of energy for the case (c). This plot provides a key motivation for the drive for going towards lower dimensional systems for lasers.

1.4. We will learn later that current conduction can occur not only by negatively charged electrons, but also positively charged holes. A sample of Ge has both electrons and holes carrying the current. When a Hall measurement is done, there is no Hall effect! If the mobility of electrons in germanium is 3500 cm^2/V-s and that of holes is 1500 cm^2/V-s, what fraction of the current is carried by electrons?

1.5. Consider a 2-dimensional electron gas with the dispersion relation

$$E_n(k_x, k_y) = E_n + \frac{\hbar^2 k_x^2}{2m_{xx}} + \frac{\hbar^2 k_y^2}{2m_{yy}}.$$

Show that the density of states has the same form as for a "spherical" dispersion case except that the density of states mass is $\sqrt{m_{xx}m_{yy}}$. What is the position of the Fermi level in terms of the carrier concentration?

1.6. The conductivity of Cu at room temperature is 6×10^6 (Ω cm)$^{-1}$. The Cu crystal has a free electron concentration of 8.47×10^{22} cm^{-3}. What is the mobility and scattering time τ? Assume a value of Fermi energy equal to 7.0 eV and use $v_F = \sqrt{2E_F/m}$ to calculate the mean free path.

1.7. In GaAs, once the channel dimensions are less than 1000 Å, much of the transport occurs without scattering. In such ballistic transport, the electron climbs up along the E vs. $\boldsymbol{k}$ diagram in accordance with the effective Newton's equation of motion. Assume a parabolic band relation

$$E = \frac{\hbar^2 k^2}{2m^*}$$

with $m^* = 0.067m_0$. Calculate the electron transit time and final energy for a transit length of 0.1 μm and an electric field of 10^3 V/cm, 10^4 V/cm, and 10^5 V/cm.

1.8. Consider a quantum dot of GaAs of dimensions $L \times L \times L$. Assume infinite potential barriers and calculate the separation of the ground and excited state energies in the conduction band as a function of L. If an energy separation of $k_B T$ is needed to observe 3-dimensional confinement effects, what is the maximum box size required to see these effects at 4 K and at 300 K?

1.8   REFERENCES

- **Drude Model; Sommerfeld Model**

  - A good reference is Ashcroft, N. W. and N. D. Mermin, *Solid State Physics* (Holt, Reinhart and Winston, New York, 1976), chaps. 1 and 2.

- **Carrier Statistics**

  - Most books on thermodynamics have derivations of the Boltzmann, Fermi–Dirac and Bose–Einstein statistics. An example is Zemanksky, M. W., *Heat and Thermodynamics* (McGraw–Hill, New York, 1968).

  - A very enlightening discussion about fermions and bosons is given in Feynmann, R. P., R. B. Leighton and M. Sands, *Lectures on Physics* (Addison–Wesley, New York, 1964), vol. 3, chaps. 3 and 4.

  - Joyce, W. B. and R. W. Dixon, Appl. Phys. Lett., **31**, 354 (1977).

CHAPTER 2

PERIODICITY: CRYSTAL STRUCTURES

Solid state physics represents an attempt to unravel the mysteries of physical phenomena occurring in solids. Inherently, this is an extremely difficult task because of the very large number of interacting particles. However, when the solid is a crystalline material, an enormous degree of simplification occurs in the problem. Thus, while most physical properties of crystals are very well understood, for amorphous or non-crystalline materials even simple properties are not clear. Indeed, it is difficult to conceive of what the state of solid state physics and solid state electronics would be, if solids did not occur as crystals. Crystals are made up of identical building blocks, the blocks being an atom or a group of atoms. It is easy to conceptualize why the lowest energy configuration of the solid would involve some symmetric arrangement of atoms, but it is extremely difficult to analyze what symmetry a given solid would acquire. While in natural crystals the crystalline symmetry is fixed by nature, new advances in crystal growth techniques are allowing scientists to produce artificial crystals with modified crystalline structure. These advances depend upon being able to place atomic layers with exact precision and control during growth, leading to superlattices. The underlying periodicity of crystals is the key which controls the properties of the electrons inside the material. Thus by altering crystalline structure artificially, one is able to alter electronic properties. This ability to tailor properties is an important driving force behind modern electronics.

2.1 PERIODICITY OF A CRYSTAL

The intrinsic property of a crystal is that the environment around a given atom or group of atoms is exactly the same as the environment around another atom or similar group of atoms.

The building block which is repeated infinitely, to produce the crystal, may be quite simple, such as a single atom for many metals (such as copper, gold, aluminum, etc.) or could be quite complex (as in some proteins). In $NaCd_2$ there are 1192 atoms in the basic building block. In man-made superlattices the number can be arbitrary. For almost all natural semiconductors, the building block consists of two atoms. To understand and define the crystal structure, two important concepts are introduced, the lattice and the basis.

The *lattice* represents a set of points in space which form a periodic structure. Each point sees exactly the same environment. The lattice is, by itself, a mathematical abstraction. A building block of atoms, called the *basis*, is then attached to each lattice point, yielding the crystal structure.

An important property of a lattice is the ability to define three vectors, a_1, a_2, a_3, such that any lattice point $R^{'}$ can be obtained from any other lattice point R by a translation

$$R^{'} = R + m_1 a_1 + m_2 a_2 + m_3 a_3, \tag{2.1}$$

where m_1, m_2, and m_3 are integers. Such a lattice is called a Bravais lattice. The entire lattice can be generated by choosing all possible combinations of the integers m_1, m_2, m_3. The crystal structure is now produced by attaching the basis to each of these lattice points.

$$\boxed{\text{lattice } + \text{ basis } = \text{ crystal structure}}$$

The translation vectors a_1, a_2, and a_3 are called primitive, if the volume of the cell formed by them is the smallest possible. There is no unique way to to choose the primitive vectors. One choice is to select

1. a_1 to be the shortest period of the lattice,

2. a_2 to be the shortest period not parallel to a_1,

3. a_3 to be the shortest period not coplanar with a_1 and a_2.

Figures 2.1 and 2.2 illustrate the basic functions described above.

In our discussions we will usually deal with infinite lattices, ignoring the effects of boundaries and interfaces which break the periodicity. The boundaries and interfaces do play very important roles in real semiconductors and their devices, as we shall discuss later.

It is possible to define more than one set of primitive vectors for a given lattice, and often the choice depends upon convenience. The volume cell enclosed by the primitive vectors is called the *primitive unit cell* .

Because of the periodicity of a lattice, it is useful to define the symmetry of the structure. The symmetry is defined via a set of point group operations which involve a set of operations applied around a point of the lattice. The operations consist of rotations, reflections, and inversions. The symmetry plays a very important role in the electronic properties of the crystal. An important

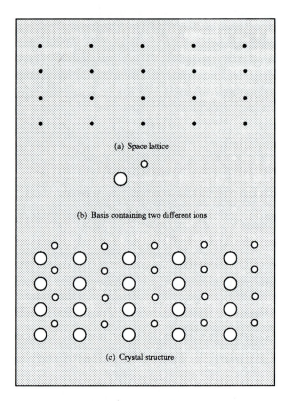

(a) Space lattice

(b) Basis containing two different ions

(c) Crystal structure

Figure 2.1: How a crystal structure is formed. One starts with a lattice, which is simply a collection of periodically arranged points (a). Then an arbitrarily complex basis consisting of atoms, oriented in a particular manner to each other (b), are placed at each lattice point (c), in exactly the same order to form the crystal structure.

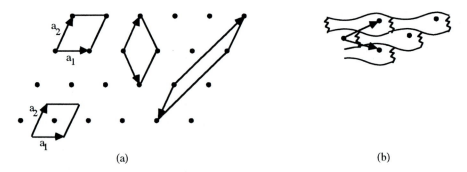

(a)   (b)

Figure 2.2: Different ways to choose the primitive lattice vectors and the primitive unit cell in a two-dimensional lattice. The actual choice may depend upon the special mathematical simplicity associated with one particular choice.

Voltage produced by piezoelectric effect

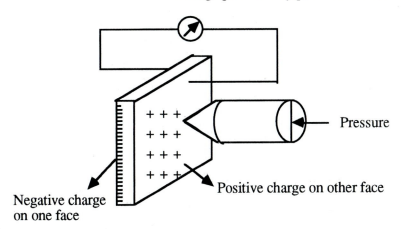

Pressure

Positive charge on other face

Negative charge
on one face

Figure 2.3: The piezoelectric effect is produced when a crystal, lacking inversion symmetry, is strained. An electric field develops across the crystal faces due to charges that accumulate on the faces. This effect is often used for pressure sensors.

manifestation of the symmetry properties are the degeneracies at certain points (i.e., several electron wave functions having the same energy). For example, the conduction band of silicon is 6-fold degenerate corresponding to the symmetry in the lattice between the directions x, $-x$, y, $-y$, z, $-z$.

The point group operations are defined by the following operations, along with the commonly used symbols.

Rotation, C_n: This involves a rotation by an angle $2\pi/n$ about the specified axis. The rotation sense is often chosen to be that of a right–handed screw.

Inversion, I: In this operation, each point at the position (x, y, z) in the reference frame is transformed to the point $(-x, -y, -z)$. A central, fixed point is defined as the origin. The inversion symmetry is extremely important and many physical properties of semiconductors are tied to the presence or absence of this symmetry. For example, in the diamond structure (Si, Ge, C, etc.) inversion symmetry is present, while in the zinc–blende structure (GaAs, AlAs, InAs, etc.) it is absent. Because of this lack of inversion symmetry, these semiconductors are piezoelectric, i.e., when they are strained an electric potential is developed (Figure 2.3) across the opposite faces of the crystal. In crystals with inversion symmetry, where the two faces are identical, this is not possible.

Reflection, σ: This operation involves a reflection across a plane chosen in the reference frame.

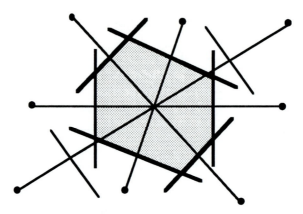

Figure 2.4: The procedure to form the Wigner–Seitz cell.

Improper Rotation, S_n: This involves a rotation C_n followed by (or following) a reflection σ about a plane normal to the rotation axis.

2.1.1   The Wigner–Seitz Cell

A very useful way to define a unit cell is the procedure given by Wigner and Seitz. The procedure involves:

1. Drawing lines to connect a given lattice point to all neighboring points;

2. Drawing bisecting lines or planes to the previous lines.

The volume enclosed within the bisections is called the Wigner–Seitz cell. This manner of defining the unit cell proves to be a very useful one when we examine the electronic states in periodic structures. Figure 2.4 illustrates this procedure.

2.2   BASIC LATTICE TYPES

The various kinds of lattice structures possible in nature are described by the symmetry group that describes their properties. Rotation is one of the important symmetry groups. Lattices can be found which have a rotational symmetry of 2π, $2\pi/2$, $2\pi/3$, $2\pi/4$, and $2\pi/6$. The rotational symmetries are denoted by $n = 1$, 2, 3, 4, and 6. No other rotation symmetries exist, e.g. $2\pi/5$ or $2\pi/7$ are not allowed because such a structure could not fill up an infinite space. This can be simply seen by examining Figure 2.5.

Consider points A and A' on the Bravais lattice and collinear with them, the points C and D. The spacing between the points is a as shown. If we perform a rotation of C and D around A and A', we get points B and B'. If ϕ is a

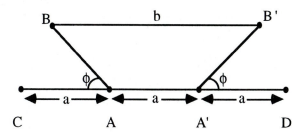

Figure 2.5: Geometric construction to prove that only certain rotation symmetries are allowed in a space filling lattice.

symmetry allowed rotation, B and B' are also lattice points and BB' must be parallel to AA' and the distance BB' should be an integral multiple of a

$$b = a + 2a\cos\phi$$
$$= ja \qquad\qquad (2.2)$$

or

$$\cos\phi = \frac{j-1}{2}$$
$$= i/2. \qquad\qquad (2.3)$$

Table 2.1 shows the allowed values of ϕ consistent with Equation 2.3.

i	$\cos\phi$	ϕ
-2	-1	π
-1	$-1/2$	$2\pi/3$
0	0	$\pi/2$
1	$1/2$	$\pi/3$
2	1	0

Table 2.1: Allowed rotation symmetry angles for space filling lattices.

2.2.1 Two–Dimensional Lattices

In two-dimensional surfaces there can be an infinite set of lattice classes, since there is no restriction on the length of the translation vectors or the angle between them. There are five basic classes of Bravais lattices in two dimensions:

1. General oblique,

2. Square,

System	Number of lattices	Restrictions on conventional cell axes and angles
Triclinic	1	$a_1 \neq a_2 \neq a_3$ $\alpha \neq \beta \neq \gamma$
Monoclinic	2	$a_1 \neq a_2 \neq a_3$ $\alpha = \gamma = 90° \neq \beta$
Orthorhombic	4	$a_1 \neq a_2 \neq a_3$ $\alpha = \beta = \gamma = 90°$
Tetragonal	2	$a_1 = a_2 \neq a_3$ $\alpha = \beta = \gamma = 90°$
Cubic	3	$a_1 = a_2 = a_3$ $\alpha = \beta = \gamma = 90°$
Trigonal	1	$a_1 = a_2 = a_3$ $\alpha = \beta = \gamma < 120°, \neq 90°$
Hexagonal	1	$a_1 = a_2 \neq a_3$ $\alpha = \beta = 90°$ $\gamma = 120°$

Table 2.2: The 14 Bravais lattices in three dimensional systems and their properties.

3. Hexagonal,

4. Rectangular,

5. Centered rectangular.

These basic classes are illustrated in Figure 2.6.

2.2.2   Three–Dimensional Lattices

There are 14 types of lattices in three dimensions. The general lattice is triclinic ($\alpha \neq \beta \neq \gamma$; $a_1 \neq a_2 \neq a_3$) and there are 13 special lattices. Table 2.2 provides the basic properties of these three-dimensional lattices. We will focus on the cubic lattice which is the structure taken by all semiconductors. Figure 2.7 shows the various allowed Bravais lattices.

There are three kinds of cubic lattices: simple cubic, body–centered cubic, and face–centered cubic. The simple cubic lattice is generated by the primitive vectors

$$
\begin{aligned}
\boldsymbol{a}_1 &= a\hat{x} \\
\boldsymbol{a}_2 &= a\hat{y} \\
\boldsymbol{a}_3 &= a\hat{z}
\end{aligned}
\tag{2.4}
$$

where the $\hat{x}$, $\hat{y}$, $\hat{z}$ are unit vectors.

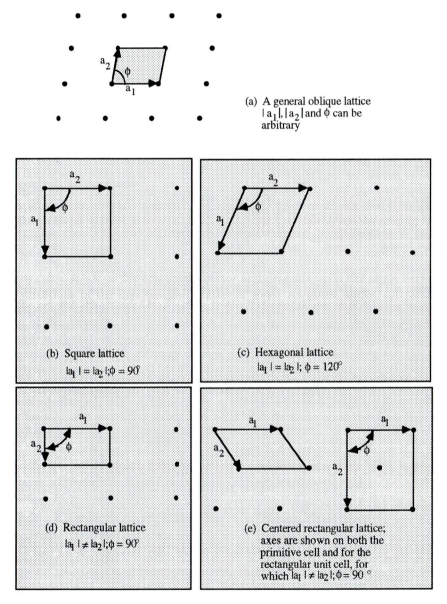

(a) A general oblique lattice
$|a_1|, |a_2|$ and ϕ can be arbitrary

(b) Square lattice
$|a_1| = |a_2|; \phi = 90°$

(c) Hexagonal lattice
$|a_1| = |a_2|; \phi = 120°$

(d) Rectangular lattice
$|a_1| \neq |a_2|; \phi = 90°$

(e) Centered rectangular lattice;
axes are shown on both the
primitive cell and for the
rectangular unit cell, for
which $|a_1| \neq |a_2|; \phi = 90°$

Figure 2.6: The five classes of two-dimensional Bravais lattices. The figure (a) shows a general oblique lattice. The figures (b) through (e) show various special two-dimensional lattices.

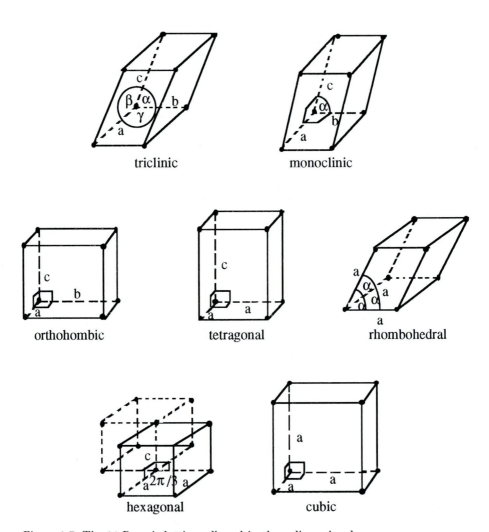

Figure 2.7: The 14 Bravais lattices allowed in three-dimensional space.

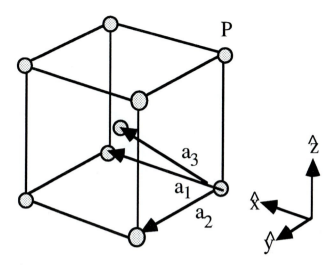

Figure 2.8: Three primitive vectors, specified in Equation 2.5, for the body-centered cubic Bravais lattice. The lattice is formed by taking all linear combinations of the primitive vectors with integral coefficients. The point P, for example is $P = -a_1 - a_2 + 2a_3$.

The body centered cubic (bcc) lattice can be generated from the simple cubic structure by placing an atom at the center of the cube. If $\hat{x}$, $\hat{y}$, and $\hat{z}$ are three orthogonal unit vectors, then a set of primitive vectors for the body-centered cubic lattice could be (Figure 2.8):

$$
\begin{aligned}
\boldsymbol{a}_1 &= a\hat{x} \\
\boldsymbol{a}_2 &= a\hat{y} \\
\boldsymbol{a}_3 &= \frac{a}{2}\left(\hat{x} + \hat{y} + \hat{z}\right).
\end{aligned}
\tag{2.5}
$$

A more symmetric set for the bcc lattice is (see Figure 2.9):

$$
\begin{aligned}
\boldsymbol{a}_1 &= \frac{a}{2}\left(\hat{y} + \hat{z} - \hat{x}\right) \\
\boldsymbol{a}_2 &= \frac{a}{2}\left(\hat{z} + \hat{x} - \hat{y}\right) \\
\boldsymbol{a}_3 &= \frac{a}{2}\left(\hat{x} + \hat{y} - \hat{z}\right).
\end{aligned}
\tag{2.6}
$$

It is important to convince oneself both geometrically and analytically that these sets do indeed generate the bcc Bravais lattice.

Another equally important lattice for semiconductors is the face-centered cubic (fcc) Bravais lattice. To construct the face-centered cubic Bravais lattice add to the simple cubic lattice an additional point in the center of each square face (Figure 2.10). For ease in description think of each cube in the simple cubic lattice as having horizontal bottom and top faces, and four vertical side faces

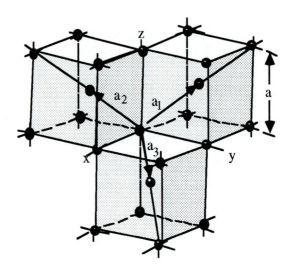

Figure 2.9: A more symmetric set of primitive vectors, specified in Equation 2.6, for the body-centered cubic Bravais lattice.

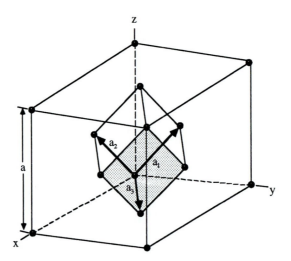

Figure 2.10: Primitive basis vectors for the face centered cubic lattice.

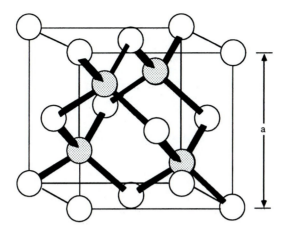

Figure 2.11: The zinc–blende crystal structure. The structure consists of the inter-penetrating fcc lattices, one displaced from the other by a distance $(a/4)(111)$ along the body diagonal. The underlying Bravais lattice is fcc with a two atom basis. The positions of the two atoms are (000) and $(a/4)(111)$.

facing north, south, east, and west. A symmetric set of primitive vectors for the face-centered cubic lattice (see Figure 2.10) is

$$
\begin{aligned}
\boldsymbol{a}_1 &= \frac{a}{2}\,(\hat{y}+\hat{z})\\
\boldsymbol{a}_2 &= \frac{a}{2}\,(\hat{z}+\hat{x})\\
\boldsymbol{a}_3 &= \frac{a}{2}\,(\hat{x}+\hat{y})\,.
\end{aligned}
\tag{2.7}
$$

The face-centered cubic and body-centered cubic Bravais lattices are of great importance, since an enormous variety of solids crystallize in these forms with an atom (or ion) at each lattice site. Essentially all semiconductors of interest for electronics and opto-electronics have the fcc structure.

2.2.3 The Diamond and Zinc–Blende Structures

As just stated, essentially all semiconductors of interest for electronics and opto-electronics have an underlying fcc lattice. However, they have two atoms per basis. The coordinates of the two basis atoms are (000) and $(a/4)(111)$. Since each atom lies on its own fcc lattice, such a two atom basis structure may be thought of as two inter-penetrating fcc lattices, one displaced from the other by a translation along a body diagonal of $(a/4)(111)$.

Figure 2.11 gives details of this important structure. If the two atoms of the basis are identical, the structure is called the diamond structure. Semiconductors such as Si, Ge, and C, fall into this category. If the two atoms are different, the structure is called the zinc–blende structure. Semiconductors such as GaAs, AlAs, and CdS, fall into this category. Semiconductors with the diamond structure are often called elemental semiconductors, while the zinc–blende semiconductors are called compound semiconductors. The compound semiconductors are also denoted by the position of the atoms in the periodic chart, e.g., GaAs, AlAs, and InP are called III–V (three–five) semiconductors while CdS, CdSe, and CdTe, are called II–VI (two–six) semiconductors.

2.2.4   Notation to Denote Planes and Points in a Lattice: Miller Indices

A simple scheme is used to describe lattice planes, directions and points. For a plane, we use the following procedure:

1. Define the x, y, z axes (primitive vectors).

2. Take the intercepts of the plane along the axes in units of lattice constants.

3. Take the reciprocal of the intercepts and reduce them to the smallest integers.

The notation (hkl) denotes a family of parallel planes. The notation $\{hkl\}$ denotes a family of equivalent planes. To denote directions, we use the smallest set of integers having the same ratio as the direction cosines of the given direction. In a cubic system the Miller indices of a plane are the same as the direction perpendicular to the plane. The notation [ ] is used for a set of parallel directions, while the notation <> is used for a set of equivalent directions. Figure 2.12 shows some examples of the use of the Miller indices to define planes.

2.3   THE RECIPROCAL LATTICE

The crystal lattices we have been discussing so far have involved working in real space. Real space is obviously the physical space of interest. However, for many applications it is very useful to work in k-space or reciprocal space. The reasons for examining k-space will be fully understood when we discuss the problem of X-ray diffraction and bandstructure of crystals, but we already know that even when we solved the Schrödinger equation for free electrons, our eigenfunctions were in k-space. For example, the wavefunction $\exp(i\boldsymbol{k}\cdot\boldsymbol{r})$ is spread over all space with equal probability and the electron has a well defined momentum $\hbar\boldsymbol{k}$.

A simple transformation is carried out to map the lattices we discussed before in real space into lattices in k-space. The motivation for choosing this transformation will become clear when we discuss X-ray diffraction. Using the primitive vectors $\boldsymbol{a}_1$, $\boldsymbol{a}_2$, $\boldsymbol{a}_3$ of the direct (i.e., real space) lattice we construct a new set of vectors

$$\boldsymbol{b}_1 = 2\pi\frac{\boldsymbol{a}_2 \times \boldsymbol{a}_3}{\boldsymbol{a}_1 \cdot \boldsymbol{a}_2 \times \boldsymbol{a}_3}$$

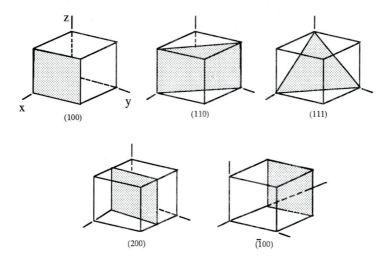

Figure 2.12: Some important planes in the cubic system along with their Miller indices.

$$b_2 = 2\pi \frac{a_3 \times a_1}{a_1 \cdot a_2 \times a_3}$$

$$b_3 = 2\pi \frac{a_1 \times a_2}{a_1 \cdot a_2 \times a_3} \tag{2.8}$$

The new vectors b_1, b_2, b_3 are the primitive vectors of the reciprocal lattice and using them, we can form the reciprocal lattice. The particular transformation to obtain the b vectors from the a vectors provides a special property to the vectors, i.e.:

$$b_i \cdot a_j = 2\pi\delta_{ij}. \tag{2.9}$$

A general vector

$$G = v_1 b_1 + v_2 b_2 + v_3 b_3 \tag{2.10}$$

where the v's are integers, is called a reciprocal lattice vector.

From now on when we think of a particular crystal structure, we will always associate both the direct and reciprocal lattices with it. If we had the ability to see atoms, we could look at a crystal and see its direct lattice. On the other hand, if we looked at the screen when an image of the crystal was formed by X-rays, we would see the reciprocal lattice. It is worth noting that because of the special relation (Equation 2.9) between direct and reciprocal primitive vectors, we have the relation:

$$\exp(iG \cdot T) = 1 \tag{2.11}$$

where G is a reciprocal lattice vector and T is a direct lattice vector.

As in direct lattices, we have unit cells in the reciprocal lattice. A very important definition of the unit cell is the Brillouin zone which is the Wigner–Seitz cell of the reciprocal lattice. The importance of the Brillouin zone will be discussed when we consider X-ray diffraction and bandstructure.

Let us now consider the reciprocal lattices of a few simple crystal structures.

2.3.1   Reciprocal Lattice of the sc Lattice

The primitive translation vectors of a simple cubic lattice may be taken as the set

$$
\begin{aligned}
\boldsymbol{a}_1 &= a\hat{x} \\
\boldsymbol{a}_2 &= a\hat{y} \\
\boldsymbol{a}_3 &= a\hat{z}.
\end{aligned}
\tag{2.12}
$$

Here $\hat{x}$, $\hat{y}$, $\hat{z}$ are orthogonal vectors of unit length. The volume of the cell is $\boldsymbol{a}_1 \cdot \boldsymbol{a}_2 \times \boldsymbol{a}_3 = a^3$. The primitive translation vectors of the reciprocal lattice are found from the standard prescription of Equation 2.8:

$$
\begin{aligned}
\boldsymbol{b}_1 &= \frac{2\pi}{a}\hat{x} \\
\boldsymbol{b}_2 &= \frac{2\pi}{a}\hat{y} \\
\boldsymbol{b}_3 &= \frac{2\pi}{a}\hat{z}.
\end{aligned}
\tag{2.13}
$$

Here the reciprocal lattice itself is a simple cubic lattice, now of lattice constant $2\pi/a$. The boundaries of the first Brillouin zone are the planes normal to the six reciprocal lattice vectors $\pm\boldsymbol{b}_1$, $\pm\boldsymbol{b}_2$, $\pm\boldsymbol{b}_3$, at their midpoints:

$$
\begin{aligned}
\pm\frac{1}{2}\boldsymbol{b}_1 &= \pm\frac{\pi}{a}\hat{x} \\
\pm\frac{1}{2}\boldsymbol{b}_2 &= \pm\frac{\pi}{a}\hat{y} \\
\pm\frac{1}{2}\boldsymbol{b}_3 &= \pm\frac{\pi}{a}\hat{z}.
\end{aligned}
\tag{2.14}
$$

The six planes bound a cube of edge $2\pi/a$ and of volume $(2\pi/a)^3$; this cube is the first Brillouin zone of the simple cubic crystal lattice.

2.3.2   Reciprocal Lattice of the bcc Lattice

The primitive translation vectors of the bcc lattice (Figure 2.9) are

$$
\begin{aligned}
\boldsymbol{a}_1 &= \frac{a}{2}\left(\hat{y} + \hat{z} - \hat{x}\right) \\
\boldsymbol{a}_2 &= \frac{a}{2}\left(\hat{z} + \hat{x} - \hat{y}\right) \\
\boldsymbol{a}_3 &= \frac{a}{2}\left(\hat{x} + \hat{y} - \hat{z}\right)
\end{aligned}
\tag{2.15}
$$

where a is the side of the conventional cube and $\hat{x}$, $\hat{y}$, $\hat{z}$ are orthogonal unit vectors parallel to the cube edges. The volume of the primitive cell is

$$\begin{aligned} V &= |\boldsymbol{a}_1 \cdot \boldsymbol{a}_2 \times \boldsymbol{a}_3| \\ &= \frac{1}{2}a^3. \end{aligned} \qquad (2.16)$$

The primitive vectors of the reciprocal lattice are defined by (Equation 2.7). We have

$$\begin{aligned} \boldsymbol{b}_1 &= \frac{2\pi}{a}(\hat{y} + \hat{z}) \\ \boldsymbol{b}_2 &= \frac{2\pi}{a}(\hat{z} + \hat{x}) \\ \boldsymbol{b}_3 &= \frac{2\pi}{a}(\hat{x} + \hat{y}). \end{aligned} \qquad (2.17)$$

Note by comparison with Figure 2.10 that these are just the primitive vectors of an fcc lattice, so that *an fcc lattice is the reciprocal lattice of the bcc lattice.*

The general reciprocal lattice vector is, for integers v_1, v_2, v_3,

$$\begin{aligned} \boldsymbol{G} &= v_1\boldsymbol{b}_1 + v_2\boldsymbol{b}_2 + v_3\boldsymbol{b}_3 \\ &= \frac{2\pi}{a}[(v_2 + v_3)\hat{x} + (v_3 + v_1)\hat{y} + (v_1 + v_2)\hat{z}]. \end{aligned} \qquad (2.18)$$

The shortest $\boldsymbol{G}$'s are the following 12 vectors, where all choices of sign are independent:

$$\frac{2\pi}{a}(\pm\hat{y} \pm \hat{z}); \ \frac{2\pi}{a}(\pm\hat{z} \pm \hat{x}); \ \frac{2\pi}{a}(\pm\hat{x} \pm \hat{y}). \qquad (2.19)$$

The primitive cell of the reciprocal lattice is the parallelepiped described by the $\boldsymbol{b}_1$, $\boldsymbol{b}_2$, $\boldsymbol{b}_3$ defined by Equation 2.17. The volume of this cell in reciprocal space is $|\boldsymbol{b}_1 \cdot \boldsymbol{b}_2 \times \boldsymbol{b}_3| = 2(2\pi/a)^3$. The cell contains one reciprocal lattice point, because each of the eight corner points is shared among eight parallelepipeds. Each parallelepiped contains one-eighth of each of eight corner points.

In solid state physics we take the central (Wigner–Seitz) cell of the reciprocal lattice as the first Brillouin zone. Each such cell contains one lattice point at the central point of the cell. This zone (for the bcc lattice) is bounded by the planes normal to the 12 vectors of Equation 2.19 at their midpoints. The zone is a regular 12-faced solid, a rhombic dodecahedron, as shown in Figure 2.13. The vectors from the origin to the center of each face are:

$$\frac{\pi}{a}(\pm\hat{y} \pm \hat{z}); \ \frac{\pi}{a}(\pm\hat{z} \pm \hat{x}); \ \frac{\pi}{a}(\pm\hat{x} \pm \hat{y}). \qquad (2.20)$$

All choices of sign are independent, giving 12 vectors.

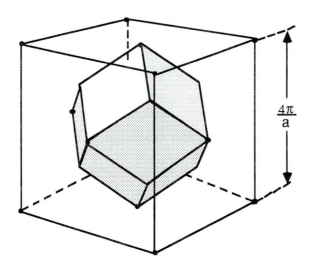

Figure 2.13: First Brillouin zone of the body-centered cubic lattice. The figure is a regular rhombic dodecahedron.

2.3.3 Reciprocal Lattice of the fcc Lattice

The primitive translation vectors of the fcc lattice of Figure 2.10 are:

$$
\begin{aligned}
\boldsymbol{a}_1 &= \frac{a}{2}\left(\hat{y} + \hat{z}\right) \\
\boldsymbol{a}_2 &= \frac{a}{2}\left(\hat{z} + \hat{x}\right) \\
\boldsymbol{a}_3 &= \frac{a}{2}\left(\hat{x} + \hat{y}\right).
\end{aligned}
\tag{2.21}
$$

The volume of the primitive cell is

$$
\begin{aligned}
V &= |\boldsymbol{a}_1 \cdot \boldsymbol{a}_2 \times \boldsymbol{a}_3| \\
&= \frac{1}{4}a^3.
\end{aligned}
\tag{2.22}
$$

The primitive translation vectors of the lattice reciprocal to the fcc lattice are

$$
\begin{aligned}
\boldsymbol{b}_1 &= \frac{2\pi}{a}\left(-\hat{x} + \hat{y} + \hat{z}\right) \\
\boldsymbol{b}_2 &= \frac{2\pi}{a}\left(\hat{x} - \hat{y} + \hat{z}\right) \\
\boldsymbol{b}_3 &= \frac{2\pi}{a}\left(\hat{x} + \hat{y} - \hat{z}\right).
\end{aligned}
\tag{2.23}
$$

These are primitive translation vectors of a bcc lattice, so that the *bcc lattice is reciprocal to the fcc lattice.* The volume of the primitive cell of the reciprocal lattice is $4(2\pi/a)^3$.

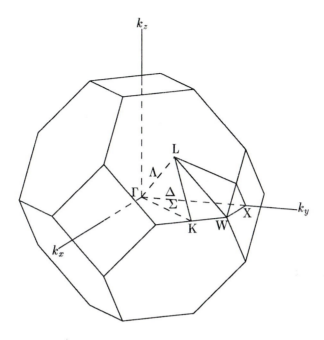

Figure 2.14: The Brillouin zone of the fcc lattice. This complicated unit cell along with its symmetries is extremely important in semiconductor physics. The inset gives the locations of certain high symmetry points in the Brillouin zone.

The shortest G's are the eight vectors

$$\frac{2\pi}{a}\left(\pm\hat{x}\pm\hat{y}\pm\hat{z}\right). \qquad (2.24)$$

The boundaries of the central cell in the reciprocal lattice are determined, for the most part, by the eight planes normal to these vectors at their midpoints. But the corners of the octahedron thus formed are cut by the planes that are the perpendicular bisectors of six other reciprocal lattice vectors:

$$\frac{2\pi}{a}\left(\pm2\hat{x}\right);\ \frac{2\pi}{a}\left(\pm2\hat{y}\right);\ \frac{2\pi}{a}\left(\pm2\hat{z}\right). \qquad (2.25)$$

Note that $(2\pi/a)(2\hat{x})$ is a reciprocal lattice vector because it is equal to $b_2 + b_3$. The first Brillouin zone is the smallest bounded volume about the origin, the truncated octahedron shown in Figure 2.14. The six planes bound a cube of edge $4\pi/a$ and of volume $(4\pi/a)^3$. Figure 2.14 represents the most important k-space volume in semiconductor physics. We will return to the properties of this Brillouin zone repeatedly during this text.

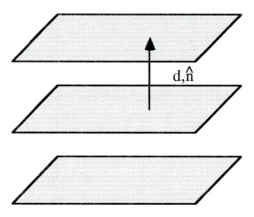

Figure 2.15: Parallel lattice planes in direct space are shown. The smallest spacing between these planes is d and $\hat{n}$ and a unit vector perpendicular to the planes.

We will now establish a theorem relating the direct and reciprocal lattices which is quite useful in understanding X-ray diffraction.

Theorem: For any family of direct lattice planes separated by distance d, there are reciprocal lattice vectors perpendicular to the planes, and the shortest of these has a length $2\pi/d$. Conversely, for any reciprocal lattice vector $\boldsymbol{G}$, there is a family of direct lattice planes normal to $\boldsymbol{G}$, and separated by distance d, where $2\pi/d$ is the length of the smallest vector parallel to $\boldsymbol{G}$.

Let $\hat{n}$ be a unit vector perpendicular to the planes in the direct lattice (see Figure 2.15). To prove that a vector $\boldsymbol{G} = (2\pi/d)\hat{n}$ is a reciprocal lattice vector, we will show that $\exp(i\boldsymbol{G} \cdot \boldsymbol{R}) = 1$ for all lattice points $\boldsymbol{R}$.

We can choose $\exp(i\boldsymbol{G} \cdot \boldsymbol{R}) = 1$ on one of the direct planes points. Since $\boldsymbol{G}$ is perpendicular to the plane, $\exp(i\boldsymbol{G} \cdot \boldsymbol{R})$ must be unity at all points of this plane. When $\boldsymbol{r}$ is translated by $\hat{n}d$, the additional phase is:

$$\begin{aligned}
\exp(i\boldsymbol{G} \cdot \hat{n}d) &= \exp(i2\pi d/d) \\
&= 1. \qquad\qquad\qquad (2.26)
\end{aligned}$$

Thus all points on other lattice planes also must satisfy $\exp(i\boldsymbol{G} \cdot \boldsymbol{R}) = 1$. In general,

$$\boldsymbol{G} = \frac{2\pi m}{d}\hat{n}. \qquad\qquad (2.27)$$

It is easy to see that if any smaller value of $\boldsymbol{G}$ is chosen (say $\hat{n}\pi/d$), $\exp(i\boldsymbol{G} \cdot \boldsymbol{R})$ will not remain unity on all planes. This theorem is useful to establish the equivalence of the Bragg and von-Laue conditions for X-ray diffraction in Chapter 3.

2.4 ARTIFICIAL STRUCTURES: SUPERLATTICES

So far in this chapter we have discussed crystal structures that are present in natural semiconductors. These structures are the lowest free energy configuration of the solid state of the atoms. Since the electronic and optical properties of the semiconductors are completely determined by the crystal structure, scientists have been intrigued with the idea of fabricating artificial structures or superlattices. Since mid-1970s, these ideas have been gaining ground, inspired by the pioneering work of Esaki and Tsu at IBM. The key to growing artificial structures with tailorable crystal structure and hence tailorable optical and electronic properties has been the progress in heteroepitaxy. Heteroepitaxial crystal growth techniques such as molecular beam epitaxy (MBE) and metal-organic chemical vapor deposition (MOCVD) have made a tremendous impact on semiconductor physics and technology. From very high speed, low noise electronic devices used for satellite communications to low threshold lasers for communication and computing, semiconductor devices are being made by these techniques. Although only compound semiconductors have benefitted from these growth techniques, so far, it appears that silicon technology is on the threshold of using heteroepitaxy for faster devices, by combing Si with Si–Ge alloys.

MBE or MOCVD are techniques which allow monolayer ($\sim$ 3 Å) control in the chemical composition of the growing crystal. Figure 2.16 shows a schematic of a typical MBE growth system. The basic components of the system are banks of Knudson cells containing the charges for the various elements to be deposited. Materials for the host crystal as well as the dopants are contained here. Highly reliable and fast shutters are mounted in front of the cells to allow abrupt change in chemical composition of the crystal. The crystal grows at a rate of about one monolayer per second or about a micron per hour. The substrate on which the growth occurs is heated to an appropriate level. For optimum control and calibration, in situ monitoring techniques, such as Reflection High Energy Electron Diffraction (RHEED), a gun is mounted. This technique will be discussed in the next chapter.

Nearly every semiconductor extending from zero bandgap (α-Sn, HgCdTe) to large bandgap materials such as ZnSe, CdS, etc., has been grown by epitaxial techniques such as MBE and MOCVD. In MBE, atoms or molecules of the species to be grown impinge upon the substrate in high vacuum. In MOCVD, the impinging species are complex molecules containing the atoms which are to form the crystal and a dissociative chemisorption reaction occurs at the surface. In either case, since the incoming species are impinging randomly, the growing surface will become very rough unless atoms can move rapidly on the surface to establish the surface free energy minimum configuration. If this free energy minimum configuration is atomically flat, it is possible to grow atomically flat heterostructures.

Since the new heteroepitaxial techniques allow one to grow heterostructures with atomic control, one can change the periodicity of the crystal in the growth direction. This leads to the concept of superlattices where two (or more)

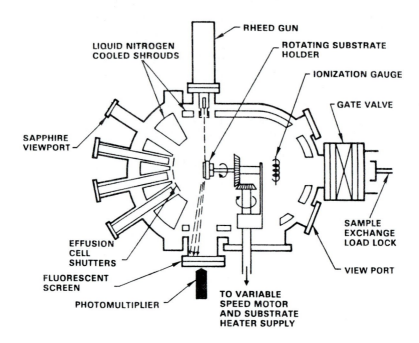

Figure 2.16: A schematic of the MBE growth system. In situ monitoring capabilities are often standard components of the system.

semiconductors A and B are grown alternately with thicknesses d_A and d_B respectively. The periodicity of the lattice in the growth direction is then $d_A + d_B$, A $(GaAs)_2(AlAs)_2$ superlattice is illustrated in Figure 2.17. It is a great testimony to the precision of the new growth techniques that values of d_A and d_B as low as one monolayer have been grown. The presence of these superlattices is revealed in X-ray diffraction, to be discussed in the next chapter, as well as in the new electronic and optical properties.

Superlattices that have been grown can be placed in three general categories: i) lattice matched, ii) strained, and iii) strained with intermediate substrate. In the lattice matched superlattices (e.g. GaAs/AlAs, HgTe/CdTe), there is a very good match between the two components forming the superlattice. Thus, there is no significant distortion in the individual unit cells making up the superlattice. These superlattices are easiest to grow and the highest quality superlattices fall in this category. The strained lattices can be classified as those where the components A and B have different lattice constants and are grown on a substrate B. In this case the thickness of the coherent superlattice is limited by the competition between the strain energy in the A region and the dislocation formation energy. These issues will be discussed in more detail in Chapter 6. For a coherent or pseudomorphic (i.e., the substrate crystallinity is maintained) structure, the region A is under strain which distorts the cubic sym-

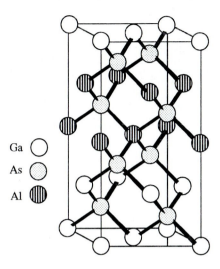

Figure 2.17: Crystal structure of a $(GaAs)_2(AlAs)_2$ superlattice.

metry. These distortions play a very important role, as will be discussed later. Figure 2.18 shows the geometrical effects of such distortion.

The strained superlattice discussed above can be grown only up to a limited thickness (critical thickness) before dislocations are generated. When the dislocations are generated, there is no longer a one-to-one correspondence between the atoms across various planes of the structure. This leads to undesirable changes in the electrical and optical properties. To avoid this problem and still utilize the benefits of built-in strain, one uses a substrate with an intermediate lattice constant. The A-B superlattice is grown on a substrate C with a lattice constant a_C which is the weighted average $(a_C = (\ell_A a_A + \ell_B a_B)/(\ell_A + \ell_B))$ of the lattice constants a_A and a_B. In this case the regions A and B are both distorted, but there is no limit to the thickness to which the crystal can be grown. Often, the substrates that are available are limited. In this case one starts with a substrate D and grows a thick buffer ($\sim$ 2–5 μm) of material C. Dislocations are then generated near the C–D interface and eventually the overlayer has the bulk lattice constant of C. This, now, may be used as a substrate on which the strained superlattice can be grown. The generation of dislocations and strain considerations will be explored in Chapter 18. Since the concept of superlattice allows one to tailor the direct space lattice, a corresponding tailorability is produced in the reciprocal space. Thus, one has a new Brillouin zone with its own high symmetry points as shown in Figure 2.19 for a superlattice along the z-direction. Note that while the period along the z-axis is increased in direct space, the period is decreased in reciprocal space.

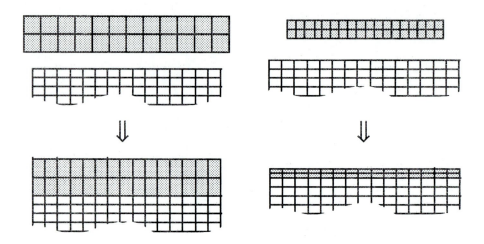

Figure 2.18: The distortion produced when an overlayer with a lattice constant different from the substrate is grown below critical thickness. The lattice of the strained layer is no longer cubic. For the case on the left-hand side, one has compression in the plane and expansion in the growth direction. For the case on the right-hand side, the expansion occurs in the growth plane and compression in the growth direction.

2.5 SURFACES: IDEAL VERSUS REAL

So far we have only considered infinite crystals with no boundaries. In reality, of course, the semiconductors are finite and have surfaces which play a very important role in their properties. Obviously, as a semiconductor structure is being grown, growth occurs at its surface. Also, when contacts are placed on semiconductors to make connection to the outside world, the nature of the surface is extremely important. In fact, in both of these cases mentioned above, apparently minor changes in the surface structure can drastically alter the physical properties.

Naively, it may appear that as long as the semiconductor is clean (no impurities), the surface structure should simply be defined by the bulk crystal structure. One simply needs to disconnect the bonds along a surface to form the surface structure. Such a surface would be called the ideal surface, and almost never occurs in nature. Upon a little reflection, it is not surprising that this is the case. The bulk crystal structure is decided by the internal chemical energy of the atoms forming the crystal with a certain number of nearest neighbors, second nearest neighbors, etc. At the surface, the number of neighbors is suddenly altered. Thus the spatial geometries which were providing the lowest energy configuration in the bulk may not provide the lowest energy configuration at the surface. Thus, there is a readjustment or reconstruction of the surface bonds towards an energy minimizing configuration.

An example of such a reconstruction is shown for the GaAs surface in

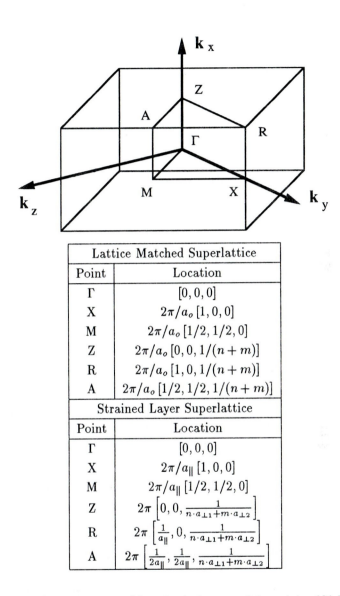

Figure 2.19: The Brillouin zone and location in k-space of the points of high symmetry in the Brillouin zone for superlattices made of n layers of material 1 and m layers of material 2, can be characterized by a parallel lattice constant and two different perpendicular lattice constants.

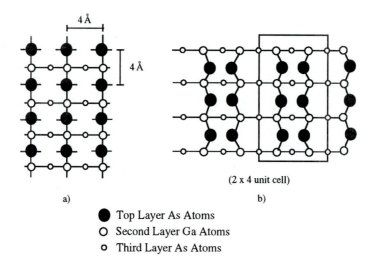

(2 x 4 unit cell)

a)   b)

● Top Layer As Atoms
○ Second Layer Ga Atoms
o Third Layer As Atoms

Figure 2.20: The structure (a) of the unreconstructed GaAs (001) arsenic-rich surface. The missing dimer model (b) for the GaAs (001) (2 × 4) surface. The As dimers are missing to create a 4-unit periodicity.

Figure 2.20. The figure (a) shows an ideal (001) surface where the top-most atoms form a square lattice. The surface atoms have two nearest neighbor bonds (Ga–As) with the layer below, four second neighbor bonds (e.g., Ga–Ga or As–As) with the next lower layer, and four second neighbor bonds within the same layer. In a real surface, the arrangement of atoms is far more complex. We could denote the ideal surface by the symbol C(1 × 1), representing the fact that the surface periodicity is one unit by one unit of the square lattice along [110] and [$\bar{1}$10]. The reconstructed surfaces that occur in nature are generally classified as C(2 × 8) or C(2 × 4), representing the increased periodicity along the [$\bar{1}$10] and [110] respectively. The C(2 × 4) case is are shown schematically in Figure 2.20b, for an arsenic stabilized surface (i.e., the top monolayer is As). The As atoms on the surface form dimers (along [$\bar{1}$10]) on the surface to strengthen their bonds. In addition, rows of missing dimers cause a longer range ordering as shown to increase the periodicity along the [110] direction to cause a C(2 × 4) or C(4 × 2) unit cell. The surface periodicity is directly reflected in the diffraction pattern to be discussed in the next chapter.

A similar effect occurs for the (110) surface of GaAs. This surface has both Ga and As atoms (the cations and anions) on the surface. A strong driving force exists to move the surface atoms, as shown in Figure 2.21c, to minimize the surface energy. Reconstruction effects also occur in silicon surfaces, where depending upon surface conditions a variety of reconstructions are observed. Surface reconstructions are very important, since often the quality of the epitaxial crystal growth depends critically on the surface reconstruction.

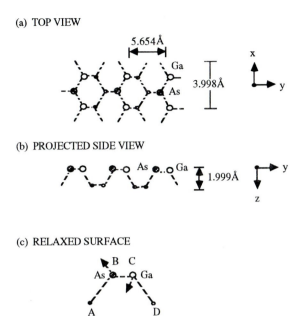

Figure 2.21: Schematic diagram showing the ideal (110) surface of GaAs in (a) and (b). Figure (c) shows the movement of the Ga and As atoms at the surface to lower the energy.

2.6 INTERFACES

Like surfaces, interfaces are an integral part of semiconductor devices. We have already discussed the concept of heterostructures and superlattices which involve interfaces between two semiconductors. These interfaces are usually of high quality with essentially no broken bonds (except for dislocations in strained structures). There is nevertheless an interface roughness of one or two monolayers which is produced because of either nonideal growth conditions or imprecise shutter control in the switching of the semiconductor species. The general picture of such a rough interface is, as shown in Figure 2.22, for epitaxially grown interfaces. The crystallinity and periodicity in the underlying lattice is maintained, but the chemical species have some disorder on interfacial planes. Such a disorder is quite important in many opto-electronic devices.

One of the most important interfaces is the Si/SiO_2 interface. This interface and its quality is responsible for essentially all of the modern consumer electronic revolution. This interface represents a situation where two materials with very different lattice constants (Figure 2.23) and crystal structures are brought together. However, in spite of these large differences the interface quality is quite good. It appears that the interface has a region of a few monolayers

AlAs (perfect crystal)

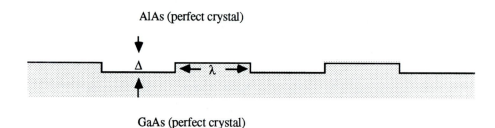

GaAs (perfect crystal)

Figure 2.22: A schematic picture of the interfaces between materials with similar lattice constants such as GaAs/AlAs. No loss of crystalline lattice and long–range order is suffered in such interfaces. The interface is characterized by islands of height Δ and lateral extent λ.

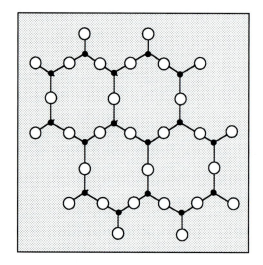

Figure 2.23: In SiO_2, the Si—O distance is 1.62 Å. Each Si atom is surrounded tetra-hedrally by four oxygen atoms. Each O atom is bonded by two Si atoms. The O—O distance is $\sim$2.65 Å(white circles – O; dark circles – Si). The figure is showing a 2-D projection of the SiO_2 network. In the Si crystal, the crystal structure is a diamond and the interatomic separation is $\sim$2.34 Å. Due to the mismatched structures, the Si/SiO_2 interface has some disorder present.

of amorphous or disordered Si—SiO_2 region creating fluctuations in the chemical species (and consequently in potential energy) across the interface. This interface roughness is responsible for reducing mobility of electrons and holes in metal–oxide–semiconductor (MOS) devices. It can also lead to trap states.

Finally, we have the interfaces formed between metals and semiconductors. Structurally, these important interfaces are hardest to characterize. These interfaces are usually produced in presence of high temperatures and involve diffusion of metal elements along with complex chemical reactions. The interfacial region usually extends over several hundred Angstroms and is a complex, non-crystalline region.

In this chapter we have learned a great deal about the periodicity and order present in crystals, in surfaces, and in interfaces. How does one really know what the order is? How does one know the atomic spacings and the complex reconstructions at the surfaces? This is the subject of the next chapter.

As a final note on this chapter, a great deal of activity is now focusing on producing lateral (i.e., in the plane *perpendicular* to the growth direction) patterning to achieve not just one-dimensional superlattice discussed above, but to produce patterned and periodic structures in two and three dimensions. This could lead to "quantum wires" and "quantum dots." The fabrication processes involved for such patterning are far more complex than the simple opening and closing of shutters for the superlattices discussed above. Thus, progress is somewhat slow. However, there are strong driving forces which will eventually allow such structures to be fabricated with high precision. Most of these driving forces come from the density of states concept discussed in Chapter 1 and its dependence on dimensionality of the structure.

2.7   FOR THE TECHNOLOGIST IN YOU

As this text develops, we will see how central the crystalline nature of semiconductors is to all our studies. The ability to fabricate high quality crystals is also critical to the success of any device fabrication technology. Clean rooms are maintained to ensure that extremely high purity is present in all phases of device fabrication. A class 10 clean room (one particle per cubic foot) is necessary for critical steps of lithography while less stringent requirements are placed on other steps.

In high quality crystals, with well-developed technologies, a perfection of one part in 100 billion can be achieved. Semiconductor device technology becomes unreliable if the level of perfection falls below one part in 10 million. This is one of the key reasons (along with doping problems) for the difficulty in fabricating devices from semiconductors such as SiC, GaN, C, etc. (all large gap materials for high power/high temperature electronics) or InSb, HgCdTe, InAs, etc. (all narrow gap semiconductors). In such semiconductors, the growth process is still not under complete control, resulting in "defective" crystals.

The device fabrication engineers and the crystal growers are famous for their love/hate relationships. Poor device characteristics are blamed on poor crystals by one and on poor processing by the other. The crystal grower is often not given his or her due in semiconductor technology, but anyone who has seen the patience and care with which a good grower "nurtures" his crystal, develops a tremendous respect for the grower. As we move through this text, it is important to appreciate that without high quality crystals, there would be no semiconductor physics or technology as we presently have it.

Over 95 percent of all semiconductor devices manufactured are fabricated in silicon. In Figure 2.24 we show the four common types of 3 inch silicon wafer used in industry. The four types are

1. (100), n-type

2. (111), n-type

3. (100), p-type

4. (111), p-type.

The figure shows how these wafers are ground with identifying flats on their edges to allow the determination of the conductivity type and crystallographic orientation which a given wafer has. The type of device or circuit to be made and the fabrication process, determines which type of wafer will be used. For example, a circuit in which the critical elements are n-channel MOS (NMOS) transistors, will be made on a (100) p-type wafer. Here, the (100) orientation is used, because it has a lower interface charge density at the Si-SiO$_2$ interface. Sometimes, the oxidation and diffusion characteristics, available in the (111) wafer are preferable. For example, in a bipolar technology, interface charge is may not be so critical. In this case, shallow junction, high speed devices can be made with (111) wafers. Oxide will grow faster on a (111) Si wafer than on a (100) wafer, resulting in less diffusion of dopants during the growth of a given thickness of oxide. In particular, this allows very narrow base widths to be maintained throughout the fabrication process.

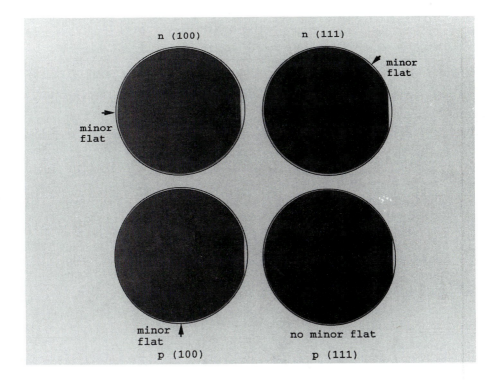

Figure 2.24: Standard wafer identification. The relative position of the minor flat with respect to the major flat serves to identify both the conductivity (either n-type or p-type) and the crystallographic orientation (either (100) or (111)). The four wafers shown here are 3 inch silicon wafers. A circle has been drawn closely around each one to help show the presence of the minor flat. The major flat is positioned on the right, for each wafer, and identifies the $< 110 >$ direction.

2.8 PROBLEMS

2.1. Find the angles between the tetrahedral bonds of a diamond lattice.

2.2. Consider a semiconductor with the zinc–blende structure (such as GaAs).

  (a) Show that the (100) plane is made up of either cation or anion type atoms.

  (b) Draw the positions of the atoms on a (110) plane assuming no surface reconstruction.

  (c) Show that there are two types of (111) surfaces: one where the surface atoms are bonded to three other atoms in the crystal, and another where the surface atoms are bonded to only one. These two types of surfaces are called the *A* and *B* surfaces, respectively.

2.3. In this chapter we have considered only the fcc Bravais lattice, since most semiconductors have this underlying structure. However, some semiconductors have the hexagonal closed packed structure. Semiconductors such as BN, AlN, GaN, InN, SiC, etc. crystallize in this structure.

Material	$c(\text{Å})$	$a(\text{Å})$
BN	4.08	2.55
AlN	4.98	3.11
GaN	5.13	3.16
InN	5.7	3.54

The hexagonal close-packed (hcp) structure is formed as shown in Figure 2.25a. A close-packed layer of spheres is formed with centers at points *A*. A second layer of spheres is placed on top of this with centers at points *B*. The third layer can be placed on points *A* (giving rise to the hcp structure) or points *C* (giving rise to the fcc structure). The hcp has the primitive cell of the hexagonal lattice with a two atom basis as shown in Figure 2.25b. The primitive cell has primitive vectors $a_1 = a_2$ and the *c*-axis (vector a_3 is parallel to *c*) normal to the a_1, a_2 plane. One atom is at the origin and the other at the point

$$r = \frac{2}{3}a_1 + \frac{1}{3}a_2 + \frac{1}{2}a_3$$

Show that the ratio c/a, $(a = a_1, a_2)$ is given by $\sqrt{8/3} = 1.633$. The values of these lattice constants for several semiconductors are given below. These semiconductors are often said to have the wurtzite structure.

2.4. Suppose that identical solid spheres are placed in space so that their centers lie on the atomic points of a crystal and the spheres on the neighboring sites touch each other. Assuming that the spheres have unit density, show that density of such spheres is the following for the various crystal structures:

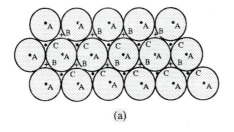

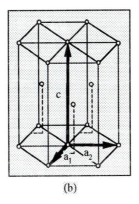

Figure 2.25: Hexagonal close-packed structure.

$$\begin{array}{ll} \text{fcc:} & \sqrt{2}\pi/6 = 0.74 \\ \text{bcc:} & \sqrt{3}\pi/8 = 0.68 \\ \text{sc:} & \pi/6 = 0.52 \\ \text{diamond:} & \sqrt{3}\pi/16 = 0.34 \end{array}$$

2.5. Show that the Brillouin zone of the fcc lattice can be reduced to 1/48 its original volume and by symmetry this irreducible zone contains all the information that the full Brillouin zone contains. This reduction is very useful since it greatly simplifies calculations for the semiconductors (see Figure 2.14 for clues).

2.6. Calculate the number of unit cells per unit volume in GaAs ($a = 5.65$ Å). Si has a 4% smaller lattice constant. What is the unit cell density for Si?

2.7. A GaAs wafer is nominally oriented along the (001) direction, but is found to be cut 2° off, towards the (110) axis. This off axis cut produces "steps" on the surface which are one monolayer high. What is the lateral spacing between the steps of the 2° off-axis wafer?

2.8. Conduct a literature search to find out what the lattice mismatch is between GaAs and AlAs at 300 K and 800 K. Calculate the mismatch between GaAs and Si at the same temperatures.

2.9. In high purity Si crystals, defect densities can be reduced to levels of 10^{13} cm^{-3}. On an average, what is the spacing between defects in such crystals? In heavily doped Si, the dopant density can approach 10^{19} cm^{-3}. What is the spacing between defects for such heavily doped semiconductors?

2.10. A surface emitting laser (SEL) structure is produced by epitaxially growing a reflector on either side of an active laser region. The reflector called a distributed Bragg reflector, consists of a periodic array of GaAs and AlGaAs layers, the periodicity, a, being given by $2a = \lambda$. In an SEL, $\lambda = 8000$ Å and the total SEL thickness is $54\lambda + 1.0$ μm. If the flux of cations (Ga, Al) is 5×10^{14} cm^{-2}s^{-1}, and all the atoms get incorporated to form the crystal, how long will it take to grow the SEL? Assume that the As atoms are present in sufficient quantity and the growth rate is controlled by cation flux only.

2.9 REFERENCES

- **Crystal Structures**

    - Buerger, M. J., *Introduction to Crystal Geometry* (McGraw–Hill, New York, 1971).

    - Lax, M., *Symmetry Principles in Solid State and Molecular Physics* (John Wiley and Sons, New York, 1974). Has a good description of the Brillouin zones of several structures in Appendix E.

    - Nye, J. F., *Physical Properties of Crystals* (Oxford, London, 1985).

    - Phillips, F. C., *An Introduction of Crystallography* (John Wiley and Sons, New York, 1971).

- **Crystal Growth; Heterostructures**

    - Cho, A. Y., J. Vac. Sci. Technol, **8**, 531, (1971).

    - Rosenberger, F., *Fundamentals of Crystal Growth* (Springer–Verlag, New York, 1979).

    - Singh, J., Rev. Sol. St. Sci., **4**, 785 (1990).

    - Wood, C. E. C., in *Physics of Thin Films* (edited by G. Haas and M. H. Francombe, Academic Press, New York, 1980).

CHAPTER
3

WAVE
DIFFRACTION
IN PERIODIC
STRUCTURES

We have been discussing crystal structures of materials in the previous chapter. How do we know the structure of a given material? We certainly cannot see the arrangements of atoms directly. Since the spacing between atoms is ~ 1 Å, we need to use a tool which has a very fine resolution. The wave properties of photons, neutrons, and electrons provide such a tool. These particles can be described by a wave picture and their wavelengths can be chosen to be in the < 1 Å range. Figure 3.1 shows the energy vs. wavelength relation for these particles.

From Figure 3.1 we see that for electrons, the energy required to make the electrons behave like 1 Å wavelength waves is ~ 100 eV, while for photons or electromagnetic waves it is $\sim 10^4$ eV. For the much heavier neutrons, the energy is only ~ 0.1 eV. All three of these tools are widely used to characterize periodic structures and the basic theory of how these tools work is qualitatively the same.

The idea behind using waves to characterize periodicity is borrowed from optics, where it is well known that if light passes through a periodic diffraction grating, well defined peaks are observed at a detector placed behind the grating. The spacing of these peaks (i.e., the order of diffraction) depends upon the grating period and the wavelengths of light. Normally, one works with visible light with $\lambda \sim 4000$–8000 Å and the diffraction grating period is of this order. When X-rays were first discovered by Roentgen in 1895, attempt was made (see for example Leighton, 1959) to use very narrow slits to find their wavelength. These attempts were only marginally successful and only gave an order of magnitude estimate. The theorist M. Laue was the first to conceive, in 1912, of the possibility of using crystals as a diffracting medium. In collaboration with Friedrich and

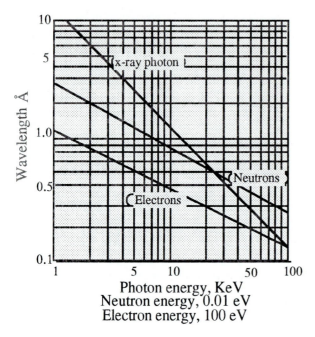

photons: $E = \dfrac{hc}{\lambda}$

finite mass particles: $p = \dfrac{h}{\lambda}$

Figure 3.1: Wavelength versus particle energy for photons, neutrons, and electrons.

Knipping, he was able to succeed in obtaining a diffraction pattern from rock salt. Thus a very precise means was available to find the wavelength if the crystal lattice was known or vice versa. This was the birth of a most important technique in solid state physics. The father and son team of W. H. Bragg and W. L. Bragg conducted very detailed work on crystal structure and established the framework to obtain crystal structure from X-ray diffraction patterns. We will see that if the wavelength of the impinging particles is comparable to lattice spacings, diffracted beams emerge in directions quite different from those given by simple reflection and refraction laws, and give us detailed information on the lattice.

3.1 BRAGG'S LAW

We will now derive the Bragg law for diffraction from a crystal. Consider a plane wave to be incident on a series of parallel lattice planes separated by a distance d. We assume that after diffraction, *the energy of the X-rays is not altered* (i.e., we have elastic scattering). The optical path difference for rays reflected from adjacent planes is $2d \sin \theta$, where θ is measured from the plane as shown in Figure 3.2. Constructive interference between these waves occurs when the path difference satisfies the relation

$$2d \sin \theta = n\lambda. \tag{3.1}$$

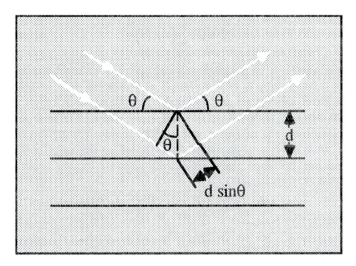

Figure 3.2: Derivation of the Bragg equation $2d\sin\theta = n\lambda$; here d is the spacing of parallel atomic planes and $2\pi n$ is the difference in phase between reflections from successive planes. The reflecting planes are not the surface planes bounding the particular specimen, and represent the planes inside the crystal.

This equation has solutions only if $\lambda < 2d$. If this condition is satisfied then for a given set of lattice planes, the X-ray diffraction pattern will be strong for values of θ_1, θ_2, ... for choices of $n = 1$, 2 .... In general, if the X-rays are incident on a crystal, diffraction spots can be seen on a fluorescent screen or a film, since there are some lattice planes for which the diffraction condition will be satisfied.

As an example of Bragg conditions, say $\lambda = 1.54$ Å, and we have a cubic structure with lattice constants of 4 Å

$$
\begin{aligned}
\theta_1 &= \sin^{-1}(\lambda/2d) = 11.1° \\
\theta_2 &= \sin^{-1}(\lambda/d) = 22.6° \\
\theta_3 &= 35.3°, \text{ etc.}
\end{aligned}
\tag{3.2}
$$

Remember, however, that in the cubic structure there are other lattice planes such as (110), (111), (211), ..., which are separated by distances different from the 4 Å lattice constant. All of these planes will also cause Bragg diffraction, but at different angles from the ones calculated above. So the interpretation of the X-ray pattern is not that simple. We will later do an explicit example to see how one gets the information about the lattice structure. So far, we have not mentioned anything about a basis in the crystal structure. The presence of two or more atoms on each lattice site makes the diffraction pattern even more complex. A more useful representation of the diffraction conditions, which is extended by complicated structures with ease, is given by the Laue equations discussed next.

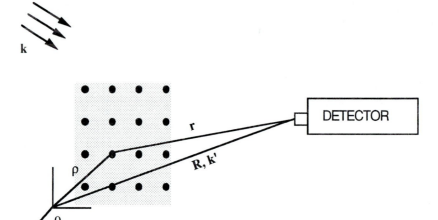

Figure 3.3: Geometry showing a plane wave with wave vector k impinging upon a crystal. The scattered wave with wave vector k' is detected by a detector at point R. The detector position is far compared to the size of the crystal.

3.2 LAUE CONDITIONS

We will now discuss the alternate derivation of the diffraction theory using scattering theory for optical waves. This approach is more suitable for developing a simple picture for interpreting complex diffraction data and also establishes the importance of the reciprocal lattices discussed in Chapter 2.

Consider a plane wave described by a field

$$\boldsymbol{F}(\boldsymbol{r}) = \boldsymbol{F}_0 \exp i \left(\boldsymbol{k} \cdot \boldsymbol{r} - \omega t\right) \tag{3.3}$$

impinging on a periodic arrangement of atoms. According to the scattering theory, the incident wave interacts with the atoms, which then send off a scattered *spherical* wave which has a value at point $\boldsymbol{R}$ given by

$$
\begin{aligned}
\boldsymbol{F}_{sc}(\boldsymbol{r}) &= f\boldsymbol{F}(\rho)\frac{e^{ikr}}{r} \\
&= f\boldsymbol{F}_0 \frac{e^{i\boldsymbol{k}\cdot\rho}e^{i(kr-\omega t)}}{r}
\end{aligned}
\tag{3.4}
$$

where

$$r \approx R - \rho \cos\left(\rho, \boldsymbol{R}\right). \tag{3.5}$$

Here f is a scattering factor representing the fraction of the incident wave that is scattered by an atom. $\boldsymbol{R}$ represents the position of a detector far from the crystal and $\boldsymbol{r}$ is the coordinate of the atom causing the scattering (see Figure 3.3).

Since

$$\begin{aligned}
|\boldsymbol{R}| &> |\boldsymbol{\rho}| \\
r &\approx R
\end{aligned} \tag{3.6}$$

and we can replace r in the denominator of Equation 3.5 by R. However, we cannot make this approximation in the phase term, which becomes

$$e^{i[\mathbf{k}\cdot\rho+kr]} = e^{i[\mathbf{k}\cdot\rho+kR-k\rho\cos(\rho,\mathbf{R})]} \tag{3.7}$$

Here we replace $k\rho\cos(\boldsymbol{\rho}, \boldsymbol{R})$ by $\boldsymbol{k}' \cdot \boldsymbol{\rho}$, where $\boldsymbol{k}'$ is the scattered wave along the direction $\boldsymbol{R}$. This gives

$$\begin{aligned}
e^{i[\mathbf{k}\cdot\rho+kr]} &= e^{ikR}e^{i[\mathbf{k}\cdot\rho-\mathbf{k}'\cdot\rho]} \\
&= e^{ikR}e^{-i\rho\cdot\Delta\mathbf{k}}
\end{aligned} \tag{3.8}$$

where

$$\Delta\boldsymbol{k} = \boldsymbol{k}' - \boldsymbol{k} \tag{3.9}$$

is the change in the wave vector.

We now sum the signal from all atoms on the lattice sites

$$\boldsymbol{F}_{sc}(\boldsymbol{R}) = \sum_{m,n,p} \left(\boldsymbol{F}_0 \frac{e^{ikR}e^{-i\omega t}}{R} \right) \left[\exp\left(-i\boldsymbol{\rho}_{mnp} \cdot \Delta\boldsymbol{k}\right) f_{mnp} \right] \tag{3.10}$$

where m, n, p represent the coordinates of the lattice site at point $\boldsymbol{\rho}$. The scattering amplitude can be written as

$$\boldsymbol{F}_{sc}(\boldsymbol{R}) = \boldsymbol{F}_0 \frac{e^{ikR}e^{-i\omega t}}{R} \sum_{m,n,p} f_{mnp} \exp\left(-i\boldsymbol{\rho}_{mnp} \cdot \Delta\boldsymbol{k}\right). \tag{3.11}$$

If we assume that f_{mnp} is the same for all sites (we will discuss the effect of more than one type of atom basis later), the summation is nonzero (for a large number of sites) if

$$\boldsymbol{\rho}_{mnp} \cdot \Delta\boldsymbol{k} = 2\pi n \tag{3.12}$$

where n is any integer. However, this is the definition of a reciprocal lattice vector. Thus $\Delta\boldsymbol{k}$ or the scattering vector has to be a reciprocal lattice vector, (see Equation 2.11), for non-zero scattered intensity. *The condition for strong diffraction intensity is satisfied only when the wave vector is scattered by a reciprocal lattice vector.* This is an extremely important representation of the diffraction conditions from the periodic arrangement of atoms. Remember that this condition depended upon the relation

$$\sum_i e^{i\mathbf{G}\cdot\mathbf{R}_i} = 0 \tag{3.13}$$

unless

$$\boldsymbol{G} \cdot \boldsymbol{R}_i = 2\pi, \text{ for all } i. \tag{3.14}$$

3.2.1   Equivalence of Bragg and Laue Diffraction Conditions

A simple examination of the Bragg and Laue conditions shows that the two are equivalent. For this we make use of the theorem proven in Chapter 2 (see Equations 2.26 and 2.27). Remembering that the scattering angle $\phi = 2\theta$, where θ is the Bragg angle, we have (see Figure 3.10 for details):

$$G = k - k'$$
$$\Rightarrow |G| = 2|k|\sin(\phi/2) \qquad (3.15)$$

since $|G| = 2\pi n/d$, and $|k| = 2\pi/\lambda$, we get

$$2d\sin\theta = n\lambda \qquad (3.16)$$

which is the Bragg law.

3.3   DIFFRACTION FROM RANDOM SCATTERERS

If the arrangement of atoms is totally *random* the phases from different sites will cancel each other producing a much smaller scattered intensity. To appreciate this, let us take the square of the scattered amplitude to get the scattered intensity

$$I_{sc} \propto \left| \sum_i e^{i G \cdot R_i} \right| \cdot \left| \sum_j e^{-i G \cdot R_j} \right| \qquad (3.17)$$

or

$$I_{sc} \propto \left| \sum_i e^{i G \cdot R_i} e^{-i G \cdot R_i} + \sum_i \sum_{j \neq i} e^{i G \cdot (R_i - R_j)} \right| \qquad (3.18)$$

The first term is equal to N, the number of sites that are causing the scattering. The second term involves the correlations of terms from different sites. If we have the condition

$$G \cdot (R_i - R_j) = G \cdot R_{ij}$$
$$= 2\pi n \qquad (3.19)$$

for all scattering sites, the second term is equal to $N(N-1) \approx N^2$. Thus, for a perfectly periodic lattice where reciprocal lattice vectors exist and satisfy the condition of Equation 3.19, we get

$$I_{sc} \propto N^2 \qquad (3.20)$$

On the other hand, if the atoms are randomly distributed, the second term in Equation 3.18 gives no contribution and the intensity is simply

$$I_{sc} \propto N \qquad (3.21)$$

Although these relations are based on very simple concepts, they are extremely important in the general theory of scattering. Here we are discussing scattering from a perfect arrangement of atoms, which leads to very strong scattered intensity every time the Laue conditions are satisfied. In transport theory, we will discuss scattering of electrons from random impurities, where each scattering site scatters independently of other sites. In a real crystal, the atoms are not arranged perfectly on a lattice, but may have some fluctuations away from the periodic sites. This may be for a variety of reasons, such as extrinsic defects, strain fields, and imperfect growth techniques. The general position of the atom is then

$$R_i = R_i^0 + \Delta R_i \tag{3.22}$$

where ΔR_i is a small fixed (i.e. time independent) deviation away from the perfect lattice site. Very often, in epitaxial growth, small tilts are produced because of small mismatch in material properties of the substrate and the overlayer. In such a case, ignoring the uncorrelated scattering term in the intensity, we get

$$I_{sc} \propto \sum_i \sum_j e^{i\Delta k \cdot (R_i - R_j)} \tag{3.23}$$

where $\Delta k = k - k'$ is the scattering vector and depends upon the angle between the directions of the incident and scattered wave. As noted above, for random arrangement of the atoms, the scattered intensity will have no angular dependence (Figure 3.4a). For the perfect arrangement, the sum will be large only for Δk equaling a reciprocal lattice vector. For the case where there are deviations from the perfect structure, the scattered intensity will have a dependence shown schematically in Figure 3.4b. Focusing on a particular diffraction peak, the scattered intensity may be written as

$$
\begin{aligned}
I_{sc} \quad &\propto \quad \sum_i \sum_j e^{i\Delta k \cdot (R_i - R_j)} \\
&= \quad \sum_i \sum_j e^{i\Delta k \cdot R_{ij}^0} \cdot e^{i\Delta k \cdot \Delta R_{ij}}
\end{aligned}
\tag{3.24}
$$

where

$$\Delta R_{ij} = \Delta R_i - \Delta R_j. \tag{3.25}$$

If we write

$$\Delta k = G^0 + \Delta G \tag{3.26}$$

where G^0 is a reciprocal lattice vector for the perfect lattice. We can define the ratio

$$
\begin{aligned}
\frac{I_{sc}(G^0 + \Delta G)}{I_{sc}(G^0)} \quad &= \quad \frac{\sum_j e^{iG^0 \cdot R_{ij}^0} \, e^{iG^0 \cdot \Delta R_{ij}} \, e^{i\Delta G \cdot R_{ij}^0} \, e^{i\Delta G \cdot \Delta R_{ij}}}{\sum_j e^{iG^0 \cdot R_{ij}^0} \, e^{iG^0 \cdot \Delta R_{ij}}} \\
&= \quad \frac{\sum_{i,j} e^{iG^0 \cdot \Delta R_{ij}} \, e^{i\Delta G \cdot R_{ij}^0} \, e^{i\Delta G \cdot \Delta R_{ij}}}{\sum_{i,j} e^{iG^0 \cdot \Delta R_{ij}}}.
\end{aligned}
\tag{3.27}
$$

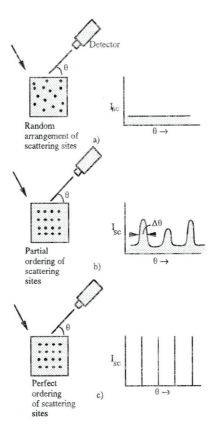

Figure 3.4: Effect of structural randomness on the scattering intensity dependence on scattering angle.

To proceed any further quantitatively, we must have more detailed understanding of ΔR_{ij}. In general, even for $\Delta G \neq 0$, we will get a finite intensity leading to a width in the diffraction peak as illustrated in Figure 3.4b.

Consider, for example, the case of amorphous semiconductors like amorphous silicon (a-Si), an important material for low-cost solar cell technology. This material has no long-range order, but does have strong short-range correlation. This means qualitatively, that if the position of an atom in a-Si is known, one is able to predict the position of the neighboring 10–12 atoms quite accurately, but one has no definitive way of predicting, say, an atom 100 Å away. In spite of this loss of the long-range order, the X-ray diffraction of such materials are *not featureless* and can provide very useful information.

The width ($\Delta\theta$ of Figure 3.4b) is a very important property of a particular crystal and provides information on how "perfect" the crystal is. This information is often obtained by carrying out rocking curve measurements to be described later. This width is also particularly useful in studying how perfect the artificial

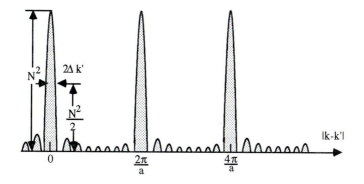

Figure 3.5: Plot of the function $\sin^2(N\Delta ka/2)/\sin^2(\Delta ka/2)$ as a function of $(k-k')/k$.

superlattices discussed in Chapter 2 are.

Before continuing with our study of perfect and *infinite* crystals, let us examine another source of the broadening of the X-ray peaks. Even if the crystal is perfect, but has a *finite* size, the diffraction conditions are somewhat relaxed. Normally, this would not be an important concern, since the number of atoms in most crystals is very large. However, with new epitaxial techniques and ability to fabricate nanostructures (of dimensions $\sim$100 Å – 1000 Å), finite size effects are important. For simplicity, consider a chain of N atoms separated by a distance a. The scattering amplitude has a phase term given by

$$
\begin{aligned}
S &= \sum_{n=0}^{N-1} \exp(in\Delta ka) \\
&= \frac{1 - \exp(iN\Delta ka)}{1 - \exp(i\Delta ka)} \\
&= \frac{\exp(iN\Delta ka/2)\sin(N\Delta ka/2)}{\exp(i\Delta ka/2)\sin(\Delta ka/2)}.
\end{aligned}
\tag{3.28}
$$

The intensity is then

$$
I_{sc} \propto \frac{\sin^2(N\Delta ka/2)}{\sin^2(\Delta ka/2)}.
\tag{3.29}
$$

This expression is plotted in Figure 3.5. The maxima of this function lie at points given by

$$
\begin{aligned}
\frac{\Delta ka}{2} &= \frac{(k-k')a}{2} \\
&= m\pi
\end{aligned}
\tag{3.30}
$$

where m is an integer. The value of the intensity at these maxima are given by taking the ratio of the derivatives of the numerator and denominator (l'Hopital's rule) and is just N^2. The condition of Equation 3.30 is just the Laue condition.

However, since N is finite, the peaks have a finite width. The width at half intensity is given by solving for $\Delta k'$, in the equation

$$\frac{\sin^2(N\Delta k' a/2)}{\sin^2(\Delta k' a/2)} = \frac{N^2}{2}. \tag{3.31}$$

Since $\Delta k'$ is expected to be small, we can write approximately, for the equation,

$$\frac{\sin^2\left(N\Delta k' a/2\right)}{\sin^2\left(\Delta k' a/2\right)} \approx \frac{\sin^2\left(N\Delta k' a/2\right)}{\left(\Delta k' a/2\right)^2}$$

$$\approx \frac{N^2}{2}. \tag{3.32}$$

This equation is of the form

$$\sin^2 x = \frac{x^2}{2}$$

with

$$x = \frac{N\Delta k' a}{2} \tag{3.33}$$

The solution of this equation is $x \approx 1.38$ so that

$$\Delta k' a = \frac{2.76}{N} \tag{3.34}$$

Clearly, if N is large, the width of the peak goes to zero.

This general formalism is also applicable when the crystal is made up of microcrystallites (or has short-range order). Each microcrystal would have a small number of atoms leading to an X-ray diffraction with broadened peaks.

3.3.1   Scattering Factor f_{mnp}

So far we have assumed that the scattering factor f_{mnp} is the same for all the scatterings and that there is only one atom per basis. We know, of course, that for semiconductors, there are at least two atoms per basis. For artificially fabricated superlattices, there are a large number of atoms per basis. We will now generalize the conditions for diffraction peaks for such cases.

In the scattering theory derivation of Laue conditions, we carried out a sum over all lattice sites assuming a single atom on each site. Let us now assume that there are n atoms per basis and the positions of the atoms we described by the two sets of coordinates (see Figure 3.6):

1. ρ_{mnp} for the position of a unit cell.

2. ρ_j for the position of an atom j in the unit cell.

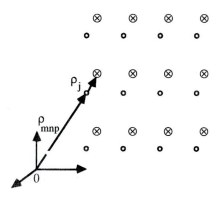

Figure 3.6: Scattering from a crystal with more than one atom per basis. The vector ρ_{mnp} represents the position to the (mnp) cell, and ρ_j represents the coordinates of the atoms within a given cell.

Going back to our derivation for the scattered amplitude, we get

$$F(k, k', R) = F_0 \frac{e^{i(kR-\omega t)}}{R} \sum_{mnp} \sum_j f_j \exp\left[-i(\rho_{mnp} + \rho_j) \cdot \Delta k\right] \qquad (3.35)$$

where we describe the scattering from each of the basis atoms by f_j which are, in general, different for different atoms.

The summation over phases is separated into two summations – one over the lattice sites and one over the atoms in the basis:

$$F(k, k', R)_{sc} = F_0 \frac{e^{i(kR-\omega t)}}{R} \sum_{mnp} \exp\left[-i\rho_{mnp} \cdot \Delta k\right]$$

$$\times \sum_j f_j \exp\left[-i\rho_j \cdot \Delta k\right]. \qquad (3.36)$$

The first summation gives us the condition $\Delta k = G$, a reciprocal lattice vector, as before. The second sum within the unit cell is called the structure factor, S_G:

$$S_G = \sum_j f_j \exp\left[-i\rho_j \cdot G\right]. \qquad (3.37)$$

Thus the X-ray diffraction pattern is obtained by *first considering only the lattice points and then modulating the results by the structure factor.*

We will now examine the structure factors for a few simple lattices. A good example for calculating the structure factor and the diffraction conditions is the diamond lattice. As we have discussed earlier, since the diamond lattice is not a Bravais lattice, one has to describe it by an fcc lattice with a two atom basis. The two atoms can be defined by

$$\rho_1 = 0$$
$$\rho_2 = \frac{a}{4}(\hat{x} + \hat{y} + \hat{z}). \qquad (3.38)$$

We also know that the reciprocal lattice vectors are those of a bcc lattice with primitive vectors:

$$
\begin{aligned}
\boldsymbol{b}_1 &= \frac{2\pi}{a}\left(-\hat{x}+\hat{y}+\hat{z}\right) \\[4pt]
\boldsymbol{b}_2 &= \frac{2\pi}{a}\left(\hat{x}-\hat{y}+\hat{z}\right) \\[4pt]
\boldsymbol{b}_3 &= \frac{2\pi}{a}\left(\hat{x}+\hat{y}-\hat{z}\right).
\end{aligned}
\tag{3.39}
$$

and the general reciprocal vector (equal to scattered vectors, $\boldsymbol{k}'-\boldsymbol{k}$, for diffraction peaks) is

$$
\boldsymbol{G} = n_1\boldsymbol{b}_1 + n_2\boldsymbol{b}_2 + n_3\boldsymbol{b}_3.
\tag{3.40}
$$

In an fcc crystal with one atom basis, all values of n_1, n_2, n_3 would lead to a diffraction peak. Let us consider the diamond lattice now. The structure factor is

$$
\begin{aligned}
S_{\boldsymbol{G}} &= f\left(1+\exp\left[\frac{i\pi}{2}(n_1+n_2+n_3)\right]\right) \\[4pt]
&= 2f, \quad\quad\; \text{if } n_1+n_2+n_3 \text{ is twice an even number,} \\[4pt]
&= (1\pm i)f, \; \text{if } n_1+n_2+n_3 \text{ is odd,} \\[4pt]
&= 0, \quad\quad\quad\; \text{if } n_1+n_2+n_3 \text{ is twice an odd number.}
\end{aligned}
\tag{3.41}
$$

We thus see that the diffraction conditions for the diamond lattice are the same as that for the fcc lattice, *except* for the peak which would have occurred when $n_1+n_2+n_3$ is equal to twice an odd number. The diamond lattice thus has *missing diffraction spots* as compared to the fcc lattice.

In this discussion, we have assumed that for the diamond lattice (Si, Ge, etc.), the factor f is the same for the two atoms of the basis. However, if we have a zinc–blende structure, this factor will be different for the two atoms in general. Although it is difficult to calculate f directly, it is important to identify its origin.

The factor f introduced in our discussion is called the atomic form factor and represents how the atom scatters the X-ray impinging upon it. The electric field of the X-ray interacts with the Coulombic charge density $\rho(\boldsymbol{r})$ of the atom. In general, the atomic factor has the form

$$
f_j(\boldsymbol{k},\boldsymbol{k}') = \frac{1}{e}\int d^3r\; e^{i(\boldsymbol{k}-\boldsymbol{k}')\cdot\boldsymbol{r}}\rho_j(\boldsymbol{r}).
\tag{3.42}
$$

The factor $1/e$ is simply to make the factor dimensionless. Since the internal charge distribution is different for different atoms, the form factor will also be different. Note that we have not proven Equation 3.42. This equation is based upon scattering theory which we will discuss in Chapter 11.

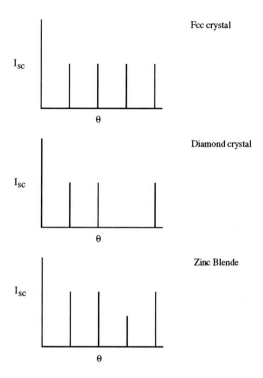

Figure 3.7: Schematic illustration of the effect of structure factor in eliminating some diffraction peaks in the diamond lattice and reducing their intensity in the zinc–blende structure.

Coming back now to the structure factor of the zinc–blende structure with the two atoms having the atomic form factors f_1 and f_2, in analogy to Equation 3.41, we get

$$
\begin{aligned}
S_{\mathbf{G}} &= \left(f_1 + f_2 \exp\left[\frac{i\pi}{2}(n_1 + n_2 + n_3) \right] \right) \\
&= f_1 + f_2, \quad \text{if } n_1 + n_2 + n_3 \text{ is twice an even number} \\
&= f_1 \pm i f_2, \quad \text{if } n_1 + n_2 + n_3 \text{ is odd} \\
&= f_1 - f_2, \quad \text{if } n_1 + n_2 + n_3 \text{ is twice an odd number.} \quad (3.43)
\end{aligned}
$$

Since $f_1 \neq f_2$ in general, diffraction conditions for all $\mathbf{G}$'s are allowed. The zinc–blende structure, therefore, has the same diffraction spots as the fcc lattice except that some of the peaks are very weak. Figure 3.7 illustrates these concepts schematically.

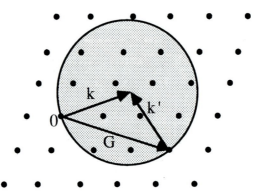

Figure 3.8: The Ewald construction. The scattered vector k' satisfies the Laue condition.

3.4 DIFFRACTION METHODS

3.4.1 The Ewald Construction

Based on the Laue conditions that require that the scattered wavevector ($\Delta k = k - k'$) be equal to the reciprocal lattice vector, a very simple geometric construction was developed by Ewald. We start with working in the reciprocal space and drawing out the reciprocal lattice points. Choosing one of these lattice points as origin, we draw the wave vector k (magnitude $= 2\pi/\lambda_{X-ray}$) of the incident X-rays, centered on the origin (Figure 3.8). Now we draw a sphere with its origin at the tip of the k–vector. Now there will be some vector k' satisfying the Laue conditions *if the surface of the sphere intersects with any reciprocal lattice points.* If this does occur, there will be a diffracted beam corresponding to the reciprocal lattice vector G of Figure 3.8. Note, however, that one still needs to calculate the structure factor S_G to check the intensity of the diffracted peak.

The various experimental techniques to carry out X-ray diffraction studies can now be understood quite simply on the basis of the Ewald construction.

3.4.2 The Laue Method

In this technique, the crystal is placed on a fixed holder and the X-ray source is also at a fixed position. For a single wavelength source, such a configuration may not give any diffraction peak in general. But in the Laue method, the X-ray source has wavelengths over a continuous range from λ_0 to λ_1. The Ewald sphere is thus expanded from a single surface to a region between two spheres of radius $|k_0| = 2\pi/\lambda_0$ to $|k_1| = 2\pi/\lambda_1$ as shown in Figure 3.9. There is, therefore, a good probability of finding some reciprocal lattice vector and a corresponding scattered X-ray wavevector that satisfies the Laue condition. The spread in the wavelengths between λ_0 and λ_1 is kept small so that only a few diffraction conditions are created, so that the data can be interpreted simply.

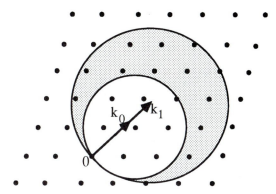

Figure 3.9: The Laue Method. Any reciprocal lattice point lying in the shaded area will give a diffraction spot.

The Laue method is probably best suited for determining the orientation of a single crystal specimen whose structure is known, since, for example, if the incident direction lies along a symmetry axis of the crystal, the pattern of spots produced by the Bragg reflected rays will have the same symmetry. Since solid state physicists generally do study materials of known crystal structure, the Laue method is probably the one of greatest practical interest.

3.4.3 The Rotating Crystal Method

In this technique, the crystal is placed on a holder which can be rotated with great precision. The X-ray source is fixed and has only a single wavelength. As the crystal is rotated, at some angle, Bragg conditions are satisfied and a diffraction pattern is observed. In the Ewald construction, this is equivalent to rotating the reciprocal lattice vectors about the axis of rotation of the crystal and checking out the procedure for diffraction conditions by the Ewald construction. As long as the X-ray wave vector is not too small, at some angles of rotation, a reciprocal lattice vector will intersect the Ewald sphere.

3.4.4 The Powder or Debye–Scherrer Method

This method is extremely useful for crystals which are available in powder forms or have microcrystallites. As shown in Figure 3.10, the X-rays are incident upon the sample, which is on a fixed holder and the diffraction pattern is recorded on a film strip. It may appear that since one has small crystals randomly oriented in the powder, it would be impossible to determine the crystal structure since all the diffraction patterns will merge with each other. However, this is not the case as will be seen shortly.

In the powder method, the scattering angle ϕ is observed by recording the

Figure 3.10: The use of the powder method to study the crystal structure. The scattering angles ϕ are recorded on a film as shown.

diffraction pattern. From Figure 3.10, we can see that the Laue condition is

$$\begin{aligned} \Delta k &= 2k\sin(\phi/2) \\ &= G \end{aligned} \tag{3.44}$$

where G is the length of a reciprocal lattice vector of the crystals in the powder. If one has some idea of the general nature of the crystal structure (i.e., fcc, diamond, etc.), one can then find the crystal properties, as discussed in the following example. Let us calculate the *first four* scattering angles for an fcc crystal, a diamond structure, and a zinc-blende structure. Note that the scattering angle ϕ is twice the Bragg angle θ of Equation 3.1.

According to Equation 3.44, we have

$$\sin\frac{\phi_1}{2} : \sin\frac{\phi_2}{2} : \sin\frac{\phi_3}{2} : \sin\frac{\phi_4}{2}\ldots\sin\frac{\phi_N}{2} = G_1 : G_2 : G_3 : G_4\ldots G_N \tag{3.45}$$

where $G_1\ldots G_N$ are the magnitudes of the first N reciprocal lattice vectors of the crystal being considered. *Remember, however, that one has to check the structure factors $S_{\mathbf{G}}$ to make sure that the diffraction intensity is nonzero.* For the fcc lattice, the reciprocal lattice unit vectors are

$$\begin{aligned} \mathbf{b}_1 &= \frac{2\pi}{a}(-\hat{x} + \hat{y} + \hat{z}) \\[2mm] \mathbf{b}_2 &= \frac{2\pi}{a}(\hat{x} - \hat{y} + \hat{z}) \\[2mm] \mathbf{b}_3 &= \frac{2\pi}{a}(\hat{x} + \hat{y} - \hat{z}). \end{aligned} \tag{3.46}$$

and a general reciprocal vector is

$$\mathbf{G} = n_1\mathbf{b}_1 + n_2\mathbf{b}_2 + n_3\mathbf{b}_3. \tag{3.47}$$

A sequence of reciprocal lattice vectors with increasing magnitude is

$$\begin{aligned} n_1 = 0; \quad n_2 = 0; \quad n_3 = 1 \;&\Rightarrow\; G_1 = 2\pi\sqrt{3}/a \\ n_1 = 1; \quad n_2 = 1; \quad n_3 = 0 \;&\Rightarrow\; G_2 = 4\pi/a \\ n_1 = 1; \quad n_2 = 2; \quad n_3 = 1 \;&\Rightarrow\; G_3 = 4\pi\sqrt{2}/a \\ n_1 = 2; \quad n_2 = 1; \quad n_3 = 0 \;&\Rightarrow\; G_4 = 2\pi\sqrt{11}/a \\ n_1 = 2; \quad n_2 = 0; \quad n_3 = 0 \;&\Rightarrow\; G_5 = 4\pi\sqrt{3}/a, \end{aligned} \tag{3.48}$$

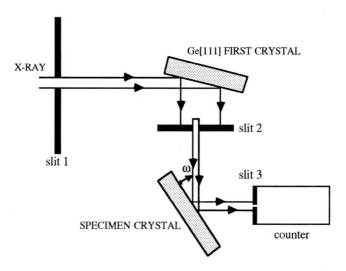

Figure 3.11: Geometry of X-ray double–crystal diffractometer.

and so on. Thus the ratio of the Equation 3.45 becomes

$$\sin\frac{\phi_1}{2} : \sin\frac{\phi_2}{2} : \sin\frac{\phi_3}{2} : \sin\frac{\phi_4}{2} = 1 : 1.5 : 1.63 : 1.91 . \tag{3.49}$$

For the fcc structure, all these angles are allowed since no structure factor is involved. For the diamond lattice, from Equation 3.41 we know that $S_{\mathbf{G}_2} = 0$, so that the ratio of the first few observed diffraction spots is

$$\sin\frac{\phi_1}{2} : \sin\frac{\phi_2}{2} : \sin\frac{\phi_3}{2} = 1 : 1.63 : 1.91 . \tag{3.50}$$

On the other hand, for the zinc–blende case, the structure factor for $S_{\mathbf{G}_2}$ is not zero but is very small. Thus, in this case, the same angles will be observed as for the fcc lattice, but the intensity of the second peak will be weak. The example above shows how one has to systematically analyze and obtain the crystal structure.

3.4.5 Double Crystal Diffraction

This is an extremely powerful measurement technique which is often used to study very detailed aspects of crystalline materials. Due to its sensitivity, it is often used to study heterostructures where it can detect small strain values, non-epitaxial regions, and different thicknesses making up the heterostructure. A typical setup for this technique is shown in Figure 3.11. A high quality crystal (Ge in the figure) is used as the first crystal. A diffracted beam from this crystal is now selected to impinge upon the sample crystal being studied. When the Bragg angles for the two crystals are identical, very narrow diffraction peaks are observed. To obtain the rocking curves, which provide information on the long-range structural order of the crystal, the specimen is rotated by a small angle ω, and the differential beam intensity is recorded. High quality crystals have peaks with widths of a few seconds of an arc. This technique is particularly useful for epitaxial layers grown on a thick substrate. In general, for such cases, two diffraction peaks are observed, one from the substrate and one from the epilayer. The difference $\Delta\omega$ in the crystal setting angle for Bragg reflection of the substrate and layer has two components, $\Delta\theta$ and $\Delta\phi$. The difference in the lattice plane spacing $\Delta d/d$ for corresponding lattice planes of layer and substrate causes a difference in Bragg angle $\Delta\theta$. The second component of $\Delta\omega$ is the difference $\Delta\phi$ in the inclination with the surface of corresponding lattice planes of layer and substrate.

3.5   TEMPERATURE DEPENDENT EFFECTS

In the discussions we have had so far for diffraction, we assumed that the positions of the scattering atoms are fixed. In reality, of course, we know that the atoms are vibrating, due to the finite temperature of the crystal. In fact, even at $T = 0$ K, there is some vibration of the crystals, according to quantum mechanics. What effect does this vibration have on the X-ray diffraction? It may seem initially that as the atoms vibrate, the diffraction pattern will gradually smear out since the periodicity is being destroyed. However, a more careful examination shows that this is not the case.

Let us assume that the position of an atom is given by

$$\rho(t) = \rho_0 + u(t) \tag{3.51}$$

where ρ_0 represents the periodic (fixed) position of the atom and $u(t)$ represents a time dependent lattice vibration shown schematically in Figure 3.12. Note that in the lattice vibrations we are talking about, $u(t)$ is small and represents a time averaged smearing of the periodic lattice points. We are not discussing the case of a molten material where $u(t)$ may be very large.

As before we can write the scattered amplitude as

$$
\begin{aligned}
\boldsymbol{F}_{sc} &= \boldsymbol{F}_0 f \frac{e^{ikR}}{R} \sum_{\rho} e^{-i\Delta\mathbf{k}\cdot\rho} \\
&= \boldsymbol{F}_0 f \frac{e^{ikR}}{R} \sum_{\rho} e^{-i\Delta\mathbf{k}\cdot\rho_0} \, e^{-i\Delta\mathbf{k}\cdot\mathbf{u}(t)}
\end{aligned}
\tag{3.52}
$$

Any measurement process will obtain the time averaged value of the scattered waves, since $u(t)$ will typically vibrate with a frequency 10^{12}s^{-1}. Denoting the average by $< \ldots >$, we get

$$< \exp(-i\Delta\mathbf{k} \cdot \mathbf{u}) > = 1 - i < \Delta\mathbf{k} \cdot \mathbf{u} > - \frac{1}{2} < (\Delta\mathbf{k} \cdot \mathbf{u})^2 > + \ldots \tag{3.53}$$

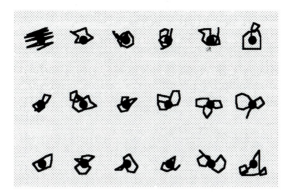

Figure 3.12: The atoms in a "perfect" crystal vibrate about their perfect lattice positions with an amplitude $u(t)$. In spite of these vibrations, the Laue conditions is still satisfied for diffraction peaks.

Since $u(t)$ is varying around ρ_0,

$$< \Delta k \cdot u >= 0 \qquad (3.54)$$

Also

$$< (\Delta k \cdot u)^2 >= \frac{1}{3}(\Delta k)^2 < u^2 > \qquad (3.55)$$

where the factor 1/3 comes from the geometric averaging. Thus

$$\begin{aligned} < \exp(-i\Delta k \cdot u) > &\approx 1 - (\Delta k)^2 < u^2 > /6 \\ &\approx \exp\left(-(\Delta k)^2 < u^2 > /6\right). \end{aligned} \qquad (3.56)$$

The scattered amplitude is then

$$F_{sc} = F_0 f \frac{e^{ikR}}{R} \sum_\rho e^{-i\Delta k \cdot \rho_0} \, e^{-(\Delta k)^2 < u^2 > /6} \qquad (3.57)$$

The scattered intensity is the square of the amplitude. Once again Δk must be equal to a reciprocal lattice vector corresponding to the *mean lattice points* ρ_0, for diffraction spots. The intensity is thus

$$I_{sc} = I_0 e^{-(\Delta k)^2 < u^2 > /3} \qquad (3.58)$$

where I_0 is the intensity from the perfect lattice with points ρ_0.

We will now estimate the *decrease* in the intensity caused by the finite temperature. It is important to note that *the diffraction conditions ($\Delta k = G$) have not changed because of the atomic vibrations*. We will evaluate $< u^2 >$ using classical concepts.

The average energy $< E >$ of a classical oscillator is $3k_BT/2$. Representing the atom of mass m as oscillating with a force constant C and angular frequency ω,

$$
\begin{aligned}
< E > \; &= \; C < u^2 > /2 \\
&= \; m\omega^2 < u^2 > /2 \\
&= \; 3k_BT/2 \\
\Rightarrow < u^2 > \; &= \; \frac{3k_BT}{m\omega^2}.
\end{aligned}
\tag{3.59}
$$

Thus,

$$
I_{sc}(G) = I_0 \exp\left[-\frac{k_BTG^2}{m\omega^2} \right].
\tag{3.60}
$$

The vibration frequency of the atoms is $\omega/2\pi \sim 10^{13} - 10^{14} \, \text{s}^{-1}$. To calculate I_0, let us examine the situation at $T = 0$, where quantum mechanics tells there will be some lattice energy. The kinetic energy is known from quantum mechanics to be

$$
\begin{aligned}
< E > \; &= \; m\omega^2 < u^2 > /2 \\
&= \; 3\hbar\omega/4
\end{aligned}
\tag{3.61}
$$

or

$$
< u^2 > = \frac{3\hbar}{2m\omega}
\tag{3.62}
$$

This gives us

$$
I_0 = I_{0R} \exp\left[-\frac{\hbar G^2}{2m\omega} \right]
\tag{3.63}
$$

where I_{0R} is the intensity for a rigid classical lattice.

This implies that even at $T = 0$, the intensity measured in an experiment is smaller than the one calculated by the rigid lattice method. If $G = 10^9 \text{cm}^{-1}$; $\omega = 2\pi \times 10^{14} \text{s}^{-1}$; $m = 10^{-22} \text{gm}$,

$$
\frac{I_0}{I_{0R}} \approx 0.997.
\tag{3.64}
$$

The results of this section are extremely important since they tell us that wave diffraction can be used at fairly high temperatures. This allows one to use diffraction in an MBE growth chamber to monitor the quality of the crystal being grown. Electrons are used in this technique known as reflection high energy electron diffraction (RHEED). RHEED has become one of the most useful in-site monitoring techniques for hetero-epitaxial growth.

3.5.1 Reflection High Energy Electron Diffraction

RHEED is one of the most widely used techniques to study surface quality during growth of epitaxial layers. It has become a standard feature of most MBE growth systems and is used for studying crystal orientation, growth rate calibration, growth quality check, and surface lattice parameters. As discussed in Chapter 2, the surface of a real semiconductor undergoes reconstruction and these reconstructions are often a strong function of growth conditions (temperature, overpressure, etc.). Since growth quality is very much dependent upon these reconstructions, it is important to monitor the precise reconstruction.

RHEED involves sending a high energy electron (5–50 keV) beam at a grazing angle of 1° to 3° to the surface of the substrate. The RHEED pattern is formed by the elastic scattering of the electron waves from the surface structure of the crystal, the penetration depth of the electron waves being only ~ 0.1 Å. The formalism developed in this chapter continues to hold for the surface diffraction conditions. There is relaxation of the Laue condition normal to the surface since only the topmost monolayer causes the diffraction. The diffraction condition $\Delta k = G_s$ imposes constraints on only the change in the X-ray wavevector parallel to the surface since G_s is now a two-dimensional vector. Thus the condition becomes

$$\begin{aligned} \Delta k_\parallel &= k_\parallel' - k_\parallel \\ &= G_s. \end{aligned} \tag{3.65}$$

To use the Ewald construction for the surface diffraction, it is useful to introduce the concept of reciprocal rods. One considers a usual three-dimensional crystal lattice whose period perpendicular to the surface of interest is expanded without limit. In the reciprocal space, this causes the reciprocal lattice points along this axis to move closer together and in the limit form a "rod." The rods are normal to the surface plane, where they intersect at the surface reciprocal lattice points. As shown in Figure 3.13, the diffraction pattern can be visualized as an intersection of the Ewald sphere with the set of reciprocal rods.

The diffraction condition reduces to Bragg's law which gives the RHEED spacing related to the lattice spacing:

$$\begin{aligned} 2d_h \sin \theta &= \lambda \\ d_h &= \frac{\lambda}{2 \sin \theta} \\ &= \frac{\lambda L}{2D} \end{aligned} \tag{3.66}$$

where d_h is the surface lattice spacing, λ is the de Broglie wavelength (for 10 keV electrons $\lambda \sim 0.1$ Å), L is the distance to the phosphor screen, and D is the rod separation on the screen. The incident electron beam does in actuality penetrate slightly into the bulk crystal, thus a refraction correction should be used to Bragg's law. Also, this means that at various azimuths, the RHEED pattern is

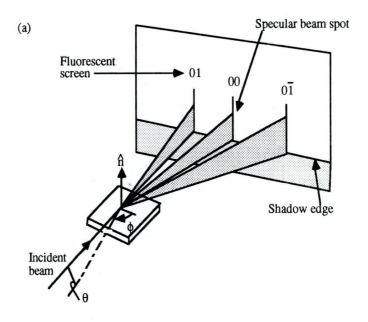

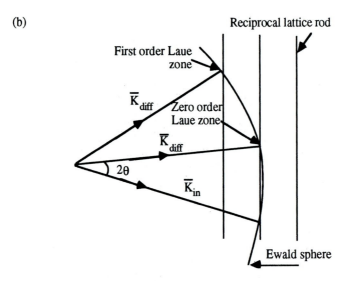

Figure 3.13: Schematic diagram of RHEED geometry (a) showing incident beam at an angle θ to the surface plane, azimuthal angle ϕ. Ewald circle construction (b) appropriate for a qualitative explanation of the formation of streaks in RHEED patterns. The wave vector K_{in} is very large compared with the inter-rod spacing. (Reproduced with permission, P. K. Larsen, et al., *Dynamical Phenomena at Surfaces, Interfaces, and Superlattices,* Springer-Verlag, New York, 1984.)

a superposition of the bulk structure and the surface reconstruction. RHEED analysis is widely used to determine the surface reconstruction (e.g., C(2 × 8) or (2 × 4) reconstruction) before growth of epitaxial films is initiated.

3.5.2 RHEED Oscillations

It is possible to explore some features of the growth dynamics of MBE, by monitoring temporal variations in the intensity of various features in the RHEED pattern. It has been found that damped oscillations in the intensity of both the specular and diffracted beams occur immediately after initiation of growth. The period of oscillation corresponds exactly to the growth of a single monolayer, (i.e. a complete layer of Ga and As atoms $(a_0/2)$, in the [001] direction), and is consequently independent of the azimuth of the incident beam and of the particular diffraction features being measured. The amplitude, however, is strongly dependent on both of these parameters. For evaluation of growth dynamics most of the information is contained in the specular beam, so the subsequent discussion will be limited to specular beam oscillations.

If now we equate changes in intensity of the specular beam in the RHEED pattern with changes in surface roughness, the equilibrium surface is smooth corresponding to high reflectivity. Any roughening of this surface during growth can be related to local growth rate differences, although the overall growth rate is not varying and is determined only by the Ga flux. On application of the driving force (i.e., at commencement of growth) clusters are formed at random positions on the crystal surface, leading to a decrease in the reflectivity. This decrease can be predicted for purely optical reasons, since the de Broglie wavelength of the electrons is ~ 0.12 Å while the bilayer step height is ~ 2.8 Å (i.e., the wavelength is at least an order of magnitude less than the size of the scatterer) so diffuse reflectivity will result. The RHEED intensity from such a growing surface is given by

$$I = \left| \sum_j \exp\left[i \left(\boldsymbol{k} - \boldsymbol{k}' \right) \cdot \boldsymbol{r}_j \right] \right|^2 \tag{3.67}$$

where $\boldsymbol{k}$ is the momentum vector of the incident electrons which form a collimated beam, $\boldsymbol{k}'$ is the momentum vector in the direction of the detector, and $\boldsymbol{r}_j$ is the position of the jth surface atom. The summation in Equation 3.67 is restricted to the surface atomic sites since the de Broglie wavelength for the electrons is ~ 0.1 Å. It is easy to see that away from the Bragg angle, the intensity from surface atoms on successive monolayers will interfere destructively. Thus, under conditions in which the growth is taking place in a layer-by-layer mode and the surface profile is changing (i.e., if one is growing on-axis with no surface steps), one should expect the RHEED intensity to oscillate as shown in Figure 3.14. These oscillations will eventually die out because of the increasing surface roughness and because of flux non-uniformities. If the flux non-uniformities are negligible, then the magnitude of the oscillation is representative of the quality of the growth front. Growth is not restricted to a single layer, but can recur

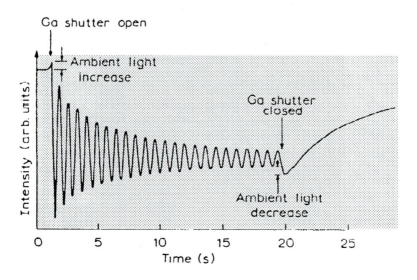

Figure 3.14: Typical intensity oscillations of the specular beam in the RHEED pattern from a GaAs (001) (2×4) reconstructed surface ([110] azimuth). The period corresponds to the growth rate of a single Ga+As layer, and the amplitude gradually decreases as the surface gets rougher and rougher.

before the preceding layer is complete. In the early stages, however, one layer is likely to be almost complete before the next layer starts, so the reflectivity will increase as the surface again becomes smooth on the atomic scale, but with subsequent roughening as the next layer develops. This repetitive process will cause the oscillations in reflectivity gradually to be damped as the surface becomes statistically distributed over several incomplete atomic layers.

3.6   FOR THE TECHNOLOGIST IN YOU

X-ray and electron diffraction have become important tools in semiconductor manufacturing technology. Semiconductor device manufacturing usually starts with large (up to several kilograms) crystals, called boules, being grown by bulk crystal growth techniques. X-ray diffraction is important in determining orientations in these boules and the subsequent wafers which are cut with saws. The wafers are typically cut $\sim 500 \mu$m thick and then thinned down to ~ 200-300μm to remove saw damage. The orientation of the wafers is critical. Essentially all technology using compound semiconductors is based on nominally (100) oriented wafers. This choice is due to processing considerations. Not only is growth by epitaxial techniques better understood and controlled for (100) growth, it is easy to cleave the wafer along say the (110) direction to eventually separate devices or circuits. The wafers are thus sold with one or two flats ground on their peripheries to denote the crystal orientation (the flats also indicate the doping type, either *n*-type or *p*-type).

Silicon technology usually utilizes the (111) growth direction in processes requiring epitaxy (e.g. in bipolar technology) but use (100) direction for MOS related processes, since the interface states are believed to be of lower concentration for this orientation. Special purpose growth is often carried out on other growth orientations for a variety of applications. For example, strained heteroepitaxy growth is often carried out on slightly misoriented substrates (e.g.$\sim$ 2° or 4° of the (100) plane) to better control dislocations. Thus X-ray diffraction is an invaluable tool not only for studying crystal structure and its quality, but also to orient the device fabrication steps.

RHEED has become an invaluable tool in high vacuum techniques, such as MBE. RHEED is widely used to determine the surface reconstruction and surface quality of the wafer before starting growth. A correct surface reconstruction is found to be essential for high quality crystals and therefore, high quality devices. The oscillations in the RHEED spots have also become important tools in heterostructure technology. In high quality growth, one can count the monolayers deposited by counting the pulsations in the RHEED pattern. Since in MBE, the growth rate is typically one monolayer per second, the RHEED oscillations can literally be seen by eye on a fluorescent screen. Imagine seeing the effect of each atomic layer by the naked eye! A pair of low and high intensity RHEED patterns are shown in Figure 3.15. The individual diffraction lines are clearly visible in the high intensity pattern, corresponding to the growth of a complete monolayer. The low intensity pattern shown, was obtained at a point in the growth, when the growing surface was only a partially completed monolayer. As the growth proceeds, the diffraction cycles between these two cases, as shown in Figure 3.14.

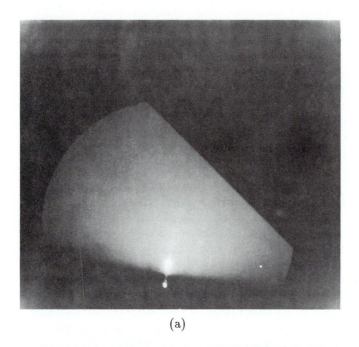

(a)

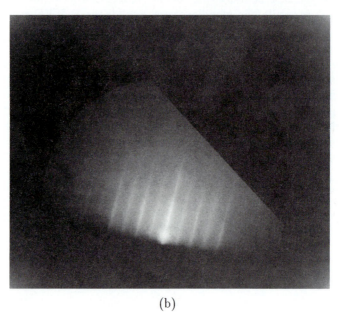

(b)

Figure 3.15: Low and high intensity RHEED patterns formed during MBE layer growth. The photographs were taken when there is partial coverage (a) and full coverage (b), respectively, of a monolayer, during growth.

3.7 PROBLEMS

3.1. In his first investigations of X-rays, Roentgen found that they undergo almost no refraction or reflection when they enter a medium. In fact, dispersion theory predicts that the index of refraction differs from unity in X-rays only by a few parts per million. According to the dispersion theory, if there are N_i oscillators of frequency ν_i per unit volume in a medium, the refractive index n is given by

$$n^2 - 1 = \frac{e^2}{\pi m} \sum_i \frac{N_i}{\nu_i^2 - \nu^2}$$

where e is the charge of the oscillator and m its mass. For X-rays, ν is extremely high and we have

$$n^2 - 1 = \frac{-e^2}{\pi m \nu^2} \sum_i N_i$$

$$= \frac{-e^2 N_{tot}}{\pi m \nu^2}.$$

Thus, n is slightly less than one. Referring to Figure 3.16, show that the externally measured angles and wavelength which satisfy Bragg's Law are related by

$$m\lambda = 2d \sin\theta \left[1 + \frac{4(n-1)d^2}{m^2 \lambda^2} \right].$$

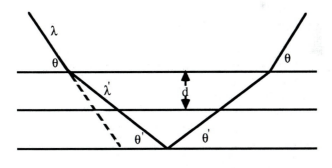

Figure 3.16: The refraction of X-rays upon entering and leaving a crystal.

3.2. Powder specimens of three different cubic crystals are analyzed with a Debye-Scherrer camera. It is known that one sample is face-centered cubic, one is body-centered cubic, and one has the diamond structure. The approximate positions of the first four diffraction rings in each case are (see Figure 3.10)

A	B	C
42.2°	28.8°	42.8°
49.2°	41.0°	73.2°
72.0°	50.8°	89.0°
87.3°	59.6°	115.0°

(a) Identify the crystal structures of A, B, and C.

(b) If the wavelength of the incident X-ray beam is 1.5 Å, what is the length of the side of the conventional cubic cell in each case?

(c) If the diamond structure were replaced by a zinc–blende structure with a cubic unit cell of the same side, at what angles would the first four rings now occur?

3.3. Find the width of the first order diffraction peaks for a linear array of atoms with spacing $a = 2$ Å when the number of atoms N is 20, 100, 1000. Assume a wavelength of 1.5 Å.

3.4. When a careful crystal diffraction is carried out on a GaAs crystal, it is found that the rocking curves have a width of 1.0 seconds. Assuming that the crystal quality can be defined by a spatial order parameter l, over which distance, the crystal is essentially perfect, what is an approximate value for l for our sample? Assume a wavelength of 1.5 Å.

3.5. An amorphous silicon sample is analyzed by X-ray diffraction. It is seen that the first two rings in a powder experiment are well-defined and the width of the first ring is 1°. If the root-mean-squared (rms) fluctuation of Si atoms from the perfect sites is $|\Delta r|^2$, what do you expect Δr to be in this sample? Assume a wavelength of 1.5 Å.

3.6. GaAs and AlAs have essentially the same lattice constants ($a \sim 5.65$ Å). A $(GaAs)_4(AlAs)_5$ superlattice is grown by an epitaxial crystal crystal growth technique. Assuming that Ga and Al atoms have a different atomic form factors, how will you detect the evidence of the superlattice in an X-ray diffraction study? Plot the scattering angles for diffraction for GaAs and the superlattice structure. Assume a wavelength of 1.5 Å.

3.7. The oscillations in the Reflection High Energy Electron Diffraction (RHEED) or Reflection Difference Spectroscopy (RDS) can be used to calculate the precise growth rates in epitaxial techniques. In MOCVD growth, the high background pressure allows only RDS as a useful probe. In RDS, light with cross-polarized beams impinges on the surface and the difference in their reflectivity is obtained. As the surface monolayer coverage changes, the dipoles on the surface change orientation causing this difference and thus oscillations in the RDS signal. In the growth of the alloy AlGaAs, the GaAs growth is calibrated to give an oscillation spacing of 1 second. How would you go about setting up conditions so that the composition $Al_{0.25}Ga_{0.75}As$ is grown?

3.8. The concept of Bragg reflection is used to produce distributed Bragg reflectors (DBRs) widely used in optoelectronic devices. A DBR is made up of multilayers of GaAs and AlAs with refractive indices 3.6 and 2.96, respectively. Show that if the optical thickness (nd) of each layer is $\lambda/4$, the structure acts as a mirror, for normally incident light.

3.9. A rigorous treatment of this problem (e.g. "Optics," M. Born and E. Wolf, Pergamon Press, New York, (1987) p. 69) shows that if light enters from GaAs into GaAs, separated by N periods of AlAs/GaAs quarter wave stacks, the reflectivity is:

$$R = \left(\frac{1 - \left(\frac{n_{AlAs}}{n_{GaAs}} \right)^{2N}}{1 + \left(\frac{n_{AlAs}}{n_{GaAs}} \right)^{2N}} \right)^2 .$$

What is the thickness of the stacks if a 99% reflectivity is required for a 0.8 μm GaAs laser?

3.8 REFERENCES

- **X-ray Diffraction: General**

  - Ashcroft, N. W., and N. D. Mermin, *Solid State Physics* (Holt, Rinehart and Winston, New York, 1976).
  - Leighton, R. B., *Principles of Modern Physics* (McGraw–Hill, New York, 1959).
  - Segmueller, A. and A. E. Blakeslee, J. Appl. Crystallogr., **6**, 19 (1973).
  - Warren, B. E., *X-ray Diffraction* (Addison–Wesley, New York, 1969).

- **Diffraction from Surfaces and Crystal Growth; RHEED**

  - Gourley, P. L. and R. M. Biefeld, J. Vac. Sci. Technol. B, **1**, 383 (1983).
  - Joyce, B. A., Rep. Prog. Phys., **48**, 1637 (1985).
  - Joyce, B. A., J. H. Neave, P. J. Dobson and P. K. Larsen, Phys. Rev. B, **29**, 814 (1984).
  - Kim, J. Y., P. Chen, F. Voillet and A. Madhukar, Appl. Phys. Lett., **50**, 739 (1987).
  - Larsen, P. K., in *Dynamical Phenomenon at Surfaces, Interfaces and Superlattices* (edited by F. Nizzoli, K. H. Rieder and R. F. Willis, Springer–Verlag, New York, 1989), p. 197.
  - Pashley, M. D., K. W. Kaberern, W. Friday and J. M. Woodall, Phys. Rev. Lett., **60**, 2176 (1988).

- Ploog, K., *Crystal Growth and Properties* (Springer–Verlag, New York, 1980).

- Tsang, W. T., *Semiconductors and Semimetals* (edited by R. K. Willardson and A. C. Beer, Academic Press, New York, 1985), vol. 22, part A.

- Van Hove, J. M., P. R. Pukite, G. J. Whaley, A. M. Worchak, and P. I. Cohen, J. Vac. Sci. Technol. B, **3**, 1116 (1985).

CHAPTER
4

ELECTRONS
IN PERIODIC
STRUCTURES

Electrons are elementary particles carrying charge which, depending on the situation, may be described by either simple classical physics, the quantum mechanical Schrödinger equation, or the relativistic Dirac equation. For most practical energies encountered in solid state electronic devices, the Schrödinger equation and often even the classical equations, describe the electrons quite adequately. The electron's properties are described in quantum mechanics by operators (e.g., the kinetic energy operator, potential energy operator, momentum operator, etc.), the wavefunction (eigenfunction or state), and the expectation values of the operators for a given electronic state. While in principle, this is a simple problem to solve if one knows the external potentials (or forces) that the electron feels, in practice, this is a very complex problem and solutions are known only for a handful of problems. The systems where exact solutions are known are the hydrogen atom, the square well, and the harmonic oscillator problem, which are usually described in quantum mechanics books. Compared to these simple problems, the real-life problem of an electron moving in a silicon device and "feeling" the ionic potential of the fixed ions appears to be extremely complex. The situation, indeed, seems to be hopeless, since even classical problems cannot be easily solved for more than a two or three body interaction (i.e., two or three particles moving under the influence of each other's forces). In a real device, we may need to describe the energy of the electrons and their response to external perturbations, under a very complex set of internal interactions. Thus we may wish to solve the simple Newton's equation of motion

$$\frac{d\boldsymbol{p}}{dt} = \boldsymbol{F}_{ext} + \boldsymbol{F}_{int} \tag{4.1}$$

for the electrons, where $\boldsymbol{p}$ is the electron momentum, $\boldsymbol{F}_{ext}$ the external (known) force, and $\boldsymbol{F}_{int}$ represents the internal forces seen by the electron inside the

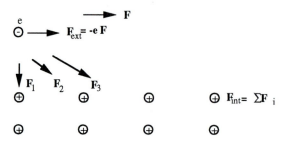

Figure 4.1: A schematic showing the motion of an electron in a crystal with a background of positively charged ions. In addition to the external electric field shown, the electron sees the internal forces of other ions as well as other electrons.

material as shown schematically in Figure 4.1. $\boldsymbol{F}_{int}$ will obviously change from material to material. Such a complex equation is almost impossible to solve because of the large number of interacting particles involved through the $\boldsymbol{F}_{int}$ term. In fact, the problem would be totally hopeless were it not for a simplifying feature of the internal interactions.

The simplifying feature, which allows us to describe electrons inside devices, is the periodic nature of the background internal potential. This periodicity, which is due to the crystalline nature of the semiconductors, is responsible in allowing us to rewrite Equation 4.1 as

$$\frac{d\boldsymbol{p}_{eff}}{dt} = \boldsymbol{F}_{ext} \tag{4.2}$$

where $\boldsymbol{p}_{eff}$ is an effective momentum of the electron and takes into account the internal interactions and, for all practical purposes, represents the response of the electrons to external forces. What $\boldsymbol{p}_{eff}$ is, what its relation is to the electron energy, and how it is related to the material properties are questions to be answered in this and the next chapter. It is worth noting that in systems where periodicity is not present, e.g., glasses and amorphous semiconductors, the electron problem is extremely complex and the understanding of such materials is still quite far from complete.

4.1   PERIODICITY AND BLOCH'S THEOREM

In the Drude model for electron conductivity, we assumed that the electrons are scattered by the rigid ions as they move between them. This seems like a very reasonable and intuitively correct scenario. However, in this section we will establish that *electrons move in periodic structures without any scattering whatsoever*. This idea is at the heart of all solid state electronics. The importance of this idea is something all of us have experienced and it may be worthwhile examining a simple everyday situation that highlights the importance of periodicity. In many cities there are synchronized traffic lights. The traffic light, in principle, represents a "scattering center," i.e., it can stop you or slow you down. As all of us have experienced at one time or another, with the synchronized lights, if we drive our car at some specific speeds, we can travel as if the traffic lights do not exist at all. Thus, in certain range of speeds, the cars can be driven as if they were "free." The synchronization, or periodicity, is what allows us to realize this scattering-free movement.

The Bloch theorem provides a mathematical basis for the description of electrons in a periodic potential. Its importance lies in the fact that it provides us a well-defined form for the electron wavefunction (out of an infinite set of possible forms) inside the crystal.

The Bloch theorem states that an eigenfunction of the Schrödinger equation for a periodic potential is the product of a plane wave $\exp(i\mathbf{k} \cdot \mathbf{r})$ times a function $u_{\mathbf{k}}(\mathbf{r})$ which has the *same periodicity as the periodic potential*. Thus,

$$\psi_{\mathbf{k}}(\mathbf{r}) = e^{i\mathbf{k} \cdot \mathbf{r}} u_{\mathbf{k}}(\mathbf{r}) \tag{4.3}$$

is the form of the electronic function. The significance of $\mathbf{k}$ and $u_{\mathbf{k}}(\mathbf{r})$ will be clear later. If the potential energy $U(\mathbf{r})$ has the property

$$U(\mathbf{r} + \mathbf{R}) = U(\mathbf{r}) \tag{4.4}$$

where $\mathbf{R}$ represents a lattice vector, then

$$u(\mathbf{r} + \mathbf{R}) = u(\mathbf{r}) \tag{4.5}$$

It is important to note that the Bloch theorem *does not* assert that the electrons *wavefunction* is periodic in space, and, in fact, the wavefunction does change from one unit cell to another. However, the *probability* of finding the electron in each cell (i.e., $|\psi|^2$) is periodic as should be expected. This situation is illustrated in Figure 4.2.

We will now discuss a proof of the Bloch theorem by examining the periodic potential wave equation for electrons in k-space (or Fourier space). It often turns out that some problems in mathematics are more tractable or more revealing in k-space rather than in r-space (i.e, real space). Writing the Schrödinger equation in k-space also allows us to develop the concepts of energy bands, bandgaps and crystal momentum (the quantity $\mathbf{k}$ in Equation 4.3) in a very natural manner.

The real space Schrödinger equation for the electron is

$$\left[\frac{-\hbar^2}{2m} \nabla^2 + U(\mathbf{r}) \right] \psi(\mathbf{r}) = E\psi(\mathbf{r}) \tag{4.6}$$

where the first term represents the kinetic energy operator for the electron and $U(\mathbf{r})$ is the periodic potential energy seen by the electron. The potential U may include the background ionic potential as well as any electron–electron interactions in general. Since the potential is periodic when a lattice translation is made as described by Equation 4.4, it can be expanded in a Fourier series

$$U(\mathbf{r}) = \sum_{\mathbf{G}} U_{\mathbf{G}} e^{i\mathbf{G} \cdot \mathbf{r}} \tag{4.7}$$

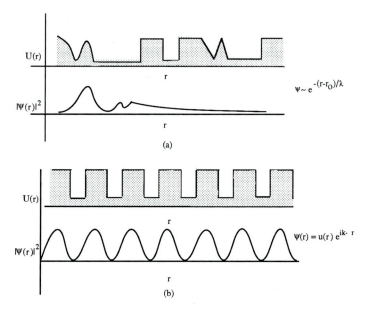

Figure 4.2: (a) Potential and electron probability value of a typical electronic wave-function in a random material. (b) The effect of a periodic background potential on an electronic wavefunction. The Bloch theorem allows us to choose the form of the wavefunction from an infinite set of possible forms.

where only the reciprocal lattice vectors G are required in the Fourier expansion. Note that such an expansion obviously satisfies Equation 4.4 since

$$
\begin{aligned}
U(\boldsymbol{r} + \boldsymbol{R}) &= \sum_{\boldsymbol{G}} U_{\boldsymbol{G}} e^{i\boldsymbol{G}\cdot(\boldsymbol{r}+\boldsymbol{R})} \\
&= \sum_{\boldsymbol{G}} U_{\boldsymbol{G}} e^{i\boldsymbol{G}\cdot\boldsymbol{r}} \\
&= U(\boldsymbol{r})
\end{aligned} \tag{4.8}
$$

as $\exp(i\boldsymbol{G}\cdot\boldsymbol{R}) = 1$. Usually only a few Fourier expansion coefficients are required in the series and the summation of Equation 4.7 then only contains a few terms. Since the potential energy term is real we must enforce the condition

$$
U_{\boldsymbol{G}}^{*} = U_{-\boldsymbol{G}}. \tag{4.9}
$$

To express the wavefunction in k-space we impose periodic boundary conditions on the wavefunction

$$
\psi(\boldsymbol{r}) = \psi(\boldsymbol{r} + \boldsymbol{L}) \tag{4.10}
$$

where L is the length of the sample under consideration, (L is much greater than the interatomic spacing). The Fourier series expansion of the wavefunction is then

$$\psi(\boldsymbol{r}) = \sum_{\mathbf{k}} C_{\mathbf{k}} \, e^{i\mathbf{k}\cdot\mathbf{r}} \tag{4.11}$$

where $\boldsymbol{k}$ is of the form $k_x = 2\pi n_x/L$, $k_y = 2\pi n_y/L$, $k_z = 2\pi n_z/L$, with n_x, n_y, n_z being integers. The expansion in Equation 4.11 is quite general and *does not impose any restrictions on the wavefunction*. In its present form, the electron wavefunction does not satisfy Bloch's theorem. However, we will show that for the periodic potential problem, only a few terms in the summation of Equation 4.11 actually survive to describe the electrons in a given state.

The kinetic energy term in the Schrödinger equation can be written in k-space as

$$\frac{-\hbar^2}{2m}\nabla^2\psi(\boldsymbol{r}) = \frac{\hbar^2}{2m}\sum_{\mathbf{k}} C_{\mathbf{k}} \, k^2 \, e^{i\mathbf{k}\cdot\mathbf{r}} \tag{4.12}$$

while the potential energy term in the k-space is

$$\left(\sum_{\mathbf{G}} U_{\mathbf{G}} e^{i\mathbf{G}\cdot\mathbf{r}}\right)\psi(\boldsymbol{r}) = \sum_{\mathbf{G}}\sum_{\mathbf{k}} U_{\mathbf{G}} \, e^{i\mathbf{G}\cdot\mathbf{r}} \, C_{\mathbf{k}} \, e^{i\mathbf{k}\cdot\mathbf{r}}. \tag{4.13}$$

The wave equation then becomes

$$\sum_{\mathbf{k}} \frac{-\hbar^2}{2m}k^2 \, C_{\mathbf{k}} \, e^{i\mathbf{k}\cdot\mathbf{r}} + \sum_{\mathbf{G}}\sum_{\mathbf{k}} U_{\mathbf{G}} \, C_{\mathbf{k}} \, e^{i(\mathbf{G}+\mathbf{k})\cdot\mathbf{r}} = E\sum_{\mathbf{k}} C_{\mathbf{k}} \, e^{i\mathbf{k}\cdot\mathbf{r}}. \tag{4.14}$$

This series of equations can be vastly simplified if we now use the orthogonality properties of the $\exp(i\boldsymbol{k}\cdot\boldsymbol{r})$ terms, i.e.,

$$\frac{1}{V}\int e^{-i\mathbf{k}'\cdot\mathbf{r}} e^{i\mathbf{k}\cdot\mathbf{r}} d^3r = \delta(\boldsymbol{k}' - \boldsymbol{k}). \tag{4.15}$$

Thus, if we multiply both sides of the Equation 4.14 by $\exp(-i\boldsymbol{k}'\cdot\boldsymbol{r})$ and integrate over space the summation over $\boldsymbol{k}$ can be eliminated giving us

$$\frac{\hbar^2}{2m}k'^2 C_{\mathbf{k}'} + \sum_{\mathbf{G}} U_{\mathbf{G}} \, C_{\mathbf{k}'-\mathbf{G}} = E \, C_{\mathbf{k}'}. \tag{4.16}$$

We point out that the indices like $\boldsymbol{k}'$, $\boldsymbol{G}$, etc., are dummy indices and can be replaced by other symbols. We can replace $\boldsymbol{k}'$ by $(\boldsymbol{k} - \boldsymbol{G}')$ and define the kinetic energy for the component $\boldsymbol{k}$ as

$$\lambda_{\mathbf{k}} = \frac{\hbar^2 k^2}{2m}. \tag{4.17}$$

We then get a compact equation for the Schrödinger equation in k-space in a periodic potential

$$\left(\lambda_{\mathbf{k}-\mathbf{G}'} - E\right) C_{\mathbf{k}-\mathbf{G}'} + \sum_{\mathbf{G}} U_{\mathbf{G}} \, C_{\mathbf{k}-\mathbf{G}-\mathbf{G}'} = 0. \tag{4.18}$$

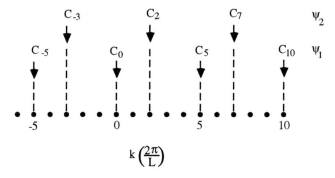

Figure 4.3: The periodic boundary conditions force the wavefunction to be expanded in k's which are integral multiples of $2\pi/L$. The Bloch theorem tells us that not all expansion coefficients are nonzero. For example, for a case of $L = 5a$, a particular wavefunction has nonzero expansion coefficients which have k's differing by a reciprocal lattice vector. The figure shows two such wavefunctions, ψ_1 and ψ_2 which involve a different set of C's in their expansions.

Once again making the sequence of changes $G' \leftrightarrow G$; then $G' \to G' - G$ we get

$$\left(\lambda_{\mathbf{k-G}} - E\right) C_{\mathbf{k-G}} + \sum_{\mathbf{G'}} U_{\mathbf{G'-G}} C_{\mathbf{k-G'}} = 0. \qquad (4.19)$$

Note that the summations over G' or $G' - G$ are the same. This equation represents a series of couple equations and is called the central equation or the secular equation.

We must realize that so far, we have simply recast the differential equation for the electrons (Equation 4.6) in k-space. We have not yet obtained any solutions for the electronic states. The solution of the equation now involves obtaining the values of $C_{\mathbf{k}}$. However, the Equation 4.19 brings out an extremely important feature of the solution: while our general solution given by Equation 4.11 for the wavefunctions involved *all* possible values of k in the summation ($k_x = 2\pi n_x/L$, etc.), in fact, we find that in the periodic problem, for a given value of k, only those expansion coefficients C's are involved *which differ from k by a reciprocal lattice vector*. Thus the wavefunction for the electron state involves a much more restrictive summation over the reciprocal lattice vectors G as shown in Figure 4.3

$$\psi_{\mathbf{k}}(\mathbf{r}) = \sum_{\mathbf{G}} C_{\mathbf{k-G}} e^{i(\mathbf{k-G})\cdot\mathbf{r}}. \qquad (4.20)$$

The subscript k chosen to describe the wavefunction is arbitrary in that it could be replaced by $k - G_1$, or $k - G_2$ (G_1, G_2 being reciprocal lattice vectors). It is convenient, however, to chose the value of k to describe the wavefunction as being in the first Brillouin zone.

Before we actually solve the Equation 4.19 which is an infinite set of coupled equations (i.e., for different values of $k - G$), it is important to examine the form of the general wavefunctions given by Equation 4.20. We can rearrange Equation 4.20 as follows

$$
\begin{aligned}
\psi_{\mathbf{k}}(\mathbf{r}) &= \left(\sum_{\mathbf{G}} C_{\mathbf{k}-\mathbf{G}} e^{-i\mathbf{G}\cdot\mathbf{r}} \right) e^{i\mathbf{k}\cdot\mathbf{r}} \\
&= e^{i\mathbf{k}\cdot\mathbf{r}} u_{\mathbf{k}}(\mathbf{r})
\end{aligned}
\tag{4.21}
$$

where

$$
u_{\mathbf{k}}(\mathbf{r}) = \sum_{\mathbf{G}} C_{\mathbf{k}-\mathbf{G}} e^{-i\mathbf{G}\cdot\mathbf{r}}.
\tag{4.22}
$$

Because of the form of $u_{\mathbf{k}}(\mathbf{r})$ we have

$$
u_{\mathbf{k}}(\mathbf{r}) = u_{\mathbf{k}}(\mathbf{r} + \mathbf{R})
\tag{4.23}
$$

where $\mathbf{R}$ is a translation vector of the lattice. This result is the statement of the Bloch theorem, i.e., the electron wavefunction is the product of $e^{i\mathbf{k}\cdot\mathbf{r}}$ and a function which has the periodicity of the lattice. A state (or wavefunction) of the form 4.16 is called a Bloch function. The result represented by Equation 4.20 is perhaps the most important result in solid state physics since it establishes a unique form of the solution of the electrons inside crystals. It is important to examine the significance of the vector $\mathbf{k}$ that appears in the Bloch function. Although a real appreciation of $\mathbf{k}$ will emerge when we actually study the electronic transport and optical properties in semiconductors, some important properties can be anticipated now.

The solution of the Schrödinger equation will be discussed later, but this solution will give the value of the electron energy for a given value of $\mathbf{k}$, along with the values of $C_{\mathbf{k}}$, $C_{\mathbf{k}-\mathbf{G}_1}$, ... etc. The time dependent part of this Schrödinger equation is

$$
i\hbar \frac{\partial \psi}{\partial t} = E\psi
\tag{4.24}
$$

and for a given E, has the general form

$$
\psi \sim e^{-iEt/\hbar} = e^{-i\omega t}
\tag{4.25}
$$

where $\omega = E/\hbar$. The general solution then has the form

$$
\psi(\mathbf{r}, t) = u_{\mathbf{k}}(\mathbf{r}) e^{i(\mathbf{k}\cdot\mathbf{r}-\omega t)}
\tag{4.26}
$$

which represents a traveling wave. The phase velocity of this wave is ω/k. Notice that this *solution is the same as the one we discussed in Chapter 1 for free electrons except that it is modulated by the function* $u_{\mathbf{k}}(\mathbf{r})$.

4.2 SIGNIFICANCE OF *k*: CRYSTAL MOMENTUM

For free electrons moving in space there are two very important laws which are used to describe their properties: i) Newton's second law of motion which tells us how the electron's trajectory evolves in presence of an external force; and ii) the law of conservation of momentum which allows us to determine the electron's trajectory when there is a collision. We are obviously interested in finding out what the analogous laws are when an electron is inside a crystal and not in free space.

4.2.1   Equation of Motion

An extremely important implication of the Bloch theorem is that in the perfectly periodic background potential that the crystal presents, *the electron propagates without scattering.* The electronic state ($\sim \exp(i\boldsymbol{k} \cdot \boldsymbol{r})$) is an extended wave which *occupies the entire crystal.* This conceptual picture of the electron inside the crystal is quite different from that developed in the Drude model where the background ions were expected to provide scattering centers.

Although we have shown that the electrons in the perfect crystal do not suffer scattering we still need to derive an equation of motion for the electrons which tells us how electrons will respond to external forces. The equation of motion

$$\frac{d\boldsymbol{p}}{dt} = \boldsymbol{F}_{ext} + \boldsymbol{F}_{int} \qquad (4.27)$$

is quite useless for a meaningful description of the electron because it includes the internal forces on the electron. We need a description which does *not* include the evaluation of the internal forces. We will now give a simple derivation for such an equation of motion. The equation of motion also provides a conceptual understanding of the vector $\boldsymbol{k}$ that has been introduced by the Bloch theorem.

Since the Bloch function is a plane wave which extends over all the crystalline space, we examine a localized wavepacket which is made up of wavefunctions near a particular $\boldsymbol{k}$ value. Using our understanding of waves, we can define the group velocity of this wavepacket as

$$\boldsymbol{v}_g = \frac{d\omega}{d\boldsymbol{k}} \qquad (4.28)$$

where ω is the frequency associated with the electron of energy E, i.e., $\omega = E/\hbar$:

$$\begin{aligned} \boldsymbol{v}_g &= \frac{1}{\hbar}\frac{dE}{d\boldsymbol{k}} \\ &= \frac{1}{\hbar}\nabla_{\boldsymbol{k}}E(\boldsymbol{k}) \end{aligned} \qquad (4.29)$$

The dependence of E on $\boldsymbol{k}$ is obtained, for example, by the solution of the crystal equation or by other techniques described in the next chapter. In this E vs. $\boldsymbol{k}$ relation, all the effects of the background crystal potential are contained.

If we have an electric field $\boldsymbol{F}$ present, the work done on the electron during a time interval δt is

$$\delta E = -e\boldsymbol{F} \cdot \boldsymbol{v}_g \delta t \qquad (4.30)$$

we may also write in general

$$\delta E = \left(\frac{dE}{d\mathbf{k}}\right)\delta\mathbf{k}$$

$$= \hbar v_g \cdot \delta\mathbf{k}. \tag{4.31}$$

Comparing the two equations for δE, we get

$$\delta\mathbf{k} = -\frac{e\mathbf{F}}{\hbar}\delta t \tag{4.32}$$

giving us the relation

$$\hbar\frac{d\mathbf{k}}{dt} = -e\mathbf{F}. \tag{4.33}$$

In general, we may write

$$\hbar\frac{d\mathbf{k}}{dt} = \mathbf{F}_{ext}. \tag{4.34}$$

This equation looks identical to Newton's second law of motion,

$$d\mathbf{p}/dt = \mathbf{F}_{ext}$$

in free space, if we associate the quantity $\hbar\mathbf{k}$ with the momentum of the electron in the crystal. The term $\hbar\mathbf{k}$ responds to the *external forces* as if it is the momentum of the electron, although, as can be seen by comparing the true Newton's equation of motion Equation 4.27 and Equation 4.34, it is clear that $\hbar\mathbf{k}$ contains the effects of the internal crystal potentials and is therefore not the true electron momentum. Often $\hbar\mathbf{k}$ is called the crystal momentum and represents a tremendous simplification of the electron problem in crystalline materials. Once the E vs. $\mathbf{k}$ relation is established, we can for all practical purposes forget about the background potential $U(\mathbf{r})$, and treat the electrons as if they are free and obey the effective Newton's equation of motion.

The crystal momentum not only responds to external forces as if it were the effective momentum of the electrons on scattering processes, also, it usually behaves as though it obeyed momentum conservation laws.

4.2.2   Conservation Laws for Collision Processes

In wave mechanics, the collision processes are described by the square of a matrix element of the form

$$M_{\mathbf{k}\mathbf{k}'} \sim \int d^3r\ \psi_{\mathbf{k}'}^*(\mathbf{r})\ V(\mathbf{r})\ \psi_{\mathbf{k}}(\mathbf{r}) \tag{4.35}$$

where $V(\mathbf{r})$ is the scattering potential. For scattering from phonons (discussed later), for example, the matrix element takes the form (suppressing details)

$$M_{\mathbf{k}\mathbf{k}'} \sim \int d^3r\ u_{\mathbf{k}'}^*(\mathbf{r})\ u_{\mathbf{k}}(\mathbf{r})\ e^{i(\mathbf{k}+\mathbf{q}-\mathbf{k}')\cdot\mathbf{r}}$$

$$= \sum_{\{\mathbf{R}\}} e^{i(\mathbf{k}+\mathbf{q}-\mathbf{k}')\cdot\mathbf{R}}$$

$$\times \int_{\text{unit cell}} d^3r \; u_{\mathbf{k}'}^*(\mathbf{r}) \; u_{\mathbf{k}}(\mathbf{r}) \; e^{i(\mathbf{k}+\mathbf{q}-\mathbf{k}')\cdot\mathbf{r}} \qquad (4.36)$$

where $\mathbf{q}$ is the phonon wave vector and $\mathbf{k}$ and $\mathbf{k}'$ are the initial and final vectors describing the electron state. Since the product $u_{\mathbf{k}'}^*(\mathbf{r}) \; u_{\mathbf{k}}(\mathbf{r})$ is periodic in the crystal lattice, the summation vanishes unless

$$\mathbf{k} + \mathbf{q} = \mathbf{k}' + \mathbf{G} \qquad (4.37)$$

when $\mathbf{G}$ is a reciprocal lattice vector. If $\mathbf{G} = 0$, Equation 4.37 resembles the momentum conservation law for free electron collisions. For most scattering processes the restriction $\mathbf{G} = 0$ does hold and such processes are called normal or N-processes. However, since the periodicity of the crystal involves a finite minimum distance, the conservation law is not exactly obeyed and processes with $\mathbf{G} \neq 0$, the so called Umklapp (German for flipping over) or U-processes are allowed. In semiconductors these processes usually do not play a significant role in electron scattering, since the integrand in Equation 4.36 is rapidly varying for $\mathbf{G} \neq 0$, significantly reducing the value of the integral.

Once again it is important to note that just like $\hbar\mathbf{k}$ is not the true momentum of the electron, the apparent violation of momentum conservation is not a real violation. *Total* momentum is, of course, *conserved*, even in Umklapp processes.

4.3 ELECTRON STATES IN A WEAK PERIODIC POTENTIAL

We will now attempt to solve for the electronic states inside the crystal, i.e., obtain the energies E and the coefficients C's for the wavefunction given by Equation 4.20.

The k-space technique that we developed to establish Bloch's theorem is very useful to bring out the concepts of bandgaps, effective masses, etc. The approach is particularly useful when the background periodic potential is weak. While for most semiconductors this is not true, and other bandstructure techniques are employed, the approach described below is conceptually very useful.

We know that the electrons will, in general, see a background of fixed ion potentials in the crystal. The electrons that we are interested in are the valence electrons and these electrons see a potential that has been strongly "screened" by the core electrons. The potential is further screened by the other conduction electrons. Thus, for some applications, it is reasonable to assume that the potential is weak enough to apply perturbation theory. The general spirit of perturbation theory is that once we know the solution of a problem for a particular set of parameters (say a given Hamiltonian), then if the set of parameters are "slightly" altered, the new solution can be expressed in terms of the old solution in a simple manner. In this particular case, we know the solution of the problem when there is *no* background potential, i.e., for the free electron case.

Let us return to the general Bloch function

$$\psi_{\mathbf{k}}(\mathbf{r}) = \sum_{\mathbf{G}} C_{\mathbf{k-G}} \, e^{i(\mathbf{k-G})\cdot\mathbf{r}} \tag{4.38}$$

along with the Schrödinger equation

$$\left(\frac{\hbar^2}{2m}|\mathbf{k} - \mathbf{G}|^2 - E\right) C_{\mathbf{k-G}} + \sum_{\mathbf{G'}} U_{\mathbf{G'-G}} \, C_{\mathbf{k-G'}} = 0. \tag{4.39}$$

If there is no background potential, all $U_{\mathbf{G}}$ are zero (we can choose U_0 to be zero) and the Schrödinger equation becomes

$$\left(E^0_{\mathbf{k-G}} - E\right) C_{\mathbf{k-G}} = 0 \tag{4.40}$$

where

$$E^0_{\mathbf{k-G}} = \frac{\hbar^2}{2m}|\mathbf{k} - \mathbf{G}|^2 \,. \tag{4.41}$$

In order for this equation to be satisfied, we must have either

$$C_{\mathbf{k-G}} = 0 \tag{4.42}$$

or

$$\left(E^0_{\mathbf{k-G}} - E\right) = 0. \tag{4.43}$$

Let us assume that for a particular value of reciprocal vector, say $\mathbf{G}_1$,

$$
\begin{aligned}
E^0_{\mathbf{k-G}_1} &= E \\
&= \frac{\hbar^2}{2m}|\mathbf{k} - \mathbf{G}_1|^2 \\
C_{\mathbf{k-G}_1} &= 1
\end{aligned} \tag{4.44}
$$

while for all other reciprocal vectors

$$C_{\mathbf{k-G}} = 0. \tag{4.45}$$

This gives the solution

$$
\begin{aligned}
E &= \frac{\hbar^2}{2m}|\mathbf{k} - \mathbf{G}_1|^2 \\
C_{\mathbf{k-G}_1} &= 1 \\
\psi_{\mathbf{k}}(\mathbf{r}) &= e^{i(\mathbf{k-G}_1)\cdot\mathbf{r}}
\end{aligned} \tag{4.46}
$$

which is essentially the same as for the *free electron* problem, except that in the free electron case, we had $\mathbf{G}_1 = 0$. The choice of the k-space origin will be

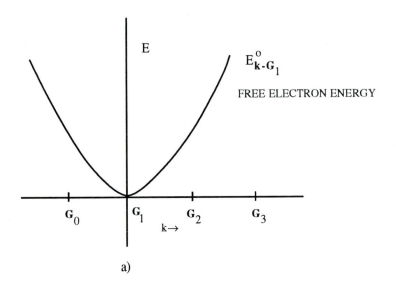

a)

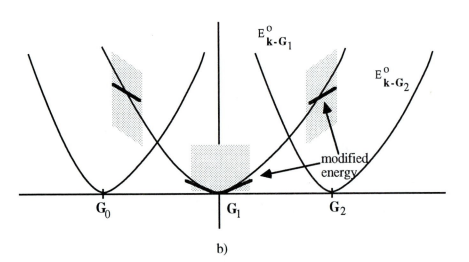

b)

Figure 4.4: (a) The free electron parabola centered around a reciprocal lattice vector G_1 ($E^0_{\mathbf{k}-\mathbf{G}_1} = \hbar^2|k-G_1|^2/(2m)$). (b) When the background potential is turned on, the parabolas centered around different reciprocal vectors interact with each other. The effect on the shaded region is discussed in Case 1 of the text.

discussed in detail later on. We note that in the choice made above, we have assumed that only one reciprocal vector G_1 has the proper free electron energy. For some energy values there may be other reciprocal lattice vectors for which the energy $E^0_{k-G_1}$ and $E^0_{k-G_m}$ are the same. This is shown in Figure 4.4. At these points of degeneracies corresponding to G_m, the coefficients C_{k-G_m} need not be zero, as we shall see below.

Case 1: Let us first examine the situation where the free energy value $E^0_{k-G_1}$ is far removed from any other energy E^0_{k-G} ($G \neq G_1$). We will now introduce the periodic background potential and assume that the potential is much smaller than $|E^0_{k-G_1} - E^0_{k-G}|$. Thus, Case 1 will be dealing with the shaded regions of Figure 4.4.

When the background potential is zero

$$\left. \begin{array}{rcl} E &=& E^0_{k-G_1} \\ C_{k-G_1} &=& 1 \end{array} \right\} \text{ and } C_{k-G} = 0 \text{ for } G \neq G_1. \tag{4.47}$$

We will now find corrections to this solution for small U values. The k-space Schrödinger equation is (for $G = G_1$)

$$\left(E - E^0_{k-G_1} \right) C_{k-G_1} = \sum_{G} U_{G-G_1} C_{k-G} \tag{4.48}$$

we assume $U_0 = 0$ since U_0 is just a constant addition to the energy solutions. Thus, $G = G_1$ is not included in the summation on the right-hand side.

If the k-space Schrödinger equation is written for $G' \neq G_1$, we get

$$\left(E - E^0_{k-G'} \right) C_{k-G'} = U_{G_1-G'} C_{k-G_1} + \sum_{G} U_{G-G'} C_{k-G} \tag{4.49}$$

where $G = G_1$ is again not included in the sum on the right-hand side.

$$C_{k-G'} = \frac{U_{G_1-G'} C_{k-G_1}}{E - E^0_{k-G'}} + \sum_{G} \frac{U_{G-G'} C_{k-G}}{E - E^0_{k-G'}} \tag{4.50}$$

with $G \neq G_1$ in the summation.

We know that the electron energy E is close to $E^0_{k-G_1}$ (since we are restricting k to such values), and $U_{G-G'} \ll |E^0_{k-G_1} - E^0_{k-G'}|$. Thus, since we expect C_{k-G} for $G \neq G_1$ to be small, the second term on the right-hand side is of second order in U and will be ignored. To first order, we have for $G' \neq G_1$

$$\begin{aligned} C_{k-G'} &= \frac{U_{G_1-G'} C_{k-G_1}}{E - E^0_{k-G'}} \\ &\approx \frac{U_{G_1-G'} C_{k-G_1}}{E^0_{k-G_1} - E^0_{k-G'}} \end{aligned} \tag{4.51}$$

where in the last approximation we have replaces E by $E^0_{k-G_1}$ in the denominator. The error produced by this approximation is very small compared to the energy term in the denominator.

Substituting this value of the general expansion coefficient in the k-space equation for G_1, in Equation 4.48 we get

$$\left(E - E^0_{\mathbf{k}-\mathbf{G}_1}\right) C_{\mathbf{k}-\mathbf{G}_1} = \sum_{\mathbf{G}} \frac{U_{\mathbf{G}-\mathbf{G}_1} U_{\mathbf{G}_1-\mathbf{G}}}{E^0_{\mathbf{k}-\mathbf{G}_1} - E^0_{\mathbf{k}-\mathbf{G}}} C_{\mathbf{k}-\mathbf{G}_1} \tag{4.52}$$

or

$$E = \underbrace{E^0_{\mathbf{k}-\mathbf{G}_1}}_{\text{free electron energy}} + \underbrace{\sum_{\mathbf{G}} \frac{\left|U_{\mathbf{G}-\mathbf{G}_1}\right|^2}{E^0_{\mathbf{k}-\mathbf{G}_1} - E^0_{\mathbf{k}-\mathbf{G}}}}_{\text{effect of background potential}} \tag{4.53}$$

where use has been made of $U_{\mathbf{G}_1-\mathbf{G}} = U^*_{\mathbf{G}-\mathbf{G}_1}$. The sum on the right-hand side of Equation 4.53 excludes $\mathbf{G} \neq \mathbf{G}_1$.

The effect of the perturbation due to the background potential is to give a *negative* contribution to the free electron energy when $E^0_{\mathbf{k}-\mathbf{G}}$ is above $E^0_{\mathbf{k}-\mathbf{G}_1}$, and a *positive* contribution when the value of $E^0_{\mathbf{k}-\mathbf{G}}$ is below $E^0_{\mathbf{k}-\mathbf{G}_1}$. This is illustrated in Figure 4.4b.

At a particular value of $\mathbf{k}$, only one term in the summation of Equation 4.53 will be important. As can be seen from the figure, midway between $\mathbf{G}_1$ and $\mathbf{G}_2$ or $\mathbf{G}_1$ and $\mathbf{G}_3$, the sign of the correction (perturbation) switches. It appears as if there is a discontinuity in the E vs. k relation. Our analysis does not hold close to the midway between $\mathbf{G}_1$ and $\mathbf{G}_2$ or $\mathbf{G}_1$ and $\mathbf{G}_3$ because we can no longer assume that $U_{\mathbf{G}-\mathbf{G}_1} \ll |E^0_{\mathbf{k}-\mathbf{G}_1} - E^0_{\mathbf{k}-\mathbf{G}_2}|$. We will have to re-derive our results at these near degenerate points.

Case 2: We will now develop the formalism necessary for the electron energy solutions for k values where $E^0_{\mathbf{k}-\mathbf{G}_1}$ is close to $E^0_{\mathbf{k}-\mathbf{G}_M}$, but is still separated from $\mathbf{G}_1 \neq \mathbf{G}_M$ (shaded area of Figure 4.5):

$$\begin{aligned} |E^0_{\mathbf{k}-\mathbf{G}_1} - E^0_{\mathbf{k}-\mathbf{G}_i}| &\gg U \\ \mathbf{G}_i &\neq \mathbf{G}_1 \text{ or } \mathbf{G}_M. \end{aligned} \tag{4.54}$$

In general, $\mathbf{G}_M$ may represent more than one reciprocal lattice vector which have free energy parabolas degenerate with $\mathbf{G}_1$. However, for simplicity we will assume that there is only one such vector. We will now examine separately the k-space Schrödinger equation for $\mathbf{G}_1$ and $\mathbf{G}_M$ and for a general vector $\mathbf{G}$ which is different from $\mathbf{G}_1$ and $\mathbf{G}_M$.

For $\mathbf{G}_1$ or $\mathbf{G}_M$ we have ($\mathbf{G}_i$ is $\mathbf{G}_1$ or $\mathbf{G}_M$)

$$\left(E - E^0_{\mathbf{k}-\mathbf{G}_i}\right) C_{\mathbf{k}-\mathbf{G}_i} = \sum_{\mathbf{G}_j = \mathbf{G}_1,\, \mathbf{G}_M} U_{\mathbf{G}_j-\mathbf{G}_i} C_{\mathbf{k}-\mathbf{G}_j}$$

$$+ \sum_{\mathbf{G} \neq \mathbf{G}_1,\, \mathbf{G}_M} U_{\mathbf{G}-\mathbf{G}_i} C_{\mathbf{k}-\mathbf{G}} \tag{4.55}$$

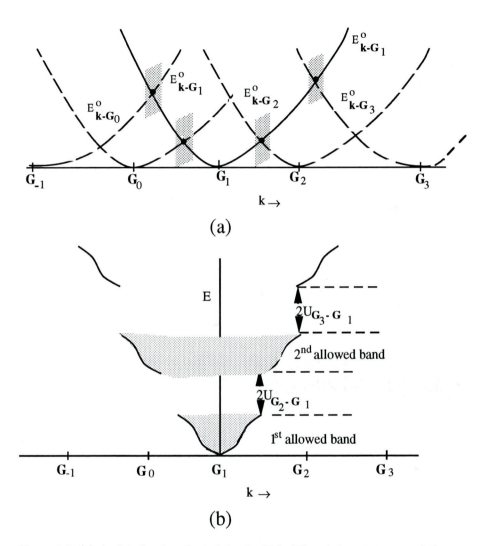

Figure 4.5: (a) A plot showing the points at which different free energy parabolas are degenerate. The points of degeneracy are the zone edges. (b) As discussed in Case 2 of the text, bandgaps are produced at the zone edges.

As before, the coefficients $C_{\mathbf{k}-\mathbf{G}}$ where $\mathbf{G}$ is not $\mathbf{G}_1$ or $\mathbf{G}_M$, are given by the approximation (see Equation 4.51)

$$C_{\mathbf{k}-\mathbf{G}} = \frac{1}{E^0_{\mathbf{k}-\mathbf{G}_1} - E^0_{\mathbf{k}-\mathbf{G}}} \sum_{\mathbf{G}_j=\mathbf{G}_1,\,\mathbf{G}_M} U_{\mathbf{G}_j-\mathbf{G}}\, C_{\mathbf{k}-\mathbf{G}_j} \qquad (4.56)$$

Substitution of these coefficients in Equation 4.55 gives us the coupled set of equations

$$\left(E - E^0_{\mathbf{k}-\mathbf{G}_i}\right) C_{\mathbf{k}-\mathbf{G}_i} = \sum_{\mathbf{G}_j=\mathbf{G}_1,\mathbf{G}_M} U_{\mathbf{G}_j-\mathbf{G}_i} C_{\mathbf{k}-\mathbf{G}_j}$$

$$+ \sum_{\mathbf{G}_j=\mathbf{G}_1,\mathbf{G}_M} \left(\sum_{\mathbf{G}\neq\mathbf{G}_1,\mathbf{G}_M} \frac{U_{\mathbf{G}-\mathbf{G}_i} U_{\mathbf{G}_j-\mathbf{G}}}{E^0_{\mathbf{k}-\mathbf{G}_1} - E^0_{\mathbf{k}-\mathbf{G}}} \right) C_{\mathbf{k}-\mathbf{G}_j}, \text{ for } i = 1, M. \quad (4.57)$$

There are two such coupled equations which need to be solved to obtain the values of E. If we make the approximation that the second term on the right hand side is small, since it is second order in $U/(E^0_{\mathbf{k}-\mathbf{G}_1} - E^0_{\mathbf{k}-\mathbf{G}})$, with $\mathbf{G} \neq \mathbf{G}_1, \mathbf{G}_M$, we get the simpler set of equations

$$\left(E - E^0_{\mathbf{k}-\mathbf{G}_i}\right) C_{\mathbf{k}-\mathbf{G}_i} = \sum_{\mathbf{G}_j=\mathbf{G}_1,\,\mathbf{G}_M} U_{\mathbf{G}_j-\mathbf{G}_i} C_{\mathbf{k}-\mathbf{G}_j}, \text{ for } i = 1, M. \qquad (4.58)$$

We will now solve this set of coupled equations when only two free energy levels are close to each other. In this case the set of equations gives the two coupled equations, letting $M = 2$:

$$\begin{aligned}
\left(E - E^0_{\mathbf{k}-\mathbf{G}_1}\right) C_{\mathbf{k}-\mathbf{G}_1} &= U_{\mathbf{G}_2-\mathbf{G}_1} C_{\mathbf{k}-\mathbf{G}_2} \\
\left(E - E^0_{\mathbf{k}-\mathbf{G}_2}\right) C_{\mathbf{k}-\mathbf{G}_2} &= U_{\mathbf{G}_1-\mathbf{G}_2} C_{\mathbf{k}-\mathbf{G}_1}.
\end{aligned} \qquad (4.59)$$

We must note that the infinite series of coupled equations has been reduced to the above two coupled equations because we are examining special points in the k-space where the coupling from other reciprocal lattice vectors is minimal. Let us define

$$\begin{aligned}
\mathbf{q} &\equiv \mathbf{k} - \mathbf{G}_1 \\
\mathbf{G} &\equiv \mathbf{G}_2 - \mathbf{G}_1
\end{aligned} \qquad (4.60)$$

we then get

$$\begin{aligned}
\left(E - E^0_{\mathbf{q}}\right) C_{\mathbf{q}} - U_{\mathbf{G}}\, C_{\mathbf{q}-\mathbf{G}} &= 0 \\
-U_{-\mathbf{G}}\, C_{\mathbf{q}} + \left(E - E^0_{\mathbf{q}-\mathbf{G}}\right) C_{\mathbf{q}-\mathbf{G}} &= 0.
\end{aligned} \qquad (4.61)$$

Such equations are called eigenvalue equations and can be solved by the usual matrix techniques by rewriting the equations in the matrix vector product form

$$\begin{bmatrix} E - E^0_{\mathbf{q}} & -U_{\mathbf{G}} \\ -U_{-\mathbf{G}} & E - E^0_{\mathbf{q}-\mathbf{G}} \end{bmatrix} \begin{bmatrix} C_{\mathbf{q}} \\ C_{\mathbf{q}-\mathbf{G}} \end{bmatrix} = 0. \qquad (4.62)$$

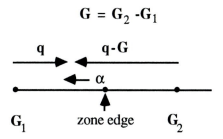

Figure 4.6: The vectors q and α defined near the Brillouin zone edge.

For nontrivial solutions (i.e., for solutions where $C_{\mathbf{q}}, C_{\mathbf{q-G}} \neq 0$) we require that, (putting $U_{-\mathbf{G}} = U_{\mathbf{G}}{}^*$):

$$\begin{vmatrix} E - E_{\mathbf{q}}^0 & -U_{\mathbf{G}} \\ -U_{\mathbf{G}}{}^* & E - E_{\mathbf{q-G}}^0 \end{vmatrix} = 0 \qquad (4.63)$$

which gives us the equation

$$E^2 - E\left(E_{\mathbf{q}}^0 + E_{\mathbf{q-G}}^0\right) - |U_{\mathbf{G}}|^2 + E_{\mathbf{q}}^0 E_{\mathbf{q-G}}^0 = 0 \qquad (4.64)$$

or

$$E = \frac{1}{2}\left(E_{\mathbf{q}}^0 + E_{\mathbf{q-G}}^0\right) \pm \left[\left(\frac{E_{\mathbf{q}}^0 + E_{\mathbf{q-G}}^0}{2}\right)^2 + |U_{\mathbf{G}}|^2\right]^{1/2}. \qquad (4.65)$$

The resulting E vs. $\mathbf{k}$ relation is shown schematically in Figure 4.5b.

This simple result of Equation 4.65 provides us with a forum to discuss the basic effects of a background periodic potential, namely, effective mass and bandgap. Let us examine the solution we have obtained near the Brillouin zone edge defined by the bisection of the reciprocal lattice vector $\mathbf{G}_1 - \mathbf{G}_2$.

At the zone edge (see Figure 4.6),

$$\begin{aligned} |q| &= |G|/2 \\ &= |q - G| \end{aligned} \qquad (4.66)$$

or

$$E_{\mathbf{q}}^0 = E_{\mathbf{q-G}}^0. \qquad (4.67)$$

The energy eigenvalue solutions then become

$$E = E_{\mathbf{G}/2}^0 \pm |U_{\mathbf{G}}|. \qquad (4.68)$$

Remembering that in absence of the background potential the energy was $E_{\mathbf{G}/2}^0$ at the zone edge, we now realize that a *discontinuity* has arisen in the

E vs. k relation at the zone edge. The magnitude of this "bandgap" is $2\,|U_{\mathbf{G}}|$. It is interesting to study the energy solutions near the zone edge. Let us write

$$q = \frac{\mathbf{G}}{2} + \alpha$$

$$q - \mathbf{G} = \alpha - \frac{\mathbf{G}}{2} \tag{4.69}$$

where α is very small and measures the wavevector from the zone edge. The energy solutions are now

$$
\begin{aligned}
E &= \frac{\hbar^2}{2m}\left(\frac{G^2}{4} + \alpha^2\right) \pm \left[\left(\frac{\hbar^2}{2m}\mathbf{G}\cdot\alpha\right)^2 + |U_{\mathbf{G}}|^2\right]^{1/2} \\
&\approx E^0_{\mathbf{G}/2} + \frac{\hbar^2\alpha^2}{2m} \pm \left[|U_{\mathbf{G}}| + \frac{\hbar^4 G^2\alpha^2}{8m^2\,|U_{\mathbf{G}}|}\right] \\
&= E^0_{\mathbf{G}/2} \pm |U_{\mathbf{G}}| + \frac{\hbar^2\alpha^2}{2}\left[\frac{1}{m} \pm \frac{\hbar^2 G^2}{4m^2\,|U_{\mathbf{G}}|}\right].
\end{aligned}
\tag{4.70}
$$

Below the bandedge, we have

$$E = E^0_{\mathbf{G}/2} - |U_{\mathbf{G}}| + \frac{\hbar^2\alpha^2}{2m}\left[1 - \frac{\hbar^2 G^2}{4m\,|U_{\mathbf{G}}|}\right] \tag{4.71}$$

and above the bandedge, we have

$$E = E^0_{\mathbf{G}/2} + |U_{\mathbf{G}}| + \frac{\hbar^2\alpha^2}{2m}\left[1 + \frac{\hbar^2 G^2}{4m\,|U_{\mathbf{G}}|}\right]. \tag{4.72}$$

If the energy is measured from the *zone edge* bandedges, we have for the lower band:

$$E = \frac{\hbar^2\alpha^2}{2m^*_L} \tag{4.73}$$

where

$$\frac{1}{m^*_L} = -\frac{1}{m}\left[\frac{\hbar^2 G^2}{4m\,|U_{\mathbf{G}}|} - 1\right] \tag{4.74}$$

since $(\hbar^2 G^2)/(4m)$ is much larger than $|U_{\mathbf{G}}|$ for the nearly free electron problem being discussed, the mass m^*_L is negative. For the upper band we have

$$E = \frac{\hbar^2\alpha^2}{2m^*_U} \tag{4.75}$$

where

$$\frac{1}{m^*_U} = \frac{1}{m}\left[\frac{\hbar^2 G^2}{4m\,|U_{\mathbf{G}}|} + 1\right]. \tag{4.76}$$

Thus it appears that the energy versus momentum measured from the zone edge (or the energy bandedge) has a *free electron-like* parabolic behavior. The quantities m_L^* and m_U^* called the effective masses since α (or q or k) behaves as an effective momentum of the electron as far as external forces or collisions are concerned, as discussed in the beginning of this chapter.

The solutions discussed near the "bandedges," have introduced a most important concept. This is the concept of the effective mass. Notice that near the bandgap, the electrons behave with a bandstructure which has a negative mass at the lower bandedge and positive mass above the bandedge. This effective mass depends upon the bandgap (through U_G, since $E_{gap} = 2U_G$), and the energy at the zone edge. We have already shown that, in general, the electron group velocity is

$$v_g = \frac{1}{\hbar} \frac{dE}{dk} \tag{4.77}$$

and near the bandedge,

$$v_g = \frac{\hbar \alpha}{m^*} \tag{4.78}$$

where m^* denotes the effective mass m_L^* or m_U^* discussed above.

If we take a time derivative of the velocity above, we get

$$\begin{aligned} \frac{dv_g}{dt} &= \frac{1}{\hbar} \frac{d^2E}{dkdt} \\ &= \frac{1}{\hbar} \nabla_k^2 E \frac{dk}{dt}. \end{aligned} \tag{4.79}$$

We also know that $\hbar dk/dt = F_{ext}$. Thus

$$\frac{dv_g}{dt} = \left(\frac{1}{\hbar^2} \nabla_k^2 E \right) F_{ext} \tag{4.80}$$

or

$$F_{ext} = \left(\frac{\hbar^2}{\nabla_k^2 E} \right) \frac{dv_g}{dt}. \tag{4.81}$$

Identifying this equation with the form of the Newton's equation of motion, we get a generalized definition of the effective mass

$$\frac{1}{m^*} = \frac{1}{\hbar^2} \nabla_k^2 E. \tag{4.82}$$

We will see later that E vs. k is, in general, not isotropic and in some cases has strong k-direction dependence. In this case we will define the effective mass as a tensor with different components. Figure 4.7 illustrates schematically, what the Bloch theorem has been able to do, to describe the electrons in a crystalline structure.

To fully solve the problem of electrons in the periodic potential, it is important to obtain the eigenfunctions of the electrons as well as the eigenenergies. Let us again focus on the zone edge. Since

$$E = E_q^0 \pm |U_G|, \tag{4.83}$$

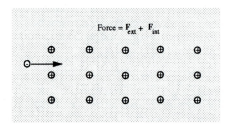

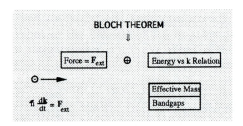

Figure 4.7: A schematic of how the complex problem of an electron in a crystalline material moving in internal and external forces is simplified by Bloch's theorem to a "free electron"–like problem with an effective energy–momentum relation.

we must have from Equation 4.61:

$$C_{\mathbf{q}} = \pm \frac{U_{\mathbf{G}}}{|U_{\mathbf{G}}|} C_{\mathbf{q}-\mathbf{G}} \tag{4.84}$$

all other coefficients in the wavefunction being negligible. The Bloch function is then

$$
\begin{aligned}
\psi_{\mathbf{k}}(\mathbf{r}) &= \sum_{\mathbf{G}'} C_{\mathbf{k}-\mathbf{G}'} \, e^{i(\mathbf{k}-\mathbf{G}')\cdot\mathbf{r}} \\
&= C_{\mathbf{q}} \, e^{-i\mathbf{G}_1\cdot\mathbf{r}} \left[1 \pm \frac{U_{\mathbf{G}}}{|U_{\mathbf{G}}|} \, e^{-i\mathbf{G}\cdot\mathbf{r}} \right] e^{-i\mathbf{k}\cdot\mathbf{r}}
\end{aligned}
\tag{4.85}
$$

where the periodic part of the Bloch function is

$$u_{\mathbf{k}}(\mathbf{r}) = C_{\mathbf{q}} \exp\left[-i\left(\frac{\mathbf{G}_1 - \mathbf{G}_2}{2} \right) \cdot \mathbf{r} \right] \left[e^{i\mathbf{G}\cdot\mathbf{r}/2} \pm \frac{|U_{\mathbf{G}}|}{U_{\mathbf{G}}} \, e^{-i\mathbf{G}\cdot\mathbf{r}/2} \right]. \tag{4.86}$$

It is interesting to examine the probability of the electron in a unit cell given by the square of the central cell part of the wavefunction: If $U_{\mathbf{G}}$ is real and positive,

$$\text{above the gap: } |u_{\mathbf{k}}(\mathbf{r})|^2 \propto \cos^2 \frac{\mathbf{G} \cdot \mathbf{r}}{2}; \ E = E_{\mathbf{q}}^0 + |U_{\mathbf{G}}|$$

$$\text{below the gap: } |u_{\mathbf{k}}(\mathbf{r})|^2 \propto \sin^2 \frac{\mathbf{G} \cdot \mathbf{r}}{2}; \ E = E_{\mathbf{q}}^0 - |U_{\mathbf{G}}|. \qquad (4.87)$$

On the other hand, if $U_{\mathbf{G}}$ is real and negative,

$$\text{above the gap: } |u_{\mathbf{k}}(\mathbf{r})|^2 \propto \sin^2 \frac{\mathbf{G} \cdot \mathbf{r}}{2}; \ E = E_{\mathbf{q}}^0 + |U_{\mathbf{G}}|$$

$$\text{below the gap: } |u_{\mathbf{k}}(\mathbf{r})|^2 \propto \cos^2 \frac{\mathbf{G} \cdot \mathbf{r}}{2}; \ E = E_{\mathbf{q}}^0 - |U_{\mathbf{G}}|. \qquad (4.88)$$

The $\cos^2$ function is called an s–like function since it is nonzero at $r = 0$ or at the lattice points. The $\sin^2$ function is p–like since it vanishes at the lattice points.

If we consider the periodic part of the wavefunction, say for positive, real $\mathbf{G}$, we see that at the top of the bandgap the electrons bunch up at the lattice sites where they see the high potential energy, while below the bandgap they move away towards regions between the lattice sites seeing a lower potential energy. This leads to an energy discontinuity. The wavefunctions are shown schematically in Figure 4.8.

In the discussions so far, it seems like we have somehow chosen the reciprocal vector $\mathbf{G}_1$ as unique from other reciprocal vectors. In fact, this is not the case. The bandstructure we have obtained is actually periodic in reciprocal lattice space due to the special nature of the Bloch functions. Everything that has been said about the vector $\mathbf{G}_1$ can be repeated for any other reciprocal lattice vectors. The bandstructure E vs. $\mathbf{k}$ and wavefunctions are periodic in the reciprocal lattice space.

The wave vector $\mathbf{k}$, appearing in the Bloch function, is, in general, extending over all k-space, but it can be restricted to the first Brillouin zone. This can be done as shown in the Figure 4.9 by a simple transformation which brings a vector into the first Brillouin zone by addition of a reciprocal lattice vector

$$\mathbf{k}' = \mathbf{k} + \mathbf{G}. \qquad (4.89)$$

The wavefunctions corresponding to $\mathbf{k}$ and $\mathbf{k}'$ are the same for the same values of $u_{\mathbf{k}}(\mathbf{r})$ as can be seen by examining the Bloch functions

$$\psi_{\mathbf{k}}(\mathbf{r}) = \sum_{\mathbf{G}'} C_{\mathbf{k}-\mathbf{G}'} e^{i(\mathbf{k}-\mathbf{G}')\cdot\mathbf{r}}$$

$$= \sum_{\mathbf{G}'} C_{\mathbf{k}'-\mathbf{G}-\mathbf{G}'} e^{i(\mathbf{k}'-\mathbf{G}-\mathbf{G}')\cdot\mathbf{r}}. \qquad (4.90)$$

Putting $\mathbf{G} + \mathbf{G}' = \mathbf{G}''$, we get

$$\psi_{\mathbf{k}}(\mathbf{r}) = \sum_{\mathbf{G}''} C_{\mathbf{k}'-\mathbf{G}''} e^{i(\mathbf{k}'-\mathbf{G}'')\cdot\mathbf{r}}$$

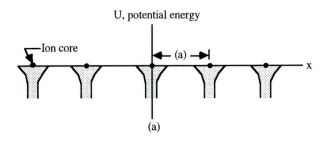

(a)

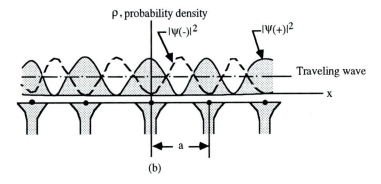

(b)

Figure 4.8: (a) Variation of potential energy of a conduction electron in the field of the ion cores of a linear lattice. (b) Distribution of probability density ρ in the lattice for $|\psi(-)|^2 \propto \sin^2 \pi x/a$; $|\psi(+)|^2 \propto \cos^2 \pi x/a$; and for a traveling wave. The wavefunction $\psi(+)$ piles up electronic charge on the cores of the positive ions, thereby lowering the potential energy in comparison with the average potential energy seen by a traveling wave. The wavefunction $\psi(-)$ piles up charge in the region between the ions, thereby raising the potential energy in comparison with that seen by a traveling wave.

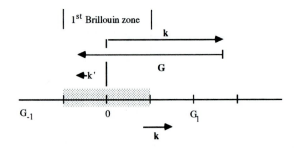

Figure 4.9: A simple transformation to fold a vector k into the first Brillouin zone.

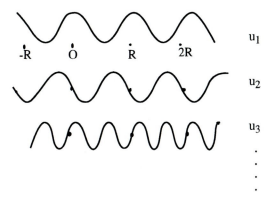

Figure 4.10: Various periodic functions $u_{\mathbf{k}}(\mathbf{r})$ leading to multiple bands in the E vs. k picture.

$$= \psi_{\mathbf{k}'}(\mathbf{r}). \qquad (4.91)$$

Thus, for a given band, i.e. for the same form of $\sum_{\mathbf{G}} C_{\mathbf{k}-\mathbf{G}} \exp(-i\mathbf{G}\cdot\mathbf{r})$, the wave functions are periodic in reciprocal lattice vectors. *The energy and momentum are thus periodic in reciprocal lattice space.*

The term, bands, that we used earlier needs to be further explained. For each value of $\mathbf{k}$, there are a number of energy eigenvalues. The difference between the wavefunction of each such eigenvalue is the symmetry of the $u_{\mathbf{k}}(\mathbf{r})$, the cell periodic parts of the wavefunction. As we know, in general,

$$\psi_{\mathbf{k}}(\mathbf{r}) = u_{\mathbf{k}}(\mathbf{r})\, e^{i\mathbf{k}\cdot\mathbf{r}}. \qquad (4.92)$$

If we substitute this in the Schrödinger equation, we get an equation for $u_{\mathbf{k}}(\mathbf{r})$,

$$\begin{aligned}
H_{\mathbf{k}} u_{\mathbf{k}}(\mathbf{r}) &= \left(\frac{\hbar^2}{2m}(-i\nabla + \mathbf{k})^2 + U(\mathbf{r}) \right) u_{\mathbf{k}}(\mathbf{r}) \\
&= E_{\mathbf{k}} u_{\mathbf{k}}(\mathbf{r}).
\end{aligned} \qquad (4.93)$$

The boundary condition on the solution for $u_{\mathbf{k}}(\mathbf{r})$ is $u_{\mathbf{k}}(\mathbf{r}) = u_{\mathbf{k}}(\mathbf{r}+\mathbf{L})$. With this boundary condition, the solutions of $u_{\mathbf{k}}(\mathbf{r})$ will be numerous as shown schematically in Figure 4.10.

$$p\psi \rightarrow i\hbar\nabla\psi = e^{i\mathbf{k}\cdot\mathbf{r}}\, \hbar(\mathbf{k} - i\nabla)u_{\mathbf{k}}(\mathbf{r}). \qquad (4.94)$$

Each solution gives a discrete energy level which belongs to a "band." As $\mathbf{k}$ varies continuously, the energies of each band change continuously tracing out the various bands. From the above discussion, we can draw the bandstructure of an electron in a one-dimensional periodic potential as shown below.

The discussion in this section has allowed us to introduce some very important concepts. The more important and the central concept in solid state

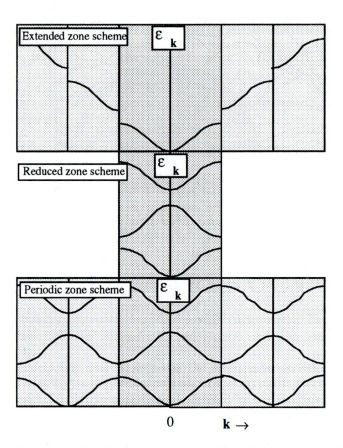

Figure 4.11: Three energy bands of a linear lattice plotted in the extended (Brillouin), reduced, and periodic zone schemes.

electronics is the concept of the bandstructure or E vs. k relation. As we noted in this section, we can draw the bandstructure around a single reciprocal lattice vector and allow k to go from 0 to ∞. This description is called the extended zone scheme and is shown in the top of Figure 4.11. We also know, however, that the bandstructure is periodic in reciprocal lattice vectors and using this property we have the periodic zone scheme as shown in the bottom of Figure 4.11. As can be seen from the periodic zone scheme, the bandstructure in each Brillouin zone is simply a repetition. Thus all of the relevant bandstructure information is actually contained in the first Brillouin zone. Thus, in the reduced zone scheme, one only displays the bandstructure in the first Brillouin zone. This is the standard way of displaying bandstructure. In a three-dimensional Brillouin zone, one usually displays the bandstructure along certain high symmetry directions. In the next chapter we will discuss realistic bandstructures of many semiconductors.

4.4 A SIMPLE DESCRIPTION OF BAND FILLING

We have developed a simple picture of allowed bands and forbidden gaps in the energy-momentum relationship of electrons in a periodic potential. We have, of course, not yet discussed the actual presence of electrons in these energy bands. When electrons are placed in the energy bands, their distribution has very profound effects on the electronic properties of the material. To find the electron distribution, we need to know how many electrons a given band can hold. We find this number for a simple case, although the results are true for more complex structures.

Consider a linear crystal having N unit cells with spacing of a. The total length is $L = N/a$. The k-states allowed in the first Brillouin zone which extends from $-\pi/a$ to $+\pi/a$ are:

$$k = 0, \ \pm \frac{2\pi}{L}, \ \pm \frac{4\pi}{L} \ldots \frac{N\pi}{L}. \tag{4.95}$$

This gives a total of N allowed k-states. Thus each unit cell contributes one electron state to each energy band. If we count the spin degeneracy, there are $2N$ allowed electron states in each energy band. Remember that we only need to worry about states in the first Brillouin zone, since states outside are just degenerate states in the first Brillouin zone. For a given material system we could have the following possible scenarios:

1. The crystal has one atom per cell. This implies that at $T = 0K$, the band is half-full.

2. One atom per cell and two electrons per atom. This will ensure that the band is full, there is a bandgap, and the next band is empty.

3. There are two atoms per cell and each atom contributes at least one electron. Once again the band is full, there is a bandgap, and the next band is empty.

For cases which are in the category i discussed above, i.e., if they have a half-filled band, the material is metallic and has a high conductivity even at very low temperatures.

For materials which fall in the categories ii or iii, the lower band is full (this band is called the valence band) while the upper band is empty (this is called the conduction band). In such materials the conductivity essentially goes to zero at low temperature. Figure 4.12 illustrates these concepts.

The above description is usually correct unless there is overlap of bands in energy in which case materials which may normally be semiconductors according to above arguments, may be metallic. This is shown schematically in Figure 4.13.

The definitions given above are based upon a very simple observation, namely, a completely filled band does not carry current. Thus, even when there

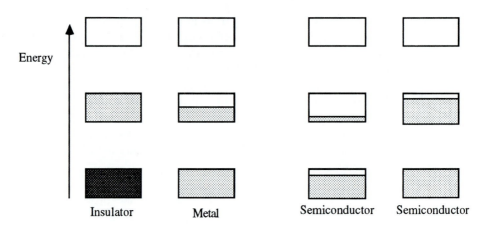

Figure 4.12: A schematic description of electron occupation of the bands in an insulator, a metal, and two semiconductors at finite temperature. At zero temperature, the semiconductor bands look like those in an insulator.

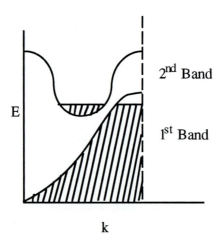

Figure 4.13: A schematic of a case of two bands which overlap in energy. The system will be metallic.

is a very large number of electrons in a filled band, there is *no net current being carried*.

The current in a completely filled band is

$$
\begin{aligned}
\boldsymbol{j} &= qn\boldsymbol{v} \\
&= -e \int N(E) \, f(E) \, \boldsymbol{v}(E) \, dE \times \text{spin degeneracy} \\
&= -e \int \frac{d^3k}{(2\pi)^3} \frac{1}{\hbar} \frac{\partial E}{\partial \boldsymbol{k}} \times 2.
\end{aligned}
\tag{4.96}
$$

The distribution function $f(E)$ is unity for the filled band.

We know from our discussion that $E(\boldsymbol{k})$ is a periodic function in k-space and the integral over k-space is over the first Brillouin zone. Since $E(\boldsymbol{k})$ is periodic in reciprocal lattice space, the integral

$$
I(\boldsymbol{k}') = \int_{1stBZ} E(\boldsymbol{k} + \boldsymbol{k}') \, d^3k
\tag{4.97}
$$

is independent of $\boldsymbol{k}'$. Thus the derivative of the integral with respect to $\boldsymbol{k}'$ or $\boldsymbol{k}$ is zero:

$$
\begin{aligned}
\frac{\partial}{\partial \boldsymbol{k}'} I(\boldsymbol{k}') &= 0 \\
&= \int_{1stBZ} \nabla_{\boldsymbol{k}'} E(\boldsymbol{k} + \boldsymbol{k}') \, d^3k \\
&= \int_{1stBZ} \nabla_{\boldsymbol{k}} E(\boldsymbol{k} + \boldsymbol{k}') \, d^3k.
\end{aligned}
\tag{4.98}
$$

Thus the current in a filled band (for which the Fermi–Dirac probability $f(E) = 1.0$) is zero. Physically, the current is zero since as many electrons contribute positive current as do negative current. This result is very important since it tells us that despite a very large number of electrons present in a filled band, there is no net contribution to current. Current conduction can only take place if the distribution function $f(E)$ is such that the band is partially filled. This also leads to another important concept, namely, that of holes in semiconductors.

4.5 HOLES IN SEMICONDUCTORS

Semiconductors are defined as materials in which the valence band is full and the conduction band is empty at $T = 0K$. At finite temperatures some of the electrons leave the valence band and occupy the conduction band. The valence band is then left with some unoccupied states. Let us consider the situation as shown in Figure 4.14 where an electron with momentum $\boldsymbol{k}_e$ is missing from the valence band.

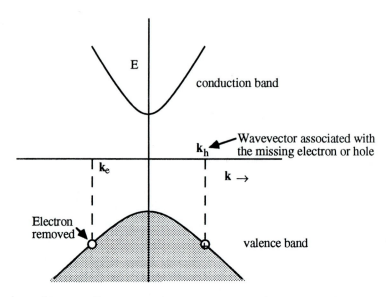

Figure 4.14: Diagram illustrating the wavevector of the missing electron k_e. The wavevector of the system with the missing electron is $-k_e$, which is associated with the hole.

When all the valence band states are occupied the sum over all wavevector states is zero, i.e.

$$\sum k_i = 0$$
$$= \sum_{k_i \neq k_e} k_i + k_e. \qquad (4.99)$$

This result is just an indication of the inversion symmetry of the Brillouin zone. Now in the situation where the electron at wavevector k_e is missing, the total wavevector is

$$\sum_{k_i \neq k_e} k_i = -k_e. \qquad (4.100)$$

The missing state is called a hole and the wavevector of the system $-k_e$ is attributed to it. It is important to note that the electron is missing from the state k_e and the momentum associated with the hole is at $-k_e$. The position of the hole is depicted as that of the missing electron. But in reality the hole wavevector k_h is $-k_e$.

$$k_h = -k_e \qquad (4.101)$$

Let us now consider the energy of the hole and its relation to the energy of the electronic state that is empty. If we choose the energy origin at the top of the valence band, the energy of the system with the missing electron is positive compared to the system with all filled states. The lower the energy of the electron below the top of the valence band, the higher the energy of the state with the missing electron. Since the hole is the system with the missing electron, if the electron is missing from a state $\boldsymbol{k}_e$, with energy $E_e(\boldsymbol{k}_e)$, the energy of the hole is

$$E_h(\boldsymbol{k}_h) = -E_e(-\boldsymbol{k}_e). \tag{4.102}$$

Also, if the band is symmetric and $E_e(\boldsymbol{k}_e) = E_e(-\boldsymbol{k}_e)$, we have

$$E_h(\boldsymbol{k}_h) = -E_e(\boldsymbol{k}_e). \tag{4.103}$$

We have seen that near the top of the valence band, as $\boldsymbol{k}$ is changed, the electronic energies decrease. However, the result above shows that if we talk about the hole band, the band energies increase away from the valence bandedge. This is illustrated in Figure 4.15.

The two relations established above also show that the velocity of the hole is the same as the velocity of the electronic state from which the electron is missing, since

$$
\begin{aligned}
\hbar v_h &= \nabla_{\boldsymbol{k}_h} E_h(\boldsymbol{k}_h) \\
&= -\nabla_{\boldsymbol{k}_e}(-E_e(\boldsymbol{k}_e)) \\
&= \nabla_{\boldsymbol{k}_e}(E_e(\boldsymbol{k}_e)) \\
&= \hbar v_e
\end{aligned}
\tag{4.104}
$$

or

$$v_h = v_e \tag{4.105}$$

It is also clear from our band description of the electrons and holes that

$$m_h^* = -m_e^* \tag{4.106}$$

Thus, for most materials the electron effective mass near the valence bandedge is negative, but the hole effective mass is positive.

Finally, let us examine the equation of motion obeyed by the holes. In presence of an electric and magnetic field, the equation of motion of the Bloch electrons is

$$\hbar \frac{dk_e}{dt} = -e\left(\boldsymbol{F} + \frac{1}{c}v_e \times \boldsymbol{B}\right). \tag{4.107}$$

Substituting $-\boldsymbol{k}_h$ for $\boldsymbol{k}_e$, and v_h for v_e we get the equation describing the holes,

$$\hbar \frac{dk_h}{dt} = e\left(\boldsymbol{F} + \frac{1}{c}v_h \times \boldsymbol{B}\right). \tag{4.108}$$

Thus the equation of motion of holes is that of a particle with a *positive* charge e. It is important to recognize that we do not actually have a positively charged particle. The holes behave as if they had a positive charge. This occurs because all of the occupied states in the valence band respond to the external forces with

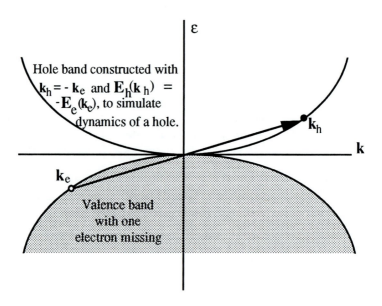

Figure 4.15: The upper half of the figure shows the hole band that simulates the dynamics of a hole, constructed by inversion of the valence band in the origin. The wavevector and energy of the hole are equal, but opposite in sign, to the wavevector and energy of the empty electron orbital in the valence band. We do not show the deposition of the electron removed from the valence band at k_e.

a proper negative charge response, but the missing electron state responds with a positive charge response. This is schematically illustrated in Figure 4.16.

Because of the equation of motion discussed above, in an electric field the electrons in the conduction band move in a direction opposite to the direction of holes in the valence band. However, because they effectively carry a positive charge, the direction of the current produced is the same as shown in Figure 4.17.

4.6   FOR THE TECHNOLOGIST IN YOU

The Bloch theorem and the resulting bandstructure of electrons in crystals were the major conceptual breakthroughs which allowed scientists to understand and

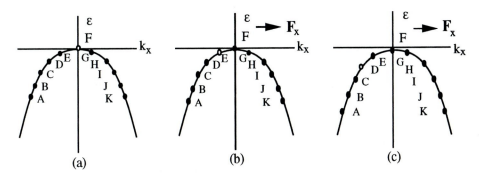

Figure 4.16: (a) At $t = 0$ all states are filled except F at the top of the band; the velocity v_x is zero at F because $dE/dk_x = 0$. (b) An electric field F_x is applied in the $+k_x$ direction. The force on the electrons is in the $-k_x$ direction and all electrons make transitions together in the $-k_x$ direction, moving the hole to the state E. (c) After a further interval of time, the electrons move farther along in k- space and the hole is now at D.

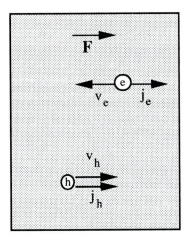

Figure 4.17: Motion of electrons in the conduction band and holes in the valence band in the electric field F. The hole and electron drift velocities are in opposite directions, but their electric currents are in the same direction, the direction of the electric field.

predict the myriad of physical phenomena seen in semiconductors. In high quality crystals at low temperatures, electrons can cross up to 10^4 unit cells without scattering! Indeed, ballistic transport devices are being conceived and demonstrated in which electrons move without any scattering effect, as they would in vacuum tubes.

The concept of holes is an extremely important one and one which requires a great deal of time to fully digest. The observation of holes by Hall effect discussed in Chapter 1 was one of the driving forces for bandstructure theories. Holes are active charge carriers in a number of electronic devices such as bipolar transistors, complimentary logic device, etc. They are also an active ingredient in almost all opto-electronic devices.

The concept of effective mass is one of the more difficult concepts in solid state physics. It is hard to see physically how an electron enters a semiconductor and behaves as if it had a different mass. The electron can be thought of as moving freely if it properly "meshes" with the periodicity of the crystal lattice. In some sense, this is like a pinion gear rolling on a rack, as shown schematically in Figure 4.18. Where the pitch of the gear matches that of the rack, it moves smoothly, despite the fact that the rack is not a smooth surface. On the other hand, when the gear's pitch does not match that of the rack, then the motion is impeded. Similarly, an electron with the right periodicity (Bloch function) is able to move freely through the periodic lattice. Development of high speed electronics is of course one of the driving forces for the search for smaller effective mass materials.

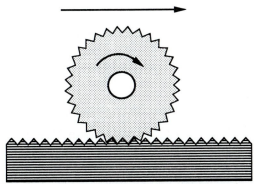

Matching of periodicity results in smooth motion.

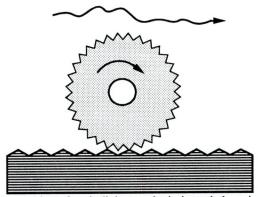

Mismatching of periodicity results in impeded motion.

Figure 4.18: Schematic illustration of pinion gear meshing with a rack. Where the periodicity of the gear's teeth and of the rack's match, the motion is smooth, despite the fact that the rack is not smooth. Where the periodicities mismatch, the motion is impeded. This is similar to the free motion of an electron in a crystal. If the electron is correctly periodic (having a cell periodic part of its Bloch function), then it will move freely throughout the crystal. A state without this periodicity cannot be an eigenstate of the system.

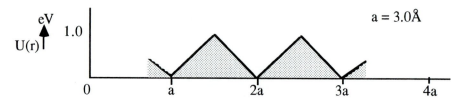

Figure 4.19: One-dimensional potential for Problem 4.1.

4.7 PROBLEMS

4.1. Consider a 1-dimensional periodic background potential having the form shown in Figure 4.19.

    (a) Find the energy widths (in eV) of the first two bandgaps and the allowed bands.

    (b) Find the effective masses just below and just above the first bandgap.

    (c) Find the effective masses just below and just above the second bandgap.

4.2. Consider a square lattice in two dimensions with a background potential

$$U(x,y) = U_0 \cos \frac{2\pi x}{a} \cos \frac{2\pi y}{a}$$

where $U_0 = 2.0$ eV. Set up a 2×2 secular equation to calculate the bandgap at the point $(\pi/a, \pi/a)$ of the Brillouin zone.

4.3. GaAs has a conduction band that can be described near the band edge by an expression in the term

$$E(k) = \frac{\hbar^2 k^2}{2m^*}$$

where $m^* = 0.067 m_0$. An electric field of 10 kV/cm (along the x-axis is applied at time $t = 0$ to an electron at the bottom of the conduction band. What is the energy of the electron after a time interval of 1, 2, 10 picoseconds? Remember that the bandstructure is periodic in the reciprocal lattice space.

4.4. In GaAs, once the channel dimensions are less than 1000 Å, much of the transport occurs without scattering. In such ballistic transport, the electron climbs up along the E vs. k diagram in accordance with the effective

Newton's equation of motion. Assume a parabolic band relation

$$E = \frac{\hbar^2 k^2}{2m^*}$$

with $m^* = 0.067 m_0$. Calculate the electron transit time and final energy for a transit length of 0.1 μm and an electric field of 10^3 V/cm, 10^4 V/cm and 10^5 V/cm.

4.5. We have seen from the solution of the Schrödinger equation in periodic structures, that bandgaps appear at the Brillouin zone edges. The wavefunctions at the zone edges represent standing waves. These standing waves are similar to those produced by placing reflecting barriers in a cavity. Away from the zone edge, the waves can be considered as made up of two waves proceeding in opposite directions with unequal amplitudes. Study the paper by H. Kogelnik and C. V. Shank, "Coupled–Wave Theory of Distributed Feedback Lasers," J. Appl. Phys., **45**, 2327, (1972), to see how this concept is used in improving the tunability of lasers.

4.6. Using the concept of conservation of total crystal momentum in normal processes, show that in a semiconductor, the transitions of electrons from the valence band to the conduction band involve only vertical transitions in the E vs. k diagram. Thus only direct gap semiconductors have strong optical interactions near the bandedge. (Hint: The photon momentum is almost zero.)

4.8 REFERENCES

- **General**

    - Ashcroft, N. W. and N. D. Mermin, *Solid State Physics* (Holt, Reinhart and Winston, New York, 1976).
    - Kittel, C., *Introduction to Solid State Physics* (John Wiley and Sons, New York, 1986).

CHAPTER
5

SEMICONDUCTOR
BANDSTRUCTURE

In the previous chapter, we have been able to establish the most important concept in solid state physics. The apparently complex problem of how electrons move through a crystal has been greatly simplified. None of the expected complications of electrons colliding with the ions as they struggle along, materialized. In fact, the electrons move through the crystal as if they were in free space, i.e., without collisions. The electrons also respond to external forces and collision processes just like free particles. The quantity $\hbar k$, where k is the parameter describing the wavefunction, behaves like an effective momentum for the electron. The only (and, of course, a very important) effect of the periodic potential is that the E vs. k relation for the electrons is not a simple free electron-like parabola but, in fact, is quite complex. We had looked at the nearly free electron picture where the background potential was weak and saw the concepts of effective mass, bandgaps, and allowed bands, being manifested. While very instructional, the bandstructure (the E vs. k picture) of real semiconductors is too complex to be described by the nearly free electron picture. In this chapter we will look at realistic methods for the bandstructure calculation in semiconductors.

There are two main categories of realistic bandstructure calculation for semiconductors:

1. Methods which describe the entire valence and conduction bands.

2. Methods which describe near bandedge bandstructures.

The techniques in the second category are simpler and considerably more accurate if one is interested only in phenomena near the bandedges. Techniques such as the tight binding method, the pseudopotential method, and the orthogonalized plane wave methods fall in the first category. On the other hand, perturbative techniques (the so called $k \cdot p$ methods) fall in the second category. We will develop the tight binding method and the $k \cdot p$ method in some detail, since both

126

of these techniques are widely used for describing real semiconductors and their heterostructures.

Before examining the various semiconductors it is extremely useful to examine the atomic structure of some of the elements which make up the various semiconductors.

IV Semiconductors

C $\quad 1s^2 \underbrace{2s^2 2p^2}$

Si $\quad 1s^2 2s^2 2p^6 \underbrace{3s^2 3p^2}$

Ge $\quad 1s^2 2s^2 2p^6 3s^2 3p^6 3d^{10} \underbrace{4s^2 4p^2}$

III–V Semiconductors

Ga $\quad 1s^2 2s^2 2p^6 3s^2 3p^6 3d^{10} \underbrace{4s^2 4p^1}$

As $\quad 1s^2 2s^2 2p^6 3s^2 3p^6 3d^{10} \underbrace{4s^2 4p^3}$

A very important conclusion can be drawn about the elements making up the semiconductors: The outermost valence electrons are made up of electrons in either the s-type or p-type orbitals. While this conclusion is strictly true for the elements in the atomic form, it turns out that even in the crystalline semiconductors the electrons in the valence and conductor band retain this s- or p-type character, even though they are "free" Bloch electrons. It is extremely important to appreciate this simple feature since it plays a key role in optical and transport processes in semiconductors.

5.1 THE TIGHT BINDING METHOD

The tight binding method is a powerful empirical technique (the empirical nature will become clear later on) to study the bandstructure of real semiconductors. It not only is capable of providing a reasonably good description of the bandstructure but can also be used to study defects in semiconductors. Additionally, it allows us to determine the nature of the eigenstates (the Bloch functions) near the band edges in semiconductors, thus facilitating the development of the perturbative $\boldsymbol{k} \cdot \boldsymbol{p}$ methods.

We remind ourselves that regardless of the method used for calculating the bandstructure, the eigenfunctions of the electrons must be Bloch functions. In the previous chapter the Bloch functions were developed from plane wave functions, i.e., they were written in the plane wave basis. Another basis set could be the atomic orbitals which describe the elements making up the crystal. The periodic part of the Bloch function would thus be represented by some combination of the atomic orbitals centered at the lattice points. If $\phi_n(\boldsymbol{r} - \boldsymbol{R})$ represents such an orbital centered at $\boldsymbol{R}$, we could write a Bloch function of the form:

$$\psi_{\mathbf{k}}(\boldsymbol{r}) = \sum_{\mathbf{R}_n} \phi_n(\boldsymbol{r} - \boldsymbol{R}) \exp(i\boldsymbol{k} \cdot \boldsymbol{R}_n). \qquad (5.1)$$

In this expansion, the periodic part of the Bloch function is expanded in terms of the atomic-like orbitals of the atoms of the unit cell (index n in the summation). We remind ourselves that, in principle, the Bloch wavefunction can be expanded in terms of *any complete set of basis states*. The choice of a particular set of basis is motivated by:

- ease of mathematical manipulation of the basis set,

- and more importantly, a judicious choice such that, to a good approximation, only a few states of the basis set are required for the description.

The second point mentioned above is the driving force for using the atomic-like orbitals for the basis set to describe the electrons in semiconductors. In the example discussed in the previous chapter (nearly free electron case), the expansion was carried out in terms of the simple Fourier basis set. While the same procedure can, in principle, be applied to semiconductors by using the orthogonal plane wave method, the description in terms of atomic orbitals is more physical and simple, and often requires fewer basis functions.

As noted earlier, the elements making up all the semiconductors of interest have the valence electrons described by s- or p-type atomic orbitals. The core electrons are usually not of interest as will be clear later on, except of some special characterization-type experiments. As the atoms of the elements making up the semiconductors are brought together to form the crystal, the valence electronic states are perturbed by the presence of neighboring atoms (see Figure 5.1). The core electron states are strongly bound (i.e., the wavefunctions are more localized around the nucleus) and do not sense the neighboring atoms much. While the original atomic functions describing the valence electrons are, of course, no longer eigenstates of the problem, they can be used as a good approximate set of basis states to describe the "crystalline" electrons. This is the motivation for the tight binding method. We develop a simple mathematical description for the tight binding method and then discuss some details of the application of the method to real semiconductors.

We assume the solution of the atomic problem

$$H_{\text{at}}\psi_n = E_n\psi_n \qquad (5.2)$$

is already known for the atoms forming the crystalline material. This solution leads to the description of the electronic structure of the various atoms. One could construct a Bloch state given by

$$\psi_{\mathbf{k}}(\boldsymbol{r}) = \sum_{n,\mathbf{R}} e^{i\mathbf{k}\cdot\mathbf{R}}\psi_n(\boldsymbol{r} - \boldsymbol{R}) \qquad (5.3)$$

but this state does not describe the new problem of the crystalline material where now we have

$$H_{\text{cryst}} = H_{\text{at}} + \Delta U(\boldsymbol{r}) \qquad (5.4)$$

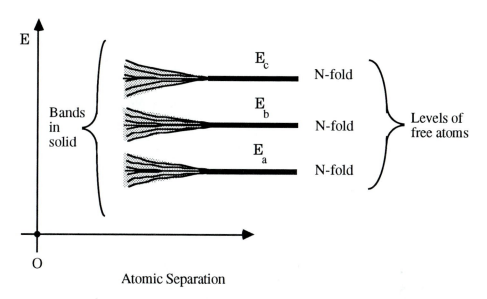

E

Bands
in
solid

E_c

N-fold

E_b

N-fold

E_a

N-fold

Levels of
free atoms

O

Atomic Separation

Figure 5.1: Atomic levels spreading into bands as the atoms come together. When the atoms are far apart, the electron levels are discrete and N-fold degenerate (N is the number of atoms). As the atoms are brought closer, the discrete levels form bands.

where $\Delta U(\boldsymbol{r})$ is the additional perturbation coming in, due to the interaction of neighboring atoms as shown in Figure 5.2.

The new wavefunctions are now chosen as the more general wavefunction (they must, of course, satisfy Bloch's Theorem):

$$\Psi_{\mathbf{k}}(\boldsymbol{r}) = \sum_{\mathbf{R}} e^{i\mathbf{k}\cdot\mathbf{R}}\phi(\boldsymbol{r} - \boldsymbol{R}) \tag{5.5}$$

where $\phi(\boldsymbol{r})$ are not the atomic functions, but can be constructed out of the atomic functions. We will shortly discuss the more general form for the case where there is more than one atom in the basis. Expanding $\phi(\boldsymbol{r})$ in terms of the atomic eigenfunctions $\psi_n(\boldsymbol{r})$ we have

$$\phi(\boldsymbol{r}) = \sum_{n=1}^{N} b_n \psi_n(\boldsymbol{r}). \tag{5.6}$$

In the tight binding method, we will only include a finite number, N, of orbitals in terms of which $\phi(\boldsymbol{r})$ is described. The Schrödinger equation now involves the unknown coefficients b_n of Equation 5.6 and to solve for them we first derive a set of N–coupled equations, by using the orthonormal properties of the basis set ψ_n. The Schrödinger equation is now

$$H\Psi_{\mathbf{k}} = E(\boldsymbol{k})\Psi_{\mathbf{k}}. \tag{5.7}$$

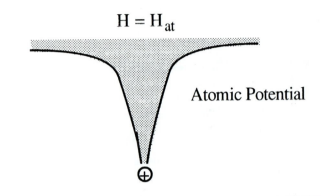

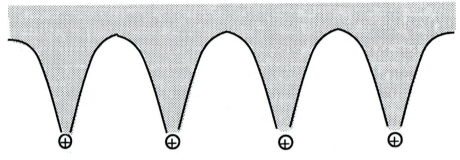

Figure 5.2: The effect of the neighboring atoms in a crystal is to alter the potential an electron experiences from that of an atomic potential (top figure) by an additional potential $\Delta U(r)$.

Using Equations 5.5 and 5.6 for the eigenfunction Ψ_n and multiplying by $\psi_m^*(r)$ and integrating over space we get:

$$\int d^3r \; \psi_m^*(r) \left\{ [H_{at} + \Delta U(r)] \sum_{R,n} b_n \; e^{ik \cdot R} \; \psi_n(r - R) \right. \\ \left. - E(k) \sum_{R,n} b_n \; e^{ik \cdot R} \; \psi_n(r - R) \right\} = 0. \tag{5.8}$$

Since the atomic functions are orthogonal, we have

$$\int d^3r \; \psi_m^*(r) \; \psi_n(r) = \delta_{mn}. \tag{5.9}$$

However, the atomic functions centered at different sites are not orthogonal, i.e.

$$\int d^3r \; \psi_m^*(r) \; \psi_n(r - R) \neq \delta_{mn} \text{ for } R \neq 0. \tag{5.10}$$

In the summation over lattice vectors we separate the terms with $\boldsymbol{R} = 0$ and $\boldsymbol{R} \neq 0$ to get,

$$
\begin{aligned}
(E(\boldsymbol{k}) &- E_m)b_m \\
&= -(E(\boldsymbol{k}) - E_m) \sum_{n=1}^{N} \left(\sum_{\boldsymbol{R} \neq 0} \int \psi_m^*(\boldsymbol{r})\, \psi_n(\boldsymbol{r} - \boldsymbol{R})\, e^{i\boldsymbol{k}\cdot\boldsymbol{R}}\, d^3r \right) b_n \\
&\quad + \sum_{n=1}^{N} \left(\int \psi_m^*(\boldsymbol{r})\, \Delta U(\boldsymbol{r})\, \psi_n(\boldsymbol{r})\, d^3r \right) b_n \\
&\quad + \sum_{n=1}^{N} \left(\sum_{\boldsymbol{R} \neq 0} \int \psi_m^*(\boldsymbol{r})\, \Delta U(\boldsymbol{r})\, \psi_n(\boldsymbol{r} - \boldsymbol{R})\, e^{i\boldsymbol{k}\cdot\boldsymbol{R}}\, d^3r \right) b_n .
\end{aligned}
\tag{5.11}
$$

Note that we have used the equality

$$
\int \psi_m^*(\boldsymbol{r})\, H_{\text{at}}\, \psi_n(\boldsymbol{r})\, d^3r = E_m\, \delta_{mn} .
\tag{5.12}
$$

It may be pointed out that the atomic energies E_m may not correspond to the isolated atomic energies. This is due to the modifications arising from the neighboring atoms. As we will discuss later, the E_m are retained as fitting parameters. In tight binding methods, we also make the following approximation:

$$
\int \psi_m^*(\boldsymbol{r})\, \psi_n(\boldsymbol{r} - \boldsymbol{R})\, e^{i\boldsymbol{k}\cdot\boldsymbol{R}}\, d^3r \approx 0 .
\tag{5.13}
$$

This approximation assumes that there is negligible overlap between neighboring atomic functions, i.e, the atomic functions are tightly bound to the atoms.

The quantity

$$
\int \psi_m^*(\boldsymbol{r})\, H\, \psi_n(\boldsymbol{r})\, d^3r = E_m + \int \psi_m^*(\boldsymbol{r})\, \Delta U(\boldsymbol{r})\, \psi_m(\boldsymbol{r})\, d^3r
\tag{5.14}
$$

is called the on-site matrix element. For most potentials, the on-site integral:

$$
\int \psi_m^*(\boldsymbol{r})\, \Delta U(\boldsymbol{r})\, \psi_n(\boldsymbol{r})\, d^3r \text{ vanishes for } m \neq n .
\tag{5.15}
$$

The secular equation (Equation 5.11) for the eigenvalues $E(\boldsymbol{k})$ and eigenfunctions (whose coefficients are the b_m) is an $N \times N$ coupled set of equations whose solution is derived from an $N \times N$ secular equation. For each value of $\boldsymbol{k}$, there will be N solutions, which will provide the E vs. $\boldsymbol{k}$ relation or the bandstructure. It is illustrative to examine a simple s-band problem to develop an understanding of the method. We will then discuss the extension to the general zinc–blende structure.

5.1.1 Bandstructure Arising From a Single Atomic s-Level

Since there is only one atomic level, the coefficients $\{b_m\}$ are zero except for the s-level where $b_s = 1$. A single equation results in this case. Equation 5.11

becomes

$$
\begin{aligned}
E(k) - E_s \;=\;& -(E(k) - E_s) \sum_{\mathbf{R} \neq 0} \int \psi_s^*(\mathbf{r}) \, \psi_s(\mathbf{r} - \mathbf{R}) \, e^{i\mathbf{k}\cdot\mathbf{R}} \, d^3r \\
& + \int \psi_s^*(\mathbf{r}) \, \Delta U(\mathbf{r}) \, \psi_s(\mathbf{r}) \, d^3r \\
& + \sum_{\mathbf{R} \neq 0} \int \psi_s^*(\mathbf{r}) \, \Delta U(\mathbf{r}) \, \psi_s(\mathbf{r} - \mathbf{R}) \, e^{i\mathbf{k}\cdot\mathbf{R}} \, d^3r.
\end{aligned}
\tag{5.16}
$$

Let us choose the following symbols for the integrals

$$
\begin{aligned}
\alpha(\mathbf{R}) \;&=\; \int \psi_s^*(\mathbf{r}) \, \psi_s(\mathbf{r} - \mathbf{R}) \, d^3r \\
\beta_s \;&=\; -\int \psi_s^*(\mathbf{r}) \, \Delta U(\mathbf{r}) \, \psi_s(\mathbf{r}) \, d^3r \\
\gamma(\mathbf{R}) \;&=\; -\int \psi_s^*(\mathbf{r}) \, \Delta U(\mathbf{r}) \, \psi_s(\mathbf{r} - \mathbf{R}) \, d^3r.
\end{aligned}
\tag{5.17}
$$

As discussed before, in the tight binding method we choose $\alpha(\mathbf{R}) = 0$. This gives us

$$
E(k) = E_s - \beta_s - \sum_{\mathbf{R}} \gamma(\mathbf{R}) \, e^{i\mathbf{k}\cdot\mathbf{R}}.
\tag{5.18}
$$

The off-site integrals $\gamma(\mathbf{R})$ drop rapidly as the separation $\mathbf{R}$ increases. We will consider the case where we only have nearest neighbor interaction and all other off-site integrals are zero. Also, note that because of symmetry $\gamma(-\mathbf{R}) = \gamma(\mathbf{R})$. Let us solve the problem for the fcc lattice. The twelve nearest neighbors for an fcc point are at:

$$
\frac{a}{2}(\pm 1, \pm 1, 0); \frac{a}{2}(\pm 1, 0, \pm 1); \frac{a}{2}(0, \pm 1, \pm 1).
\tag{5.19}
$$

The energy equation then becomes

$$
\begin{aligned}
E(k) \;=\;& E_s - \beta_s - \gamma \left[e^{i(k_x + k_y)a/2} + e^{i(k_x - k_y)a/2} \right. \\
& \left. + e^{i(-k_x + k_y)a/2} + e^{i(k_x - k_y)a/2} + \dots \right] \\
=\;& E_s - \beta_s - 4\gamma \left[\cos \frac{k_x a}{2} \cos \frac{k_y a}{2} \right. \\
& \left. + \cos \frac{k_y a}{2} \cos \frac{k_z a}{2} + \cos \frac{k_z a}{2} \cos \frac{k_x a}{2} \right].
\end{aligned}
\tag{5.20}
$$

We will now examine this band in the first Brillouin zone of the fcc lattice. The Brillouin zone has certain high symmetry points, which in units of $2\pi/a$, have the following coordinates (Figure 5.3):

- Γ point: $(0, 0, 0)$, is the zone center,

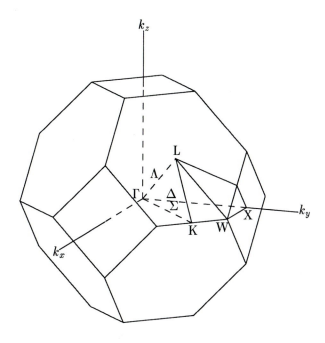

Figure 5.3: Brillouin zone and high symmetry points for the fcc lattice which forms the underlying Bravais lattice for diamond and zinc–blende structures.

- X point: $(1, 0, 0)$ and the five other equivalent points,

- L point: $(1/2, 1/2, 1/2)$ and the seven other equivalent points,

- K point: $(3/4, 3/4, 0)$,

- W point: $(1, 1/2, 0)$.

The opposite L points are connected by a reciprocal lattice vector and therefore the real degeneracy is only 4-fold, instead of 8-fold. Similarly, the X point contributes only three distinct points to the first Brillouin zone, instead of six.

If we examine the energy along various symmetry directions, we get the bandstructure:

$$\gamma = 1.0 \text{ eV} \qquad E_s + \beta = 0$$

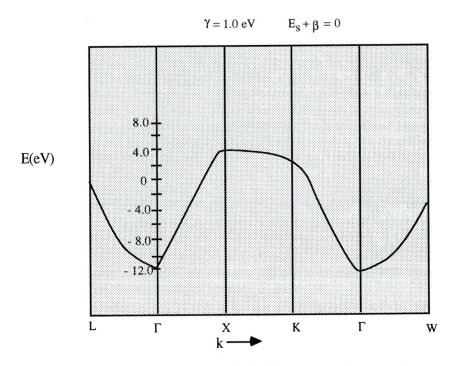

Figure 5.4: Bandstructure of the s–band model with parameters chosen as shown.

Along ΓX $k_x = 2\pi\alpha/a$ $0 \le \alpha \le 1$

$k_y = k_z = 0$

$E(\mathbf{k}) = E_s - \beta_s - 4\gamma(1 + 2\cos\pi\alpha)$

Along ΓL $k_x = k_y = k_z = 2\pi\alpha/a$ $0 \le \alpha \le 1/2$

$E(\mathbf{k}) = E_s - \beta_s - 12\gamma\cos^2\pi\alpha)$

Along ΓK $k_x = k_y = 2\pi\alpha/a$ $0 \le \alpha \le 3/4$

$k_z = 0$

$E(\mathbf{k}) = E_s - \beta_s - 4\gamma(\cos^2\pi\alpha + 2\cos\pi\alpha)$

Figure 5.4 shows a plot of these results. This is a standard technique to plot bandstructures on a two-dimensional figure. In the result shown here, for each value of $\mathbf{k}$, there is only one energy level. Contrast this to the nearly free electron problem of Chapter 4, where for each $\mathbf{k}$-value we had an infinite number of energy levels. This is because we are focusing on only one band by choosing a single s-band description.

The width of the band shown in Figure 5.3 is 16γ and as the overlap integral γ increases, the bandwidth increases. It is illustrative to examine the bandstructure near the Γ point, where ka is small.

Putting $k_x^2 = k_y^2 = k_z^2 = k^2/3$, we have ($ka \ll 1$)

$$E(\mathbf{k}) = E_s - \beta_s - 12\gamma + \gamma k^2 a^2. \qquad (5.21)$$

Comparing with the free electron problem solution

$$E(p) = E_0 + \frac{p^2}{2m} \tag{5.22}$$

we write

$$E(k) = E_s - \beta_s - 12\gamma + \frac{\hbar^2 k^2}{2m^*} \tag{5.23}$$

where

$$m^* = \frac{\hbar^2}{2\gamma a^2}$$

$$\gamma = \frac{\Delta W}{16} \tag{5.24}$$

If we choose $\gamma = 1.0$ eV and $a = 4$ Å we find that $m^* \approx 0.2 m_0$. Thus, in this simple model the effective mass is determined by the parameters γ and a. Of course, these parameters are related to each other. We expect that as a increases, the value of γ will decrease, until at large values of a, γ goes to zero and we get back a discrete level, with infinite *effective* mass.

5.1.2 Bandstructure of Semiconductors

As we have discussed earlier, the atomic functions required to describe the outermost electrons in semiconductors are the s, p_x, p_y, and p_z type. Moreover, since there are two atoms per basis in a semiconductor, we require eight functions to describe the central cell part of the Bloch functions. Once again, we choose a state of the form

$$\Psi(k, r) = \sum_{R_i} \sum_{m=1}^{4} \sum_{j=1}^{2} C_{mj}(k)\, \phi_{mj}(r - r_m - R_i) \tag{5.25}$$

where the sum R_i is over unit cells, m are the different atomic functions ϕ_{mj} being used in the basis, and j are the atoms in each unit cell.

Once the expansion set for the crystal states has been chosen, the coefficients C, of the expansion remain to be determined. These are then used to get the tight binding crystal wave function, and the associated eigenvalues to determine the electronic bandstructure. To this end, the Schrödinger equation is cast in the form of a secular determinant:

$$\left| < \phi_{m'j'} \,|H - E|\, \Psi(k) > \right| = 0. \tag{5.26}$$

Here, H is the crystal Hamiltonian.

In theory, one can calculate the matrix elements in the secular determinant, Equation 5.26, from the first principles, by determining the crystal potential. This can be very difficult, however, because of the complexity of the problem.

From cation center		From anion center	
First nearest neighbor	Second nearest neighbor	First nearest neighbor	Second nearest neighbor
$a_0(+\hat{x}+\hat{y}+\hat{z})/4$	$a_0(+\hat{x}+\hat{y})/2$	$a_0(-\hat{x}-\hat{y}-\hat{z})/4$	$a_0(+\hat{x}+\hat{y})/2$
$a_0(+\hat{x}-\hat{y}-\hat{z})/4$	$a_0(+\hat{x}-\hat{y})/2$	$a_0(-\hat{x}+\hat{y}+\hat{z})/4$	$a_0(+\hat{x}-\hat{y})/2$
$a_0(-\hat{x}+\hat{y}-\hat{z})/4$	$a_0(-\hat{x}+\hat{y})/2$	$a_0(+\hat{x}-\hat{y}+\hat{z})/4$	$a_0(-\hat{x}+\hat{y})/2$
$a_0(-\hat{x}-\hat{y}+\hat{z})/4$	$a_0(-\hat{x}-\hat{y})/2$	$a_0(+\hat{x}+\hat{y}-\hat{z})/4$	$a_0(-\hat{x}-\hat{y})/2$
	$a_0(+\hat{x}+\hat{z})/2$		$a_0(+\hat{x}+\hat{z})/2$
	$a_0(+\hat{x}-\hat{z})/2$		$a_0(+\hat{x}-\hat{z})/2$
	$a_0(-\hat{x}+\hat{z})/2$		$a_0(-\hat{x}+\hat{z})/2$
	$a_0(-\hat{x}-\hat{z})/2$		$a_0(-\hat{x}-\hat{z})/2$
	$a_0(+\hat{y}+\hat{z})/2$		$a_0(+\hat{y}+\hat{z})/2$
	$a_0(+\hat{y}-\hat{z})/2$		$a_0(+\hat{y}-\hat{z})/2$
	$a_0(-\hat{y}+\hat{z})/2$		$a_0(-\hat{y}+\hat{z})/2$
	$a_0(-\hat{y}-\hat{z})/2$		$a_0(-\hat{y}-\hat{z})/2$

Table 5.1: Relative locations of first and second nearest neighbors to anion and cation atoms in zinc–blende semiconductors.

Slater and Koster were the first to advocate the use of the tight binding method as an empirical technique, instead of an ab initio technique. In their formalism, the symmetry of the lattice is preserved in the Bloch sums, while the energy interactions in the matrix elements of the secular determinant are treated as disposable constants. Measured or accurately calculated levels in the bandstructure can be fit to by adjusting the disposable constants. Some techniques have been proposed to make good guesses at the constants for particular semiconductors. After this, a numerical fit is usually performed.

In the sp^3 second nearest neighbor approximation for zinc–blende crystals, there will be eight basis functions, an s and three p orbitals, p_x, p_y, and p_z, for each of the two atoms within the Wigner–Seitz cell. This approximation assumes that there is spin degeneracy in the bandstructure of the crystal. If the effects of the breaking of spin degeneracy are being considered, one would need a basis which includes the spin–up and spin–down variants of each orbital. That is, both spin–up and spin–down (i.e. $s \rightarrow s \uparrow$ and $s \downarrow$, etc.) orbitals for each atom in the Wigner–Seitz cell would need to be included in the basis. This results in a requirement of a sixteen function basis for zinc–blende semiconductors.

In order to determine the tight binding matrix elements, the positions of the neighboring atoms with respect to each atom must be known. In the zinc–blende structure, the positions of the neighbors are different for the cation and the anion. The directions to the first and second nearest neighbors are given in Table 5.1.

Since one has the freedom to choose an origin at any point within the crystal, as well as the crystal orientation, the directions to the first nearest neighbors

$$\begin{vmatrix}
(s^0 \mid s^0) & (s^0 \mid p_x^0) & (s^0 \mid p_y^0) & (s^0 \mid p_z^0) & (s^0 \mid s^1) & (s^0 \mid p_x^1) & (s^0 \mid p_y^1) & (s^0 \mid p_z^1) \\
(p_x^0 \mid s^0) & (p_x^0 \mid p_x^0) & (p_x^0 \mid p_y^0) & (p_x^0 \mid p_z^0) & (p_x^0 \mid s^1) & (p_x^0 \mid p_x^1) & (p_x^0 \mid p_y^1) & (p_x^0 \mid p_z^1) \\
(p_y^0 \mid s^0) & (p_y^0 \mid p_x^0) & (p_y^0 \mid p_y^0) & (p_y^0 \mid p_z^0) & (p_y^0 \mid s^1) & (p_y^0 \mid p_x^1) & (p_y^0 \mid p_y^1) & (p_y^0 \mid p_z^1) \\
(p_z^0 \mid s^0) & (p_z^0 \mid p_x^0) & (p_z^0 \mid p_y^0) & (p_z^0 \mid p_z^0) & (p_z^0 \mid s^1) & (p_z^0 \mid p_x^1) & (p_z^0 \mid p_y^1) & (p_z^0 \mid p_z^1) \\
(s^1 \mid s^0) & (s^1 \mid p_x^0) & (s^1 \mid p_y^0) & (s^1 \mid p_z^0) & (s^1 \mid s^1) & (s^1 \mid p_x^1) & (s^1 \mid p_y^1) & (s^1 \mid p_z^1) \\
(p_x^1 \mid s^0) & (p_x^1 \mid p_x^0) & (p_x^1 \mid p_y^0) & (p_x^1 \mid p_z^0) & (p_x^1 \mid s^1) & (p_x^1 \mid p_x^1) & (p_x^1 \mid p_y^1) & (p_x^1 \mid p_z^1) \\
(p_y^1 \mid s^0) & (p_y^1 \mid p_x^0) & (p_y^1 \mid p_y^0) & (p_y^1 \mid p_z^0) & (p_y^1 \mid s^1) & (p_y^1 \mid p_x^1) & (p_y^1 \mid p_y^1) & (p_y^1 \mid p_z^1) \\
(p_z^1 \mid s^0) & (p_z^1 \mid p_x^0) & (p_z^1 \mid p_y^0) & (p_z^1 \mid p_z^0) & (p_z^1 \mid s^1) & (p_z^1 \mid p_x^1) & (p_z^1 \mid p_y^1) & (p_z^1 \mid p_z^1)
\end{vmatrix}$$

Figure 5.5: Arrangement of the tight binding secular determinant.

of the cations and anions may be interchanged, but once chosen, should be held consistently in the analysis thereafter. The first nearest neighbors of a cation will be an anion, and vice versa. The second nearest neighbors of a cation will be a cation, and similarly for an anion, the second nearest neighbor will be another anion.

One possible arrangement which can be used to set up the secular determinant, for the calculation without spin, is shown in Figure 5.5. The upper left quarter of the determinant will contain matrix elements between cation centers and cation neighbors. These will be self–interactions and second nearest neighbor interactions. The upper right quarter of the determinant will contain matrix elements between anion centers and cation neighbors. These will be first nearest neighbor interactions. An example of the derivation of a particular matrix element is now given for the $< s^0|H|p_x^1 >$ term. Here, the superscript "0" refers to a cation and the superscript "1" refers to an anion atom. The ket corresponds to the state of the center atom and the bra corresponds to the state of the neighbor atom.

Figure 5.6 shows the spatial relations of the anion center p_x orbital to its cation first nearest neighbor's orbitals. There will be four terms in this element due to the interaction with each of the first nearest neighbors. After pulling the Bloch phase out of each term, the element will be given by

$$\begin{aligned}
&< s^0|H|p_x^1 > \\
&= \exp\left(i\mathbf{k} \cdot \tfrac{a_0}{4}(-\hat{x} - \hat{y} - \hat{z})\right) < s^0 \left(\tfrac{a_0}{4}(-\hat{x} - \hat{y} - \hat{z})\right) |H|p_x^1 > \\
&+ \exp\left(i\mathbf{k} \cdot \tfrac{a_0}{4}(-\hat{x} + \hat{y} + \hat{z})\right) < s^0 \left(\tfrac{a_0}{4}(-\hat{x} + \hat{y} + \hat{z})\right) |H|p_x^1 > \\
&+ \exp\left(i\mathbf{k} \cdot \tfrac{a_0}{4}(+\hat{x} - \hat{y} + \hat{z})\right) < s^0 \left(\tfrac{a_0}{4}(+\hat{x} - \hat{y} + \hat{z})\right) |H|p_x^1 > \\
&+ \exp\left(i\mathbf{k} \cdot \tfrac{a_0}{4}(+\hat{x} + \hat{y} - \hat{z})\right) < s^0 \left(\tfrac{a_0}{4}(+\hat{x} + \hat{y} - \hat{z})\right) |H|p_x^1 > .
\end{aligned}$$
(5.27)

By symmetry, it can be demonstrated that the energy integrals in Equation 5.27 are all related. This relation assumes that the interaction between two orbitals, separated by a fixed distance, varies by the directional cosines of the vector between the orbitals. There are three directional cosines, denoted l,

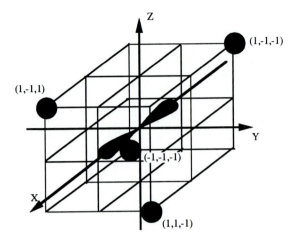

Figure 5.6: Spatial relation of the cation center p_x orbital to the first nearest neighbor anion s orbitals.

m, and n. These three constants have the values of the cosine of the angle between the vector, r, which points from the central atom to its neighbor, and the x, y, and z axes, respectively. For the matrix element in Equation 5.27, we are interested in the interaction between an s orbital and a p_x orbital. Since the s orbital has no angular dependence and the p_x orbital is only dependent upon the orientation of the x-axis, we write the interaction between an s orbital at location r with respect to a p_x orbital as

$$< s^0(r)|H|p_x^1 >= lsp_\sigma^{01} \qquad (5.28)$$

where l is the cosine of the angle between r and the x-axis, and sp_σ^{01} is the interaction energy between first nearest neighbor cation s orbitals and central anion p orbital. We use the value of sp_σ^{01} as a disposable constant. After some elementary algebra, Equation 5.27 can then be reduced to

$$< s^0|H|p_x^1 > \;=\; 4\frac{sp_\sigma^{01}}{\sqrt{3}}\left[\cos\left(\frac{k_x a_0}{4}\right)\sin\left(\frac{k_y a_0}{4}\right)\sin\left(\frac{k_z a_0}{4}\right)\right.$$
$$\left. +i\sin\left(\frac{k_x a_0}{4}\right)\cos\left(\frac{k_y a_0}{4}\right)\cos\left(\frac{k_z a_0}{4}\right)\right]. \quad (5.29)$$

To evaluate this matrix element, one has to choose a position within the Brillouin zone, shown in Figure 5.3. After choosing a particular value for k, evaluation of the matrix elements is then straightforward.

Tabulating all of the different disposable constants which one gets in the second nearest neighbor sp^3 approximation yields seventeen different constants. Four are self–interaction energies which go on the diagonal of the secular determinant and set the relative energies of the orbitals. There are five first nearest

Self interaction energies	First nearest neighbor interaction energies	Second nearest neighbor interaction energies
E_{s0}	ss_{σ}^{01}	ss_{σ}^{00}
E_{p0}	sp_{σ}^{01}	sp_{σ}^{00}
E_{s1}	sp_{σ}^{10}	pp_{σ}^{00}
E_{p1}	pp_{σ}^{01}	pp_{π}^{00}
	pp_{π}^{01}	ss_{σ}^{11}
		sp_{σ}^{11}
		pp_{σ}^{11}
		pp_{π}^{11}

Table 5.2: List of interaction energies in second nearest neighbor sp^3 tight binding calculation for zinc–blende semiconductors.

neighbor interaction energies, and eight second nearest neighbor interaction energies. These constants are listed in Table 5.2. The angular dependence of the energy portion of the matrix elements is constructed from the symmetry of the orbitals. Equation 5.30 serves to characterize the angular dependence of the energy portion of all of the matrix elements. Permutation of indices can be used to determine the relations for each of the 64 matrix elements.

$$
\begin{aligned}
< s|H|s > &= ss_{\sigma} \\
< s|H|p_x > &= l sp_{\sigma} \\
< p_x|H|p_x > &= l^2 pp_{\sigma} + (1 - l^2)pp_{\pi} \\
< p_x|H|p_y > &= lm pp_{\sigma} + lm pp_{\pi}.
\end{aligned}
\tag{5.30}
$$

These equations predict that the interaction energy between a p_x orbital and a neighboring p_y orbital in the $(a_0/2)(\hat{x} + \hat{z})$ location will be zero. While this is true to first order approximation, some studies allow this and similar constants to be nonzero. This would increase the number of constants available to fit the bandstructure. A set of the tight binding matrix elements for a number of semiconductors is given by Talwar and Ting (1982).

As was mentioned before, the tight binding method is used empirically. That is, the seventeen constants are never calculated from first principles, but are fit numerically in order to get a bandstructure which matches up in certain respects to either measured or ab initio calculations. The bandstructure parameters which are fit are the band levels at high symmetry points and effective masses or band curvatures. In performing this fit, one usually finds that it is impossible to simultaneously match all of the available data. It is, therefore, necessary to decide exactly what features in the bandstructure are most important

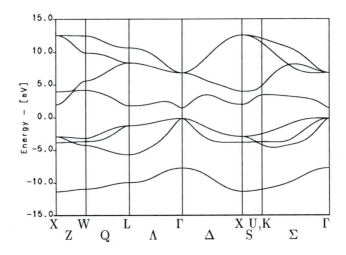

Figure 5.7: Calculated tight binding bandstructure for GaAs without the effects of spin–orbit coupling. (From M. D. Jaffe, 1989).

for the particular study being done, and to concentrate on fitting to them. For example, it is possible to accurately fit the levels of most of the bands at the high symmetry points. However, if this is done, the effective masses are usually far from what is desired. Alternatively, one can concentrate on the first conduction band, and the top valence bands, coercing their levels and their effective masses to conform to measured data. When this is done, the other bands above and below usually are not accurate.

A typical bandstructure calculated with the tight binding method is shown in Figure 5.7. Care has been taken to fit the bandgap and other high symmetry points in the Brillouin zone. However, it is known that the bandstructure of GaAs is quite different from this calculation especially at the top of the valence band. According to the tight binding method, the top of the valence band is 3-fold degenerate, corresponding to the degeneracy of (p_x, p_y, p_z). This degeneracy is 6-fold if spin is included. It is well known that in semiconductors, the top of the valence band is 2-fold (4-fold with spin) degenerate with another band (a 2-fold degenerate band) at a small energy below the valence bandedge. These effects can be incorporated only if relativistic effects are included in the problem. These effects are called the spin–orbit coupling.

5.2   THE SPIN–ORBIT COUPLING

The electron is a fermion with spin 1/2 (in units of $\hbar$). The concept of spin is a quantum mechanical concept that does not exist in classical mechanics. In classical mechanics a point particle must rotate about an axis to have an angular momentum ($= \boldsymbol{r} \times \boldsymbol{p}$). However, in quantum mechanics, a point particle can have discretely quantized intrinsic values of angular momentum called spin. The spin provides the electron with a means to interact with the magnetic field produced through its orbital motion. An electron in the p-state has an orbital angular momentum of $\hbar$. Thus there is a strong interaction of the spin with the orbital motion of the electron. As we will see later, the top of the valence bandedge states are primarily p-type. Thus the spin–orbit coupling has a strong effect there. While it is possible to calculate spin–orbit coupling in isolated atoms, it is difficult to do so in crystals. Thus, a general form of the interaction is assumed with a fitting parameter which is adjusted to experimentally observed effects. The spin–orbit interaction is quite small and one adds its effect in a perturbative approach.

For example, to the tight binding Hamiltonian, one adds the spin–orbit interaction energy. Thus the total Hamiltonian becomes

$$H = H_{\text{tb}} + H_{\text{so}}. \tag{5.31}$$

The matrix elements arising from the spin–orbit component of the Hamiltonian can couple states of different spin. To calculate these terms, the spin–orbit interaction is written as

$$H_{\text{so}} = \lambda \boldsymbol{L} \cdot \boldsymbol{S}. \tag{5.32}$$

Here, $\boldsymbol{L}$ represents the operator for orbital angular momentum, $\boldsymbol{S}$ is the operator for spin angular momentum, and we can treat λ as a constant. The addition of the spin and orbital angular momentum is the total angular momentum, $\boldsymbol{J}$, which can be expressed in the following form

$$\begin{aligned} \boldsymbol{J}^2 &= (\boldsymbol{L} + \boldsymbol{S})^2 \\ &= \boldsymbol{L}^2 + \boldsymbol{S}^2 + 2\boldsymbol{L} \cdot \boldsymbol{S} \end{aligned} \tag{5.33}$$

thus

$$\begin{aligned} <\boldsymbol{L} \cdot \boldsymbol{S}> &= \frac{1}{2} <\boldsymbol{J}^2 - \boldsymbol{L}^2 - \boldsymbol{S}^2> \\ &= \frac{\hbar^2}{2} \left[j(j+1) - l(l+1) - s(s+1) \right]. \end{aligned} \tag{5.34}$$

Here, j, l, and s are the quantum numbers for the operators $\boldsymbol{J}$, $\boldsymbol{L}$, and $\boldsymbol{S}$ respectively. This gives a straightforward technique for evaluating the spin–orbit interaction energy, but it is only applicable to pure angular momentum states, that is, one needs to know the total angular momentum of the states to which Equation 5.34 is applied. States like $p_x \uparrow$ are mixed states, that is they are made up of a combination of pure states. To determine the spin–orbit interaction energy, the basis must first be decomposed into states of pure angular momentum.

The first step in such a decomposition is to define what is meant by states like $p_x \uparrow$. The original three p states, p_x, p_y, p_z, are well-known simple linear combinations of the three p states of pure angular momentum, $\phi_{1,1}$, $\phi_{1,-1}$, $\phi_{1,0}$. That is,

$$p_x = \frac{1}{\sqrt{2}} \left(-\phi_{1,1} + \phi_{1,-1} \right)$$

$$p_y = \frac{i}{\sqrt{2}}(\phi_{1,1} + \phi_{1,-1})$$

$$p_z = \phi_{1,0}. \tag{5.35}$$

The ϕ_{ij} are eigenfunctions of L^2 and L_z with respective quantum numbers $l = i$ and $l_z = j$ (e.g. $L^2\phi_{1,-1} = \hbar^2(1)(1+1)\phi_{1,-1} = 2\hbar^2\phi_{1,-1}$ and $L_z\phi_{1,-1} = -1\hbar\phi_{1,-1}$).

$$\phi_{1,\pm 1} \equiv Y_{1,\pm 1}(\theta, \varphi) = \mp\sqrt{\tfrac{3}{8\pi}} \sin\theta e^{\pm i\varphi}$$

$$\phi_{1,0} \equiv Y_{1,0}(\theta, \varphi) = \sqrt{\tfrac{3}{4\pi}} \cos\theta. \tag{5.36}$$

By using a natural extension of these equations, similar definitions for the spin–up and spin–down p-states can be made as exemplified by

$$p_x \uparrow = \frac{1}{\sqrt{2}}(-\phi_{1,1} + \phi_{1,-1}) \uparrow. \tag{5.37}$$

This formulation, however, is still in terms of mixed states. To decompose these mixed states into states of pure angular momentum, we must perform the addition of the spin and the orbital angular momentum to obtain the total angular momentum states. Applying the standard Clebsch–Gordan technique for the addition of angular momentum to the ϕ states plus the spin states yields the following six equations (see Appendix D):

$$\Phi_{3/2,3/2} = \phi_{1,1} \uparrow$$

$$= \frac{-1}{\sqrt{2}}(p_x + ip_y) \uparrow$$

$$\Phi_{3/2,1/2} = \frac{1}{\sqrt{3}}\phi_{1,1} \downarrow + \frac{\sqrt{2}}{\sqrt{3}}\phi_{1,0} \uparrow$$

$$= \frac{-1}{\sqrt{6}}[(p_x + ip_y) \downarrow - 2p_z \uparrow]$$

$$\Phi_{3/2,-1/2} = \frac{\sqrt{2}}{\sqrt{3}}\phi_{1,0} \downarrow + \frac{1}{\sqrt{3}}\phi_{1,-1} \uparrow$$

$$= \frac{1}{\sqrt{6}}[(p_x - ip_y) \uparrow + 2p_z \downarrow]$$

$$\Phi_{3/2,-3/2} = \phi_{1,-1} \downarrow$$

$$= \frac{1}{\sqrt{2}}(p_x - ip_y) \downarrow$$

$$\Phi_{1/2,1/2} = \frac{-1}{\sqrt{3}}\phi_{1,0} \uparrow + \frac{\sqrt{2}}{\sqrt{3}}\phi_{1,1} \downarrow$$

$$= \frac{-1}{\sqrt{3}}[(p_x + ip_y) \downarrow + p_z \uparrow]$$

$$\Phi_{1/2,-1/2} = \frac{-\sqrt{2}}{\sqrt{3}}\phi_{1,-1} \uparrow + \frac{1}{\sqrt{3}}\phi_{1,0} \downarrow$$

$$= \frac{-1}{\sqrt{3}} [(p_x - ip_y) \uparrow -p_z \downarrow]. \tag{5.38}$$

These six equations must be inverted to find the states like $\phi_{1,0} \uparrow$ in terms of the total angular momentum states. Once this is done, we can substitute back into the definitions for the basis states, exemplified by Equation 5.37, to get them in terms of the total angular momentum states. This procedure results in the following six equations:

$$p_x \uparrow = \frac{1}{\sqrt{2}} \left[-\Phi_{3/2,3/2} + \frac{1}{\sqrt{3}} \Phi_{3/2,-1/2} - \frac{\sqrt{2}}{\sqrt{3}} \Phi_{1/2,-1/2} \right]$$

$$p_x \downarrow = \frac{1}{\sqrt{2}} \left[-\frac{1}{\sqrt{3}} \Phi_{3/2,1/2} - \frac{\sqrt{2}}{\sqrt{3}} \Phi_{1/2,1/2} + \Phi_{3/2,-3/2} \right]$$

$$p_y \uparrow = \frac{i}{\sqrt{2}} \left[\Phi_{3/2,3/2} + \frac{1}{\sqrt{3}} \Phi_{3/2,-1/2} - \frac{\sqrt{2}}{\sqrt{3}} \Phi_{1/2,-1/2} \right]$$

$$p_y \downarrow = \frac{i}{\sqrt{2}} \left[\frac{1}{\sqrt{3}} \Phi_{3/2,1/2} + \frac{\sqrt{2}}{\sqrt{3}} \Phi_{1/2,1/2} + \Phi_{3/2,-3/2} \right]$$

$$p_z \uparrow = \frac{\sqrt{2}}{\sqrt{3}} \Phi_{3/2,1/2} - \frac{1}{\sqrt{3}} \Phi_{1/2,1/2}$$

$$p_z \downarrow = \frac{\sqrt{2}}{\sqrt{3}} \Phi_{3/2,-1/2} + \frac{1}{\sqrt{3}} \Phi_{1/2,-1/2}. \tag{5.39}$$

The phases used in the above expressions of Φ_{j,m_j} in terms of $p_x \uparrow, \ldots, p_z \downarrow$, result from the use of the standard phase conventions in the derivation of the Clebsch–Gordan coefficients. However, the overall phase of a state is arbitrary and has no effect on the physical predictions. This admits the possiblity of other phase conventions for the expressions of Φ_{j,m_j} in terms of $p_x \uparrow, \ldots, p_z \downarrow$. One such convention which is in widespread use is that used by Luttinger and Kohn (1955):

$$\Phi_{3/2,3/2}^{LK} = -\Phi_{3/2,3/2}^{CG}$$

$$= \frac{1}{\sqrt{2}} (p_x + ip_y) \uparrow$$

$$\Phi_{3/2,1/2}^{LK} = -i\Phi_{3/2,1/2}^{CG}$$

$$= \frac{i}{\sqrt{6}} [(p_x + ip_y) \downarrow -2p_z \uparrow]$$

$$\Phi_{3/2,-1/2}^{LK} = \Phi_{3/2,-1/2}^{CG}$$

$$= \frac{1}{\sqrt{6}} [(p_x - ip_y) \uparrow +2p_z \downarrow]$$

$$\Phi_{3/2,-3/2}^{LK} = i\Phi_{3/2,-3/2}^{CG}$$

$$= \frac{i}{\sqrt{2}} (p_x - ip_y) \downarrow$$

$$\Phi^{LK}_{1/2,1/2} = -\Phi^{CG}_{1/2,1/2}$$

$$= \frac{1}{\sqrt{3}} [(p_x + ip_y) \downarrow + p_z \uparrow]$$

$$\Phi^{LK}_{1/2,-1/2} = i\Phi^{CG}_{1/2,-1/2}$$

$$= \frac{-i}{\sqrt{3}} [(p_x - ip_y) \uparrow - p_z \downarrow], \qquad (5.40)$$

where the superscript LK identifies the states with the Luttinger–Kohn phase and the superscript CG identifies the states with the standard Clebsch–Gordan phase.

With these decompositions, the evaluation of terms like $< p_x \uparrow |H_{so}|p_y \downarrow >$ becomes straightforward. By combining Equations 5.32 and 5.34, we can write the spin–orbit Hamiltonian as:

$$H_{so} = \frac{\lambda\hbar^2}{2} [j(j+1) - l(l+1) - s(s+1)]. \qquad (5.41)$$

For p-type electron orbitals, $l = 1$ and $s = 1/2$. j is given by the first index of Φ in the decompositions of the states, Equation 5.39. Because the pure states are orthogonal, many of the terms will be zero. Evaluation of all possible terms gives nonzero results only in the following cases:

$$< p_x \uparrow |H_{so}|p_y \uparrow > = -i\frac{\Delta}{3}$$

$$< p_x \uparrow |H_{so}|p_z \downarrow > = \frac{\Delta}{3}$$

$$< p_y \uparrow |H_{so}|p_z \downarrow > = -i\frac{\Delta}{3}$$

$$< p_x \downarrow |H_{so}|p_y \downarrow > = i\frac{\Delta}{3}$$

$$< p_x \downarrow |H_{so}|p_z \uparrow > = -\frac{\Delta}{3}$$

$$< p_y \downarrow |H_{so}|p_z \uparrow > = -i\frac{\Delta}{3} \qquad (5.42)$$

as well as the cases which are reflections about the diagonal of these terms which are the conjugates of the values given. The parameter Δ is the spin–orbit splitting $\Delta = \Delta_{so} = 3\lambda\hbar^2/2$. The values of Δ_{so} for several semiconductors is listed in Table 5.3.

If the spin–orbit effects are included in the bandstructure, the top of the valence band loses part of its degeneracy shown earlier in Figure 5.7. The effect is easier to demonstrate in the total angular momentum basis instead of the p_x, p_y, p_z basis. In the total angular momentum basis, the p-states (with spin) can be written as the six states (already discussed) $|j, m >$ where j and m take the values: $|3/2, +3/2 >$; $|3/2, -3/2 >$; $|3/2, +1/2 >$; $|3/2, -1/2 >$; $|1/2, +1/2 >$; $|1/2, -1/2 >$. As can be seen from the equations for the spin–orbit perturbation,

Semiconductor	Δ (eV)
Si	0.044
Ge	0.29
GaAs	0.35
InAs	0.41
InSb	0.82
InP	0.14
GaP	0.094

Table 5.3: Spin–orbit splitting for different semiconductors.

there is a splitting between the $j = 3/2$ states and the $j = 1/2$ states. This splitting in energy is simply Δ_{so}. The general valence bandedge of semiconductors then has a form shown in Figure 5.8. One has a doubly degenerate state (4-fold with spin) at the zone center and a split-off state (2-fold degenerate with spin). The degenerate states at the zone center have different curvatures and are called the light hole (LH) and the heavy hole (HH) state. Figure 5.9 shows the bandstructure of GaAs with spin–orbit coupling. Contrast this to Figure 5.7, where the spin–orbit coupling was ignored.

It is extremely useful to examine the nature of the central cell states of the Bloch functions at the high symmetry points in the Brillouin zone. These symmetries are extremely important for determining selection rules for optical

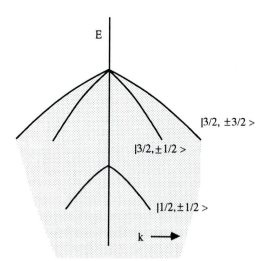

Figure 5.8: The general form of the valence bandstructure after including the effects of spin–orbit coupling. The states are described by pure angular momentum states only at $k = 0$. The splitting between the $j = 3/2$ and $j = 1/2$ states is Δ.

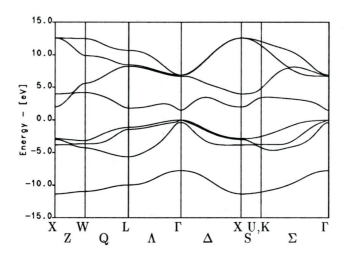

Figure 5.9: Calculated tight binding bandstructure for GaAs after including spin–orbit coupling. (From M. D. Jaffe, 1989).

transitions.

5.3 SYMMETRY OF CONDUCTION BANDEDGE STATES

It is useful to distinguish the conduction bandedge states for the direct bandgap materials such as GaAs and InAs, from the indirect bandgap materials such as Si and Ge. In direct gap semiconductors, the conduction band minima states occur at the Γ-point and have a central cell periodic part which is spherically symmetric. It is described as being made up of s-type states at the bandedge. Of course, as one examines the states away from the edge, there is an increasing p-type contribution that is mixed in the eigenfunction. Because of this predominant s-type nature of the wavefunction, very important selection rules for optical transitions arise. This will be discussed in detail later.

For indirect bandgap materials such as Si (with conduction bandedge near the X-point and a 6-fold degeneracy) and Ge (with an edge at the L-point) there is a strong anisotropy of the wavefunction. The anisotropy is described by appropriate combinations of the s, p_x, p_y, and p_z type functions. If the strain tensor is anisotropic, the degeneracies at these edges can be lifted causing significant changes in transport and optical properties associated with the bandedges. In Figure 5.10, we show schematically the nature of the bandedge states.

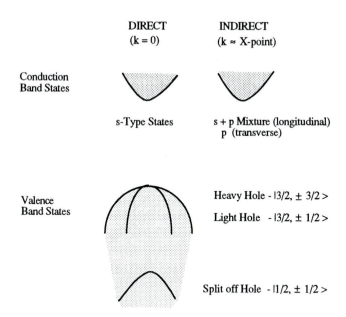

Figure 5.10: A schematic description of the nature of central cell states in direct and indirect bandgap materials.

5.4 SYMMETRY OF VALENCE BANDEDGE STATES

The character of the valence bandedge states of most semiconductors is quite similar. The central cell part of the wavefunction is primarily p-type. This makes the spin–orbit interaction very important. In absence of this interaction, the top of the valence band is 3-fold degenerate (6-fold if spin degeneracy is included). However, in presence of the spin–orbit coupling, the degeneracy is lifted as shown in Figure 5.8 leaving a 4-fold degeneracy and a 2-fold degeneracy. The 4-fold degenerate (at the top of the valence band) state consists of two heavy hole (HH) and two light hole (LH) bands while the other 2-fold bands are the split-off bands. Since optical transitions depend critically upon the nature of the hole states, it is useful to describe these states in terms of angular momentum states $\phi_{l,m}$ (l = total angular momentum, m = projection of the angular momentum along the z-axis) and spin state ($\uparrow= +1/2$, $\downarrow= -1/2$). The relationship between the total angular momentum states and the orbital angular momentum states has been discussed earlier and is the following.
Heavy hole states:

$$\Phi_{3/2,3/2} = \frac{-1}{\sqrt{2}} (|p_x > +i|p_y >) \uparrow$$

$$\Phi_{3/2,-3/2} = \frac{1}{\sqrt{2}} (|p_x > -i|p_y >) \downarrow \qquad (5.43)$$

Light hole states:

$$\Phi_{3/2,1/2} \;=\; \frac{-1}{\sqrt{6}}\left[(|p_x> +i|p_y >)\downarrow -2|p_z >\uparrow\right]$$

$$\Phi_{3/2,-1/2} \;=\; \frac{1}{\sqrt{6}}\left[(|p_x> -i|p_y >)\uparrow +2|p_z >\downarrow\right] \tag{5.44}$$

Split–off hole states:

$$\Phi_{1/2,1/2} \;=\; \frac{-1}{\sqrt{3}}\left[(|p_x> +i|p_y >)\downarrow +|p_z >\uparrow\right]$$

$$\Phi_{1/2,-1/2} \;=\; \frac{-1}{\sqrt{3}}\left[(|p_x> -i|p_y >)\uparrow +|p_z >\downarrow\right]. \tag{5.45}$$

This description of the hole states in terms of the total angular momentum states is extremely useful in calculating the optical properties of semiconductors. It is also useful to remember that the pure description of the hole states is strictly valid only at $k = 0$ (center of the Brillouin zone) since at $k \neq 0$ the HH and LH states mix strongly.

We have discussed the tight binding method in some detail in this chapter since it is a relatively simple technique to study bandstructures of materials. It also provides a good conceptual picture of the nature and symmetry of Bloch functions at high symmetry points of the Brillouin zone. Nevertheless, it must be realized that it is expected to be a reliable approach only for bands originating from well localized atomic orbitals. This is often not a good approximation especially for the higher-lying conduction band states which are more free electron like. The technique can be improved by adding more orbitals (e.g. high s-levels, d-levels, etc.). Of course, as more orbitals are added, the size of the matrix equation that needs to be solved also increases making the solutions more complex. However, with ease of access to computer math libraries, that is not a problem. If the matrix elements of the tight binding method are to be evaluated ab initio, the method becomes extremely unreliable. Integrals such as

$$\int \phi_m(\boldsymbol{r}-\boldsymbol{R}_1)\,V(\boldsymbol{r})\,\phi_n(\boldsymbol{r}-\boldsymbol{R}_2)\,d^3r \tag{5.46}$$

are extremely sensitive to the nature of the crystal potential and are difficult to evaluate directly. One modification, that has been suggested, is to not start with the atomic orbitals, but use some "distorted" orbitals, which satisfy the Schrödinger equation of an atom together with the potential of the neighboring atoms. These distorted orbitals will then reflect the symmetry of the crystal and improve the reliability of the method.

In the method introduced in this chapter the matrix elements are used simply as fitting parameters. This approach has proven to be very useful for providing semiquantitative description of semiconductors.

We will briefly discuss two other approaches used for bandstructure calculation. The first, the orthogonalized plane wave method, is the approach used in

Chapter 4, in discussing the nearly free electron problem with some important modifications. The second, the pseudopotential method, is probably the most useful technique when more quantitative description of bands is required.

5.5 THE ORTHOGONALIZED PLANE WAVE METHOD

In Chapter 4 we had discussed the general problem of electrons in a periodic structure by writing the problem in k-space and using a plane wave basis. The plane wave basis is an attractive basis but has difficulty because too many plane waves are needed to describe the problem adequately. For example, we have seen that the potential has to be expanded in reciprocal lattice vectors

$$V(\boldsymbol{r}) = \sum_{\mathbf{G}} V_{\mathbf{G}} e^{i\mathbf{G}\cdot\mathbf{r}}. \tag{5.47}$$

If the potential is short-ranged, a large number of reciprocal lattice vectors are required to describe it. This makes the size of the secular equation to be solved correspondingly large. The orthogonalized plane wave (OPW) method is an approach to avoid having to deal with a very large number of plane wave states. The basic idea is that the valence and conduction band states are orthogonal to the core states of the crystal and this fact should be utilized in the selection of the plane waves. This simple imposition greatly simplifies the problem.

As discussed in Chapter 4, the general form of the Bloch function in k-space is

$$\Psi(\boldsymbol{k}, \boldsymbol{r}) = \sum_{m} C_{m}(\boldsymbol{k}) \, e^{i(\mathbf{k}+\mathbf{G}_m)\cdot\mathbf{r}}. \tag{5.48}$$

In general one should include a normalization factor $1/\sqrt{Nr_0}$ where N is the number of unit cells, and r_0 is the volume of the unit cell. The secular equation to be solved has the form

$$||< \phi_{\mathbf{k},m}|H - E|\phi_{\mathbf{k},n} >|| = 0 \tag{5.49}$$

where $\phi_{\mathbf{k},n}$, $\phi_{\mathbf{k},m}$ are the plane waves

$$\phi_{\mathbf{k},m} = \frac{1}{\sqrt{Nr_0}} \, e^{i(\mathbf{k}+\mathbf{G}_m)\cdot\mathbf{r}}. \tag{5.50}$$

Instead of working with the general plane wave basis set, one uses the fact that the core states are known and the conduction and valence band states are orthogonal to them. To incorporate this property, one defines the orthogonal states

$$\chi_{\mathbf{k},m} = \phi_{\mathbf{k},m} - \sum_{c} < \psi_c|\phi_{\mathbf{k},m} > \psi_c \tag{5.51}$$

where ψ_c are the core states. The Bloch functions are now expanded in the orthogonalized states χ and one gets a secular equation

$$||< \chi_{\mathbf{k},m} |H - E| \chi_{\mathbf{k},n} >|| = 0. \tag{5.52}$$

This matrix equation only gives the eigenvalues corresponding to the valence and conduction bands, since the core states have been eliminated from the basis being used. This allows for easier convergence of the problem. The general form of the Schrödinger equation in k-space was derived in Chapter 4. To be able to solve the problem one needs three ingredients:

1. the form of the background atomic potentials which is then written as a Fourier series;

2. the form of the core states so that the orthogonal states can be determined. Usually the isolated atomic core states are used since the presence of other neighboring atoms is not expected to alter the core states;

3. the crystal structure which is, of course, known.

Once all this information is there, the solution of the problem is straightforward. Of course, detailed knowledge of the atomic potential in the crystal is difficult to obtain and one may have to resort to consulting the experimental results for high symmetry points and develop an approach similar to the tight binding method where the matrix elements are adjusted to obtain good fits with some known points in the bandstructure.

5.6   THE PSEUDOPOTENTIAL METHOD

The pseudopotential is a powerful technique to solve for bandstructures of semiconductors and is often used as a benchmark for comparison of other techniques. We will describe the spirit of the method without going into its details. Like the orthogonal plane wave method, the pseudopotential method makes use of the information that the valence and conduction band states are orthogonal to the core states. However, this information is not just used in the construction of the Bloch states, but is included in an ingenious manner in the Hamiltonian itself. Thus the background periodic potential is replaced by a new "pseudopotential," which is obtained by subtracting out the effects of the core levels. The pseudopotential then has a smooth spatial dependence and yet includes all the relevant information to give the valence and conduction band bandstructure. The following formal equations define the procedure. The Schrödinger equation for the valence or conduction band states is

$$\left[\frac{p^2}{2m} + V(\boldsymbol{r})\right] \Psi_v(\boldsymbol{k}, \boldsymbol{r}) = E_v \Psi_v(\boldsymbol{k}, \boldsymbol{r}) \qquad (5.53)$$

with the orthogonality condition

$$\langle \Psi_c | \Psi_v \rangle = 0 \qquad (5.54)$$

where Ψ_c are the core states. This condition is explicitly incorporated into the definition of the valence band states by defining new states $\phi_v(\boldsymbol{k}, \boldsymbol{r})$ where

$$\Psi_v(\boldsymbol{k}, \boldsymbol{r}) = \phi_v(\boldsymbol{k}, \boldsymbol{r}) - \sum_c \langle \Psi_c | \phi_v \rangle \Psi_c. \qquad (5.55)$$

The equation for $\phi_v(\boldsymbol{k}, \boldsymbol{r})$ then becomes

$$\left[\frac{p^2}{2m} + V(\boldsymbol{r})\right] \phi_v(\boldsymbol{k}, \boldsymbol{r}) - \sum_c [E_v(\boldsymbol{k}) - E_c] \langle \Psi_c | \phi_v \rangle \Psi_c = E_v(\boldsymbol{k}) \; \phi_v(\boldsymbol{k}, \boldsymbol{r}) \quad (5.56)$$

where E_c are the known core level energies. The Schrödinger equation for $\phi_v(\boldsymbol{k}, \boldsymbol{r})$ has the same eigenvalues as the original equation for $\Psi_v(\boldsymbol{k}, \boldsymbol{r})$ together with the orthogonality condition, but with a new background potential. The original potential $V(\boldsymbol{r})$ is replaced by the operator

$$V(\boldsymbol{r})\Psi_v(\boldsymbol{k}, \boldsymbol{r}) \Rightarrow \left[V(\boldsymbol{r}) \; \phi_v(\boldsymbol{k}, \boldsymbol{r}) + \sum_c [E_v(\boldsymbol{k}) - E_c] \langle \Psi_c | \phi_v \rangle \Psi_c \right] = V_p. \quad (5.57)$$

The new potential operator which involves subtraction of the core energies weighted with $\phi_v(\boldsymbol{k}, \boldsymbol{r})$ from the eigenvalues $E_v(\boldsymbol{k})$ is called the pseudopotential. Of course, there is no simplification as yet since the new equation is as difficult to solve as the starting equation. The pseudopotential V_p is a nonlocal eigenvalue dependent operator.

The problem is simplified due to the realization that the pseudopotential is much smoother (see Figure 5.11) than the original starting potential since the term $-E_c \langle \Psi_c | \phi_v \rangle$ is a position dependent term which subtracts the strong core effects near the atomic sites leaving the potential in the regions between atoms unchanged. The pseudopotential is thus equivalent to a constant potential plus a weak background potential as far as the valence and conduction band states are concerned. The solution can then be expanded in terms of plane waves as discussed in Chapter 3. Usually about 50 plane wave states (i.e., 50 reciprocal lattice vectors) are required for convergence. This involves including up to third neighbor reciprocal lattice vectors in the Fourier transforms of the pseudopotential. A number of clever approximations are made to simplify the problem and the interested reader is referred to the references given at the end of this chapter.

5.7   THE **k · p** METHOD

In the bandstructure techniques we have described so far, the emphasis has been on being able to describe the bandstructure in the entire Brillouin zone. Thus a fairly large basis set was used to describe the central cell part of the Bloch function. Once the bandstructure has been calculated, it usually turns out that at and near the bandedges, the central cell part has a fairly simple form, as discussed previously. In the **k · p** method, one starts with the known form of the bandstructure problem at the bandedges and using perturbation theory attempts to describe the bands away from the high symmetry points. Since for the central cell functions, we only expand around the high symmetry points in terms of known functions, the problem is considerably simplified, often leading to analytical results. The **k · p** techniques are also particularly useful for evaluating

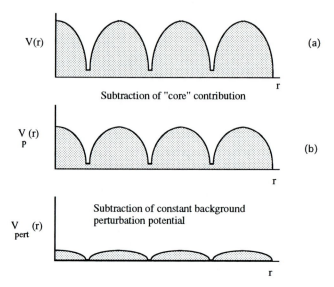

Figure 5.11: Schematic steps in the application of the pseudopotential formalism. The true potential $V(r)$ along with the orthogonality condition (a) is rewritten in terms of a pseudopotential (b) which is much smoother. The problem can then be solved perturbatively by separating the $[p^2/(2m) + V(0)]$ term in the Hamiltonian.

bandstructures in heterostructures and will be the key tools used in the next two chapters.

Let us consider how the $\mathbf{k} \cdot \mathbf{p}$ method works for a semiconductor (with a bandedge at $\mathbf{k}_0$). We assume that the eigenvalues and Bloch functions are known for the bandedge; i.e., the equation

$$\left[\frac{p^2}{2m} + V(\mathbf{r})\right] \psi_n(\mathbf{k}_0, \mathbf{r}) = E_n(\mathbf{k}_0)\, \psi_n(\mathbf{k}_0, \mathbf{r}) \qquad (5.58)$$

is known. In most applications $\mathbf{k}_0$ is the Γ-point ($= [000]$) in the Brillouin zone. We can expand the general solutions away from the known $\mathbf{k} = \mathbf{k}_0$ solutions in the basis set $\exp[i(\mathbf{k} - \mathbf{k}_0) \cdot \mathbf{r}]$. Thus we have

$$\psi(\mathbf{k}, \mathbf{r}) = \sum_n b_n(\mathbf{k})\, \psi_n(\mathbf{k}_0, \mathbf{r})\, e^{i(\mathbf{k} - \mathbf{k}_0) \cdot \mathbf{r}} \qquad (5.59)$$

where b_n are the expansion coefficients, that are to be determined by the standard eigenvalue solution method. This general approach is shown in Figure 5.12. The secular equation has the usual form, formally represented by

$$\left\| < e^{i(\mathbf{k} - \mathbf{k}_0) \cdot \mathbf{r}} \psi_{n'}(\mathbf{k}_0, \mathbf{r}) | H - E | e^{i(\mathbf{k} - \mathbf{k}_0) \cdot \mathbf{r}} \psi_n(\mathbf{k}_0, \mathbf{r}) > \right\| = 0. \qquad (5.60)$$

A simple expansion allows us to rewrite this equation for just the central cell

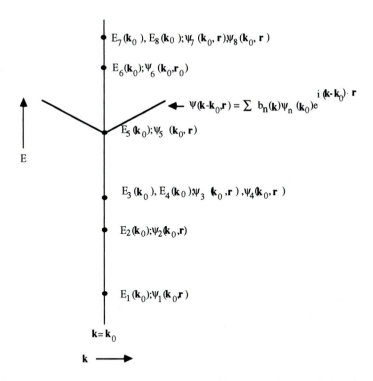

Figure 5.12: A schematic of the $k \cdot p$ approach. The eigenvalues and eigenfunctions of the crystalline material are known at some point $k = k_0$. The states away from k_0 are expanded in terms of the known k_0-states.

part of the Bloch states. Remembering that $p = -i\hbar\nabla$,

$$
\left[\frac{p^2}{2m} + V(r)\right] e^{i(k-k_0)\cdot r}\psi_n(k_0, r)
$$

$$
= e^{i(k-k_0)\cdot r}\left[\frac{\{p + \hbar(k-k_0)\}^2}{2m} + V(r)\right]\psi_n(k_0, r)
$$

$$
= e^{i(k-k_0)\cdot r}\left[\frac{\hbar^2}{2m}(k-k_0)^2 + \frac{\hbar}{m}(k-k_0)\cdot p + E_n(k_0)\right]\psi_n(k_0, r). \quad (5.61)
$$

The eigenvalue determinant then becomes

$$
\left\|\left\langle\left[\frac{\hbar^2}{2m}(k-k_0)^2 + E_n(k_0) - E\right]\delta_{n'n} + \frac{\hbar}{m}(k-k_0)\cdot P_{n'n}(k_0)\right\rangle\right\| = 0 \quad (5.62)
$$

where $P_{n'n}$ is the momentum matrix element between the different bandedge states

$$
P_{n'n} = \int \psi_{n'}^*(k_0, r)\, p\, \psi_n(k_0, r)\, d^3r. \quad (5.63)
$$

If the matrix elements are known, the eigenvalue problem can be easily solved for $E(k_0)$ and $b_n(k)$. The momentum matrix elements can usually be written in terms of a small number of parameters by using symmetry properties of $\psi_n(k_0, r)$. As discussed in the previous section, the zone edge central cell functions have well-defined symmetry properties. Another way to rewrite the matrix elements and utilize the symmetry of the states is to use the relationship

$$
\begin{aligned}
[H, r] &= Hr - rH \\
&= \frac{i\hbar}{m}p.
\end{aligned}
\tag{5.64}
$$

This gives, for $n \neq n'$,

$$
\begin{aligned}
P_{n'n}(k_0) &= \frac{m}{i\hbar}\left[E_{n'}(k_0) - E_n(k_0)\right] \\
&\times \int \psi_{n'}^*(k_0, r)\, r\, \psi_n(k_0, r)\, d^3r.
\end{aligned}
\tag{5.65}
$$

The integral in Equation 5.65 is nonzero only for certain symmetries of $\psi_{n'}(k_0, r)$ and $\psi_n(k_0, r)$. It is this reduction in the number of independent parameters, together with the fact that near a particular energy $E_n(k_0)$, only bands which have the energy difference $E_{n'}(k_0) - E_n(k_0)$ small (see Equation 5.69), will contribute significantly, that makes the $k \cdot p$ method so attractive. Usually the matrix elements $P_{n'n}$ are used as fitting parameters and adjusted to fit measured quantities such as carrier masses, etc.

Consider, for example, the $k \cdot p$ description of the nondegenerate bands (e.g., conduction bandedge or the split-off band in the valence band for the case of large spin–orbit coupling). In this case one can use the perturbation theory to obtain the energy and wavefunctions away from k_0. For simplicity, let us assume $k_0 = 0$. The Schrödinger equation for the perturbation Hamiltonian is simply

$$
(H_0 + H_1 + H_2)\, u_{nk} = E_{nk}\, u_{nk}
\tag{5.66}
$$

where

$$
\begin{aligned}
H_0 &= \frac{p^2}{2m} \\
H_1 &= \frac{\hbar}{m} k \cdot p \\
H_2 &= \frac{\hbar^2 k^2}{2m}
\end{aligned}
$$

In the perturbation approach, H_1 is a first order term in k, and H_2 is a second order term. The u_{nk} are the central cell part of the Bloch functions $\psi_n(k)$. To zero order, we then have (see Appendix E)

$$
\begin{aligned}
u_{nk} &= u_{n0} \\
E_{nk} &= E_n(0).
\end{aligned}
\tag{5.67}
$$

To first order we have

$$u_{n\boldsymbol{k}} = u_{n0} + \frac{\hbar}{m} \sum_{n' \neq n} \boldsymbol{k} \cdot \frac{< n0|\boldsymbol{p}|n0 >}{E_n(0) - E_{n'}(0)} u_{n0}$$

$$E_{n\boldsymbol{k}} = E_n(0) + \frac{\hbar}{m} \boldsymbol{k} \cdot < n'0|\boldsymbol{p}|n0 > . \qquad (5.68)$$

If the states $|n0 >$ or u_{n0} have inversion symmetry, the first order matrix element is zero because $\boldsymbol{p}$ has an odd parity. This would occur in crystals with inversion symmetry (e.g., Si, Ge, and C). For crystals lacking inversion symmetry, the functions $|n0 >$ may not have a well-defined parity leading a small correction to energy proportional to $\boldsymbol{k}$. This correction is usually very small and leads to a small band warping, i.e., the energy is not an extrema at the high symmetry point.

Notice that even though the first order correction to energy is zero (or negligible), there is an important correction to the central cell part of the Bloch function. This correction is proportional to the momentum matrix element and inversely proportional to the energy separation of the bands. As an example, the conduction bandedge of the direct band semiconductors is s-type at the zone center, but will have an increasing p-type mixture as one moves away from the zone center. The p-type mixture is coming from the valence bandedge states which are p-type.

To second order, the energy becomes

$$E_n(\boldsymbol{k}) = E_n(0) + \frac{\hbar^2 k^2}{2m} + \frac{\hbar^2}{m^2} \sum_{n' \neq n} \frac{|\boldsymbol{k} \cdot < n'0|\boldsymbol{p}|n0 > |^2}{E_n(0) - E_{n'}(0)}. \qquad (5.69)$$

This equation can be expressed in terms of an effective mass m^*

$$E_n(\boldsymbol{k}) = E_n(0) + \sum_{i,j} \frac{\hbar^2}{m^*_{i,j}} k_i \cdot k_j \qquad (5.70)$$

where

$$\frac{m}{m^*_{i,j}} = \delta_{i,j} + \frac{2}{m} \sum_{n' \neq n} \frac{< n0|p_i|n'0 >< n'0|p_j|n0 >}{E_n(0) - E_{n'}(0)}. \qquad (5.71)$$

This equation is valid for the conduction bandedge and the split–off bands. For the conduction band, retaining only the valence bandedge bands in the summation, we get

$$E_c(\boldsymbol{k}) = E_c(0) + \frac{\hbar^2 k^2}{2m^*_c} \qquad (5.72)$$

with

$$\frac{1}{m^*_c} = \frac{1}{m} + \frac{2p_{cv}}{m^2} \frac{1}{3} \left(\frac{2}{E_{g\Gamma}} + \frac{1}{E_{g\Gamma} + \Delta} \right)$$

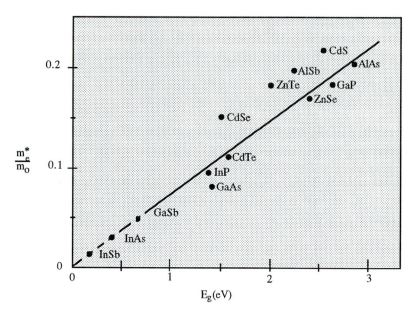

Figure 5.13: Electron effective mass, m^* as a function of the lowest–direct gap E_g for various III–V compounds.

where $E_{g\Gamma}$ is the gap at the zone center and Δ is the HH–SO band separation. The momentum matrix element p_{cv} is of great importance and will be discussed in greater detail shortly. For the SO band we have

$$E_{so} = -\Delta - \frac{\hbar^2 k^2}{2m^*_{so}}$$

$$\frac{1}{m^*_{so}} = \frac{-1}{m} + \frac{2p_{cv}^2}{3m^2(E_{g\Gamma} + \Delta)}. \tag{5.73}$$

Notice that in the SO band mass we have no contribution from the HH, LH bands in this simple treatment since the momentum matrix elements are zero, by symmetry. However, a more accurate treatment using the determinant equation shows important coupling between the LH, HH, and SO band, particularly for small Δ.

In the case of the conduction band mass for direct gap semiconductors, one can see that as the bandgap decreases, the carrier effective mass also decreases. This result holds quite well as can be seen by examining the effective masses of a range of semiconductors as shown in Figure 5.13.

For degenerate states that occur at the valence bandedge, the formalism above based on nondegenerate perturbation theory is obviously invalid. In this case one has to examine the eigenvalue determinant. The HH, LH states at the valence bandedge are made from p-type states and are represented by either $p_x \uparrow, p_x \downarrow, p_y \uparrow, p_y \downarrow, p_z \uparrow, p_z \downarrow$ states or more conveniently by the angular momentum states $|3/2,\pm 3/2>$, $|3/2,\pm 1/2>$, and $|1/2,\pm 1/2>$. If one ignores the effects of the conduction band in the determinant equation, one then gets a 6×6 eigenvalue secular equation. Symmetry considerations are then used to select the form and nonzero matrix elements of this matrix equation. A treatment which has proven very valuable is due to Kohn and Luttinger. The matrix equation, with the Luttinger and Kohn phases, is of the form (see discussion given with Equation 5.40):

j:	$3/2$	$3/2$	$3/2$	$3/2$	$1/2$	$1/2$
m_j:	$3/2$	$1/2$	$-1/2$	$-3/2$	$1/2$	$-1/2$

$$
H = - \begin{bmatrix}
H_{hh} & b & c & 0 & ib/\sqrt{2} & -i\sqrt{2}c \\
b^* & H_{lh} & 0 & c & -iq & i\sqrt{3}b/\sqrt{2} \\
c^* & 0 & H_{lh} & -b & -i\sqrt{3}b^*/\sqrt{2} & -iq \\
0 & c^* & -b^* & H_{hh} & -i\sqrt{2}c^* & -ib^*/\sqrt{2} \\
-ib^*/\sqrt{2} & iq & i\sqrt{3}b/\sqrt{2} & i\sqrt{2}c & H_{so} & 0 \\
i\sqrt{2}c^* & -i\sqrt{3}b^*/\sqrt{2} & iq & ib/\sqrt{2} & 0 & H_{so}
\end{bmatrix}
$$

$$(5.74)$$

The elements in the Hamiltonian are given by

$$
H_{hh} = \frac{\hbar^2}{2m_0} \left[(\gamma_1 + \gamma_2)\left(k_x^2 + k_y^2\right) + (\gamma_1 - 2\gamma_2)k_z^2 \right]
$$

$$
H_{lh} = \frac{\hbar^2}{2m_0} \left[(\gamma_1 - \gamma_2)\left(k_x^2 + k_y^2\right) + (\gamma_1 + 2\gamma_2)k_z^2 \right]
$$

$$
H_{so} = (H_{hh} + H_{lh})/2 + \Delta_0
$$

$$
b = \frac{-\sqrt{3}i\hbar^2}{m_0}\gamma_3 \left(k_x - ik_y\right) k_z
$$

$$
c = \frac{\sqrt{3}\hbar^2}{2m_0} \left[\gamma_2 \left(k_x^2 - k_y^2\right) - 2i\gamma_3 k_x k_y \right]
$$

$$
q = (H_{hh} - H_{lh})/\sqrt{2}. \qquad (5.75)
$$

In most semiconductors with large spin–orbit coupling, the 6×6 matrix equation can be separated into a 4×4 and a 2×2 equation. The appropriate equation defining the HH and LH states is then

$$
- \begin{bmatrix}
H_{hh} & b & c & 0 \\
b^* & H_{lh} & 0 & c \\
c^* & 0 & H_{lh} & -b \\
0 & c^* & -b^* & H_{hh}
\end{bmatrix}
\begin{bmatrix}
\Phi_{(3/2,3/2)} \\
\Phi_{(3/2,1/2)} \\
\Phi_{(3/2,-1/2)} \\
\Phi_{(3/2,-3/2)}
\end{bmatrix}
= E
\begin{bmatrix}
\Phi_{(3/2,3/2)} \\
\Phi_{(3/2,1/2)} \\
\Phi_{(3/2,-1/2)} \\
\Phi_{(3/2,-3/2)}
\end{bmatrix}
\qquad (5.76)
$$

where the coefficients H_{hh}, H_{lh}, c, b are the same as above and γ_1, γ_2 and γ_3 are the Kohn–Luttinger parameters. These can be obtained by fitting experimentally obtained hole masses. The eigenstates of the Kohn–Luttinger Hamiltonian are the angular momentum states which are related to the p states. The Kohn–Luttinger matrix can be extended very easily to the quantum well problem in a manner to be discussed in the next chapter. It may be noted that the 4 × 4 matrix equation can be reduced to two 2 × 2 matrix equations (see Problem 5.7 and Broido and Sham, 1985), and the E vs. k relations can be solved analytically.

Near the valence bandedge, the HH, LH states can be represented by an energy momentum relation of the following form

$$E_v(\mathbf{k}) = \frac{-\hbar^2}{2m} \left\{ Ak^2 \pm \left[Bk^4 + C \left(k_x^2 k_y^2 + k_y^2 k_z^2 + k_z^2 k_x^2 \right) \right]^{1/2} \right\} \qquad (5.77)$$

where A, B, and C are dimensionless parameters. The upper sign is for HH and the lower one is for the LH states. As an example for Si, we have $A = 4.0$, $B = 1.1$, and $C = 4.1$ with $m_{HH}^* = 0.49m_0$, $m_{LH}^* = 0.16m_0$. For Ge we have $A = 13.1$, $B = 8.3$, and $C = 12.5$, giving $m_{HH}^* = 0.29m_0$, $m_{LH}^* = 0.047m_0$. It is important to note that Ge has one of the lowest masses for the hole bands of any semiconductor. This leads to excellent hole transport properties.

Let us examine the momentum matrix element p_{cv}, in terms of which, the conduction band masses are expressed in the $\mathbf{k} \cdot \mathbf{p}$ formalism. We note that the conduction bandedge state for direct gap semiconductors has an s-type symmetry, and is denoted by $| + \sigma >$ (spin up) and $| - \sigma >$ (spin down).

The valence band states have been written in the orbital angular momentum–spin representation

$$\Phi_{3/2,3/2} = \frac{-1}{\sqrt{2}} (|p_x > +i|p_y >) \uparrow$$

$$\Phi_{3/2,-3/2} = \frac{1}{\sqrt{2}} (|p_x > -i|p_y >) \downarrow$$

$$\Phi_{3/2,1/2} = \frac{-1}{\sqrt{6}} [(|p_x > +i|p_y >) \downarrow -2|p_z >\uparrow]$$

$$\Phi_{3/2,-1/2} = \frac{1}{\sqrt{6}} [(|p_x > -i|p_y >) \uparrow +2|p_z >\downarrow]. \qquad (5.78)$$

The matrix elements of interest are of the form $< r|P|\sigma >$; $r = x, y, z$. From parity considerations $< x|P_x|\sigma >=< y|P_y|\sigma >=< z|P_z|\sigma >$ are the only nonzero matrix elements while the rest of the elements are zero.

The nonvanishing matrix elements are

$$< \pm 3/2|P_x| \pm \sigma > = \frac{1}{\sqrt{2}} < x|P_x|\sigma >$$

$$< \pm 1/2|P_x| \mp \sigma > = \frac{1}{\sqrt{6}} < x|P_x|\sigma >$$

$$< \pm 3/2|P_z| \pm \sigma > = \frac{2}{\sqrt{6}} < x|P_x|\sigma > . \qquad (5.79)$$

We define a quantity

$$E_p = \frac{2}{m} |< x|P_x|\sigma >|^2$$

$$= \frac{2}{m} p_{cv}^2. \qquad (5.80)$$

Devices	Region of Bandstructure of Importance Measured from Bandedge (in eV)
• Transistors (Source Gate) Low Field Region	$\sim 2k_BT$ ($\sim$ 50meV at $T = 300$K)
• Transistors High Field Region (Gate-Drain Region)	~ 0.5 eV
• Power Transistors Avalanche Detectors and Other Devices Involving Breakdown	$\sim E_{\mathrm{gap}} \sim 1.0$eV
• Lasers	$\sim 2 - 3k_BT$ ($\sim 50 - 75$meV at $T = 300$K)
• Detectors	Variable, depending upon photon wavelength

Table 5.4: Various electronic and optoelectronic devices and the range of bandstructure that is important for their performance.

The following are the values of E_p for various semiconductors in (eV) (Lawaetz, 1971).

GaAs	25.7
InP	20.4
InAs	22.2
CdTe	20.7

5.8 SELECTED BANDSTRUCTURES

We will now examine special features of some semiconductors. Of particular interest are the bandedge properties since they dominate the transport and optical properties. In this context, it is important to appreciate the range of energies away from the bandedges which control various physical properties of devices. These energies are shown in Table 5.4 for various kinds of electronic and optical devices. As can be seen, the region of interest varies depending upon the kind of devices one is interested in. In any case, one should be quite familiar with semiconductor bandstructures about a bandgap away from the bandedges. We will examine Si and GaAs as two important representatives of semiconductors.

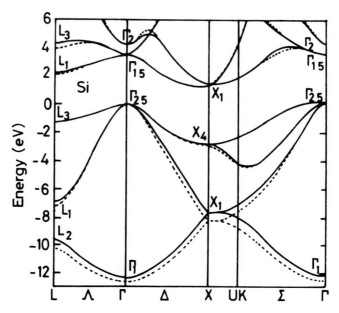

Figure 5.14: Bandstructure of Si. Although the bandstructure of Si is far from ideal, having an indirect bandgap, high hole masses, and small spin–orbit splitting, processing related advantages make Si the premier semiconductor for consumer electronics. (Reproduced with permission, J. R. Chelikowsky, et al., Phys. Rev. B, **14**, 556 (1984).)

5.8.1   Silicon

Silicon is the most important semiconductor for electronics industry. Its premier position is not so much due to the special bandstructure it possesses, but its other material properties such as its robustness, availability in nature, ease of processing, and most importantly, the availability of an oxide (SiO_2), which is an insulator. The Si–SiO_2 interface is also of high quality and is very stable. More than anything, this interface has given the silicon technology the boost it needed to take over the premiership of electronics industry from the earlier semiconductor of importance–Germanium.

The bandstructure of silicon is shown in Figure 5.14. The semiconductor has an indirect bandgap (i.e., the top of the valence and bottom of the conduction band are at different k-points). This fact greatly limits the applications of Si in optical devices, particularly for light emitting devices. The bottom of the conduction band in Si is close to the X-point of the Brillouin zone ($\sim (2\pi/a)(0.85, 0.0)$). Due to the symmetry of the fcc lattice, there are six degenerate X-points and consequently six conduction bandedge valleys. The central cell part of the Bloch functions near the bandedge is a strong mixture of s and p_x functions along the x-axis (the longitudinal axis) and p_y and p_z along the transverse direction from the bandedge. The near bandedge bandstructure can be represented by ellipsoids of energy with simple E vs. k relations of the form (for examples for the [100]

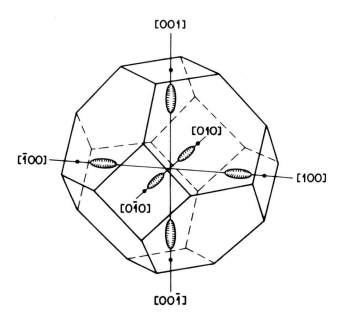

Figure 5.15: Constant energy ellipsoids for Si conduction band. There are six equivalent valleys in Si at the bandedge resulting in a very high bandedge density of states.

valley)

$$E(\mathbf{k}) = \frac{\hbar^2 k_x^2}{2m_l^*} + \frac{\hbar^2 \left(k_y^2 + k_z^2 \right)}{2m_t^*} \tag{5.81}$$

where we have two masses, the longitudinal and transverse. The constant energy surfaces of Si are ellipsoids according to Equation 5.81 and the six such surfaces are shown in Figure 5.15.

The longitudinal mass m_l^* is approximately $0.98m_0$, while the transverse mass is approximately $0.19m_0$. Keep in mind that for the conduction bandedge near $(2\pi/a)[100]$, the longitudinal direction is x-axis and the transverse plane is the y-z plane, but for, say, the valley at $(2\pi/a)[010]$, the longitudinal direction is y-axis while the transverse plane is the x-z. Thus, even though there is strong anisotropy in each valley, there is not as much of an anisotropy in properties such as transport of electrons which involve the electrons moving in all of the valleys.

The next valley in the conduction band is the L-point valley, which is about 0.5 eV above the bandedge. Above this is the Γ-point edge. The direct bandgap of Si is ~ 2.2 eV. This direct gap is quite important for optical transitions since, as we shall see later, the absorption coefficient for photons above this energy is very strong. It is important to note that due to the 6-fold degeneracy of the conduction bandedge, the electron transport in Si is quite poor. This is because of the very large density of states near the bandedge leading to a high scattering rate.

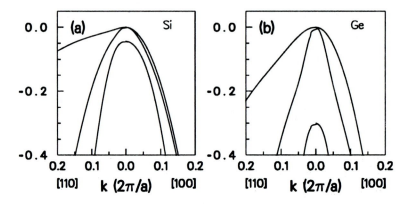

Figure 5.16: The valence bandstructure of Si and Ge. Notice the lower hole masses for Ge and the very large spin–orbit splitting. Ge has perhaps the best hole properties of any semiconductor.

The top of the valence band has the typical features seen in all semiconductor valence bands. One has the HH, LH degeneracy at the zone edge. The split-off (SO) band is also very close for Si since the split-off energy is only 44 meV. This is one of the smallest split off energies of any semiconductors. The HH, LH bands can be described by Equation 5.77. The valence bandstructure is quite anisotropic as shown in Figure 5.16. One can see a very large effective mass for the HH band along the [110] direction. It is very instructive to examine the constant energy surfaces of Si valence band states. These are shown in Figures 5.17, 5.18, and 5.19. One can see the inadequacy of a simple spherical parabolic band to describe these bands particularly the HH band. Due to the large hole mass and the closeness of the SO band, the hole transport properties of Si are quite poor, as we will discuss later.

As we can see from this discussion, the electronic properties of Si are far from ideal. Several important considerations save the day for Si. Most important are the material properties, i.e., ease of processing and availability of SiO_2 as an insulator. Another important reason is that most electronic devices operate at very high electric fields ($F \geq 20kV/cm$). At such high fields, the response of the electrons to field in almost all semiconductors is nearly the same.

(a)

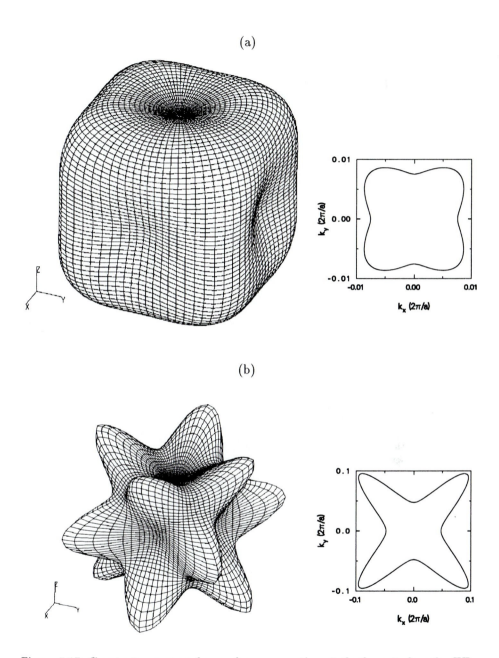

(b)

Figure 5.17: Constant energy surface and a cross section at the $k_z = 0$ plane for HH bands in Si at (a) 1 meV and (b) 40 meV away from the bandedge. Notice how the band becomes extremely nonparabolic at the higher energy. (From J. M. Hinckley, 1990).

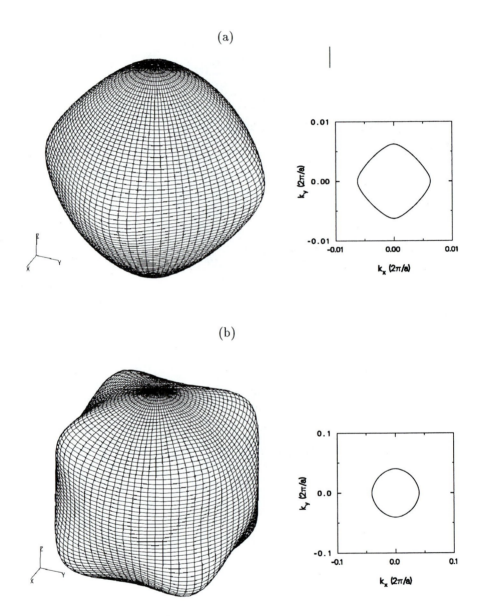

Figure 5.18: Constant energy surfaces and their cross-section in the $k_z = 0$ plane for the LH bands in Si at (a) 1 meV and (b) 40 meV away from the bandedge value. (From J. M. Hinckley, 1990).

(a)

(b)

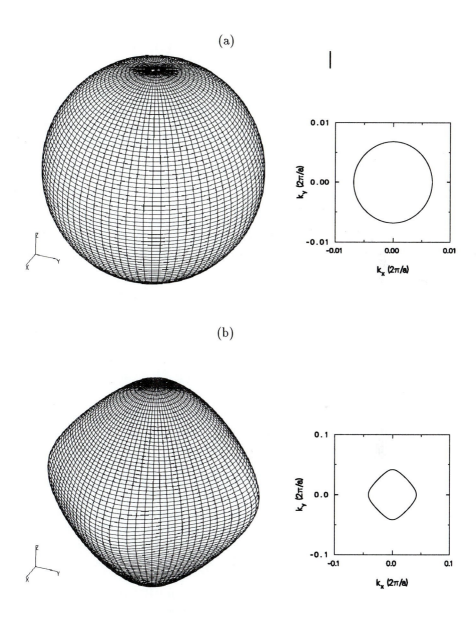

Figure 5.19: Constant energy surfaces and their cross-section with the $k_z = 0$ plane for the split-off bands in Si at (a) 45 meV and (b) 84 meV from the valence bandedge. The split-off band is much more isotropic and parabolic than the HH or LH bands. (From J. M. Hinckley, 1990).

5.8.2   GaAs

After Si, GaAs has become one of the most important semiconductors. Unlike Si, this semiconductor has its success based upon its superior electronic bandstructure. However, it suffers from several drawbacks related to its material properties. GaAs does not have an oxide which could form a high quality insulator-semiconductor interface. It is much more difficult to process which is an inherent problem of compound semiconductors. The basis consists of two atoms which makes it easier to introduce defects (e.g., a Ga atom on the As sublattice, the so called antisite defect). In spite of these drawbacks, GaAs is making steady inroads into the technology.

The bandstructure of GaAs was shown in Figure 5.9. The bandgap is direct, which is the chief attraction of GaAs. The direct bandgap ensures excellent optical properties of GaAs as well as superior electron transport in the conduction band. The conduction bandedge states have an s-type symmetry of the central cell. The bandedge E vs. k relation is quite isotropic leading to spherical equal energy surfaces. The bandstructure can be represented by the relation

$$E = \frac{\hbar^2 k^2}{2m^*} \tag{5.82}$$

with $m^* = 0.067m_0$. A better relationship is the nonparabolic approximation

$$E(1 + \alpha E) = \frac{\hbar^2 k^2}{2m^*} \tag{5.83}$$

with $\alpha = 0.67$ eV^{-1}.

For high electric field transport, it is important to note that the valleys above Γ point are the L-valleys. There are eight L-points, but since half of them are connected by a reciprocal lattice vector, there are four valleys. The separation $\Delta E_{\Gamma L}$ between the Γ and L minima is 0.29 eV. The L valley has a much larger effective mass than the Γ valley. For GaAs, $m_L^* \sim 0.25m_0$. This difference in masses is extremely important for high electric field transport and leads to negative differential resistance. Above the L-point in energy is the X-valley with $\Delta E_{\Gamma L} \sim 0.48$ eV. The mass of the electron in the X-valley is also quite large ($m_X^* \sim 0.6m_0$). At high electric fields, electrons populate both the L and X valleys in addition to the Γ-valley, making these regions of bandstructure quite important.

The valence band of GaAs has the standard HH, LH, and SO bands. Due to the large spin–orbit splitting, for most purposes, the SO band does not play any role in electronic or optoelectronic properties.

The Kohn-Luttinger parameters for GaAs are

$$
\begin{aligned}
\gamma_1 &= 6.85 \\
\gamma_2 &= 2.1 \\
\gamma_3 &= 2.9
\end{aligned}
\tag{5.84}
$$

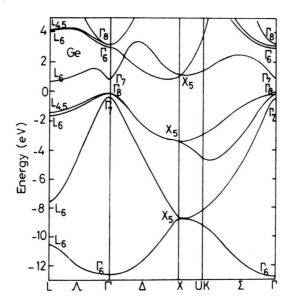

Figure 5.20: Bandstructure of Ge. Like Si, Ge is an indirect semiconductor. The bottom of the conduction band occurs at the L point. There are eight L points, but only four of them are independent since the other four are connected by a reciprocal lattice vector. The hole properties of Ge are the best of any semiconductor with extremely low hole masses. Ge was initially the semiconductor of choice, but because of processing considerations lost out to Si. (Reproduced with permission, J. R. Chelikowsky, et al., Phys. Rev. B, **14**, 556 (1984).)

leading to the density of states hole masses of $m^*_{HH} = 0.45m_0$; $m^*_{LH} = 0.08m_0$. As discussed in the case of Si, the effective masses and E vs. k relation for holes is highly anisotropic. The constant energy surfaces have the same general form as shown in Figures 5.17–5.19.

GaAs has excellent electronic properties. It has far superior properties when compared to Si and, of course, most importantly, the direct bandgap allows one to make solid state lasers from it. Its larger bandgap also ensures better high temperature performance and better radiation hardness (i.e., better immunity from α particles and γ-rays).

The bandstructures of several other semiconductors are shown in Figures 5.20–5.22, along with brief comments about their important properties.

It is also important to note that the bandgap of semiconductors in general decreases as the temperature increases. The bandgap of GaAs, for example, is 1.51 eV at $T = 0K$ and 1.43 eV at room temperature. These changes have very important consequences for both electronic and optoelectronic devices. The temperature variation alters the laser frequency in solid state lasers, and alters

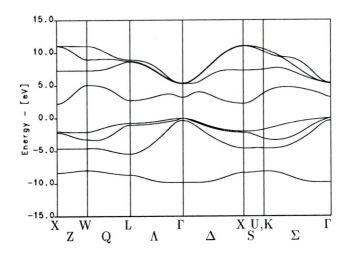

Figure 5.21: Bandstructure of AlAs. AlAs in an important III–V semiconductor because of its excellent lattice matching to GaAs. The material is indirect bandgap and is usually used as an AlGaAs alloy for barrier materials in GaAs/AlGaAs heterostructures. (From M. D. Jaffe, 1989).

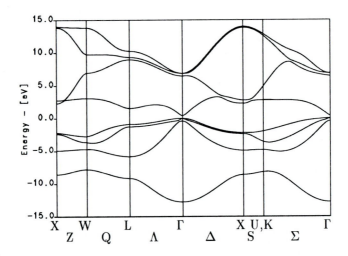

Figure 5.22: Bandstructure of InAs. InAs is a very narrow bandgap semiconductor with exceptional electronic properties. The electron mass is very low and the Γ–L, Γ–X intervalley separations are very large giving superior transport properties. Since no good substrate matches InAs directly, it is often used as an alloy (InGaAs, InAlAs, etc.) for most devices. (From M. D. Jaffe, 1989).

Compound	Type of Bandgap	Experimental Bandgap E_G (eV)		Temperature Dependence of Bandgap $E_G(T)$ (eV)
		0 K	300 K	
AlP	Indirect	2.52	2.45	$2.52 - 3.18 \times 10^{-4}T^2/(T+588)$
AlAs	Indirect	2.239	2.163	$2.239 - 6.0 \times 10^{-4}T^2/(T+408)$
AlSb	Indirect	1.687	1.58	$1.687 - 4.97 \times 10^{-4}T^2/(T+213)$
GaP	Indirect	2.338	2.261	$2.338 - 5.771 \times 10^{-4}T^2/(T+372)$
GaAs	Direct	1.519	1.424	$1.519 - 5.405 \times 10^{-4}T^2/(T+204)$
GaSb	Direct	0.810	0.726	$0.810 - 3.78 \times 10^{-4}T^2/(T+94)$
InP	Direct	1.421	1.351	$1.421 - 3.63 \times 10^{-4}T^2/(T+162)$
InAs	Direct	0.420	0.360	$0.420 - 2.50 \times 10^{-4}T^2/(T+75)$
InSb	Direct	0.236	0.172	$0.236 - 2.99 \times 10^{-4}T^2/(T+140)$

Table 5.5: Bandgaps of binary III–V compounds. (From Casey and Panish, 1978).

the response of modulators and detectors. It also has effects on intrinsic carrier concentration in semiconductors. While the general theory to explain the change of bandgap is quite complex, the key effects that alter the bandgap are:

1. thermal expansion which changes the crystal potential and weakens the overlap matrix elements;

2. smearing of the periodic background potential. We discussed this effect in relationship to the X-ray diffraction peak reduction in presence of lattice vibrations;

3. mutual repulsion of the intraband electronic states via electron-phonon coupling; and

4. the same effect for states within the same band.

The thermal expansion term is usually quite small and the electron-phonon effects dominate the band shrinkage. In general, the bandgap changes for several semiconductors are given by Table 5.5.

5.9 DENSITY OF STATES IN SEMICONDUCTORS

We have earlier discussed the concept of density of states for parabolic bands. As we can see from the bandstructure of semiconductors, the bands are not parabolic in general. We will now develop a more general formalism for the density of states. The number of electrons in the energy interval E and $E + dE$

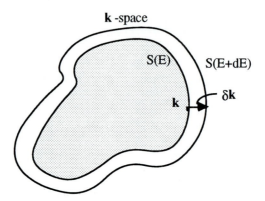

Figure 5.23: Constant energy surfaces $S(E)$ and $S(E+dE)$ separated by energy dE, and a k-vector dk as shown.

are $N(E)dE$ (per unit volume), where $N(E)$ is the density of states:

$$N(E)dE = \frac{2}{V} \times \text{ (number of allowed } k\text{-vectors between } E \text{ and } E+dE). \quad (5.85)$$

The k-space volume per state is $\Delta k = (2\pi)^3/V$. Thus,

$$N(E)dE = \int \frac{d^3k}{4\pi^3} \times \begin{cases} 1 & \text{if } E \leq E(k) \leq E+dE \\ 0 & \text{otherwise.} \end{cases} \quad (5.86)$$

To evaluate the integral, we define a surface of constant energy $S(E)$ where all surface points have the energy E. Around it we have a different surface $S(E+dE)$ where the k-space points have energy $E+dE$ as shown in Figure 5.23. The volume element in k-space can be written as

$$d^3k = dS \cdot \delta k \quad (5.87)$$

where δk is the perpendicular distance between $S(E)$ and $S(E+dE)$ at the point k and dS is the surface element on the constant energy surface.

We may write

$$E + dE = E + |\nabla_k E(k)| \cdot \delta k(k)$$

or

$$\delta k(k) = \frac{dE}{|\nabla_k E(k)|}$$

Thus

$$N(E) = \int_{S(E)} \frac{dS}{4\pi^3} \frac{1}{|\nabla_k E(k)|} \quad (5.88)$$

If the E vs. k relation is simple, the integral can be evaluated analytically. In general, however, one has to carry out a numerical integration.

We note that in the E vs. $\boldsymbol{k}$ relation, there may be regions where $\nabla_{\boldsymbol{k}} E(\boldsymbol{k})$ approaches zero. At these points the density of states increases rapidly giving spikes in the density of states. Such points are called van Hove singularities. The van Hove singularities occur around high symmetry points and since most physical properties of the semiconductor are determined by the density of states, their presence is reflected in these properties.

In this chapter we have discussed the most important aspect of semiconductor physics: bandstructure. Essentially every property of the semiconductor is controlled by the bandstructure.

The energy versus crystal momentum relations are quite complex in semiconductors but for many important processes one can use the simplifications that arise near the bandedges. Near bandedges one can describe the E vs. $\boldsymbol{k}$ relation by simple relations, the simplest of which is the free electron parabolic relation with an effective mass. The effective mass and bandgap of semiconductors are an intrinsic property of the material crystalline structure and the atomic potentials and until the 1970s were considered a given from nature. All this is now changed and, as we shall see in the next two chapters, a tremendous flexibility now exists to modify the bandstructure.

5.10   FOR THE TECHNOLOGIST IN YOU

The bandstructure of a semiconductor is the most important manifestation of the semiconductor's electronic and optical properties and as such has a direct impact on devices. There are many different reasons for preferring materials with different bandstructure. In Table 5.6 we show some of the key physical phenomena which are desirable for applications, their impact on devices of various types and what the optimum choice of bandstructure properties would be.

It can be seen that the choice of bandstructure depends very much on what device applications one has in mind. The variety of semiconductors provide a wide range of materials to choose from for specific applications. Of course, in reality one has to contend with the growth and processing problems. A semiconductor which may look great as far as the bandstructure is concerned, may have serious processing problems. Key examples in this category are very low gap semiconductors (e.g. InAs and InSb) and very large gap materials (e.g. GaN, AlN, SiC and C). The growth, doping, processing of these materials is extremely problematic. The low gap materials are usually very "soft" and are easy to damage. The large gap materials are hard to grow defect free and very difficult to dope reliably. However, if the need for the technology is strong, these problems are usually overcome.

Often the motivation for a particular bandstructure comes indirectly. An example is the loss in glass fibers used for optical communication, shown in Figure 5.24a. The loss minimas at 1.55 μm and 1.3 μm have determined which semiconductors are useful for long haul communication. Similarly, the microwave losses in the atmosphere shown in Figure 5.24b determine the needs for advanced

Desired Physical Effect	Impact on Devices	Preferred Bandstructure
Superior Low Field Mobility	Source Resistance in FETs; Base Resistance in HBTs	Low Effective Mass
High Peak Velocity at Intermediate F-Fields	Short Transit Times	Large Intervalley Separation
Negative Resistance Region in Velocity– Field Relations	Microwave Devices Based on Gunn Effect Based on Gunn Effect	Low Energy, Low Mass /High Energy, High Mass Valleys
High Temperature / High Breakdown Voltage	High Temperature Electronics; Power Devices	Large Bandgap
Optically Active Material	Lasers; Detectors	Direct Gap Materials
Long Wavelength Detection	Night Vision Devices; Thermal Imagers	Narrow Bandgap
Long Haul Communication Low Loss Lasers	Fiber–Optic Communication Technology	Bandgap Tuned to Low Loss Energies $(1.55\mu m; 1.3\mu m)$

Table 5.6: Semiconductor physical phenomena and their applications.

microwave devices for satellite communications.

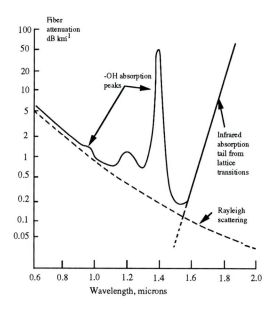

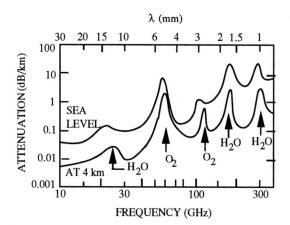

Figure 5.24: (a) Optical attenuation vs. wavelength for an optical fiber. Primary loss mechanisms are identified as absorption and scattering. (After Wilson and Hawkes, *Optoelectronics: An Introduction*, Prentice–Hall, 1983). (b) Millimeter wave attenuation vs. frequency for the atmosphere. Primary loss mechanisms are absorption by water and oxygen. The degree of attentuation depends on the many factors, with a primary one being the altitutde. (After Sze, *High Speed Semiconductor Devices*, Wiley).

5.11   PROBLEMS

5.1. Using the relation

$$\sum_{\mathbf{k}} e^{i\mathbf{k}\cdot\mathbf{R}} = N\delta_{\mathbf{R},0}$$

use the orthonormality of the Bloch functions to show that the Wannier functions $\phi_n(\mathbf{r})$ at different sites are orthogonal, i.e.

$$\int \phi_n^*(\mathbf{r}-\mathbf{R})\, \phi_{n'}(\mathbf{r}-\mathbf{R}')\, d^3r \propto \delta_{n,n'}\, \delta_{\mathbf{R},\mathbf{R}'}.$$

5.2. In the text we had discussed the bandstructure of an s-band model in an fcc lattice. What is the bandstructure in a bcc lattice? Assume only nearest neighbor interaction $\gamma = 1.0$ eV. What is the effective mass near the bottom of the band and the top of the band? Assume a lattice constant of 4 Å.

5.3. If in the s-band model discussed in the text one includes a second neighbor interaction γ_2, what is the expression for the bandstructure? What is the electron effective mass at the bottom of the band if $\gamma_1 = 1.0$ eV; $\gamma_2 = 0.2$ eV? Assume a lattice constant of 4 Å.

5.4. Consider a cubic lattice with an s, p_x, p_y, p_z basis. Write down the 4×4 eigenvalue equation for the system. Assume only nearest neighbor interactions and make use of the following symmetries of the tight binding matrix elements (use the notation $s \to 1$, $p_x \to 2$, $p_y \to 3$, $p_z \to 4$)

$$\int d^3r\, \phi_1(x,y,z)\, \Delta U\, \phi_1(x-a,y,z) \;=\; V_{ss\sigma}$$

$$\int d^3r\, \phi_1(x,y,z)\, \Delta U\, \phi_2(x-a,y,z) \;=\; V_{sp\sigma}$$

$$\int d^3r\, \phi_1(x,y,z)\, \Delta U\, \phi_2(x,y-a,z) \;=\; 0$$

$$\int d^3r\, \phi_2(x,y,z)\, \Delta U\, \phi_1(x-a,y,z) \;=\; V_{sp\sigma}$$

$$\int d^3r\, \phi_2(x,y,z)\, \Delta U\, \phi_3(x,y-a,z) \;=\; V_{pp\pi}$$

$$\int d^3r\, \phi_2(x,y,z)\, \Delta U\, \phi_3(x-a,y,z) \;=\; 0$$

Show that the matrix elements in the 4×4 secular determinant are (E_{s0}, E_{p0} are on-site matrix elements),

$$\begin{aligned}
H_{1,1} &= \;<s|H|s> \\
&= \; E_{s0} + 2V_{ss\sigma}[\cos k_x a + \cos k_y a + \cos k_z a]
\end{aligned}$$

$$
\begin{aligned}
H_{1,2} &= \ <p_x|H|s> \\
&= \ 2iV_{sp\sigma}\sin k_x a \\
H_{2,2} &= \ <p_x|H|p_x> \\
&= \ E_{p0} + 2V_{pp\sigma}\cos k_x a + 2V_{pp\pi}[\cos k_y a + \cos k_z a] \\
H_{3,2} &= \ <p_y|H|p_x> \\
&= \ 0.
\end{aligned}
$$

Other elements are generated by cyclical permutations. What are the solutions of the problem at $k = 0$?

5.5. Write out the matrix elements for the diamond structure using the tight binding approach. Without spin–orbit coupling, compare your results to the matrix elements given in the classic paper of Slater and Koster (1954), (reference above). Note that there is a misprint of the matrix elements in the original paper.

5.6. Include spin–orbit coupling in the tight binding matrix using an sp^3 basis per site. A good source of matrix elements for the tight binding for a variety of semiconductors is Talwar and Ting (1982).

5.7. Express the heavy hole and light hole masses along [001], [011], and [111] directions in terms of the Kohn–Luttinger parameters. Hint: The 4×4 $\mathbf{k} \cdot \mathbf{p}$ matrix (Equation 5.70) can be reduced to two doubly degenerate (in the absence of external fields) 2×2 equations of the form

$$
\left| \begin{array}{cc} H_{hh} & b - ic \\ (b - ic)^* & H_{lh} \end{array} \right| \psi = E\psi,
$$

where ψ is a 1×2 vector, (Broido and Sham, 1985).

5.8. In Si electron transport, the intervalley scattering is very important. Two kinds of intervalley scatterings are important: in the g–scattering an electron goes from one valley (say a [001] valley) to an opposite valley ([00$\bar{1}$]), while in an f–scattering, the electron goes to a perpendicular valley ([001] to [010], for example). The extra momentum for the transitions is provided by a phonon and may include a reciprocal lattice vector. Remembering that Si valleys are not precisely at the X–point, calculate the phonon vector which allows these scatterings.

5.9. Assuming k conservation, what is the phonon wavevector which can take an electron in the GaAs Γ–valley to the L–valley?

5.12　REFERENCES

- **General Bandstructure**

  - Bassani, F., in *Semiconductors and Semimetals* (edited by R. K. Willardson and A. C. Beer, Academic Press, New York, 1966), vol. 1, p. 21.

  - For general electronic properties a good reference is: Casey, H. C., Jr. and M. B. Panish, *Heterostructure Lasers, Part A, Fundamental Principles* and *Part B, Materials and Operating Characteristics* (Academic Press, New York, 1978).

  - Fletcher, G. C., *Electron Band Theory of Solids* (North-Holland, Amsterdam, 1971).

  - Harrison, W. A., *Electronic Structure and Properties of Solids* (W. H. Freeman, San Francisco, 1980).

  - Kane, E. O., *Semiconductors and Semimetals* (edited by R. K. Willardson and A. C. Beer, Academic Press, New York, 1966), vol. 1, p. 81.

  - Phillips, J. C., *Bonds and Bands in Semiconductors* (Academic Press, New York, 1973).

- **Tight Binding Method**

  - Bassani, F., in *Semiconductors and Semimetals* (edited by R. K. Willardson and A. C. Beer, Academic Press, New York, 1966), vol. 1, p. 21.

  - Chadi, D. and M. L. Cohen, Phys Stat. Sol. B, **68**, 404 (1975).

  - Jaffe, M. D., *Studies of the Electronic Properties and Applications of Coherently Strained Semiconductors*, Ph.D. Thesis, (The University of Michigan, Ann Arbor, 1989).

  - Slater, J. C. and G. F. Koster, Phys. Rev., **94**, 1498 (1959).

  - Talwar, D. N. and C. S. Ting, Phys. Rev. B, **25**, 2660 (1982).

- **Spin–Orbit Effects**

  - Chadi, D., Phys. Rev. B, **16**, 790 (1977).

  - Dresselhaus, D., A. F. Kip, and C. Kittel, Phys. Rev., **98**, 368 (1955).

  - Kane, E. O., in *Semiconductors and Semimetals* (edited by R. K. Willardson and A. C. Beer, Academic Press, New York, 1966), vol. 1, p. 81.

  - Luttinger, J. and W. Kohn, Phys. Rev., **97**, 869 (1955).

  - Sakurai, J. J., *Advanced Quantum Mechanics* (Addison–Wesley, New York, 1982).

– Slater, J. C., *Quantum Theory of Solids* (McGraw–Hill, New York, 1965), vol. 2.

• **The OPW Method**

– Woodruff, T. O., Solid State Physics, **4**, 367 (1957).

• **The Pseudopotential Method**

– Chelikowsky, J. R. and M. L. Cohen, Phys. Rev. B, **14**, 556 (1976).

– Cohen, M. H. and V. Heine, Phys. Rev., **122**, 1821 (1961).

– Harrison, W. A., *Pseudopotentials in the Theory of Metals* (W. A. Benjamin, New York, 1966).

– Phillips, J. C. and L. Kleinmann, Phys. Rev., **116**, 287 (1959).

• **The $k \cdot p$ Method**

– Broido, D. A. and L. J. Sham, Phys. Rev. B, **31**, 888 (1985).

– Hinckley, J. M., *The Effect of Strain in Pseudomorphic p-$Si_{1-x}Ge_x$: Physics and Modelling of the Valence Bandstructure and Hole Transport*, Ph.D. Thesis, (The University of Michigan, Ann Arbor, 1990).

– Kane, E. O., J. Phys. Chem. Solids, **8**, 38 (1959).

– Kane, E. O., in *Semiconductors and Semimetals* (edited by R. K. Willardson and A. C. Beer, Academic Press, New York, 1966), vol. 1, p. 81.

– Lawaetz, P., Phys. Rev. B, **4**, 3460 (1971).

– Luttinger, J., Phys. Rev., **102**, 1030 (1956).

– Luttinger, J. and W. Kohn, Phys. Rev., **97**, 869 (1955).

CHAPTER
6

BANDSTRUCTURE MODIFICATIONS: ALLOYS AND HETEROSTRUCTURES

In the previous chapter we have seen how the intrinsic properties of a semiconductor as reflected by its chemical composition and crystalline structure lead to the phenomenon of bandstructure. Since essentially all the electronic and optical properties of semiconductor devices are dependent upon the bandstructure, an obvious question that arises is: Can the bandstructure of a material be changed? The ability to tailor the bandstructure at will can obviously become a powerful tool in the hands of an insightful electrical engineer. Novel devices can be conceived and designed for superior and tailorable performance. The answer to the question above is an emphatic yes. The bandstructure of semiconductors can, indeed, be changed and over the last decade this has become one of the driving forces in semiconductor physics. In fact, it can be argued that without the new concepts in band tailoring, new research in semiconductor physics would have come to a halt. However, while the ability to modify bandstructure provides a new and exciting dimension in device design, it also places a tremendous burden on the electrical engineer. Without the ability to modify the bandstructure, the knowledge base required by a typical electrical engineer was limited to properties of "naturally" occurring semiconductors, e.g., Si, GaAs, and Ge. With revolutionary advances in bandstructure modification, the electrical engineer must learn quantum mechanical concepts governing the modifications and their control. This, of course, makes life a great deal more exciting for the electrical engineer.

In the next two chapters we will establish some of the physical concepts which are responsible for bandstructure modifications. Although, in principle, many physical phenomena can modify the electronic bandstructure, we will discuss three important ones, since these are widely used for band tailoring (or engineering).

These three phenomena involve:

1. alloying of two or more semiconductors;

2. use of heterostructures to cause quantum confinement or formation of "superlattices";

3. use of built-in strain via lattice mismatched epitaxy.

These three concepts are increasingly being used for improved performance in electronic and optical devices and their importance is expected to become greater with each passing year. The first two issues will be discussed in this chapter while the effect of strain will be discussed in Chapter 7.

6.1 BANDSTRUCTURE OF SEMICONDUCTOR ALLOYS

Alloying of two materials is one of the oldest techniques to modify properties of materials. We are all familiar with the "Bronze Age." Bronze is an alloy between copper and tin. Alloys have been used for centuries to improve material properties.

In semiconductors the concept of randomly mixing two or more semiconductors is motivated by two main objectives:

1. Alter the bandgap of the material to a prechosen value. This motivation drives a great deal of alloy studies in the laser/detector area. The bandgap essentially determines the energy of the light emitted in a laser, and often fiber optics communication constraints, for example, force scientists to design systems with a particular wavelength to ensure low loss. Similarly, desire for night vision drives one toward very small bandgap materials. Some of the common alloys used are HgCdTe for infrared detectors; InGaAsP for lasers; and AlGaAs for confining layers in lasers.

2. To create a material with a proper lattice constant to match or mismatch with an available substrate. For example, one uses $In_{0.53} Ga_{0.47}As$ alloy since it is lattice matched with InP substrates, which are easily available.

Along with these main motivations there are, of course, potential advantages of improved carrier transport, fabrication of heterostructures, etc.

When two semiconductors A and B are mixed via an appropriate growth technique, one must have the following information regarding the structure of the alloy:

1. The crystalline structure of the lattice: in most semiconductors the two (or more) components of the alloy have the same crystal structure so that

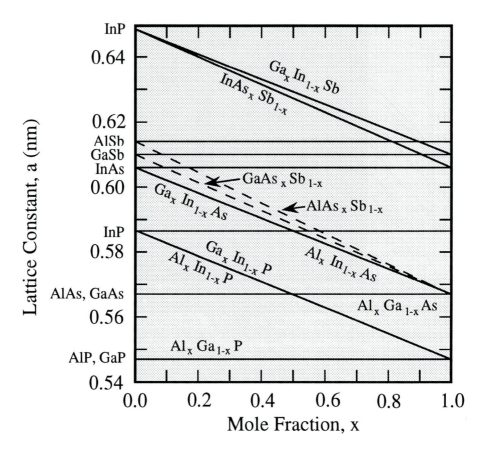

Figure 6.1: Lattice constant as a function of composition for ternary III–V crystalline solid solutions. Vegard's law is assume to be obeyed in all cases. The dashed lines show regions where miscibility gaps are expected. (Reproduced with permission, H. C. Casey Jr., et al., *Heterostructure Lasers*, Academic Press, New York, 1978.)

the final alloy also has the same crystalline structure. However, mixing a diamond lattice material (e.g., Ge) with a zinc–blende material (e.g., GaAs) can lead to some very interesting structures. For the same lattice structure materials, the lattice constant obeys Vegard's law:

$$a_{\text{alloy}} = x a_A + (1 - x) a_B. \tag{6.1}$$

Lattice constants for some alloys are shown in Figure 6.1 (after Casey and Panish), assuming Vegard's law.

2. The ordering of the atoms: if an alloy $A_x B_{1-x}$ is formed, an important question is what is the arrangement of the atoms A and B in the alloy. One could have several extreme cases, namely:

(a) All of the A atoms are localized in one region while the B atoms are localized in another region. Such alloys are called *phase separated*.

(b) The probability that an atom next to an A-type atom is A is x and the probability that it is B is $(1 - x)$. Such alloys are called *random alloys*.

(c) The A and B atoms form a well-ordered periodic structure, leading to a *superlattice*.

The ordering of the atoms in the alloy is extremely important since the bandstructure depends strongly on the ordering. Most semiconductor alloys used in the electronics/optoelectronics industry are grown with the intention of making perfectly random alloys. Usually, deviations from this randomness leads to deterioration in device performance.

The two structural properties mentioned above are, in general, determined by the free energy minimum of the solution of the two components A and B of the alloy. The free energy F, in general, has the form

$$F = U - TS \qquad (6.2)$$

where U is the internal energy, T the temperature at which the alloy is grown and S is the entropy of the system. The totally random system has the highest entropy since it provides the most disordered state. The totally phase separated and totally ordered state have negligible entropy terms. A simple picture provides a conceptual understanding of the forces that determine the nature of the alloy.

In Figure 6.2 we show the bond energies in an A–B alloy. There are three kinds of bond energies: the like atom bond energies V_{AA} and V_{BB}; and the unlike atom energy V_{AB}. The parameter

$$\Delta = \frac{1}{2} (V_{AA} + V_{BB}) - V_{AB} \qquad (6.3)$$

represents the preferential energy between an arrangement where atoms are surrounded by like atoms versus unlike atoms. Thus, we have the following qualitative cases:

1. $|\Delta| \approx k_B T$, in which case there is no particular preference for that atomic arrangement and the alloy is random;

2. $|\Delta| \gg k_B T$ and $\Delta < 0$, in which case the like atom bonding energy is much stronger (remember that the bond energy is negative) than the unlike atom bond energy, leading to a phase separated or clustered alloy. In this case, one often says there is a miscibility gap in the alloy;

3. $|\Delta| \gg k_B T$ and $\Delta > 0$, in which case an atom prefers to be surrounded by an unlike atom. This can lead to natural ordering in the alloy with important consequences for electronic properties.

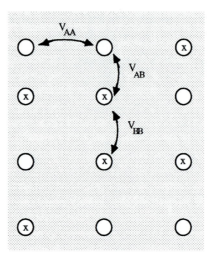

Figure 6.2: A conceptual picture showing the bond energies for an A–B alloy. The relative strengths of the like bond energies (V_{AA}, V_{BB}) and the unlike bond energy (V_{AB}) determines whether the alloy is clustered, random, or ordered.

Figure 6.3 gives a simple schematic of these three cases.

Semiconductor alloys provide cases falling in all three categories listed above. Before discussing a few examples, it is important to note that the free energy considerations discussed above are valid, if the crystal growth technique is a close to equilibrium growth technique. Techniques such as liquid phase epitaxy are carried out close to equilibrium, while techniques such as MBE, MOCVD and sputtering, can operate in a wide range of parameter space, ranging from near equilibrium to very far from equilibrium. Thus, these non-equilibrium techniques can overcome the constraints dictated by thermodynamics.

Since clustering plays an important role in carrier mobility in alloys, we define the Warren–Cowley order parameters, which describe the order in the atomic distribution of the alloys. For an alloy $A_x B_{1-x}$, the definition is:

$$
\begin{aligned}
C_\tau &= 1 - x \quad \text{if the atom at site } \tau \text{ is A–type} \\
&= x \qquad \text{if the atom at site } \tau \text{ is B–type}
\end{aligned}
\tag{6.4}
$$

The order parameters are then defined as

$$
\alpha_\tau = \sum_{\tau'}^{N} \frac{C_{\tau'} C_{\tau'+\tau}}{Nx(1-x)}
\tag{6.5}
$$

It can be easily seen that $\alpha_0 = 1$ and for a random alloy, $\alpha_{\tau \neq 0} = 1/N$.

In general, the scattering rate for nonrandom scattering can be calculated in terms of the quantities α_τ. Usually, clustering increases the scattering rates, unless the alloy is an ordered superlattice.

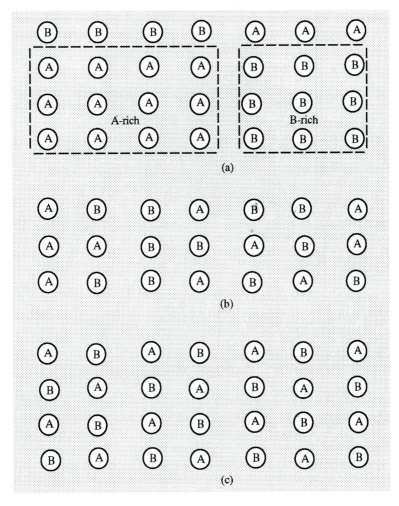

Figure 6.3: A schematic example of (a) a clustered, (b) a random, and (c) an ordered alloy.

The bandstructure calculations for alloys are very complex although a first order approximation can be obtained quite simply and is used for most applications. The reason for this complexity is that even though the alloys are crystalline material, the randomness of the atom on any site means that other than the case of a superlattice (or ordered alloy) there is *no periodicity* in the background crystalline potential. This means that we can no longer use Bloch's theorem to describe the electronic wavefunctions. The electronic states, in general, are not the simple traveling waves but are much more complex with position dependent probabilities. Because of the inherent disorder in the alloy, there is a finite probability even in a random alloy that a finite region of volume V is

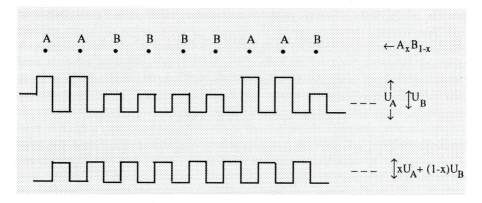

Figure 6.4: Motivation for the virtual crystal approximation. The uppermost section of this figure shows the arrangements of A- and B-type atoms on a lattice. Associated with these atoms are the corresponding short-ranged atomic potentials, U_A and U_B. In the virtual crystal approximation it is assumed that the extended states see an "average" weighted potential $xU_A + (1 - x)U_B$ which is then considered to be periodic.

rich in material A. This region can trap the electron, i.e., form a localized wavefunction. Such states will not be conducting at very low temperatures, except through tunneling. In fact, the electronic states can be classified as either localized or extended. The extended states extend throughout the material although they may not be Bloch states and may not have finite probability everywhere in space. The energy separating the localized and extended states is often called the mobility edge in contrast to the bandedge in a single semiconductor. We will discuss the localized states further in Chapter 18.

A simple approximation is usually made to study the bandstructure of alloys and is motivated by Figure 6.4. The figure shows the atomic potentials distributed in real space. The randomness of the potentials seen by the electrons is obvious. However, in the virtual crystal approximation the random potential is replaced by an average periodic potential as shown

$$U_{\mathrm{av}}(\boldsymbol{r}) = xU_A(\boldsymbol{r}) + (1 - x)U_B(\boldsymbol{r}). \tag{6.6}$$

For example, an implementation of this approach in the tight binding method involves taking the weighted average of the matrix elements. For direct bandgap materials (bandedges are at Γ–point or at $\boldsymbol{k} = 0$) this implies that the bandgaps are also weighted linearly, since the bandedges at $\boldsymbol{k} = 0$ are linear sums of the tight binding matrix elements.

$$E_g^{\mathrm{alloy}} = xE_g^A + (1 - x)E_g^B. \tag{6.7}$$

In most alloys, however, there is a bowing effect arising from the increasing disorder due to the alloying. In fact, it can be physically seen that there is a small probability of finding regions with bandgaps as small as the smallest bandgap in

Compound	Direct Energy Gap E_g (eV)
$Al_xIn_{1-x}P$	$1.351 + 2.23x$
$Al_xGa_{1-x}As$	$1.424 + 1.247x$[a]
	$1.424 + 1.455x$[b]
$Al_xIn_{1-x}As$	$0.360 + 2.012x + 0.698x^2$
$Al_xGa_{1-x}Sb$	$0.726 + 1.129x + 0.368x^2$
$Al_xIn_{1-x}Sb$	$0.172 + 1.621x + 0.43x^2$
$Ga_xIn_{1-x}P$	$1.351 + 0.643x + 0.786x^2$
$Ga_xIn_{1-x}As$	$0.36 + 1.064x$
$Ga_xIn_{1-x}Sb$	$0.172 + 0.139x + 0.415x^2$
GaP_xAs_{1-x}	$1.424 + 1.150x + 0.176x^2$
$GaAs_xSb_{1-x}$	$0.726 - 0.502x + 1.2x^2$
InP_xAs_{1-x}	$0.360 + 0.891x + 0.101x^2$
$InAs_xSb_{1-x}$	$0.18 - 0.41x + 0.58x^2$

Table 6.1: Compositional dependence of the energy gaps of the binary III–V solid solutions at 300 K. (After Casey and Panish, 1978).

the components of the alloy. One usually defines the bandgap described by the mobility edge as

$$E_g^{alloy} = a + bx + cx^2 \qquad (6.8)$$

where c is the bowing parameter. In Figure 6.5 we show how the bandgaps of various material combinations change as alloys are made. The solid lines represent direct bandgap regions and the dotted lines the indirect gap regions. Table 6.1 gives the composition dependence of the energy gaps of several semiconductor alloys at room temperature.

In the virtual crystal approximation it can be easily seen that the bandedge masses scale as

$$\frac{1}{m_{alloy}^*} = \frac{x}{m_A^*} + \frac{1-x}{m_B^*}, \qquad (6.9)$$

since

$$\begin{aligned}
E_{alloy}(k) &= \frac{\hbar^2 k^2}{2m_{alloy}^*} \\
&= \frac{x\hbar^2 k^2}{2m_A^*} + \frac{(1-x)\hbar^2 k^2}{2m_B^*}.
\end{aligned} \qquad (6.10)$$

It is quite clear from the discussion above that semiconductor alloys offer a tremendous range of bandstructures. Both bandgaps and lattice constants can

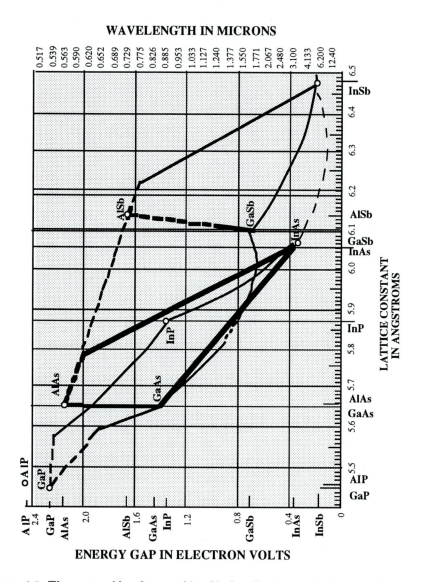

Figure 6.5: The range of bandgaps achievable by alloy formation in some III–V compound semiconductors. (After P. K. Tien.)

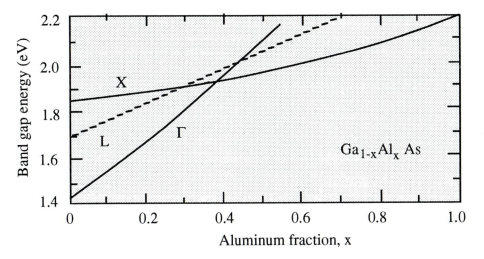

Figure 6.6: The variation of conduction band valleys in AlGaAs as a function of composition at 300 K.

be altered by using the concept of alloys. Several important alloys have made extremely important contributions in electronics and optoelectronics. We will briefly discuss a few specific cases, which highlight the versatility of alloys.

6.1.1 GaAs–AlAs Alloy

The AlGaAs system is perhaps the most important alloy system. It has become an important component of high speed electronic devices (the modulation doped field effect transistors or MODFETs) and optoelectronic devices (modulators, detectors, and lasers). Because of its excellent lattice match to GaAs substrates, it has also been a component of nearly all kinds of "exotic" quantum well structures. The alloy also has very interesting switching of the bandgap from direct to indirect. Figure 6.6 shows the composition dependence of the conduction band valleys. Since the material becomes indirect for Al fraction above ∼35%, most device structures use a composition below this value. Close to this transition composition, the alloy does develop some problems related to the deep level dubbed the "D–X center." This deep level seems to be connected to the merging of the Γ, X, and L valleys in energy and has been an area of intense research over the last decade. The presence of this level has disastrous effects on AlGaAs based devices at low temperature, due to the carrier trapping behavior of this D–X center. An excellent source for the properties of the AlGaAs alloy is the review article by Adachi (1985).

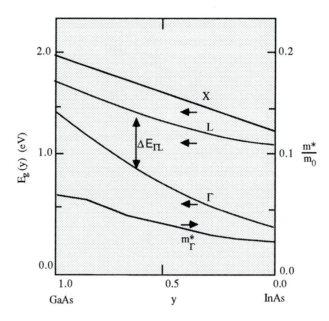

Figure 6.7: Variation of the principal gap energy levels in the alloy of InAs and GaAs. Also shown is the effective mass in the alloy.

6.1.2   InAs–GaAs Alloy

InAs and GaAs span a bandgap range of 0.39 eV to 1.5 eV and have a lattice mismatch of 7%. The special properties of the $In_xGa_{1-x}As$ alloy have made it an active ingredient of very high speed transistors as well as for fiber optic communication lasers. A lattice matched composition often used is $In_{0.53}Ga_{0.47}As$ ($E_g = 0.8$ eV) which matches to InP. The alloy can then form a quantum well with InP ($E_g = 1.35$ eV) or $In_{0.52}Al_{0.48}As$ ($E_g = 1.45$ eV) as barriers. Other compositions that have become increasingly favorable are the lattice mismatched compositions of $In_xGa_{1-x}As$ (grown on GaAs) and $In_{0.53+x}Ga_{0.47-x}As$ (grown on InP). These "strained" structures have remarkable properties which are being exploited for high speed electronics and optoelectronics and will be discussed in detail in the next chapter. The $In_{0.53}Ga_{0.47}As$ alloy has found a niche in high speed electronics because of its small effective mass ($m_e^* = 0.04m_0$) and high Γ–L and Γ–X separation which lead to excellent low and high field transport properties. Like AlGaAs alloys, InGaAs alloys can be grown free of clustering effects. Figure 6.7 shows the bandstructure of this alloy.

6.1.3   HgTe–CdTe Alloy

The HgCdTe system offers one of the most versatile alloys. The two components are very well lattice matched, do not show any miscibility gap, and most importantly, span a bandgap of 0 to 1.5 eV, remaining direct throughout the

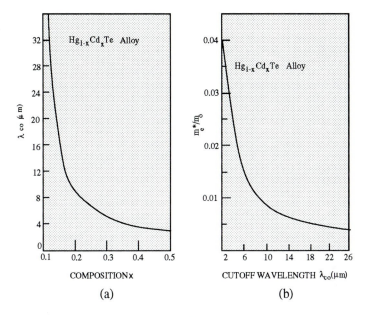

Figure 6.8: (a) Cutoff wavelength for alloy HgCdTe as a function of composition, (b) electron effective mass as a function of cutoff wavelength for HgCdTe alloy. (Reproduced with permission, D. L. Smith, et al., Journal de Physique, **C5**, 509, (1984).)

composition range. The chief attraction of this alloy is for very small bandgap device applications. These primarily involve night vision applications, thermal imaging in industrial and medical applications, imaging through dense fog, etc. The alloy also has the advantage that it can be grown on both CdTe, ZnTe, and even Si and GaAs substrates. This allows for the possibility of integrating long wavelength detectors with high speed GaAs devices and high density silicon circuitry.

The HgTe system has a "negative" bandgap, i.e., the Γ–point of the s-type states normally associated with conduction band in other semiconductors lies below the p-type Γ–point states. As the alloy composition is changed, one can obtain a wide range of bandgaps. The electron masses can also be extremely small which offer attractive possibilities of very high speed devices. The bandgap of the alloy $Hg_{1-x}Cd_xTe$ is given by the relation

$$E_g(x) = -0.3 + 1.9x \text{ eV} \tag{6.11}$$

In Figure 6.8 we show the wavelength corresponding to the alloy bandgap as well as the carrier mass for the HgCdTe alloy.

6.1.4 Si–Ge Alloy

Silicon and Germanium have a lattice mismatch of ∼4% so that it is difficult to find a good substrate to grow this alloy on. Also, since the alloy composition remains indirect, there is little motivation from optoelectronic device considerations to grow the alloy. However, recently there has been an increasing interest in this alloy since it can be a component of Si–SiGe structures and allow heterostructure concepts to be realized in Si technology.

The conduction band minima of Si is at X–point while that of Ge is at the L–point. The alloy retains an X–point character for the bandedge up to 85% Ge and then changes its character to L–like.

6.2   BANDSTRUCTURE MODIFICATIONS BY HETEROSTRUCTURES

Since the 1970s, there have been spectacular advances in thin film epitaxial growth techniques. While earlier growth methods could grow high quality single crystals, it was difficult for these techniques to abruptly change semiconductors during growth. Epitaxial techniques such as molecular beam epitaxy (MBE) and metal organic chemical vapor deposition (MOCVD) are able to produce abruptness, in growth of two semiconductors, approaching one monolayer ($\sim$3 Å). In MBE, for example, elements making up the heterostructure (e.g., Ga, As, and Al), if GaAs/AlAs structures are to be grown, are heated in cells (essentially Knudson cells) and the generated vapor impinges on a substrate (usually a rotating substrate to ensure uniform growth). In the path of the vapor are shutters, which can allow or prevent a particular species from impinging . Since growth rates are maintained at about one monolayer per second, the shutters can easily control the amount of a given species deposited to better than one monolayer. Similar controls can be obtained in MOCVD techniques.

It must be realized, however, that simply depositing a controlled amount of material of a semiconductor does not make a good heterostructure. An important aspect is the quality of the heterostructure interface. Since the motivation of most heterostructures is to modify the electronic properties by using quantum effects, the spatial extent of the chemical modulation should be $\sim$100 Å, i.e., $\sim$30–90 monolayers. If the interface roughness is more than a couple of monolayers, many of the advantages of the heterostructures are lost. Since the atoms or molecules impinging on the substrate do so randomly, without additional kinetic processes, the surface will develop a Gaussian roughness which will continue to grow as the film growth continues. This will, of course, cause an extremely rough interface.

To ensure a reliable and repeatable atomically abrupt interface between two semiconductors, the following conditions must be assured:

1. The free energy minimum of the two-dimensional surface of the heterostructure must be atomically flat.

2. Since the impinging flux is random, the atoms must have sufficient kinetics to reach surface thermodynamic equilibrium.

It is important to emphasize that the kinetics should not be so great that mixing occurs through bulk diffusion with the resulting destruction of the interface.

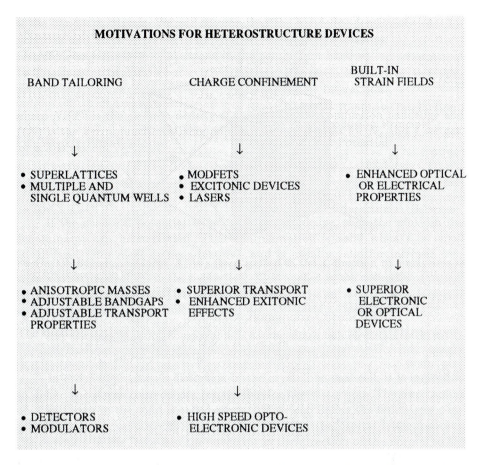

Figure 6.9: Semiconductor heterostructure material features and types of devices whose design takes advantage of these features.

The success of a crystal growth experiment thus depends upon the ability of the crystal grower to realize these conditions. This is often not easy. However, a number of heterostructure combinations are now available for the semiconductor scientists.

The heterostructures discussed above provide a chemical modulation in the growth direction. This can be utilized to fabricate quantum wells and superlattices where confinement effects are realized in one dimension. In Figure 6.9, we show some of the motivations spurring the heterostructure technology. Increased efforts are being dedicated to realizing confinement in two dimensions (quantum wires) and all three dimensions (quantum dots). While the epitaxial techniques for one-dimensional confinement are well-established and conceptually simple, confinement in other directions involves difficult and cumbersome epitaxial or processing technologies. We will focus our attention on the one-dimensional con-

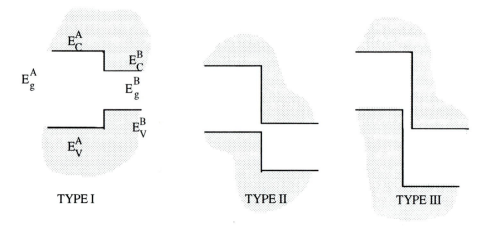

Figure 6.10: Various possible bandedge lineups in heterostructures.

finement.

One of the most important issues to be addressed when two semiconductors are brought together abruptly to form an interface is how the bandedges of the two materials line up at the interface. In principle, several possibilities could exist if a semiconductor A with bandgap E_g^A and edges E_v^A and E_c^A is grown with a semiconductor B with gap E_g^B and edges E_v^B and E_c^B. A number of possible band lineups can then arise, as shown in Figure 6.10. Each of these will have unique and special bandstructure and device applications. The bandgap distribution is thus most important in heterostructures. This simple piece of information is unfortunately not so easy to obtain. In fact, for the GaAs/AlAs system, one of the most studied systems, for almost six years, it was believed that 85% of the discontinuity was in the conduction band and 15% in the valence band. This information which was obtained from fitting optical data was later on revised (after almost six years!) to the 60:40 discontinuity distribution rule.

A key reason why it has been so difficult to assign the band discontinuities is that the relative positions of the ground states (to be discussed shortly) are not very sensitive to the band offsets. For example, interband level energy differences between the HH and the electron ground states for GaAs/Al$_{0.3}$Ga$_{0.7}$As quantum wells for a 100 Å well, assuming a 80:20 versus a 50:50 discontinuity distribution, is only ∼3 meV. For a 50 Å well, the difference increases to ∼10 meV. As can be seen, this difference is relatively insensitive to the band offsets assumed. On the other hand, the properties within a particular band, say the conduction band inter-subband energies are quite sensitive to the band offset. Thus experiments which have measured properties within a single band have been more successful in ascertaining the offsets.

On the theoretical side, there has been a great deal of effort to develop formalisms that can describe the band offset problem. Early on, simple approaches were developed, but it soon became clear that the band offset problem was not a simple one. More detailed theories have evolved and this subject is still an area of active research. The practitioner in the field has learned to rely more on experiments than on theoretical predictions in this particular instance. We will briefly review simplest of these theories since the more complex formalisms are beyond the scope of this chapter.

6.2.1 The Electron Affinity Rule

Electron affinities are the energies required to remove an electron from the bottom of the conduction band to the outside of the semiconductor (commonly referred to as the vacuum level). The electron affinity rule asserts that the conduction-band offset at an abrupt heterojunction is equal to the difference in electron affinities between the two semiconductors, with the signs chosen such that the semiconductor with the smaller affinity has the higher conduction band at the interface:

$$\begin{aligned} \Delta E_c &= E_{c2} - E_{c1} \\ &= \chi_1 - \chi_2 \end{aligned} \tag{6.12}$$

where χ is the electron affinity. Since the ionization energy ϕ is the sum of χ and E_g, it follows that

$$\begin{aligned} \Delta E_v &= E_{v2} - E_{v1} \\ &= \phi_1 - \phi_2 \\ \Delta E_c + \Delta E_v &= \Delta E_g. \end{aligned} \tag{6.13}$$

Unfortunately, this simple rule does not work very well in real semiconductors. The apparent problem lies with the fact that when two semiconductors are brought together, there is a charge transfer across the interface due to the dissimilar nature of the chemical bonds. This short ranged dipole at the interface can readjust the band offsets away from the simple electron affinity rule. Many of the more sophisticated theories have tried to estimate this charge transfer across the interface.

6.2.2 The Common Anion Rule

This rule has been an important reason why the earlier band offset results for GaAs/AlGaAs system ($\Delta E_c : \Delta E_v = 85:15$) went unchallenged for so many years. The motivation for this rule is the following. The valence band states of most semiconductors are made up of anion atomic functions. It thus appears that if one has semiconductor heterostructures made up of components which have the same anion (e.g., GaAs/AlAs and CdTe/HgTe), there should be little or no band offset in the valence band. Once again this rule is only marginally satisfied. It does appear, however, that in common anion heterostructures, the conduction band discontinuity is larger than the valence band discontinuity.

6.2.3   Transitivity of Band Discontinuities

Many bandedge lineup theories assume that there is a specific absolute energy associated with the bandedges of every semiconductor, and that the band offsets are simply the difference between the relevant absolute band energies of the semiconductor pair. This means that these theories assume that

$$\Delta E_v(A/B) = E_v(B) - E_v(A). \tag{6.14}$$

Such theories are called linear theories. If linear theories are valid, we have the following relationship

$$\Delta E_v(A/B) + \Delta E_v(B/C) + \Delta E_v(C/A) = 0. \tag{6.15}$$

This property is referred to as "transitivity." The transitivity property may also be used to test for experimental accuracy and consistency. For example, for three pairs of lattice-matched semiconductors, Ge on ZnSe, ZnSe on GaAs, and Ge on GaAs, the measured ΔE_v values follow the transitivity property

$$\Delta E_v \text{ (Ge/ZnSe) } + \Delta E_v \text{ (ZnSe/GaAs) } - \Delta E_v \text{ (Ge/GaAs)}$$
$$= -1.52 \text{ eV } + 0.96 \text{ eV } + 0.53 \text{ eV}$$
$$= -0.03 \text{ eV}.$$

The algebraic sum of -0.03 eV is very small and is below the accuracy of measurements and it appears that transitivity is a sound assumption for well-prepared heterostructures.

In Figure 6.11 we show some band offsets for a variety of material combinations. Although virtually any structural configuration can be realized by heterostructure concepts, two important categories of heterostructures are quantum wells and superlattices. In quantum wells the electronic states in the well region (the narrow bandgap region for Type I structures) are bound in the direction of the confining potential. In the superlattice a periodic arrangement of the semiconductors is imposed with a periodicity W in the growth direction. Due to the periodicity, the wavefunctions retain their Bloch character (i.e. traveling wave form) in the new structure. We will now discuss some of the effects of the potential modulation in real space on the bandstructure.

6.3   BANDSTRUCTURE IN QUANTUM WELLS

To calculate the bandstructure in quantum wells, we recall the nature of the energy levels and wavefunctions near the edges of the bandgap, since the quantum well problem is described in terms of these wavefunctions. We will discuss the case where the well region is made up of a direct bandgap material. In this case, the conduction band states are s-type and valence band states are p-type. It is straightforward to extend these results to other quantum wells. The simple quantum well structure such as shown in Figure 6.12 is one of the most studied heterostructures. Its simple square well shape allows for easy solutions which are

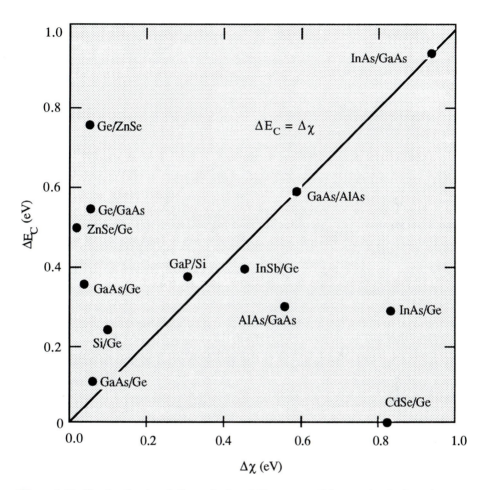

Figure 6.11: Conduction band discontinuity ΔE_C measured by core level photoelectron spectroscopy using the bandgaps given in Milnes and Feucht (1972). The materials are listed with the substrate semiconductor written first, and the deposited overlayer written second. While the growth conditions vary widely among these results, no systematic trend is obtained when the electron affinity rule $\Delta E_C = \Delta \chi$ is applied by plotting the offsets as a function of electron affinity difference $\Delta \chi$. (From tables in Milnes and Feucht, 1972, and from Bauer et al., 1983.)

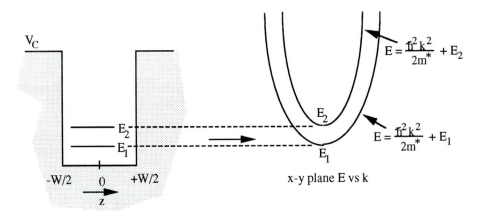

Figure 6.12: Schematic of a quantum well and the subband levels. In the x–y plane the subbands can be represented by parabolas.

quite accurate and can be used to do first order comparisons with many experiments. If the barrier thickness is sufficiently thick (≥ 100 Å) and the potential barrier V_c sufficiently high, multiquantum wells are essentially uncoupled. The Schrödinger equation for the electron states in the quantum well can be written in a simple approximation as

$$\left[-\frac{\hbar^2}{2m^*}\nabla^2 + V(z) \right] \Psi = E\Psi \tag{6.16}$$

where m^* is the effective mass of the electron. The wavefunction Ψ can be separated into its z and ρ (in the x–y plane) dependence and the problem is much simplified

$$\Psi(x, y, z) = e^{ik_x \cdot x} \cdot e^{ik_y \cdot y} f(z) \tag{6.17}$$

where $f(z)$ satisfies

$$\left[-\frac{\hbar^2}{2m^*}\frac{\partial^2}{\partial z^2} + V(z) \right] f(z) = E_n f(z). \tag{6.18}$$

This simple 1–D problem is solved in undergraduate quantum mechanics books. If one assumes an infinite barrier approximation, the values of $f(z)$ are simply (W is the well size)

$$\begin{aligned} f(z) &= \cos\frac{\pi n z}{W}, \text{ if } n \text{ is even} \\ &= \sin\frac{\pi n z}{W}, \text{ if } n \text{ is odd} \end{aligned} \tag{6.19}$$

with energies

$$E_n = \frac{\pi^2 \hbar^2 n^2}{2m^* W^2}. \tag{6.20}$$

The energy of the electron bands are then

$$E = E_n + \frac{\hbar^2 k_{\parallel}^2}{2m^*} \tag{6.21}$$

leading to bands as shown in Figure 6.12.

If the barrier potential V_c is not infinite, the wavefunction decays exponentially into the barrier region, and is a sine or cosine function in the well. By matching the wavefunction and its derivative at the boundaries one can show that the energy and the wavefunctions are given by the solution to the transcendental equations

$$\alpha \tan \frac{\alpha W}{2} = \beta$$

$$\alpha \cot \frac{\alpha W}{2} = -\beta \tag{6.22}$$

where

$$\alpha = \sqrt{\frac{2m^* E}{\hbar^2}}$$

$$\beta = \sqrt{\frac{2m^*(V_c - E)}{\hbar^2}}.$$

These equations can be solved numerically.

The subband structure represented by Equation 6.21 has important consequences for optical and transport properties of heterostructures. An important manifestation of this subband structure is the density of states (DOS) of the electronic bands. The density of states figures importantly in both electrical and optical properties of any system, as was discussed for the simple parabolic bands in Chapter 1. We will review the form of the density of states.

If we assume a simple parabolic relation $E = (\hbar^2 k^2)/(2m^*)$, we can immediately see that the density of states per unit volume in a 3–D system are

$$
\begin{aligned}
N(E)\, dE &= N(k) d^3 k \\
&= \frac{m^{*3/2} E^{1/2}}{\sqrt{2}\pi^2 \hbar^3} \times 2\, dE.
\end{aligned} \tag{6.23}
$$

Thus the density of states increases as $E^{1/2}$ away from the bandedge. For a 2–D system the density of states is given by

$$N(E)\, dE = \frac{m^*}{2\pi\hbar^2} \times 2\, dE, \tag{6.24}$$

i.e., the density of states is independent of energy. Remember that each subband contributes a step in the density of states given by Equation 6.24. In Chapter 1

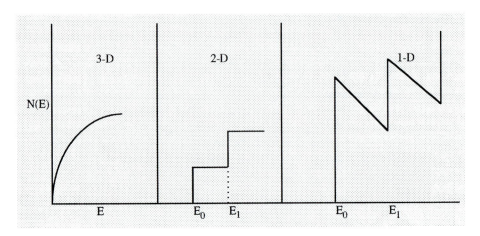

Figure 6.13: Schematic of density of states in a 3–, 2– and 1–dimensional system with parabolic energy momentum relations.

we also discussed the density of states for the 1–dimensional problem. In Figure 6.13 we show schematically the density of states for the three dimensions. In the sub-3–D systems the subband structure results in sharp discontinuity in the DOS. These sharp structures in the density of states are partly responsible for some unusual properties of heterostructures.

In the simple discussion for the quantum well structure, we have assumed that the conduction band state is a pure s-type state and we have used a very simple-minded effective mass theory to understand the quantum well bandstructure. A more sophisticated calculation can be done where one retains the full description of the bandstructure of the individual components (e.g., an eight–band model discussed in Chapter 5). When this is done, it turns out that the results for the conduction band states are not very much affected. Figure 6.14 gives a comparison of the 8–band model and the simple model discussed above. As can be seen, the wavefunction has a small p-type character. The subband levels are not too much affected.

6.3.1   The Valence Bandstructure in Quantum Wells

The description of the quantum well bandstructure and the density of states presented above is quite valid for electron states since, as noted earlier, the electron states in direct bandgap materials are adequately described by a single s-type band. However, the valence band states are formed from p-type states leading to HH and LH states. Unfortunately, while the HH($3/2, \pm 3/2$) and LH $(3/2, \pm 1/2)$ states are pure states at $k = 0$, they strongly mix away from $k = 0$. Thus, as far as subband level positions are concerned, the starting energies of the subbands can be solved for just as for the electron case, i.e., independently for the HH and LH. However, the dispersion relation for the hole states in the

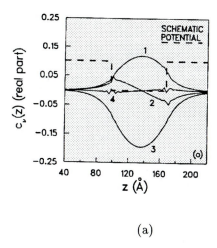

(a)

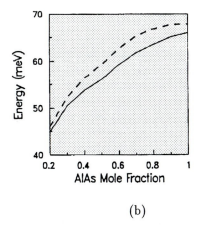

(b)

Figure 6.14: (a) The conduction band subband wavefunction using an 8–band tight binding model. The s-components are denoted by indices 1 and 3. As can be seen, there is a small mixture of p-type bands in the solution. Results are for a 70 Å GaAs quantum well with $Al_{0.3}Ga_{0.7}As$ barriers. (b) Variation of the first subband energy level in a 70 Å GaAs quantum well for different alloy compositions of the barrier (solid line). The dotted line is the corresponding result obtained from a secular solution based on simple effective mass theory and parabolic dispersions. (From Sankaran and Singh, 1991.)

x–y plane is only approximately given by

$$E(\mathbf{k}) = E_{n,i} + \frac{\hbar^2 k^2}{2m_i^*} \tag{6.25}$$

where i denotes the HH or LH band. A better description of the hole states is given by solving the Kohn–Luttinger form of the Schrödinger equation

$$[H + V_p]\Psi = E\Psi \tag{6.26}$$

which for the HH, LH system is a 4 × 4 coupled equation given by the Kohn–Luttinger Hamiltonian discussed earlier. Treating the z component of the momentum as an operator $(k_z = -i(\partial/\partial z))$, we get the following new expressions for the matrix elements.

$$H_{hh} = -\frac{\hbar^2}{2m_0}\left[(\gamma_1 + \gamma_2)\left(k_x^2 + k_y^2\right) - (\gamma_1 - 2\gamma_2)\frac{\partial^2}{\partial z^2}\right] + V_p(z)$$

$$H_{lh} = -\frac{\hbar^2}{2m_0}\left[(\gamma_1 - \gamma_2)\left(k_x^2 + k_y^2\right) - (\gamma_1 + 2\gamma_2)\frac{\partial^2}{\partial z^2}\right] + V_p(z)$$

$$c = \frac{\sqrt{3}\hbar^2}{2m_0}\left[\gamma_2\left(k_x^2 - k_y^2\right) - 2i\gamma_3 k_x k_y\right]$$

$$b = -i\frac{\sqrt{3}\hbar^2}{m_0}\left(-k_y - ik_x\right)\gamma_3\frac{\partial}{\partial z} \tag{6.27}$$

where $V_p(z)$ represents the potential profile due to the quantum well. In the presence of biaxial strain, additional terms are to be included and will be discussed later. The general hole solutions can be written as

$$\Psi_h^m(\mathbf{k}_\parallel, z) = \sum_v g_m^v(z)\, U^v(\mathbf{r})\, e^{i\mathbf{k}_\parallel \cdot \rho} \tag{6.28}$$

where $g_m^v(z)$ is the z-dependent function arising from the confinement of the potential, v is the index representing the total angular momentum of the state, m index for each subband in the well, and $U^v(\mathbf{r})$ is the valence band central cell state for the v-spin component in the bulk material.

In the absence of the off-diagonal mixing terms in the Kohn–Luttinger Hamiltonian (the so-called diagonal approximation), the hole problem is as simple to solve as the electron problem. However, in real semiconductors, the off-diagonal mixing is quite strong and must be included for quantitative comparison to experiments.

A technique commonly employed to solve for the hole eigenfunctions and dispersion relations is to solve the problem variationally. Although this approach has been shown to work quite well, it has the usual disadvantages of variational techniques, viz. considerable insight is required to choose the form of the starting wave function and the techniques become increasingly complex for excited states. In fact, the hole dispersion relations need not be solved variationally. The

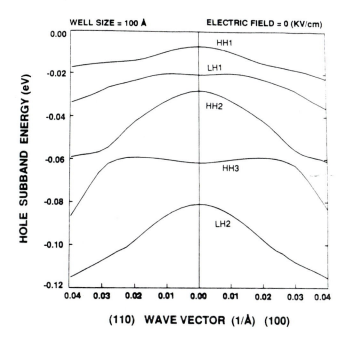

Figure 6.15: Hole dispersion relations in a 100 Å GaAs/Al$_{0.3}$Ga$_{0.7}$As quantum well assuming the same Kohn–Luttinger parameters in the well and barrier.

equation can be written in a finite difference form as an eigenvalue problem and then solved by matrix solving techniques (see Appendix F).

In Figure 6.15 we show a typical valence bandstructure dispersion relation in a quantum well. As can be seen quite clearly, the valence band dispersion relation is highly nonparabolic. It is also interesting to note that the first light hole band has a curvature opposite the normal valence bandstructure, i.e., the hole state has a negative mass near the zone edge. The character of the hole states is represented by pure angular momentum states at the zone center, but there is a strong mixing of states as one proceeds away from the zone center.

6.4 BANDSTRUCTURE IN SUPERLATTICES

The quantum well structures we considered above have a thick barrier region surrounding the well. If a number of quantum wells are placed next to each other, separated by thin barriers, one gets to the next level of heterostructures called superlattices. The superlattice concept allows one to extend the region of periodicity from a primitive cell (for a single semiconductor) to an arbitrary value. We had discussed the structural aspects of the superlattices in Chapter 2. This increase in the real space periodicity distance has very important consequences for the bandstructures. In Figure 6.16 we show the arrangement of

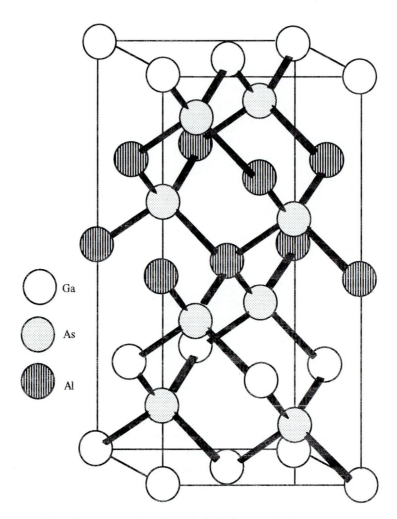

Figure 6.16: Crystal structure of a $(GaAs)_2(AlAs)_2$ superlattice.

atoms in a two monolayer/two monolayer superlattice of GaAs/AlAs. As can be seen in the plane of the growth ((100) in this case), the periodicity distance is still given by the fcc unit cell. However, in the growth direction, the periodicity has increased to four times the previous value. As shown in Figure 6.17, this means that the k-space periodicity or the reciprocal lattice vector in the x-direction has *decreased* by the same factor. The extent of the first Brillouin zone has therefore decreased. The high symmetry points in the lattice matched and strained superlattice, of this type are shown in Table 6.2.

In Chapter 3, we discussed how the presence of a periodic potential causes the formation of bandgaps at the Brillouin zone edges. The same concept holds here. The imposition of the background periodic potential causes the formation

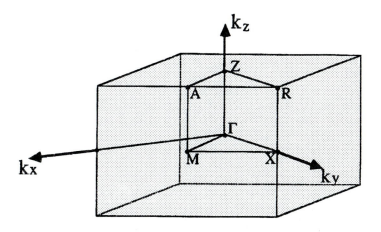

Figure 6.17: Brillouin zone for a superlattice.

of new bandgaps and also alters the effective mass of the composite material.

A simple way to address the superlattice problem is to use the effective mass theory via the so called Kronig–Penney model. This model is very useful to introduce the concepts of minibands and zone folding which are important driving forces behind superlattice research. In the Kronig–Penney model, we assume that the electron is described by an effective mass corresponding to the conduction band or valence band of the semiconductor A or B forming the superlattice, and it simply sees a superimposed periodic potential as shown in Figure 6.18. The periodic potential is determined by the band offsets in the same manner as the quantum well problem discussed earlier.

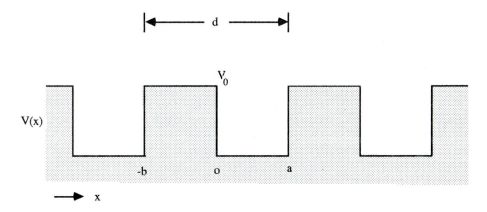

Figure 6.18: The periodic potential produced by a superlattice in one dimension.

Lattice Matched Superlattice	
Point	Location
Γ	$[0, 0, 0]$
X	$2\pi/a_o \, [1, 0, 0]$
M	$2\pi/a_o \, [1/2, 1/2, 0]$
Z	$2\pi/a_o \, [0, 0, 1/(n + m)]$
R	$2\pi/a_o \, [1, 0, 1/(n + m)]$
A	$2\pi/a_o \, [1/2, 1/2, 1/(n + m)]$
Strained Layer Superlattice	
Point	Location
Γ	$[0, 0, 0]$
X	$2\pi/a_\parallel \, [1, 0, 0]$
M	$2\pi/a_\parallel \, [1/2, 1/2, 0]$
Z	$2\pi \left[0, 0, \frac{1}{n \cdot a_{\perp 1} + m \cdot a_{\perp 2}} \right]$
R	$2\pi \left[\frac{1}{a_\parallel}, 0, \frac{1}{n \cdot a_{\perp 1} + m \cdot a_{\perp 2}} \right]$
A	$2\pi \left[\frac{1}{2a_\parallel}, \frac{1}{2a_\parallel}, \frac{1}{n \cdot a_{\perp 1} + m \cdot a_{\perp 2}} \right]$

Table 6.2: Location in k-space of the points of high symmetry for the Brillouin zone for superlattices made of n layers of material 1 and m layers of material 2. The strained layer superlattice must be characterized by a parallel lattice constant and two different perpendicular lattice constants.

The general Schrödinger equation is of the form

$$\left[-\frac{\hbar^2}{2m} \frac{\partial^2}{\partial x^2} + V(x) \right] \psi(x) = E\psi(x) \tag{6.29}$$

where $V(x)$ is the background potential of Figure 6.18. We use a symbol m for the mass of the electron. This is the effective mass appropriate for the material at x and can, in general, be different for different regions. Note that we have suppressed the Schrödinger equation in the plane perpendicular to the superlattice potential. The energy due to the momentum in this perpendicular plane is simply given by

$$E_\parallel(k_\parallel) = \frac{\hbar^2 k_\parallel}{2m} \tag{6.30}$$

and has to be added on to the results obtained by the solution of Equation 6.29. Due to the periodic nature of the potential $V(x)$, the solution of Equation 6.29 must satisfy Bloch theorem, i.e.

$$\psi(x + d) = e^{i\phi}\psi(x) \tag{6.31}$$

where

$$\phi = k_x d.$$

In the period $-b < x < a$, let

$$\psi(x) = \begin{cases} Ae^{i\beta x} + Be^{-i\beta x}, & \text{if } -b < x < 0 \\ De^{i\alpha x} + Fe^{-i\alpha x}, & \text{if } 0 < x < a \end{cases} \tag{6.32}$$

where

$$\beta = \sqrt{\frac{2m(E - V_0)}{\hbar^2}}$$

$$\alpha = \sqrt{\frac{2mE}{\hbar^2}}.$$

Then, in the following period, $a < x < a + d$,

$$\psi(x) = e^{i\phi} \begin{cases} Ae^{i\beta(x-d)} + Be^{-i\beta(x-d)}, & \text{if } a < x < d \\ De^{i\alpha(x-d)} + Fe^{-i\alpha(x-d)}, & \text{if } d < x < a + d. \end{cases} \tag{6.33}$$

From the continuity conditions at $x = 0$ and at $x = a$, the following system of equations is obtained

$$
\begin{aligned}
A + B &= D + F \\
\beta(A - B) &= \alpha(D - F) \\
e^{i\phi}(Ae^{-i\beta b} + Be^{i\beta b}) &= De^{i\alpha a} + Fe^{-i\alpha a} \\
\beta e^{i\phi}(Ae^{-i\beta b} - Be^{i\beta b}) &= \alpha(De^{i\alpha a} - Fe^{-i\alpha a}).
\end{aligned}
\tag{6.34}
$$

Non-trivial solutions for the variables A, B, D, and F are obtained only if the determinant of their coefficients vanishes, which gives the condition

$$
\begin{aligned}
\cos \phi &= \cos a\alpha \cosh b\delta - \frac{\alpha^2 - \delta^2}{2\alpha\delta} \sin a\alpha \sinh b\delta, \quad \text{if } 0 < E < V_0 \\
&= \cos a\alpha \cos b\beta - \frac{\alpha^2 + \beta^2}{2\alpha\delta} \sin a\alpha \sin b\beta, \quad \text{if } E > V_0
\end{aligned}
\tag{6.35}
$$

where

$$\delta = \sqrt{\frac{2m(V_0 - E)}{\hbar^2}}.$$

Now the energy E, which appears in (6.39) through α, β, and δ, is physically allowed only if

$$-1 \leq \cos \phi \leq +1. \tag{6.36}$$

We distinguish two cases:

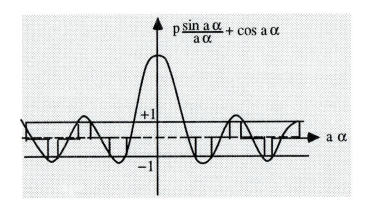

Figure 6.19: A graphical method to see the positions of the allowed bands in a super-lattice.

1. $0 < E < V_0$. To get a picture of the structure of the energy spectrum we look at the particular case for which $b \to 0$, $\delta \to \infty$, in such a manner that $b\delta^2$ remains finite. With the notation

$$P = \lim_{b \to 0, \delta \to \infty} \frac{ab\delta^2}{2}$$

Equation 6.36 becomes

$$-1 \leq P \frac{\sin a\alpha}{a\alpha} + \cos a\alpha \leq +1. \tag{6.37}$$

From Figure 6.19, where $P = 3\pi/2$, it can be seen that the energy spectrum consists of a series of separate regions, inside each of which, the energy of the particle can vary continuously. These regions are the "allowed bands," or "minibands," and the ones between them the "forbidden bands." It can be seen that the width of the allowed bands increases as the energy increases.

2. $E > V_0$. The possible values of the energy are determined by the condition

$$-1 \leq f(E) \leq +1, \tag{6.38}$$

where

$$
\begin{aligned}
f(E) &= \cos a\alpha \, \cos b\beta - \frac{\alpha^2 + \beta^2}{2\alpha\beta} \sin a\alpha \, \sin b\beta \\
&= \cos(a\alpha + b\beta) - \frac{(\alpha - \beta)^2}{2\alpha\beta} \sin a\alpha \, \sin b\beta. \tag{6.39}
\end{aligned}
$$

The energy spectrum will also, in this case, have a band structure. The relation $a\alpha + b\beta = n\pi$, $n = 0$, 1, 2, ..., which would lead to a discrete spectrum does not satisfy the inequality of Equation 6.36. Substituting $a\alpha = n(\pi/2) - \phi$ and $b\beta = (\pi/2) + \phi$ into Equation 6.39, we find that

$$
\begin{aligned}
f(E) &= 1 + \frac{(\alpha - \beta)^2}{2\alpha\beta} \sin^2\phi > 1 \quad \text{for } n \text{ even,} \\
&= -1 - \frac{(\alpha - \beta)^2}{2\alpha\beta} \cos^2\phi < -1 \text{ for } n \text{ odd.} \quad (6.40)
\end{aligned}
$$

In general the solutions for Equation 6.36 or Equation 6.40 can be obtained by a simple computer program. As the barrier width increases, the miniband width decreases until we simply have discrete levels, as in the case of the quantum well problem discussed earlier. It is also important to know that the E vs. k_x ($= \phi/d$) relation obtained from the superlattice gives a new effective mass in the superlattice direction. When the barriers are very thin, this mass is just the starting mass m used in the Equation 6.29. But in the extreme limit of large barriers, the mass becomes infinite, i.e., the electron becomes "bound" in the quantum well. Finally, it is important to note that even though we have the "minibands" in the 1-D superlattice, the real superlattices are 3-D structures. When the transverse energy $E_\parallel$ of Equation 6.30 is added to the bandstructure, there is no "real energy gap" in the bandstructure. However, if an electron is moving in the x-direction, and *does not suffer any scattering*, i.e., does not change its wavevector, it will see a discontinuity in the E vs. k_x relation and consequently will be affected as if there was an energy gap present.

An important concept that can be understood easily on the basis of the Kronig–Penney model is the concept of "zone folding." This phenomenon was seen when we discussed the nearly free electron problem in Chapter 4. In Figure 6.20 we show how the starting well semiconductor's bandstructure $E = (\hbar^2 k^2)/(2m)$ is modified by the periodic potential. The bandstructure of the superlattice is shown in the folded zone scheme (discussed in Chapter 3). We see that the superlattice potential has "folded" the parabolic band on to the zone center point (the Γ-point) and introduced bandgaps at the new zone edge. The states that were originally at $k \neq 0$ points can thus be brought on to the new $k = 0$ state. This concept is particularly attractive since it can, in principle, change an indirect bandedge to a "direct bandedge." This is, of course, not a truly direct state, only a $k_x = 0$ state, which means the phase difference across the new periodicity distance d is zero. In a true direct gap state, the phase difference between points that are a "unit cell" apart is zero. Nevertheless, this way of making indirect materials into direct materials is attractive and can increase certain optical transitions.

The Kronig–Penney model is a very simple description of the superlattice bandstructure. There are many improvements to this model, many of them using the $k \cdot p$ description. A method that is often used for accurate calculations is the tight binding method which was discussed in Chapter 5. Although the details are

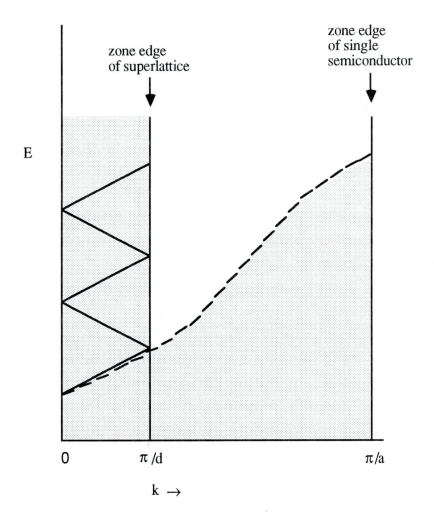

Figure 6.20: The concept of zone folding. The superlattice increases the real space periodicity from a to d causing a reduced Brillouin zone. The original band is thus "folded" into this new zone. States that were originally at $k \neq 0$ values are now at $k = 0$ values.

more tedious, the tight binding Hamiltonian can be formulated for superlattices exactly as it was for bulk crystals. The major difference is that the minimal cell of the superlattice has $2n$ atoms in it where n is the total number of monolayers in one superlattice period. If the sp^3 basis is used as before, there will be $8n$ basis functions. With improvements in computer availability it is possible to carry out tight binding analysis for up to 100 monolayers. To set up the tight binding Hamiltonian, the locations of each of the neighbors of each atom within the unit cell must be calculated. It is somewhat more difficult to choose the tight binding constants for the superlattice. For interactions between atoms in a given layer, it is assumed that the tight binding constants will be the same as they are for the given bulk material. We thus have two complete sets of constants, one for each layer. For interactions between two atoms of different layers, the tight binding constants are often averaged. Spin–orbit interactions have to be included and put into superlattice bandstructure calculations in exactly the same manner as they are for bulk semiconductors.

One additional unknown parameter, the bandedge lineup at heterointerfaces, is needed in order to complete the tight binding formalism. This parameter shows up in the original tight binding formalism in the self-interaction energies listed in Chapter 5. If a fixed energy is added to each of these four constants, it would have the effect of shifting all of the bands, but not effecting their relative levels or curvatures. Since only relative energies are important, in the bulk bandstructures, the self-interaction energies are altered so that the energy at the top of the valence band came out to be zero. At a heterointerface, the relative levels of the bands in each material set the bandedge discontinuity. By adding a constant to the portion of the diagonal of the superlattice Hamiltonian which characterizes the bands of one of the two layer materials, the bandedge offset can be simulated at an arbitrary value.

Examples of superlattice bandstructures are shown in Figure 6.21 for the $(GaAs)_1(InAs)_1$ superlattice, and Figure 6.22 for the $(GaAs)_2(InAs)_2$ superlattice. These figures are for an assumed offset ratio of 70:30. As can be seen, the zone center features of superlattice bandstructure are similar to the zone center features of bulk semiconductors. They are both direct bandgap materials. The features at the valence band maxima as well as the masses of both the conduction and valence bands are somewhat similar to those of bulk materials. There are many more bands in the vicinity of the bandgap in the superlattice bandstructure than in the bulk bandstructure due to the large number of atoms in the minimal cell. For superlattices with thicker periods, the number of bands increases even more due to the zone folding.

It is important to note that in this full 3–D bandstructure one does not really have "mini-bandgaps" as would result in the 1–D problem. The density of states is zero only between the top of the valence band and the bottom of the conduction band. This real bandgap can be quite different from the gap of the random alloy produced if the superlattice is mixed up randomly to form an alloy. This has been one of the attractions for using superlattices for replacing alloys in devices. The superlattice is also ordered and so, in principle, will not

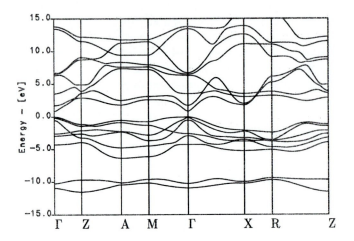

Figure 6.21: Bandstructure of a $(GaAs)_1(InAs)_1$ superlattice. (From Jaffe, 1989.)

suffer from random alloy scattering (discussed in Chapter 11). The superlattice transport is also expected to be highly anisotropic since the bandstructure is quite anisotropic.

We have seen how the bandstructure of semiconductor structures can be dramatically altered by using the concept of heterostructures. The band tailoring achievable is virtually limitless and is only limited by our imagination.

6.5   FOR THE TECHNOLOGIST IN YOU

At the end of Chapter 5, we examined some of the driving forces behind some of the technologies. The use of alloys and heterostructures adds a tremendous versatility to the available parameter space to exploit. Semiconductor alloys are already an integral part of many advanced technology systems. Consider the following examples.

- The HgCdTe alloy is the most important high-performance imaging material for long wavelength applications $(10 - 14 \ \mu m)$. These applications include night vision, seeing through fog, thermal imaging of the human body parts for medical applications, and a host of special purpose applications involving thermal tracking.

- The AlGaAs alloy is an important ingredient in GaAs/AlGaAs heterostructure devices which drive a multitude of technologies including microwave circuits operating up to 100 GHz, lasers for local area networks, and compact disc players.

- InGaAs and InGaAsP alloy systems are active ingredients of MMICs operating above 100 GHz and long-haul optical communication lasers.

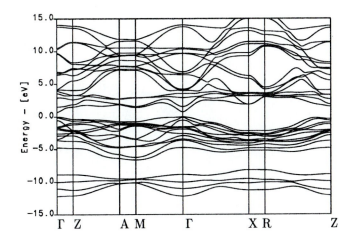

Figure 6.22: Bandstructure of a $(GaAs)_2(InAs)_2$ superlattice. (From Jaffe, 1989.)

While alloys are important ingredients of many technologies, it must be emphasized again that alloys are not perfectly periodic structures. This results in random potential fluctuations which leads to an important scattering mechanism that limits certain performances. For example, the low temperature low field mobility is severely affected by alloy scattering as is the exciton linewidth of optical modulators (discussed in Chapters 11 and 16). The growth and fabrication issues in alloy systems are also sometimes serious due to miscibility gaps that may be present.

Technologies based on the heterostructure concepts are also evident in many high performance systems in use today. The most important heterostructure based devices are the MODFET, the HBT, and the quantum well laser. These devices are the driving force behind advances in MMICs operating above 100 GHz and low power optoelectronic systems. However, it must be emphasized that while the heterostructures can produce an extremely broad range of physical phenomena, not all of these effects can result in real devices. These concepts are explored in Chapter 19. Over the last decade, hundreds of proposals, many seemingly very attractive, have been made for devices using heterostructure physics. Only a handful have made it into systems. However, even the rest of the ideas have certainly made life very exciting for the proponents of the ideas!

(a)

HgCdTe HYBRID FOCAL PLANE ARRAY

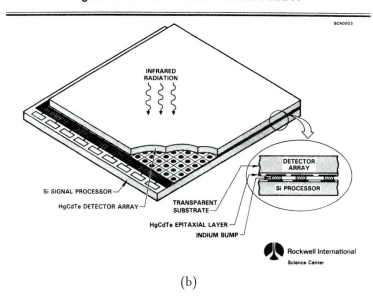

(b)

Figure 6.23: The HgCdTe system is one of the most important semiconductor systems for "night vision" applications. Shown is a 640 × 480 pixel HgCdTe array with Si readout circuitry. The schematic shows the details of the array. (Courtesy Rockwell International.)

6.6 PROBLEMS

6.1. Consider the alloy system $Si_{1-x}Ge_x$. Using the virtual crystal approximation, calculate the positions of the Γ, X, and L point energies in the lowest conduction band. Use the top of the valence band as a reference. At what Ge composition does the conduction bandedge change from X-like to L-like?

6.2. Using the bandstructure of GaAs and AlAs, calculate the conduction band minima at Γ, X, L points in $Al_xGa_{1-x}As$ alloy, as x varies from 0 to 1.

6.3. Glass fibers have a minimum loss window for light transmission at 1.3 μm and 1.55 μm. These wavelengths determine the laser materials of choice for long distance optical communication. List the various semiconductor combinations that can be used for lasers and detectors in such a system. List only those materials that can be grown on GaAs or InP substrates with a strain of less than 2%. Do not be concerned with the effects of strain on the bandgap which is the topic of study in Chapter 7. Using the virtual crystal approximation, estimate the electron effective masses of these materials.

6.4. Consider the GaAs/$Al_xGa_{1-x}As$ ($0 \leq x < 1$). Assume that the band discontinuity distribution between the conduction and valence band is given by

$$\Delta E_c = 0.6\Delta E_g \text{ (direct)}$$
$$\Delta E_v = 0.4\Delta E_g \text{ (direct)}$$

where ΔE_g(direct) is the bandgap discontinuity between AlGaAs (*even if the material is indirect*) and GaAs. Calculate the valence and conduction band offsets as a function of Al composition. Notice that the conduction band offset starts to decrease as Al composition increases beyond $\sim$0.4.

6.5. Show that the heterostructure $Al_xGa_{1-x}As/Al_yGa_{1-y}As$ ($x < y$) can be type II (i.e., valence band maxima is in $Al_xGa_{1-x}As$ and conduction band minima (X-type) is in $Al_yGa_{1-y}As$).

6.6. Calculate the first and second subband energy levels for the conduction band in a GaAs/$Al_{0.3}Ga_{0.7}As$ quantum well as a function of well size. Assume a 60:40 rule for $\Delta E_c{:}\Delta E_v$. Also, calculate the energy levels if an infinite barrier approximation was being used.

6.7. Calculate the first two valence subband levels for heavy hole and light hole states in a GaAs/$Al_{0.3}Ga_{0.7}As$ quantum well as a function of the well size. Note that to find the subband levels (at $k_\parallel = 0$), one does not need to include the coupling of the heavy hole and light hole states.

6.8. Using the eigenvalue method described in Appendix F, write the valence band 4×4 Schrödinger equation (using the Kohn–Luttinger formalism discussed in the text) as a difference equation. Write a computer program to solve this $4N \times 4N$ matrix equation where N is the number of grid points used to describe the region of the well and the barrier. Using the parameter values $\gamma_1 = 6.85$, $\gamma_2 = 2.1$, and $\gamma_3 = 2.9$, calculate the E vs. $k_\parallel$ diagram for the valence band in a 100 Å GaAs/Al$_{0.3}$Ga$_{0.7}$As quantum well. You will need to find a proper mathematical library through your computer center to diagonalize the large matrix.

6.9. Using the Kronig–Penney model calculate the miniband dispersion relation for electrons and holes for a GaAs (20 Å) AlAs (20 Å) superlattice. Assume that the bandgap of GaAs is 1.5 eV and the direct gap of AlAs is 2.9 eV (use the direct gap for your calculations). Assume the electron effective mass in the bulk crystals is $0.067m_0$ and hole mass is $0.4m_0$. What is the new "effective mass" of the electrons and holes near the bandedges in the superlattice?

6.10. Superlattices of (AlAs)$_m$(GaAs)$_n$ are grown with $\{m, n\}$ equal to $\{10$ Å, 20 Å$\}$, $\{20$ Å, 40 Å$\}$, and $\{30$ Å, 60 Å$\}$. Assume that the simple Kronig–Penney model can be used: equal masses = $0.067m_0$; E_g (GaAs) = 1.5 eV; E_g (AlAs) = 2.9 eV for the relevant direct bandgap. Calculate the effective bandgap and effective mass of the electron in the superlattice. How do the bandgaps compare with the virtual crystal approximation of Chapter 6?

6.11. Show that in a parabolic potential well, the spacing between the energy levels is constant. In semiconductors, parabolic potential wells are often produced by using narrow square potential wells where the well to barrier width ratio gradually changes. Use the virtual crystal approximation to design a GaAs/AlAs parabolic well where the level spacing for the electron is approximately 10 meV. Hint: This is the "harmonic oscillator" problem.

6.12. Even in high quality glasses made for optical filters, small particulates of semiconductors (e.g. CdS) are suspended. The particle size can be altered by fabrication parameter variations from several hundred Angstroms to several tens of Angstroms in radius. Assuming an electron and hole mass of 0.07 m_0 and 0.2 m_0, calculate the effect on the bandgap of confinement in these "quantum dots" if the particle size is 20 Å, 100 Å and 500 Å in radius.

6.13. Show that in a superlattice with miniband width of Δ and superlattice period of d, the *approximate* mass along the superlattice axis is

$$m^*_{SL} = \frac{2\hbar^2}{\Delta d^2}.$$

6.14. Consider a 10 Å/20 Å AlAs/GaAs superlattice. Solve for the energy minibands for the electrons, assuming

$$\frac{\Delta E_c}{\Delta E_v} = 0.65$$

and the relevant energy gaps and masses are

$$
\begin{aligned}
E_g^\Gamma(\text{AlAs}) &= 2.9 \text{ eV} \\
E_g^\Gamma(\text{GaAs}) &= 1.5 \text{ eV} \\
m^*(\text{AlAs}) &= 0.1 m_0 \\
m^*(\text{GaAs}) &= 0.067 m_0.
\end{aligned}
$$

Use the Kronig–Penney method with the modified boundary conditions

$$\psi|_{x+} = \psi|_{x-}$$

and

$$\frac{1}{m^*}\frac{d\psi}{dx}\bigg|_{x+} = \frac{1}{m^*}\frac{d\psi}{dx}\bigg|_{x-}$$

Present the miniband widths and energy positions for the first two bands. Obtain the same information assuming that the mass in AlAs is the same as in GaAs. Compare the two results.

6.15. Consider a quantum dot of GaAs of dimensions $L \times L \times L$. Assume infinite potential barriers and calculate the separation of the ground and excited state energies in the conduction band as a function of L. If an energy separation of $k_B T$ is needed to observe 3-dimensional confinement effects, what is the maximum box size required to see these effects at 4 K and at 300 K, in the conduction band?

6.7 REFERENCES

- **Semiconductor Alloys: Electronic Properties**

    - S. Adachi, J. Appl. Phys., **58**, R–1 (1985).

    - For general alloy property values a good reference text is Casey, H. C., Jr. and M. B. Panish, *Heterostructure Lasers, Part A, Fundamental Principles, Part B, Materials and Operating Characteristics* (Academic Press, New York, 1978).

    - For details of various methodologies beyond the virtual crystal approximation a good text is Economou, E. N., *Green's Functions in Quantum Physics* (Springer–Verlag, New York, 1979).

    - Smith, D. L. and T. C. McGill, J. de Physique, **45**, C5–509 (1984).

- **Semiconductor Alloys: Structural Properties**

  – Hong, W. P., A. Chin, N. Debbar, J. M. Hinckley, P. K. Bhattacharya, J. Singh and R. Clarke, J. Vac. Sci. Technol. B, **5**, 800 (1987).

  – Jen, H. R., M. J. Cherng and G. B. Stringfellow, Appl. Phys. Lett., **48**, 782 (1986).

  – Kuan, T. S., T. F. Keuch, W. I. Wang and E. L. Wilkie, Phys. Rev. Lett., **54**, 201 (1985).

  – Mbaye, A. A., A. Zunger and D. M. Wood, Appl. Phys. Lett., **49**, 782 (1986).

  – Srivastara, G. P., J. L. Martins and A. Zunger, Phys. Rev. B, **31**, 2561 (1985).

- **Heterojunctions: Band Offsets**

  – Bauer, R. S., P. Zurcher and H. W. Sang, Appl. Phys. Lett. 43, 663 (1983).

  – Harrison, W. A., J. Vac. Sci. Technol., **14**, 1016 (1977).

  – Kroemer, H., in *Molecular Beam Epitaxy and Heterostructures*, edited by L. L. Chang and K. Ploog (NATO ASI Series E, No. 87, Martinus Nijhoff, Dordrecht, Netherlands, 1985).

  – Mayer, J. W. and S. S. Lau, *Electronic Material Science: For Integrated Circuits in Si and GaAs* (Macmillan, New York, 1990).

  – Milnes, A. G. and D. L. Feucht, *Heterojunctions and Metal Semiconductor Junctions* (Academic Press, New York, 1972).

  – Tersoff, J., Phys. Rev. Lett., **56**, 2755 (1986).

  – Van de Welle, C. G. and R. M. Martin, J. Vac. Sci. Technol. B, **4**, 1055 (1986).

- **Bandstructure in Quantum Wells**

  – For the simple quantum well energy levels, any quantum mechanics book would do. An example is Schiff, L. I., *Quantum Mechanics* (McGraw–Hill, New York, 1968). For more detailed treatment of quantum wells, see the following references.

  – Akera, H., S. Wakahana and T. Ando, Surf. Sci., **196**, 694 (1988).

  – Bangerk, E. and G. Landwehr, Superlattices and Microstructures, **1**, 363 (1985).

  – Broido, D. A. and L. J. Sham, Phys. Rev. B, **31**, 888 (1985).

  – Hong, S. C., M. Jaffe and J. Singh, IEEE J. Quant. Electron., **QE–23**, 2181 (1987).

  – Sanders, G. D. and Y. C. Chang, Phys. Rev. B, **31**, 6892 (1985).

- Sankaran, V. and J. Singh, Appl. Phys. Lett., **59**, 1963 (1991).
- Ukenberg, U. and M. Altarelli, Phys. Rev. B, **30**, 3569 (1984).

• **Bandstructures in Superlattices**

- Bastard, G., Phys. Rev. B, **25**, 7584 (1982).
- Jaffe, M. D., *Studies of the Electronic Properties and Applications of Coherently Strained Semiconductors*, Ph.D. Thesis, (The University of Michigan, Ann Arbor 1989).
- Jaffe, M. and J. Singh, IEEE Trans. Elect. Dev., **ED–34**, 2540 (1987).
- Nara, S., Jap. J. Appl. Phys., **26**, 690 (1987).
- Osbourn, G., J. Vac. Sci. Technol. B, **1**, 379 (1983).
- Schulman, J. N. and Y. C. Chang, Phys. Rev. B, **31**, 2056 (1985).
- Schulman, J. N. and T. C. McGill, Phys. Rev. B, **19**, 6341 (1979).

CHAPTER 7

BANDSTRUCTURE MODIFICATIONS THROUGH STRAIN

For several decades, there have been careful studies on the role of strain on electronic and optical properties of semiconductors. Such studies have been extremely important in developing a better theoretical understanding of the bandstructure of semiconductors by identifying symmetries of energy states involved in optically observed transitions. The studies have also been important since they allow determination of deformation potentials that are important in understanding electronic transport in presence of lattice scattering. Until recently, the strain in the semiconductor was introduced by external means, using sophisticated apparatus such as diamond anvil cells, and the experiments were done primarily to clarify the physics of semiconductors. Although it may have been realized that certain physical properties of semiconductors can be tailored, essentially no work was devoted to considering device related benefits of strain. This is understandable since it is difficult to consider a technology based on using the diamond anvil cell as an ingredient.

7.1 CRITICAL THICKNESS

Since the late 1970s the situation has changed rapidly and the use of strain to modify device performance has become an important area of research. The driving force behind this development has been the gradual mastery of the art of strained hetero-epitaxy. By growing a semiconductor overlayer on top of a thick substrate, a large strain can be built into the overlayer, while still maintaining crystallinity and long-range order. The basic understanding behind this pseudomorphic growth was provided by Frank and Van der Merwe in their classic papers

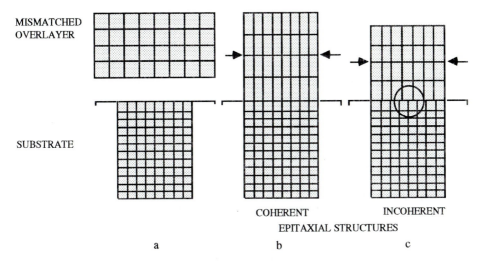

MISMATCHED
OVERLAYER

SUBSTRATE

COHERENT   INCOHERENT

EPITAXIAL STRUCTURES

a   b   c

Figure 7.1: (a) A strained layer structure is formed by forcing a mismatched over-layer into interfacial coherence with a substrate. When below the critical thickness for strained layer stability, the resulting coherent structure is shown in (b). If the overlayer is thick enough that the coherent structure is unstable, the mismatch will partially be accommodated by lattice strain and partially by introduction of misfit dislocations (c).

in the late 1940s. These theories were extended by later workers and this area is still being researched actively. In essence, these theories show that as long as the lattice misfit is below approximately 10%, it is possible to grow an epitaxial film which is in complete registry with the substrate (i.e., it is pseudomorphic up to a thickness called critical thickness). A discussion of the critical thickness issues and dislocation generation is presented in Chapter 18. Beyond the critical thick-ness, dislocations are produced and the strain relaxes. It is important to note that the pseudomorphic films below critical thickness are thermodynamically stable, i.e., even though they have strain energy, the relaxed state with dislocations has a higher free energy. This allows one to have large built-in strain without serious concern that the film will somehow "disintegrate" after some time. These ideas are schematically illustrated in Figure 7.1, where we show how an overlayer with a lattice constant larger than or smaller than the substrate grows below critical thickness. Above critical thickness thermodynamics favors dislocation generation as shown in Figure 7.1. While it may be possible to grow a strained structure above critical thickness, such a structure is inherently metastable and may trans-form into an incoherent structure with dislocations. The critical thickness can be large enough that heterostructure concepts such as quantum wells, etc., can be realized along with large strain. In Figure 7.2, we show the critical thickness for growth of $In_xGa_{1-x}As$ on GaAs. The basic tools to study the bandstructure changes due to the built-in strain are already present in the literature and involve the use of the deformation potential theory. Very important changes occur in the

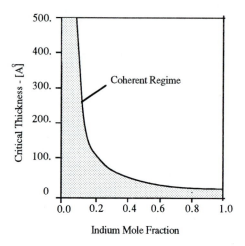

Figure 7.2: Critical thickness of $In_x Ga_{1-x} As$ grown pseudomorphically on GaAs.

electronic and optical properties of such strained quantum well structures which can be exploited for numerous optical and opto-electronic devices. This chapter will examine strain related effects bandstructure focusing on the built-in strain produced in pseudomorphic films. Also, since the motivations of such studies are largely technologically oriented (e.g., low threshold lasers, enhanced electro-optic effects, superior detectors, etc.) we will focus on near bandedge phenomenon. In Table 7.1 we show lattice constants for some semiconductors.

In the next sections, we will review important issues in stress–strain relations, the deformation potential theory and its use in understanding the role of strain on bandstructure of semiconductors. We will present an overview of important bandstructure changes arising from the built-in strain in heterostructures.

Material	Lattice Constant (Å)
C	3.5668
Si	5.4309
GaP	5.4495
GaAs	5.6419
Ge	5.6461
AlAs	5.6611
InP	5.8687
InAs	6.0584

Table 7.1: Lattice constants for several common group IV materials and III-V compounds which take the diamond or zinc–blende crystal structure.

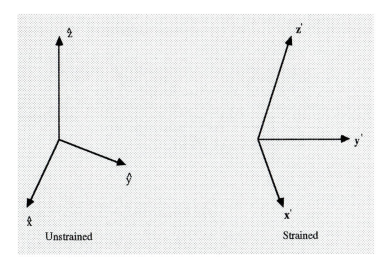

Figure 7.3: Effect of deformation on a coordinate system x, y, z.

7.2 ELASTIC STRAIN

In this section we will establish some basic expressions for strain in crystalline materials. We will confine ourselves to small values of strain. In order to define the strain in a system we imagine that we have a set of ortho-normal vectors $\hat{x}$, $\hat{y}$, $\hat{z}$ in the unstrained system. Under the influence of a uniform deformation these axes are distorted to x', y', z', as shown in Figure 7.3. The new axes can be related to the old one by

$$
\begin{aligned}
x' &= (1 + \epsilon_{xx})\hat{x} + \epsilon_{xy}\hat{y} + \epsilon_{xz}\hat{z} \\
y' &= \epsilon_{yx}\hat{x} + (1 + \epsilon_{yy})\hat{y} + \epsilon_{yz}\hat{z} \\
z' &= \epsilon_{zx}\hat{x} + \epsilon_{zy}\hat{y} + (1 + \epsilon_{zz})\hat{z}.
\end{aligned}
\tag{7.1}
$$

The coefficients $\epsilon_{\alpha\beta}$ define the deformation in the system. The new axes are not orthogonal in general. Let us consider the effect of the deformation on a point r which in the unstrained case is given by

$$
r = x\hat{x} + y\hat{y} + z\hat{z}.
\tag{7.2}
$$

After the distortion the new vector is given by

$$
r' = xx' + yy' + zz'.
\tag{7.3}
$$

Note that by definition the coefficients x, y, z of the vector are unchanged. The displacement of the deformation is then

$$\begin{aligned}
\boldsymbol{R} &= \boldsymbol{r}' - \boldsymbol{r} \\
&= x(\boldsymbol{x}' - \hat{\boldsymbol{x}}) + y(\boldsymbol{y}' - \hat{\boldsymbol{y}}) + z(\boldsymbol{z}' - \hat{\boldsymbol{z}})
\end{aligned} \tag{7.4}$$

or

$$\begin{aligned}
\boldsymbol{R} &= (x\epsilon_{xx} + y\epsilon_{yx} + z\epsilon_{zx})\hat{\boldsymbol{x}} \\
&+ (x\epsilon_{xy} + y\epsilon_{yy} + z\epsilon_{zy})\hat{\boldsymbol{y}} \\
&+ (x\epsilon_{xz} + y\epsilon_{yz} + z\epsilon_{zz})\hat{\boldsymbol{z}}
\end{aligned} \tag{7.5}$$

or by defining quantities u, v, w

$$\boldsymbol{R}(\boldsymbol{r}) = u(\boldsymbol{r})\hat{\boldsymbol{x}} + v(\boldsymbol{r})\hat{\boldsymbol{y}} + w(\boldsymbol{r})\hat{\boldsymbol{z}}. \tag{7.6}$$

For a general nonuniform distortion one must take the origin of $\boldsymbol{r}$ close to the point and define a position dependent strain. In the small strain limit:

$$x\epsilon_{xx} = x\frac{\partial u}{\partial x} \; ; \; y\epsilon_{yy} = y\frac{\partial v}{\partial y} \; ; \; z\epsilon_{zz} = z\frac{\partial w}{\partial z}, \text{ etc.} \tag{7.7}$$

Rather than using the ϵ_{xx} to describe the distortion we will use the strain components which are defined as

$$e_{xx} = \epsilon_{xx} = \frac{\partial u}{\partial x} \; ; \; e_{yy} = \epsilon_{yy} = \frac{\partial v}{\partial y} \; ; \; e_{zz} = \epsilon_{zz} = \frac{\partial w}{\partial z}. \tag{7.8}$$

The off-diagonal terms are

$$e_{xy} = \boldsymbol{x}' \cdot \boldsymbol{y}' \approx \epsilon_{yx} + \epsilon_{xy} = \frac{\partial u}{\partial y} + \frac{\partial v}{\partial x} \tag{7.9}$$

$$e_{yz} = \boldsymbol{y}' \cdot \boldsymbol{z}' \approx \epsilon_{zy} + \epsilon_{yz} = \frac{\partial v}{\partial z} + \frac{\partial w}{\partial y} \tag{7.10}$$

$$e_{zx} = \boldsymbol{z}' \cdot \boldsymbol{x}' \approx \epsilon_{zx} + \epsilon_{xz} = \frac{\partial u}{\partial z} + \frac{\partial w}{\partial x}. \tag{7.11}$$

The off-diagonal terms define the angular distortions of the strain.

It is useful to define the net fractional change in the volume produced by the distortion. This quantity is called dilation. The initially cubic volume of unity after distortion has a volume

$$\begin{aligned}
V' &= \boldsymbol{x}' \cdot (\boldsymbol{y}' \times \boldsymbol{z}') \\
&= \begin{vmatrix}
1 + \epsilon_{xx} & \epsilon_{xy} & \epsilon_{xz} \\
\epsilon_{yx} & 1 + \epsilon_{yy} & \epsilon_{yz} \\
\epsilon_{zx} & \epsilon_{zy} & 1 + \epsilon_{zz}
\end{vmatrix} \\
&\approx 1 + e_{xx} + e_{yy} + e_{zz}.
\end{aligned} \tag{7.12}$$

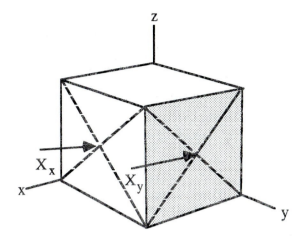

Figure 7.4: Stress component X_x is a force applied in the x-direction to a unit area of a plane whose normal lies in the x-direction; X_y is applied in the x-direction to a unit area of a plane whose normal lies in the y-direction.

The dilation is then

$$\delta = \frac{V' - V}{V} \approx e_{xx} + e_{yy} + e_{zz}. \qquad (7.13)$$

In order to produce a distortion in the crystalline unit cell, it is important to define the stress components responsible for the distortion. The force acting on a unit area in the solid is called stress and we can define the nine stress components X_x, X_y, X_z, Y_x, Y_y, Y_z, Z_x, Z_y, Z_z. Here the capital letter indicates the direction of the force and the subscript is the direction of the normal to the plane on which the stress is acting as shown in Figure 7.4. The number of stress components reduces to six if we impose the condition, on a cubic system, since there is no torque in the system (i.e., the stress does not produce angular acceleration). Then, $X_y = Y_x$; $Y_z = Z_y$; $Z_x = X_z$. We then have the six independent components: X_x, Y_y, Z_z; Y_z, Z_x, X_y.

7.3   THE ELASTIC CONSTANTS

The elastic constants are defined through the Hooke's Law which states that for small distortion the strain is proportional to the stress.

$$
\begin{aligned}
e_{xx} &= s_{11}X_x + s_{12}Y_y + s_{13}Z_z + s_{14}Y_z + s_{15}Z_x + s_{16}X_y \\
e_{yy} &= s_{21}X_x + s_{22}Y_y + s_{23}Z_z + s_{24}Y_z + s_{25}Z_x + s_{26}X_y \\
e_{zz} &= s_{31}X_x + s_{32}Y_y + s_{33}Z_z + s_{34}Y_z + s_{35}Z_x + s_{36}X_y \\
e_{yz} &= s_{41}X_x + s_{42}Y_y + s_{43}Z_z + s_{44}Y_z + s_{45}Z_x + s_{46}X_y \\
e_{zx} &= s_{51}X_x + s_{52}Y_y + s_{53}Z_z + s_{54}Y_z + s_{55}Z_x + s_{56}X_y \\
e_{xy} &= s_{61}X_x + s_{62}Y_y + s_{63}Z_z + s_{64}Y_z + s_{65}Z_x + s_{66}X_y.
\end{aligned} \qquad (7.14)
$$

Conversely, the stress components are linear functions of the strain components:

$$
\begin{aligned}
X_x &= c_{11}e_{xx} + c_{12}e_{yy} + c_{13}e_{zz} + c_{14}e_{yz} + c_{15}e_{zx} + c_{16}e_{xy} \\
Y_y &= c_{21}e_{xx} + c_{22}e_{yy} + c_{23}e_{zz} + c_{24}e_{yz} + c_{25}e_{zx} + c_{26}e_{xy} \\
Z_z &= c_{31}e_{xx} + c_{32}e_{yy} + c_{33}e_{zz} + c_{34}e_{yz} + c_{35}e_{zx} + c_{36}e_{xy} \\
Y_z &= c_{41}e_{xx} + c_{42}e_{yy} + c_{43}e_{zz} + c_{44}e_{yz} + c_{45}e_{zx} + c_{46}e_{xy} \\
Z_x &= c_{51}e_{xx} + c_{52}e_{yy} + c_{53}e_{zz} + c_{54}e_{yz} + c_{55}e_{zx} + c_{56}e_{xy} \\
X_y &= c_{61}e_{xx} + c_{62}e_{yy} + c_{63}e_{zz} + c_{64}e_{yz} + c_{65}e_{zx} + c_{66}e_{xy}.
\end{aligned} \quad (7.15)
$$

The 36 elastic constants can be reduced in real structures by invoking various symmetry arguments. Let us examine the elastic energy of the system. The energy is a quadratic function of the strain, and can then be written as

$$
U = \frac{1}{2} \sum_{\lambda=1}^{6} \sum_{\mu=1}^{6} \tilde{c}_{\lambda\mu}\, e_\lambda\, e_\mu \quad (7.16)
$$

where $1 = xx$; $2 = yy$; $3 = zz$; $4 = yz$; $5 = zx$; $6 = xy$. The $\tilde{c}$'s are related to the c's defined above.

The stress component is found by taking the derivative of U with respect to the associated strain component.

$$
\begin{aligned}
X_x &= \frac{\partial U}{\partial e_{xx}} \\
&\equiv \frac{\partial U}{\partial e_1} \\
&= \tilde{c}_{11}e_1 + \frac{1}{2}\sum_{\beta=2}^{6}(\tilde{c}_{1\beta} + \tilde{c}_{\beta 1})\, e_\beta.
\end{aligned} \quad (7.17)
$$

Note that we will always get the combination $(\tilde{c}_{\alpha\beta} + \tilde{c}_{\beta\alpha})/2$ in the stress-strain relations. It follows that the elastic stiffness constants are symmetrical.

$$
\begin{aligned}
c_{\alpha\beta} &= \frac{1}{2}(\tilde{c}_{\alpha\beta} + \tilde{c}_{\beta\alpha}) \\
&= c_{\beta\alpha}.
\end{aligned} \quad (7.18)
$$

Thus the 36 constants reduce to 21.

The number of force constants is further reduced if one examines the cubic symmetrics. We will show that for cubic systems, in the elastic energy U, the only terms that occur are

$$
\begin{aligned}
U &= \frac{1}{2}c_{11}\left(e_{xx}^2 + e_{yy}^2 + e_{zz}^2\right) + c_{44}\left(e_{yz}^2 + e_{zx}^2 + e_{xy}^2\right) \\
&\quad + c_{12}(e_{yy}e_{zz} + e_{zz}e_{xx} + e_{xx}e_{yy}).
\end{aligned} \quad (7.19)
$$

Other terms of the form

$$
(e_{xx}e_{xy} + \ldots), (e_{yz}e_{zx} + \ldots), (e_{xx}e_{yz} + \ldots), \text{ etc.}
$$

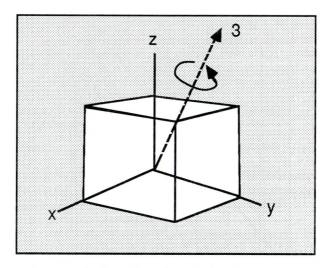

Figure 7.5: Rotation by $2\pi/3$ about the axis marked 3 changes $x \to y$; $y \to z$; $z \to x$.

do not occur.

If one examines a cubic system, the structure has a 4-fold symmetry. Focusing on the [111] and equivalent directions, if we rotate by $2\pi/3$ we get the following transformations (see Figure 7.5):

$$
\begin{array}{ccccccc}
x & \to & y & \to & z & \to & x \\
-x & \to & z & \to & -y & \to & -x \\
x & \to & z & \to & -y & \to & x \\
-x & \to & y & \to & z & \to & -x
\end{array}
\tag{7.20}
$$

The terms in the energy density must be invariant under these transformations. Note that

$$
e_{xx}e_{xy} \to -e_{xx}e_{x(-y)}
\tag{7.21}
$$

and therefore any term which is odd in any of the indices will vanish.

$$
\begin{aligned}
\frac{\partial U}{\partial e_{xx}} &= X_x \\
&= c_{11}e_{xx} + c_{12}(e_{yy} + e_{zz})
\end{aligned}
\tag{7.22}
$$

comparing the various terms

$$
c_{12} = c_{13}; c_{14} = c_{15} = c_{16} = 0.
\tag{7.23}
$$

Also since

$$
\begin{aligned}
\frac{\partial U}{\partial e_{xy}} &= X_y \\
&= c_{44}e_{xy}
\end{aligned}
\tag{7.24}
$$

upon comparison with the stress-strain relation

$$c_{61} = c_{62} = c_{63} = c_{64} = c_{65} = 0; \; c_{66} = c_{44}. \tag{7.25}$$

Thus, from Equations 7.23 and 7.25 we find that the array of values of the elastic stiffness constants is reduced for a cubic crystal to the matrix

$$
\begin{array}{c|cccccc}
 & e_{xx} & e_{yy} & e_{zz} & e_{yz} & e_{zx} & e_{xy} \\
\hline
X_x & c_{11} & c_{12} & c_{12} & 0 & 0 & 0 \\
Y_y & c_{12} & c_{11} & c_{12} & 0 & 0 & 0 \\
Z_z & c_{12} & c_{12} & c_{11} & 0 & 0 & 0 \\
Y_z & 0 & 0 & 0 & c_{44} & 0 & 0 \\
Z_x & 0 & 0 & 0 & 0 & c_{44} & 0 \\
X_y & 0 & 0 & 0 & 0 & 0 & c_{44}
\end{array}
\tag{7.26}
$$

For cubic crystals the stiffness and compliance constants are related by

$$
\begin{aligned}
c_{44} &= 1/s_{44} \\
c_{11} - c_{12} &= (s_{11} - s_{12})^{-1} \\
c_{11} + 2c_{12} &= (s_{11} + 2s_{12})^{-1}.
\end{aligned}
\tag{7.27}
$$

These relations follow on evaluating the inverse matrix to Equation 7.26.

Consider the uniform dilation $e_{xx} = e_{yy} = e_{zz} = \delta/3$. For this deformation the energy density (Equation 7.19) of a cubic crystal is

$$U = \frac{1}{6}(c_{11} + 2c_{12})\delta^2. \tag{7.28}$$

We may define the *bulk modulus* B by the relation

$$U = \frac{1}{2}B\delta^2 \tag{7.29}$$

which is equivalent to the definition $-V\,dp/dV$. For a cubic crystal

$$B = \frac{1}{3}(c_{11} + 2c_{12}). \tag{7.30}$$

The compressibility K is defined as $K \equiv 1/B$. In most semiconductors, $c_{11} \approx 2c_{12}$ and $c_{12} \approx c_{44}$. For example, in GaAs, $c_{11} = 1.188 \times 10^{12}$ dynes cm^{-2}; $c_{12} = 0.538 \times 10^{12}$ dynes cm^{-2} and $c_{44} = 0.594 \times 10^{12}$ dynes cm^{-2}.

7.4 STRAIN TENSOR IN LATTICE MISMATCHED EPITAXY

In order to study the effect of strain on electronic properties of semiconductors, it is first essential to establish the strain tensor produced by epitaxy. The work of Frank and van der Merwe and of Matthews and Blakeslee demonstrated that

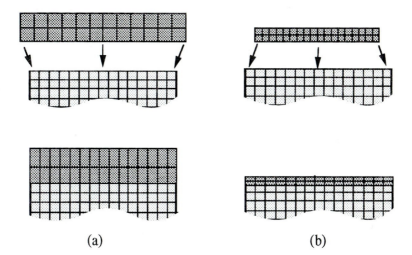

(a)   (b)

Figure 7.6: Pseudomorphic strain produced by epitaxy of an overlayer with a bulk lattice constant larger (a), or smaller (b) than the substrate. The overlayer must match the in-plane lattice constant of the substrate.

careful growth of an epitaxial layer whose lattice constant is close, but not equal, to the lattice constant of the substrate can result in a coherent strain, as opposed to polycrystalline or amorphous incoherent growth. If the strain is incorporated into the epitaxial crystal coherently, the lattice constant of the epitaxial layer in the directions parallel to the interface is forced to be equal to the lattice constant of the substrate. The lattice constant of the epitaxial perpendicular to the substrate will be changed by the Poisson effect. If the parallel lattice constant is forced to shrink, or a compressive strain is applied, the perpendicular lattice constant will grow. Conversely, if the parallel lattice constant of the epitaxial layer is forced to expand under tensile strain, the perpendicular lattice constant will shrink. These two cases are depicted in Figure 7.6. This type of coherently strained crystal is called pseudomorphic.

For systems of interest in the present work, the epitaxial semiconductor layer is biaxially strained in the plane of the substrate, by an amount $\epsilon_\parallel$, and uniaxially strained in the perpendicular direction, by an amount $\epsilon_\perp$. For a thick substrate, the in-plane strain of the layer is determined from the bulk lattice constants of the substrate material, a_S, and the layer material, a_L:

$$
\begin{aligned}
e_\parallel &= \frac{a_S}{a_L} - 1 \\
&= \epsilon.
\end{aligned}
\tag{7.31}
$$

Since the layer is subjected to no stress in the perpendicular direction, the perpendicular strain, $\epsilon_\perp$, is simply proportional to $\epsilon_\parallel$:

$$\epsilon_\perp = \frac{-\epsilon_\parallel}{\sigma} \tag{7.32}$$

where the constant σ is known as Poisson's ratio.

Noting that there is *no stress* in the direction of growth it can be simply shown that for the strained layer grown on a (001) substrate (Osbourn, 1982 and Hinckley and Singh, 1990),

$$
\begin{aligned}
\sigma &= \frac{c_{11}}{2c_{12}} \\
\epsilon_{xx} &= \epsilon_\parallel \\
\epsilon_{yy} &= \epsilon_{xx} \\
\epsilon_{zz} &= \frac{-2c_{12}}{c_{11}}\epsilon_\parallel \\
\epsilon_{xy} &= 0 \\
\epsilon_{yz} &= 0 \\
\epsilon_{zx} &= 0
\end{aligned}
\tag{7.33}
$$

while in the case of strained layer grown on a (111) substrate

$$
\begin{aligned}
\sigma &= \frac{c_{11} + 2c_{12} + 4c_{44}}{2c_{11} + 4c_{12} - 4c_{44}} \\
\epsilon_{xx} &= \left[\frac{2}{3} - \frac{1}{3}\left(\frac{2c_{11} + 4c_{12} - 4c_{44}}{c_{11} + 2c_{12} + 4c_{44}} \right) \right]\epsilon_\parallel \\
\epsilon_{yy} &= \epsilon_{xx} \\
\epsilon_{zz} &= \epsilon_{xx} \\
\epsilon_{xy} &= \left[\frac{-1}{3} - \frac{1}{3}\left(\frac{2c_{11} + 4c_{12} - 4c_{44}}{c_{11} + 2c_{12} + 4c_{44}} \right) \right]\epsilon_\parallel \\
\epsilon_{yz} &= \epsilon_{xy} \\
\epsilon_{zx} &= \epsilon_{yz}.
\end{aligned}
\tag{7.34}
$$

The general strain tensor for arbitrary orientation is shown in Figure 7.7. In general, the strained epitaxy causes a distortion of the cubic lattice and, depending upon the growth orientation, the distortions produce a new reduced crystal symmetry as shown in Figure 7.8. It is important to note that for (001) growth, the strain tensor is diagonal while for (111), and several other directions, the strain tensor has nondiagonal terms. The nondiagonal terms can be exploited to produce built-in electric fields in certain heterostructures as discussed in Section 7.6.

7.5   DEFORMATION POTENTIAL THEORY

Once the strain tensor is known, we are ready to apply the deformation potential theory to calculate the effects of strain on various eigenstates in the Brillouin

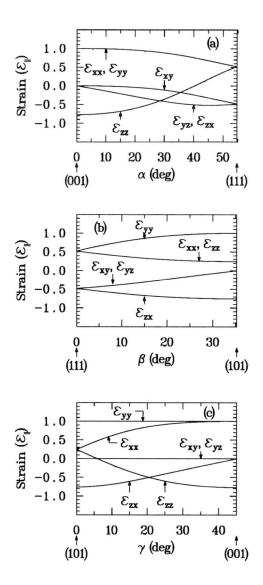

Figure 7.7: The general strain tensor produced when an overlayer is grown on different substrate orientations. The strain between the two materials is $\epsilon_\parallel$.

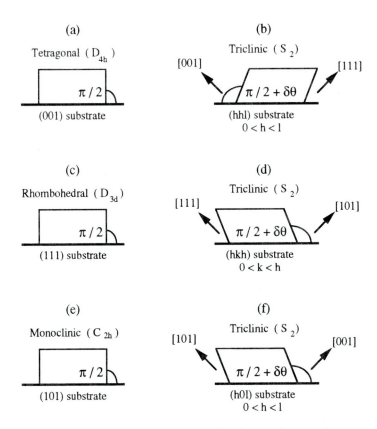

Figure 7.8: Schematic edge view of distortion of film lattice due to epitaxy on various substrate orientations. (From Hinckley, 1990.)

zone. The strain perturbation Hamiltonian is defined and its effects are calculated in the simple first order perturbation theory. In general we have

$$H_\epsilon^{\alpha\beta} = \sum_{ij} D_{ij}^{\alpha\beta} \epsilon_{ij} \tag{7.35}$$

where D_{ij} is the deformation potential operator which transforms under symmetry operations as a second rank tensor. $D_{ij}^{\alpha\beta}$ are the matrix elements of D_{ij}.

The deformation potential is not calculated in an ab initio manner, but is usually fitted to experimental results. As in the case of the force constants, the number of independent elements in the deformation potential can also be reduced based on the symmetry of the wavefunctions.

Let us consider the matrix elements of the strain tensor (Equation 7.35) which defines the perturbation Hamiltonian for the strain. We are interested in the $(\alpha\beta)$ element of the matrix where α and β represent the basic functions being used for the unperturbed crystal. The symmetry of the basis states is

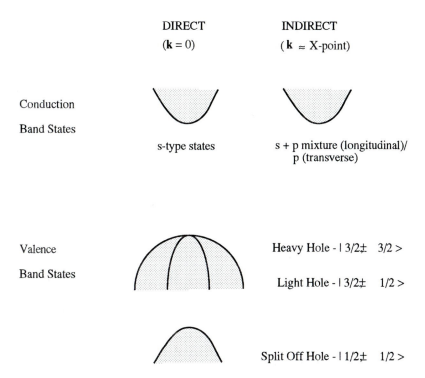

Figure 7.9: A schematic showing the nature of the central cell symmetry at the band-edges of direct and indirect semiconductors.

critical in simplifying the number of independent deformation potential elements. Figure 7.9 is a schematic of the nature of the symmetries encountered at the bandedges of direct and indirect semiconductors. We will discuss the deformation potentials realizing that we are primarily interested in seeing the effect of the strain on bandedge states.

Case 1: Let us first examine the nondegenerate Γ_2' state which represents the conduction bandedge of direct bandgap semiconductors. This state is an s-type state and has the full cubic symmetry associated with it. Let us perform the following two steps to establish the independent number of deformation potentials for this state:

Step 1: Rotate by $120°$ about (111). This causes the following transformation in the new axes (primes).

$$
\begin{aligned}
x' &= y \\
y' &= z \\
z' &= x
\end{aligned}
\tag{7.36}
$$

Consequently, we have

$$\left. \begin{array}{rcl} D_{xx} & = & D_{z'z'} \\ D_{yy} & = & D_{x'x'} \\ D_{zz} & = & D_{y'y'} \end{array} \right\} \Rightarrow D_{xx} = D_{yy} = D_{zz} \tag{7.37}$$

$$\left. \begin{array}{rcl} D_{xy} & = & D_{z'x'} \\ D_{zx} & = & D_{y'z'} \\ D_{yz} & = & D_{x'y'} \end{array} \right\} \Rightarrow D_{xy} = D_{yz} = D_{zx} \tag{7.38}$$

Step 2: Rotate about (001) by 90° leading to the transformation

$$\begin{array}{rcl} x' & = & y \\ y' & = & -x \\ z' & = & z \end{array}$$

$$\tag{7.39}$$

The deformation potentials transform as

$$\begin{array}{rcl} D_{xy} & = & -D_{y'x'} \\ & = & -D_{x'y'}. \end{array} \tag{7.40}$$

Thus, $D_{xy} = 0$, and by symmetry, $D_{xy} = Dyz = D_{zx} = 0$.

Thus for Γ_2' states there is only one deformation potential and the effect of the strain is to produce a shift in energy.

$$\begin{array}{rcl} \delta E^{(000)} & = & H_\epsilon \\ & = & D_{xx}(\epsilon_{xx} + \epsilon_{yy} + \epsilon_{zz}). \end{array} \tag{7.41}$$

Conventionally we write

$$D_{xx} = \Xi_d^{(000)} \tag{7.42}$$

where $\Xi_d^{(000)}$ represents the dilation deformation potential for the conduction band (000) valley.

Case 2: States along the (100) direction in k-space or Δ_1 symmetry states. We again carry out the following symmetry transformation.

Step 1: Rotate by 90° about the (100) axis, producing the transformation

$$\begin{array}{rcl} x' & = & x \\ y' & = & z \\ z' & = & -y \end{array} \tag{7.43}$$

The deformation potentials transform as

$$\begin{array}{l} D_{xx} = D_{x'x'} \\ \left. \begin{array}{l} D_{yy} = D_{z'z'} \\ D_{zz} = D_{y'y'} \end{array} \right\} \Rightarrow D_{yy} = D_{zz} \\ \left. \begin{array}{l} D_{xy} = -D_{x'z'} \\ D_{zx} = D_{x'y'} \end{array} \right\} \Rightarrow D_{xy} = -D_{x'y'} \\ D_{yz} = -D_{z'y'} \Rightarrow D_{yz} = 0. \end{array} \tag{7.44}$$

Thus,

$$\delta E^{(100)} = D_{xx}\epsilon_{xx} + D_{yy}(\epsilon_{yy} + \epsilon_{zz}) \tag{7.45}$$

Once again we write

$$
\begin{aligned}
D_{yy} &= \Xi_d^{(100)} \\
D_{xx} &= \Xi_d^{(100)} + \Xi_u^{(100)}
\end{aligned}
\tag{7.46}
$$

where d and u represent dilation and uniaxial portions. This gives

$$\delta E^{(100)} = \Xi_d^{(100)}(\epsilon_{xx} + \epsilon_{yy} + \epsilon_{zz}) + \Xi_u^{(100)}\epsilon_{xx}. \tag{7.47}$$

By symmetry we can write

$$\delta E^{(010)} = \Xi_d^{(100)}(\epsilon_{xx} + \epsilon_{yy} + \epsilon_{zz}) + \Xi_u^{(100)}\epsilon_{yy} \tag{7.48}$$

$$\delta E^{(001)} = \Xi_d^{(100)}(\epsilon_{xx} + \epsilon_{yy} + \epsilon_{zz}) + \Xi_u^{(100)}\epsilon_{zz} \tag{7.49}$$

We note that if the strain tensor is such that the diagonal elements are unequal (as is the case in strained epitaxy), the strain will split the degeneracy of the Δ_1 branches.

Case 3: The L_1 symmetry or states along (111) direction in k-space.

Step 1: Rotate by 120° about (111) axis causing the transformation

$$
\begin{aligned}
x' &= y \\
y' &= z \\
z' &= x.
\end{aligned}
\tag{7.50}
$$

The deformation potentials transform as for the Γ_2' case giving

$$D_{xx} = D_{yy} = D_{zz} \tag{7.51}$$

$$D_{xy} = D_{yz} = D_{xz}. \tag{7.52}$$

Thus we get a perturbation

$$\delta E^{(111)} = D_{xx}(\epsilon_{xx} + \epsilon_{yy} + \epsilon_{zz}) + 2D_{xy}(\epsilon_{xy} + \epsilon_{yz} + \epsilon_{zx}). \tag{7.53}$$

Conventionally, we write

$$
\begin{aligned}
D_{xx} &= \Xi_d^{(111)} + \frac{1}{3}\Xi_u^{(111)} \\
D_{xy} &= \frac{1}{3}\Xi_u^{(111)}.
\end{aligned}
\tag{7.54}
$$

By similar transformation we find that

$$
\begin{aligned}
\delta E^{(11\bar{1})} &= D_{xx}(\epsilon_{xx} + \epsilon_{yy} + \epsilon_{zz}) + 2D_{xy}(\epsilon_{xy} - \epsilon_{yz} - \epsilon_{zx}) \\
\delta E^{(1\bar{1}1)} &= D_{xx}(\epsilon_{xx} + \epsilon_{yy} + \epsilon_{zz}) + 2D_{xy}(-\epsilon_{xy} - \epsilon_{yz} + \epsilon_{zx}) \\
\delta E^{(\bar{1}11)} &= D_{xx}(\epsilon_{xx} + \epsilon_{yy} + \epsilon_{zz}) + 2D_{xy}(-\epsilon_{xy} + \epsilon_{yz} - \epsilon_{zx}).
\end{aligned}
\tag{7.55}
$$

Case 4: The triple degenerate states describing the valence bandedge.

The valence band states are defined (near the bandedge) by primarily p_x, p_y, p_z (denoted by x,y,z) basis states. Consider a matrix element H_ϵ^{xx}.

$$
\begin{aligned}
H_\epsilon^{xx} &= \langle x \,|H_\epsilon|\, x \rangle \\
&= \sum_{ij} D_{ij}^{xx} \epsilon_{ij}
\end{aligned}
$$

Step 1: Rotate by 90° about (100). This causes the transformation

$$
\begin{aligned}
x' &= x \\
y' &= z \\
z' &= -y
\end{aligned}
\tag{7.56}
$$

Using arguments similar to those used before

$$
\begin{aligned}
D_{xx}^{xx} &= D_{x'x'}^{x'x'} = \ell \\
\left.\begin{array}{l}
D_{yy}^{xx} = D_{z'z'}^{x'x'} \\
D_{zz}^{xx} = D_{y'y'}^{x'x'}
\end{array}\right\} &\Rightarrow D_{yy}^{xx} = D_{zz}^{xx} = m \\
\left.\begin{array}{l}
D_{xy}^{xx} = -D_{x'z'}^{x'x'} \\
D_{xz}^{xx} = D_{x'y'}^{x'x'}
\end{array}\right\} &= 0 \\
D_{yz}^{xx} = -D_{z'y'}^{x'x'} &= 0.
\end{aligned}
\tag{7.57}
$$

Also examining terms like H_ϵ^{xy}, we rotate by 90° about (001). Then it is easy to see that

$$
\left.\begin{array}{l}
D_{xx}^{xy} = -D_{y'y'}^{x'y'} \\
D_{yy}^{xy} = -D_{x'x'}^{x'y'}
\end{array}\right\} \Rightarrow D_{xx}^{xy} = -D_{yy}^{xy}
\tag{7.58}
$$

These are zero if we consider a reflection through $x = y$.

$$
D_{zz}^{xy} = -D_{z'z'}^{x'y'} = 0
\tag{7.59}
$$

$$
D_{zz}^{xy} = -D_{z'z'}^{x'y'} = 0
\tag{7.60}
$$

$$
\left.\begin{array}{l}
D_{xz}^{xy} = D_{y'z'}^{x'y'} \\
D_{yz}^{xy} = -D_{x'z'}^{x'y'}
\end{array}\right\} \Rightarrow D_{xz}^{xy} = D_{yz}^{xy} = 0
\tag{7.61}
$$

Thus the unique deformation potentials are

$$
\begin{aligned}
D_{xx}^{xx} &= \ell \\
D_{yy}^{xx} &= m \\
D_{xy}^{xy} &= n.
\end{aligned}
\tag{7.62}
$$

We often use the related definition which is more useful for the angular momentum basis

$$a = \frac{\ell + 2m}{3}$$

$$b = \frac{\ell - m}{3}$$

$$d = \frac{n}{\sqrt{3}}. \tag{7.63}$$

We have already discussed the strain tensor in epitaxial growth. For (001) growth which has been the main growth direction studied because of its compatibility with technology of processing we have

$$\epsilon_{xx} = \epsilon_{yy} = \epsilon$$

$$\epsilon_{zz} = -\frac{2c_{12}}{c_{11}}\epsilon. \tag{7.64}$$

Let us evaluate the matrix elements in the angular momentum basis instead of the p_x, p_y, p_z basis, since the angular momentum basis is used to describe the heavy hole, light hole states (for a diagonal tensor produced by (001) epitaxy).

$$\begin{aligned}
\langle \tfrac{3}{2}, \tfrac{3}{2} | H_\epsilon | \tfrac{3}{2}, \tfrac{3}{2} \rangle &= \frac{1}{2} \langle p_x - i p_y | H_\epsilon | p_x + i p_y \rangle \\
&= \frac{1}{2} [\langle p_x | H_\epsilon | p_x \rangle + i \langle p_x | H_\epsilon | p_y \rangle \\
&\quad - i \langle p_y | H_\epsilon | p_x \rangle + \langle p_y | H_\epsilon | p_y \rangle] \\
&= \frac{1}{2} [\ell \epsilon_{xx} + m(\epsilon_{yy} + \epsilon_{zz}) + \ell \epsilon_{yy} + m(\epsilon_{zz} + \epsilon_{xx})] \\
&= \frac{1}{2} [\epsilon_{xx}(\ell + m) + \epsilon_{yy}(\ell + m) + 2m\epsilon_{zz}]. \tag{7.65}
\end{aligned}$$

In terms of the deformation potentials, a, b, d,

$$m = a - b$$

$$\ell = a + 2b$$

$$n = \sqrt{3}d \tag{7.66}$$

$$\begin{aligned}
\langle \tfrac{3}{2}, \tfrac{3}{2} | H_\epsilon | \tfrac{3}{2}, \tfrac{3}{2} \rangle &= \frac{1}{2} [\epsilon_{xx}(2a + b) + \epsilon_{yy}(2a + b) + \epsilon_{zz}(2a - 2b)] \\
&= a(\epsilon_{xx} + \epsilon_{yy} + \epsilon_{zz}) + \frac{b}{2}(\epsilon_{xx} + \epsilon_{yy} - 2\epsilon_{zz}). \tag{7.67}
\end{aligned}$$

If we examine the case where growth is along the (001) direction, as noted earlier,

$$\epsilon_{xx} = \epsilon_{yy} = \epsilon$$

$$\epsilon_{zz} = -\frac{2c_{12}}{c_{11}}\epsilon \tag{7.68}$$

we then obtain

$$\langle \tfrac{3}{2}, \tfrac{3}{2} | H_\epsilon | \tfrac{3}{2}, \tfrac{3}{2} \rangle = 2a \frac{(c_{11} - c_{12})}{c_{11}} \epsilon + b \left(\frac{c_{11} + 2c_{12}}{c_{11}} \right) \epsilon. \tag{7.69}$$

Remember that in our definition

$$\epsilon = \frac{a_S}{a_L} - 1. \tag{7.70}$$

In a similar manner it can be shown that

$$\langle \tfrac{3}{2}, \pm \tfrac{1}{2} | H_\epsilon | \tfrac{3}{2}, \pm \tfrac{1}{2} \rangle = 2a \frac{(c_{11} - c_{12})}{c_{11}} \epsilon - b \left(\frac{c_{11} + 2c_{12}}{c_{11}} \right) \epsilon \tag{7.71}$$

Restricting ourselves to the HH and LH states, the strain Hamiltonian can be written as (the state ordering is $|3/2, 3/2\rangle$, $|3/2, -1/2\rangle$, $|3/2, 1/2\rangle$, and $|3/2, -3/2\rangle$)

$$H_\epsilon = \begin{bmatrix} H_{hh}^\epsilon & H_{12}^\epsilon & H_{13}^\epsilon & 0 \\ H_{12}^{\epsilon*} & H_{lh}^\epsilon & 0 & H_{13}^\epsilon \\ H_{13}^{\epsilon*} & 0 & H_{lh}^\epsilon & -H_{12}^\epsilon \\ 0 & H_{13}^{\epsilon*} & -H_{12}^{\epsilon*} & H_{hh}^\epsilon \end{bmatrix} \tag{7.72}$$

where the matrix elements are given by

$$
\begin{aligned}
H_{hh}^\epsilon &= a(\epsilon_{xx} + \epsilon_{yy} + \epsilon_{zz}) - b \left[\epsilon_{zz} - \frac{1}{2}(\epsilon_{xx} + \epsilon_{yy}) \right] \\
H_{lh}^\epsilon &= a(\epsilon_{xx} + \epsilon_{yy} + \epsilon_{zz}) + b \left[\epsilon_{zz} - \frac{1}{2}(\epsilon_{xx} + \epsilon_{yy}) \right] \\
H_{12}^\epsilon &= -d(\epsilon_{xz} - i\epsilon_{yz}) \\
&= \langle \tfrac{3}{2}, \tfrac{3}{2} | H_\epsilon | \tfrac{3}{2}, \tfrac{1}{2} \rangle \\
H_{13}^\epsilon &= \frac{\sqrt{3}}{2} b(\epsilon_{yy} - \epsilon_{xx}) + id\epsilon_{xy} \\
&= \langle \tfrac{3}{2}, \tfrac{3}{2} | H_\epsilon | \tfrac{3}{2}, \tfrac{-1}{2} \rangle.
\end{aligned}
\tag{7.73}
$$

Here, the quantities a, b, and d are valence band deformation potentials. As discussed earlier, strains achieved by lattice mismatched epitaxial growth along (001) direction can be characterized by $\epsilon_{xx} = \epsilon_{yy} = \epsilon$, and $\epsilon_{zz} = -(2c_{12}/c_{11})\epsilon$. All of the diagonal strain terms are zero. Using this information, we get

$$H_{hh}^\epsilon = \left[2a \left(\frac{c_{11} - c_{12}}{c_{11}} \right) + b \left(\frac{c_{11} + 2c_{12}}{c_{11}} \right) \right] \epsilon \tag{7.74}$$

$$H_{lh}^\epsilon = \left[2a \left(\frac{c_{11} - c_{12}}{c_{11}} \right) - b \left(\frac{c_{11} + 2c_{12}}{c_{11}} \right) \right] \epsilon \tag{7.75}$$

with all other terms zero. If the hole dispersion is to be described in a quantum well, the hole states $|m, \boldsymbol{k}\rangle$ can be written as

$$\langle \boldsymbol{r}_h | m, \boldsymbol{k} \rangle = \frac{e^{i\boldsymbol{k} \cdot \rho_h}}{2\pi} \sum_v g_m^v(\boldsymbol{k}, z_h) U_0^v(\boldsymbol{r}_h) \tag{7.76}$$

where k is the in-plane two-dimensional wave vector, ρ_h is the in-plane radial coordinate, z_h is the coordinate in the growth direction, the U_0^v are the zone-center Bloch functions having spin symmetry v, and m is a subband index. The envelope functions $g_m^v(k, z_h)$ and subband energies $E_m(k)$ satisfy the Kohn–Luttinger equation along with the strain effect

$$
-\begin{bmatrix}
H_{hh} - \frac{1}{2}\delta & b & c & 0 \\
b^* & H_{lh} + \frac{1}{2}\delta & 0 & c \\
c^* & 0 & H_{lh} + \frac{1}{2}\delta & -b \\
0 & c^* & -b^* & H_{hh} - \frac{1}{2}\delta
\end{bmatrix}
\begin{bmatrix}
g_m^{3/2,3/2}(k, z_h) \\
g_m^{3/2,1/2}(k, z_h) \\
g_m^{3/2,-1/2}(k, z_h) \\
g_m^{3/2,-3/2}(k, z_h)
\end{bmatrix}
$$

$$
= E_m(k)
\begin{bmatrix}
g_m^{3/2,3/2}(k, z_h) \\
g_m^{3/2,1/2}(k, z_h) \\
g_m^{3/2,-1/2}(k, z_h) \\
g_m^{3/2,-3/2}(k, z_h)
\end{bmatrix}
$$

(7.77)

The δ is the separation of the HH and LH states in a bulk material due to the strain and is given by Equations 7.74 and 7.75. For the $In_yGa_{1-y}As$ system it is given by $\delta = -5.966\epsilon$ eV. Note that the function $g_m^v(k, z_h)$ depends on k as well as z_h and that the energy bands are not, in general, parabolic. The matrix entries in Equation 7.77 are given by

$$
H_{hh} = \frac{\hbar^2}{2m_0}\left[(k_x^2 + k_y^2)(\gamma_1 + \gamma_2) - (\gamma_1 - 2\gamma_2)\frac{\partial^2}{\partial z_h^2}\right] - V^h(z_h)
$$

$$
H_{lh} = \frac{\hbar^2}{2m_0}\left[(k_x^2 + k_y^2)(\gamma_1 - \gamma_2) - (\gamma_1 + 2\gamma_2)\frac{\partial^2}{\partial z_h^2}\right] - V^h(z_h)
$$

$$
c = \frac{\sqrt{3}\hbar^2}{2m_0}\left[\gamma_2(k_x^2 - k_y^2) - 2i\gamma_3 k_x k_y\right]
$$

$$
b = -\frac{\sqrt{3}\hbar^2}{m_0}(k_x - ik_y)\gamma_3\frac{\partial}{\partial z_h}
$$

where m_0 is the free-electron mass, V_h is the potential profile for the hole, and for GaAs $\gamma_1 = 6.85$, $\gamma_2 = 2.1$, and $\gamma_3 = 2.9$.

Equation 7.77 can be solved by writing it in finite-difference form and diagonalizing the resulting matrix to obtain the in-plane band structure. For GaAs, InAs type systems, the values of a and b are such that the net effect is that the $(3/2, \pm3/2)$ state moves a total of 5.96ϵ eV and the $(3/2, \pm1/2)$ state moves by energy equal to 12.0ϵ eV (Kato et al, 1986).

The relationships between the deformation potentials used in the discussion above and what is measured from a hydrostatic pressure measurement are described as follows

$$
\Xi_d^{(000)} = \Xi_{hyd}^{(000)} + a
$$

$$\Xi_d^{(100)} = \Xi_{hyd}^{(100)} - \frac{1}{3}\Xi_u^{(100)} + a$$

$$\Xi_d^{(111)} = \Xi_{hyd}^{(111)} - \frac{1}{3}\Xi_u^{(111)} + a \qquad (7.78)$$

From hydrostatic compression

$$\delta E_g(\bar{k}) = \Xi_{hyd}^{(\bar{k})}\left(\epsilon_{xx} + \epsilon_{yy} + \epsilon_{zz}\right)$$

$$\Xi_{hyd}^{(\bar{k})} = -\frac{1}{3}\left(c_{11} + 2c_{12}\right)\frac{dE_g}{dP} \qquad (7.79)$$

The elastic stiffness constants, c_{11}, c_{12}, and the hydrostatic pressure coefficient of the bandgap, dE_g/dP, are fairly accurately measured by various experiments and we thus get the values of the individual deformation potentials for different bands.

The effect of strain on bandstructure for both conduction band and valence band states is illustrated by examining the direct bandgap material $In_xGa_{1-x}As$ grown on GaAs and the indirect bandgap material Ge_xSi_{1-x} alloy grown on Si. For direct bandgap materials conduction bands, the strain tensor only moves the position of the bandedge and has a rather small effect on the carrier mass. The results shown in Figure 7.10 are from calculations done for the unstrained and strained system using tight binding method adapted to include the deformation potential theory and show that the mass decrease occurs due to addition to Indium. The strain does not directly affect the mass significantly.

In the case of the indirect bandgap $Si_{1-x}Ge_x$ alloy grown on Si, the conduction band also is significantly affected according to Equations 7.47–7.49. For (001) growth there is splitting in the 6 equivalent valleys. The results on the bandedge states are shown in Figure 7.11. Note that the biaxial compressive strain causes a lowering of the four-fold in-plane valleys below the 2 two-fold out of plane valleys (People, 1986). The carrier masses are not expected to change significantly.

The effect of strain on the valence bandstructure is much more dramatic. In Figure 7.12 we show how the valence bandstructure of GaAs is modified as it is subjected to the biaxial tensile and compressive strain. Notice that there is a large change in the curvature of the bands along with the splittings of the HH-LH state. In Chapter 6, we showed some results on the constant energy surfaces of Si valence bands. We show these results again in Figures 7.13 through 7.16 but under biaxial strain as produced by (001) growth on a substrate. The same values of the energy are used, but notice that the k-space intersections are quite different due to the change in the band curvatures. To emphasize this point more we show in Figure 7.17 the density of states at the valence bandedge for Si and Ge and some of their unstrained alloys. Notice that the density of states decreases as the Ge content increases since Ge has very low hole masses. In Figure 7.18 we show the density of states for a Si under strain of +1% or −1%. The lattice mismatch between Si and Ge is 4%, so a 1% strain is produced by addition of 25% Ge into Si and growing on a Si substrate (compressive strain) or

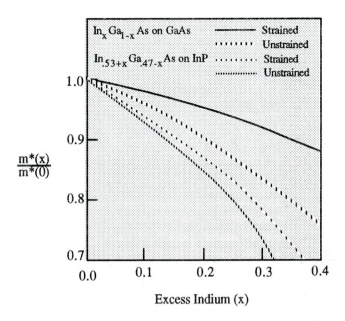

Figure 7.10: Results of an eight band tight binding model for the effect of excess In (and consequent strain) on carrier mass (Jaffe, 1989).

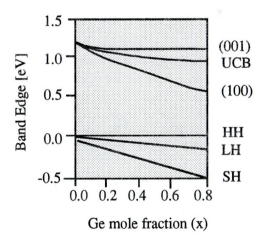

Figure 7.11: Splittings of the conduction band and valence band are shown as a function of alloy composition. UCB: unstrained conduction band, HH: heavy hole, LH: light hole, SH: split-off hole.

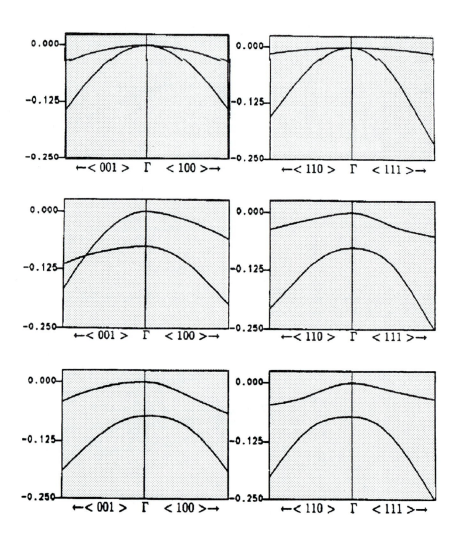

Figure 7.12: Hole band dispersions for (top) unstrained GaAs, (middle) GaAs under 1% biaxial tension, and (bottom) GaAs under 1% biaxial compression.

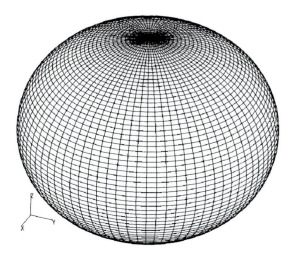

Figure 7.13: Biaxially tensilely strained (+1%) Si HH constant energy surface at 1 meV. (From Hinckley, 1990.)

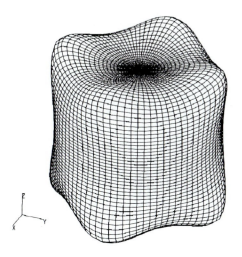

Figure 7.14: Biaxially tensilely strained (+1%) Si HH constant energy surface at 40 meV. (From Hinckley, 1990.)

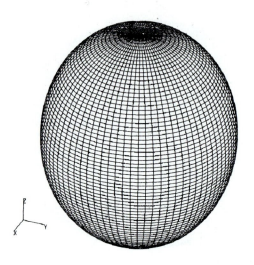

Figure 7.15: Biaxially compressively strained (−1%) Si HH constant energy surface at 40 meV. (From Hinckley, 1990.)

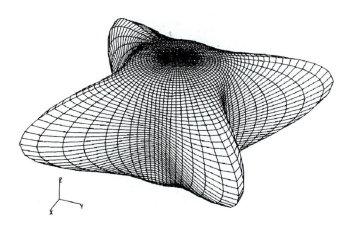

Figure 7.16: Biaxially compressively strained (−1%) Si HH constant energy surface at 1 meV. (From Hinckley, 1990.)

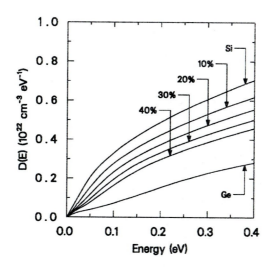

Figure 7.17: Effect of alloying on valence band density of states. (From Hinckley, 1990.)

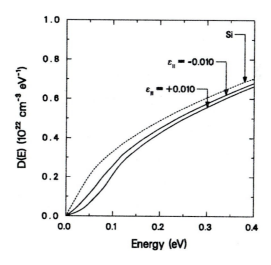

Figure 7.18: Strained Si valence band density of states. (From Hinckley, 1990.)

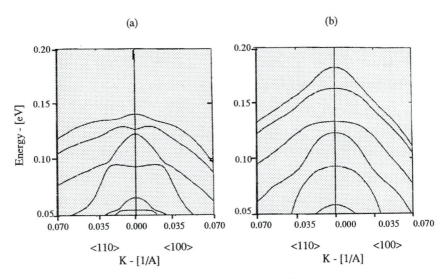

Figure 7.19: Hole subband dispersion curves for a 100 Å wide quantum well in the (a) $Al_{0.30}Ga_{0.70}As/GaAs$ material system and the (b) $Al_{0.30}Ga_{0.70}As/In_{0.1}Ga_{0.9}$ system.

on a $Si_{0.5}Ge_{0.5}$ substrate (tensile strain). Notice that there is a large reduction in the density of states, especially up to 100 meV near the valence bandedge. Such decreases occur in III-V compounds as well and represent important changes in the electronic properties of the semiconductors.

The effects of strain on the valence bandstructure can also be seen if we examine the dispersion relations of a 100 Å $GaAs/Al_{0.3}Ga_{0.7}As$ quantum well and a 100 Å $In_{0.1}Ga_{0.9}As/Al_{0.3}Ga_{0.7}As$ well as shown in Figure 7.19. The sharp decrease in the hole curvature is quite obvious from these curves. As the In content is increased and the strain builds up, the near bandedge masses can decrease by up to a factor of 3.

It is interesting to note that the degeneracy lifting produced by quantum confinement of HH and LH states can be restored if the well is under tensile strain. This is illustrated schematically in Figure 7.20 along with the hole in-plane dispersion curves. The density of hole states becomes extremely large in this case with important implications for optical devices. Figure 7.20 also shows the high in-plane hole masses for a $GaAs/In_{0.06}Ga_{0.57}Al_{0.37}As$ 150 Å quantum well where the tensile strain has merged the HH and LH bands.

It is quite evident from the discussions in this section that strain can significantly affect the bandstructure of semiconductors. The level of strain we have considered can be incorporated in the semiconductor reasonably easily through strained epitaxy. Degeneracy splittings in the valence band can be of the order of 100 meV, accompanied by large changes in band curvatures. It is important to appreciate that such large uniaxial strains are extremely difficult to obtain by external apparatus. It is important to identify whether or not the changes

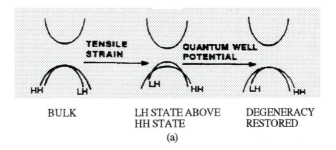

BULK   LH STATE ABOVE   DEGENERACY
            HH STATE   RESTORED

(a)

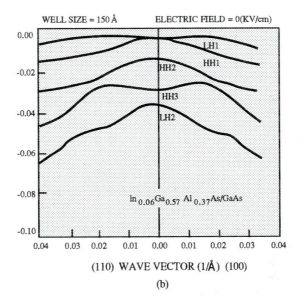

(110) WAVE VECTOR (1/Å) (100)

(b)

Figure 7.20: Effect of biaxial tensile strain: (a) schematic of the effect of biaxial strain and quantum confinement on conduction and valence band states; (b) hole dispersion relations for GaAs/In$_{0.06}$Ga$_{0.57}$Al$_{0.37}$As 150 Å quantum well with degenerate heavy and light hole states.

produced by the strain have any impact on the physical properties of the semiconductors. These consequences will be explored later in the chapters on transport and optical properties. The effects are, indeed, found to be significant.

The changes in the bandstructure have several implications for devices. We will discuss two important ones here postponing other implications to the chapters on transport and exciton physics.

7.6   BANDGAP ALTERATION

We discussed earlier how the bandedges of semiconductors respond to the strain tensor. The controlled variation in the bandgap was the first motivation for strained epitaxy. A great deal of theoretical and experimental effort has carried out to establish the value of strain for bandgap tailoring. Pioneering effort in this area has been conducted at the Sandia Labs where the initial work on utilizing strain to control bandgap was carried out by Osbourn and co-workers.

To obtain complete flexibility in semiconductor combinations that could be exploited for tailoring bandgap, most of the strained detector work has used the *intermediate buffer concept*. In this scheme one starts with the best available substrate material, and grows on it a thick (several micron) buffer of a composition which has the *average* lattice constant of the active heterostructure to be grown later. The buffer is much thicker than the critical thickness and a network of dislocations is generated. The art and science of the crystal growth is to localize the dislocations near the buffer-substrate region, so that the buffer surface is free of defects. Now when the active region is grown, the buffer acts as a substrate with a lattice constant which is the weighted average of two semiconductors which form the active heterostructure. In this concept, the two semiconductors are alternately in compression and tension. A very large range of bandgaps can be reached by such techniques. Two examples are shown in Figures 7.21 and 7.22, displaying the great flexibility in band tailoring.

In Figure 7.21, we show the calculated bandgap as a function of lattice constant for $GaAs_xP_{1-x}/GaAs_yP_{1-y}$ *strained layer superlattices* obtained by varying layer thicknesses and composition. If one were to use the *unstrained* bulk GaAsP, only the upper bound of the shaded area would be achievable. Similar results for $In_xGa_{1-x}As/In_yGa_{1-y}As$ structures are shown in Figure 7.22. Numerous experimental results have verified such predictions and it is quite clear that strain can play an important role in detector technology. The problems that still need to be overcome from a technological point of view relate to the generation and control of dislocations.

7.7   BUILT-IN ELECTRIC FIELDS IN STRAINED QUANTUM WELLS

As we have seen in Figure 7.7, for (100) growth, pseudomorphic epitaxy produces a strain tensor which is diagonal. However, the other directions can have off-diagonal shear terms. Semiconductors which do not have inversion symmetry (e.g. compound semiconductors) respond to shear strain by producing a dipole of charge which leads to an electric field. Thus, in pseudomorphic epitaxy, one can have strong built-in fields which can be used for a number of device applications.

The general polarization developed due to strain is given by

$$P_i = \sum_{k,l} e_{ikl}\, s_{kl}. \qquad (7.80)$$

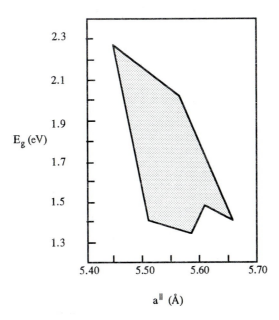

Figure 7.21: Calculated range of bandgaps vs. lattice constant for $GaAs_xP_{1-x}$ /$GaAs_yP_{1-y}$ (100) strained-layer superlattices obtained by varying layer thicknesses and layer compositions. The obtainable gaps are contained in the shaded area. The upper bound of this area coincides with the gap vs. lattice constant curve for bulk GaAsP. (From Osbourn, 1983.)

It was shown by Nye (1957) that for zinc–blende structures, only one piezo-electric constant exists and in the reduced representation ($xx \Rightarrow 1$; $yy \Rightarrow 2$; $zz \Rightarrow 3$; $yz \Rightarrow 4$; $zx \Rightarrow 5$; $xy \Rightarrow 6$;), e_{ikl} can be written as e_{im}(m = 1 to 6). The nonzero piezoelectric coefficients are

$$e_{14} = e_{25} = e_{36}. \tag{7.81}$$

Thus, only for shear strain does one have a finite polarization. For (111) growth of strained layers, one thus gets a strong dipole moment across a quantum well producing an electric field profile as shown in Figure 7.23, as was pointed out by Mailhiot and Smith (1987). The electric field is given by the equation

$$F = \sqrt{3}\frac{4\pi e_{14}\epsilon_{xy}}{\epsilon_s} \text{ esu / cm}$$

or

$$F = \sqrt{3}\frac{e_{14}\epsilon_{xy}}{\epsilon_0\epsilon_s} \text{ V/m} \tag{7.82}$$

where e_{14} is the piezoelectric coefficient (usually in the range of ~ 0.1 C/m^2), ϵ_{xy} is the off-diagonal strain component (see Figure 7.7), and ϵ_s is the dielectric constant of the semiconductor. A straightforward evaluation shows that a strain

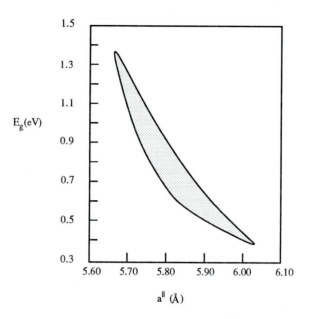

Figure 7.22: Calculated range of bandgaps vs. lattice constant for $In_x Ga_{1-x} As$ /$In_y Ga_{1-y} As$(100) strained-layer superlattices obtained by varying the layer thicknesses and layer compositions. The obtainable gaps are contained in the shaded area. The upper bound of this area coincides with the gap vs. lattice constant curve for bulk InGaAs. (from Osbourn (1983)).

ϵ_{xy} of about 1% can easily produce an electric field of the range 10^5 V/cm. This strong built-in electric field can have numerous applications ranging from optoelectronic modulators to electronic devices (see Laurich et al, 1989).

7.8   FOR THE TECHNOLOGIST IN YOU

Since the 1980s, as strained epitaxy has become reliable, there has been an increasing interest in incorporating strain in active semiconductor devices. Semiconductor lasers have particularly benefitted from this, as the strain can dramatically modify valence bandstructure and allow the "inversion" needed for lasing at low current injection. This results in low threshold lasers. Additionally, the emission frequency can be tuned since stain offers another tunable parameter.

High frequency microwave devices have also benefitted, indirectly, from the incorporation of strain. For example, $In_x Ga_{0.47-x} As$ (on GaAs substrates) and $In_{0.53+x} Ga_{1-x} As$ (on InP substrates) provide high mobility channels for transistors. In these devices, the strain does not play a direct role. The improvements come from the high indium content of the channel and its smaller bandgap. However, the ability to grow high quality strained layers has allowed the use of high indium content, low bandgap materials in these devices.

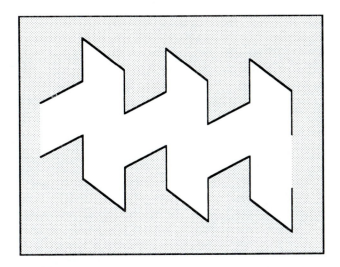

Figure 7.23: Since the strain tensor in (111) growth has nondiagonal shear components, in materials with lack of inversion symmetry strong built-in fields are generated. Here we show a schematic of such fields in a quantum well structure where the well and barrier are under opposite strain.

Strain has also been used in detectors, particularly in long wavelength infra-red detectors. However, the material problems have not been completely overcome, yet. The main reason is that, while in lasers or modulation doped field effect transistors (MODFETs), the strained region is ≤ 100 Å, in detectors, the active regions have to be a few microns thick, requiring much greater care and material control.

When strained layer devices were initially studied, there was considerable apprehension in regard to the device reliability and lifetime. Careful studies now seem to suggest that, provided the strained regions are not above the thickness where dislocation generation is favored (critical thickness), there is no problem with reliability. In the case of strained lasers, it even appears that the device lifetime improves, as strain appears to "repel" defects from the active device region.

The effect of strain on the electronic properties of materials was used for pressure sensing devices long before pseudomorphic devices and strained epitaxy came into the scene. Here, the strain is mechanically induced on the device by the environment being sensed. These sensors form an important class of devices with numerous applications in automotive engineering, medical science, and other fields.

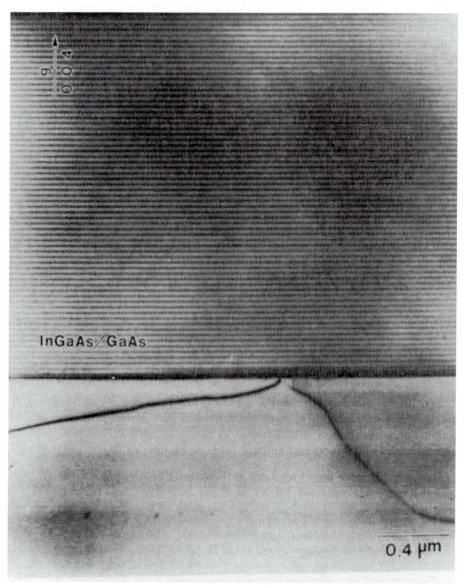

Figure 7.24: Cross-sectional transmission electron microscopy (TEM) micrograph of an $In_{0.07}Ga_{0.97}As/GaAs$ multiquantum well (MQW) structure.

7.9 PROBLEMS

7.1. Consider the (001) strained epitaxy of $In_xGa_{1-x}As$ on GaAs. The mismatch between InAs and GaAs is 7% (InAs has a larger lattice constant). Given the constraint that no dislocations are produced, i.e.

$$\epsilon_{xx} = \epsilon_{yy} = \epsilon_\|,$$

show that the minimum energy of the epitaxial overlayer occurs when

$$\epsilon_{zz} = -\frac{2c_{12}}{c_{11}}\epsilon_\|.$$

Hint: Off diagonal terms are zero.

7.2. Calculate the elastic strain energy stored per unit cell when $In_{0.2}Ga_{0.8}As$ is grown pseudomorphically on a GaAs substrate along the (001) direction. Compare it to the bond strength of semiconductors of ~ 1 eV.

7.3. Using the deformation potentials provided in Appendix L, calculate the splitting of the 6-fold degenerate X-valleys when $Ge_{0.2}Si_{0.8}$ is grown on a (001) Si substrate pseudomorphically.

7.4. Calculate the splitting between the heavy hole and light hole states at the zone edge when $In_{0.2}Ga_{0.8}As$ is grown lattice matched to GaAs.

7.5. Consider a 100 Å $GaAsP/Al_{0.3}Ga_{0.7}As$ quantum well. At what composition of P will be zone center heavy hole and light hole states merge?

7.6. Consider a 100 Å $In_xGa_{1-x}As/Al_{0.3}GA_{0.7}As$ (001) quantum well structure. Calculate the heavy hole effective mass near the zone edge along the (100) and (110) direction as x goes from 0 to 0.3, by solving the Kohn–Luttinger equation. You may write the Kohn–Luttinger equation in the difference form and solve it by calling a matrix solving subroutine from your computer library.

7.7. The piezoelectric constant e_{14} for several semiconductors are listed below (after Adachi, J. Appl. Phys., **58**, (Aug. 1985)):

Material	e_{14} (C/m^2)
AlAs	-0.23
GaAs	-0.16
GaSb	-0.13
GaP	-0.10
InAs	-0.05
InP	-0.04

Plot the electric field profile when a 100 Å /100 Å $GaAs/In_{0.2}Ga_{0.8}As$ multiquantum well structure is grown on a (111) GaAs substrate. You can use the weighted average of e_{14} for the alloy.

7.10   REFERENCES

- **Strain in Materials: General**

  - Kittel, C., *Introduction to Solid State Physics* (John Wiley and Sons, New York, 1971), 4th edition. New editions of this book do not have a chapter on this subject.

  - Huntington, H. B., *Elastic Constants of Crystals* Sol. St. Phys., **7**, 213 (1958).

  - Nye, J. F., *Physical Properties of Crystals: Their Representation by Tensors and Matrices* (Clarendon Press, Oxford, 1957).

- **Strain Tensor in Lattice Mismatched Epitaxy**

  - Hinckley J. M. and J. Singh, Phys Rev. B, **42**, 3546 (1990).

  - Osbourn,G.C., J. Appl. Phys., **53**, 1586 (1982).

- **Deformation Potential Theory**

  - Hinckley, J. M., *The Effect of Strain in Pseudomorphic p-$Si_{1-x}Ge_x$: Physics and Modelling of the Valence Bandstructure and Hole Transport*, Ph.D. Thesis, (The University of Michigan, Ann Arbor, 1990).

  - Picus, G. E. and G. E. Bir, Sov. Phys. Sol. St., **1**, 1502 (1959).

  - Picus, G. L. and G. E. Bir, *Symmetry and Strain Induced Effects in Semiconductors* (John Wiley and Sons, New York, 1974).

- **Bandstructure Modification by Epitaxially Produced Strain**

  - Hinckley, J. M., *The Effect of Strain in Pseudomorphic p-$Si_{1-x}Ge_x$: Physics and Modelling of the Valence Bandstructure and Hole Transport*, Ph.D. Thesis, (The University of Michigan, Ann Arbor, 1990).

  - Hinckley, J. M. and J. Singh, Phys. Rev. B, **42**, 3546 (1990).

  - Jaffe, M. D., *Studies of the Electronic Properties and Applications of Coherently Strained Semiconductors*, Ph.D. Thesis, (The University of Michigan, Ann Arbor 1989).

  - Kato, H., N. Iguchi, S. Chika, M. Nakayama, and N. Sano, Jap. J . Appl. Phys., **25**, 1327 (1986).

  - Laurich, B. K., K. Elcess, C. G. Fonstad, J. G. Berry, C. Mailhiot and D. L. Smith, Phys. Rev. Lett., **62**, 649 (1989).

  - Mailhiot, C. and D. L. Smith, J. Vac. Sci. Technol. A, **5**, 2060 (1987).

  - Mailhiot, C. and D. L. Smith, Phys. Rev. B, **35**, 1242 (1987).

  - O'Reilly, E. P., Semicond. Sci. Technol., **4**, 121 (1989).

  - Osbourn, G. C., J. Appl. Phys., **53**, 1586 (1982).

– Osbourn, G. C., J. Vac. Sci. Technol. B, **1**, 379 (1983).

– Osbourn, G. C., J. Vac. Sci. Technol. B, **3**, 1586 (1985).

– People, R., IEEE J. Quant. Electron., **QE–22**, 1696 (1986).

CHAPTER
8

DOPING OF
SEMICONDUCTORS

We discussed in the previous chapters that a semiconductor is characterized by the fact that at zero degrees Kelvin, the valence band is completely occupied while the conduction band is completely empty. We also showed that a completely full band does not conduct charge. Thus, at low temperatures the pure semiconductor offers an extremely high resistance to current transport. As the temperature is raised, the Fermi distribution function smears out as discussed in Chapter 1, and some electrons are emitted from the valence band into the conduction band. When this happens, there are electrons in the conduction band and holes in the valence band which can carry current. However, such current-carrying electrons produced by raising the temperature are known as intrinsic carriers, and are not useful in semiconductor devices and often are a nuisance. The intrinsic carriers often are a source of limitation for high temperature operation of devices, since they cannot be controlled effectively by electric fields.

A controllable manner of introducing carriers into semiconductors is called "doping." Doping allows one to vary the electron concentration over a very large range (say from 10^{14}cm^{-3} to 10^{20}cm^{-3}) thus altering the conductivity also over a similarly large range. The carrier concentration can also be varied spatially quite accurately, thus producing p–n junctions and built in electric fields. Essentially all electronic devices, from switches and memories to semiconductor lasers, incorporate dopants as a crucial ingredient of the device structure. In this chapter we will study the physics behind dopants in both bulk semiconductors and quantum well structures.

8.1 INTRINSIC CARRIER CONCENTRATION

The intrinsic carrier concentration refers to the electrons (holes) present in the conduction band (valence band) of a pure semiconductor. The intrinsic carrier concentration depends upon the bandgap and temperature as well as the details of the bandedge masses. We will assume that the bandedge density of states for electrons and holes originate from parabolic E vs. k relationships.

The concentration of electrons in the conduction band is

$$n_c = \int_{E_c}^{\infty} N_e(E)\, f(E)\, dE \tag{8.1}$$

where $N_e(E)$ is the electron density of states near the conduction bandedge and $f(E)$ is the Fermi function. Using appropriate expressions for N_e and f we get, for a 3-D system

$$n_c = \frac{1}{2\pi^2} \left(\frac{2m_e}{\hbar^2} \right)^{3/2} \int_{E_c}^{\infty} \frac{(E - E_c)^{1/2}\, dE}{\exp\left(\frac{E-\mu}{k_B T} \right) + 1}. \tag{8.2}$$

If the chemical potential is far from the bandedge, then the unity in the denominator can be neglected. This approximation is valid when n is small ($\leq 10^{16} \text{cm}^{-3}$ for most semiconductors), and is usually valid for intrinsic concentrations. Then we get

$$
\begin{aligned}
n_c &= \frac{1}{2\pi^2} \left(\frac{2m_e}{\hbar^2} \right)^{3/2} \exp\left(\frac{\mu}{k_B T} \right) \int_{E_c}^{\infty} (E - E_c)^{1/2} \exp\left(-E/k_B T \right) dE \\
&= 2 \left(\frac{m_e k_B T}{2\pi\hbar^2} \right)^{3/2} \exp\left[(\mu - E_c)/k_B T \right] \\
&= N_c \exp\left[(\mu - E_c)/k_B T \right]
\end{aligned}
\tag{8.3}
$$

where N_c is known as the effective density of states at the conduction bandedge.

The carrier concentration is known *when μ is calculated*. To find the intrinsic carrier concentration, this requires finding the hole concentration p as well.

The hole distribution function f_h is given by

$$
\begin{aligned}
f_h &= 1 - f_e \\
&= 1 - \frac{1}{\exp\left(\frac{E-\mu}{k_B T} \right) + 1} \\
&= \frac{1}{\exp\left[\frac{(\mu - E)}{k_B T} \right] + 1} \\
&\approx \exp\left[\frac{(E - \mu)}{k_B T} \right].
\end{aligned}
\tag{8.4}
$$

The approximation is again based on our assumption that $\mu - E \gg k_B T$, which is a good approximation for pure semiconductors. Carrying out the mathematics similar to that for electrons, we find that

$$
\begin{aligned}
p_v &= 2 \left(\frac{m_h k_B T}{2\pi\hbar^2} \right)^{3/2} \exp\left[(E_v - \mu)/k_B T \right] \\
&= N_v \exp\left[(E_v - \mu)/k_B T \right]
\end{aligned}
\tag{8.5}
$$

where N_v is the effective density of states for the valence bandedge.

In intrinsic semiconductors, the electron concentration is equal to the hole concentration. If we multiply the electron and hole concentrations, we get

$$n_c p_v = 4 \left(\frac{k_B T}{2\pi\hbar^2} \right)^3 (m_e m_h)^{3/2} \exp\left(-E_g/k_B T\right) \tag{8.6}$$

and since for the intrinsic case $n_i = p_i$ (denoting $n_c = n_i$, $p_v = p_i$ for the intrinsic case),

$$
\begin{aligned}
n_i &= p_i \\
&= 2 \left(\frac{k_B T}{2\pi\hbar^2} \right)^{3/2} (m_e m_h)^{3/4} \exp\left(-E_g/2k_B T\right).
\end{aligned}
\tag{8.7}
$$

If we set $n = p$ we also obtain the chemical potential

$$\exp(2\mu/k_B T) = (m_h/m_e)^{3/2} \exp\left(E_g/k_B T\right) \tag{8.8}$$

or

$$\mu = \frac{1}{2} E_g + \frac{3}{4} k_B T \, \ln\left(m_h/m_e\right). \tag{8.9}$$

Thus, the chemical potential of an intrinsic material lies close to the midgap.

In the expression above, it is important to note that the relevant masses are the density of states masses. For an ellipsoidal energy surface, (e.g. conduction band of Si or Ge) the density of states mass is

$$m_{\mathrm{de}} = (m_1 m_2 m_3)^{1/3} \tag{8.10}$$

where m_1, m_2, m_3 are the masses along the principle axes. In addition, the total density of states is M_c times the density of states obtained from the above mass, where M_c is the number of valleys at the bandedge (6 in silicon).

For holes where one has the light hole, heavy hole degeneracy, the density of states mass to be used is (the degeneracy is included)

$$m_{\mathrm{dh}} = (m_{lh}^{3/2} + m_{hh}^{3/2})^{2/3} \tag{8.11}$$

where $m_{lh}^{3/2}$ and $m_{hh}^{3/2}$ are the light hole and heavy hole masses.

We note that the carrier concentration increases exponentially as the bandgap decreases. Results for the intrinsic carrier concentrations for some semiconductors are shown in Figure 8.1. The presence of intrinsic carriers is detrimental to devices where current has to be modulated by some means. The concentration of intrinsic carriers is fixed by the temperature and therefore these carriers are detrimental to device performance. Once the intrinsic carrier concentration increases to $\sim 10^{15} \mathrm{cm}^{-3}$, the material becomes unsuitable for electronic devices. A growing interest in high bandgap semiconductors such as diamond (C), SiC, etc.,

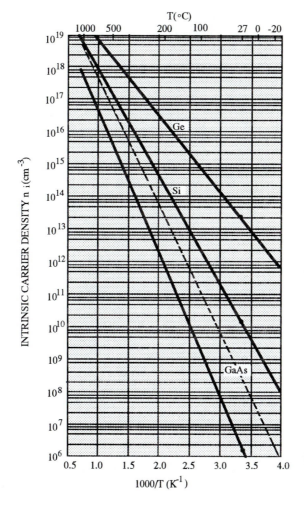

Figure 8.1: Intrinsic carrier densities of Ge, Si, and GaAs as a function of reciprocal temperature. (After Thurmond, 1975.)

is partly due to the potential applications of these materials for high temperature devices, where due to their larger gap, the intrinsic carrier concentration remains low up to very high temperatures.

We note that the product np calculated above is independent of the chemical potential μ. This is an expression of the law of mass action. This result is valid not only for the intrinsic case but also when we have dopants. The assumption made for the particular derivation simply required that μ is far from the band-edges. At room temperature, the np product is $2.1 \times 10^{19} \text{cm}^{-6}$, $2.89 \times 10^{26} \text{cm}^{-6}$, and $6.55 \times 10^{12} \text{cm}^{-6}$ for Si, Ge, and GaAs respectively.

The fact that the np product is constant at a given temperature is often utilized to produce high resistive (insulating) materials from impure semiconductors. Consider, for example, impure GaAs with $n = 10^{16} \text{cm}^{-3}$ and $p = 10^5 \text{cm}^{-3}$ giving a total free carrier density $n + p = 10^{16} \text{cm}^{-3}$, and an np value of 10^{21}cm^{-3} (e.g., at 180° C). If the p-type carrier concentration is now increased (by doping) to 10^{10}cm^{-3}, the $n + p$ value becomes $\sim 3 \times 10^{10} \text{cm}^{-3}$ since np product must remain the same. This greatly reduces the material conductivity. This technique is called compensation. It must be remembered, of course, that the np product is constant only when the system is *in equilibrium.*

It is quite clear from the discussion above that pure semiconductors have a very low concentration of carriers that can conduct current. One must compare the room temperature concentrations of $\sim 10^{11} \text{cm}^{-3}$ to the carrier concentrations of $\sim 10^{21} \text{cm}^{-3}$ for metals. Indeed, pure semiconductors would have little use by themselves. It was observed experimentally in the 1920s that the conductivity of semiconductors could change by several orders of magnitude if the semiconductor had some impurities. For some time these "impure" materials were looked upon with disdain by solid state physicists till the theory behind doping was understood. Now, of course, doping is exploited as the most versatile technique to modify the properties of semiconductors. The physics behind dopants can be understood on the basis of the simple effective mass theory. We will first introduce the physics behind the effective mass theory according to which, for certain physical phenomenon, it is sufficient to forget about the full crystal bandstructure by simply representing the crystal by a bandedge effective mass.

8.2   THE EFFECTIVE MASS EQUATION FOR SHALLOW LEVELS

When a dopant (impurity) atom is introduced in a crystal, the perfect periodicity of the crystal is destroyed. At a particular atomic site the background potential of the host lattice is replaced by the potential of the impurity. Under certain conditions the problem of the electronic levels associated with the impurity can be greatly simplified. This simplification results in the levels associated with dopants to be described by a simple hydrogen atom-like problem. We will now derive the conditions under which this is possible. The problem we wish to address can be written in the form

$$[H_0 + V] \psi(\boldsymbol{r}) = E_I \psi(\boldsymbol{r}) \tag{8.12}$$

where H_0 is the Hamiltonian associated with the perfect crystal and V is the potential energy distortion due to the impurity. We assume that we know the solution of the perfect crystal Hamiltonian.

$$H_0 \phi_{\boldsymbol{k}\ell} = E_\ell(\boldsymbol{k}) \phi_{\boldsymbol{k}\ell} \tag{8.13}$$

where ℓ is the band index and

$$\phi_{\boldsymbol{k}\ell} = u_{\boldsymbol{k}\ell}(\boldsymbol{r}) e^{i\boldsymbol{k}\cdot\boldsymbol{r}}. \tag{8.14}$$

We will assume that the band is not degenerate. The impurity potential wavefunction can, in general, be written in terms of the Bloch functions using expansion coefficients $C_{\mathbf{k}'\ell}$

$$\psi(\mathbf{r}) = \sum_{\mathbf{k}'\ell'} C_{\mathbf{k}'\ell'} \, \phi_{\mathbf{k}'\ell'}. \tag{8.15}$$

This solution is substituted in the impurity problem and we take a scalar product with $\phi^*_{\mathbf{k}\ell}$ to get the secular equation

$$E_\ell C_{\mathbf{k}\ell} + \sum_{\mathbf{k}'\ell'} C_{\mathbf{k}'\ell'} \, \langle \phi_{\mathbf{k}\ell} | V | \phi_{\mathbf{k}'\ell'} \rangle = E_I C_{\mathbf{k}\ell}. \tag{8.16}$$

We now write the impurity potential in a Fourier series

$$V = \sum_{\mathbf{q}} V_{\mathbf{q}} \, e^{i \mathbf{q} \cdot \mathbf{r}}. \tag{8.17}$$

The matrix element of V then becomes

$$\langle \phi_{\mathbf{k}\ell} | V | \phi_{\mathbf{k}'\ell'} \rangle = \sum_{\mathbf{q}} V_{\mathbf{q}} \int d^3r \, e^{i\left(\mathbf{k}'-\mathbf{k}+\mathbf{q}\right)\cdot \mathbf{r}} \, u^*_{\mathbf{k}\ell} \, u_{\mathbf{k}'\ell'}. \tag{8.18}$$

Since $u^*_{\mathbf{k}\ell} \, u_{\mathbf{k}'\ell'}$ is periodic in the direct lattice, the integral vanishes unless

$$\mathbf{k} = \mathbf{k}' + \mathbf{q} + \mathbf{G} \tag{8.19}$$

where $\mathbf{G}$ is a reciprocal lattice vector. We will be dealing with small values of $\mathbf{k}$, $\mathbf{k}'$, and $\mathbf{q}$ so that only $\mathbf{G} = 0$ will be included in the matrix element. The assumption of small values of $\mathbf{q}$, $\mathbf{k}$, $\mathbf{k}'$ are due to the assumed long-range nature of the potential V and the wavefunction ψ. Thus, this approach is not valid for short-range potentials.

The secular equation then becomes

$$E_\ell \, C_{\mathbf{k}\ell} + \sum_{\mathbf{q}\ell'} V_{\mathbf{q}} \int d^3r \, u^*_{\mathbf{k}\ell} \, u_{\mathbf{k}-\mathbf{q},\ell'} \, C_{\mathbf{k}-\mathbf{q}} = E_I \, C_{\mathbf{k}\ell}. \tag{8.20}$$

We call the integral over the central cell $\Delta^{\ell\ell'}_{\mathbf{k}-\mathbf{q},\mathbf{k}}$. We know that as $|\mathbf{q}| \to 0$

$$\Delta^{\ell\ell'}_{\mathbf{k}-\mathbf{q},\mathbf{k}} \to \delta_{\ell\ell'}. \tag{8.21}$$

In the limit of $\mathbf{q} \to 0$ the secular equation becomes

$$E_\ell(\mathbf{k}) \, C_{\mathbf{k}\ell} + \sum_{\mathbf{q}} V_{\mathbf{q}} \, C_{\mathbf{k}-\mathbf{q},\ell} = E_I \, C_{\mathbf{k}\ell}. \tag{8.22}$$

The chief approximation in this analysis is the assumption $\Delta^{\ell\ell'}_{\mathbf{k}-\mathbf{q},\mathbf{k}} \to \delta_{\ell\ell'}$. This assumption allows us to write the secular equation for a single band with *no coupling to other bands.* If the secular equation is transformed to real-space and we define

$$F_\ell(r) = \sum_k e^{ik \cdot r} \, C_{k\ell} \tag{8.23}$$

the real space equation for $F_\ell(r)$ is

$$[E_\ell + V(r)] \, F_\ell(r) = E_I F_\ell(r). \tag{8.24}$$

If this equation is solved for $F_\ell(r)$, the expansion coefficients $C_{k\ell}$ can be obtained as

$$C_{k\ell} = \int d^3r \, e^{-ik \cdot r} \, F_\ell(r) \tag{8.25}$$

and the impurity wavefunction becomes

$$\psi_\ell(r) = \sum_k \phi_{k\ell}(r) \int d^3r' \, F_\ell(r') \, e^{-ik \cdot r'}. \tag{8.26}$$

If we assume that the central cell part of the Bloch function does not depend much on k over the range of k which are significant in the solution, then we can write

$$u_{k\ell} \approx u_{0\ell} \tag{8.27}$$

and

$$\begin{aligned}
\psi_\ell(r) &= u_{0\ell}(r) \int d^3r' \, F_\ell(r') \sum_k e^{ik \cdot (r-r')} \\
&= u_{0\ell}(r) \, F_\ell(r)
\end{aligned} \tag{8.28}$$

since

$$\sum_k e^{ik \cdot (r-r')} = \delta(r - r'). \tag{8.29}$$

In this derivation we have assumed that there is no interband coupling. This is a good approximation for impurity levels which are weakly bound, i.e., which are near bandedges.

To solve the donor (or acceptor problem) within this approximation, we consider a donor atom on a crystal lattice site. The donor atom could be a pentavalent atom in silicon or a Si atom on a Ga site in GaAs. Focusing on the pentavalent atom in Si, four of the valence electrons of the donor atom behave as they would in a Si atom, the remaining fifth electron now sees a positively charged ion to which it is attracted as shown in Figure 8.2. The ion has a charge of unity and the attraction is simply a Coulombic attraction suppressed by the dielectric constant of the material.

Using

$$V(r) = \frac{e^2}{\epsilon r} \tag{8.30}$$

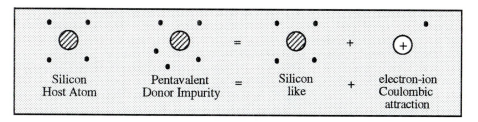

Figure 8.2: A schematic showing the approach one takes to understand donors in semiconductors. The donor problem is treated as the host atom problem together with a Coulombic interaction term.

and

$$E_\ell(\boldsymbol{k}) \equiv E_\ell + \frac{\hbar^2}{2m^*}k^2$$

$$\equiv \frac{-\hbar^2}{2m_\ell^*}\nabla^2 + E_\ell \tag{8.31}$$

we get the effective mass equation for the donor level

$$\left[\frac{-\hbar^2}{2m_\ell^*}\nabla^2 + \frac{e^2}{\epsilon r}\right]F_\ell(\boldsymbol{r}) = (E_I - E_\ell)\,F_\ell(\boldsymbol{r}). \tag{8.32}$$

This equation will be considered for the *conduction bandedge* since this is the only band which produces a level in the bandgap region.

This equation is now essentially the same as an electron in the hydrogen atom problem. The only difference is that the electron mass is m^* and the Coulombic potential is reduced by $1/\epsilon$.

The energy solutions for this problem are

$$E_I = E_d$$

$$= E_c - \frac{e^4 m^*}{2\epsilon^2 \hbar^2}\frac{1}{n^2},\ n = 1, 2, 3, \dots. \tag{8.33}$$

A series of energy levels are produced, with the ground state energy level being at

$$E_d = E_c - \frac{e^4 m^*}{2\epsilon^2 \hbar^2}. \tag{8.34}$$

Note: In MKS units, the equation for the donor binding energy is

$$E_d = E_c - \frac{e^4 m^*}{2(4\pi\epsilon_0)^2 \epsilon^2 \hbar^2}.$$

Since

$$\frac{e^4 m}{2\hbar^2} = 13.6 \text{ eV}.$$

$$E_d = E_c - 13.6\left(\frac{m^*}{\epsilon^2 m}\right) \text{ eV} \tag{8.35}$$

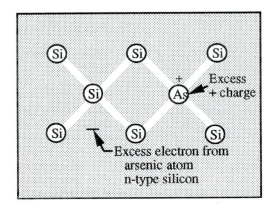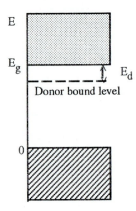

Figure 8.3: Charges associated with an arsenic impurity atom in silicon. Arsenic has five valence electrons, but silicon has only four valence electrons. Thus, four electrons on the arsenic form tetrahedral covalent bonds similar to silicon, and the fifth electron is available for conduction. The arsenic atom is called a donor because when ionized it donates an electron to the conduction band.

The ground state is schematically shown in Figure 8.3 and the values of the donor energy are shown for some conductors in Table 8.1.

The wavefunction of the ground state is

$$F_c(\boldsymbol{r}) = \frac{1}{\sqrt{\pi a^3}} e^{-r/a} \tag{8.36}$$

where a is the donor Bohr radius and is given by

$$
\begin{aligned}
a &= \frac{\epsilon \hbar^2}{m_l^* e^2} \\
&= 0.53 \frac{\epsilon}{(m^*/m)} \text{ Å}. \tag{8.37}
\end{aligned}
$$

For most semiconductors the donor energies are a few meV's below the conduction bandedge and the Bohr radius is $\sim$100 Å.

The effective mass that is to be used in the expressions above is the conductivity or constant energy surface effective mass. For direct bandgap materials like GaAs, this is simply the effective mass. For materials like Si the mass is

$$m^* = 3 \left(\frac{2}{m_t^*} + \frac{1}{m_l^*} \right)^{-1} \tag{8.38}$$

According to the simple picture of the donor impurity discussed above, the donor energy levels depend only upon the host crystal (through E and m^*) and *not* on the nature of the dopant. According to Equation 8.35, the donor energies for Ge, Si and GaAs should be 0.006 eV, 0.025 eV, and 0.007 eV, respectively.

Material	Impurity (Donor)	Shallow Donor. Energy (meV).	Impurity (Acceptor)	Shallow Acceptor Energy (meV)	
GaAs	Si	5.8	C	26	
	Ge	6.0	Be	28	
	S	6.0	Mg	28	
	Sn	6.0	Si	35	
Si	Li	33.	B	45	
	Sb	39.	Al	67	
	P	45.	Ga	72	
	As	54.	In	160	
Ge	Li	9.3	B	10	
	Sb	9.6	Al	10	
	P	12.	Ga	11	
	As	13.	In	11	

Table 8.1: Shallow level energies in some semiconductors.

However, as can be seen from Table 8.1, there is a small deviation from these numbers, depending upon the nature of the dopant. This difference occurs because the real impurity potential perturbation (Figure 8.4) is not simply the Coulombic potential as assumed by us, but has a central cell short-range correction which depends upon the dopant impurity atom. More accurate theories for the donor levels include this potential to get a better agreement with the experiments.

Another important class of intentional impurities are the acceptors. Just as donors are defect levels which are neutral when an electron occupies the defect level and positively charged when unoccupied, the acceptors are neutral when empty and negatively charged when occupied by an electron. The acceptor levels are produced when impurities which have a similar core potential as the atoms in the host lattice but have one less electron in the outermost shell. Thus, group III elements can form acceptors in Si or Ge, while Si could be an acceptor if it replaces As in GaAs. An example is shown for B in Si in Figure 8.5.

The acceptor impurity potential could now be considered to be equivalent to a host atom potential together with a *negatively* charged Coulombic potential. The "hole" (i.e., the absence of an electron) can then bind to the acceptor potential. The effective mass equation can again be used since only the bands at the top of the valence band are of interest in the shallow acceptor level problem. However, in this case one cannot use the scalar Schrödinger equation to describe the valence bandedge accurately. As we discussed in the $k \cdot p$ method discussions of Chapter 5, the Schrödinger equation becomes

$$[H_0 + V(r)] \Psi = E_I \Psi \tag{8.39}$$

where H_0 could be, for example, the 4x4 Kohn–Luttinger representation of the

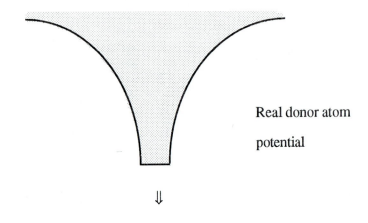

Real donor atom

potential

$\Downarrow$

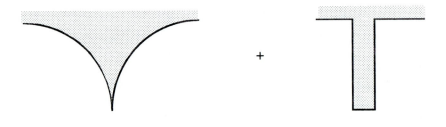

Coulombic potential

$$V(r) = \frac{-e^2}{\epsilon\, r}$$

central cell correction,

dependent upon the impurity

Figure 8.4: The real donor potential is not simply a Coulombic interaction, but consists of a short-range central cell correction. The central cell correction can cause serious corrections for some impurities.

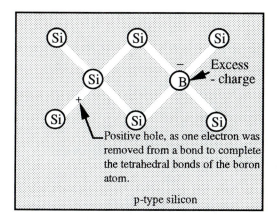
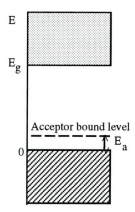

Figure 8.5: Boron has only three valence electrons; it can complete its tetrahedral bonds only by taking an electron from a Si-Si bond, leaving behind a hole in the silicon valence band. The positive hole is then available for conduction. The boron atom is called an acceptor because when ionized it accepts an electron from the valence band. At $T = 0$ K the hole is bound, remember that holes float.

hole states. The solution is not as straightforward as the simple scalar, isotropic "hydrogen atom" solution used for the donor states. The problem can be solved numerically or variationally. The results are usually not in very good agreement with the experiments especially when the acceptor core potential is very different from the host atom's potential. This is because of the increased importance of the central cell correction in acceptors. The Bohr radius for acceptor levels is usually a factor of 2 to 3 smaller than that for donors, and the wavefunction is quite sensitive to the details of the central cell corrections. An *approximate value* for the double degenerate acceptor level energy can be obtained by using the *heavy hole mass*.

From the discussions above, it is clear that while in group IV semiconductors, the donor- or acceptor-like nature of an impurity is well-established, in compound semiconductors, the dopants can be "amphoteric." For example, Si can act as a donor in GaAs if it replaces a Ga atom, while it can act as an acceptor if it replaces an As atom. In many compound semiconductors, "auto doping" can occur if one element replaces another. For example, in HgCdTe alloy, the replacement of a Hg or Cd atom by a Te atom can cause donor levels. The amphoteric nature of some dopants can be exploited by a clever crystal grower to produce a p–n junction by using the same dopant but changing growth conditions at the junction. Usually the doping character (say in GaAs) is determined by whether the growth conditions are "As-rich"(i.e., the surface of the growing crystal is mostly As) or "Ga-rich."

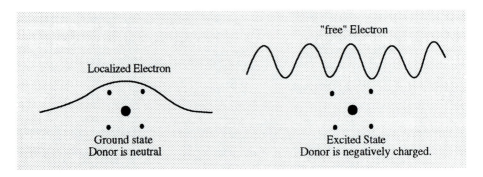

Figure 8.6: An electron band to a donor does not contribute to charge conduction. However, if the donor is "ionized," the electron becomes free and can contribute to the charge transport.

8.3   EXTRINSIC CARRIERS

In the lowest energy state of the donor atom, the extra electron of the donor is localized at the donor site. Such an electron cannot carry any current and is not useful for changing the electronic properties of the semiconductor. At very low temperatures, the donor electrons are, indeed, tied to the donor sites and this effect is called carrier freeze-out. At higher temperatures, however, the donor electron is "ionized" and resides in the conduction band as a free electron as shown in Figure 8.6. Such electrons can, of course, carry current and modify the electronic properties of the semiconductor. The ionized donor atom is negatively charged and offers a scattering center for the free electrons. We will discuss the scattering in a later chapter.

The ionization of the dopants will now be calculated, along with some expressions for extrinsic carrier properties. Because of the doping, we no longer have the equality between electrons and holes, i.e.

$$n_c - p_v = \Delta n \neq 0. \tag{8.40}$$

However, the law of mass action still holds (the value of the product changes at high doping levels as will be discussed later)

$$n_c p_v = \text{constants} = n_i^2. \tag{8.41}$$

If we eliminate p_v in these equations we get

$$n_c = \frac{1}{2}\Delta n + \frac{1}{2}(\Delta n^2 + 4n_i^2)^{1/2}. \tag{8.42}$$

Similarly, we have for the holes

$$p_v = -\frac{1}{2}\Delta n + \frac{1}{2}(\Delta n^2 + 4n_i^2)^{1/2}. \tag{8.43}$$

We also note that using the approximation that the distribution function can be replaced by a Boltzmann-like function $(f(E) = \exp(-(E - \mu)/k_B T)$ we get

$$\frac{n_c}{n_i} = e^{(\mu-\mu_i)/k_B T} \tag{8.44}$$

and

$$\frac{p_v}{n_i} = e^{-(\mu-\mu_i)/k_B T} \tag{8.45}$$

where μ is the chemical potential corresponding to the doped semiconductor. This gives us the simple equation:

$$\frac{n_c - p_v}{n_i} = \frac{\Delta n}{n_i}$$

$$= 2\sinh\left(\frac{\mu - \mu_i}{k_B T}\right). \tag{8.46}$$

8.4 POPULATION OF IMPURITY LEVELS, CARRIER FREEZE-OUT

At very low temperatures we expect all the electrons to be bound to the donor atoms, and occupying the ground state of the system. At finite temperature, the electrons will occupy higher energy states and in particular will go into the conduction band which is separated from the donor ground state by an energy E_d. The fraction of the electrons that are bound to the donors cannot be calculated by simply applying the distribution function $f(E - \mu)$ because of the multiplicity of states the electron could be in. The electron + donor system can be in one of the following states:

1. the electron is free;

2. there is one electron attached to the donor with spin up or spin down;

3. there are two electrons attached to a donor.

While in principle the latter condition is allowed, the repulsion energy for two electrons on the same donor is so large that the third condition is not allowed. Thus, two electrons each with opposite spin cannot be bound to a donor. In such cases it is useful to use the general thermodynamic expression for probability of the electrons being bound to the donor.

$$< n > = \frac{\sum_{j, N_j \neq 0} N_j e^{-(E_j - \mu N_j)/k_B T}}{\sum_{j, \text{all states}} e^{-(E_j - \mu N_j)/k_B T}} \tag{8.47}$$

The energy E_j and number of electrons in the state j are illustrated for the three different physical possibilities discussed in Figure 8.7.

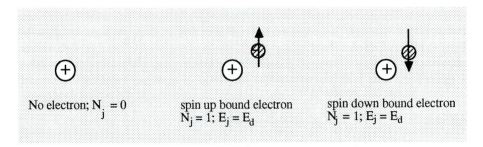

No electron; $N_j = 0$ spin up bound electron   spin down bound electron
                                $N_j = 1; E_j = E_d$ $N_j = 1; E_j = E_d$

Figure 8.7: Three possible allowed states of the donor atom + electron complex.

Using the bound state occupation for probability expression we get

$$
\begin{aligned}
<n> &= \frac{e^{-(E_d-\mu)/k_BT} + e^{-(E_d-\mu)/k_BT}}{1 + e^{-(E_d-\mu)/k_BT} + e^{-(E_d-\mu)/k_BT}} \\
&= \frac{1}{\frac{1}{2}e^{(E_d-\mu)/k_BT} + 1}
\end{aligned}
\tag{8.48}
$$

or

$$
\begin{aligned}
n_d &= \text{number density of electrons bound to the donors} \\
&= \frac{N_d}{\frac{1}{2}e^{(E_d-\mu)/k_BT} + 1} \\
&\approx 2N_d e^{-(E_d-\mu)/k_BT} \text{ for } (E_d - \mu)/k_BT \gg 1.
\end{aligned}
\tag{8.49}
$$

Here N_d is the number density of the donor energies. The number of free electrons is consequently

$$
n_c = \frac{N_d}{1 + 2e^{-(E_d-\mu)/k_BT}} \sim N_d \text{ for } (E_d - \mu)/k_BT \gg 1.
\tag{8.50}
$$

This represents the free electron density due to the donors. One has to add to this the "intrinsic" component as well. In general, one has to do the problem self-consistently so that μ is adjusted to the position where

$$
\begin{aligned}
n_{\text{free}} &= n_{\text{free}}(\text{donor}) + n_{\text{free}}(\text{intrinsic}) \\
p_{\text{free}} &= n_{\text{free}}(\text{intrinsic}) \\
n_{\text{free}}(\text{donor}) &= N_d - <n_d> .
\end{aligned}
\tag{8.51}
$$

If acceptors are also present, they have to be accounted for also in the self-consistent determination of μ. In most cases, one usually is able to make simple approximations to avoid a fully self-consistent treatment described above.

8.4.1 Ionization of Acceptor Levels

An analysis similar to the one for acceptors above gives (note that the acceptor levels are doubly degenerate since the valence band is doubly degenerate)

$$p_a = \frac{N_a}{\frac{1}{4} \exp\left(\frac{(\mu - E_a)}{k_B T}\right) + 1} \tag{8.52}$$

where p_a is the density of holes trapped at acceptor levels.

8.4.2 Equilibrium Density of Carriers in Doped Semiconductors

In general, a semiconductor will have both donors and acceptors as impurities. To find the carrier density one has to relax the constraint $n_c = p_v$ and replace it with some equation that can then be used to calculate the position of the chemical potential. Let us first examine the problem at $T = 0$, where the physical picture is quite simple. If we assume that $N_d > N_a$, then at $T = 0$, the valence band states are all free, and the N_a of the donor atoms will fall into the acceptor levels. The remaining $N_d - N_a$ of the electrons will then be bound to the donors. There are no electrons in the conduction band at $T = 0$.

At finite temperatures, the electrons will be redistributed, but their numbers will be the same. Thus, we have the equation

$$n_c + n_d = N_d - N_a + p_v + p_a \tag{8.53}$$

where

$$
\begin{aligned}
n_c &= \text{free electrons in the conduction band} \\
n_d &= \text{electrons bound to the donors} \\
p_v &= \text{free holes in the valence band} \\
p_a &= \text{holes bound to the acceptors.}
\end{aligned}
$$

This equation along with the explicit form of n_c, n_d, p_v, and p_a allow us to calculate μ at a given temperature. The general analysis requires numerical techniques, but in some cases, one can make simple approximations. The most commonly used approximation is that the donors and acceptors are ionized. In this case, which occurs when the temperature is moderately high so that the impurities ionize, but not so high that intrinsic carrier density is larger than the dopant density, we have

$$\Delta n = n_c - p_v = N_d - N_a \tag{8.54}$$

Using Equations 8.42, 8.43, and 8.46, we get

$$\left\{ \begin{array}{c} n_c \\ p_v \end{array} \right\} = \frac{1}{2} \left[(N_d - N_a)^2 + 4n_i^2 \right]^{1/2} \pm \frac{1}{2} \left[N_d - N_a \right] \tag{8.55}$$

$$\frac{N_d - N_a}{n_i} = 2\sinh\left(\frac{\mu - \mu_i}{k_B T}\right).$$ (8.56)

If $n_i \gg N_d - N_a$, i.e. if the doping levels are low or the material is compensated ($N_d \sim N_a$),

$$\left\{\begin{array}{c} n_c \\ p_v \end{array}\right\} \approx n_i \pm \frac{1}{2}(N_d - N_a)$$ (8.57)

If $n_i \ll N_d - N_a$

$$\left.\begin{array}{ccc} n_c & \approx & N_d - N_a \\ p_v & \approx & \dfrac{n_i^2}{N_d - N_a} \end{array}\right\} \quad \text{if} \quad N_d > N_a$$

$$\left.\begin{array}{ccc} n_c & \approx & \dfrac{n_i^2}{N_a - N_d} \\ p_v & \approx & N_a - N_d \end{array}\right\} \quad \text{if} \quad N_a > N_d$$ (8.58)

In general, there are three regions of interest for extrinsic semiconductors. At very low temperatures, the electrons are trapped at the donor levels and the free carrier density goes to zero. This region is called the freeze-out range (see Figure 8.8). At higher temperatures, the shallow levels are ionized and there is little change in free carrier density. This region is called the saturation range. Finally, at very high temperatures, the intrinsic carrier density exceeds the doping levels and the carrier density ($n \approx p$) increases exponentially as for an intrinsic material. The higher the bandgap, the higher the temperature where this regime takes over. As discussed earlier, electronic devices cannot operate in this regime.

8.5 HEAVILY DOPED SEMICONDUCTORS

In the theory discussed so far, we have made several important assumptions which are valid only when the doping levels are low:

1. we assumed that the bandstructure of the host crystal is not seriously perturbed and the bandedge states are still described by simple parabolic bands;

2. the dopants are assumed to be independent of each other and their potential is thus a simple Coulombic potential.

These assumptions become invalid as the doping levels become higher. The Bohr radius of the impurity states is of the order of 100 Å. Thus, when the average spacing of the impurity atoms reaches this level, the potential seen by the impurity electron is influenced by the neighboring impurities. In a sense this is like the problem of electrons in atoms. When the atoms are far apart, we get discrete atomic levels. However, when the atomic separation reaches a few Angstroms as in a crystal, we get electronic bands. At high doping levels we get impurity bands. Several other important effects occur at high doping levels. All these effects require us to abandon our simple one electron picture that has worked well for low

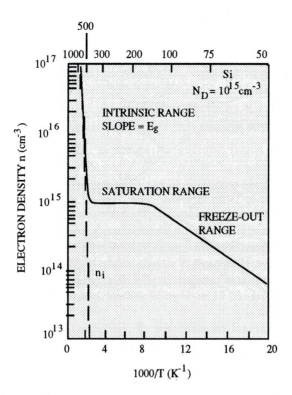

Figure 8.8: Electron density as a function of temperature for a Si sample with donor impurity concentration of $10^{15} cm^{-3}$. (Reproduced with permission, S. M. Sze, *Physics of Semiconductor Devices*, 2nd ed., John Wiley and Sons, New York, 1981.)

doping levels. The many body effects which self-consistently include the effects of other free electrons present in the three-dimensional system at high doping levels are an important area of research. This is probably so for low-dimensional systems such as quantum wells and quantum wires. We will only qualitatively summarize some of the results. For details, a series of references are listed in this chapter.

8.5.1 Screening of Impurity Potential

As the doping levels are increased, the background mobile electron density also increases. This background density adjusts itself in response to the impurity potential causing a screening of the potential. We will discuss this screening in Chapter 11, but in essence the $1/r$ long-range potential is reduced by an exponential factor in the simplest theory. This effect shown schematically in Figure 8.9 lowers the binding energy of the electron to the donor.

The reduction in the donor ionization energy causes the donor level to move toward the conduction bandedge E_c as the donor concentration is gradually

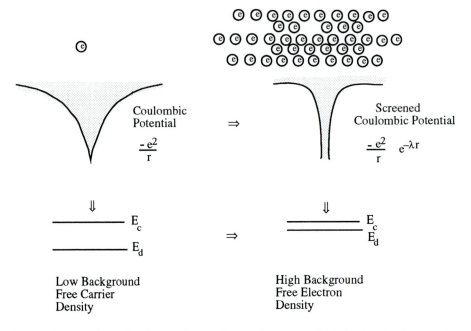

Figure 8.9: A schematic of many body effects arising from high doping levels. The free carrier affect the donor energy level E_d.

increased and ultimately merges into the conduction band. Measurements of the ionization energy of arsenic in germanium have shown that E_d can be expressed by the following empirical relation

$$E_d = E_{d0} \left[1 - (N_d/N_{\text{crit}})^{1/3} \right] \qquad (8.59)$$

where E_{d0} is the ionization energy in a lightly doped crystal and $N_{\text{crit}} = 2 \times 10^{17}$ cm^{-3} is the critical donor concentration at which the ionization energy will vanish. From the known value of $E_{d0} = 0.0127$ eV for arsenic, and using Bohr's model for an electron attached to the donor atom, it can be shown that E_d drops to zero when the average spacing between the arsenic atoms is about $3r_0$, where r_0 is the ground state Bohr radius of the electron attached to the arsenic atom. Note that the electron donor interaction causes only a shift in the donor level toward E_c, but no change occurs in the position of bandedges E_c and E_v so that the energy gap E_g remains unchanged.

8.5.2   Electron–Electron Interaction

The bandstructure calculations we discussed in earlier chapters define the position of the valence and conduction bandedges for the situation where the valence band is full and the conduction band is empty. When a large number of electrons are introduced in the conduction band (or a large number of holes in the valence band), the electrons which are Fermions interact strongly with each other.

Electron-electron interaction results on a downward shift in the conduction band edge E_c. This shift is caused by electron exchange energy which evolves from the Pauli exclusion principle. When the electron concentration in the semiconductor becomes sufficiently large, their wavefunctions begin to overlap. Consequently, the Pauli exclusion principle becomes operative, and the electrons spread their momenta in such a way that the overlapping of the individual electron wavefunctions is avoided. The Bloch states that we devised earlier are thus modified by the presence of the other electrons. In general, the electron-electron interaction can be represented by the usual Coulombic interaction and the exchange interaction. The latter comes about due to the constraint of the Pauli exclusion principle which forces any multiparticle electronic wavefunction to be antisymmetric in the exchange of two electrons. The average Coulombic energy between an electron with other electrons and with the background positive charge cancels out. The exchange term which "keeps the electrons away from each other," then lowers the energy of the system. This lowering has been studied in 3-D systems in great detail and is an area of continuing research in sub-3-D systems. For bulk GaAs the electron–electron interaction results in a lowering of the bandgap which is given by (H. Casey and F. Stern, 1976),

$$E_g = E_{g0} - 1.6 \times 10^{-8}(p^{1/3} + n^{1/3}) \text{ eV} \tag{8.60}$$

where E_{g0} is the bandgap at zero doping and n and p are the electron and hole densities. As can be seen at background charge levels of $\sim 10^{18}\text{cm}^{-3}$, the bandgap can shrink by $\sim$16 meV.

8.5.3 Band Tailing Effects

In addition to the band shrinkage that occurs when a semiconductor is heavily doped, another important effect occurs near the bandedge. This effect occurs because of the disordered arrangement of the impurity atoms on the host lattice. As shown schematically in Figure 8.10, the randomly placed impurity atoms cause a random fluctuation in the effective bandedge. Deep well regions as indicated in the figure are produced which lead to low-energy electronic states. The random nature of the potential fluctuation leads to a bandedge tail in the density of states. The underlying reasons behind the effect of disorder will be discussed in Chapter 18.

In view of the various effects discussed above, the "optical bandgap" of the semiconductor changes as the doping changes. The optical bandgap is defined from the optical absorption versus photon energy data and represents the energy separation where the valence and conduction band density of states are significant. In addition, one often defines artificially an electrical bandgap. This is defined from the np product discussed earlier. According to this definition

$$np = n_i^2$$

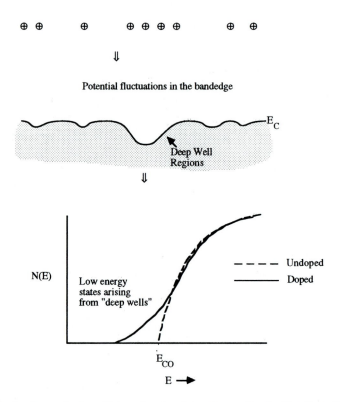

Figure 8.10: A schematic description showing how the randomly distributed impurities cause band tail states.

$$= C \exp\left(-\frac{E_g^{\text{elect}}}{k_B T}\right). \tag{8.61}$$

This definition has only a mathematical significance and does not represent any real physical property. The electrical bandgap is usually smaller than the optical bandgap.

8.6 MODULATION DOPING

We already discussed how doping is an integral part of semiconductor devices. The purpose behind doping of semiconductors is to controllably change the free carrier density in the semiconductor. This requires that the dopant be ionized and thus positively charged. This fixed charged center causes scattering for the free electron and the ionized impurity scattering is an important scattering mechanism. An obvious question that arises is whether one can have a controllable free electron density *without* a scattering. The answer to this question is yes and this is realized through the concept of modulation doping. Before addressing

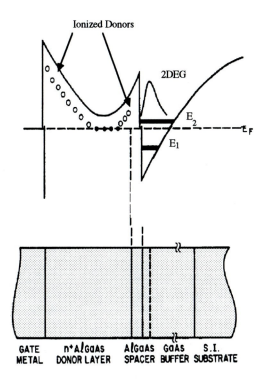

Figure 8.11: A modulation doped heterostructure showing the band profile and the layer sequence. The electrons are transferred to the narrow gap semiconductor where one has a 2-dimensional electron gas (2DEG).

this concept, it is worth remarking that the modulation doping also overcomes another problem with doping, the carrier freeze-out problem. As we discussed in the previous section, at low temperatures, the electrons are localized at the donor sites thus reducing the free carriers available for conduction. This effect can negate some of the benefits of operating devices at low temperatures. The concept of modulation doping is able to overcome this problem as well.

Modulation doping can be understood by examining Figure 8.11. A heterostructure is grown (say GaAs/AlGaAs) and the high bandgap material is doped. In equilibrium the electrons associated with the donors see lower lying energy states in the narrow bandgap material and thus transfer to the well region. This spatial separation of the positively charged donors and negatively charged electrons produces an electric field profile governed by the Poisson equation which causes a band bending as shown in Figure 8.11. Usually the dopants are placed some distance away from the heterointerface by including an undoped "spacer" region. The ionized impurity is essentially eliminated by this physical separation between the mobile electrons and the fixed ionized scattering centers. Also since the electrons are at energy positions lower than the localized ground

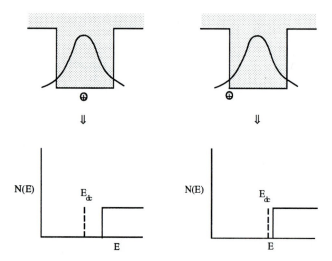

Figure 8.12: A schematic showing how the position of a dopant in a quantum well can alter the value of the donor binding energy. The overlap between the ground state wavefunction in the well and the impurity Coulombic potential changes as the dopant position changes.

state of the donor atoms, the electrons remain mobile even at the lowest temperatures provided the material quality is pure. Extremely high sheet charge density of electrons ($\geq 10^{12}$ cm^{-2}) can thus be maintained at low temperatures. Transistors based on such concepts (modulation doped field effect transistors or MODFETs) can operate at low temperatures and are often used for detection of very weak signals from space and in other applications where low noise devices are required.

8.7 HYDROGENIC IMPURITIES IN QUANTUM WELLS

The modulation doping concept discussed above is one extreme of doping in heterostructures. The free electron that is transferred to the lower bandgap region has essentially no interaction with the dopant. If, on the other hand, the dopant is placed in a quantum well, the donor binding energy can be increased above the bulk binding energy. In fact, the binding energy for donors in the quantum wells is a continuous function of the position of the dopant in the quantum well. This is illustrated schematically in Figure 8.12. The electronic states in the quantum well are already confined in the growth direction as discussed in Chapter 6. This confinement can be on a scale smaller than the Bohr radius of the bulk donor level. Thus, there can be a strong overlap between the electronic state and the donor Coulombic potential. This overlap is largest for a center doped case as shown and decreases as the dopant moves towards the edge. The donor (or acceptor) level is, therefore, a function of both the well size and the position of the donor in the well. Thus, for a uniformly doped quantum well one expects a donor band. The origin of this impurity band is different from the impurity band created at high doping levels. The general donor problem can be expressed by the Hamiltonian

$$H = H_0 - \frac{e^2}{\epsilon \left[\rho^2 + (z - z_i)^2\right]^{1/2}} \tag{8.62}$$

where H_0 is the Hamiltonian representing the bandedge states and $V_B(z)$ is the potential barrier of the quantum well. For example, if the barrier height in a square potential well is V_0, the value of $V_B(z)$ is

$$
\begin{aligned}
V_B(z) &= 0 \text{ for } |z| \le L/2 \\
&= V_0 \text{ for } |z| > L/2,
\end{aligned}
\tag{8.63}
$$

where L is the well size. For acceptor levels, H and H_0 involve the usual four-band $k \cdot p$ description. The donor or acceptor level cannot be solved exactly as was the case for the hydrogen atom problem in the bulk semiconductors. One must resort to numerical techniques. A popular approach is to use the variational approach in which one assumes an impurity wavefunction and obtains the variational parameters by finding the minimum of energy. Another approach is to write the impurity problem in k-space and then using the fact that the impurity potential is limited in k-space, write the equation as a finite matrix equation that can then be diagonalized.

In the limit that the potential barrier is infinite and the well size goes to zero, the 2-dimensional donor binding energy goes to four times the 3-dimensional value if a scalar fixed effective mass equation is used. The binding energies in realistic quantum wells do not go as high. In Figure 8.13 we show some results for the well size dependence of a center doped donor level. The results are shown in units of the bulk Bohr radius for the well size and the Rydberg for the binding energy.

In Chapters 6 and 7 we discussed in detail how the valence bandstructure is affected by both quantum confinement and strain. The strain in particular has a dramatic effect on the valence bandstructure. One way to monitor these changes is to obtain the hole masses experimentally. This is usually a very difficult experiment to carry out and interpret.

The changes in the valence bandstructure are also reflected on the hydrogenic acceptor levels in the pseudomorphic layers. In fact, the acceptor level energies are easier to monitor than the hole masses and thus provide an easy probe for the effect of strain on the valence bandstructure. A detailed theory for the acceptor level energies in strained quantum well structures has been presented in literature, and measurements for the acceptor level energies for both compressive and tensile strain have been carried out. Figures 8.14 and 8.15 show the results of the acceptor level energies along with calculated values. The results in Figure 8.14 are for quantum wells doped at the center of the well where

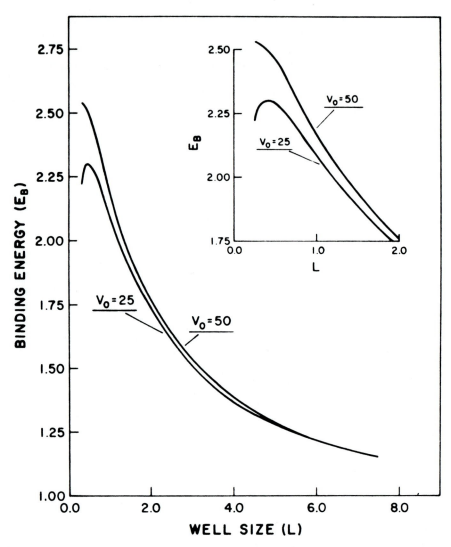

Figure 8.13: Variation of the binding energy of the ground state (EB) of a donor as a function of the GaAs well size (L) for two different potential barriers. All energies are expressed in terms of an effective Rydberg (R) and all distances in terms of Bohr radius, a, as given by Equations 8.35 and 8.37. (Reproduced with permission, K. K. Bajaj, et al., J. Vac. Sci. Technol., **B1**, 391 (1983).)

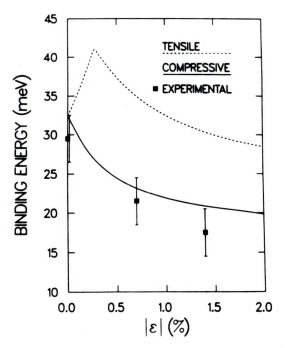

Figure 8.14: Lowest energy acceptor level as a function of lattice mismatch ϵ in a 100 Å $In_yGa_{1-y}As/Al_{0.3}Ga_{0.7}As$ quantum well (after Loehr et al., 1990).

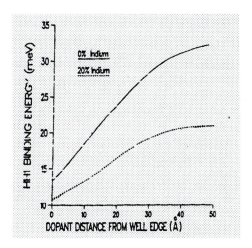

Figure 8.15: Heavy hole ground state acceptor-level binding energy as a function of position of the dopant in a 100 Å $GaAs/Al_{0.3}Ga_{0.7}As$ (solid curve) and $In_{0.2}Ga_{0.8}As/Al_{0.3}Ga_{0.7}As$ (dotted curve) quantum well (after Loehr and Singh, 1990).

the binding energy is maximum. As can be seen from Figure 8.14, for a compressive strain the acceptor energy steadily decreases as the strain increases. The decrease in the energy is not as rapid as the zone edge mass because the acceptor level probes k-space bandstructure up to ~ 0.05 Å^{-1}, where the bands begin to develop a higher mass. For the tensile strain, one sees a large increase in the acceptor energy initially, corresponding to the merger of the HH and LH states and the very high density of states at the bandedge. As the tensile strain is further increased, the binding energy steadily decreases as the LH state goes above HH state, and the density of states start decreasing. The effect of the dopant position dependence for strained and unstrained quantum wells is shown in Figure 8.15.

In this chapter we discussed the very important concept of doping in semiconductors. Without doping, the semiconductors are essentially useless for electronic devices. Thus, a great deal of effort has focussed on understanding the properties of dopants. The area of heavily doped semiconductors is not only of great significance technologically, but also offers an area where many body theory predictions can be checked. Heterostructure technology has opened new areas of research and devices where new doping concepts are playing a very important role. As discussed in this chapter, the problems associated with carrier freeze-out and background scattering can be avoided.

8.8   FOR THE TECHNOLOGIST IN YOU

As has been noted in this chapter, semiconductors are of little use without the ability to dope them. The inability to dope semiconductors reliably can stunt the development of a technology. A number of compound semiconductor technologies suffer particularly from this problem. Very often an anti– site defect (e.g. a cation or anion on the wrong lattice) can act as a dopant which is uncontrollable. To a large extent the success of large bandgap lasers and electronic devices hinges on doping control which is a serious problem at present.

Doping is usually carried out by using either,

1. epitaxial techniques, in which the dopant is introduced during growth,

2. ion implantation, where high energy dopant ions are implanted into the semiconductor, or

3. diffusion, where a "lump" of the dopant material is placed on the semiconductor and is annealed causing a diffusion of the dopant atoms into the semiconductor.

The epitaxial incorporation of dopants particularly in techniques like MBE and MOCVD produces very abrupt doping profiles and leads to very controllable dopant profiles. In fact, one can use pulse doping where dopants can be placed on a single monolayer of the material. An interesting phenomenon occurs in epitaxial doping of compound semiconductors such as GaAs where a Si atom could be an n–type (if it replaces Ga) or p–type (if it replaces As) dopant. It is possible to alter growth conditions so that in one region of the material one has n–type doping while in another the same dopant acts as a p–type dopant. This can be done efficiently by using special directions of growth such as the 311A surface in GaAs. The amphoteric nature of dopants in compound semiconductors also causes serious problems in certain materials since a great deal of compensation can occur with the dopant producing both n and p–type dopants in the same region of the crystal.

Ion implantation is the most widely used doping technique for commercial electronics. The energy of the dopant ions can be tailored to produce a prechosen doping profile although the control is certainly not the same as in epitaxial techniques. An important consideration in doping by ion implantation is the crystal orientation. One prefers a direction where there are open "channels" in the lattice so that the ions can enter the crystal without creating too much damage. Nevertheless, damage is created and the crystal has to be annealed to eliminate the damage and activate the dopants.

Introduction of dopant by diffusion is widely used to produce ohmic contacts where a very heavily doped region is created to allow electrons to be injected into the conduction band (or holes into the valence band) without encountering any significant barrier. For example in GaAs a common "recipe" used involves a Au–Ge which is deposited on the semiconductor and then annealed according to some "magic" formula. The Ge diffuses into the material providing a good source of dopants. Researchers often spend months coming up with a good recipe and then guard it valiantly!

8.9   PROBLEMS

8.1. Calculate the intrinsic carrier concentration of Si, Ge, and GaAs as a function of temperature. The bandgap dependence on temperature may be written as

$$E_g(T) = E_g(0) - \alpha T^2/(T + \beta)$$

where for,

Si: $E_g(0)$ =1.17 eV; α =4.73 × 10^{-4} K^{-1}; β =636 K
Ge: $E_g(0)$ =0.744 eV; α =4.77 × 10^{-4} K^{-1}; β =235 K
GaAs: $E_g(0)$ =1.519 eV; α =5.4 × 10^{-4} K^{-1}; β =204 K

8.2. Calculate the donor and acceptor binding energies in Si and GaAs assuming an average conductivity mass. Use the information provided in Appendix L.

8.3. A Si sample is doped n-type with 10^{17} atoms cm^{-3}. Calculate the free electron carrier concentration between 10 K and 1000 K. How does the position of the Fermi level change with temperature? Assume a donor energy level of 0.03 eV.

8.4. Repeat Problem 3 for a GaAs sample doped n-type at 10^{17} cm^{-3}? Assume a donor energy of 0.007 eV.

8.5. A GaAs sample is doped p-type at 10^{17} cm^{-3}. What is the free hole density at 77 K?

8.6. A uniformly doped sample of GaAs has a donor concentration of 10^{16} cm^{-3} and an acceptor concentration of 5 × 10^{15}cm^{-3}. Calculate the free electron and free hole concentrations at 77 K and 300 K. Assume a donor binding energy of 0.007 eV and an acceptor binding energy of 0.05 eV.

8.7. At what n–type doping density does the Fermi level enter the conduction band in (a) GaAs at 300 K, (b) Si at 300 K? What are the corresponding p–type doping limits for GaAs and Si?

8.8. Assume that N_c and N_v are 1.04 × 10^{19} cm^{-3} and 0.49 × 10^{19} cm^{-3} for Ge at room temperature (300 K). What is the corresponding electron and hole density of states mass? The corresponding values for Si are 2.8 × 10^{19} cm^{-3} and 1.05 × 10^{19} cm^{-3}. What are the electron and hole masses in Si?

8.9. Calculate the intrinsic carrier concentrations and resistivities in Ge, Si, and GaAs at 300 K. Use the mobility data given in Appendix L.

8.10. Assume that the condition for degeneracy is defined by the relation

$$E_F - E_c > 3k_B T.$$

Calculate the electron concentrations at which the bands are degenerate in GaAs, Si, and InAs at room temperature.

8.10 REFERENCES

- **Intrinsic and Extrinsic Carriers**

  - Ashcroft, N. W. and N. D. Mermin, *Solid State Physics* (Holt, Rinehart and Winston, New York, 1976).
  - Blakemore, J. S., Electron. Commun., **29**, 131 (1952).
  - Blakemore, J. S., *Semiconductor Statistics* (Pergamon Press, New York, 1962, and reprinted by Dover, New York, 1988).
  - Kittel, C., *Quantum Theory of Solids* (John Wiley and Sons, New York, 1987), Chap. 14.
  - Seeger, K., *Semiconductor Physics: An Introduction* (Springer–Verlag, Berlin, 1985).
  - Sze, S. M., *Physics of Semiconductor Devices* (John Wiley and Sons, New York, 1981).
  - Thurmond, C. D., J. Electrochem. Soc. **122**, 1133 (1975).
  - Tyagi, M. S., *Introduction to Semiconductor Materials and Devices* (John Wiley and Sons, New York, 1991).
  - Wang, S., *Fundamentals of Semiconductor Theory and Device Physics* (Prentice Hall, New Jersey, 1989).

- **Heavily Doped Semiconductors**

  - Casey, H. C., Jr. and F. Stern, J. Appl. Phys. **47**, 631 (1976).
  - Kane, E. O., Solid State Electron. **28**, 3 (1985).
  - Lee, D. S. and J. G. Fossun, IEEE Trans. Elect. Dev., **ED–30**, 626 (1983).
  - Mott, N. F. and W. D. Twose, Advan. Phys., **10**, 107 (1961).
  - Pantelides, S. T., A Selloni and R. Car, Sol. St. Electron., **28**, 17 (1985).
  - Van Overstraeten, R. J. and R. P. Mertens, Sol. St. Electron., **30**, 1077 (1987).

- **Modulation Doping**

  - Delagebeaudeuf, D. and N. Linh, IEEE Trans. Electron Devices, **ED–29**, 955 (1982).
  - "Molecular Beam Epitaxy and the Technology of Selectively Doped Heterostructure Transistors," by Hendel, R. H., C. W. Tu and R. Dingle, in *Gallium Arsenide Technology* edited by D. K. Ferry (Howard W. Sams and Co., Indianapolis, 1985).
  - Jaffe, M. and J. Singh, J. Appl. Phys., **65**, 329 (1989).

– Norris, G., D. Look, W. Koop, J. Klem and H. Morkoc, Appl. Phys. Lett., **47**, 423 (1985).

– Solomon, P. and H. Morkoc, IEEE Trans. Electron Dev., **ED–31**, 1015 (1984).

• **Hydrogenic Impurities in Quantum Wells**

– Andeani, L. C., S. Fraizzoli and A. Pasquarello, Phys. Rev. B, **42**, 7641 (1990).

– Chang, Y. C., Physica, **146–B**, 137 (1987).

– Green, R. and K. K. Bajaj, J. Vac. Sci. Technol. B, **1**, 391 (1983).

– Loehr, J. P., *Theoretical Studies of Pseudomorphic Quantum Well Optoelectronic Devices*, Ph.D. Thesis, (The University of Michigan, Ann Arbor, 1991).

– Loehr, J. P. and J. Singh, Phys. Rev. B, **41**, 3695 (1990).

– Loehr, J. P., Y. Chen, D. Biswas, P. Bhattacharya and J. Singh, Appl. Phys. Lett., **57**, 180 (1990).

– Maselink, W. T., Y. C. Chang and H. Morkoc, Phys. Rev. B, **28**, 7373 (1983).

– Miller, R. C., A. C. Gossard, W. T. Tsang and O. Munteanu, Phys. Rev. B, **25**, 3871 (1982).

CHAPTER
9

LATTICE VIBRATIONS: PHONONS

In our discussions for the bandstructure we assumed that the atoms in the crystal are at fixed and periodic positions. The background potential is thus rigid, periodic, and does not have any time dependence. This was the key assumption in being able to derive the Bloch's theorem and the bandstructure of crystals. Just to remind ourselves of the outcome of the Bloch's theorem, we note that the wavefunction

$$\psi_{\mathbf{k}}(\boldsymbol{r}, t) = u_n(\boldsymbol{k}) \, e^{i(\mathbf{k} \cdot \mathbf{r} - \omega t)} \tag{9.1}$$

represents an eigenfunction of an electron and if an electron has a momentum $\boldsymbol{k}$ at one instance of time it always stays in the same state.

In actual materials the background ions forming the crystal are not fixed rigidly but vibrate. The vibration increases as the temperature is increased and at high enough temperature the material may melt or evaporate, i.e., there is no underlying lattice. We will be interested in temperatures which are quite a bit lower than the melting temperature but nevertheless the atoms will be vibrating. In such a case, fortunately, one need not throw out the concept of bandstructure entirely. As shown schematically in Figure 9.1, the concept of bandstructure is still a valid one, but an electron placed in a momentum state $\boldsymbol{k}$ need not stay in the same state indefinitely. Scattering will occur due to the potential disturbances by the lattice vibration. Before we can answer the question regarding how lattice vibrations cause scattering, we must understand some basic properties of these vibrations.

We discussed in previous chapters the arrangement of atoms in a crystalline material in some detail. We have not, however, discussed what causes some atoms to form one kind of crystal while others form a different crystal. While there is no simple theory for crystal structures, it is useful to examine the nature of forces which cause isolated atoms to bind together to form nice periodic crystals. The

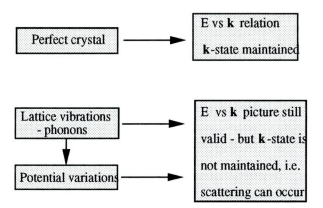

Figure 9.1: The effect of imperfections caused by either lattice vibrations or other potential fluctuations lead to scattering of electrons.

crystals obviously represent a free energy minimum configuration of the system. Any distortion causes a restoring force to be operative much like a pendulum which is disturbed.

In Table 9.1 we characterize some of the important forces that bind crystals.

9.1 CONSIDERATIONS FOR CRYSTAL BINDING

The considerations for crystal binding are:

- Keep the positively charged ions apart

- Keep the negatively charged electrons apart

- Keep electrons close to the ions

- Keep electron kinetic energy low by spreading the electrons

This results in the requirement that $U_{\mathrm{crystal}} - U_{\mathrm{free}} < 0$ where U_{crystal} and U_{free} are the energy of the atoms in the crystal and when they are free respectively.

We will not go into any detail of the precise nature of the forces that cause crystals to bind, but will simply outline some of these forces in Table 9.1. The binding forces are, of course, electronic in nature, but the problem is complex because of the difficulty in accurately treating the details of the electron-electron many body interactions. When the atoms are separated by large distances ($\geq$

Nature of Crystal	Binding Forces
Inert Gas Crystals	
• Transparent Insulators	Long Range → Attractive van der Waal Dipole Interaction
	Short Range → Repulsive Interaction due to Pauli Exclusion Principle
⇒ Weakly Bound Atoms	Lennard–Jones Potential
	$U(R) = 4\epsilon \left[\left(\frac{\sigma}{R} \right)^{12} - \left(\frac{\sigma}{R} \right)^{6} \right]$
Ionic Crystals	
• NaCl, CsCl	Electrostatic Interactions Between Ions (Madelung Energy)
⇒ Strong Binding	
• Crystals such as GaAs, AlAs, etc. are *partially ionic*.	
Covalent Crystals	
• Si, C, Ge	Homopolar Chemical Bond
⇒ Very strong bonding comparable to ionic bonds. Semiconductors with high melting temperatures.	Atoms share two electrons each with anti-parallel spin.
Metallic Crystal	
• Metallic	Bonding Due to Conduction Electrons
High Electrical Conductivity ⇒ Not as strong binding as ionic crystals. Crystal structure hcp, fcc, bcc.	

Table 9.1: A brief outline of the nature of the forces which bind various kinds of crystals. Most semiconductors are bound by covalent bonds and in case of compound semiconductors by additional ionic bonds.

2 Å), there is an attraction between them. Depending upon the nature of the atoms, this attraction can involve a variety of forms. We will briefly discuss each of these cases.

9.1.1   Inert Gas Crystals

These are the simplest of crystals with electron distributions in the crystal very close to the free atom case. Since the electrons form a complete shell in the individual atoms, there is very weak binding between the atoms. The crystals are transparent and are all fcc type. The electron distribution is slightly distorted due to the presence of other atoms. This slight distortion leads to a dipole–

dipole interaction which is called the van der Waal interaction. This attractive interaction has the form

$$\Delta U_a(R) = \frac{-A}{R^6} \tag{9.2}$$

where R is the interatomic separation.

As the two atoms are brought closer their charge distribution starts to overlap and a repulsion occurs primarily because of the Pauli exclusion principle. This principle ensures that only one electron can occupy a given state. As the atoms are brought closer, a portion of the electrons must occupy higher energy states of the atom and thus increase the electron energy. The repulsive potential has the form

$$\Delta U_r(R) = \frac{B}{R^{12}}. \tag{9.3}$$

The total potential is usually then written as

$$U(R) = 4\epsilon \left[\left(\frac{\sigma}{R}\right)^{12} - \left(\frac{\sigma}{R}\right)^6 \right] \tag{9.4}$$

where $4\epsilon\sigma^2 = A$ and $4\epsilon\sigma^{12} = B$. This potential is known as the Lennard–Jones potential. The equilibrium separation of the atoms is given by the condition

$$\frac{dU}{dR} = 0 \tag{9.5}$$

which leads to

$$R_0 = 1.09\sigma \tag{9.6}$$

for the inert gases.

9.1.2 Ionic Crystals

Crystals such as NaCl, LiF, etc., can be represented by positive and negative ions since there is a near complete transfer of an electron from the anion to the cation. Crystals such as compound semiconductors are partially ionic and can be represented by an effective charge e^* which we will calculate later on in our discussion of polar optical phonons. Thus part of the binding energy of these ionic semiconductors comes from the ionic interaction and the rest comes from the covalent bond energy to be discussed next. The main contribution to the binding from the ionic part comes from the simple electrostatic interaction and is called the Madelung energy. To evaluate this energy we assume a potential energy from between two atoms at sites i and j as

$$\begin{aligned} U_{ij} &= \lambda \exp(-R/\rho) - \frac{q^2}{R} \quad \text{(for nearest neighbor)} \\ &= \pm \frac{q^2}{r_{ij}} \quad \text{(otherwise).} \end{aligned} \tag{9.7}$$

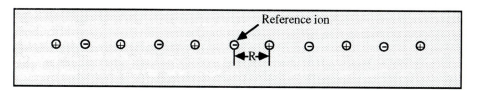

Figure 9.2: Line of ions of alternating signs, with distance R between ions.

The nearest-neighbor term has a repulsive term along with the attractive interaction. The arrangement of the positive and negative charges is shown schematically in Figure 9.2. We define $r_{ij} = p_{ij} R$. The total energy is

$$
\begin{aligned}
U &= N U_i \\
&= N \left(z \lambda e^{-R/\rho} - \alpha \frac{e^2}{R} \right)
\end{aligned}
\tag{9.8}
$$

where

$$
\alpha = \sum_j{}' \frac{(\pm)}{p_{ij}}
\tag{9.9}
$$

is called the Madelung constant and z is the number of nearest neighbors. The Madelung constant is of central importance in the binding energy of ionic crystals. For most crystals one employs computers to evaluate α. For a simple chain of atoms shown in Figure 9.2, one has

$$
\alpha = 2 \left[1 - \frac{1}{2} + \frac{1}{3} - \frac{1}{4} + \cdots \right].
\tag{9.10}
$$

Using the expansion

$$
\ln(1 + x) = x - \frac{x^2}{2} + \frac{x^3}{3} - \frac{x^4}{4} + \cdots
\tag{9.11}
$$

at $x = 1$, we then get

$$
\alpha = 2 \ln 2.
\tag{9.12}
$$

For 3-D systems, the problem is far more complex. Some typical values of α are given below.

- Zinc–blende crystals: $\alpha = 1.6381$

- Sodium chloride: $\alpha = 1.747565$.

As noted earlier, a number of important semiconductors have an important ionic contribution to their binding energy. However, another important binding comes from electron sharing leading to the covalent bond.

9.1.3 Covalent Crystals

The covalent crystals such as Si, Ge, C, etc., are bound together with the covalent bond in which atoms lower their energy by sharing electrons from their outermost orbitals. We discussed the outer shell electrons in Chapter 5. For most semiconductors these are the sp^3 orbitals. The bonding is carried out by two electrons, one from each atom. The electrons localize in the region between the bonds and have *antiparallel* spins. This spin configuration has the lowest energy because of the Pauli exclusion principle.

In semiconductors there is a continuous range of crystals extending between totally covalent (the group IV semiconductors) to highly ionic compound semiconductors. In Table 9.2 we show the ionicity of the several semiconductors from the work of J. C. Phillips, who developed a very successful semi-empirical theory for the fractional ionic character of a crystal.

Figure 9.3 shows the general energy versus atomic spacing curve for most semiconductors. There is an attractive component to the total energy which dominates at larger spacing and a strong repulsive component at shorter spacings. The total energy goes through a minima as shown. This minima gives the equilibrium spacings of the atoms.

9.1.4 Metallic Bonds

Another important class of materials is the metals which usually crystallize in a close-packed structure like fcc, bcc, or hcp and not in loosely packed structures such as diamond. The main contribution to the metallic bond comes from the valence band electrons which are able to reach a lower energy state due to inter-

Crystal	Fractional Ionic Character
Si	0.0
SiC	0.18
Ge	0.0
ZnSe	0.63
ZnS	0.62
CdSe	0.70
InP	0.42
InAs	0.36
InSb	0.32
GaAs	0.31
GaSb	0.26

Table 9.2: Fractional ionic character of some semiconductors (from J. C. Phillips, 1973).

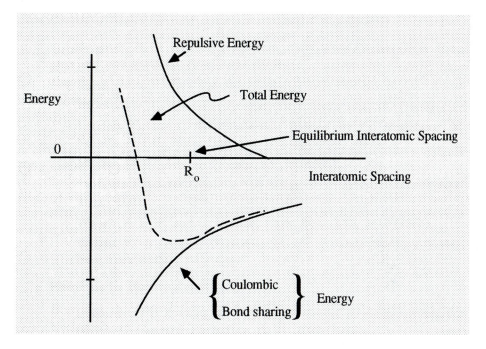

Figure 9.3: General form of the binding energy versus atomic distance of a crystal. In the case of most semiconductors, the long-range attraction is due to either electrostatic interactions of the ions or the bond sharing energy of the covalent bond.

action with the neighboring atoms. There is also a significant contribution from the interaction between the ion cores and the conduction electrons.

Regardless of the nature of the crystal we have seen that the binding energy versus atomic separation curve shows a minimum which corresponds to the equilibrium separation R_0 of the crystal, as shown in Figure 9.3.

9.1.5 Restoring Force

In general we can expand the crystal binding energy around the point R_0 as follows:

$$U(R) = U(R_0) + \left(\frac{dU}{dR}\right)_{R_0} \Delta R + \frac{1}{2}\left(\frac{d^2U}{dR^2}\right)_{R_0} \Delta R^2 + \dots \qquad (9.13)$$

The second term is zero since R_0 is the equilibrium interatomic separation. Retaining terms to the second order in ΔR (this is called the harmonic approximation), we get

$$U(R) = U(R_0) + \frac{1}{2}C(\Delta R)^2 \qquad (9.14)$$

Name	Field
Electron	——
Photon	Electromagnetic wave
Phonon	Elastic wave
Plasmon	Collective electron wave
Magnon	Magnetization wave
Polaron	Electron + elastic deformation
Exciton	Polarization wave

Figure 9.4: Important elementary excitations in solids. The second quantization procedure allows one to describe the fields in terms of particles.

where

$$C = \frac{\partial^2 U}{\partial R^2} \tag{9.15}$$

is the force constant of the material. The restoring force is then

$$\text{Force} = -C\Delta R. \tag{9.16}$$

Due to this restoring force the atoms in the crystal vibrate as a particle attached to a spring would do. It is important to note that the force constant C used in this chapter is obtained from the elastic stiffness constants of Chapter 7 by dividing the stiffness constant by the interatomic separation. We will now discuss such vibrations for two different classes of crystals, monatomic and diatomic. The two cases yield qualitatively different results.

9.2 CRYSTAL VIBRATIONS FOR A MONATOMIC BASIS

When the atoms in a crystal vibrate, the vibrations are expressed in terms of a traveling wave solution because of the periodicity in the system. In fact, one can derive a dispersion curve, i.e., energy of vibration vs. wave vector k relation in a manner similar to the one used for bandstructure of electrons. These lattice vibrations known as phonons, when quantized, are part of a more general set of excitations found in solid state physics. In Figure 9.4 several such excitations are listed. The procedure for obtaining these "particles" from the wave description is called second quantization.

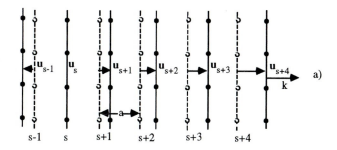

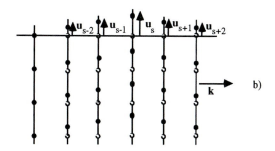

Figure 9.5: (a) Dashed lines: planes of atoms when in equilibrium; Solid lines: planes of atoms when displaced as for a longitudinal wave. The coordinate u measures the displacement of the planes. (b) Planes of atoms when displaced during passage of a transverse wave.

For crystals with underlying cubic structure, the dispersion relations are simplest along the high symmetry directions [100], [110], and [111] since for these directions the problem can be expressed as a scalar or one-dimensional problem. For a lattice vibration with k-vector in these directions, because of symmetry, entire planes of atoms vibrate in phase. Thus, one only needs to describe the amplitude of vibration of any one atom on the plane. For any wave vector the atoms can vibrate along k (longitudinal mode) or perpendicular to k (transverse modes). The one longitudinal mode and two mutually perpendicular transverse modes give three independent modes of vibration for each k.

We will assume that the restoring force for any displacement is proportional to the displacement, which is equivalent to saying that the potential energy has only second-order terms in displacement (the harmonic approximation). We will denote the displacement of the sth plane from the equilibrium lattice point position by u_s (see Figure 9.5). The total force on the atom on plane s is then

$$F_s = \sum_p C_p(u_{s+p} - u_s). \qquad (9.17)$$

We will assume that the force constant is only due to neighboring atoms and is equal to a constant value C.

$$\boldsymbol{F}_s = C(\boldsymbol{u}_{s+1} - \boldsymbol{u}_s) + C(\boldsymbol{u}_{s-1} - \boldsymbol{u}_s). \tag{9.18}$$

In general, the force constant will be different for longitudinal and transverse modes.

We can now write the equation of motion for the atoms on the plane s.

$$M\frac{d^2\boldsymbol{u}_s}{dt^2} = C(\boldsymbol{u}_{s+1} + \boldsymbol{u}_{s-1} - 2\boldsymbol{u}_s) \tag{9.19}$$

where M is the mass of the atoms. We consider a traveling wave solution of the term

$$\boldsymbol{u}_{s+p} = \boldsymbol{u}\,\exp\left[i(s+p)ka\right]\exp(-i\omega t) \tag{9.20}$$

where a is the spacing between planes and where we have introduced the quantities k and ω which represent the wave vector and frequency of the vibrations. With this solution the equation becomes

$$\begin{aligned} -M\omega^2 u\exp(iska) \;=\; & C\{\exp\left[i(s+1)ka\right] \\ +\;& \exp\left[i(s-1)ka\right] - 2\exp\left[iska\right]\} \end{aligned} \tag{9.21}$$

or

$$M\omega^2 = -C\left[\exp(ika) + \exp(-ika) - 2\right] \tag{9.22}$$

or

$$\omega^2 = \frac{2C}{M}(1 - \cos ka). \tag{9.23}$$

This is the dispersion relation for the lattice vibrations and once again we only need to be concerned with $\boldsymbol{k}$ in the first Brillouin zone as shown in Figure 9.6. At the Brillouin zone edge $(k = \pm\pi/a)$, the atoms vibrate according to

$$\begin{aligned} \boldsymbol{u}_s \;=\; & \boldsymbol{u}\exp\left(\pm is\pi\right) \\ =\; & \boldsymbol{u}(-1)^s, \end{aligned} \tag{9.24}$$

i.e., they vibrate in opposite phase to their neighbors. The wave is a standing wave at the zone edge, i.e., a wave produced when a plane wave is reflected upon itself. We have encountered this sort of a situation in Bragg reflection of X-rays as well as in talking about the bandstructure at Brillouin zone edge.

9.2.1 Group Velocity

As in the case of E vs. $\boldsymbol{k}$ in electronic bandstructure, the wavefunction describing a lattice wave extends over all space since it is a plane wave. One has to develop a wavepacket description to actually describe how such waves carry energy from

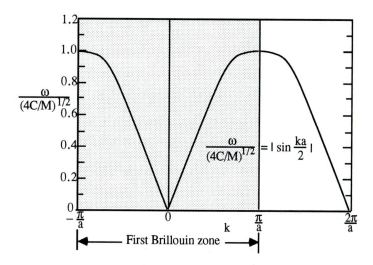

Figure 9.6: Plot of ω versus k. The region of $k < \pi/a$ or $\lambda > a$ corresponds to the continuum approximation; here ω is directly proportional to k. The shaded area is the first Brillouin zone.

one region in space to another. The rate at which such a wavepacket moves in space is given by the group velocity

$$v_g = \frac{d\omega}{dk} \tag{9.25}$$

which becomes for our dispersion relation

$$v_g = \left(\frac{Ca^2}{M}\right)^{1/2} \cos\left(\frac{ka}{2}\right). \tag{9.26}$$

The group velocity is plotted in Figure 9.7 and at the Brillouin zone edge the velocity becomes zero corresponding to the standing wave discussed above.

9.2.2 Acoustic Waves

In the limit of $k \to 0$ (long wavelength) the dispersion relation for lattice vibrations of the monatomic crystal becomes

$$\omega^2 = \frac{C}{M}k^2a^2$$

or

$$\omega = \sqrt{\frac{C}{M}}ka. \tag{9.27}$$

We have a linear $\omega - k$ relation which gives us the group velocity which is

$$v_g = v_{\text{sound}}$$

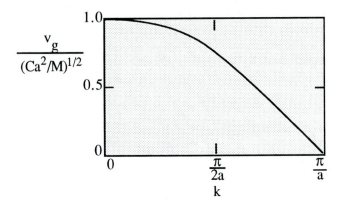

Figure 9.7: Group velocity v_g versus k. At the zone boundary, the group velocity is zero.

$$= \sqrt{\frac{C}{M}} a. \tag{9.28}$$

These results are the same as the results from the continuum theory of elastic waves, the theory that gives the description of sound waves.

We note that we have assumed that the force constants only contribute in the equation of motion for the nearest-neighbor planes. This is not true for ionic crystals where long-range restoring forces come into the picture. The theory can be easily generalized to cover these cases. We also reiterate that, in general, the transverse and longitudinal branches will have different dispersion relations, since the force constants will, in general, be different.

9.3   CRYSTAL VIBRATIONS FOR A DIATOMIC BASIS

When the primitive basis of a crystal has more than one atom (as is the case for all the semiconductors), the lattice vibrations have a qualitatively different dispersion from what we have discussed. We will now discuss the dispersion relation for a two atom basis crystal under the assumption that the plane of atoms vibrate in phase. This again is true only for high symmetry directions, such as [100] and [111] for the diamond lattice. We assume that the force constant is nonzero only for nearest-neighbor interactions and that the masses of the two atoms of the basis, are M_1 and M_2. If u_s and v_s represent the displacements of the two kinds of atoms of the unit cell on plane s (see Figure 9.8), we get the following equations of motion for the atomic planes

$$M_1 \frac{d^2 u_s}{dt^2} = C(v_s + v_{s-1} - 2u_s)$$

$$M_2 \frac{d^2 v_s}{dt^2} = C(u_{s+1} + u_s - 2v_s) \tag{9.29}$$

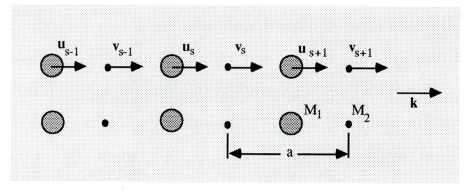

Figure 9.8: A zinc–blende crystal structure with masses M_1, M_2 connected by force constant C between adjacent planes. The displacements of atoms M_1 are denoted by u_{s-1}, u_s, u_{s+1}, ..., and of atoms M_2 by v_{s-1}, v_s, v_{s+1}. The periodicity is a in the direction of the wave vector k.

with M_1, M_2, $C > 0$.

Note that we have assumed that there is no ionic charge on the atoms. As we have discussed previously, for compound semiconductors we have ionic charge on each atom. This produces a long-range force which we will discuss later on in this chapter. The present discussion would pertain to covalent semiconductors, such as silicon and germanium. Note that for silicon and germanium, $M_1 = M_2$.

We look for solutions of the traveling wave form but with different amplitudes u and v on alternating planes

$$
\begin{aligned}
u_s &= u \, \exp(iska) \, \exp(-i\omega t) \\
v_s &= v \, \exp(iska) \, \exp(-i\omega t).
\end{aligned}
\tag{9.30}
$$

We note that a is the distance between nearest identical planes and not nearest planes, i.e., it is the minimum distance of periodicity in the crystal as shown in Figure 9.8. Equations 9.30 when substituted in Equation 9.29 give

$$
\begin{aligned}
-\omega^2 M_1 u &= Cv\,[1 + \exp(-ika)] - 2Cu \\
-\omega^2 M_2 v &= Cu\,[\exp(ika) + 1] - 2Cv.
\end{aligned}
\tag{9.31}
$$

These are again coupled eigenvalue equations which can be solved by the matrix method.

$$
\begin{vmatrix}
2C - M_1\omega^2 & -C\,[1 + \exp(-ika)] \\
-C\,[1 + \exp(ika)] & 2C - M_2\omega^2
\end{vmatrix}
= 0
\tag{9.32}
$$

or

$$
M_1 M_2 \omega^4 - 2C(M_1 + M_2)\omega^2 + 2C^2(1 - \cos ka) = 0.
\tag{9.33}
$$

This gives the solution

$$
\omega^2 = \frac{2C(M_1 + M_2) \pm \left[4C^2(M_1 + M_2)^2 - 8C^2(1 - \cos ka)M_1 M_2\right]^{1/2}}{2M_1 M_2}.
\tag{9.34}
$$

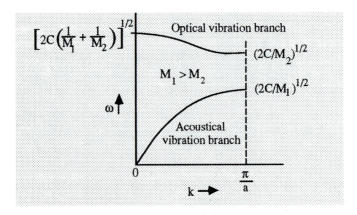

Figure 9.9: Optical and acoustical branches of the dispersion relation for a diatomic linear lattice, showing the limiting frequencies at $k = 0$ and $k = K_{max} = \pi/a$.

It is useful to examine the results at two limiting cases. For small k, we get the two solutions,

$$\omega^2 \approx 2C \left(\frac{1}{M_1} + \frac{1}{M_2} \right) \tag{9.35}$$

and

$$\omega^2 \approx \frac{C/2}{M_1 + M_2} k^2 a^2. \tag{9.36}$$

Near the Brillouin zone we get

$$\omega^2 = 2C/M_2 \tag{9.37}$$

$$\omega^2 = 2C/M_1 \tag{9.38}$$

The general dependence of ω on k is shown in the Figure 9.9. Two branches of lattice vibrations can be observed in the results. The lower branch, which is called the acoustic branch, has the property that as for the monatomic lattice, ω goes to zero as k goes to zero. The upper branch, called the optical branch, has a finite ω even at $k = 0$.

It is important to examine the eigenfunctions (i.e., u_s) for the optical branch and the acoustic branch of the dispersion relation. For $k = 0$, for the optical branch, we have after substituting

$$\omega^2 = 2C \left(\frac{1}{M_1} + \frac{1}{M_2} \right) \tag{9.39}$$

in the equation of motion

$$u = \frac{-M_2}{M_1} v. \tag{9.40}$$

The two atoms vibrate against each other, but their center of mass is fixed. If we examine the acoustic branch, we get $u = v$ in the long wavelength limit.

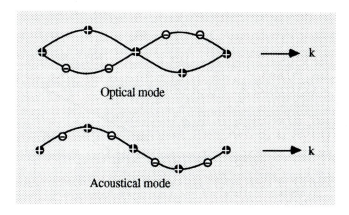

Figure 9.10: Transverse optical and transverse acoustical waves in a diatomic linear lattice, illustrated by the particle displacements for the two modes at the same wavelength.

This is shown schematically in Figure 9.10. The vibration of the atoms in the optical mode, if the atoms are charged, can produce a long-range electric field. Photons can interact with this electric field and this is the reason the mode is called optical mode.

9.4   PHONONS: QUANTIZATION OF LATTICE VIBRATIONS

In the previous discussions we evaluated the dispersion relation ω vs. k for a set of coupled harmonic oscillator equations. If we consider a single harmonic oscillator problem in quantum mechanics with the Hamiltonian (Appendix C)

$$H = \frac{P^2}{2m} + \frac{1}{2}Cx^2 \tag{9.41}$$

the energy of the vibrating particles is quantized and is given by

$$\epsilon_n = \left(n + \frac{1}{2}\right)\hbar\omega \tag{9.42}$$

where $n = 0, 1, 2 \ldots$.

The frequency ω is just the classical frequency $(2C/M)^{1/2}$. In classical physics the energy of the oscillator can be continuous and corresponds to a continuously increasing amplitude of vibration. The quantum oscillator has a minimum energy $\hbar\omega/2$ and the energy changes in steps of $\hbar\omega$. In the language of second quantization one says that the number n of Equation 9.42 represents the number of "particles" in the system or the occupation number of the system. One uses the term *phonon* to describe the lattice vibrations once they are treated as particles. For a single oscillator the frequency ω is fixed, but if we have a series of coupled oscillators as is the case for the atoms in a crystal, the frequency varies and we can introduce the phase determining vector $\boldsymbol{k}$ and get an ω vs. $\boldsymbol{k}$ relation of the form we derived. However, at each frequency $\omega_{\mathbf{k}}$ one can solve the harmonic oscillator problem in quantum mechanics and find that the energy is quantized and given by

$$\epsilon_{\mathbf{k}} = \left(n_{\mathbf{k}} + \frac{1}{2} \right) \hbar \omega_{\mathbf{k}} \tag{9.43}$$

In the context of lattice vibrations the number $n_{\mathbf{k}}$ denotes the number of phonons in the mode $\omega_{\mathbf{k}}$. To find out how many phonons are in a given mode one needs to define the statistics for phonons which we will discuss later, in Section 9.7.

The wave vector $\boldsymbol{k}$ can take on the values given by

$$|\boldsymbol{k}| = \frac{2\pi n}{Na}; \text{ for } n = 0, \pm 1, \ldots, \pm \frac{N-1}{2}, \frac{N}{2} \tag{9.44}$$

where N is the number of unit cells in the system. This leads to $3N$ (N longitudinal and $2N$ transverse) modes of vibration for the system. Each such mode can have a number n for its occupation number as given by the phonon statistics.

9.4.1   Conservation Laws in Scattering of Particles Involving Phonons

A phonon with a wave vector $\boldsymbol{k}$ will interact with particles such as electrons and photons and change their momentum as if its momentum was $\hbar \boldsymbol{k}$. Remember that in the case of electrons, the relevant electron momentum is $\hbar \boldsymbol{k}$ (wave vector) and not the true momentum of the electron. The phonons actually do not carry any momentum, they just behave as if they had a momentum. The actual physical momentum of the lattice vibrations is zero. Physically, this is obvious since the atoms are moving against each other, the crystal as a whole is not moving. Mathematically this can be seen as follows. The momentum of the crystal is

$$\boldsymbol{p} = M \frac{d}{dt} \sum_s \boldsymbol{u}_s. \tag{9.45}$$

Due to the nature of the solution for the vibration $\boldsymbol{u}_s$, this quantity is zero as one expects. This situation is quite similar to the discussions we when we discussed the crystal momentum of the electrons. In that context we had noted that even though $\hbar \boldsymbol{k}$ was not the momentum of the electrons, one could use it as if it were the electron momentum. We had also discussed the conservative laws for crystal momentum. The same holds for phonon momentum. When we discuss electron-phonon interactions in Chapter 12, we will see that one has, in general, the conservation laws

$$\boldsymbol{k}_i = \boldsymbol{k}_f + \boldsymbol{q} \tag{9.46}$$

$$E_i = E_f \pm \hbar w_{\mathbf{q}} \qquad (9.47)$$

where $\mathbf{k}_i$ and $\mathbf{k}_f$ are the initial and final electron momenta, $\mathbf{q}$ is the phonon momenta, E_i, E_f, $\hbar w_{\mathbf{q}}$ are the corresponding energies. In more complex scattering problems where more phonons are involved, the conservation laws get appropriately modified.

9.5 POLAR OPTICAL PHONONS

In our discussions of optical phonons, we have ignored the fact that in some semiconductors, the atoms carry positive and negative charges (the anions and cations). This is not true only of group IV semiconductors like Si, Ge, C, etc. Due to this ionic nature of compound semiconductors, there is an additional restoring force due to the long-range polarization fields that are produced in the lattice vibrations. These polarization fields are only produced in the longitudinal modes and not in the transverse modes as can be seen from Figure 9.11. Due to this additional restoring force, there is a difference between the longitudinal and transverse frequencies. We will examine these differences in two approaches. The first one is extremely simplistic and only brings out the physical concepts. We will work in the relative vector

$$\mathbf{u}_r = \mathbf{u} - \mathbf{v} \qquad (9.48)$$

which represents the relative displacement between the positively and negatively charged ion lattices. The equation of motion for the transverse vibrations which do not produce any polarizations is

$$M\ddot{\mathbf{u}}_r + M\omega_t^2 \mathbf{u}_r = 0 \qquad (9.49)$$

where M is the reduced mass of the two atoms and ω_t is the transverse optical phonon frequency. In a longitudinal vibration mode, an addition electric field is produced due to the polarization produced by the vibrations. The equation of motion is given by the restoring force, which is the sum of the force in Equation 9.49 and the electric field force. The equation for the longitudinal vibration is

$$-\omega_l^2 M\mathbf{u}_r = -\omega_t^2 M\mathbf{u}_r + \mathbf{F}_i e^* \qquad (9.50)$$

when $\mathbf{F}_i$ is the internal electric field due to the polarization, and e^* is an effective electronic charge per ion. If n is the number of unit cells per unit volume, the polarization is

$$\mathbf{P} = ne^* \mathbf{u}_r \qquad (9.51)$$

and the electric field is

$$\begin{aligned} \mathbf{F}_i &= -4\pi \mathbf{P} \\ &= -4\pi ne^* \mathbf{u}_r. \qquad (9.52) \end{aligned}$$

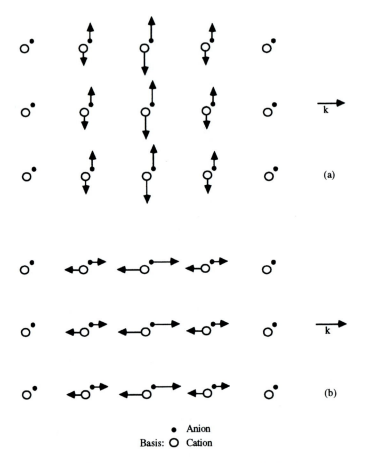

Basis: ● Anion
○ Cation

Figure 9.11: Optical modes of vibration of an ionic crystal. During transverse modes, (a) the vibrations do not produce any polarization effects, while long-range electric fields due to polarization are produced in longitudinal modes (b).

The longitudinal frequency is then

$$\omega_l^2 = \omega_t^2 + \frac{4\pi n e^{*2}}{M} \tag{9.53}$$

The effective charge, e^*, will be discussed again in Chapter 12, when we discuss polar optical phonon scattering.

We will now develop a second, somewhat more involved, macroscopic theory for the phonon frequency ω_l, by expressing the restoring force due to the polarization in terms of physical quantities ϵ_0 and ϵ_∞, the low frequency and high frequency dielectric constants. The dielectric constant of ionic semiconductors has, in general, two components. The most important component is the electronic component coming from the electrons in the valence band. The electrons are able to respond very fast to any external electric field and thus this component is present at low as well as high frequencies. The second component is due to the dipole between atoms. This part contributes only at low frequencies and is absent from ϵ_∞ since at high frequencies the heavy atoms cannot respond to the rapidly varying fields. In general, the equation of motion of the relative displacement

$$u_r = (u - v) \tag{9.54}$$

is given from the Lagrangian density (see for example, Kittel, 1987),

$$\mathcal{L} = \frac{1}{2}M u_r^2 - \frac{1}{2}\left(\gamma_{11}\, u_r^2 - \gamma_{12}\, u_r \cdot F - \frac{1}{2}\gamma_{22}\, F^2\right)$$

$$M\ddot{u}_r + \gamma_{11}\, u_r - \gamma_{12}\, F = 0 \tag{9.55}$$

where γ_{11} and γ_{12} are parameters to be determined later. The equation of motion comes from a restoring force proportional to u_r and a component proportional to the electric field of the polarization. The Hamiltonian density is

$$H = \frac{1}{2}M\dot{u}_r^2 + \frac{1}{2}\gamma_{11}\, u_r^2 - \gamma_{12}\, u_r \cdot F - \frac{1}{2}\gamma_{22}\, F^2 \tag{9.56}$$

leading to a polarization

$$
\begin{aligned}
P &= -\frac{\partial H}{\partial F} \\
&= \gamma_{12} u_r + \gamma_{22} F.
\end{aligned}
\tag{9.57}
$$

The transverse optical phonons do not involve any electric field and have the equation of motion

$$\ddot{u}_r + \gamma_{11} u_r = 0 \tag{9.58}$$

with

$$\gamma_{11} = \omega_t^2. \tag{9.59}$$

Now under static conditions, $\ddot{u}_r = 0$ leading to

$$u_r = \frac{\gamma_{12}}{\gamma_{11}} F \tag{9.60}$$

for the longitudinal mode.

This gives a value for the polarization

$$
\begin{aligned}
P &= \left[\frac{\gamma_{12}^2}{\gamma_{11}} + \gamma_{22}\right] F \\
&\equiv \frac{\epsilon_0 - 1}{4\pi} F
\end{aligned}
\tag{9.61}
$$

where by definition, ϵ_0 is the static dielectric constant. At very high frequencies, the heavy atoms cannot follow the electric field and u_r approaches zero giving us from Equation 9.57

$$
\begin{aligned}
P &= \gamma_{22} F \\
&= \frac{\epsilon_\infty - 1}{4\pi} F
\end{aligned}
\tag{9.62}
$$

where ϵ_∞ is the high frequency dielectric constant coming only from the electronic part. This gives

$$\gamma_{22} = \frac{\epsilon_\infty - 1}{4\pi} \tag{9.63}$$

and

$$\gamma_{12} = \left(\frac{\epsilon_0 - \epsilon_\infty}{4\pi} \right)^{1/2} \omega_t \tag{9.64}$$

Since $\boldsymbol{D} = \boldsymbol{F} + 4\pi \boldsymbol{P} = 0$ in absence of any external fields

$$
\begin{aligned}
\boldsymbol{F} + 4\pi \boldsymbol{P} &= [1 + 4\pi \, \gamma_{22}] \, \boldsymbol{F} + 4\pi \, \gamma_{12} \, \boldsymbol{u}_r \\
&= 0
\end{aligned}
\tag{9.65}
$$

for longitudinal vibrations. The equation of motion for the longitudinal modes becomes

$$\ddot{\boldsymbol{u}}_r + \left(\gamma_{11} + \frac{4\pi \gamma_{12}^2}{1 + 4\pi \gamma_{22}} \right) \boldsymbol{u}_r = 0$$

or

$$
\begin{aligned}
\omega_l^2 &= \gamma_{11} + \frac{4\pi \, \gamma_{12}^2}{1 + 4\pi \, \gamma_{22}} \\
&= \frac{\epsilon_0}{\epsilon_\infty} \omega_t^2.
\end{aligned}
\tag{9.66}
$$

Note that a comparison of Equations 9.53 and 9.66 allows one to express the effective charge e^* in terms of ϵ_0 and ϵ_∞. In Chapter 12, we will explore this further while discussing electron–polar optical phonon scattering.

Since $\epsilon_0 > \epsilon_\infty$, the longitudinal optical phonon frequency is higher than the transverse phonons at small $\boldsymbol{k}$. The Figures 9.12 through 9.15 show some phonon dispersion curves for several semiconductors. For group IV semiconductors, there is, of course, no splitting at $\boldsymbol{k} = 0$ between the longitudinal and transverse phonon frequencies. However, for III-V compounds there is an important difference arising from the ionicity of the crystal. An important point to note is that the optical phonons have little dispersion near $\boldsymbol{k} = 0$, i.e., the bands are almost flat unlike the acoustic phonons. When we come to the chapter on scattering of electrons by phonons we will make the assumption that the optical phonons are dispersionless.

We will now discuss why the optical phonons are given the prefix optical by studying the interaction of phonons and photons.

9.6   OPTICAL PHONON–PHOTON INTERACTIONS

In the analysis for the optical phonon dispersion, we have neglected the presence of any external electric field. If an electromagnetic wave (photon) is incident on the semiconductor, the electric field of the optical phonons and the photons will

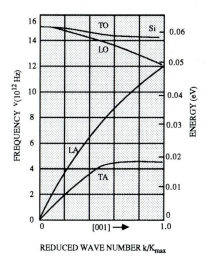

Figure 9.12: Measured phonon spectra of Si. (Reproduced with permission, B. N. Brockhouse, Phys. Rev. Lett., **2**, 256 (1959).)

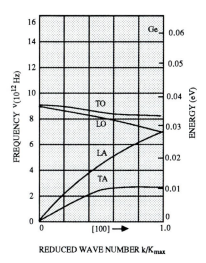

Figure 9.13: Measured phonon spectra in Ge. (Reproduced with permission, B. N. Brockhouse, et al., Phys. Rev., **111**, 747 (1958).)

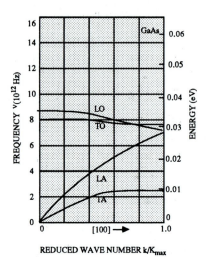

Figure 9.14: Phonon spectra of GaAs. (Reproduced with permission, J. L. T. Waugh, et al., Phys. Rev., **132**, 2410 (1963).)

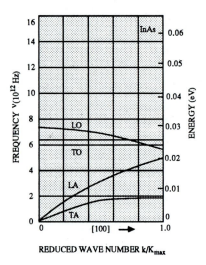

Figure 9.15: Phonon spectra in InAs. (Reproduced with permission, R. Carles, Phys. Rev. B, **22**, 4804 (1980).)

couple with each other. One has to then solve the combined phonon–phonon problem. This involves solving the following six equations (four Maxwell's equations and two phonon equations).

$$\nabla \times \boldsymbol{B} = \frac{1}{c}\left(\frac{\partial \boldsymbol{F}}{\partial t} + 4\pi \frac{\partial \boldsymbol{P}}{\partial t}\right)$$

$$\nabla \times \boldsymbol{F} = -\frac{1}{c}\frac{\partial \boldsymbol{B}}{\partial t}$$

$$\nabla \cdot \boldsymbol{B} = 0$$

$$\nabla \cdot (\boldsymbol{F} + 4\pi \boldsymbol{P}) = 0$$

$$\ddot{\boldsymbol{u}}_r + \gamma_{11}\boldsymbol{u}_r - \gamma_{12}\boldsymbol{F} = 0$$

$$\boldsymbol{P} = \gamma_{12}\boldsymbol{u}_r + \gamma_{22}\boldsymbol{F}. \tag{9.67}$$

Let us consider the $\boldsymbol{k}$-vector to be along the z-axis and look at transverse modes of vibration.

$$F_x = F_x(0)\, e^{i(\omega t - kz)} \quad ; \quad P_x = P_x(0)\, e^{i(\omega t - kz)}$$
$$u_{rx} = u_{rx}(0)\, e^{i(\omega t - kz)} \quad ; \quad B_y = B_y(0)\, e^{i(\omega t - kz)} \tag{9.68}$$

This substitution yields the following coupled equations

$$\frac{i\omega}{c}F_x - ikB_y + \frac{4\pi i\omega}{c}P_x = 0$$

$$ikF_x - \frac{i\omega}{c}B_y = 0$$

$$\gamma_{12}\,F_x + (\omega^2 - \gamma_{11})\,u_{rx} = 0$$

$$\gamma_{22}\,F_x - P_x + \gamma_{12}\,u_{rx} = 0 \tag{9.69}$$

This is solved by the usual matrix technique which tells us that for nontrivial solutions, the following determinant must vanish

$$\begin{vmatrix} \omega/c & 4\pi\omega/c & -k & 0 \\ k & 0 & -\omega/c & 0 \\ \gamma_{12} & 0 & 0 & \omega^2 - \gamma_{11} \\ \gamma_{22} & -1 & 0 & \gamma_{12} \end{vmatrix} = 0 \tag{9.70}$$

which gives the quartic equation, after making the substitutions for $\gamma_{11}, \gamma_{12}, \gamma_{22}$, from Equations 9.59, 9.63, and 9.64,

$$\omega^4 \epsilon_\infty - \omega^2 \left(\omega_t^2 \epsilon_0 + c^2 k^2\right) + \omega_t^2 c^2 k^2 = 0 \tag{9.71}$$

where ω_t is the transverse optical phonon frequency value discussed above. The solutions for ω^2 are

$$\omega^2 = \frac{1}{2\epsilon_\infty}\left(\omega_t^2 \epsilon_0 + c^2 k^2\right) \pm \left[\frac{1}{4\epsilon_\infty^2}\left(\omega_t^2 \epsilon_0 + c^2 k^2\right)^2 - \omega_t^2 k^2 \left(\frac{c^2}{\epsilon_\infty}\right)\right]^{1/2}. \tag{9.72}$$

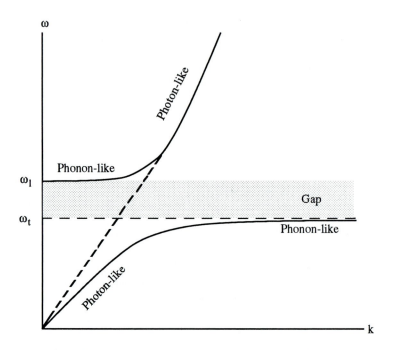

Figure 9.16: Coupled modes of photons and transverse optical phonons in an ionic crystal. The broken lines show the spectra without interaction.

These solutions take on a simple form near $k = 0$

$$
\begin{aligned}
\omega^2 &= \omega_t^2 \frac{\epsilon_0}{\epsilon_\infty} \\
&= \omega_l^2
\end{aligned}
\tag{9.73}
$$

and

$$
\omega^2 = \frac{c^2}{\epsilon_0} k^2.
\tag{9.74}
$$

For large values of k, the solutions become

$$
\omega^2 = \frac{c^2 k^2}{\epsilon_\infty}
\tag{9.75}
$$

and

$$
\omega^2 = \omega_t^2.
\tag{9.76}
$$

These solutions are shown in Figure 9.16. We can see that the lower solution has a photon-like behavior at small k and behaves like the transverse phonon at higher k-value. The upper branch is phonon-like at low k and even though the phonons are transverse, their frequency is ω_l. At high k-values, the branch becomes photon-like.

It is important to note that there is a forbidden gap in the region ω_t to ω_l. Although we have as yet only looked at transverse fields, the photons do not have a longitudinal mode and thus there is no possibility of transmitting photons with frequency between ω_t and ω_l. These photons are reflected back.

For longitudinal solution to the problem, there is no coupling between the phonons and the photon field and we simply have the longitudinal optical phonon modes as before.

9.7 PHONON STATISTICS

We have briefly discussed how the lattice vibration can be represented by particles called phonons. How many phonons are present in a given mode $\omega_{\mathbf{k}}$ at temperature T? As in the case of electrons, to get this information we need to know the distribution function. The phonons are characterized as Bosons, i.e., particles which can "share" the same quantum state. Their occupation number is given by Bose–Einstein statistics which is valid at thermal equilibrium.

The derivation of this distribution is quite simple. Consider an ensemble of identical harmonic oscillators, with their quantum states all differing in energy by $\hbar\omega$. The ratio of the oscillators in the state $n + 1$ and n^{th} state is simply

$$\frac{N_{n+1}}{N_n} = \exp\left(\frac{-\hbar\omega}{k_B T}\right). \tag{9.77}$$

Thus the fraction of oscillators having the state n (i.e. having energy $(n\hbar\omega + 1/2)$ or n phonons) is

$$\begin{aligned} <n> &= \frac{\sum_{p=0}^{\infty} p\, N_p}{\sum_{p=0}^{\infty} N_p} \\ &= \frac{\sum_{p=0}^{\infty} p\, \exp(-p\hbar\omega/k_B T)}{\sum_{p=0}^{\infty} \exp(-p\hbar\omega/k_B T)}. \end{aligned} \tag{9.78}$$

Using the summations

$$\begin{aligned} \sum_p x^p &= \frac{1}{1-x} \\ \sum_p p x^p &= \frac{x}{(1-x)^2} \\ x &= \exp(-\hbar\omega/k_B T) \end{aligned} \tag{9.79}$$

we get

$$\langle n_\omega \rangle = \frac{1}{\exp\frac{\hbar\omega}{k_B T} - 1} \tag{9.80}$$

which is called the Planck's or Bose-Einstein distribution. In Figure 9.17 we show a plot of this distribution function. As can be seen, unlike the Fermi–Dirac

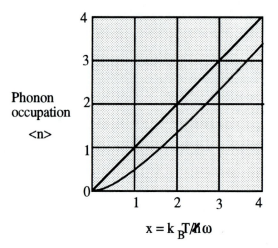

Figure 9.17: Plot of the Bose–Einstein distribution function. At high temperatures the occupancy of a state is approximately linear in the temperature. The function $\langle n \rangle + 1/2$, which is not plotted, approaches the upper line as asymptote at high temperatures. The upper straight line is a classical limit.

function, for occupancy of electron states, phonon occupancy can be larger than unity. The higher the temperature, the larger the vibration of the lattice atoms and larger the value of $\langle n_\omega \rangle$. It is also important to note that at low temperatures, the occupancy of the optical phonons is going to be very small since the optical phonons have a large energy for any value of k. On the other hand, the acoustic phonons exist with very small $\hbar\omega$ (at low k values) and are thus present even at very low temperatures. Thus at low temperatures, the optical phonons do not play as important a role. One can see that in the limit

$$\hbar\omega \ll k_B T$$
$$\langle n \rangle \approx \frac{k_B T}{\hbar\omega}. \qquad (9.81)$$

The total energy of the lattice vibrations is given by (ignoring the zero point energy)

$$U = \sum_{k,\rho} \langle n_{k,\rho} \rangle \, \hbar\omega_{k,\rho} \qquad (9.82)$$

where k is the wavevector and ρ represents the polarization of the mode.

9.7.1 Density of Modes

As in the case of the electron dispersion results, it is useful to describe and use the concept of density of states. The formal expressions for the density of states are exactly the same since the lattice vibration and the electronic state

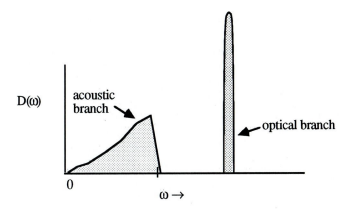

Figure 9.18: A schematic of the density of phonons for a simple 1-D lattice. The optical branch gives a high density of states because of the nature of the optical phonon w vs. k dispersion.

are both described by a planewave $(\exp(i\boldsymbol{k} \cdot \boldsymbol{r}))$ form. Once again we remind ourselves that the k-space volume occupied by each state is $(2\pi/L)^d$ where d is the dimensionality and L is the length of the crystal being considered.

For a 1–D problem the density of states is

$$D(\omega)d\omega = \frac{2L}{2\pi} \left| \frac{dk}{d\omega} \right| \cdot d\omega$$

$$= \frac{L}{\pi} \frac{d\omega}{|(d\omega/dk)|}$$

$$D(\omega)d\omega = \frac{L}{\pi} \frac{1}{|(d\omega/dk)|}. \tag{9.83}$$

In one-dimension both dk and $-dk$ are counted so that we have a factor L/π and not $L/(2\pi)$ in the expression. The density of states has to be summed for all polarizations.

In a 3-D system with volume V, the density of modes is

$$D(\omega) = \frac{d}{d\omega} \left[\frac{4\pi}{3} k^3 \times \left(\frac{L}{2\pi} \right)^3 \right]$$

$$D(\omega) = \frac{V}{2\pi^2} k^2 \frac{dk}{d\omega} \tag{9.84}$$

As in the case of the electron density of states, one has, in general, regions where $d\omega/dk$ vanishes leading to singularities in the density of states. In fact, in our simple dispersion curves obtained for monatomic or diatomic lattices, there are singularities at the Brillouin zone. A schematic density of states is shown in Figure 9.18 for a typical dispersion curve. The optical phonon branch has little dispersion and has a sharp peak in the density of states at the optical phonon energy.

It is important to note certain guidelines for the total number of modes present in material for each unit cell. For s–nonequivalent ions in the unit cell, there are 3 branches (one longitudinal, 2 transverse) which are acoustic in nature, i.e., the frequency goes to zero as k goes to zero. Additionally, there are $3(s-1)$ optical branches. Also, the value of k is to be restricted to the first Brillouin zone, otherwise one simply recounts the same modes. Thus, if there are N unit cells, there are $3Ns$ modes of vibrations. These guidelines are useful when one develops simpler descriptions of the phonon dispersion curves to understand the heat capacity of solids. Two such models are the Debye model and the Einstein model.

9.8   MODELS FOR PHONON ENERGY

9.8.1   Debye Model

A useful concept in phonon studies is the concept of Debye temperature. Debye assumed that the dispersion of the lattice vibrations was simply

$$\omega = vk. \tag{9.85}$$

The density of modes is then

$$D(\omega) = V \frac{\omega^2}{2\pi^2 v^3}. \tag{9.86}$$

Note that this is also the density of modes for photons. If there are N primitive cells in the system, the integral

$$N = \int_0^{\omega_D} D(\omega) \, d\omega \tag{9.87}$$

sets an upper limit of the frequency of vibration. We note that in reality, of course, the upper limit is determined by the Brillouin zone edge, but then the ω vs. k relation is more complex. In the simpler Debye model we get from Equations 9.86 and 9.87 the upper frequency limit for the phonon

$$\omega_D^3 = 6\pi^2 v^3 \frac{N}{V}. \tag{9.88}$$

Correspondingly, there is a cutoff wave vector k_D

$$
\begin{aligned}
k_D &= \frac{\omega_D}{v} \\
&= \left(6\pi^2 \frac{N}{V} \right)^{1/3}.
\end{aligned}
\tag{9.89}
$$

The quantity $\hbar\omega_D/k_B$ is called the Debye temperature T_D. This upper limit will, in general, be different from the Brillouin zone edge because of our incorrect choice of the ω vs. k relation. The thermal energy for each polarization is now

$$U = \int d\omega \, D(\omega) \, \langle n_\omega \rangle \, \hbar\omega$$
$$= \int_0^{\omega_D} d\omega \left(\frac{V\omega^2}{2\pi^2 v^3} \right) \left(\frac{\hbar\omega}{\exp(\hbar\omega/k_B T) - 1} \right). \tag{9.90}$$

If we assume that the velocity of the phonons is independent of the polarization, the total energy is simply three times the above result.

$$U = \frac{3V\hbar}{2\pi^2 v^3} \int_0^{\omega_D} d\omega \, \frac{\omega^3}{\exp(\hbar\omega/k_B T) - 1}. \tag{9.91}$$

Writing

$$x = \frac{\hbar\omega}{k_B T}$$

and

$$x_D = \frac{\hbar\omega_D}{k_B T},$$

we get

$$U = \frac{3V k_B^4 T^4}{2\pi^2 v^3 \hbar^3} \int_0^{x_D} dx \, \frac{x^3}{e^x - 1}$$
$$= 9Nk_B T \left(\frac{T}{T_D} \right)^3 \int_0^{x_D} dx \, \frac{x^3}{e^x - 1}. \tag{9.92}$$

At low temperatures, we can extend the limit on the integral to ∞ without any loss of accuracy. We then use the value of the integral

$$\int_0^\infty dx \, \frac{x^3}{e^x - 1} = \frac{\pi^4}{15}$$

to get

$$U = 3\pi^4 N k_B T^4 / 5T_D^3 \tag{9.93}$$

for $T \ll T_D$ and the specific heat then has the form

$$C_V = \frac{\partial U}{\partial T}$$
$$= \frac{12\pi^4}{5} N k_B \left(\frac{T}{T_D} \right)^3. \tag{9.94}$$

This is called the Debye T^3 law, and is a fairly good approximation at low temperatures. In the Debye model, the optical phonons are completely ignored. In the Einstein model to be discussed next, we effectively include only the optical modes.

9.8.2   Einstein Model

A quite different model was proposed by Einstein, in which he argued that it is not the acoustic modes but the optical modes that are important for the specific heat. The rationale for this is that although the acoustic modes are much more heavily populated, they really do not store much energy since their frequency is so low. On the other hand, even the weakly populated optical modes will store significant energy as their frequency is very high. In the Einstein model, use is made of the fact that the dispersion curve for optical phonons is relatively flat, so that the spectrum is approximately constant, and the density of states then becomes

$$D(\omega) = N\delta(\omega - \omega_0), \tag{9.95}$$

where ω_0 is the optical mode frequency. Then the total energy in the optical modes is just

$$
\begin{aligned}
U &= 3N \langle n(\omega_0) \rangle \hbar\omega_0 \\
  &= 3N\, k_B T \frac{x_0}{\exp(x_0) - 1},
\end{aligned}
\tag{9.96}
$$

where $x_0 = \hbar\omega_0/k_B T$. The specific heat is then generated as (again, the derivative is taken prior to introducing the reduced coordinate x_0)

$$C_v = 3Nk_B \frac{x_0^2 \exp(x_0)}{[\exp(x_0) - 1]^2}. \tag{9.97}$$

The behavior of Equation 9.97 at low temperatures is very similar to that of the Debye model, but its magnitude is slightly smaller.

9.8.3   Anharmonic Effects

In the analysis that has been carried out so far, we have made the harmonic approximation, i.e., retained only second order term in the potential energy versus atomic displacement relation. While this is adequate for most purposes (particularly scattering of electrons from phonons), it does create serious difficulties in interpreting some known observations. The most important deficiencies are:

1. There is no thermal expansion in solids!

2. Phonons do not interact with each other. Thus a phonon can remain indefinitely in a crystal without decaying.

3. The elastic constants have no pressure or temperature dependence.

In this text the issues listed above are not a major concern so we will not go into the much more complex discussions of anharmonic effects.

9.9   PHONON DISPERSION MEASUREMENT TECHNIQUES

A number of important measurement techniques exist for obtaining phonon dispersion of materials. The key ones are: neutron scattering, Brillouin scattering, and Raman scattering. All of these techniques are extremely important characterization tools, with Raman scattering becoming a key tool for characterization of semiconductors and superlattices.

9.9.1   Neutron Scattering

In this technique, neutrons with energy $E = p^2/2m_n$ $(m_n = 1.67 \times 10^{-24}$ gm) are incident upon the crystal. The outcoming neutrons emerge at energy E' and momentum p'. The phonon dispersion is mapped out by exploiting the energy and momentum conservation laws.

If $\Delta n_{\mathbf{k}s}$ is the change in the phonon occupancy we have

$$E' - E = -\sum_{\mathbf{k},s} \hbar\omega_{\mathbf{k}s}\Delta n_{\mathbf{k}s} \tag{9.98}$$

The momentum conservation requires

$$p' - p = -\sum_{\mathbf{k},s} \hbar\mathbf{k}\Delta n_{\mathbf{k}s} + \hbar\mathbf{G} \tag{9.99}$$

where $\mathbf{G}$ is a reciprocal lattice vector. We note that because of the finite periodicity of the crystal, the conservation law can involve a nonzero reciprocal lattice vector. Scattering without involving a reciprocal lattice vector is called a normal scattering, in contrast to the name Umklapp, for a scattering event where a nonzero reciprocal lattice vector is involved. Using the two conservation laws, one can map out the phonon dispersion. In principle, several kinds of scattering processes may occur, i.e., zero, one, two, or more phonons could be involved.

9.9.2   Zero Phonon Scattering

If no phonon is emitted or absorbed, we have an elastic scattering and the problem is that discussed in our chapter on X-ray diffraction. We have

$$p' - p = \hbar\mathbf{G} \tag{9.100}$$

which is simply the Laue condition. This kind of scattering only provides information on the crystal structure.

9.9.3   One Phonon Scattering

These scattering events are most useful for obtaining information on the phonon spectra. We have the possibility of a phonon absorption or emission with the conditions,

- Absorption:

$$E^{'} = E + \hbar\omega_s(\boldsymbol{k}) \tag{9.101}$$

$$\boldsymbol{p}' = \boldsymbol{p} + \hbar\boldsymbol{k} + \hbar\boldsymbol{G} \tag{9.102}$$

where $\boldsymbol{k}$ and s are the wave vector and branch index of the phonon.

- Emission:

$$E^{'} = E - \hbar\omega_s(\boldsymbol{k}) \tag{9.103}$$

$$\boldsymbol{p}' = \boldsymbol{p} - \hbar\boldsymbol{k} + \hbar\boldsymbol{G}. \tag{9.104}$$

For either case, we can express the phonon momentum in terms of $\boldsymbol{p}' - \boldsymbol{p}$. Also, since

$$\omega_s(\boldsymbol{k} \pm \boldsymbol{G}) = \omega_s(\boldsymbol{k}) \tag{9.105}$$

i.e., the phonon spectra is periodic in reciprocal lattice vector, one can ignore the additional reciprocal lattice vector in the expression for $\hbar\boldsymbol{k}$ in terms of $(\boldsymbol{p}' - \boldsymbol{p})$. We have,

- Absorption:

$$\frac{p^{'2}}{2m_n} = \frac{p^2}{2m_n} + \hbar\omega_s\left(\frac{\boldsymbol{p} + \boldsymbol{p}'}{\hbar}\right) \tag{9.106}$$

- Emission:

$$\frac{p^{'2}}{2m_n} = \frac{p^2}{2m_n} - \hbar\omega_s\left(\frac{\boldsymbol{p} - \boldsymbol{p}'}{\hbar}\right). \tag{9.107}$$

In a particular experiment we can have the knowledge of E, $\boldsymbol{p}$, $E^{'}$, $\boldsymbol{p}'$ which allows one to map out the ω vs. $\boldsymbol{k}$ relation for the phonons.

In general, the scattered neutrons will not satisfy the energy–momentum conditions for any arbitrary value of scattering angle. Only some particular angles will have scattered phonons for a fixed incident beam of monochromatic neutrons. This sharp peak will be observed. This is in contrast to the multiphonon scattering processes where since two or more phonons are involved, the scattered neutrons emerge with a broad distribution rather than a peak. This allows one to distinguish the one phonon processes.

9.9.4 Light Scattering

When photons from a laser are scattered from a crystal with an emission or absorption of phonons, the energy shifts of the photons are small, but can be measured by interferometric techniques. Usually, the photon wave vectors are very small ($\sim 10^5$ cm^{-1} for a ~ 1 eV photon) compared to the size of the Brillouin zone ($\sim 10^8$ cm^{-1}) so that the interactions are only with zone center phonons. Thus, one can have interaction with either the zone center acoustic phonons or the optical phonons. The interaction with acoustic phonons is called

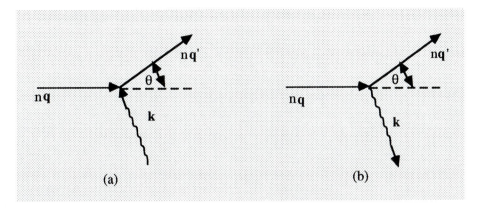

Figure 9.19: The scattering of a photon through an angle θ from free-space wave vector q to free-space wave vector q' with (a) the absorption of a phonon of wave vector k (anti-Stokes) and (b) the emission of a phonon of wave vector k (Stokes). The photon wave vectors in the crystal are nq and nq', where n is the index of refraction.

Brillouin scattering while the interaction with optical phonons is called Raman scattering.

Once again, as with the neutron scattering, one can write the conservation laws for energy and momentum. It must be remembered that the wave vector in the crystal is different from the free space photon wavevectors by the refractive index.

$$\hbar\omega' = \hbar\omega \pm \hbar\omega_s(\boldsymbol{k}) \tag{9.108}$$

$$\hbar\eta q' = \hbar\eta q \pm \hbar\boldsymbol{k} + \hbar\boldsymbol{G} \tag{9.109}$$

where n is the refractive index and $\boldsymbol{q}$ and $\boldsymbol{q}'$ are the photon wavevectors in free space. The upper sign corresponds to a phonon absorption (the process is called anti-Stokes scattering) while the lower sign corresponds to an emission (Stokes scattering). Since $\boldsymbol{q}$ and $\boldsymbol{q}'$ are very small, $\boldsymbol{G}$ has to be zero. The anti-Stokes and Stokes scattering are shown in Figure 9.19. The momentum conservation is represented by Figure 9.20. Since the energy of the phonons involved in scattering is ~ 10 meV, while the photon energy is ~ 1 eV, the process is essentially elastic and we have

$$|\boldsymbol{q}| \sim |\boldsymbol{q}'| \tag{9.110}$$

Thus, the phonon vector $\boldsymbol{k}$ is given by

$$\begin{aligned} \boldsymbol{k} &= 2\eta q \sin\frac{\theta}{2} \\ &= 2\frac{\omega\eta}{C}\sin\frac{\theta}{2} \end{aligned} \tag{9.111}$$

where θ is the scattering angle for the one-phonon scattering. The corresponding phonon frequency is determined by the change in photon frequency $\Delta\omega$. This allows one to obtain information on the phonon dispersion.

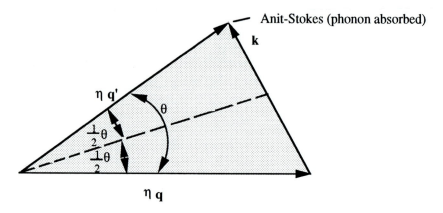

Figure 9.20: Conditions imposed by momentum conservation in photon–phonon scattering. Since the energy of the phonon is very small compared to that of the photon, $|q| \approx |q'|$.

9.10 PHONONS IN HETEROSTRUCTURES

In Chapter 6 we discussed the electronic bandstructure in heterostructures. The concepts of quantum wells, superlattices, etc., have important consequences on the phonon dispersion just like they do for electronic spectra. The main difference between the two cases is qualitative. For electrons, the band offsets in semiconductors are such that superlattice effects start becoming important as long as the barrier and well thicknesses are $\leq 20-30$ Å. Thus the electron wavefunction decay length is of the order of 30 Å or so. On the other hand, for most semiconductors the changes in force constants (the equivalent of band offsets) is so large that the lattice wave usually decays within a monolayer or so. The area of study of phonons in heterostructures has been an active one, although not to as much degree as the electronic properties in heterostructures. We will briefly recall some qualitative features of phonons in superlattices. These phonons can be characterized in three categories (see references at the end of this chapter for more details).

9.10.1 Folded Phonons

We have discussed how the superlattice produces the "folded" bands for the electronic dispersion. The same effect occurs for phonons. In particular, the acoustic phonon branch gets folded due to the decrease in the first Brillouin zone dimension. The folded phonons are just the optical phonon branches of the superlattice and can be accessed by Raman scattering. These phonons occur over the range over which the constituents materials of the superlattice overlap. For example, for GaAs and AlAs this range extends from 0 to 220 cm^{-1} (see Figure 9.21).

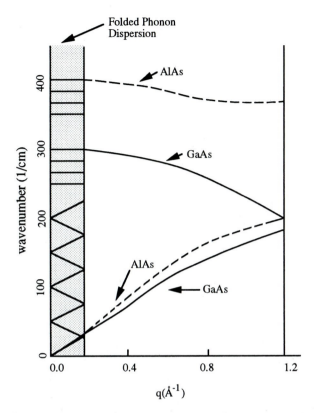

Figure 9.21: Folded phonon dispersion curve. Linear-chain model calculation of phonon dispersion curves for small longitudinal modes. Large zone: bulk GaAs (solid lines) and AlAs (dashed lines). Small zone: 5 monolayer (ml) GaAs, 4 ml AlAs superlattice. q is given in Å^{-1}. Note: there are 9-folded LA modes, 5-confined GaAs and 4-confined AlAs LO modes (after Colvard et al., 1985).

9.10.2 Confined Optical Phonons

Since the lattice waves decay rapidly when the material composition is altered (due to the large change in the atomic mass and force constants), in a superlattice, the optical phonons are confined to the individual components. For example, the optical phonon dispersion curves of GaAs and AlAs do not overlap and, therefore, the optical modes of one material cannot propagate into the other. These modes are confined within their respective layers. The picture of confined phonons is similar to the case of a particle in an infinite square well. The allowed wave vectors of these modes are:

$$|k_n| = \frac{n}{2d} \quad ; \text{for } n = 1, 2, 3, \ldots \qquad (9.112)$$

where d is a thickness of the GaAs or AlAs layer. The energy of these modes has been found to follow the dispersion curve of the bulk material fairly well. In other words, $E(k)$ is nearly the same whether one is looking at the continuous values of k for, say, GaAs or the discrete values of k dictated by Equation 9.112. Figure 9.21 shows the optical phonons which are confined.

9.10.3   Interface Phonons

In superlattices, there are also modes in the optical region that have their largest amplitude at the interfaces between two semiconductors. These interface modes carry a macroscopic electric field and can be discussed in terms of a simple electrostatic model.

The interface phonon modes have amplitudes which decay rapidly away from the interface. They are expected to play an important role in charge transport in extremely thin confinement regions (≤ 50 Å).

In this chapter we have discussed the vibration properties of the atoms forming the crystal. The mathematics of these excitations is very similar to that of the electronic bandstructure. While the phonons are not actively used in any semiconductor devices directly, they play a very important role via scattering processes. Electron phonon scattering is one of the most important scattering phenomenon which control electronic device performance. Phonon studies are also extremely important characterization tools since the lattice modes are directly related to intrinsic material properties such as crystal binding energy.

9.11   FOR THE TECHNOLOGIST IN YOU

By and large, phonons are a source of poor performance for electronic devices. As we shall see in Chapter 12, the electrons scatter from phonons resulting in poorer transport properties. A driving force for cryogenic electronics is to reduce the phonons present in a system. However, there are some areas where phonons play a very positive role. The effects of phonons in Raman spectroscopy as well as many other characterization techniques is very important. These techniques are widely used in obtaining material properties. Phonons are also important in allowing optical absorption in Si near the bandedge. This effect, discussed in Chapter 15 is of great importance since it allows Si to be used as a detector material. The near bandedge optical processes are forbidden in Si. Because of its indirect bandgap and requirement of momentum conservation (remember that the momentum of a 1.1 eV photon is almost zero). The presence of phonons allows these transitions by providing the appropriate momentum. The absorption strength is quite weak, but nevertheless, it is enough to allow detection of photons.

9.12 PROBLEMS

9.1. Consider a crystal which can be represented by a simple linear chain as far as the acoustic phonon spectra is concerned. If the sound velocity in this material is 3×10^5 cm/s, what is the phonon frequency at the zone edge $(a = 5.6$ Å$)$?

9.2. Calculate the Debye frequency for GaAs where the sound velocity is 5.6×10^5 cm/s. Assume that the volume of the unit cell is 4.39×10^{-23} cm^{-3}.

9.3. The optical phonon energies of GaAs and AlAs are 36 meV and 50 meV respectively at the zone center. What is the occupation probability of these optical phonons at 77 K and 300 K?

9.4. Consider a crystal of GaAs in which the sound velocity is 5.6×10^5 cm/s and the optical phonon energy is 36 meV and is assumed to have no dispersion. Using the Debye model for the acoustic phonon energy and the Einstein model for the optical phonons, calculate the lattice vibration energy per cm^3 at 77 K, 300 K and 1000 K. If the Ga–As bond energy is 1 eV, compare the phonon energy with the crystal binding energy per cm^3.

9.5. In Si electron transport, the intervalley scattering is very important. Two kinds of intervalley scatterings are important: in the g–scattering an electron goes from one valley (say a [001] valley) to an opposite valley ([00$\bar{1}$]), while in an f–scattering, the electron goes to a perpendicular valley ([001] to [010], for example). The extra momentum for the transitions is provided by a phonon and may include a reciprocal lattice vector. Remembering that Si valleys are not precisely at the X–point, calculate the phonon vectors which allow these scatterings.

9.6. Assuming k conservation, what is the phonon wavevector which can take an electron in the GaAs from the Γ–valley to the L–valley?

9.7. In the text, we solved the problem of phonon dispersion in a two atom basis system assuming that the force constants are the same between the M_1–M_2 bonds and the M_2–M_1 bonds. This is true for longitudinal modes, but not for transverse modes. Assume two force constants f_1 and f_2 and show that the phonon solutions are given by the equation

$$\omega^4 - \frac{M_1 + M_2}{M_1 M_2}(f_1 + f_2)\omega^2 + \frac{2f_1 f_2}{M_1 M_2}(1 - \cos\frac{ka}{2}) = 0$$

and

$$\frac{u_2}{u_1} = \frac{(f_1 + f_2 \exp(ika/2))/\sqrt{M_1 M_2}}{\frac{f_1 + f_2}{M_2} - \omega^2}.$$

9.8. The optical phonon zone center energy for GaAs is 36 meV and for AlAs it is 50 meV. Calculate the force constants for the two materials, assuming a simple linear chain model. Based on these results, what are the sound velocities in the two semiconductors?

9.9. Based on a simple linear chain model, calculate the phonon dispersion in a 2 monolayer/2 monolayer GaAs/AlAs superlattice. Use the information obtained from the previous problem.

9.10. Estimate the rms fluctuation of the atoms in an fcc structure with a bulk modulus of 7.5×10^{11} erg cm^{-2} at a temperature of 300 K. Assume that each unit cell has a thermal energy of $\sim k_B T/2$.

9.13 REFERENCES

- **Crystal Bonding**

    - Ashcroft, N. W. and N. D. Mermin, *Solid State Physics* (Holt, Rinehart and Winston, New York, 1976).

    - Kittel, C., *Introduction to Solid State Physics* (John Wiley and Sons, New York) 1986.

    - Pauling, L., *The Nature of the Chemical Bond* (Cornell, 1960).

    - Phillips, J. C., *Bonds and Bands in Semiconductors* (Academic Press, New York, 1973).

- **Lattice Vibrations in Crystals**

    - Ashcroft, N. W. and N. D. Mermin, *Solid State Physics* (Holt, Rinehart and Winston, New York, 1976).

    - Born, M. and K. Huang, *Dynamical Theory of Crystal Lattices* (Oxford University Press, London, 1954).

    - Cochran, W., *Dynamics of Atoms in Crystals* (Crane, Russak, New York, 1973).

- **Quantization of Lattice Vibrations**

    - Most quantum mechanics books have detailed discussions on the second quantization procedure which allows one to treat classical fields as particles. An example is Schiff, L. I., *Quantum Mechanics* (McGraw Hill, New York, 1968).

- **Polar Optical Phonons**

    - Kittel, C., *Quantum Theory of Solids* (John Wiley and Sons, New York, 1987).

    - Ziman, J. M., *Principles of the Theory of Solids* (Cambridge, 1972).

- **Phonon Dispersion: Measurements and Calculations**

  - Ashcroft, N. W. and N. D. Mermin, *Solid State Physics* (Holt, Rinehart and Winston, New York, 1976).
  - Brockhouse, B. N., Phys. Rev. Lett., **2**, 256 (1959).
  - Brockhouse, B. N. and P. Iyengar, Phys. Rev., **111**, 747 (1958).
  - Landolt-Bornstein, *Semiconductors* (edited by O. Madelung, M. Schultz, and H. Weiss, Springer–Verlag, Berlin, 1982).
  - Martin, D. H., Adv. in Physics, **14**, 39 (1965).
  - "Vibration Spectra of Solids," by Mitra, S. S., in Solid State Physics, **13**, (1962).
  - Waugh, J. L. T. and G. Dolling, Phys. Rev., **132**, 2410 (1963).
  - Wright, G. B., editor, *Scattering Spectra of Solids* (Springer–Verlag, New York, 1969).

- **Phonons in Heterostructures**

  - Colvard, C., T. A. Gant, M. V. Klein, R. Merlin, R. Fischer, H. Morkoc and A. C. Gossard, Phys. Rev. B, **31**, 2080 (1985).
  - Huang, K. and B. F. Zhu, Phys. Rev. B, **38**, 13377 (1988).
  - Ridley, B. K., Phys. Rev. B, **39**, 5282 (1989).
  - Rytov, S. M., Sov. Phys. JETP, **2**, 466 (1956).
  - Sawaki, N., J. Phys. C, **19**, 4965 (1986).
  - Stroscio, M. A., K. W. Kim and M. A. Littlejohn, in *Physical Concepts of Materials for Novel Optoelectronic Device Applications II: Device Physics and Applications* (edited by M. Razeghi, SPIE vol. 1362, 1990), p. 566.
  - Tamura, S. and J. P. Wolfe, Phys. Rev. B, **35**, 2528 (1987).
  - Tsu, R. and S. S. Jha, Appl. Phys. Lett, **20**, 16 (1972).

CHAPTER
10

TRANSPORT: GENERAL FORMALISM

An important concept that has emerged from our understanding of the band-structure is that even though the electron sees a complex background potential in a crystal, it *suffers no collision during its motion through the structure.* This is evident from the Bloch theorem according to which the electron is described by a plane wave function and the equation of motion for the electron (i.e., $\hbar \, dk/dt = \boldsymbol{F}_{ext}$) which describes motion without scattering as shown in Figure 10.1. However, the Bloch theorem is dependent upon the perfect periodicity of the crystalline potential, a property which is never realized in real crystals.

Various imperfections exist in a real crystal and these are responsible for scattering of the electrons between the Bloch states. The impurities could be intentional such as dopants introduced to alter the conductivity of the semiconductor as well as unintentional such as impurities and, of course, phonons or lattice vibrations. Imperfections are also present in alloys due to the inherent randomness of the atoms making up the alloy. We will now calculate the effects of these imperfections on the electron transport. It is important to remember that we use first order perturbation theory which gives us the Fermi golden rule. The rates given by the golden rule are calculated for Bloch states. Very often it is necessary to describe the electron by states that are well-defined in position space as well as momentum space. This is done by the wavepacket description. However, one ignores the uncertainty relation

$$\Delta x \Delta k \approx 1 \tag{10.1}$$

for the wavepacket. In this quasiclassical treatment the electron is then described as having a well-defined *position and momentum* while the *transition rates* are calculated using Bloch states. For most semiconductors this requires that the

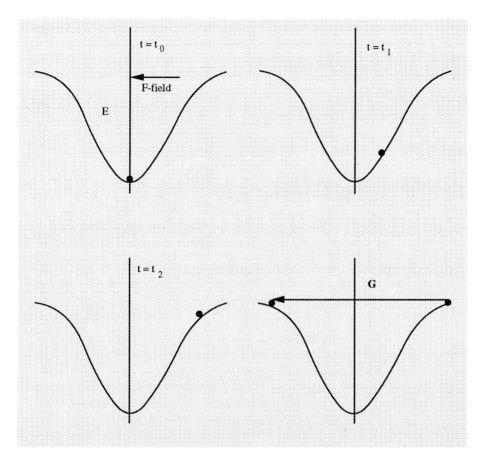

Figure 10.1: A schematic of how electrons move in absence of any imperfections in a crystal. An electron gains crystal momentum according to the equation $\hbar \, dk/dt = eF$. The electron climbs up the band until it reaches a zone edge and in the reduced zone scheme the electron appears as if it has been scattered by a reciprocal lattice vector.

region of transport be larger than about 1000 Å. For small transit regions, the uncertainty in Δk given by Equation 10.1 is too large to obtain the scattering rates by the golden rule.

In order to calculate the scattering rates using the Fermi golden rule, one must identify the scattering potential and evaluate its matrix elements between an initial state $|k\rangle$ and final state $|k^{'}\rangle$ where

$$
\begin{aligned}
|k\rangle &= u_{nk} \exp(ik \cdot r) \\
|k^{'}\rangle &= u_{n'k'} \exp(ik^{'} \cdot r).
\end{aligned}
$$

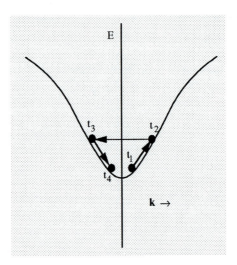

Figure 10.2: In presence of scattering the electron moves in the band in a random manner. The presence of an electric field produces a net drift.

The matrix element is then (see Appendix I)

$$H_{\mathbf{kk'}} = \frac{1}{V} \int e^{-i\mathbf{k'}\cdot\mathbf{r}} \, U_s(\mathbf{r}) \, e^{i\mathbf{k}\cdot\mathbf{r}} \, d^3r \, I(\mathbf{k},\mathbf{k'}) \qquad (10.2)$$

where $I(\mathbf{k},\mathbf{k'})$ is the overlap integral $\int_{\text{central cell}} u_{n\mathbf{k}} u_{n\mathbf{k'}} d^3r$ of the central cell part of the Bloch function. The overlap integral is extremely important especially in cases of scattering between states with different symmetries. We will discuss this integral separately and for now we will assume $I(\mathbf{k},\mathbf{k'}) = 1$.

The scattering rate is then according to the Fermi golden rule

$$W(\mathbf{k},\mathbf{k'}) = \frac{2\pi}{\hbar} \left| H_{\mathbf{kk'}} \right|^2 \delta \left(E(\mathbf{k'}) - E(\mathbf{k}) - \Delta E \right) \qquad (10.3)$$

where ΔE is the energy change during scattering.

We will evaluate $W(\mathbf{k},\mathbf{k'})$ for several important scattering processes in the next few chapters.

10.1   RELAXATION TIMES

If electrons, in a beam, initially have a momentum $\mathbf{p}_0(= \hbar \mathbf{k}_0)$ at time $t = 0$, then due to the scattering processes, they will suffer change in their states as shown in Figure 10.2. Several important time scales are of significance.

We can define a total scattering rate as

$$W_{tot} \quad = \quad \frac{1}{\tau(\mathbf{k}_0)}$$

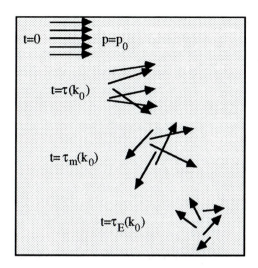

Figure 10.3: Illustration of how collisions affect a group of electrons injected at $t = 0$ with momentum p_0.

$$= \sum_{k'} W(k_0, k') \qquad (10.4)$$

which simply describes the rate (or time) taken for electrons to scatter from the state with momentum $\hbar k_0$ to any other state with momentum $\hbar k'$. Since many important scattering mechanisms have an anisotropy favoring small angle scatterings, in time $\tau(k_0)$, the electrons may not have lost all memory of their initial state. In order to understand how the momentum of the ensemble is altered, one adds a weighting factor and defines a time τ_m:

$$\frac{1}{\tau_m(k_0)} = \sum_{k'} W(k_0, k') \left(1 - \frac{|k'|}{|k_0|} \cos \theta \right) \qquad (10.5)$$

where θ is the scattering angle. τ_m is called the momentum relaxation time and represents the time over which the momentum is randomized.

Another important time scale involves the randomization of energy and is defined through,

$$\frac{1}{\tau_E(k_0)} = \sum_{k'} W(k_0, k') \left(1 - \frac{E(k')}{E(k_0)} \right) \qquad (10.6)$$

These various time scales are illustrated schematically in Figure 10.3.

10.2   THE BOLTZMANN TRANSPORT EQUATION

Given the nature of the scattering potential, it is reasonably straightforward to calculate the scattering rate. However, this information by itself does not tell us how an electron gas will move through a material. In order to describe the transport properties of an electron gas, we need to know the distribution function of the electron gas. The distribution would tell us how electrons are distributed in k-space (and E-space) and from this information all of the transport properties can be evaluated. We know that at equilibrium the distribution function is simply the Fermi-Dirac function

$$f(E) = \frac{1}{\exp\left(\dfrac{E - \mu}{k_B T}\right) + 1}. \tag{10.7}$$

This distribution function describes the equilibrium electron gas and is *independent* of any collisions that may be present. While the collisions will continuously remove electrons from one k-state to another, the net distribution of electrons is always given by the Fermi-Dirac function as long as there are no external influences to disturb the equilibrium.

To describe the distribution function in presence of external forces, we develop the Boltzmann transport equation. Let us denote by $f_{\mathbf{k}}(\mathbf{r})$ the local concentration of the electrons in state $\mathbf{k}$ in the neighborhood of $\mathbf{r}$. The Boltzmann approach begins with an attempt to determine how $f_{\mathbf{k}}(\mathbf{r})$ changes with time. There are three possible reasons for the change in the electron distribution in k-space and r-space:

1. Due to the motion of the electrons (diffusion), carriers will be moving into and out of any volume element around $\mathbf{r}$

2. Due to the influence of external forces, electrons will be changing their momentum (or $\mathbf{k}$-value) according to $\hbar \, d\mathbf{k}/dt = \mathbf{F}_{ext}$

3. Due to scattering processes, electrons will move from one $\mathbf{k}$-state to another.

We will now calculate these three individual changes by evaluating the partial time derivative of the function $f_{\mathbf{k}}(\mathbf{r})$ due to each source.

10.2.1 Diffusion Induced Evolution of $f_{\mathbf{k}}(\mathbf{r})$

If $\mathbf{v_k}$ is the velocity of a carrier in the state $\mathbf{k}$, in a time interval t, the electron moves a distance $t \, \mathbf{v_k}$. Thus the number of electrons in the neighborhood of $\mathbf{r}$ at time δt is equal to the number of carriers in the neighborhood of $\mathbf{r} - \delta t \, \mathbf{v_k}$ at time 0, as shown in Figure 10.4.

We can thus define the following equality due to the diffusion

$$f_{\mathbf{k}}(\mathbf{r}, \delta t) = f_{\mathbf{k}}(\mathbf{r} - \delta t \, \mathbf{v_k}, 0) \tag{10.8}$$

or

$$f_{\mathbf{k}}(\mathbf{r}, 0) + \frac{\partial f_{\mathbf{k}}}{\partial t} \cdot \delta t = f_{\mathbf{k}}(\mathbf{r}, 0) - \frac{\partial f_{\mathbf{k}}}{\partial \mathbf{r}} \cdot \delta t \, \mathbf{v_k}$$

$$\left. \frac{\partial f_{\mathbf{k}}}{\partial t} \right|_{\text{diff}} = -\frac{\partial f_{\mathbf{k}}}{\partial \mathbf{r}} \cdot \mathbf{v_k}. \tag{10.9}$$

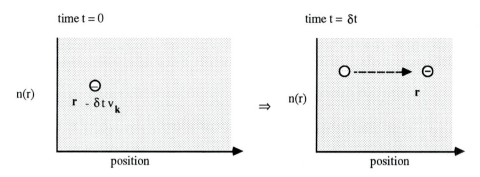

Figure 10.4: At time $t = 0$ particles at position $r - \delta t v_{\mathbf{k}}$ reach the position r at a later time δt. This simple concept is important in establishing the Boltzmann transport equation.

10.2.2 External Field Induced Evolution of $f_{\mathbf{k}}(r)$

The crystal momentum $\mathbf{k}$ of the electron evolves under the action of external forces according to Newton's equation of motion. For an electric and magnetic field ($\mathbf{F}$ and $\mathbf{B}$), the rate of change of $\mathbf{k}$ is given by

$$\dot{\mathbf{k}} = \frac{e}{\hbar}\left[\mathbf{F} + \frac{v_{\mathbf{k}} \times \mathbf{B}}{c}\right]. \tag{10.10}$$

In analogy to the diffusion induced changes, we can argue that particles at time $t = 0$ with momentum $\mathbf{k} - \dot{\mathbf{k}}\,\delta t$ will have momentum $\mathbf{k}$ at time δt and

$$f_{\mathbf{k}}(r, \delta t) = f_{\mathbf{k}-\dot{\mathbf{k}}\delta t}(r, 0) \tag{10.11}$$

which leads to the equation

$$\left.\frac{\partial f_{\mathbf{k}}}{\partial t}\right|_{\text{ext. forces}} = -\dot{\mathbf{k}}\frac{\partial f_{\mathbf{k}}}{\partial \mathbf{k}}$$

$$= \frac{-e}{\hbar}\left[\mathbf{F} + \frac{v \times \mathbf{B}}{c}\right] \cdot \frac{\partial f_{\mathbf{k}}}{\partial \mathbf{k}}. \tag{10.12}$$

10.2.3 Scattering Induced Evolution of $f_{\mathbf{k}}(r)$

We will assume that the scattering processes are *local* and *instantaneous* and change the state of the electron from $\mathbf{k}$ to $\mathbf{k}'$. Let $W(\mathbf{k}, \mathbf{k}')$ define the rate of scattering from the state $\mathbf{k}$ to $\mathbf{k}'$ if the state $\mathbf{k}$ is occupied and $\mathbf{k}'$ is empty. By principle of microscopic reversibility, we have the relation

$$W(\mathbf{k}, \mathbf{k}') = W(\mathbf{k}', \mathbf{k}) \tag{10.13}$$

i.e., the rate at which electrons are scattered from the state $\mathbf{k}$ to $\mathbf{k}'$ is the same as the rate at which they are scattered back to $\mathbf{k}$ from $\mathbf{k}'$. This principle does not mean that carriers cannot preferentially go from one state to another. To find the actual rate of transfer one must weigh the effect of occupation probability. The rate of change of the distribution function $f_{\mathbf{k}}(\mathbf{r})$ due to scattering is

$$\left.\frac{\partial f_{\mathbf{k}}}{\partial t}\right)_{\text{scattering}} = \int \left[f_{\mathbf{k}'} \left(1 - f_{\mathbf{k}}\right) W(\mathbf{k}', \mathbf{k}) - f_{\mathbf{k}} \left(1 - f_{\mathbf{k}'}\right) W(\mathbf{k}, \mathbf{k}') \right] d^3 k'.$$
(10.14)

The first term in the integral represents the rate at which electrons are coming from an occupied $\mathbf{k}'$ state (hence the factor $f_{\mathbf{k}'}$) to an unoccupied $\mathbf{k}$-state (hence the factor $(1 - f_{\mathbf{k}})$). The second term represents the loss term.

Using the principle of microscopic reversibility and simplifying the expression

$$\left.\frac{\partial f_{\mathbf{k}}}{\partial t}\right)_{\text{scattering}} = \int (f_{\mathbf{k}'} - f_{\mathbf{k}}) \, W(\mathbf{k}, \mathbf{k}') \, d^3 k'.$$
(10.15)

Under steady-state conditions, there will be no net change in the distribution function and the total sum of the partial derivative terms calculated above will be zero.

$$\left.\frac{\partial f_{\mathbf{k}}}{\partial t}\right)_{\text{scattering}} + \left.\frac{\partial f_{\mathbf{k}}}{\partial t}\right)_{\text{fields}} + \left.\frac{\partial f_{\mathbf{k}}}{\partial t}\right)_{\text{diffusion}} = 0.$$
(10.16)

Let us define

$$g_{\mathbf{k}} = f_{\mathbf{k}} - f_{\mathbf{k}}^0$$
(10.17)

where $f_{\mathbf{k}}^0$ is the equilibrium distribution.

We will attempt to calculate $g_{\mathbf{k}}$, which represents the deviation of the distribution function from the equilibrium case.

Substituting for the partial time derivatives due to diffusion and external fields we get

$$- v_{\mathbf{k}} \cdot \nabla_r f_{\mathbf{k}} - \frac{e}{\hbar} \left(\mathbf{F} + \frac{v_{\mathbf{k}} \times \mathbf{B}}{c} \right) \cdot \nabla_k f_{\mathbf{k}} = \left. \frac{-\partial f_{\mathbf{k}}}{\partial t} \right)_{\text{scattering}}$$
(10.18)

Substituting $f_{\mathbf{k}} = f_{\mathbf{k}}^0 + g_{\mathbf{k}}$

$$
\begin{aligned}
&-v_{\mathbf{k}} \cdot \nabla_r f_{\mathbf{k}}^0 - \frac{e}{\hbar} \left(\mathbf{F} + \frac{1}{c} v_{\mathbf{k}} \times \mathbf{B} \right) \nabla_k f_{\mathbf{k}}^0 \\
&= \left. -\frac{\partial f_{\mathbf{k}}}{\partial t} \right)_{\text{scattering}} + v_{\mathbf{k}} \cdot \nabla_r g_{\mathbf{k}} + \frac{e}{\hbar} \left(\mathbf{F} + \frac{1}{c} v_{\mathbf{k}} \times \mathbf{B} \right) \cdot \nabla_k g_{\mathbf{k}}.
\end{aligned}
$$
(10.19)

We remind ourselves that

$$v_{\mathbf{k}} = \frac{1}{\hbar} \frac{\partial E}{\partial k}$$
(10.20)

and

$$f_{\mathbf{k}}^0 = \frac{1}{\exp\left[\dfrac{E_{\mathbf{k}} - \mu}{k_B T}\right] + 1}$$
(10.21)

Thus

$$\nabla_r f^0 = \frac{-\left[\exp\left(\frac{E-\mu}{k_B T}\right)\right]}{\left[\exp\left(\frac{E-\mu}{k_B T}\right)+1\right]^2} \nabla_r \left(\frac{E-\mu(r)}{k_B T(r)}\right)$$

$$= k_B T \cdot \frac{\partial f^0}{\partial E}\left[-\frac{\nabla\mu}{k_B T} - \frac{(E-\mu)}{k_B T^2}\nabla T\right]$$

$$\nabla_r f^0 = \frac{\partial f^0}{\partial E}\left[-\nabla\mu - \frac{(E-\mu)}{T}\nabla T\right]. \tag{10.22}$$

Also

$$\nabla_k f^0 = \frac{\partial f^0}{\partial E}\cdot\nabla_k E$$

$$= \hbar v_{\mathbf{k}}\frac{\partial f^0}{\partial E}. \tag{10.23}$$

Substituting these terms and retaining terms only to second order in electric field (i.e., ignoring terms involving products $g_{\mathbf{k}}\cdot\boldsymbol{F}$), we get

$$-\frac{\partial f^0}{\partial E}\cdot v_{\mathbf{k}}\cdot\left[-\frac{(E-\mu)}{T}\nabla T + e\boldsymbol{F} - \nabla\mu\right]$$

$$= -\frac{\partial f}{\partial t}\bigg)_{\text{scattering}} + v_{\mathbf{k}}\cdot\nabla_r g_{\mathbf{k}} + \frac{e}{\hbar}(v_{\mathbf{k}}\times\boldsymbol{B})\cdot\nabla_k g_{\mathbf{k}}. \tag{10.24}$$

We note that the magnetic force term on the left-hand side of Equation 10.19 is proportional to

$$v_{\mathbf{k}}\cdot\frac{e}{\hbar}(v_{\mathbf{k}}\times\boldsymbol{B})$$

and is thus zero. The equation derived above is the Boltzmann transport equation.

While the Boltzmann equation looks quite simple in its form, in fact it is an extremely complex integral equation. Remember we wish to solve for $f_{\mathbf{k}}$ or $g_{\mathbf{k}}$, which are involved in the $\partial f/\partial t_{\text{scatt.}}$ term in the integrand of the scattering integral. For some simple cases one is able to make reasonable approximations and solve the equation. Often, however, the problem can become so complex that one often studies the transport problem completely bypassing the Boltzmann equation and using computer simulation techniques.

We will now apply the Boltzmann equation to derive some simple expressions for conductivity, mobility, etc., in semiconductors. We will attempt to relate the microscopic scattering events to the measurable macroscopic transport properties. Let us consider the case where we have a uniform electric field $\boldsymbol{F}$ in an infinite system maintained at a uniform temperature.

The Boltzmann equation becomes

$$
\begin{aligned}
-\frac{\partial f^0}{\partial E} \boldsymbol{v_k} \cdot e\boldsymbol{F} &= \left.-\frac{\partial f_{\mathbf{k}}}{\partial t}\right)_{\text{scattering}} \\
&= \int \left(f_{\mathbf{k}} - f_{\mathbf{k}'}\right) W(\boldsymbol{k}, \boldsymbol{k}') \, d^3 k' \\
&= \int \left(g_{\mathbf{k}} - g_{\mathbf{k}'}\right) W(\boldsymbol{k}, \boldsymbol{k}') \, d^3 k'. \qquad (10.25)
\end{aligned}
$$

Note that only the deviation $g_{\mathbf{k}}$ from the equilibrium distribution function above contributes to the scattering integral.

As mentioned earlier, this equation, although it looks simple, is a very complex equation which can only be solved analytically under fairly simplifying assumptions. We make an assumption that the scattering induced change in the distribution function is given by

$$
\left.-\frac{\partial f_{\mathbf{k}}}{\partial t}\right)_{\text{scattering}} = \frac{g_{\mathbf{k}}}{\tau}. \qquad (10.26)
$$

We have introduced a time constant τ whose physical interpretation can be understood when we consider what happens when the external forces have been removed. In this case the perturbation in the distribution function will decay according to the equation

$$
\frac{-\partial g_{\mathbf{k}}}{\partial t} = \frac{g_{\mathbf{k}}}{\tau}
$$

or

$$
g_{\mathbf{k}}(t) = g_{\mathbf{k}}(0) e^{-t/\tau}. \qquad (10.27)
$$

The time τ thus represents the time constant for relaxation of the perturbation as shown schematically in Figure 10.5. The approximation which allows us to write such a simple relation is called the relaxation time approximation (RTA).

According to this approximation

$$
\begin{aligned}
g_{\mathbf{k}} &= \left.-\frac{\partial f_{\mathbf{k}}}{\partial t}\right)_{\text{scattering}} \cdot \tau \\
&= \frac{-\partial f^0}{\partial E} \tau \boldsymbol{v_k} \cdot e\boldsymbol{F}. \qquad (10.28)
\end{aligned}
$$

Note that we have not defined how τ is to be calculated. We have merely introduced a simpler unknown that still needs to be determined. In the RTA

$$
\begin{aligned}
f_{\mathbf{k}} &= f_{\mathbf{k}}^0 + g_{\mathbf{k}} \\
&= f_{\mathbf{k}}^0 + \left(\frac{-\partial f^0}{\partial E}\right) \cdot \tau \boldsymbol{v_k} \cdot e\boldsymbol{F} \\
&= f^0 \left(E - e\tau \boldsymbol{v_k} \cdot \boldsymbol{F}\right). \qquad (10.29)
\end{aligned}
$$

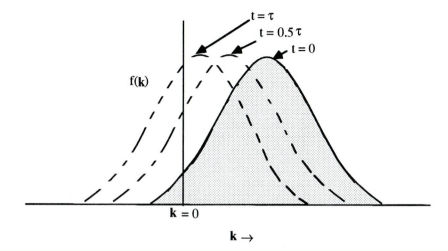

Figure 10.5: This figure shows that at time $t = 0$, the distribution function is distorted by some external means (e.g., on electric field). If the external force is removed, the electrons recover to the equilibrium distribution by collisions. In the relaxation time approximation, this recovery time is $\approx \tau$.

The distribution function thus has the *same* form as the equilibrium distribution function except that it's origin has been *shifted*. It is as if the electric field has provided an excess energy $e\tau v_\mathbf{k} \cdot \mathbf{F}$ to the electron gas. A similar form can be written in k-space.

$$
\begin{aligned}
f_\mathbf{k} &= f_\mathbf{k}^0 - \left(\frac{\partial f_\mathbf{k}^0}{\partial E}\right) e\tau v_\mathbf{k} \cdot \mathbf{F} \\
&= f_\mathbf{k}^0 - (\nabla_k f_\mathbf{k}^0) \cdot \frac{\partial k}{\partial E} \cdot e\tau v_\mathbf{k} \cdot \mathbf{F} \\
&= f_\mathbf{k}^0 - (\nabla_k f_\mathbf{k}^0) \cdot \frac{e\tau \mathbf{F}}{\hbar} \quad\quad (10.30)
\end{aligned}
$$

since

$$
\frac{1}{\hbar}\frac{\partial k}{\partial E} \cdot v_\mathbf{k} = 1
$$

$$
f_\mathbf{k} = f_\mathbf{k}^0 \left(k - \frac{e\tau \mathbf{F}}{\hbar}\right). \quad\quad (10.31)
$$

Once again, in k-space the effect of the electric field is to shift the origin of the k-space by an amount $e\tau \mathbf{F}/\hbar$. As shown in Figure 10.6, it is as if this excess k-value has been provided to the electron gas by the field. To relate the relaxation time t to the measured transport characteristics, we make the following analogy. The electron has gained an energy from the field equal to

$$
\delta E_\mathbf{k} = e\tau v_\mathbf{k} \cdot \mathbf{F}. \quad\quad (10.32)
$$

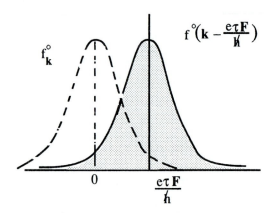

Figure 10.6: The displaced distribution function shows the effect of the applied electric field. The system behaves as if the electrons acquire a mean momentum of $e\tau F$ from the field.

This is the same energy that a classical electron gas will gain from the field if it moved through the field for a time τ. The excess drift velocity during this time will be such that

$$\delta v \cdot \frac{\partial E}{\partial v} = ev \cdot F\tau. \tag{10.33}$$

Assuming a parabolic relation $\left(E = m^* v^2/2\right)$ so that $\partial E/\partial v = m^* v$, we get

$$\delta v = \frac{e\tau F}{m^*}. \tag{10.34}$$

If the electrons concentration is n, the current density is

$$\begin{aligned} J &= ne\,\delta v \\ &= \frac{ne^2 \tau F}{m^*} \end{aligned} \tag{10.35}$$

or the conductivity of the system is

$$\sigma = \frac{ne^2 \tau}{m^*}. \tag{10.36}$$

Compare this expression to the result from the Drude model discussed in Chapter 1. Notice that we have an effective mass in Equation 10.36, but the general form for σ is the same. This equation allows us to relate a microscopic quantity τ to a macroscopic quantity σ.

So far we have introduced the relaxation time τ but not described how it is to be calculated. We will now relate it to the scattering rate $W(k, k')$ which can be calculated by using the Fermi Golden Rule. The simple form of the Boltzmann equation is

$$\frac{-\partial f^0}{\partial E} v_k \cdot eF = \int (g_k - g_{k'})\, W(k, k') d^3 k'$$

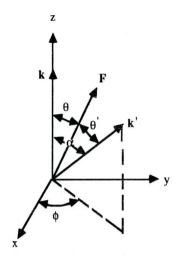

Figure 10.7: Coordinate system illustrating a scattering event. The incident carrier has momentum $\hbar k$, the scattered carrier has momentum $\hbar k^{'}$, and the applied force is F.

$$= \left. \frac{-\partial f}{\partial t} \right)_{\text{scattering}} \tag{10.37}$$

The relaxation time was defined through

$$g_{\mathbf{k}} = \left(\frac{-\partial f^0}{\partial E} \right) e\mathbf{F} \cdot \mathbf{v_k} \cdot \tau$$

$$= \left. \frac{-\partial f}{\partial t} \right)_{\text{scattering}} \cdot \tau. \tag{10.38}$$

Substituting this value in the integral on the right-hand side, we get

$$\frac{-\partial f^0}{\partial E} \mathbf{v_k} \cdot e\mathbf{F} = \frac{-\partial f^0}{\partial E} e\tau \mathbf{F} \cdot \int (\mathbf{v_k} - \mathbf{v_{k'}})\, W(k, k^{'})\, d^3 k^{'} \tag{10.39}$$

or

$$\mathbf{v_k} \cdot \mathbf{F} = \tau \int (\mathbf{v_k} - \mathbf{v_{k'}})\, W(k, k^{'})\, d^3 k^{'} \cdot \mathbf{F} \tag{10.40}$$

and

$$\frac{1}{\tau} = \int W(k, k^{'}) \left[1 - \frac{\mathbf{v_{k'}} \cdot \mathbf{F}}{\mathbf{v_k} \cdot \mathbf{F}} \right] d^3 k^{'}. \tag{10.41}$$

In general, this is a rather complex integral to solve. However, it becomes considerably simplified for certain simple cases. Consider, for example, the case of isotropic parabolic bands and elastic scattering. In Figure 10.7 we show a geometry for the scattering process. We choose a coordinate axis where the initial momentum is along the z-axis and the applied electric field is in the y-z plane.

The wavevector after scattering is given by $\boldsymbol{k}'$ represented by the angles α and ϕ. Since the scattering is elastic and the bands are isotropic, $|\boldsymbol{v_k}| = |\boldsymbol{v_{k'}}|$. We thus get

$$\frac{\boldsymbol{v_{k'}} \cdot \boldsymbol{F}}{\boldsymbol{v_k} \cdot \boldsymbol{F}} = \frac{\cos \theta'}{\cos \theta}. \tag{10.42}$$

We can easily see from Figure 10.7 that

$$\cos \theta' = \sin \theta \sin \alpha \sin \phi + \cos \theta \cos \alpha \tag{10.43}$$

or

$$\frac{\cos \theta'}{\cos \theta} = \tan \theta \sin \alpha \sin \phi + \cos \alpha. \tag{10.44}$$

When this term is integrated over ϕ to evaluate τ, the term involving $\sin \phi$ will integrate to zero for isotropic bands since $W(\boldsymbol{k}, \boldsymbol{k}')$ does not have a ϕ dependence, only an α dependence. Thus,

$$\frac{1}{\tau} = \int W(\boldsymbol{k}, \boldsymbol{k}') \left(1 - \cos \alpha\right) d^3 k'. \tag{10.45}$$

This weighting factor $(1 - \cos \alpha)$ confirms the apparent fact that large-angle scatterings are much more important in determining transport properties than small-angle scatterings. Forward-angle scatterings ($\alpha = 0$) in particular have no detrimental effect on σ or μ.

We have so far assumed that the incident electron is on a well-defined state. This has allowed us to define a relaxation time for that state and the corresponding relation

$$\boldsymbol{J} = \frac{ne^2 \tau}{m^*} \cdot \boldsymbol{F}. \tag{10.46}$$

10.3   AVERAGING PROCEDURES

In a realistic system the electron gas will have an energy distribution and τ, in general, will depend upon the energy of the electron. Thus, it is important to address the appropriate averaging procedure for τ. We will now do so under the assumptions that the drift velocity due to the electric field is much smaller than the average thermal speeds so that the energy of the electron gas is still given by $3k_B T/2$.

Let us evaluate the average current in the system.

$$\boldsymbol{J} = \int e \, \boldsymbol{v_k} \, g_{\boldsymbol{k}} \, \frac{d^3 k}{(2\pi)^3}. \tag{10.47}$$

The perturbation in the distribution function is

$$\begin{aligned} g_{\boldsymbol{k}} &= \frac{-\partial f^0}{\partial E} \tau \boldsymbol{v_k} \cdot e\boldsymbol{F} \\ &\approx \frac{f^0}{k_B T} \boldsymbol{v_k} \cdot e\boldsymbol{F}. \end{aligned} \tag{10.48}$$

If we consider a field in the x-direction, the average current in the x-direction is from Equation 10.47 and 10.48

$$\langle J_x \rangle = \frac{e^2}{k_B T} \int \tau \, v_x^2 \, f^0 \, \frac{d^3 k}{(2\pi)^3} \, F_x. \tag{10.49}$$

The assumption made on the drift velocity ensures that $v_x^2 = v^2/3$, where v is the total velocity of the electron. Thus we get

$$\langle J_x \rangle = \frac{e^2}{3 k_B T} \int \tau \, v^2 \, f^0(k) \, \frac{d^3 k}{(2\pi)^3} \, F_x. \tag{10.50}$$

Now we note that

$$\frac{1}{2} m^* \langle v^2 \rangle = \frac{3}{2} k_B T$$
$$\Rightarrow k_B T = m^* \langle v^2 \rangle / 3 \tag{10.51}$$

also

$$\langle v^2 \, \tau \rangle = \frac{\int v^2 \, \tau \, f^0(k) \, d^3 k / (2\pi)^3}{\int f^0(k) \, d^3 k / (2\pi)^3}$$
$$= \frac{\int v^2 \, \tau \, f^0(k) \, d^3 k / (2\pi)^3}{n}. \tag{10.52}$$

Substituting in the right-hand side of Equation 10.50, we get (using Equation 10.51 for $k_B T$)

$$\langle J_x \rangle = \frac{n e^2}{m^*} \frac{\langle v^2 \tau \rangle}{\langle v^2 \rangle} F_x$$
$$= \frac{n e^2}{m^*} \frac{\langle E \tau \rangle}{\langle E \rangle} F_x. \tag{10.53}$$

Thus, for the purpose of transport, the proper averaging for the relaxation time is

$$\langle\langle \tau \rangle\rangle = \frac{\langle E \tau \rangle}{\langle E \rangle}. \tag{10.54}$$

Here the double brackets represent an averaging with respect to the perturbed distribution function while the single brackets represent averaging with the equilibrium distribution function.

For calculations of low-field transport where the condition $v_x^2 = v^2/3$ is valid, one has to use the averaging procedure given by Equation 10.54 to calculate mobility or conductivity of the semiconductors. For most scattering processes, one finds that it is possible to express the energy dependence of the relaxation time in the form

$$\tau(E) = \tau_0 (E/k_B T)^s \tag{10.55}$$

where τ_0 is a constant and s is an exponent which is characteristic of the scattering process. We will be calculating this energy dependence for various scattering processes in the next two chapters. When this form is used in the averaging of Equation 10.54, we get, using a Boltzmann distribution for $f^0(k)$

$$\langle\langle\tau\rangle\rangle = \tau_0 \frac{\int_0^\infty [p^2/(2m^*k_BT)]^s \ \exp[-p^2/(2m^*k_BT)] \ p^4 \ dp}{\int_0^\infty \exp[-p^2/(2m^*k_BT)] \ p^4 \ dp} \qquad (10.56)$$

where $p = \hbar k$ is the momentum of the electron.

Substituting $y = p^2/(2m^*k_BT)$, we get

$$\langle\langle\tau\rangle\rangle = \tau_0 \frac{\int_0^\infty y^{s+(3/2)} e^{-y} dy}{\int_0^\infty y^{3/2} e^{-y} dy}. \qquad (10.57)$$

In mathematics, one has the Γ-functions which have the properties

$$
\begin{aligned}
\Gamma(n) &= (n-1)! \\
\Gamma(1/2) &= \sqrt{\pi} \\
\Gamma(n+1) &= n \ \Gamma(n)
\end{aligned}
\qquad (10.58)
$$

and have the integral value

$$\Gamma(a) = \int_0^\infty y^{a-1} e^{-y} dy. \qquad (10.59)$$

In terms of the Γ-functions we can then write

$$\langle\langle\tau\rangle\rangle = \tau_0 \frac{\Gamma(s+5/2)}{\Gamma(5/2)}. \qquad (10.60)$$

Some typical exponents for important scattering processes are shown in Table 10.1. We have also listed the so called "Hall factor" which we will discuss shortly.

The conductivity mobility obtained by measuring the rate of drift of carriers in an electric field is the drift velocity leading to the drift mobility. This has to be contrasted with the Hall mobility which will be discussed shortly. A number of techniques exist to find the drift mobility the most well known being the classic Haynes-Shockley experiment which measures the drift mobility of the minority carriers in a semiconductor. Another popular technique is the time of flight method. We will briefly describe these techniques before discussing the differences between drift and Hall mobility.

10.4 MOBILITY MEASUREMENT TECHNIQUES

10.4.1 Haynes-Shockley Experiment

A schematic diagram of the experimental arrangement is shown in Figure 10.8. For p-type mobility the sample consists of a bar of an n-type semiconductor with

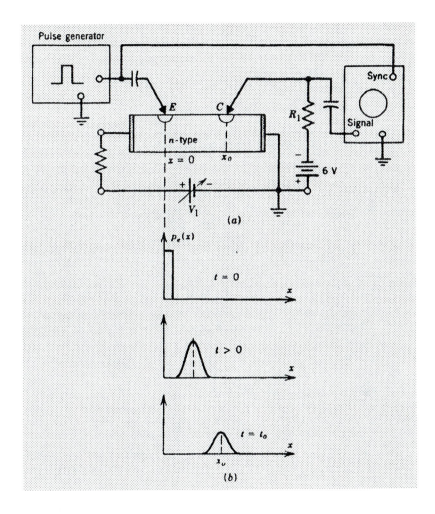

Figure 10.8: The Haynes-Shockley experiment: (a) schematic diagram and (b) development of minority carrier pulse during its drift toward the collector. (Reproduced with permission, M. S. Tyagi, *Introduction to Semiconductor Materials and Devices*, John Wiley and Sons, New York, 1991.)

Scattering Mechanism	Exponent s	Hall Factor
Acoustic phonon	$-1/2$	1.18
Ionized impurity (weakly screened)	$+3/2$	1.93
Ionized impurity (strongly screened)	$-1/2$	1.18
Neutral impurity	$-1/2$	1.18
Piezoelectric	$+1/2$	1.10
Alloy scattering	$-1/2$	1.18

Table 10.1: Exponents of some important scattering mechanisms.

ohmic contacts at the two ends. Two rectifying contacts (E and C) are placed on the bar. The contact E is used to inject minority carriers into the semiconductor, and C is used to collect them. The variable dc voltage V_1 provides the electric field for the drift of minority carriers. A pulsed voltage source is connected between E and the ground, and the contact C is reverse biased through a resistance R_1.

A positive pulse is applied to the contact E which leads to a positive pulse on the oscilloscope because of the voltage-dividing action of the bar. Thus, the initiation time of the pulse can be noted from the oscilloscope. The positive pulse at E causes injection of holes into the semiconductor, and to maintain the space-charge neutrality an equal number of electrons is drawn through the ohmic contact at the end of the bar. The electron-hole cloud initiated around E moves toward the collector contact C. As these carriers drift down the bar, the total number of carriers in the pulse decreases because of electron-hole pair recombination. In addition, holes diffuse to both sides of the original pulse, and the rectangular pulse spreads into a bell-shaped curve as shown in the lower two sketches in Figure 10.8b. When the pulse passes under the contact C, holes are collected by the contact causing a current in the resistor R_1. The voltage drop across R_1, as a function of time, is displayed on the oscilloscope as a bell-shaped curve.

The arrival time of the center of the pulse determines the mobility, and the pulse spread can be used to calculate the diffusion coefficient of the minority carriers. If $t = 0$ is the time when the pulse is applied at the emitter contact $(x = 0)$, x_0 the spacing between the emitter and the collector contacts, and t_0 the time of the arrival of the pulse center at the collector, the average drift velocity of holes is then obtained as

$$
\begin{aligned}
v_d &= \mu_p F \\
&= \frac{x_0}{t_0}
\end{aligned}
\tag{10.61}
$$

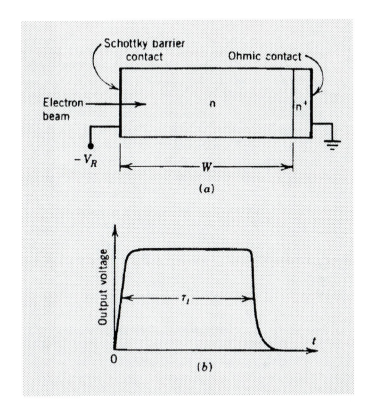

Figure 10.9: The time-of-flight method for measuring the drift velocity of carriers: (a) schematic cross-section and (b) the output voltage waveform. (Reproduced with permission, M. S. Tyagi, *Introduction to Semiconductor Materials and Devices*, John Wiley and Sons, New York, 1991.)

and since $F = V_1/l$, we get

$$\mu_p = \frac{l\, x_0}{V_1\, t_0} \tag{10.62}$$

where l is the length of the bar.

10.4.2   The Time of Flight Method

In this method, the carrier drift velocity is determined by measuring the transit time of the carriers through a region of uniform electric field. Figure 10.9a shows a typical structure that uses an n-type semiconductor. The device is fabricated by making a Schottky barrier contact at one end and producing an n^+-region at the other end of the semiconductor to which an ohmic contact is made. A similar

structure with one rectifying and the other p–p^+ contact can also be made on a
p-type semiconductor.

The n-region in Figure 10.9 is completely depleted by applying a large reverse bias to the left-hand side contact. When the bias voltage is large compared to the punch-through voltage, the field in the whole region becomes nearly constant. A very short pulse of high energy ($1 - 10$ keV) electrons from an electron gun now bombards the sample through the reverse-biased contact. The electrons dissipate their energy by creating secondary electron-hole pairs in the n-region close to the rectifying contact. The generated holes are collected at the metal contact while the electrons drift toward the n^+-region. The drift of electrons into the n-region induces a current in the external circuit that continues to flow until the electrons are collected at the n$^+$-contact. Consequently, the duration of the current pulse is essentially equal to the transit time of the electrons through the n-region. A typical output waveform may look like the one shown in Figure 10.9. The field-dependent transit time $\tau_t(F)$ is obtained as the half-amplitude width of the curve shown in the figure, and the electron drift velocity is given by

$$v_d(F) = \frac{W}{\tau_t(F)} \tag{10.63}$$

where W is the width of the drift region. The same structure can be used to determine the hole drift velocity if the n^+-face is exposed to the pulsed beam. In that case, the secondary electrons are collected at the n^+-contact, but the holes drift to the other contact and induce a current in the external circuit. This technique has been widely used to measure the electron and hole drift velocities as a function of electric field in Si and GaAs.

In the discussion above we have obtained the recipe for the averaging that needs to be carried out on the relaxation time τ ($\langle\langle\tau\rangle\rangle = \langle E\tau\rangle/\langle E\rangle$) to get the drift velocity of an ensemble of electrons. The drift mobility is, of course, of interest for most device applications. However, a common technique that is used to obtain information on the semiconductor structures is the Hall effect discussed briefly in Chapter 1. Hall effect is a powerful method which can be used to obtain information on free carrier density and "mobility." The mobility obtained by Hall effect is, however, different from the drift mobility. Although we will discuss magnetic field effects in semiconductors in more detail in Chapter 17, we will outline here the basic differences between Hall mobility and drift mobility.

10.5   TRANSPORT IN A WEAK MAGNETIC FIELD: HALL MOBILITY

The Hall effect experiment is shown schematically in Figure 10.10. One applies an electric field $\boldsymbol{F}$ and a magnetic field $\boldsymbol{B}$ in the geometry shown in the figure. The conductivity of the sample is then measured as a function of the magnetic field. The electric field is maintained at a very low value (a few V/cm) and the analysis

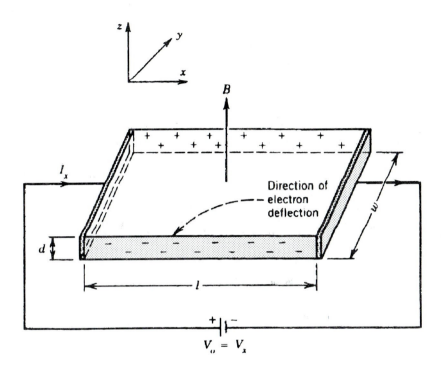

Figure 10.10: A rectangular Hall sample of an n-type semiconductor.

we will discuss below will also assume a low magnetic field. A more complete analysis of the effects of magnetic field in semiconductors will be presented in Chapter 17.

The Boltzmann equation is now

$$v \cdot \nabla_{\mathbf{r}} f + e \left[\mathbf{F} + \frac{v}{c} \times \mathbf{B} \right] \cdot \nabla_{\mathbf{p}} f = -\frac{g_f}{\tau} \tag{10.64}$$

where we are again making the relaxation time approximation. The perturbation in the distribution function g_f can be assumed to be made up of two parts: g_f' due to the electric field and g_f'' due to the magnetic field. The total perturbation is the sum of these two by the superposition principle as long as the applied forces are not strong. We already know that the effect of the electric field is to produce a distribution function

$$f(E) = f^0 \left(E - e\tau \boldsymbol{v} \cdot \boldsymbol{F} \right). \tag{10.65}$$

To evaluate the effect of the magnetic field we need to evaluate the $\nabla_p f$ term. Note that as shown by Equation 10.23

$$\nabla_p f^0(E) = \boldsymbol{v} \frac{\partial f^0}{\partial E}. \tag{10.66}$$

so that the magnetic field term $[\boldsymbol{v} \times \boldsymbol{B}] \cdot \nabla_p f$ is zero if we replace f by f^0. To the next order we replace f by Equation 10.65 so that

$$\nabla_p f = e\tau \frac{\partial f^0}{\partial E} \cdot \nabla_p \left(\boldsymbol{v} \cdot \boldsymbol{F} \right). \tag{10.67}$$

For parabolic isotropic bands we get

$$\nabla_p f \approx \frac{\partial f^0}{\partial E} \frac{e\tau \boldsymbol{F}}{m^*}. \tag{10.68}$$

We then get

$$g_f' = -e\tau \boldsymbol{F} \tag{10.69}$$

as before, and

$$g_f'' = \frac{e^2 \tau^2}{m^*} \frac{\partial f^0}{\partial E} \left(\boldsymbol{F} \cdot \boldsymbol{v} \times \boldsymbol{B} \right). \tag{10.70}$$

Now we use the identity $(\boldsymbol{A} \cdot \boldsymbol{B} \times \boldsymbol{C} = \boldsymbol{B} \cdot \boldsymbol{C} \times \boldsymbol{A})$ to get

$$g_f'' = \frac{e^2 \tau^2}{m^*} \frac{\partial f^0}{\partial E} \boldsymbol{v} \cdot \left(\boldsymbol{B} \times \boldsymbol{F} \right). \tag{10.71}$$

The current density is now simply

$$\boldsymbol{J} = e \int \frac{d^3 k}{2\pi^3} \, \boldsymbol{v} \left(g_f' + g_f'' \right). \tag{10.72}$$

The term with g_f' was already evaluated and gives our averaging procedure for τ and the result

$$\boldsymbol{J}' = \sigma' \boldsymbol{F} \tag{10.73}$$

where σ' is the diagonal conductivity tensor. To evaluate the magnetic field component $\boldsymbol{J}''$ we use the alternating unit tensor ϵ_{ijk} to represent the elements of the cross product, i.e., the ith component of the cross product in Equation 10.70 is

$$(\boldsymbol{B} \times \boldsymbol{F})_i = \epsilon_{ijk} B_j F_k \tag{10.74}$$

where

$$\begin{aligned}
\epsilon_{ijk} &= 1 &&\text{for } i, j, k \text{ in cyclical order } (123; 231; 312) \\
&= -1 &&\text{for anticyclic } i, j, k \ (321; 213; 132) \\
&= 0 &&\text{otherwise.}
\end{aligned} \tag{10.75}$$

Now the ith component of the current $\boldsymbol{J}^{''}$ from the magnetic field is

$$\boldsymbol{J}^{''} = e \int \frac{d^3k}{2\pi^3} \, \tau^2 \, \frac{e^2}{m^*} \, \frac{\partial f^0}{\partial E} \, v_i \, v_m \, \epsilon_{mnj} \, B_n \, F_j. \tag{10.76}$$

This can be expressed by a conductivity tensor $\sigma_{ij}^{''}$ where

$$\sigma_{ij}^{''} = e \int \frac{d^3k}{2\pi^3} \, \tau^2 \, \frac{e^2}{m^*} \, \frac{\partial f^0}{\partial E} \, v_i \, v_m \, \epsilon_{mnj} \, B_n. \tag{10.77}$$

It is easy to see that diagonal terms in this tensor are zero. For example, consider the terms involving $v_1 v_m$ in $\sigma_{11}^{''}$. The only terms that can occur (because of ϵ_{mnj}) are $v_1 v_2$ or $v_1 v_3$ which both integrate to zero. However, off-diagonal components are nonzero in general. Consider $\sigma_{12}^{''}$

$$\sigma_{12}^{''} = - \left[e \int \frac{d^3k}{2\pi^3} \, \tau^2 \, \frac{e^2}{m^*} \, \frac{\partial f^0}{\partial E} \, v_1^2 \right] B_3. \tag{10.78}$$

The term in the parenthesis requires the same kind of averaging as we did for the drift mobility except that we are averaging τ^2 *instead of* τ.

The integration gives

$$\sigma_{12}^{''} = -\sigma_0 \, \mu_H \, B_3 \tag{10.79}$$

where

$$\sigma_0 = ne\mu \tag{10.80}$$

where μ is the drift mobility calculated earlier and

$$\begin{aligned} \mu_H &= \frac{\langle\langle \tau^2 \rangle\rangle}{\langle\langle \tau \rangle\rangle^2} \, \mu \\ &= r_H \, \mu. \end{aligned} \tag{10.81}$$

Once again

$$\langle\langle A \rangle\rangle \Rightarrow \langle EA \rangle \tag{10.82}$$

where the double-bracket averaging is over the actual perturbed distribution function and the single-bracket averaging is over the *equilibrium distribution function*. If we assume as before that the scattering time τ has an energy dependence

$$\tau = \tau_0 \left(\frac{E}{k_B T} \right)^s \tag{10.83}$$

we see that

$$r_H = \frac{\Gamma\left(2s + 5/2\right) \Gamma\left(s/2\right)}{\left[\Gamma\left(s + 5/2\right)\right]^2}. \tag{10.84}$$

We had listed some of the Hall factors in Table 10.1. As we can see, the Hall mobility can be quite different from the drift mobility, depending on which scattering mechanism dominates.

From the discussions above we see that, in general, in presence of both electric and magnetic fields we have

$$J_i = \sigma_{ij}(B) F_j \tag{10.85}$$

where

$$[\sigma(B)] = \sigma_0 \begin{bmatrix} 1 & -\mu_H B_3 & \mu_H B_2 \\ \mu_H B_3 & 1 & -\mu_H B_1 \\ -\mu_H B_2 & \mu_H B_1 & 1 \end{bmatrix}. \tag{10.86}$$

In Chapter 17 we will discuss how the electronic states respond to magnetic field when the field is strong and the bandstructure of the electrons is itself seriously perturbed. It is important to realize that while magnetic field is not usually actively used in devices due to the difficulty in obtaining magnetic fields in the miniature dimensions required by microelectronics, it is an extremely important tool to study semiconductor physics.

10.6 SOLUTION OF THE BOLTZMANN TRANSPORT EQUATION

We have seen that for elastic scattering in parabolic isotropic bands, the relaxation time approximation gives an easy way to solve for the transport properties. However, for most semiconductors, the scattering process is not always elastic or isotropic and the RTA itself fails at high electric fields. Numerous approaches have been developed to address the transport problem in such cases. We will discuss the iterative approach and the balance equation approach in this chapter. Another powerful technique, the Monte Carlo method, will be discussed in Chapter 13.

10.6.1 The Iterative Approach

We will discuss an approach which is quite successful for the solution of steady state, homogeneous Boltzmann equation. The equation is

$$
\begin{aligned}
e\boldsymbol{F} \cdot \nabla_{\mathbf{p}} f &= \int \frac{d^3 k^{'}}{(2\pi)^3} W(\boldsymbol{k}, \boldsymbol{k}^{'}) f(\boldsymbol{k}^{'}) - \int \frac{d^3 k^{'}}{(2\pi)^3} W(\boldsymbol{k}, \boldsymbol{k}^{'}) f(\boldsymbol{k}) \\
&= I(\boldsymbol{k}) - \frac{f(\boldsymbol{k})}{\tau(\boldsymbol{k})}
\end{aligned}
\tag{10.87}
$$

where we have defined

$$I(\boldsymbol{k}) = \int \frac{d^3 k^{'}}{(2\pi)^3} W(\boldsymbol{k}, \boldsymbol{k}^{'}) f(\boldsymbol{k}^{'}) \tag{10.88}$$

$$\frac{1}{\tau(\boldsymbol{k})} = \int \frac{d^3 k^{'}}{(2\pi)^3} W(\boldsymbol{k}, \boldsymbol{k}^{'}). \tag{10.89}$$

We then obtain

$$f(\boldsymbol{k}) = \tau(\boldsymbol{k}) \left[I(\boldsymbol{k}) - e\boldsymbol{F} \cdot \nabla_{\mathbf{p}} f \right]. \tag{10.90}$$

This integral equation contains the unknown distribution function $f(\boldsymbol{k})$ on both sides of the equation. To solve this equation, one makes an intelligent guess for $f(\boldsymbol{k})$ and then calculates the next order $f(\boldsymbol{k})$ iteratively. If $f^n(\boldsymbol{k})$ is the nth iterative value for $f(\boldsymbol{k})$, the $n+1$ value is

$$f^{n+1}(\boldsymbol{k}) = \tau(\boldsymbol{k}) \left[I^n(\boldsymbol{k}) - e\boldsymbol{F} \cdot \nabla_{\mathbf{p}} f^n \right] \tag{10.91}$$

In actual practice, one discretizes the k-space into a grid and uses the difference method to calculate $I^n(\boldsymbol{k})$ and the gradient term

$$\nabla_{\mathbf{p}} f^n(\boldsymbol{k}) = \frac{f^n(\boldsymbol{p} + \Delta\boldsymbol{p}_i) - f^n(\boldsymbol{p})}{\Delta p_i} \hat{x}_i \tag{10.92}$$

with $p_i = \hbar k_i$, $i = x,y,z$.

It is interesting to note that if the starting distribution is chosen to be the equilibrium distribution, one gets upon the first iteration

$$f^2(\boldsymbol{k}) = \tau(\boldsymbol{k}) \left[I'(\boldsymbol{k}) - e\boldsymbol{F} \cdot \nabla_{\mathbf{p}} f^0 \right] \tag{10.93}$$

and

$$I'(\boldsymbol{k}) = \int \frac{d^3k}{2\pi)^3} W(\boldsymbol{k}, \boldsymbol{k}') f^0(\boldsymbol{k}') \tag{10.94}$$

which by detailed balance at equilibrium is equal to

$$\begin{aligned} I'(\boldsymbol{k}) &= \int \frac{d^3k}{2\pi)^3} W(\boldsymbol{k}, \boldsymbol{k}') f^0(\boldsymbol{k}) \\ &= \frac{f^0(\boldsymbol{k})}{\tau(\boldsymbol{k})}. \end{aligned} \tag{10.95}$$

Thus

$$\begin{aligned} f^2(\boldsymbol{k}) &= f^0(\boldsymbol{k}) - e\tau \boldsymbol{F} \cdot \nabla_{\mathbf{p}} f^0 \\ &= f^0(\boldsymbol{k} - \frac{e\tau \boldsymbol{F}}{\hbar}) \end{aligned} \tag{10.96}$$

which is the result we obtained earlier (Equation 10.31). However, to obtain better results, one has to continue the iteration until the results for transport properties such as drift velocity converge.

10.6.2   The Balance Equation Approach

The Boltzmann equation is extremely difficult to solve except under very simplifying conditions, e.g., conditions of very low fields. These simplifying conditions usually breakdown for realistic devices where fields can be quite high and non-uniform. Very often in these cases one has to resort to computer simulation techniques based on Monte Carlo methods which will be discussed later. However, it is useful to develop additional numerical approaches since Monte Carlo methods are very computer intensive. These methods often use Monte Carlo method results as checks or for determination of certain quantities, but are then used for realistic device simulations. The Boltzmann equation can be written in the form of balance equations which prove to be very useful for such treatments.

Consider a physical quantity $n_g(r, t)$ defined by the average value (in a unit volume)

$$n_g(r, t) = \frac{1}{(2\pi)^3} \int g(k) \, f(r, k, t) \, d^3k. \tag{10.97}$$

This quantity represents the average value of g in the system. The factor $1/(2\pi)^3$ comes from the k-space per unit state. By choosing various values of $g(k)$, one can get different physical quantities of interest. The general balance equation is produced when we take the Boltzmann equation, multiply it by $g(k)$ and integrate over k-space. We get the equation

$$\begin{aligned}
\int g(k) \frac{\partial f}{\partial t} \, d^3k + \int g(k) \, v \cdot \nabla_r f \, d^3k + \int g(k) e F \cdot \nabla_p f \, d^3k \\
= \int g(k) \left. \frac{\partial f}{\partial t} \right|_{\text{coll.}} d^3k
\end{aligned} \tag{10.98}$$

where F is the electric field.

From the definition of n_g we have for the first term

$$\int g(k) \frac{\partial f}{\partial t} \, d^3k = \frac{\partial}{\partial t} n_g(r, t) \tag{10.99}$$

since g has no time dependence. The second term in Equation 10.98 becomes

$$\int g(k) \, v \cdot \nabla_r f \, d^3k = \nabla \cdot F_g(r, t)$$

where

$$F_g(r, t) = \int g(k) \, v \, f \, d^3k. \tag{10.100}$$

The function F_g represents a flux associated with n_g.

The electric field term of Equation 10.98 becomes

$$e F \cdot \int g(k) \, \nabla_p f \, d^3k = e F \cdot \int \nabla_p (gf) \, d^3k - e F \cdot \int f \, \nabla_p g \, d^3k. \tag{10.101}$$

The first term can be represented by a surface integral which equals zero since $f(k)$ goes to zero at large k. We now define a generation term G_g

$$\begin{aligned}
G_g &= -e F \cdot \int g(k) \, \nabla_p f \, d^3k \\
&= e F \cdot \int f \, \nabla_p g \, d^3k.
\end{aligned} \tag{10.102}$$

Finally coming to the collision term in the general balance equation, we note that the collisions are responsible for destroying momentum and can be physically represented by a recombination term R_g.

$$
\begin{aligned}
R_g &= -\int g(\mathbf{k}) \left.\frac{\partial f}{\partial t}\right|_{\text{coll.}} d^3k \\
&\equiv \langle\langle\frac{1}{\tau_g}\rangle\rangle \left[n_g(\mathbf{r},t) - n_g^0(\mathbf{r},t)\right]
\end{aligned}
\tag{10.103}
$$

where n_g^0 is the equilibrium value of n evaluated with the Fermi function. The relation for R_g defines a quantity $\langle\langle 1/\tau_g\rangle\rangle$ which represents a relaxation rate for the ensemble. Collecting these terms we get the final balance equation

$$
\frac{\partial n_g(\mathbf{r},t)}{\partial t} = -\nabla \cdot \mathbf{F}_g + G_g - R_g.
\tag{10.104}
$$

By substituting different physical quantities for g, we get different balance equations. The equations that are important for most semiconductor devices are the equations pertaining to carrier density, momentum, and energy.

The balance equation for the carrier density is obtained by putting $g(\mathbf{k}) = 1$ so that $n_g = n$, the carrier density. The flux term is just the particle flux $(= \mathbf{J}/e)$. The electric field term G_g and the collision term R_g are both just zero. The balance equation becomes

$$
\frac{\partial n}{\partial t} = -\frac{1}{e}\nabla \cdot \mathbf{J}
\tag{10.105}
$$

which is just the current continuity equation.

To obtain the momentum balance equation, we use $g(\mathbf{k}) = p_z$ (for the z-component of the momentum). The quantity n_g is now

$$
\begin{aligned}
n_g &= \int \frac{d^3k}{(2\pi)^3} p_z f \\
&= \langle p_z \rangle \\
&= n\, m^*\, v_{dz}
\end{aligned}
\tag{10.106}
$$

where m^* is the carrier mass and v_{dz} is the z-component of the average velocity (i.e., the drift velocity). The flux term associated with the momentum is

$$
\mathbf{F}_g = \int \frac{d^3k}{(2\pi)^3} \mathbf{v}\, p_z\, f.
\tag{10.107}
$$

Denoting the x,y,z components of this flux by the index i, we can write

$$
F_{g,i} = 2\, W_{iz}
\tag{10.108}
$$

where W_{iz} is an element of the kinetic energy tensor defined in Equation 10.113, below. The generation term from the electric field is

$$
G_g = enF_z.
\tag{10.109}
$$

The momentum loss rate is ($p_z^0 = 0$)

$$R_g = \langle\langle\frac{1}{\tau_m}\rangle\rangle p_z .$$ (10.110)

Collecting these terms we get the momentum balance equation

$$\frac{dp_z}{dt} = -\frac{\partial}{\partial x_i}(2 W_{iz}) + neF_z - \langle\langle\frac{1}{\tau_m}\rangle\rangle p_z ,$$ (10.111)

or in general

$$\frac{\partial \boldsymbol{p}}{\partial t} = -2\nabla \cdot W + ne\boldsymbol{F} - \langle\langle\frac{1}{\tau_m}\rangle\rangle \boldsymbol{p}$$ (10.112)

where the i,j components of the kinetic energy tensor are

$$W_{ij} = \frac{1}{2}\int \frac{d^3k}{(2\pi)^3} \, v_i \cdot p_j \, f$$ (10.113)

and the derivative $\nabla \cdot W$ is the vector

$$\nabla \cdot W \equiv \sum_{ij} \frac{\partial}{\partial x_i} W_{ij} \, \hat{x}_j .$$ (10.114)

If the bandstructure of the electron is parabolic

$$\boldsymbol{J} = \frac{e\boldsymbol{p}}{m^*} .$$ (10.115)

Thus, for such a case, the current density equation can be written as

$$\frac{\partial \boldsymbol{J}}{\partial t} = -2e\frac{\nabla \cdot W}{m^*} + \frac{e^2 n\boldsymbol{F}}{m^*} - \langle\langle\frac{1}{\tau_m}\rangle\rangle \boldsymbol{J} .$$ (10.116)

If we define the mobility as

$$\mu = \frac{e}{m^* \langle\langle 1/\tau_m\rangle\rangle} ,$$ (10.117)

and assume that the current is not changing very rapidly during the time $1/\langle\langle 1/\tau_m\rangle\rangle$, we get

$$\boldsymbol{J} = ne\mu\boldsymbol{F} - 2\mu\nabla \cdot W .$$ (10.118)

The kinetic energy contains terms due to the random motion of the electrons as well as the drift components. We assume that the drift components are negligible (valid at low fields), and that the kinetic energy tensor is diagonal. We then get

$$\begin{aligned} W_{ij} &= \frac{nk_B T_c}{2} \delta_{ij} \\ &= \frac{w}{3} \delta_{ij} \end{aligned}$$ (10.119)

where T_c defines the carrier temperature, and

$$w = \frac{3}{2} n \, k_B \, T_c. \tag{10.120}$$

With this description of the kinetic energy we get,

$$
\begin{aligned}
\boldsymbol{J} &= ne\mu \boldsymbol{F} - \frac{2}{3} \mu \nabla w \\
&= ne\mu \boldsymbol{F} - eD \nabla n - e S \nabla T_c
\end{aligned}
\tag{10.121}
$$

where D is the diffusion coefficient

$$D = \frac{k_B T_c}{e} \mu \tag{10.122}$$

and S is the Soret coefficient

$$S = \mu \frac{k_B}{e} n \tag{10.123}$$

This is the drift-diffusion equation and shows that a current may flow due to an electric field, a concentration gradient, or a temperature gradient.

Let us now go to the energy balance equation which is quite useful in understanding high field transport. Choosing $g(\boldsymbol{k}) = E(\boldsymbol{k})$ the particle energy, we get

$$
\begin{aligned}
n_g &= \int \frac{d^3 k}{(2\pi)^3} E(\boldsymbol{k}) \, f \\
&= w
\end{aligned}
\tag{10.124}
$$

where w is defined in Equation 10.119.

The associated flux is

$$
\begin{aligned}
\boldsymbol{F}_g &= \int \frac{d^3 k}{(2\pi)^3} \boldsymbol{v} \, E(\boldsymbol{k}) \, f \\
&= \boldsymbol{F}_E
\end{aligned}
\tag{10.125}
$$

which represents an energy flux. The energy supplied to the carriers is due to the electric field generation term

$$
\begin{aligned}
G_g &= e\boldsymbol{F} \cdot \int \frac{d^3 k}{(2\pi)^3} \nabla_{\mathbf{p}} E(\boldsymbol{k}) \, f \\
&= \boldsymbol{J} \cdot \boldsymbol{F}
\end{aligned}
\tag{10.126}
$$

since $\nabla_{\mathbf{p}} E(\boldsymbol{k})$ is the carrier velocity. The energy is lost through the collision terms

$$R_g = \langle\langle \frac{1}{\tau_E} \rangle\rangle (w - w^0). \tag{10.127}$$

The energy balance equation is then

$$\frac{\partial w}{\partial t} = -\nabla \cdot \boldsymbol{F}_E + \boldsymbol{J} \cdot \boldsymbol{F} - \langle\langle\frac{1}{\tau_E}\rangle\rangle(w - w^0). \tag{10.128}$$

We had earlier mentioned the carrier temperature T_c in discussing the drift-diffusion equation. We will now formalize this concept. As the electric field is increased, the carriers gain energy from the field and a balance is established between this energy increase and the loss due to collisions. The distribution function describing the electrons is no longer the Fermi-Dirac function. It is sometimes useful to define this distribution function by a carrier temperature which is, in general, higher than the lattice temperature. In general, the carrier velocities can be written as

$$\boldsymbol{v} = \boldsymbol{v}_d + \boldsymbol{v}_r \tag{10.129}$$

where $\boldsymbol{v}_d$ is the drift velocity and $\boldsymbol{v}_r$ is the random velocity component. The kinetic energy is

$$w = \frac{1}{2} n \, m^* \, v_d^2 + \frac{1}{2} n \, m^* \, \langle v_r^2 \rangle. \tag{10.130}$$

Note that there is no cross term since $\langle \boldsymbol{v}_r \rangle = 0$. The first term in the energy, w, is the drift term, while the second term is due to the random thermal motion of the carriers, though not at the lattice temperature, in general. We define the carrier temperature by this thermal part of the kinetic energy

$$\frac{3}{2} n \, k_B \, T_c = \frac{1}{2} m^* \, n \, \langle v_r^2 \rangle. \tag{10.131}$$

For simplicity we will assume that the carrier temperature is represented by a diagonal tensor. The momentum balance equation can now be represented in terms of a carrier temperature

$$\frac{\partial p_j}{\partial t} = -\frac{\partial(n \, m^* \, v_{di} \, v_{dj} + n \, k_B \, T_c)}{\partial x_i} + neF_j - \langle\langle\frac{1}{\tau_m}\rangle\rangle \, p_j. \tag{10.132}$$

Finally, to write the energy balance equation in terms of a carrier temperature, we consider the energy flux

$$\boldsymbol{F}_E = \frac{n \, m^*}{2} \langle v^2 \boldsymbol{v} \rangle. \tag{10.133}$$

Once again we separate the energy flux coming from the thermal motion by defining

$$\boldsymbol{\theta} = \frac{n \, m^*}{2} \langle v_r^2 \boldsymbol{v}_r \rangle. \tag{10.134}$$

By the definition of the velocity $\boldsymbol{v}$, we get

$$\begin{aligned}
\boldsymbol{F}_E &= \frac{n \, m^*}{2} \langle v^2 \rangle \boldsymbol{v}_d + \frac{n \, m^*}{2} \langle v^2 \boldsymbol{v}_r \rangle \\
&= w \boldsymbol{v}_d + \frac{n \, m^*}{2} \langle \left(v_d^2 + 2\boldsymbol{v}_d \cdot \boldsymbol{v}_r + v_r^2 \right) \boldsymbol{v}_r \rangle
\end{aligned} \tag{10.135}$$

The term to be averaged on the right-hand side has three terms, the first of which averages to zero, the second is related to the carrier temperature, and the third is the heat flux. Thus

$$F_E = wv_d + v_d \cdot nk_B T_c + \theta. \qquad (10.136)$$

If we write

$$\theta = -H\nabla T_c \qquad (10.137)$$

where H is the thermal conductivity, we get the following energy balance equation

$$\frac{\partial w}{\partial t} = \sum_i \left(-\frac{\partial}{\partial x_i} \left[(w + nk_B T_c)v_{di} - H\frac{\partial T_c}{\partial x_i} \right] + J_i F_i \right)$$
$$- \langle\langle \frac{1}{\tau_E} \rangle\rangle (w - w^0). \qquad (10.138)$$

The advantage of writing the balance equations in terms of the carrier temperatures is that the relationship between T_c and the applied electric field may be available from either some simplifications or from Monte Carlo methods. Once this is known, the balance equations can be solved, as discussed later in Section 13.7.

10.7 FOR THE TECHNOLOGIST IN YOU

In this chapter we have developed some of the formalism required to describe electronic transport in semiconductors. Of course, so far we have not discussed the most important input, the scattering rates $W(k, k')$. These will be discussed for several scattering potentials in the next two chapters. It must be realized, however, that the evaluation of scattering rates is relatively simple compared to obtaining information on macroscopic properties of the material (μ, σ, etc.). As discussed in this chapter, this is because of the difficulty in calculating the distribution function. We have formulated in this chapter some approximate schemes to obtain this information. It must be realized that our entire discussion is based on the quasiclassical approach, i.e., the electrons can be treated as point particles while the scattering rates are determined by their plane wave description. As discussed in the beginning of this chapter, this assumption breaks down for structure which are only a few hundred Angstroms wide. Quantum transport approaches are required for such structures. For a vast majority of devices used today, the quasiclassical approach works quite well and has been the foundation of our transport understanding.

The transport of electrons (holes) in semiconductors is of course the most important material property that determines the device performance. We will discuss the specific details of how transport at different electric fields depends upon material parameters in the next three chapters. In high purity materials, at low temperature, the mean free path of electrons can approach several microns.

Thus electrons can move thousands of lattice sites without scattering! This is in marked contrast to what we expect from Drude's model. Low electric field mobilities as high as several hundred thousand V cm^2 s^{-1} in bulk semiconductors, and several million in heterostructures has been obscured at low temperatures. However, it is important to realize that most devices do not rely only on high mobility alone for superior performance. Usually, the device with best performance has a mediocre low field mobility as will be clear from our discussions in Chapter 19.

10.8 PROBLEMS

10.1. Using the Maxwell-Boltzmann distribution function at equilibrium show that the average kinetic energy of an electron is given by $3k_BT/2$. Show that for a displaced Maxwell-Boltzmann distribution the average kinetic energy is given by

$$\frac{1}{2}m^*v_d^2 + \frac{3}{2}k_BT$$

where v_d is the drift velocity given by the derivations in the text (Equation 10.34).

10.2. Consider a sample of GaAs with electron effective mass of 0.067 m_0. If an electric field of 1 kV/cm is applied, what is the drift velocity produced if

(a) $\tau = 10^{-13}$s

(b) $\tau = 10^{-12}$s

(c) $\tau = 10^{-11}$s ?

How does the drift velocity compare to the average thermal speed of the electrons?

10.3. (a) Plot the distribution function for electrons in GaAs ($f(E)$) when a field of 0.5, 1.0, 2.0 kV/cm is applied. Assume that $\tau = 10^{-12}$s, and assume a nondegenerate case.

(b) Plot the k-space distribution function when an electric field $\boldsymbol{F} = F_0\hat{x}$ is applied to the sample of GaAs. Assume the field magnitudes and τ as given in part a.

10.4. Using Table 10.1 and Equation 10.60, calculate the average relaxation time $\langle\langle\tau\rangle\rangle$ in terms of τ_0 for all the scattering processes listed in Table 10.1.

10.5. In a semiconductor sample, the Hall probe region has a dimension of 0.5 cm by 0.25 cm by 0.05 cm thick. For an applied electric field of 1.0 V/cm, 20 mA current flows (through the long side) in the circuit. When a 10 kG magnetic field is applied, a Hall voltage of 10 mV is developed. What is the Hall mobility of the sample and what is the carrier density? If the dominant scattering mechanism is acoustic phonon scattering, what is the drift mobility?

10.6. The electron mobility of Si at 300 K is 1400 cm^2/V-s. Calculate the mean free path and the energy gained in a mean free path at an electric field of 1 kV/cm.

10.7. Show that the average energy gained between collisions is

$$\delta E_{\mathrm{av}} = \alpha m^*(\mu F)^2$$

where F is the applied electric field, and $\alpha \sim 1$. If the optical phonon energies in GaAs and Si are 36 meV and 47 meV, and the mobilities are 8000 cm^2/V-s and 1400 cm^2/V-s, respectively, what are the electric fields at which optical phonon emission can start? Note that because of the statistical nature of the scattering, a small fraction of the electrons can emit phonons at much lower electric fields.

10.9   REFERENCES

- **General**

  - "Transport: The Boltzmann Equation," by Conwell, E., in *Handbook on Semiconductors* (North–Holland, New York, 1982), vol. 1.
  - Duderstadt, J. and W. Martin, *Transport Theory* (John Wiley and Sons, New York, 1979).
  - Ferry, D. K., *Semiconductors* (Macmillan, New York) 1991.
  - Harris, S., *An Introduction to the Theory of the Boltzmann Equation* (Holt, Rinehart and Winston, New York, 1971).
  - Haynes, J. R. and W. Shockley, Phys. Rev., **81**, 835 (1951).
  - Lundstrom, M., *Fundamentals of Carrier Transport* (Modular Series on Solid State Devices, edited by G. W. Neudeck and R. P. Pierre, Addison–Wesley, New York, 1990), vol. X.
  - "Low Field Transport in Semiconductors," by Rode, D. S., in *Semiconductors and Semimetals* (edited by R. K. Willardson and A. C. Beer, Academic Press, New York, 1972), vol. 10.
  - Wolfe, C. M., N. Holonyak and G. E. Stillman, *Physical Properties of Semiconductors* (Prentice Hall, New Jersey, 1989).

CHAPTER
11

DEFECT AND
CARRIER-CARRIER
SCATTERING

In the previous chapter we discussed the Boltzmann transport theory and the approximations used to address transport problems. A key ingredient of the theory is the scattering rate $W(k, k')$ which tells us how an electron in a state k scatters into the state k'. We will use the semiclassical approach to the transport problem, where we assume the electron can be represented by a point particle but is still in a well-defined Bloch state ψ_k. The Fermi golden rule is then used to calculate the scattering rate (see Appendix I). Such an approach is valid for semiconductors as long as the device distances are greater than 1000 Å. At smaller dimensions, the extent of the wavepacket uncertainty $\Delta k_x \approx 1/\Delta x$ is too large to allow one to treat the electron as a point particle with a well-defined k-state.

As has been discussed several times now, in the perfect crystal the electron suffers no collision. It is the imperfections in the crystal that cause scattering. These imperfections can be time independent such as impurity centers, native defects (vacancies, etc.), alloy potential, or time varying due to lattice vibrations. To first order the Fermi golden rule (which is equivalent to the Born approximation for time independent perturbations) provides us with the scattering rate due to these imperfections. The general approach to the transport problem is outlined in Figure 11.1.

The first, and most important ingredient, is an understanding of the scattering potential. This may seem like a simple problem, but is, in fact, one of the most difficult parts of the problem. Consider, for example, a simple exercise where one takes a Ga atom in GaAs and replaces it by a Si atom. We have treated this problem in the discussion on donors. The potential of the impurity

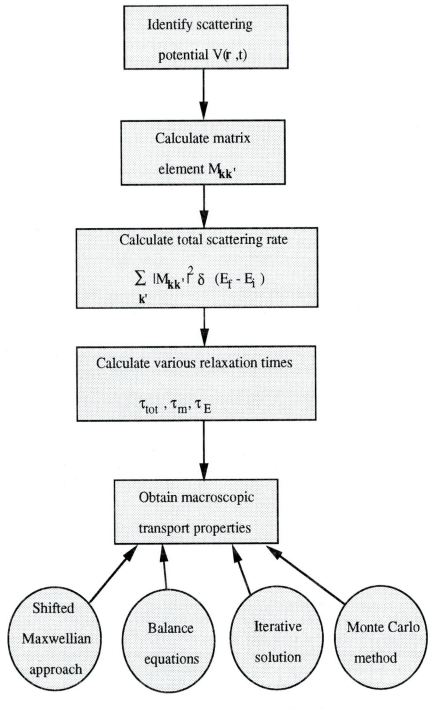

Figure 11.1: Mathematical steps in a typical transport calculation.

is represented by

$$V_{\text{imp}} = V_{\text{host}} + \frac{e^2}{\epsilon r} \tag{11.1}$$

in the donor problem. However, we will see in this chapter that the simple $e^2/(\epsilon r)$ potential does not give meaningful results for transport in doped semiconductors and needs to be modified. Similarly, drastic approximations are made to describe the alloy potential. Once the potential is known, one evaluates the scattering matrix element between the initial and final state of the electron. This effectively amounts to taking a Fourier transform of the potential since the initial and final states are essentially plane wave states. With the matrix element known one carries out an integral over all final states into which the electron can scatter and which are consistent with energy conservation. This kind of integral provides the various scattering times. Finally, one uses any of a variety of approaches to solve for the transport problem and obtain results for carrier mobility.

In this chapter we will examine two kinds of scattering mechanisms. The first involves fixed defect centers such as ionized impurity atoms (donors, acceptors) and random crystal potential disorder arising in alloys. The second kind of scattering involves the scattering of electrons from other electrons (or holes). This can be an important scattering mechanism in heavily doped semiconductors where there is a high density of background free carriers. This type of mechanism also gives rise to the important processes of impact ionization and Auger processes. The former is responsible for the breakdown of semiconductors at high electric fields while the latter is responsible for the nonradiative recombination of electrons and holes.

11.1 IONIZED IMPURITY SCATTERING

We start with the ionized impurity scattering and first develop a simple formalism for the scattering potential. The reason we do not use the bare Coulombic potential has to do with "screening" of the potential by other free carriers. These free electrons (holes) are the attractive potential and respond by changing their local density. The variation produced in the electron density reduces the effect of the ionized impurity, particularly at distances that are far from the impurity. Another way to express this is that the dielectric response of the free electron gas is such as to reduce the influence of the ionized impurity potential. We will now calculate this dielectric response.

We define the following symbols:

- $\rho_{\text{ext}}; \phi_{\text{ext}}$: the charge density and potential due to the external perturbation, e.g. , the ionized impurity.

- $\rho_{\text{ind}}; \phi_{\text{ind}}$: the charge density and potential due to the induced effects in the free carriers.

- $\rho_{\text{tot}}; \phi_{\text{tot}}$: the total charge density and potentials.

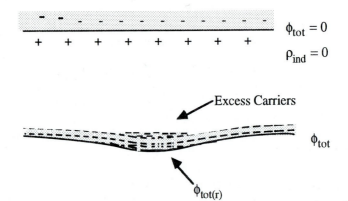

Figure 11.2: Effect of the impurity potential is to alter the uniform free charge by inducing charge. This in turn modifies the potential profile.

The dielectric response will be calculated in k-space due to the simplicity of the Poisson equation in k-space. Let us consider a particular Fourier component of the external potential

$$\rho_{\text{ext}}(\boldsymbol{k}) = \rho e^{i\mathbf{k}\cdot\mathbf{r}} \tag{11.2}$$

The Poisson equation is

$$\nabla^2 \phi = \frac{-4\pi\rho}{\epsilon} \tag{11.3}$$

and in k-space this equation becomes

$$\phi = \frac{4\pi\rho}{\epsilon k^2}. \tag{11.4}$$

The free electron charge density will be assumed to be given by the Boltzmann statistics (i.e., we will deal with nondegenerate semiconductors). If ϕ_{tot} is zero, the background ionic charge exactly balances the negative charge of the free electrons. However, since there is a net potential ϕ_{tot} which is spatially non-uniform, there will be an induced charge given by

$$\rho_{\text{ind}} = n_0 e - n_0 e \exp\left(\frac{e\phi_{\text{tot}}}{k_B T}\right) \tag{11.5}$$

where n_0 is the mean background carrier density. Figure 11.2 shows how this induced charge creates a change in the potential of the system.

If the perturbation $\phi_{\text{tot}}(\boldsymbol{r})$ is small, we can linearize the exponential and get

$$
\begin{aligned}
\rho_{\text{ind}} &= \frac{-n_0 e^2}{k_B T} \phi_{\text{tot}} \\
&= \frac{-n_0 e^2}{k_B T} \cdot \frac{4\pi}{\epsilon k^2} \rho_{\text{tot}}
\end{aligned}
\tag{11.6}
$$

using Equation 11.4.

The dielectric response is defined by

$$\epsilon_{\text{free}}(\boldsymbol{k}) \;=\; \frac{\rho_{\text{ext}}}{\rho_{\text{tot}}}$$

$$=\; \frac{\phi_{\text{ext}}}{\phi_{\text{tot}}}$$

$$=\; 1 - \frac{\rho_{\text{ind}}}{\rho_{\text{tot}}} \tag{11.7}$$

since $\rho_{\text{ext}} = \rho_{\text{tot}} - \rho_{\text{ind}}$.

Substituting from Equation 11.6

$$\epsilon_{\text{free}} \;=\; 1 + \frac{4\pi n_0 e^2}{\epsilon k_B T}\frac{1}{k^2}$$

$$=\; 1 + \frac{\lambda^2}{k^2} \tag{11.8}$$

where

$$\lambda^2 = \frac{4\pi n_0 e^2}{\epsilon k_B T}. \tag{11.9}$$

Let us now apply this formalism to the case where we have a Coulombic potential

$$\phi_{\text{ext}} = q/r. \tag{11.10}$$

In real space, the corresponding charge is

$$\rho_{\text{ext}}(\boldsymbol{r}) = q\delta(\boldsymbol{r}). \tag{11.11}$$

We will express ϕ_{ext} in Fourier space by noting that

$$\delta(\boldsymbol{r}) = \frac{1}{(2\pi)^3}\int d^3k\, e^{i\boldsymbol{k}\cdot\boldsymbol{r}} \tag{11.12}$$

i.e., the Fourier transform of $\delta(\boldsymbol{r})$ is unity. Thus

$$\rho_{\text{ext}}(\boldsymbol{k}) = q \tag{11.13}$$

and

$$\phi_{\text{ext}}(\boldsymbol{k}) = \frac{4\pi q}{k^2}. \tag{11.14}$$

Using our value of the dielectric constant, from Equation 11.8

$$\phi_{\text{tot}}(\boldsymbol{k}) = \frac{4\pi q}{\epsilon\,(k^2 + \lambda^2)}. \tag{11.15}$$

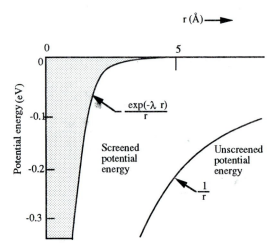

Figure 11.3: Comparison of screened and unscreened Coulomb potentials of a unit positive charge as seen by an electron. The screening length is λ^{-1}.

The real space behavior of this function can be obtained by the Fourier transform:

$$
\begin{aligned}
\phi_{\text{tot}}(\boldsymbol{r}) &= \frac{4\pi q/\epsilon}{(2\pi)^3} \int_0^\infty dk \frac{k^2}{k^2 + \lambda^2} \int_{-1}^1 d(\cos\theta)e^{ikr\cos\theta} \int_0^{2\pi} d\phi \\
&= \frac{(4\pi q/\epsilon)\cdot 2\pi}{(2\pi)^3} \int_0^\infty dk \frac{k^2}{k^2 + \lambda^2}\left[\frac{1}{ikr}e^{ikr\cos\theta}|_{-1}^1\right] \\
&= \frac{2q/\epsilon}{\pi r} \int_0^\infty dk \frac{k\sin kr}{k^2 + \lambda^2} \\
&= \frac{q}{\epsilon r}e^{-\lambda r}.
\end{aligned}
\tag{11.16}
$$

This is the screened Coulombic potential which we will use for the calculations of the scattering rate in nondegenerate semiconductors. The effect of screening is to reduce the range of the potential from a $1/r$ variation to a $\exp(-\lambda r)/r$ variation. This is an extremely important effect and is shown schematically in Figure 11.3. As we shall see later, without taking account of the screening effect, the mobility tends to zero in presence of ionized impurities.

We now calculate the matrix element for screened Coulombic potential

$$
U(\boldsymbol{r}) = \frac{Ze^2}{\epsilon}\frac{e^{-\lambda r}}{r}
\tag{11.17}
$$

where Ze is the charge of the impurity. We choose the initial normalized state as $|\boldsymbol{k}\rangle = \exp(i\boldsymbol{k}\cdot\boldsymbol{r})/\sqrt{V}$ and the final state as $|\boldsymbol{k}'\rangle = \exp(i\boldsymbol{k}'\cdot\boldsymbol{r})/\sqrt{V}$, where V is the volume of the crystal.

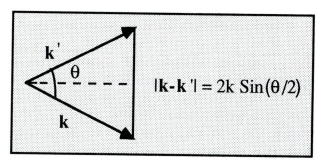

$$|k-k'| = 2k \, Sin(\theta/2)$$

Figure 11.4: As a consequence of the elastic scattering, there is a simple relation between the magnitude of the scattered wavevector and the scattering angle q.

The matrix element is then

$$M_{\mathbf{kk'}} = \frac{Ze^2}{V\epsilon} \int e^{-i(\mathbf{k'}-\mathbf{k})\cdot\mathbf{r}} \frac{e^{-\lambda r}}{r} r^2 dr \sin\theta d\theta d\phi \qquad (11.18)$$

where $|\mathbf{k'}| = |\mathbf{k}|$ since the scattering is elastic. Then, as can be seen from Figure 11.4

$$\left|\mathbf{k} - \mathbf{k'}\right| = 2k\sin(\theta/2) \qquad (11.19)$$

where θ is the polar scattering angle.

$$
\begin{aligned}
M_{\mathbf{kk'}} &= \frac{Ze^2}{\epsilon V} 2\pi \int_0^\infty r dr \int_{-1}^1 d(\cos\theta) e^{-\lambda r} e^{-i|\mathbf{k'}-\mathbf{k}|r\cos\theta} \\
&= \frac{Ze^2}{\epsilon V} 2\pi \int_0^\infty r dr e^{-\lambda r} \frac{1}{-i|\mathbf{k'}-\mathbf{k}|r} |e^{-i|\mathbf{k'}-\mathbf{k}|r\cos\theta}|_1^{-1} \\
&= \frac{Ze^2}{\epsilon V} 2\pi \int_0^\infty dr e^{-\lambda r} \frac{1}{-i|\mathbf{k'}-\mathbf{k}|} \left[e^{i|\mathbf{k'}-\mathbf{k}|r} - e^{-i|\mathbf{k'}-\mathbf{k}|r} \right] \\
&= \frac{Ze^2}{\epsilon V} 2\pi \int_0^\infty dr \frac{1}{-i|\mathbf{k'}-\mathbf{k}|} \left[e^{(-\lambda+i|\mathbf{k'}-\mathbf{k}|)r} - e^{(-\lambda-i|\mathbf{k'}-\mathbf{k}|)r} \right] \\
&= \frac{Ze^2}{\epsilon V} 2\pi \frac{1}{-i|\mathbf{k'}-\mathbf{k}|} \left[\frac{1}{-\lambda+i|\mathbf{k'}-\mathbf{k}|} - \frac{1}{-\lambda-i|\mathbf{k'}-\mathbf{k}|} \right] \\
&= \frac{Ze^2}{\epsilon V} 2\pi \frac{2}{|\mathbf{k'}-\mathbf{k}|^2 + \lambda^2} \\
&= \frac{Ze^2 4\pi}{V\epsilon} \frac{1}{4k^2 \sin^2(\theta/2) + \lambda^2}. \qquad (11.20)
\end{aligned}
$$

The scattering rate is given by the Fermi golden rule

$$W(\mathbf{k}, \mathbf{k'}) = \frac{2\pi}{\hbar} \left(\frac{4\pi Ze^2}{V\epsilon} \right)^2 \frac{\delta\left(E_{\mathbf{k}} - E_{\mathbf{k'}}\right)}{\left(4k^2 \sin^2(\theta/2) + \lambda^2\right)^2}. \qquad (11.21)$$

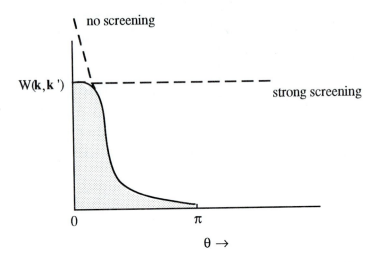

Figure 11.5: Angular dependence of the scattering by ionized impurities. The scattering has a strong forward angle preference.

One can see that in the two extremes of no screening ($\lambda \to 0$) and strong screening ($\lambda \to \infty$), the rate becomes respectively

$$W(k, k') = \frac{2\pi}{\hbar} \left(\frac{4\pi Z e^2}{V \epsilon} \right)^2 \frac{\delta \left(E_{\mathbf{k}} - E_{\mathbf{k}'} \right)}{16 k^4 \sin^4(\theta/2)} \tag{11.22}$$

and

$$W(k, k') = \frac{2\pi}{\hbar} \left(\frac{4\pi Z e^2}{V \epsilon} \right)^2 \frac{\delta \left(E_{\mathbf{k}} - E_{\mathbf{k}'} \right)}{\lambda^4}. \tag{11.23}$$

As was discussed in our derivation of relaxation time, it is important to examine the angular dependence of $W(k, k')$. This is plotted as a function of the scattering angle θ in Figure 11.5. The ionized impurity scattering has a strong forward angle bias as can be seen.

Let us now examine the relaxation time τ_i which is used to obtain the low field carrier mobility.

$$
\begin{aligned}
\frac{1}{\tau} &= \frac{V}{(2\pi)^3} \int (1 - \cos\theta)\, W(k, k')\, d^3 k' \\
&= \frac{2\pi}{\hbar} \left(\frac{4\pi Z e^2}{\epsilon} \right)^2 \frac{1}{V^2} \frac{V}{(2\pi)^3} \\
&\quad \times \int (1 - \cos\theta) \frac{\delta \left(E_{\mathbf{k}} - E_{\mathbf{k}'} \right)}{\left(4k^2 \sin^2(\theta/2) + \lambda^2 \right)^2} k'^2\, dk'\, \sin\theta\, d\theta\, d\phi \\
&= \frac{1}{2\hbar} \left(\frac{4\pi Z e^2}{\epsilon} \right)^2 \frac{1}{V}
\end{aligned}
$$

$$\times \int (1 - \cos\theta) \frac{\delta\left(E_{\mathbf{k}} - E_{\mathbf{k}'}\right)}{\left(4k^2 \sin^2(\theta/2) + \lambda^2\right)^2} N(E_{\mathbf{k}'}) \, dE_{\mathbf{k}'} \, d(\cos\theta) \, d\phi$$

$$= \frac{1}{\hbar} \left(\frac{4\pi Z e^2}{\epsilon}\right)^2 \frac{1}{V} \frac{N(E_{\mathbf{k}})}{32k^4}$$

$$\times \int (1 - \cos\theta) \frac{1}{\left[\sin^2(\theta/2) + \left(\frac{\lambda}{2k}\right)^2\right]^2} \, d(\cos\theta) \, d\phi$$

$$= F \int (1 - \cos\theta) \frac{1}{\left[\sin^2(\theta/2) + \left(\frac{\lambda}{2k}\right)^2\right]^2} \, d(\cos\theta) \, d\phi \qquad (11.24)$$

with

$$F = \frac{1}{\hbar} \left(\frac{4\pi Z e^2}{\epsilon}\right)^2 \frac{1}{V} \frac{N(E_{\mathbf{k}})}{32k^4}. \qquad (11.25)$$

Let $z = \cos\theta$, so that $\sin^2(\theta/2) = (1 - z)/2$.

$$\frac{1}{\tau} = 8\pi F \int_{-1}^{1} \frac{(1 - z)\, dz}{\left(1 + 2\left(\frac{\lambda}{2k}\right)^2 - z\right)^2}$$

$$= 8\pi F \int_{-1}^{1} \frac{dz}{\left(1 + 2\left(\frac{\lambda}{2k}\right)^2 - z\right)^2} - \int_{-1}^{1} \frac{z\, dz}{\left(1 + 2\left(\frac{\lambda}{2k}\right)^2 - z\right)^2} (11.26)$$

Let $a = 2(\lambda/2k)^2$ and $w = 1 - z + a$.

$$\frac{1}{\tau} = 8\pi F \int_{a}^{2+a} \frac{(w - a)}{w^2} \, dw$$

$$= 8\pi F \int_{a}^{2+a} \left(\frac{1}{w} - \frac{a}{w^2}\right) \, dw$$

$$= 8\pi F \left[\left(\ln|w| + \frac{a}{w}\right)\Big|_{a}^{2+a}\right]$$

$$= 8\pi F \left[\ln\left|\frac{2+a}{a}\right| - \frac{1}{1 + a/2}\right]$$

$$= 8\pi F \left[\ln\left(1 + \left(\frac{2k}{\lambda}\right)^2\right) - \frac{1}{1 + \left(\frac{\lambda}{2k}\right)^2}\right].$$

Finally

$$\frac{1}{\tau} = \frac{\pi}{4\hbar} \left(\frac{4\pi Z e^2}{\epsilon}\right)^2 \frac{N(E_{\mathbf{k}})}{V k^4}$$

$$\times \quad \left[\ln\left(1 + \left(\frac{2k}{\lambda}\right)^2\right) - \frac{1}{1 + \left(\frac{\lambda}{2k}\right)^2} \right]$$

$$N(E_{\mathbf{k}}) \quad = \quad \frac{m^{*3/2} E^{1/2}}{\sqrt{2}\pi^2\hbar^3}. \tag{11.27}$$

Note that the spin degeneracy is ignored since the ionized impurity scattering cannot alter the spin of the electron. In terms of the electron energy, $E_{\mathbf{k}}$, we have

$$\frac{1}{\tau} \quad = \quad \frac{1}{V}\frac{\pi}{\sqrt{2}}\left(\frac{Ze^2}{\epsilon}\right)^2 \frac{1}{m^{*1/2}E_{\mathbf{k}}^{3/2}}$$

$$\times \quad \left[\ln\left(1 + \left(\frac{8m^* E_{\mathbf{k}}}{\hbar^2\lambda}\right)^2\right) - \frac{1}{1 + \left(\frac{\hbar^2\lambda}{8m^* E_{\mathbf{k}}}\right)^2} \right]. \tag{11.28}$$

The average relaxation time is

$$\langle\langle\tau\rangle\rangle = \frac{\int_0^\infty E \, \tau_{\mathbf{k}} \, e^{-\beta E} \, dE}{\int_0^\infty E \, e^{-\beta E} \, dE}. \tag{11.29}$$

To a good approximation, the effect of this averaging is essentially to replace $E_{\mathbf{k}}$ by $k_B T$ in the expression for $1/\tau$.

$$\frac{1}{\langle\langle\tau\rangle\rangle} \quad = \quad \frac{1}{V}\frac{\pi}{\sqrt{2}}\left(\frac{Ze^2}{\epsilon}\right)^2 \frac{1}{m^{*1/2}(k_B T)^{3/2}}$$

$$\times \quad \left[\ln\left(1 + \left(\frac{8m^* k_B T}{\hbar^2\lambda}\right)^2\right) - \frac{1}{1 + \left(\frac{\hbar^2\lambda}{8m^* k_B T}\right)^2} \right]. \tag{11.30}$$

If there are N_i impurities per unit volume, and if we assume that they scatter electrons independently, the total relaxation time is

$$\frac{1}{\langle\langle\tau\rangle\rangle} \quad = \quad N_i \frac{\pi}{\sqrt{2}}\left(\frac{Ze^2}{\epsilon}\right)^2 \frac{1}{m^{*1/2}(k_B T)^{3/2}}$$

$$\times \quad \left[\ln\left(1 + \left(\frac{8m^* k_B T}{\hbar^2\lambda}\right)^2\right) - \frac{1}{1 + \left(\frac{\hbar^2\lambda}{8m^* k_B T}\right)^2} \right]. \tag{11.31}$$

The mobility is then

$$\mu = \frac{e\langle\langle\tau\rangle\rangle}{m^*}. \tag{11.32}$$

Note: In the MKS units, the expressions for the screening length and the scattering matrix element are

$$\lambda^2 = \frac{n_0\, e^2}{\epsilon_0\, \epsilon\, k_B T}$$

$$M_{\mathbf{kk'}} = \frac{Z e^2}{V\, \epsilon_0\, \epsilon} \frac{1}{4k^2 \sin^2(\theta/2) + \lambda^2}. \qquad (11.33)$$

Other equations can be also appropriately modified (see Appendices J and M).

The derivation of the ionized impurity scattering given above is often known as the Brooks-Herring treatment. This is by no means the only way to treat the ionized impurity problem. In fact, there are a number of other competing techniques to explain the ionized impurity scattering. The difference arises mainly due to the form of the impurity scattering potential that is assumed. Various treatments are given by Conwell and Weisskopf and Takimoto. All these results have the special $\mu \sim T^{3/2}$ behavior that is represented in Equation 11.31. This temperature dependence (the actual temperature dependence is more complex due to the other T-dependent terms of Equation 11.31) is a special signature of the ionized impurity scattering. One can understand this behavior physically by saying that at higher temperatures, the electrons are traveling faster and are less affected by the ionized impurities.

We will see in the next chapter that the phonon scattering rates increase with temperature, i.e., the mobility due to phonons decreases with temperature in contrast to the case of ionized impurity scattering. Thus, for a semiconductor with some background doping, the mobility versus temperature relation has the form shown in Figure 11.6. At low temperatures the mobility is low because of ionized impurity scattering. The mobility increases with temperature up to ~ 50 K or so, after which it starts decreasing because of phonon scattering effects. This behavior is in marked contrast to what happens in modulation doped semiconductors discussed earlier. Here, due to the remoteness of the dopants from the free electrons, the ionized impurity scattering is essentially absent. This leads to a mobility that continues to increase with decreasing temperature as shown in Figure 11.6. This will be discussed further in Chapter 14.

We finally note that the derivation given in this section is for a nondegenerate semiconductor where the Boltzmann expression was sufficient to describe the carrier density variation in presence of the external potential (Equation 11.5). For heavily doped semiconductors, one may be in the degenerate limit where the Fermi level is in the band and one needs to use the proper distribution function to represent the fluctuations in the electron density. In the high degeneracy limit, this leads to a screening parameter λ given by

$$\lambda^2 = \frac{6\pi n e^2}{\epsilon E_F} \qquad (11.34)$$

where E_F is the Fermi level energy measured from the bandedge. However, the problem of scattering in heavily doped semiconductors is a lot more complex

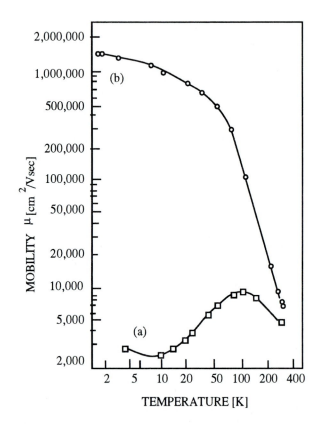

Figure 11.6: Electron mobility as a function of temperature in a uniformly doped GaAs with $N_D = 10^{17}$ cm^{-3}. The mobility drops at low temperature due to ionized impurity scattering becoming very strong. In contrast, the curve b shows the mobility in a modulation doped structure where ionized impurity is essentially eliminated. (Reproduced with permission, G. Weimann, *Two Dimensional Systems: Physics and New Devices*, Springer-Verlag, New York, 1986.)

than the screening problem mentioned above. In writing Equation 11.31, we made the assumption that each impurity center causes scattering independent of each other. While this is a reasonable assumption when the impurities are separated by a large distance (several hundred Angstroms), it is not a good approximation for inter-impurity separations less than approximately 100 Å. In general, the mobility falls faster with doping density than predicted by Equation 11.31 for heavily doped semiconductors due to the effects of multi-impurity scatterings. Figure 11.7 shows the concentration dependence of mobility for both electrons and holes in Ge, Si, and GaAs.

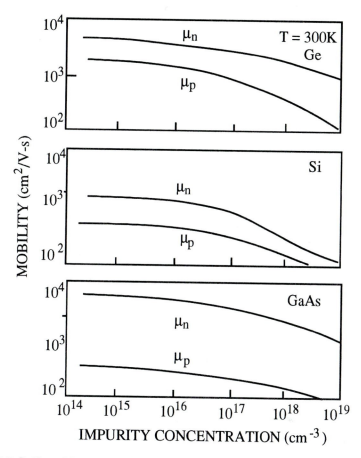

Figure 11.7: Drift mobility of Ge, Si, and GaAs as 300 K versus impurity concentration. (Reproduced with permission, S. M. Sze, *Physics of Semiconductor Devices*, 2nd ed., John Wiley and Sons, New York, 1981.)

11.2 ALLOY SCATTERING

As discussed in our chapter on bandstructures of alloys, there is no microscopic periodicity in the alloy crystal. For example, in the alloy $(AlAs)_x (GaAs)_{1-x}$ while the atom on the anion sublattice is always As, the atoms on the cation sublattice are randomly distributed between Ga and Al. In a perfectly random alloy the probability that a particular cation site is occupied by an Al atom is x and that it is occupied by a Ga atom is $(1-x)$ regardless of the neighboring composition of the site. If, on the other hand, the alloy is clustered, there are regions in space where there is a higher than x or $(1-x)$ probability of finding a particular kind of atom. Since clustering plays an important role in mobility in alloys, we define the Warren-Cowley order parameters which describe the order in the atomic

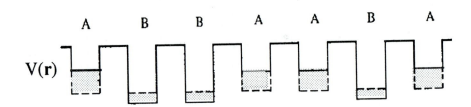

Figure 11.8: A schematic of the actual atomic potential (solid line) and the average virtual crystal potential (dashed line) of an A-B alloy. The shaded area shows the difference between the real potential and the virtual crystal approximation.

distribution of the alloys. These parameters were discussed in Chapter 6. For an alloy $A_x B_{1-x}$, we define

$$
\begin{aligned}
C_\tau &= 1 - x \quad \text{if the atom at site } \tau \text{ is A-type,} \\
&= x \qquad\ \text{if the atom at site } \tau \text{ is B-type.}
\end{aligned}
\tag{11.35}
$$

The order parameters are then

$$
\alpha_\tau = \sum_{\tau'}^{N} \frac{C_{\tau'} C_{\tau'+\tau}}{Nx(1-x)}.
\tag{11.36}
$$

It can be easily seen that $\alpha_0 = 1$ and for a random alloy

$$
\alpha_{\tau \neq 0} = \frac{1}{N}.
\tag{11.37}
$$

In general, the scattering rate for nonrandom scattering can be calculated in terms of the quantities α_τ. Usually, clustering increases the scattering rates unless the alloy is an ordered superlattice.

Let us consider the scattering processes in a perfectly random alloy where the smallest physical size over which the crystal potential fluctuates randomly is the unit cell. An electron moving in the alloy $A_x B_{1-x}$ will see a random potential schematically shown in the Figure 11.8. The average potential and the average bandstructure of the alloy is described to the lowest order by the virtual crystal approximation. In this approximation, the averaging of the atomic potentials or tight binding matrix elements is

$$
\{M\}_{\text{all}} = x\{M\}_A + (1-x)\{M\}_B
\tag{11.38}
$$

gives an average *periodic* potential represented by the dashed line in Figure 11.8. An important approximation is now made. The difference between the real potential and the assumed virtual crystal potential is represented within each unit cell by a highly localized potential. For example, for the A-type atoms, the difference is

$$
\begin{aligned}
E_{all} - E_A &= x E_A + (1-x) E_B - E_A \\
&= (1-x) [E_B - E_A] \\
&= (1-x) U_{all}.
\end{aligned}
\tag{11.39}
$$

Similarly, for the B atom, the difference is

$$
\begin{aligned}
E_B - E_{all} &= x [E_B - E_A] \\
&= x U_{all}.
\end{aligned}
\tag{11.40}
$$

The quantities E_A, E_B, E_{all} are not well-defined in the current scattering theory. They represent some energy level corresponding to the different species, but it is not clear which one. For example, it is not evident if $[E_B - E_A] = U_{all}$ should be the difference in electron affinities, difference in bandgap of the two species, or difference in band offsets if a heterostructure was made from the two systems. Usually $[E_B - E_A]$, often called the alloy potential, is adjusted to fit experimental data.

The scattering potential is chosen to be of the form

$$
\begin{aligned}
\Delta U(r) &= U_0 \quad \text{for } |r| \leq r_0 \\
&= 0 \quad \text{for } |r| > r_0
\end{aligned}
\tag{11.41}
$$

where r_0 is the interatomic distance and $U_0 = U_{all}$. If we use the Fermi golden rule to calculate the scattering rate, we have

$$
W(k) = \frac{2\pi}{\hbar} \sum_{k'} |M_{kk'}|^2 \delta(E_k - E_{k'})
$$

and

$$
M_{kk'} = \int e^{i(k-k')\cdot r} \Delta U(r) \, d^3 r.
\tag{11.42}
$$

We will now use the fact that the scattering potential only extends over a unit cell and over this small distance

$$
e^{i(k-k')\cdot r} \approx 1.
\tag{11.43}
$$

Thus

$$
M_{kk'} = \frac{4\pi}{3} r_0^3 U_0
\tag{11.44}
$$

and

$$
\begin{aligned}
W(k) &= \frac{2\pi}{\hbar} \left(\frac{4\pi}{3} r_0^3 U_0 \right)^2 \frac{1}{(2\pi)^3} \int \delta(E_k - E_{k'}) \, d^3 k' \\
&= \frac{2\pi}{\hbar} \left(\frac{4\pi}{3} r_0^3 U_0 \right)^2 N(E_k),
\end{aligned}
\tag{11.45}
$$

since

$$r_0 = \frac{\sqrt{3}}{4}a$$

where a is the cube edge for an fcc lattice

$$\left(\frac{4\pi}{3}r_0^3\right)^2 = \frac{3\pi^2}{16}V_0^2 \tag{11.46}$$

where $V_0 = a^3/4$ is the volume of the unit cell. We finally obtain for the scattering rate

$$W(k) = \frac{2\pi}{\hbar}\left(\frac{3\pi^2}{16}V_0^2\right)U_0^2\,N(E_k). \tag{11.47}$$

We will now assume that all scattering centers cause incoherent scattering so that we can simply sum the scattering rates. For the A-type atoms, the scattering rate is

$$W_A(k) = \frac{2\pi}{\hbar}\left(\frac{3\pi^2}{16}V_0^2\right)(1-x)^2\,U_0^2\,N(E_k). \tag{11.48}$$

For the B-type atoms, the rate is

$$W_A(k) = \frac{2\pi}{\hbar}\left(\frac{3\pi^2}{16}V_0^2\right)x^2\,U_0^2\,N(E_k). \tag{11.49}$$

There are x/V_0 A-type atoms and $(1-x)/V_0$ B-type atoms in the unit volume and under the assumption of incoherent scattering, the total scattering rate is

$$\begin{aligned}
W_{\text{tot}} &= \frac{2\pi}{\hbar}\left(\frac{3\pi^2}{16}V_0\right)U_0^2\,N(E_k)\left[x\,(1-x)^2 + (1-x)\,x^2\right] \\
&= \frac{3\pi^3}{8\hbar}V_0\,U_0^2\,N(E_k)\,x\,(1-x). \tag{11.50}
\end{aligned}$$

Several important points are to be noted about the alloy scattering. The first is that the matrix element has no k, k' dependence, i.e., there is no angular dependence of the matrix element. If the density of states is isotropic, there will be no angular dependence of the scattering rate $W(k, k')$. This is in contrast to the impurity scattering which had a strong forward angle scattering preference. The relaxation time for the alloy scattering is quite simple (see Equation 10.60)

$$\frac{1}{\langle\langle\tau\rangle\rangle} = \frac{3\pi^3}{8\hbar}V_0U_0^2 x(1-x)\frac{m^{*3/2}(k_BT)^{1/2}}{\sqrt{2}\pi^2\hbar^3}\frac{1}{0.75} \tag{11.51}$$

according to which the mobility due to alloy scattering is

$$\mu_0 \propto T^{-1/2}. \tag{11.52}$$

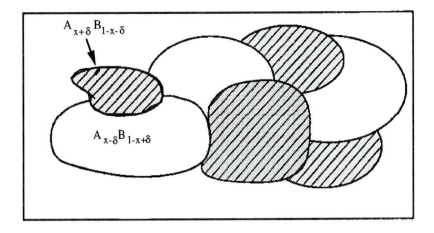

Figure 11.9: A clustered A_xB_{1-x} alloy with A-rich and B-rich regions.

Thus, in 3-D systems the mobility decreases with temperature. This is again in contrast to the situation for the ionized impurity scattering. The quantity U_0 is not known with any certainty from the scattering theory discussed here. Its value is usually obtained by carefully fitting the temperature dependent mobility data. The value of U_0 is usually in the range of 0.5 eV and because of clustering effects in alloys, is difficult to quantify.

Alloy	U_0 (eV)
AlGaAs	0.2
InGaAs	0.5
InAlAs	0.5
InAsP	0.4

In the discussions above we assumed that the alloy was cluster-free and the smallest region in which the disorder occurred was the unit cell. However, in some alloys one can expect alloy clustering as shown schematically in Figure 11.9. Here we show a macroscopic alloy A_xB_{1-x} made up of microscopic regions with compositions $A_{x+\delta}B_{1-x-\delta}$ and $A_{x-\delta}B_{1-x+\delta}$. We can no longer calculate the total scattering rate assuming independent scattering from each unit cell. Atoms within a cluster size r_c will now scatter coherently making the problem more complex. One approximation for the alloy shown in Figure 11.9 to is to use a scattering potential

$$\Delta U(r) = U_{\text{all}} \cdot \delta \text{ for } |r| \leq r_c \qquad (11.53)$$
$$= 0 \text{ for } |r| > r_c, \qquad (11.54)$$

where we have used a potential with a smaller value but a larger spatial extent. Now in the matrix element evaluation we can no longer make the constant phase approximation, (Equation 11.43) since r_c is a large value. In fact, the matrix element now depends critically on the value of $|k - k'|$, reaching a maximum when $|k - k'| \approx 1/r_c$. The scattering rate and mobility is, therefore, very much dependent upon the cluster size and temperature which determines the effective value of k and k'.

11.3   CARRIER-CARRIER SCATTERING

So far in this chapter we have studied the scattering processes from fixed impurities or defects. Another important class of scattering is that between the carriers themselves. Since electrons and holes are both charged particles there can be scattering between them. Also, there can be scattering between electrons themselves. The scattering between electrons is somewhat more complex due to the fact that they are identical Fermions. This introduces special features which we will discuss in this section. Both electron-hole and electron-electron scattering is quite important especially in heavily doped semiconductors.

11.3.1   Electron-Hole Scattering

The scattering of electrons (holes) from ionized impurities is an extremely important process, which controls low field mobility in most semiconductors. However, it is not the only Coulombic scattering present in semiconductors. Two additional scattering mechanisms dependent upon the Coulombic interaction are the e-h and e-e scattering. For example, the electron transport in heavily p-doped materials (e.g., in the base of an n-p-n transistor) is dominated by e-h scattering which is comparable to e-impurity scattering.

This scattering mechanism is closely related in essence to the charged impurity scattering discussed earlier. Electron-hole scattering can be a significant factor in determining the resistivity of narrow-gap intrinsic semiconductors, such as InSb at room temperature.

We can approximate the interaction once again by a screened Coulombic potential between two point particles and obtain the rate in the Born approximation as done previously. The interaction occurs as particle 1, with the initial wavevector k_1, collides with particle 2, with initial wavevector k_2. The collision causes a change in the wavevectors of both particles. Particle 1 leaves the interaction with a final wavevector k'_1 and particle 2 leaves with a final wavevector k'_2. This interaction is schematically shown in Figure 11.10 and is described by the matrix element

$$
\begin{aligned}
\langle k'_1 k'_2 |eV| k_1 k_2 \rangle &= I(k_1, k'_1)I(k_2, k'_2) \\
&\times \frac{1}{V^2} \int \int d^3 r_1 d^3 r_2 e^{-i(k'_1 \cdot r_1 + k'_2 \cdot r_2)} \\
&\times \frac{e^2 \exp(-\lambda|r_1 - r_2|)}{\epsilon|r_1 - r_2|} e^{i(k_1 \cdot r_1 + k_2 \cdot r_2)} \quad (11.55)
\end{aligned}
$$

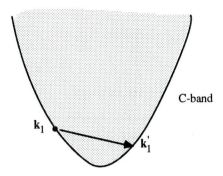

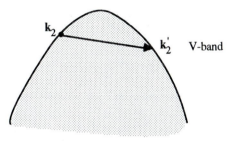

Figure 11.10: Scattering of an electron and hole. Each particle remains in the same band after scattering.

where $I(\boldsymbol{k}_1, \boldsymbol{k}_1'), I(\boldsymbol{k}_2, \boldsymbol{k}_2')$ are the overlap integrals over the unit cell involving the cell-periodic parts of the Bloch functions

$$I(\boldsymbol{k}_1, \boldsymbol{k}_1') \, I(\boldsymbol{k}_2, \boldsymbol{k}_2') = \int_{\text{cell}} u_{\boldsymbol{k}_1'}^*(\boldsymbol{r}_1) \, u_{\boldsymbol{k}_1}(\boldsymbol{r}_1) \, d^3 r_1$$

$$\times \int_{\text{cell}} u_{\boldsymbol{k}_2'}^*(\boldsymbol{r}_2) \, u_{\boldsymbol{k}_2}(\boldsymbol{r}_2) \, d^3 r_2. \qquad (11.56)$$

For scattering events in which all wavevectors lie close to the bandedges, the integrals are usually assumed to be unity. In general, they are less than unity, especially for the hole states.

The interaction depends only on the separation distance of the particles, so it is convenient to transform the problem to a frame of reference in which the center of mass of the two particles is at rest. The transformation (nonrelativistic) to the center-of-mass frame is affected by converting to the new coordinates given by

$$\boldsymbol{K} = \boldsymbol{k} - \boldsymbol{k}_{cm}$$
$$\boldsymbol{k}_{cm} = \frac{1}{2} (\boldsymbol{k}_1 + \boldsymbol{k}_2)$$

$$K_{12} = \frac{1}{2}(k_1 - k_2)$$

or

$$k_1 = k_{cm} + K_{12}$$
$$k_2 = k_{cm} - K_{12}. \qquad (11.57)$$

The corresponding transformation of spatial coordinates is

$$R = r - r_{cm}$$
$$r_{cm} = \frac{m_1^* r_1 + m_2^* r_2}{m_1^* + m_2^*}$$
$$r_{12} = r_1 - r_2$$

leading to

$$r_1 = r_{cm} + \frac{m_2^*}{m_1^* + m_2^*} r_{12} \qquad (11.58)$$

$$r_2 = r_{cm} - \frac{m_1^*}{m_1^* + m_2^*} r_{12}. \qquad (11.59)$$

The integral for the matrix element now splits into a product of two integrals, one over r_{cm} and the other over r_{12}. The former gives unity and ensures the conservation of momentum. The integral over r_{12} is

$$\langle K_{12}' | eV(r_{12}) | K_{12} \rangle = \frac{1}{V} \int \exp(-iK_{12}' \cdot r_{12})$$

$$\times \frac{e^2 \exp(-\lambda r_{12})}{\epsilon r_{12}} \exp(iK_{12} \cdot r_{12}) \, d^3r_{12}$$

$$= \frac{e^2}{\epsilon V} \frac{1}{\left| K_{12}' - K_{12} \right|^2 + \lambda^2}. \qquad (11.60)$$

as for the case of the ionized impurity scattering. The problem is exactly similar to the collision of a particle of mass $\overline{m}^*$, equal to the reduced mass of the two particles, with a fixed center. Thus one can use the calculations carried out for the ionized impurity scattering to obtain the angular dependence of the scattering rate.

The transformation from relative to absolute coordinates is usually facilitated in reality by the disparity between electron and hole masses. In most cases, the hole mass exceeds the electron mass significantly, and consequently the hole can be considered to be at rest and the problem of electron-hole scattering reduces to that for the charged impurity scattering.

In minority carrier transport, e.g., electrons moving in p-type semiconductors, the electron gets scattered from acceptors and holes with the result that if $m_h^* \gg m_e^*$, the scattering rate simply becomes *twice* that from the impurities alone. This approximation works quite well for most semiconductors.

11.3.2 Scattering of Identical Particles

In quantum mechanics, the interactions of identical particles introduces some very important consequences which have direct experimental implications. In classical physics, whether two particles are distinguishable or not, does not have bearing on the physics. However, because of the probabilistic nature of the quantum description, this is not the case in quantum mechanics.

Consider the following experimental facts. Two particles, A and B, scatter from each other and we measure their scattering rates by placing detectors as shown in Figure 11.11. We will look for the angular distribution of the probability that some particle arrives at the detector D_1. We will work in the center of mass system and denote by $f(\theta)$ the amplitude that the particle A is scattered by angle θ. We have to consider the two possibilities, shown in the figure, where the particles are exchanged. The amplitude of scattering for the second case is $f(\pi - \theta)$. The following is observed experimentally.

- If the particles are distinguishable the probability of *some* particle appearing as D_1 is
$$|f(\theta)|^2 + |f(\pi - \theta)|^2 \,. \tag{11.61}$$

- If the particles are indistinguishable and are bosons (e.g. α-particles, photons, mesons) the probability of one of the particles appearing is D_1 is
$$|f(\theta) + f(\pi - \theta)|^2 \,. \tag{11.62}$$

- If the particles are identical but are fermions (e.g. electrons, neutrinoes, protons, neutrons) the probability is
$$|f(\theta) - f(\pi - \theta)|^2 \,. \tag{11.63}$$

Note that if the two particles are electrons but have different spins, and the scattering is not supposed to alter the spin, then the probability is given by the *distinguishable* case. In general, if we have a multitude of processes leading to scattering, one has to add the amplitude of each process and then square the total amplitude to get the probability. In the case of distinguishable particles where there is no phase coherence between the direct and exchange state, this is simply equivalent to summing the individual probabilities. However, for identical particles, there is a well-defined relationship between the direct state and the exchanged state.

In general, the direct and exchange states would have an amplitude of scattering $f(\theta)$ and $\exp(i\delta)f(\pi - \theta)$, respectively. If one carries out the exchange again from the exchanged state the new amplitude is $\exp(2i\delta)f(\theta)$. But this is equal to $f(\theta)$ so that $\exp(i\delta)$ is $+1$ or -1. It was shown by Pauli that for fermions the choice of the phase factor is -1 and for bosons it is $+1$. In fact, in general, the wavefunction describing a set of fermions must be such that it is *antisymmetric* (changes sign) to any permutation or interchange of two particles. Similarly, for bosons the wavefunction is *symmetric* to such a permutation.

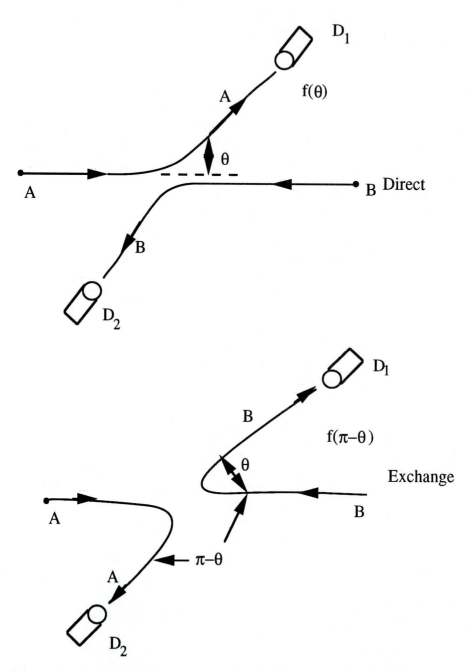

Figure 11.11: Scattering of two particles in the center of mass system. The detector D_1 is able to detect any particle being scattered at the angle.

It is also important to examine composite particles where two or more particles are bound together. If the composite is made up of an even number of fermions (e.g., an α-particle or an exciton), and the binding of these internal particles is strong enough that during the interaction of the composites, there is negligible possibility of any exchange of the internal constituents, then the composite will act as a *boson*. However, if the binding is weak, permitting interchange of the constituents, the composite may act as a *fermion*.

11.3.3 Electron-Electron Scattering

The e-h system discussed previously constitutes distinguishable particles. On the other hand, the e-e system involves indistinguishable particles and, in general, this introduces important differences in the scattering calculations as discussed above. In general, we have to include the direct and exchange terms and add the scattering amplitudes with the prescription discussed above. Figure 11.12 shows the various possible scattering processes for both the indistinguishable (i.e., same spins) and distinguishable (opposite spins) cases.

We can essentially use the formalism we have already developed for the e-h collisions and apply it to the e-e case. The processes (1) and (2) are totally indistinguishable and will interfere. The matrix element we calculated earlier for e-h case is M_{12}

$$
\begin{aligned}
M_{12} &= \langle \boldsymbol{K}'_{12} | V | \boldsymbol{K}_{12} \rangle \\
&= \frac{4\pi e^2}{\epsilon V} \frac{1}{\left| \boldsymbol{K}'_{12} - \boldsymbol{K}_{12} \right|^2 + \lambda^2}
\end{aligned}
\tag{11.64}
$$

where

$$
\left| \boldsymbol{K}'_{12} - \boldsymbol{K}_{12} \right| = 2K_{12} \sin(\theta/2).
$$

The process (2) changes $\theta \to \pi - \theta$

$$
M_{21} = \frac{4\pi e^2}{\epsilon V} \frac{1}{\left| \boldsymbol{K}'_{12} - \boldsymbol{K}_{12} \right|^2 + \lambda^2}
\tag{11.65}
$$

where

$$
\left| \boldsymbol{K}'_{12} - \boldsymbol{K}_{12} \right| = 2K_{12} \cos(\theta/2).
$$

Since these two processes are indistinguishable, they interfere destructively (since the electrons are fermions) at the amplitude level. The processes (3) and (4) are distinguishable and therefore do not interfere. One has to square and add the contributions separately. The total matrix element squared is now

$$
\begin{aligned}
|M|^2 &= \frac{1}{2} \left[|M_{12}|^2 + |M_{21}|^2 + |M_{12} - M_{21}|^2 \right] \\
&= |M_{12}|^2 + |M_{21}|^2 - \frac{1}{2} \left(M_{21} M_{12}^* + M_{21}^* M_{12} \right).
\end{aligned}
\tag{11.66}
$$

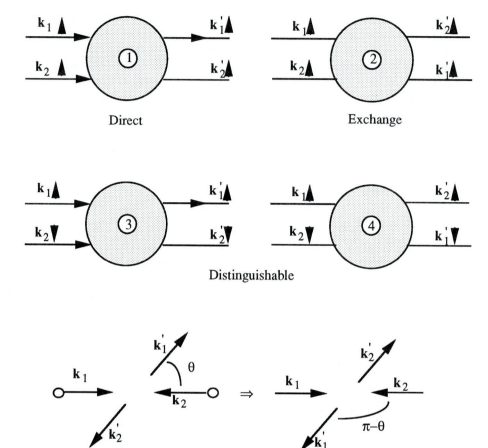

Figure 11.12: A schematic showing the direct and exchange scattering processes for identical particle scattering. When the spins of the two particles are the same, the two processes (1 and 2) are indistinguishable. When the spins are different, the two processes (3 and 4) are distinguishable.

The factor 1/2 arises because in half the collisions the spins are aligned and in half they are opposed.

Following the arguments for the e-h case, or the ionized impurity case, we can write for the differential cross section in the center of mass frame (taking the overlap integrals to be unity)

$$
\sigma(\theta) \;=\; \left(\frac{e^2}{4\epsilon E_{12}}\right)^2 \left[\frac{1}{\left\{\sin^2(\theta/2) + \left(\frac{\lambda}{2K_{12}}\right)^2\right\}^2}\right.
$$

$$+ \frac{1}{\left\{ \cos^2(\theta/2) + \left(\frac{\lambda}{2K_{12}} \right)^2 \right\}^2}$$

$$- \frac{1}{\left\{ \sin^2(\theta/2) + \left(\frac{\lambda}{2K_{12}} \right)^2 \right\} \left\{ \cos^2(\theta/2) + \left(\frac{\lambda}{2K_{12}} \right)^2 \right\}} \Bigg] \quad (11.67)$$

where θ is the angle between $\boldsymbol{K}_{12}$ and $\boldsymbol{K}'_{12}$.

$$K_{12} = \left| \frac{\boldsymbol{K}_1 - \boldsymbol{K}_2}{2} \right|$$

$$E_{12} = \frac{\hbar^2 K_{12}^2}{2\overline{m}^*}$$

$$\overline{m}^* = \frac{m^*}{2}. \quad (11.68)$$

The total cross section is derived by integrating over all angles

$$\sigma = \left(\frac{e^2}{4\epsilon E_{12}} \right)^2 8\pi \left[\frac{1}{(\lambda/2K_{12})^2 \{1 + (\lambda/2K_{12})^2\}} \right.$$

$$+ \left. \frac{1}{1 + 2(\lambda/2K_{12})^2} \ln \left\{ \frac{(\lambda/2K_{12})^2}{1 + (\lambda/2K_{12})^2} \right\} \right]. \quad (11.69)$$

A momentum relaxation cross section can be found by multiplying the first term in Equation 11.67 by $(1 - \cos\theta)$, second term by $(1 + \cos\theta)$, and the third term by $(1 - \cos\theta)(1 + \cos\theta)$. With $x = (\hbar^2\lambda^2)/(2\overline{m}^* E_{12})$

$$\frac{1}{\tau_m} = \frac{2\pi e^4}{\epsilon^2 V \sqrt{2\overline{m}^*} E_{12}^{3/2}} \left[\ln\left(1 + \frac{4}{x}\right) - \frac{1}{1 + x} - \frac{\pi}{2} \left\{ \frac{1}{1 + x\left(1 + \frac{x}{4}\right)} \right\} \right]. \quad (11.70)$$

This scattering rate is usually too small for carrier concentrations of less than 10^{17} cm^{-3}. However, at higher values of carrier density, this rate becomes comparable to the phonon scattering rates and must be accounted for in any transport calculation.

11.4 AUGER PROCESSES AND IMPACT IONIZATION

The scattering processes we have discussed so far mainly influence the mobility of the carriers without altering the *number* of free carriers. Two additional important processes relying on carrier-carrier scattering are the Auger process and the impact ionization. In both these processes, the number of free carriers before and after scattering are altered. Figure 11.13 shows a schematic of four important Auger processes. For example, in the direct process an electron recombines

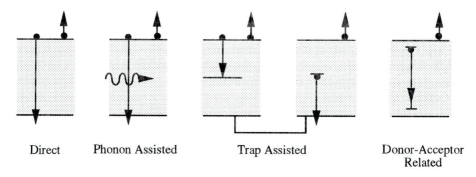

Direct   Phonon Assisted   Trap Assisted   Donor-Acceptor Related

Figure 11.13: Various processes that contribute to Auger recombination. In direct band-gap materials of high purity, one needs to be concerned about the direct process alone.

with a hole and the extra energy is absorbed by another electron. In this process, the electron hole recombination does not produce a photon as would be the case for radiative transitions (discussed later). Such processes are very important in narrow bandgap lasers where this process causes carrier recombination without producing useful photons. In addition to the processes shown for electrons, we have the processes for holes (where the energy of recombination is transferred to a hole). These processes are all mediated by the Coulombic interactions and involve e-e scattering. We will be only interested in the direct process shown in Figure 11.13.

Under very high electric fields, electrons gain energy larger than the band-gap of the semiconductor. When this happens, impact ionization, which is the reverse process of the Auger scattering, can occur. Thus a high energy electron in the conduction band scatters from an electron in the valence band. The second electron is raised to the conduction band, resulting in two electrons in the conduction band and a hole in the valence band. This causes carrier multiplication and the current in the semiconductor increases dramatically. This results in the breakdown of the semiconductor and limits the high performance behavior of electronic devices. Impact ionization is also exploited in avalanche photodetectors for very high gains. We will study these processes using the electron-electron interaction discussion above, except that the process now involves carriers in the valence and conduction bands.

First, we will discuss the Auger recombination analysis. The matrix element M_{12} for the scattering in the direct process is as before (see Figure 11.14)

$$
\begin{aligned}
M_{12} ={}& \frac{1}{V^2} \int\int d^3r_1\, d^3r_2\, \frac{e^2 \exp(-\lambda|\boldsymbol{r}_1 - \boldsymbol{r}_2|)}{\epsilon|\boldsymbol{r}_1 - \boldsymbol{r}_2|} \\
& \times\ u^*_{v\boldsymbol{k}'_1}(\boldsymbol{r}_1)\, \exp(-i\boldsymbol{k}'_1 \cdot \boldsymbol{r}_1)\, u^*_{c\boldsymbol{k}'_2}(\boldsymbol{r}_2)\, \exp(-i\boldsymbol{k}'_2 \cdot \boldsymbol{r}_2) \\
& \times\ u^*_{c\boldsymbol{k}_1}(\boldsymbol{r}_1)\, \exp(i\boldsymbol{k}_1 \cdot \boldsymbol{r}_1)\, u^*_{c\boldsymbol{k}_2}(\boldsymbol{r}_2)\, \exp(i\boldsymbol{k}_2 \cdot \boldsymbol{r}_2).
\end{aligned}
\tag{11.71}
$$

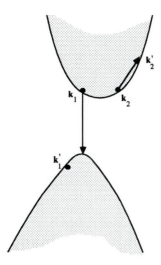

Figure 11.14: A schematic of the states of the electrons before and after an Auger scattering. The reverse of this process is the impact ionization process. This particular process is called CHCC (Conduction-Heavy hole-Conduction-Conduction).

We have assumed a screened Coulombic potential here. Here we assume that the initial electrons are in the conduction band while the one of the final states is in the valence band as shown in Figure 11.14. Transforming to the center of mass system gives us the conservation of momentum

$$k_1 + k_2 = k_1' + k_2'. \tag{11.72}$$

As before, we have

$$M_{12} = \left(\frac{4\pi e^2}{\epsilon V}\right) \frac{I(k_1, k_1')\, I(k_2, k_2')}{\left|k_1' - k_1\right|^2 + \lambda^2}. \tag{11.73}$$

The relevant overlap integrals are

$$
\begin{aligned}
I(k_1, k_1') &= \int_{\text{cell}} d^3 r_1 \, u_{vk_1'}^*(r_1)\, u_{ck_1}^*(r_1) \\
I(k_2, k_2') &= \int_{\text{cell}} d^3 r_2 \, u_{ck_2'}^*(r_2)\, u_{ck_2}^*(r_2).
\end{aligned}
\tag{11.74}
$$

Here we have used the fact that

$$K_{12} = \frac{1}{2}\left|k_1 - k_2\right|$$

so that due to momentum conservation

$$\left|K_{12}' - K_{12}\right|^2 = \left|k_1' - k_1\right|^2. \tag{11.75}$$

For the exchange process

$$M_{21} = \left(\frac{4\pi e^2}{\epsilon V}\right) \frac{I(\mathbf{k}_1, \mathbf{k}_2')I(\mathbf{k}_2, \mathbf{k}_1')}{\left|\mathbf{k}_1' - \mathbf{k}_2\right|^2 + \lambda^2}. \tag{11.76}$$

and

$$I(\mathbf{k}_1, \mathbf{k}_2') = \int_{\text{cell}} d^3r_1 u^*_{c\mathbf{k}_2'}(\mathbf{r}_1)u_{c\mathbf{k}_1}(\mathbf{r}_1)$$

$$I(\mathbf{k}_2, \mathbf{k}_1') = \int_{\text{cell}} d^3r_2 u^*_{v\mathbf{k}_1'}(\mathbf{r}_2)u_{c\mathbf{k}_2}(\mathbf{r}_2). \tag{11.77}$$

As discussed for the case of the e-e scattering we have to consider the four processes of Figure 11.12 which give us the total matrix element squared

$$|M|^2 = \left[|M_{12}|^2 + |M_{21}|^2 + |M_{12} - M_{21}|^2\right]. \tag{11.78}$$

To calculate the Auger rates we must discuss the occupation statistics of the various electrons and hole states involved in the process. We need to weigh the rate with the probability that state $\mathbf{k}_2$ is full, $\mathbf{k}_1'$ is empty and $\mathbf{k}_1$ is full. If we assume nondegenerate statistics, the occupation factor becomes

$$P(\mathbf{k}_1, \mathbf{k}_2, \mathbf{k}_1') = f(\mathbf{k}_1)\, f(\mathbf{k}_2) \left(1 - f(\mathbf{k}_1')\right) \tag{11.79}$$

where

$$f(\mathbf{k}_1) = \frac{n}{N_c} \exp\left(\frac{-E_{c\mathbf{k}_1}}{k_B T}\right)$$

$$f(\mathbf{k}_2) = \frac{n}{N_c} \exp\left(\frac{-E_{c\mathbf{k}_2}}{k_B T}\right)$$

$$1 - f(\mathbf{k}_1') = \frac{p}{N_v} \exp\left(\frac{-E_{v\mathbf{k}_1'}}{k_B T}\right). \tag{11.80}$$

Here n and p are the electron and hole carrier densities and N_c, N_v are the conduction and valence band effective density of states.

This gives the total probability factor

$$P(\mathbf{k}_1, \mathbf{k}_2, \mathbf{k}_1') = \frac{np}{N_c N_v} \frac{n}{N_c} \exp\left(-\frac{E_{c\mathbf{k}_2} + E_{v\mathbf{k}_1'} + E_{c\mathbf{k}_1}}{k_B T}\right)$$

$$\approx \frac{n}{N_c} \exp\left(-\frac{E_g + E_{c\mathbf{k}_2} + E_{v\mathbf{k}_1'} + E_{c\mathbf{k}_1}}{k_B T}\right). \tag{11.81}$$

We have assumed that the state $\mathbf{k}_2'$ is always available since it is a high energy electron state in the conduction band.

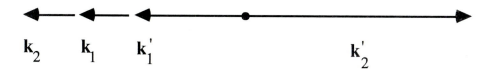

Figure 11.15: Procedure for finding the maximum in probability for Auger rates. This procedure is also used to find the threshold energy for the impact ionization process to occur. The threshold is reached when the high energy electron k_2' has its wavevector lined up opposite to those of the low energy electrons as shown.

It is useful to examine the energy at which this term maximizes. This involves finding the extremum of the expression (in the parabolic band approximation)

$$\frac{k_1^2}{2m_c^*} + \frac{k_2^2}{2m_c^*} + \frac{k_1'^2}{2m_v^*} = \frac{1}{2m_c^*}\left[k_1^2 + k_2^2 + \mu k_1'^2\right] \tag{11.82}$$

where

$$\mu = \frac{m_c^*}{m_v^*}. \tag{11.83}$$

The probability factor will maximize for the lowest energy values of k_1, k_1' and k_2 which are consistent with energy and momentum conservation. Since k_2' is the largest vector, we line up k_1, k_1', and k_2 with k_2' in the opposite direction as shown in Figure 11.15. Thus we choose

$$k_1 + k_1' + k_2 = -k_2'. \tag{11.84}$$

We also write

$$\begin{aligned} k_1 &= ak_1' \\ k_2 &= bk_1'. \end{aligned} \tag{11.85}$$

We now have from conservation of energy

$$k_2'^2 = (a^2 + b^2 + \mu)k_1'^2 + K_g^2 \tag{11.86}$$

where

$$E_g = \frac{\hbar^2 K_g^2}{2m_c^*}. \tag{11.87}$$

Also the conservation of momentum gives us

$$k_2' = (a + b + 1)k_2'$$

or

$$k_2'^2 = (a^2 + b^2 + 1 + 2ab + 2a + 2b)k_1'^2. \tag{11.88}$$

Eliminating $k_2'^2$ from Equations 11.86 and 11.88 we get

$$k_1'^2(1 + 2ab + 2a + 2b - \mu) = K_g^2. \tag{11.89}$$

The quantity to be minimized for maximum Auger rate or the impact ionization threshold is

$$k_1^2 + k_2^2 + \mu k_1'^2 = k_1'^2(a^2 + b^2 + \mu).$$

Substituting for $k_1'^2$ from Equation 11.89 we get

$$(a^2 + b^2 + \mu)k_1'^2 = \frac{a^2 + b^2 + \mu}{1 + 2ab + 2a + 2b - \mu} K_g^2. \tag{11.90}$$

This quantity minimizes when

$$a = b = \mu. \tag{11.91}$$

This gives us the energy values

$$
\begin{aligned}
E_{c\mathbf{k}_1} &= E_{c\mathbf{k}_2} \\
&= \mu E_{v\mathbf{k}_1'} \\
&= \left(\frac{\mu^2}{1 + 3\mu + 2\mu^2}\right) E_g. \tag{11.92}
\end{aligned}
$$

The maximum probability function is now

$$P(\mathbf{k}_1, \mathbf{k}_2, \mathbf{k}_1') = \frac{n}{N_c} \exp\left(-\frac{1 + 2\mu}{1 + \mu}\frac{E_g}{k_B T}\right) \tag{11.93}$$

and the energy of the high energy electron is

$$E_{c\mathbf{k}_2'} = \frac{1 + 2\mu}{1 + \mu} E_g. \tag{11.94}$$

If $\mu \ll 1$, we have the approximation

$$E_{c\mathbf{k}_2'} \approx (1 + \mu)E_g. \tag{11.95}$$

The value for $E_{c\mathbf{k}_2'}$ represents the threshold for the inverse process of impact ionization.

In the simple discussion above, we assumed an isotropic and parabolic band to get the maximum probability function for the Auger rate and the threshold for impact ionization. In general, we know that the hole bands are highly anisotropic with masses which vary considerably as a function of the wavevector angle. The general threshold condition then requires a graphical or numerical solution to find the minimum value for $E_{c\mathbf{k}_2'}$ which is consistent with the conservation of energy and momentum. In general, the momentum needs to be conserved only to within a reciprocal lattice vector. The threshold energies are then very much dependent upon the angle of k_2'. Also since the bands are highly nonparabolic for the conduction band, the Equation 11.95 only provides an approximate condition.

For example, the threshold energy for an electron in the Si conduction band is 1.18 eV if the electron is moving along the (100) direction initially and 3.1 eV if it is moving along the (111) direction. Similarly, for a conduction band electron moving along the (100) direction in GaAs, the threshold energy is 2.1 eV and for the trajectory along (110), it is 1.7 eV. These details can be accounted for in a Monte Carlo approach to the impact ionization problem, but one needs to carry out an averaging procedure for other analytical approaches.

To solve the general integral for the Auger rates (or the impact ionization process), one needs to evaluate the multiple integral (these are rates for a particular electron at k_1; the total rate over all electrons will involve a further integral over k_1, as well)

$$
\begin{aligned}
W_{\text{Auger}} \;=\; & 2\left(\frac{2\pi}{\hbar}\right)\left(\frac{4\pi e^2}{\epsilon}\right)^2 \frac{1}{(2\pi)^6} \\
& \times \int d^3k_2 \int d^3k_1' \int d^3k_2' \, |M|^2 \, P(k_1, k_2, k_1') \\
& \times \; \delta(E_{ck_1} + E_{ck_2} - E_{vk_1'} - E_{ck_2'}).
\end{aligned}
\tag{11.96}
$$

The matrix element $|M|^2$ has been discussed before and for most purposes it is adequate to use $\lambda = 0$. In general, one has to explicitly evaluate the overlap integrals by using an accurate bandstructure description. Typical results for such a calculation are shown in Figure 11.16 where we show the Auger recombination rate for the narrow bandgap material $In_{0.53}Ga_{0.47}As$ ($E_g \approx 0.8$ eV) which is widely used for long-distance optical communication lasers. The Auger rate is approximately proportional to n^3 (for the laser $n = p$), and is often written in the form

$$
\begin{aligned}
W \;=\; & R_{\text{Auger}} \\
\;=\; & F n^3.
\end{aligned}
\tag{11.97}
$$

where F is the Auger coefficient. This relation is, however, only approximate and breaks down at high injection where the statistics change from nondegenerate Boltzmann-like to degenerate Fermi-Dirac statistics.

An approximate treatment for the Auger rates can be made if one assumes parabolic bands and a simple form for the overlap integrals as discussed below.

If we assume that the overlap integrals vary slowly with energy, since the energies of k_1 and k_2 are quite similar, we have

$$
I(k_1, k_1') = I(k_2, k_1')
$$

and

$$
I(k_2, k_2') = I(k_1, k_2').
\tag{11.98}
$$

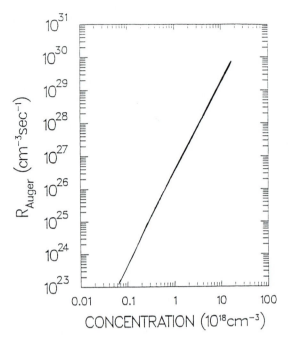

Figure 11.16: Auger rates calculated for $In_{0.53}Ga_{0.47}As$ at room temperature. The important process involves the final state with one hole in the split off band. The term CHHS (Conduction-Heavy hole-Heavy hole-Split off hole) is used for such events (after J. Loehr, 1991).

As a consequence of this and the result that $k_1 \approx k_2$

$$M_{12} \approx M_{21} \tag{11.99}$$

which implies that we can neglect the collisions between like spins, and

$$|M|^2 = 2|M_{12}|^2 \tag{11.100}$$

$$
\begin{aligned}
W_{\text{recomb}} &= \frac{4\pi}{\hbar}\left(\frac{e^2}{2\pi^2\epsilon}\right)^2 \frac{np}{N_c N_v} \int\int \left|I(\boldsymbol{k}_1, \boldsymbol{k}_1')I(\boldsymbol{k}_2, \boldsymbol{k}_2')\right|^2 \\
&\quad \times \frac{\exp\left\{-(E_{c\boldsymbol{k}_2} + E_{v\boldsymbol{k}_1'})/(k_B T)\right\}}{\left(|\boldsymbol{k}_1' - \boldsymbol{k}_1|^2\right)^2} \\
&\quad \times \delta(E_{c\boldsymbol{k}_2'} - E_g - E_{v\boldsymbol{k}_1'} - E_{c\boldsymbol{k}_1} - E_{c\boldsymbol{k}_2})d^3k_2 d^3k_1' \tag{11.101}
\end{aligned}
$$

where we have set $\lambda = 0$, as mentioned above.

When both states lie in the same band, it is reasonable to take the overlap integral to be unity. However, for integrals like

$$I(\boldsymbol{k}_1, \boldsymbol{k}_1') = \int_{\text{cell}} d^3 r_1 \, u_{v\boldsymbol{k}_1'}^*(\boldsymbol{r}_1) \, u_{c\boldsymbol{k}_1}(\boldsymbol{r}_1)$$

one cannot make such an approximation. We can go back to the $\boldsymbol{k} \cdot \boldsymbol{p}$ theory to get an approximate value for these integrals. We showed in Chapter 5 (see Equation 5.68) that

$$u_{c\boldsymbol{k}_1} = u_{c0} + \frac{\hbar}{m} \frac{\boldsymbol{P}_{cv} \, u_{v0} \cdot \boldsymbol{k}_1}{E_g} \tag{11.102}$$

and

$$u_{v\boldsymbol{k}_1'} = u_{v0} - \frac{\hbar}{m} \frac{\boldsymbol{P}_{cv} \, u_{c0} \cdot \boldsymbol{k}_1}{E_g}, \tag{11.103}$$

so that

$$I(\boldsymbol{k}_1, \boldsymbol{k}_1') = \frac{\hbar}{m} \frac{\boldsymbol{P}_{cv}}{E_g} \left| \boldsymbol{k}_1 - \boldsymbol{k}_1' \right| \tag{11.104}$$

and

$$
\begin{aligned}
\left| I(\boldsymbol{k}_1, \boldsymbol{k}_1') \right|^2 &= \frac{\hbar^2}{m^2} \frac{P_{cv}^2}{E_g^2} \left| \boldsymbol{k}_1 - \boldsymbol{k}_1' \right|^2 \\
&= \frac{\hbar^2}{2E_g} \left(\frac{1}{m} + \frac{1}{m_v^*} \right) \left| \boldsymbol{k}_1 - \boldsymbol{k}_1' \right|^2.
\end{aligned}
\tag{11.105}
$$

If we ignore the effect of screening

$$
\begin{aligned}
W_{\text{recomb}} &= \frac{2\pi}{\hbar} \left(\frac{e^2}{2\pi^2\epsilon} \right)^2 \frac{\hbar^2}{E_g} \left(\frac{1}{m} + \frac{1}{m_v^*} \right) \frac{np}{N_c N_v} \\
&\times \int\int \frac{\exp\left\{ -\left(E_{c\boldsymbol{k}_2} + E_{v\boldsymbol{k}_1'} \right) / k_B T \right\}}{\left| \boldsymbol{k}_1' - \boldsymbol{k}_1 \right|^2} \\
&\times \delta\left(E_{c\boldsymbol{k}_2'} - E_g - E_{v\boldsymbol{k}_1'} - E_{c\boldsymbol{k}_1} - E_{c\boldsymbol{k}_2} \right) \, dk_2 \, dk_1'. \quad (11.106)
\end{aligned}
$$

This is the result for the recombination process. It is not possible to do all the integrals without making significant approximations now. However, if we assume that

$$m_c^* \ll m_v^*$$
$$k_1' \gg k_1.$$

The integral can be simplified to obtain

$$W_{\text{recomb}} = \frac{(4\pi)^2 e^4 m_c^* (k_B T)^{3/2} \left(\frac{m_c^*}{m} + \mu \right)}{4\pi^{5/2} \epsilon^2 \hbar^3 (1 + \mu)^{1/2} E_g^{3/2}} \exp\left\{ -\frac{(1 + \mu)E_g}{k_B T} \right\}. \tag{11.107}$$

The Auger rates increase exponentially as the bandgap is decreased. They also increase exponentially as the temperature increases. These are direct results of the energy and momentum conservation constraints and the carrier statistics. Auger processes are more or less unimportant in semiconductors with bandgaps larger than approximately 1.5 eV (e.g., GaAs, AlGaAs, InP). However, they become quite important in narrow bandgap materials such as $In_{0.53}Ga_{0.47}As$ ($E = 0.8$ eV) and HgCdTe ($E < 0.5$ eV), and are thus a serious hindrance for the development of long wavelength lasers.

The full calculation for the impact ionization rates also involves the knowledge of the entire bandstructure. This implies a complicated numerical solution. However, we can obtain reasonable results by using the same approximations for the overlap integral and the carrier bandstructure as were used for the Auger rates. The impact ionization rate can be written as

$$W_{impact}(E_{\mathbf{k}_1}) = \frac{4\pi}{\hbar} \left(\frac{e^2}{2\pi\epsilon} \right)^2 \frac{\hbar^2 P_{cv}^2}{m^2 E_g^2} \int \frac{(k_{2,max}^2 - k_{2,min}^2)}{\left| \mathbf{k}_1 - \mathbf{k}_1' \right|^3} k_1'^2 \, dk_1 \, d(\cos\theta).$$

(11.108)

Here $\mathbf{k}_{2,max}$ and $\mathbf{k}_{2,min}$ are the maximum and minimum values of the valence electron wavevector consistent with energy and momentum conservation. The term $(k_{2,max}^2 - k_{2,min}^2)$ gives us the threshold for the impact ionization process. The integral in Equation 11.108 can be numerically integrated. It is illustrative to examine the threshold condition if the bands are parabolic. In this case, the impact ionization threshold energy is as discussed before

$$E_{\mathbf{k}_1} = \frac{1 + 2\mu}{1 + \mu} E_g.$$

(11.109)

In Figures 11.17 and 11.18 we show some typical impact ionization rates for GaAs and $In_{0.53}Ga_{0.47}As$. These results are calculated assuming the conduction band states to be described by the nonparabolic relation

$$(1 + \alpha E)E = \frac{\hbar^2 k^2}{2m^*}$$

(11.110)

where the nonparabolicity factor is $\alpha = 0.67$ eV^{-1} for GaAs and $\alpha = 1.0$ eV^{-1} for $In_{0.53}Ga_{0.47}As$. The hole band is chosen to be parabolic with an averaged mass of $m_{HH}^* = 0.45m$. One can see from these figures how the ionization rate increases once the initial electron has an energy larger than the threshold.

If the electron and hole bands are assumed to be parabolic, it is possible to obtain a simple analytic expression for the impact ionization rate (Ridley, 1982)

$$
\begin{aligned}
W_{imp} &= 4.139 \times 10^{16} \text{sec} \\
&\times \left\{ \frac{4\sqrt{m_c^* m_v^*}}{m} \left(\frac{m_c^*}{m} + \mu \right) \left(\frac{1}{\epsilon} \right)^2 \left[\frac{E_{c\mathbf{k}_2'}}{E_g} - (1 + \mu) \right] \right\}.
\end{aligned}
$$
(11.111)

The impact ionization process becomes important in semiconductor devices when they are operated at high electric fields (several hundred kV/cm). It

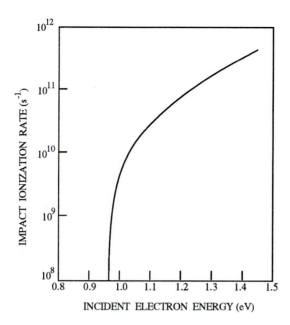

Figure 11.17: Impact ionization rates for $In_{0.53}Ga_{0.47}As$ ($E_g = 0.8$ eV) calculated using an isotropic bandstructure. The hole bands are represented by a parabolic density of states mass.

causes breakdown in semiconductor structures and thus limits the high power application of transistors. The impact ionization process (or avalanche process) is, however, exploited in avalanche detectors where a photo-generated carrier causes carrier multiplication by impact ionization and thus provides a high gain detector.

11.5 FOR THE TECHNOLOGIST IN YOU

In this chapter we have discussed some very important scattering processes. These processes play an important role in affecting the transport of carriers in semiconductors. As we noted in this chapter, at low temperatures, the defect scattering becomes a limiting factor in transport. As the temperature is raised, the effects of lattice vibrations starts to become important. We will discuss these effects in the next chapter.

The scattering processes discussed in this chapter play a major role in electronic device performance. The desire to control these processes or to exploit them has been a key driving force for new device designs and the search for new material systems. As discussed in this chapter, ionized impurity scattering is an important source of scattering and becomes even more dominant at low temperature. The use of the modulation doping concept essentially eliminates this source of scattering in FET structures and is a major reason for superior

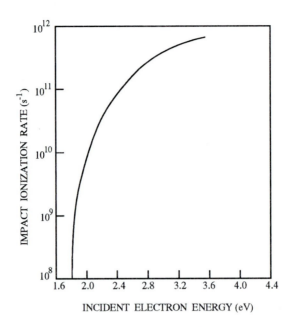

Figure 11.18: Impact ionization rates for GaAs ($E_g = 1.4$ eV) calculated using an isotropic bandstructure.

performance of the MODFET as compared to a MESFET.

The electron-hole scattering plays a very important role in the minority carrier transport in the base of bipolar devices. On the one hand, a high base doping is necessary to reduce the base resistance and, on the other hand, the minority carrier transit time is increased because of this. Usually, however, the improvements due to lower base resistance are more dominant.

The impact ionization process limits the power output of most electronic devices. This is a particularly serious problem for high frequency devices based on narrow bandgap semiconductors such as InGaAs. The need for higher power output devices is very serious for applications such as radar transmitters, satellite communications, broadcasting, etc. This need drives research in high gap materials such as SiC, C, GaN, AlN, etc.

The impact ionization process is not always undesirable. It is exploited for devices such as high gain avalanche photodetectors and microwave devices such as IMPATTs.

Auger processes in narrow bandgap semiconductor lasers are the main limitation for high temperature operation of such lasers. The need for semiconductor lasers operating at room temperature and above is very real. Unfortunately, the higher temperatures also mean higher Auger rates which means more of the current goes into nonradiative processes causing further increase in operating temperatures.

11.6 PROBLEMS

11.1. Calculate and plot the screening length λ^{-1} as a function of free carrier density from $n_{\text{free}} = 1 \times 10^{14}$ cm^{-3} to 1×10^{18} cm^{-3} at 77 K and 300 K for GaAs and Si.

11.2. Plot the angular dependence of the scattering rate (like Figure 11.5) due to ionized impurities when the background ionized donors are 10^{15} cm^{-3} and 10^{17} cm^{-3} at room temperature for GaAs. Assume an electron energy of $k_B T$.

11.3. Calculate the ionized impurity limited mobility ($N_D = 10^{16}$ cm^{-3}; 10^{17} cm^{-3}) in GaAs from 77 K to 300 K.

11.4. Calculate the alloy scattering limited mobility in In$_{0.53}$Ga$_{0.47}$As as a function of temperature from 77 K to 400 K. Assume an alloy scattering potential of 1.0 eV.

11.5. Assume that the holes are much heavier than electrons in GaAs. Calculate the room temperature minority carrier mobility of electrons moving in a p-type base of an HBT where the base acceptor doping level is 10^{17} cm^{-3}. Remember that the electrons will scatter from the holes as well as the acceptors.

11.6. Calculate the energy dependence of the impact ionization rate in GaAs and InAs using Equation 11.111.

11.7. Assume that the scattering potential of neutral, or un-ionized impurities, in a semiconductor can be represented by a form similar to that used for the alloy scattering potential. What is the room temperature electron mobility in GaAs, due to 10^{15} neutral impurities per cm^3, each having a potential of 1.0 eV and a radial extent of 10 Å?

11.8. In a clustered alloy, the scattering potential is represented by

$$
\begin{aligned}
V(r) &= V_0 \quad \text{for } r \leq r_c \\
&= 0 \quad \text{for } r > r_c,
\end{aligned}
$$

where r_c is the cluster radius. Explain why the temperature dependence of the alloy scattering limited mobility shows a peak at high temperatures.

11.9. In the text, when considering impurity scattering, we considered each scatterer to be independent. It is found experimentally that at high doping, the mobility is much lower than the theoretical value. Explain this qualitatively.

11.10. In our discussions of impact ionization, we continued to use the Fermi golden rule or Born approximation for the scattering rates. At the high energies encountered in impact ionization, the total scattering rates may approach 10^{13} s^{-1} or even 10^{14} s^{-1}. Discuss the effects this may have in terms of the energy conservation rule used in the scattering rate derivation.

11.11. Show that while in a 3-dimensional and 2-dimensional system, it is possible for electron-electron scattering to randomize the energy distribution of hot electrons, in a strictly 1-dimensional system, this is not possible.

11.12. In the lucky drift model for impact ionization, it is assumed that some lucky carriers are accelerated ballistically to energies above threshold, causing impact ionization. Assume that the average relaxation time is 0.01 ps. At approximately what electric fields will 0.1% of the electrons acquire threshold energy in GaAs?

11.7   REFERENCES

- **Screening and Dielectric Constant**

    - Ashcroft, N. W. and N. D. Mermin, *Solid State Physics* (Holt, Rinehart and Winston, New York, 1976).
    - Kittel, C., *Introduction to Solid State Physics* (John Wiley and Sons, New York, 1986).
    - Ziman, J. M., *Principles of the Theory of Solids* (Cambridge University Press, Cambridge, 1972).

- **Electron-Ionized Impurity Scattering: Theory**

    - Brooks, H., Phys. Rev., **83**, 879 (1951).
    - Conwell, E. M. and V. Weisskopf, Phys. Rev., **77**, 388 (1950).
    - Lundstrom, M., *Fundamentals of Carrier Transport* (Modular Series on Solid State Devices, edited by G. W. Neudeck and R. F. Pierret, Addison-Wesley, Reading, 1990), vol. X.
    - Ridley, B. K., *Quantum Processes in Semiconductors* (Clarendon Press, Oxford, 1982).
    - Takimoto, N., J. Phys. Soc. Japan, **14**, 1142 (1959).

- **Impurity Dependence of Mobility: Experiments**

    - Anderson, D. A., N. Aspley, P. Davies and P. L. Giles, J. Appl. Phys., **58**, 3059 (1985).
    - Casey, H. C., Jr. and M. B. Panish, *Heterostructure Lasers* (Academic Press, New York, 1978).
    - "Modulation Doping of Semiconductor Heterostructures," by Gossard, A. C., in *Proceeding of NATO School of MBE and Heterostructures* at Erice, Italy, (Nijhoft, Holland, 1983).

- Prince, M. B., Phys. Rev., **92**, 681 (1953).

- Sze, S. M., *Physics of Semiconductor Devices* (John Wiley and Sons, New York, 1981).

• **Alloy Scattering**

- Ferry, D. K., *Semiconductors* (Macmillan, New York, 1991).

- Harrison, J. W. and J. Hauser, Phys. Rev. B, **1**, 3351 (1970).

- Makowski, L. and M. Glicksman, J. Phys. Chem. Sol., **34**, 487 (1976).

• **Consequences of Alloy Clustering**

- Cowley, J. M., Phys. Rev., **77**, 669 (1950)

- Hall, G. L., Phys. Rev., **116**, 604 (1959).

- Hong, W. P., P. Bhattacharya and J. Singh, Appl. Phys. Lett., **50**, 618 (1987).

- Hong, W. P., A. Chin, N. Debbar, J. M. Hinckley, P. Bhattacharya and J. Singh, J. Vac. Sci. Technol. B, **5**, 800 (1987).

- Marsh, J., Appl. Phys. Lett., **4**, 732 (1982).

- Nordheim, L., Ann. Physik, **9**, 607 (1931).

• **Electron-Electron Scattering**

- Feynman, R. P., R. B. Leighton and M. Sands, *The Feynman Lectures on Physics* (Addison-Wesley, Reading, 1965). Volume III has an excellent discussion on identical particle scattering.

- Pines, D., Rev. Mod. Phys., **28**, 184 (1956).

- Ridley, B. K., *Quantum Processes in Semiconductors* (Clarendon Press, Oxford, 1982).

• **Auger Processes**

- Beattie, A. R. and P. T. Landsberg, Proc. Roy. Soc. A, **249**, 16 (1958).

- Beattie, A. R., J. Phys. Chem. Solids, **49**, 589 (1988).

- Haug, A., J. Phys. Chem. Solids, **49**, 599 (1988).

- Loehr, J. P., *Theoretical Studies of Pseudomorphic Quantum Well Optoelectronic Devices*, Ph.D. Thesis, (The University of Michigan, Ann Arbor, 1991).

- Suemune, I., Appl. Phys. Lett., **55**, 2579 (1989).

• **Impact Ionization**

- Ferry, D. K., *Semiconductors* (Macmillan, New York, 1991).

- Hess, K., *Advanced Theory of Semiconductor Devices* (Prentice-Hall, Englewood Cliffs, 1988).

- Kane, E. O., Phys. Rev., **159**, 624 (1967).

- Ridley, B. K., *Quantum Processes in Semiconductors* (Clarendon Press, Oxford, 1982).

- Robbins, D. J., Phys. Status Solidi B, **97**, 9 (1980).

- Shichijo, H. and K. Hess, Phys. Rev. B, **23**, 4197 (1981).

CHAPTER 12

PHONON SCATTERING

Scattering of electrons from phonons is one of the most important processes to be considered in the transport of electrons in semiconductors. In our discussion of electronic bandstructure, we assumed a time-independent background periodic lattice of atoms which led to our bandstructure picture. The problem of lattice vibrations, on the other hand, led us to the phonons and their dispersion. The ability to separate in the first order the lattice vibrations from the electronic spectra is dependent upon the so called adiabatic approximation which can be applied to a time-dependent problem. This approximation is applicable when the time variation of the Hamiltonian is slow enough that the problem can be treated as a stationary state (time-independent) problem at each instant in time. Of course, as we have seen from our discussions on phonon frequencies, the term slow variation is only relative, since the atoms move at frequencies of several terrahertz (10^{12} Hz)! Nevertheless, since the electron masses are so much smaller than the atomic masses, the adiabatic approximation works quite well. Thus, we are able to treat the problem in two steps:

1. Electronic states in a perfect lattice (bandstructure).

2. Interaction of electrons with lattice vibrations (phonon scattering).

We have already addressed the first step. We are now going to address the second one.

12.1 GENERAL FORMALISM

We have already discussed some important properties of the lattice vibrations or phonons. In semiconductors which have two atoms per basis, we have acoustic phonons which have an essentially linear ω vs. k relation near $k = 0$ and optical phonons which have essentially no dispersion (i.e. variation of ω) near $k = 0$.

The optical phonons represent opposing motion of the two atoms within a unit cell. For both acoustic and optical phonons we have longitudinal and transverse modes of vibration. The motion of the lattice atoms produces strain in the crystal which according to the deformation potential theory produces perturbation in the electronic states. This relationship was examined in detail in our chapter on bandstructure modification by strain (Chapter 7). The effect of optical phonon strain was not examined there but can be understood on the basis of a similar formalism.

We briefly outline the nature of the perturbation produced by phonons.

Phonons	Properties
Acoustic Phonons	• Displacement of atoms produces energy fluctuations.
	• Can produce piezoelectric effect in semiconductors which lack inversion symmetry.
Optical Phonons	• Relative displacement of atoms produces energy fluctuations.
	• In polar materials, these can produce polarization fluctuations which cause polar optical phonon scattering.

The electrons see the energy fluctuations produced by the phonons as shown schematically in Figure 12.1 and scatter from them. To address this scattering problem we need to

1. Identify the nature of the electron-phonon interaction.

2. Use the Fermi golden rule to evaluate the scattering rate.

3. Use an appropriate transport theory to calculate macroscopic quantities such as mobility, drift velocity, etc.

We will first develop a general formalism for scattering rate and then apply it to the specific case of acoustic optical or polar optical phonons.

In general, the electron-phonon interaction will depend directly upon the displacement u of the atoms in the crystal. For example, as we shall see later, the form of the perturbation potential is

$$\begin{aligned} \text{Acoustic phonons} \qquad & U_{AP} \sim D\partial u/\partial x \\ \text{Optical phonons} \qquad & U_{OP} \sim D_0 u \\ \text{Polar optical phonons} \qquad & U_{OP} \sim e^* u \end{aligned}$$

where e^* is an effective charge which we will evaluate later and was discussed in Chapter 9 in connection with longitudinal polar optical phonons.

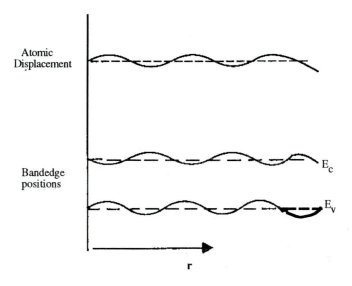

Figure 12.1: A schematic showing the effect of atomic displacement on bandedge energy levels in real space.

It is easy to conceptualize the differences between the acoustic and optical phonon interactions with electrons. The acoustic phonons represent the atoms moving in the same direction but with a relative phase $\exp(i\boldsymbol{q} \cdot \boldsymbol{r})$. Thus, it is the gradient ∇u of the displacement that causes the energy fluctuation. On the other hand, for optical phonons where atoms vibrate against each other, the atomic displacement directly causes the energy fluctuations seen by the electrons.

In order to discuss the electron-phonon interaction we will need to use the quantum theory of the harmonic oscillator (discussed in Appendix C). This connection between the classical lattice vibrations and the quantum picture of lattice vibrations as phonons was discussed in Chapter 9. The displacement of the harmonic oscillator is represented in quantum mechanics by operators which are called creation and destruction operators. (See Figure 12.2). The creation operator in the electron-phonon interaction would then lead to scattering processes in which a phonon is created after scattering (phonon-emission process). The destruction operator, on the other hand, would lead to processes where a phonon is destroyed (phonon absorption) in the scattering.

In general, the lattice vibrations represent coupled oscillators, and the displacement u representing the deformation of the unit cell or of the two atoms in the unit cell, must be represented in "normal coordinates" where the different modes are uncoupled. The conversion of real displacement to the normal coordinate description involves a simple transformation, and the normal modes can

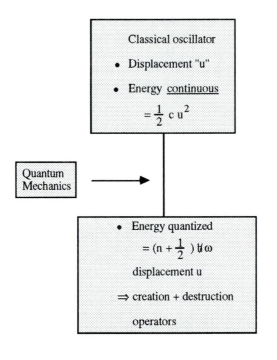

Creation operator $a^\dagger \mid \psi_n > \; \to \; \mid \psi_{n+1} >$

Destruction operator $a \mid \psi_n > \; \to \; \mid \psi_{n-1} >$

Figure 12.2: A schematic description of how the harmonic oscillator problem evolves from a classical picture to a quantum picture.

then be described by the harmonic oscillator quantum mechanics. In general

$$u = \frac{1}{\sqrt{N}} \sum_q [\theta_{qb} \, b_q \, \exp(iq \cdot R) + \text{ c.c.}] \qquad (12.1)$$

where c.c. is the complex conjugate of the first term, N is the number of unit cells, θ_{qb} are the normal coordinate displacements for wavevector q and polarization b, and b_q is the polarization vector.

The normal coordinate displacement can now be written in terms of the phonon creation and destruction operators $a^\dagger$ and a as (see Appendix C)

$$\theta_{qb} = \sqrt{\frac{\hbar}{2 \, m \, \omega_{qb}}} \left(a^\dagger_{-q} + a_q \right). \qquad (12.2)$$

In the scattering problem of interest we consider the initial state of the electron-phonon system where the electron has a state $|k\rangle$ and the phonons are described by the product state $\prod |n_{qb}(\theta)\rangle$ which describes the phonon distribution. In the final state, the electron is in the state $|k'\rangle$ and the phonons are described by a new product state where the number of phonons may have changed due to scattering. We thus have the initial and final states of the electron- phonon system written as

$$\Psi_i = \psi_k(r) \prod_{qb} |n_{qb}(\theta)\rangle$$

$$\Psi_f = \psi_{k'}(r) \prod_{qb} |n'_{qb}(\theta)\rangle. \tag{12.3}$$

In evaluating the scattering matrix element, we will examine the phonon part and the electronic part of the matrix element separately for the sake of clarity. The phonon part is for a particular normal mode q and polarization b

$$\prod_{q'',b''} \prod_{q',b'} \langle n_{q''b''} | \theta_{qb} | n_{q'b'} \rangle. \tag{12.4}$$

We remind ourselves that θ consists of terms $(a^\dagger_{-q} + a_q)$ as seen by Equation 12.2 and these operators will only mix states according to the following rules

$$\langle n_{qb} - 1 | a_q | n_{qb} \rangle = \sqrt{n_{qb}}$$

$$\langle n_{-qb} + 1 | a^\dagger_{-q} | n_{-qb} \rangle = \sqrt{n_{qb} + 1}. \tag{12.5}$$

The matrix element involving θ_{qb} will only involve the above states resulting in a term

$$\sqrt{\frac{\hbar}{2 m \omega_{qb}}} \, \delta_{q,q',q''} \, \delta_{b,b',b''} \left[\sqrt{n_{qb}} \, \delta_{n'-1,n} + \sqrt{n_{qb} + 1} \, \delta_{n'+1,n} \right]. \tag{12.6}$$

The first term in the brackets involves removing a phonon from the initial state during scattering and is the phonon absorption term. The second term involves adding an extra phonon to the final state and is the phonon emission term. Notice the difference in the coefficients involving absorption and emission. The absorption process involves the number of phonons already present in the initial state and will be zero if no phonons are initially present. On the other hand, the emission process involves the $(n_{-qb} + 1)$ term and is nonzero even if there are no initial phonons present. At equilibrium the phonon occupation is simply given by the phonon statistics discussed in Chapter 9. A similar result will be encountered when we discuss the electron-photon interaction to study optical interactions in semiconductors.

We will now consider the electronic part of the matrix element. If we write the general electron-phonon interaction as

$$H_{ep} = \sum_q \left[H_{qb}\, \theta_{qb}\, e^{iq \cdot R} + \text{c.c.} \right] \tag{12.7}$$

then the electronic part of the matrix element for a particular mode (qb) is

$$\frac{1}{V} \int u^*_{n'k'}\, e^{-ik \cdot r}\, H_{qb}(r)\, e^{\pm iq \cdot R}\, u_{nk}\, e^{ik \cdot r}\, d^3r. \tag{12.8}$$

The r-space interaction can be broken up into a sum over all lattice sites R, and an integral over a unit cell. This gives

$$\frac{1}{V} \int_{cell} \Psi^*_{n'k'}\, H_{qb}\, \Psi^*_{nk}\, d^3r \sum_R \exp\left[i(k \pm q - k') \cdot R \right]. \tag{12.9}$$

We assume that over the small size of the unit cell $\exp[i(k-k') \cdot r] \approx 1$. The lattice sum is given by the same equality we used in deriving X-ray diffraction conditions

$$\sum_R \exp\left[i(k \pm q - k') \cdot R \right] = \delta_{k \pm q - k', G} \tag{12.10}$$

where G is a reciprocal vector. In a scattering process, if $G = 0$ the process is the normal process. If $G = 0$, the process is an Umklapp process. The matrix element can now be written as

$$M^{electronic}_{k,k'} = \frac{1}{V}\, C_{qb}\, G(k, k')\, \delta_{k \pm q - k', G} \tag{12.11}$$

where

$$C_{qb}\, G(k, k') = \int_{cell} \Psi^*_{n'k'}\, H_{qb}\, \Psi^*_{nk}\, d^3r. \tag{12.12}$$

In most phonon scattering problems H_{qb} does not vary over the unit cell and the equality in Equations 12.9–12.12 can be written as

$$C_{qb}G(k, k') = H_{qb}G(k, k') \tag{12.13}$$

where

$$G(k, k') = \frac{1}{2} \sum_{\mu,\mu'} I_{\mu,\mu'}(k, k')$$

$$I_{\mu,\mu'}(k, k') = \langle n'k'\mu' | nk\mu \rangle$$

$$\begin{aligned} n \quad &\text{is the band index} \\ k \quad &\text{is the electron wavevector} \\ \mu \quad &\text{is the electron spin.} \end{aligned}$$

i.e., $G(k, k')$ represents the overlap of the cell periodic part of the initial and final electron states.

The overlap integral $G(k, k')$ imposes important selection rules especially for scattering involving different initial and final bands. As we have discussed in the chapter on bandstructure, the bottom of conduction band for direct bandgap material is essentially s-type in which case the overlap integral for scattering within the conduction band would be unity. However, because of the small p-type mixture, the integral is given by (Fawcett et al., 1970)

$$G(k, k') = \frac{\left\{ \sqrt{1 + \alpha E_{k'}} \sqrt{1 + \alpha E_k} + \alpha \sqrt{E_{k'} E_k} \cos \theta_k \right\}^2}{(1 + 2\alpha E_{k'})(1 + 2\alpha E_k)} \qquad (12.14)$$

where α is the non-parabolicity factor given by $\hbar^2 k^2 / (2m^*) = E(1 + \alpha E)$, and θ_k is the angle between k and k'. The hole bands are p-type in nature with strong angular dependence of the overlap integral. For scattering within the same bands (e.g. heavy hole to heavy hole), the integral is approximately

$$G(k, k') = \frac{1}{4}(1 + 3 \cos^2 \theta_k) \qquad (12.15)$$

while for interband scattering (e.g. heavy hole to light hole)

$$G(k, k') = \frac{3}{4} \sin^2 \theta_k. \qquad (12.16)$$

A more accurate numerical analysis shows that the overlap functions for hole scattering are, in fact, quite complex and are shown in Figure 12.3 .

The electron-phonon matrix element becomes for normal processes

$$|\langle f|H_{\text{ep}}|i\rangle|^2 = \frac{\hbar}{2NM} \frac{C_{\text{qb}}^2 \, G(k, k')}{\omega_{\text{qb}}} \left(n(\omega_{\text{qb}}) + \frac{1}{2} \mp \frac{1}{2} \right) \delta_{k \pm q - k', 0} \qquad (12.17)$$

where the upper sign is for phonon absorption and the power sign is for phonon emission. The scattering rate, according to the golden rule, is then

$$W(k) = \frac{1}{8\pi^2 NM} \int \frac{C_{\text{qb}}^2 \, G(k, k')}{\omega_{\text{qb}}} \left(n(\omega_{\text{qb}}) + \frac{1}{2} \mp \frac{1}{2} \right)$$
$$\times \delta_{k \pm q - k', 0} \, \delta \left(E_{k'} - E_k \mp \hbar \omega_{\text{qb}} \right) \, d^3 k'. \qquad (12.18)$$

12.2 LIMITS ON PHONON WAVEVECTORS

It is important to consider the consequences of the energy and momentum conservation imposed by the δ-functions. These restrictions are important in the evaluation of the integrals.

In normal processes involving phonon scattering, both energy and momentum are conserved, i.e.

$$E(k') = E(k) \pm \hbar \omega(q). \qquad (12.19)$$

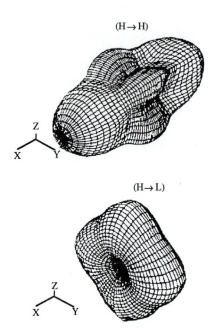

Figure 12.3: Polar plots of representative heavy hole overlap functions, $G_{n,n'}(k,k')$, as a function of the direction of the final wavevector. In all cases shown, the initial wavevector is in the [100] (X) direction and both the initial and final energies are -0.15 eV relative to the top of the heavy hole band. Results are for GaAs and are typical of the complex behavior found in the valence bands.

For parabolic electron bands we have

$$\frac{\hbar^2 k'^2}{2m^*} = \frac{\hbar^2 k^2}{2m^*} \pm \hbar\omega(q) \tag{12.20}$$

and

$$k' = k \pm q. \tag{12.21}$$

As seen from Figure 12.4, this gives

$$
\begin{aligned}
k'^2 &= k^2 + q^2 \pm 2k \cdot q \\
     &= k^2 + q^2 \pm 2kq\cos\theta.
\end{aligned}
\tag{12.22}
$$

Substituting Equation 12.20

$$\frac{\hbar^2 k'^2}{2m^*} = \frac{\hbar^2 k^2}{2m^*} + \frac{\hbar^2 q^2}{2m^*} \pm \frac{\hbar^2 kq\cos\theta}{m^*}$$

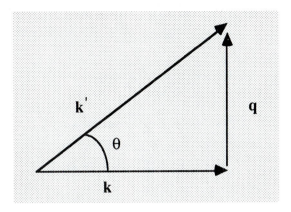

Figure 12.4: Wavevectors of the electron and phonon in a scattering event.

$$= \frac{\hbar^2 k^2}{2m^*} \pm \hbar\omega$$

thus

$$\frac{\hbar^2 q^2}{2m^*} = \mp \frac{\hbar^2 kq \cos\theta}{m^*} \pm \hbar\omega \qquad (12.23)$$

or

$$\hbar q = \hbar k \left[\mp 2\cos\theta \pm \frac{2\omega m^*}{\hbar kq} \right]$$

$$= \hbar k \left[\mp 2\cos\theta \pm \frac{2\omega}{v(k)q} \right] \qquad (12.24)$$

where $v(k) = \hbar k/m^*$ is the electron velocity. The value of $\cos\theta$ is restricted between ± 1 and this imposes limits on the wavevectors of the phonons involved in the scattering. It is useful to consider the restriction arising from the momentum and energy conservation relations for various kinds of phonons. It must be kept in mind that typical phonon energies are of the order of a few meV's across the Brillouin zone. This is in contrast to electron energies which are much larger. We will first consider the scattering of electrons within the same valley by acoustic and optical phonons.

12.2.1 Intravalley Acoustic Phonon Scattering

For acoustic phonons $\omega/q = v_s$, the sound velocity, and Equation 12.24 gives

$$\hbar q = 2\hbar k \left[\mp \cos\theta \pm \frac{v_s}{v(k)} \right]. \qquad (12.25)$$

The upper limit on the phonon vector involved in a scattering is given by $\theta = \pi$ for phonon absorption and by $\theta = 0$ for phonon emission. The upper limits are

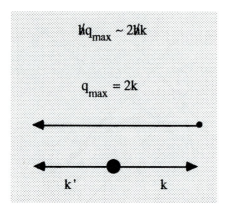

Figure 12.5: A scattering event in which the electron is scattered backwards. This defines the maximum limit for the phonon vector.

then

$$\hbar q_{\max} = 2\hbar k \left[1 \pm \frac{v_s}{v(\boldsymbol{k})}\right] \qquad (12.26)$$

since $v_s \sim 10^5$ cm/sec and typically $v(\boldsymbol{k}) \sim 10^6 - 10^7$ cm/sec. This corresponds to a backward scattering of the electron as shown in Figure 12.5. Acoustic phonon scattering is important at low temperatures or low electric fields where the electron k-vectors are close to the zone center. This means that the maximum acoustic phonon wavevectors are also close to the zone center and energy change produced by these phonons is

$$
\begin{aligned}
\Delta E_{\max} &= \hbar \omega_{\max} \\
&\sim \hbar q_{\max} v_s \\
&\sim 10^{-4} \text{ eV.}
\end{aligned}
\qquad (12.27)
$$

Since the energy change is so small, one usually takes the acoustic phonon scattering to be elastic since $\Delta E_{\max}$ is so much smaller than the electron energy. This approximation is valid down to temperatures where $k_B T$ starts to approach the energy given by Equation 12.27, i.e., $T \sim 10\text{--}20$ K.

12.2.2 Intravalley Optical Phonon Scattering

For optical phonons the energy is more or less independent of q near the zone center. For constant frequency ω_0, we can solve for q in Equation 12.23 to get

$$\hbar q = \hbar k \left[-\cos\theta + \sqrt{\cos^2\theta \pm \frac{\hbar \omega_0}{E(\boldsymbol{k})}}\right]. \qquad (12.28)$$

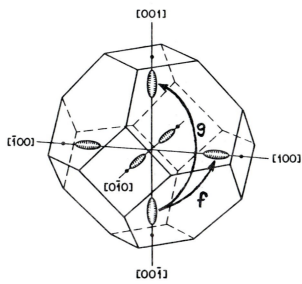

Figure 12.6: The six equivalent valleys in the conduction band of silicon with the f and g intervalley scatterings shown.

The maximum phonon vector is then, $(\cos \theta = -1)$

$$\hbar q_{max} = \hbar k \left[1 + \sqrt{1 \pm \frac{\hbar \omega_0}{E(\boldsymbol{k})}} \right].$$ (12.29)

This equation tells us:

1. Since q_{max} has to be positive and real, that carriers cannot scatter by emitting a phonon unless their initial energy is larger than the optical phonon energy.

2. Once again we see that q_{max} is a small number and close to the zone center.

12.2.3 Intervalley Phonon Scattering

An extremely important scattering process in semiconductors is the intervalley phonon scattering which often is a dominant source of scattering, particularly at high electric fields. A variety of important intervalley or interband scattering processes are induced by phonons. Figure 12.6 shows the important processes in Silicon electron transport. As has been discussed in detail in earlier chapters, Si has 6 equivalent X-valleys. Scattering between opposite valleys, e.g., $< 100 >$ to $< \bar{1}00 >$ is called a g-process and that between non-opposite valleys is called an f-process (e.g., between $< 100 >$ and $< 010 >$. Once again, we must maintain momentum conservation to *within a reciprocal lattice vector*. In Si scattering, the intervalley scattering involves an Umklapp process. The reciprocal lattice vector

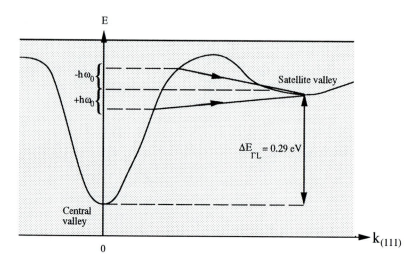

Figure 12.7: Scattering process involving intervalley scattering in GaAs. Electrons in Γ-valley can scatter into the L-valley (or even the X-valley) by absorbing or emitting an appropriate phonon. This scattering process is important at high electric fields and leads to the negative differential resistance in GaAs.

involved in the g-process is G_{100} and for an f-process it is G_{111}. It must be remembered that the minimum of the conduction band in Si is *not* at the zone edge (X-point) but is only 85% to the zone edge. Thus, an additional phonon of wavevector 0.3 times the X-point zone edge value $2\pi/a(100)$ is required for a g-process. For the f-process one needs a phonon with the wave vector along the Σ_1 symmetry line (11° off a $< 100 >$ direction) and with the zone edge magnitude is required.

In Figure 12.7 we show the intervalley scattering processes in GaAs . This is typical of intervalley scattering in direct bandgap semiconductors. In GaAs, the lowest valley for electron transport is the Γ-valley and the next valley is the L-valley with a separation of 0.36 eV. The X-valleys are slightly higher in energy at ∼ 0.5 eV above the Γ-point. Energy conservation ensures that an electron cannot scatter from the Γ- valley to the L-valley unless the electron energy is equal to at least $E_i = \Delta E_{\Gamma L} - \hbar\omega$, in which case the electron can absorb a phonon and move to the upper valley. The momentum of the phonon has to be close to the zone edge value to provide the electron the momentum difference between the Γ and the L-valleys. Due to the high energy required, before intervalley scattering can occur, the electron must be provided this energy by either a high electric field or by a high energy laser source. The scattering process also takes the electron from a low mass Γ-valley ($m^* \approx 0.067\ m_0$) to a high mass L-valley ($m^* \approx 0.35\ m_0$). This results in a negative differential mobility in the high field transport of semiconductors like GaAs, InGaAs, etc. This effect is absent in semiconductors such as Si, Ge, or AlAs which do not have such a transfer from low mass to high

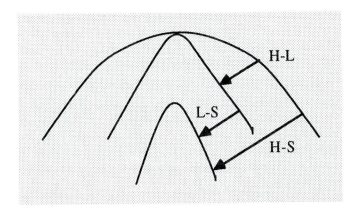

Figure 12.8: Interband scattering between the hole bands is one of the most important scattering processes which limits the hole transport phenomenon. At low fields the heavy hole to light hole (H-L), and vice versa, scattering dominates. At very high fields the scattering to the split off bands also plays an important role.

mass valleys.

Finally, one has, as shown in Figure 12.8, the scattering between the various hole bands. These scattering processes are very strong and involve taking the hole from, say, the HH band to the LH or SO band. The interband scatterings are important at both low and high electric fields, because of the degeneracy of the HH and LH bands at the zone center. In most semiconductors, the SO band is separated from the HH and LH bands by an energy of several hundred meV's, so that scattering into the SO band does not occur until high electric fields. However, for Si, this is not the case since the SO band is only 44 meV away from the top of the valence band. This is one of the reasons that hole transport in Si is comparatively poor.

Another important consideration for interband hole scattering is the role of the overlap function $G(k, k')$ between the central cell part of the hole states. Since the hole states are primarily p-type, they have a strong direction dependence. This direction dependence is also reflected in the angular dependence of the overlap functions. Since the overlap function between various bands vanishes for zero angle scattering and increases for orthogonal angle scattering, the interband scattering causes serious disturbance in the hole transport. Figure 12.3 shows some of the angular dependencies of the overlap function.

As pointed out in Chapter 6, the degeneracies of various high symmetry points can be lifted by uniaxial strain as produced, for example, by strained epitaxy. We noticed in particular that the valence bandedge degeneracies are lifted by strained epitaxy. This can greatly reduce the interband scattering for holes and is a key motivation for studies of strained structures for p-type transport improvements. A discussion of such improvements will be presented in Chapter 13.

Valley		Phonons Allowed in First Order Scattering
Γ_1,	(CB)	LA
X_1,	(CB)	LA, TA
L_1,	(CB)	LA, TA, LO, TO
Γ_{15},	(VB)	LA, TA, LO, TO

Table 12.1: Selection rules for intra-valley electron- phonon scattering in valleys with different symmetries. Polar optical phonons, which cause long range electric fields from which electrons scatter, are not listed here, nor in Table 12.2.

12.3   SELECTION RULES FOR PHONON SCATTERING

We will mainly be discussing lowest order scattering by phonons involving simply an emission or absorption of a single phonon. As we discussed in Chapter 7, the effect of the lattice distortion on the electronic states is given by the deformation potential theory. This formalism provides us with selection rules for the electron-phonon interactions in various valleys. The selection rules are determined by the symmetry of the electronic states and the nature of the strain tensor produced by the lattice vibration. In general, the energy distortion for the electrons is

$$\Delta E = \sum_{ij} D_{ij} \, \epsilon_{ij}. \qquad (12.30)$$

As noted in Chapter 7, the distortions produce energy shifts which are different for different valley symmetries. For example, the Γ-valley in direct bandgap semiconductors is affected only by the trace of the strain tensor. Shear strain or other strains which leave the trace of the strain zero have no effect on the Γ-valley. Thus, only LA phonons are effective in scattering in this valley. The general selection rules are given in Tables 12.1 and 12.2. Deformation optical phonons which leave the trace of the strain unaffected do not affect the electron to the first order. Polar optical phonons, on the other hand, which interact via polarization fields are, of course, very important for electron scattering in zinc-blende materials, and effect scatterings in all valleys.

We will now focus on the various scattering mechanisms and their scattering rates. In these calculations, we will assume that the overlap function is unity. The results including the deviations from non-unity overlap integral are listed in Chapter 13 for all important scattering rates. Numerical values for the scattering rates are presented in Appendix M.

Material	Initial Valley	Final Valley	Allowed Phonons	
Zinc-blende & Si	Γ_1	L_1	LO, LA	
Zinc-blende	X_1	X_1	LO,	if $M_V < M_{III}$
			LA,	if $M_V > M_{III}$
Si	Δ_1	Δ_1	LO,	g scattering
			LA, TO,	f scattering
Zinc-blende & Si	L_1	L_1	LO, LA	
Zinc-blende	L_1	X_1	LO,	if $M_V < M_{III}$
			LA,	if $M_V > M_{III}$
Si	L_1	Δ_1	LO, LA	

Table 12.2: Selection rules for phonons in inter-valley conduction band scattering processes. M_V and M_{III} are the masses of the group V and group III atoms in the compound semiconductors.

12.4 ACOUSTIC PHONON SCATTERING

In the case of acoustic phonons, the electronic energy perturbation is related to the strain in the crystal ∇u and is given by the deformation potential theory as

$$
\begin{aligned}
H_{ep} &= D\frac{\partial u}{\partial r} \\
&= \frac{1}{\sqrt{N}} \sum_q [i\,\theta_{qb}\, D\, b_q \cdot q\, \exp(iq \cdot R) + \text{c.c.}]
\end{aligned}
\tag{12.31}
$$

where D is the deformation potential for the particular valley of interest. Thus, for acoustic phonons we have from Equation 12.12

$$
C_{qb}^2 = D^2 q^2.
\tag{12.32}
$$

Also for acoustic phonons the phonon dispersion relation is simply

$$
\omega_q = v_s q,
\tag{12.33}
$$

where v_s is the sound velocity. In addition since the low energy phonons will dominate the scattering process

$$
\begin{aligned}
n(\omega_q) &= \frac{1}{\exp\left(\hbar\omega_q/k_B T\right) - 1} \\
&\approx \frac{k_B T}{\hbar\omega_q}.
\end{aligned}
\tag{12.34}
$$

Finally, assuming that the overlap integral is unity, we get for the scattering rate

$$W(\mathbf{k}) = \frac{V}{8\pi^2 N M}$$

$$\times \int d^3k' \frac{D^2 q^2}{\omega_q} \, \delta(\mathbf{k} \pm \mathbf{q} - \mathbf{k}') \, \delta(E_{\mathbf{k}'} - E_{\mathbf{k}} \mp \hbar\omega_q)$$

$$\times \left(n + \frac{1}{2} \mp \frac{1}{2}\right). \tag{12.35}$$

Note that $M = \rho V/N$, where ρ is the mass density. We also ignore $1/2$ in comparison to the occupation number n, which is a good approximation except at very low temperatures (≤ 50 K).

With these approximations, we find that the acoustic phonon scattering rate is

$$W(\mathbf{k}) = \frac{D^2 k_B T}{8\pi^2 \hbar \rho v_s^2} \int d^3k' \, \delta(\mathbf{k} \pm \mathbf{q} - \mathbf{k}') \, \delta(E_{\mathbf{k}'} - E_{\mathbf{k}} \mp \hbar\omega_q). \tag{12.36}$$

Ignoring $\hbar\omega$ in the energy δ function (i.e., assuming elastic scattering) and using the definition of the density of states

$$\frac{1}{8\pi^3} \int d^3k = N(E_{\mathbf{k}}),$$

we get

$$W(\mathbf{k}) = \frac{\pi \, D^2 \, k_B T \, N(E_{\mathbf{k}})}{\hbar \rho v_s^2}. \tag{12.37}$$

The total scattering is the sum of emission and absorption rates which for acoustic scattering (under our assumptions) are the same. Thus, the total rate is we get

$$W_{\mathrm{ac}}(\mathbf{k}) = \frac{2\pi \, D^2 \, k_B T \, N(E_{\mathbf{k}})}{\hbar \rho v_s^2}. \tag{12.38}$$

The acoustic phonon scattering is obviously proportional to the temperature as one may expect. This linear dependence arises from the assumption of Equation 12.34 which is valid for $k_B T$ greater than the typical acoustic phonon energies relevant in scattering processes. As noted earlier, this is valid for temperatures above 50 K. One must also note that, in general, the various acoustic modes will have different velocities although usually one uses the average sound velocity for v_s of Equation 12.38.

In our discussions on the Boltzmann equation we noted that from the point of view of transport, it is not just the scattering rate that is important, but even more important is the scattering angle. A small scattering angle is far less effective in reducing mobility (remember the $(1 - \cos\theta)$ factor in the definition of relaxation time).

In general, the scattering rates for transitions from a band n to a band n' are given by the expression,

$$W_{n,n'}(\mathbf{k}) = \frac{V}{(2\pi)^3} \frac{2\pi}{\hbar} \int d^3k' \left|M_{n,n'}(\mathbf{k}, \mathbf{k}')\right|^2 \delta(E_n - \Delta E - E_{n'}') \tag{12.39}$$

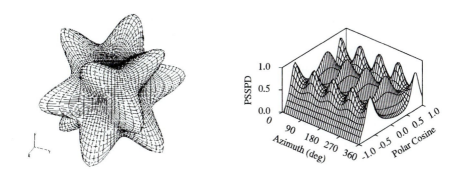

Figure 12.9: The complex nature of the hole bands reflects itself in the angular dependence of the scattering rate. On the left is shown the HH density of states (at 10 meV) and on the right is shown the normalized angular dependence for acoustic phonon scattering of an electron at 10 meV energy traveling along the [100] direction in Si (from Hinckley,1990).

which may be written as $(d\Omega' = d(\cos\theta')d\phi')$

$$W_{n,n'}(\mathbf{k}) = \int d\Omega' \frac{dW_{n,n'}(\mathbf{k})}{d\Omega'} \qquad (12.40)$$

where $d^3k' = d\Omega' k'^2 dk'$. The integrand $dW_{n,n'}(\mathbf{k})/d\Omega'$ is referred to as a differential scattering rate and gives information on the angular dependence of the scattering process. For simple isotropic parabolic bands, this angular dependence is simply given by the matrix element since the density of states does not vary with angle. Therefore, the angular dependence of the scattering is determined entirely by the angular dependence of $|M|^2$. In the present case of acoustic phonon scattering, $|M|^2$ has no angular dependence; therefore the scattering is isotropic. Other scattering processes in the parabolic conduction band may have a dependence on the polar angle θ, but will generally be independent of the azimuthal angle ϕ. For the warped valence bands, the situation is quite different. In the valence band, the density of states is strongly anisotropic. As an example, we show in Figure 12.9 the plot of the quantity

$$P(\cos\theta, \phi) = \left(\frac{dW_{n,n'}(\mathbf{k})}{d\Omega'} / \max \frac{dW_{n,n'}(\mathbf{k})}{d\Omega'}\right). \qquad (12.41)$$

This quantity represents the post-scattering state probability distribution (PSSPD) and Figure 12.9 shows the results for acoustic phonon scattering for a hole with energy of 10 meV traveling in the [100] direction in Si. The plots show the scattering rate dependence on the cosine of the polar scattering angle θ and on the azimuthal angle ϕ. Also shown in Figure 12.9 is the density of states for the heavy hole band at 10 meV. By comparison, an isotropic density of states would appear as a sphere when plotted in this way. The post-scattering state probability distribution is seen to have twelve maxima which corresponds to the twelve maxima in the density of states in the [110] directions. As can be seen, this complex angular dependence for the scattering processes in the hole bands make it extremely difficult to calculate the scattering rate analytically. For accurate results one needs to develop numerical techniques to evaluate the scattering integral. However, reasonable results can be obtained if one uses instead an isotropic band which has the same density of states as the warped bands. The difficulties mentioned for the hole bands are present not just for the acoustic phonons, but also the ionized impurity scattering, alloy scattering, etc., and make the study of hole transport quite difficult compared to the study of the electron transport. In Figures 12.10 and 12.11 we show the acoustic phonon scattering rates as a function of energy for silicon for both electrons and holes.

12.5   DEFORMATION POTENTIAL OPTICAL PHONON SCATTERING

For the acoustic phonon scattering, we made the assumption that the scattering was elastic. This is a good approximation because of the relatively low frequency of the acoustic phonons. For optical phonons we cannot make this assumption, since the zone center optical phonons have energies which are several tens of meVs. The interaction Hamiltonian for the optical phonons is

$$H_{\text{ep}} = D_0 \cdot u \tag{12.42}$$

where D_0 is the optical deformation potential, and u is the relative displacement of the two atoms in the basis. The interaction in Equation 12.42 is strictly valid only for the diamond lattice in which the two atoms on the basis have the same mass. However, deformation optical phonon scattering is primarily an important process only for diamond lattice structures since in zinc-blende structures, the polar optical phonons (to be discussed later) are more important. Also, the deformation optical phonon scattering is not allowed in the lowest order for the (Γ-valley) conduction band of direct bandgap materials by selection rule considerations.

Once again, expanding in terms of the normal coordinates, the interaction Hamiltonian is

$$H_{\text{ep}} = \frac{1}{\sqrt{N}} \sum_{\mathbf{q}} \{\theta_{\mathbf{qb}} \exp(i\mathbf{q} \cdot \mathbf{R}) + \text{ c.c.}\} D_0 \cdot \mathbf{b_q} \tag{12.43}$$

and the appropriate coupling coefficient is

$$C_{\mathbf{q}}^2 = D_0^2 \tag{12.44}$$

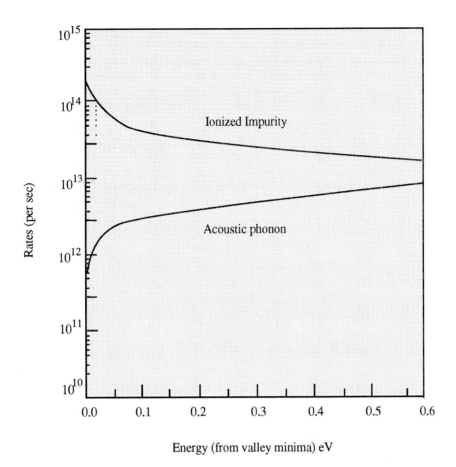

Figure 12.10: Acoustic phonon scattering rates in silicon as a function of energy. For comparison we also show the ionized impurity scatterings rates at a very high doping level of 10^{18} cm^{-3}. All results are at 300 K.

where $b_{\mathbf{q}}$ represents the polarization vector. We remind ourselves that the optical phonon frequencies near the zone center have very little dispersion. Therefore, we make the assumption that the optical phonon frequency is fixed with no q dependence. We also recall from Chapter 9 that for diamond structure the transverse and longitudinal phonons have the same frequency at the zone center. This is not the case for the zinc-blende structures, but the differences are quite small and can be ignored. With this dispersionless ω approximation, the energy conserving δ- function in the Fermi golden rule for the scattering rate (Equation 12.18) becomes independent of the scattering angle and one is simply left with an integration over the final energy states. This simply gives the final state

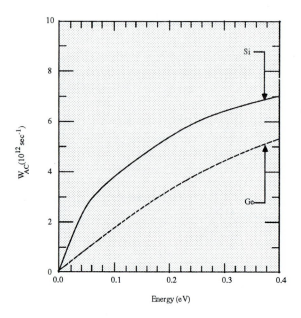

Figure 12.11: Acoustic phonon scattering rates for holes in Si at 300 K. For comparison, the rates are also shown for Ge. Ge has a very low hole mass and excellent hole transport properties (from Hinckley, 1990).

density of states. Thus, the scattering rate becomes

$$
\begin{aligned}
W(k) &= \frac{\pi D_0^2}{\rho \omega_0} \left[n(\omega_0) \, N(E_k + \hbar \omega_0) \right] \qquad \text{(absorption)} \\
&= \frac{\pi D_0^2}{\rho \omega_0} \left[(n(\omega_0) + 1) \, N(E_k - \hbar \omega_0) \right] \quad \text{(emission)} \qquad (12.45)
\end{aligned}
$$

where $N(E_k)$ is the density of states (without spin degeneracy). For parabolic bands this is given by the usual analytical formula, but once again for hole bands one has to carry out a numerical integration over the warped bands for the density of states. We have also assumed that $G(k, k')$, the overlap integral, is unity. This approximation also has to be removed for the hole bands.

In Figure 12.12 we show a typical form of the scattering of electrons from optical phonons. The scattering rates have two distinct regions. At low electron energies the electrons scatter only by absorption of the phonons. This scattering rate is proportional to $n(\omega_0)$, the occupation probability, and is thus very sensitive to the lattice temperature. At higher electron energy, the scattering is dominated by the phonon emission process with the factor $(n(\omega_0) + 1)$. Phonons can be emitted even if $n(\omega_0)$ is zero, provided the starting electron has an energy at least equal to the phonon energy $\hbar \omega_0$.

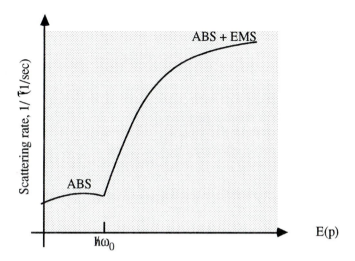

Figure 12.12: A schematic of the inelastic phonon scattering (e.g., optical phonon scattering–deformation type or polar type). The absorption (ABS) process can occur at low energies, but the emission process (EMS) can only start once the electron has an energy equal to $\hbar\omega_0$.

12.6 POLAR OPTICAL PHONON SCATTERING

In polar materials such as GaAs, InAs, etc., when the cation and anion vibrate against each other in a longitudinal optical phonon mode, a polarization field is created. This causes a strong perturbation for the electrons resulting in the polar optical phonon scattering. In general, the dipole produced by this perturbation is

$$\delta p = e^* u \tag{12.46}$$

where e^* is an effective charge in the cation or anion. However, since it is not possible to directly measure e^*, we will relate it to physically observable properties of the semiconductor (see Chapter 9). The dielectric constant of the semiconductor has a contribution from the electronic levels (the dominant contribution) and the lattice dipole moments. At low frequencies both of these are important. However, at high frequencies only the electronic contribution is present since the lattice response is too slow. The polarization of the medium is given by

$$p_{\text{tot}}(0) = \frac{1}{4\pi}\left(\frac{\epsilon_s - 1}{\epsilon_s}\right) D \quad \text{(low frequency)}$$

$$p_{\text{tot}}(\infty) = \frac{1}{4\pi}\left(\frac{\epsilon_\infty - 1}{\epsilon_\infty}\right) D \quad \text{(high frequency)} \tag{12.47}$$

where ϵ_s is the low frequency (static) dielectric constant, ϵ_∞ is the high frequency dielectric constant, and D is the displacement vector. The difference in polarization is due to the lattice dipoles, which is then given by

$$
\begin{aligned}
\boldsymbol{p}_{\text{lattice}} &= \boldsymbol{p}_{\text{tot}}(0) - \boldsymbol{p}_{\text{tot}}(\infty) \\
&= \frac{1}{4\pi} \left(\frac{1}{\epsilon_\infty} - \frac{1}{\epsilon_s} \right) \boldsymbol{D}.
\end{aligned}
\tag{12.48}
$$

The lattice vibrations causing the dipole satisfy the equation

$$
\bar{m} \left(\frac{\partial^2 \boldsymbol{u}}{\partial t^2} + \omega_0^2 \boldsymbol{u} \right) = \boldsymbol{F}
\tag{12.49}
$$

where $\boldsymbol{F}$ is the applied force and $\bar{m}$ is the reduced mass. The polarization is given by

$$
\boldsymbol{p}_{\text{lattice}} = \frac{e^* \boldsymbol{u}}{V_0}
\tag{12.50}
$$

where V_0 is the unit cell volume and e^* is the effective charge. The equation for the polarization is then (force $= e^* \boldsymbol{D}$);

$$
\frac{\bar{m} V_0}{e^*} \left(\frac{\partial^2 \boldsymbol{p}}{\partial t^2} + \omega_0^2 \boldsymbol{p} \right) = e^* \boldsymbol{D}.
\tag{12.51}
$$

The value of the polarization is for static case (no time dependence)

$$
\boldsymbol{p}_{\text{lattice}} = \frac{e^{*2} \boldsymbol{D}}{\bar{m} \, V_0 \, \omega_0^2}.
\tag{12.52}
$$

Equating these two values from Equations 12.48 and 12.52, we get (see Chapter 9, Section 5 for a discussion of e^*)

$$
e^{*2} = \frac{\bar{m} \, V_0 \, \omega_0^2}{4\pi} \left(\frac{1}{\epsilon_\infty} - \frac{1}{\epsilon_s} \right)
\tag{12.53}
$$

ϵ_∞ and ϵ_s can be measured experimentally so that e^* can be evaluated.

We are now ready to calculate the scattering rate from the polar optical phonons. Firstly we consider the interaction Hamiltonian. The basic energy interaction energy is

$$
H_{\text{ep}} = \int \rho(\boldsymbol{R}) \, \phi(\boldsymbol{R}) \, d^3 R
\tag{12.54}
$$

where $\rho(\boldsymbol{R})$ $(= \nabla \cdot \boldsymbol{D}/4\pi)$ is the electronic charge density and $\phi(\boldsymbol{R})$ is the electric potential due to the polarization in the unit cell at $\boldsymbol{R}$. The polarization, as before, is

$$
p(\boldsymbol{R}) = \frac{e^* \boldsymbol{u}(\boldsymbol{R})}{V_0}.
\tag{12.55}
$$

Only longitudinal modes will result in such a polarization fields as discussed in Chapter 9 and also shown in Figure 12.13.

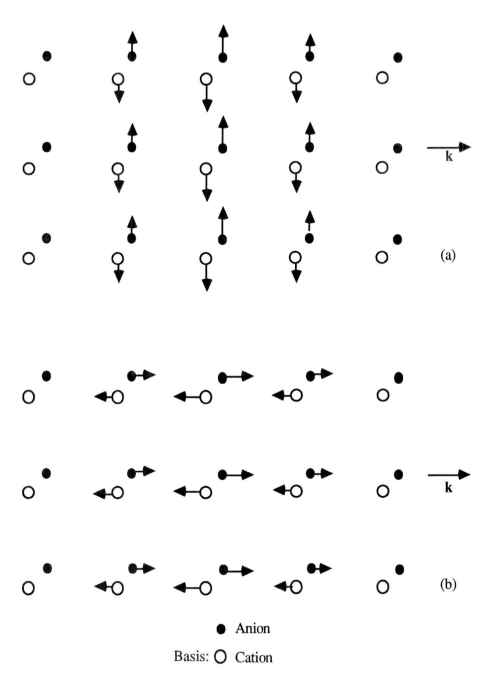

Figure 12.13: Optical modes of vibration of an ionic crystal. During transverse modes (a), the vibrations do not produce any polarization effects, while long range electric fields due to polarization are produced in longitudinal modes (b).

To calculate H_{ep}, we evaluate the integral

$$
\begin{aligned}
H_{\text{ep}} &= \frac{1}{4\pi} \int \{\nabla \cdot \boldsymbol{D}(\boldsymbol{R})\} \, \phi(\boldsymbol{R}) \, d^3R \\
&= -\frac{1}{4\pi} \int \boldsymbol{D}(\boldsymbol{R}) \cdot \nabla\phi(\boldsymbol{R}) \, d^3R \\
&= \frac{1}{4\pi} \int \boldsymbol{D}(\boldsymbol{R}) \cdot \boldsymbol{F}(\boldsymbol{R}) \, d^3R
\end{aligned}
\tag{12.56}
$$

where $\boldsymbol{D}(\boldsymbol{R})$ is the electric displacement associated with the charge and $\boldsymbol{F}(\boldsymbol{R})$ is the field associated with the polarization.

The electric displacement at a point $\boldsymbol{R}$ due to an electron at a point $\boldsymbol{r}$ is

$$
\boldsymbol{D}_e(\boldsymbol{R}) = -\nabla\left(\frac{e}{|\boldsymbol{r} - \boldsymbol{R}|}\right).
\tag{12.57}
$$

In the presence of screening, the displacement is suppressed by a screening factor $\exp(-\lambda\,|\boldsymbol{r} - \boldsymbol{R}|)$ as discussed in the case of ionized impurity scattering. Thus, we have

$$
\boldsymbol{D}(\boldsymbol{R}) = -\nabla\left\{\frac{e}{|\boldsymbol{r} - \boldsymbol{R}|}\,e^{-\lambda|\boldsymbol{r} - \boldsymbol{R}|}\right\}
\tag{12.58}
$$

Substituting the normal coordinate form for the lattice displacement

$$
\boldsymbol{u}(\boldsymbol{R}) = \frac{1}{\sqrt{N}} \sum_{\mathbf{q},\mathbf{b}} \{\theta_{\mathbf{q},\mathbf{b}}\, b_{\mathbf{q}}\, \exp(i\boldsymbol{q} \cdot \boldsymbol{R}) + c.c.\}
\tag{12.59}
$$

and using the expression 12.58 for the displacement we get (remember that $\boldsymbol{F}(\boldsymbol{R}) = -4\pi\boldsymbol{P}/\epsilon_0$)

$$
H_{\text{ep}} = \frac{1}{\sqrt{N}}\frac{ee^*}{V_0} \sum_{\mathbf{q},\mathbf{b}} \int \left\{\nabla\left[\frac{\exp(-\lambda\,|\boldsymbol{r} - \boldsymbol{R}|)}{|\boldsymbol{r} - \boldsymbol{R}|}\right] e^{i\mathbf{q}\cdot\boldsymbol{R}}\, \theta_{\mathbf{q},\mathbf{b}}\, b_{\mathbf{q}} + c.c.\right\} d^3R.
\tag{12.60}
$$

The spatial integral has the same form as the integral solved by us in ionized impurity scattering.

The resulting value for the electron-polar optical phonon interaction is

$$
H_{\text{ep}} = -\frac{4\pi}{\sqrt{N}}\frac{ee^*}{V_0} \sum_{\mathbf{q}} \frac{q}{q^2 + \lambda^2} \{i\,\theta_{\mathbf{q}}\, \exp(i\boldsymbol{q} \cdot \boldsymbol{r}) + c.c.\}.
\tag{12.61}
$$

The scattering rate then becomes

$$
\begin{aligned}
W(\boldsymbol{k}) &= \frac{V_0}{8\pi^2\bar{m}\omega_0}\left(\frac{4\pi ee^*}{V_0}\right)^2 \int_0^{q_{max}} \int_{-1}^{1} \int_0^{2\pi} \frac{q^4}{(q^2 + \lambda^2)^2}\delta_{\mathbf{k}\pm\mathbf{q}+\mathbf{k}',0} \\
&\quad \times \left(n\left(\omega_0\right) + \frac{1}{2} \mp \frac{1}{2}\right) \delta\left(E_{\mathbf{k}'} - E_{\mathbf{k}} \mp \hbar\omega_0\right) \, dq \, d(\cos\theta) \, d\phi.
\end{aligned}
\tag{12.62}
$$

As for the case of the deformation optical phonon scattering, we assume that the polar optical phonon frequency is dispersionless. The scattering rate depends explicitly on q making this integral more difficult than the ones encountered in the case of deformation scattering. The momentum and energy δ- functions put constraints on the phonon vector as was discussed through Equations 12.19 through 12.24, and summarized for optical phonons in Equations 12.28 and 12.29. The scattering rate integral then becomes for parabolic bands

$$
W(\mathbf{k}) = \frac{V_0}{4\pi\,\bar{m}\,\omega_0} \left(\frac{4\pi ee^*}{V_0}\right)^2 \frac{1}{\hbar v} \left[n(\omega_0) \int_{q_{min,a}}^{q_{max,a}} \frac{q^3}{(q^2+\lambda^2)^2}\,dq \right.
$$
$$
\left. + (n(\omega_0)+1) \int_{q_{min,e}}^{q_{max,e}} \frac{q^3}{(q^2+\lambda^2)^2}\,dq \right] \tag{12.63}
$$

where v is the electron velocity and q_{min} and q_{max} are the limits on the phonon wavevector. We will now proceed assuming no screening effect ($\lambda = 0$), in which case the integrals are simple

$$
W(\mathbf{k}) = \frac{V_0}{2\pi\,\bar{m}\,\hbar\,\omega_0\,v}\left(\frac{4\pi ee^*}{V_0}\right)^2
$$
$$
\times \left[n(\omega_0)\,\ln\left(\frac{q_{max}}{q_{min}}\right) + (n(\omega_0)+1)\,\ln\left(\frac{q_{max}}{q_{min}}\right) \right]. \tag{12.64}
$$

$$
q_{max} = k\left(1 + \sqrt{1 \pm \frac{\hbar\omega_0}{E(\mathbf{k})}}\right) \tag{12.65}
$$

and

$$
q_{min} = k\left(\mp 1 \pm \sqrt{1 \pm \frac{\hbar\omega_0}{E(\mathbf{k})}}\right) \tag{12.66}
$$

where the upper sign corresponds to phonon emission ($q_{max,e}$, $q_{min,e}$) and the lower sign corresponds to phonon absorption ($q_{max,a}$, $q_{min,a}$).

Using the identity

$$
\sinh^{-1}(x) = \ln\left[x + \sqrt{1 + x^2}\right] \tag{12.67}
$$

we get for the final scattering rate

$$
W(\mathbf{k}) = \frac{V_0}{2\pi\,\bar{m}\,\hbar\,\omega_0\,v}\left(\frac{4\pi ee^*}{V_0\epsilon_0}\right)^2 \left[n(\omega_0)\,\sinh^{-1}\left(\frac{E_{\mathbf{k}}}{\hbar\omega_0}\right)^{1/2} \right.
$$
$$
\left. + (n(\omega_0)+1)\,\sinh^{-1}\left(\frac{E_{\mathbf{k}}}{\hbar\omega_0} - 1\right)^{1/2} \right] \tag{12.68}
$$

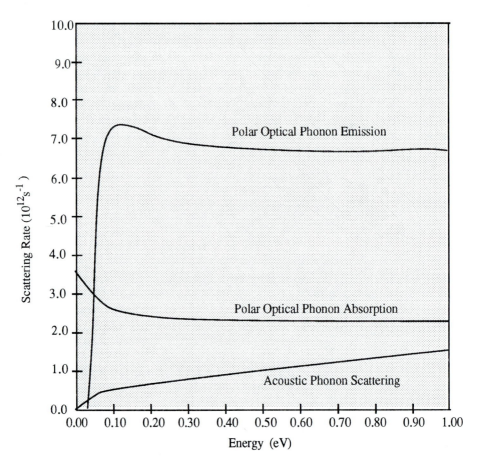

Figure 12.14: A comparison of the polar optical phonon scattering and acoustic phonon scattering in GaAs at room temperature.

The emission rate is zero unless $E_\mathbf{k} > \hbar\omega_0$. Substituting for the value of effective charge we get

$$W(\mathbf{k}) = \frac{4\pi e^2 \omega_0}{2\pi\hbar v}\left(\frac{1}{\epsilon_\infty} - \frac{1}{\epsilon_s}\right)\left[n(\omega_0)\ \sinh^{-1}\left(\frac{E_\mathbf{k}}{\hbar\omega_0}\right)^{1/2}\right.$$
$$\left. +(n(\omega_0)+1)\ \sinh^{-1}\left(\frac{E_\mathbf{k}}{\hbar\omega_0} - 1\right)^{1/2}\right]. \qquad (12.69)$$

In Figure 12.14 we show a plot of the polar optical phonon scattering for electrons in GaAs at room temperature. This scattering is not very important at low temperature since the occupation probability $n(\omega_0)$ is small, but is a dominant scattering mechanism in compound semiconductors at room temperature. If the electrons are "hot" due to the application of a strong electric field, the polar optical phonon emission becomes a dominant scattering mechanism even at low temperatures.

To evaluate the momentum relaxation time for the polar optical phonons, one has to weigh each scattering by the change in momentum $\mp (q/k)\cos\theta$

$$\frac{q}{k}\cos\theta = \cos\theta\sqrt{\cos^2\theta + \left(\frac{k'^2}{k^2} - 1\right)} - \cos^2\theta \quad \text{(absorption)}$$

$$\frac{-q}{k}\cos\theta = \pm\cos\theta\sqrt{\cos^2\theta - \left(1 - \frac{k'^2}{k^2}\right)} - \cos^2\theta \quad \text{(emission)}. \quad (12.70)$$

This gives

$$\frac{1}{\tau_m} = \frac{4\pi e^2\omega_0}{4\pi\hbar v}\left(\frac{1}{\epsilon_\infty} - \frac{1}{\epsilon_s}\right). \quad (12.71)$$

This leads to the following expression

$$\begin{aligned}
\frac{1}{\tau_m} = & \frac{e^2\omega_0}{4\pi\hbar v}\left(\frac{1}{\epsilon_\infty} - \frac{1}{\epsilon_s}\right) \\
& \times \left(n(\omega_0)\left(1 + \frac{\hbar\omega_0}{E_{\mathbf{k}}}\right)^{1/2} + (n(\omega_0) + 1)\left(1 - \frac{\hbar\omega_0}{E_{\mathbf{k}}}\right)^{1/2}\right. \\
& + \frac{\hbar\omega_0}{E_{\mathbf{k}}}\left[-n(\omega_0)\sinh^{-1}\left(\frac{E_{\mathbf{k}}}{\hbar\omega_0}\right)^{1/2}\right. \\
& + \left.\left.(n(\omega_0) + 1)\sinh^{-1}\left(\frac{E_{\mathbf{k}}}{\hbar\omega_0} - 1\right)^{1/2}\right]\right). \quad (12.72)
\end{aligned}$$

Note: In MKS units, the values of the effective charge e^* and the scattering rate are

$$e^{*2} = \bar{m}\,V_0\,\omega^2\,\epsilon_0\left(\frac{1}{\epsilon_\infty} - \frac{1}{\epsilon_s}\right)$$

$$\begin{aligned}
W(\mathbf{k}) = & \frac{e^2\omega_0}{2\pi\hbar v}\left(\frac{1}{\epsilon_\infty} - \frac{1}{\epsilon_s}\right)\left[n(\omega_0)\sinh^{-1}\left(\frac{E_{\mathbf{k}}}{\hbar\omega_0}\right)^{1/2}\right. \\
& + \left.(n(\omega_0) + 1)\sinh^{-1}\left(\frac{E_{\mathbf{k}}}{\hbar\omega_0} - 1\right)^{1/2}\right]. \quad (12.73)
\end{aligned}$$

Before proceeding with other types of phonon scattering, we will digress a little and consider the scattering of electrons from plasmons since the mathematics and the results are exactly the same as the case of polar optical phonons discussed above.

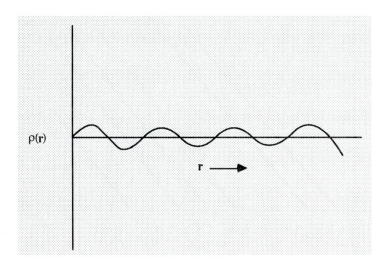

Figure 12.15: A schematic of the local charge density $\rho(r)$ produced in the collective oscillation of the free charge against the fixed positive background charge.

12.7 ELECTRON-PLASMON SCATTERING

When the density of the free carriers exceeds certain limits (determined by the scattering time as discussed below), there are new excitations in the semiconductor system. These excitations, known as plasmons, involve the collective vibration of the free electrons against the fixed background of positive charges. Figure 12.15 shows such a vibration. Just like the longitudinal polar optical phonons, these vibrations create a long-range electric field from which the electrons can scatter. This scattering rate is given by the same expressions derived by us for polar optical phonon scattering except that we do not need to worry about the effective charge e^*. We simply need to find the frequency of the plasmons.

As shown in Figure 12.15, as the electron gas moves as a whole with respect to the positive ion background, the displacement $\boldsymbol{u}$ creates an displacement field

$$\boldsymbol{D} = \frac{4\pi \, ne\boldsymbol{u}}{\epsilon} \tag{12.74}$$

where n is the electron density. This creates a restoring force on the electrons. The equation of motion then becomes

$$
\begin{aligned}
nm^* \frac{d^2\boldsymbol{u}}{dt^2} &= -ne\boldsymbol{D} \\
&= -\frac{4\pi \, n^2}{\epsilon} e^2 \boldsymbol{u}. \tag{12.75}
\end{aligned}
$$

This gives a plasma frequency ω_p, where

$$\omega_p = \left(\frac{4\pi \, ne^2}{\epsilon m^*} \right)^{1/2}. \tag{12.76}$$

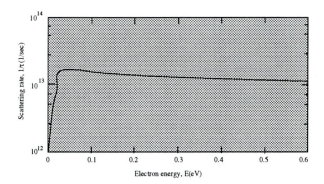

Figure 12.16: Electron-plasmon scattering rate versus energy for electrons in GaAs at room temperature. The electron density is $n_0 = 1.0 \times 10^{17}$ cm^{-3}.

The scattering from these plasmon fields has the same form as that of the polar optical phonon scattering. Thus, the scattering rate is

$$W_p(k) = \frac{e^2 \omega_p \left(N(\omega_p) + \frac{1}{2} \mp \frac{1}{2} \right)}{\epsilon \hbar v} \ln \left[\frac{q_c/(2k)}{\mp 1 \pm \sqrt{1 \pm (\hbar \omega_p / E_k)}} \right]. \qquad (12.77)$$

Here q_c is either the maximum value of the phonon vector given by Equation 12.65 or is the inverse of the screening length (λ^{-1}), whichever is smaller. For plasma oscillations to be sustained, we must have $\omega_p \tau \gg 1$, where τ is the relaxation time for the scattering electrons. This tells us that the plasma oscillations can only be sustained for the carrier concentration $n > 10^{17}$ cm^{-3} since $\tau \sim 10^{-13}$ s. In Figure 12.16 we show typical values of plasma scattering at room temperature for GaAs with a carrier concentration of 10^{17} cm^{-3}. As can be seen from these rates, this scattering is quite strong at such high carrier concentrations.

Note: The plasma frequency and the plasma scattering rates in MKS units are

$$\omega_p = \left(\frac{ne^2}{\epsilon m^*} \right)^{1/2}$$

$$W_p(k) = \frac{e^2 \omega_p \left(N(\omega_p) + \frac{1}{2} \mp \frac{1}{2} \right)}{4\pi \epsilon \hbar v} \ln \left[\frac{q_c/(2k)}{\mp 1 \pm \sqrt{1 \pm (\hbar \omega_p / E_k)}} \right]. \qquad (12.78)$$

12.8   PIEZOELECTRIC SCATTERING

As discussed above, the source of the polar optical phonon scattering is the lack of inversion symmetry in the zinc-blende or wurtzite crystal. The presence of lattice vibrations produces an electric field not only for the optical phonons, but also for the acoustic phonons. The polarization field due to acoustic phonons leads to the piezoelectric scattering. Although not very important at room temperature, the piezoelectric phonon scattering can be important at very low temperatures in very pure semiconductors.

The derivation of the piezoelectric scattering is similar to that of polar optical phonon scattering except that the perturbation depends upon the acoustic strain and not the optical displacement. To define the scattering matrix element we write the equation relating the electric displacement D to the electric field F and the acoustic strain field S.

$$D_i = \sum_j \epsilon_{ij} \, F_j + \sum_{k,\ell} e_{ik\ell} \, S_{k\ell} \tag{12.79}$$

where ϵ is the permittivity tensor and e is the piezoelectric tensor. The second term in Equation 12.79 is the polarization produced by the strain

$$P_i = \frac{1}{\epsilon} \sum_{k,\ell} e_{ik\ell} \, S_{k\ell} \tag{12.80}$$

and the interaction energy is as in Equation 12.56

$$H_{\text{ep}} = -\int D(R) \cdot P(R) \, dR \tag{12.81}$$

and

$$D(R) = -\nabla \left\{ \frac{e}{|r-R|} e^{-\lambda|r-R|} \right\}. \tag{12.82}$$

The polarization is given by the acoustic strain and is nonzero only for the *shear* components of the strain in zinc-blende structures. In terms of the normal coordinates, the polarization becomes

$$P_1 = \frac{1}{\sqrt{N}} \sum_{\mathbf{q}} \frac{e_{pz}}{\epsilon} \left\{ i \left(a_2 q_3 + a_3 q_2 \right) \theta_{\mathbf{q}} \, \exp(i q \cdot R) + c.c. \right\} \tag{12.83}$$

where e_{pz} is the piezoelectric constant for the material. After carrying out the integral for the interaction Hamiltonian we get

$$H_{\text{ep}} = \frac{4\pi \, e e_{pz}}{\sqrt{N}} \sum_{\mathbf{q}} \frac{q^2}{q^2+\lambda^2} \left\{ 2i(a_1\beta\gamma + a_2\gamma\alpha + a_3\alpha\beta)\theta_{\mathbf{q}} \exp(i q \cdot r) + c.c. \right\}$$

$$\tag{12.84}$$

where α, β, γ are the direction cosines of the wave with respect to the crystal axes. The coupling constant for the electron- phonon matrix element is

$$C_{\mathbf{q}}^2 = \left(\frac{4\pi \, e e_{pz}}{\epsilon} \right)^2 \frac{q^4}{(q^2+\lambda^2)^2} \, 4 \left(a_1\beta\gamma + a_2\gamma\alpha + a_3\alpha\beta \right)^2. \tag{12.85}$$

As can be seen from Equation 12.85, a fairly complex directional averaging is required to evaluate the matrix element. A number of workers have used different approaches for this averaging (see, for example, B. K. Ridley, *Quantum Processes in Semiconductors*). It can be shown that for longitudinal waves we have

$$\langle C_{\mathbf{q}\ell}^2 \rangle = \frac{12}{35} \left(\frac{4\pi \, ee_{pz}}{\epsilon} \right)^2 \frac{q^4}{(q^2 + \lambda^2)^2} \tag{12.86}$$

and for transverse waves

$$\langle C_{\mathbf{q}t}^2 \rangle = \frac{16}{35} \left(\frac{4\pi \, ee_{pz}}{\epsilon} \right)^2 \frac{q^4}{(q^2 + \lambda^2)^2}. \tag{12.87}$$

12.9 INTERVALLEY SCATTERING

Intervalley scattering is not only an important scattering mechanism for indirect gap materials like Si and Ge, it is also very important for direct bandgap materials like GaAs. Once the electrons in a direct gap material become heated by an electric field (or by an optical perturbation), they reach energies in the Γ-valley equal to or greater than the Γ-L or Γ-X, valley separation. These electrons can scatter by appropriate phonons (discussed earlier in this chapter) to go from the Γ-valley to the X-valley (and vice versa). The mathematical treatment of intervalley scattering is done in a very simple phenomenological manner by simply postulating a deformation potential-like interaction

$$H_{ep} = D_{if} \, U \tag{12.88}$$

where D_{if} is the intervalley deformation potential that scatters the electron from the valley i to f. In a sense this choice is like that for a deformation optical phonon scattering. In general, the scattering could involve an acoustic phonon, but one still chooses the expression in Equation 12.88 and simply redefines D_{ij}. The value of D_{ij} is usually found by fitting to experimental data. By analogy with the nonpolar optical phonon scattering (Equation 12.45), we have for the scattering rate

$$W(k) = \frac{\pi D_{ij}^2 Z_f}{\rho \, \omega_{ij}} \left(n(\omega_{ij}) + \frac{1}{2} \mp \frac{1}{2} \right) N \left(E \pm \hbar\omega_{ij} - \Delta E_{fi} \right) \tag{12.89}$$

where $N(E)$ is the density of states in the final valley (*without* spin degeneracy), Z_f is the number of equivalent final valleys, ΔE_{fi} is the energy separation between the initial and final valley (= 0 for Si and 0.3 eV for Γ to L valley transfers and -0.3 eV for L to Γ valley transfers in GaAs). The frequency of the phonons responsible for scattering is ω_{ij}. In Figures 12.17 and 12.18 we plot some typical results for the intervalley scattering in Si and GaAs. In this and the last chapter we have discussed a variety of important scattering processes in semiconductors. The results discussed have been for bulk semiconductors. Important changes occur in the scattering rates when heterostructure concepts such

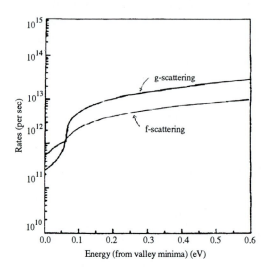

Figure 12.17: The g and f intervalley scattering rates in Si at 300 K.

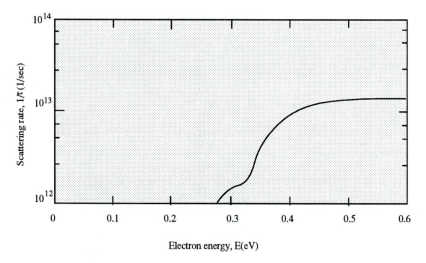

Figure 12.18: Intervalley scattering rates for electrons in Γ-valley scattering into the L-valley in GaAs at 300 K.

as quantum confinement, minibands, strain related effects, etc., are introduced. These effects will be discussed in Chapter 14. We will end this chapter by noting that the Fermi golden rule tells us that the scattering rate is proportional to the final state density of states. We have mostly assumed parabolic bands in deriving our final density of states. Often it is useful to describe the bandstructure by the general nonparabolic band

$$\frac{p^2}{2m^*} = \gamma(E(\boldsymbol{p}))$$
(12.90)

where m^* is the effective mass near $p = 0$. A particularly useful form of Equation 12.90 is the equation

$$\gamma(E) = E(1 + \alpha E).$$
(12.91)

The density of states in such cases is, in general, different from the usual parabolic density of states and can be easily shown to be of the form

$$N(E) = \frac{\left(2(m^*)^{3/2}\right)^{3/2}}{4\pi^2\hbar^3} \sqrt{\gamma(E)} \left.\frac{d\gamma}{dE'}\right|_{E'=E}$$
(12.92)

If $\gamma(E) = E$, this reduces to the usual 3-D density of states. In the next chapter, where we discuss high field transport, it is important to use the density of states given by Equation 12.92 in the scattering rates. Heterostructures also alter the density of states and thereby affect the scattering process as discussed in Chapter 14.

12.10 THE POLARON

In this chapter we focussed primarily on the electron-phonon interaction from the point of view of causing scattering between electronic states. The electron phonon interaction can also cause shifts in the energy values and thus cause changes in the mass of the electron. The electron is a negatively charged particle which can be considered to cause a polarization of its local environment. This results in a local lattice perturbation, and one says that the electron is "dressed." The electron has a cloud of virtual phonons which can cause a considerable increase in the electron mass over the one obtained from the bandstructure calculations of Chapter 5.

The shift in perturbation in the electron energy of the state $|k\rangle$ can be obtained from the second order perturbation theory as follows

$$E_{\mathbf{k}} = E_{\mathbf{k}0} + \sum_{\mathbf{q}} \left(\frac{|M_{\mathbf{q},\text{em}}|^2}{E_{\mathbf{k}} - E_{\mathbf{k}-\mathbf{q}} - \hbar\omega_{\mathbf{q}}} + \frac{|M_{\mathbf{q},\text{abs}}|^2}{E_{\mathbf{k}} - E_{\mathbf{k}-\mathbf{q}} + \hbar\omega_{\mathbf{q}}} \right)$$
(12.93)

where $M_{\mathbf{q},\text{em}}$ and $M_{\mathbf{q},\text{abs}}$ are the matrix elements for emission and absorption respectively and have been derived in detail in this chapter for various kinds of phonons. In general, these matrix elements have a strong temperature dependence through the phonon occupation number $n(\omega_q)$, and thus the energy shifts have a strong temperature dependence. It can be shown that the effect of the electron-phonon interaction can be written in the form (see, for example, Ridley, 1982)

$$E_k = \Delta E_{ep} + E_{k0} \left(1 - \frac{\alpha_{ep}}{6}\right) \qquad (12.94)$$

where ΔE_{ep} is a shift in the energy and α_{ep} is a parameter related to the change in the electron effective mass by

$$\frac{1}{m^*} = \frac{1}{m_0^*} \left(1 - \frac{\alpha_{ep}}{6}\right). \qquad (12.95)$$

The coupling strength α_{ep} is responsible for causing a higher effective mass than the "bandstructure" effective mass by dressing the electron. The values of α_{ep} is ~ 0.03 for acoustic and optical phonons which has quite negligible effects. Also, in most compound semiconductors, α_{ep} has a value of ~ 0.1 for polar optical phonons and piezoelectric phonons. This changes the effective mass by a few percent. However, for highly polar materials α_{ep} can approach and even exceed unity. In this case the electron is trapped by its own lattice distortions and conduction occurs by hopping.

12.11   FOR THE TECHNOLOGIST IN YOU

Phonon scattering is one of the limiting scattering processes for electronic transport. This is especially true for high field transport where phonon emission is the most dominant scattering process. This emission process has little temperature dependence (because of its $(n(T) + 1)$ dependence) and therefore is significant even at low temperatures. Thus, while the low temperature low-field mobility can be greatly improved by lowering temperature, the improvement in high field transport is not as dramatic. Nevertheless, there are certainly improvements in device performance if the device operating temperature is lowered. The use of low temperature to eliminate scattering has also spawned the cryogenic instrumentation technology. Cryostats are an important part of any well-equipped laboratory. Usually these cryostats use liquid nitrogen or liquid helium (often pumped to reach milli-Kelvin temperatures) to reach low temperatures. However, while this is possible for characterization type techniques, it is not possible to rely on these methods for a viable technology. However, advances in refrigeration based on the Peltier effect have now made available very compact units that can be easily interfaced with existing electronic systems. Thus, cryogenic electronics is an important part of high performance electronic and optoelectronic technology.

12.12 PROBLEMS

12.1. Calculate and plot the total scattering rate for acoustic phonons as a function of electron energy in GaAs and Si at 77 K and 300 K. Plot the results for electron energies between 0.0 and 0.5 eV.

12.2. Calculate and plot the total scattering rate for polar optical phonons in GaAs for electron energy between 0 and 300 meV, at 77 K and 300 K. Calculate the results separately for the absorption and emission of the optical phonon.

12.3. Calculate the optical phonon scattering rates in Si at 77 K and 300 K as a function of electron energy between 0 and 300 meV.

12.4. Using momentum conservation considerations (i.e. momentum is conserved to within a reciprocal vector), identify the phonon vectors necessary for intervalley scattering in (a) GaAs for Γ-X and Γ-L scattering; (b) in Si for g and f scattering and in (c) in Ge for L-X scattering.

12.5. Calculate the $\Gamma \rightarrow$L and L$\rightarrow \Gamma$ intervalley scattering rate for GaAs electrons as a function of energy at 77 K and 300 K.

12.6. Calculate the f- and g-type scattering rates for Si as a function of electron energy at 77 K and 300 K.

12.7. Using GaAs and $In_{0.53}Ga_{0.47}As$ bandstructure plots, estimate the magnitude of the phonon vectors needed to cause Γ-L and Γ-X intervalley scatterings.

12.8. In the text, the optical phonon density is assumed to be given by the thermodynamic lattice temperature. At high fields, the electrons emit optical phonons at a very high rate, causing "hot phonon" related effects. Estimate the optical phonon generation rate in GaAs at electron energies of 200 meV. If the optical phonons cannot dissipate rapidly, the phonon occupancy $n(\omega_0)$ becomes large. What effect will this have in terms of hot carrier relaxation?

12.9. Calculate the energy dependence of f- and g-type scattering rates in Si. If an alloy $Si_{1-x}Ge_x$ is grown on Si(001), there is a splitting of the four in-plane valleys ([100], [$\bar{1}$00], [010], [0$\bar{1}$0]) and the two out of plane valleys. What would the f- and g-type scattering rates be as a function of energy for the $Si_{0.8}Ge_{0.2}$ alloy? You can use the results in Chapter 6 for the splitting values.

12.10. The static and high frequency dielectric constants in GaAs are 13.2 and 10.9, respectively. The transverse optical phonon frequency is $\omega_t = 5.4 \times 10^{13}$ rad s^{-1} and the ionic masses are $M_{Ga} = 69.7\ M$, $M_{As} = 69.7\ M$ ($M = 1.67 \times 10^{-24}$ gm). What is the ionic charge on the Ga atom?

12.11. Calculate and plot the energy dependence of acoustic and polar optical phonon scattering rates in GaAs at 77 K and at 300 K. It is observed experimentally that when temperature is lowered, the low field mobility improves but the high field mobility remains almost unaffected. Do your results explain this behavior?

12.12. In many experiments, electron (and hole) carrier distributions are specially prepared by laser pulses. Thus, at time zero, the electrons have a well-defined energy. In such experiments, the time- dependent optical spectroscopy of such monoenergetic particles show "phonon replicas." Discuss the source of such phonon replicas.

NOTE: You can use material parameters listed in Table 13.2 for your calculations.

12.13 REFERENCES

- **General**

    - "High Field Transport in Semiconductors," by Conwell, E. M., in *Solid State Physics* (edited by F. Seitz, D. Turnbull and H. Ehrenreich, Academic Press, New York, 1967), vol. Suppl. 9.

    - Fawcett, W., A. D. Boardman and S. Swain, J. Phys. Chem. Solids, **31**, 1963 (1970).

    - Ferry, D. K., *Semiconductors* (Macmillan, New York, 1991).

    - Frohlich, H., Proc. Roy Soc. A, **160**, 230 (1937).

    - Hinckley, J. M., *The Effect of Strain on Pseudomorphic p- $Si_x Ge_{1-x}$: Physics and Modeling of the Valence Bandstructure and Hole Transport*, Ph.D. Thesis, (The University of Michigan, Ann Arbor, 1990).

    - Lundstrom, M., *Fundamentals of Carrier Transport* (Modular Series on Solid State Devices, edited by G. W. Neudeck and R. F. Pierret, Addison-Wesley, Reading, 1990), vol. X.

    - Ridley, B. K., *Quantum Processes in Semiconductors* (Clarendon Press, Oxford, 1982).

    - "Low Field Electron Transport," by Rode, D. L., in *Semiconductors and Semimetals* (edited by R. K. Willardson and A. C. Beer, Academic Press, New York, 1975), vol. 10.

    - Ziman, J. M., *Electrons and Phonons* (Clarendon Press, Oxford, 1980).

CHAPTER
13

THE VELOCITY-FIELD
RELATIONS

In the last two chapters we examined the effect of various kinds of scatterings on the free electron. In an experimental situation, all of these scattering mechanisms may be simultaneously present. The response of the free carriers to an external electric field is represented by the velocity versus electric field relationship. This relationship which obviously depends upon temperature, doping, etc., contains the information which is vital to the understanding of electronic devices. There are three regions of the electric field which are important in charge transport:

1. The low electric field region where the velocity-field relation is linear and is defined by the mobility μ through the relation

$$v = \mu \boldsymbol{F}. \tag{13.1}$$

2. A higher electric field (usually $F \geq 1$ kV/cm), where the v-F relation is no longer linear but can be extremely complex involving negative resistance regions as in the case of many direct bandgap semiconductors. To understand the transport in this region one usually requires numerical methods including those based on computer simulations.

3. Finally, at extremely high electric fields ($F \geq 10^5$ V/cm), the semiconductor "breaks down" either due to impact ionization or due to electrons tunneling from the valence band to the conduction band. Most electronic devices such as transistors, diodes, etc., operate below this upper field limit, after which the electric current shows a runaway behavior. However, some devices such as avalanche detectors do exploit the impact ionization phenomenon for high gain detection of photons.

The steady state v-F relationships require an electron to undergo several (usually at least several tens) collisions before reaching steady state. Most collision times are of the order of a picosecond, and since electron velocities are of the order of 10^7 cm/s, it takes an electron ~ 1000 Å of travel before scattering occurs. Transport in regions which are submicron in length is therefore not described by the usual v-F curves. This region of transport is described by the transient velocity-field curves and for extremely short distances the electron moves "ballistically" (i.e., without scattering). While several numerical approaches have been developed to describe this region, it is best described the computer simulation techniques based on Monte Carlo methods.

To address all of these important regions of transport in detail will not be possible in just one chapter, so we will only discuss some of the important techniques and the important results which illustrate the diverse and rich phenomenon of transport in semiconductors.

13.1   LOW FIELD TRANSPORT

This area of transport is the easiest one to understand, since the assumptions made in Chapter 10 to obtain the result for mobility

$$\mu = \frac{e < \tau >}{m^*} \tag{13.2}$$

are valid for most cases of interest. At low fields, the first order solution of the Boltzmann equation is quite valid and the distribution function in presence of an electric field is simply

$$f(\boldsymbol{k}) = f^0 \left(\boldsymbol{k} + \frac{e\tau \boldsymbol{F}}{\hbar} \right). \tag{13.3}$$

In case the carrier density is small, the distribution function is adequately given by a displaced Maxwellian function and as discussed in Chapter 10, the relaxation time appearing in Equation 13.2 for the mobility is simply

$$\ll \tau \gg = \frac{\langle E\tau \rangle}{\langle E \rangle} \tag{13.4}$$

where τ is the momentum relaxation time. We have already calculated these times for various scattering processes in the previous two chapters.

In most cases, one does not have a single scattering process present during carrier transport. If the various scattering processes are independent of each other, the total scattering rate is just the sum of the individual scattering rates. Thus, we have

$$\frac{1}{\tau_{\text{tot}}} = \sum_i \frac{1}{\tau_i} \tag{13.5}$$

Now, *if* the various scattering rates have the *same* energy dependence, then when one carries out the averaging of the Equation 13.4, the final mobility is simply given by

$$\frac{1}{\mu_{\text{tot}}} = \sum \frac{1}{\mu_i} \tag{13.6}$$

This is known as the Mathieson's rule and is strictly valid only when all the scattering mechanisms have the same energy dependence. As we have seen in the previous chapters, this is usually not true, so Equation 13.6 is not strictly valid. However, Mathieson's rule is widely used because of its ease of application and reasonable accuracy.

In Chapter 10 we showed that if a scattering mechanism has an energy dependence given by

$$\tau(E) = \tau_0 \left(\frac{E}{k_B T}\right)^s \tag{13.7}$$

the the averaging of Equation 13.4 simply gives

$$\ll \frac{1}{\tau} \gg = \frac{1}{\tau_0} \frac{\Gamma(5/2)}{\Gamma(s + 5/2)}. \tag{13.8}$$

As an example, let us consider the ionized impurity scattering and the acoustic phonon scattering. The ionized impurity scattering momentum relaxation time can be written approximately as

$$\tau(\boldsymbol{k}) = \tau_0 \left(\frac{E(\boldsymbol{k})}{k_B T}\right)^{3/2}. \tag{13.9}$$

We recall that the real energy dependence is somewhat more complex because of the energy dependence in the logarithmic terms. However, Equation 13.9 represents the dominant energy dependence. Here

$$\tau_0 = \frac{16\sqrt{2m^*}\pi\epsilon^2\epsilon_0^2}{N_I e^4}(k_B T)^{3/2} \left[\ln(1 + \gamma^2) - \frac{\gamma^2}{1 + \gamma^2}\right]^{-1}. \tag{13.10}$$

The term γ has an energy dependence which is weak and is evaluated at the value of energy which maximizes the value of $\ll \tau \gg$. This value is, in general, $E_m = (s + 3/2)k_B T = 3k_B T$. Thus, the value of γ is

$$\gamma_m = \frac{2}{\hbar\lambda}\sqrt{6m^* k_B T} \tag{13.11}$$

and the mobility is given by

$$\mu_I = \frac{128\sqrt{2\pi}\epsilon^2\epsilon_0^2(k_B T)^{3/2}}{e^3\sqrt{m^*}N_I\left[\ln(1 + \gamma_m^2) - \gamma_m^2/(1 + \gamma_m^2)\right]}. \tag{13.12}$$

As noted earlier, the mobility increases with temperature, a distinguishing signature of the ionized impurity scattering.

In the case of acoustic phonon scattering we have from Chapter 12

$$\tau(E) = \tau_0 \left(\frac{E}{k_B T}\right)^{-1/2} \tag{13.13}$$

with (see Chapter 12 for the details)

$$\tau_0 = \frac{2\pi\hbar^4 c_\ell}{D^2}(2m^* k_B T)^{-3/2} \tag{13.14}$$

The mobility then becomes

$$\begin{aligned} \mu_{AP} &= \frac{e\tau_0}{m^*}\frac{\Gamma(2)}{\Gamma(5/2)} \\ &= \frac{2\sqrt{2}\pi\,e\,\hbar^4\,c_\ell}{3D^2\,(m^*)^{5/2}\,(k_B T)^{3/2}}. \end{aligned} \tag{13.15}$$

The mobility limited by acoustic phonons decreases with temperature and has a characteristic $T^{-3/2}$ dependence. Mobilities due to other scattering mechanisms can be similarly determined from the results of Chapters 11 and 12 and the total mobility can then be determined by the Mathieson's rule. We will now examine the low field transport in a few semiconductors.

13.1.1   Low Field Mobility in Silicon

Si has a rather poor low field mobility as compared to the mobilities in direct bandgap materials. Fortunately, in electronic devices high field transport dominates the device performance allowing Si devices to be reasonably good. In Figure 13.1 we show typical mobilities for Si as a function of temperature and doping. For high quality samples, the mobility continues to increase as the temperature decreases since ionized impurity scattering is absent and the acoustic phonon scattering has a $T^{-3/2}$ behavior. However, for doped samples the mobility shows a peak at low temperatures and then decreases.

13.1.2   Low Field Mobility in GaAs

The electrons in GaAs have a superior low field mobility as compared to the case in Si. This is mainly due to the lower density of states at the bandedge. Room temperature mobilities in high quality GaAs samples are ~ 8500 cm^{2}V^{-1}s^{-1} compared to only ~ 1500 cm^{2}V^{-1}s^{-1} for Si. Figure 13.2 shows a typical plot of mobility versus temperature for GaAs. Also shown are the relative contributions of ionized impurity, acoustic phonons and polar optical phonons to the mobility. The polar optical phonon scattering is the dominant scattering for temperatures above 100 K.

Another semiconductor of considerable importance for high speed devices is In$_{0.53}$Ga$_{0.47}$As. This material has a very high room temperature mobility of ~ 11000 cm^{2}V^{-1}s^{-1}. However, at low temperatures the mobility is dominated by alloy scattering effects.

In Table 13.1 we show mobilities for electrons and holes for a number of semiconductors. There is no influence of impurity scattering in these results. Additional results are also provided in Appendix M.

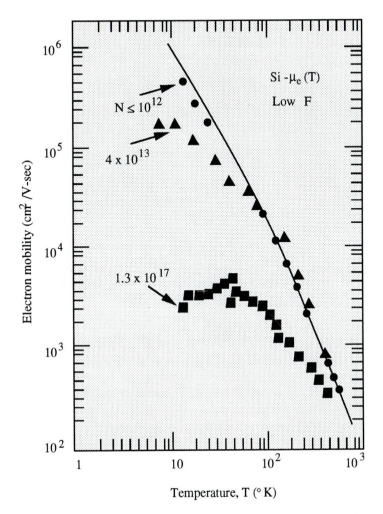

Figure 13.1: Low-field mobility of electrons in silicon as a function of temperature. (Reproduced with permission, C. Jacoboni, et al., Sol. St. Electron., **20**, 177 (1977).)

13.2 HIGH FIELD TRANSPORT

Unlike the low field transport region where analytical results are available for the velocity field dependence, at higher electric fields it is not possible to make any simple approximations which could lead to analytical results. As a result, one needs fairly complex numerical techniques to address the problem. One of the most powerful ones is the Monte Carlo, based computer simulation. Due to the accuracy and versatility of this approach, it is often the technique of choice for transport studies. However, since it is fairly computer intensive, key parameters are extracted from Monte Carlo runs and then used in less computer-intensive

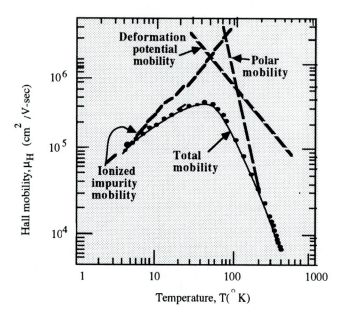

Figure 13.2: Low-field Hall mobility of electrons in GaAs as a function of temperature. The material has an ionized impurity concentration of 7×10^{13} cm^{-3}. (Reproduced with permission, G. E. Stillman, et al., J. Phys. Chem. Sol., **31**, 1199 (1970).)

Semiconductor	Bandgap (eV)		Mobility at 300 K (cm^2/V-s)	
	300 K	0 K	Elec.	Holes
C	5.47	5.48	1800	1200
Ge	0.66	0.74	3900	1900
Si	1.12	1.17	1500	450
α-SiC	3.00	3.30	400	50
GaSb	0.72	0.81	5000	850
GaAs	1.42	1.52	8500	400
GaP	2.26	2.34	110	75
InSb	0.17	0.23	80000	1250
InAs	0.36	0.42	33000	460
InP	1.35	1.42	4600	150
CdTe	1.48	1.61	1050	100
PbTe	0.31	0.19	6000	4000

Table 13.1: Bandgaps along with electron and hole mobilities in several semiconductors.

techniques such as in balance equations. Because of the importance of the Monte Carlo method, we will examine this approach in some detail now.

13.3 MONTE CARLO SIMULATION OF CARRIER TRANSPORT

The Monte Carlo approach is based upon an attempt to simulate the electron (hole) as it moves in a semiconductor. The technique is very flexible and powerful since it can incorporate local variations in electric field, charge density, etc., which occur in a real device. It is also useful to study transient transport properties in submicron channels. Such transport, which may involve overshoot and undershoot phenomena, is very poorly described by the Boltzmann transport equation approximations.

In the Monte Carlo process, the electron is considered as a point particle (like in a localized wavepacket description) whose scattering rates are given by the Fermi golden rule expressions. The Monte Carlo approach comes in because of the probabilistic value of the transport phenomenon. The Monte Carlo method involves carrying out a computer simulation to represent as closely as possible the actual physical phenomena occurring during the carrier transport. In general, the computer simulation involves the following physical processes:

1. Particle Injection into the Region of Study: The particles under study are injected into the region (say from a contact) with a prechosen distribution of carrier momenta. The carrier momentum distribution may be simply Maxwellian or could be more complex if, for example, the electrons were injected from a tunneling-type contact. Monte Carlo methods described below are used to generate the appropriate probability distribution.

2. Free Flight of the Carrier: This is an important component of the Monte Carlo method. In the Monte Carlo approach, the scattering event is considered to be instantaneous and between the scattering process the electron simply moves in the electric field according to the "free particle" equation of motion.

3. Scattering Event: A specific prescription is used in the Monte Carlo method to determine the time between scattering events. At the end of a free flight a scattering occurs which alters the flight pattern of the electron.

4. Selection of the Scattering Event: Since a number of scattering processes will be simultaneously present one has to decide which event was responsible for the scattering that occurred. This choice is again based on the Monte Carlo method.

5. State of the Electron After Scattering: Finally, one uses the Monte Carlo method to determine the momentum of the electron immediately after the collision has occurred. Remember that the collision duration is assumed

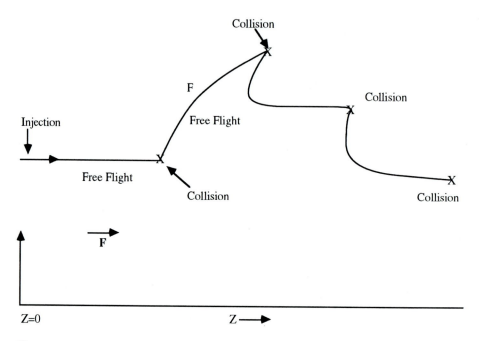

Figure 13.3: A schematic of processes involved in the physical picture used in Monte Carlo methods.

    to be zero. To determine the final state after collision one needs detailed information on the scattering process.

Once the final state is known, the procedure is simply repeated with a new free flight. Figure 13.3 illustrates the Monte Carlo approach schematically while Figure 13.4 gives a general flowchart for the Monte Carlo computer simulation program.

13.3.1   Simulation of Probability Functions by Random Numbers

The Monte Carlo approach is an extremely versatile technique which is not only used to study carrier transport, but all kinds of diverse physical phenomenon such as crystal growth, melting of solids, solution of complex integrals, etc. The heart of any Monte Carlo program is the generation of "random" numbers which are cleverly used to simulate random physical events. Since the random numbers are actually generated by some computer program, they are not really random since the entire sequence of numbers is predictable. Nevertheless, if the random number generation code is good, there should be little correlation between the random numbers. Such random numbers generated by computer codes are called pseudorandom numbers. It is, of course, possible to generate random numbers through "noise" in actual devices, but this approach is usually not used in actual

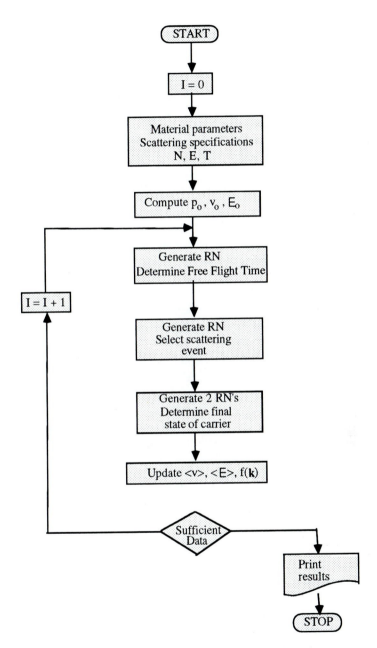

Figure 13.4: A flowchart of the Monte Carlo program to study carrier transport.

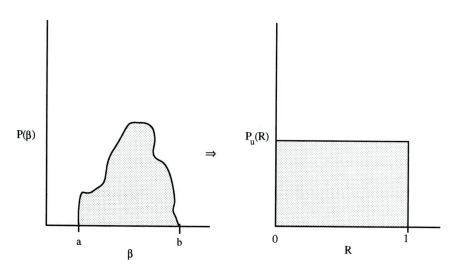

Figure 13.5: Mapping of a random probability function to a randomly generated number from a uniform random number generator.

computer simulations. The pseudo-random numbers are more convenient than truly random numbers since they are repeatable and therefore the computer program can be debugged.

If $P(\beta)$ is a probability distribution of some variable β in a range a to b, the question one asks in the Monte Carlo methods is the following: What are the different values of β if the events are chosen randomly? For example, $P(\beta)$ may be the probability that an electron scatters by an angle β. In this case we would be interested, for example, in finding the scattering angle during successive random collisions. This choice is made by generating a random number which has a uniform distribution, say between 0 and 1. As shown in Figure 13.5 we are then interested in mapping the probability function for the random number $P_u(R)$ to the probability function $P(\beta)$. The following equation is used for this mapping

$$\int_0^{R_n} P_u(R)dR = \int_0^{\beta_n} P(\beta)d\beta \tag{13.16}$$

where R_n is the random number generated in the nth try. The left-hand side of the Equation 13.16 is simply R_n. In many cases the right-hand side can be expressed analytically in terms of β_n, in which case once R_n is known, β_n is also known, at least implicitly. In some cases, it is difficult to evaluate the integral on the right-hand side and other approaches are then used to evaluate β. Some of these approaches will be discussed here.

Let us now examine the various components of the Monte Carlo program as outlined in Figures 13.3 and 13.4.

13.3.2 Injection of Carriers

The steady state v-F relations should not be dependent upon the initial conditions under which an electron is injected into the semiconductor. However, for transient transport studies or study of transport in small structures, the initial conditions of injection are quite important. While, in principle, the injecting contact can be quite complex, especially in heterostructure devices, usually the contact is simply a heavily doped semiconductor region (an ohmic contact) where the electrons simply reside with nearly an equilibrium distribution. For a nondegenerate case the equilibrium distribution is simply a Maxwellian distribution according to which the probability of finding the velocity between v and $v + dv$ is

$$P(v) = A^3 \exp\left[\frac{-m^*}{2k_BT}\left(v_x^2 + v_y^2 + v_z^2\right)\right] \qquad (13.17)$$

with

$$A^3 = \left(\frac{m^*}{2\pi k_BT}\right)^{3/2}.$$

If the electrons are to be injected, say, into the device along the z-axis, we are only interested in electrons with positive velocities which provide the current into the device. The x- and y-direction velocities can be positive or negative since the current flow is along the z-axis. These are then given by the Monte Carlo prescription, (e.g. for v_x)

$$\int_0^{R_n} P_u(R)dR = \int_{-\infty}^{v_{xn}} A \exp\left[\frac{-m^*}{2k_BT}v_x^2\right] dv_x. \qquad (13.18)$$

Two random numbers are therefore used to get v_x and v_y.

To find the velocity along the z-axis one makes the approximation that the current is given by the velocities along the z-direction only, i.e.

$$\frac{J}{e} = \int v_z\, f(v_z)\, dv_z. \qquad (13.19)$$

The flux between the velocity v_z and $v_z + dv_z$ is just

$$P(v_z)\, dv_z = v_z\, f(v_z)\, dv_z. \qquad (13.20)$$

Then the z-direction velocity is weighted into the probability function. The Monte Carlo method gives

$$\int_0^{R_n} P_u(R)dR = \frac{\int_0^{v_{zn}} v_z \exp\left[-m^*v_z^2/(2k_BT)\right] dv_z}{\int_0^{\infty} v_z \exp\left[-m^*v_z^2/(2k_BT)\right] dv_z}. \qquad (13.21)$$

The denominator is present to ensure that the probability is normalized. The right-hand side can now be integrated to get

$$v_{zn} = \sqrt{\frac{-2k_BT\ln(1 - R_n)}{m^*}} \qquad (13.22)$$

The term $-\ln(1 - R_n)$ is positive since $0 \leq R_n \leq 1$. The z-direction velocity then has only a positive value.

If the contact injects the electrons according to some other distribution, the Monte Carlo method has to simulate that particular distribution.

13.3.3 Free Flight

The Monte Carlo approach treats the transport problem as a series of free flights followed by scattering events. During the free flight the electron simply moves in the electric field according to the free electron equations of motion

$$\frac{d\boldsymbol{p}}{dt} = e\boldsymbol{F}. \tag{13.23}$$

If the electric field is along the z-axis, we have the following changes in the various properties of the electron (the time interval for free flight is typically 10^{-13} s so that on can linearize the equations):

Momentum after time t

$$
\begin{aligned}
p_x(t) &= p_x(0) \\
p_y(t) &= p_y(0) \\
p_z(t) &= p_z(0) + eFt.
\end{aligned}
\tag{13.24}
$$

Position after time t

$$
\begin{aligned}
x(t) &= x(0) + \frac{p_x(0)}{m^*}t \\
y(t) &= y(0) + \frac{p_y(0)}{m^*}t \\
z(t) &= z(0) + \frac{E(t) - E(0)}{eF}
\end{aligned}
\tag{13.25}
$$

where the energy change is given by

$$E(t) - E(0) = \frac{p^2(t)}{2m^*} - \frac{p^2(0)}{2m^*}. \tag{13.26}$$

13.3.4 Scattering Times

One of the most important parameters to be evaluated in the Monte Carlo method is the time interval between collisions. To evaluate this, we note that:

1. The total scattering rate is given by the Fermi golden rule

$$
\begin{aligned}
W(\boldsymbol{k}) &= \frac{2\pi}{\hbar} \sum_{\boldsymbol{k}'} \left| M_{\boldsymbol{k},\boldsymbol{k}'} \right|^2 \delta(E_f - E_i) \\
R_{\text{tot}} &= \sum_{i=1}^{m} W_i(\boldsymbol{k})
\end{aligned}
\tag{13.27}
$$

where R_{tot} represents the sum of all scattering rates due to the m scattering processes.

2. The angular dependence of the scattering process is given by

$$W(\boldsymbol{k}, \boldsymbol{k}') = \frac{2\pi}{\hbar} |M_{\mathbf{kk'}}|^2 \, \delta(E_f - E_i). \tag{13.28}$$

If $\lambda(\boldsymbol{k}, t)$ is the total scattering rate for an electron with momentum $\boldsymbol{k}(t)$, the probability that the electron will drift without scattering for time t and then scatter in time Δt is

$$P(t)\Delta t = \lambda(\boldsymbol{k}, t)\, \Delta t \; x \; [1 - \lambda(\boldsymbol{k}_i, t_i)\Delta t]^n \tag{13.29}$$

with

$$
\begin{aligned}
n\Delta t &= t \\
i\Delta t &= t_i \\
\boldsymbol{k}_i &= \boldsymbol{k}(t_i).
\end{aligned}
$$

The first term in Equation 13.29 is the probability of having a collision in time Δt and the second term in the parenthesis is the combined probability of not having a collision in n time intervals of Δt. If Δt is small or n is large, Equation 13.27 becomes

$$P(t) = \lambda(\boldsymbol{k}, t) \exp\left[-\int_0^t \lambda(\boldsymbol{k}, t')dt' \right]. \tag{13.30}$$

In general, $\lambda(\boldsymbol{k})$ will be different from R_{tot} defined in Equation 13.27 as we shall see below. We use the Monte Carlo approach to find the times interval t_f between collisions. We have

$$\int_0^{R_n} P_u(r)dr = \int_0^{t_f} P(t)dt \tag{13.31}$$

or

$$R_n = \int_0^{t_f} \lambda(t) \exp\left\{ -\int_0^t \lambda(t')dt' \right\} dt. \tag{13.32}$$

Noting that

$$\frac{-d}{dt} \exp\left\{ -\int_0^t \lambda(t)'dt' \right\} = \lambda(t) \exp\left\{ -\int_0^t \lambda(t)'dt' \right\} \tag{13.33}$$

we get

$$R_n = \left[-\exp\left(-\int_0^t \lambda(t)'dt' \right) \right]\Big|_0^{t_f} \tag{13.34}$$

or

$$R_n = 1 - \exp\left(-\int_0^t \lambda(t)'dt' \right). \tag{13.35}$$

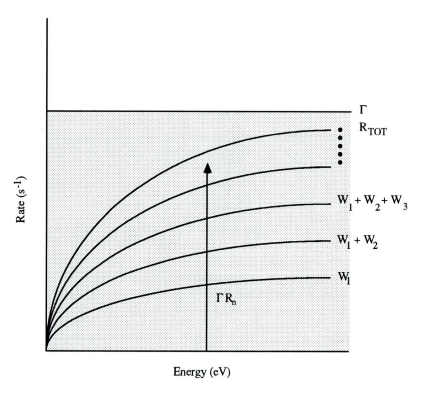

Figure 13.6: A schematic showing how a random number allows one to determine the scattering mechanism responsible for scattering.

In principle this equation can be used to generate various values of t_f. However, if $\lambda(t)$ is equal to R_{tot}, it has a fairly complex energetic and, therefore, temporal dependence, which makes it difficult to evaluate the integral. One possibility is to develop elaborate look up tables after having solved the problem numerically. However, a simple and ingenious way is based on the concept of self-scattering as shown in Figure 13.6. We define a scattering rate

$$\Gamma \equiv \lambda = R_{\text{tot}} + \lambda_0 \qquad (13.36)$$

where λ_0 is such that Γ is a constant scattering rate. The λ_0 part of the scattering rate is just a fictitious scattering rate called the self-scattering rate which does not cause any real scattering. With this choice we get

$$
\begin{aligned}
R_n &= 1 - \exp\left[-\int_0^{t_f} \Gamma dt\right] \\
&= 1 - e^{-\Gamma t_f}
\end{aligned}
$$

or

$$t_f = \frac{-1}{\Gamma} \ln(1 - R_n). \qquad (13.37)$$

Equation 13.37 allows us to find the free flight time during which the electron simply accelerates in the presence of the electric field. At the end of the free flight time the electron scatters. Now a (hopefully) small fraction of the electrons will "self scatter," i.e., here no real scattering. In this case the electron is simply allowed to continue accelerating in the field.

13.3.5 Identification of the Scattering Event

After the free flight, all the properties of the electron are updated. This requires us to know which particular mechanism is responsible for scattering. This is determined as shown schematically in Figure 13.6 and requires a single random number, R, which is used to identify the scattering mechanism ℓ which satisfies the inequality

$$\sum_{i=1}^{\ell-1} W_i(\boldsymbol{k}) < \Gamma R \leq \sum_{i=1}^{\ell} W_i(\boldsymbol{k}). \tag{13.38}$$

It is clear that one has to be quite judicious in the choice of Γ. Γ should be larger than R_{tot}, but not by too much, otherwise a larger number of scattering events will be self-scattering events which just consume extra computer time.

13.3.6 Particle Energy and Momentum After Scattering

Once the scattering event is identified one has to define the electron's energy and momentum just after the scattering event. Since the scattering time is assumed to be zero, the position of the electron is unaffected by the scattering event. The scattering process immediately tells us how much the energy has changed as a result of scattering. For example, we have the following results:

Ionized impurity:	$\Delta E = 0$
Alloy scattering:	$\Delta E = 0$
Polar optical phonon absorption:	$\Delta E = \hbar\omega_0$
Polar optical phonon emission:	$\Delta E = -\hbar\omega_0$
Acoustic phonon scattering:	$\Delta E \approx 0.$

The determination of the particle momentum after scattering is somewhat more complex. If the energy–momentum relation is isotropic, it is straightforward to determine the magnitude of the momentum since the energy after scattering is known. If the bands are more complex, as in the case of holes or in the case of electrons in very high field studies ($F > 10^5$ V/cm), the problem is more complex and will be discussed briefly later.

The updating of the momentum (direction) requires further generation of random numbers. It is convenient to find the scattered angle in the coordinate system where the z-axis is along the direction of the original momentum $\boldsymbol{k}$. This is done since all the angular dependencies calculated (see Chapters 11 and 12), are in this system. Of course, eventually we will describe the final momentum in the coordinate system where the z-axis is along the electric field. This will require

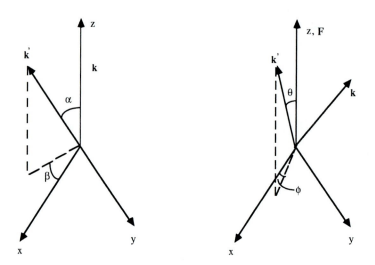

Figure 13.7: The two coordinate systems used in Monte Carlo method. One uses the system (left) where the momentum before scattering is along the z-axis to determine the final state after scattering. This has then to be transformed in the fixed-coordinate system (right) where the F-field is along the z-axis.

a simple transformation. The two coordinate systems are shown in Figure 13.7. The angles β and α represent the azimuthal and polar angles of scattering in the initial momentum coordinate system while ϕ and θ are the scattering angles in the F-field coordinate system.

The determination of the azimuthal angle β after scattering is given by the probability that k' lies between azimuthal angles β and $\beta + d\beta$

$$P(\beta)d\beta = \frac{d\beta \int_0^\infty \int_0^\pi W(k, k') \, \sin\alpha \, d\alpha \, k'^2 \, dk'}{\int_0^{2\pi} d\beta \int_0^\infty \int_0^\pi W(k, k') \, \sin\alpha \, d\alpha \, k'^2 \, dk'}. \tag{13.39}$$

Since $W(k, k')$ does not depend upon β for any of the isotropic band scattering rates, we simply have

$$P(\beta)d\beta = \frac{d\beta}{2\pi}. \tag{13.40}$$

Thus, one simply generates a random number, R_n, and determines β by the equation

$$\beta = 2\pi R_n. \tag{13.41}$$

The azimuthal angle is then uniformly distributed between 0 and 2π.

In general, the scattering rate has a polar angle dependence so that the determination of the polar angle α is somewhat more involved. We have

$$P(\alpha)d\alpha = \frac{\sin\alpha \, d\alpha \int_0^\infty \int_0^{2\pi} W(k, k') \, d\beta \, k'^2 \, dk'}{\int_0^\pi \int_0^{2\pi} \int_0^\infty \sin\alpha \, d\alpha \, W(k, k') \, d\beta \, k'^2 \, dk'} \tag{13.42}$$

Let us first examine isotropic scattering where $W(k, k')$ has no α dependence. This case occurs for acoustic phonon scattering, alloy scattering (with no clustering), etc. In this case we have

$$P(\alpha)d\alpha = \frac{\sin \alpha \, d\alpha}{2} a. \qquad (13.43)$$

In the Monte Carlo approach, a random number is generated and we have

$$\begin{aligned} R_n &= \frac{1}{2} \int_0^\alpha \sin \alpha' \, d\alpha' \\ &= \frac{1}{2}(1 - \cos \alpha) \end{aligned} \qquad (13.44)$$

or

$$\cos \alpha = 1 - 2R_n. \qquad (13.45)$$

Note that even though the scattering is isotropic, the average value of α is $\pi/2$. This is due to the number of available states between α and $\alpha + d\alpha$ which peak at $\pi/2$ as shown in Figure 13.8.

A number of scattering mechanisms have strong angular dependencies. We will now examine a few of these.

Ionized Impurity Scattering

In this case the scattering matrix element has a strong angular dependence given by

$$W(k, k') \propto \frac{1}{\left[4k^2 \sin^2(\alpha/2) + \lambda^2\right]^2} \qquad (13.46)$$

where λ is the inverse screening length. The integration for $P(\alpha)$ can be carried out and the scattering angle is given by

$$\cos \alpha = 1 - \frac{2(1 - R_n)}{1 + 4\frac{E}{E_\beta}R_n} \qquad (13.47)$$

where

$$E_\beta = \frac{\hbar^2 \lambda^2}{2m^*}$$

and

$$E = \frac{\hbar^2 k^2}{2m^*}.$$

It is easy to see that if $\lambda \to 0$, i.e., there is no screening, the scattering angle goes towards zero. On the other hand, if the screening is very strong, the scattering becomes randomizing, as in the case of alloy scattering. These cases are shown in Figure 13.9. The ionized impurity scattering rate, $W(k)$, is usually the strongest ($\sim 10^{13}$–10^{14} s^{-1}) of any of the scattering processes. However, its effect is not correspondingly as strong because the scattering is dominantly forward-directed and thus not as effective in momentum randomization.

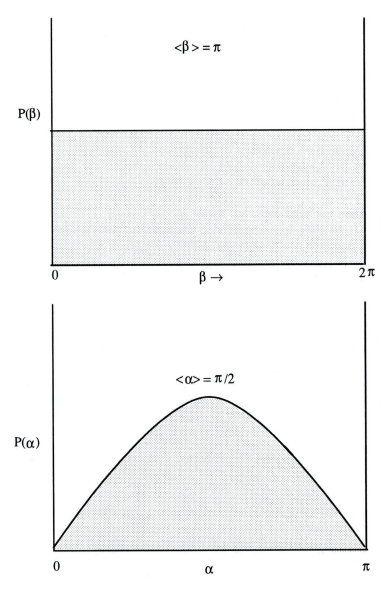

Figure 13.8: The probability of the azimuthal and polar scattering angles in the case of an isotopic scattering involving a randomizing scattering.

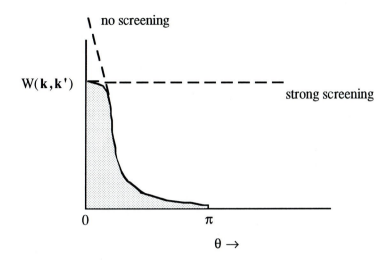

Figure 13.9: Angular dependence of the scattering by ionized impurities. The scattering has a strong forward angle preference.

Polar Optical Phonon Scattering

Another important nonrandomizing scattering is the polar optical phonon scattering. In this case the scattering matrix element has a dependence given by

$$W(\mathbf{k}, \mathbf{k}') \propto \frac{1}{\left|\mathbf{k} - \mathbf{k}'\right|^2}. \tag{13.48}$$

For a parabolic energy momentum relation

$$\frac{\hbar^2 k^2}{2m^*} = E,$$

we get

$$P(\alpha)d\alpha = \frac{\left[\frac{\sin\alpha\, d\alpha}{E+E'-2(EE')^{1/2}\cos\alpha}\right]}{\int_0^\pi \frac{\sin\alpha\, d\alpha}{E+E'-2(EE')^{1/2}\cos\alpha}}. \tag{13.49}$$

Using the Monte Carlo approach

$$\begin{aligned}
R_n &= \int_0^\alpha P(\alpha')\, d\alpha' \\
&= \frac{\ln\left[1 + f(1 - \cos\alpha)\right]}{\ln\left[1 + 2f\right]}
\end{aligned}$$

where

$$f = 2(EE')^{1/2}\left[E^{1/2} - E'^{1/2}\right]^{-2}. \tag{13.50}$$

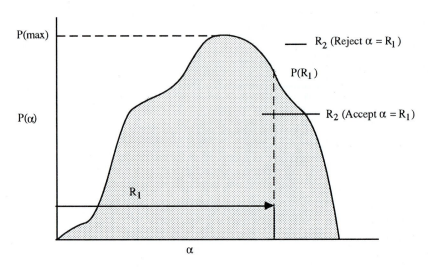

Figure 13.10: The procedure for using the von Neumann method to generate an arbitrary probability function.

Thus, the polar angle is given by

$$\cos \alpha = \frac{\left[(1 + f) - (1 + 2f)^{R_n}\right]}{f}. \tag{13.51}$$

When nonparabolic effects are included in the evaluation of $W(\mathbf{k}, \mathbf{k}')$ and its polar angle distribution, it is often not possible to evaluate the $P(\alpha)d\alpha$ integral in terms of a random number. This may also occur whenever the bandstructure is complex. In such cases, a technique due to von Neumann is used to obtain α from an arbitrary $P(\alpha)$. In this technique, random numbers are generated in pairs, the first number R_1 representing the value of $\cos \alpha$ in the range -1 to 1, i.e., the limits for $\alpha = 0$ and π. The second number, R_2, is generated between 0 and $P(max)$, where $P(max)$ is the maximum value of the probability. If $P(R_1)$ is less than R_2, the value of R_1 ($= \cos \alpha$) is not accepted and another pair of random numbers is generated until $P(R_1)$ is larger than R_2. In this case the value of $\cos \alpha$ will then mimic $P(\alpha)$. Figure 13.10 shows schematically how the von Neumann technique works.

Once α and β are known, a simple rotational transformation is made to obtain the angles ϕ and θ in the electric field coordinate system. This is straightforward, since the orientation of the vector $\mathbf{k}$ just before scattering and the electric field are known. This updates the momentum of the electron after each scattering event. The Monte Carlo procedure described here is repeated thousands of times (typically steady state conditions require $\sim 10^5$ scattering events). This makes the approach quite computer intensive. However, since the trajectory of the electron is followed in real space, as well as energy and momentum space, a tremendous insight is gained. The k-space distribution for the electron ensemble can be mapped out by constructing a k-space grid and determining the relative time spent by the electron around each grid point. Once the distribution function is known, essentially all physical quantities of interest can be determined. However, often it is useful to determine certain physical quantities directly. For example, the drift velocity in the jth valley is determined from the relation

$$
\begin{aligned}
v_j &= \frac{1}{k_j} \sum \int_{k_{zi}}^{k_{zf}} \frac{1}{\hbar} \frac{\partial E(k)}{\partial k_z} dk_z \\
&= \frac{1}{\hbar k_j} \sum (E_f - E_i).
\end{aligned}
\tag{13.52}
$$

Here k_{zi} and k_{zf} are the initial and final k-vectors in a free flight, the summation is over all free flights and E_i and E_f are the energies of the electron at the beginning and end of a free flight. The vector k_j is the total length in the direction of the k-space trajectory in the valley and is given by

$$
k_j = \frac{T_j e |\mathbf{F}|}{\hbar}
\tag{13.53}
$$

where T_j is the total time spent in the valley and $\mathbf{F}$ is the electric field. The relative population of the electron in different valleys is determined by simply the relative time spent by the electron in different valleys.

The only missing ingredient to carry out the Monte Carlo simulation is the material parameters. These are listed for GaAs and Si in Table 13.2. We also briefly list the total scattering rate $W(k)$ and differential scattering rates $W(k, k')$ for electron transport in direct gap semiconductors below. The results for the Γ-valley assume a nonparabolic band.

Ionized Impurity Scattering

$$
\begin{aligned}
W(k) &= 4\pi F \left(\frac{2k}{\lambda} \right)^2 \left[\frac{1}{1 + (\lambda/2k)^2} \right] \\
F &= \frac{1}{\hbar} \left[\frac{Ze^2}{\epsilon} \right]^2 \frac{N(E_{\mathbf{k}})}{32k^4} \cdot N_I.
\end{aligned}
\tag{13.54}
$$

Angular dependence

$$
\frac{1}{4k^2 \sin^2(\theta/2) + \lambda^2} \sin\theta d\theta.
\tag{13.55}
$$

Alloy scattering in Alloy $A_x B_{1-x}$

$$
\begin{aligned}
W(k) &= \frac{3\pi^3}{8\hbar} V_0 \, U_{\text{all}}^2 \, N(E_{\mathbf{k}}) \, x \, (1 - x) \\
V0 &= \text{volume of the unit cell.}
\end{aligned}
\tag{13.56}
$$

Angular dependence: randomizing.

Parameter	Symbol	Value in Si	Value in GaAs
Mass density (g/cm^3)	ρ	2.329	5.36
Lattice constant (Å)	a_0	5.43	5.642
Low frequency dielectric constant	ϵ_0	11.7	12.90
High frequency dielectric constant	ϵ_∞	—	10.92
Piezoelectric constant (C/m^2)	e_{PZ}	—	0.160
Longitudinal acoustic velocity $(\times 10^5 \text{ cm/sec})$	v_l	9.04	5.24
Transverse acoustic velocity $(\times 10^5 \text{ cm/sec})$	v_t	5.34	3.0
Longitudinal optical phonon energy (eV)	$\hbar\omega_0$	0.063	0.03536
Electron effective mass (lowest valley) (m_0)	m^* m_l^*, m_t^*	— 0.916, 0.19 (X)	0.067 (Γ) —
Electron effective mass (upper valley) (m_0)	m^* m^* m_l^*, m_t^*	— — 1.59, 0.12 (L)	0.222 (L) 0.58 (X) —
Nonparabolicity parameter (eV^{-1})	α	0.5 (X)	0.610 (Γ) 0.461 (L) 0.204 (X)
Energy separation between valleys (eV)	$\Delta E_{\Gamma L}$ $\Delta E_{\Gamma X}$	— —	0.29 0.48

Table 13.2: Material parameters for Silicon and Gallium Arsenide, (from Jacoboni and Reggiani, 1983, Hess, 1988).

Parameter	Symbol	Value in Si	Value in GaAs
Electron acoustic deformation potential (eV)	D_A	9.5	7.0 (Γ) 9.2 (L) 9.0 (X)
Electron optical deformation potential ($\times 10^8$ eV/cm)	D_0	—	3.0 (L)
Optical phonon energy (eV)	ω_0	0.0642	0.0343
Hole acoustic deformation potential (eV)	D_A	5.0	3.5
Hole optical deformation potential (eV/cm)	D_0	6.00	6.48
Intervalley parameters, g-type (X–X) ($\times 10^8$ eV/cm), (eV)	D_y, E_y	0.5, 0.012 (TA) 0.8, 0.019 (LA) 11.0, 0.062 (LO)	—
Intervalley parameters, f-type (X–X) ($\times 10^8$ eV/cm), (eV)	D_y, E_y	0.3, 0.019 (TA) 2.0, 9.947 (LA) 2.0, 0.059 (LO)	—
Intervalley parameters, (X–L) ($\times 10^8$ eV/cm), (eV)	D_y, E_y	2.0, 0.058 2.0, 0.055 2.0, 0.041 2.0, 0.017	—
Intervalley deformation potential ($\times 10^8$ eV/cm)	$D_{\Gamma L}, D_{\Gamma X}$ D_{LL}, D_{LX} D_{XX}	—	10.0, 10.0 10.0, 5.0 7.0
Intervalley phonon energy (eV)	$E_{\Gamma L}, E_{\Gamma X}$ E_{LL}, E_{LX} E_{XX}	—	0.0278, 0.0299 0.0290, 0.0293 0.0299

Table 13.2: continued.

Polar Optical Phonon Scattering

In Chapter 12 we discussed the polar optical phonon scattering assuming unity overlap integral and a parabolic band. The polar optical phonon is usually the most important scattering mechanism for high field transport. At these high fields the electron energies are quite large and nonparabolic effects quite important. We will, therefore, give the rates for nonparabolic bands (Fawcett, et al., 1970). The angular dependence of the scattering rate is given by

$$
W(\mathbf{k}, \mathbf{k}') = \frac{2\pi}{\hbar} \cdot \frac{2\pi e^2 \hbar \omega_0}{V \left| \mathbf{k} - \mathbf{k}' \right|^2} \left(\frac{1}{\epsilon_\infty} - \frac{1}{\epsilon_s} \right) G(\mathbf{k}, \mathbf{k}')
$$

$$
\times \begin{cases} n(\omega_0)\, \delta(E(\mathbf{k}') - E(\mathbf{k}) - \hbar\omega_0) & \text{(absorption)} \\ (n(\omega_0) + 1)\, \delta(E(\mathbf{k}') - E(\mathbf{k}) + \hbar\omega_0) & \text{(emission)} \end{cases} \quad (13.57)
$$

where $n(\omega_0)$ is the occupation probability for the optical phonons, ϵ_∞, ϵ_s are the high frequency and static dielectric constants, and ω_0 is the optical phonon frequency. If a nonparabolic energy band is assumed with the relation

$$
\frac{\hbar^2 k^2}{2m^*} = E(1 + \alpha E) \quad (13.58)
$$

the overlap integral is given by

$$
G(\mathbf{k}, \mathbf{k}') = \left[a_{\mathbf{k}} a_{\mathbf{k}'} + c_{\mathbf{k}} c_{\mathbf{k}'} \cos \beta \right]^2 \quad (13.59)
$$

where β is the angle between $\mathbf{k}$ and $\mathbf{k}'$ and

$$
a_{\mathbf{k}} = \left[\frac{1 + \alpha E(\mathbf{k})}{1 + 2\alpha E(\mathbf{k})} \right]^{1/2}
$$

$$
c_{\mathbf{k}} = \left[\frac{\alpha E(\mathbf{k})}{1 + 2\alpha E(\mathbf{k})} \right]^{1/2} . \quad (13.60)
$$

Also, $a_{\mathbf{k}'}$ and $c_{\mathbf{k}'}$ are the same corresponding functions of $E(\mathbf{k})$.

If α is 0, the overlap integral is unity. The total scattering rate is

$$
W(\mathbf{k}) = \frac{e^2 m^{*1/2} \omega_0}{\sqrt{2}\hbar} \left(\frac{1}{\epsilon_\infty} - \frac{1}{\epsilon_s} \right) \frac{1 + 2\alpha E'}{\gamma^{1/2}(E)} F_0(E, E')
$$

$$
\times \begin{cases} n(\omega_0) & \text{(absorption)} \\ (n(\omega_0) + 1) & \text{(emission)} \end{cases} \quad (13.61)
$$

where

$$
\begin{aligned} E' &= E + \hbar\omega_0 \text{ for absorption} \\ &= E - \hbar\omega_0 \text{ for emission} \end{aligned}
$$

$$\gamma(E) = E(1 + \alpha E)$$

$$F_0(E, E') = C^{-1}\left(A\ln\left|\frac{\gamma^{1/2}(E) + \gamma^{1/2}(E')}{\gamma^{1/2}(E) - \gamma^{1/2}(E')}\right| + B\right)$$

$$A = \left[2(1 + \alpha E)(1 + \alpha E') + \alpha\{\gamma(E) + \gamma(E')\}\right]^2$$

$$B = -2\alpha\gamma^{1/2}(E)\,\gamma^{1/2}(E')$$
$$\times\left[4(1 + \alpha E)(1 + \alpha E') + \alpha\{\gamma(E) + \gamma(E')\}\right]$$

$$C = 4(1 + \alpha E)(1 + \alpha E')(1 + 2\alpha E)(1 + 2\alpha E'). \qquad (13.62)$$

Although the results look quite complicated, it is straightforward to use them in the Monte Carlo method. The angular dependence of the momentum after scattering requires the von Neumann technique discussed earlier.

Acoustic Phonon Scattering

The acoustic phonon scattering is an important scattering mechanism at low electric fields especially at low temperatures where the optical phonon occupation number is very small. The total scattering rate is

$$W(k) = \frac{(2m^*)^{3/2}\,k_B T\,D_{ac}^2}{2\pi\rho v_s^2\hbar^4}\gamma^{1/2}(E)(1 + 2\alpha E)F_a(E)$$

$$F_a(E) = \frac{(1 + \alpha E)^2 + \frac{1}{3}(\alpha E)^2}{(1 + 2\alpha E)^2}. \qquad (13.63)$$

Once again if $\alpha = 0$, we recover the results of Chapter 12. The angular dependence of the acoustic phonon scattering is randomizing if the overlap integral is unity, but is otherwise given by the angular dependence of $G(k, k')$ as given by Equations 13.59 and 13.60.

It is important to include the nonparabolicity effects in the polar optical phonon scattering for the Γ-valley in electron transport in GaAs, InGaAs etc. However, for transport in the L-valley or X-valley, one need not use the nonparabolic effects except at fields close to breakdown fields ($F > 10^5$ V/cm). The acoustic and polar optical phonon scattering are then simply obtained by $\alpha = 0$ and are the same as the cases discussed in Chapter 12.

Intervalley Scattering

As noted in Chapter 12, the intervalley scattering is simply treated as a deformation potential scattering described by a deformation potential D_{ij}. The total scattering rate is for equivalent valleys

$$W(k) = \frac{(Z_e - 1)\,m^{*3/2}D_{ij}^2}{\sqrt{2}\pi\rho\,\omega_{ij}\hbar^3}E'^{1/2}\begin{cases} n(\omega_{ij}) & \text{(absorption)} \\ (n(\omega_{ij}) + 1) & \text{(emission)} \end{cases} \qquad (13.64)$$

where

$$E' = \begin{cases} E(\boldsymbol{k}) + \hbar w_{ij} & \text{(absorption)} \\ E(\boldsymbol{k}) - \hbar w_{ij} & \text{(emission)} \end{cases} \tag{13.65}$$

Z_e is the number of equivalent valleys and ω_{ij} is the phonon frequency which allows the intervalley scattering. The angular dependence of the scattering rate is randomizing.

For non-equivalent intervalley scattering (e.g., $\Gamma \rightarrow L$) the scattering rate has a similar form except the factor $(Z_e - 1)$ is replaced by the number of final valleys available for scattering (e.g., 4 for $\Gamma \rightarrow L$ scattering; 1 for $L \rightarrow \Gamma$ scattering; 6 for $\Gamma \rightarrow X$ scattering, etc.). Since the electrons will have a fairly high energy in the Γ-valley for a $\Gamma \rightarrow L$ scattering ($\sim$ 300–500 meV), it is important to include nonparabolic band effects for the Γ-valley. The scattering rate for the transfer of the electron form i to j valley in this case is

$$W(\boldsymbol{k}) = \frac{Z_j m_j^{*3/2} D_{ij}^2}{\sqrt{2}\pi \rho \omega_{ij} \hbar^3} \gamma_j^{1/2} (E')(1 + 2\alpha_j E') G_{ij}(E, E')$$

$$\times \begin{cases} n(\omega_{ij}) & \text{(absorption)} \\ (n(\omega_{ij}) + 1) & \text{(emission)} \end{cases} \tag{13.66}$$

where

$$G_{ij}(\boldsymbol{k}, \boldsymbol{k}') = \frac{\left[1 + \alpha_i E_i(\boldsymbol{k})\right]\left[1 + \alpha_j E_j(\boldsymbol{k}')\right]}{\left[1 + 2\alpha_i E_i(\boldsymbol{k})\right]\left[1 + 2\alpha_j E_j(\boldsymbol{k}')\right]}$$

and

$$E_j' = \begin{cases} E_i - \Delta_j + \Delta_i + \hbar w_{ij} & \text{(absorption)} \\ E_i - \Delta_j + \Delta_i - \hbar w_{ij} & \text{(emission)}. \end{cases}$$

It is now straightforward to follow the flowchart of Figure 13.4 and write a computer program to simulate carrier transport in semiconductors. Some important material parameters for GaAs and Si are given in Table 13.2. Numerical values for some of the scattering rates are also listed in Appendix M. The approach discussed here is extremely versatile since it can be easily generalized to address any of the following problems:

1. Steady state v–F relations along with information on carrier distribution in $\boldsymbol{k}$-space, electron temperature, valley occupation, etc.

2. Transient v–F relations and its dependence on transit length, scattering processes, injection conditions, etc.

3. Dependence of transit time in a fixed channel on the field distribution which could be calculated in a self-consistent way with the Poisson equation and current continuity equation.

4. Noise in electronic transport can also be studied from the carrier distribution information.

The Monte Carlo approach can also be used for understanding ultrafast optical experiments where carriers are excited by a fast laser and their relaxation is then studied. The above list is by no means complete and is simply included to point out the extreme versatility of the Monte Carlo method. We will now discuss some typical results for transport of electrons in electric fields below the breakdown fields.

13.4 ELECTRON TRANSPORT MONTE CARLO CALCULATIONS

13.4.1 GaAs, Steady State

GaAs has been a semiconductor for which numerous Monte Carlo studies have been carried out. We will give some representative results for the electron transport, which can be physically understood on the basis of the two valley model. At low electric fields the electron moves in the high mobility, low mass ($m^*/m_0 = 0.067$) Γ-valley and has an excellent v– F relationship with a room temperature mobility ~ 8000 cm^2/V-s, for pure GaAs. The peak velocity in pure GaAs is $\sim 2 \times 10^7$ cm/s at room temperature, at an electric field of ~ 3.5 kV/cm. Up to this field, most of the electrons are in the Γ-valley as their energy is less than the Γ-L energy separation. However, at higher electric fields there is a transfer of electrons from the Γ to L valley where the electron mass is very large ($m^*/m_0 \sim 0.22$). This causes the negative differential resistance which is a special feature of most direct bandgap semiconductors. The negative differential resistance is exploited to produce charge domains resulting from instabilities and leading to Gunn oscillations.

In Figure 13.11 we show the doping dependence of the v- F relations in GaAs at room temperature. The temperature dependence of the v–F relations is shown in Figure 13.12. It is interesting to note that while the low field mobility increases rapidly as the temperature is lowered, the high field velocity does not show such a pronounced temperature dependence. This is because the low field mobility, which is dominated by acoustic phonons, and polar optical phonon *absorption*, shows improvement due to the suppression of these scattering processes. The high field transport, on the other hand, is dominated by polar optical phonon emission and intervalley scattering which do not have much lattice temperature dependence.

In Figure 13.13 we show the Γ valley occupation fraction for the electrons as a function of the electric field. As we can see at high fields the electrons transfer out of the Γ-valley. Also shown are the electron temperatures as a function of the electric field.

While the Monte Carlo calculations are computer intensive, they can be used to develop simple analytical descriptions for the v–F curves which could

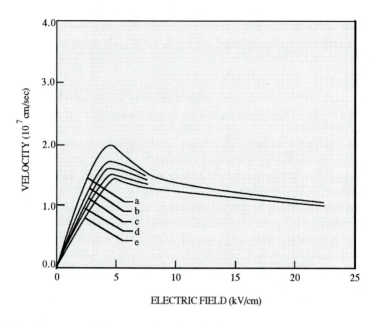

Figure 13.11: Electron velocity as a function of electric field in a GaAs. The impurity density for the different curves is (a) $N_D = 0$; (b) $N_D = 1.0 \times 10^{17}$ cm^{-3}; (c) $N_D = 2.0 \times 10^{17}$ cm^{-3}; (d) $N_D = 4.0 \times 10^{17}$ cm^{-3}; (e) $N_D = 8.0 \times 10^{17}$ cm^{-3}.

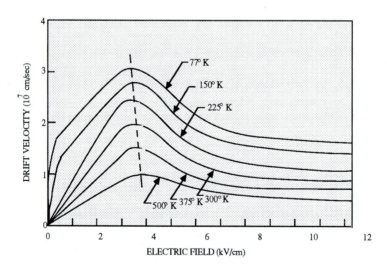

Figure 13.12: Dependence of the velocity–field relations on temperature for GaAs electrons. (Reproduced with permission, J. G. Ruch, et al., J. Appl. Phys., **41**, 3843, (1970).)

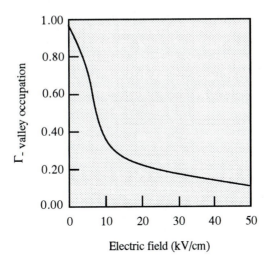

Figure 13.13: Occupation of the Γ-valley in GaAs electron transport as a function of electric field.

be used for certain device simulations. For example, one can use the following function for the field dependence of the mobility (Chang and Felterman, 1986)

$$\mu(\boldsymbol{F}) = \frac{\mu^0}{\left[1 + \theta(F - F_0)\left\{(F - F_0)/F_{\mathrm{cr}}^2\right\}^2\right]} \tag{13.67}$$

where μ^0 is the low field mobility, $F_{\mathrm{cr}} = v_{\mathrm{sat}}/\mu^0$ and

$$F_0 = \frac{1}{2}\left[F_{\mathrm{th}} + \sqrt{F_{\mathrm{th}}^2 - 4F_{\mathrm{cr}}^2}\right] \tag{13.68}$$

where F_{th} is the electric field where the velocity peaks. The function $\theta(F - F_0)$ is a step function which is zero for fields below F_0 and 1 otherwise. Similarly, the saturation velocity has a temperature dependence given by (Jacoboni, et al., 1977)

$$v_{\mathrm{sat}} = \frac{2.4 \times 10^7}{1 + 0.8\exp(T_L/600)} \text{ cm/s.} \tag{13.69}$$

where T_L is the lattice temperature in K.

13.4.2   GaAs, Transient Behavior

The steady state results discussed above are valid when the electrons have sufficient time to suffer several scattering events to reach a steady state distribution. This usually requires a few picoseconds or a transit distance of ≥ 1000 Å. When transit distances are smaller than ≈ 1000 Å, the electron can move ballistically. This has been demonstrated by an ingenious experiment using the Tunneling

Hot Electron Transistor (THETA). In this structure, shown schematically in Figure 13.14, electrons are injected through a tunneling contact into a drift region (the base of the transistor) and those carriers having energies above the collect side barrier as shown are collected by the carrier contact. The height of the carrier contact barrier can be adjusted by the collector bias. The experiments are done as a function of base width and provide a spectroscopy of the energy distribution of the injected carriers (which are essentially mono-energetic) after drifting a fixed distance. These experiments have shown that when the drift distances are ~ 1000 Å, the electrons suffer essentially no collisions during transit.

In the ballistic regime the electrons simply more according to the equation

$$\frac{\hbar \, d\boldsymbol{k}}{dt} = e\boldsymbol{F}. \tag{13.70}$$

In the case of GaAs in the presence of a strong electric field, the electrons would simply "climb up" on the E vs. $\boldsymbol{k}$ curve in the Γ-valley reading extremely high velocities. However, as time passes, the intervalley scattering starts to occur reducing the velocity towards the steady state value.

In Figure 13.15 we show some typical results for this "velocity overshoot" at various electric fields. It is important to note that the velocity overshoot persists up to a few picoseconds which is the transit time in many modern submicron GaAs devices. The Monte Carlo method is ideally suited to understanding the nonstationary transport in the transient regime. However, since it is usually very computer intensive, especially for device simulations, key parameters (e.g., average momentum and energy relaxation time, carrier temperature, etc.) are extracted from Monte Carlo methods and then used in simpler numerical techniques. We will discuss some of these aspects later on.

The results described for GaAs are typical of electron transport in most direct bandgap semiconductors. A material system that has become very important for high frequency microwave devices is $In_{0.53}Ga_{0.47}As$. This material has a very small carrier mass ($m^*/m_0 = 0.04$) and a large intervalley separation ($\Delta E_{L-X} \sim 0.55$ eV) which gives it a superior v–F relation than that of GaAs. Also, the velocity overshoot effects persist up to longer transit times and are also much stronger than in GaAs. Some results for this important system are shown in Figure 13.16.

13.5 HIGH FIELD ELECTRON TRANSPORT IN Si

In Si the electron transport is essentially described by the six equivalent valleys since the upper valleys are not occupied unless one is at extremely high fields ($F \geq 10^5$ V/cm). There is no negative differential resistance region. The transport is much poorer than in GaAs or InGaAs due to the very large density of states involved and the corresponding high scattering rate. Typical results for Si are shown in Figure 13.17.

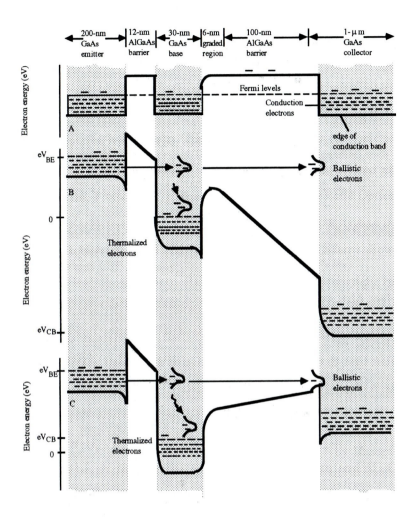

Figure 13.14: Energy band diagrams of the THETA device show how the ballistic electrons are launched, collected, and measured. When no voltages are applied to the emitter, base, and collector (A), none of the thermal electrons can flow across the AlGaAs barriers. When a voltage is applied across the emitter base barrier, the potential of the conduction electrons is raised so that they can tunnel through the AlGaAs barrier and enter the base at high energy (B). Some may collide with the crystal lattice and lose energy; others may travel through ballistically and enter the collector. Researchers have used this transistor as a spectrometer to measure the distribution of ballistic electrons by biasing the collector–base junction negatively (C), thus raising the potential barrier at the collector side. By adjusting the voltage, more and more electrons can be blocked and their distribution in energy can be measured. (Reproduced with permission, M. I. Nathan, et al., IEEE Spectrum, **22**, 45 (1986).)

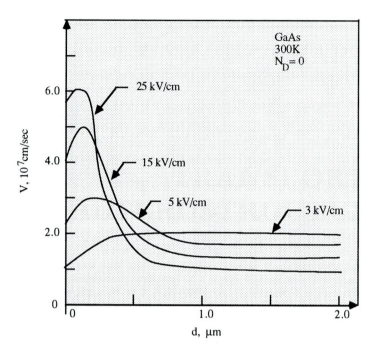

Figure 13.15: Velocity as a function of distance for electrons in GaAs at 300 K. It takes about 0.4 μm for the electrons to reach steady state. (Reproduced with permission, T. J. Maloney, et al., J. Appl. Phys., **48**, 781 (1977).)

13.6 HOLE TRANSPORT MONTE CARLO CALCULATIONS

In the Monte Carlo techniques described so far, the bandstructure and scattering rates involved in the simulation are available in analytic form. However, in the case of hole transport (or electron transport near breakdown) the above approximations and techniques are no longer viable as means to describe the system. Owing to the anisotropy of the valence band states (dominantly p-like and the small energy separation between the heavy, light, and split-off hole bands, completely numerical methods must be employed in determining both the bandstructure and the scattering rates. The bandstructure itself, is calculated from the valence band secular equation as described in Chapter 5. The scattering rates depend upon the initial trajectories and are obtained by numerically integrating the differential scattering rates over the final constant energy surface. The differential scattering rates, themselves, depend upon both the initial and final trajectories, separately.

The transport simulation procedure is a sequence of particle free flights under an accelerating electric field followed by a scattering event, repeated until a stable value of drift velocity is obtained. The duration of the free flight of the

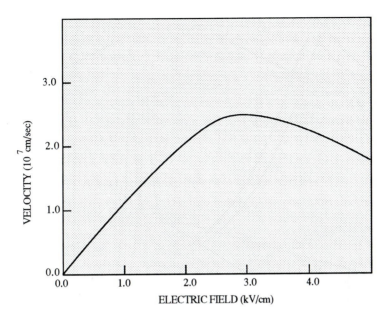

Figure 13.16: The velocity–field relations for $In_{0.53}Ga_{0.47}As$.

hole is determined in the usual way, with the aid of a self- scattering mechanism. However, the determination and resolution of the scattering event requires a detailed treatment.

Transport in, and coupling between, all three of the top valence bands (heavy hole, light hole, and split-off hole) have to be accounted for in general. The split-off band in Si (zone center spin–orbit splitting = 0.044 eV) influences transport both by strongly coupling with the heavy and light hole bands and thus affecting the bandstructure and by carrying a certain amount of the current at high fields. The inclusion of the split-off band, along with the heavy and light hole bands, leads to the consideration of three intra-band and six inter-band modes of scattering for each type of scattering process, such as acoustic phonon scattering.

The scattering rate for each mechanism (e.g. heavy hole to light hole via acoustic phonon scattering), is calculated on a mesh in k-space, which is designed to efficiently account for both the anisotropy and the symmetry of the system. On a particular mesh site, a calculated rate corresponds to the rate of scattering by the specified mechanism, of a particle whose initial wavevector terminates on the mesh site's position in reciprocal space. In materials with cubic O_h symmetry, such as unstrained Si and unstrained Ge, the scattering rates need only be calculated within an irreducible sector of the Brillouin zone such as that bounded by the Δ, Σ, and Λ axes, which corresponds to 1/48 of the full Brillouin zone. The scattering rate for a particle whose wavevector lies outside the irreducible sector may be obtained by transforming the particle's wavevector into the irreducible

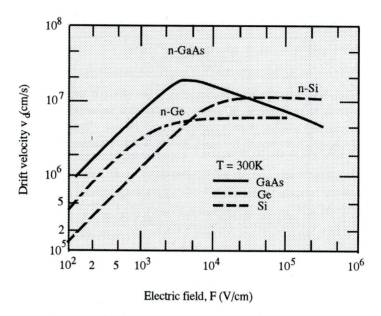

Figure 13.17: Velocity–field relation for Si, Ge and GaAs. Note that both Ge and Si have higher saturation velocities than GaAs. (after Jacoboni, et al, (1977); P. Smith, et al (1980); Ruch and Kino (1967)).

sector via one of the symmetry operations of the cubic O_h symmetry group, and then determining the rate from those calculated at specific wavevectors within this sector. Within each sector, specific radial axes or rays, which originate at the center of the Brillouin zone, are chosen. In the cubic system, for example, such rays might be the Δ([001]) axis, the Σ ([101]) axis, and the Λ ([111]) axis. Along each ray, mesh points are chosen to correspond to equal steps in particle energy. These mesh points may, therefore, be viewed as determining concentric constant energy surfaces. The set of rays constitutes an angular mesh in reciprocal space, while the set of mesh points at each energy increment along each ray constitutes a radial mesh. The two meshes are used together to divide the reciprocal space into prism shaped elements, bounded on the corners by mesh points at which are calculated the scattering rates.

The scattering rate associated with a particle after a simulated free flight is determined during Monte Carlo operation, by interpolation within the prism which contains the particle's wavevector. The interpolation is a weighted sum of the scattering rates on the six bounding mesh points. Each weighting factor is a product of two terms. The first term effects a linear interpolation in energy between the two triangular faces of the prism. The second term is formed by locating the position of the particle wavevector in the interior of the triangular prism face and dividing the prism face into three subtriangles $1'$, $2'$, $3'$. The three triangles are formed by drawing lines from the point at which the wavevector intersects the prism face to each of the three corners of the prism face. The weighting of a mesh point of the corner of the prism (e.g. corner 1) is then taken as the ratio of the area of the subtriangle opposite to this corner (e.g., subtriangle $1'$) to the total area of the prism face. This area ratio, multiplied by the factor of linear interpolation in energy, is used as a weighting factor for each of the six scattering rates on the bounding mesh points. The weighted scattering rates are then added to obtain the resulting scattering rate value for the given wavevector.

Once all of the relevant scattering rates have been determined for a given particle, the acting scattering mechanism is chosen in the standard way with the aid of the self-scattering mechanism, as outlined already. This determines the change in particle energy and possibly band, as a result of scattering. The second state of resolving a scattering event involves determining the orientation of the particle trajectory (i.e., wavevector) after scattering. For a given process (initial band, final band, scattering mechanism) and initial wavevector, the final particle trajectory is obtained with the aid of a post-scattering state probability distribution $P(\cos\theta_s, \phi_s)$, which is proportional to the differential scattering rate $dW_{m;n,n'}(\mathbf{k}, \mathbf{k}')/d\Omega'$

$$P(\cos\theta_s, \phi_s) = \left(dW_{m;n,n'}(\mathbf{k}, \mathbf{k}')/d\Omega'\right) / \max\left(dW_{m;n,n'}(\mathbf{k}, \mathbf{k}')/d\Omega'\right) \quad (13.71)$$

where the maximum is over all final wavevectors $\mathbf{k}'$, which lie on the constant final energy surface. The explicit dependence of the probability distribution on the scattering azimuth ϕ_s, must be retained since, generally, there is significant variation in $dW_{m;n,n'}(\mathbf{k}, \mathbf{k}')/d\Omega'$ for constant θ_s. The scattering angles θ_s and ϕ_s are chosen by the standard von Neumann method, using two random numbers to pick $\cos\theta_s$ and ϕ_s, and a third to accept or reject the chosen $(\cos\theta_s, \phi_s)$ pair. After the scattering angles are chosen, the final trajectory is determined by operating on the final wavevector by the inverse of the symmetry operation which carried the initial wavevector into the irreducible sector of the Brillouin zone.

As illustrations of hole transport, we will now discuss results based on Monte Carlo method for Si and Ge. Si has one of the poorest hole transports due to the very small spin–orbit splitting which results in a very high bandedge density of states. Ge on the other hand, has perhaps the best hole transport in semiconductors due to the small carrier mass and large spin–orbit splitting. In Figure 13.18 we show the population distribution for holes at various electric fields (along [100] direction) in Si and Ge at 300 K. The dashed line gives the thermodynamic equilibrium distribution (nondegenerate) at zero field. We see that the holes in Si remain very close to the thermodynamic value even at fairly high fields. In case of Ge, however, the hole distribution is broadened out considerably more.

While the previous results included the sum of the heavy, light, and split-off band distributions, it is found that the population is dominantly comprised of heavy holes. The relative occupations of the three bands are shown in Figures 13.19a (Si) and b (Ge). For Si, approximately 10% of the holes are in the

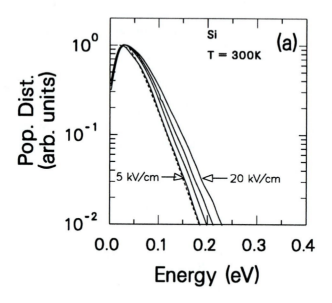

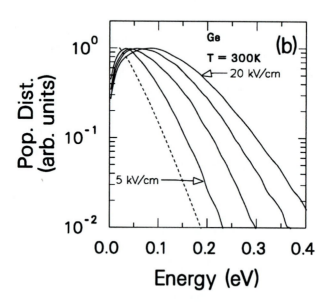

Figure 13.18: Si and Ge hole population energy distributions, at various electric fields in steps of 5 kV/cm, (from J. M. Hinckley and J. Singh, 1990).

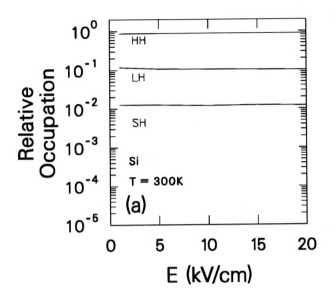

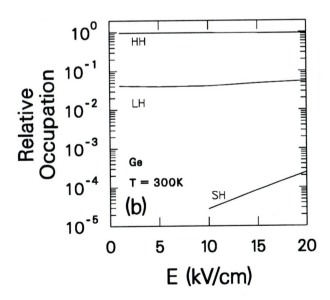

Figure 13.19: Bulk Si and Ge valence band occupation fractions as a function of electric field, (from J. M. Hinckley, 1990).

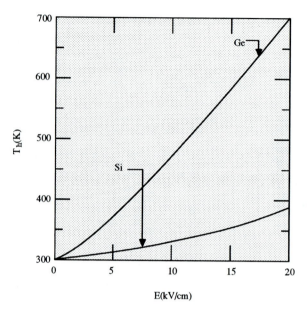

Figure 13.20: Effective hole temperature, for Si and Ge, (from J. M. Hinckley and J. Singh, 1990).

light hole band, 1% are in the split-off band, with the remainder being in the heavy hole band. Negligible variation is found with respect to electric field in the range studied. In the case of Ge, only approximately 5% of the holes are in the light hole band and virtually all of the rest are in the heavy hole band. Due to the larger spin–orbit splitting in Ge (0.28 eV in Ge vs. 0.044 eV in Si), the split-off band is negligibly populated, even at the highest field of 20kV/cm, where approximately 0.02% of the holes are in the split-off band. Although negligible in terms of transport characteristics, it is worth noting that the monotonic increase of an order of magnitude in the split-off band occupation between 10kV/cm and 20kV/cm corresponds closely to the order of magnitude increase in the population energy distribution at 0.28 eV between 10kV/cm and 20kV/cm. In contrast, the energy distribution between 1 and $2k_BT$ from the valence bandedge does not exhibit an order of magnitude variation with electric fields in the range considered. Thus, the occupation of the light and heavy hole bands in Ge and all three bands in Si are relatively invariant with electric field. The effective hole temperatures also represent the change of the carrier distributions and are shown for Si and Ge in Figure 13.20.

Finally, in Figure 13.21 we show the v–F relations for the holes in Si and Ge along with some experimentally measured results.

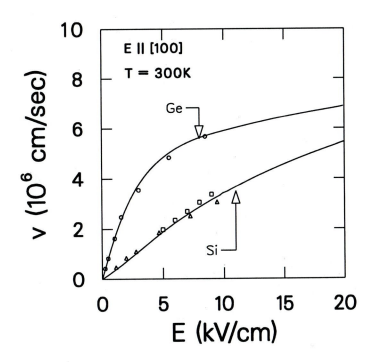

Figure 13.21: Si and Ge drift velocity vs. electric field relations. Also shown are experimental points, (from J. M. Hinckley and J. Singh, 1990; Experimental points: circles, triangles, Ryder, 1953; squares, Quaranta, et al., 1968).

13.7 BALANCE EQUATION APPROACH TO HIGH FIELD TRANSPORT

In the previous sections we discussed in some detail the Monte Carlo approach to study transport and some of the important results. The Monte Carlo approach provides the most versatile technique for transport studies at high fields not only for bulk semiconductors, but also for heterostructures as will be discussed in the next chapter. However, due to the computer intensive character of the Monte Carlo method, other numerical tools have been developed to study high field transport. These techniques are particularly useful for device simulations where the necessity of self-consistency forces one to study transport iteratively which requires numerous field dependent transport studies. In Chapter 10, we discussed some of the approximate methods to solve the Boltzmann transport equation. In particular we developed the balance equations for carrier density, carrier momentum, and carrier energy. These equations are extremely useful in providing a simple description of the high field transport in semiconductors. We will only give a flavor of these approximate approaches since this field of study is quite broad and is motivated more by fast convergence of results and therefore has numerous mathematical details which we shall not address.

An approach often used is dependent on the momentum and energy balance equations written for the displaced Maxwellian carrier distribution. The carrier distribution in turn is described by the carrier temperature as discussed in Chapter 10. We will briefly recall some of those results and describe the approach used for high field transport. The displaced Maxwellian distribution function has the general form

$$f \approx e^{-|\mathbf{p}-m^*\mathbf{v}_d|^2/(2m^*k_BT_C)} \tag{13.72}$$

where T_C is the carrier temperature. In Chapter 10, we showed that the energy argument of Equation 13.72 can be expanded to give

$$
\begin{aligned}
f &= e^{-(p^2-2m^*\mathbf{p}\cdot\mathbf{v}_d+m^{*2}v_d^2)/(k_BT_C)} \\
&\approx \exp\left\{-\left[p^2/(2m^*k_BT_C)\right]\right\}\left[1+\frac{\mathbf{p}\cdot\mathbf{v}_d}{k_BT_C}\right].
\end{aligned} \tag{13.73}
$$

This simplification is valid if the drift part of the energy, $m^*v_d^2/2$, is small compared to the total energy of the electron distribution. This is usually true since $v_d \sim 10^7$ cm s^{-1}, i.e., $m^*v_d^2/2$ is of the order of 20–30 meV while the average energy of the electron is approximately 200–300 meV at high fields. As shown by Equation 10.120, the kinetic energy is given essentially by the carrier temperature

$$W_{zz} = \frac{1}{2}k_BT_C. \tag{13.74}$$

The diffusion coefficient also takes on a simple form (Equation 10.122)

$$D = \frac{k_BT_C}{e}\mu. \tag{13.75}$$

The approach based on the drifted Maxwellian assumptions are called the electron temperature approach since the unknown is the electron temperature. The balance equations for energy and momentum are used to solve the problem. The velocity under steady state conditions with uniform electric field is (Equation 10.117)

$$v_z = \frac{e}{m^* \ll 1/\tau_m \gg}F_z. \tag{13.76}$$

The energy balance equation then gives for steady state conditions

$$\frac{J_zF_z}{n} = \ll \frac{1}{\tau_E} \gg \left(\frac{3}{2}k_BT_C - \frac{3}{2}k_BT_L\right) \tag{13.77}$$

which gives us for the carrier temperature

$$\frac{T_C}{T_L} = 1 + \frac{2e^2}{3k_B T_L m^*} \frac{F_z^2}{\ll 1/\tau_m \gg \ll 1/\tau_E \gg}. \tag{13.78}$$

To solve for the drift velocity and the carrier temperature, one has to evaluate the averaged relaxation times which further requires the knowledge of the distribution function. In the displaced Maxwellian approach by ignoring the drift part, the relaxation times can be calculated in terms of the carrier temperature. For example, we showed that if a particular scattering process has a energy dependence given through the scattering time of

$$\tau = \tau_0 \left(\frac{E}{k_B T_C} \right)^s \tag{13.79}$$

then we have

$$\ll \frac{1}{\tau_m} \gg = \frac{1}{\tau_0} \frac{\Gamma(5/2)}{\Gamma(s + 5/2)}. \tag{13.80}$$

A similar solution can be obtained for the energy relaxation time. Iterative self-consistent approaches can then be developed to solve the balance equations. Usually one has to compare the results of the balance equation with the Monte Carlo results to make sure that the assumptions made are valid.

It is illustrative to examine the dependence of mobility of carriers on carrier temperature and electric field in the electron temperature approach. While this approach is not as accurate as the Monte Carlo approach, it provides good semi-quantitative fits. Consider the case where the transport is limited by acoustic phonon scattering. The scattering time is given by

$$\begin{aligned}
\tau_m &= \frac{\pi \hbar^4 c_\ell}{\sqrt{2}\,(m^*)^{3/2}\,D^2} \frac{E^{-1/2}}{k_B T_L} \\
&= \frac{\pi \hbar^4 c_\ell}{\sqrt{2}\,(m^*)^{3/2}\,D^2} \frac{1}{(k_B T_L)^{3/2}} \left(\frac{T_L}{T_C} \right)^{1/2} \left[\frac{E}{k_B T_C} \right]^{-1/2} \\
&= \tau_0(T_C) \left[\frac{E}{k_B T_C} \right]^{-1/2} \tag{13.81}
\end{aligned}$$

The constant $\tau_0(T_C)$ is given by

$$\tau_0(T_C) = \tau_0(T_L) \sqrt{\frac{T_L}{T_C}}. \tag{13.82}$$

We then have

$$\ll \frac{1}{\tau_m} \gg = \ll \frac{1}{\tau_m^0} \gg \sqrt{\frac{T_C}{T_L}}$$

or

$$\mu(T_C) = \mu_n^0 \sqrt{\frac{T_L}{T_C}}. \tag{13.83}$$

The mobility thus decreases as the carriers get hotter.

In the case of mobility limited by ionized impurity scattering, the energy dependence is $E^{3/2}$ for the scattering time. The use of the electron temperature approach then gives

$$\mu_n(T_C) = \mu_n^0 \left[\frac{T_C}{T_L}\right]^{3/2} \tag{13.84}$$

and the mobility increases with carrier temperature. It must be remembered that these expressions are valid in case the density of states does not alter with increased energy in a manner other than $E^{1/2}$. In the case of III–V direct bandgap materials, we know that the presence of the satellite valleys can abruptly alter the density of states so that the equations would be invalid once the electrons transfer to the upper valleys.

For electrons in materials like Si, where intervalley scattering dominates transport, the energy relaxation time can be estimated to be given by

$$\ll \frac{1}{\tau_E} \gg \approx \frac{2}{3} \frac{C}{k_B T_L} \sqrt{\frac{T_L}{T_C}} \tag{13.85}$$

where C $\sim 10^{-8}$ W for Si. Using the energy balance Equation 13.78 and a momentum relaxation time given by acoustic phonons, one gets

$$\frac{T_C}{T_L} = 1 + \frac{e\mu^0 F^2}{C} \tag{13.86}$$

Defining a field

$$F_{\rm cr} = \sqrt{\frac{C}{e\mu^0}} \tag{13.87}$$

which has a value of 7 kV/cm for Si, we get

$$\frac{T_L}{T_C} = 1 + \left(\frac{F}{F_{\rm cr}}\right). \tag{13.88}$$

The corresponding mobility is then

$$\mu(\boldsymbol{F}) = \frac{\mu^0}{\sqrt{1 + (F/F_{\rm cr})}}. \tag{13.89}$$

The mobility decreases as $1/F$ at high electric fields, causing the velocity to saturate. The interested reader is advised to use the references listed in this chapter to study more details of how the balance equation approach is used in transport studies.

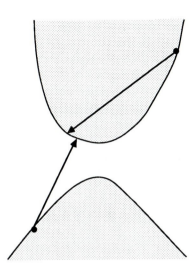

Figure 13.22: The impact ionization process where a high energy electron scatters from a valence band electron producing two conduction band electrons and a hole. Hot holes can undergo a similar process.

13.8 IMPACT IONIZATION IN SEMICONDUCTORS

In the discussions on transport so far we have assumed that the charged carrier remains in the same band. At very high fields ($F > 10^5$ V/cm), this assumption breaks down. We discussed the problem of impact ionization in Chapter 11. As shown in Figure 13.22, in this process hot electrons (holes) scatter from holes (electrons) via the Coulombic interaction to excite the hole (electron) from the valence band (construction band) to the conduction band (valence band). The number of excess free carriers thus increases (called carrier multiplication) causing a runaway current. This is often called the breakdown phenomenon.

The impact ionization process can be included in a Monte Carlo approach just as another scattering mechanism. While this is simple in principle, it is somewhat tedious in practice. The reason for the difficulty is that the energies required for the impact ionization to start is quite high as shown in Chapter 11. At these high energies the bandstructure is no longer described by simple analytical methods. One needs to use a numerical approach such as the one described in our section on hole transport. While this can be carried out, there are other important changes in the physics of the problem which make the results somewhat questionable. The bandstructure itself, at such high electric fields, may be distorted. Also the collision rates are so high at such high carrier energies that the use of the Fermi golden rule becomes questionable. The δ-function in the golden rule arises from the assumption that the perturbation exists for a long time. One has to relax the energy conservation rule for very short duration collisions at high rates. Also the assumption that the collision time is essentially zero during which the electric field has no influence on the electrons, becomes questionable at such high electric fields. This effect (intracollisional field effect) also causes the simple Monte Carlo method to develop inaccuracies. Nevertheless, reasonable results which shed light on the impact ionization phenomenon can be obtained by Monte Carlo methods.

For device applications, one is usually interested in the impact ionization coefficient defined by the equation

$$\frac{\partial I}{\partial t} = \alpha_t I$$

or

$$\frac{\partial I}{\partial Z} = \alpha_z I \tag{13.90}$$

where I is the current and a represents an average rate of ionization per unit time (α_t) or unit distance (α_z). The average is taken over the distribution function.

$$\alpha_t = \frac{\int_{-\infty}^{\infty} d^3k f(\mathbf{k})/\tau_I}{\int_{-\infty}^{\infty} d^3k f(\mathbf{k})} \tag{13.91}$$

where $1/\tau_I$ is the impact ionization rate given in Chapter 11. For the steady state case, with uniform time and space dependence

$$\alpha_z = \alpha_\tau/v_d. \tag{13.92}$$

Because of the high energy required for impact ionization only the high energy tail of the distribution function is responsible for the impact ionization coefficient. The scattering processes are extremely important in determining this high energy tail. For example, in the presence of very strong scattering, the electrons will find it difficult to reach the higher energies required and the material will not breakdown. While Monte Carlo techniques can adequately address the impact ionization problem, a number of analytical and numerical theories have been developed to describe the high energy part of the electron distribution. Since once the electron reaches energies above threshold, it has a very high probability to impact ionize, these theories are able to describe the semiquantitative features of the breakdown phenomenon. We will not discuss the details of these approximation schemes, but will simply provide the functional dependence of the ionization coefficient on the applied electric field.

In the first theoretical work on impact ionization coefficients, Wolff assumed that electrons experience only two types of collisions: collisions with optical phonons and collisions with the lattice that produce impact ionization. In his solution of the Boltzmann equation, Wolff argued that the mean free path for ionizing collisions would be much smaller than that for phonon collisions. This would tend to keep the electron velocity distribution almost spherically symmetric (that is, a displaced Maxwellian distribution), especially at high electric fields.

For some parabolic bands and phonon scattering, we can, therefore, use the carrier temperature as given earlier. However, this approach is not self-consistent since we need to include impact ionization itself as a scattering mechanism. In other words, one needs to include an average energy loss due to impact ionization into the energy balance equation. If the electrons lose all their energy due to the ionization (which is only approximately true) the loss is given by

$$\int_{-\infty}^{+\infty} d^3k \, \frac{E}{\tau_I} \, f_0(\boldsymbol{k}). \tag{13.93}$$

This term can be evaluated using τ_I from Chapter 11, and can then be added to the energy balance equation. Following this approach, one finds

$$\alpha_t \propto \exp(-\text{const}/F^2) \tag{13.94}$$

where the square of the electric field enters due to its relation to the carrier temperature. This result is found to be valid only for large F.

For small F a large number of experimental results exhibit a dependence

$$\alpha_t \propto \exp(-\text{const}/F). \tag{13.95}$$

This dependence was explained by Shockley. Shockley's idea was that only those electrons that do not interact with phonons contribute to impact ionization. This means that impact ionization is not caused by the spherical part of the distribution function, or by high electron temperature, but by those electrons that do not scatter until they are at the ionization threshold where they ionize instantaneously. The probability P that an electron is not scattered is given by Equation 13.28. We can write

$$
\begin{aligned}
\frac{dE}{dt} &= \frac{dE}{dk}\frac{dk}{dt} \\
&= \frac{dE}{dk} \cdot \frac{e\boldsymbol{F}}{\hbar}.
\end{aligned}
\tag{13.96}
$$

This gives, with the definition of the total scattering rate by phonons $1/\tau_{\text{tot}}^{\text{ph}}$, the probability for the electron to survive up to threshold energy

$$P = \exp\left\{ -\frac{\hbar}{eF} \int_0^{E_{\text{th}}} \left(\frac{dE}{dk}\right)^{-1} \frac{1}{t_{\text{tot}}^{\text{ph}}(E)} dE \right\}. \tag{13.97}$$

Shockley assumed that the electrons start over at $k = 0$ at $t = 0$. However, the general solution of the equation of motion is

$$\boldsymbol{k} = e\boldsymbol{F}t/\hbar + \boldsymbol{k}_0. \tag{13.98}$$

so that the electron does not start from $k = 0$ but rather from $k = \boldsymbol{k}_0$, corresponding to some average energy E of the electrons in the electric field. Overall a heated electron gas is established in which the electrons at the upper energy tail cause avalanche (so-called "lucky" electrons). Since the electrons do not start at $E = 0$ but rather at some average energy that in GaAs and Si is typically 1 eV at $F = 500$ kV/cm. One must replace the lower limit of integration in Equation 13.97 by an average energy equal to $3k_BT_C/2$, where T_C is approximately the carrier temperature.

The coefficient α_z is, according to Equation 13.90, the inverse of the mean free distance L_I^* that an electron travels without ionizing. The distance L_I that is necessary to reach threshold without scattering is obtained from

$$E_{\text{th}} = e \int_0^{L_I} F(z)dz. \tag{13.99}$$

To proceed we need to specify the z-dependence of the electric field F, which is determined by the device configuration. To avoid the complications of z-dependent F, which also enters Equation 13.88, we neglect the z-dependence here ($F = \text{constant}$) and discuss its consequences briefly below. Then we have

$$L_I = E_{\text{th}}/eF. \tag{13.100}$$

If we divide L_I by the probability that an electron travels without collision, we obtain L_I^* and α_z

$$\begin{aligned} \alpha_z &= 1/L_I^* \\ &= \frac{eF}{E_{\text{th}}} \exp\left\{ \frac{\hbar}{eF} \int_{\frac{3}{2}kT_C}^{E_{\text{th}}} \left(\frac{dE}{dk}\right)^{-1} \frac{1}{\tau_{\text{tot}}^{\text{ph}}(E)} dE \right\}. \end{aligned} \tag{13.101}$$

A physical expression for the ionization rate is given by

$$\alpha(F) = (eF/E_{th}) \exp\left\{ -F_I / [F(1 + F/F_p) + F_{kT}] \right\} \tag{13.102}$$

where E_I is the high field, effective ionization threshold energy, and F_{kT}, F_p, and F_I are threshold fields for carriers to overcome the decelerating effects of thermal, optical phonon, and ionization scattering, respectively. Over a limited field range, Equation 13.102 can be reduced to

$$\begin{aligned} \alpha(F) &= (eF/E_{th}) \exp(-F_I/F) &&, \text{if } F_p > F > F_{kT} \\ &= (eF/E_{th}) \exp(-F_I F_p/F^2), &&\text{if } F > F_p \\ &&&\text{and } F > \sqrt{F_p F_{kT}}. \end{aligned} \tag{13.103}$$

Figure 13.23a shows the experimental results of the ionization rates for Ge and Si. Figure 13.23b shows the measured ionization rates of GaAs and a few other III–V binary and ternary compounds. These results are obtained by using photomultiplication measurements on p-n junctions. Note that for certain semiconductors, such as GaAs, the ionization rate is a function of crystal orientation. Note that

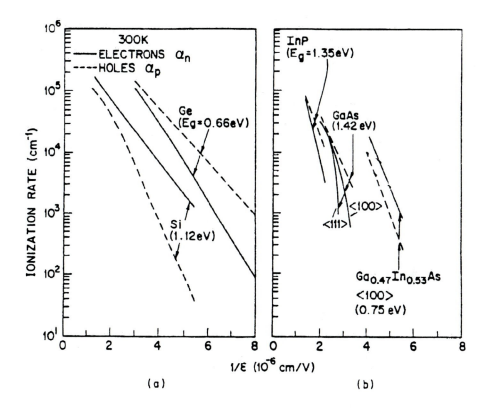

Figure 13.23: Ionization rates at 300 K versus reciprocal electric field for Ge, Si, GaAs, $In_{0.53}Ga_{0.47}As$, and InP. (After Logan and Sze (1966); Grant (1973); Pearsall et al (1978); Umebu et al (1980); Pearsall (1980)).

Equation 13.103 is applicable to most semiconductors shown in Figure 13.23, except GaAs and GaP, for which Equation 13.103 is applicable.

The temperature dependence of the ionization rate can be studied by extending theoretical work by Baraff (1962, 1964). Baraff introduced a three parameter model. The parameters are: E_{th}, the ionization threshold energy; λ, the optical phonon mean free path; and $< E_p >$, the average energy loss per phonon scattering. The values λ and $< E_p >$ are given by

$$\lambda = \lambda_0 \tanh\left(\frac{E_p}{2k_BT}\right) \tag{13.104}$$

$$< E_p >= E_p \tanh\left(\frac{E_p}{2k_BT}\right) \tag{13.105}$$

and

$$\frac{\lambda}{\lambda_0} = \frac{< E_p >}{E_p} \qquad (13.106)$$

where E_p is the optical phonon energy, and λ_0 is the high- energy low-temperature asymptotic value of the phonon mean free path. Since the electrons suffer more collisions as temperature increases, the impact ionization coefficient decreases with temperature. It must be noted, though, that the bandgap decreases with temperature, as well. This tends to increase the coefficient. Overall, however, it is seen that the impact ionization rate does, indeed, decrease with temperature.

13.9   ZENER-BLOCH OSCILLATIONS

In the discussion so far on transport, we discussed the effects of scattering on the response of electrons to an electric field. It is interesting to look at the electron response in absence of any scattering. We briefly mentioned this in the discussion of ballistic transport. The equation of motion is simply

$$\frac{\hbar d\mathbf{k}}{dt} = e\mathbf{F}. \qquad (13.107)$$

In the absence of any collisions the electron will simply start from the bottom of the band (Figure 13.24) and go along the E vs. $\mathbf{k}$ curve until it reaches the Brillouin zone edge. As discussed in Chapter 4, the bandstructure E vs $\mathbf{k}$ is represented within the first Brillouin zone since it is periodic in k-space. The electron at the zone edge is thus "reflected" as shown in Figure 13.26c and now starts to lose energy in its motion in the field. The k-direction of the electron changes sign as the electron passes through the zone edge representing oscillations in k-space and consequently in the real space. These oscillations are called the Zener-Bloch oscillations.

If the electric field is along the direction of the reciprocal vector $\Gamma = 2\pi/a$, the frequency of this oscillation is

$$\omega = \frac{eFa}{\hbar}. \qquad (13.108)$$

The oscillation frequency is quite high and can easily be in the several terrahertz regime. Due to this possibility of high frequency oscillations, there is a tremendous interest in this phenomenon. Unfortunately, since the scattering mechanisms are usually strong enough to cause the electron to scatter before it can go through a complete oscillation, it has not been possible to observe these oscillations. Also, at high electric fields, the tunneling between bands is quite strong, reducing the possibility of oscillations.

The Bloch oscillations are localized in space and the electron function is centered on a particular unit cell. The simple plane wave description is no longer adequate since the presence of the electric field causes a perturbation in the bands making $\mathbf{k}$ in the direction of the field no longer a good quantum number. It is

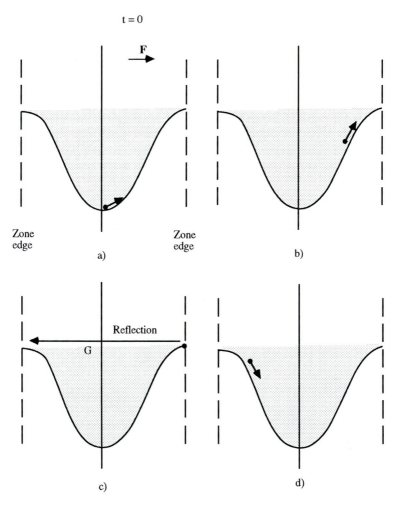

Figure 13.24: A schematic showing how an electron starting at $t = 0$ at the bottom of the Γ-valley travels up the E vs. k diagram and gets reflected at the zone edge.

easy to see the nature of the state in presence of the field by using perturbation theory. The equation satisfied by the electron is

$$(H_0 - e\boldsymbol{F} \cdot \boldsymbol{r})\psi_b = E_b \psi_b \qquad (13.109)$$

where H_0 is the Hamiltonian that leads to the zero-field bandstructure and E_b are the energy levels (say, measured from the bandedge). The general wavefunction is

$$\psi_b = \frac{1}{\sqrt{V}} \sum_{\mathbf{k}} C_{\mathbf{k}} \, \phi_{\mathbf{k}}(\boldsymbol{r}) \qquad (13.110)$$

where $\phi_{\mathbf{k}}(\boldsymbol{r})$ are the unperturbed Bloch functions for the crystal. Substituting

ψ_b in Equation 13.109 and taking a dot product with $\phi_{\mathbf{k}'}$ we have

$$C_{\mathbf{k}'} = \sum_{\mathbf{k}} \frac{C_{\mathbf{k}} \langle \mathbf{k}' | (-e\mathbf{F} \cdot \mathbf{r}) | \mathbf{k} \rangle}{E_b - E_{\mathbf{k}'}}. \tag{13.111}$$

The matrix element to be determined is

$$M_{\mathbf{kk}'} = -\frac{e\mathbf{F}}{(2\pi)^3} \cdot V \int d^3k \; e^{-i\mathbf{k}' \cdot \mathbf{r}} \; C_{\mathbf{k}} \; \mathbf{r} \; e^{i\mathbf{k} \cdot \mathbf{r}}. \tag{13.112}$$

We use the identity

$$\mathbf{r} e^{i\mathbf{k} \cdot \mathbf{r}} = -i \nabla_{\mathbf{k}} e^{i\mathbf{k} \cdot \mathbf{r}} \tag{13.113}$$

and integrate by parts using the orthogonality of the plane waves to get

$$\sum_{\mathbf{k}} C_{\mathbf{k}} \langle \mathbf{k}' | (-e\mathbf{F} \cdot \mathbf{r}) | \mathbf{k} \rangle = -e\mathbf{F} \; \nabla_{\mathbf{k}} C_{\mathbf{k}} \; \delta_{\mathbf{kk}'}.$$

This gives upon substitution in Equation 13.111

$$\frac{dC_{\mathbf{k}}}{d\mathbf{k}} = \frac{i(E_b - E_{\mathbf{k}})C_{\mathbf{k}}}{e F}$$

or

$$C_{\mathbf{k}} = C_0 \exp \left\{ \int \frac{i(E_b - E_{\mathbf{k}})}{e F} d\mathbf{k} \right\}. \tag{13.114}$$

We recall that $E_{\mathbf{k}}$ is periodic in k-space. The localized function ψ_b must be periodic in unit cells, i.e., for the same value of E_b measured from the bandedge there have to be series of degenerate energy levels which are simply centered around different unit cells. To retain this periodicity, the function $C_{\mathbf{k}}$ must be periodic.

Choosing

$$E_{\mathbf{k}} = E_0 + E(\mathbf{k}) \tag{13.115}$$

where E_0 is the bandedge, we get a periodic value for C_0 if

$$E_b - E_0 = -eFna \tag{13.116}$$

where n is an integer and a is the unit cell dimension. Thus, the wavefunction which has an energy E_b is centered around the unit cell at the point na ($= r_0$). This gives us

$$C_{\mathbf{k}} = C_0 \exp \left\{ -(\mathbf{k} \cdot \mathbf{r}_0) + \int \frac{E(\mathbf{k})}{e F} d\mathbf{k} \right\} \tag{13.117}$$

and the wavefunction is

$$\psi_b = \frac{1}{\sqrt{V}} C_0 \sum_{\mathbf{k}} u_{\mathbf{k}}(\mathbf{r}) \exp \left\{ i \int \frac{E(\mathbf{k})}{e F} d\mathbf{k} - i\mathbf{k} \cdot (\mathbf{r}_0 - \mathbf{r}) \right\} \tag{13.118}$$

where $u_{\mathbf{k}}(\mathbf{r})$ is the central cell part of the states.

Let us examine a simple s-band tight-binding case considered for a simple cubic structure (see discussions in Chapter 3). We use for the bandstructure the relation

$$E(\boldsymbol{k}) = \frac{-E_B}{2} \cos ka \text{ for } \frac{-\pi}{a} < k < \frac{\pi}{a} \tag{13.119}$$

where E_B is the width of the bandwidth. For the s-band case the central cell part $u(\boldsymbol{r})$ has no k-dependence. We get

$$\begin{aligned}
\psi_b &= \frac{1}{\sqrt{V}} C_0 \, u(\boldsymbol{r}) \sum_{\boldsymbol{k}} \exp\left\{ -\frac{iE_B}{2eFa} - i\boldsymbol{k} \cdot (\boldsymbol{r} - \boldsymbol{r}_0) \right\} \\
&= C \, J_m(E_B/2eFa)
\end{aligned} \tag{13.120}$$

where C is a constant and $m = (x_0 - x)/a$, and the field is along the x-axis. The J's are Bessel functions, which can be written in the series form

$$J_m(z) = z^m \sum_{\ell=0}^{\infty} \frac{(-1)^\ell \, z^{2\ell}}{2^{2\ell+m} \, \ell! \, (m+\ell)!} \tag{13.121}$$

when $m = (x_0 - x)/a$ is a large number we get an asymptotic limit, with $L_b = E_B/2eF$

$$J_m\left(\frac{L_b}{a}\right) \approx \frac{(-1)^{|x_0-x|/a}}{2\pi \left[|x_0 - x|/a\right]^{1/2}} \left[\frac{e_n L_b}{2 |x_0 - x|}\right] \tag{13.122}$$

i.e., the function rapidly decays. For small m, the function has a maxima $a |x_0 - x| = L_b/2$. The general nature of these functions is shown in Figure 13.25. The form of the wavefunction is similar to that of the harmonic oscillators with the functions peaked at the classical turning points as shown.

Due to the potential applications of the Bloch oscillations, a considerable amount of work has focussed on their realization. However, these attempts have not been successful. The reason for this is the scattering processes and interband transitions which do not allow the coherent movement of the electrons that is necessary for the oscillations to occur. A reduction in the width of a band can reduce the spatial distance L_b the electrons must transit during the oscillations. The frequency ω_b is correspondingly larger and the conditions

$$\omega_b \tau_{SC} \geq 1 \tag{13.123}$$

where τ_{SC} is the scattering time can, therefore, be satisfied more easily thus allowing the oscillations to occur. The width of the band can be reduced by using superlattice concepts as we discussed in Chapter 6. This possibility has been one of the many motivations to study superlattices.

In the last several chapters we discussed transport issues in bulk semiconductors. Transport is controlled by the scattering mechanisms which, in turn, depend upon the scattering potential and the bandstructure via the density of states. Both of these can be altered by using heterostructure concepts. In the next chapter we will discuss how transport is altered in the heterostructures.

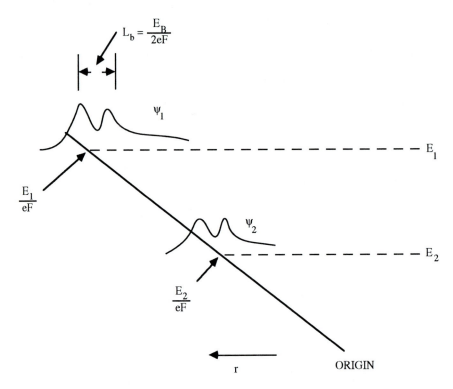

Figure 13.25: A schematic of the wavefunctions at different energy levels. The functions have a form similar to the harmonic oscillator and represent the oscillation in real space with periods of $L_b = E_B/(2eF)$ where E_B is the width of the band.

13.10   FOR THE TECHNOLOGIST IN YOU

The velocity–field relations for electrons (holes) in a semiconductor are the most important manifestation of the semiconductor properties as far as speed of electronic devices is concerned. Of course, as discussed in the text for submicron devices, there is no one-to-one correspondence between velocity and local electric field. It is useful to examine the field profiles under which electrons (holes) move in two important device structures: a) the unipolar devices where modulation of current is carried out by a gate using depletion of change (e.g. MESFETs, MOSFETs, i.e., field effect transistors) and b) the bipolar devices where current modulation is carried out by changing the barrier which the electrons (holes) have to cross to flow to from the emitter to the collector. These field profiles are shown schematically in Figure 13.26.

In the case of the FET structure, the electric field is low in the source–gate region and reaches very high fields (up to 105 V/cm, depending upon the source–drain bias and the device dimensions) near the gate–drain region.

In the n-p-n HBT, the field through which electrons move in the base region

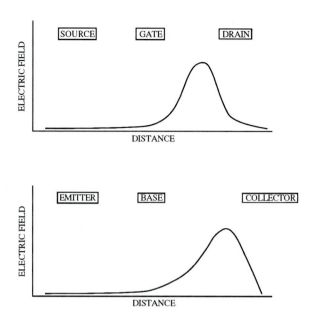

Figure 13.26: A schematic of the electric field strength as a function of distance in a typical FET and HBT structure. Low field transport can be significantly improved by using materials with lower carrier mass and/or low-temperature operation. (Reproduced with permission, H. Hasegawa, et al., *Ext. Abs. 16*[th] *Int. Conf. Sol. St. Dev. Mat.*, Kobe, Japan, (1984).)

is quite low while it becomes quite high as the electrons reaches the collector region. The majority carrier transport in the base is at low electric fields as well.

From our discussions in this chapter we have seen that low electric field transport is very sensitive to material properties and can be improved considerably by removing scattering processes such as ionized impurity scattering, acoustic phonons, etc. Thus, one can improve the transport in the low field regions of devices by going to faster materials and/or low temperatures. Of course, one must ensure that carrier freezeout is not a problem at low temperatures. The high field transport (steady state) is relatively independent of material systems and temperature. Thus, there is not as much improvement in this region of the device if material system is changed or temperature is lowered.

For the submicron devices where overshoot effects are important, the transport in low and high field regions are strongly coupled and therefore improvements are present at both low and high fields if one uses a "faster" material or lower temperature.

Let us discuss a few specific issues which are of great importance in device technology.

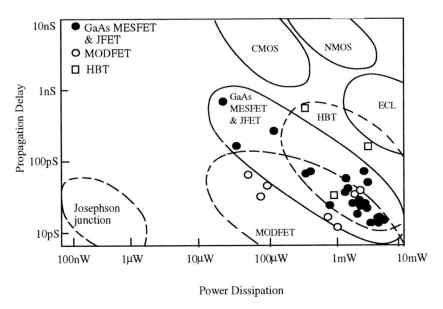

Figure 13.27: Power and delay time for different high speed technologies, (from H. Hasegawa, et al, 1984).

13.10.1   Some Device-Related Issues

Power–Speed Issues in Digital Technology

An extremely important issue in high density digital technology is the power dissipated in a transistor and the switching speed. The power– speed issue is an important parameter in the success of new technologies. To minimize the power dissipated, the drain bias is kept as small as possible. This consideration gives GaAs an advantage over Si, due to the difference in their v–F curves. Consider for example, a device biased at 0.25 V and having a device dimension of 1.0 μm. The average channel field is then 2.5 kV/cm, so that the Si channel velocity is approximately 1×10^6 cm/s while for GaAs it is approximately 2×10^7 cm/s. The channel transit time for Si is then approximately 0.1 ns, while for GaAs it is approximately 5 ps. These advantages grow as the device dimensions shrink, since GaAs displays significant velocity overshoot effects for short channels. Of course, one must remember that Si has a great advantage due to the ease of processing. Also, in Si, one can use CMOS technology which uses n- and p-type devices. The CMOS dissipates power only during switching. Thus, for static (e.g. memory) applications, CMOS is difficult to beat. However, for high speed applications, GaAs has the advantage over Si.

The power–delay relationship for a number of device technologies is shown in Figure 13.27. As can be seen, considerable improvement is achieved as one moves from Si to GaAs and then to MODFETs. The best performance occurs in Josephson junction devices which, however, have to be cooled to temperatures of ~ 15–20 K. Advances in high temperature superconductors may have an important impact in making the Josephson technology suitable for digital applications.

Power Output–High Frequency Operation in Field Effect Transistors

One of the important applications of transistors is power amplification. Power amplifiers seek to maximize output power at high frequencies. In the field effect transistor (FET), this translates into driving the transistor at as high a source–drain voltage, V_{DS}, as possible (see Chapter 19 for a brief description of the FET). The maximum voltage that can be applied is determined by the breakdown electric field. An additional consideration for such amplifiers is the cutoff frequency f_T which is approximately given by

$$f_T = \frac{v_s}{2\pi L_{\text{eff}}} \tag{13.124}$$

where v_s is the saturation velocity for the electrons and L_{eff} is the effective channel length between the source and the drain. Assuming for simplicity that the field inside the channel is uniform (actually the field is highly non-uniform and a proper numerical simulation need to be done to get accurate results), the product of the maximum V_{DS} ($= V_B$) and the cutoff frequency is

$$
\begin{aligned}
V_B f_T &= \frac{V_B}{L_{\text{eff}}} \frac{v_s}{2\pi} \\
&\approx \frac{F_m v_s}{2\pi}
\end{aligned}
\tag{13.125}
$$

where F_m is the maximum field at which the breakdown phenomenon becomes significant (say at the field where $\alpha \approx 10^4$ cm^{-1}). The values of F_m depend upon the bandgap and to some extent, doping. As doping increases, the scattering also increases, reducing the probability that electrons will be able to overcome the threshold energy for impact ionization. In Figure 13.28 we show the approximate values of the maximum allowable voltage as a function of cutoff frequency for several semiconductors. The results are based on the work of Geis, et al., 1988, and clearly show the advantages of materials like diamond and SiC for high frequency power amplifiers.

Carrier Multiplication and Noise in Avalanche Photodetectors

An important detector configuration for measuring optical signals is a *p-i-n* diode biased under strong reverse bias. The applied bias is so strong that any electron or hole created can impact ionize, causing multiplication and consequently a very high gain can be achieved. An important concern in this device is the noise introduced by the carrier multiplication process. The noise generated in the avalanche photodetector (APD) is strongly controlled by the α/β ratio in the

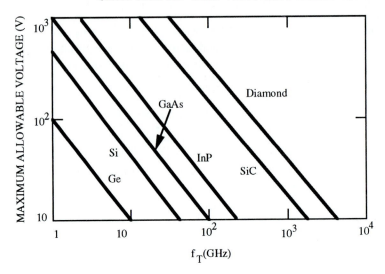

Figure 13.28: Maximum allowable junction voltage as a function of cutoff frequency.

semiconductor. Some of the motivation for using MQW structures to alter α/β discussed in Chapter 14 comes from the desire to suppress noise.

An important source of noise in devices is the shot noise which comes about due to the random and discrete nature of the electron flow. If a device has a mean current $\bar{I}$ flowing through it and one probes the number of electrons passing through a cross section of the device in a time Δt, on an average, this number is

$$\bar{n}(\Delta t) = \frac{\bar{I}\,\Delta t}{e}. \tag{13.126}$$

However, since the current is carried by the discrete electrons which are flowing randomly, one has a fluctuation in this number. As a result, the current has a root mean square fluctuation, called shot noise, I_{sh}. The noise value depends upon the measurement time Δt or the bandwidth Δf. If the bandwidth increases, the fluctuations are more significant. Simple statistical arguments show that the shot noise is given by

$$I_{sh} = \sqrt{2e\bar{I}\,\Delta f}. \tag{13.127}$$

In an APD, this is the noise level if no carrier multiplication occurs. The multiplication process introduces further noise. We will consider a steady state situation in which an electron current $i_e(0)$ is injected into a depletion layer of width W at $x = 0$, as shown in Figure 13.29. We assume that there is no photogeneration in the depletion region where only charge multiplication produces additional carriers. The rate of generation of the current (we assume that all the charges move at saturation velocity) is

$$\frac{di_e(x)}{dx} = \alpha i_e(x) + \beta i_h(x) \tag{13.128}$$

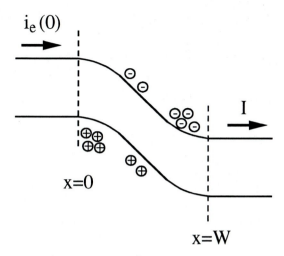

Figure 13.29: The depletion region with high field in an APD. Electrons are injected at $x = 0$ and the impact ionization causes carrier multiplication. The device has high gain as a result, although the random processes involved cause a high noise level.

where i_e and i_h are the electron and hole currents, respectively. The total current I is a constant

$$i_e(x) + i_h(x) = I. \tag{13.129}$$

Using this equality, we get

$$\frac{di_e(x)}{dx} = \frac{i_e(0) + \int_0^x \beta I \exp[-\int_0^{x'} (\alpha - \beta) dx''] dx'}{-\int_0^x (\alpha - \beta) dx'}. \tag{13.130}$$

The electron multiplication factor is defined as

$$M_e = \frac{I}{i_e(0)}. \tag{13.131}$$

If no holes are injected at $x = W$, $i_e(0) = I$ and we have

$$M_e = \frac{i_e(W)}{i_e(0)}. \tag{13.132}$$

This gives

$$M_e = \frac{i_e(0) + i_e(W) \int_0^W \beta \exp[-\int_0^{x'} (\alpha - \beta) dx''] dx'}{i} {}_e(0) - \int_0^x (\alpha - \beta) dx'. \tag{13.133}$$

Evaluation of this expression gives (Gowar, J., *Optical Communication Systems* Prentice-Hall, (1984))

$$M_e = \frac{1}{1 - \int_0^W \alpha \exp[-\int_0^{x'} (\alpha - \beta) dx''] dx'}. \tag{13.134}$$

For device breakdown, the denominator has to vanish (i.e. $M_e \to \infty$). If the field in the depletion region is uniform, α and β become independent of the space and we get (with $k \equiv \beta/\alpha$)

$$M_e = \frac{1-k}{\exp[-(1-k)\alpha W] - k}. \tag{13.135}$$

If $k \to 1$, $M_e \to 1/(1 - \alpha W)$.

The effect of the multiplication is also to increase the shot noise present in the initial signal $i_e(0)$ by a factor of F_e. The noise factor is given by

$$F_e = \frac{2 + [kM_e^2 + 2kM_e - (1-k)]}{M_e}. \tag{13.136}$$

For large values of M_e, this expression approaches

$$F_e = kM_e \tag{13.137}$$

so that the noise factor increases as k. A small k is thus desirable for low noise. Note that if the holes were being injected into the depletion region for detection, the noise would be minimized by a large k. Usually, the value of k approaches unity as the electric field increases. Since high speed devices require a short depletion width and a high electric field, the noise level in high speed APDs becomes large.

13.11 PROBLEMS

13.1. Calculate and plot the average speed of electrons in GaAs and Si between 10 K and 400 K. How do these speeds compare to the saturation drift velocities?

13.2. Calculate the low field mobility in undoped and doped ($N_D = 10^{17}$ cm-3) Si between 77 K and 300 K. Assume that all the donors are ionized.

13.3. Calculate the low field mobility in pure GaAs and In$_{0.53}$Ga$_{0.47}$As at 10 K and 300 K. Note that the room temperature mobility in In$_{0.53}$Ga$_{0.47}$As is higher than in GaAs, but at 10 K, this is not the case. What is the key reason for this turnaround? Assume an alloy scattering potential of 1.0 eV.

13.4. Calculate and plot the energy dependence of the various scattering rates listed in section 13.3 for electrons in GaAs from 0 to 400 meV. Examine carefully the relative strengths of the various scattering processes.

13.5. Write a Monte Carlo computer program based on the flowchart of Figure 13.4 and using the scattering rates and their angular dependence for GaAs based upon the Γ-L ordering. Compare the output of your results with the results presented in the paper by Fawcett, et al., (1970). Note that in their paper they had used a Γ-X ordering of the valleys.

13.6. Develop a Monte Carlo computer program to study electron transport in Si using the six equivalent X-valleys model and without including any other valleys. Examine the differences in the electron transport if you use an isotropic band with the density of states mass for the E vs. k relation or if you use the longitudinal and transverse mass relation, i.e.

$$E(k) = \frac{\hbar^2 k^2}{2m^*_{dos}}$$

vs.

$$E(k) = \frac{\hbar^2 k_l^2}{2m^*_l} + \frac{\hbar^2 k_t^2}{2m^*_t}.$$

13.7. Use your Monte Carlo program developed for GaAs to study the transient electron transport. Compare your results to the results in the paper by Maloney and Frey.

13.8. Study the transient transport in Si using your Monte Carlo program. How small would Si devices have to be before transient effects become important. Compare this to the case for GaAs devices.

13.9. When devices operate at high frequency, the conductivity of the semiconductor material changes. The propagation of the signal is then described by the description used in Chapter 15 for electromagnetic waves. Using the equation of motion for the drift velocity,

$$\frac{d\langle v \rangle}{dt} = -\frac{\langle v \rangle}{\tau} + \frac{F}{m}$$

show that the conductivity has the frequency dependent form

$$\sigma(\omega) = \frac{\sigma_0}{1 + i\omega\tau}$$

where σ_0 is the dc conductivity. Using $\mu = 8000$ cm^2/V-sec for GaAs, plot the frequency dependence of the conductivity up to a frequency of 200 GHz.

13.10. Using a Monte Carlo method, calculate the electron temperature as a function of electric field for GaAs. Study the temperature up to a field of 10^5 V/cm.

13.12 REFERENCES

- **Low Field Transport**

    - "Transport: The Boltzmann Equation," by Conwell, E. M., in *Handbook on Semiconductors* (North Holland, Amsterdam, 1982), vol. 1.

    - Jacoboni, C., C. Canali, G. Ottoviani and A. Alberigi- Quaranta, Sol. St. Electron., **20**, 77 (1977).

    - Lundstrom, M., *Fundamentals of Carrier Transport* (Modular Series on Solid State Devices, edited by G. W. Neudeck and R. F. Pierret, Addison-Wesley, Reading, 1990), vol. X.

    - "Low Field Electron Transport," by Rode, D. L., in *Semiconductors and Semimetals* (edited by R. K. Willardson and A. C. Beer, Academic Press, New York, 1975), vol. 10.

    - Stillman, G. E., C. M. Wolfe and J. O. Dimmock, J. Phys. Chem. Solids, **31**, 1199 (1970).

- **Monte Carlo Method**

    - Fawcett, W., A. D. Boardman and S. Swain, J. Phys. Chem. Solids, **31**, 1963 (1970).

    - Ferry, D. K., *Semiconductors* (Macmillan, New York, 1991).

    - Hess, K., *Advanced Theory of Semiconductor Devices* (Prentice-Hall, Englewood Cliffs, 1988).

    - Hockney, R. W. and J. W. Eastwood, *Computer Simulation Using Particles* (McGraw-Hill, New York, 1981).

- Jacoboni, C. and P. Lugli, *The Monte Carlo Method for Semiconductor Device Simulation* (Springer-Verlag, New York, 1989).

- Jacoboni, C. and L. Reggiani, Rev. Mod. Phys., **55**, 645 (1983).

- Lundstrom, M., *Fundamentals of Carrier Transport* (Modular Series on Solid State Devices, edited by G. W. Neudeck and R. F. Pierret, Addison-Wesley, Reading, 1990), vol. X.

- **General High Field Transport**

  - Chang, C. S. and H. R. Felterman, Sol. St. Electron., **29**, 1295 (1986).

  - Jacoboni, C., C. Canali, G. Ottoviani and A. Alberigi- Quaranta, Sol. St. Electron., **20**, 77 (1977).

  - Jacoboni, C. and L. Reggiani, Adv. in Phys., **28**, 493 (1979).

  - Nag, B. R., *Electron Transport in Compound Semiconductors* (Springer-Verlag, New York, 1980).

  - Omar, M. A. and L. Reggiani, Sol. St. Electron., **30**, 693 (1987).

  - Ruch, J. G. and G. S. Kino, Appl. Phys. Lett., **10**, 40 (1967).

  - Ruch. J. G. and G. S. Kino, Phys. Rev., **174**, 921 (1968).

  - Seeger, K., *Semiconductor Physics* (Springer-Verlag, New York, 1985).

  - Smith, P., M. Inoue and J. Frey, Appl. Phys. Lett., **37**, 797 (1980).

- **Transient Transport Issues**

  - A good review is provided in IEEE Spectrum, February 1986. Excellent articles by J. M. Poate and R. C. Dynes; by L. Eastman; and by M. I. Nathan and M. Heiblum cover important issues in ballistic transport and its use in devices.

  - Glisson, T. H., C. K. Williams, J. R. Hauser and M. A. Littlejohn, in *VLSI Electronics: Microstructure Science* (Academic Press, New York, 1982), vol. 4.

  - Hays, J. R., A. F. J. Levy and W. Wiegmann, Electron. Lett., **20**, 851 (1984).

  - Heiblum, M., M. L. Nathan, D. C. Thomas and C. M. Knoedler, Phys. Rev. Letts., **55**, 2200 (1985).

  - Maloney, T. J. and J. Frey, J. Appl. Phys., **48**, 781 (1977).

  - "The HEMT: A Superfast Transistor," by Morkoc, H. and P. M. Solomon, IEEE Spectrum, **21**, 28 (February 1984).

- **Transport of Holes**

  - Alberigi-Quaranta, A., M. Martini, G. Ottoviani, G. Radgelli and G. Zangarini, Sol. St. Electron., **11**, 685 (1968).

- Hinckley, J. M. and J. Singh, Phys. Rev. B., **41**, 2912 (1990).

- Hinckley, J. M., *The Effect of Strain on Pseudomorphic p- $Si_x Ge_{1-x}$: Physics and Modeling of the Valence Bandstructure and Hole Transport*, Ph.D. Thesis, (The University of Michigan, Ann Arbor, 1990).

- Madarasz, F. L. and F. Szmulowicz, Phys. Rev. B, **24**, 4611 (1981).

- Ryder, E. J., Phys. Rev., **90**, 766 (1953).

- "Mobility of Holes in III-V Compounds," by Wiley, J. D., in *Semiconductors and Semimetals* (edited by R. K. Willardson and A. C. Beer, Academic Press, New York, 1975), vol. 10, chap. 2.

- **Balance of Approach**

  - Baccarani, G. and M. R. Wordeman, Sol. St. Electron., **28**, 407 (1985).

  - Blotekjaar, K. IEEE Trans. Electron. Dev., **ED-17**, 38 (1970).

  - "High Field Transport in Semiconductors," by Conwell, E. M., in *Solid State Physics* (edited by F. Seitz, D. Turnbull and H. Ehrenreich, Academic Press, New York, 1967), vol. Suppl. 9.

  - Liboff, R. L., *Kinetic Equations* (Gordon and Breech, New York, 1971).

  - Lundstrom, M., *Fundamentals of Carrier Transport* (Modular Series on Solid State Devices, edited by G. W. Neudeck and R. F. Pierret, Addison-Wesley, Reading, 1990), vol. X.

- **Impact Ionization Coefficients**

  - Baraff, G. A., Phys. Rev., **128**, 2507 (1962).

  - Baraff, G. A., Phys. Rev., **133**, A26 (1964).

  - Bartelink, D. J., J. L. Moll and N. Meyer, Phys. Rev., **130**, 972 (1963).

  - Ferry, D. K., *Semiconductors* (Macmillan, New York, 1991).

  - Grant, W. N., Sol. St. Electron., **16**, 1189 (1973).

  - Hess, K., *Advanced Theory of Semiconductor Devices* (Prentice-Hall, Englewood Cliffs, 1988).

  - Logan, R. A. and S. M. Sze, *Proc. Int. Conf. Phys. Semicond., Kyoto* J. Phys. Soc. Japan, **Suppl. 21**, 434 (1966).

  - Moll, J. L. and R. van Overstraeten, Sol. St. Electron., **6**, 147 (1963).

  - Pearsall, T. P., F. Capasso, R. E. Nahory, M. A. Pollack and J. R. Chelikowsky, Sol. St. Electron., **21**, 297 (1978).

  - Pearsall, T. P., Appl. Phys. Lett., **36**, 218 (1980).

  - Ridley, B. K., J. Phys. C, **16**, 3373 (1983).

  - Ridley, B. K., J. Phys. C, **16**, 4733 (1983).

- Shichijo, H. and K. Hess, Phys. Rev. B, **23**, 4197 (1981).

- Shockley, W., Sol. St. Electron., **2**, 35 (1961).

- Stillman, G. E. and C. M. Wolfe, in *Semiconductors and Semimetals* (edited by R. K. Willardson and A. C. Beer, Academic Press, New York, 1977), vol 12.

- Umebu, I., A. N. M. M. Chaudhury and P. N. Robson, Appl. Phys. Lett., **36**, 302 (1980).

- Wolff, P. A., Phys. Rev., **95**, 1415 (1954).

- **Zener-Bloch Oscillations**

- Bassani, F. and G. P. Parravicini, *Electronic States and Optical Transitions in Solids* (Pergamon, New York, 1975).

- Iafrate, G. J., *The Physics of Submicron/Ultrasubmicron Dimensions in Gallium Arsenide Technology* (edited by D. K. Ferry, Howard W. Sans and Co., Indianapolis, 1985).

- R. K. Reich, R. O. Gorondin, D. K. Ferry and G. J. Iafrate, IEEE Elect. Dev. Lett., **EDL-3**, 381 (1982).

- Ridley, B. K., *Quantum Processes in Semiconductors* (Clarendon Press, Oxford, 1982).

- Zener, C., Proc. Roy. Soc. A, **145**, 523 (1934).

- **Device Performance**

- Geis, M. W., N. N. Efremow and D. D. Rathman, J. Vac. Sci. Technol. A, **6**, 1953 (1988)

- "GaAs LSI/VLSI: Advantages and Applications," by Hasegawa, H., M. Abe, P. M. Asbeck, A. Higashizaka, Y. Koto and M. Ohmori, in *Extended Abstracts of the 16th International Conference on Solid State Devices and Materials* (Kobe, Japan, 1984), p. 41.

CHAPTER
14

TRANSPORT IN
HETEROSTRUCTURES

The last four chapters provided a glimpse of the diversity and complexity of the transport phenomenon in bulk semiconductors. This complexity arises in spite of the fact that we used a semiclassical picture to describe the transport phenomenon. In this picture the quantum mechanical nature of the electron is invoked only to calculate the scattering rates. The particle transport itself is described by classical ideas of point particle electrons. For most cases of interest, this approach works quite well and the results obtained in Chapter 13 are quite adequate to describe transport phenomenon in bulk semiconductors. There are certain areas, especially those involving transport in ultra small structures, where the semiclassical approach starts to fail. When the area of study moves from bulk to heterostructure semiconductors, the transport problem acquires a new dimension of complexity. The transport issues in heterostructures have formed an area of intense research and many of the problems are still being actively researched. Nevertheless, a great deal of semiquantitative and, in some cases, quantitative information has been assembled in this important area. It is impossible to discuss all of the interesting problems of heterostructure transport in this chapter because of the essentially infinite ways the bandstructure and scattering processes can be manipulated, but we will examine some generic problems.

It is useful to divide the general problem of heterostructure transport into two regimes:

1. Transport where the electrons are essentially moving with energies outside the bandgap region, i.e., tunneling phenomenon is not important.

2. Transport where tunneling through "forbidden gaps" is important. In absence of tunneling, the extension of transport studies to heterostructures is conceptually simple.

The effect of the heterostructures as discussed in Chapter 6 is to modify the electron wavefunction which modifies the scattering matrix elements. The den-

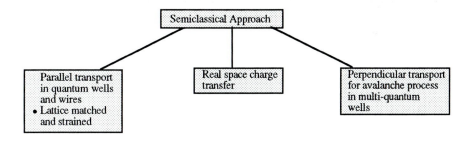

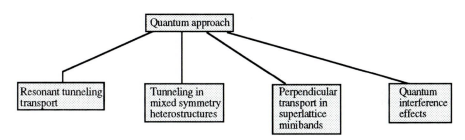

Figure 14.1: Problems to be addressed in this chapter. The problems fall in two classes: i) problems which can be addressed by semiclassical approaches developed in previous chapters, and, ii) problems which require quantum treatment.

sity of states is also modified by quantum confinement effects. However, in most cases one can still use the semiclassical approach to describe the transport phenomenon. Transport in electronic devices such as modulation doped field effect transistors (MODFETs), multiquantum well avalanche photodetectors, etc. can thus be understood with little new conceptual input. However, in structures such as resonant tunneling diodes, superlattice "Bloch oscillators," quantum interference devices, etc., the transport phenomenon requires a totally different conceptual level of understanding. Transport in such structures can be understood semiquantitatively by using relatively simple quantum mechanical concepts (such as tunneling and time dependent solutions of the Schrödinger equation). However, a quantitative understanding of such transport continues to be a subject of theoretical research. While quantum transport equations have been formulated in principle, their solution in realistic structures with real scattering processes has proven to be a very difficult problem. In general, unlike the case of the bulk transport where a single theory was able to tractably address a vast range of transport phenomenon in different material systems, in heterostructures one has to use makeshift formalisms for each different kind of heterostructure. In Figure 14.1 we show some of the areas of heterostructure transport that we will address in this chapter. These areas should not be regarded as being complete in describing the tremendous range of transport phenomenon observed in het-

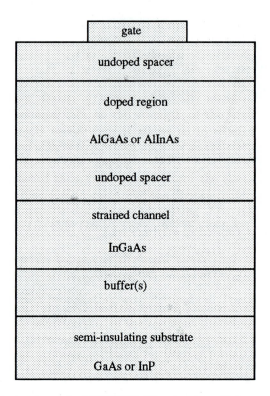

Figure 14.2: Layer structure of a MODFET. The structure shows a general case where the active channel is strained (InGaAs).

erostructures. However, these areas have been studied in some detail both theoretically and experimentally and are of considerable technological importance.

14.1 PARALLEL TRANSPORT IN QUANTUM WELLS AND MODFETS

The first, and perhaps the most important, application of transport in heterostructures has been in transport in quantum wells. This area of transport has been largely studied in the context of MODFETs, which have become the highest speed devices for digital and microwave applications. A general MODFET structure is shown in Figure 14.2. The structure consists of a substrate on which an undoped narrow bandgap material is grown epitaxially. A larger bandgap material is next grown and after leaving an undoped spacer region, the larger bandgap material is doped (modulation doped). The electrons from the donors transfer into the narrow bandgap material leaving behind the positively charged donors. The spatial separation between the donors and the free negative charge causes a non-uniform electric field which results in a quantum well being formed where the electrons are confined. To find the precise shape of this quantum well, one has to solve self-consistently the Schrödinger equation and the Poisson equations which are written as

$$\left[-\frac{\hbar^2}{2m^*}\nabla^2 + V_c(z) \right] \psi(z) = E\psi(z) \tag{14.1}$$

where the in-plane wavefunction is suppressed as we did for the quantum well problem discussed in Chapter 6. $V_c(z)$ is the conduction band profile to be calculated by using the Poisson equation

$$\frac{\partial^2}{\partial z^2}V_c(z) = -\frac{\rho(z)}{\epsilon(z)}. \tag{14.2}$$

The charge density, $\rho(z)$, is the sum of the doping charge, the free charge, and the quantum confined charge. This can be written as

$$\rho(z) = q\left(N_d^*(z) - N_a^*(z) - n_{\text{free}}(z) + p_{\text{free}}(z) - \sum_n n_n\,\phi_n^*(z)\,\phi_n(z) \right) \tag{14.3}$$

where N_a^* and N_d^* are the effective doping levels, n_{free} and p_{free} are the free carrier concentrations, and the sum is over n two-dimensionally confined subbands whose normalized envelope functions are ϕ_n and in which the occupation is n_n (or p_n for the hole case). The effective doping levels, N_d^* and N_a^*, are the concentration of ionized dopants. It is important to determine the percentage of the dopants which are ionized when, for example, the conduction band dips down close to the Fermi level. When this happens, the donor levels begin to fill. A filled, or unionized, donor site is charge neutral, and does not contribute a free electron. Writing

$$N_d^* = N_d(1 - < n_d >) \tag{14.4}$$

where N_d is the total real concentration of donor atoms and $< n_d >$ is the average occupation of a donor level. The effective donor concentration can be written as (see Chapter 8)

$$N_d^* = N_d\left(\frac{1}{1 + 2\exp\left(\frac{E_d - E_F}{k_B T}\right)} \right) \tag{14.5}$$

Here, E_d is the donor level which is usually at a fixed energy below the conduction band.

For a parabolic band case, the electron density in the nth band is simply

$$n_n = \frac{m_\parallel^*}{\pi\hbar^2}k_B T \ln\left[1 + \exp\left(\frac{-(E_n - E_F)}{k_B T}\right)\right]. \tag{14.6}$$

The formalism for modeling the p-type MODFET is conceptually similar, but much more complicated numerically. The complication arises out of the

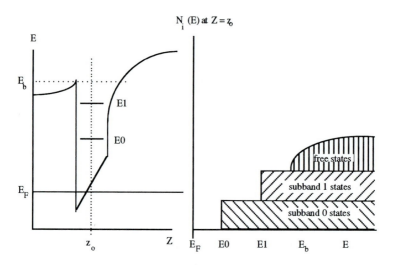

Figure 14.3: Conduction band profile and density of states at a point inside of the confining well. Free electron states appear above the confining potential.

fact that there are two degenerate hole bands. Thus, instead of the one band Schrödinger equation which we had for electrons, we must instead represent the hole bands with a Hamiltonian matrix capable of describing the full hole bandstructure in the presence of quantum confinement and possibly strain. We discussed in Chapters 5 and 6 how this can be done using the Kohn-Luttinger formalism. The self-consistent solution is straightforward.

In Figure 14.3 we show a typical band profile that results in a MODFET structure. The electron gap is confined in a quantum well which has a triangular shape. The density of states of the electron can be regarded as two-dimensional for the first few subbands, but becomes three-dimensional in nature as the well widens and the excited states become more extended. In Figure 14.4 we show some typical wavefunctions for the confined states in a MODFET. One can see that the first few states are strongly confined.

In the MODFET quantum well and other similar quantum well structures, the transport of carriers along the channel is adequately described by the semi-classical picture that has been used by us to describe transport in 3-D systems. However, there are several important differences.

Form of the Wavefunctions: The first important difference is the nature of the electron wavefunction. As shown in Figure 14.4 for the MODFET structure and as discussed in detail in Chapter 6, in the growth direction (say the z-direction), the quantum well wavefunctions are confined and do not have a plane wave form. Thus, in the evaluation of the scattering matrix elements one has to use an appropriate form of the type

$$\psi = \frac{1}{\sqrt{A}}\, g_n(z)\, e^{i\mathbf{k}_\parallel \cdot \rho} \tag{14.7}$$

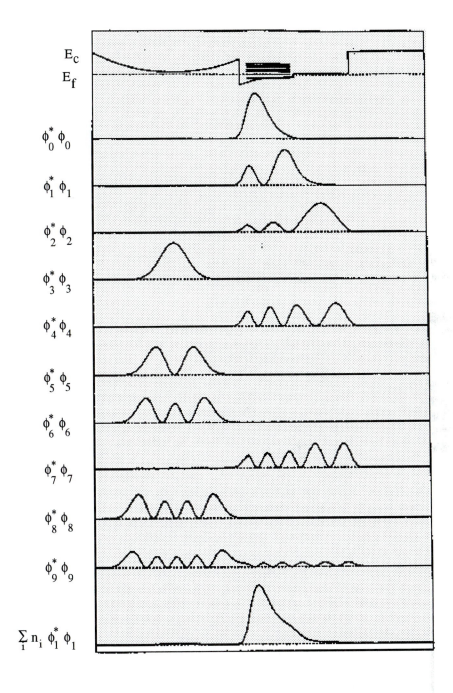

Figure 14.4: Envelope functions for the first ten subbands in a pseudomorphic MOD-FET, (from Jaffe, 1989).

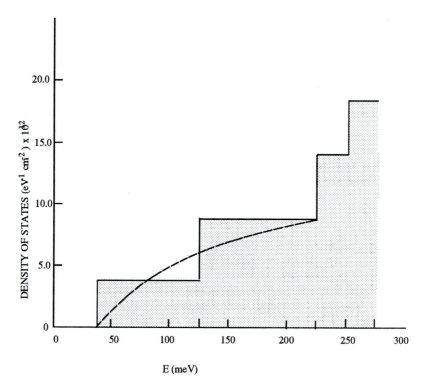

Figure 14.5: The density of states in a 100 Å GaAs/Al$_{0.3}$Ga$_{0.7}$As quantum well. Also shown (curved line) is 3-D density of states multiplied by the well size. At higher excited levels, the wavefunction is confined over regions much larger than the well size giving an appearance of high density of 2-D states. The 3-D density of states is artificially placed at the same origin as the 2-D density of states for an easier comparison.

as discussed in Chapter 6. Here $g_n(z)$ are (normalized) envelope functions for the nth subband. As discussed in Chapter 6, for the conduction band, one can use a single basis description for the wavefunction, while for the valence band one requires a larger basis (say a 4-band basis of HH and LH states). In any case, the change in the wavefunctions does not present any conceptual difficulty, it simply changes the integrals that need to be solved for the matrix element.

Density of States: Another important effect of quantization is that the density of states of the quasi-2-D system is quite different from that of the 3-D system. We have derived the 2-D density of states (as well as the 1-D density of states) earlier and for parabolic bands these have the step function form shown in Figure 14.5. Also shown in Figure 14.5 is the 3-D density of states (divided by the well size to represent it in the same units). We can see that at low energies there is a marked difference in the density of states. This is especially true for electron energies below the second subband. This has important consequences for the nature of the scattering rates since the density of states appear directly

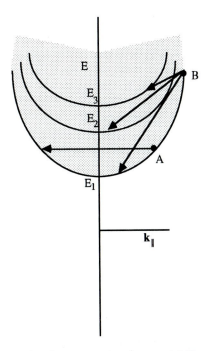

Figure 14.6: A schematic showing scattering in quasi-2-D systems. For low energy electrons (A), the scattering can only occur within the same band. However, for high energy electrons (B), the scattering rates are increased because of the inter-subband scattering.

in the Fermi golden rule. At low energies in the 2-D system the electron can only scatter within the same subband since the energy is too low for inter-subband scattering. However, when the electrons acquire higher energies, they can scatter within the same band as well as into other subbands as shown in Figure 14.6. Since the 3-D and 2-D density of states are essentially similar for higher energies, the scattering processes are quite similar, too. For single subband scattering an important manifestation of the constant density of states in 2-D systems vs. $E^{1/2}$ dependence in 3-D systems is the temperature dependence of the scattering. As discussed in Chapter 12, the temperature dependence comes from the energy dependence of the scattering rate. The carrier mass dependence of the 2-D density is also different from that in the 3-D density of states.

The brief discussion presented here suggests that at high temperatures (where several subbands are occupied) or high fields (where electrons are hot), there may be little difference in transport properties of quasi-2-D and 3-D systems. However, at low temperatures and low fields there may be important differences. This is, indeed, borne out of detailed theoretical and experimental studies.

Scattering Potential Differences: The final important parameter that controls the scattering process is the scattering potential. One of the main motivations for the MODFET structure is the reduction in the ionized impurity scattering potential. Due to the physical separation of the ionized impurities from the free electrons the scattering potential is drastically reduced. For structures where the separation is ≥ 100 Å, the effect of ionized impurity is almost completely eliminated except at liquid He temperatures.

A scattering mechanism that is not of importance in 3-D systems but which can play an important role in quantum well transport is the interface roughness scattering. In our discussions on quantum well structures we have so far assumed that the structure is perfect and there is abrupt transition between one material and the next. In reality, this is not the case, and the random nature of most techniques producing heterostructures produces chemical disorder (or interface roughness) in the quantum well structures.

Before heterostructures were fabricated by epitaxial techniques, the Si/SiO$_2$ interface provided a quantum well structure and detailed models were developed to understand the nature of the interface roughness and its consequences on transport. This approach has been the basis for developing an understanding of interface roughness scattering. For the Si/SiO$_2$ interface, the displacement of the real interface from the perfect interface is assumed to be described by a random function $\Delta(\rho)$, where ρ is a 2-D position vector on the interface. The interface potential fluctuations are described by expanding the surface potential in terms of $\Delta(\rho)$ as

$$
\begin{aligned}
V_{IR}(\rho, z) &= V(z + \Delta(\rho)) - V(z) \\
&= eF(z)\Delta(\rho)
\end{aligned}
\tag{14.8}
$$

where $F(z)$ is the field in the well near the interface. The random fluctuation $\Delta(\rho)$ is described by its correlation in the interface plane (Goodrich, et al., 1985).

$$
< \Delta(\rho)\, \Delta(\rho' - \rho) > = \Delta^2 \exp\left(-\frac{\rho'^2}{L^2}\right)
\tag{14.9}
$$

so that Δ is the rms height of the fluctuations in the interface and L is the extent of the fluctuation.

For most epitaxially given interfaces, the model for the interface roughness is schematically shown in Figure 14.7. The interface region between two materials, A and B, is to the first order defined by a region of width Δ, where the A and B material islands are placed randomly. The lateral extent of these islands is given by a parameter r_0 ($= L/2$ of Figure 14.7b). The interface potential due to each such island is now given by the following

$$
\begin{aligned}
V_{IR}(\rho, z) &= V_0 \quad \rho < r_0; |z| \leq \Delta/2 \\
&= 0 \quad \text{otherwise.}
\end{aligned}
$$

It is straightforward to calculate the scattering rates from such a potential.

The phonon scatterings in quasi-2-D systems can be quite complex if an accurate self-consistent approach is to be used. This is because, as discussed

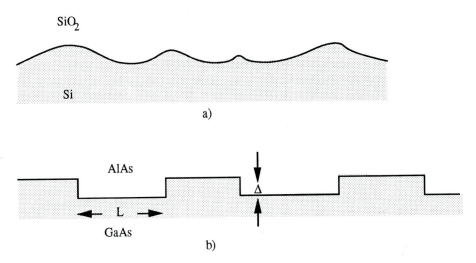

SiO$_2$

Si

a)

AlAs

L

Δ

GaAs

b)

Figure 14.7: A schematic of an interface produced by (a) an ex-situ technique such as O–diffusion in Si/SiO$_2$ interface; and (b) an in situ epitaxial technique such as MBE or MOCVD growth of GaAs/AlAs.

briefly in Chapter 9, the phonon spectra itself is altered in quasi-2-D systems. Just as one has confined modes for electrons, one has confined phonon modes except that the phonon modes can be confined to a few monolayers. In quantum wells this produces interfacial modes which are restricted to regions close to the interface and modes which are extended throughout the width of the quantum well. The effect of these two kinds of phonons on carrier scattering is an area of continued research. However, it appears that the interface and extended phonon modes produce a scattering rate not too different from the ones obtained by simply using bulk phonons, unless the quantum well is below 50 Å wide.

We will now list some of the important scattering rates for quasi-2-D systems. We will discuss the scattering rates only for the situation where the electron is in the first subband. Once scattering is allowed into several subbands, the transport becomes very similar to that of bulk materials.

14.2 MOBILITY IN A MODFET QUANTUM WELL

The MODFET quantum well has a triangular form as seen from Figure 14.3. The exact triangular well has wavefunctions which are given by Airy functions. However, often simpler variational forms are assumed so that the scattering matrix elements can be evaluated. The simplest of such variational functions for the ground state is the Fang-Howard function

$$g(z) = \left(\frac{b^3}{2}\right)^{1/2} z e^{bz/2} \qquad (14.10)$$

The average penetration of the charge in the narrow gap semiconductor is

$$Z_0 = 3/b. \tag{14.11}$$

The variational parameter b is found by evaluating the energy of the electrons in the ground state and minimizing it for a fixed carrier concentration. This procedure gives

$$b = \left[\frac{48\pi m^* e^2 N^*}{\epsilon_s \hbar^2} \right]^{1/3} \tag{14.12}$$

with

$$N^* = N_{\text{depl}} + \frac{11}{32} N_s \tag{14.13}$$

where N_{depl} is the concentration of fixed depletion charge in the channel and N_s is the two-dimensional mobile sheet charge. Other single parameter variational functions have also been proposed and one which is a better approximation to the exact results is of the form, (Ando, 1982)

$$g(z) = \left(\frac{3}{2} b^3 \right)^{1/2} z \exp \left\{ -\frac{1}{2} (bz)^{3/2} \right\}. \tag{14.14}$$

As an example of a multiparameter function often used is

$$\begin{aligned} g(z) &= B \, b^{1/2} \, (bz + B) \, \exp\left(-bz/2\right) \text{for } z > 0 \\ &= B' \, b'^{1/2} \, \exp\left(b'z/2\right) \qquad \text{for } z < 0 \end{aligned} \tag{14.15}$$

where b, b', B, and B' are variational parameters. Regardless of the function used, the final mobilities are quite close. The derivation of the mobilities is based on the same formalisms discussed in the last four chapters, except that the mathematical details are different because of the quasi-2-D nature of the wavefunctions. We will now list the low temperature mobility expressions limited by various scattering rates.

14.2.1 Remote Impurity Scattering

A number of workers have carried out detailed studies for the scattering of carriers from remote ions in the MODFET structure. These theories often differ in the screening factors used (e.g., 3-D, quasi-2-D, 2-D, etc.), as well as the statistics used to describe the carriers. A useful expression that appears to fit the observed mobility data quite well is given by Lee, et al., 1983,

$$\mu_{RI} = \frac{64\pi \, \hbar^3 \, \epsilon \, S_0^2 \, (2\pi N_s)^{3/2}}{e^3 \, m^{*2}} \left[\frac{1}{L_0^2} - \frac{1}{L_0'^2} \right]^{-1} \tag{14.16}$$

where S_0 is the inverse 2-D screening length from the carriers in the subband, and is given in the degenerate limit by

$$S_0 = \frac{2e^2 m^*}{4\pi\epsilon\hbar^2}. \tag{14.17}$$

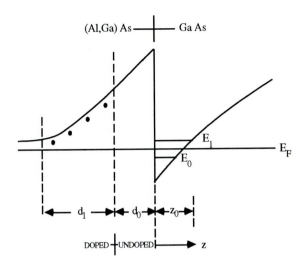

Figure 14.8: A schematic of the band profile of a MODFET and the length scales used in the remote ionized impurity scattering.

In the nondegenerate limit the screening length is

$$S_0 = \frac{e^2 n_s}{2\epsilon k_B T}. \tag{14.18}$$

The various length scales are defined in Figure 14.8. The distances L_0 and L_0' are given by

$$
\begin{aligned}
L_0 &= d_0 + z_0 \\
L_0' &= d_0 + z_0 + d_1
\end{aligned}
\tag{14.19}
$$

where d_0 is the spacer length, z_0 is the width of the well, and d_1 is the distance of the depletion width as shown.

14.2.2 Acoustic Phonon Scattering

Once again a number of workers have provided theoretical treatments for the scattering of quasi-2-D electrons from acoustic phonons. A simple expression that gives a good description of the mobility is (Arora and Naeem, 1985, also Riddock and Ridley,1984, and Price, 1984)

$$\mu_{\text{acc}} = \frac{2e\hbar^3 \rho_d \, u^2 \, b}{3m^{*2} D^2 k_B T} \tag{14.20}$$

where ρ_d is the crystal density, u is the longitudinal sound velocity, b is the effective width of the well, and D is the deformation potential. Once again this value of mobility is for scattering within a single subband. These results which are valid for low temperature show that the mobility in a quasi-2-D system is related to the bulk acoustic phonon limited mobility by the relation

$$\frac{\mu_{2D}(\text{acoustic})}{\mu_{3D}(\text{acoustic})} = \frac{b}{2\pi^{1/2}\lambda_D} \tag{14.21}$$

where

$$\lambda_D^{-1} = \frac{\hbar}{(2m^* k_B T)^{1/2}}. \tag{14.22}$$

For a GaAs well with size of 100 Å at 100 K, the mobility decreases to 35% of the bulk value.

14.2.3 Polar Optical Phonon Scattering

A careful treatment by Ridley (1982) has shown that, for the polar optical phonon absorption process, the mobility is given by

$$\mu_{p0} = \frac{4\pi \, \epsilon_p \, \hbar^2}{e \, \omega_0 \, n(\omega_0) \, m^{*2} \, b} \tag{14.23}$$

where

$$\frac{1}{\epsilon_p} = \frac{1}{\epsilon_\infty} - \frac{1}{\epsilon_s}$$

$$n(\omega_0) = \frac{1}{\exp(\hbar\omega_0/k_B T) - 1}. \tag{14.24}$$

For emission and absorption, it has been shown by Arora and Naeem (1985) that

$$\mu = \mu_{p0} \left[1 - \delta e^{-x0} + \delta^2 e^{\delta} \, E_1 \left(x_0 + \delta \right) \right] \tag{14.25}$$

where

$$\delta = 8 \frac{n(\omega_0) + 1}{n(\omega_0)} \frac{\xi_0}{k_B T}$$

$$x_0 = \frac{\hbar\omega_0}{k_B T}$$

$$\xi_0 = \frac{\pi^2 \hbar^2}{2m^* b^2}$$

$$E_1(x) \approx e^{-x}/x. \tag{14.26}$$

14.2.4 Alloy Scattering

Alloy scattering plays an important role in transport in MODFET structures involving InGaAs alloys which are the fastest electronic transistors at the moment. The mobility in this case is given by

$$\mu_{\text{all}} \approx \frac{e\hbar^3 z_0}{(m^*)^2 \, x \, (1 - x) \, U_{\text{all}}^2 \, \Omega_0} \tag{14.27}$$

where Ω_0 is the volume of the unit cell and z_0 is shown in Figure 14.8.

14.2.5 Interface Roughness Scattering

As mentioned earlier, the interface roughness effects are not present in the 3-D systems discussed in the previous chapter. We will briefly discuss a model for interface roughness scattering which has been used to understand the role of this scattering in transport in MODFETs.

An epitaxially grown interface A-B (material A grown on material B) formed under optimized growth conditions is characterized by the surface profile of B at the instant when the interface is formed. Since under optimized growth conditions, the growth of material B occurs by the two-dimensional (2-D) nucleation and growth mode (rather than three-dimensional island mode), the surface of material B at any instant can be defined by 2-D islands which are of height Δ (a few monolayers) and of lateral extent L. The inset of Figure 14.9 shows an example of interfaces in heterostructures. The lateral extent is determined by the average distance traveled by the group III atoms (e.g., In, Ga, and Al atoms) between impingement from vapor and final incorporation in the crystal. This distance for optimum growth conditions is of the order of 100 Å.

The interface model discussed above will produce a scattering potential given by

$$
\begin{aligned}
V_{IR}(\rho, \theta) &= V_0, \text{ for } \rho < r_0 \\
&= 0, \text{ for } \rho > r_0.
\end{aligned}
\tag{14.28}
$$

It is assumed that on an average the interface structure is made up of these two dimensional steps as shown in the inset of Figure 14.9. To calculate the scattering of the electrons from this interface profile, one needs to evaluate the matrix element.

$$
M(\boldsymbol{k}, \boldsymbol{k}') = \int dz \int d\rho \, \psi^*(\rho, z) \, V_{IR}(\rho, \theta) \, \psi(\rho, z).
\tag{14.29}
$$

The z-integration is simplified by expressing V_{IR} in terms of the electric field as in Equation 14.8. The electric field can then be expressed in terms of N_s, the 2-D electron carrier density and N_{acc}, the accumulation layer charge density. Performing the z, ρ (in integral above) integral

$$
M(\boldsymbol{k}, \boldsymbol{k}') = \Delta r_0 \frac{8\pi^2 e^2}{\epsilon_s} \left(N_{\text{acc}} + \frac{N_s}{2} \right) \frac{J_1(qr_0)}{q}
\tag{14.30}
$$

where $q = |\boldsymbol{k} - \boldsymbol{k}'|$ and J_1 is the first order Bessel function. Assuming an equal density of 2-D islands as flat regions (see inset of Figure 14.9), the scattering rate can be expressed as (Hong, et al., 1986)

$$
\frac{1}{\tau(k_F)} = \frac{4\pi e^4 m^*}{\hbar^3 \epsilon_s^2} \left(N_{\text{acc}} + \frac{N_s}{2} \right)^2 \Delta^2 \int_0^\infty J_1(k_F L \sin \phi)^2 d\phi.
\tag{14.31}
$$

In Figure 14.9, $1/\tau$ for the $In_{0.52}Al_{0.48}As/In_{0.53}Ga_{0.47}As$ interface calculated according to Equation 14.31 for $\Delta = 1$ monolayer and for three different values

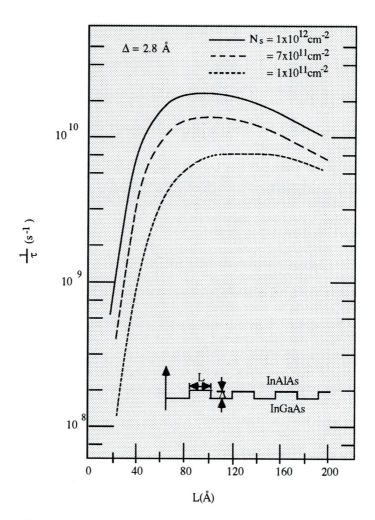

Figure 14.9: Dependence of calculated inverse scattering time due to interface roughness on 2-D island size, (from Hong, et al., 1985).

of N_s ($N_{\mathrm{acc}} \ll N_s$) as a function of L ($= 2r_0$) are plotted. It is important to realize that as L increases there is initially a sharp increase in $1/\tau$ (sharp decrease in mobility), but beyond $L \sim 50$ Å, $1/\tau$ becomes independent of L and eventually begins to decrease (mobility starts to increase). Physically this means that once the roughness scale increases beyond $1/k_F$, the electrons do not "see" the surface roughness as much.

14.2.6 Mobility

It is illustrative to apply these various formulae to study the mobility in a MOD-FET structure. We show such a case study for an $In_{0.53}Ga_{0.47}As/In_{0.52}Al_{0.48}As$ structure. The structure has a spacer region of 80 Å and is doped at 2×10^{18} cm^{-3}. The distances d_1 and z_0 for the remote impurity scattering turn out to be 100 Å and 42.5 Å respectively with a sheet charge of $\sim 1.5 \times 10^{12}$ cm^{-2}. In Figure 14.10 we show the measured results, limiting mobilities due to various scattering rates, and the theoretical mobilities according to Matheison's rule. In this particular system, the alloy scattering dominates the mobility below 77 K and the acoustic phonon scattering appears to dominate up to 200 K. Above 200 K, the results start deviating from the theory because of the importance of inter-subband scattering which is ignored. In fact, around 300 K, the mobility is very close to the bulk mobility in the $In_{0.53}Ga_{0.47}As$ alloy.

14.3 HIGH TEMPERATURE / HIGH FIELD TRANSPORT

The overview discussed above is valid only for the cases where the transport is in a single subband. Once the electrons are heated, either by temperature or by an electric field, the inter-subband scattering starts occurring. Tomizawa, et al. (1984) have carried out detailed calculations for the high field transport in quantum well structures and compared the results with transport in bulk materials. A typical result is shown in Figure 14.11. As can be seen, the low field transport in the quantum well is superior to that in the bulk material with a similar carrier density ($N_D = 1 \times 10^{18}$ cm^{-3}). However, most of this improvement is due to the reduction in the ionized impurity scattering in the MODFET. If the results are compared with the $N_D = 0$ bulk case one finds that the 2-D and 3-D cases have similar mobilities. Also at high fields the transport is essentially the same for the 2-D and 3-D systems. However, there are differences in the peak velocity for the 2-D and 3-D system.

14.4 EFFECT OF STRAIN ON TRANSPORT

In Chapter 7 we discussed in some detail the advances being made in pseudomorphic growth and its consequences for tailoring the bandstructure. We showed that for direct bandgap semiconductors, the strain produced by mismatched epitaxy

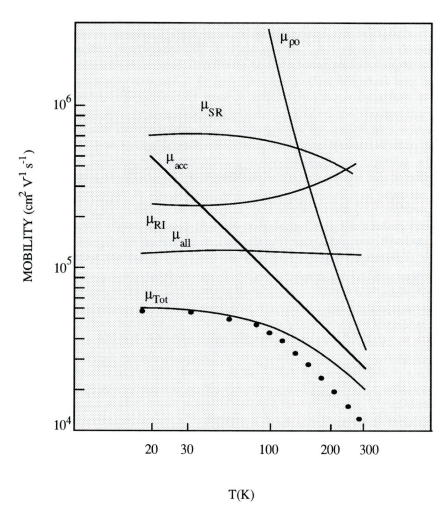

Figure 14.10: Calculated mobility in an $In_{0.53}Ga_{0.47}As/In_{0.52}Al_{0.43}As$ MODFET with an 80 Å spacer and a doping level of 2×10^{18} cm^{-3}. The experimental points are also shown. A one monolayer ($\Delta = 2.8$ Å, $L = 100$ Å) surface roughness is assumed.

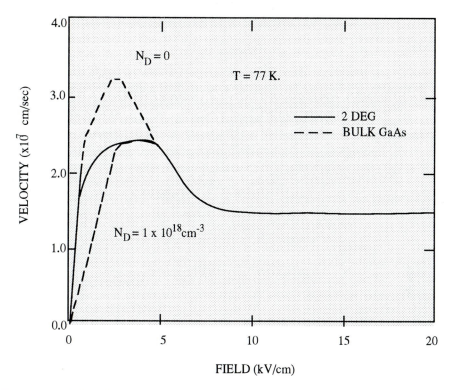

Figure 14.11: The velocity field relations calculated for a two dimensional system. Also shown are the bulk results for zero and 10^{18} background ionized impurity scattering. (Reproduced with permission, M. Tomizawa, et al., IEEE Electron Dev. Lett., **5**, 464 (1984).)

is such that the conduction bandedge simply moves in energy without any serious change in the bandedge masses. Thus, one expects little change in transport properties. This seems to be borne out by experimental studies. However, there is a great deal of interest in n-type pseudomorphic MODFETs and improvements in device performance have been observed. This appears to be linked more to the *higher carrier density*, which is possible for the narrower bandgap strained channel, rather than any improvements in the material properties.

The effect of uniaxial strain produced by mismatched epitaxy on the valence band is quite profound and has been discussed in some detail in Chapter 7. From these discussions, it is clear that a compressive strain in the growth plane can reduce the in-plane hole effective mass and thus offer improved performance for p-type devices. Material systems of interest in this regard are $In_x Ga_{1-x}As$ on GaAs, $In_{0.53+x}Ga_{0.47-x}As$ on InP, $Si_{1-x}Ge_x$ on Si, etc. Figures 14.12 and 14.13 show some typical results for the band profile and in-plane bandstructure for the lattice matched and strained MODFET structures. As can be seen, the hole band curvature is considerably sharper for the pseudomorphic case. The effects

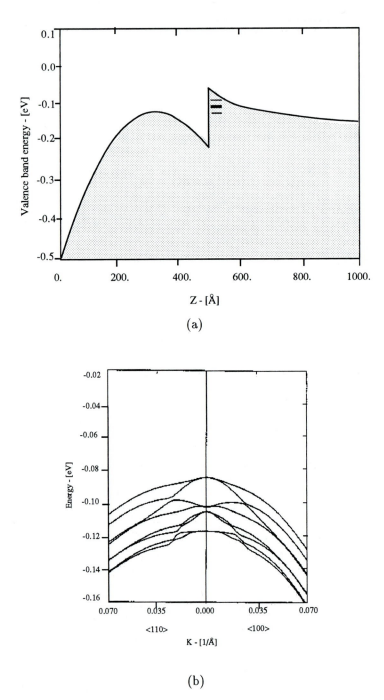

Figure 14.12: (a) Valence band profile in a p-type AlGaAs/GaAs MODFET. (b) Hole subbands in a p-type AlGaAs/GaAs MODFET.

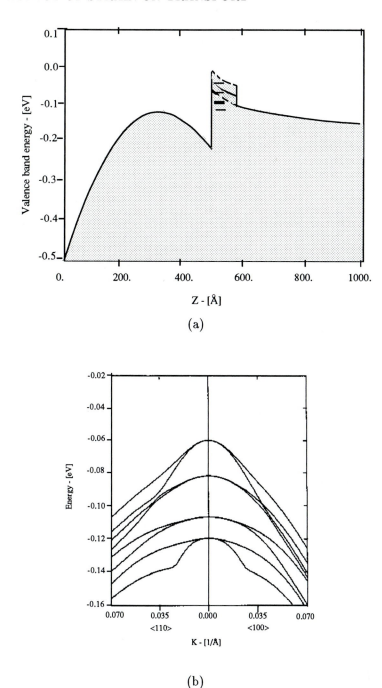

(a)

(b)

Figure 14.13: (a) Valence band profile in a p-type pseudomorphic MODFET $In_{0.12}Ga_{0.88}As$ channel. (b) Hole subbands in a p-type pseudomorphic MODFET with an $In_{0.12}Ga_{0.88}As$ channel.

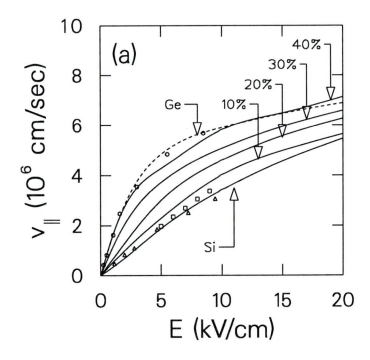

Figure 14.14: Calculated velocity–field relations in the $Si_{1-x}Ge_x$ alloy which are pseudomorphically grown on the (001) Si substrate. Also shown for comparison are results in bulk Si and Ge (see Figure 13.21). The transport improvements are primarily due to the strain in the system, (from Hinckley and Singh, 1990).

of strain on p-type device performance have been documented by several workers and considerable improvements have been reported. Monte Carlo studies for p-type transport in strained structures have also been carried out. An unknown in these calculations is the alloy scattering potential and interface scattering which may partially negate some of the benefits of strain. Without these effects one expects significant improvements in the hole velocity–field relations. As an example, we show results for the $Si_{1-x}Ge_x$ alloy grown pseudomorphically on Si. These results shown for increasing compositions of Ge are shown in Figure 14.14.

14.5 TRANSPORT IN QUANTUM WIRES

There has been considerable interest in pursuing research in quasi-1-D structures because of their exciting potential. This potential is mainly due to the nature of the eigenstates, eigenenergies, and density of states. In a quasi-1-D wire, the electron function is confined in two dimensions and is "free" only in one direction. For a simple rectangular wire of dimensions L_x and L_y, the wavefunction is of the form

$$\psi_{\mathbf{k}} = \frac{1}{\sqrt{L_z}} g_n(x)\, g_\ell(y)\, e^{ik_z z} \qquad (14.32)$$

where the envelope functions for an infinite barrier case have the usual form

$$g_n(x) = \sqrt{\frac{2}{L_x}} \cos\left(\frac{n\pi x}{L_x}\right), \quad \text{for } n \text{ odd}$$

$$g_n(x) = \sqrt{\frac{2}{L_x}} \sin\left(\frac{n\pi x}{L_x}\right), \quad \text{for } n \text{ even} \qquad (14.33)$$

where the well extends from $x = -L_x/2$ to $x = +L_x/2$. Similar eigenfunctions pertain for $g_\ell(y)$.

The electron energies are

$$E_{n,\ell} = \frac{\hbar^2}{2m^*}\left\{ \left(\frac{n\pi}{L_x}\right)^2 + \left(\frac{\ell\pi}{L_y}\right)^2 \right\} + \frac{\hbar^2 k_z^2}{2m^*}. \qquad (14.34)$$

As discussed earlier in Chapter 1, such a dispersion relation produces a density of states of the form

$$N(E) = \sum_n \frac{\sqrt{2}m^{*1/2}}{\pi\hbar}(E - E_{n\ell})^{-1/2} \qquad (14.35)$$

where the $E_{n\ell}$ are the various subband levels. An important effect of this quantization is that once L_x and L_y approach 100 Å or less, there is enough inter-subband separation (≥ 50 meV) that there is no inter-subband scattering. The scattering in the same subband is severely restricted for the 1-D system as can be seen from Figure 14.15 where elastic scattering is considered. The only possible final state for elastic scattering is k or $-k$ unlike for the 2-D or 3-D system. Scattering to the state k has no influence on transport while scattering to $-k$ state requires a very short ranged potential to conserve momentum. Overall this results in a severe suppression of scattering and mobilities as high as 10^7 cm^2 V^{-1}s^{-1} have been predicted.

The experimental picture of superior transport in 1-D systems has not been very rosy so far. This appears to be linked to the growth and fabrication difficulties. Unlike quantum wells, the fabrication of quantum wires usually involves complex etching/regrowth steps which probably introduce serious defects which affect the transport properties.

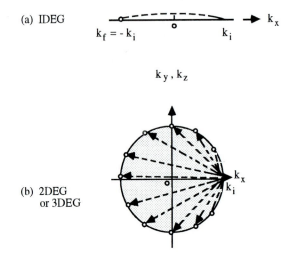

Figure 14.15: Equal energy surface of a 1-DEG (a) in comparison with that of 2-DEG or 3-DEG (b) in k-space. Note that scattering of a 1-DEG takes place only between k and $-k$, whereas for the 2-D or 3-D system the electron can be scattered into various states. (Reproduced with permission, H. Sakaki, Jap. J. Appl. Phys., **19**, L735 (1980).)

14.6   REAL SPACE CHARGE TRANSFER

This is another area of transport in heterostructures which can be understood on the basis of our semiclassical transport theory. As we discussed in Chapter 13, for materials like GaAs, one sees a negative differential resistance region in the velocity–field relation. This occurs when the low mass, high mobility Γ-electrons, transfer to the high mass, low mobility L-electrons at high fields. The negative differential resistance is of great use for designing microwave devices. Normally, in a bulk semiconductor, this effect is produced only by such a k-space transfer of electrons. Thus, this effect is an intrinsic property of the semiconductor. However, in a heterostructure, a similar effect can be realized by using the concept of real space charge transfer. The concept can be understood on the basis of Figure 14.16. Here we simply show a $GaAs/Al_xGa_{1-x}As$ quantum well structure. The electron mobility in GaAs is higher than that in the $Al_xGa_{1-x}As$ alloy (because of the increased carrier mass and alloy scattering). At low electric fields, the electrons are confined in the high mobility GaAs region. However, as the electric field is increased, the electrons become "hot" and a certain fraction gets transferred in real space to the low mobility $Al_xGa_{1-x}As$ alloy. This transfer in real space produces a similar effect in the velocity–field relations as the transfer in k-space. The electrons switch from having high mobility to having low mobility as a result of being heated by the imposed electric field. Thus, one can achieve a negative differential resistance region. Since the quantum well barrier discontinuity can be altered, the velocity–field curves can be tailored. The Monte

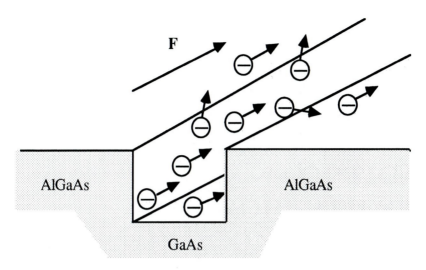

Figure 14.16: A schematic of the real space charge transfer effect where electrons can move in real space from one material (say, the well material) to another (barrier) as they are heated by an electric field.

Carlo method is ideally suited for calculating these relationships. However, one has to include the solution of the Poisson equation explicitly for accurate results. At low fields, the electrons are in the quantum well and the space charge effects are negligible. However, at high electric fields the electrons transfer out of the well into the barrier region creating a space charge region and perpendicular electric fields. In Figure 14.17 we show some results for the velocity field relations for GaAs/Al$_x$Ga$_{1-x}$As quantum well structures obtained by Littlejohn, et al. (1983).

An approach that has been used to obtain reasonable semiquantitative results for the velocity–field results is to use the carrier temperature approach. In this approach the distribution function is depicted by the shifted Maxwellian function described by the carrier temperature. The carrier temperatures as a function of the electric field are assumed to be known, say, from a Monte Carlo method or the balance equation. At low electric fields, the carrier temperature is simply the lattice temperature T_L. The relative carrier density occupation in the well and the barrier region is simply

$$\frac{n_w}{n_B} \approx \exp(\Delta E_c / k_B T_L) \tag{14.36}$$

where we assume a barrier discontinuity ΔE_c. In presence of an electric field, the relevant temperature in Equation 14.36 is T_c, the carrier temperature. It is clear that as T_c increases, the relative occupation of the barrier region is increased. The velocity is then calculated by the expression

$$v(F) = \frac{v_w(F)\, n_w\, W_w + v_B(F)\, n_B\, W_B}{n_w\, W_w + n_B\, W_B} \tag{14.37}$$

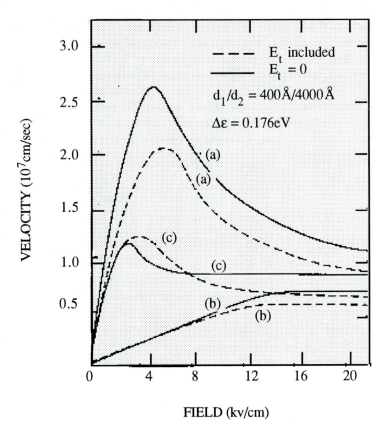

Figure 14.17: Velocity–field characteristics for a real space transfer device. The solid curves include a transverse field while the dotted curves are for $F_T = 0$. Curves (a) are for GaAs region; curves (b) are in AlGaAs only; curves (c) are for the total device. (Reproduced with permission, M. A. Littlejohn, et al., J. Vac. Sci. Technol., **B1**, 445 (1983).)

where W_w and W_B are the widths of the well and the barrier region, and v_w and v_B are given by the velocity–field relations of the individual materials. The more accurate calculations are complicated by the need to solve the equation self-consistently with the Poisson equation.

14.7 AVALANCHE PROCESSES IN QUANTUM WELL STRUCTURES

We discussed the impact ionization (avalanching) process in Chapters 11 and 13. In bulk semiconductors the avalanche process is simply controlled by the material bandgap and scattering processes and can not be altered. As we have mentioned several times, the avalanche process is a limiting process for the high power

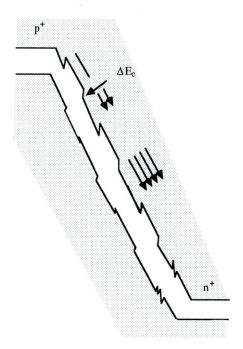

Figure 14.18: A schematic showing how the presence of a large conduction band discontinuity can enhance the electron impact ionization rate.

operation of electronic devices and is to be avoided in these devices. However, for avalanche photodetectors, this process is utilized for producing high gain devices. An important consideration in these devices is the ratio of the electron impact ionization coefficient (α) to the hole impact ionization coefficient (β). This ratio should be large (or small) to minimize the noise in the avalanche process.

The α/β ratio is normally a fixed material property in bulk semiconductors. However, it was suggested by Chin, et al. (1980) and by Capasso, et al. (1982) that this ratio could be altered in a multiquantum well structure for carrier transport perpendicular to the growth plane. These expectations were verified experimentally by several groups and have led to extremely low noise avalanche photodetectors.

The early explanations offered for the ability to tune the α/β ratio were based on intuitive ideas which only provided part of the explanation. For example, the increase in the α/β ratio in AlGaAs/GaAs multiquantum well structures was explained in the following manner. Referring to Figure 14.18, the electrons impinging from the high bandgap AlGaAs side gain an energy ΔE_c (the conduction band discontinuity) as they enter the GaAs region. The holes, on the other hand, gain an energy ΔE_v (the valence band discontinuity). Since $\Delta E_c > \Delta E_v$, the electron gains a comparatively higher energy and therefore has a higher prob-

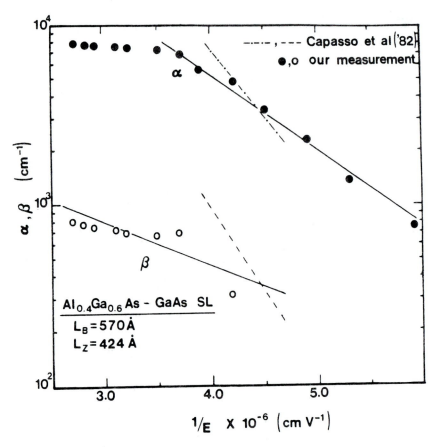

Figure 14.19: Measured α and β in GaAs/AlGaAs multi-quantum wells with large L_Z and L_B, (from F. Y. Juang, 1987).

ability of impact ionizing. At the time the explanation was offered, the 85:15 rule ($\Delta E_c = 0.85\Delta E_g$, $\Delta E_v = 0.15\Delta E_g$) was accepted. The currently accepted value is closer to 60:40.

More quantitative information has emerged from Monte Carlo methods which are based on using either the barrier bulk material parameters or the well bulk parameters. This is obviously a strong approximation especially for thin period multiquantum well structures. However, it does provide a greater insight into the problem. It appears that the enhanced α/β ratio in AlGaAs/GaAs multiquantum wells has more to do with reduced β values than increased α values. The value of β appears to decrease because the presence of discontinuities slows down the rate at which the holes can gain energy from the electric field.

Detailed experimental studies have been carried out by Juang and Bhattacharya on studying the variation of α and β in multiquantum well structures. Some of their results are reproduced in Figures 14.19 and 14.20.   One can see

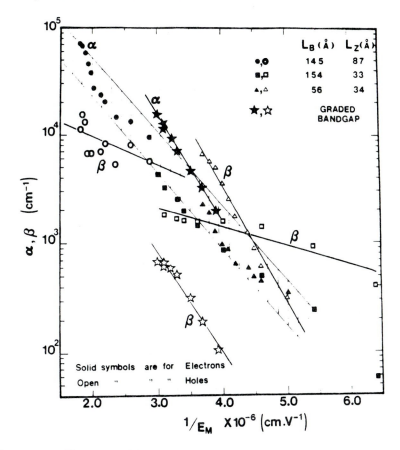

Figure 14.20: Electron and hole impact ionization coefficients in GaAs/AlGaAs super-lattices with varying L_Z and L_B, (from F. Y. Juang, 1987).

that the variation in the quantum well parameters affects β much more than α.

14.8 QUANTUM TRANSPORT

The various cases of transport in heterostructures discussed so far have required only semiclassical approaches for their understanding (Figure 14.1). While the semiclassical approach has questionable validity, especially for vertical transport in multiquantum wells, it provides a reasonable representation if the electron transport is over the barriers. The next class of transport problems, referred to as quantum transport, we will discuss cannot be understood at all unless the wave nature of the electrons is invoked. We have chosen four problems in this category as outlined in Figure 14.1. The full theoretical understanding of transport in these cases is not yet complete, and is an ongoing area of research. In particular, there are serious difficulties in including scattering processes in quantum transport. In our discussions we will not attempt to develop the complex and usually insolvable formalism necessary to address these problems. We will develop the simplest approach which provides the physical insight into the phenomenon and contains sufficient physics in that experimental results are semiquantitatively explained.

14.9　RESONANT TUNNELING

Resonant tunneling is a quantum mechanical concept that manifests itself in particles tunneling through a sequence of classically forbidden regions sandwiching a classically allowed region. The classically forbidden region must be thin enough so that particles can tunnel through it and the classically allowed region should be thick enough to allow the existence of eigenenergy states, referred to as quasibound states. Particles with certain energies can then penetrate the sequence of classically forbidden regions without attenuation.

Resonant tunneling devices have potential for very high speed applications and are therefore being studied in great detail. The operation of a resonant tunneling structure is understood conceptually by examining Figure 14.21. At zero bias, point A, no current flows through the structure. At point B, when the Fermi energy lines up with the quasibound state, a maximum amount of current flows through the structure. Further increasing the bias results in the structure of point C, where the current through the structure has decreased with increasing bias (negative resistance). Applying a larger bias results in a strong thermionic emission current and thus the current increases substantially as shown at point D.

A variety of modeling tools have been developed to understand the operation of the resonant tunneling structure. The simplest ones are based on quantum mechanical tunneling approaches developed in most textbooks and provide the basic underlying physics. However, these theories do not give very good agreement with experimental results. The discrepancies arise from several sources, the main ones are:

1. Lack of self-consistency between the Poisson equation and the Schrödinger equation.

2. Lack of scattering processes in the solution.

3. Use of single particle picture to calculate the current flow.

Varying levels of complexities have been introduced to overcome these problems and it seems that even with a simple approach a self-consistent solution gives a good agreement with experiments. We will discuss the simplest approach, similar to the one used by Tsu and Esaki (1973) in their first proposal for the resonant tunneling structure. In this approach, known as the transfer matrix approach, the potential profile (say, the conduction band lineup) is divided into regions of constant potential. The Schrödinger equation is solved in each region and the corresponding wavefunction in each region is matched at the boundaries

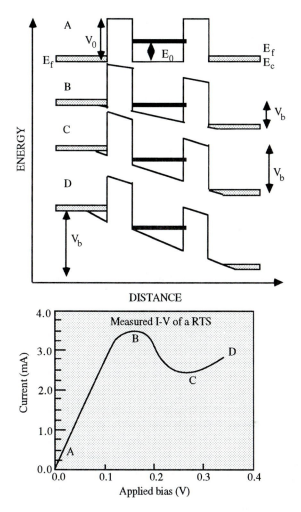

Figure 14.21: Schematic explanation of the operation of resonant tunneling devices showing the energy band diagram for different bias voltages and the corresponding measured current–voltage characteristic of the diode.

with the wavefunctions in the adjacent regions. For simplicity the electronic wavefunction is expanded in terms of a single band on either side of a barrier and the Schrödinger equation is separated into a parallel and perpendicular part. The one-dimensional Schrödinger's equation for the direction perpendicular to a barrier interface can be written as

$$\left[-\frac{\hbar^2}{2m}\frac{d^2}{dz^2} + V(z) - E \right] \psi_E(z) = 0. \tag{14.38}$$

When the potential $V(z)$ is constant in a given region, the general solution of Equation 14.38 has the form (see Figure 14.22)

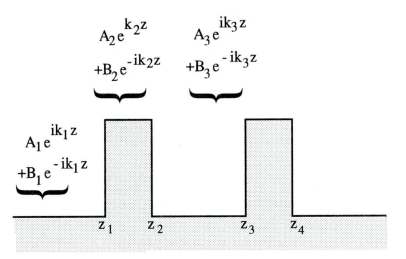

Figure 14.22: The form of the electron wavefunctions in different regions of a resonant tunneling structure.

$$\psi(z) = A \exp[ikz] + B \exp[-ikz],\qquad(14.39)$$

with

$$\frac{\hbar^2 k^2}{2m} = E - V.\qquad(14.40)$$

When $E - V > 0$, k is real, and the wave functions are plane waves. When $E - V < 0$, k is imaginary and the wave functions are growing and decaying waves. Thus, the overall wavefunction for a single barrier profile is an exponentially decaying wave for the barrier region and a plane-wave everywhere else.

At the boundaries between two materials one applies the boundary conditions

$$\psi(z^-) = \psi(z^+)\qquad(14.41)$$

and

$$\frac{1}{m_1}\frac{d\psi}{dz}\bigg|_{z^-} = \frac{1}{m_2}\frac{d\psi}{dz}\bigg|_{z^+}\qquad(14.42)$$

where m_1 and m_2 are the masses in the two regions. The second boundary condition ensures current continuity across the interface. The boundary conditions at the interface then determine the coefficients A and B (the subscripts denote the different regions) and can be described by a 2 × 2 matrix, M, such that

$$\begin{bmatrix} A_1 \\ B_1 \end{bmatrix} = M \begin{bmatrix} A_2 \\ B_2 \end{bmatrix}\qquad(14.43)$$

where M is known as the transfer matrix. It can be written as

$$M = \frac{1}{2k_1 m_2} \begin{bmatrix} C \exp[i(k_2 - k_1)z_1] & D \exp[-i(k_2 + k_1)z_1] \\ D \exp[i(k_2 + k_1)z_1] & C \exp[-i(k_2 - k_1)z_1] \end{bmatrix}\qquad(14.44)$$

where $C = (k_1 m_2 + k_2 m_1)$ and $D = (k_1 m_2 - k_2 m_1)$.

This method has been used by Kane (1969) for the case of more than one interface, assuming a uniform particle mass. In general, if the potential profile consists of n , characterized by the potential values V_x and the masses m_x separated by $n - 1$ interfaces at positions z_x then

$$
\begin{bmatrix} A_1 \\ B_1 \end{bmatrix} = [M_1 \cdots M_{n-1}] \begin{bmatrix} A_n \\ B_n \end{bmatrix}
\tag{14.45}
$$

The elements of M_x are

$$
M_x(1,1) = \left(\frac{1}{2} + \frac{k_{x+1}}{2k_x} \frac{m_x}{m_{x+1}} \right) \exp\left[i(k_{x+1} - k_x)z_x \right]
$$

$$
M_x(1,2) = \left(\frac{1}{2} - \frac{k_{x+1}}{2k_x} \frac{m_x}{m_{x+1}} \right) \exp\left[-i(k_{x+1} + k_x)z_x \right]
$$

$$
M_x(2,1) = \left(\frac{1}{2} - \frac{k_{x+1}}{2k_x} \frac{m_x}{m_{x+1}} \right) \exp\left[i(k_{x+1} + k_x)z_x \right]
$$

$$
M_x(2,2) = \left(\frac{1}{2} + \frac{k_{x+1}}{2k_x} \frac{m_x}{m_{x+1}} \right) \exp\left[-i(k_{x+1} - k_x)z_x \right]
$$

If an electron is incident from the left only a transmitted wave will appear in region n, and therefore $B_n = 0$.

A simple application of this formalism is the tunneling of electrons through a single barrier of height V_0 and width d. The tunneling probability is given by

$$
\begin{aligned}
T(E) &= \left| \frac{A_3}{A_1} \right|^2 \\
&= \frac{4E(V_0 - E)}{V_0^2 \sinh^2(qd) + 4E(V_0 - E)}
\end{aligned}
\tag{14.46}
$$

with

$$
q = \frac{1}{\hbar} \sqrt{2m(V_0 - E)}.
\tag{14.47}
$$

This tunneling probability does not have any useful features as shown in Figure 14.23. On the other hand, the double barrier structure has very interesting behavior in its tunneling probability. The calculated transmission probability as a function of longitudinal electron energy for a typical RTD is shown in Figure 14.24 (solid curve). For this calculation the barriers are assumed to be 1.2 eV and 26 Å wide. The well is 50 Å wide. The mass of the particle is taken to be $0.15m_0$ in the barriers and $0.042m_0$ outside of the barriers. The sharp peaks in the transmission probability correspond to resonant tunneling through the quasi-bound states in the quantum well formed between the two barriers. Note the relative widths of the ground and first resonant state. Also note that the transmission probability reaches unity. The tunneling probability reaches unity

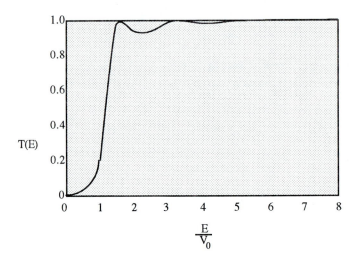

Figure 14.23: The transmission coefficient of a square barrier as a function of particle energy for $mV_0a^2/\hbar^2 = 8$.

at energies corresponding to the quasi-bound states in the quantum well, of width W, formed by the barriers. These energies are approximately

$$E_n = \frac{\pi^2\hbar^2 n^2}{2mW^2}. \tag{14.48}$$

Although the transfer-matrix method was developed for rectangular barriers, it can be generalized to profiles of arbitrary shape, by dividing the barrier into steps of infinitesimal width. This enables one to calculate the probability of transmission through the double barrier structure in the presence of an applied field. This is shown in Figure 14.24 (dashed curve). In contrast with the zero-field case (rectangular symmetrical barriers) the probability does not reach unity, because of the asymmetry introduced by the electric field. This calculation can be used to study the effect of various device design parameters such as the barrier height, barrier width, and well width. These parameters can be varied to optimize the tunneling probability. However, the tunneling probability is not readily verifiable experimentally. The parameter commonly measured and of interest for device applications is the I–V characteristic of the structure. However, in order to calculate the current the tunneling probability must be known.

The current in the system is given by

$$
\begin{aligned}
\boldsymbol{J} &= ne\boldsymbol{v} \\
&= \frac{e}{4\pi^3\hbar} \int_0^\infty dk_\ell \int_0^\infty d^2k_t \left[f(E) - f(E') \right] T(E_\ell) \frac{\partial E}{\partial k_\ell} \tag{14.49}
\end{aligned}
$$

where the longitudinal velocity is

$$\boldsymbol{v} = \frac{1}{\hbar} \frac{\partial E}{\partial \boldsymbol{k}_\ell} \tag{14.50}$$

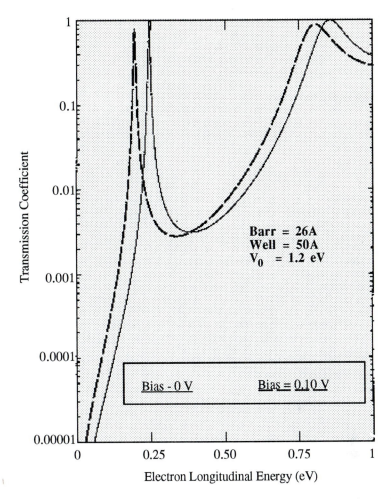

Figure 14.24: Transmission coefficient vs. electron longitudinal energy for a double barrier structure at zero bias (solid curve) and with an applied voltage (dashed curve).

and the net current is due to the electrons going from the left-hand side with energy E and from the right-hand side with energy $E' = E + eFl = E + eV$ where F is the electric field and l is the distance between the contacts on the two sides.

$$
\begin{aligned}
J &= \frac{e}{4\pi^3\hbar} \int dk_\ell T(E_\ell) \frac{\partial E}{\partial k_\ell} \int d^2k_t \left[\frac{1}{\exp\left[(E_t + E_\ell - E_F)/k_BT\right] + 1} \right. \\
&\quad \left. - \frac{1}{\exp\left[(E_t + E_\ell + eV - E_F)/k_BT\right] + 1} \right].
\end{aligned}
\tag{14.51}
$$

The transverse momentum integral can be simplified by noting that

$$
\begin{aligned}
d^2k_t &= k_t \, dk_t \, d\phi \\
&= \frac{m^* \, dE_t \, d\phi}{\hbar^2}.
\end{aligned}
$$

The current then becomes

$$
\begin{aligned}
J &= \frac{em^*}{2\pi^2\hbar^3} \int dE_\ell T(E_\ell) \int_0^\infty dE_t \left[\frac{1}{\exp\left[(E_t + E_\ell - E_F)/k_BT\right] + 1} \right. \\
&\qquad \left. - \frac{1}{\exp\left[(E_t + E_\ell + eV - E_F)/k_BT\right] + 1} \right] \\
&= \frac{em^*}{2\pi^2\hbar^3} \int_0^\infty T(E_\ell) \ln\left[\frac{1 + \exp\left[(E_F - E_\ell)/k_BT\right]}{1 + \exp\left[(E_F - E_\ell - eV)/k_BT\right]} \right] dE_\ell. \quad (14.52)
\end{aligned}
$$

The current shows peaks because of the peaks in the tunneling probability. The reader is advised to be careful to distinguish between $T(E_\ell)$, the tunneling probability and T, the temperature.

While the formalism described above does provide the qualitative features observed in the I–V characteristics of the resonant tunneling diodes, it does not provide good quantitative agreement. We already discussed some of the reasons for this disagreement. Approaches based on Wigner formulation, self-consistent treatments, as well as somehow including scattering effects, have been used to improve the agreement between experiments and theory. The techniques are too complex to be discussed here. Nevertheless, the need for such complexity shows how electronic devices have approached the regime where simpler quantum mechanics concepts are not adequate. In Figure 14.25 we show some typical results for the I–V characteristics of resonant tunneling structures.

14.10 TUNNELING IN HETEROSTRUCTURES WITH SPATIALLY VARYING CENTRAL CELL SYMMETRY

In the usual tunneling problems addressed in quantum mechanics textbooks, the electron wavefunction is simply represented by plane waves. We have used such an approach in the previous section. Of course, we know from Bloch's theorem, that in semiconductors the wavefunction is not simply a plane wave but consists of a central cell part as well. The central cell part depends upon the k-space point under consideration and the symmetry of the state. For example, we have discussed earlier that the conduction band minima in direct band materials have an s-type central cell function while indirect bandgap materials have an s-p mixture describing the central cell part. If the tunneling problem involves a band lineup where the central cell symmetry of the minimum energy states does not change appreciably, one can simply suppress the central cell part and the kind of treatment discussed in the previous section becomes valid. However,

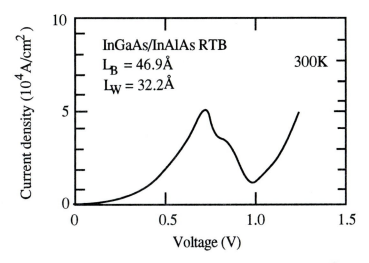

Figure 14.25: Static current–voltage characteristics of an InGaAs/InAlAs RTB diode at room temperature for $L_W = 46.9$ Å and $L_B = 32.2$ Å. Bias shown was negative to substrate. (Reproduced with permission, Y. Sugiyama, et al., Appl. Phys. Lett., **52**, 314 (1988).)

if the quantum structure involves combinations of direct and indirect bandgap materials, the role of the central cell symmetry becomes critical.

The GaAs/AlGaAs system is one in which a complex range of tunneling problems can be studied. In this system, discussed in detail in Chapter 6, the $Al_xGa_{1-x}As$ alloy remains a direct bandgap material up to an Al composition of $\sim 35\%$ and then becomes indirect with the band minima at the X-point. The heterostructure discontinuity between the $Al_xGa_{1-x}As/Al_yGa_{1-y}As$ heterostructure is given by the rule

$$\frac{\Delta E_c}{\Delta E_v} \approx \frac{0.65 \, \Delta E_{g\Gamma}}{0.35 \, \Delta E_{g\Gamma}} \tag{14.53}$$

where $\Delta E_{g\Gamma}$ is the bandgap discontinuity between the direct gaps of the heterostructure. This allows some very interesting conduction band discontinuities in this system as shown in Figure 14.27. The various conduction band discontinuities are given by the following equations

$$\begin{aligned}
\Delta E_c^{\Gamma-\Gamma}(x,y) &\approx 0.9 \, (y-x) \text{ eV} \\
\Delta E_c^{X-X}(x,y) &\approx -0.3 \, (y-x) \text{ eV} \\
\Delta E_c^{L-L}(x,y) &\approx 0.2 \, (y-x) \text{ eV}.
\end{aligned} \tag{14.54}$$

As can be seen from these equations, and from Figure 14.26, one can have a situation where the Γ-Γ discontinuity is extremely high, while Γ-X discontinuity is very small. The question then arises for tunneling processes whether the

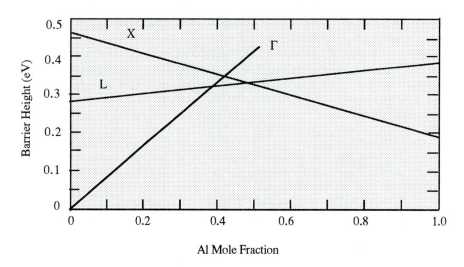

Figure 14.26: Barrier heights between GaAs (Γ-point) and Al$_x$Ga$_{1-x}$As heterostructures. The heights are shown for Γ-Γ, Γ-L, and Γ-X discontinuities. The barrier heights for any other structure Al$_y$Ga$_{1-y}$As/As$_x$Ga$_{1-x}$As can be found by the transitivity rule.

electron tunnels through the Γ-Γ barrier or the smaller Γ-X barrier.

Detailed experimental studies have been carried out for the tunneling and thermionic emission processes in the GaAs/Al$_x$Ga$_{1-x}$As heterostructure systems. These studies involve tunneling through "thick" Al$_x$Ga$_{1-x}$As barriers as a function of the Al composition. The significance of thick barriers will become clear soon. The experimental findings are represented in Figure 14.27 where we show the tunneling prefactor and effective barrier height for the tunneling process as a function of the Al composition. When the barriers are direct, the tunneling prefactor is the one given by simple tunneling formalism (e.g., the WKB approximation) for an electron tunneling through a thick barrier under an electric field F

$$T = \exp\left(-\frac{4\sqrt{2m^*}\left(\Delta E_c\right)^{3/2}}{3\hbar e F}\right) \qquad (14.55)$$

where $2m^*$ is the effective mass in the barrier and ΔE_c is the barrier discontinuity. The tunneling barrier is simply the $\Delta E_c^{\Gamma-\Gamma}$ discontinuity when the Al composition in the barrier increases above 35% making the AlGaAs barrier indirect, it is found that the prefactor drops precipitously and the tunneling barrier approaches the $\Delta E_c^{\Gamma-X}$ discontinuity. Thus, electrons are tunneling through the X-point minima which, of course, gives the lower discontinuity.

However, another interesting feature of the tunneling emerges in this regime and is brought out by Figure 14.28. As we have discussed for the case of Si, the X-valley has a large longitudinal mass and a small transverse mass. Tunneling through the small mass transverse x,y valleys will, of course, be much faster than the larger mass z valley (for (001) growth). However, the electron needs to

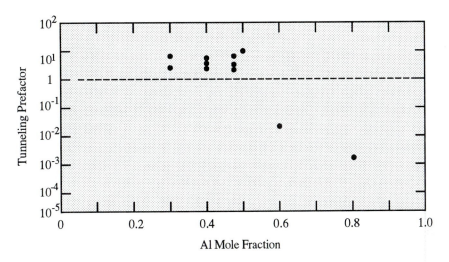

Figure 14.27: Tunneling prefactors obtained from tunneling studies in GaAs /Al_xGa_{1-x}As structures. The barriers are thick, (after Solomon, et al., 1986).

scatter to the x or y valleys. This does appear to occur for the thick barriers and as shown in Figure 14.28, the relevant mass to fit the tunneling expression is the lighter transverse mass.

For thin barriers, the situation is quite different. It is found that regardless of the Al composition in the barrier, the tunneling is dominated by the $\Delta E_c^{\Gamma-\Gamma}$ discontinuity. Thus, the central cell symmetry is *preserved during tunneling without scattering*. Clearly to understand such tunneling processes, the central cell function has to be explicitly retained in the problem. An elegant way to approach such problems is to study the time evolution of a quasi-bound state, say, in a GaAs well through an Al_xGa_{1-x}As barrier by solving the time dependent Schrödinger equation. The Schrödinger equation is not scalar but has to be a multiband equation to describe the correct symmetry of the central cell state. Ando, et al. (1989) proposed a method which allows one to extend the envelope function method to multiband wavefunctions. Envelope functions arising from dissimilar band extrema are matched at interfaces using local tight binding or pseudopotential calculations. Another approach is to solve the time dependent multiband Schrödinger equation. This approach does not require any matching conditions at the interfaces and provides more physical insight into the tunneling process since the actual time evolution of an electron is studied.

An example of the time dependent study is the approach used by Sankaran and Singh (1991) who use an 8-band tight binding representation for the electronic states.

An initial electron state is prepared from the stationary state solutions of the problem as in the wavepacket description discussed in Appendix A. This multiband state is chosen so that the electron is localized in a particular region

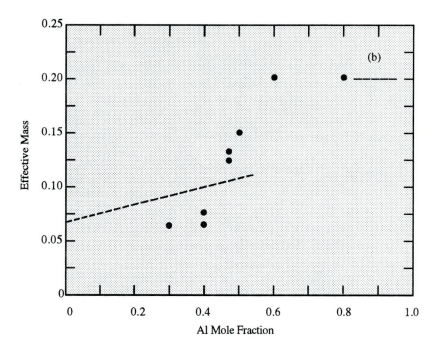

Figure 14.28: The effective masses in the barrier obtained from tunneling studies in GaAs/Al$_x$Ga$_{1-x}$As structures. At low Al composition the mass is essentially that of the direct gap alloy (dashed line). For high composition the mass corresponds to the transverse X-valley mass (dashed line), (after Solomon, et al., 1986).

of the structure, e.g. in a quantum well. The multiband state is then allowed to evolve in time.

For a scalar Schrödinger equation, a formal solution to the time evolution of a wavepacket in a time-independent potential is given by

$$\psi(\mathbf{r}, t) = e^{-iHt/\hbar}\,\psi(\mathbf{r}, 0). \tag{14.56}$$

The details of solving this equation by discretizing the time interval of interest into infinitesimal steps δt are given by Goldberger, et al. (1967). For δt sufficiently small, we can approximate

$$\exp(-iH\delta t/\hbar) \approx 1 - iH\delta t/\hbar. \tag{14.57}$$

However, this approximation is not unitary, and probability is not conserved. A better approximation which is unitary and also correct to second order in δt is the Cayley form

$$\exp(-iH\delta t/\hbar) \approx \frac{1 - iH\delta t/2\hbar}{1 + iH\delta t/2\hbar}. \tag{14.58}$$

To this approximation we have

$$\psi(r, t + \delta t) = \frac{1 - iH\delta t/2\hbar}{1 + iH\delta t/2\hbar} \psi(r, t). \tag{14.59}$$

Furthermore, any instability in the procedure arising from numerical round off errors is suppressed by rewriting the above equation in the implicit form

$$(1 + iH\delta t/2\hbar) \, \psi(r, t + \delta t) = (1 - iH\delta t/2\hbar) \, \psi(r, t). \tag{14.60}$$

This approach can be easily extended to multiband wave functions.

Assuming that the tunneling escape of carriers can be described by an exponential decay law, tunneling times τ are obtained from the initial decay rate of probability in the starting well

$$\tau = \frac{P(0)}{(\Delta P/\Delta t)} \tag{14.61}$$

This may be taken as the definition of the tunneling times.

In Figure 14.29 we show the time evolution of a $k_\parallel = 0$ wavefunction from a 84 Å GaAs well through a 56 Å $Al_{0.3}Ga_{0.7}As$ barrier ($\Delta E_c^{\Gamma - \Gamma} = 0.2$ eV). The indices 1 and 2 represent the s and p_z coefficients on the cation while 3 and 4 represent the same for the anion. As can be seen there is significant p-type mixing in the starting wavefunction. For comparison when the barrier is changed to $Al_{0.6}Ga_{0.4}As$ so that $\Delta E_c^{\Gamma - X} = 0.2$ eV, the same barrier height as for the case of the previous figure, but a different symmetry, there is essentially no evolution of the wavefunction out of the barrier. When the barrier is reduced to 28 Å $Al_{0.6}Ga_{0.4}As$, the wavefunction evolves as shown in Figure 14.30. The tunneling times calculated for an $Al_{0.3}Ga_{0.7}As$ and AlAs barriers are shown in Figure 14.31. These results show that the valley symmetry is *conserved* during scattering free tunneling.

An important area of tunneling involving initial and final states with very dissimilar central cell symmetries is the area of tunneling of electrons from the valence band into the conduction band under the influence of a strong electric field. In many semiconductor systems, this is an important source of breakdown (in addition to impact ionization breakdown). This phenomenon, called Zener tunneling, is also the basis of tunnel diodes, where the band-to-band tunneling produces negative differential resistance in the I–V characteristics (e.g. Esaki, 1958; Sze, 1981). The problem of band-to-band tunneling is usually treated by the WKB method without special considerations for the symmetry of the initial and final states. In Figure 14.32 we show a typical band profile of the conduction and valence bands in a p-n junction which is reverse biased. In this figure the E vs. k curves are superimposed on top of the E-x profile of the semiconductor. Due to the band bending electrons in the valence band at point x, for example, are aligned in energy with electrons at point x_2 and can thus tunnel through the forbidden barrier which may be treated as a triangular barrier. If the symmetry

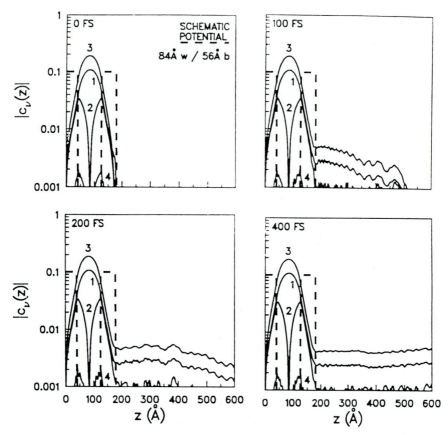

Figure 14.29: Time evolution of a multiband electron wave from a 84 Å GaAs well through a 56 Å $Al_{0.3}Ga_{0.7}As$ barrier, (from Sankaran and Singh, 1991).

of the initial and final states is ignored, the tunneling probability can be written as (e.g. Sze, 1981)

$$T_t = \exp\left[\frac{4}{3}\frac{\sqrt{2m^*}}{eF\hbar}\left(\frac{E_g}{2} - eFx\right)^{3/2}\right]\Bigg|_{-x_1}^{x_2}. \qquad (14.62)$$

Also since at

$$x = x_2; \left(\frac{E_g}{2} - eFx\right) = 0 \qquad (14.63)$$

and at

$$x = -x_1; \left(\frac{E_g}{2} - eFx\right) = E_g \qquad (14.64)$$

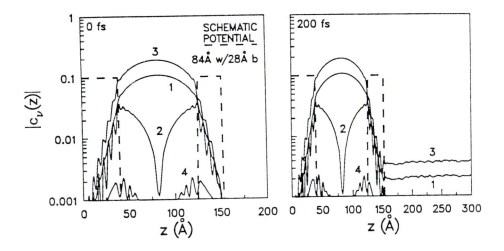

Figure 14.30: Time evolution of envelope functions for an electron tunneling from the first quasibound level of an 84 Å (30 monolayer) GaAs well through a 28 Å (10 monolayer) $Al_{0.6}Ga_{0.4}As$ (indirect) barrier, (from Sankaran and Singh, 1991).

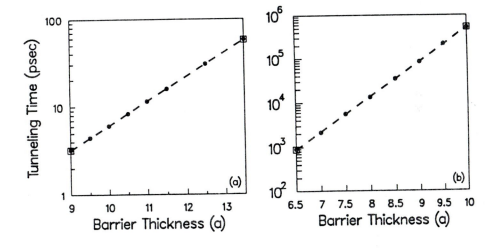

Figure 14.31: Tunneling times as a function of barrier thickness for quasibound electrons escaping from a 56 Å GaAs quantum well through barriers of (a) $Al_{0.3}Ga_{0.7}As$ and (b) AlAs. Barrier thickness is in units of the lattice constant. Bullets mark the results of computations while the dotted line is an exponential fit through them, (from Sankaran and Singh, 1991).

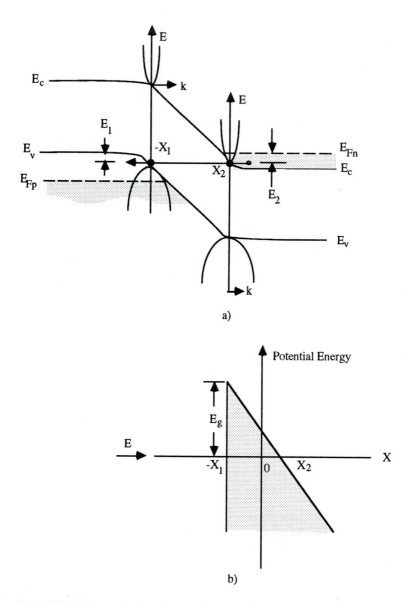

Figure 14.32: (a) A schematic showing the $E-x$ and E vs. k diagram for a p-n junction. An electron in the valence band can tunnel into an unoccupied state in the conduction band or vice-versa. (b) The potential profile seen by the electron during the tunneling process.

the tunneling probability is

$$T_t \approx \exp\left(-\frac{4\sqrt{2m^*}E_g^{3/2}}{3e\hbar F}\right). \tag{14.65}$$

Other treatments of this problem involve the use of parabolic barriers or other forms of the barrier profile. Nevertheless, these treatments are usually not too accurate in defining the tunneling current. There is a growing interest in these problems with the advent of heterostructures and the greater appreciation of the need to consider the cell symmetric part of the wavefunction in tunneling.

14.11 PERPENDICULAR TRANSPORT IN SUPERLATTICES

In our discussion on avalanche processes in multiquantum well structures we used the semiclassical transport theory to understand the transport phenomenon. The reason this theory is adequate in that case is that there is essentially no tunneling and the electron always moves in the region of allowed states in the individual bulk material. We know from our discussions in Chapter 6 that when the barrier regions of multiquantum wells become very thin, the superlattice acquires a totally new bandstructure with minibands in the direction (k-space) of the growth. While the bandstructure in a real superlattice is quite complex, as can be seen from Chapter 6, a simple picture of transport can be developed by using the concepts in Figure 14.33. It is useful to consider the transport in two regimes: in the absence of scattering, and in the presence of scattering.

In the absence of any scattering events, the formalism discussed in Chapter 13 for electron transport and Bloch-Zener oscillations is most relevant in describing the electron transport. We showed in that discussion that an electron simply undergoes an oscillatory motion in both real space and k-space. As shown in those discussions, the oscillation frequency is given by

$$\omega \approx \frac{eFa}{\hbar} \tag{14.66}$$

where F is the applied electric field and a is a period of the superlattice. These oscillations simply represent the successive reflections of the electron once they reach the miniband edge. The main difference between the superlattice and the bulk material discussions of Chapter 13 is the details of the miniband width. The bandwidth will be quite a bit smaller in the case of the superlattice and thus there is a higher probability that the conditions for the Bloch oscillations to occur, viz.

$$\omega\tau_{sc} \geq 1 \tag{14.67}$$

will be satisfied (τ_{sc} = scattering time). The frequency of these oscillations can be tailored to be in the 100–1000 GHz making them very important sources of

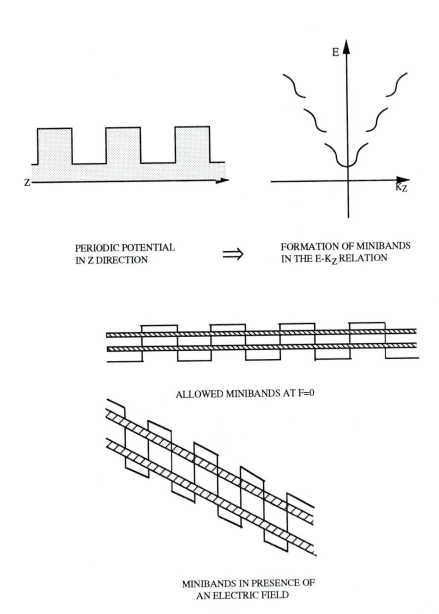

PERIODIC POTENTIAL $\Longrightarrow$ FORMATION OF MINIBANDS
IN Z DIRECTION   IN THE E-K_Z RELATION

ALLOWED MINIBANDS AT F=0

MINIBANDS IN PRESENCE OF
AN ELECTRIC FIELD

Figure 14.33: Formation of minibands in one-dimensional periodic potential, and effect of an electric field on minibands in MQW.

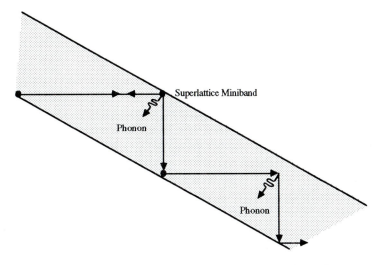

Figure 14.34: A schematic view of how an electron would physically move across a superlattice. Phonon emission is required for the electron to avoid zone edge reflection.

microwave radiation. While several groups have made serious attempts to observe Bloch oscillations, there has been no success so far. However, coherent oscillations in a coupled quantum well system have been observed. In this experiment an electron is injected by a short pulse laser in *one* of the quantum wells of an asymmetric quantum well structure. The short pulse produces an electron wavepacket selectively in one quantum well and this electron oscillates in the two quantum wells as long as there is no scattering . The observation of coherent oscillations suggests that it may be possible to see Bloch oscillations as well.

In the presence of scattering processes one does not expect the Bloch oscillations to occur. Nevertheless, there is a great deal of very interesting transport phenomenon. For the electron to traverse a region of a semiconductor and reach from one contact to another, it should be able to have inelastic scattering and "go down" to the bottom of the miniband by emitting a phonon. Once the electron is at the bottom of the miniband, it can again proceed to travel under the influence of the electric field. The ability to emit a phonon is thus crucial to the transport process and the current–voltage characteristics. The transport process is shown schematically in Figure 14.34. Experimentally a tremendous richness is observed in the current–voltage characteristics in thin period superlattices.

14.12 QUANTUM INTERFERENCE EFFECTS

In our discussion of wave diffraction in crystals in Chapter 3, we discussed the diffraction of electrons. Under certain conditions the electrons are described by their wave character and they produce the same sort of phenomenon that optical waves do. For example, effects like interference, diffraction, etc., which occur

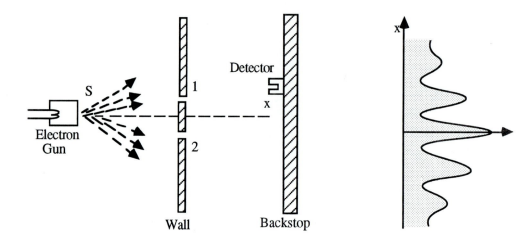

Figure 14.35: A schematic of the double slit interference experiment done with electrons. If coherence is maintained between the electrons coming from the electron gun (contact for semiconductor devices), the electron waves interfere producing a highly modulated intensity as shown.

in optics can occur in electronics as well. An important consideration for these effects to occur is lack of scattering so that the electron (or photon) can maintain its k-state (or coherence) over different paths. In case of photons, scattering is usually not a serious problem since the photon carries no charge and is relatively immune to material disturbances. However, for electrons, the scattering process is quite strong, and only at low temperatures in short channel structures can one expect there to be no scattering. However, with fine line lithography it is now possible to make semiconductor structures with dimensions where electrons can retain coherence in their phases from one contact to the other. This opens the possibility of studying and utilizing effects that are based on interference phenomenon. The classic interference effect in optics is described by the two slit experiment shown in Figure 14.35. Here electrons (photons) from a single source go through two slits and interfere on a screen at a distance d from the slits. The electron intensity across the screen is modulated and is given by the sum of the individual amplitudes at a particular point of the electrons coming from two different paths

$$I = \left| \psi_0 \, e^{i k \cdot d_1} + \psi_0 \, e^{i k \cdot d_2} \right|^2 . \tag{14.68}$$

If the photon wavelength could be modulated by some means, the intensity at a particular point on the screen could also be modulated. A similar concept could be used in electron waves where the charge density could be similarly modulated. It is reasonably easy to modulate the effective electronic wavelength, say, in a MODFET structure. The electron wavelength at the Fermi level is simply given in a 2-D system by the expression (assuming a single subband occupation)

$$\lambda_F \approx \sqrt{\frac{2\pi}{n_s}} \tag{14.69}$$

where n_s is the sheet charge density. The sheet charge density is readily modulated by the gate on the MODFET.

A large number of electronic devices can be now conceived which can utilize the interference effects. These devices can be switched (i.e., the interference pattern can be modified) with only a small change in n_s or λ_F (unlike the normal transistors where n_s has to undergo a large modulation), therefore, they promise low-power high-speed switching. Of course, these devices must operate under conditions of no scattering which may cause loss of phase coherence. It may be noted that certain kinds of fixed center scattering (e.g. defect scattering) do not cause phase memory loss. Thus, these quantum devices are expected to operate only at very low temperatures ($\geq$ 10–15 K), where phonon effects are negligible.

In absence of any potential fluctuations (due to defects) and inelastic scattering, the charge transport of electron waves can be based on the knowledge developed in optics. However, even at low temperatures, where inelastic processes can be suppressed, there will be defects which are randomly placed in the path of the electron wave. The electron transport through these potential fluctuations must be treated in the same manner as we treated the transport in the resonant tunneling structure. Thus, one must talk in terms of transmission (or tunneling) probabilities through the randomly arranged defects. Such transport is described best by a formalism developed by Landauer and will be discussed in more detail in Chapter 18 where we introduce disordered and mesoscopic structures. As devices become smaller, the effect of phase correlations between different paths taken by electrons to get from one contact to another become important leading a very rich range of transport phenomenon. In our discussions on X-ray diffraction in nonperiodic structures (Chapter 3), we went into some detail on the averaging process. We showed that for uncorrelated scattering one could find the transmitted intensity by simply summing the *square* of the transmitted wave from each individual scatterer. However, if there are correlations in the scattered waves (as is the case for X-ray diffraction from nonrandom structures), one must sum the individual amplitudes and *then* square them. The richness in X-ray diffraction patterns (or RHEED patterns) arises from such correlated sums. In the transport theory developed in Chapters 10 through 13 we always assumed that individual scattering events are random. This assumption breaks down in very small structures where phase information is correlated throughout the size of the structure. Such structures are called mesoscopic structures and the transport phenomenon in these structures shows a richness not unlike that seen in X-ray diffraction.

14.13   DENSITY MATRIX FORMALISM

We will end this chapter by presenting a very brief discussion of quantum transport formalism to describe transport in small structures (we will discuss the Landauer formalism in Chapter 18). It is not possible to describe all the intricacies of the quantum transport, especially those dealing with its applications for real semiconductor structures. In fact, the approaches described here have been applied only to simple model systems with strong approximations as far as scattering processes are concerned. Also, in many cases the results that one obtains are not too different from those obtained by the Boltzmann equation using a classical distribution function. As we discussed in Chapter 10, the classical distribution function assumes a point particle approach, an approach which breaks down once the electron's de Broglie wavelength becomes comparable to the device dimensions. In the absence of scattering, one can still estimate the charge transport, for example, as we did in the resonant tunneling problem, by assuming that the electrons are in thermal equilibrium with the contact regions even though there is no scattering in the active device structure. However, to include scattering effects one must use the quantum transport equations.

In a quantum mechanical system electrons are described by the eigenfunctions and eigenenergies of the appropriate Hamiltonian. However, in an ensemble of carriers, the electrons do not all occupy a single state but are distributed in various states. Thus, for example, one may be able to say no more than that the quantum system has non-negative probabilities, p_α, p_β, ... for being in states $|\alpha\rangle$, $|\beta\rangle$, etc. Thus, a statistical picture needs to be developed in analogy to the classical situation. The density matrix approach serves this purpose.

We recall that a pure classical state is represented by a single particle moving in phase space, with definite values of position and momenta. The statistical state in the classical situation is represented by a non-negative density function, $\rho(x_1 \ldots x_f, p_1 \ldots p_f)$ such that the probability that a system is found in the interval $dp_1 \ldots dp_f$ is simply $\rho \, dp_1 \ldots dp_f$. This ρ is, of course, the distribution function f used in the Boltzmann transport equation. The analog of the classical density (or distribution) function is the density operator or its representation in a basis which is called the density matrix.

Before defining the density operator, it is useful to define the projection operators in quantum mechanics. Consider a pure state $|\alpha\rangle$ which can be written as

$$
\begin{aligned}
|\alpha\rangle &= \sum_\mu |\mu\rangle\langle\mu|\alpha\rangle \\
&= \sum_\mu P_\mu |\alpha\rangle
\end{aligned}
\tag{14.70}
$$

where P_μ is called a projection operator and is given by

$$
P_\mu = |\mu\rangle\langle\mu|.
\tag{14.71}
$$

If the states $|\mu\rangle$ are eigenstates of an operator Ω, so that

$$\Omega|\mu\rangle = w_\mu|\mu\rangle, \tag{14.72}$$

then the state $P_\mu|\mu\rangle$ is also an eigenstate of Ω with eigenvalue w_μ. Thus, an arbitrary state $|\alpha\rangle$ can be written as a generalized sum of eigenstates of any operator Ω by using the projection operators. P_μ is called the projection operator since it projects out of any state $|\alpha\rangle$ the part that is a particular eigenstate of Ω. The projector operations contain the same information as the eigenstates and are useful in describing the average properties of a quantum system.

The expectation value of an operator Ω in a normalized state $|\alpha\rangle$ is

$$\begin{aligned}
\langle\alpha|\Omega|\alpha\rangle &= \langle\alpha|i\rangle\langle i|\Omega|j\rangle\langle j|\alpha\rangle \\
&= \langle i|\Omega|j\rangle\langle j|P_\alpha|i\rangle
\end{aligned} \tag{14.73}$$

where P_α is the projection operation $|\alpha\rangle\langle\alpha|$. Remember that

$$\begin{aligned}
\sum_i |i\rangle\langle i| &\equiv |i\rangle\langle i| \\
&= 1.
\end{aligned} \tag{14.74}$$

The right-hand side of Equation 14.73 can be written as $\langle i|\Omega P_\alpha|i\rangle$, and we have

$$\begin{aligned}
\langle\alpha|\Omega|\alpha\rangle &= \mathrm{Tr}(\Omega P_\alpha) \\
&= \mathrm{Tr}(P_\alpha\Omega).
\end{aligned} \tag{14.75}$$

Note that $P_\alpha^2 = P_\alpha$ and $\mathrm{Tr}(P_\alpha) = 1$.

The quantum equation of motion for the projection operator is given simply by the Schrödinger equation

$$\begin{aligned}
i\hbar\frac{d}{dt}P_\alpha &= i\hbar\left(\frac{d}{dt}|\alpha\rangle\right)\langle\alpha| + i\hbar|\alpha\rangle\left(\frac{d}{dt}\langle\alpha|\right) \\
&= H|\alpha\rangle\langle\alpha| - |\alpha\rangle\langle\alpha|H \\
&= [H, P_\alpha]
\end{aligned} \tag{14.76}$$

since

$$i\hbar\frac{d}{dt}|\alpha\rangle = H|\alpha\rangle$$

and

$$i\hbar\frac{d}{dt}\langle\alpha| = -\langle\alpha|H.$$

The density operator is now defined in terms of the projection operator by the relation

$$\begin{aligned}
\rho &\equiv \sum_\alpha p_\alpha P_\alpha \\
&= \sum_\alpha |\alpha\rangle p_\alpha\langle\alpha|
\end{aligned} \tag{14.77}$$

whereas the p_α are the probabilities of finding the system in the state $|\alpha\rangle$. It follows from Equations 14.77 and 14.75 that the average expectation value of Ω that corresponds to these probabilities is

$$
\begin{aligned}
\langle \Omega \rangle_{\text{av}} &= \sum_\alpha p_\alpha \langle \alpha | \Omega | \alpha \rangle \\
&= \text{Tr}(\Omega \rho) \\
&= \text{Tr}(\rho \Omega).
\end{aligned}
\tag{14.78}
$$

We also have the conditions

$$
\begin{aligned}
\text{Tr}(\rho) &= 1 \\
\text{Tr}(\rho^2) &= \sum_\alpha p_\alpha^2 \leq 1.
\end{aligned}
\tag{14.79}
$$

The equation of motion for the density operator is now simply

$$
i\hbar \frac{d\rho}{dt} = [H, \rho].
\tag{14.80}
$$

We note that in the coordinate representation the density matrix is given by

$$
\begin{aligned}
\rho(x, x') &= \langle x | \rho | x' \rangle \\
&= \langle x | \psi \rangle \langle \psi | x' \rangle \\
&= \psi(x)\, \psi(x').
\end{aligned}
\tag{14.81}
$$

The diagonal terms $\rho(x, x)$ simply represent the particle density at point x. The off-diagonal elements $\rho(x, x')$ represent transitions between $|x'\rangle$ and $|x\rangle$. There is a simple relation between the current in a structure and the density matrix. In quantum mechanics the current is given by

$$
J = \frac{e\hbar}{2im^*} \left[\psi^*(x) \frac{\partial \psi(x)}{\partial x} - \psi(x) \frac{\partial \psi^*(x)}{\partial x} \right].
\tag{14.82}
$$

Now consider

$$
\begin{aligned}
\text{Im}\,\rho(x, x') &= \text{Im}\left[\psi(x)\psi^*(x') \right] \\
&= \frac{\psi(x)\, \psi^*(x') - \psi^*(x)\, \psi(x')}{2i}.
\end{aligned}
\tag{14.83}
$$

Let

$$
\begin{aligned}
\eta &= \frac{x + x'}{2} \\
\xi &= x - x'.
\end{aligned}
\tag{14.84}
$$

Then

$$\left. \frac{\partial \mathrm{Im}\left(\rho(x,x')\right)}{\partial \xi}\right|_{\xi=0} = \left[\frac{\partial x}{\partial \xi}\frac{\partial \mathrm{Im}\left(\rho(x,x')\right)}{\partial x} + \frac{\partial x'}{\partial \xi}\frac{\partial \mathrm{Im}\left(\rho(x,x')\right)}{\partial x'}\right]_{x=x'}$$

$$= \frac{1}{2i}\left[\psi^*(x)\frac{\partial \psi(x)}{\partial x} - \psi(x)\frac{\partial \psi^*(x)}{\partial x}\right]. \qquad (14.85)$$

Thus, the current is

$$J = \frac{e\hbar}{m^*}\left[\frac{\partial \mathrm{Im}\left(\rho(x,x')\right)}{\partial \xi}\right]_{\xi=0}. \qquad (14.86)$$

The time-dependent quantum Liouville equation, given by Equation 14.80 can be used to study time evolution of the charge density. However, this equation is conservative and does not have any dissipative terms due to collisions. In order to describe a system in contact with a dissipative reservoir (say, an ohmic contact), a phenomenological relaxation term is added to give

$$i\hbar \frac{\partial \rho}{\partial t} = [H, \rho] - i\hbar \frac{(\rho - \rho_0)}{\tau} \qquad (14.87)$$

where ρ_0 is the equilibrium density operator and τ is a relaxation time. The quantity τ is usually not calculated as was done for the semiclassical transport (using the Fermi golden rule) and a considerable effort is being currently spent to develop methods to obtain τ. The solution of Equation 14.87 can now be obtained by the numerical algorithm

$$\rho(t + \Delta t) = \rho(t) + \Delta t \left\{\left(\frac{1}{i\hbar}\right)[H, \rho(t)] - \frac{\rho(t) - \rho_0}{\tau}\right\} \qquad (14.88)$$

This algorithm is often highly unstable because $\rho(t + \Delta t)$ is not unitary (see our discussion on tunneling). However, for very short times (10–20 fs) the above algorithm yields useful results. More stable algorithms can be used (like the one used in our discussion of wavepacket tunneling) to obtain results valid over longer time scales.

There is another approach to quantum transport based on a different distribution function called the Wigner distribution. This formalism is quite attractive because since it has all the essential quantum mechanics information about the system, yet has an appearance of a classical picture. The Wigner distribution function is defined in terms of the generalized coordinates and momenta of the system as

$$P_w(x_1 \cdots x_n, p_1 \cdots p_n) = \frac{1}{(2\pi\hbar)^n}\int_{-\infty}^{\infty} dy_1 \cdots dy_n$$

$$\times \ \Psi^*\left(x_1 + \frac{y_1}{2}, \cdots, x_n + \frac{y_n}{2}\right)$$

$$\times \quad \Psi\left(x_1 - \frac{y_1}{2}, \cdots, x_n - \frac{y_n}{2}\right)$$

$$\times \quad e^{i(p_1 y_1 + \cdots + p_n y_n)/\hbar}. \tag{14.89}$$

However, for simplicity, we will discuss the properties of a single coordinate and momentum function

$$p_w(x, p) = \frac{1}{2\pi\hbar} \int_{-\infty}^{\infty} dy \, \Psi^*\left(x + \frac{y}{2}\right) \Psi\left(x - \frac{y}{2}\right) e^{ipy/\hbar} \tag{14.90}$$

where $\Psi(x)$ represents the state of the system in the coordinate representation. The adaptation of this formalism to include mixed states is accomplished through the generalization

$$p_w(x, p) = \sum_n p_n \left[\frac{1}{2\pi\hbar} \int_{-\infty}^{\infty} dy \, \Psi_n^*\left(x + \frac{y}{2}\right) \Psi_n\left(x - \frac{y}{2}\right) e^{ipy/\hbar}\right] \tag{14.91}$$

where p_n is the probability to be in state n.

The distribution function (Equation 14.90) has interesting properties in that integration over all coordinates leads to the probability density in momentum space

$$\begin{aligned} \int_{-\infty}^{\infty} p_w(x, p) \, dx &= \frac{1}{2\pi\hbar} \int_{-\infty}^{\infty} dy \int_{-\infty}^{\infty} dx \, \Psi^*\left(x + \frac{y}{2}\right) \Psi\left(x - \frac{y}{2}\right) e^{ipy/\hbar} \\ &= \phi^*(p) \, \phi(p) \end{aligned} \tag{14.92}$$

where

$$\phi(p) = \frac{1}{\sqrt{2\pi\hbar}} \int_{-\infty}^{\infty} e^{ipx/\hbar} \, \Psi(x) \, dx. \tag{14.93}$$

As for the density function ρ, the average of an operator Ω is given by

$$\langle \Omega \rangle = \int \Omega \, p_w(x, p) \, dx \, dp. \tag{14.94}$$

However, unlike the density matrix, the Wigner distribution should not be viewed as a quantum analog of the classical distribution function since it uses a phase space description (x, p) of particles. However, in quantum mechanics the position and momentum do not commute. This results in often negative and nonunique values of p_w.

The Wigner distribution function satisfies a transport equation quite analogous to the semiclassical Boltzmann equation. It has been shown by Wigner that this equation for a Hamiltonian $H = p^2/(2m) + V(x)$ is

$$\frac{\partial P_w}{\partial t} + \frac{p}{m} \frac{\partial P_w}{\partial x} + \theta \cdot P_w = 0 \tag{14.95}$$

where

$$\theta \cdot P_w = -\frac{2}{\hbar} \sum_{n=0}^{\infty} (-1)^n \frac{(\hbar/2)^{2n+1}}{(2n+1)!} \frac{\partial^{2n+1} V(x)}{\partial x^{2n+1}} \frac{\partial^{2n+1} P_w(x, p)}{\partial p^{2n+1}}. \tag{14.96}$$

Alternately, $\theta \cdot P_w$ can be expressed as

$$\theta \cdot P_w = -\frac{2}{\hbar} \left[\sin \frac{\hbar}{2} \left\{ \frac{\partial}{\partial x} \frac{\partial}{\partial p} \right\} \right] V(x) P_w(x,p) \qquad (14.97)$$

where it is understood that the position gradient operates only on the potential energy $V(x)$. In the limit $\hbar \to 0$, $\theta \cdot P_w = -(\partial V/\partial x)(\partial P_w/\partial p)$ and Equation 14.95 reduces to the classical collisionless Boltzmann equation.

Once again the collision terms are included in an ad hoc manner to give the equation

$$\frac{\partial P_w}{\partial t} + \frac{p}{m} \frac{\partial P_w}{\partial x} + \theta \cdot P_w = \left(\frac{\partial P_w}{\partial t} \right)_{\text{coll.}} . \qquad (14.98)$$

This equation can be formally solved by the moments method discussed in Chapters 10 and 13 for the Boltzmann equation. However, it must be admitted that application of this and other quantum transport equations in real device structures has been very difficult. This arises partly from the breakdown of the single band effective mass theory in structures of dimensions ~ 50 Å. Use of an 8-band Schrödinger equation makes the problem a lot harder as our discussion on tunneling made evident.

In this chapter we have examined issues of transport in heterostructures. As we have seen there are two classes of transport phenomenon. For problems in the first class, the semiclassical approaches developed in Chapters 10–13 are reasonably adequate and experimental observations are explained relatively easily. In the second class the quantum mechanical nature of the electrons is so dominant that semiclassical treatments breakdown. The understanding of transport in this regime is far from complete. It is also clear that future electronic devices will need this understanding more and more.

14.14 FOR THE TECHNOLIGIST IN YOU

14.14.1 Some Device Related Issues

Negative Resistance and Charge Instabilities

In this chapter, one of the physical phenomena that we studied was in the resonant tunneling structure. The I–V characteristics of this device show a negative resistance region which is due to the tunneling phenomenon. The tunnel diode also shows this negative resistance phenomenon. Another instance where we see negative resistance is in materials like GaAs. We saw in Chapter 13 that the velocity–field relationship in GaAs (and InP, InGaAs, etc.) has a negative mobility region due to the transfer of electrons from the high mobility Γ-valley to an upper low mobility valley. Negative resistance can also be created by causing a time delay between an applied potential and the resulting current. This is done in devices such as impact ionization avalanche transit time devices (IMPATTs). To understand the reason behind the interest in creating negative resistance structures, one has to look at charge fluctuations in a system where there is negative resistance (or negative differential mobility). The charge fluctuation could originate spontaneously in the material, due to noise or due to an externally applied signal. If the material resistance is positive as is usually the case, the fluctuations die out. However, if the resistance is negative, these fluctuations can grow in time and space.

Let us first consider a simple description of the charge fluctuation in a semiconductor. Describing the semiconductor by a equivalent RC circuit, the resistance of the material of area A and length L is

$$R = \frac{L}{en\mu A} \tag{14.99}$$

and the capacitance is

$$C = \frac{\epsilon A}{L}. \tag{14.100}$$

Here n is the electron density and μ is the electron mobility. If a charge fluctuation develops, it will decay with a time constant of RC. This time is the dielectric response time τ_d

$$\tau_d = \frac{\epsilon}{en\mu} \tag{14.101}$$

and the charge fluctuation has a temporal response

$$\Delta Q = \Delta Q(0) \exp(-t/\tau_d). \tag{14.102}$$

If τ_d is negative (i.e. if μ is negative), the fluctuation actually grows in time, instead of decaying.

To study this effect more rigorously, consider the solutions of the Poisson equation and the current flowing in the semiconductor. The Poisson equation is

$$\frac{\partial F}{\partial x} = -\frac{e(n - n_D)}{\epsilon}. \tag{14.103}$$

The total current is

$$I = e\mu n F + eDn\frac{\partial n}{\partial x} + \epsilon\frac{\partial F}{\partial t} \tag{14.104}$$

where F is the electric field, which may be changing in time, giving rise to a displacement current (the last term of the current equation).

If the electric field is uniform in space, and constant in time, the carrier density and field are simply

$$\begin{aligned} n_0 &= N_D \\ F_0 &= \frac{I}{e\mu N_D}. \end{aligned} \tag{14.105}$$

Let us now assume a solution of the general problem to be given by

$$\begin{aligned} n &= n_0 + n_1 \exp[i(\omega t - kx)] \\ F &= F_0 + F_1 \exp[i(\omega t - kx)]. \end{aligned}$$

$$\tag{14.106}$$

Substituting these equations in the original Poisson equation and current equation, gives (for first order in n_1 and F_1)

$$-ikF_1 + \frac{e}{\epsilon}n_1 = 0$$

$$(e\mu n_0 + i\epsilon\omega)F_1 + (e\mu F_0 - ikeDn_0)n_1 = 0. \tag{14.107}$$

For nontrivial solutions, the determinant of the coupled equations should vanish. This gives us the condition on the allowed values of ω

$$\omega = -k\mu F_0 + i\left[\frac{e\mu n_0}{\epsilon} + k^2Dn_0\right]. \tag{14.108}$$

Writing

$$\tau_d = \frac{\epsilon}{e\mu n_0}$$

$$= \frac{\epsilon}{en_0(dv/dF)} \tag{14.109}$$

we get

$$\omega = -k\mu F_0 + i\left[\frac{1}{\tau_d} + Dn_0k^2\right]. \tag{14.110}$$

The real part of ω determines the frequency of the fluctuation waves

$$\text{Re}(\omega) = -k\mu F_0 \tag{14.111}$$

and the imaginary part determines the time decay of the fluctuations

$$\text{Im}(\omega) = \frac{1}{\tau_d} + Dn_0k^2 \tag{14.112}$$

If $\text{Im}(\omega)$ is positive, the fluctuation decays in time, while if it is negative, the fluctuation grows in time. The condition for the instability growth is then

$$0 \le k \le \frac{1}{(Dn|\tau_d|)^{1/2}}. \tag{14.113}$$

The quantity k describes the spatial evolution of the fluctuation. We see from Equation 14.106 that

$$\text{Re}(k) = -\frac{\omega}{\mu F}$$

$$\text{Im}(k) = \frac{1}{\tau_d\mu F}, \tag{14.114}$$

assuming no diffusion effects (i.e. $D = 0$). If the sample length is L, the growth of the instability over the sample length is given by

$$Q(L) = Q(0)\exp[\text{Im}(k)]. \tag{14.115}$$

Thus, if the resistance of the sample is negative, the initial fluctuation grows in space and time. This can be used to produce amplification as well as microwave power devices (oscillators) by appropriate choice of sample length and/or using resonant microwave cavities. Thus, devices which can generate tailorable negative resistance are of great interest.

Negative resistance devices can also be used to provide efficient digital logic circuits. Many circuits based on the saturated transistor logic can be greatly simplified by the negative resistance devices.

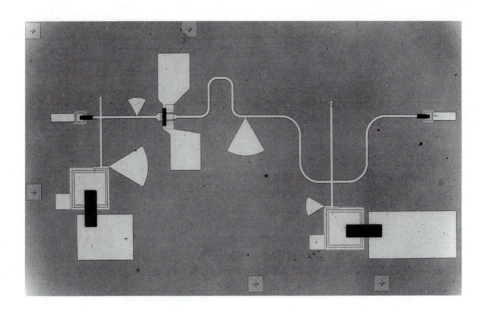

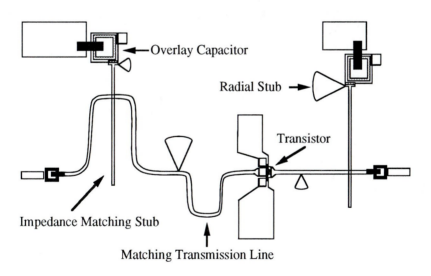

Figure 14.36: A monolithic microwave integrated circuit based on submicron In-GaAs/InAlAs MODFET technology. The circuit is designed to act as a frequency doubler for an input signal at 90 GHz. (Courtesy of the Solid State Electronics Laboratory, University of Michigan.)

14.15   REFERENCES

- **Quantum Wells and MODFETs**

  - Ando, T., J. Phys. Soc. Japan, **51**, 3900 (1982).
  - Arora, V. K. and A. Naeem, Phys. Rev. B, **31**, 3887 (1985).
  - Bastard, G., Appl. Phys. Lett., **43**, 591 (1983).
  - Basu, P. K. and B. R. Nag, Phys. Rev. B, **22**, 4849 (1980).
  - Basu, P. K. and B. R. Nag, Appl. Phys. Lett., **43**, 689 (1983).
  - Hong, W. P., J. Singh and P. K. Bhattacharya, IEEE Elect. Dev. Lett., **EDL-7**, 480 (1986).
  - Jaffe, M. D., *Studies of the Electronic Properties and Applications of Coherently Strained Semiconductors*, Ph.D. Thesis, (The University of Michigan, Ann Arbor, 1989).
  - Lee, J. and M. O. Vassell, Jap. J. Appl. Phys., **23**, 1086 (1984).
  - Lee, K., M. S. Shur, T. J. Drummond and H. Morkoc, J. Appl. Phys., **54**, 6432 (1983).
  - Price, P. J., Surface Science 143, 145 (1984).
  - Riddoch, F. A. and B. K. Ridley, Surf. Sci., **142**, 260 (1984).

- **Transport in Strained Structures**

  - Hinckley, J. M. and J. Singh, Appl. Phys. Lett., **53**, 785 (1988).
  - Hinckley, J. M. and J. Singh, Phys. Rev. B., **41**, 2912 (1990).
  - Lee, C. P., H. T. Wang, G. T. Sullivan, N. H. Sheng, and D. L. Miller, IEEE Elect. Dev. Lett., **EDL-8**, 85 (1987).
  - Ziperian, T. E., L. R. Dawson, T. J. Drummond, J. E. Schinber, I. J. Fritz, Appl. Phys. Lett., **52**, 975 (1988).

- **Quantum Wire Structures**

  - Arakawa, Y. and H. Sakaki, Appl. Phys. Lett., **40**, 939 (1982).
  - Sakaki, H., Jap. J. Appl. Phys., **19**, L735 (1980).

- **Real Space Charge Transfer**

  - Hess, K., *Advanced Theory of Semiconductor Devices* (Prentice-Hall, Englewood Cliffs, 1988).
  - Hess, K., H. Morkoc, H. Shichijo, and G. B. Streetman, Appl. Phys. Lett., **35**, 469 (1979).
  - Littlejohn, M. A., W. M. Kwapien, T. H. Glisson, J. R. Hauser and K. Hess, J. Vac. Sci. Technol. B, **1**, 445 (1983).

- **Avalanche Processes in Quantum Wells**

  - Bhattacharya, P. K., Y. Zebda, and J. Singh, Appl. Phys. Lett., **58**, 2791 (1991).

  - Capasso, F., W. T. Tsang, A. L. Hutchinson, and G. F. Williams, Appl. Lett., **40**, 38 (1982).

  - Capasso, F. W. T. Sang, and G. F. Williams, IEEE Trans. Electron, Dev., **ED-30**, 381 (1983).

  - Chin, R., N. Holonyak, Jr., G. E. Stillman, J. Y. Tang, and K. Hess, Electron. Lett., **16**, 467 (1980).

  - Juang, F. Y., *Molecular Beam Epitaxial Growth and Characterization of Superlattice Avalanche Photodetectors*, Ph.D. Thesis, (The University of Michigan, Ann Arbor, 1987).

  - Juang, F. Y., U. Das, Y. Nashimoto, and P. K. Bhattacharya, Appl. Phys. Lett., **47**, 972 (1985).

- **Resonant Tunneling**

  - Kane, E. O., *Tunneling Phenomenon in Solids* (Plenum, New York, 1969).

  - Price, P. J., IEEE Trans. Electron. Dev., **36**, 2340 (1989).

  - Sollner, T. C. L. G., W. D. Goodhue, C. D. Parker, T. E. Tannenwald and D. D. Peck, Appl. Phys. Lett., **43**, 588 (1983).

  - Sugiyama, Y., T. Inata, S. Muto, Y. Nakata, and S. Hiyamizu, Appl. Phys. Lett., **52**, 314 (1988).

  - Tsu, R. and L. Esaki, Appl. Phys. Lett., **22**, 562 (1973).

  - YaAzbel, M., Phys. Rev. B, **28**, 4106 (1983).

- **Tunneling in Heterostructures with Spatially Varying Central Cell Symmetry**

  - Ando, T. and H. Akera, Phys. Rev. B, **40**, 11619 (1989).

  - Esaki, L., Phys. Rev., **109**, 603 (1958).

  - Goldberg, H. M. Schey, and J. L. Schwartz, Am. J. Phys., **35**, 177 (1967).

  - Hall, R. N., IRE Trans. Electron. Dev., **ED-7**, 1 (1960).

  - Mailhiot, C., T. C. McGill, and J. W. Schulman, J. Vac. Sci. Technol. B, **1**, 439 (1983).

  - Osbourn, G. C., J. Vac. Sci. Technol., **19**, 592 (1981).

  - Sankaran, V. and J. Singh, Phys. Rev. B, **44**, 3175 (1991).

  - Sankaran, V. and J. Singh, Appl. Phys. Lett., **59**, 1969 (1991).

– Solomon, P. M., S. L. Wright, and C. Lanza, Superlattices and Microstructures, **2**, 521 (1986).

– Sze, S. M., *Physics of Semiconductor Devices* (John Wiley and Sons, New York, 1981).

- **Quantum Interference Effects**

  – Ismail, K., GaAs and Related Compounds, Inst. Phys. Conf. Ser. No. 106, pp. 837 (1989).

  – Tsubaki, K., T. Fukui, Y. Tokura, H. Saito, and N. Susa, Electron. Lett., **25**, 728 (1989).

  – "Quantum Interference Effects in Condensed Matter Physics," by Webb, R. A., in *Nanostructure Physics and Fabrication* (edited by M. A. Reed and W. P. Kirk, Academic Press, New York, 1989). Also see other articles in this book.

- **Transport in Superlattices; Coherent Oscillations**

  – Capasso, F., A. Y. Cho, and P. W. Foy, Electron. Lett., **20**, 635 (1984).

  – Leo, K., J. Shah, E. O. Göbel, and T. C. Damen, *Subpicosecond Transient-Grating Experiments: A Novel Method to Study Coherent Resonant Tunneling* (presented at the 5th International Conference on the Physics of Electro-Optic Microstructures and Microdevices, July 30–Aug. 3, 1990, Heraklion, Greece).

- **Density Matrix Formalism, Wigner Distribution, Quantum Transport**

  – An excellent collection of articles on quantum transport are presented in *Nanostructure Physics and Fabrication* (edited by M. A. Reed and W. P. Kink, Academic Press, New York, 1989).

  – Frenseley, J., J. Vac. Sci. Technol. B, **3**, 1261 (1985).

  – Goodnick, S. M., D. K. Ferry, C. W. Wilmsen, Z. Lilienthal, D. Fathy and O. L.Krivanek, Phys. Rev. B, **32**, 8171 (1985).

  – Iafrate, G. I., *The Physics of Submicron/Ultrasubmicron Dimensions in Gallium Arsenide Technology* (edited by D. K. Ferry, Howard W. Sams and Co., Indianapolis, 1985).

  – Lee, J. and M. O. Vassell, Jap. J. Appl. Phys., **23**, 1086 (1984).

  – Ridley, B. K., J. Phys. C, **15**, 5899 (1982).

  – Schiff, L. I., *Quantum Mechanics* (McGraw-Hill, New York, 1968).

  – Tomizawa, M., K. Yokoyama, and A. Yoshii, IEEE Elect. Dev. Lett. **EDL-5**, 464 (1984).

  – Wigner, E., Phys. Rev. **40**, 749 (1932).

CHAPTER
15

INTERACTIONS OF
PHOTONS WITH
SEMICONDUCTORS

We have so far been discussing the effect of imperfections on scattering of electrons. Perturbations such as ionized impurities, phonons, etc., cause scattering of an electron from an initial Bloch state to another state. Electromagnetic radiation or photons cause a similar scattering process and the problem can be treated by using time dependent perturbation theory as we treated the electron-phonon scattering problem provided the photon intensities are not too high. The photons can introduce scattering within a band as well as between bands as shown in the Figure 15.1. The interband scattering involving valence and conduction band states is, of course, most important for optical devices such as lasers and detectors. In addition to the band-to-band transitions, increasing interest has recently focussed on excitonic states especially in quantum well structures. The exciton-photon interaction in semiconductor structures contains important physics and is also of great technical interest for high speed modulation devices and optical switches.

We will briefly review some important concepts in electromagnetic theory and then discuss the interactions between electrons and photons. We will focus on the special aspects of this interaction for semiconductor electrons, especially those relating to selection rules.

The areas that will be covered in this and the next chapter are briefly listed in Figure 15.2. We will first discuss a macroscopic theory for the optical effects in materials. In this formalism the details of the Bloch states and the bandstructure are ignored and are, instead, represented by macroscopic quantities such as conductivity, dielectric constant, etc. We will also discuss a simple picture for the dielectric response of materials based on the Drude-Zener picture of atoms. The Kramers-Kronig relation and the associated sum rules will also be discussed. Next, we will discuss the one-electron picture of optical-semiconductor interac-

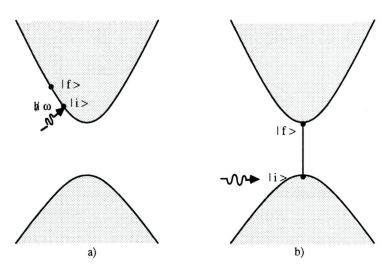

Figure 15.1: Intraband and interband scattering of an electron from an initial state $|i\rangle$ to a final state $|f\rangle$.

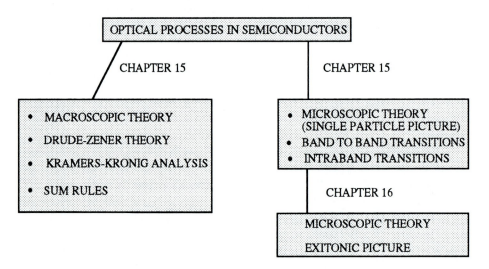

Figure 15.2: A flow-chart of our approach to the photon semiconductor interactions in this and the next chapter.

tions where the details of the Bloch states and the bandstructure are critical. Band-to-band and intraband absorption coefficients will be discussed. Both 3-dimensional and 2-dimensional systems will be covered. We will also focus on the selection rules and "gain" in semiconductor structures, considerations which are extremely important in solid state lasers.

While the single electron picture which gives us the E vs. k relation provides a good description of optical processes for photon energies above the bandgap, just below the bandgap there are extremely important optical interactions involving the electron-hole system. These processes known as excitonic processes are becoming increasingly important for technological applications such as high speed switches and modulators. We will discuss the exciton-related effects in Chapter 16.

15.1 MAXWELL EQUATIONS, VECTOR POTENTIAL, AND GAUGE TRANSFORMATIONS

We start by reviewing certain important properties of electromagnetic radiation or photons. Electromagnetic phenomenon and its interaction with materials is described by four Maxwell's equations. Apart from the electric (F) and magnetic (B) fields and velocity of light, the effects of the material are represented by the dielectric constant, permeability (we will assume $\mu = 1$), electrical conductivity, etc. Often, instead of working in the F-field and B-field representation, it is convenient to work in a different representation. This representation is non-unique and allows certain useful simplifications for easier manipulation of electron-photon interactions. We start with the four Maxwell equations

$$
\begin{aligned}
\nabla \times \boldsymbol{F} + \frac{1}{c}\frac{\partial \boldsymbol{B}}{\partial t} &= 0 \\
\nabla \times \boldsymbol{H} - \frac{1}{c}\frac{\partial \boldsymbol{D}}{\partial t} &= \frac{4\pi}{c}\boldsymbol{J} \\
\nabla \cdot \boldsymbol{D} &= 4\pi\rho \\
\nabla \cdot \boldsymbol{B} &= 0
\end{aligned}
\tag{15.1}
$$

where $\boldsymbol{F}$ and $\boldsymbol{H}$ are the electric and magnetic fields, $\boldsymbol{D} = \epsilon\boldsymbol{F}$, $\boldsymbol{B} = \mu\boldsymbol{H}$, $\boldsymbol{J}$, and ρ are the current and charge densities. In dealing with the electron-photon interactions, it is convenient to work with the vector and scalar potentials $\boldsymbol{A}$ and ϕ respectively, which are defined through the equations

$$
\begin{aligned}
\boldsymbol{F} &= -\frac{1}{c}\frac{\partial \boldsymbol{A}}{\partial t} - \nabla\phi \\
\boldsymbol{B} &= \nabla \times \boldsymbol{A}.
\end{aligned}
\tag{15.2}
$$

The first and fourth Maxwell equations are automatically satisfied by these definitions. The potentials $\boldsymbol{A}$ and ϕ are not unique, but can be replaced by a new set of potentials $\boldsymbol{A}'$ and ϕ' given by

$$
\begin{aligned}
\boldsymbol{A}' &= \boldsymbol{A} + \nabla\chi \\
\phi' &= \phi - \frac{1}{c}\frac{\partial\chi}{\partial t}.
\end{aligned}
\tag{15.3}
$$

The new choice of potentials does not have any effect on the physical fields $\boldsymbol{F}$ and $\boldsymbol{B}$. To at least partially remove the arbitrariness of the potentials $\boldsymbol{A}$ and ϕ, we define certain gauge transformations which restrict them. Before considering these transformations let us rewrite the Maxwell equations in terms of $\boldsymbol{A}$ and ϕ.

The second and third Maxwell equations become

$$
\begin{aligned}
\nabla\times\nabla\times\boldsymbol{A} + \frac{1}{c^2}\frac{\partial^2\boldsymbol{A}}{\partial t} + \frac{1}{c}\nabla\frac{\partial\phi}{\partial t} &= \frac{4\pi}{c}\boldsymbol{J} \\
\frac{1}{c}\frac{\partial}{\partial t}\nabla\cdot\boldsymbol{A} + \nabla^2\phi &= -4\pi\rho.
\end{aligned}
\tag{15.4}
$$

Now

$$
\nabla\times\nabla\times\boldsymbol{A} = \nabla(\nabla\cdot\boldsymbol{A}) - \nabla^2\boldsymbol{A}
\tag{15.5}
$$

giving us

$$
\nabla\left(\nabla\cdot\boldsymbol{A} + \frac{1}{c}\frac{\partial\phi}{\partial t}\right) - \nabla^2\boldsymbol{A} + \frac{1}{c^2}\frac{\partial^2\boldsymbol{A}}{\partial t^2} = \frac{4\pi}{c}\boldsymbol{J}
\tag{15.6}
$$

$$
\frac{1}{c}\frac{\partial}{\partial t}(\nabla\cdot\boldsymbol{A}) + \nabla^2\phi = -4\pi\rho.
\tag{15.7}
$$

We will now impose certain restrictions on $\boldsymbol{A}$ and ϕ to further simplify these equations. Note that these restrictions have no implications on $\boldsymbol{F}$ and $\boldsymbol{B}$ fields as can be easily verified from their descriptions in terms of $\boldsymbol{A}$ and ϕ. The purpose of working in different gauges is mathematical elegance and simplicity.

Since the vector potential $\boldsymbol{A}$ is defined in terms of its curl: $\boldsymbol{B} = \nabla\times\boldsymbol{A}$, its divergence ($\nabla\cdot\boldsymbol{A}$) is arbitrary. Choice of a particular gauge is equivalent to the choice of the the value of $\nabla\cdot\boldsymbol{A}$.

In the Lorentz gauge, widely used in relativistic electrodynamics, we choose

$$
\nabla\cdot\boldsymbol{A}' + \frac{1}{c}\frac{\partial\phi'}{\partial t} = 0
\tag{15.8}
$$

This is equivalent to imposing the following restriction on the arbitrary quantity χ.

$$
\nabla^2\chi - \frac{1}{c^2}\frac{\partial^2\chi}{\partial t^2} = -\left(\nabla\cdot\boldsymbol{A} + \frac{1}{c}\frac{\partial\phi}{\partial t}\right).
\tag{15.9}
$$

With this choice of χ we get for the Maxwell equations

$$
\begin{aligned}
\nabla^2\boldsymbol{A} - \frac{1}{c^2}\frac{\partial^2\boldsymbol{A}}{\partial t^2} &= \frac{-4\pi}{c}\boldsymbol{J} \\
\nabla^2\phi - \frac{1}{c^2}\frac{\partial^2\phi}{\partial t^2} &= -4\pi\rho.
\end{aligned}
\tag{15.10}
$$

This form of Maxwell's equations is extremely useful for generalizing to relativistic electrodynamics. In dealing with electron-photon interactions, a most useful gauge is the Radiation or Coulomb gauge. If $J = 0$ and $\rho = 0$, we can choose the constant background potential $\phi' = 0$. In addition we can choose $\nabla \cdot A' = 0$. In this case the solutions for the vector potential are represented by plane wave transverse electromagnetic waves. We will be working in this gauge. It is useful to establish the relation between the vector potential A and the photon density which represents the optical power. The time dependent solution for the vector potential solution of Equation 15.10 with $J = 0$ is

$$A(r, t) = A_0 \left\{ \exp\left[i(k \cdot r - \omega t)\right] + \text{c.c.} \right\}$$ (15.11)

The corresponding electric and magnetic fields are

$$
\begin{aligned}
F &= \frac{-1}{c} \frac{\partial A}{\partial t} \\
&= -2\frac{\omega}{c} A_0 \sin(k \cdot r - \omega t) \\
B &= \nabla \times A \\
&= -2k \times A_0 \sin(k \cdot r - \omega t).
\end{aligned}
$$ (15.12)

The Poynting vector S representing the optical power is

$$
\begin{aligned}
S &= \frac{c}{4\pi}(F \times H) \\
&= \frac{vk^2 |A_0|^2}{\pi\mu} \sin^2(k \cdot r - \omega t)\hat{k}
\end{aligned}
$$ (15.13)

where v is the velocity of light in the medium $(= c/\sqrt{\epsilon\mu})$ and $\hat{k}$ is a unit vector in the direction of k. The time averaged value of the power is

$$
\begin{aligned}
< S >_{\text{time}} &= \hat{k}\frac{vk^2 |A_0|^2}{2\pi\mu} \\
&= \frac{v\,\epsilon\,\omega^2}{2\pi c^2\mu} |A_0|^2 \,\hat{k}
\end{aligned}
$$ (15.14)

since

$$|k| = \omega/v.$$ (15.15)

The energy density is then

$$\left|\frac{S}{v}\right| = \frac{\epsilon\,\omega^2 |A_0|^2}{2\pi c^2\mu}.$$ (15.16)

Also, if the number of photons in a volume V is n, the energy density is

$$\frac{n\hbar\omega}{V}.$$ (15.17)

Equating these two, we get

$$|A_0|^2 = \frac{2\pi\hbar n c^2 \mu}{V\epsilon\omega}. \tag{15.18}$$

The phonon number density n/V is a physically measurable quantity which according to this relation tells us the strength of the vector potential. Equation 15.18 is extremely useful since it allows us to relate the photon number density to the vector potential $\boldsymbol{A}$ which appears in the electron-photon interaction as we will see later in this chapter.

Having established these basic equations for the electromagnetic field, we will now develop a macroscopic picture of the photon-material interactions. Going back to the Maxwell's equations and writing $\boldsymbol{J} = \sigma\boldsymbol{F}$, we get the wave equation for the electric field (after eliminating the $\boldsymbol{B}$-field)

$$\nabla^2\boldsymbol{F} = \frac{\epsilon\mu}{c^2}\frac{\partial^2\boldsymbol{F}}{\partial t^2} + \frac{4\pi\sigma\mu}{c^2}\frac{\partial\boldsymbol{F}}{\partial t} \tag{15.19}$$

This represents a wave propagating with dissipation. The general solution can be chosen to be of the form

$$\boldsymbol{F} = \boldsymbol{F}_0 \exp\left\{i(\boldsymbol{k}\cdot\boldsymbol{r} - \omega t)\right\} \tag{15.20}$$

so that k is given by

$$-k^2 = -\epsilon\mu\frac{\omega^2}{c^2} - \frac{4\pi\sigma\mu i\omega}{c^2} \tag{15.21}$$

or

$$k = \frac{\omega}{c}\left(\epsilon\mu + \frac{4\pi\sigma\mu i}{\omega}\right)^{1/2}. \tag{15.22}$$

In general k is a complex number. In free space where $\sigma = 0$ we simply have ($\epsilon = 1$)

$$k = \omega/c. \tag{15.23}$$

In a medium, the phase velocity is modified by dividing c by a complex refractive index given by

$$n = \left(\epsilon\mu + \frac{4\pi\sigma\mu i}{\omega}\right)^{1/2}. \tag{15.24}$$

The macroscopic theory of optical properties can be represented by N. We can write the complex refractive index in terms of its real and imaginary parts

$$N = n + i\beta \tag{15.25}$$

so that

$$k = \frac{n\omega}{c} + i\beta\frac{\omega}{c}. \tag{15.26}$$

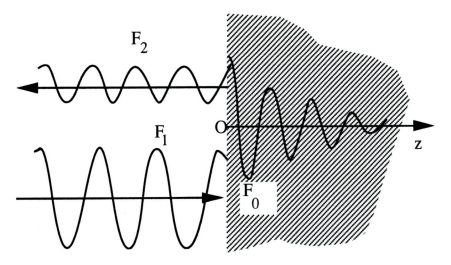

Figure 15.3: Schematic showing the incident, reflected, and transmitted waves.

The electric field wave Equation 15.20 now becomes (for propagations in the +z direction)

$$\boldsymbol{F} = \boldsymbol{F}_0 \exp\left\{i\omega\left(\frac{nz}{c} - t\right)\right\} \exp\left(\frac{-\beta\omega z}{c}\right). \qquad (15.27)$$

The velocity of the wave is reduced by n to c/n and its amplitude is damped exponentially by a fraction $\exp(-2\pi\beta/n)$ per wavelength. The damping of the wave is associated with the absorption of the electromagnetic energy. The absorption coefficient α is described by the absorption of the intensity (i.e. square of Equation 15.27)

$$\alpha = \frac{2\beta\omega}{c}. \qquad (15.28)$$

The absorption coefficient can be measured for any material system and it provides information on β. Another quantity which can be easily measured is the reflection coefficient R. If we consider a normally incident wave as shown in Figure 15.3, impinging on a medium at $z = 0$, we have a reflected wave. For $z > 0$ we can write

$$\boldsymbol{F}_x = \boldsymbol{F}_0 \exp\left\{i\omega\left(\frac{Nz}{c} - t\right)\right\} \qquad (15.29)$$

and for $z < 0$ we have

$$\boldsymbol{F}_x = \boldsymbol{F}_1 \exp\left\{i\omega\left(\frac{z}{c} - t\right)\right\} + \boldsymbol{F}_2 \exp\left\{-i\omega\left(\frac{z}{c} + t\right)\right\} \qquad (15.30)$$

corresponding to a wave with amplitude $\boldsymbol{F}_1$ traveling to the right and a reflected wave to the left. Matching the boundary conditions we have

$$\boldsymbol{F}_0 = \boldsymbol{F}_1 + \boldsymbol{F}_2 \qquad (15.31)$$

and for B_y, we get using Maxwell's equation

$$- N\boldsymbol{F}_0 = \boldsymbol{F}_2 - \boldsymbol{F}_1. \tag{15.32}$$

These give for the reflection coefficient

$$
\begin{aligned}
R &= \left| \frac{F_2}{F_1} \right|^2 \\
&= \left| \frac{1 - N}{1 + N} \right|^2 \\
&= \frac{(n-1)^2 + \beta^2}{(n+1)^2 + \beta^2}.
\end{aligned} \tag{15.33}
$$

The measurement of the reflection coefficient and absorption coefficient give us the optical constants n and β of the material. Of course, we have not calculated n and β from any microscopic information on the semiconductor as yet.

15.2 DRUDE-ZENER THEORY

One simple macroscopic theory to describe the optical constants of a material is by the Drude-Zener theory. This approach is strictly valid only for metals where the free electron response dominates the optical properties. In nondegenerate semiconductors, the interband transitions dominate the optical processes and one must turn to the microscopic theory discussed later. In heavily doped semiconductors, where a high density of free electrons exist, the Drude-Zener theory is applicable to describe the free electron contribution to the optical constants.

The dielectric constant ($\epsilon = N^2$) is given from Equation 15.24 as (we choose both μ and the static ϵ to be unity)

$$\epsilon(\omega) = 1 + \frac{4\pi i}{\omega}\sigma(\omega). \tag{15.34}$$

The Drude-Zener theory develops a simple picture for $\sigma(\omega)$ in the relaxation time approximation. We start with the linearized Boltzmann equation discussed in Chapter 10

$$
\begin{aligned}
\frac{\partial g}{\partial t} &= e\boldsymbol{F} \cdot \boldsymbol{v}\frac{\partial f^0}{\partial E} + \boldsymbol{v} \cdot \frac{\partial f^0}{\partial \boldsymbol{r}} \\
&= \frac{-g}{\tau}
\end{aligned} \tag{15.35}
$$

where f^0 is the equilibrium distribution function, g is the perturbation, and τ is the relaxation time. We assume that the wavelength of $\boldsymbol{F}$ is large enough to neglect any spatial variations over a microscopic region. We also assume that g has the same frequency response $\exp(i\omega t)$ as the $\boldsymbol{F}$-field. We get

$$i\omega g - e\boldsymbol{F} \cdot \boldsymbol{v}\frac{\partial f^0}{\partial E} = -\frac{g}{\tau}. \tag{15.36}$$

The effect of the nonzero frequency is then simply to replace the dc conductivity σ_0 by replacing τ^{-1} by $(\tau^{-1} + i\omega)$. Thus

$$\sigma(\omega) = \frac{\sigma_0}{1 + i\omega\tau}. \tag{15.37}$$

If σ_1 and σ_2 are the real and imaginary part of the conductivity, we have

$$
\begin{aligned}
\sigma_1 &= \frac{\sigma_0}{1 + \omega^2\tau^2} \\
\sigma_2 &= -\frac{\omega\tau\sigma_0}{1 + \omega^2\tau^2}.
\end{aligned}
\tag{15.38}
$$

The optical constants can now be derived from the conductivity if we know the relaxation times. We have from Equations 15.24 to 15.26 (with $\epsilon = 1$)

$$
\begin{aligned}
n^2 - \beta^2 &= 1 + \frac{4\pi}{\omega}\sigma_2 \\
n\beta &= \frac{2\pi}{\omega}\sigma_1.
\end{aligned}
\tag{15.39}
$$

We know that the dc conductivity is given by

$$\sigma_0 = \frac{ne^2\tau}{m^*}. \tag{15.40}$$

The mass m^* is the effective mass only for low frequency phonons, since at high frequencies the lattice is unable to respond to the electric signal and the mass approaches the free electron mass. This mass is called the optical mass. We now have

$$n^2 - \beta^2 = 1 - \frac{\omega_p^2\tau^2}{1 + \omega^2\tau^2} \tag{15.41}$$

and

$$2n\beta = \frac{\omega_p^2\tau}{\omega(1 + \omega^2\tau^2)} \tag{15.42}$$

where

$$\omega_p = \sqrt{\frac{4\pi ne^2}{m^*}} \tag{15.43}$$

is the plasma frequency discussed in Chapter 11.

It is useful to examine certain limits of these equations. For low frequencies $(\omega\tau \ll 1)$ we have

$$(n + \beta)(n - \beta) \approx 1 - \omega_p^2\tau^2 \tag{15.44}$$

$$2n\beta = \frac{\omega_p^2\tau}{\omega} \tag{15.45}$$

Thus, n and β increase indefinitely as $\omega \to 0$ and since $1 - \omega_p^2\tau^2$ is independent of ω, the two constants become equal

$$
\begin{aligned}
n \;&\approx\; \beta \\
&\approx\; \sqrt{\frac{\omega_p^2\tau}{2\omega}} \\
&=\; \sqrt{\frac{2\pi\sigma_0}{\omega}}.
\end{aligned} \tag{15.46}
$$

The skin depth δ is defined by the distance at which the incident wave is attenuated to $1/e$ times its original value. From Equation 15.46, we have

$$
\begin{aligned}
\delta \;&=\; \frac{c}{\omega\beta} \\
&=\; \sqrt{\frac{c^2}{2\pi\sigma_0\omega}}.
\end{aligned} \tag{15.47}
$$

Another region of interest is one where $\omega\tau \gg 1$. In this case we have (ϵ_1 and ϵ_2 are the real and imaginary parts of the dielectric constant)

$$
\begin{aligned}
\epsilon_1 \;&=\; n^2 - \beta^2 \\
&\approx\; 1 - \left(\frac{\omega_p}{\omega}\right)^2 \\
\epsilon_2 \;&=\; 2n\beta \\
&\approx\; \frac{\omega_p^2}{\omega^3\tau}.
\end{aligned} \tag{15.48}
$$

If the plasma frequency is in this range, at the plasma edge we have

$$
\begin{aligned}
n^2 - \beta^2 \;&=\; 0 \\
2n\beta \;&=\; \frac{1}{\omega\tau} \ll 1.
\end{aligned} \tag{15.49}
$$

Both n and β are close to zero and the reflection coefficient R becomes unity, as can be seen from Equation 15.33 For the case $\omega \ge \omega_p$, we have $2n\beta \approx 0$, but $n^2 - \beta^2 < 0$, so that β increases faster than n as the frequency is lowered. The reflection coefficient is close to unity. For $\omega > \omega_p$, $n^2 - \beta^2 > 0$ while $\beta = 0$. Thus, above the plasma frequency the material is essentially transparent. In Figure 15.4 we show a typical plot for n and β.

As mentioned earlier, the theory discussed above is strictly valid for metals or very heavily doped semiconductors. In case of semiconductors, the relation

$$
\epsilon(\omega) = 1 + \frac{4\pi i}{\omega}\sigma(\omega) \tag{15.50}
$$

should be replaced by

$$
\epsilon(\omega) = \epsilon^0(\omega) + \frac{4\pi i}{\omega}\sigma(\omega) \tag{15.51}
$$

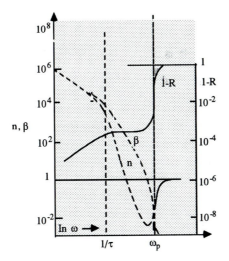

Figure 15.4: Schematic behavior of optical properties of metals, showing real and imaginary parts of dielectric constant and reflection coefficient.

where $\epsilon^0(\omega)$ is the contribution to the dielectric constant due to the filled band. For example $\epsilon^0(\omega) \approx 12$ for GaAs. $\epsilon^0(\omega)$ is determined by the interband transitions and the polarizability of ionic crystals.

15.3 OPTICAL MODES IN IONIC CRYSTALS

In Chapter 9, on phonons, we discussed in detail how electromagnetic waves interact with the lattice modes in ionic crystals. We found a strong interaction of the longitudinal optical phonons with photons leading to a very interesting dispersion relation for the photon-phonon or polarization modes. In Figure 15.5 we reproduce the dispersion relation shown in Chapter 9. We remind ourselves of the equations derived in that chapter

$$\frac{\omega_L^2}{\omega_T^2} = \frac{\epsilon(0)}{\epsilon(\infty)} \tag{15.52}$$

where ω_L and ω_T are the longitudinal and transverse optical phonon frequencies at $k = 0$, and $\epsilon(0)$ and $\epsilon(\infty)$ are the static and high frequency dielectric constants. These two are related by the equation derived earlier by

$$\left(\frac{e^*}{e}\right)^2 \approx 3\left(\frac{1}{\epsilon(\infty)} - \frac{1}{\epsilon(0)}\right) \tag{15.53}$$

where e^* is the effective charge on the ionic crystal.

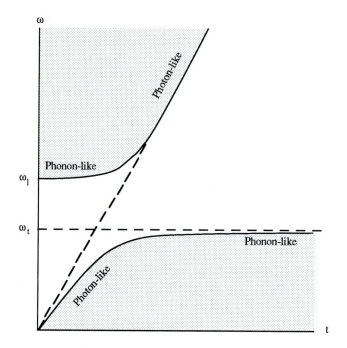

Figure 15.5: Coupled modes of photons and transverse optical phonons in an ionic crystal. The broken lines show the spectra without interaction.

15.4   KRAMERS-KRONIG RELATION

The optical constants n and β discussed above are not independent of each other but are related by dispersion relations based on Kramers-Kronig relations. The Kramers-Kronig relations are general relations which relate the real and imaginary parts of a response function. To emphasize their generality we develop the general Kramers-Kronig analysis for the current–electric field response via conductivity which can then be generalized for the electric displacement–electric field response via the dielectric constant.

The general relation between current and applied electric field is

$$j(\omega) = \sigma(\omega)\, F(\omega). \tag{15.54}$$

In general the conductivity is complex

$$\sigma = \sigma_1 + i\sigma_2 \tag{15.55}$$

where σ_1 and σ_2 are real. On the other hand, this complex nature is purely formal and the actual current

$$j(t) = \frac{1}{2\pi} \int_{-\infty}^{\infty} \sigma(\omega)\, e^{i\omega t}\, F(\omega)\, d\omega \tag{15.56}$$

must be real on the application of a real electric field. As a result, in the convolution of the expression

$$j(t) = \int_{-\infty}^{\infty} \sigma(t - t') \, F(t') \, dt' \qquad (15.57)$$

the quantity

$$\sigma(t) = \frac{1}{2\pi} \int_{-\infty}^{\infty} \sigma(\omega) \, e^{-i\omega t} \, dt \qquad (15.58)$$

must be real. This implies that

$$\sigma(-\omega) = \sigma^*(\omega) \qquad (15.59)$$

i.e.

$$\begin{aligned} \sigma_1(-\omega) &= \sigma_1(\omega) \\ \sigma_2(-\omega) &= -\sigma_2(\omega). \end{aligned} \qquad (15.60)$$

The central point in obtaining the Kramers-Kronig relations is the "causality principle," that the effect cannot precede the cause, $j(t)$ cannot depend on $F(t')$ if $t < t'$. As a result

$$\sigma(t) = 0 \text{ if } t < 0 \qquad (15.61)$$

and we can write the inverse Fourier transform of $\sigma(t)$ as

$$\sigma(\omega) = \int_0^{\infty} \sigma(t) \, e^{i\omega t} \, dt. \qquad (15.62)$$

We may note from Equation 15.57 that if $F(t')$ is a delta-function impulse, $j(t) = \sigma(t)$, i.e. $\sigma(t)$ is the current produced by a unit impulse of electric field at $t = 0$. We shall also use the physically obvious result that

$$\lim_{\omega \to \infty} \sigma(\omega) = 0 \qquad (15.63)$$

We will now exploit some simple relations from complex plane integration (see for example, Kreyszig, 1962). The good behavior of $\sigma(t)$ has the consequence that, if ω has complex values, $\sigma(\omega)$ has no zeros or singularities in the upper-half of the complex-plane, and since Equation 15.63 holds, $\sigma(\omega)$ vanishes over the semi-circle at infinity at this plane. Consider therefore the contour C shown in Figure 15.6, and the integral

$$\oint_c \frac{\sigma(\xi) \, d\xi}{\xi - \omega} = 0. \qquad (15.64)$$

The integral is zero since the contour contains no poles and, since the integrand vanishes over the semi-circle at infinity, can also be written

$$P \int_{-\infty}^{\infty} \frac{\sigma(\xi)}{\xi - \omega} \, d\xi - i\pi\sigma(\omega) = 0, \qquad (15.65)$$

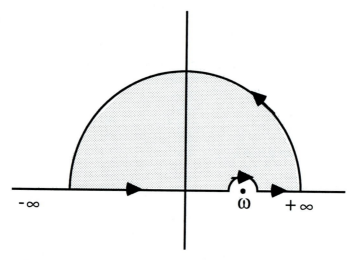

Figure 15.6: Form of the contour used in the integral in Equation 15.64.

the second term on the left-hand side being the contribution to the integral over the infinitesimal semi-circle about the simple pole at $\xi = \omega$, and the P in front of the integral sign showing that the principal value is taken. Taking real and imaginary parts of Equation 15.65 we immediately find

$$\sigma_1(\omega) = \frac{1}{\pi} P \int_{-\infty}^{\infty} \frac{\sigma_2(\xi)}{\xi - \omega} \, d\xi,$$

$$\sigma_2(\omega) = -\frac{1}{\pi} P \int_{-\infty}^{\infty} \frac{\sigma_1(\xi)}{\xi - \omega} \, d\xi. \qquad (15.66)$$

These are the Kramers-Kronig relations, often rewritten as

$$\sigma_1(\omega) = \frac{2}{\pi} P \int_0^{\infty} \frac{\xi \, \sigma_2(\xi)}{\xi^2 - \omega^2} \, d\xi,$$

$$\sigma_2(\omega) = \frac{2\omega}{\pi} P \int_0^{\infty} \frac{\sigma_1(\xi)}{\xi^2 - \omega^2} \, d\xi \qquad (15.67)$$

which forms are easily obtained from Equation 15.66 by using the fact that $\sigma_1(\omega)$ is even and $\sigma_2(\omega)$ is odd, as seen in Equation 15.60.

   The analysis discussed above can be generalized to any response relation of the type given by Equation 15.54. Minor modifications may be required depending upon special properties of the physical observables involved. We are interested in the relation between the real and imaginary part of the dielectric constant defined by $\boldsymbol{D} = \epsilon \boldsymbol{F}$. In this case we note that the quantity $\epsilon(t)$ has a δ-function singularity at $t = 0$, i.e.

$$\epsilon(t) = \frac{1}{2\pi} \int_{-\infty}^{\infty} \epsilon'(\omega) e^{i\omega t} \, dt + \epsilon_1(\infty)\delta(t), \qquad (15.68)$$

because a δ-function impulse in $\mathbf{F}(t)$ induces a d-function impulse in $D(t)$. As a result, $\epsilon_1(\infty) \neq 0$ (although $\epsilon_2(\infty) = 0$). We therefore separate the dielectric constant as

$$\epsilon(\omega) = \epsilon'(\omega) + \epsilon_1(\infty) \qquad (15.69)$$

so that

$$\epsilon'(\infty) = 0 \qquad (15.70)$$

and the analysis applied to $\sigma(\omega)$ is applicable to $\epsilon'(\omega)$, so that we obtain, instead of Equation 15.67. Note that in the model considered by us in Section 15.2, $\epsilon_1(\infty) = 1$, as seen from Equation 15.41

$$\epsilon_1(\omega) - \epsilon_1(\infty) = \frac{2}{\pi} P \int_0^\infty \frac{\xi \epsilon_2(\xi)}{\xi^2 - \omega^2} d\xi$$

$$\epsilon_2(\omega) = -\frac{2\omega}{\pi} P \int_0^\infty \frac{\epsilon_1(\xi) - \epsilon_1(\infty)}{\xi^2 - \omega^2} d\xi. \qquad (15.71)$$

These are the Kramers-Kronig relations for the optical constants. If the absorption coefficient is known at all frequencies, then the optical constants n and β are known. We will use this relation in evaluating the electro-optic coefficients in quantum well structures in the next chapter. Note that the only assumption required for the Kramers-Kronig relation is that the principle of causality is satisfied.

An important outcome of the Kramers-Kronig relation is the sum rules which are very useful in calculations of optical constants. We note from Equations 15.41 and 15.42 that for frequencies far above the ω_p (the resonant plasma frequency), $\beta \to 0$ and the dielectric constant becomes

$$\epsilon(\omega) = 1 - \frac{\omega_p^2}{\omega^2}$$

$$\equiv \epsilon_1(\infty) - \frac{\omega_p^2}{\omega^2}. \qquad (15.72)$$

The imaginary part of the dielectric constant falls to zero (see Figure 15.4). The plasma frequency can, in fact, be defined by

$$\omega_p^2 = \lim_{\omega \to \infty} \left\{ \omega^2 \left(1 - \epsilon(\omega)\right) \right\}. \qquad (15.73)$$

If the imaginary part of $\epsilon(\omega)$ falls to zero faster than $1/\omega^3$ as $\omega \to \infty$, we have from the first of Equation 15.71

$$\omega_p^2 = \frac{2}{\pi} \int_0^\infty \xi \mathrm{Im}\, \epsilon(\xi)\, d\xi. \qquad (15.74)$$

This rule is known as the sum rule for oscillator strengths.

Another sum rule arises from the second of Equation 15.71. With the assumption that

$$[\mathrm{Re}\, \epsilon(\xi) - 1] = -\frac{\omega_p^2}{\xi^2} + O\left(\frac{1}{\xi^4}\right) \qquad (15.75)$$

for

$$\xi > \omega_N. \tag{15.76}$$

One can see from the second part of Equation 15.71, that for $\omega > \omega_N$

$$\text{Im } \epsilon(\omega) = \frac{2}{\pi\omega} \left\{ -\frac{\omega_p^2}{\omega_N} + \int_0^{\omega_N} [\text{Re } \epsilon(\xi) - 1] \, d\xi \right\}. \tag{15.77}$$

Since Im $\epsilon(\omega)$ vanishes for large ω, the expression in the curly brackets must vanish and we have

$$\frac{1}{\omega_N} \int_0^{\omega_N} \text{Re } \epsilon(\xi) \, d\xi = 1 + \frac{\omega_p^2}{\omega_N^2} \tag{15.78}$$

and for $\omega \to \infty$, the right-hand side becomes unity.

We will now proceed to derive a microscopic theory for the optical processes in semiconductors. We will focus on the photon energies close to the bandgap of the semiconductor since most optoelectronic devices cater to this energy range. Thus, our formalism, while general, will focus on the physics behind devices such as solid state detectors and lasers. The approach we use will be based on the perturbation theory in which we evaluate the scattering rate for electrons to scatter among various Bloch states. The transitions could be interband or intraband.

15.5   ELECTRONS IN AN ELECTROMAGNETIC FIELD

The Hamiltonian describing the interactions between a charge, e, and the electromagnetic field is

$$\begin{aligned}
H &= \frac{1}{2m}\left(p - \frac{eA}{c}\right)^2 + e\phi + V(r) \\
&= \frac{p^2}{2m} - \frac{e}{2mc}(p \cdot A + A \cdot p) + \frac{e^2}{2mc^2}A^2 + e\phi + V(r). \tag{15.79}
\end{aligned}$$

Here A is the vector potential and $V(r)$ is any background crystal potential.

We use the general commutation result

$$\begin{aligned}
[f(r), p] &= f(r)p - pf(r) \\
&= i\hbar \frac{\partial}{\partial r} f(r) \tag{15.80}
\end{aligned}$$

which can be explicitly verified by using $f(r) = x;\ x^2$, etc. This then allows us to write

$$\frac{e}{2mc} p \cdot A = \frac{eA \cdot p}{2mc} - \frac{ie\hbar}{2mc} \nabla \cdot A. \tag{15.81}$$

The Hamiltonian becomes

$$H = \frac{p^2}{2m} - \frac{e}{mc}\boldsymbol{A}\cdot\boldsymbol{p} + \frac{ie\hbar}{2mc}\nabla\cdot\boldsymbol{A} + \frac{e^2}{2mc^2}\boldsymbol{A}^2 + e\phi + V(\boldsymbol{r}) \qquad (15.82)$$

We will now use the perturbation theory to study the effect of the electromagnetic radiation on the electron. We will first discuss the semiclassical theory of radiation which is quite simple, but does not give rigorously correct results for spontaneous emission of photons. The quantum theory of radiation involves an approach similar to that used by us for electron-phonon interactions. In this approach the electromagnetic field is written in terms of creation and destruction operators as was done for the phonon problem using the harmonic oscillator analogy. We will only outline this approach often called the second quantization approach.

The Schrödinger equation to be solved is

$$ih\frac{\partial\psi}{\partial t} = \left[-\frac{\hbar^2}{2m}\nabla^2 + \frac{ie\hbar}{mc}\boldsymbol{A}\cdot\nabla + \frac{ie\hbar}{2mc}(\nabla\cdot\boldsymbol{A})\right.$$
$$\left. + \frac{e^2}{2mc^2}\boldsymbol{A}^2 + e\phi + V(\boldsymbol{r})\right]\psi. \qquad (15.83)$$

We will work in the radiation gauge ($\nabla\cdot\boldsymbol{A} = \phi = 0$), and use the time dependent theory which results in scattering rates given by the Fermi golden rule. We assume that the optical power and consequently A is small, so that the ratio

$$\left|\frac{ie\hbar}{mc}\boldsymbol{A}\cdot\nabla\right| : \left|\frac{\hbar^2}{2m}\nabla^2\right| \approx \left|\frac{e^2\boldsymbol{A}^2}{2mc^2}\right| : \left|\frac{ie\hbar}{mc}\boldsymbol{A}\cdot\nabla\right|$$
$$\approx \frac{eA}{cp} \qquad (15.84)$$

where p is the particle momentum.

For an optical power of 1 watt/cm^2 the photon density of a 1eV energy beam is $\sim 10^9$ cm^{-3}. Using an electron velocity of 10^6 cm/s, one finds that

$$\frac{eA}{cp} \sim 10^{-5}. \qquad (15.85)$$

Thus, even for an optical beam carrying 1 MW/cm^2, the value of eA/cp is small enough that perturbation theory can be used. We will, therefore, only retain the first order term in $\boldsymbol{A}$.

The Schrödinger equation is now written as

$$ih\frac{\partial\psi}{\partial t} = (H_0 + H')\psi \qquad (15.86)$$

where

$$H_0 = -\frac{\hbar}{2m}\nabla^2 + V(\boldsymbol{r}) \qquad (15.87)$$

and

$$H' = \frac{ie\hbar}{mc} \boldsymbol{A} \cdot \nabla. \tag{15.88}$$

In some cases, especially for forbidden transitions, the higher order term needs to be included. We will first address the problem assuming simple plane wave states for the electronic unperturbed problem. Later we will discuss the effect of Bloch central cell terms on the photon emission and absorption. The central cell terms play a crucial role in optical interactions in semiconductors, and, among other things, determine the selection rules.

The first order time dependent perturbation theory gives us the transition rates from the initial electron state $|i\rangle$ to the final state $|f\rangle$ by the golden rule

$$W(i) = \frac{2\pi}{\hbar} \sum_f \left| \langle f|H'|i\rangle \right|^2 \delta \left(E_f - E_i \mp \hbar\omega \right) \tag{15.89}$$

where the upper sign is for photon absorption and the lower one is for emission. For the scattering rate to have physical significance, we need to define the final state as having either a spread in the electronic states or a spread in the photonic states.

In case of absorption process, the final electronic states have a spread given by the concept of the density of states. For emission of photons, the spread is in the photon spectra. If we assume that the photons are spread over a range of frequency with width $d\omega$, we can write the photon density as

$$N_{\text{ph}} = n \, \rho(\hbar\omega) \, d(\hbar\omega) \tag{15.90}$$

where n is the photon occupation and $\rho(\hbar\omega)$ is the photon density of states for a 3-dimensional volume of space is given by

$$\rho(\hbar\omega) = \frac{\omega^2}{2\pi^2 \hbar v^3} \tag{15.91}$$

where

$$v = c \text{ if } \epsilon = 1.$$

The vector potential is then given from Equation 15.18 by

$$\begin{aligned}
|\boldsymbol{A}_0|^2 &= \frac{2\pi\hbar N_{\text{ph}} c^2}{\omega\epsilon} \\
&= \frac{2\pi\hbar c^2 n \, \rho(\omega) \, d\omega}{\omega\epsilon}.
\end{aligned} \tag{15.92}$$

Expressing the final state density of states in terms of photon density of states we then get the absorption rate, after substituting for H' and $\boldsymbol{A}_0$ in the Fermi golden rule

$$W_{\text{abs}}(\omega) = \frac{4\pi^2 e^2 n \rho(\omega)}{m^2 \omega\epsilon} \left| \int \psi_{\boldsymbol{k}'}^* \, \exp(i\boldsymbol{k}_{\text{ph}} \cdot \boldsymbol{r}) \, p_a \, \psi_{\boldsymbol{k}} \, d^3r \right|^2 \tag{15.93}$$

where ψ_k and $\psi_{k'}$ represent the initial and final states of the electron and k_{ph} is the photon wavevector. p_a is the momentum operator in the direction of the vector A. We note that the photon intensity $I(\omega)$ per unit *frequency* interval is

$$I(\omega) = V\hbar^2 \omega n \rho(\omega),\tag{15.94}$$

so that the absorption rate can also be written as

$$W_{abs} = \frac{4\pi^2 e^2 I(\omega)}{m^2 V \omega^2 \hbar^2 \epsilon} \left| \int \psi_{k'}^* \exp(i k_{ph} \cdot r)\, p_a\, \psi_k\, d^3r \right|^2 \tag{15.95}$$

In a similar manner, the emission rate is given by

$$W_{em} = \frac{4\pi^2 e^2 n \rho(\omega)}{m^2 \omega \epsilon} \left| \int \psi_{k'}^* \exp(i k_{ph} \cdot r)\, p_a\, \psi_k\, d^3r \right|^2 .\tag{15.96}$$

The transition rates can be written in terms of final state electron density of states $N(E_f)$ instead of photonic density of states $\rho(\omega)$, giving the transition rates

$$W_{abs} = \frac{4\pi^2 e^2 \hbar}{m^2 \epsilon} \frac{1}{\hbar \omega} n\, |a \cdot p_{if}|^2\, N(E_f)\tag{15.97}$$

$N(E_f)$ is the *reduced density* of states since the transition energy is governed by ($k_{ph} \sim 0$ making the transitions "vertical")

$$\begin{aligned} \hbar\omega &= \frac{\hbar^2 k^2}{2}\left(\frac{1}{m_e^*} + \frac{1}{m_h^*}\right)\\ &= \frac{\hbar^2 k^2}{2m_r^*}. \end{aligned}\tag{15.98}$$

The quantity p_{if} is the momentum matrix element between the initial and final states. A similar term for emission of photons can be written.

In the expressions derived above, the emission and absorption theory are both proportional to n, the photon occupation. This result is modified when a proper quantum theory for the perturbation theory is used. As in the case of phonons, the general approach goes as follows:

Perturbation	$eA \cdot p/mc$
Quantization of EM field	$A \rightarrow a^\dagger + a$
	$a^\dagger =$ creation operator for photons
	$a =$ destruction operator of photon
Emission matrix element	$\langle n+1|a^\dagger|n\rangle \rightarrow (n+1)^{1/2}$
Absorption matrix element	$\langle n-1|a|n\rangle \rightarrow n^{1/2}$.

With this approach we get the following rates written in terms of either photon or electron final state density of states. The main difference is that as with phonon emission, the emission process has a factor $(n+1)$ instead of n. Thus, photons can be emitted (spontaneous emission) even if there are no photons already present.

Final photon density of states

$$W_{\text{abs}} = \frac{4\pi^2 e^2 \hbar}{m^2 \epsilon} \frac{1}{\hbar\omega} n \left| \boldsymbol{a} \cdot \boldsymbol{p}_{\text{if}} \right|^2 \rho(\hbar\omega)$$

$$W_{\text{em}} = \frac{4\pi^2 e^2 \hbar}{m^2 \epsilon} \frac{1}{\hbar\omega} (n+1) \left| \boldsymbol{a} \cdot \boldsymbol{p}_{\text{if}} \right|^2 \rho(\hbar\omega)$$

$$\rho(\hbar\omega) = \frac{\omega^2}{2\pi^2 \hbar v^3}$$

$$v = \frac{c}{\sqrt{\epsilon}}. \tag{15.99}$$

Final electron density of states

$$W_{\text{abs}} = \frac{4\pi^2 e^2 \hbar}{m^2 \epsilon} \frac{1}{\hbar\omega} n \left| \boldsymbol{a} \cdot \boldsymbol{p}_{\text{if}} \right|^2 N(E_f)$$

$$W_{\text{em}} = \frac{4\pi^2 e^2 \hbar}{m^2 \epsilon} \frac{1}{\hbar\omega} (n+1) \left| \boldsymbol{a} \cdot \boldsymbol{p}_{\text{if}} \right|^2 N(E_f). \tag{15.100}$$

The electronic density of states depends upon the material bandstructure and dimensionality, as we have discussed several times.

It may seem from the discussions above that the absorption or emission rates could be very different depending upon whether the photon or electron density of states are used. These two densities are obviously very different leading to very different rates. However, as shown in Figure 15.7, there is no inconsistency between these two rates. In a scattering process involving electrons and photons, we may be interested in the transition rate of either a particular photon or a particular electronic state. For example, in discussing absorption coefficient we are interested in the rate at which *photons* at a particular energy are absorbed. We do not care which electronic states are involved in the absorption process. Thus, we integrate over the electronic density of states. On the other hand, in emission processes we focus on the rate at which an electron in a given state in the conduction band recombines with a hole. In this case, we do not care about the particular nature of the photon emitted and, therefore, integrate over the final photon density of states. Of course, this is the usual way of defining absorption and emission process. One is perfectly free to use alternate descriptions, but one has to be careful to compare these rates with experimental results.

15.6 SELECTION RULES FOR OPTICAL PROCESSES

A number of selection rules which determine whether or not electron-photon interactions will take place can be derived by using simple symmetry arguments. We will examine these selection rules by examining the matrix element

$$\left| \boldsymbol{a} \cdot \boldsymbol{p}_{\text{if}} \right|^2 = \left| \int \psi_f^* \, p_a \, \psi_i \, e^{i\mathbf{q}\cdot\mathbf{r}} \, d^3r \right|^2 \tag{15.101}$$

ELECTRON - PHOTON SYSTEM

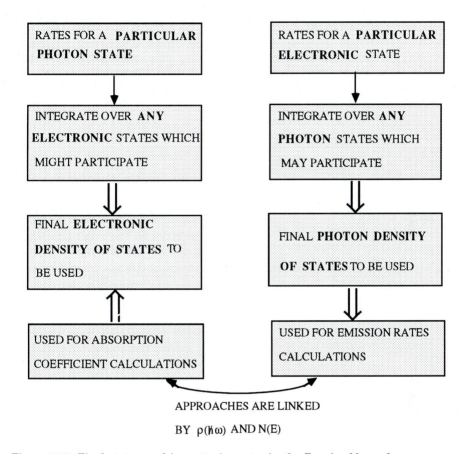

Figure 15.7: Final states used in scattering rates in the Fermi golden rule.

where p_a is the momentum component along the polarization direction. In most problems the relevant dimensions of the integration are such that $\exp(i\boldsymbol{q} \cdot \boldsymbol{r})$ can be taken as a constant ($=$ unity) in the integral. This approximation is called the dipole approximation. We can write

$$\frac{1}{m}\langle f|\boldsymbol{p}|i\rangle = \frac{d}{dt}\langle f|\boldsymbol{r}|i\rangle. \qquad (15.102)$$

The time dependence of the initial and final states can be written as

$$|i(t)\rangle = |i(0)\rangle e^{iE_i t/\hbar} \qquad (15.103)$$

$$|f(t)\rangle = |f(0)\rangle e^{iE_f t/\hbar} \qquad (15.104)$$

so that

$$\frac{d}{dt}\langle f|\boldsymbol{r}|i\rangle = i\,\omega_{\text{if}}\langle f|\boldsymbol{r}|i\rangle \tag{15.105}$$

where

$$\omega_{\text{if}} = \frac{E_i - E_f}{\hbar}. \tag{15.106}$$

Note that in this derivation we have used the Schrödinger picture where the time dependence is only in the wavefunctions and not in the operation. We then get for the matrix element

$$\boldsymbol{p}_{\text{if}} = i\,m\,\omega_{\text{if}}\langle f|\boldsymbol{r}|i\rangle. \tag{15.107}$$

Thus, the momentum matrix element is equivalent to a matrix element of the dipole along the polarization. If the matrix element $\langle f|\boldsymbol{r}|i\rangle$ is zero, the transition is called a forbidden transition. If, on the other hand, $\langle f|\boldsymbol{r}\exp(i\boldsymbol{q}\cdot\boldsymbol{r})|i\rangle$ is zero, the transition is called strictly forbidden.

The conditions on ψ_f and ψ_i, for which the transitions are not forbidden, give us the selection rules for emission or absorption of photons. Let us now consider the initial and final states which have the Bloch function form. The momentum matrix element is in the dipole approximation

$$\boldsymbol{p}_{\text{if}} = -i\hbar \int \psi^*_{\boldsymbol{k}'\ell'}\,\nabla\psi_{\boldsymbol{k}\ell}\,d^3r \tag{15.108}$$

where we choose

$$\begin{aligned}
|i\rangle &= \psi_{\boldsymbol{k}\ell} \\
&= e^{i\boldsymbol{k}\cdot\boldsymbol{r}}u_{\boldsymbol{k}\ell} \\
|f\rangle &= \psi_{\boldsymbol{k}'\ell'} \\
&= e^{i\boldsymbol{k}'\cdot\boldsymbol{r}}u_{\boldsymbol{k}'\ell'}
\end{aligned} \tag{15.109}$$

where $u_{\boldsymbol{k}\ell}$ is the cell periodic part of the Bloch state and ℓ, ℓ' are the band indices. Carrying out the differentiation we can write

$$\boldsymbol{p}_{\text{if}} = \hbar\boldsymbol{k}\int \psi^*_{\boldsymbol{k}'\ell'}\,\psi_{\boldsymbol{k}\ell}\,d^3r - i\hbar\int u^*_{\boldsymbol{k}'\ell'}\,(\nabla u_{\boldsymbol{k}\ell})\,e^{i(\boldsymbol{k}-\boldsymbol{k}')\cdot\boldsymbol{r}}\,d^3r. \tag{15.110}$$

In the next section, we will examine the selection rules explicitly, for semiconductor systems of interest.

15.7   INTERBAND TRANSITIONS

15.7.1   Interband Transitions in Bulk Semiconductors

Let us consider the selection rules for *band-to-band* transitions in direct gap semiconductors. We will now use our understanding of the nature of conduction and valence band state central cell functions. The first term on the right-hand side of the matrix elements is zero because of orthogonality of Bloch states. The second term requires ($u^*_{\mathbf{k}'\ell'} \nabla u_{\mathbf{k}\ell}$ is periodic)

$$\mathbf{k} - \mathbf{k}' = 0 \tag{15.111}$$

so that the interband transitions are "vertical" transitions (we will not discuss Umklapp processes since they are not relevant for most optoelectronic devices). The interband matrix element is, therefore

$$\langle u_{c\mathbf{k}}|\mathbf{p}_a|u_{v\mathbf{k}}\rangle \tag{15.112}$$

where $u_{c\mathbf{k}}$ and $u_{v\mathbf{k}}$ represent the conduction band and valence band central cell states.

For near bandedge transitions we will assume that $u_{c\mathbf{k}}$ and $u_{v\mathbf{k}}$ are given by their zone center values. We remind ourselves that in this case the central cell states are (See Chapter 5 for a discussion on the $\mathbf{k} \cdot \mathbf{p}$ formalism),

- Conduction band:

$$u_{c0} = |s\rangle \tag{15.113}$$

where $|s\rangle$ is a spherically symmetric state.

- Valence band:

$$
\begin{aligned}
\text{Heavy hole states:} \quad |3/2, 3/2\rangle &= \frac{-1}{\sqrt{2}}\left(|p_x\rangle + i|p_y\rangle\right)\uparrow \\
|3/2, -3/2\rangle &= \frac{1}{\sqrt{2}}\left(|p_x\rangle - i|p_y\rangle\right)\downarrow \\
\text{Light hole states:} \quad |3/2, 1/2\rangle &= \frac{-1}{\sqrt{6}}\left[\left(|p_x\rangle + i|p_y\rangle\right)\downarrow - 2|p_z\rangle\uparrow\right] \\
|3/2, -1/2\rangle &= \frac{1}{\sqrt{6}}\left[\left(|p_x\rangle - i|p_y\rangle\right)\uparrow + 2|p_z\rangle\downarrow\right].
\end{aligned}
\tag{15.114}
$$

From symmetry we see that *only* the matrix elements of the form

$$\langle p_x|p_x|s\rangle = \langle p_y|p_y|s\rangle = \langle p_z|p_z|s\rangle$$

are nonzero. Thus, for band-to-band transition, the only allowed transitions have the following matrix elements

$$\langle \text{HH}|p_x|s\rangle = \langle \text{HH}|p_y|s\rangle = \frac{1}{\sqrt{2}}\langle p_x|p_x|s\rangle \tag{15.115}$$

$$\langle \text{LH}|p_x|s\rangle = \langle \text{LH}|p_y|s\rangle = \frac{1}{\sqrt{6}}\langle p_x|p_x|s\rangle \tag{15.116}$$

and

$$\langle \text{LH}|p_z|s\rangle = \frac{2}{\sqrt{6}}\langle p_x|p_x|s\rangle. \tag{15.117}$$

Semiconductor	E_p (eV)
GaAs	25.7
InP	20.9
InAs	22.2
CdTe	20.7

Table 15.1: Values of E_p for different semiconductors.

It is important to note that

$$\langle HH|p_z|s\rangle = 0. \tag{15.118}$$

It is very useful to examine the matrix element square for light polarized along various orientations. This polarization dependence is accentuated in quantum wells because the HH and LH states are no longer degenerate in that case.

$$
\begin{array}{lll}
\textit{z-polarized light:} & \text{No HH} \rightarrow \text{c-band coupling} & \\
& \text{LH} \rightarrow \text{c-band:} & |\boldsymbol{p}_{\text{if}}|^2 = \frac{2}{3}\,|\langle p_x|p_x|s\rangle|^2 \\
\textit{x-polarized light:} & \text{HH} \rightarrow \text{c-band:} & |\boldsymbol{p}_{\text{if}}|^2 = \frac{1}{2}\,|\langle p_x|p_x|s\rangle|^2 \\
& \text{LH} \rightarrow \text{c-band:} & |\boldsymbol{p}_{\text{if}}|^2 = \frac{1}{6}\,|\langle p_x|p_x|s\rangle|^2 \\
\textit{y-polarized light:} & \text{HH} \rightarrow \text{c-band:} & |\boldsymbol{p}_{\text{if}}|^2 = \frac{1}{2}\,|\langle p_x|p_x|s\rangle|^2 \\
& \text{LH} \rightarrow \text{c-band:} & |\boldsymbol{p}_{\text{if}}|^2 = \frac{1}{6}\,|\langle p_x|p_x|s\rangle|^2 .
\end{array}
\tag{15.119}
$$

We see that the z-polarized light has no coupling to the HH states. Of course, the states have the pure form only at $\boldsymbol{k} = 0$. Away from $\boldsymbol{k} = 0$, the HH state and LH states have some mixture. For x-y polarized light the light couples three times as strongly to the HH states as to the LH states. In quantum well structures where the HH, LH degeneracy is lifted, the selection holes have important consequences for lasers and detectors and their polarization dependent properties.

It is important to remember that the momentum matrix elements that appear in the photon-semiconductor interactions in this chapter are the same that appeared in the $\boldsymbol{k} \cdot \boldsymbol{p}$ formalism discussed in Chapter 5. As discussed in Chapter 5, the momentum matrix elements were responsible for the carrier masses near the bandedges.

It is convenient to define a quantity

$$E_p = \frac{2}{m}\,|\langle p_x|p_x|s\rangle|^2 \tag{15.120}$$

which is related to a matrix element appearing in the $\boldsymbol{k} \cdot \boldsymbol{p}$ theory. The values of E_p for several semiconductors (Lawaetz, 1971), are given in Table 15.1.

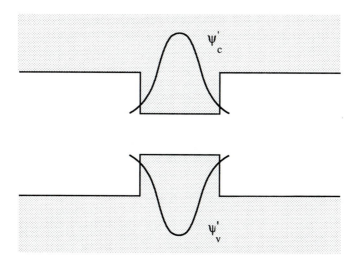

Figure 15.8: A schematic of the electron and hole ground state wavefunctions. The valence band state is actually more accurately a four-band state.

15.7.2 Interband Transitions in Quantum Wells

The formalism developed so far can be extended in a straightforward manner to the case of the quantum well structures. The central cell functions in the quantum wells are relatively unaffected by the presence of the confining potential. The two changes that occur are the nature of the wavefunctions, which for the low lying states are confined to the well region, and the density of states which have the usual step-like form for parabolic 2-dimensional bands.

The absorption rates are calculated only for the well region since the barrier material has a higher bandgap and does not participate in the optical process till the photon energies are much higher. As shown in Figure 15.8, the quantum well conduction and valence band states are given in the envelope function approximation by

$$\psi_c^n = \frac{1}{\sqrt{AW}} \, e^{i\mathbf{k}_e \cdot \rho} \, g_c^n(z) \, u_{c\mathbf{k}_e}^n$$

$$\psi_v^m = \frac{1}{\sqrt{AW}} \, e^{i\mathbf{k}_h \cdot \rho} \sum_\nu g_v^{\nu m}(z) \, u_{v\mathbf{k}_h}^{\nu m}. \tag{15.121}$$

Here W is the well size and A is the area considered and we have used as before the scalar description of the conduction band states and a multiband (indexed by ν) description of the valence band. The envelope functions g_c^n and $g_v^{\nu m}$ correspond to the n and m subband levels in the conduction and valence bands respectively. If we ignore the band mixing effects between the HH and LH states, i.e., ignore the off-diagonal terms in the Kohn-Luttinger Hamiltonian, we obtain simple analytic results for the absorption and emission rates. Note that the momentum matrix element now undergoes the following change when we go from our 3-dimensional calculation to a quasi-2-dimensional one

$$p_{if}^{3D} = \frac{1}{V} \int e^{i(\mathbf{k}_e - \mathbf{k}_h)\cdot \mathbf{r}} \langle u_v^\nu | p_a | u_c \rangle \, d^3 r$$

$$\to p_{if}^{2D} = \frac{1}{AW} \sum_\nu \langle g_v^{\nu m} | g_c^n \rangle \int e^{i(\mathbf{k}_e - \mathbf{k}_h)\cdot \rho} \langle u_v^{\nu m} | p_a | u_c \rangle \, d^2 \rho \quad (15.122)$$

where $\langle g_v^{\nu m} | g_c^n \rangle$ denotes the overlap between the z-dependent envelope functions of the conduction and valence bands. For symmetrical potentials one has the approximate condition that

$$\sum_\nu \langle g_v^{\nu m} | g_c^n \rangle \approx \delta_{nm}. \tag{15.123}$$

This condition is not exact and can be changed if there is any asymmetry present (e.g. if there is a transverse electric field present).

When expressing the photon absorption rate in terms of the final electronic density of states, the changes discussed above can be represented by a modified density of states which for parabolic bands are given by

$$N_{cv}^{3D}(\hbar\omega) = \frac{\sqrt{2}\, m_T^{3/2} (\hbar\omega - E_g)^{1/2}}{\pi \hbar^3} \tag{15.124}$$

to be replaced by

$$\frac{N_{cv}^{2D}(\hbar\omega)}{W} = \frac{m_r}{\pi \hbar^2 W} \sum_{nm} \langle g_v^m | g_c^n \rangle \, \theta(E_{nm} - \hbar\omega)$$

$$E_{nm} = E_{gap} + E_c^n + E_v^m. \tag{15.125}$$

Here m_r is the reduced electron hole mass. The θ-function is the Heaviside step function. In the emission process, if we are interested in the recombination of an electron hole (for well-defined $\mathbf{k}_e = \mathbf{k}_h$), we integrate over the final density of photon states. In general, one can alter the photon density of states as well in heterostructures. If this is done, the recombination rate can change in quantum well structures. In fact, considerable work is being carried out to modify photon density of states by using specially tailored heterostructures. In this chapter we will assume that the photons are still 3-dimensional, with the dispersion relation $\omega = vk$.

Before summarizing and comparing the results for the optical absorption and electron-hole recombination in bulk and quantum well structures, we will briefly relate the absorption coefficient to the absorption rate. It is useful to talk about absorption coefficient rather than the rate at which a photon is absorbed. If we consider a beam of photons traveling along the x-axis, we can write the continuity equation for the photon density

$$\frac{dn}{dt} = \left. \frac{\partial n}{\partial t} \right|_{vol} + \frac{\partial(vn)}{\partial x} \tag{15.126}$$

where the first term represents the absorption rate of photons and the second term represents the photons leaving due to the photon current. Here v is the velocity of light. In steady state we have, in general

$$n(x) = n_0 \exp(-\alpha x) \tag{15.127}$$

which defines the absorption coefficient. Also

$$\frac{\partial n}{\partial t} = W_{\text{abs}} \tag{15.128}$$

and in steady state we have

$$W_{\text{abs}} = \alpha v n$$

or

$$\alpha = \frac{W_{\text{abs}}}{v n}. \tag{15.129}$$

Let us now summarize the absorption coefficients for interband and inter-sub-band transitions discussed above. Some typical numerical values are discussed in Appendix L.

Bulk Semiconductors: Interband Transitions

$$\alpha(\hbar\omega) = \frac{4\pi^2 e^2 \hbar}{m^2 c\eta} \frac{1}{(\hbar\omega)} |\boldsymbol{a} \cdot \boldsymbol{p}_{\text{if}}|^2 N(\hbar\omega)$$

with

$$N(\hbar\omega) = \frac{\sqrt{2} \, (m_r)^{3/2} \, (\hbar\omega - E_g)^{1/2}}{\pi^2 \hbar^3} \tag{15.130}$$

for parabolic electron-hole bands. The polarization dependence of the absorption coefficient is contained in the matrix element $|\boldsymbol{a} \cdot \boldsymbol{p}_{\text{if}}|^2$. η is the refractive index of the material.

Quantum Well: Interband Transitions

$$\alpha(\hbar\omega) = \frac{4\pi^2 e^2 \hbar}{m^2 c\eta} \frac{1}{(\hbar\omega)} |\boldsymbol{a} \cdot \boldsymbol{p}_{\text{if}}|^2 \frac{N_{2D}(\hbar\omega)}{W} \sum_{n,m} f_{nm} \, \theta(E_{nm} - \hbar\omega). \tag{15.131}$$

Here, for parabolic bands, we have

$$N_{2D} = \frac{m_r}{\pi \hbar^2} \tag{15.132}$$

and f_{nm} represents the overlap between the n and m subband overlap functions. This function is close to unity for $n = m$ and close to zero, otherwise.

The recombination rates for an electron to recombine with a hole is given for the bulk system by

$$W_{\text{em}} = \frac{4\pi^2 e^2 \hbar}{m^2 \hbar \omega \epsilon} (n+1) |\boldsymbol{a} \cdot \boldsymbol{p}_{\text{if}}|^2 \rho_a(\hbar\omega) \tag{15.133}$$

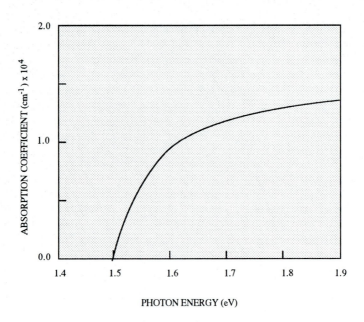

Figure 15.9: Absorption coefficient for GaAs. In a real situation, the effects of the e-h interaction discussed in Chapter 16 causes the absorption coefficient to be finite at the bandedge.

where ρ_a is the photon density of states for the polarization $\boldsymbol{a}$. The total photon density of states is given by (there are 2 transverse modes for each $\boldsymbol{k}$ value)

$$\rho(\hbar\omega) = \frac{2\omega^2}{2\pi^2\hbar v^3} \tag{15.134}$$

for photons emitted in the 3-dimensional space. For a given polarization, the photon density of states is one third of the value in Equation 15.134. For quantum well structures the rate is simply modified by the overlap of the envelope functions of the electron and hole states.

It is useful to examine some numerical values of the absorption coefficient and the recombination time for, say, a common system like GaAs. In Figures 15.9 and 15.10 we show the absorption coefficient for GaAs and a 100 Å GaAs /Al$_{0.3}$Ga$_{0.7}$As quantum well structure. In the bulk semiconductor the absorption coefficient starts at $\hbar\omega = E_g$, with a zero value and initially increases as $(\hbar\omega - E_g)^{1/2}$. It also has a $1/\hbar\omega$ behavior which only influences the absorption coefficients at high energies where the density of states is not parabolic anymore. Because of the degeneracy of the HH and LH states, there is no polarization dependence of the absorption coefficient near the bandgap region.

The absorption coefficient in the quantum well structure is quite distinct from the bulk case mainly because of the density of states function. Another difference arises because of the lifting of the HH, LH degeneracy which makes the absorption coefficient strongly polarization dependent as discussed earlier.

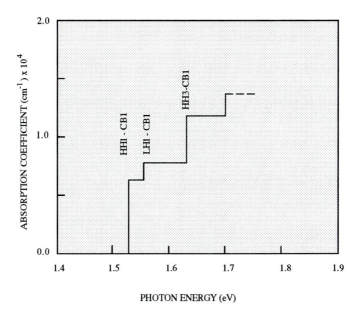

Figure 15.10: Absorption coefficient in a 100 Å GaAs/Al$_{0.3}$Ga$_{0.7}$As quantum well structure for in-plane polarized light. The HH transition is about three times stronger than the LH transition in this polarization. The higher subbands become closer spaced and eventually one gets the 3-D absorption coefficient.

The 1/W dependence of the absorption coefficient is quite interesting and somewhat misleading. We note that this dependence came from our assumption that the wavefunction is localized a distance equal to the well size. The 1/W dependence suggests that the absorption coefficient can be increased indefinitely by decreasing W, the well size. This is, however, not true. As shown schematically in Figure 15.11, as the well size is narrowed, the wavefunctions of the electron and hole no longer are confined to the well size. The region of interest for the electrons starts increasing beyond W. Also, because of the different masses of the electron and hole, the electron function starts spreading beyond the well at a larger well size making the overlap from less than unity. Thus, depending upon the material, the optimum well size is ∼ 50 Å (for GaAs) to 80 Å (for In$_{0.53}$Ga$_{0.47}$As). The recombination time τ_r (= $1/W_{em}$) for an electron and hole is in the range of ∼ 0.5 ns for most direct gap semiconductors. Because τ_r decreases with the photon energy, near the bandgap the recombination time is shorter for larger bandgap materials. It is important to note that the value ∼ 0.5 ns mentioned above is calculated for the case the electron with momentum k_e is present in the conduction band and a hole with momentum $k_h = k_e$ is also present. In many experiments carriers are pumped into the conduction band by a short pulse laser and their recombination is studied by observing the photons coming out. As will be discussed in the next section, in such experiments the occupation probability

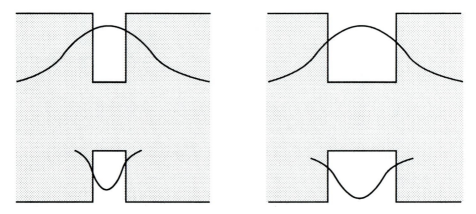

Figure 15.11: Schematic representation of the effect of well size on electron and hole wavefunctions and the associated overlap integrals.

for the initial electron and final hole can greatly influence the recombination time. Such recombination times can range from nanoseconds to even milliseconds! In such cases, it is extremely important to specify the carrier concentration when discussing recombination times.

15.8 OPTICAL PROCESSES IN SEMICONDUCTOR LASERS

In the formalism for interband transitions discussed so far, we have assumed that the initial electron state is occupied with unity probability while the final state is empty. In actual experimental situations this may, of course, not be true. In this section we will discuss the important optical properties in semiconductor lasers viz. gain and recombination rates.

In a typical semiconductor laser (bulk or quantum well), the semiconductor structure has a configuration shown in Figure 15.12. In the bulk or double heterostructure laser (say, a GaAs/AlGaAs laser) the large bandgap material forms the n and p regions from which electrons and holes are injected under forward bias conditions into the narrower bandgap region (GaAs). The electrons and holes recombine in the active region emitting photons. The purpose of the larger barrier regions is to provide a confining index step for the optical waves by providing a waveguide. The active region thickness is typically ~ 1 μm so that no quantum confinement effects occur for the electronic states.

A typical quantum well structure is shown in Figure 15.12b. In this structure there is a separate confining structure for the optical wave and a separate one for the electronic states. The electronic states thus have a two-dimensional density of states, a feature that greatly improves the laser performance. For the operation of the semiconductor laser, electrons and holes are pumped into the active region where they recombine producing photons. These photons are par-

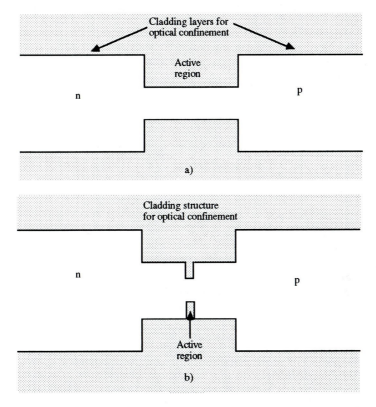

Figure 15.12: Typical band profiles used for (a) double heterostructure and (b) quantum well lasers. The active region dimensions in the quantum well laser is ≤ 100 Å while in the double heterostructure laser it is ≥ 0.1 μm.

tially lost either by absorption or by loss to the outside world. For the lasing action to occur the emission rate should exceed the losses in the laser cavity. Once this occurs, the emission term is dominated by the photon occupation n in the emission rate term $(n + 1)$. The stimulated emission now takes over producing photons with well-defined phase and polarization in contrast to spontaneous emission which produces incoherent photons.

The two important processes in the laser are thus gain and recombination rate. The definition of gain is simply

$$g(\hbar\omega) = -\alpha(\hbar\omega) \tag{15.135}$$

where α is the absorption coefficient discussed earlier but with a key difference, due to the occupation number. In our previous derivation we assumed that all valence band states are occupied while all conduction band states are empty. In the case of an injection laser, the occupation of the conduction and valence bands is given by the quasi-Fermi levels, given by the relations for the electron and hole density

$$n = \int_{E_c}^{\infty} N_e(E) \, f_e(E) \, dE$$

$$p = \int_{-\infty}^{E_v} N_h(E) \, f_h(E) \, dE \qquad (15.136)$$

where $N_e(E)$ and $N_h(E)$ are the conduction and valence band density of states and the f_e and f_h are the distribution functions related to the quasi-Fermi levels μ_e and μ_h by

$$f_e(E) = \frac{1}{\exp\left(\frac{E-\mu_e}{k_B T}\right) + 1}$$

$$f_h(E) = 1 - \frac{1}{\exp\left(\frac{E-\mu_h}{k_B T}\right) + 1}. \qquad (15.137)$$

The gain spectra is now given by emission minus the absorption coefficient

$$g(\hbar\omega) = \frac{4\pi^2 e^2 \hbar}{\eta c m^2 \hbar\omega} \int \frac{d^3k}{(2\pi)^3} |\boldsymbol{a} \cdot \boldsymbol{p}_{\mathrm{if}}|^2 \, N_r(E)$$

$$\times \; \left[f_e(E^e(\boldsymbol{k})) + f_h(E^h(\boldsymbol{k})) - 1 \right]$$

$$\times \; \delta\left(E^e(\boldsymbol{k}) - E^h(\boldsymbol{k}) - \hbar\omega \right). \qquad (15.138)$$

In case $f_e(E^e(\boldsymbol{k}))$ and $f_h(E^h(\boldsymbol{k}))$ are zero, we simply recover the results obtained for the absorption coefficient (with a negative sign). The gain can exceed zero when $f_e + f_h$ are larger than unity. This condition is called population inversion. The gain spectra for the quantum well system is given by the expression

$$g_{nm}(\hbar\omega) = \frac{4\pi^2 e^2 \hbar}{\eta c m^2 W \hbar\omega} \int \frac{d^2k}{(2\pi)^2} \sum_{\sigma} |\boldsymbol{a} \cdot \boldsymbol{p}_{\mathrm{n}}|^2$$

$$\times \; \left[f_e(E_n^e(\boldsymbol{k})) + f_h(E_m^h(\boldsymbol{k})) - 1 \right]$$

$$\times \; \delta\left(E_n^e(\boldsymbol{k}) - E_m^h(\boldsymbol{k}) - \hbar\omega \right) \qquad (15.139)$$

where we have used σ to denote the various angular momentum states making up the hole states. In case of the diagonal approximation one need not worry about the mixing of LH and HH states and the summation of σ can be eliminated. The indices n and m denote the electron and hole subband index. The matrix element is as before

$$p_{nm} = \sum_{\nu} \int g_c^{*n}(z) \, g_v^{\nu m}(k,z) \, dz \cdot \langle s | p_a | u_v^h \rangle \qquad (15.140)$$

where the integral over the envelope functions gives approximate unity for $n = m$ and the central cell momentum matrix element is the one we evaluated earlier in Equation 15.119. The polarization rules discussed for absorption are also valid for the gain spectra. The total gain in the quantum well structure is obtained by summing the gain from different subband level combinations. Usually a broadening function $\Delta(E)$ is introduced to account for thermal or other inhomogeneous broadening sources. The total gain is then

$$g(\hbar\omega) = \int dE' \sum_{nm} g_{nm}(E') \, \Delta(E' - \hbar\omega). \tag{15.141}$$

At energies much larger than the bandgap, the occupation of electrons and holes is negligible and the gain curves are simply given by

$$g(\hbar\omega) = -\alpha(\hbar\omega). \tag{15.142}$$

The gain is negative corresponding to the photon absorption process dominating the emission process. However, at finite injection, near the bandedges, the electron occupation is greater than zero while the same holds for hole occupation. Then the term $f_e - f_h$ becomes positive giving a positive gain, or possibility of light amplification as the electromagnetic wave travels through the medium. The condition for lasing is that the gain should be able to overcome the losses in the cavity, i.e.

$$\Gamma_g = \alpha_{\text{loss}}. \tag{15.143}$$

The parameter Γ is the optical confinement factor which represents the fraction of optical intensity in the active region. For quantum well lasers, where the active region is only 50–100 Å, Γ can be quite small (a few percent). The cavity loss is made of two parts, the loss α_0 due to any absorption in the cladding regions and the loss term arriving from the fact that the photons are escaping from the laser facets. If L is the laser cavity length and R is the facet reflectivity, we have

$$\alpha_{loss} = \frac{1}{L} \ln\left(\frac{1}{R}\right) + \alpha_0. \tag{15.144}$$

The challenge for a laser physicist is to reach the lasing condition with as low an injection density (and currents) as possible. This involves increasing the product Γ_g which is the effective cavity gain. The optical confinement factor is obtained by solving the optical equation which takes the form

$$\frac{d^2 F_{mk}(z)}{dz^2} + \left(\frac{\epsilon_m(z)\,\omega^2}{c^2} - k^2\right) F_{mk}(z) = 0 \tag{15.145}$$

where F_{mk} is the z-dependent (confinement direction) electric field, k is the photon wavenumber, and $\epsilon_m(z)$ is the z-dependent dielectric constant. The role of the cladding layers is to confine the optical wave by producing a spatial variation in ϵ. The index m represents the waveguide mode. In Figure 15.13 we show the

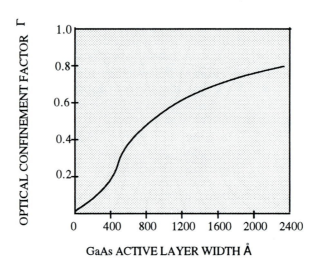

Figure 15.13: A typical optical confinement factor Γ as a function of the well size in a GaAs/AlGaAs separate confinement quantum well laser structure.

value of Γ in a typical separate confinement structure of $GaAs/Al_{0.3}Ga_{0.7}As$ as a function of well size. We note that when the well size region increases above $\sim 0.15\,\mu m$, the value of Γ does not change much. For smaller well sizes, $\Gamma \sim 1/W$.

Once the quantum well is thick enough that it has essentially a bulk density of states, we are in the range where the *3-dimensional carrier density* to reach the same gain value is *independent of the well size*. Thus, the carrier density *per unit area*, n_A, for the same gain is related by

$$\frac{n_A(W_1)}{n_A(W_2)} = \frac{W_1}{W_2} \qquad (15.146)$$

where W_1 and W_2 are the active region size.

Since the current injected is proportional to n_A, $(J = n_A/\tau_{recomb})$, and Γ, the optical confinement factor does not vary strongly with the well size for large well sizes, the threshold current decreases with well size.

For the cases where only the first subband levels are occupied when the lasing condition is satisfied, the gain can be very high at a very low injected carrier density. This is due to the nature of the 2-dimensional density of states as shown in Figure 15.14. Because of the abrupt increase of the density of states near the bandedges, a smaller carrier concentration is able to create inversion $(f_e - f_h > 0)$, providing a high gain. By the same token, in 1-dimensional systems (quantum wires) the density of states has a peak at the bandedge allowing inversion to be reached at even lower injected carrier density. In fact, the 1-dimensional density of states is ideal for the laser since one can reach a very high gain at the bandedge with a very small injection. We note that the *maximum*

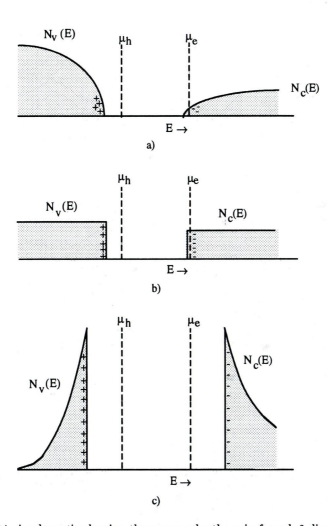

Figure 15.14: A schematic showing the reason why the gain for sub-3-dimensional systems is higher than the bulk case. The enhanced joint density of states at the bandedge ensures a higher absorption coefficient which means that a higher gain can be obtained with less carrier inversion.

gain is simply given by

$$g_{\max}(\hbar\omega) = \alpha(\hbar\omega) \qquad (15.147)$$

where $\alpha(\hbar\omega)$ is the absorption coefficient derived in the previous section. Since $\alpha(\hbar\omega)$ is highest near the bandedge for a 1-dimensional system, and lowest for a 3-dimensional system, the march towards lower-dimensional system for lasers is natural. We note that in quantum wells as for the absorption coefficient, there is a lower limit to the thickness of the well that continues to improve the injection density at threshold conditions.

Before ending the discussion on gain, it is important to discuss the effects of strain on the gain spectra. We have discussed how the biaxial compressive strain lowers the bandedge hole density of states. The lighter hole mass allows the hole Fermi level to penetrate deeper towards the valence band as shown schematically in Figure 15.15. This greatly affects improved gain of the strained structure. In addition, the compressive strain also pushes the LH state away from the valence bandedge. Since only the LH state couples to the TM mode (z-polarized light), the TM mode gain is severely suppressed. In Figures 15.16 and 15.17 we show the TE and TM mode gain curves for a 50 Å GaAs/Al$_{0.3}$Ga$_{0.7}$As and In$_{0.2}$Ga$_{0.8}$As/Al$_{0.3}$Ga$_{0.7}$As quantum well structures for various injection levels. We can see that the TE mode gain is much higher (and steeper) than that for the lattice matched case.

We have also discussed in Chapter 7, that compressive strain can cause a large separation of the HH and LH states in a quantum well. This greatly reduces the TM gain. Results for the 50 Å structure of Figure 15.16 structure are shown in Figure 15.17 for the TM gain.

Spontaneous Emission Rate

When electrons and holes are pumped into the conduction and valence bands of a semiconductor, they recombine with each other as we have discussed earlier. In absence of any photon density in the cavity (i.e. $n = 0$), the emission rate is the spontaneous emission rate which we had calculated to be $\sim 1/(0.5\text{ ns})$ provided an electron is present in the state $\boldsymbol{k}$ and a hole is present in the same state $\boldsymbol{k}$ in the valence band. As for the case of gain, we have to include the distribution functions for electrons and holes and integrate over all possible electronic states. Thus, the recombination rate *per unit area* is (D is the width of the active region)

$$
\begin{aligned}
R_{\text{spon}} &= \frac{2}{3} \int d(\hbar\omega) \frac{2e^2\eta\hbar\omega}{m^2c^3\hbar^2} \left[\int \frac{1}{(2\pi)^3} d^3k \, |p_{\text{if}}|^2 \right. \\
&\times \quad \delta(E^e(\boldsymbol{k}) - E^h(\boldsymbol{k}) - \hbar\omega) \\
&\times \quad \left. f_e(E^e(\boldsymbol{k})) f_h(E^h(\boldsymbol{k})) \right] \times D.
\end{aligned}
\qquad (15.148)
$$

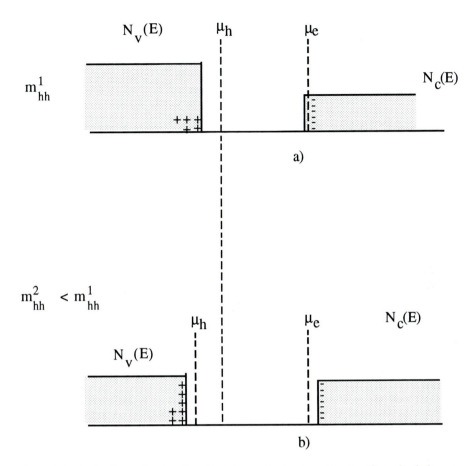

Figure 15.15: A schematic showing the reason for improved gain when the hole mass decreases. The lower density of hole states due to the reduced hole mass forces the chemical potential μ_n to get closer to the bandedge allowing stronger inversion and increasing the gain.

The integral over $d(\hbar\omega)$ is to find the rate for all photons emitted and the integration over d^3k is to get the rate for all the occupied electron and hole states. The prefactor 2/3 comes about since we are considering emission into any photon polarization so that we average the matrix element square $|\boldsymbol{a} \cdot \boldsymbol{p}_{if}|^2$.

The extension to quantum well structures is the usual one giving

$$R_{\text{spon}} = \frac{2}{3} \int d(\hbar\omega) \frac{2e^2\eta\hbar\omega}{m^2c^3\hbar^2} \sum_{nm} \left[\int \frac{d^2k}{(2\pi)^2} |p_{if}|^2 \right.$$
$$\times \quad \delta(E_n^e(\boldsymbol{k}) - E_m^h(\boldsymbol{k}) - \hbar\omega)$$

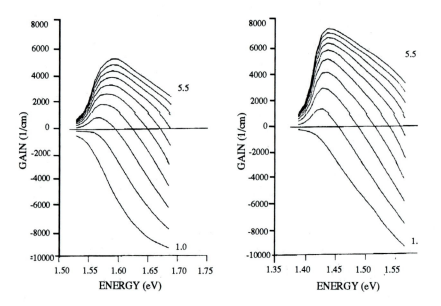

Figure 15.16: TE mode material gain in a 50 Å (left fig) GaAs/Al$_{0.3}$Ga$_{0.7}$As (on GaAs); and (right fig) In$_{0.2}$Ga$_{0.8}$As/Al$_{0.3}$Ga$_{0.7}$As (on GaAs) quantum well at 300 K for various carrier injections. Injections are given in (10^{12} carriers cm^2) in steps of 0.5×10^{12} cm^2.

$$\times \quad f_e\left(E_n^e(\boldsymbol{k})\right)f_h\left(E_m^h(\boldsymbol{k})\right) \Bigg] . \tag{15.149}$$

The spontaneous emission rate can be considered in two limiting cases. One where the injected carrier density is low so that the Boltzmann statistics are applicable. The integral over $f_e f_h$ then simply gives a term proportional to $n_e n_h$ ($= n_e^2$ if $n_e = n_h$). The emission rate depends on the joint probability of finding an electron and a hole. In the other extreme of high injection, the Fermi levels are in the bands and the spontaneous rate is simply proportional to n_e (or n_h). In the high injection case, which usually holds true near threshold for lasers, we can write

$$R_{\text{spon}} = \frac{n_e}{\tau_0} \tag{15.150}$$

where τ_0 is the time calculated in earlier section (i.e.~ 0.5 ns) assuming a unity electron and hole occupation. In absence of any nonradiative recombination processes involving either defects or Auger processes discussed in Chapter 11, the current flowing in the laser is simply given by

$$J = eR_{\text{spon}}. \tag{15.151}$$

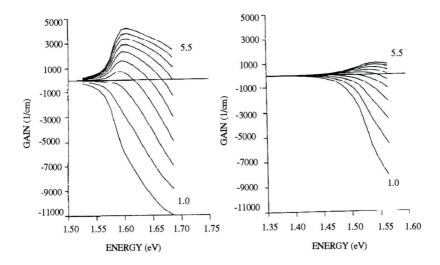

Figure 15.17: TM mode material gain in a 50 Å (left fig) GaAs/Al$_{0.3}$Ga$_{0.7}$As (on GaAs); and (right fig) In$_{0.2}$Ga$_{0.8}$As/Al$_{0.3}$Ga$_{0.7}$As (on GaAs) quantum well at 300 K for various carrier injections. Injections are given in (10^{12} carriers cm^2) in steps of 0.5×10^{12} cm^2.

The threshold current where the lasing action starts is given by $R_{\rm spon}(n_{th})$, where n_{th} is the carrier concentration at the point where $\Gamma_g = \alpha_{\rm loss}$. In the presence of Auger processes, the Auger recombination rate has to be included and the current value increases. The Auger rates were discussed in detail in Chapter 11. Based upon the considerations discussed in this section, it is simple to see the driving forces behind attempts to reduce the threshold current in lasers. It is easy to see that the threshold current of a laser drops steadily as the size of the active region is decreased. The current stabilizes when the well size is such that only the first subband of the well is involved in the lasing action. Further decrease of the well size can increase the current because the gain can decrease since the electron wavefunction is no longer confined to the well size for narrow wells. We can also see how the inclusion of compressive strain enhances the gain and reduces the threshold current. The strain reduces the hole density of states as discussed in Chapter 7, and allows the inversion to occur at a lower injection. In Figure 15.18 we show the calculated decrease of the threshold current for the In$_x$Ga$_{1-x}$As / Al$_{0.3}$Ga$_{0.7}$As structure (50 Å well). Similar results for the In$_{0.53+x}$Ga$_{0.47-x}$As/In$_{0.52}$Al$_{0.48}$As system have also been reported.

15.9 INDIRECT INTERBAND TRANSITIONS

In the previous section we discussed the interactions between photons and electrons in direct bandgap material where vertical transitions in k-space are allowed.

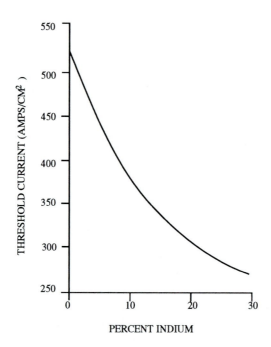

Figure 15.18: Calculated threshold current density J_{th} for a 50 Å $In_x Ga_{1-x}As$ /$Al_{0.3}Ga_{0.7}As$ (on GaAs) quantum well as a function of excess In percentage, x. The actual threshold current in a particular structure may differ because of different cavity losses, but the trend of the decrease in current with strain should remain.

However, photons also cause interband transitions in indirect semiconductors where the bandedges are at different k-points. Thus, optical absorption is observed in Si and Ge although the absorption rate is far weaker than for GaAs.

Transitions between electron states that are not vertical in k-space are called indirect transitions and they involve a phonon interaction. The phonons are required to ensure momentum conservation in the process.

A typical process in the interband transition is shown in Figure 15.19. The process is second order in which the electron is first scattered by a photon to the direct band conserving momentum and then scattering to the indirect band by a phonon. While momentum is conserved in the intermediate process, *the energy is not conserved since this process is virtual and the time–energy uncertainty ensures that there is no energy conservation requirement.* The overall process, however, does conserve energy. The scattering rate is again given by the Fermi golden rule except that the matrix element is the second order matrix element

$$W = \frac{2\pi}{\hbar} \int \left| \frac{\sum \langle f|H_{\mathrm{per}}|n\rangle \langle n|H_{\mathrm{per}}|i\rangle}{E_i - E_n} \right|^2 \delta(E_f - E_i) \frac{d^3k}{(2\pi)^3} \qquad (15.152)$$

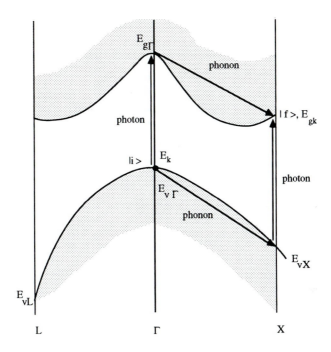

Figure 15.19: Typical processes responsible for optical absorption in indirect bandgap semiconductors. The photon energy need not be equal to the vertical energy since the intermediate transitions are virtual.

where $|n\rangle$ is an intermediate state, and the perturbation is

$$H_{\text{per}} = H_{\text{ph}} + H_{\text{ep}} \qquad (15.153)$$

where H_{ph} is the electron-photon interaction discussed so far and H_{ep} is the electron-phonon interaction discussed in Chapter 12. In general, the processes shown in Figure 15.19 can contribute to the scattering process. However, the processes which involve first a photon interaction are stronger since the denominator is smaller for them (denominator is $\sim$ direct bandgap), than for the processes involving the phonon first (denominator is $\sim |E_{v\Gamma} - E_{vX}|$ or $|E_{v\Gamma} - E_{vL}|$). The scattering rate is then

$$W(\boldsymbol{k}) = \frac{2\pi}{\hbar} \int_f \left\{ |M_{\text{em}}|^2 + |M_{\text{abs}}|^2 \right\} \delta(E_f - E_i) \frac{d^3k}{(2\pi)^3}. \qquad (15.154)$$

The matrix elements M_{em} and M_{abs} correspond to the cases where first a photon is absorbed and then a phonon is either emitted or absorbed. Note that the photon energy $\hbar\omega$ is smaller than the direct bandgap, but the intermediate transition can occur since energy need not be conserved. The form of the matrix elements is

$$
M_{\text{abs}} = \frac{\left|\langle c, \boldsymbol{k} + \boldsymbol{q}|H_{\text{ep}}^{\text{abs}}|c, \boldsymbol{k}\rangle\right|^2 \left|\langle c, \boldsymbol{k}|H_{\text{ph}}^{\text{abs}}|v, \boldsymbol{k}\rangle\right|^2}{(E_{g\Gamma} - \hbar\omega)^2}
$$

$$
M_{\text{em}} = \frac{\left|\langle c, \boldsymbol{k} - \boldsymbol{q}|H_{\text{ep}}^{\text{em}}|c, \boldsymbol{k}\rangle\right|^2 \left|\langle c, \boldsymbol{k}|H_{\text{ph}}^{\text{em}}|v, \boldsymbol{k}\rangle\right|^2}{(E_{g\Gamma} - \hbar\omega)^2}. \tag{15.155}
$$

We have already evaluated the matrix element M_{ph} for the photon absorption process. The phonon scattering is the intervalley scattering discussed in Chapter 13. Its matrix element is

$$
M_q^2 = \frac{\hbar D_{ij}^2}{2\rho V \omega_{ij}} \left\{ \begin{array}{c} n(\omega_{ij}) \\ n(\omega_{ij}) + 1 \end{array} \right\} \tag{15.156}
$$

for the absorption and emission processes respectively, and ω_{ij} is the phonon frequency. Here D_{ij} is the deformation potential, ρ is the mass density, and ω_{ij} is the phonon frequency which connects the Γ valley to the zone edge valley. It is useful to point out that due to the *indirect* nature of the transition, the rates calculated earlier for direct gap semiconductors are essentially *lowered* by a factor equal to

$$
\frac{M_q^2}{(E_{g\Gamma} - \hbar\omega)^2}.
$$

This factor is typically 10^{-2} to 10^{-3}. For direct gap transitions, for a given initial state $|i\rangle$, there was only one final state $|f\rangle$ which had the same $\boldsymbol{k}$-value. For a given photon energy one then had the states $N_{cv}(\hbar\omega)d(\hbar\omega)$ in energy interval $\hbar\omega$ to $\hbar(\omega + d\omega)$ which contributed with N_{cv} given by Equation 15.130. In case of indirect transitions, for a given initial states $|v, \boldsymbol{k}\rangle$, there is a spread in the final states due to the phonon scattering. The scattering rate sums over this spread, giving

$$
\begin{aligned}
W(\boldsymbol{k}) = {} & \frac{2\pi}{\hbar} \frac{M_{\text{ph}}^2}{(E_{g\Gamma} - \hbar\omega)^2} \frac{\hbar D_{ij}^2}{2\rho\omega_{ij}} J_v \\
& \times \ [n(\omega_{ij}) \, N_c(E_1 + \hbar\omega_{ij}) \\
& + \ \{n(\omega_{ij}) + 1\} \, N_c(E_1 - \hbar\omega_{ij})]
\end{aligned} \tag{15.157}
$$

where J_v is the number of equivalent valleys, N_c is the density of states for a given spin in a valley, and

$$
E_1 = \hbar\omega - E_{g\boldsymbol{k}'} - E_{\boldsymbol{k}} \tag{15.158}
$$

where $E_{g\boldsymbol{k}'}$ is the *indirect gap* and the $E_{\boldsymbol{k}}$ is the energy of the initial electron measured from the top of the valence band.

To find the absorption coefficient we need to sum the above rate over all possible starting states which could absorb a photon with energy $\hbar\omega$. This means we must sum over all possible initial states from $E_k = 0$ to E_{kmax} where

$$
\begin{aligned}
E_{kmax} &= \hbar\omega - E_{gk'} + \hbar\omega_{ij} \text{ (phonon absorption)} \\
E_{kmax} &= \hbar\omega - E_{gk'} - \hbar\omega_{ij} \text{ (phonon emission).}
\end{aligned}
\tag{15.159}
$$

We multiply W(k) by $2V N_v(E_k)dE_k$ where N_v is the single spin density of states in the valence band and iterate from 0 to E_{kmax}. For parabolic bands the integral is simple and we get

$$
\begin{aligned}
W_{\text{abs}}(\hbar\omega) &= \frac{M_{\text{ph}}^2 \, D_{ij}^2 \, J_v \, (m_c m_v)^{3/2}}{8\pi^2 (E_{g\Gamma} - \hbar\omega)^2 \, \hbar^6 \, \rho \, \omega_{ij}} \\
&\quad \times \left[n(\omega_{ij}) \left(\hbar\omega - E_{gk'} + \hbar\omega_{ij} \right)^2 \right. \\
&\quad \left. + \{ n(\omega_{ij}) + 1 \} \left(\hbar\omega - E_{gk'} - \hbar\omega_{ij} \right)^2 \right]
\end{aligned}
\tag{15.160}
$$

and from our earlier calculations

$$
M_{\text{ph}}^2 = \frac{2\pi e^2 \hbar n_{\text{ph}} \, |\alpha \cdot p_{\text{if}}|^2}{m^2 \epsilon \omega}.
\tag{15.161}
$$

The absorption coefficient is then given by $W_{\text{abs}}/(n_{\text{ph}} \, v_{\text{ph}})$ (see Equation 15.129). We note that once the threshold photon energy is reached the absorption coefficient increases as $(\hbar\omega - E_{\text{th}})^2$ in contrast to the direct gap case where the energy dependence was $(\hbar\omega - E_g)^{1/2}$.

In Figure 15.20 we show typical absorption measurements for Si and compare it to results in GaAs. We note the low absorption coefficient at near the bandgap in Si. Once the photon energies reach the direct gap region, the absorption coefficient increases rapidly since direct transitions are possible.

15.10   INTRABAND TRANSITIONS

In direct bandgap materials it is possible to satisfy both momentum and energy conservation laws for an optical interband transition to occur in first order. This is not possible for intraband transitions in bulk semiconductors. However, as we shall discuss shortly, in quantum well structures, it is possible to have strong intraband transitions making quantum well structures quite exciting for long wavelength optical devices.

15.10.1   Intraband Transitions in Bulk Semiconductors

For bulk semiconductors, the intraband transitions must involve a phonon or some other scattering mechanism (ionized impurity, defects, etc.) discussed in

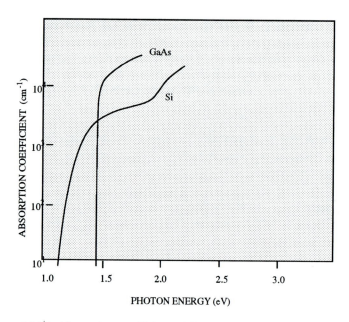

Figure 15.20: Absorption coefficient of Si and GaAs. For the direct gap material, the absorption coefficient is very strong once the photon energy exceeds the bandgap. For indirect materials the absorption coefficient rises much more gradually.

Chapters 11 and 12 to ensure momentum conservation. The second order process is essentially similar to the one we dealt with for indirect processes. The free carrier absorption, as absorption due to intraband transitions is called, is quite important particularly for lasers since it is responsible for losses in the cladding layers of the laser. We will not calculate the free carrier absorption rates in detail here. A good source for their evaluation is B. K. Ridley (1982). We will only note that for acoustic phonon assisted processes the absorption coefficient is

$$\alpha(\hbar\omega) \approx \frac{128 \, \alpha_{\rm f} \, e \, \hbar \, n_e}{g \, \eta \, (m_c^*)^2 \, \omega^2 \, \mu_{ac}} \tag{15.162}$$

where $\alpha_{\rm f}$ is the fine structure constant ($\approx 1/137$), n_e is the free carrier density, η the refractive index, and μ_{ac} the mobility due to acoustic phonon scattering. The absorption coefficient is inversely proportional to the square of the frequency.

15.10.2 Intraband Transitions in Quantum Wells

As we have seen in this chapter, quantum well structures can produce remarkable changes in the optical properties of semiconductor structures. Nowhere are the changes more impressive than in the area of intraband transitions. As we have seen, the intraband transitions in bulk semiconductors are forbidden in the first order. This is because it is not possible to obey both energy and momentum conservation in such transitions. The momentum conservation is due to the plane wave part of the Bloch states. In quantum well structures, the electronic states are no longer of the plane wave form in the growth direction making it possible to have intraband transitions for certain polarizations of light. Since the intraband (or inter-subband) transition energy can be easily varied by changing the well size, these transitions have great importance for far infrared detectors and modulators.

Let us consider the intraband (inter-subband) transitions for the quantum well case. Due to the confinement in the z-direction, the subband functions can be written as (say, the first two functions)

$$
\begin{aligned}
\psi^1(\mathbf{k}, z) &= g^1(z)\, e^{i\mathbf{k}\cdot\boldsymbol{\rho}}\, u^1_{n\mathbf{k}}(\mathbf{r}) \\
\psi^2(\mathbf{k}, z) &= g^2(z)\, e^{i\mathbf{k}\cdot\boldsymbol{\rho}}\, u^2_{n\mathbf{k}}(\mathbf{r}).
\end{aligned}
\tag{15.163}
$$

We are once again interested in vertical transitions since the photon momentum is very small. The functions g^1 and g^2 are orthogonal and to a good approximation the central cell functions are same for the different subbands (this especially true for the conduction band). Thus, the momentum matrix element is given by

$$
\mathbf{P}_{\mathrm{if}} = -\frac{i\hbar}{W} \int g^{2*}(z)\, e^{-i\mathbf{k}\cdot\boldsymbol{\rho}}\, \mathbf{a}\cdot\nabla g^1(z)\, e^{i\mathbf{k}\cdot\boldsymbol{\rho}}\, d^2\rho\, dz
\tag{15.164}
$$

where W is the well width.

As in the case of the 3-dimensional system, the momentum matrix element is zero if the polarization vector (or the ∇ function) is in the $\boldsymbol{\rho}$-plane. Thus, for the x-y polarized light, the *transitions rate is still zero*. (If there is strong mixing of the central cell functions as in the valence bands, this condition can be relaxed.) However, if the light is z-polarized we get

$$
\mathbf{P}_{\mathrm{if}} = \frac{-i\hbar}{W} \int g^{2*}(z)\, \hat{z}\, \frac{\partial}{\partial z} g^1(z)\, dz.
\tag{15.165}
$$

Since $g^1(z)$ and $g^2(z)$ have even and odd parities respectively, as shown in Figure 15.21, $g^2(z)$ and $\partial g^1(z)/\partial z$ both have odd parity. The momentum matrix element for z-polarization is then approximately

$$
|\mathbf{P}_{\mathrm{if}}| \approx \frac{\hbar}{W}.
\tag{15.166}
$$

This result is reasonably accurate if both the ground and excited states are confined to the well size. Often the excited state may have less confinement than the ground state in which case one has to explicitly evaluate the integral in Equation 15.165.

If we make a simple parabolic approximation, we see that the dispersion relations of the two subbands are essentially parallel and shifted by the subband energy levels difference $E_2 - E_1$. In principle, therefore, the joint density of states is a δ-function with infinite density of states at the transition energy. However, at this point we must include the statistics and broadening into the problem.

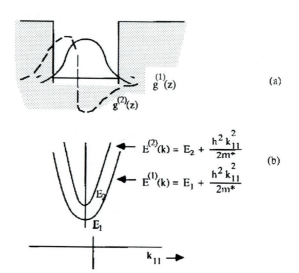

(a)

(b)

$$E^{(2)}(k) = E_2 + \frac{h^2 k_{11}^2}{2m^*}$$

$$E^{(1)}(k) = E_1 + \frac{h^2 k_{11}^2}{2m^*}$$

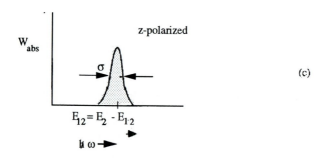

(c)

Figure 15.21: A schematic presentation of the (a) envelope functions; (b) bandstructure, and (c) absorption rate for z-polarized light in a quantum well.

For interband transitions it was reasonable to assume that the initial state (in the valence band) is occupied and the final state (in the conduction band) is empty. However, in intraband transitions discussed above (the inter-subband transitions), the electrons have to be introduced by doping the material so that the electrons are present in the first subband and hopefully not present in the second subband. Introducing the Fermi factors, we get for the absorption process

$$W_{\text{abs}} = \frac{4\pi^2 e^2 n}{m^2 \omega \epsilon} \frac{1}{W} \sum_f |p_{\text{if}}|^2 \, \delta \left(E_f - E_i - \hbar \omega \right) f(E_i) \left[1 - f(E_f) \right] \quad (15.167)$$

with

$$|p_{\text{if}}| \approx \frac{\pi \hbar}{W}.$$

If we assume that the second subband is empty, the sum over the final states is zero except at resonance where we have

$$\sum_f \delta(E_f - E_i - \hbar \omega) \, f(E_i) = N_c \quad (15.168)$$

where N_c is the electron concentration in the first subband. The density of states at resonance is infinite for the simple parabolic band giving an infinite absorption rate. However, in reality the nonparabolicity and scattering mechanisms introduce some broadening in the density of states. If we assume a Gaussian broadening, the two-dimensional density of states becomes

$$N(E) = \frac{N_c \exp \left(-\frac{(E - E_{12})^2}{1.44\sigma^2} \right)}{\sqrt{1.44\pi} \sigma} \quad (15.169)$$

where σ is the linewidth of the transition. The linewidth may have contributions from both homogeneous (phonon related) and inhomogeneous (structural imperfections) effects.

The absorption coefficient for the z-polarized light now becomes

$$\alpha(\hbar\omega) = \frac{4\pi^2 e^2 \hbar}{m^2 c \eta \, (\hbar\omega)} \frac{|p_{\text{if}}|^2}{W} \frac{N_c \exp \left(-\frac{(\hbar\omega - E_{12})^2}{1.44\sigma^2} \right)}{\sqrt{1.44\pi} \sigma} \quad (15.170)$$

with

$$|p_{\text{if}}|^2 \sim \frac{\pi^2 \hbar^2}{W^2}.$$

The absorption coefficient increases rapidly with decreasing well size although it is important to note again that as the well size becomes very small, the electronic states are no longer confined to the well size as assumed by us. For a transition which is only 1–2 meV wide, the absorption coefficient could reach 10^4 cm^{-1}, making such transitions useful for detectors or modulators.

In this chapter we have studied how photons interact with electrons in semiconductors. These interactions are responsible for optoelectronic devices which are now becoming as important in technology as electronic devices. Lasers, detectors, and modulators have already taken a stronghold in the area of communication. Optoelectronics also represents an area where quantum well structures are already making significant impact on the technology. We note that in this chapter we have only touched upon a few areas in the vast optical-electron phenomenon. Nonlinear effects, for example, have not been discussed at all. Many novel devices are based on these exotic phenomenon. However, fortunately the physics discussed in this chapter does adequately describe the physical phenomenon in important devices such as lasers and detectors. The one electron picture used in this chapter is quite sufficient to describe phenomenon where the photon energies are above the bandgap. However, there are some important physical effects that occur below the bandedge which require one to consider the interactions between electrons and holes. This is the subject of the next chapter.

15.11   FOR THE TECHNOLOGIST IN YOU

The area of optoelectronics is perhaps the most important driving force for compound semiconductor solid state electronics. Not only are high speed lasers and detectors making new strides in communication systems, but they are also producing new custom integrated circuit markets for Si and GaAs technology. The success and inroads of optoelectronics is evident in the rapid transference of sound recording medium to compact discs, the use of lasers to scan bar codes in stores, and the use of fiber optics in telephone calls and cable television. For communication of information and storage and reading of information, optoelectronics is undoubtedly an acknowledged force already. In fact, this is perhaps the single most important reason for research and development in compound semiconductors.

In the beginning of the 1980s, as optoelectronic integrated circuits (OEICs) started to come into the picture, visions of "optical computers" seemed to be in everybody's mind. The blue-sky dream of computing with "the speed of light" was and still is extremely appealing. This area will be explored further in Chapter 16 and the reasons for a scale back of expectations will be mentioned in Chapter 19. Notwithstanding this reassessment of optoelectronics and the difficulties in beating electronics at the game of computing, optoelectronics has made great contributions to the quality of life.

The basic workhorses of optoelectronics continue to be the laser and detector system. The modulation in communication systems is provided by electronic circuitry. Research in laser/detector systems is driven by several motivations, some of which are:

1. Shorter wavelength lasers. This development is motivated by being able to store and use higher density information on compact discs. Access to a blue-green laser, which has been demonstrated in the laboratory, will also be important for displays.

2. Higher modulation speed lasers for higher bandwidth communications.

3. Lower threshold laser which could be driven by less electrical power.

4. Lasers operating at higher temperature for applications in real life, such as temperatures encountered near machinery, etc.

These motivations drive research into new materials (strained and unstrained), new processing techniques for growth and efficient doping, and of course, new concepts.

15.11.1 Some Device Related Issues

Electron-Hole Recombination Rates in an LED and a Laser Diode

Light emission devices are an increasingly important part of modern technology. Semiconductor based optical devices such as lasers promise not only to be a source of optical signals, but may also become important devices for logic applications, light amplification, etc. An important parameter in such devices is the electron-hole recombination rate. This rate plays an important role in the speed at which the device can operate.

Two important light emitting devices are the light emitting diode (LED) and the laser diode. The light emitting diode is a simple p-n diode which is forward biased to inject current so that there is an excess electron and hole concentration in the device. These carriers recombine as discussed in this chapter and emit photons. The recombination process is controlled by the *spontaneous* emission rate and under high injection is given by Equation 15.150:

$$
\begin{aligned}
R_{\text{spon}} &= \frac{n}{\tau_0} \\
&= \frac{p}{\tau_0}
\end{aligned}
\tag{15.171}
$$

where n is the injected charge and τ_0 is the spontaneous emission time which approaches ~ 0.5 ns. The photon density in a given mode remains very small in an LED structure since the photons emitted escape. As a result, the factor n in the $(n + 1)$ of Equation 15.100 does not play a role in the emission rate. The term proportional to the photon number is the stimulated emission which can become very important in a laser.

In a laser, the active emission region is surrounded by a mirror so that a build-up takes place in the number of photons in a given mode. The laser operation can loosely be divided into two parts: below threshold and above threshold. Below threshold, the gain in the device is less than the loss suffered by the light so that significant photon build up does not occur. If I_{inj} is the current injected in a laser with cross section A, in this regime

$$
\begin{aligned}
I_{\text{ph}} &= R_{\text{spon}} \\
&= A\frac{n}{\tau_0} \\
&= \frac{I_{\text{inj}}}{e}
\end{aligned}
\tag{15.172}
$$

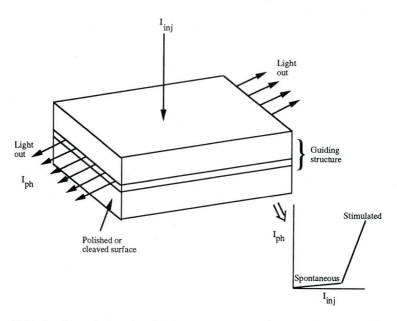

Figure 15.22: In a laser, below threshold the injected charge recombines via spontaneous emission of photons as in an LED. Above threshold, the light guiding structure and the mirrors ensure a high photon flux in the cavity and a dominance of stimulated emission.

where n is the injected charge per unit area, I_{ph} is the photon flux. For focus, consider a laser structure (see Figure 15.22) with dimensions 10 μm × 200 μm. In state of the art GaAs/AlGaAs quantum well lasers, the threshold current is $\sim$ 500 A/cm^2 at room temperature. The threshold current for our case is therefore 10 mA. Assuming $\tau_0 \approx 0.6$ ns, the charge injected at threshold is

$$n_{th} = 1.9 \times 10^{12} \ \mathrm{cm}^2. \tag{15.173}$$

Once threshold is reached in a laser, the stimulated emission starts to dominate so that carrier concentration *does not* increase much beyond n_{th}, even as I_{inj} is increasing. The current is related to the charge by the relation

$$\frac{I_{\mathrm{inj}}}{e} = A\frac{n_{th}}{\tau_{st}}\beta \tag{15.174}$$

where τ_{st} is the stimulated emission rate (for above threshold biasing). The factor β represents the fraction of the carriers which are emitting into the lasing modes. This factor is determined by the laser cavity design and can be anywhere from 10^{-2} to 10^{-5}. For example, in our case, if the laser is biased at 20 mA and $\beta = 10^{-2}$, the electron-hole recombination time is $\tau_{st} \approx 30$ ps. The photon output, for the lasing mode, has thus increased 20 times (compared to an LED). Thus, for high speed small signal laser modulation, the laser is biased at as high a bias current as possible. Of course, there are practical limitations to this due to device heating effects, reduced efficiency of recombination, etc.

It is important to point out that the assumption that electron and hole densities are given by quasi-Fermi levels starts to break down at high recombination rates, encountered in lasers. This leads to gain suppression effects which also limit the high speed performance of lasers.

Lasers and Photonic Bandstructure

The electron-hole spontaneous emission rate is an extremely important quantity for semiconductor lasers and LEDs. In the discussions in this chapter, we have calculated this rate based upon a very important assumption. We assumed that the density of photon states applicable to the emitting photon is (see Equation 15.133 and 15.148)

$$\rho(\hbar\omega) = \frac{\omega^2}{2\pi^2\hbar v^3} \qquad (15.175)$$

which is the 3-D density of photons. What role does this assumption play in semiconductor lasers and is it appropriate to assume that we should use a 3-D density of photon states? This is an issue which is becoming increasingly important for advanced laser concepts.

The photons obey the Helmholtz equation

$$\nabla^2 \boldsymbol{F} + \frac{\epsilon\omega^2}{c^2}\boldsymbol{F} = 0 \qquad (15.176)$$

and have the standard plane wave solutions $F \sim \exp[i(\boldsymbol{k}\cdot\boldsymbol{r} - \omega t)]$ if ϵ is constant in space. To produce a high quality laser, it is important that when electron-hole recombination produces photons, for at least one mode, the emitted photons do not escape the cavity. For such modes, the photon density can increase so that eventually, stimulated emission can occur.

The usual laser diode structure is a Fabry-Perot guide with cavity length L. This structure is usually so large (say $W = 10\ \mu\text{m}$, $L = 50\text{–}200\ \mu\text{m}$) that the photon modes that can be excited are essentially 3-dimensional. However, for the resonant modes, the photon density can increase, to cause simulated emission. As shown in Figure 15.23a, the mode spacing ($\Delta k_z = 2\pi/L$) is very small and thus a number of modes can in principle lase. Thus, the mode selectivity of a Fabry-Perot laser is not very good. As the laser is pumped harder, one or two modes which coincide with the peak in the gain curve start to become stronger and stronger.

An important advance in laser frequency purity was to use the Bragg reflection (discussed in Chapter 4) to provide the necessary reflection to provide the feedback for lasing. In Chapter 4, we saw that if a structure has a periodicity a in real space, then bandedges appear whenever the wavevector has values π/a, $2\pi/a$, …. At these bandedges, the wave is essentially a stationary state In other words, when $k = \pi/a$, the wave suffers a reflection due to the periodic structure. For $k \neq \pi/a$, the wave does not suffer such a reflection. This concept is used to

ALLOWED STATIONARY
PHOTON MODES ($\Delta k = 2\pi/L$)

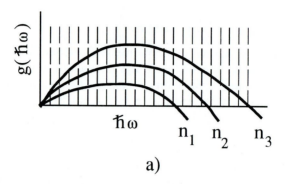

a)

FABRY-PEROT LASER CAVITY

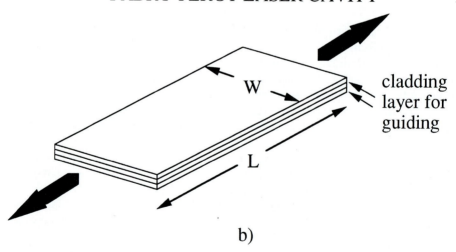

b)

Figure 15.23: a) The gain versus energy curves for various injection levels. Also shown are the positions of various modes for which the Fabry-Perot guide produces stationary states; b) A schematic of the Fabry-Perot guiding structure.

produce distributed feedback (DFB) and distributed Bragg reflectors (DBR) as shown in Figure 15.24. The DFB structure allows only those photons for which $\lambda = 2a$ to get to feedback necessary for stimulated emission. As a result, the output of a DFB laser is much more monchromatic than that of a Fabry-Perot laser. The DBR concept is used to provide an external reflector whose optical periodicity, ηa can be altered by external means, such as current flow or applied field. This allows one to tune the laser output frequency.

Another use of the DBR concept is in the surface emitting laser (SEL), whose vertical DBRs are placed to allow photon build-up so that light is emitted vertically.

In the above concepts, the cavity is tailored to allow one to select a particular photon mode with preference. However, the allowed photon modes for emission are essentially 3-dimensional. If the structure of Figure 15.24c is made smaller (say 3–5 μm) in width, a microcavity is produced which starts to resemble a quantum dot for electrons. This small 3-dimensional structure has allowed photon modes which are not 3-dimensional. In particular, the photon modes are discretely spaced. In such a case, the spontaneous emission can be drastically affected. It may even be possible that there *is only one photon mode allowed in the entire region of the laser emission spectra*, in which case, an extremely low threshold lasing can be achieved. These concepts are driving some of the recent research into microcavity photonics.

Another approach to tailoring photonic bandstructure is to construct 3-D lattices in which the dielectric constant is periodic, so that the spectrum develops bandgaps (just like for the electronic spectrum in crystals). In principle, then the electron-hole recombination and photon emission into these bandgaps will be forbidden, once again modifying the spontaneous emission rate.

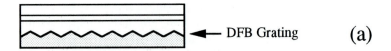

Distributed Feedback Structure

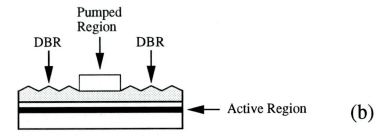

Distributed Bragg Reflector Structure

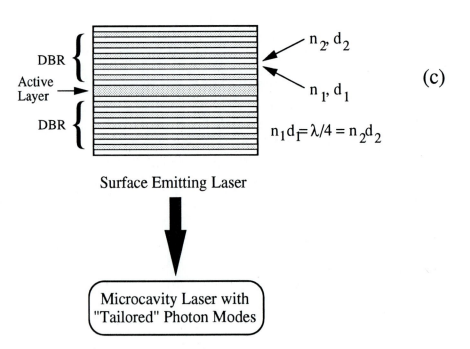

Surface Emitting Laser

Microcavity Laser with "Tailored" Photon Modes

Figure 15.24: Various techniques to tune photon spectra. (a) The distributed feedback structure, (b) the distributed Bragg reflector, (c) the surface emitting laser structure with DBR.

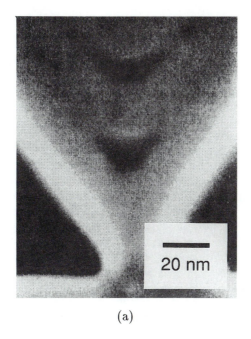

(a)

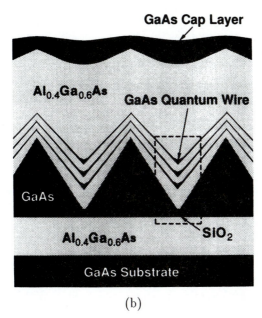

(b)

Figure 15.25: The desire for low threshold lasers is leading scientists to explore quantum wire structures of the kind shown here. The growth and fabrication of such structures is a major challenge. (Courtesy of the University of Tokyo.)

15.12   PROBLEMS

15.1. Calculate and plot the optical absorption coefficients in GaAs, InAs, and InP as a function of photon energy assuming a parabolic density of states.

15.2. Consider a 100 Å GaAs/Al$_{0.3}$Ga$_{0.7}$As quantum well structure. Assuming that the problem can be treated as that with an infinite barrier, calculate the absorption spectra for in-plane and out-of-plane polarized light for $E \leq 100$ meV from the effective bandedge. Assume the simple uncoupled model for the HH and LH states.

15.3. Calculate and plot the overlap of an electron and heavy hole ground state envelope function in a GaAs/Al$_{0.3}$Ga$_{0.7}$As quantum well as a function of well size from 20 Å to 200 Å. Assume a 60:40 value for $\Delta E_c{:}\Delta E_v$. At what well size does the overlap significantly differ from unity?

15.4. Calculate the gain in a GaAs region as a function of injected carrier density at room temperature. Plot your results in the form of Figure 15.16.

15.5. Calculate and plot the 300 K recombination rate in GaAs as a function of electron (hole) carrier density. Cover the electron (hole) density range from 10^{14} cm^{-3} to 10^{18} cm^{-3} in your calculations. Estimate the carrier density dependence of the recombination rate in the low carrier density and high carrier density regime.

15.6. Estimate the strength of the intraband transitions in a 100 Å GaAs /Al$_{0.3}$Ga$_{0.7}$As quantum well structure at an electron carrier concentration of 10^{12} cm^{-2}. Assume an infinite barrier model and a linewidth (full width at half maximum) of 1 meV for the transition.

15.7. We have seen from the solution of the Schrödinger equation in periodic structures, that bandgaps appear at the Brillouin zone edges. The wavefunctions at the zone edges represent standing waves. These standing waves are similar to those produced by placing reflecting barriers in a cavity. Away from the zone edge, the waves can be considered as made up of two waves proceeding in opposite directions with unequal amplitudes. Study the paper by H. Kogelnik and C. V. Shank, "Coupled-Wave Theory of Distributed Feedback Lasers," J. Appl. Phys., **45**, 2327 (1972), to see how this concept is used in improving the tunability of lasers.

15.8. Develop a computer program to calculate the gain versus carrier density ($n = p$) for a bulk semiconductor GaAs laser at 300 K and at 77 K. Assuming an active layer thickness of 1 μm and complete optical confinement, calculate the threshold current at room temperature and at 77 K. Assume a cavity loss of 10 cm^{-1}.

15.9. Develop a computer program to calculate the gain versus injection density of carriers for a 100 Å GaAs/Al$_{0.3}$Ga$_{0.7}$As quantum well laser at 300 K and at 77 K. Assume an uncoupled model for the heavy hole ($m^* = 0.35m_0$) and light hole ($m^* = 0.08m_0$) bands. What is the threshold current at the two temperatures, if the optical confinement factor is 2.0% and the cavity loss is 50 cm^{-1}?

15.10. Consider a pseudomorphically strained $In_{0.2}Ga_{0.8}As/Al_{0.3}Ga_{0.7}As$ quantum well laser (oriented along the [001] direction). If the hole mass is decreased from $m^*_{HH} = 0.35m_0$ to $m^*_{HH} = 0.15m_0$, due to the strain, calculate the gain curves for the laser, assuming a single electron band and single hole band. What is the 300 K threshold current if the optical confinement factor is 2% and the cavity loss is 50 cm^{-1}? What is the polarization of the light?

15.13 REFERENCES

- **Maxwell's Equations; Gauge Transformation**

  - Jackson, J. D., *Classical Electrodynamics* (John Wiley and Sons, New York, 1975).

- **Macroscopic Theory of Optical Processes**

  - Jackson, J. D., *Classical Electrodynamics* (John Wiley and Sons, New York, 1975).

  - Jones, W. and N. H. March, *Theoretical Solid State Physics* (Dover, New York, 1973), vol. 2.

  - Kreyszig, E., *Advanced Engineering Mathematics* (John Wiley and Sons, New York, 1962).

  - "Elementary Theory of the Optical Properties of Solids," by Stern, F., *Solid State Physics* (Academic Press, New York, 1963), vol. 15.

  - Ziman, J. M., *Principles of the Theory of Solids* (Cambridge, 1972).

- **Microscopic Theory of Optical Processes in Semiconductors**

  - Bassani, F. and G. P. Parravicini, *Electronic States and Optical Transitions in Solids* (Pergamon Press, New York, 1975).

  - Jones, W. and N. H. March, *Theoretical Solid State Physics* (Dover, New York, 1973), vol. 2.

- **Optical Processes in Quantum Wells**

  - Hong, S. and J. Singh, Superlattices and Microstructures, **3**, 645 (1987).

  - Miller, R. C., D. A. Kleinman, W. A. Nordland, and A. C. Gossard, Phys. Rev. B, **22**, 863 (1980).

– Sanders, G. D. and Y. C. Chang, Phys. Rev. B, **31**, 6892 (1985).

– Weiner, J. S., D. A. B. Miller, D. S. Chemla, T. C. Damen, C. A. Burrus, T. H. Wood, A. C. Gossard, and W. Wiegman, Appl. Phys. Lett., **47**, 1148 (1985).

- **Optical Processes in Semiconductor Lasers**

  – Agrawal, G. P. and N. K. Dutta, *Long wavelength Semiconductor Lasers* (Van Nostrand Reinhold, New York, 1986).

  – Kressel, H. and J. K. Butler, *Semiconductor Lasers and Heterojunction LEDs* (Academic Press, Orlando, 1977).

  – Thompson, G. H. B., *Physics of Semiconductor Laser Devices* (John Wiley and Sons, New York, 1980).

- **Effect of Strain on Laser Performance**

  – Adams, A. R., Electron. Lett., **22**, 249 (1986).

  – Ahn, D. and S. L. Chuang, IEEE J. Quant. Electron., **QE-24**, 2400 (1988).

  – Loehr, J. P. and J. Singh, IEEE J. Quant. Electron., **QE-27**, 708 (1991).

  – Yablanovitch, E. and E. O. Kane, IEEE J. Lightwave Technol., **4**, 504 (1986).

- **Optical Processes in Indirect Semiconductors**

  – Bassani, F. and G. P. Parravicini, *Electronic States and Optical Transitions in Solids* (Pergamon, New York, 1975).

  – Dash, W. C. and R. Newman, Phys. Rev., **99**, 1151 (1955).

  – Phillip, H. R. and E. A. Taft, Phys. Rev., **113**, 1002 (1959).

  – Phillip, H. R. and E. A. Taft, Phys. Rev. Lett., **8**, 13 (1962).

- **Intraband Transitions in Quantum Wells**

  – Coon, D. D. and R. P. G. Karunasiri, Appl. Phys. Lett., **45**, 649 (1984).

  – Harwitt, A. and J. S. Harris, Appl. Phys. Lett., **50**, 685 (1987).

  – Lavine, B. F., K. K. Choi, C. G. Bathea, J. Walker and R. J. Malik, Appl. Phys. Lett., **50**, 1092 (1987).

CHAPTER 16

OPTICAL PROPERTIES IN SEMICONDUCTORS: EXCITONIC TRANSITIONS

In our discussion of transport and optical properties of semiconductors we made the independent electron approximation. The energy spectrum of the electrons is independent of the presence of other electrons. The effect of other electrons is only manifested through the occupation probabilities without altering the eigenvalues of the electronic problem. This approach is usually valid for many important physical phenomena like transport in nondegenerate semiconductors or optical absorption away from the bandedges. However, some very important properties are modified by electron-electron (or electron-hole) interactions. We already mentioned the effects of strong electron-charged impurity interactions in heavily doped semiconductors. The electron-hole interaction is also important for bandgap narrowing in lasers and other devices with strong charge injection. The full theory of the electron-electron interaction depends upon many body theory, which is beyond the scope of this text. However, fortunately, there is one important problem, that of excitonic effects in semiconductors, that can be addressed by simpler theoretical techniques.

The exciton problem can be motivated by the simple schematic of Figure 16.1. On the left-hand side, we show the bandstructure of a semiconductor with a full valence band and an empty conduction band. Under these conditions there are no allowed states in the bandgap. Now consider the case where there is one electron in the conduction band and one hole in the valence band. In this new configuration, the Hamiltonian describing the electronic system has changed. We now have an additional Coulombic interaction between the electron

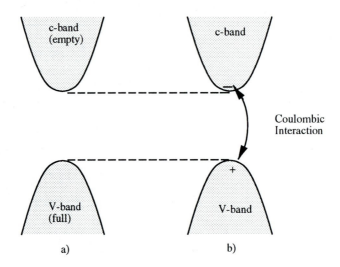

Figure 16.1: (a) The bandstructure in the independent electron picture and (b) the Coulombic interaction between the electron and hole which would modify the band picture.

and the hole. The electronic bandstructure should thus be modified to reflect this change. In fact, the problem is somewhat similar to the case of a dopant where the electron-ionized impurity interaction modified the electronic states by introducing impurity levels in the forbidden gap region. The electron-hole system, coupled through the Coulombic interaction, is called the exciton and will be the subject of this chapter.

Excitonic states have been known to exist in crystals since 1931, when Frenkel first provided the concepts to describe such excitations. Further work was done by Peirls and Wannier. In semiconductors, a great deal of work was done by Elliot and Knox. In bulk semiconductors, excitons are usually observable optically, only in very high purity samples, due to their rather small binding energies. In poorer quality samples, the excitonic optical resonances often merge with the band-to-band transitions. These transitions were, therefore, mainly studied from the point of view of material characterization. However, with the advent of heterostructure technology, the study of excitonic transitions in quantum wells has become an extremely important area, both from the point of view of new physics and of new technology. We will see in this chapter, that due to quantum confinement, the exciton binding energy is greatly increased. This and improved oscillator strength, allows one to observe extremely sharp resonances in quantum well optical spectra. Moreover, the energy position, or strength, of these resonances can be controlled easily by simple electronics or optics. This ability allows one to use the excitonic transitions for high speed modulation of optical signals, as well as for optoelectronic switches, which could serve important functions in future information processing systems.

Two important approaches have emerged to control the excitonic transitions:

1. By application of a transverse electric field—the Quantum Confined Stark Effect (QCSE).

2. "Bleaching" of the exciton resonance by high electron-hole density.

The physics behind the QCSE is relatively simple and will be discussed in this chapter. This approach, being compatible with electronics, promises versatile devices. The "bleaching" of the exciton by high density of carriers requires concepts from many-body theory, if a detailed quantitative understanding is to be obtained. We will only briefly describe some interesting aspects of this problem, without addressing the details.

In the following, we will first describe a simple effective mass theory of the excitonic states. This approach allows us to predict the energy levels of the semiconductor in the exciton picture. However, this approach is not suitable to calculate the optical properties related to the excitonic resonances. For this, we need to generalize the exciton problem. This will be done later. The electron-hole coupled system moving in the background crystal potential can be described by an envelope function (to be calculated below), which gives the relative probability distribution. Note that the Hamiltonian is still periodic in the presence of the Coulombic interaction so that the exciton wavefunction should have a Bloch form.

16.1 EXCITONIC STATES IN SEMICONDUCTORS

Two important classes of excitons exist depending upon the extent of the periodic envelope function. When the envelope function is confined to just a few unit cells, the excitons are classified as Frenkel excitons. Due to their restricted spatial extent, the Heisenberg uncertainty principle indicates that their treatment necessitates dealing with the full bandstructure of the semiconductors. On the other hand, if the envelope function extends over several hundred Angstroms, near bandedge electron and hole states can be used to describe them. Such excitons are called Mott excitons and are responsible for the excitonic physics in semiconductors (see Figure 16.2). The effective mass theory can be used to describe these excitons and accordingly the problem is represented by the following Schrödinger equation

$$\left[-\frac{\hbar^2}{2m_e^*}\nabla_e^2 - \frac{\hbar^2}{2m_h^*}\nabla_h^2 - \frac{e^2}{\epsilon \left| \boldsymbol{r}_e - \boldsymbol{r}_h \right|} \right] \psi_{ex} = E\psi_{ex}. \qquad (16.1)$$

Here m_e^* and m_h^* are the electron and hole effective masses and $\left| \boldsymbol{r}_e - \boldsymbol{r}_h \right|$ is the difference in coordinates defining the Coulombic interaction between the electron and the hole. We will shortly discuss in more detail the makeup of the exciton

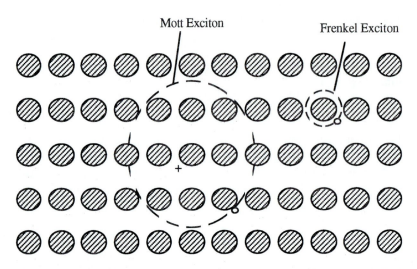

Figure 16.2: A conceptual picture of the periodic envelope function extent of the Frenkel and Mott excitons. The Frenkel exciton periodic function is of the extent of a few unit cells while the Mott exciton function extends over many unit cells. We will focus on the Mott excitons in this chapter.

wavefunction ψ_{ex}. The problem is now the standard two-body problem, which can be written as a one-body problem, by using the following transformation

$$
\begin{aligned}
\boldsymbol{r} &= \boldsymbol{r}_e - \boldsymbol{r}_h \\
\boldsymbol{k} &= \frac{m_e^* \boldsymbol{k}_e + m_h^* \boldsymbol{k}_h}{m_e^* + m_h^*} \\
\boldsymbol{R} &= \frac{m_e^* \boldsymbol{r}_e + m_h^* \boldsymbol{r}_h}{m_e^* + m_h^*} \\
\boldsymbol{K} &= \boldsymbol{k}_e - \boldsymbol{k}_h.
\end{aligned}
\tag{16.2}
$$

The Hamiltonian then becomes

$$
H = \frac{\hbar^2 K^2}{2(m_e^* + m_h^*)} + \left\{ \frac{\hbar^2 k^2}{2\mu} - \frac{e^2}{\epsilon \, |\boldsymbol{r}|} \right\}
\tag{16.3}
$$

where μ is the reduced mass of the electron-hole system. The Hamiltonian consists of two parts, the first term giving the description for the motion of center of mass of the electron-hole system, while the second term describing the relative motion of the electron-hole system. The first term gives a plane wave solution

$$
\psi_{\text{cm}} = e^{i \boldsymbol{K} \cdot \boldsymbol{R}}
\tag{16.4}
$$

while the solution to the second term satisfies

$$
\left(\frac{\hbar^2 k^2}{2\mu} - \frac{e^2}{\epsilon \, |\boldsymbol{r}|} \right) F(\boldsymbol{r}) = E F(\boldsymbol{r}).
\tag{16.5}
$$

This is the usual hydrogen atom problem and $F(r)$ can be obtained from the mathematics of that problem. The general exciton solution is now (writing $K_{ex} = K$)

$$\psi_{nK_{ex}} = e^{iK_{ex}\cdot R}\, F_n(r)\, \phi_c(r_e)\, \phi_v(r_h) \tag{16.6}$$

where ϕ_c and ϕ_v represent the central cell nature of the electron and hole band-edge states used in the effective mass theory. The excitonic energy levels are then

$$E_{nK_{ex}} = E_n + \frac{\hbar^2}{2(m_e^* + m_h^*)} K_{ex}^2 \tag{16.7}$$

with E_n being the eigenvalues of the hydrogen atom-like problem

$$E_n = -\frac{\mu e^4}{2\epsilon^2\hbar^2}\frac{1}{n^2} \tag{16.8}$$

and the second term in Equation 16.7 represents the kinetic energy of the center of mass of the electron-hole pair.

The energy of the excitonic state is measured with respect to the energy of the state without the Coulomb interaction, i.e., the bandgap. Thus, excitonic levels appear slightly below the bandgap since typical values for E_1 are ~2-6 meV for most semiconductors. The dispersion then looks as shown in Figure 16.3.

This dispersion relation looks quite different from the usual E vs. k relation we are used to. This is because we are describing the system not in terms of the electron crystal momentum, but the electron-hole crystal momentum K_{ex}. This is obviously the appropriate quantum number to describe the problem once the electron-hole Coulombic interaction is turned on. If the Coulombic interaction is turned off, the parabolas below the bandgap (bond states) all disappear and we simply have the free electron-hole dispersion which is the same as the bandstructure discussed in earlier chapters except that we plot the dispersion in a $k_e - k_h$ description.

We notice now that unlike the cases discussed in Chapter 15 where the electron-hole joint density of states started at the bandedge position, we now have a density of states below the bandedge energies. However, not all these states will couple to the photon because of momentum conservation.

In order to examine the absorption spectra of excitonic transitions in semiconductors, it is useful to examine the problem in a little greater detail. As discussed earlier, the independent electron picture provides us the conduction and valence band states. The Coulombic interaction of the electron-hole pairs will now be treated as a perturbation, and the new wavefunction can be expressed in terms of the independent electron wavefunction basis. The general form of the excitonic problem is given by the Hamiltonian

$$H_e = H_0 + \frac{1}{2}\sum_{i\neq j}\frac{e^2}{\epsilon\,|r_i - r_j|} \tag{16.9}$$

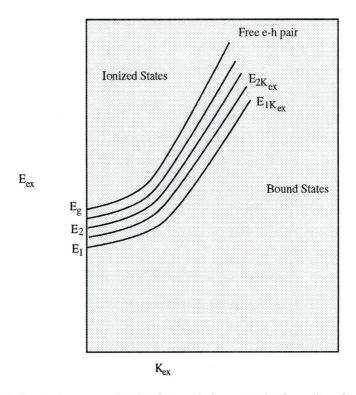

Figure 16.3: Dispersion curves for the electron-hole system in the exciton framework.

where H_0 is the independent electron Hamiltonian giving rise to the usual band-structure. The indices i and j represent the different electron pairs, with the factor 1/2 to prevent double counting.

Since the Hamiltonian has the symmetry of the crystal, the Bloch theorem applies to the wavefunction, which must satisfy the condition

$$\psi_{\text{ex}}(\boldsymbol{r}_1 + \boldsymbol{R}, \boldsymbol{r}_2 + \boldsymbol{R}, \boldsymbol{r}_3 + \boldsymbol{R}, \ldots) = e^{i\mathbf{K}_{\text{ex}}\cdot\mathbf{R}} \, \psi_{\text{ex}}(\boldsymbol{r}_1, \boldsymbol{r}_2, \boldsymbol{r}_3, \ldots) \qquad (16.10)$$

where $\boldsymbol{R}$ is a lattice vector of the crystal.

The exciton state can be written in terms of a basis function $\Phi_{c,\mathbf{k}_e,S_e;v,\mathbf{k}_h,S_h}$ which represents a state where an electron, with momentum $\boldsymbol{k}_e$ and spin S_e, is in the conduction band and a hole, with momentum and spin $\boldsymbol{k}_h$ and S_h, is in the valence band, as shown in Figure 16.4. The difference $\boldsymbol{k}_e - \boldsymbol{k}_h$ represents the momentum of the exciton state. The exciton state is made up of a proper expansion of the Φ states. However, because of the Bloch theorem, the combination $\boldsymbol{k}_e - \boldsymbol{k}_h$ in the expansion must be constant for any given excitonic state. This greatly simplifies our exciton wavefunction, which can now be written as

$$\psi_{\text{ex}}^{n\ell m} = \sum_{\mathbf{k}} A_{n\ell m}(\boldsymbol{k}) \, \Phi_{c,\mathbf{k}+\mathbf{K}_{\text{ex}}/2,S_e;v,\mathbf{k}-\mathbf{K}_{\text{ex}}/2,S_h}^{n\ell m}. \qquad (16.11)$$

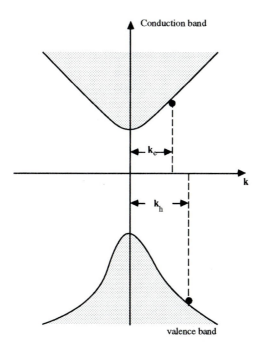

Figure 16.4: Schematic picture of an exciton in the Bloch representation. The state $\Phi_{c,\mathbf{k}_e,S_e;v,\mathbf{k}_h,S_h}$ represents an extra electron of wave vector k_e and spin S_e in the conduction band and a hole of wave vector k_h and spin S_h in the valence band.

Here n is the energy eigenvalue index (see Equation 16.8), ℓ and m are angular momentum indices representing the multiplicity of the excitonic state and $A_{n\ell m}(\mathbf{k})$ are the expansion coefficients. The exciton solution is given with the determination of $A_{n\ell m}(\mathbf{k})$. Since we are dealing with large envelope functions (order of $\sim$100 Å), the coefficients $A_{n\ell m}(\mathbf{k})$ are expected to be localized sharply in k-space. We can define the Fourier transform of $A_{n\ell m}(\mathbf{k})$ as

$$F_{n\ell m}(\mathbf{r}) = \sum_{\mathbf{k}} A_{n\ell m}(\mathbf{k})\, e^{i\mathbf{k}\cdot\mathbf{r}}. \tag{16.12}$$

This real space envelope function $F_{n\ell m}(\mathbf{r})$ is the same as we introduced in our simple derivation earlier and which obeys the hydrogen atom-like equation (ignoring exchange interactions):

$$\left[E_{\mathrm{cv}}(-i\nabla, \mathbf{K}_{\mathrm{ex}}) - \frac{e^2}{\epsilon} \right] F_{n\ell m}(\mathbf{r}) = E_{\mathrm{ex}} F_{n\ell m}(\mathbf{r}). \tag{16.13}$$

Here $E_{\mathrm{cv}}(-i\nabla, \mathbf{K}_{\mathrm{ex}})$ represents the operator obtained by expanding $E_c(\mathbf{k}+\mathbf{K}_{\mathrm{ex}}/2) - E_v(\mathbf{k} - \mathbf{K}_{\mathrm{ex}}/2)$ in powers of $\mathbf{k}$ and replacing $\mathbf{k}$ by $-i\nabla$. The exchange term is usually very small and will be ignored. The dielectric constant, in general, can be quite complicated, especially if the free carrier density is large. At low carrier densities ($n < 10^{14}$ cm^{-3}), the static dielectric constant is a good approximation to ϵ. It is important to note that this effective mass like equation is valid only if $F_{n\ell m}(\boldsymbol{r})$ is extended in space, i.e., $A_{n\ell m}(\boldsymbol{k})$ is peaked in k-space.

For a simple parabolic band, we have already discussed the solution of the exciton problem. The exciton energy levels are

$$
\begin{aligned}
E_n^{\mathrm{ex}} &= E_g - \frac{\mu e^4}{2\hbar^2 \epsilon^2} \frac{1}{n^2} \\
&= E_g - \frac{R_{\mathrm{ex}}}{n^2}
\end{aligned}
\tag{16.14}
$$

where R_{ex} denotes the exciton Rydberg. The kinetic energy of the electron-hole pair is to be added to Equation 16.14 for the total exciton energy.

The exciton envelope functions are the hydrogen atom-like functions, e.g., the ground state is

$$
F_{100}(\boldsymbol{r}) = \frac{1}{\sqrt{\pi a_{\mathrm{ex}}^3}} e^{-r/a_{\mathrm{ex}}}
\tag{16.15}
$$

with $a_{\mathrm{ex}} = (\epsilon m/\mu)\, a_B$ (a_B = Bohr radius = 0.529 Å). The exciton radius a_{ex} is $\sim$100 Å for most semiconductors. Thus, the exciton is spread over a large number of unit cells, and the use of the effective mass equation is justified.

16.2   OPTICAL PROPERTIES WITH INCLUSION OF EXCITONIC EFFECTS

Excitonic effects have very dramatic consequences for the optical properties of semiconductors, especially near the bandedges. Below the bandedge, there is a strong and sharp excitonic absorption/emission transition. Above the bandgap, there is a strong enhancement of the absorption process especially in 3-D systems.

As discussed earlier, in absence of excitonic effects, the absorption coefficient can be written as

$$
\alpha(\hbar\omega) = \frac{4\pi^2 e^2}{m^2 c\eta} \frac{\hbar}{\hbar\omega} \int \frac{2\, d^3k}{(8\pi^3)} \left| a \cdot p_{\mathrm{if}}(\boldsymbol{k}) \right|^2 \, \delta(E_c(\boldsymbol{k}) - E_v(\boldsymbol{k}) - \hbar\omega).
\tag{16.16}
$$

For allowed transitions we can assume that p_{if} is independent of $\boldsymbol{k}$ giving us the absorption coefficient

$$
\begin{aligned}
\alpha(\hbar\omega) &= 0 && \text{if } \hbar\omega < E_g \\
&= \frac{4\pi^2 e^2}{m^2 c\eta} \frac{\hbar}{\hbar\omega} \left| a \cdot p_{\mathrm{if}} \right|^2 \cdot N_{\mathrm{cv}}(\hbar\omega) && \text{if } \hbar\omega \geq E_g
\end{aligned}
\tag{16.17}
$$

where $N_{\mathrm{cv}}(\hbar\omega)$ is the joint density of states.

If the excitonic effects are accounted for, these expressions are modified. We will again work in the dipole approximation and consider a transition from the ground state (all electrons are in the valence band) to the excited exciton state. This transition rate is, according to the Fermi golden rule

$$W(\psi_0 \rightarrow \psi_{\mathbf{K}_{ex}}) = \frac{2\pi}{\hbar} \left(\frac{eA}{mc}\right)^2 \delta_{\mathbf{K}_{ex}} \left|\sum_{k} A(k)\, \mathbf{a} \cdot \mathbf{p}_{cv}(k)\right|^2 \delta(E_{ex} - E_0 - \hbar\omega)$$

(16.18)

where E_0 is the energy corresponding to the ground state.

Once again, if we assume $\mathbf{p}_{cv}(\mathbf{k})$ is independent of $\mathbf{k}$

$$W(\psi_0 \rightarrow \psi_{\mathbf{K}_{ex}}) = \frac{2\pi}{\hbar} \left(\frac{eA}{mc}\right)^2 \delta_{\mathbf{K}_{ex}} |\mathbf{a} \cdot \mathbf{p}_{if}(0)|^2 \left|\sum_{k} A(k)\right|^2 \delta(E_{ex} - E_0 - \hbar\omega).$$

(16.19)

From the definition of the Fourier transform $F_{n\ell m}$, we see that from Equation 16.12,

$$F_{n\ell m}(0) = \sum_{k} A_{n\ell m}(k). \tag{16.20}$$

We also know from the theory of the hydrogen atom problem that $F_{n\ell m}(0)$ is nonzero only for s-type states, and, in general

$$F_{n\ell m}(0) = \frac{1}{\sqrt{\pi a_{ex}^3 n^3}} \, \delta_{\ell,0}\delta_{m,0}. \tag{16.21}$$

Thus, the absorption rate is given by

$$W(\psi_0 \rightarrow \psi_{\mathbf{K}_{ex}}) = \frac{2\pi}{\hbar} \left(\frac{eA_0}{mc}\right)^2 \delta_{\mathbf{K}_{ex}} |\mathbf{a} \cdot \mathbf{p}_{if}(0)|^2 \frac{\delta(E_{ex}^n - E_0 - \hbar\omega)}{\pi a_{ex}^3 n^3}. \tag{16.22}$$

Comparing this result with the case for free band-to-band transitions, we note that the density of states in the free case is replaced by the term

$$N_{cv}(\hbar\omega) \rightarrow \frac{\delta(E_{ex}^n - E_0 - \hbar\omega)}{\pi a_{ex}^3 n^3}, \tag{16.23}$$

with the δ-function eventually being replaced by a broadening function. If, for example, we assume a Gaussian broadening, we have

$$\delta(\hbar\omega - E) \rightarrow \frac{1}{\sqrt{1.44\pi}\, \sigma} \exp\left(\frac{-(\hbar\omega - E)^2}{1.44\, \sigma^2}\right). \tag{16.24}$$

This result suggests that the excitonic transitions occur *as if* each exciton has a spatial extent of $1/(\pi a_{ex}^3 n^3)$. However, we note that this is not really the correct picture, since the excitons are extended states. We also note that since only the $\mathbf{K}_{ex} = 0$ state of the exciton is optically active, the transitions are *discrete*, even though the exciton density of states is *continuous*. The strength of the successive

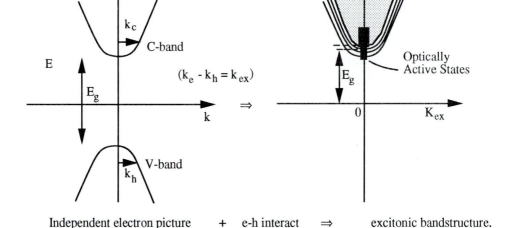

Independent electron picture   +   e-h interact $\Rightarrow$ excitonic bandstructure.

Figure 16.5: The effect of the electron-hole Coulombic interaction is to create exciton bands as shown. Only $K_{ex} = 0$ states are optically active.

transitions decreases as $1/n^3$, so that the $n = 2$ resonance has one-eighth the strength of the $n = 1$ transition.

It is useful to examine again the independent electron picture and the exciton picture. This is done in Figure 16.5. On the left-hand side we show the usual bandstructure with the valence and conduction band. The presence of the Coulomb interaction causes us to use $k_e - k_h = K_{ex}$ as an appropriate quantum number for the description. As discussed earlier, this leads to the exciton bands below the bandgap and free states above the bandgap. Due to the momentum conservation, only the $K_{ex} = k_e - k_h = 0$ states are optically active. Above the bandgap, these states are just the ones we considered earlier, in the band-to-band transitions. However, below the bandgap, these are the discrete excitonic resonances. Strong changes in the optical properties occur near the bandedge.

As one approaches the bandedge, the exciton lines become closer and closer and (see Equation 16.8), even though each transition becomes weaker, the absorption over an infinitesimal energy range reaches a finite value. In fact, the concept of the density of states of $K_{ex} = 0$ states becomes a meaningful concept. This density of states is from Equation 16.8 or Equation 16.14

$$
\begin{aligned}
D_{ex}(E) &= 2\frac{\partial n}{\partial E} \\
&= \frac{n^3}{R_{ex}}.
\end{aligned}
\tag{16.25}
$$

Extending the expression for the transition rates (Equation 16.19), by including a final state density of excitonic states we get

$$
\begin{aligned}
W(\psi_0 \rightarrow \psi_{\text{ex}}) &= \frac{2\pi}{\hbar} \left(\frac{eA_0}{mc} \right)^2 \delta_{\mathbf{K}_{\text{ex}}} |\mathbf{a} \cdot \mathbf{p}_{\text{if}}(0)|^2 \\
&\quad \times \sum_n \left| \sum_{\mathbf{k}} A(\mathbf{k}) \right|^2 \delta \left(E_{\text{ex}}^n - E_0 - \hbar\omega \right) \\
&= \frac{2\pi}{\hbar} \left(\frac{eA_0}{mc} \right)^2 |\mathbf{a} \cdot \mathbf{p}_{\text{if}}(0)|^2 \frac{1}{\pi a_{\text{ex}}^3} \frac{1}{R_{\text{ex}}}.
\end{aligned} \tag{16.26}
$$

This expression is valid near the bandedge. If we compare this expression with the free electron-hole absorption rate near the bandedge, we see that the difference is that the density of states has been replaced by $1/(\pi a_{\text{ex}}^3 R_{\text{ex}})$ or, near the bandedge, the absorption coefficient is

$$
\alpha_{\text{ex}}(\hbar\omega \approx E_g) = \alpha_F \cdot \frac{2\pi R_{\text{ex}}^{1/2}}{(\hbar\omega - E_g)^{1/2}} \tag{16.27}
$$

where α_F is the absorption without excitonic effects. Thus, instead of α going to zero at the bandedge, it *becomes a constant*. By examining the nature of the "free" hydrogen atom-like states for the exciton *above* the bandedge, it can be shown that the absorption coefficient is given by the relation

$$
\alpha_{\text{ex}}(\hbar\omega > E_g) = \alpha_F \cdot \frac{\pi x \, e^{\pi x}}{\sinh \pi x} \tag{16.28}
$$

where

$$
x = \frac{R_{\text{ex}}}{(\hbar\omega - E_g)^{1/2}}.
$$

When $E_g - \hbar\omega \gg R_{\text{ex}}$, the results reduce to the band-to-band transitions calculated in Chapter 15. These effects are shown in Figure 16.6.

From these discussions it is clear that the excitonic transitions greatly modify the independent electron absorption spectra, especially near the bandedges. In Figure 16.7, we show a low temperature measurement of the excitonic and band-to-band absorption in GaAs. The excitonic peak is clearly resolved here. The binding energy of the exciton in GaAs is ~ 4 meV. Since the exciton line is broadened by background impurity potential fluctuations, as well as phonons, it is possible to see such transitions only in high purity semiconductors, at low temperatures. In fact, the observation of excitons in bulk semiconductors is a good indication of the quality of the sample. For narrow bandgap semiconductors like $In_{0.53}Ga_{0.47}As$, the excitons are difficult to observe, because of the even small binding energy. In such materials, the exciton-related transitions are seen better in low temperature luminescence experiments. In these experiments, carriers are pumped into the material with a laser. The carriers relax into the low lying excitonic states in extremely short time scales (picoseconds) and then recombine,

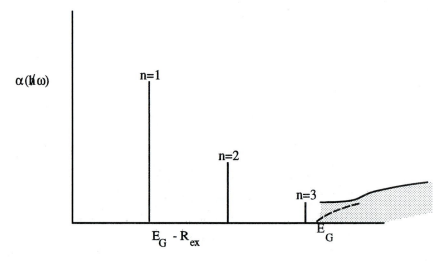

Figure 16.6: A schematic picture of the absorption spectra with (solid line) and without (dashed line) excitonic effects.

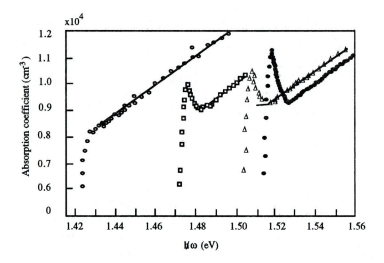

Figure 16.7: Measured excitonic and band-to-band spectra in GaAs: at o–294 K; □–186 K; △–90 K, and ●–21 K. As can be seen, the excitonic peak essentially merges with the band-to-band absorption onset at room temperature. (Reproduced with permission, M. D. Sturge, Phys. Rev., **127**, 768 (1962).)

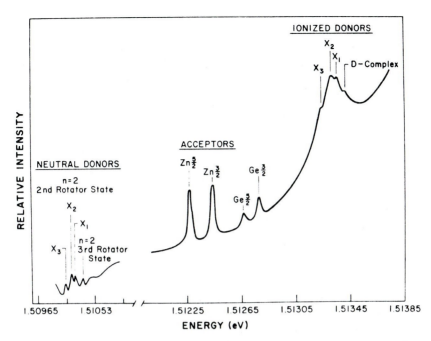

Figure 16.8: Typical high resolution luminescence spectrum in GaAs. A number of transitions below the free exciton are observed and represent the bound exciton states where excitons are coupled to a variety of defects, (from Reynolds, et al., 1982).

emitting photons with appropriate energies. At low temperatures, the band-to-band transitions are eliminated, since the electrons and holes thermalize into the excitonic states, from where they recombine. A typical luminescence spectrum is shown in Figure 16.8. In such a spectrum, one sees not just the "free" exciton, which arises from the electron-hole system discussed above, but also various kinds of "bound" excitons. These bound excitons do not have the $\exp(i\boldsymbol{K}_{ex} \cdot \boldsymbol{R})$ dependence in their wavefunctions and are bound to local impurities such as donors or acceptors.

16.3 EXCITONIC STATES IN QUANTUM WELLS

The ability to fabricate quantum well structures, where the electrons and holes can be strongly confined in the growth direction, has allowed excitonic resonances to assume an important technological aspect. The motivation for exciton studies is based equally between material characterization, pure physics, and "optical information processing." The highly controllable nature of the excitonic resonances lends itself to many versatile devices. The main reason for the interest in excitonic resonances in quantum well structures is the enhanced binding energy of the confined electron-hole system. Simple variational calculations show that the binding energy of a 2-dimensional electron-hole system with Coulombic interaction is four times that of the 3-dimensional system. In reality, of course, a quantum well system is not a 2-dimensional system, but is a quasi-2-dimensional system. The actual binding energy is, therefore, somewhat smaller than the $4 R_{ex}$ value. Nevertheless, the increased binding energy allows the excitonic transitions to persist up to high temperatures.

We address the exciton problem in the quantum well in the same manner as we addressed the 3-dimensional problem. The exciton state is again a Bloch state, with K_{ex} being a 2-dimensional quantum number in the plane of the quantum well. The kinetic energy of the exciton has the same form as for the 3-D problem. The relative coordinate problem is then given by the Hamiltonian

$$
H = \frac{-\hbar^2}{2\mu} \left(\frac{1}{\rho} \frac{\partial}{\partial p} \rho \frac{\partial}{\partial p} + \frac{1}{\rho^2} \frac{\partial^2}{\partial \phi^2} \right) - \frac{\hbar^2}{2m_e} \frac{\partial^2}{\partial z_e^2} - \frac{\hbar^2}{2m_h} \frac{\partial^2}{\partial z_h^2}
$$

$$
- \frac{e^2}{\epsilon |r_e - r_h|} + V_{ew}(z_e) + V_{hw}(z_h). \tag{16.29}
$$

Here V_{ew}, V_{hw} are the confining potentials, m_e and m_h are the in-plane effective masses of the electron and the hole, and μ is the reduced mass. The first term is the kinetic energy operator in the plane of the quantum well. The dielectric constant ϵ is the static dielectric constant, if there are no free carriers present. Otherwise, it is the screened dielectric constant, of the form used by us in the ionized impurity scattering problem. We will return to the screening problem later.

Unlike the 3-D problem, the Hamiltonian of Equation 16.29 has no simple analytical solution, even if one assumes that the electron and hole states have a parabolic bandstructure. While the parabolic approximation is a good approximation for the electrons, it is a very poor approximation for the hole states, as can be seen from the in-plane valence bandstructure in a 100 Å GaAs/Al$_{0.3}$Ga$_{0.7}$As quantum well structure shown in Figure 16.9. As can be seen, the valence subbands are highly parabolic and the light hole state (LH1) even has a "negative" curvature at the zone center making the zone center reduced mass very large. It is possible to include these nonparabolic effects by using simple expressions of the form

$$
E_h(k) = \alpha k^2 + \beta k^4 \tag{16.30}
$$

where α and β can be fit to a calculated subband structure and then identifying k by $-i\nabla_\rho$. The function $F(\rho)$, describing the relative motion envelope, cannot be directly obtained. This function is usually obtained by assuming its form to be an exponential, or Gaussian or some combination of Gaussian functions, etc., with some variational constants which are then adjusted to minimize the energy

$$
E = \frac{\int \psi_{ex}^* H \psi_{ex} \, dz_e \, dz_n \, \rho \, d\rho \, d\phi}{\int \psi_{ex}^* \psi_{ex} \, dz_e \, dz_n \, \rho \, d\rho \, d\phi}. \tag{16.31}
$$

This approach gives quite reliable results, with the effects of choosing different forms of variational functions being no more than ~10% of the exciton

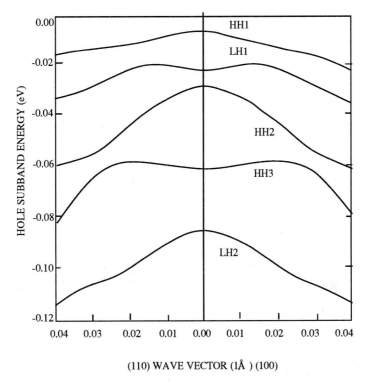

Figure 16.9: In plane valence band dispersion relations for a 100 Å GaAs /Al$_{0.3}$Ga$_{0.7}$As quantum well. Notice the strong nonparabolicity of the LH1 state.

binding energies. In Figure 16.10, we show the effect of well size on the ground state excitonic states in GaAs/Al$_{0.3}$Ga$_{0.7}$As quantum well structures. As can be seen, the exciton binding energies can increase by up to a factor of ~2.5 in optimally designed quantum well structures.

A useful approach to solve the exciton problem is to work in *k*-space instead of the real space. This approach is more appropriate, since then the hole kinetic energy need not be represented by any complicated real space differential operator. Instead, the bandstructure could be used with all nonparabolic effects included. This approach is also more useful when screening effects are to be included in the exciton problem. The important consideration in casting the exciton problem in *k*-space is to write the Coulombic interaction in the *k*-space basis of the free electron and hole states. If these states were simply the plane wave states, this would simply involve Fourier transforming the 1/r potential. The presence of the envelope functions and the central cell functions modifies the result slightly. Writing the electron and hole functions as

$$|n, \boldsymbol{k}\rangle \ = \ f_n(z_e) \, e^{i\boldsymbol{k}\cdot\rho_e}$$

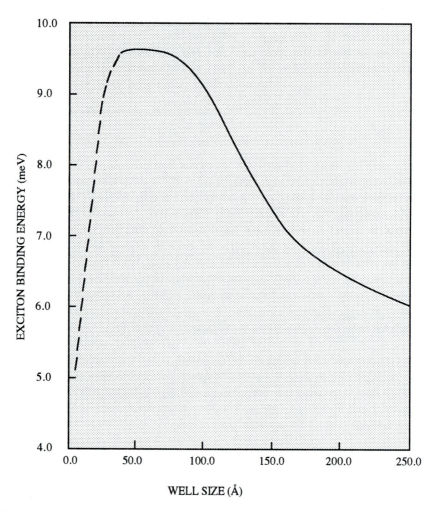

Figure 16.10: Variation of the heavy-hole exciton binding energy as a function of well size in GaAs/Al$_{0.3}$Ga$_{0.7}$As wells. The binding energy of the infinite barrier well should approach 16 meV as the well size goes to zero. However, in a real structure the binding energy starts to decrease below 50 Å well size.

$$|m, k\rangle = \sum_v g_m^v(k, z_h) \, e^{i\mathbf{k}\cdot\rho_h} \qquad (16.32)$$

respectively, we need to evaluate the matrix elements of the Coulombic potential

$$V(\rho_e, z_e; \rho_h, z_h) = \frac{-e^2}{\epsilon \left[|\rho_e - \rho_h|^2 + (z_e - z_h)^2 \right]^{1/2}} \qquad (16.33)$$

in the electron-hole product state basis. The k-space representation can be shown to have the form

$$V(k - k'; z_e, z_h) = \frac{1}{(2\pi)^2} \int d^2\rho_e \, e^{-i(\mathbf{k}-\mathbf{k}')\cdot\rho_e} \, V(\rho_e, z_e; 0, z_h)$$

$$= \frac{-e^2}{2\pi\epsilon_r |k - k'|} \, e^{|k-k'| \, |z_e - z_h|}. \qquad (16.34)$$

The full Hamiltonian in k-space is now

$$H = H_e^0 + H_h^0 + V \qquad (16.35)$$

where H_e^0 and H_h^0 simply give the E vs. k relations for the electron and hole subbands. The exciton wavefunction then obeys the equation

$$H|\psi^{\text{ex}}\rangle = E^{\text{ex}}|\psi^{\text{ex}}\rangle. \qquad (16.36)$$

The optically active exciton function (i.e., $K_{\text{ex}} = 0$), is expanded as usual, in the electron-hole basis with expansion coefficients $G_{nm}(k)$, the indices n,m representing various subband levels

$$|\psi^{\text{ex}}\rangle = \sum_n \sum_m \int d^2 k \, |n, k\rangle \, |m, -k\rangle \, G_{nm}(k). \qquad (16.37)$$

An eigenvalue equation can now be set up for the $G_{nm}(k)$ by taking matrix elements of Equation 16.36 between states $|n, k\rangle|m, -k\rangle$ and $|n'k'\rangle|m', -k'\rangle$, using Equation 16.34 for the Coulombic potential matrix elements. Additionally, for narrow quantum wells ($W \approx 150$ Å) it is also reasonable to assume that the intersubband coupling is weak, i.e.

$$\langle n, k| \langle m, -k|V|n'k'\rangle \, |m', -k'\rangle = 0 \qquad (16.38)$$

unless $m = m'$, $n = n'$. This results in an eigenvalue equation

$$\left[E^{\text{ex}} - E_n^e(k) + E_m^h(-k) \right] G_{nm}(k) =$$

$$\int d^2k' \int dz_e \int dz_h \, f_n^*(z_e) \, f_n(z_e)$$

$$\sum_v g_m^{*v}(-k, z_h) \, g_m^v(-k', z_h) \, V(k - k'; z_e, z_h) \, G_{nm}(k'). \qquad (16.39)$$

This equation can be solved numerically, by discretizing k-space and using the fact that the exciton function has a finite extent in k-space (~ 0.01 Å^{-1}). Alternately, the problem can be solved by variational techniques. Once the coefficients $G_{nm}(k)$ are known, the real-space dependence of the exciton function can be obtained by Fourier transformation, i.e.

$$\psi_{nm}^{\mathrm{ex}}(\rho, z_e, z_h) = \frac{1}{2\pi} f_n(z_e) \int d^2k \, e^{ik\cdot\rho} \sum_v g_m^v(-k, z_h) \, G_{nm}(k). \qquad (16.40)$$

In Figure 16.11 we show the CB1-HH1 (ground state) exciton wavefunction. Both the k-space and real-space functions are shown. We note that $G(\rho)$ has an exponential dependence $\psi^{\mathrm{ex}} \sim \exp(-\rho/a_{\mathrm{ex}})$, where a_{ex} can be used to define the exciton Bohr radius. It is interesting to note that the exciton radius decreases steadily as the well size is decreased. This is consistent with the increasing binding energy of the exciton.

16.4   EXCITONIC ABSORPTION IN QUANTUM WELLS

The absorption spectra in quantum wells is given by the same formalism that was used for the case of bulk semiconductors. We simply need to represent the exciton envelope function by the function appropriate for the quantum well. The absorption coefficient is given by

$$\alpha_{nm}^{\mathrm{ex}}(\hbar\omega) = \frac{4\pi^2 e^2 \hbar}{\eta m^2 cW \hbar\omega} \left| \sum_{k,n,m} G_{nm}(k) \, a \cdot p_{nm}(k) \right|^2 \delta\left(\hbar\omega - E_{nm}^{\mathrm{ex}}\right). \qquad (16.41)$$

The matrix elements $p_{nm}(k)$ are given by the central cell part used for the 3-dimensional problem, as well as the overlap of the envelope function as used in the Chapter 15 for band-to-band absorption

$$p_{nm}(k) = \sum_{v,\mu} \int d^2r \, U_0^v(r) \, p \, U_0^\mu(r) \int dz \, f_n^\mu(z) \, g_m^v(k, z). \qquad (16.42)$$

The selection rules and polarization dependencies discussed in Chapter 15 for band to band transitions, still hold for the excitonic transitions.

The absorption coefficient is often also written in terms of oscillator strengths f_{nm} as

$$\alpha_{nm}(\hbar\omega) = \sum_{nm} \frac{4\pi^2 e^2 \hbar}{\eta mcW} f_{nm} \, \delta\left(E_{nm}^{\mathrm{ex}} - \hbar\omega\right) \qquad (16.43)$$

where the oscillator strength per unit area is defined by

$$f_{nm} = \frac{2}{m E_{nm}^{\mathrm{ex}} (2\pi)^2} \left| \int d^2k \, G_{nm}(k) \, a \cdot p_{nm}(k) \right|^2. \qquad (16.44)$$

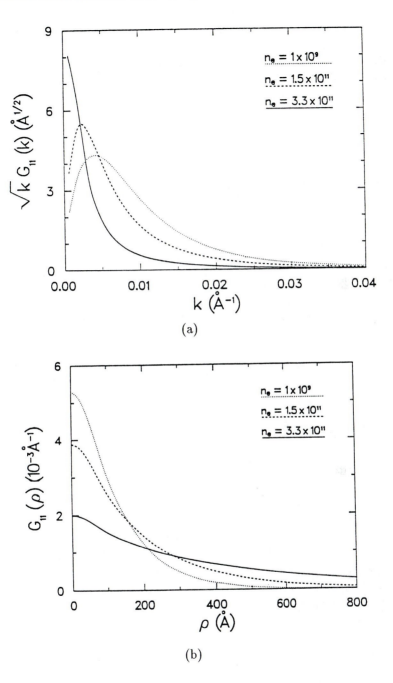

Figure 16.11: The (a) k-space and (b) real space exciton wavefunction defined by $\sqrt{k}G_{11}(k)$ and $G_{11}(\rho)$ for the CB1-HH1 exciton in a 100 Å GaAs/Al$_{0.3}$Ga$_{0.7}$As quantum well structure, (from Loehr, 1991).

The oscillator strength is a better measure of the excitonic absorption because it does not involve the δ-function. The δ-function will eventually be replaced by a broadening function whose value will be sample and temperature dependent as we will see below. Since quantum confinement decreases the spatial extent of the exciton function, the oscillator strength increases as the exciton is confined.

16.5   EXCITON BROADENING EFFECTS

We have seen from the previous discussions that the exciton absorption resonance has a δ-function. In real systems the δ-function is always broadened. This line broadening or linewidth is extremely important from both a physics and a technological point of view. In general, the peak of the exciton absorption is inversely proportional to the linewidth of the resonance. This puts a tremendous premium on reducing the exciton linewidth (in a reliable manner). Unfortunately, small variations in growth of quantum wells can change the exciton linewidth by as much as 100%! In fact, the exciton linewidth is one of the serious hurdles in using exciton based devices in reliable technology.

The excitonic transitions are broadened by two important kinds of fluctuations: inhomogeneous and homogeneous. The inhomogeneous linewidth is due to local potential fluctuations which arise due to imperfections in the structure. Homogeneous broadening, on the other hand, is due to fluctuations which are extended in nature and influence the entire excitonic spectra. The main inhomogeneous broadening sources are:

1. Interface roughness.

2. Alloy potential fluctuations.

3. Well to well fluctuations in multiquantum well spectra.

4. Background impurity broadening.

In high purity materials the impurity broadening is usually negligible (if background density $< 10^{15} \text{cm} - 3$). The homogeneous broadening mechanisms are:

1. Acoustic phonon scattering.

2. Optical phonon scattering.

3. Other mechanisms which may affect the exciton lifetime such as tunneling, recombination, etc.

The treatment of inhomogeneous broadening usually follows the approach developed to study electronic states in disordered materials. This approach will be described in a more detail in Chapter 18.

Line broadening arises due to spatially localized fluctuations which are capable of shifting the excitonic emission energy. In general, one may describe these fluctuations by concentration fluctuations in the mean compositions C_A^0 and C_B^0 of the structure. For example C_A^0 and C_B^0 may represent the fraction of the islands and the valleys representing interface roughness in a quantum well, or the mean composition of the alloy in the treatment of alloy broadening. The width of the concentration fluctuation occurring over a region β (which is an area for interface roughness treatment and a volume for the treatment of alloy broadening) is given by (Lifshitz, 1969):

$$\delta P = 2\sqrt{\frac{1.4\, C_A^0\, C_B^0\, \alpha}{\beta}} \qquad (16.45)$$

where α is the smallest extent over which the fluctuation can take place. Again for the treatment of interface roughness, α is the average area of the two-dimensional islands representing the interface roughness and for alloy broadening, α is the volume of the smallest cluster in the alloy. For a perfectly random alloy, this is the volume per cation.

The shift in the excitonic energy due to this fluctuation is then

$$\sigma(\beta) = \delta P \, |\Psi|_\beta^2 \, \frac{\partial E_{\text{ex}}}{\partial C} \qquad (16.46)$$

where $|\Psi|_\beta^2$ is the fraction of the exciton sensing the region β, and $\partial E_{\text{ex}}/\partial C$ represents the rate of change in the exciton energy with change in the concentration. To obtain the linewidth of the absorption, one needs to identify the volume (or area) β. For interface roughness broadening, this area is $\sim 3r_{\text{ex}}^2$ and the linewidth is given by

$$\sigma_{\text{IR}} = 2\sqrt{\frac{1.4\, C_A^0\, C_B^0\, a_{2\text{-D}}}{3r_{\text{ex}}^2\, \pi}} \cdot \left.\frac{\partial E_{\text{ex}}}{\partial W}\right|_{W_0} \cdot \delta_0 \qquad (16.47)$$

where $a_{2\text{D}}$ is the real extent of the two-dimensional islands representing the interface roughness, δ_0 their height, and r_{ex} is the exciton Bohr radius in the lateral direction parallel to the interface. $\partial E_{\text{ex}}/\partial W$ is the change of the exciton energy as a function of well size.

Apart from interface roughness fluctuations in the same well, often one has to contend with intra-well fluctuations. Most optical devices using excitonic transitions use more than one well, i.e., use multiquantum wells that are produced by opening and shutting off fluxes of one or other chemical species. There is invariably a monolayer or so of variation in the well sizes across a stack of quantum wells. For a 100 Å GaAs/Al$_{0.3}$Ga$_{0.7}$As quantum well, a monolayer fluctuation can produce ~ 1.5 meV change in the exciton resonance energy. This change arises almost entirely from the changes in subband levels since the *exciton binding energy* does not vary significantly with a monolayer change in the well size. In high quality GaAs/AlGaAs multiquantum well samples, an absorption linewidth of 3–4 meV is achievable.

In the GaAs based system, the well material is a binary material with no alloy scattering. In cases like In$_{0.53}$Ga$_{0.47}$As/InP or In$_{0.53}$Ga$_{0.47}$As/In$_{0.52}$Al$_{0.48}$As, one additionally has alloy broadening effects. These effects can also be of the order of 3–5 meV and are given by similar treatments. If C_A^0 and C_B^0 are the mean concentrations of the two alloy components and V_C is the average alloy cluster size (= unit cell for random alloy), the linewidth is given approximately by

$$\sigma_{\text{alloy}}^{\text{internal}} = 2\sqrt{\frac{1.4\,C_A^0\,C_B^0\,V_C}{3\pi r_{\text{ex}}^2 W_0}} \cdot \left.\frac{\partial E_{\text{ex}}}{\partial C_A}\right|_{C_A^0} \tag{16.48}$$

where $\partial E_{\text{ex}}/\partial C_A$ represents the change in the exciton resonance with changes in composition. If the barrier material is also an alloy, there is a contribution to the linewidth from the barrier as well

$$\sigma_{\text{alloy}}^{\text{external}} = 2\sqrt{\frac{1.4\,C_A^0\,C_B^0\,V_C}{3\pi r_{\text{ex}}^2 L_{\text{eff}}}} \cdot \left.\frac{\partial E_{\text{ex}}}{\partial C_A}\right|_{C_A^0} \tag{16.49}$$

where L_{eff} is an effective length to which the exciton wavefunction penetrates in the barrier and has to be calculated numerically. L_{eff} is approximately equal to twice the distance over which the exciton wavefunction falls to $1/e$ of its initial value. Typically this is on the order of a few monolayers. The well size dependence of the exciton linewidth is quite apparent from the results of Figure 16.12 and are due to the increase in $\partial E_{\text{ex}}/\partial W$ with decreasing well size.

It is important to note that for systems such as GaAs/AlGaAs modulators where the interface roughness dominates the linewidth, the quantity $\partial E_{\text{ex}}/\partial W|_{W_0}$ increases rapidly with electric field. Thus, the inhomogeneous broadening increases as the electric field is increased. It must be noted that a one monolayer change produces a shift of ~1.5 meV, 2.0 meV, and 2.2 meV in the heavy hole exciton energy of a 100 Å GaAs/AlGaAs quantum well at 0 kV/cm, 30 kV/cm, and 70 kV/cm respectively.

Finally, to examine the homogeneous broadening note that the exciton state is optically created at the $\boldsymbol{K}_{\text{ex}} = 0$ state. The acoustic and optical phonons interact with the exciton causing either a transition to a $\boldsymbol{K}_{\text{ex}} \neq 0$ state in the same quantum level or even ionization of the exciton. This homogeneous broadening effect can be calculated in a manner similar to the one used for electron-phonon scattering. The linewidth is given approximately by

$$\sigma = \frac{1}{W(\boldsymbol{K}_{\text{ex}} = 0)} \tag{16.50}$$

and has the form

$$\sigma = \alpha T + \frac{\beta}{\exp\left(\hbar\omega_0/k_B T\right) - 1}. \tag{16.51}$$

At room temperature the homogeneous linewidth due to phonons is ~3–4 meV, implying that the exciton lifetime is ~ 0.2 ps.

The consequences of the exciton linewidth on devices cannot be emphasized enough. While the homogeneous linewidths are controlled by the temperature or

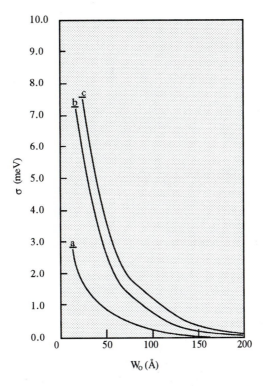

Figure 16.12: Variation of exciton linewidth as a function of well size for a one mono-layer interface roughness. The half width σ is given for slant size extents of (a) 20 Å; (b) 80ÃÅA; (c) 100 Å for the GaAs/Al$_{0.3}$Ga$_{0.7}$As system.

other controllable effects, the inhomogeneous effects are dependent upon sample quality. This places a heavy burden on the crystal grower. In this context, it is useful to compare the effect of, say, one-monolayer fluctuation in the interface quality on an MODFET versus an exciton based device. The effect on room temperature mobility of a MODFET is less than 1%, while the effect on exciton linewidth at room temperature is ~30%!

In Figure 16.13 we show the comparison of the excitonic spectra in a 100 Å GaAs/Al$_{0.3}$Ga$_{0.7}$As and 100 Å In$_{0.53}$Ga$_{0.47}$As/In$_{0.52}$Al$_{0.48}$As quantum well structure. The large reduction in the InGaAs spectra is primarily due to the alloy broadening of the exciton peak.

16.6 MODULATION OF EXCITONIC TRANSITIONS: QUANTUM CONFINED STARK EFFECT

We have seen that by confining the excitonic wavefunction in a quantum well, the binding energy greatly increases along with the oscillator strength. This has

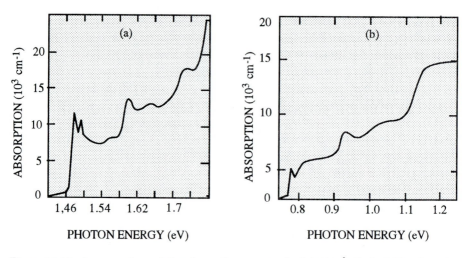

Figure 16.13: A comparison of the absorption spectra in (a) 100 Å GaAs /Al$_{0.3}$Ga$_{0.7}$As and (b) In$_{0.53}$Ga$_{0.47}$As /In$_{0.52}$Al$_{0.48}$As quantum wells. The excitons in InGaAs suffer alloy broadening which reduces their clarity. The absorption peak is also lower because of the lower binding energy of the excitons in InGaAs.

allowed excitonic transitions to persist up to high temperatures without merging into the band-to-band transitions. When static electric fields are applied to a 3-D semiconductor, the energy term

$$eFz_e - eFz_h$$

must be added to the exciton Hamiltonian to solve the problem. The electric field ionizes the exciton state by pulling apart the electron hole pair. This causes a broadening of the exciton peak and also shifts the peak somewhat by the Stark effect. This effect is known as Franz-Keldysh effect and was first discovered theoretically in 1958, and later workers made contributions to the excitonic problem. The shift of the absorption to lower energies can be understood as due to tunneling of an electron between the top of the valence band and bottom of the conduction band due to a photon. In fact, all energies are in principle possible for these transitions along the electric field since the energy gap between the valence and conduction band is a triangular potential well whose height is the energy gap and the width is $z = E_g/(eF)$ where F is the electric field. In presence of a photon of energy $\hbar\omega$, the barrier height becomes $(E_g - \hbar\omega)$ and the tunneling probability depends exponentially on this parameter. Thus, even when the photon energy approaches zero, there is a finite probability of such transitions.

We will not address the details of the Franz-Keldysh effect in 3-D systems. This effect is not of much technological importance although a particular feature of this effect is often used to characterize the precise electric field in a region of a material. The absorption coefficient develops an oscillatory behavior with

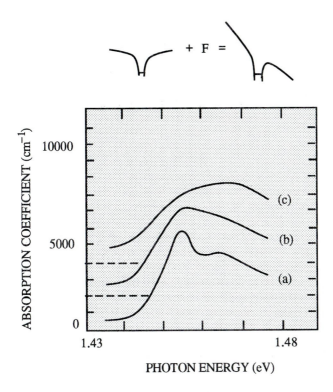

Figure 16.14: Absorption spectra at various electric fields for the parallel field (a) 0 V/cm; (b) 1.6×10^4 V/cm; (c) 4.8×10^4 V/cm. The insert shows schematically the distortion of the Coulomb potential of electron and applied field. The zeroes are displaced as shown by the dashed line clarity. (Reproduced with permission, D. S. Chemla, *Nonlinear Optics: Materials and Devices*, Springer-Verlag, New York, 1986.)

respect to photon energy and the period of this oscillation is given by

$$\left(\frac{9\pi^2 \hbar^2 e^2}{8} \frac{E^2}{\mu} \right) \tag{16.52}$$

where μ is the reduced mass.

We will focus our attention to the absorption spectra in quantum wells in presence of an electric field. The electric field can be either longitudinal (in the plane of the well) or transverse (in the growth direction). The longitudinal field problem is similar to the bulk problem and the excitonic transition essentially disappears at at fairly low field (≤ 10 kV/cm) as shown in Figure 16.14. The absorption edge shifts to lower energy as in the case of the bulk problem.

The transverse field problem is of great interest since the exciton does not field ionized since the electron and hole states are confined because of the high barriers of the potential well. As a result, exciton transitions can persist up to electric fields of greater than 100 kV/cm. This effect is known as Quantum

Confined Stark Effect (QCSE) and has been used to design new optoelectronic devices ranging from modulators to switches. The QCSE can be understood on the basis of the same formalism as the one discussed for the exciton and band to band transitions in absence of the electric field as long as one can assume that the quantum well subband levels are reasonably confined states. In principle, the quantum well states are quasi-bound states in presence of the field with the wavefunction primarily peaked in the quantum well region. Electrons and holes created in the form of a wavepacket in the well will eventually tunnel out of the well. In the addressing exciton problem one assumes that the subband states are localized in the well and the exciton can be made up of only the confined states. There are several effects that occur in the presence of the transverse electric field:

1. The intersubband separations change. The field pushes the electron and hole functions to opposite sides making the ground state intersubband separation smaller. This effect is the dominant term in changing the exciton resonance energy.

2. Due to the separation of the electron and hole wavefunction, the binding energy of the exciton decreases. This effect is shown in Figure 16.15.

In Figure 16.16 and Figure 16.17 we show the variation in the intersubband separation and exciton binding energies with applied fields. As can be seen from these figures, the change in the exciton binding energy is only ~2–3 meV while the intersubband energies are altered by up to 20 meV. The QCSE is, therefore, primarily determined by the intersubband effect.

While the exact calculation of the intersubband separation requires numerical techniques, one can estimate these changes by using perturbation theory. This approach gives reasonable results for low electric fields. The problem can be defined by the Hamiltonian

$$H = H_0 + eFz \qquad (16.53)$$

where H_0 is the usual quantum well Hamiltonian. The eigenfunctions of H_0 are ψ_n and in the square quantum well, the ground state function ψ_1 has an even parity so that the first order correction to the subband energy is

$$\Delta E^{(1)} = \langle \psi_1 | eFz | \psi_1 \rangle \qquad (16.54)$$

which is zero. Thus, one has to calculate the second order perturbation by using the usual approach. For the infinite barrier quantum well, the states ψ_n are known and it is, therefore, possible to calculate the second order correction. If the field is small enough such that

$$|eFW| \ll \frac{\hbar^2 \pi^2}{2m^* W^2} \qquad (16.55)$$

i.e., the perturbation is small compared to the ground state energy then it can be shown that the ground state energy changes by

$$\Delta E_1^{(2)} = \frac{1}{24\pi^2} \left(\frac{15}{\pi^2} - 1 \right) \frac{m^* e^2 F^2 W^4}{\hbar^2}. \qquad (16.56)$$

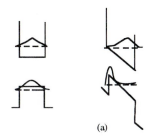

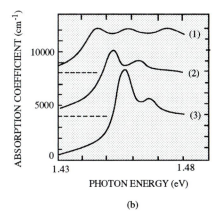

Figure 16.15: Absorption spectra at various electric fields for the parallel field (a) 0 V/cm; (b) 1.6×10^4 V/cm; (c) 4.8×10^4 V/cm. The insert shows schematically the distortion of the Coulomb potential of electron and applied field. The zeroes are displaced as shown by the dashed line clarity. (Reproduced with permission, D. S. Chemla, *Nonlinear Optics: Materials and Devices*, Springer-Verlag, New York, 1986.)

One sees that the second order effect increases with m^* and has a strong well size dependence. This would suggest that for best modulation one should use a wide well. However, in wide wells the exciton absorption decreases and also the HH, LH separation becomes small. Optimum well sizes are of the order of ~100 Å for modulators.

In Figure 16.18 we show the calculated effects of applied electric field on the absorption spectra of a 100 Å $GaAs/Al_{0.3}Ga_{0.7}As$ quantum well structure. It is interesting to note that not only do the HH1 and LH1 exciton shift to lower energies, but some of the "forbidden" transitions become observable. These transitions are forbidden because of parity considerations in the square quantum well (e.g., the HH1-C1 transition). However, in the presence of the electric field, the quantum well is no longer symmetric and these transitions become stronger. In fact, as some "allowed" transitions weaken, other transitions become stronger in accordance to the sum rules for absorption.

As can be seen from Figure 16.18, an optical beam with a frequency near

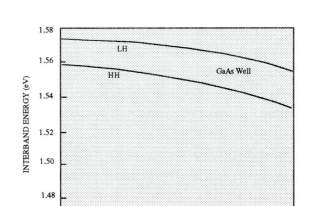

Figure 16.16: Variation of the ground state HH and LH (to conduction band ground state) intersubband transition energies as a function of electric field.

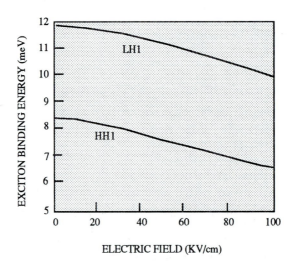

Figure 16.17: The variation in the exciton binding energy in a 100 Å GaAs /Al$_{0.3}$Ga$_{0.7}$As quantum well as a function of electric field. The HH and LH exciton results are shown.

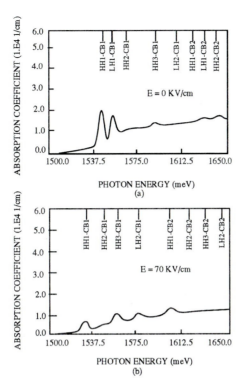

Figure 16.18: Total absorption coefficient calculated for a 100 Å GaAs /Al$_{0.3}$Ga$_{0.7}$As quantum well. Cases: (a) $F = 0$; (b) $F = 70$ kV/cm, (from Hong and Singh, 1987).

the exciton resonance can be modulated by applying an electric field across, say, a p-i (MQW) -n region. This is an obvious use of the QCSE. In fact, a number of devices can also be designed on this basis. For example, the photocurrent through the p-i (MQW) -n structure is determined by the electron-hole pairs generated and since the absorption coefficient varies with electric field, the photocurrent can also show the same variation. This effect, schematically shown in Figure 16.19 can lead to negative differential resistance and can be exploited in logic switches. The first example of such a device is the self-electro-optic effect device (SEED), in which switching of a device occurs as the optical power is changed. We note that the matrix element in the excitonic absorption obeys the same polarization selection rules as the ones we discussed in Chapter 15 for band to band transitions. In Figure 16.20 we show the TE and TM absorption spectra calculated for a 100 Å GaAs/Al$_{0.3}$Ga$_{0.7}$As quantum well. As can be seen, in the TE mode, the LH exciton strength is approximately a third of the HH exciton strength. In the TM mode on the other hand, there is no HH transition allowed in accordance with our discussions in Chapter 15. Measured dependent spectra in similar structures is shown in Figure 16.21.

In the context of polarization dependence of the absorption spectra, it is

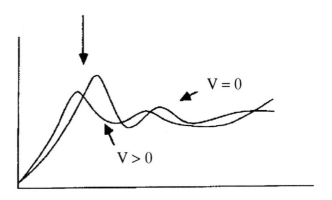

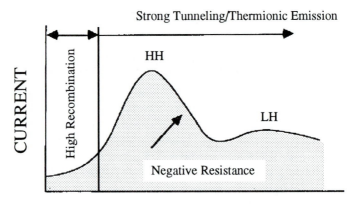

Figure 16.19: The change in the absorption profile of the excitonic spectra with applied electric field produces a photocurrent-voltage characteristics which can have a negative resistance region. The optical beam has an energy denoted by the arrow.

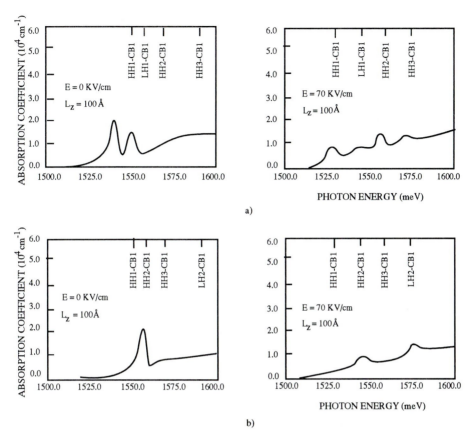

Figure 16.20: Calculated absorption coefficients for TE and TM modes in a 100 Å GaAs/AlGaAs quantum well structure at (a) $F = 0$ and (b) $F = 70$ kV/cm, (from Hong and Singh, 1987).

very interesting to see the effect of strain on the spectra. We noted in Chapter 7 that epitaxial strain can lift the degeneracy between the HH and LH states. In fact, a compressive in-plane strain pushes the LH below the HH state while a tensile strain does the opposite. Now the quantum confinement also pushes the LH state below the HH state. Thus, in principle a properly chosen tensile strain can cause a *merger* of the HH and LH states at the zone center in a quantum well. In Figure 16.22 we show a schematic sketch of this possibility along with the valence bandstructure in a 150 Å GaAs/$In_{0.06}Ga_{0.57}Al_{0.37}As$ well where we assume that the GaAs well and the barrier share the lattice mismatch to put the well under tensile strain. As can be seen, the LH and HH states are degenerate at the zone center with a very high hole density of states at the bandedge.

This HH, LH merger can produce a large enhancement of the absorption peak in quantum wells. The merger of HH and LH excitonic resonances by strain

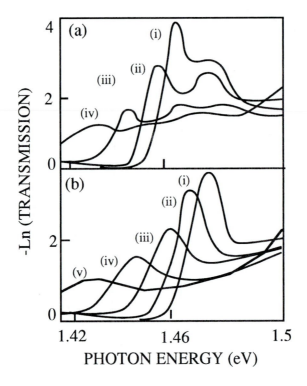

Figure 16.21: Measured polarization dependent transmittances in GaAs/AlGaAs (100 Å) multiquantum well structures when light is coming in the waveguide geometry. (a) Incident polarization parallel to the plane of the layers for fields of (i) 1.6×10^4 V/cm, (ii) 1.0×10^5 V/cm, (iii) 1.3×10^5 V/cm, and (iv) 1.8×10^5 V/cm. (b) Incident polarization perpendicular to the plane of the layers for fields of (i) 1.6×10^4 V/cm, (ii) 1.0×10^5 V/cm, (iii) 1.4×10^5 V/cm, (iv) 1.8×10^5 V/cm, and (v) 2.2×10^5 V/cm, (from Miller, et al., 1986).

has been verified experimentally in two kinds of structures:

1. In the GaAs/InAlGaAs system, where the substrate is removed so that the strain is distributed between the well and the barrier. This puts the well under a compressive strain and the barrier under a tensile strain.

2. In the GaAsP/AlGaAs system, the tensile strain can be directly produced in the well without substrate removal problems (see Figure 16.23).

16.7   EXCITON QUENCHING

In the previous section we discussed an extremely powerful approach used to modulate the excitonic transitions in quantum wells. There are several other

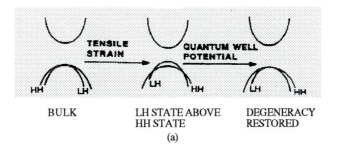

BULK   LH STATE ABOVE   DEGENERACY
            HH STATE   RESTORED

(a)

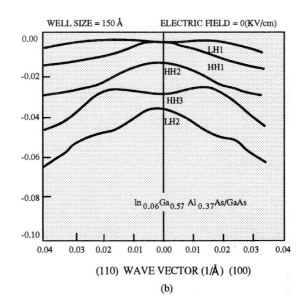

(b)

Figure 16.22: Biaxial tensile strain can be adjusted to produce a HH, LH degeneracy in a quantum well. The valence bandedge mass is extremely high in this case as shown by the dispersion relation. (Reproduced with permission, D. A. B. Miller, et al., IEEE J. Quant. Electron., **22**, 1816 (1986).)

approaches which can also modulate the exciton spectra and have been used to design various devices. Two important categories of these techniques are:

1. Quenching of the exciton by free carriers.

2. Quenching of the exciton by creation of a high density of excitons by high optical intensity.

In the first approach, a high density of free electrons (or holes) is introduced into the quantum well. The free carriers screen the Coulombic interaction between the electron and hole, weakening the exciton binding energy and reducing the exciton

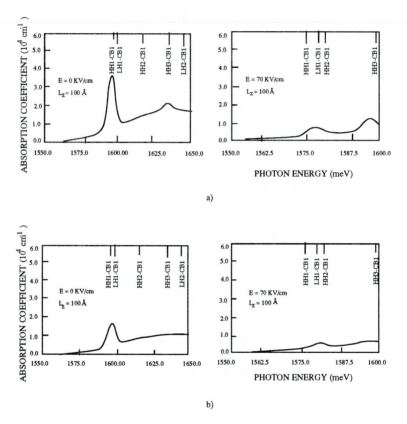

Figure 16.23: Calculated absorption spectra for (a) TE and (b) TM polarization in the case of a 100 ÅGaAs$_{0.947}$P$_{0.053}$/Al$_{0.3}$Ga0.7As quantum well (matched to GaAs substrate). The strain is chosen to merge the HH, LH excitonic states.

oscillator strength. The physics behind the second approach is quite complex and a number of important phenomenon including bandgap renormalization, exciton phase space filling, and screening effects participate to cause the modulation of the exciton resonance. Since we are not fully equipped to treat these phenomenon which require many body theory we will only summarize the current state of knowledge.

The screening of the exciton is relatively simple to understand and has been used to design high speed modulators. An example is the field effect transistor optical modulator (FETOM) in which the optical beam passes under the gate of a MODFET and has an energy equal to the exciton resonance energy in the undoped well of the device. The gate is used to inject free electrons into the channel where they screen the electron-hole interaction thus quenching the exciton transition .

In Chapter 10 we discussed how the potential of an ionized impurity is screened by free carriers. We found that the Coulomb potential had the form

$$V(r) = \frac{e^2}{\epsilon r} e^{-\lambda r} \tag{16.57}$$

where

$$\lambda^2 = 4\pi e^2 N(E_F)$$

and $N(E_F)$ is the density of states at the Fermi energy E_F.

We need to extend the effect of the dielectric response to the general quasi-2-D problem. It is useful to work in the k-space as we had discussed earlier for the exciton problem. The Coulombic potential in presence of the free carriers is given by

$$V(\boldsymbol{k} - \boldsymbol{k}'; z_e, z_h) = \frac{V_{\text{bare}}(\boldsymbol{k} - \boldsymbol{k}'; z_e, z_h)}{\epsilon(\boldsymbol{k} - \boldsymbol{k}')}. \tag{16.58}$$

Here $\epsilon(\boldsymbol{q})$ is given by

$$\epsilon(\boldsymbol{q}) = 1 + \frac{4\pi e^2}{\epsilon_r} \Delta(\boldsymbol{q}) \int dz_e \int dz_e' \, |f_1(z_e)|^2 \left(-\frac{e^{-q|z_e - z_e'|}}{2q} \right) |f_1(z_e')|^2 \tag{16.59}$$

with

$$\Delta(\boldsymbol{q}) \equiv \frac{2}{(2\pi)^2} \int d^2 k' \, \frac{f^0 \left[E_1^e(\boldsymbol{k}') \right] - f^0 \left[E_1^e(\boldsymbol{k}' + \boldsymbol{q}) \right]}{E_1^e(\boldsymbol{k}') - E_1^e(\boldsymbol{k}' + \boldsymbol{q})} \tag{16.60}$$

where f^0 is the Fermi-Dirac occupation function.

The bare potential is as in Equation 16.34

$$\begin{aligned} V_{|\text{bare}}(\boldsymbol{k} - \boldsymbol{k}'; z_e, z_h) &= \frac{1}{(2\pi)} \int d^2\rho_e \, e^{-i(\boldsymbol{k}-\boldsymbol{k}')\cdot\rho_e} \, V(\rho_e, z_e; 0, z_h) \\ &= \frac{-e^2}{2\pi\epsilon_r|\boldsymbol{k} - \boldsymbol{k}'|} e^{|\boldsymbol{k}-\boldsymbol{k}'| \, |z_e - z_h|}. \end{aligned} \tag{16.61}$$

If only a single subband (E_1^e) is occupied we may write

$$\mu = E_1^e(0) + k_B T \, \ln \left(\exp \left[\frac{E_F - E_1^e(0)}{k_B T} \right] - 1 \right) \tag{16.62}$$

where

$$E_F = E_1^e(0) + \frac{\hbar^2 k_F^2}{2m^*}$$

and

$$k_F = \sqrt{2\pi n_e}.$$

Here n_e is the two-dimensional electron concentration (electrons/cm^2). Note that these results require the conduction band envelope functions $f_n(z_e)$ to be independent of the in-plane wavevector $\boldsymbol{k}$.

Assuming parabolic conduction bands and $T = 0$, Equation 16.60 can be evaluated analytically and the result is

$$
\begin{aligned}
\Delta(\boldsymbol{q}) &= -\frac{m^*}{\pi\hbar^2}, \text{ if } q \leq 2k_F \\[2mm]
&= -\frac{m^*}{\pi\hbar^2}\left\{1 - \sqrt{1 - \left(\frac{2k_F}{q}\right)^2}\right\}, \text{ if } q > 2k_F.
\end{aligned}
\tag{16.63}
$$

Note that $\Delta(\boldsymbol{q})$ depends only on $|\boldsymbol{q}|$ and that as $n_e \epsilon 0$, $\Delta(\boldsymbol{q}) \to 0$ hence $\epsilon(\boldsymbol{q}) \to 1$. For large electron concentrations at $T = 300$ K, though, $\Delta(\boldsymbol{q})$ differs significantly from its $T = 0$ value and Equation 16.60 must be evaluated numerically.

To observe the effects of screening, we plot the function $q\epsilon(\boldsymbol{q})$ versus q for various electron concentrations for $T = 0$ in Figure 16.24a and for $T = 300$ K in Figure 16.24b. This function is a useful indicator of the screening effects, since one notes from Equation 16.58 and Equation 16.61 that the screened potential takes the form

$$V(\boldsymbol{q}; z_e, z_h) = \frac{-e^2}{2\pi\epsilon_r} e^{q|z_e - z_h|} \frac{1}{q\epsilon(\boldsymbol{q})}. \tag{16.64}$$

Clearly, the denominator $q\epsilon(\boldsymbol{q})$ strongly influences the behavior of the potential. When there is no screening ($\epsilon(\boldsymbol{q}) = 1$) the denominator is zero at $q = 0$ making the potential infinite there. The presence of screening electrons, though, removes this singular behavior by making the denominator nonzero. In addition, it is clear that the screening effects at $T = 300$ K are reduced from those at $T = 0$ especially at low q values. This results from the increased kinetic energy of the electrons at high temperatures which renders them less susceptible to the influence of the Coulomb potential. Once the screened potential is known, the exciton problem may be addressed as discussed before.

In Figure 16.25 we show how the exciton binding energy changes as a function of carrier density for a 100 Å GaAs/Al$_{0.3}$Ga$_{0.7}$As quantum well structure. Also shown in Figure 16.25 is the exciton radius as a function of carrier density for the same structure. We can see that the exciton essentially "disappears" once the background carrier density approaches 2–3×10^{11}cm^{-2}. This is a fairly low density and can be easily injected at high speeds into a quantum well. Since the injected charge removes the exciton peak, the absorption coefficient can be modulated rapidly by this process. We note that in addition to the effect noted above, the injected carriers also renormalize the bandgap by shrinking the gap somewhat. At the carrier concentrations of $\sim 10^{11}$cm^{-2}, the screening effects are, however, more dominant. This phenomenon has been used in creating electronic devices which can modulate an optical signal by charge injection.

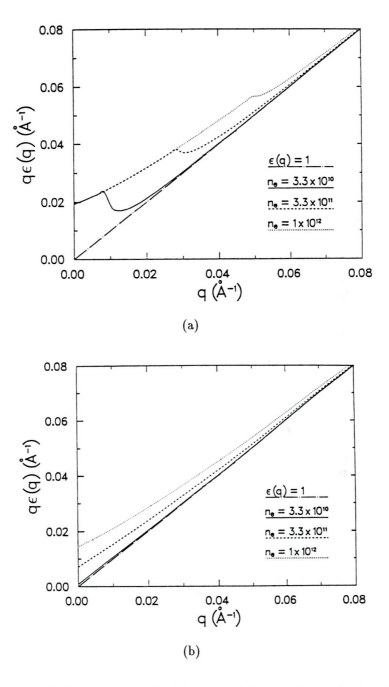

Figure 16.24: The denominator $q\epsilon(q)$ of the screened Coulomb interaction in a 100 Å GaAs/Al$_{0.3}$Ga$_{0.7}$As quantum well at (a) $T = 0$ and (b) $T = 300$ K; the case $\epsilon(q) = 1$ is plotted for reference, (from Loehr, 1991).

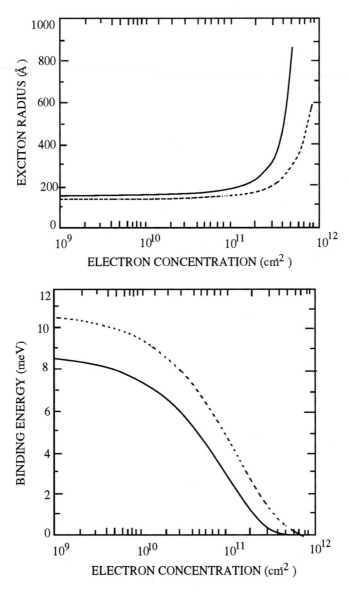

Figure 16.25: (a) Exciton radii a_{ex} in a 100 Å $GaAs/Al_{0.3}Ga_{0.7}As$ quantum well verses electron concentration n_e at $T = 300$ K. The solid curve is for the CB1-HH1 exciton, the dashed curve is for the CB1-LH1 exciton. (b) Also shown is the exciton binding energy as a function of the carrier concentration, (from Loehr, 1991).

Another area of intense research in exciton physics is the area of nonlinear effects. At low optical intensity, the optical constants of the material are essentially independent of the optical intensity. However, as the optical intensity is increased, excess carriers are generated and these carriers affect the optical constants causing them to be highly dependent upon the intensity. A number of devices have been proposed on the basis of such effects. In this text we will not attempt to describe the physics behind the optical nonlinearities. We will simply review a few cases.

When the optical intensity generates electron-hole pairs, the optical absorption is affected by phase space filling. In the case of the free electron-hole pairs, this effect is simply due to the band filling effects manifested in the product term $f^e(E) \cdot f^h(E)$ which we discussed when discussing the gain in a laser. While the free electron-hole pairs, which are Fermions, clearly obey the exclusion principle, the situation for the excitonic states, which are bound states, is not as clear. These composite particles are essentially bosons when their concentration is small, but obey Fermi statistics when their concentration is high. Thus, phase space filling effects occur in the case of excitons once the exciton density starts approaching $\sim 10^{12} \text{cm}-2$.

In addition to the phase space filling effects, the free electron-hole pairs, as well as excitons, cause the screening of the Coulombic interaction as discussed already and thus reduce the absorption coefficient. As discussed earlier, this causes the exciton wavefunction to increase in real space causing a decrease in the oscillator strength.

The effects of optical intensity on the absorption spectra are shown in Figure 16.26 where we show experimental results comparing the absorption spectra of an unexcited (i.e., low intensity) multiquantum well structure to the spectra after excitation by an ultrashort pump pulse at resonance with the heavy hole exciton. The zero time is measured from the time the peak power of the pulse hits the sample, so that the absorption is affected at negative times. While the decrease in the absorption is quite evident, there is a great deal of dynamical information in such experiments which the interested reader can find in the references presented at the end of this chapter.

16.8 REFRACTIVE INDEX MODULATION DUE TO EXCITON MODULATION

So far in this chapter we considered how the exciton transitions affect the absorption coefficient. We also addressed the issue of how the exciton absorption can be modulated. While this provides an excellent means to modulate an optical signal with energy at the exciton resonance, the signal is modulated by absorption. In many applications, the absorption of the optical signal is not desirable. Particular examples are the "directional coupler" and the Mach-Zender interferometer shown in Figure 16.27. In the directional coupler, for example, an optical beam is fed into a waveguide and is brought close to another waveguide which is close

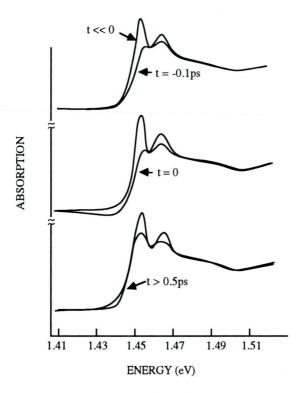

ENERGY (eV)

Figure 16.26: A comparison of the absorption spectra of an unexcited GaAs/AlGaAs multiquantum well structure with the spectra produced after being pulsed by a high intensity ultra short pulse at the HH exciton resonance. (Reproduced with permission, D. S. Chemla, *Nonlinear Optics: Materials and Devices*, Springer-Verlag, New York, 1986.)

enough that the evanescent wave can couple with the other guide. The picture is very similar to two coupled pendulums. The optical energy sloshes back and forth between the waveguides and can come out from the other end via either of the two guides depending upon the coupling coefficient, the distance traveled, and the variation in the refractive index of the two guides. For unit input into one guide, the crossover intensity (efficiency) into the second guide is given by

$$\eta = \frac{1}{1 + (\delta/\Delta K)^2} \, \sin^2 \left\{ CL \left[1 + (\delta/\Delta K)^2 \right]^{1/2} \right\} \qquad (16.65)$$

where

$$\delta = \frac{2\pi}{\lambda} \frac{(N_2 - N_1)}{2}$$

$$= \frac{\Delta K}{2}$$

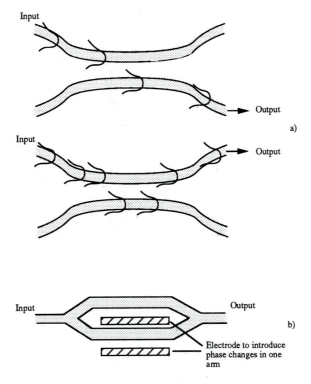

Figure 16.27: A schematic of optical devices which rely upon changes produced in refractive index and phase for switching optical signals. (a) A directional coupler; (b) the Mach-Zender interferometer.

$$
\begin{aligned}
L &= \text{length of interaction} \\
C &= \text{coupling coefficient per unit length} \\
K &= \text{wavevector of the radiation} \\
N_1, N_2 &= \text{indices of refraction in the interferometer arms.} \\
\Delta K &= \text{wavevector difference between two interferometer arms.}
\end{aligned}
$$

For identical waveguides ($\delta = 0$), the coupling efficiency is given by

$$\eta = \sin^2 CL. \tag{16.66}$$

Thus, a complete crossover takes place when

$$CL = \frac{n\pi}{2}; n \text{ is odd.} \tag{16.67}$$

The distance $\ell = (n\pi)/(2C)$ is called the transfer length. If somehow the refractive index in one or the other guides can be modulated, a mismatch in the refractive index can be induced and the optical beam can be allowed to go straight through if

$$CL \left[1 + \left(\frac{\delta}{K} \right)^2 \right]^{1/2} = \pi. \qquad (16.68)$$

Now if CL is chosen to be $\pi/2$, this allows the straight through state if

$$\delta = \sqrt{3}K. \qquad (16.69)$$

The change in $(N_2 - N_1)$ can be induced by using any of the modulation schemes discussed above, i.e., electric field, free carrier screening, or high intensity bleaching effects. Of course, the structure is useful if the modulating force is reasonable and can be applied in a simple manner.

In bulk semiconductors, the electro-optic effect described by the electric fields required to alter δ enough to cause switching are extremely high, making them unable to compete with materials like Lithium Niobate for waveguide switching. However, in quantum well structures, since the exciton peak is so strong and can be modulated easily, large changes in the refractive index can be produced. Additionally, since there are strong selection rules for TE and TM modes in quantum wells and, in particular, for strained quantum wells, one can exploit these for altering the polarization of the transmitted light. In quantum well structures, the electro-optic effect is essentially controlled by the Stark effect shift of the excitonic and band-to-band transitions. The effect has been studied by a number of workers and utilized for devices. To determine the effect of excitonic and band-to-band absorption on the refractive index we use the Kramers-Kronig transform yielding the result, (Weiner, et al., 1987).

$$n(\omega_0) - 1 = \frac{c}{\pi} P \int_0^\infty \frac{\alpha(\omega)\, d\omega}{\omega^2 - \omega_0^2}. \qquad (16.70)$$

It has been observed experimentally that the total area under the absorption curve (for energies slightly above the bandgap) remains constant with the application of electric field. This reflects the sum rules that hold for excitonic and band-to-band absorption: as the electric field breaks the reflection symmetry of the potential, the parity-allowed transitions have their absorption strengths decreased and the parity-forbidden transitions start increasing in strength causing the total area to remain approximately constant.

The effect of the strain has been studied assuming that the excitonic broadening to be a Lorentzian function with half-width Γ

$$\Delta(\omega - \omega') = \frac{\Gamma}{\pi \left[(\omega - \omega')^2 + \Gamma^2 \right]}. \qquad (16.71)$$

The Kramers-Kronig transform is then carried out by using the result

$$P \int_0^\infty d\omega \, \frac{\Delta(\omega - \omega')}{\omega^2 - \omega_0^2} = - \frac{ - \left[\omega_0^2 - \omega'^2 + \Gamma^2 \right] }{ \left[\omega_0^2 - \omega'^2 + \Gamma^2 \right]^2 - 4\omega_0^2 \omega'^2 } \qquad (16.72)$$

obtained by contour integration. A number of groups have examined the electro-optic effect including the effect of strain. One can see a strong quadratic effect corresponding to the quadratic Stark effect. The inclusion of strain separates the LH state making the effect stronger. It is to be noted that other modulation approaches such as free carrier screening and high optical intensity bleaching can also alter the refractive index in the same manner.

16.9   STRAIN INDUCED ELECTRIC FIELDS FOR ENHANCED OPTICAL MODULATION

In square quantum wells, the Stark effect is a quadratic effect and is consequently quite small at low electric fields. Thus, if the device is operated at higher electric fields, a larger change in the excitonic peak position would result for the same swing in the electric field. This idea has led to the conception and demonstration of optoelectronic devices which utilize strain to produce a built-in electric field in a quantum well. As shown in Figure 7.7 for (100) growth, the strain tensor is diagonal and there is no piezoelectric effect. However, for other orientations, the strain tensor is not diagonal and strong shear components are present which can be exploited to produce built-in electric fields. The general polarization developed due to strain is given by

$$P_i = \sum_{k,l} e_{ikl} \, \epsilon_{kl}. \tag{16.73}$$

It was shown by Nye (1957) that for zinc-blende structures, only one piezo-electric constant exists and in the reduced representation ($xx \rightarrow 1$; $yy \rightarrow 2$; $zz \rightarrow 3$; $yz \rightarrow 4$; $zx \rightarrow 5$; $xy \rightarrow 6$), e_{ikl} can be written as e_{im} ($m = 1$ to 6). The nonzero piezoelectric coefficients are: $e_{14} = e_{25} = e_{36}$.

Thus, only for shear strain does one have a finite polarization. For (111) growth of strained layers, one thus gets a strong dipole moment across a quantum well producing an electric field profile as shown in Figure 16.28 as was first pointed out by Smith (1986).

The electric field is given by the equation

$$F = \sqrt{3} \frac{e_{14} \epsilon_{xy}}{\epsilon} \tag{16.74}$$

where e_{14} is the piezoelectric coefficient (usually in the range of ~ 0.05 C/m^2), ϵ_{xy} is the off-diagonal strain component and ϵ is the dielectric constant of the semiconductor. A straightforward evaluation shows that a strain ϵ_{xy} of about 1% can easily produce an electric field of the range 10^5 V/cm. This strong built in electric field can have numerous applications ranging from optoelectronic modulators to electronic devices.

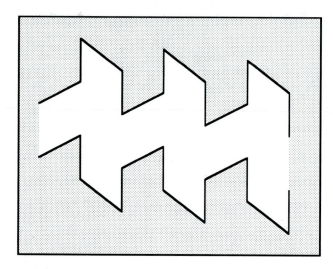

Figure 16.28: Electric field profile produced in a strained multiquantum well grown along the (111) direction.

16.10   RADIATIVE RECOMBINATION FROM EXCITONIC STATES

We end this chapter by discussing the seemingly simple but actually quite complex problem of the radiative exciton lifetime. In Chapter 15 we discussed the free electron-hole recombination time. In that case the concept of density of the electron-hole states which conserved momentum was quite clear and the problem was quite simple. In the case of the exciton, the problem is quite complex for the following reasons. When we examine the absorption coefficient of the exciton state, we notice that the absorption is due to a single exciton state (i.e., with $K_{ex} = 0$). In reality, this state is broadened, but nevertheless unlike the density of states available in the band-to-band (free e-h) transitions, in the case of the exciton a single state provides the high oscillator strength for the transition. This is because the exciton-oscillator strength is derived from *all* the independent electron states in the valence and conduction band as is clear from the exciton wavefunction. It is clear that if the exciton was to recombine in the ideal system (no broadening), the recombination rate would be extremely high (approaching infinity) just as the absorption coefficient in the unbroadened exciton transition would approach infinite at $\hbar\omega = E_{ex}$. However, in real structures, just as the absorption coefficient does not approach infinity, the recombination time also does not approach infinity. To obtain a realistic description of the absorption spectra or the emission rate one must introduce the linewidth of the exciton states and thus bring in the concept of exciton density of states. In the case of absorption this was rather simple as it merely involved writing the δ-function as a Gaussian or Lorentzian function. In the case of emission, this is somewhat more involved, and requires using concepts from the theory of disordered systems which is not as precise. One argues that the $K_{ex} = 0$ oscillator strength is now shared among different exciton states, each with a slightly different energy and with a coherence length in real space which is finite. In fact, the coherence length is related to the exciton linewidth σ since we have

$$\Delta x \Delta K \sim 1$$
$$\frac{\hbar^2 \Delta K^2}{2M} = \sigma \tag{16.75}$$

where Δx is the spatial coherence length, ΔK is momentum broadening for the exciton state, and $M = m_e + m_h$. The exciton recombination lifetime can now be written in the form

$$\frac{1}{\tau_{ex}} \approx \frac{1}{\tau_0} \frac{\Delta x^2}{A_{ex}} \tag{16.76}$$

where τ_0 is the band-to-band recombination time calculated in Chapter 15, and A_{ex} is the exciton area in the relative coordinates. Replacing Δx by its value in terms of the exciton linewidth we get

$$\tau_{ex} = \tau_0 \frac{2 A_{ex} M \sigma}{\hbar^2}. \tag{16.77}$$

The exciton linewidth is of the order of 3–4 meV in most quantum well structures at low temperature. The area A_{ex} is dependent upon the well size and as discussed in this chapter, decreasing with decreasing well size. For a fixed linewidth we expect the recombination time to increase with well size. This has, indeed, been observed.

In this chapter we have examined some of the physics in the excitonic phenomenon in bulk and quantum well structures. The enhanced excitonic binding energy and the modulation techniques that can be applied in quantum well structures have made this area of research very exciting. The physics of excitons in low-dimensional systems is by no means exhausted. In fact, exciton physics in quantum wires and quantum dots is at a very nascent stage at present. In these structures, the exciton effects are expected to be even stronger and more versatile than for the quantum well structures.

Before ending this chapter, we would just like to point out one feature of the excitonic transitions which often creates an enormous problem in design and control of exciton based devices. This is the temperature dependence of the excitonic resonance. The temperature dependence comes from the variation of the bandgap with temperature and as shown in Figure 16.29 is approximately -0.5 meV/K at room temperature. This variation is very strong and since the exciton peak is itself only a few meV at room temperature, the variation can cause serious problems in system design and tolerances. Clearly, careful temperature control is essential if exciton based devices are to make impact in optical computation.

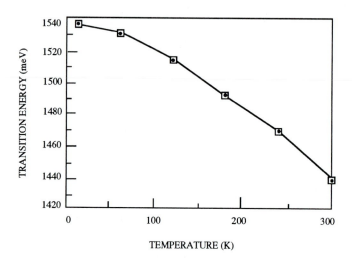

Figure 16.29: Variation of HH exciton resonance energy with temperature in a 100 Å GaAs/Al$_{0.3}$Ga$_{0.7}$As quantum well structure.

16.11   FOR THE TECHNOLOGIST IN YOU

Excitonic effects in semiconductors have long been recognized as important material characterization effects. The enhanced binding energy, higher oscillator strength, and ease of modulation of excitons in quantum well systems has added a device dimension to the excitonic phenomenon. Exciton based devices have provided a great deal of impetus to "optical computing" although some earlier predictions of immanent realization of such systems have been scaled back. While exciton based devices have had spectacular successes as individual devices, serious concerns remain.

In Table 16.1 we show a summary of some of the important physical phenomena based on excitonic effects in quantum wells, the devices that have been demonstrated using the given phenomenon, and some of the outstanding challenges facing this technology. It is important to note that monochromatic photons needed for excitonic devices are not conveniently or cheaply integrated into a system. Also, while photons can travel in free space without wires, it is not easy to focus or steer optical beams. Electrons, on the other hand, are produced relatively cheaply, and once a hardwired connection is made, there are no defocusing or misalignment problems. Excitonic devices also suffer from thermal problems, since each degree Kelvin shift in temperature shifts the exciton peak by $\sim$0.5 meV.

It must, of course, be realized that all new technology faces serious hurdles

Physical phenomenon based on excitons	Devices / circuits	Challenges
Nonlinear effects	Bistable devices, switches, gates	Need for high optical intensity; heating effects
Quantum confined Stark effect	Spatial light modulators; negative resistance based devices; logic circuits; oscillators	Thermal fluctuations; spatial nonuniformities across wafers; focusing and beam steering
Electro-optic effect	Directional couplers; switches	Need for higher electro-optic coefficient

Table 16.1: Excitonic effects and devices based on them.

and, given enough effort, seemingly insurmountable problems look simple after a few years. It appears that while an "all optical" information processing system is not likely in the near future, optoelectronics is finding niche areas in conjunction with standard electronics technology.

16.11.1 Some Device Related Issues

Excitonic Devices—Potentials and Pitfalls

In this chapter, we have studied the physics of excitonic phenomena, an area that has become extremely popular and promising since the advent of heterostructure technology. The ability to modulate the sharp excitonic resonances by electric field (QCSE) or by free carriers (electrons or holes or electron-hole pairs) or by phase space filling of excitons promises potentially exciting new devices. These devices which depend upon changing the near exciton resonance optical properties of an optical beam have been proposed and demonstrated for a variety of applications in optical computing. However, despite many spectacular demonstrations of the basic devices (some even reported in the Wall Street Journal!), the technology has not developed yet to a commercial level. Let us briefly examine some of the ideas behind the excitonic devices and also some of the pitfalls which have hindered the technology from blossoming.

One class of devices based upon excitonic modulation by electron-hole plasma or by excitonic phase space filling, depends upon the nonlinearity in the optical properties near the excitonic resonance. The absorption coefficient for example would then be dependent on the optical intensity. "All optical" devices can then be conceived where the state of an output beam can be 0 (the beam is absorbed) or 1 (the beam is transmitted) depending upon a control beam state. The response of such devices is usually in the subpicosecond domain and they are apparently quite attractive. In face, an array of logic operations have been demonstrated for such devices.

It is useful, however, to examine the optical intensity required for room temperature application of such devices. Typically, one needs an electron-hole carrier density of approximately 10^{12} cm^{-2} to "bleach" the excitonic resonance. This requires an electron-hole pair generation rate of

$$G \approx \frac{10^{12} \text{ cm}^{-2}}{10^{-9} \text{ s}}$$
$$= 10^{-21} \text{ cm}^{-2} \text{ s}^{-1}.$$

Assuming a 100 Å quantum well where the electron-hole pairs are generated and a 1% absorption of photons is incident vertically, one needs a photon flux of $\sim 10^{21}$ cm^{-2} s^{-1}. If the photon energy is ~ 1 eV, this translates to an optical power of ~ 10 kW cm^{-2}. While such power levels are not unreasonably high, they are currently difficult to obtain from semiconductor lasers in high speed operation.

The QCSE operates in the linear absorption regime and uses an applied electric field to modulate the excitonic properties. It appears to be one of the most promising approaches for optoelectronic intelligent devices. Since it allows one to couple optical and electronic effects, in principle it allows the best of optics and electronics. Typical logic devices utilize the negative resistance regions produced by the QCSE related photocurrent, as shown in Figure 16.30.

In the simple circuit, the p-i (MQW) -n diode is connected in series to a resistor and a power supply. The photocurrent–voltage characteristics have a negative resistance region, as shown. When light intensity is changed from I_1^{ph} (a low value) to I_2^{ph} (a high value), the voltage across the diode switches from V_H to V_L. Correspondingly, the diode switches from being transparent to being opaque. Numerous logic and microwave devices can be based on this simple concept. However, it is important to consider some difficulties associated with general excitonic devices, as well.

Two important concerns in excitonic devices are the temperature dependence of the excitonic peaks and the sensitivity of the excitonic absorption to the quality of the quantum wells. The excitonic peak, being related to the bandgap, shifts about 0.5 meV K^{-1}. Consider, as an example, an excitonic peak with a linewidth of 3 meV and a peak value of $\alpha_0 = 10^4$ cm-1. Let us say this is used in a modulator where the exciton peak is shifted 5 meV by an electric field. The ON/OFF ratio in a 1.0 μm modulator is ~ 2.34, assuming a Gaussian broadening. If the temperature shifts by ± 1°C, the ON/OFF ratio becomes 2.16 or 2.42. Thus, a 1°C change places an error of $\sim 6\%$ in the device output. If the temperature changes are greater, the system reliability will be completely lost. In contrast, electronic devices do not show such critical temperature dependence.

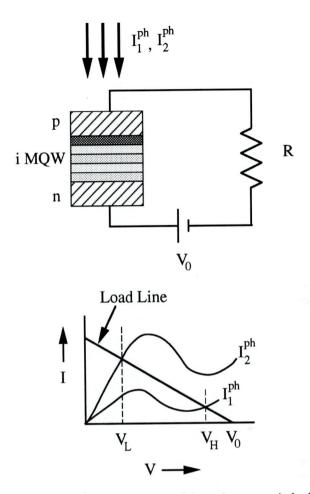

Figure 16.30: A schematic showing how optical intensity can switch the voltage (or transmittance) state of a *p-i-n* diode, using QCSE.

The excitonic linewidth has a similar devastating effect on excitonic devices. Since only one monolayer of interface fluctuations an cause ~ 2 meV broadening in the absorption peak, the control over the device fabrication has to be complete.

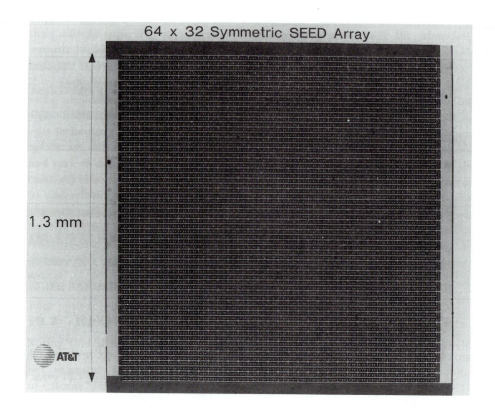

Figure 16.31: The SEED provides an elegant way to couple electronics and optics. Shown is a 64 × 32 SEED array. Such devices can be used as spatial light modulators, optical memories, and logic devices, (Courtesy of AT&T Bell Labs.)

16.12 PROBLEMS

16 1. Assume a simple parabolic density of states mass for the electrons and holes and calculate the exciton binding energies in GaAs, $In_{0.53}Ga_{0.47}As$ and InAs. What is the exciton Bohr radius in each case?

16 2. Assume a Gaussian exciton linewidth of 1 meV half-width at half maximum and plot the absorption coefficient due to the ground state exciton resonance in each of the three semiconductors of problem 1.

16 3. Assume a hydrogenic form of the ground state exciton function. Using the variational method (Appendix H) show that a 2-D exciton has four times the binding energy of the 3-D exciton. Also calculate the in-plane Bohr radius of the 2-D exciton.

16 4. Assume that the exciton radius a_{ex} scales roughly as inverse of the exciton binding energy. Using the in-plane dependence of the exciton envelope function as $\exp(-\rho/a_{ex})$, use the results of Figure 16.10 to plot the well size dependence of the exciton peak absorption strength of the heavy hole ground state exciton. Use a 4 meV (HWHM) Gaussian width. In general, the linewidth may increase with decreasing well size.

16 5. Using the results of the simple perturbation theory (Equation 16.56) calculate the electric field dependence of the HH exciton emission energy in a 100 Å GaAs quantum well. How does the position of the LH exciton (ground state) vary?

16.13 REFERENCES

- **General**

    - Bassani, F. and G. P. Parravicini, *Electronic States and Optical Transitions in Solids* (Pergamon Press, New York, 1975).

    - Dimmock, J. O., in *Semiconductors and Semimetals* (edited by R. K. Willardson and A. C. Beer, Academic Press, New York, 1967), vol. 3.

    - Elliott, R. J., in *Polarons and Excitons* (edited by C. G. Kuper and G. D. Whitfield, Plenum Press, Englewood Cliffs, 1963).

    - "Theory of Excitons," by Knox, R. S., *Solid State Physics* (Academic Press, New York, 1963), vol. Suppl. 5.

    - Onodera, Y. and Y. Toyozawa, J. Phys. Soc. Japan, **22**, 833 (1967).

    - Reynolds, D. C., C. W. Litton, E. B. Smith and K. K. Bajaj, Sol. St. Comm., **44**, 47 (1982).

    - Sturge, M. D., Phys. Rev., **127**, 768 (1962).

- **Excitons in Quantum Wells**

  – Bastard, G., E. E. Mendez, L. L. Chang and L. Esaki, Phys. Rev. B, **26**, 1974 (1982).

  – "Nonlinear Interactions and Excitonic Effects in Semiconductor Quantum Wells," by Chemla, D. S., in *Nonlinear Optics: Materials and Devices* (edited by C. Flytzanis and J. L. Oudar; Springer-Verlag, 1986).

  – Green, R. L. and K. K. Bajaj, J. Vac. Sci. Technol., **B1**, 391 (1983).

  – Loehr, J. P. and J. Singh, Phys. Rev. B, **42**, 7154 (1990).

  – Miller, R. C., D. A. Kleinman, W. A. Nordland and A. C. Gossard, Phys. Rev. B, **22**, 863 (1980).

  – Sanders, G. D. and Y. C. Chang, Phys. Rev. B, **31**, 6892 (1985).

- **Exciton Broadening Effects in Quantum Wells**

  – Lee, J., E. S. Koteles and M. O. Vassell, Phys. Rev. B, **32**, 5512 (1986).

  – Lifshitz, I. M., Adv. Phys., **13**, 483 (1969).

  – Singh, J. and K. K. Bajaj, Appl. Phys. Lett., **48**, 1077 (1986).

  – Weisbuch, C., R. Dingle, A. C. Gossard and W. Wiegmann, J. Vac. Sci. Technol., **17**, 1128 (1980).

- **Quantum Confined Stark Effect**

  – Dow, J. D. and D. Redfield, Phys. Rev. B, **1**, 3358 (1970).

  – Hong, S. and J. Singh, Superlattices and Microstructures, **3**, 645 (1987).

  – Mendez, E. E., G. Bastard, L. L. Chang and L. Esaki, Phys. Rev. B, **26**, 7101 (1982).

  – Miller, D. A. B., D. S. Chemla, T. C. Damen, A. C. Gossard, W. Wiegmann, T. H. Wood and C. A. Burrus, Phys. Rev. Lett., **53**, 2173 (1984).

  – Miller, D. A. B., J. S. Weiner and D. S. Chemla, IEEE J. Quant. Electron., **QE-22**, 1816 (1986).

  – Sanders, G. D. and K. K. Bajaj, Phys. Rev. B, **35**, 2308 (1987).

- **Exciton Quenching**

  – Flytzanis, C. and J. L. Oudar, editors, *Nonlinear Optics: Materials and Devices* (Springer-Verlag, New York, 1985).

  – Haug, H. and S. Schmitt-Rink, Prog. Quant. Electron., **9**, 3 (1984).

- Knox, W. H., R. F. Fork, M. C. Downer, D. A. B. Miller, D. S. Chemla and C. V. Shank, in *Ultrafast Phenomenon IV* (edited by D. H. Anston and K. B. Eisenthal, Springer-Verlag, 1984).

● **Electro-Optic Effect**

- Pamulapati, J., J. P. Loehr, J. Singh and P. K. Bhattacharya, J. Appl. Phys., **69**, 4071 (1991).
- Weiner, J. S., D. A. B. Miller, D. S. Chemla, T, C. Damen, C. A. Burrus, T. H. Wood, A. C. Gossard and W. Wiegmann, Appl. Phys. Lett., **47**, 1148 (1985).
- Zucker, J. E., T. L. Hendrickson and C. A. Burrus, Appl. Phys. Lett., **52**, 945 (1988).

● **Exciton Radiative Recombination**

- Feldmann, J., G. Peter, E. O. Gobal, P. Dawson, K. Moore, C. Foxon and R. J. Elliot, Phys. Rev. Lett., **59**, 2337 (1987).

CHAPTER 17

SEMICONDUCTORS IN MAGNETIC FIELDS

In this text we have addressed the problem of electrons in semiconductors and their response to external electric fields in great detail. These issues are, of course, crucial for understanding solid state electronics devices. The response of electrons in a semiconductor in a magnetic field, on the other hand, has at present little direct technological importance. Magnetic fields are difficult to produce and incorporate in current electronic chips which are based on semiconductors. Of course, magnetic memories are important components of many computational architectures, but these are based on magnetic materials which do not include semiconductors. Although magnetic field effects seem to have less technological significance, they provide a far richer insight into semiconductor physics than is possible by studying electrons in electric fields. Thus, magnetic fields have become crucial ingredients of characterization techniques used to evaluate the semiconductor physics. Techniques based on magneto- optics and magneto-transport have provided us with much of what we know about the symmetry of the electronic states in the Brillouin zone, carrier masses at bandedges, etc. The effects of magnetic field on both free Bloch states, and bound states such as impurity levels provide us with important physical insight. Effects like the quantum Hall effect have provided new details on the many- body interactions in sub-3-dimensional systems. Also, effects like the Aharonov-Bohm effect hold some promise of low power high speed switching devices.

It is difficult to discuss all the details of magnetic effects in semiconductors and its consequences. We will address some key problems in this area which are representative of several qualitatively different phenomenon. The general category of problems we will examine are sketched in Figure 17.1. It is important to realize that in many cases the physical phenomenon can qualitatively alter depending upon the strength of the magnetic field.

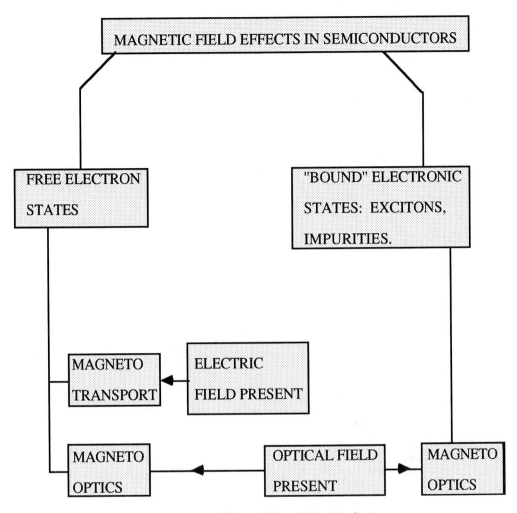

Figure 17.1: A schematic of the problems addressed in this chapter.

In Figure 17.1 we broadly differentiate between the "free" or Bloch states in semiconductors and the electron-hole coupled states like excitons or bound states. The magnetic field greatly alters the nature of the electronic states which then manifests itself in magneto-optic or magneto-transport phenomenon.

We will address the problem of electrons in the presence of a magnetic field in two steps. The first one is based on semi-classical ideas where the electron is treated as a point particle with the E vs. k relation given by the bandstructure. In this case the magnetic field is assumed to be small enough that the concept of the bandstructure, effective mass, velocity, etc., is retained. Such low fields are used in experiments such as the Hall effect. The other case we will examine becomes important as the magnetic field increases. In this case the free electron states are no longer the usual planewave-like states $(u_{nk}\exp(i\mathbf{k}\cdot\mathbf{r}))$, but are greatly modified. This results in new energy levels, different density of states, etc., and has important consequences on magneto-transport and magneto-optic phenomenon.

17.1   SEMICLASSICAL DYNAMICS OF ELECTRONS IN A MAGNETIC FIELD

In this approach we will assume that the underlying picture of the electronic bandstructure remains intact and the electrons are described by the $\mathbf{k}$-vector which is a good quantum number. The equation of motion is then

$$\frac{d\mathbf{k}}{dt} = \frac{\mathbf{F}_{\text{ext}}}{\hbar} \tag{17.1}$$

which becomes for a magnetic field force

$$\frac{d\mathbf{k}}{dt} = \frac{e}{c\hbar}\mathbf{v}\times\mathbf{B}. \tag{17.2}$$

We immediately see that the change in the $\mathbf{k}$-vector is normal to $\mathbf{B}$ and also normal to the velocity. The velocity itself is normal to the constant energy surface and is given by

$$\mathbf{v}_{\mathbf{k}} = \frac{1}{\hbar}\nabla_{\mathbf{k}}E(\mathbf{k}). \tag{17.3}$$

The magnetic field thus alters $\mathbf{k}$ along the intersection of the constant energy surface and the plane perpendicular to the magnetic field as shown in Figure 17.2. The constant energy surface can, of course, be quite simple as for the conduction band of direct semiconductors or quite complex as for the valence bands. If $\mathbf{k}$ is the (still 3-D) vector in this plane of intersection and $\boldsymbol{\rho}$ is the position of the electron, we have

$$\frac{d\mathbf{k}}{dt} = \frac{e}{c\hbar}\dot{\boldsymbol{\rho}}\times\mathbf{B} \tag{17.4}$$

where $\mathbf{v} = \dot{\boldsymbol{\rho}}$ has a component, $\dot{\boldsymbol{\rho}}_{\perp}$, perpendicular to $\mathbf{B}$ and a component, $\dot{\boldsymbol{\rho}}_{\parallel}$, parallel to $\mathbf{B}$. Equation 17.4 shows that $\dot{\mathbf{k}}$ has a component, $\dot{\mathbf{k}}_{\perp}$, perpendicular to $\mathbf{B}$, only, while $\dot{\mathbf{k}}_{\parallel} = 0$.

The value of $\boldsymbol{\rho}_{\perp}(t)$ can be simply derived by taking a cross product of both sides of Equation 17.4 with a unit vector $\hat{B}$ parallel to the magnetic field. This gives

$$\begin{aligned}
\hat{B}\times\dot{\mathbf{k}} &= \frac{eB}{c\hbar}\left[\dot{\boldsymbol{\rho}} - \hat{B}\left(\hat{B}\cdot\dot{\boldsymbol{\rho}}\right)\right] \\
&= \frac{eB}{c\hbar}\dot{\boldsymbol{\rho}}_{\perp}. \tag{17.5}
\end{aligned}$$

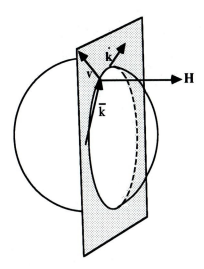

Figure 17.2: A schematic showing the orbit of an electron in a magnetic field. The electron moves on a constant energy surface in a plane perpendicular to the magnetic field.

Integrating we get

$$\boldsymbol{\rho}_\perp(t) = \frac{c\hbar}{eB} \boldsymbol{k}_\perp(t) + \pi/2 \text{ rotation.} \tag{17.6}$$

where the 90deg rotation is included since the cross product of a unit vector with a perpendicular vector simply gives the second vector rotated by 90deg. If the constant energy surface is spherical, as shown in Figure 17.2, then the value of $\boldsymbol{\rho}_\parallel(t)$ may be determined as well. Because no electric field is applied, the wavevector moves on a constant energy surface, where $\boldsymbol{\rho}_\parallel = \boldsymbol{v}_\parallel = 1/\hbar \hat{B} \cdot \nabla_{\boldsymbol{k}} E(\boldsymbol{k})$ is constant. Thus, by integration, $\boldsymbol{\rho}_\parallel(t) = \boldsymbol{v}_\parallel \cdot t + \boldsymbol{\rho}_\parallel(0)$. If the constant $\boldsymbol{v}_\parallel$ is nonzero, the electron moves in a helical trajectory under the application of a magnetic field.

Let us now consider the frequency of the electron around the constant energy surface. We examine two orbits in $\boldsymbol{k}$-space with energies E and $E + dE$ as shown in Figure 17.3. The $\boldsymbol{k}$-space separation of the orbits is

$$
\begin{aligned}
\delta k &= \frac{dE}{|\nabla_{\boldsymbol{k}} E|} \\
&= \frac{\delta E}{\hbar |\boldsymbol{v}_{\boldsymbol{k}}|} \\
&= \frac{\delta E}{\hbar \dot{\boldsymbol{\rho}}} .
\end{aligned}
\tag{17.7}
$$

The rate at which an electron moving along one of the orbits sweeps the

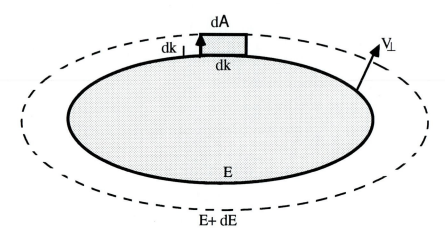

Figure 17.3: Two orbits of the electron at energies E and $E + dE$ in the magnetic field.

annulus area is given by

$$
\begin{aligned}
\frac{dk}{dt}\delta k &= \frac{e}{c\hbar^2}|\dot{\boldsymbol{\rho}} \times \boldsymbol{B}|\frac{\delta E}{|\dot{\boldsymbol{\rho}}|} \\
&= \frac{eB}{c\hbar^2}\frac{\delta E}{\ }.
\end{aligned}
\tag{17.8}
$$

This rate is constant for constant δE and if we define by T, the time period of the orbit

$$
\begin{aligned}
\delta S &= T \times \frac{eB}{c\hbar^2}\delta E \\
&= \text{area of the annulus} \\
&= \frac{dS}{dE} \cdot \delta E
\end{aligned}
\tag{17.9}
$$

where S is the area in k-space of the orbit of the electron with energy E. Thus

$$
T = \frac{c\hbar^2}{eB}\frac{dS}{dE}.
\tag{17.10}
$$

We can now define a cyclotron resonance frequency

$$
\begin{aligned}
\omega_c &= \frac{2\pi}{T} \\
&= \frac{2\pi eB}{c\hbar^2}\frac{1}{dS/dE} \\
&= \frac{eB}{m_c c}
\end{aligned}
\tag{17.11}
$$

where we have introduced the cyclotron resonance mass m_c as

$$m_c = \frac{\hbar^2}{2\pi} \frac{dS}{dE}.$$ (17.12)

The cyclotron resonance mass is a property of the entire orbit and is not the same as the effective mass in general. For a parabolic band we have

$$E = \frac{\hbar^2 k^2}{2m^*}$$ (17.13)

or

$$
\begin{aligned}
S &= \pi k^2 \\
&= \frac{2m^* \pi E}{\hbar^2}
\end{aligned}
$$ (17.14)

and

$$\frac{dS}{dE} = \frac{2m^* \pi}{\hbar^2}.$$ (17.15)

This gives

$$m_c = m^*.$$ (17.16)

For a more complex band this relation will be appropriately modified. For example, the conduction band of indirect gap materials, such as Ge and Si can be represented by an ellipsoidal constant energy surface

$$E(\boldsymbol{k}) = \hbar^2 \left(\frac{k_x^2 + k_y^2}{2m_t} + \frac{k_z^2}{2m_\ell} \right)$$ (17.17)

where m_t is the transverse mass and m_ℓ is the longitudinal mass. The velocity components are now

$$
\begin{aligned}
v_x &= \frac{\hbar k_x}{m_t} \\
v_y &= \frac{\hbar k_y}{m_t} \\
v_z &= \frac{\hbar k_z}{m_\ell}.
\end{aligned}
$$ (17.18)

If we assume that the magnetic field lies in the equatorial plane of the spheroid and is parallel to the k_x axis, we get from the equation of motion

$$\hbar \frac{dk_x}{dt} = 0$$ (17.19)

$$
\begin{aligned}
\hbar \frac{dk_y}{dt} &= \frac{eB}{c} v_z \\
&= \frac{\hbar e B}{m_\ell c} k_z
\end{aligned}
$$

or

$$\frac{dk_y}{dt} = \omega_\ell k_z, \text{ with } \omega_\ell = \frac{eB}{m_\ell c}. \tag{17.20}$$

Also,

$$\hbar \frac{dk_z}{dt} = -\frac{eB}{c} v_y$$
$$= -\hbar \frac{eB}{m_t c} k_y$$

or

$$\frac{dk_z}{dt} = -\omega_t k_y, \text{ with } \omega_t = \frac{eB}{m_t c} \tag{17.21}$$

If we differentiate Equation 17.20 with respect to time we get

$$\frac{d^2 k_y}{dt^2} = \omega_\ell \frac{dk_z}{dt}. \tag{17.22}$$

Substituting for dk_z/dt from Equation 17.21, we get

$$\frac{d^2 k_y}{dt^2} + \omega_\ell \omega_t k_y = 0 \tag{17.23}$$

which is the equation of motion of a harmonic oscillator with frequency

$$\omega_0 = (\omega_\ell \omega_t)^{1/2}$$
$$= \frac{eB}{(m_\ell m_t)^{1/2} c}. \tag{17.24}$$

It can be shown also that if $\boldsymbol{B}$ is parallel to k_z, then the frequency is simply

$$\omega_0 = \omega_t$$
$$= \frac{eB}{m_t c}. \tag{17.25}$$

In general, if the magnetic field makes an angle θ with respect to the k_z direction we have for the cyclotron mass

$$\left(\frac{1}{m_c}\right)^2 = \frac{\cos^2 \theta}{m_t^2} + \frac{\sin^2 \theta}{m_t m_\ell}. \tag{17.26}$$

Thus, by altering the magnetic field direction, one can probe various combinations of m_ℓ and m_t. In the cyclotron resonance experiment to be described later, the cyclotron frequency can be measured directly, thus allowing measuring of the carrier masses. Results of such measurements for Ge electrons and holes are shown in Figure 17.4. One can now see how powerful this technique is since it allows us to probe the detailed band curvature along various bands.

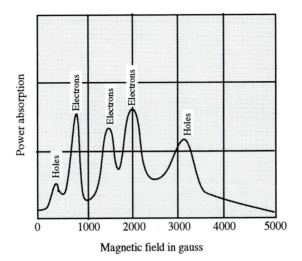

Figure 17.4: Results of cyclotron resonance absorption in germanium at 4 K, near 24 GHz. The static magnetic field is in a (110) plane at 60° from a (100) axis. Both electrons and holes are produced by illumination. The peaks correspond to the cyclotron frequency coinciding with 24 GHz. (Reproduced with permission, C. Kittel, *Introduction to Solid State Physics*, 4th ed., John Wiley and Sons, New York, 1971.)

17.2 SEMICLASSICAL THEORY OF MAGNETOTRANSPORT

The approach discussed in the previous section to describe electrons in magnetic fields is valid when the Fermi surface is not itself strongly affected by magnetic field. It is often useful in describing the important characterization experiment of the Hall effect. We discussed the transport equation in presence of magnetic and electric fields in Chapter 10. Once again in this theory we assumed that the Fermi surface was not affected by the magnetic field. We will not repeat that analysis again in this chapter. It is important to point out that the semiclassical treatment is widely used to understand the Hall effect which is one of the most important characterization techniques for semiconductors. In particular, we showed that the Hall mobility μ_H measured in presence of the magnetic field is related to the conductivity mobility μ by the following relation

$$\mu_H = r_H \mu \tag{17.27}$$

where r_H is the Hall factor and is given by

$$r_H = \frac{\langle\langle \tau^2 \rangle\rangle}{\langle\langle \tau \rangle\rangle^2} \tag{17.28}$$

where

$$\langle\langle \tau \rangle\rangle = \frac{\langle E\tau \rangle}{\langle E \rangle} \tag{17.29}$$

and τ is the scattering time for various scattering processes. In particular, if it is possible to represent the energy dependence of τ by

$$\tau = \tau_0 \left(\frac{E}{k_B T} \right)^s \tag{17.30}$$

then, for a Maxwellian distribution, we have

$$r_H = \frac{\Gamma(2s + 5/2)\Gamma(5/2)}{[\Gamma(s + 5/2)]^2} \tag{17.31}$$

where Γ is the Gamma function defined in Chapter 10. The conductivity tensor which relates the current to the applied field

$$J_i = \sigma_{ij}(\boldsymbol{B})E_j \tag{17.32}$$

is given by

$$\sigma(\boldsymbol{B}) = \sigma_0 \begin{bmatrix} 1 & -\mu_H B_3 & \mu_H B_2 \\ \mu_H B_3 & 1 & -\mu_H B_1 \\ -\mu_H B_2 & \mu_H B_1 & 1 \end{bmatrix} \tag{17.33}$$

where σ_0 is the conductivity in absence of the magnetic field.

The magnetotransport problem becomes quite a bit more complicated when the magnetic fields are strong and the Fermi surface starts to be seriously modified. This occurs when $\hbar\omega_c \geq k_B T$ and one needs to examine the electronic states by solving the Schrödinger equation in presence of the magnetic field. However, a simple model for the magneto-transport can be developed for high fields.

17.3 QUANTUM MECHANICAL APPROACH TO ELECTRONS IN A MAGNETIC FIELD

We will now address the problem of electrons in a magnetic field by including the magnetic field energy in the Schrödinger equation. We will use the effective mass equation to absorb the effect of the background crystal potential. This approach was outlined in Chapter 9 when we addressed the problem of shallow impurities. The approach is, of course, general and allows us to use the operator equivalence

$$-\frac{\hbar^2}{2m}\nabla^2 + V(r) \Rightarrow -\frac{\hbar^2}{2m^*}\nabla^2 \tag{17.34}$$

provided there are no interband couplings. Here m^* is the effective mass of a particular band. The general Hamiltonian for the electrons is

$$H = \frac{1}{2m}\left(\boldsymbol{p} - \frac{e}{c}\boldsymbol{A}\right)^2 + V_c(r). \tag{17.35}$$

This equation is now written as an effective mass equation for a band with effective mass m^* (assumed isotropic and parabolic for simplicity). The resulting equation is

$$\frac{1}{2m^*}\left(\frac{\hbar}{i}\nabla - \frac{e}{c}\boldsymbol{A}\right)^2 \psi = E\psi \tag{17.36}$$

where $\psi(\mathbf{r})$ is now to be considered the envelope function which, when multiplied by the zone edge function of the band, gives the full wavefunction. For example, as we have discussed several times, the zone edge function of the conduction band state in the direct gap materials is an s-type state. It is important to appreciate how we have simplified Equation 17.35 versus how we treated the similar equation involving the electromagnetic interaction with electrons in the semiconductor. In that problem which led to the photon absorption, we did not apply the effective mass equation to the operator

$$\frac{1}{2m^*}\left(\frac{\hbar}{i}\nabla - \frac{e}{c}\mathbf{A}\right)^2 + V_c(\mathbf{r})$$

directly since the electromagnetic field does couple various bands. The effective mass approach was only applied to the operator

$$-\frac{\hbar^2}{2m}\nabla^2 + V_c(\mathbf{r}) \left(= \frac{-\hbar^2}{2m^*}\nabla^2\right). \tag{17.37}$$

We also note that the interaction of the spin of the electron with the magnetic field is ignored at present. This interaction is $g\mu_B\boldsymbol{\sigma}\cdot\mathbf{B}$ where $\boldsymbol{\sigma}$ is the spin operator, $\mu_B = e\hbar/(2mc)$ is the Bohr magneton and the g-factor is related to the details of the state ($g = 2$ for free electrons). This interaction is just added on to our solutions and will be discussed later.

We write the vector potential in the gauge

$$\mathbf{A} = (0, Bx, 0) \tag{17.38}$$

which gives a magnetic field in the z-direction

$$B = B\hat{z} \tag{17.39}$$

The equation to be solved is

$$\frac{\partial^2\psi}{\partial x^2} + \left(\frac{\partial}{\partial y} - \frac{ieBx}{\hbar c}\right)^2\psi + \frac{\partial^2\psi}{\partial z^2} + \frac{2m^*}{\hbar^2}E\psi = 0 \tag{17.40}$$

where all energies are to be measured from the bandedges. Since our Hamiltonian does not involve y or z explicitly, the wavefunction can be written as

$$\psi(x, y, z) = \exp\{i(\beta y + k_z z)\}u(x). \tag{17.41}$$

Denoting by

$$E' = E - \frac{\hbar^2}{2m^*}k_z^2 \tag{17.42}$$

we get the equation for $u(x)$ as

$$\frac{\partial^2 u}{\partial x^2} + \left\{\frac{2m^*}{\hbar^2}E' - \left(\beta - \frac{eB}{\hbar c}x\right)^2\right\}u = 0. \tag{17.43}$$

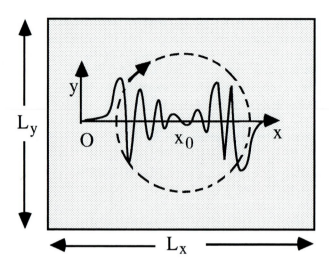

Figure 17.5: Solution of the Schrödinger equation in a magnetic field. The electron function along, say, x-axis is that of a harmonic oscillator centered around a point x_0.

We note that as in classical approach, the motion of the electron along the magnetic field is unaffected. The motion in the x-y plane is given by the Harmonic oscillator like equation

$$-\frac{\hbar^2}{2m^*}\frac{\partial^2 u(x)}{\partial x^2} + \frac{1}{2}m^*\left(\frac{eB}{m^*c}x - \frac{\hbar\beta}{m^*}\right)^2 u(x) = E^{'} u(x). \qquad (17.44)$$

This is the 1-dimensional Harmonic oscillator equation with a frequency eB/m^*c and centered around the point

$$x_0 = \frac{1}{\omega_c}\frac{\hbar\beta}{m^*}. \qquad (17.45)$$

The solution of this problem is

$$E^{'} = \left(n + \frac{1}{2}\right)\hbar\omega_c \qquad (17.46)$$

and the total energy is

$$E = \left(n + \frac{1}{2}\right)\hbar\omega_c + \frac{\hbar^2}{2m^*}k_z^2. \qquad (17.47)$$

The electron energy is quantized in the x-y plane and has the additional translational energy along the magnetic field. The schematic form of the wavefunction is shown in Figure 17.5.

Since the contributions to the energy from the x-y plane motion is so drastically affected, it is important to understand what happens to the density of states of the system. Consider a box of sides L_x, L_y, L_z. From the form of the wavefunction given by Equation 17.41, it is clear that both k_z and β are quantized in units of $2\pi/L_z$ and $2\pi/L_y$ respectively. However, the energy of the electron has no β dependence so that all allowed β values give rise to the same energy state (for constant k_z value). However, the values of β is not infinite. Note that the wavefunction is centered around the point (see Figure 17.5)

$$x_0 = \frac{1}{\omega_c} \frac{\hbar\beta}{m^*}. \tag{17.48}$$

The center x_0 must, of course, remain inside the dimensions of one system, i.e.

$$0 \le x_0 \le L_x. \tag{17.49}$$

Thus, the number of allowed values for β are

$$p = \frac{\beta_{max}}{(2\pi/L_y)} \tag{17.50}$$

where from Equations 17.48 and 17.49

$$\beta_{max} = \frac{\omega_c L_x m^*}{\hbar}. \tag{17.51}$$

Thus, the degeneracy of a level is

$$p = \frac{m^* \omega_c L_x L_y}{2\pi\hbar}. \tag{17.52}$$

One way to physically represent the effect of magnetic field is to use the schematic view in Figure 17.6. Focusing only on the k_x-k_y plane, in absence of the magnetic field, the k_x, k_y points are good quantum numbers and the various points in Figure 17.6a represent the allowed states. In presence of the magnetic field, various k_x, k_y points condense into points on circles which represent constant energy surfaces with energies $\hbar\omega_c/2$, $3\hbar\omega_c/2$, etc. This rearrangement of states does not, of course, alter the total number of states in a macroscopic volume. This can be understood by examining the number of states in the presence of the magnetic field per unit area. This number is

$$
\begin{aligned}
\frac{\partial N}{\partial E} &= \frac{p}{\hbar\omega_c} \\
&= \frac{L_x L_y}{2\pi} \frac{m^* \omega_c}{\hbar^2 \omega_c} \\
&= L_x L_y \frac{m}{2\pi\hbar^2}.
\end{aligned}
\tag{17.53}
$$

This is the same as the 2-dimensional density of states in the x- y plane. Thus, on the macroscopic energy scale the density of states is unaffected.

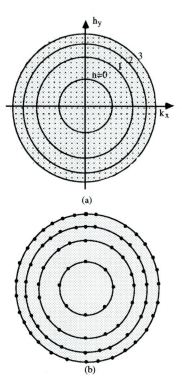

(a)

(b)

Figure 17.6: Quantization scheme for free electrons: (a) without magnetic field; (b) in a magnetic field.

The levels that are produced for a given value of the integer n are called Landau levels. The density of states of the 3-dimensional system is essentially given by the one-dimensional density of states derived in Chapter 1, weighted by the degeneracy factor p. Since k_z is still a good quantum number, the E vs. k_z given the bandstructure and the density of states. The various Landau levels are shown in Figure 17.7. In the 1-dimensional k_z space the density of states is (for a particular Landau level with energy E_n)

$$N_{1D}(E) = \frac{\sqrt{m^*}(E - E_n)^{-1/2}}{\sqrt{2}\hbar} \qquad (17.54)$$

with the total density given by multiplying this by p and running the contribution from all Landau levels with starting energies less than E,

$$N(E) = \frac{1}{4\pi^2}\left(\frac{2m^*}{\hbar^2}\right)^{3/2}\hbar\omega_c \sum_n \left[E - \left(n + \frac{1}{2}\right)\hbar\omega_c\right]^{-1/2} \qquad (17.55)$$

The density of states is shown in Figure 17.8 where we see the van Hove singularities arising from the quantization of the states. This change of the density of

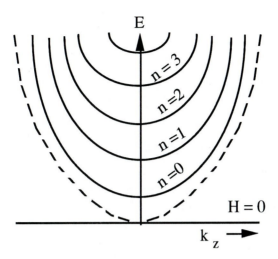

Figure 17.7: Effect of magnetic field on the bandstructure of a semiconductor. Only k_z is a good quantum number. The magnetic field produces quantization in the x-y plane leading to Landau levels. The dashed curve is for zero field.

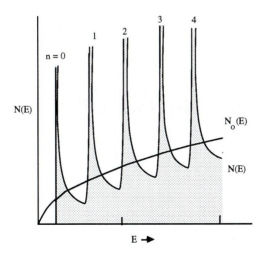

Figure 17.8: Density of states in a 3-D system in presence of a magnetic field. The density of states develops singularities due to quantization in the plane perpendicular to the magnetic field. Also shown is the zero field density of states for comparison.

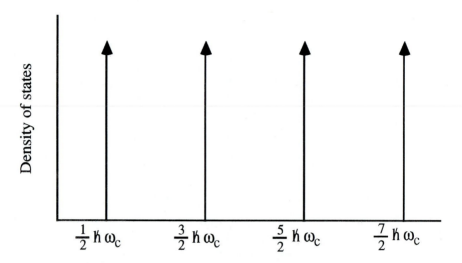

Figure 17.9: Density of states in an ideal 2-dimensional system in presence of a magnetic field.

states due to the formation of Landau levels has important effects on the physical properties of the system. As the magnetic field is altered, the separation of the Landau level changes and the Fermi level (for a fixed carrier concentration) passes through these sharp structures in the density of states. This leads to very interesting effects as will be discussed later.

The treatment discussed above for 3-dimensional systems can be easily extended to the 2-dimensional system where the effects of the magnetic field become even more interesting. If we consider the magnetic field along the z-axis or the growth (confining) axis, then k_z is not a good quantum number so that not only are the x-y energies quantized, but so are the z energies. This leads to the remarkable result that the density of states becomes a series of δ-functions as shown in Figure 17.9. The discrete energy levels are now given by

$$E_{n\ell} = E_n + \left(\ell + \frac{1}{2}\right)\frac{\hbar e B_\perp}{m_\parallel} + \frac{e B_\parallel^2}{2 m_\parallel c^2}\left[(\bar{z})^2 - (\overline{z^2})\right]. \tag{17.56}$$

Here the last term represents the diamagnetic effect of the parallel (in-plane) magnetic field which arises from first order perturbation theory using the perturbation Hamiltonian, (see Equation 15.82).

$$B' = \frac{e^2 A^2}{2mc^2}. \tag{17.57}$$

In Equation 17.56, the E_n represent the subband level energies arising from the quantization of the energy levels due to the confining potentials. Most experiments in 2-D systems are carried out with $B_\parallel = 0$.

The presence of δ-function like density of states which is broadened in real systems has some very profound effects on physical phenomenon in 2-dimensional systems. The most well-known and Nobel prize winning effect is the quantum Hall effect. Another widely used characterization test in the Shubnikov-de Haas effect which allows one to obtain carrier masses.

Before discussing some of these effects which are controlled by the changes in the electron density of states, we will introduce another important effect of magnetic field not on the energy levels, but on the wavefunction.

17.4   THE AHARONOV-BOHM EFFECT

Let us consider the effect of the magnetic field on the wavefunction of an electron. One of the reasons we wish to do so is that while most electronic devices at present depend upon the electron density (i.e., $|\psi|^2$), it is conceivable that devices based on quantum interference of electrons would depend upon the phase of the electron wavefunction. If this phase can be altered by a magnetic field one can have a switching device, in principle.

Let us consider the Schrödinger equation for an electron in presence of an electromagnetic potential described by the vector potential $\boldsymbol{A}$ and scalar potential ϕ

$$\frac{1}{2m}\left(-i\hbar\nabla - \frac{e}{c}\boldsymbol{A}\right)^2 \psi + V\psi = E\psi \tag{17.58}$$

where $V = e\phi$. We assume that $\boldsymbol{A}$ and ϕ are time independent. In a region where the magnetic field is zero we can write the solution of the problem in the form

$$\psi(x) = \psi^0(x)\exp\left[\frac{ie}{\hbar c}\int^{S(x)}\boldsymbol{A}(x')\cdot ds'\right] \tag{17.59}$$

where $\psi^0(x)$ satisfies the Schrödinger equation with the same value of ϕ but with $\boldsymbol{A}(x) = 0$. The line integral in Equation 17.59 can be along any path as long as the end point $S(x)$ is the point x and $(\nabla \times \boldsymbol{A})$ is zero along the integral. Notice that this is essentially equivalent to making the change

$$\boldsymbol{k} \rightarrow \boldsymbol{k} - \frac{e}{c\hbar}\boldsymbol{A} \tag{17.60}$$

in the usual free electron wavefunction $\exp(i\boldsymbol{k}\cdot\boldsymbol{r})$.

To prove that Equation 17.59 satisfies the Schrödinger equation we use this solution and evaluate

$$\left(-i\hbar\nabla - \frac{e}{c}\boldsymbol{A}\right)\psi = \exp\left[\frac{ie}{\hbar c}\int^{S(x)}\boldsymbol{A}(x')\cdot ds'\right]\left[\left(-i\hbar\nabla - \frac{e}{c}\boldsymbol{A}(x)\right)\psi^0\right.$$

$$\left. + \psi^0(-i\hbar)\left(\frac{ie}{\hbar c}\boldsymbol{A}(x)\right)\right]$$

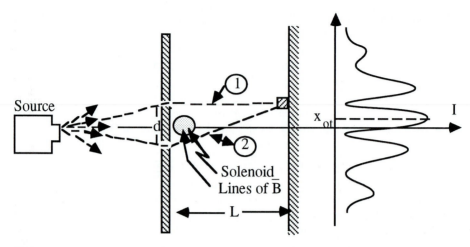

Figure 17.10: A magnetic field can influence the motion of electrons even though it exists only in regions where there is an arbitrarily small probability of finding the electrons. The interference pattern of the electrons can be shifted by altering the magnetic field.

$$= \exp\left[\frac{ie}{\hbar c}\int^{S(x)} \boldsymbol{A}(\boldsymbol{x}')\cdot d\boldsymbol{s}'\right]\left(-i\hbar\nabla\psi^0\right). \tag{17.61}$$

Similarly

$$\left(-i\hbar\nabla - \frac{e}{c}\boldsymbol{A}(\boldsymbol{x})\right)^2\psi = \exp\left[\frac{ie}{\hbar c}\int^{S(x)} \boldsymbol{A}(\boldsymbol{x}')\cdot d\boldsymbol{s}'\right]\left(-\hbar^2\nabla^2\psi^0\right). \tag{17.62}$$

Thus, $\psi(x)$ satisfies the Schrödinger equation with $\boldsymbol{A} \neq 0$ if $\psi^0(x)$ satisfies the Schrödinger equation with $\boldsymbol{A} = 0$, but with same $V(\boldsymbol{x})$.

Let us now consider the problem described by Figure 17.10. Here a beam of coherent electrons is separated into two parts and made to recombine at an interference region. This is the double slit experiment discussed in Chapter 14, except now we have a region of magnetic field enclosed by the electron paths as shown. The wavefunction of the electrons at the point where the two beams interfere is given by (we assume that phase coherence is maintained)

$$\begin{aligned}
\psi(\boldsymbol{x}) &= \psi_1^0 \exp\left[\frac{ie}{\hbar c}\int_{\text{path 1}}^{S(x)} \boldsymbol{A}(\boldsymbol{x}')\cdot d\boldsymbol{s}'\right] \\
&+ \psi_2^0 \exp\left[\frac{ie}{\hbar c}\int_{\text{path 2}}^{S(x)} \boldsymbol{A}(\boldsymbol{x}')\cdot d\boldsymbol{s}'\right].
\end{aligned} \tag{17.63}$$

The intensity or the electron density is given by

$$I(\boldsymbol{x}) = \{\psi_1(\boldsymbol{x}) + \psi_2(\boldsymbol{x})\}\{\psi_1(\boldsymbol{x}) + \psi_2(\boldsymbol{x})\}^*. \tag{17.64}$$

If we assume that $\psi_1^0 = \psi_2^0$, i.e. the initial electron beam has been divided equally along the two paths, the intensity produced after interference is

$$
\begin{aligned}
I(x) \quad &\propto \quad \cos\left[\frac{e}{\hbar c} \oint \boldsymbol{A} \cdot d\boldsymbol{s}\right] \\
&= \quad \cos\left[\frac{e}{\hbar c} \int_{\text{area}} \boldsymbol{B} \cdot \boldsymbol{n} \, da\right] \\
&= \quad \cos\frac{e\phi}{\hbar c} \quad\quad\quad\quad\quad (17.65)
\end{aligned}
$$

where we have converted the line integral over the path enclosed by the electrons to a surface integral and used $\boldsymbol{B} = \nabla \times \boldsymbol{A}$. The quantity ϕ is the magnetic flux enclosed by the two electron paths. It is interesting to note that even though the electrons never pass through the $\boldsymbol{B} \neq 0$ region, they are still influenced by the magnetic field. From Equation 17.65 it is clear that if the magnetic field is changed, the electron density will undergo modulation. This phenomenon has been observed in semiconductor structures as well as metallic structures.

For completeness, it is illustrative to examine the implications of our results in a superconductor. In superconductors, the electrons find it energetically favorable to form pairs mediated by the electron-lattice interactions. These pairs, called Cooper pairs, do not suffer collisions because of the existence of an energy gap between their energy and the energies of state where they could scatter into. We use $2e$ instead of e to describe the wavefunction of the Cooper pairs

$$
\psi(x) = \psi^0 \exp\left[\frac{2ie}{\hbar c} \int^{S(x)} \boldsymbol{A}(x') \cdot d\boldsymbol{s}'\right]. \quad\quad\quad\quad (17.66)
$$

If we consider a superconducting ring as shown in Figure 17.11 enclosing a magnetic field region, the fact that the electron wavefunction should not be multivalued if we go around the ring gives us the condition

$$
\frac{2e}{\hbar c} \oint \boldsymbol{A} \cdot d\boldsymbol{s} = 2n\pi \qu\quad\quad\quad\quad\quad (17.67)
$$

or

$$
\frac{2e\phi}{\hbar c} = 2n\pi. \qu\quad\quad\quad\quad\quad (17.68)
$$

The flux enclosed by the superconducting ring is thus quantized

$$
\phi = \frac{n\pi\hbar c}{e}. \qu\quad\quad\quad\quad\quad (17.69)
$$

This effect was used to confirm that the current in superconductors is carried by a pair of electrons rather than individual electrons.

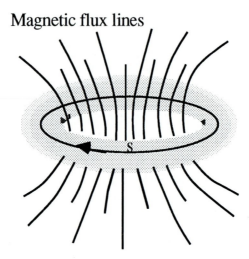

Figure 17.11: Measurements of Aharonov-Bohm effects in semiconductor structures. The variation of the device properties with magnetic field could be used in principle to serve for a low power switching device.

17.5   THE DE HAAS-VAN ALPHEN EFFECT

The changes in density of states of the electronic system in presence of magnetic fields has some very important manifestations. One important manifestation is the de Haas-van Alphen effect in which the magnetization of the electronic system shows oscillations when examined as a function of $1/B$. These oscillations can provide important information on carrier properties. The underlying reasons for these oscillations also provide the basis for understanding two other effects: the Shubnikov-de Haas effect and the quantum Hall effect, although the latter is considerably more complex due to many-body interactions.

In order that the modifications in the density of states affect physical phenomena, we must have the condition $\hbar\omega_c > k_B T$. For example, if this condition is to be satisfied for an electron effective mass of $0.1m_0$ at 12 K, one would need a magnetic field of 10^5 Gauss or 10 Tesla. Since such fields are almost at the limiting end of magnetic fields available, one has to work at liquid He temperatures.

In Figure 17.12 we show the E vs k_z relations of the Landau levels in a 3-D system. Let us focus on a slab δk_z about the momentum value k_z (shaded area). At $T = 0$, all the states below E_F are occupied and all states above it are empty. The number of electronic states in the slab in a particular Landau level are

$$\begin{aligned}
\delta N &= L_x L_y L_z \frac{e\,\delta k_z}{4\pi^2 c\hbar} B \\
&= V\xi B
\end{aligned} \tag{17.70}$$

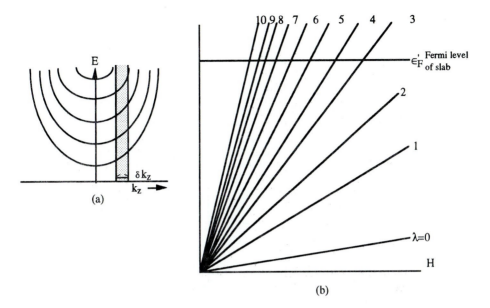

Figure 17.12: (a) The E vs. k_z relations in presence of a magnetic field. We focus on a slab of width δk_z. (b) The spectrum of the Landau levels as a function of B. As the field increases, states of lower and lower λ, pass through the Fermi level $E_{F'}$.

from Equation 17.52 using the fact that there are $L_z\, \delta k_z/(2\pi)$ states along the k_z space. Here we have defined ξ as the degeneracy per unit magnetic field per unit volume. We can include a factor of 2 per spin. At $T = 0$, all levels λ in the δk_z slice will be filled for which (see Figure 17.12)

$$\left(\lambda + \frac{1}{2}\right)\hbar\omega_c \;<\; E_F - \frac{\hbar^2}{2m}k_z^2$$
$$= \; E_F'. \tag{17.71}$$

If the highest occupied level is λ', the total number of electrons in the δk_z slice are

$$n = (\lambda' + 1)\xi B. \tag{17.72}$$

Remember that $\lambda = 0$ is a filled state. As B is increased, this number increases till abruptly the Landau level λ' crosses E_F'. An infinitesimal change then spills out the electrons in the λ' level into other levels in different δk_z slabs. This sudden spillover occurs when

$$\left(\lambda' + \frac{1}{2}\right) \;=\; \frac{E_F'}{\hbar\omega_c}$$
$$= \; \frac{mcE_F'}{\hbar eB}. \tag{17.73}$$

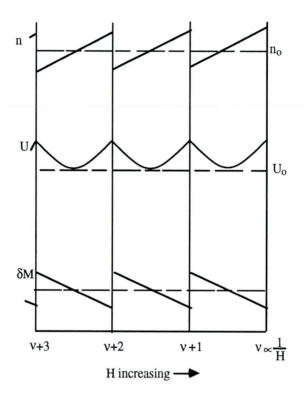

Figure 17.13: Variation of population n, energy U, and magnetic moment δM of slice δk_z, as the magnetic field is increased. The successive values of λ' are denoted by $\nu + 3$, $\nu + 2, \nu + 1, \nu, \cdots$. The horizontal scale is linear at $1/B$, which decreases to the right.

Thus, there is a fluctuation δn in the number of carriers in the slab. The δn is periodic in $1/B$ and has a period $(e\hbar)/(mcE'_F)$, as shown in Figure 17.13. The population of the slab thus oscillates with an amplitude $\pm \xi B/2$, about the value n_0 equal to the number of electrons in the slab at $B \rightarrow 0$. Let us examine the energy of the electrons in the slab. We first examine the energy at the point where there are n_0 electrons in the slab, i.e. when the magnetic field has a particular value corresponding to $n = n_0$.

$$U_0 = \xi B \hbar \omega_c \sum_{\lambda=0}^{\lambda'} \left(\lambda + \frac{1}{2}\right) + \frac{n_0 \hbar^2 k_z^2}{2m} \qquad (17.74)$$

where λ' is the highest occupied level.

We get

$$U_0 = \frac{1}{2}\xi B \hbar \omega_c \left(\lambda' + 1\right)^2 + \frac{n_0 \hbar^2 k_z^2}{2m}. \qquad (17.75)$$

Also, since

$$n_0 = \left(\lambda' + 1\right)\xi B,$$

$$U_0 = \frac{1}{2}\frac{\hbar\omega_c n_0^2}{\xi B} + n_0\frac{\hbar^2 k_z^2}{2m}. \tag{17.76}$$

If we examine a neighboring value of B, which does not change λ', the energy can be written as

$$U = \frac{1}{2}\frac{\hbar\omega_c}{\xi B}n^2 + \frac{\hbar^2 k_z^2}{2m}n + E_F(n_0 - n). \tag{17.77}$$

The last term comes from the transfer of $(n - n_0)$ excess electrons at the Fermi energy. We have thus included the effect of the transfer on the *entire Fermi sea*. We define

$$\mu \equiv \frac{e\hbar}{2mc} \tag{17.78}$$

and evaluate $U - U_0 = \delta U$

$$\begin{aligned}\delta U &= \frac{\mu}{\xi}\left(n^2 - n_0^2\right) + \left(E_F - \frac{\hbar^2 k_z^2}{2m}\right)(n_0 - n) \\ &= \frac{\mu}{\xi}\left(n^2 - n_0^2\right) + (n_0 - n)E_F'.\end{aligned} \tag{17.79}$$

Now at $n = n_0$

$$\begin{aligned}E_F &= \lambda'\hbar\omega_c + \frac{\hbar^2 k_z^2}{2m} \\ &= \frac{n_0}{\xi B}\hbar\omega_c + \frac{\hbar^2 k_z^2}{2m}\end{aligned} \tag{17.80}$$

so that

$$E_F' = \frac{n_0}{\xi B}\hbar\omega_c. \tag{17.81}$$

Thus

$$\begin{aligned}\delta U &= \left(\frac{\mu}{\xi}\right)(n - n_0)^2 \\ &> 0.\end{aligned} \tag{17.82}$$

The energy of the system thus increases away from U_0 as shown in Figure 17.13. The change in magnetization is

$$\begin{aligned}\delta M &= \frac{-\partial U}{\partial B} \\ &= -\left(\frac{2\mu}{\xi}\right)(n - n_0)\frac{dn}{dB}.\end{aligned} \tag{17.83}$$

We know from Equation 17.72 that

$$\frac{dn}{dB} = (\lambda' + 1)\xi$$

$$\approx \frac{E_F' \xi}{\hbar\omega} \tag{17.84}$$

where we have used Equation 17.73 for the approximation. Finally

$$\delta M \approx -\frac{E_F'}{B}(n - n_0). \tag{17.85}$$

Since $(n - n_0)$ oscillates between $\pm\xi B/2$, the magnetization also does the same as shown in Figure 17.13.

We need to find the response of the entire system, where, of course, total electron density is constant. This involves summing over all δk_z slices. We note that the linear variation of δM can be written in a Fourier series. We write

$$\delta M = \delta k_z \sum_{p=1}^{\infty} A_p \sin px \tag{17.86}$$

where

$$x = \frac{\pi E_F'}{\mu B}. \tag{17.87}$$

Now for $-\pi < x < \pi$

$$\delta M = -\frac{1}{2\pi}\xi E_F' x$$

$$= \frac{1}{\pi}\xi E_F' \sum_{p=1}^{\infty}(-1)^p \frac{\sin px}{p} \tag{17.88}$$

which is simply the Fourier transform of δM shown by Figure 17.13. Thus

$$A_p = \frac{1}{p\pi}E_F'(-1)^p\left(\frac{\xi}{\delta k_z}\right)$$

$$= (-1)^p \frac{e\,E_F'}{4p\pi^3 ch}. \tag{17.89}$$

We now simply sum over all δk_z

$$M = \frac{e}{4\pi^3 ch}\sum_{p=1}^{\infty}\frac{(-1)^p}{p}\int_{-k_F}^{k_F} dk_z\, E_F'\,\sin\left[\frac{p\pi}{\mu B}\left(E_F - \frac{\hbar^2 k_z^2}{2m}\right)\right]. \tag{17.90}$$

For degenerate electron gas, $\mu B \ll E_F$ and the integrand oscillates rapidly giving zero contribution unless $k_z \approx 0$. We thus replace E_F' by E_F, and bring it out of the integral. We write

$$\sin\left[\frac{p\pi}{\mu B}\left(E_F - \frac{\hbar^2 k_z^2}{2m}\right)\right] = \sin\left(\frac{p\pi}{\mu B}E_F\right)\cos\left(\frac{p\pi}{\mu B}\frac{\hbar^2 k_z^2}{2m}\right)$$
$$- \cos\left(\frac{p\pi}{\mu B}E_F\right)\sin\left(\frac{p\pi}{\mu B}\frac{\hbar^2 k_z^2}{2m}\right) \quad (17.91)$$

and we use the integral

$$\int_0^\infty dx \ \sin^2\frac{\pi x^2}{2} = \int_0^\infty dx \ \cos^2\frac{\pi x^2}{2}$$
$$= \frac{1}{2} \quad (17.92)$$

to finally obtain (with the approximation $k_F \to \infty$)

$$M = \frac{\sqrt{2}\ E_F\ em^{1/2}(\mu B)^{1/2}}{4\pi^3 c\hbar}\sum_p \frac{(-1)^p}{p^{3/2}}\sin\left(\frac{p\pi}{\mu B}E_F - \frac{\pi}{4}\right). \quad (17.93)$$

The $p = 1$ term has the dominant contribution, and we can see oscillations in the $1/B$ response of the magnetization. The period of these oscillations can provide the mass of the particles if the carrier concentration is known or vice-versa.

As the temperature is raised, the Fermi function is no longer abrupt and this causes a smearing of the oscillations. It has been shown that the pth term has to be multiplied by

$$L_p = \frac{x_p}{\sinh x_p} \quad (17.94)$$

where

$$x_p = \frac{2\pi^2 p k_B T}{\hbar\omega}. \quad (17.95)$$

This factor decreases the amplitude of the oscillation as temperature is increased. For realistic magnetic fields, the oscillations are usually observed only for $T \leq 4K$.

Another issue that is important in the observation of the oscillations is the scattering of the electronic states. The scattering introduces an uncertainty in the energy of the electrons which can be treated as an effective temperature. One can use Equation 17.95 with

$$k_B T \to k_B T + \frac{\hbar}{\pi\tau} \quad (17.96)$$

where τ is the scattering time.

17.6 THE SHUBNIKOV-DE HAAS EFFECT

The formation of Landau levels results in oscillations in the conductivity (or resistivity) of a material essentially for the same reasons as discussed above. These

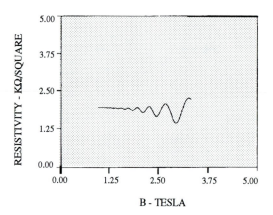

Figure 17.14: Typical Shubnikov-de Haas oscillations taken from a p-type symmetrically doped quantum well at 3.9 K, (from Jaffe, 1989).

oscillations, known as Shubnikov-de Haas effects, have become a very powerful tool to characterize the mass of electrons, especially in new heterostructures and alloys.

The Shubnikov-de Haas effect consists of oscillations in resistivity as a function of magnetic field at low temperatures. This effect was first observed in the late 1920s by L. Shubnikov and W. de Haas. The effect is caused by the fact that a magnetic field applied perpendicular to a two-dimensional electron gas causes the formation of discrete quantized orbits called Landau levels. The Landau levels increase in energy linearly with magnetic field due to the cyclotron resonance frequency, $\omega_c = eB/(m^*c)$. As the magnetic field is increased, these levels will pass through the Fermi energy causing oscillations in the conductivity.

A typical measurement of Shubnikov-de Haas oscillations is shown in Figure 17.14. These measurements were made on a p-type symmetrically doped quantum well of GaAs/Al$_{0.3}$Ga$_{0.7}$As. The resistivity can be divided up into oscillatory and non-oscillatory portions, or

$$\rho = \rho_{\text{oscillatory}} + \rho_{\text{non-oscillatory}}. \tag{17.97}$$

It is oscillatory portion of the resistivity which yields the information on effective masses, carrier concentrations, and scattering times. Thus, the theories briefly described will analyze the oscillatory portion of the resistivity.

Many authors have treated the Shubnikov-de Haas effect theoretically and although different levels of sophistication have been applied to the analysis, the typical expression used to describe the magnetoconductivity in a 2-D channel with sheet charge density N_s and scattering time τ_{SdH} is given as

$$\sigma_{xx} = \frac{N_s e^2 \tau_{\text{H}}}{m^*} \frac{1}{1 + (\omega_c \tau_{\text{H}})^2} \tag{17.98}$$

$$\times \quad \left[1 - \frac{2(\omega_c \tau_{\text{SdH}})^2}{1 + (\omega_c \tau_{\text{SdH}})^2} \cdot \frac{2\pi^2 m^* k_B T / \hbar e B}{\sinh(2\pi^2 m^* k_B T / \hbar e B)} \right.$$

$$\times \quad \left. \exp\left(-\frac{\pi}{\omega_c \tau_{\text{SdH}}}\right) \cos\left(\frac{2\pi^2 \hbar N_s}{e B}\right) \right]. \qquad (17.99)$$

The theoretical expression given in Equation 17.98 gives the conductivity while the measured quantity is always the resistivity. In a magnetic field, both conductivity and resistivity; must be expressed as two-dimensional tensors since the Hall effect yields nonzero values for ρ_{xy} and σ_{xy}. In order to obtain the theoretical expression for ρ_{xx}, the resistivity tensor must be inverted. This yields

$$\rho_{xx} = \sigma_{xx} \left(\rho_{xx}^2 + \rho_{xy}^2 \right). \qquad (17.100)$$

The Hall resistivity can be written as

$$\begin{aligned} \rho_{xy} &= R_H B \\ &= \frac{\mu_H B}{\sigma_{xx}(B=0)} \\ &= \rho_{xx}(B=0)\mu_H B. \end{aligned} \qquad (17.101)$$

Using Equation 17.101, we can write

$$\rho_{xx}^2 + \rho_{xy}^2 = \rho_{xx}^2(B=0)\left[1 + \frac{2\left(\rho_{xx} - \rho_{xx}(B=0)\right)}{\rho_{xx}(B=0)} \right.$$

$$+ \left. \frac{(\rho_{xx} - \rho_{xx}(B=0))^2}{\rho_{xx}^2(B=0)} + \mu_H^2 B^2 \right]. \qquad (17.102)$$

By assuming that

$$\mu_H B \gg \frac{\rho_{xx} - \rho_{xx}(B=0)}{\rho_{xx}(B=0)} \qquad (17.103)$$

which is a very good approximation in high mobility samples, Equation 17.102 becomes

$$\rho_{xx}^2 + \rho_{xy}^2 = \rho_{xx}^2(B=0)\left[1 + \mu_H^2 B^2 \right]. \qquad (17.104)$$

By combining Equation 17.98, Equation 17.100 and Equation 17.103, and by noting that $\omega_c \tau_H = \mu_H B$, we can write the magnetoresistivity as

$$\rho_{xx} = \frac{\rho_{xx}^2(B=0)N_s e^2 \tau_H}{m^*}$$

$$\times \quad \left[1 - \frac{2(\omega_c \tau_{\text{SdH}})^2}{1 + (\omega_c \tau_{\text{SdH}})^2} \cdot \frac{2\pi^2 m^* k_B T / \hbar e B}{\sinh(2\pi^2 m^* k_B T / \hbar e B)} \right.$$

$$\times \quad \left. \exp\left(-\frac{\pi}{\omega_c \tau_{\text{SdH}}}\right) \cos\left(\frac{2\pi^2 \hbar N_s}{e B}\right) \right]. \qquad (17.105)$$

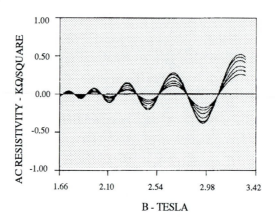

Figure 17.15: The oscillatory portion of the magnetoconductivity of a *p*-type symmetric quantum well at six different temperatures between 1.7 K and 3.2 K. As the temperature increases, the amplitude of the oscillations decreases, (from Jaffe, 1989).

Using typical values for the particle effective mass and scattering rates, we get that $\omega_c \tau_{\text{SdH}} \geq 10000$. Therefore, for magnetic fields of interest, which are usually above 0.3 Tesla, we can accurately approximate the oscillatory portion of the magnetoresistivity as

$$\rho_{xx} = C \frac{2\pi^2 m^* k_B T/\hbar e B}{\sinh(2\pi^2 m^* k_B T/\hbar e B)} \exp\left(-\frac{\pi}{\omega_c \tau_{\text{SdH}}}\right) \cos\left(\frac{2\pi^2 \hbar N_s}{e B}\right). \quad (17.106)$$

We can view this equation as an amplitude which grows with increasing magnetic field and shrinks with increasing temperature and effective mass, multiplying a cosine wave whose frequency is determined by the sheet charge and the magnetic field. Figure 17.15 shows the oscillatory portion of the resistivity as a function of effective mass at six different temperatures between 1.7 K and 3.2 K. From this figure we can see the effect of temperature on the oscillations. As the temperature increases, the amplitude of the oscillations decreases.

Equations 17.98 to 17.106 are valid for the conductivity only if a single subband is occupied. If more than one subband is occupied, the conductivity can be expressed as the sum of the conductivity in each subband. This will generate a sum of sinusoidal oscillations each of different frequency.

After obtaining $\rho_{\text{oscillatory}}$, one can obtain the effective mass by examining the variation in the amplitude of the oscillations with temperature. We begin by defining an amplitude function, A, as

$$A(B,T) \equiv C \frac{2\pi^2 m^* k_B T/\hbar e B}{sinh(2\pi^2 m^* k_B T/\hbar e B)} \exp\left(-\frac{\pi}{\omega_c \tau_{\text{SdH}}}\right). \quad (17.107)$$

The amplitude function can be measured experimentally by taking the values of $\rho_{\text{oscillatory}}$ at maxima or minima of the oscillations where the cosine term has a value of ± 1. The amplitude function can be normalized to the amplitude at a specific temperature, T_0, or

$$
\begin{aligned}
A_n(B,T) &\equiv \frac{A(B,T)}{A(B,T_0)} \\
&= \frac{T \sinh(2\pi^2 m^* k_B T_0 / \hbar e B)}{T_0 \sinh(2\pi^2 m^* k_B T / \hbar e B)}.
\end{aligned} \tag{17.108}
$$

$A_n(B,T)$ can be measured experimentally, and all of the parameters in the theoretical expression for $A_n(B,T)$ are known except for the effective mass. The effective mass can, therefore, be then obtained by the minimization of the total squared error between the measured normalized amplitudes and the calculated normalized amplitudes from Equation 17.108.

Examining Equation 17.106 shows that the oscillations should be periodic in inverse magnetic field. Information can, therefore, be obtained on the subband occupations by taking the Fourier transform of $\rho_{\text{oscillatory}}$ as a function of inverse magnetic field. If only one subband is occupied, the frequency of the peak in the Fourier transform curve will be at

$$
\Delta\left(\frac{1}{B}\right) = \frac{q}{\pi^2 \hbar N_s}. \tag{17.109}
$$

Thus, the frequency of the oscillations reveals the sheet charge concentration. The relationship between resistivity and magnetic field becomes much more complicated if more than one subband is occupied. In this case, the oscillations will look like the sum of two sine waves of different frequencies, and it will be difficult if not impossible to extract accurate measurements for effective mass. When more than one subband is occupied, the Fourier transform will show multiple peaks whose positions will give the occupation of each subband.

The exponential term in Equation 17.106 contains a time constant, τ_{SdH} which is the Shubnikov-de Haas scattering time, or the lifetime of the Landau levels. This time constant is typically smaller than the transport derived scattering time obtained from Hall measurements, $\tau_H = \mu_H m^* / q$. For silicon MOSFETs, the ratio $\tau_H / \tau_{\text{SdH}}$ is close to unity while for AlGaAs/GaAs heterostructures the value of the ratio ranges from 10 to 40. The value of τ_{SdH} can be obtained from the amplitude function at a given temperature after the effective mass has been determined.

17.7 THE QUANTUM HALL EFFECT

The quantum Hall effect is a remarkable phenomenon observed in the conductivity of high quality two-dimensional electron systems which has allowed development of new understanding of electrons in condense matter. The two-dimensional system can be the channel of a metal oxide semiconductor transistor (MOSFET) or the MODFET structure described in Chapter 14.

In Chapter 1, we discussed the equation of motion for electrons in presence of scattering processes. If τ is the average scattering time, the equation of motion is

$$\frac{d\mathbf{p}}{dt} = \mathbf{F} - \frac{\mathbf{p}}{\tau} \tag{17.110}$$

which gives for the electrons in presence of an electric and magnetic field

$$n\left(\frac{d}{dt} + \frac{1}{\tau}\right)\mathbf{v} = -e\left[\mathbf{F} + \frac{1}{c}\mathbf{v} \times \mathbf{B}\right]. \tag{17.111}$$

If we assume a magnetic field along the z-axis, we get

$$n\left(\frac{d}{dt} + \frac{1}{\tau}\right)v_x = -e\left(F_x + \frac{B}{c}v_y\right)$$

$$n\left(\frac{d}{dt} + \frac{1}{\tau}\right)v_y = -e\left(F_y - \frac{B}{c}v_x\right)$$

$$n\left(\frac{d}{dt} + \frac{1}{\tau}\right)v_z = -eF_z. \tag{17.112}$$

In steady state, the time derivatives are zero so that we have

$$v_x = -\frac{e\tau}{n}F_x - \omega_c\tau v_y$$

$$v_y = -\frac{e\tau}{n}F_y + \omega_c\tau v_x$$

$$v_z = -\frac{e\tau}{n}F_z. \tag{17.113}$$

Noting that $\mathbf{J} = -en\mathbf{v}$ and $\sigma_0 = ne^2\tau/m$, we can write these equations in the form

$$\begin{pmatrix} J_x \\ J_y \\ J_z \end{pmatrix} = \frac{\sigma_0}{1 + (\omega_c\tau)^2}\begin{pmatrix} 1 & -\omega_c\tau & 0 \\ \omega_c\tau & 1 & 0 \\ 0 & 0 & 1 + (\omega_c\tau)^2 \end{pmatrix}\begin{pmatrix} F_x \\ F_y \\ F_z \end{pmatrix}. \tag{17.114}$$

In the high magnetic field limit $(\omega_c\tau) \gg 1$, and one has

$$\sigma_{xx} \Rightarrow 0. \tag{17.115}$$

If we examine the conductivity of such a 2-D system in presence of a magnetic field, it can be written by the surface conductivity tensor σ with components

$$\sigma_{xx} = \frac{\sigma_0}{1 + (\omega_c\tau)^2}$$

$$\sigma_{xy} = \frac{-\sigma_0\,\omega_c\tau}{1 + (\omega_c\tau)^2} \tag{17.116}$$

where σ_0 is the conductivity in absence of the magnetic field and is given by

$$\sigma_0 = \frac{ne^2\tau}{m} \tag{17.117}$$

where n is the density per unit area of the electrons.

The quantum Hall effect involves carrying out the usual Hall effect at very low temperatures. The geometry used is shown in Figure 17.16. Essentially one measures the current flowing in the x-direction along with the field developed in the y-direction. In the unit of $\omega_c \tau \gg 1$, the conductivity components become

$$\sigma_{xx} = 0$$

$$\sigma_{xy} = \frac{-nec}{B}. \tag{17.118}$$

In the surface Hall measurement, the x-direction current is $I_x = J_x L_y = (nec/B)F_y L_y = (nec/B)V_y$, where V_y is the voltage developed across the y-direction. Note that $J_x = \sigma_{xy} F_y$ since σ_{xx} is zero in the limit of $\omega_c \tau \gg 1$. The Hall resistance is now

$$\rho_H = \frac{V_y}{I_x}$$

$$= \frac{B}{nec}. \tag{17.119}$$

In Figure 17.17 we show the results of the measurement of K. von Klitzing, G. Dorda, and M. Pepper [Phys. Rev. Lett., **45**, 494, (1980)] where the Hall voltage is plotted as a function of the gate voltage. The gate voltage essentially changes the carrier density in the 2-D channel. The remarkable observation from Figure 17.17 is that the Hall voltage and the voltage in the direction of the current flow goes to zero. The Hall resistivity V_H/I_x at these values is a plateau and is accurately given by $h/(e^2\nu)$ ohms. The precision in this value is so good that it has become a standard tool for obtaining a very accurate value of the fine structure constant.

Let us first consider a simplistic explanation of this phenomenon. Under strong magnetic fields we consider the description of the electronic system in terms of the Landau levels which are discrete in the 2-D system as shown in Figure 17.18a. As the gate voltage is changed to fill the Landau levels, there will be a point where one Landau level is completely full and the next one is completely empty. In this case there can be no scattering of electrons. The condition for this to occur is from our previous discussions

$$n = \nu \frac{eB}{hc} \tag{17.120}$$

where ν is an integer. The Hall resistance at this point is

$$\rho_H = \frac{B}{nec}$$

$$= \frac{h}{\nu e^2}. \tag{17.121}$$

However, the addition of a few electrons will alter this value. Thus, on this basis one does not expect plateaus in the resistance.

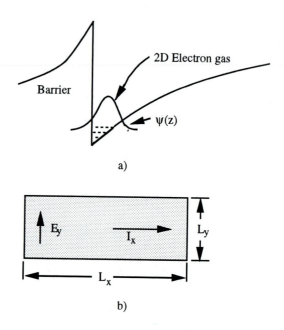

a)

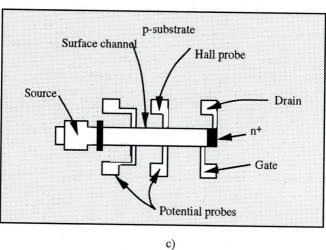

b)

c)

Figure 17.16: (a) A schematic of the band profile and the 2-D electron gas used for quantum Hall effect experiments; (b) the applied electric field and drift current orientations; (c) the actual positions of the various contacts used for quantum Hall effect.

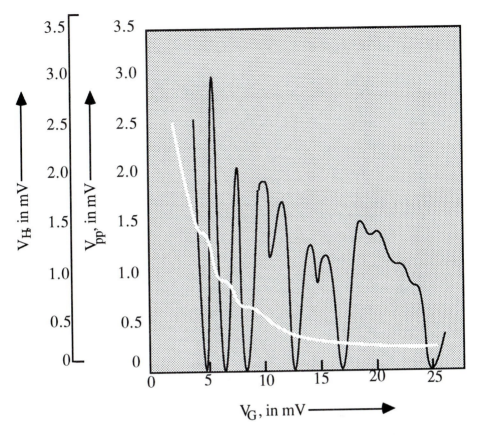

Figure 17.17: Results from the original quantum Hall effect carried out by K. von Klitzing, G. Dorda, and M. Pepper. A magnetic field of 18 T is perpendicular to the sample and measurements area done at 1.5 K. A constant current of 1 μA is forced to flow between the source and the drain. Voltages V_{pp} and V_H are plotted versus the gate voltage V_G. (Reproduced with permission, K. von Klitzing, et al., Phys. Rev. Lett., **45**, 494 (1980).)

One has to also realize that in a real 2-D system the density of states is not δ-function like, but is expected to have a form shown in Figure 17.18b. Due to the disorder present in the system, one expects extended and localized states as discussed in the next chapter. Thus, there is no reason that the Landau level will be filled (i.e., the extended states part that conducts) at precise values of the electron concentrations. This dilemma was addressed by Laughlin (1981). His arguments were based on arguments of flux quantization discussed in our treatment of superconducting rings in the section on Aharonov-Bohm effect. Laughlin divided the electronic states into extended and localized states where the localized states are unaffected by the magnetic field. The extended states enclose the magnetic flux and can be affected by it. However, if the magnetic flux

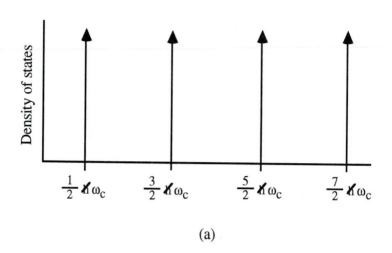

(a)

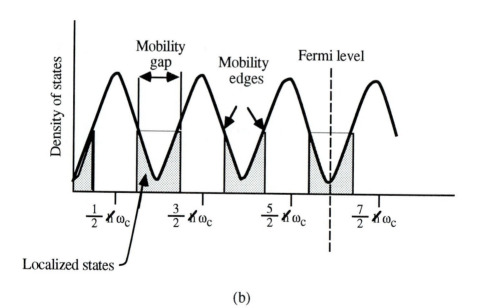

(b)

Figure 17.18: Density of states in a 2-D electron gas in a strong magnetic field: (a) ideal 2-D crystal, (b) real 2-D crystal, with impurities and imperfections.

is altered by a flux quantum $\delta\phi = ch/e$, the extended states are identical to those before the flux quantum was added. Using these arguments, Laughlin was able to show that plateaus should appear in the Hall resistance with values precisely $h/\nu e^2$ regardless of the disorder provided, of course, we still had $\omega_c\tau \gg 1$.

The quantum Hall effect has become even more complex in recent years with the observation of fractional quantum Hall effect. In these experiments, carried out at very high magnetic fields and low temperatures, one observes the Hall resistance quantized in units of $3h/e^2$ when the first Landau level is $1/3$, $2/3$, $2/5$, $3/5$, $4/5$, $2/7$ filled.

In these cases, the simple one electron picture of the Landau levels has obviously broken down and research is continuing using many-body descriptions of the electrons.

17.8 MAGNETO-OPTICS IN LANDAU LEVELS

The changes in the density of states of the electrons in presence of the magnetic field is obviously expected to alter the optical spectra. The magneto-optical studies of free carriers (we will discuss excitons and impurities later) provides very useful information, especially on the carrier masses. We will examine band-to-band transitions and use the approach used in Chapter 15.

The perturbation due to the electromagnetic radiation is

$$\frac{e}{mc}\left(\boldsymbol{p} - \frac{e\boldsymbol{A}_{\text{ext}}}{c}\right) \cdot \boldsymbol{A}_{\text{em}} \tag{17.122}$$

where $\boldsymbol{A}_{\text{ext}}$ is due to the applied magnetic field and $\boldsymbol{A}_{\text{em}}$ is due to the electromagnetic field. Using the approach similar to the one used in Chapter 15 for band-to-band transitions we get

$$\alpha(\hbar\omega, \boldsymbol{B}) = \frac{4\pi^2 e^2}{\eta m^2 \omega} \sum_{\text{all states}} |\boldsymbol{a} \cdot \boldsymbol{P}_{\text{cv}}(\boldsymbol{B})|^2 \, \delta\left(E_c(\boldsymbol{B}) - E_v(\boldsymbol{B}) - \hbar\omega\right) \tag{17.123}$$

where

$$\boldsymbol{a} \cdot \boldsymbol{P}_{\text{cv}}(\boldsymbol{B}) = \int \psi_c^*(\boldsymbol{r}, \boldsymbol{B}) \, \boldsymbol{a} \cdot \left(\boldsymbol{p} - \frac{e}{c}\boldsymbol{A}_{\text{ext}}\right) \psi_v(\boldsymbol{r}, \boldsymbol{B}) \, d^3r \tag{17.124}$$

and ψ_c, ψ_v, E_c, E_v represent the band wavefunctions and energies in presence of the magnetic field. To first order the effect of the magnetic field on the matrix element can be easily seen by neglecting $\boldsymbol{A}_{\text{ext}}$ in Equation 17.123 and using the effective mass equation for the representation of the electronic states and the density of states. In the usual approach of the effective mass theory, we may write

$$\psi(\boldsymbol{r}, \boldsymbol{B}) = F(\boldsymbol{r})\psi_n(\boldsymbol{k}_c, \boldsymbol{r}) \tag{17.125}$$

where $F(r)$ is the $\psi(x, y, z)$ of Equation 17.41, where we had suppressed the bandedge central cell function $\psi_n(k_c, r)$. The matrix elements are then in k-space

$$
\begin{aligned}
a \cdot P_{cv}(B) &= \int \left[\sum_k F_c(k)\psi_c(k, r) \right]^* a \cdot p \left[\sum_{k'} F_v(k')\psi_v(k', r) \right] d^3r \\
&= \sum_{k,k'} F_c^*(k)F_v(k')\, a \cdot p_{cv}(k)\, \delta(k - k')
\end{aligned}
\tag{17.126}
$$

where k and k' are nearly equal because of the near zero photon momentum. We also assume, as we did for the band-to-band transitions in Chapter 15, that $P_{cv}(k)$ has no dependence on k and obtain the matrix elements, in terms of the real space wavefunction

$$
a \cdot P_{cv}(B) = a \cdot M_{cv} \int F_{cn'k'}^*(r)\, F_{vnk}(r)\, d^3r.
\tag{17.127}
$$

We will assume that the bands are isotropic, in which case the envelope functions for the harmonic oscillator problem are essentially orthonormal giving the selection rule

$$
\begin{aligned}
\Delta n &= 0 \\
\Delta k &= 0.
\end{aligned}
\tag{17.128}
$$

In Figure 17.19 we show schematically the transitions in magneto-optical experiments. The sum over the δ-function in Equation 17.126 gives us the joint density of states of the electron-hole system. This joint density of states is simply

$$
N_{cv}(E, B) = \frac{2eB}{\hbar^2 c}(2\mu)^{1/2} \sum_n \left[E - E_g - \hbar\omega_0\left(n + \frac{1}{2}\right) \right]^{-1/2}
\tag{17.129}
$$

where μ is the reduced mass and $\omega_0 = eB/\mu c$. The absorption coefficient now becomes

$$
\alpha(\omega, B) = \frac{4\pi^2 e^2}{\eta m^2 \omega}\frac{2eB}{h^2 c}(2\mu)^{1/2}|a \cdot p_{cv}|^2 \sum_n \left[\hbar\omega + E_g - \hbar\omega_0\left(n + \frac{1}{2}\right) \right]^{-1/2}.
\tag{17.130}
$$

This absorption profile has sharp structures because of the structures in the density of states. The spacings between the singularities gives the reduced mass of the electron-hole system. The results can be extended to the 2-dimensional case by following the method for the 2-D density of states. These density of states are now δ-function which will be broadened by an appropriate linewidth.

The magneto-optical studies have been used to obtain carrier masses especially in material systems where it is difficult to do Shubnikov-de Haas or

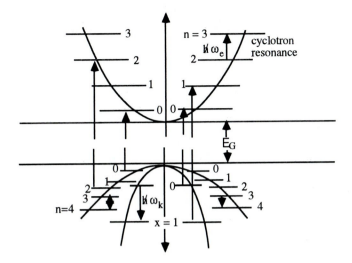

Figure 17.19: A schematic of how Landau levels are formed in presence of magnetic field. The intraband transitions are observed in cyclotron resonance experiments and interband transitions with $\Delta n = 0$ are observed in magneto-optical experiments.

cyclotron resonance measurements. Normally, if only the $\Delta n = 0$ transitions are observed, one can obtain the reduced mass of the electron-hole pair system. However, in presence of impurity scattering, it has been shown by Jones, et al. (1989), that the $\Delta n \neq 0$ transitions are also allowed. In Figure 17.20 we show then low temperature luminescence data for strained InGaAs/GaAs quantum wells. The data shows both $\Delta n = 0$ and $\Delta n \neq 0$ transitions. By following the $\Delta n \neq 0$ transitions for the same hole subband but different electron subband, it is possible to obtain the value of $\hbar\omega_e$ where $\omega_e = eB/(m_e^* c)$. Once m_e^* is known one can examine the $\Delta n = 0$ transitions to obtain the reduced mass and thus gets m_h^*.

17.9 EXCITONS IN MAGNETIC FIELD

So far in this chapter we have discussed how magnetic fields affect the independent electron Bloch states. We will now address the problem of excitons and shallow impurities in a magnetic field. The studies of excitons in semiconductors have been used to obtain accurate values of basic band parameters such as effective mass and g-values and to obtain information on symmetry of the states. One serious problem with extracting important information from the magneto-optic studies of excitons is the difficulty in interpreting the data. The theory of excitons in magnetic field is quite difficult and requires difficult numerical techniques.

The simplest exciton problem is that based on nondegenerate isotropic bands. Unfortunately, even in this simple problem, it is difficult to address the effect of the magnetic field. At low magnetic fields one can use the perturbation

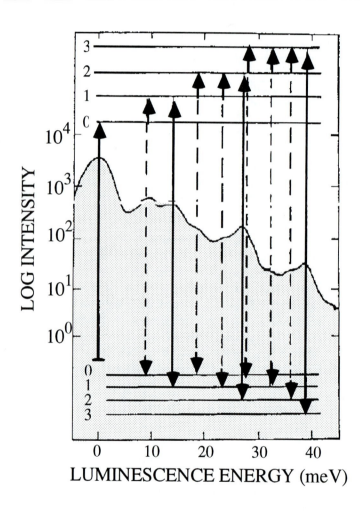

Figure 17.20: A logarithmic plot of the magnetoluminescence spectra at 5.0 T for an InGaAs/GaAs quantum well, at 4 K. The nature of the transition are indicated. Both the $\Delta n = 0$ and $\Delta n \neq 0$ transitions are observed in luminescence. The $0 \rightarrow 0$ energy is 1.395 eV. (Reproduced with permission, E. D. Jones, et al., *GaAs and Related Compounds 1989*, **106**, 435 (1989), IOP Publishing, New York.)

theory to address the problem. This treatment is valid when the magnetic energy is smaller than the exciton binding energy. However, experiments are often carried out in regimes where this is not true. Under very high fields, the adiabatic approach is used where the low frequency problem of motion in the field direction is separated from the high frequency motion in the plane perpendicular to the field. For intermediate fields the problem is quite complex and variational approaches have to be used.

The most studied excitonic problems are the ones involving semiconductors where the valence bands are degenerate. This problem is quite complex, but provides important insight into the semiconductor properties. We will first consider the problem of the simple two band excitons in a magnetic field. In this case the effective mass exciton function can be written as

$$\psi_{ex}(\boldsymbol{K}_{ex}, \boldsymbol{r}_e, \boldsymbol{r}_h) = \sum_{\boldsymbol{q}} F(\boldsymbol{q}, \boldsymbol{K}_{ex}) \, \psi_v(\boldsymbol{q}, \boldsymbol{r}_h) \, \psi_c(-\boldsymbol{q} + \boldsymbol{K}_{ex}, \boldsymbol{r}_e). \qquad (17.131)$$

The equation for the Fourier transform of $F(\boldsymbol{q}, \boldsymbol{K}_{ex})$ is

$$\left\{ \frac{1}{2m_e} \left(\boldsymbol{p}_e - \frac{e\boldsymbol{A}}{c} \right)^2 + \frac{1}{2m_h} \left(\boldsymbol{p}_h - \frac{e\boldsymbol{A}}{c} \right)^2 - \frac{e^2}{\epsilon |\boldsymbol{r}_e - \boldsymbol{r}_h|} \right\} F(\boldsymbol{r}_e, \boldsymbol{r}_h)$$

$$= E F(\boldsymbol{r}_e, \boldsymbol{r}_h) \qquad (17.132)$$

where $\boldsymbol{A}$ is the vector potential due to the magnetic field. We reduce the problem to the center of mass system by the transformation

$$\boldsymbol{R} = \frac{m_e \boldsymbol{r}_e + m_h \boldsymbol{r}_h}{m_e + m_h}$$

$$\boldsymbol{r} = \boldsymbol{r}_e - \boldsymbol{r}_h \qquad (17.133)$$

and performing the transformation

$$F(\boldsymbol{r}_e, \boldsymbol{r}_h) = \exp\left(i \left[\boldsymbol{K}_{ex} - \frac{e}{hc}\boldsymbol{A} \right] \cdot \boldsymbol{R} \right) \Phi(\boldsymbol{r}). \qquad (17.134)$$

The relative motion equation is then defined by

$$\left\{ \frac{p^2}{2\mu} + \frac{e}{c} \left(\frac{1}{m_h} - \frac{1}{m_e} \right) \boldsymbol{A} \cdot \boldsymbol{p} + \frac{e^2}{2\mu c^2} \boldsymbol{A} \cdot \boldsymbol{A} \right.$$

$$\left. - \frac{e^2}{\epsilon r} - \frac{2e\hbar}{Mc} \boldsymbol{K}_{ex} \cdot \boldsymbol{A} + \frac{\hbar^2 K_{ex}^2}{2M} \right\} \Phi(\boldsymbol{r}) = E\Phi(\boldsymbol{r}). \qquad (17.135)$$

Here μ is the electron-hole reduced mass and M is the total effective mass of the system. Using the Lorentz gauge and writing

$$\boldsymbol{A} = \frac{1}{2}\boldsymbol{B} \times \boldsymbol{r}, \qquad (17.136)$$

the various magnetic field dependent terms of the Equation 17.129 take on the following values:

- The second term can be written as

$$\frac{e}{2c}\left(\frac{1}{m_h} - \frac{1}{m_e}\right) \boldsymbol{B} \cdot \boldsymbol{L}$$

  which is the Zeeman term discussed in Appendix G.

- The third term is the diamagnetic operator,

$$\frac{e^2}{8\mu c^2}\left|\boldsymbol{B} \times \boldsymbol{r}\right|^2.$$

- The fifth term depends upon the motion of the exciton and is given by

$$-\frac{e\hbar}{Mc}(\boldsymbol{K}_{\text{ex}} \times \boldsymbol{B} \cdot \boldsymbol{r})$$

  and will be neglected due to its small value.

For optical transitions we are only interested in the $m = 0$ excitonic states (the s-states) since, as discussed in Chapter 16, these are the only allowed transitions. The equation then becomes

$$\left\{\frac{p^2}{2\mu} - \frac{e^2}{\epsilon r} + \frac{e^2 B^2}{8\mu c^2}(x^2 + y^2)\right\} \phi(\boldsymbol{r}) = E\phi(\boldsymbol{r}). \qquad (17.137)$$

In order to define the relative strengths of the Coulombic and magnetic terms one defines a parameter

$$\begin{aligned} \gamma &= \frac{\hbar\omega_c}{2R_{\text{ex}}} \\ &= \frac{\hbar^3 \epsilon B}{c\mu^2 e^3} \end{aligned} \qquad (17.138)$$

which is the ratio of the cyclotron energy and twice the exciton binding energy. In terms of γ the equation for the exciton is

$$\left\{-\nabla^2 - \frac{2}{\gamma} + \frac{\gamma^2}{4}(x^2 + y^2)\right\} \phi(\boldsymbol{r}) = E\phi(\boldsymbol{r}) \qquad (17.139)$$

where we have used $R_{\text{ex}} = \mu e^4/(2\hbar^2\epsilon^2)$ as the units of energy and the Bohr radius $a_{\text{ex}} = \hbar^2\epsilon/\mu e^2$ as the unit of length. We note that the Zeeman term coming from the electron and hole spins are not considered and can be simply added on to the solutions later. This contribution is

$$g_e \mu_0 \boldsymbol{S}_e \cdot \boldsymbol{B} + g_h \mu_0 \boldsymbol{S}_h \cdot \boldsymbol{B}. \qquad (17.140)$$

For small magnetic fields, one can treat the diamagnetic term as simply a perturbation and evaluate the effect on the excitonic states, assuming that there is no mixing of the exciton states. One finds that first order perturbation theory gives

$$E_{ex}(1s) = R_{ex}\left[-1 + \frac{1}{2}\gamma^2\right]$$

$$E_{ex}(2s) = R_{ex}\left[-\frac{1}{4} + 7\gamma^2\right]. \qquad (17.141)$$

Higher order exciton states can also lose their degeneracies by the diamagnetic correction. At higher magnetic fields one needs to use the variational methods. At very high magnetic field, the problem is somewhat simplified because the adiabatic approximation allows one to separate the motion in the plane perpendicular to the field and in the field. A number of workers have addressed these problems and the interested reader can refer to the articles suggested in the reference list at the end of this chapter. In Figure 17.21 we show results of theoretical calculations from Baldereschi and Bassani for the entire range of γ values.

17.10 SHALLOW IMPURITIES IN MAGNETIC FIELDS

The studies of shallow impurity states in magnetic fields have provided us with extremely important near bandedge properties and have shed light on the validity of theoretical models. These studies have also been crucial in understanding various impurities incorporated in crystals during growth. The impurity problem is quite similar to the exciton problem discussed above except that it is simplified since there is no electron-hole center of mass motion and the properties are described by a single band equation.

The envelope function of the impurity level satisfies the equation

$$\left\{\frac{1}{2m^*}\left(-i\hbar\nabla - \frac{e}{c}\boldsymbol{A}\right)^2 - \frac{e^2}{\epsilon r}\right\} F(\boldsymbol{r}) = EF(\boldsymbol{r}). \qquad (17.142)$$

Once again choosing the vector potential as $\boldsymbol{A} = \boldsymbol{r} \times \boldsymbol{B}/2$, one gets

$$H = H_0 + H_1 \qquad (17.143)$$

where

$$H_0 = -\frac{\hbar^2}{2m^*}\nabla^2 - \frac{e^2}{\epsilon r}$$

$$H_1 = \frac{e}{2cm^*}\boldsymbol{B}\cdot\boldsymbol{L} + \frac{e^2}{8m^*c^2}|\boldsymbol{B} \times \boldsymbol{r}|^2 \qquad (17.144)$$

where $\boldsymbol{L}$ is the orbital angular momentum operator of the impurity state. The Schrödinger equation is not separable and requires numerical techniques to solve

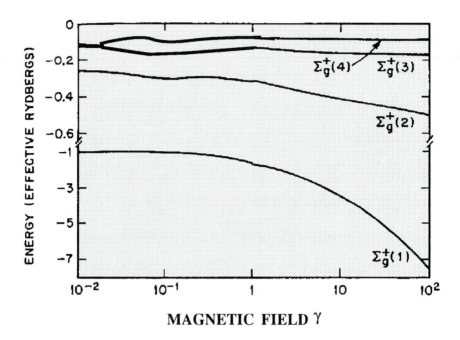

Figure 17.21: Dependence on γ of the energy of the lowest four exciton states with $m = 0$ and even parity calculated with the low-field and high-field methods explained in the text. The zero of energy is at the $N = 0$ Landau level. (Reproduced with permission, A. Baldereschi, et al., Proc. X Int. Conf. Phys. Semicond., Cambridge, (1970), pg. 191.)

it. A variety of approaches have been used to study the effects of the magnetic field on the impurity levels. In Figure 17.22 we show the variation of the impurity state energies with magnetic field in the intermediate field regime $\gamma \leq 1$. The ground state energy becomes less bound as can be seen and some of the excited states lose their degeneracy. The lifting of the degeneracies provides valuable information on the bandedge properties and the effects of central cell correction on the impurity levels.

Another important characterization technique involves studying the photoconductivity of semiconductors under fan infrared illumination. The energies of the shallow levels correspond to the fan infrared region of the spectra and the availability of sources in this region allows one to directly excite carriers from or into the impurity levels. The absorption cross sections for these transistors are such that one needs at least 10^{12} impurities/cm^2 if the absorption peaks are to be resolved. While this limit is reasonable for thick samples, for thin samples of thicknesses of a few microns, it is not possible to detect the impurity levels unless the impurity density exceeds 10^{15} cm^{-3}. This sensitivity is extended by

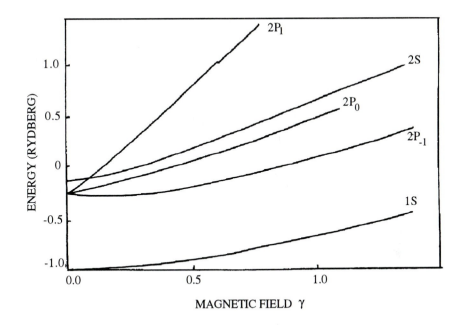

Figure 17.22: Theoretical variation of impurity states with field in intermediate field regime $\gamma \sim 1$. (Reproduced with permission, R. A. Stradling, *Theoretical Aspects and New Developments in Magneto-optics*, ed. Devreese, Plenum Press, New York, 1980.)

use of photoconductive techniques instead of transmission techniques. Thus, very high resolution spectroscopy can be carried out on very low impurity densities. These results have been used to identify uniquely the source of impurities in high quality semiconductor crystals.

17.11 MAGNETIC SEMICONDUCTORS

We conclude this chapter with a brief discussion of a very important class of semiconductors which is beginning to attract increasing interest. These are semiconductors which have intrinsic magnetic moments. Notable examples of these semiconductors are CdMnTe, ZnMnSe, and HgMnTe. These semiconductors, known as diluted magnetic semiconductors, and their heterostructures with other semiconductors can now be fabricated and they offer a unique opportunity for the combined studies of semiconductor physics and magnetism. There is a strong exchange interaction between the magnetic moments of the magnetic ions and the spins of the band electrons giving rise to large Zeeman splittings. In a heterostructure environment, the bandstructure can be tailored so that both the electronic and magnetic properties can be tailored.

The magnetic semiconductors are fabricated by the usual epitaxial techniques like MBE or MOCVD and Mn is introduced as an extra ingredient. The Mn composition is usually $\leq 20\%$. A typical structure widely used is the CdTe–CdMnTe. This is a Type I heterostructure similar to the GaAs–AlGaAs structure, and the CdTe serves as a barrier for both the electrons and holes. The CdMnTe remains a direct bandgap material even for high Mn compositions. A wide range of physical phenomenon have been observed in such heterostructures. We will not discuss these phenomenon in detail because of the vastness of the subject, but will only summarize some of the approaches used to study the physics of these structures.

17.11.1   Optical Spectroscopy

Optical techniques are the most commonly used approaches to characterize magnetic semiconductor structures. The simplest techniques are based on photoluminescence and excitation luminescence. Sharp excitonic peaks have been observed in the quantum wells and these peaks are strongly affected by the magnetic fields. The magnetic field dependence of the exciton peaks has been used to infer that excitons are localized at the interfaces in the CdTe/CdMnTe quantum well structures.

17.11.2   Spin Polarization Spectroscopy

Dynamic experiments have been carried out using pulsed lasers to see how carriers generated optically relax. Of particular interest is how the spin polarization of the carrier changes with time. In absence of magnetic ions, the electrons (holes) do not alter their spins (or alter it "very slowly") as they undergo inelastic scattering and lose their energies. But in magnetic semiconductors, the electrons can transfer their spins to the Mn ions. These processes are of great interest and have been studied in great detail.

17.11.3   Magnetic Spectroscopy

Another important experimental probe used to study magnetic semiconductors is the magnetic spectroscopy. This measurement has no counterpart in ordinary semiconductors. In these experiments the magnetization of the ions is probed as a result of their interactions with the free carriers. A variation in optical intensity can alter the free carrier density causing occupation of higher subbands. The magnetization data is, in fact, quite similar to luminescence data and contains information on the density of states, the form of the carrier wavefunction, and the spin relaxation rate.

To summarize, there is a great deal of interesting physics in studies of magnetic semiconductors. They may eventually find potential uses as devices such as memories and switches.

17.12   FOR THE TECHNOLOGIST IN YOU

Magnetic field effects in semiconductors have almost always been used for characterizing the properties of materials. While magnetic field effects in materials other than semiconductors have been used in technology (usually for information storage), this has not been the case for semiconductors. Devices have been proposed, utilizing magnetic field effects in semiconductors. A key example is the proposal to use the Aharonov-Bohm effect in MODFET channels to produce very low power switching devices at low temperatures. However, the difficulty of incorporating magnetic field effects in semiconductor chips is a major obstacle to any serious use of such devices. This may change with the use of magnetic semiconductors or the possible integration of magnetic materials on semiconductor substrates.

17.13   REFERENCES

- **Semiclassical Approach**

    - Kittel, C., *Introduction to Solid State Physics* (John Wiley and Sons, New York, 1986).

    - Kittel, C., *Quantum Theory of Solids* (John Wiley and Sons, New York, 1987).

    - Lundstrom, M., *Fundamentals of Carrier Transport* (Modular Series on Solid State Devices, edited by G. W. Neudeck and R. F. Pierret, Addison-Wesley, Reading, 1990), vol. X.

    - Ziman, J. M., *Principles of the Theory of Solids* (Cambridge, 1972).

- **Quantum Mechanical Approach**

    - Feynman, R. P., R. B. Leighton and M. Sands, *The Feynman Lectures on Physics* (Addison-Wesley, Reading, 1965), vol. 3.

    - Kittel, C., *Quantum Theory of Solids* (John Wiley and Sons, New York, 1987).

    - Ziman, J. M., *Principles of the Theory of Solids* (Cambridge, 1972).

- **Shubnikov-de Haas Effect**

    - Ando, T., J. Phys. Soc. Japan, **37**, 1233 (1974).

    - Ando, T., Fowler, A. and F. Stern, Rev. Mod. Phys., **54**, 213 (1982).

    - Grabowski, M. and A. Madhukar, Surf. Sci., **113**, 273 (1982).

    - Jaffe, M. D., *Studies on the Electronic Properties and Applications of Coherently Strained Semiconductors* Ph.D. Thesis, (The University of Michigan, Ann Arbor, 1989).

- **The Quantum Hall Effect**

    - Kittel, C., *Introduction to Solid State Physics* (John Wiley and Sons, New York, 1986).

    - Laughlin, R. B., Phys. Rev. B, **23**, 5632 (1981).

    - Stormer, H. L. and D. C. Tsui, Science, **220**, 1241 (1983).

    - Von Klitzing, K., G. Dorda and M. Pepper, Phys. Rev. Lett., **45**, 494 (1980).

- **Magneto Optics Studies**

    - Bassani, F. and G. P. Parravicini, *Electronic States and Optical Transitions in Solids* (Pergamon Press, New York, 1975).

- Jones, E. D., R. M. Biefeld, J. F. Klem and S. K. Lyo, *GaAs and Related Compounds 1989* (Inst. Phys. Conf. Ser. 106, Institute of Physics, Bristol, 1989), p. 435.

- Ziman, J. M., *Principles of the Theory of Solids* (Cambridge, 1972).

- **Excitons and Impurities in a Magnetic Field**

  - Baldereschi, A. and F. Bassani, *Proc. X Int. Conf. Phys. Semiconductors* (Cambridge, Massachusetts, 1970), p. 191.

  - "Excitons and Impurities in Magnetic Fields," by Baldereschi, A., in *Theoretical Aspects and New Developments in Magneto-Optics* (edited by J. T. Devreese, Plenum Press, New York, 1980). Also, see other articles in this book.

  - Stillman, G. E., D. M. Larsen and C. M. Wolfe, Phys. Rev. Lett., **27**, 989 (1971).

  - "Magneto-optical Studies of Impurities," by Stradling, R. A., in *Theoretical Aspects and New Developments in Magneto-Optics* (edited by J. T. Devreese, Plenum Press, New York, 1980).

- **Magnetic Semiconductors**

  - "Optical and Magnetic Properties of Diluted Magnetic Semiconductor Heterostructures," by Chang, L. L., D. D. Awschalom, M. R. Freeman and L. Vina, in *Condensed Systems of Low-Dimensionality* (edited by J. L. Beeby, Plenum Press, 1991). See other references in this article.

  - Gunsher, R. L., L. A. Kolodziejski, N. Otsuka and S. Datta, Surf. Sci., **174**, 522 (1986).

  - Kolodziejski, L. A., T. C. Bonsett, R. L. Gunshor, S. Datta, R. B. Bylsma, W. M. Becker and N. Otsuka, Appl. Phys. Lett., **45**, 440 (1989).

CHAPTER
18

DEFECTS
AND DISORDER
IN SEMICONDUCTORS

The foundation of all the various formalisms presented in this book so far is the crystalline nature of semiconductors. It is the nature of the Bloch functions that allows us to discuss the concepts of bandstructure, transport, optical, and magnetic properties. To be more precise, there are two levels where we have made important assumptions in order to describe the physical phenomena in semiconductors. The first one relates to the nature of the wavefunction being described by a Bloch state. This assumption based on perfect periodicity in the material tells us that the wavefunction is a plane wave function modulated by a unit cell periodic function. The concepts of effective mass, bandgap, etc., are all a result of periodicity. The second assumption deals with how we deal with nonperiodicity which we realize occurs in every crystal. This nonperiodicity arises from defects, phonons, etc., and is treated by perturbation theory producing simply transitions between various Bloch states. The nonperiodicity is not regarded as strong enough to alter the *energy spectrum* of the problem itself. The scattering problem is also treated in a particularly simplistic manner. We assume that the scattering rate is given by simply the number of scatterers times the individual scattering rate. As discussed in detail in Chapter 3, on X-ray diffraction from nonperiodic structures, such an assumption implies lack of phase memory between different scattering centers.

These assumptions about the unperturbed eigenstates and eigenvalues of the semiconductor and the effects of imperfections allowed us to derive the expressions for the various observables that represent semiconductor physics. Increasingly, solid state electronics is moving in a direction where such assumptions will have to be drastically modified if not totally abandoned. While the physics of noncrystalline materials has been of great interest for over several decades, the electrical engineers have not worried about these effects so much.

This has been in spite of the interest in amorphous semiconductors (particularly amorphous Si) for low cost devices, say, for solar energy conversion. However, gradually beginning in the 1980s, state of the art electronic and optoelectronic devices are moving towards sub-3-dimensional structures. Also, the structures themselves are becoming extremely small ($\leq\sim$ 1000 Å). The sub-3-dimensional structures, especially the quantum wires and dots, are usually produced by processing techniques (say etching, regrowth, etc.) which leave a significant disorder in the structure. This disorder is not unlike the interface disorder discussed in Chapter 14, except that it is on a larger scale, and can have a very profound effect on the physical properties.

As the device structures themselves become very small, the phase coherence in the electron wave between one contact and the other can be maintained. Such structures are called mesoscopic structures and are of great interest for next generation electronics. Very exciting observations on transport properties of these structures have been made. These observations suggest that our simple transport formalism must be greatly modified.

In this chapter we will address three important issues, although rather superficially, due to the complexity of the problem. First, we will discuss the effect of defects such as chemical impurities, vacancies, etc. on the electronic states. We will show how these defects can produce levels in the bandgap of the semiconductors. An important class of defects is the dislocation. The dislocations are particularly important for lattice mismatched heterostructures. We will next discuss the case of disordered semiconductors where the underlying crystalline lattice is seriously modified at nearly all sites. In this case the long-range order is lost, even though nearest neighbor bonding is maintained. Finally, we will conclude with a glimpse of exciting physics in small structures where electron phase correlation is maintained (mesoscopic structures).

18.1 POINT DEFECTS IN SEMICONDUCTORS

In Chapter 8 we discussed the issues of dopants in semiconductors. The dopant atom was treated in the effective mass theory which rendered the problem very simple. Only the bandedge states were invoked to calculate the dopant energy levels. This was possible because of the long-range and weak nature of the shallow impurity problem. Most defects create a deep short-range potential fluctuation in the host lattice. The simplest defect is a vacancy which is a missing atom, and is often known as the Schottky defect. Chemical impurities also create a point defect producing strong short-ranged potential alterations. In compound semiconductors an anion or cation appearing on a wrong sublattice (e.g. a cation on the anion sublattice) can produce a defect known as an anti-site defect. The point defects which are native (vacancies, antisites, interstitial defects, etc.) will be present in any crystal because of entropy considerations. In Figure 18.1 some simple point defects are shown. For crystals grown close to equilibrium the num-

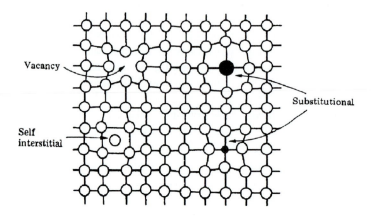

Figure 18.1: Simple native defects in a crystalline material.

ber of defects n is given by

$$n \approx N \exp\left(\frac{-E_D}{k_B T}\right) \tag{18.1}$$

where N is the total number of atomic sites, E_D is the energy cost of producing a defect, and T is the temperature of growth. Equation 18.1 suggests that the defect density could be reduced by growing the structure at low temperatures. However, this is not the case since, at low temperatures, the atoms may not have the kinetic energy necessary to reach the equilibrium crystalline sites. Thus, a compromise is used in choosing the ideal growth temperature. If a crystal is grown at 1000 K and a defect has a formation energy of 1 eV, the density of defects is $n/N \sim 10^{-5}$. Of course, in addition to entropy driven defects, one has defects arising from the chemical impurities in the background.

For the purpose of completeness we will now define some of the common terminologies for certain defects. A Frenkel defect is a vacancy-related defect in which an atom leaves its crystalline position and moves to an interstitial position. The term color center defect (often in alkali-halides) is used for a defect which absorbs visible light in a normally transparent crystal. The term F-center defect is used for a defect in alkali-halides where an electron is bound to a negative ion vacancy. The negative ion vacancy acts as a positive charge and traps an electron. It may be noted that in compound semiconductors, anti-site defects often act as a source of dopants. If the anti-site defect density is not carefully controlled, this "auto-doping" phenomenon seriously limits the use of the semiconductor. This problem is often present in many II-VI semiconductors.

The presence of point defects produces a strong perturbation in the crystal potential. We are primarily concerned with the effects of levels that are produced in the bandgap region of the semiconductor bandstructure. The electronic levels in the bandgap can produce trapping states which have important consequences for solid state electronics. We will develop a simple formalism to study the electronic levels associated with the defect. We will assume that the defect related perturbations are short-ranged, extending over only a unit cell or so.

The problem of defects and disorder is addressed most effectively by the Green function approach. In Chapter 4 and Chapter 5 we discussed the electronic bandstructure in perfect crystals. It is useful to reinterpret this information in terms of Green functions and then study the effect of defects and disorder. The problem of point defects can be addressed in a very simple manner by using the Koster-Slater model for impurities.

The Green functions are defined for a general operator equation. Consider the equation

$$L(\boldsymbol{r})\phi_n(\boldsymbol{r}) = \lambda_n \phi_n(\boldsymbol{r}) \tag{18.2}$$

where $\phi_n(\boldsymbol{r})$ are the solutions of the operator $L(\boldsymbol{r})$ with eigenvalues λ_n. For example, in Schrödinger equation, $L(\boldsymbol{r})$ is simple $H(\boldsymbol{r})$, the Hamiltonian. The Green function is defined as the solution to the equation

$$[z - L(\boldsymbol{r})]\, G(\boldsymbol{r}, \boldsymbol{r}'; z) = \delta(\boldsymbol{r} - \boldsymbol{r}'). \tag{18.3}$$

In the Dirac notation, the equations can be rewritten as

$$L|\phi_n\rangle = \lambda_n|\phi_n\rangle \tag{18.4}$$

$$(z - L)G(z) = 1. \tag{18.5}$$

Also,

$$\begin{aligned}
\langle \phi_n | \phi_m \rangle &= \delta_{nm} \\
\sum_n |\phi_n\rangle\langle\phi_n| &= 1.
\end{aligned} \tag{18.6}$$

If all eigenvalues of $z - L$ are nonzero, i.e. if $z \neq \lambda_n$ one can solve Equation 18.5 formally as

$$\begin{aligned}
G(z) &= \frac{1}{z - L} \\
&= \sum_n \frac{|\phi_n\rangle\langle\phi_n|}{z - L} \\
&= \sum_n \frac{|\phi_n\rangle\langle\phi_n|}{z - \lambda_n}.
\end{aligned} \tag{18.7}$$

The last step comes about since

$$F(L)|\phi_n\rangle = F(\lambda_n)|\phi_n\rangle. \tag{18.8}$$

This equation can be written more generally as

$$G(z) = \sideset{}{'}\sum_{n} \frac{|\phi_n\rangle\langle\phi_n|}{z - \lambda_n} + \int dn \frac{|\phi_n\rangle\langle\phi_n|}{z - \lambda_n} \tag{18.9}$$

where the sum is over the discrete values of λ_n and the integral is over the continuous values.

We assume that the operator L is hermitian, so that all the eigenvalues are real. Thus, if $g_m(z) \neq 0$, $z \neq \lambda_n$, i.e., the function $G(z)$ is an analytical function, except points on the real axis which correspond to the eigenvalues of L. At such points the Green function is defined by limiting procedures. We define two limits for such points

$$G^+(r, r'; \lambda) = \lim_{s \to 0+} G(r, r'; \lambda + iS)$$

$$G^-(r, r'; \lambda) = \lim_{s \to 0-} G(r, r'; \lambda - iS). \tag{18.10}$$

We note that

$$G^-(r, r'; \lambda) = \left[G^+(r, r'; \lambda) \right]^* \tag{18.11}$$

which shows that

$$\text{Re}\left[G^-(r, r'; \lambda) \right] = \text{Re}\left[G^+(r, r'; \lambda) \right]$$

$$\text{Im}\left[G^-(r, r'; \lambda) \right] = -\text{Im}\left[G^+(r, r'; \lambda) \right] \tag{18.12}$$

We now use the identity

$$\lim_{y \to 0} \frac{1}{x \pm iy} = P\left(\frac{1}{x}\right) \mp i\pi\delta(x) \tag{18.13}$$

where $P(1/x)$ is the principle part, to express the discontinuity

$$\tilde{G}(\lambda) = G^+(\lambda) - G^-(\lambda)$$

$$= -2\pi i \sum_{n} \delta(\lambda - \lambda_n) \, \phi_n(r) \, \phi_n^*(r'). \tag{18.14}$$

For the diagonal matrix elements we have

$$G^\pm(r, r'; \lambda) = P \sum_{n} \frac{\phi_n(r) \, \phi_n^*(r')}{\lambda - \lambda_n} \mp i\pi \sum_{n} \delta(\lambda - \lambda_n) \, \phi_n(r) \, \phi_n^*(r'). \tag{18.15}$$

Integrating over r, we get

$$\text{Tr} \, G^\pm(\lambda) = P \sum_{n} \frac{1}{\lambda - \lambda_n} \mp i\pi \sum_{n} \delta(\lambda - \lambda_n). \tag{18.16}$$

The quantity $\sum_n \delta(\lambda - \lambda_n)$ is simply the density of states $N(\lambda)$ at the point λ corresponding to the Equation 18.4. We thus have the important relation

$$N(\lambda) = \mp \frac{1}{\pi} \mathrm{Im} \left[\mathrm{Tr}\, G^{\pm}(\lambda) \right]. \tag{18.17}$$

In our particular case of the electronic states in a crystalline material, the band-structure knowledge gives us the corresponding Green functions. The use of these functions becomes clear when we next address the problem of a Hamiltonian operator of the form

$$H = H_0 + H_1. \tag{18.18}$$

The Hamiltonian H_0 corresponds to the perfectly periodic structure addressed in Chapter 3 and Chapter 4 while H_1 represents a perturbation which could represent a defect in the crystal. The Green function corresponding to H_0 is thus known and is formally

$$G_0(z) = \frac{1}{z - H_0}. \tag{18.19}$$

The Green function corresponding to H is

$$\begin{aligned}
G(z) &= \frac{1}{z - H} \\
&= \frac{1}{z - H_0 - H_1} \\
&= \left[(z - H_0) \left\{ 1 - (z - H_0)^{-1} H_1 \right\} \right]^{-1} \\
&= \left[1 - G_0 H_1 \right]^{-1} G_0. \tag{18.20}
\end{aligned}$$

Expanding $(1 - G_0 H_1)^{-1}$ in a power series, we have

$$\begin{aligned}
G &= G_0 + G_0 H_1 G_0 + G_0 H_1 G_0 H_1 G_0 + \cdots \\
&= G_0 + G_0 H_1 G. \tag{18.21}
\end{aligned}$$

This may be written as

$$G = G_0 + G_0 T G_0 \tag{18.22}$$

where

$$T = H_1 + H_1 G_0 H_1 + H_1 G_0 H_1 G_0 H_1 + \cdots. \tag{18.23}$$

We will now develop a model for the point defect problem using the tight binding approach discussed in Chapter 5. We consider a tight binding Hamiltonian whose periodicity has been destroyed at just one site (say the ℓ-site). At site ℓ, the diagonal element is $E_0 + \epsilon$, where E_0 is the perfect periodic value. The Hamiltonian is written as

$$H = H_0 + H_1 \tag{18.24}$$

where

$$H_0 = \sum_m |m\rangle E_0 \langle m| + V \sum_{nm}{}' |n\rangle \langle m| \tag{18.25}$$

which represents the on-site tight binding elements E_0 and off-site elements V. The most general Hamiltonian, of course, has several matrix elements corresponding to the basis functions used. The perturbation Hamiltonian is

$$H_1 = |\ell\rangle \epsilon \langle \ell|. \tag{18.26}$$

The equation for the T–matrix is now

$$
\begin{aligned}
T &= |\ell\rangle \epsilon \langle \ell| + |\ell\rangle \epsilon \langle \ell| G_0 |\ell\rangle \epsilon \langle \ell| + |\ell\rangle \epsilon \langle \ell| G_0 |\ell\rangle \epsilon \langle \ell| G_0 |\ell\rangle \epsilon \langle \ell| + \dots \\
&= |\ell\rangle \epsilon \left\{ 1 + \epsilon G_0(\ell, \ell) + [\epsilon G_0(\ell, \ell) + \dots]^2 \right\} \langle \ell| \\
&= |\ell\rangle \frac{\epsilon}{1 - \epsilon G_0(\ell, \ell)} \langle \ell| \tag{18.27}
\end{aligned}
$$

where

$$G_0(\ell, \ell) \equiv \langle \ell| G_0 |\ell\rangle.$$

Having obtained a closed expression for T, we have immediately G

$$
\begin{aligned}
G &= G_0 + G_0 T G_0 \\
&= G_0 + G_0 |\ell\rangle \frac{\epsilon}{1 - \epsilon G_0(\ell, \ell)} \langle \ell| G_0. \tag{18.28}
\end{aligned}
$$

The poles of $G(E)$ or $T(E)$ correspond to the discrete eigenvalues of H. For our defect problem the poles are given by

$$G_0(\ell, \ell; E_p) = \frac{1}{\epsilon} \tag{18.29}$$

as can be seen from Equation 18.28. We are interested in the effect of the defects on the states in the bandgap. The starting Hamiltonian H_0 has no states in the gap so that G_0 is real for energies in the bandgap and is simply given by

$$G(E) = \int_{-\infty}^{\infty} dE' \frac{N(E')}{E - E'} \tag{18.30}$$

where $N(E)$ is the density of states obtained from the solution of H_0 (i.e., from the perfect semiconductor bandstructure).

It is interesting to examine the condition for levels in the gap for the generic cases of 3-D, 2-D, and 1-D structures. We know, for example, that the density of states near the bandedges for a 3-D system has the form

$$N(E) = C_b \sqrt{E - E_b} \tag{18.31}$$

where E_b represents a bandedge. Due to this energy dependence, the value of $G(E_b)$ at the bandedge is finite. Also, the value of $G(E)$ falls away from the bandedge as shown in Figure 18.2. Notice that for a typical semiconductor, $G(E)$ will have a positive value just above the valence bandedge and a negative value

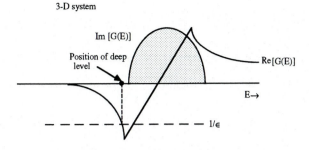

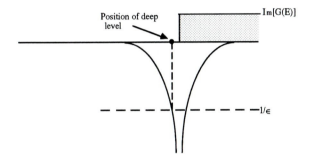

Figure 18.2: The effect of an impurity of strength E different from the host lattice on electronic spectra. In one and two dimensions a bandgap state is produced regardless of the strength of ϵ. In three dimensions a minimum strength is needed.

below the conduction bandedge. *We can see that for the 3-D case, the strength of the perturbation ϵ has to be finite before a level will appear in the bandgap.*

For the two-dimensional case, the density of states is a constant so that at the bandedges the Green function of the unperturbed Hamiltonian becomes

$$
\begin{aligned}
G_0(E) &\rightarrow \ln|E - E_\ell| \rightarrow \infty \\
E &\rightarrow E_\ell^-.
\end{aligned}
\tag{18.32}
$$

As a result there will be a level in the forbidden gap for an infinitesimally small value of the perturbation E. As the strength of E increases the level moves further into the bandgap.

For the 1-dimensional case the density of states has a $(E - E_b)^{-1/2}$ behavior which again causes $G_0(E_b)$ to go infinity. *Thus, in the 1-D problem also the smallest perturbation produces a level in the bandgap.* The effects of dimensionality discussed here are schematically sketched in Figure 18.2.

In the Koster-Slater model for the defect, the perturbation H' is considered to be local and existing only on the defect site as assumed in our derivation. A

Au levels in Si

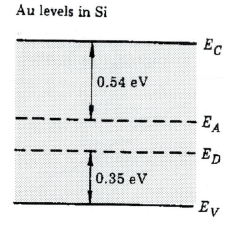

Figure 18.3: Au in Si has an acceptor state, E_A ($\sim E_c - 0.54$ eV) and a donor state, E_D ($\sim E_V + 0.35$ eV).

real defect may, of course, perturb the crystal more. However, a good semiquantitative description of the defect states is provided by the Koster-Slater picture. A vacancy level is represented by the perturbation E to be chosen as infinity, representing the inability of the electrons to physically exist at the vacancy site. Substitutional impurities are represented by the differences in the on-site tight binding matrix elements. Of course, more complex defects such as interstitial defects, defect complexes, etc., are not described in this simple picture and require more complex formalism.

In contrast to the shallow levels associated with the Coulombic potential of dopants, the deep levels in the bandgap are associated with short-ranged impurity potentials. These levels need not necessarily be near the mid-bandgap region, and, in fact, for some impurities, they could be quite close to the bandedges. However, they are not derived from the bandedge states but are affected by the *entire bandstructure* of the host crystal. A typical deep level may also have several energy levels associated with it, and these could act as donors (i.e., neutral when it captures an electron, charged positively when empty) or acceptors.

A typical example of deep levels in Si is shown in Figure 18.3 . Au in Si has an acceptor-like state which is 0.54 eV below the conduction band and a donor-like state which is 0.35 eV above the valence band. The ideal vacancy in silicon has been shown to have a deep level 0.27 eV above the valence bandedge. The corresponding levels in Ge are at 0.11 eV. In GaAs we can have the Ga vacancy denoted by V^{Ga} which has an energy at 0.02 eV and an As vacancy denoted by V^{As} which has a level at 0.71 eV and one near the conduction bandedge at 1.47 eV.

Unlike the elemental semiconductors, the compound semiconductors can have antisite defects which can often dominate the deep level spectra in high quality materials. For example, in GaAs, the deep levels observed in MBE grown samples are critically dependent upon the Ga to As pressure rations, whether As_2 or As_4 is used for growth, etc. It appears that the combination of native defects and impurities forming some defect complex is responsible for the more than a dozen deep levels seen in "high purity" GaAs.

An extremely important deep level in semiconductors is the so called D-X center which is observed widely in $Al_x Ga_{1-x} As$ and several other semiconductors where the conduction band energies at the Γ, X, L points are very close to each other. In $Al_x Ga_{1-x} As$ this occurs at x $\sim$ 0.35. The D-X center is associated with n-type donors in AlGaAs. As the Al composition is increased, an effective mass-like donor is observed up to $x \sim 0.25$. At higher values of Al, deep levels emerge and dominate the carrier concentrations in AlGaAs. The deep level, known as the D-X center, is apparently associated with the wavefunctions at the L-point and involve a donor complex. As the Al fraction is increased beyond 0.45, the bottom of the conduction band is X-like and the effect of the D-X center diminishes. The D-X center is an extremely important defect which causes serious problems in AlGaAs/GaAs MODFETs at low temperature due to trapping effects. It is also related to strong light sensitivity of these devices related to trapping and detrapping effects.

Deep levels are almost always to be avoided in semiconductors since they are usually sources of trapping, recombination, and scattering. However, in some special cases, deep levels are introduced. This is usually done for detectors to speed up the response of the device. For example, in Si detectors the electron-hole recombination time is at least 10^{-6} seconds and GaAs is $\sim 10^{-9}$ seconds (longer if the electron-hole densities are low). Thus, the device speeds are often limited unless some other method is used to remove the electrons and holes. Deep levels are often introduced to accomplish this task.

18.2 TRAPPING AND RECOMBINATION

The effects of deep levels in the electrons and holes in the conduction and valence band are manifested via two phenomena. In the first one the electron (hole) is captured from the free state into the deep level when it is localized in space. It is then re-emitted into the conduction (valence) band. This process, known as trapping, involves the electron capture and emission. On the other hand, once the electron is in the deep level, it could recombine with a hole, so that the deep level is then responsible for the electron-hole recombination. The important processes that occur in presence of deep levels are illustrated in Figure 18.4. These processes represent electrons and holes being captured and emitted from the deep levels. Also shown are the processes leading to electron-hole recombination.

The capture process of the electron (hole) into a deep level is described by the scattering formalism used in our discussions on transport and optical

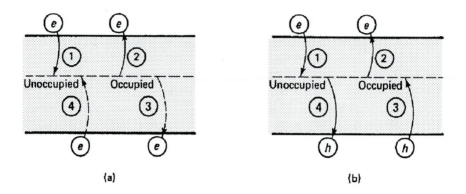

Figure 18.4: Various processes that lead to trapping and recombination via deep levels. The processes 1 and 2 in (a) represent trapping and emission of electrons while 3 and 4 represent the same for holes. The electron-hole recombination is shown in figure (b).

processes. This involves evaluating the scattering or transition matrix element between the Bloch-like electron state and the localized deep level state. Since energy is lost during the trapping process, phonons are involved in the process. Due to the complexity of this problem and the differences in the nature of the trap levels for different defects, it is useful to describe the phenomenon by a simple approach developed by Shockley and Read and by Hall. The capture process is represented by a scattering cross section σ which represents an area associated with the trap so that an electron impinging within this area is captured by the trap. If an electron in the conduction band is traveling with a velocity v, it sweeps out a volume vs per unit time and will be captured by the traps in this volume. Let us consider a semiconductor with a density of recombination centers N_t located at an energy E_t. The probability that the state is occupied is given by

$$f(E_t) = \frac{1}{1 + \exp\left(\dfrac{E_t - E_F}{k_B T}\right)}. \tag{18.33}$$

The rate at which the electrons will be captured is then

$$R_{cn} = \sigma_{cn} \, v_{th} \, n \, N_t \, (1 - f). \tag{18.34}$$

This rate is proportional to the electron density and the unoccupied trap density. We assume that the electrons are moving with the thermal velocity, v_{th}.

The electron emission rate R_{en} is proportional to the concentration $N_t f$ of the occupied traps, and can be written as

$$R_{en} = e_n \, N_t \, f \tag{18.35}$$

where the emission probability e_n depends upon the density of empty states in the conduction band and the value of E_t. We now invoke the principle of detailed balance which states that in equilibrium the rate of a physical process and its reverse have to be balanced. Thus, we have

$$R_{en} = R_{cn} \tag{18.36}$$

writing the free carrier density as

$$n = n_i \, \exp \left[\frac{E_F - E_i}{k_B T} \right] \tag{18.37}$$

where n_i is the intrinsic carrier concentration, we get

$$e_n = \sigma_{cn} \, v_{th} \, n_i \, \exp \left[\frac{E_t - E_i}{k_B T} \right]. \tag{18.38}$$

The analysis can be repeated for the holes and we have similar equations

$$R_{cp} = \sigma_{cp} \, v_{th} \, p \, N_t \, f \tag{18.39}$$

$$R_{ep} = e_p \, N_t \, (1 - f) \tag{18.40}$$

and

$$e_p = \sigma_{cp} \, v_{th} \, n_i \, \exp \left[\frac{E_i - E_t}{k_B T} \right]. \tag{18.41}$$

We see that the emission coefficient e_n increases as E_t rise towards the conduction band, while e_p increases as E_t approaches the valence band.

In Chapter 15 we discussed the radiative recombination of electron-hole pairs. The radiative recombination is accompanied by photon emission. In the case of trapping and recombination, the excess energy is simply lost as phonons. Let us consider a case where a semiconductor is illuminated optically and electron-hole pairs are generated at a rate G_L per unit volume per second. This increases the electron (hole) concentration above equilibrium and the capture rate increases correspondingly. In steady state the net rate of generation and loss are equal, i.e.

$$G_L + R_{en} - R_{cn} = 0. \tag{18.42}$$

Similarly for holes

$$G_L + R_{ep} - R_{cp} = 0. \tag{18.43}$$

This leads to the following result

$$\begin{aligned} U &= R_{en} - R_{cn} \\ &= R_{ep} - R_{cp}. \end{aligned} \tag{18.44}$$

In presence of the excess carrier concentrations the occupation probability of the trap levels will change. One can obtain this value by substituting for R_{en}, R_{cn}, R_{ep}, and R_{cp} in Equation 18.44 and solving for the occupation probability f. This gives

$$f = \frac{\sigma_{cn} \, n_1 + \sigma_{cp} \, p_1}{\sigma_{cn} \, (n + n_1) + \sigma_{cp} \, (p + p1)} \tag{18.45}$$

where

$$n_1 = n_i \exp\left(\frac{E_t - E_i}{k_B T}\right)$$

$$p_1 = n_i \exp\left(\frac{E_i - E_t}{k_B T}\right). \tag{18.46}$$

Using the value of f, we get for the generation rate

$$
\begin{aligned}
U &= R_{en} - R_{cn} \\
&= \frac{\sigma_{cp}\,\sigma_{cn}\,v_{th}\,N_t(pn - n_i^2)}{\sigma_{cn}\,(n + n_1) + \sigma_{cp}\,(p + p_1)}.
\end{aligned} \tag{18.47}
$$

We now define capture times for the electrons and holes as

$$\tau_{p0} = \frac{1}{\sigma_{cp}\,v_{th}\,N_t}$$

$$\tau_{n0} = \frac{1}{\sigma_{cn}\,v_{th}\,N_t} \tag{18.48}$$

and obtain

$$U = \frac{pn - n_i^2}{\tau_{p0}\,(n + n_1) + \tau_{n0}\,(p + p_1)}. \tag{18.49}$$

This equation gives us the rate at which the electron-hole pairs generated by light will recombine via the traps. Of course, we have assumed that there is no radiative recombination. The radiative part has to be added separately in a manner discussed in Chapter 15.

Let us consider the trap assisted recombinations (the Shockley-Read-Hall recombination) for an n-type semiconductor. The excess carrier lifetime is defined by

$$
\begin{aligned}
\tau_p &= \frac{p_n - p_{n0}}{U} \\
&= \frac{p_e}{U}
\end{aligned} \tag{18.50}
$$

where p_e is the excess carrier density (a small value) introduced by illumination. Substituting for U from Equation 18.49 we get

$$\tau_p = p_e \left[\frac{\tau_{p0}\,(n + n_1) + \tau_{n0}\,(p + p_1)}{(pn - n_i^2)}\right]. \tag{18.51}$$

We now use the relations

$$n = n_{n0} + n_e$$

$$p = p_{n0} + p_e$$

$$n_e = p_e \tag{18.52}$$

and n_{n0} is large compared to p_{n0} and p_e. This allows us to write

$$\tau_p = p_e \left[\frac{\tau_{p0} \left(n_{n0} + n_1 \right) + \tau_{n0} \left(p_e + p_1 \right)}{n_{n0}} \right]. \tag{18.53}$$

Now, if we consider the case of a heavily doped n-type semiconductor, so that n_{n0} is larger than any other carrier densities, we get

$$\begin{aligned} \tau_p &= \tau_{p0} \\ &= \frac{1}{\sigma_{cp} \, v_{th} \, N_t}. \end{aligned} \tag{18.54}$$

In this regime, the recombination time is simply determined by the hole capture since a high density of electrons are always available to recombine with the hole.

The analysis is similar for a p-type semiconductor and gives for the heavy doped case

$$\begin{aligned} \tau_n &\approx \tau_{n0} \\ &= \frac{1}{\sigma_{cn} v_{th} N_t}. \end{aligned} \tag{18.55}$$

In case the illumination level is so high that the one cannot neglect the excess carrier concentration with respect to the equilibrium values, we have, ($p_e = n_e \gg p_{n0}$)

$$\tau_p \approx \frac{\tau_{p0} \left(n_{n0} + p_e + n_1 \right) + \tau_{n0} \left(p_e + p_1 \right)}{\left(n_{n0} + p_e \right)}. \tag{18.56}$$

The value of τ_p increases over the low injection value, and eventually approaches $(\tau_{n0} + \tau_{p0})$.

The important physical property that represents the trap or deep level is the cross section associated with it. Typical values of these cross sections are in the range of 10^{-13}–10^{-15} cm^2. We note that in direct bandgap semiconductors, usually the radiative recombination is quite strong so that the electron-hole pairs choose this path for recombination unless the material quality is not good. In indirect gap semiconductors, however, the radiative recombination times are very long ($> 10^{-6}$ sec) so that even at low defect densities, the nonradiative recombination dominates.

In devices such as HBT, the recombination time must be maintained at as low a value as possible in the base region since the base recombination reduces the gain of the device. However, in many photodetectors, defects are intentionally introduced to speed up the device.

We conclude this section by mentioning that the semiconductor surface usually has a high density of defect states arising from dangling bonds, impurities, etc. These traps can also lead to a very high recombination rates for the carriers. The recombination process is usually defined via a surface recombination velocity, (say for holes)

$$v_S = \sigma_p \, v_{th} \, N_{st} \tag{18.57}$$

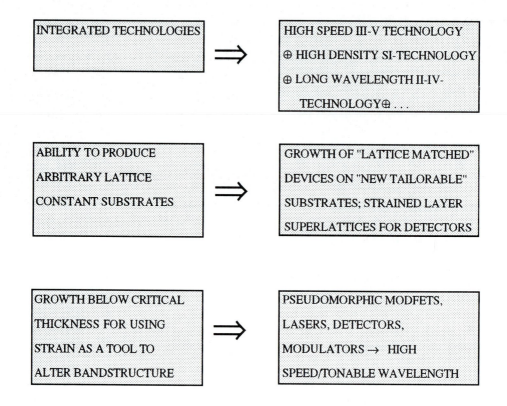

CENTRAL PROBLEM → DISLOCATION CONTROL

Figure 18.5: Driving forces for lattice mismatched epitaxy.

where N_{st} is the areal density of the surface traps. For most semiconductors, the surface recombination velocity is of the order of a few hundred cm/sec, and is quite sensitive to the surface conditions.

18.3   DISLOCATIONS AND LATTICE MISMATCHED EPITAXY

A very important class of defects are the line defects known as dislocations. These defects have assumed extreme importance because of the tremendous interest in lattice mismatched epitaxy. In Figure 18.5 we show some of the motivations for the drive towards lattice mismatched epitaxy. As one can see, the impact of lattice mismatched epitaxy could be over all aspects of electronic and optoelectronic technology. The ideal "blue-sky" chip of the future would have the properties sketched in Figure 18.6. The best properties of several different material systems

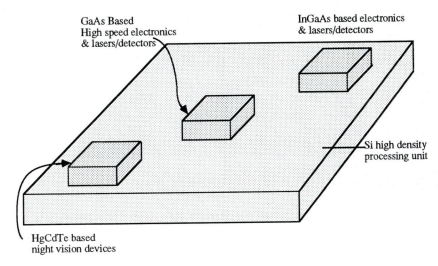

GaAs Based
High speed electronics
& lasers/detectors

InGaAs based electronics
& lasers/detectors

Si high density
processing unit

HgCdTe based
night vision devices

Figure 18.6: A schematic of the integrated circuit of the future combining the best of different material technologies on the same chip.

would be combined to produce a highly versatile integrated circuit. The main hindrance to being able to do this reliably is a lack of understanding over dislocation generation and control. In this section we will briefly review some of the properties of dislocations. Dislocations are line defects that result when part of a crystal slips relative to another part, relative to a plane in the crystal. The driving force behind such a slip is due to elastic strain energy of the crystal.

An example of a particular kind of dislocation, called edge dislocation, is shown in Figure 18.7. Such a dislocation would arise, for example, if stress is applied so that the lower half of the crystal moves to the right with respect to the upper half. An entire line of atoms (along AD of the figure) then has a broken bond along the lower plane. It is as if an extra plane of atoms (ABCD) is inserted into the upper plane. For the edge dislocations, the dislocation line is perpendicular to the slip direction.

Another important dislocation is the screw dislocation in Figure 18.8. In this case the slip direction is parallel to the dislocation line AF. As one can see, the dislocation line has atoms whose coordination is not the same as the regular crystalline atoms. Because of a series of broken bonds, it is energetically expensive to create dislocations. However, dislocations are created to relax a build up of strain energy and at least locally, the state with dislocations has a lower energy than the state with proper coordination but with strain energy. We will discuss this case for the strained epitaxy a little later.

Before discussing the special features of dislocations in the semiconductors we define an important concept that is very useful in defining dislocations. This is the concept of Burger's vector, which defines the translational or shift vector of a dislocation. The Burger's vector b is perpendicular to the dislocation line for

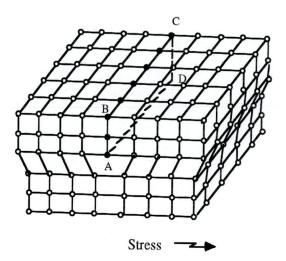

Stress

Figure 18.7: Schematic diagram of a crystal containing edge dislocation. The dislocation line AD is normal to the slip direction.

an edge dislocation and is parallel to the dislocation line for a screw dislocation. In general, one can determine the Burger's vector by comparing the circuit path (the Burger's circuit) in the perfect crystalline region with the same steps in the circuit taken along a path that encloses the dislocation line, as shown in Figure 18.9.

We list below some of the important properties of dislocations:

1. For a given dislocation, there is only one Burger's vector regardless of the shape of the dislocation line.

2. A dislocation must end on itself, thus forming a loop, or on other dislocations, thus forming a network, or on surfaces such as external surface or a ground boundary.

3. In general, dislocations in real crystals form three-dimensional networks. The sum of the Burger's vectors at the node or point of junction of the dislocation is zero.

4. The slip (or glide) plane of a dislocation contains the dislocation line and its Burger's vector.

In the case of the tetrahedrally bonded semiconductors there are some special features of the dislocations. Each atom is tetrahedrally bonded to four nearest neighbors, and the shortest lattice vector $1/2 < 110 >$ links a second-neighbor pair. The close-packed $\{111\}$ planes have a six-fold stacking sequence AaBbCcAaBb... as shown in Figure 18.10. Atoms of adjacent layers of the same letter such as Aa lie directly over each other, and planar stacking faults arising from insertion or removal of such pairs do not change the tetrahedral bonding.

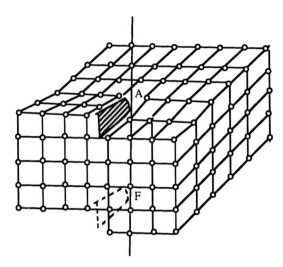

Figure 18.8: Geometry of a screw-type dislocation. The dislocation line is parallel to the slip direction.

Perfect dislocations have Burger's vector $1/2 < 110 >$ and slip on $\{111\}$ planes. They usually lie along $< 110 >$ directions at $0°$ or $60°$ to the Burger's vector as result of low core energy in those orientations. From consideration of dislocations formed by the cutting operations, two dislocation types may be distinguished. The cut may be made between layer of either different letters, e.g., aB, or the same letter, e.g., bB. Following Hirth and Lothe, the dislocations produced belong to either the glide set or the shuffle set, as denoted in Figure 18.10.

18.3.1 Strained Epitaxy and Critical Thickness

From our discussions in Chapter 7 and the discussions in this section, it is clear that epitaxy of lattice mismatched layers is of extreme importance in solid state electronics. What is the microscopic configuration of an overlayer of a semiconductor grown on top of a lattice mismatched substrate? This question has been studied for almost two generations now and continues to be of great interest. Although there are some quantitative differences between various theories, they all come to the following basic conclusions regarding the thermodynamic equilibrium state of a stained overlayer deposited on a semi-infinite substrate with misfit ϵ:

1. If ϵ is less than ϵ_{c1} ($\sim 10\%$), the first monolayer has no dislocation. If ϵ lies between ϵ_{c1} and ϵ_{c2} ($\sim 14\%$), the lowest energy state of a monolayer has dislocations running along the monolayer, although the dislocations may not be generated in a metastable state. If $\epsilon > \epsilon_{c2}$, dislocations will be always generated in the very first monolayer and the thick overlayer may

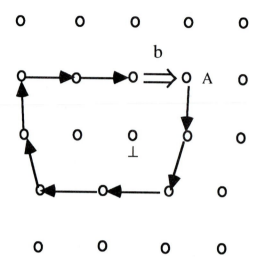

Figure 18.9: The Burger's vector of an edge dislocation is determined by drawing a Burger's circuit around a dislocation. Look along the dislocation (the symbol $\perp$ represents a dislocation going into the plane of the page) and draw a circuit (starting from atom A) in the clockwise direction. The Burger's vector b is the vector required to close the circuit.

continue growth in a different orientation than the substrate.

2. For $\epsilon < \epsilon_{c1}$, it is possible to divide the overlayer thickness d into two regimes: $d < d_c$, where the overlayer grows in coherence with the substrate (i.e., no dislocations are produced, and $d > d_c$, where dislocations are produced at the interface and overlayer grows with its own bulk lattice constant.

Numerous experiments have verified these basic conclusions although there is still some confusion regarding the precise critical thickness–misfit dependence. It must be noted, however, that the ideas discussed above are based upon the assumption that the pseudomorphic overlayer is atomically flat on top of the mismatched substrate. During growth, the overlayer may choose not to have an atomically flat profile and *may grow in a 3-dimensional island mode to minimize its strain energy.* Thus, thus concept of critical thickness is somewhat ambiguous and is more relevant for buried strained layers, which are sandwiched between thick unstrained layers.

The fact that one has a critical thickness below which the overlayer is pseudomorphic and above which it is dislocated (see Figure 18.11) is apparent from the following simple considerations of the energy of the overlayer (assuming that the overlayer has a uniform thickness). For simplicity let us consider the growth of a semiconductor on an infinite substrate. If the lattice mismatch is all absorbed via strain (i.e. growth is pseudomorphic), the strain energy per unit

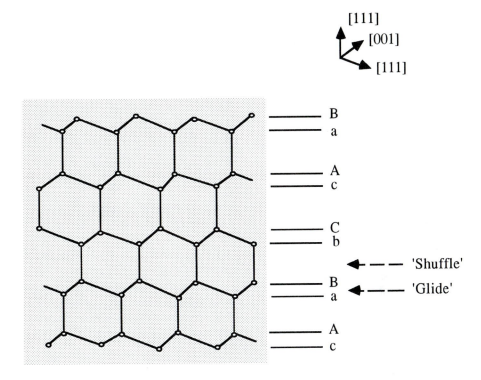

Figure 18.10: The covalent structure viewed along the [1$\bar{1}$0] direction. Note the stacking sequence of the (111) planes and the shuffle and glide planes defined in the test.

area of the film of thickness d is (see Chapter 7)

$$E = d \left[\frac{1}{2}c_{11} \left(\epsilon_{xx}^2 + \epsilon_{yy}^2 + \epsilon_{zz}^2 \right) + c_{12} \left(\epsilon_{xx}\epsilon_{yy} + \epsilon_{yy}\epsilon_{zz} + \epsilon_{zz}\epsilon_{xx} \right) \right.$$

$$\left. + \frac{1}{2}c_{44} \left(\epsilon_{xy}^2 + \epsilon_{yz}^2 + \epsilon_{zx}^2 \right) \right] \tag{18.58}$$

where c_{11}, c_{12}, and c_{44} are the force constants of the semiconductor. Now for (001) growth, the pseudomorphic growth requires that

$$\epsilon_{xx} = \epsilon_{yy} = \epsilon$$
$$\epsilon_{zz} = -\frac{2c_{12}}{c_{11}}\epsilon \tag{18.59}$$

so that the strain energy becomes

$$E_{st} = \epsilon^2 \left(c_{11} + c_{12} - \frac{2c_{12}^2}{c_{11}} \right) d$$
$$\sim 13 \, \epsilon^2 d \left(\times 10^{11} \text{ ergs / cm}^2 \right) \tag{18.60}$$

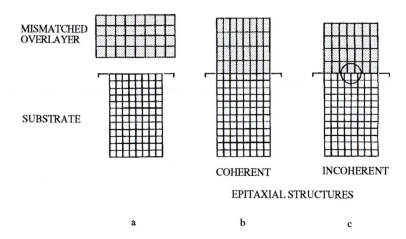

Figure 18.11: When an overlayer with a lattice constant mismatched with a substrate (a) is deposited on the substrate, below the critical thickness the overlayer is in coherence (b) with the substrate. Above critical thickness dislocations appear at the interface as shown in (c). Note that these concepts assume that the overlayer thickness is uniform, i.e., the pseudomorphic region is flat.

using typical values of the force constant (e.g. $c_{11} = 12.0 \times 10^{11}$ dynes/cm^2; $c_{12} = 5.5 \times 10^{11}$ dynes/cm^2; $c_{44} = 5 \times 10^{11}$ dynes/cm^2, for GaAs). The strain energy increases linearly with the thickness of film. On the other hand, if we consider a configuration where there is a network of dislocations separated by a distance

$$L_d = \frac{a}{\epsilon} \tag{18.61}$$

where a is the lattice constant, then there is no strain energy in the overlayer. If one assumes a very simple picture of the dislocation energy as being represented by a line of atoms with broken bonds of energy W, the areal energy density of the dislocation network is

$$E_d \approx \left(\frac{2L_d W}{a} \right) \left(\frac{1}{L_d^2} \right) \tag{18.62}$$

where the first term represents the average broken band energy in the region enclosed by the dislocation network "unit cell" as shown in Figure 18.12. It will be energetically favorable to have the dislocation network as opposed to the pseudomorphic growth when the overlayer thickness is such that

$$E_{st}(d_c) > E_d. \tag{18.63}$$

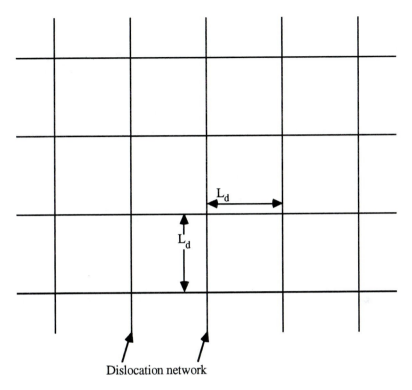

Figure 18.12: A schematic picture of a dislocation network spaced at by distance L_d.

Typical values of the bond energy are $\sim c_{11}\, a^3/2$, (i.e. ~ 1 eV per bond), so that the critical thickness is roughly

$$d_c \sim \frac{a}{2\epsilon}. \tag{18.64}$$

The above treatment provides some physical insight into the causes for the existence of the critical thickness. However, in reality, the dislocation energy is considerably more complex. A simple empirical expression has been given by Blanc according to which the critical thickness is

$$d_c \sim \frac{b}{2\epsilon} \tag{18.65}$$

where b is the magnitude of the Burger's vector of the dislocation. A more rigorous treatment of the dislocation energy has been carried out by Jesser and Kuhlmann-Wilsdorf who show that

$$E_d = \frac{\mu b}{2\pi(1-\nu)} \frac{|\epsilon + f|\,(1 - \nu \cos^2 \beta)\,\ln(qR/b)}{\cos \theta \sin \beta} \tag{18.66}$$

where μ and ν are the shear modulus and Poisson ratio, ϵ is the strain present in the film, f is the film-substrate misfit, b is the magnitude of the Burger's vector, β is the angle between the Burger's vector and the dislocation line, θ is the angle between the interface and the glide plane, q is a factor of order unity, and R is the extent of the distortion produced by a dislocation. This expression represents the case of an array of dislocations along [110] and [1$\bar{1}$0] directions on the (001) plane. The critical thickness that results from this expression is based on the criterion

$$\frac{\partial E_{\text{tot}}}{\partial \epsilon} = \frac{\partial (E_{st} + E_d)}{\partial \epsilon}\bigg|_{\epsilon=f}$$

$$= 0 \tag{18.67}$$

and gives

$$d_c = \frac{b\,(1 - \nu\cos^2\beta)}{8\pi|\epsilon|(1+\nu)\sin\beta\cos\theta}\,\ln\left(\frac{qd_c}{b}\right). \tag{18.68}$$

The logarithmic dependence is quite slow and the expression also gives $d_c \sim 1/\epsilon$ behavior. The results from the two calculations are quite similar.

A different approach to the dislocation problem was developed by Mathews and Blakeslee, who assumed that the misfit dislocations were produced by the glide of existing threading dislocations in the substrate during film growth. If f is the misfit between the substrate and overlayer, one assumes that a strain value ϵ is present in the film and a misfit δ ($= f - \epsilon$) is accommodated as dislocations. The principle of the theory is then to determine equilibrium values of f and d for a given system when the competing forces during introduction of misfit dislocations are balanced. The critical thickness from this approach turns out to be

$$d_c = \frac{b}{8\pi f}\,\frac{1 - \nu\cos^2\beta}{(1+\nu)\cos\theta}\left[\ln\frac{h_c}{b} + 1\right]. \tag{18.69}$$

This result is not too different from the earlier results although the force balance treatment is very versatile and can be applied to different mechanisms for dislocation generation. In an actual growth of a strained overlayer, the onset of critical thickness is often not abrupt and depends upon the growth conditions since growth is carried out away from equilibrium conditions.

For applications of lattice mismatched epitaxy in integrated technologies like GaAs on Si, CdTe on GaAs, etc., the key question is how the dislocation network is arranged after critical thickness has been reached. If the dislocation network is such that the dislocations are all confined to the substrate-overlayer interface, the effect of the dislocations is not felt in the active region of the overlayers where the devices are to be fabricated. However, if the dislocations thread through the growing overlayer, they will propagate in the overlayer and cause deterioration of active devices fabricated in the overlayer. This control of the dislocation network is obviously of great concern and is an area of active research. Unfortunately, the ability to control dislocation has not yet been reliably acquired.

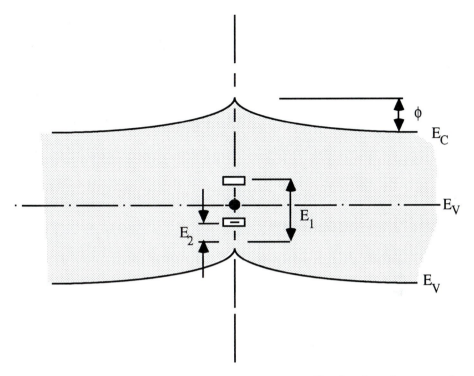

Figure 18.13: Band bending around an edge dislocation. The dangling electron at the core of the dislocation (running into the page) accepts an electron to lower its energy from E_1 (relative to E_v) to E_2, forming a positively charged space-charge region. The electron barrier ϕ is created (band bending) around the dislocation to repel the free electrons in the semiconductor, (after Matare, 1971).

18.3.2   Electronic Effects of Dislocations

Dislocations represent a line of atoms which have a missing bond with their neighbors. As discussed in the previous section, this results in deep levels in the bandgap of the semiconductor. The actual calculation of such levels is considerably more complicated than the point defect calculation. Matare has carried out a detailed investigation of the electronic levels associated with dislocations in Si and Ge. A picture schematically given by Figure 18.13 emerges from these studies.

The deep level when unoccupied has an energy E_1 with respect to the valence band. This level can, however, accept an electron from the band and get negatively charged. This produces a space charge region which is positively charged. The energy of the charged level is E_2 and the quantity ϕ defines the band bending produced. Since the spacing of the charged impurities on the dislocation line is on the order of the lattice constant, the space charge typically extends over a micron or so. Thus, when current flows through the semiconductor, the

DISORDERED SYSTEM	SOURCE OF DISORDER
• Si/SiO$_2$ interface	Distortions in bond lengths and bond angles
• GaAs/AlAs interface	Random placement of Ga and Al atoms on the interfacial planes
• Amorphous semiconductors	Bond angle, bond length fluctuations
• Alloys	Random arrangement of chemical species on the lattice
• Doping in semiconductors	Random placement of impurities
• Low temperature grown compound semiconductors	Random incorporation of defects

Table 18.1: Important examples of disordered structures in selected semiconductors and their heterostructures.

electrons encounter a winding path due to the band bending and the resistance of the material increases.

The deep levels are also a source of trapping and recombination of electrons and holes. The recombination processes are particularly important in lasers where the high recombination along dislocation lines produces dark line defects which eventually reduce the life of the laser.

18.4 DISORDERED SEMICONDUCTORS

The first eight chapters of this text dealt with the properties of the perfect crystalline structure. In Chapter 9 we introduced an important defect, the dopant atom which is a necessary defect for semiconductor technology. The effects of defects on the electronic properties were primarily described by the scattering of electrons from one state to another. In this chapter we have seen that certain defects can introduce new electronic states in the bandgap. In all of these discussions we have assumed that the density of defects is small enough that each defect can be treated as being independent of others. In this section we will deal with situations where there is some "defect" at almost every site of the crystal. This occurs in a number of important situations some of which are listed in Table 18.1.

A most important example is the Si/SiO$_2$ interface mentioned in Chapter 2. In this case, because of the lattice mismatch between Si and SiO$_2$, the interface region has an amorphous nature with small but significant distortions in the bond angles and bond lengths of the interfacial atoms. Another important example are the random alloy semiconductors, in which, even though there is a perfect underlying lattice, the atoms on each site are not well-defined leading to random potential fluctuations. Similarly the interfaces of even high quality heterostructures have interfacial disorder on the scale of a few monolayers.

The amorphous semiconductors also form an important class of materials. These semiconductors are usually grown under highly non-equilibrium growth conditions so that the growing structure is unable to reach the equilibrium crystalline structure. The advantage, of course, is that the structure is grown at a very low cost and, perhaps, can be grown over large areas. Hydrogenated amorphous silicon is a prime example of such semiconductors and offers the possibility of a cheap material for solar energy conversion. In such amorphous semiconductors, the nearest neighbor coordination is maintained, but long-range order is lost. Since often such semiconductors have broken bonds, certain additional defects are introduced in the structure to passivate the defects. For example, in amorphous silicon, hydrogen serves this purpose.

18.5 EXTENDED AND LOCALIZED STATES

In the discussion of deep levels produced by the point defects, we realized that the wavefunction associated with the point defect is not an extended state of the form

$$\psi_{\text{ex}} = \frac{1}{\sqrt{V}} u_{\mathbf{k}}(\boldsymbol{r}) e^{i\mathbf{k}\cdot\mathbf{r}} \tag{18.70}$$

but was a localized state with a finite extent in space. The defect states have a general form $\psi_{\text{loc}}(\boldsymbol{r}, \boldsymbol{r}_0)$ representing the fact that they are localized around a point $\boldsymbol{r}_0$ in space. Typical localized states may have an exponentially decaying behavior. An example of this are the donor or acceptor states which are localized around the impurity position. This concept of localized and extended states is further generalized as the extent of disorder is increased. While for point defects and dopant atoms, the associated localized states are energetically separated, as the level of disorder increases, the extended and localized states merge forming a continuum in electronic spectra.

The qualitative differences between the extended and localized states can theoretically be brought out by an approach suggested by Thouless. Consider a volume V_1 of the disordered sample. If one solves for the electronic states of the sample with boundary conditions that the wavefunctions go to zero at the boundary, then both "extended" and localized states will be confined to this volume. Now if one increases the volume, the amplitude of the "extended" states will decrease as $\sim 1/\sqrt{V_1}$ while that of the localized states will essentially remain constant. The energy points which separate the extended and localized states are called the mobility edge, the term arising from the consensus that the dc conductivity of the localized states goes to zero (at low temperatures). The effect of disorder on the nature of electronic states was first studied by Anderson in his classic paper. He showed that as the disorder is increased, the extent of the localized states increases as shown schematically in Figure 18.14.

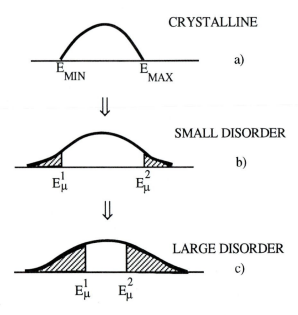

Figure 18.14: Density of states and the influence of disorder. The shaded region represents the region where the electronic states are localized in space. The mobility edges E_μ separate the region of localized and extended states.

There have been many different approaches to tackle the problem of disordered systems. These can be classified into three sets. The first involves numerical methods in which the problem of a very large number of atoms simulating the system is solved numerically. In the second category are Green function methods involving some averaging procedures. These methods may be called the effective medium methods. Methods like average T-matrix approximation (ATA), coherent potential approximation (CPA), and their variations are in this category. Finally, there are theories based upon statistical and variational principles. Techniques in the first two categories are usually capable of producing good results between the two mobility edges E_μ^1 and E_μ^2 (Figure 18.14). The eigenstates within these energies involve gross features of the material and not extreme fluctuations and thus the first two categories are able to account for them. However, the regions below E_μ^1 and above E_μ^2 (in 3-D systems) are due to extreme fluctuations and have to be treated by special statistical and variational principles. Because of the importance of these statistical methods in addressing not only the "band tail states" (i.e. states in the bandgap away from the mobility edges), but also their success in addressing problems of broadening of excitonic transitions and general effects of fluctuations, we will discuss these approaches.

Lifshitz was the first to introduce a statistical theory to attack the problem of a random A-B alloy. Figure 18.15 shows individual eigenspectra of any A and B components forming the alloy. The problem that Lifshitz addressed was to find

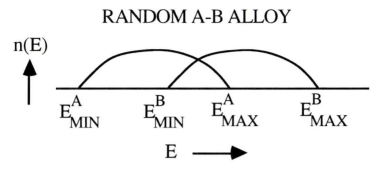

Figure 18.15: The individual eigenspectra of the A and B components forming a random alloy.

the density of states near the extremities E^A_{min} and E^B_{max}. The region of interest for statistical-variational theories is between E^A_{min}, E^B_{min} and E^A_{max}, E^B_{max}. The mean concentrations of A and B atoms are C^0_A and C^0_B, and it is assumed that no correlations exist between the atoms. Lifshitz asserted that states near E^A_{min} (in the alloy) will arise from regions in space which are purely A-like, i.e. regions which represent extreme potential fluctuations. It is now immediately clear why a statistical theory has to be invoked to find the density of states near E^A_{min}, since this density of states will be proportional to the probability of such fluctuations. The probability of a volume V_0 having a concentration C_A when the mean concentration is C^0_A is given by the usual statistical techniques

$$P(V_0) = \exp\left[-\frac{V_0}{v_0}\{C_A \ln(C_A/C^0_A) + C_B \ln(C_B/C^0_B)\}\right] \qquad (18.71)$$

where v_0 is the atomic volume.

In addition Lifshitz argued that it is the ground state of such a fluctuation which is important in determining the density of states near E^A_{min}. This argument becomes clearer due to Lloyd and Best's variational principle mentioned later. Using these prescriptions, then the probability in Equation 18.71 becomes (for $C_A = 1$)

$$P(V_0) = \exp\left[-\frac{V_0}{v_0} \ln(1/C^0_A)\right] \qquad (18.72)$$

and the energy of a localized wavefunction describing ground state may be written as

$$E = E^A_{min} + B/R^2_0 \qquad (18.73)$$

where B is a constant ($\sim h^2/m^*_A$) and $R^3_0 \sim V_0$ for 3-D. The first term in Equation 18.73 represents the lowest "potential energy" that an electron could have in the pure A environment, while the second term represents the "kinetic energy" or the energy of confining the electron to a volume V. From Equation 18.73, one then derives the relation between V_0 and E, viz.

$$V_0 = \left[\left(\frac{E - E^A_{min}}{B} \right) \right]^{-3/2} \tag{18.74}$$

and substituting in Equation 18.72, one gets

$$
\begin{aligned}
n(E) \quad &\propto \quad P(E) \\
&= \quad \exp\left[-\frac{1}{v_0} \ln(1/C_A^0) \left(\frac{E - E^A_{min}}{B} \right)^{-3/2} \right]. \tag{18.75}
\end{aligned}
$$

The density of band tail states thus depends upon the smallest volume of disorder (V_0 which is the unit cell volume for a perfectly random system or could be larger for a clustered alloy). The Lifshitz results are applicable only at the extreme end of the band tail states, since it is assumed that these states arise from regions of pure A material. In general one has to relax this condition along with the condition that the localized states result from the ground state function.

Lloyd and Best used the variational principle for energy minimization and showed that any statistical method to be used for finding the density of localized states should be coupled with a maximization principle which ensures that out of a variety of possibilities (corresponding to different fluctuations) that could lead to a localized state with the same energy, one should choose those configurations that maximize the density of states.

Using this prescription it is easy to see that the choice of using only ground states to get the density of states near E^A_{min} by Lifshitz was the correct one. The reason for this is that for an excited state to have the same energy as a ground state, the volume of the fluctuation (pure A atoms) would have to be eight times as much. Since the probability falls exponentially with volume, the contribution of excited states will be much smaller to the overall probability.

A proper incorporation of a maximization scheme in the spirit discussed was carried out by Halperin and Lax and Friedberg and Luttinger. The basic new ingredient in the theory of Halperin and Lax is that the concentration of the fluctuations which gives rise to the localized state is not assumed (as was done by Lifshitz who chose $C_A = 1$), but calculated by a maximization scheme. Friedberg and Luttinger cast the problem of band tail states into a problem of Brownian motion, but also included a maximization scheme in accordance with the variational principle. A simple extension of such approaches was also developed by Singh and Madhukar who applied the theory to the problem of interface states in Si/SiO_2. The general form of the density of states is shown in Figure 18.16 where the dashed line shows the Lifshitz limit discussed above. In general, one has exponentially decaying density of localized states, away from the mobility edge.

The theory discussed above can apply to any source of disordered potential. This includes the background impurities arranged randomly in a perfect crystal.

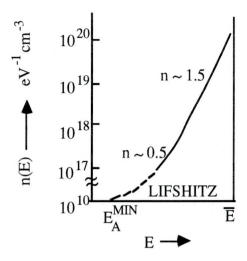

Figure 18.16: Behavior of the density of states for system with small disorder–n is the exponent in $N(E) = n_0 \exp\left\{-\left[(\bar{E}-E)/E_0\right]^n\right\}$.

Thus, the true density of states in a material is almost never one which starts out at the bandedges and is zero in the bandgap. One always has a band tail away from the bandedges. These band tail states participate in optical processes and lead to "Urbach Tails" in the absorption profile. We will discuss the optical properties of localized states later on.

18.5.1 Interface Disorder and Band Tail States

Heterointerfaces form an extremely important class of ingredients in essentially all electronic and optoelectronic devices. We have mentioned the Si/SiO$_2$ interface several times in this text and this interface obviously forms one of the most important interfaces in solid state electronics. As we mentioned in Chapter 2, this interface can be described by a region of a few monolayers where the positions of the atoms are somewhat distorted due to the mismatch between Si and SiO$_2$. This is a two-dimensional region of disorder. Interfaces which are formed from homocrystalline semiconductors or even lattice matched semiconductors, also have a region of 1–2 monolayers where the chemical species are arranged randomly. Thus, the interfacial disorder is almost always present whenever a heterointerface is prepared.

The effects of interfacial disorder are quite similar to the effects of bulk disorder. The disorder leads to the two regions of electronic spectra, viz. the localized states and the extended states. The extended states, even though they couple to the entire volume of the crystal, are *not* Bloch states. They are not the usual plane wave functions modulated by the cell periodic parts. However, in local regions of some extent λ, they can be regarded as Bloch states with a particular k-value. The distance λ is thus the region over which phase coherence is maintained. The problem of transport in the extended states can then be described by this approach. In fact, we implicitly used this approach when we discussed transport in alloys or interface roughness scattering limited transport in Chapter 11 and Chapter 15. We will come back to the problem of transport in the localized and extended states later.

The localized states in the interface region bandgap play an important role since they can behave as trapping and recombination states. Their presence can be revealed by careful capacitance-voltage measurements. The quality of the hetero-interface is reflected in the magnitude of the band tail states. In high quality interfaces, these U-shaped density of states should approach 10^{11} cm^{-2} eV^{-1} near the midgap regions.

18.5.2   Optical Properties in Disordered Semiconductors

As we discussed in the previous section, an important consequence of disorder is that the electronic states are no longer described by Bloch states. In optical properties and optical transitions, the underlying matrix element for the interband transitions has the general form

$$\int \psi_f^* \, \boldsymbol{p}_A \, \psi_i \, d^3r = \int \langle u_f | \boldsymbol{p}_A | u_i \rangle \, e^{i(\mathbf{k}_i - \mathbf{k}_f)\cdot \mathbf{r}} \, d^3r \qquad (18.76)$$

assuming that the photon momentum was negligible. This essentially results in the k-selection rules, viz. $\boldsymbol{k}_i = \boldsymbol{k}_f$ (i.e., vertical transitions). This is, of course, the reason why Si and Ge, both indirect materials, have very poor optical absorption near the bandedges. However, once the states are no longer Bloch states, it is not possible to make any such statements. In fact, we had examined the issue of the von Laue condition on X-ray diffraction

$$\boldsymbol{k}_i - \boldsymbol{k}_f = \boldsymbol{G} \qquad (18.77)$$

where $\boldsymbol{G}$ is a reciprocal lattice in some detail in Chapter 3. The issues are essentially the same. As we showed in Chapter 3, the effect of disorder was to relax the $\boldsymbol{G}$ selection rule and introduce a width to the allowed $\boldsymbol{k}_i - \boldsymbol{k}_f$ values where the scattering integral was not zero. The same concept is applicable when discussing optical absorption in disordered systems. Since the electronic states have phase coherence only over a certain length scale, $\boldsymbol{k}$-selection rules are relaxed and optical transitions can be observed even in materials which were indirect when in crystalline form. In this sense the disordered material has a positive impact on the properties of materials. This feature is, of course, particularly useful for silicon which has very poor near bandedge absorption. Amorphous silicon or microcrystallites of silicon, on the other hand, can have strong absorption profile. The effects of k-selection rule breakdown is further explored in the next section on transport.

An important aspect of disorder mentioned in Chapter 16 was in the context of inhomogeneous linewidth of excitonic transitions. As noted there the inhomogeneous linewidth of excitonic transitions is intimately tied to disorder present in the system. Due to the disorder, there are local potential fluctuations which are described by the statistical arguments presented in the context of Lifshitz theory of band tail states. The potential fluctuations over a region V then affect the local energy spectra of, for example, the excitonic states. We have already listed in Chapter 15 the results of the potential fluctuations on the excitonic linewidth where the relevant volume of the fluctuation is roughly the exciton relative coordinate volume. Both alloy disorder and interface disorder are an important source of exciton linewidth, particularly in quantum well structures as discussed in Chapter 15.

18.5.3 Transport in Disordered Semiconductors

We have seen that the presence of disorder creates a qualitative perturbation in the electronic spectra. The general electronic spectra can be described by localized and extended states. The transport properties of the electron in the localized and extended states are expected to be quite different. In the localized states, one state at an energy E has essentially no real space overlap with another state at the same energy. Thus, in some sense, the electron is trapped in a local region of the disordered material. The only way for the electron to be transported across the material is by inelastic scattering processes, whereby the electron tunnels or hops from one state to another. Thus, hopping conduction is essential for transport in localized states.

The extended states are connected throughout the volume of the disordered structure. However, k is no longer a good quantum number because the underlying periodicity has been lost. The quantity k in the Bloch states essentially describes the phase relation of the electron wave between two points in space. In the Bloch state there is perfect phase coherence throughout the crystal. In the disordered semiconductor the phase coherence exists only over a very small region in space. This region can be called the mean free path of the electron in analogy with the term used in the Boltzmann transport theory. This phase coherence distance could be very small (a few lattice constants) and obviously is dependent on the extent of disorder and how far the energy of the state is from the mobility edge. At this point, it is useful to examine the approach used to study transport in crystalline and disordered semiconductors. In the crystalline semiconductors as shown in Figure 18.17 we start with the perfect Bloch states which have long-range phase coherence and introduce defects as sources of scattering. The defects mix two states $|k\rangle$ and $|k'\rangle$, i.e. destroy phase coherence and the macroscopic properties of the system is described by the scattering time (properly averaged). This is the Boltzmann approach to transport and was used in Chapters 10 through Chapter 15.

In the case of the disordered system we calculate the electronic spectra first in presence of the disorder. This is important, as discussed earlier, because of the qualitative differences between a crystalline material with defects and a disordered material. Transport in the localized states is by hopping conduction,

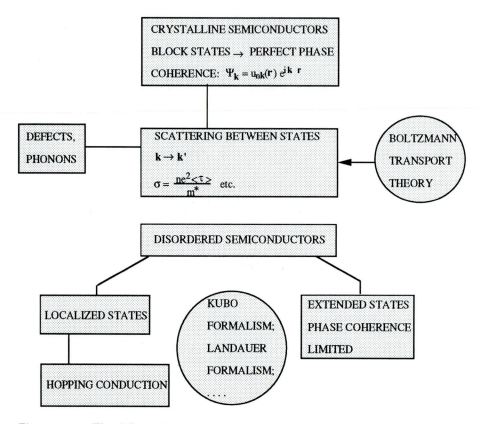

Figure 18.17: The different approaches used to address defects in almost crystalline materials versus the effect of disorder in the case where disorder is strong.

details of which we will discuss shortly. The extended states are described by a phase coherence distance and we need to develop a formalism which will connect this to the conductivity of the material. This connection is provided by the Kubo formalism which is a general approach to transport and is particularly useful for cases of strong scattering. We will present the Kubo formalism for transport now.

We will calculate the conductivity $\sigma(\omega)$ of a disordered system at frequency ω and then obtain the d_c conductivity by letting ω go to zero. Let us consider an electric field, $F \cos \omega t$, acting on a system of volume V. The probability, P, per unit time that an electron makes a transition from a state E to any of the degenerate states $E + \hbar\omega$ is

$$P = \frac{1}{4}e^2 \, F^2 \left(\frac{2\pi}{\hbar}\right) |\langle E + \hbar\omega |x| E\rangle|^2 \, V N \, (E + \hbar\omega). \tag{18.78}$$

The matrix element for the transition is

$$\langle E' | x | E \rangle = \int \psi_{E'}^* \, x \, \psi_E \, d^3x \qquad (18.79)$$

where ψ_E is the electronic state with energy E and is normalized to volume V. The states need not be a Bloch state. It is useful to rewrite the matrix element in the form.

$$\langle E + \hbar\omega | x | E \rangle = \frac{\hbar}{m\omega} \int \psi_{E+\hbar\omega}^* \frac{\partial}{\partial x} \psi_E \, d^3x. \qquad (18.80)$$

This form could be obtained if we use the perturbation potential as eA/mc instead of eFx, and use the relation $A = cF/\omega$. The transition rate is now

$$P = \frac{\pi e^2 \hbar V}{2m^2 \omega^2} \, F^2 \, |D|^2 N(E + \hbar\omega) \qquad (18.81)$$

where

$$D = \int \psi_{E+\hbar\omega}^* \frac{\partial}{\partial x} \psi_E \, d^3x.$$

We now define the conductivity of the system via the relationship between the conductivity and the rate of loss of energy per unit volume. This quantity is just $\sigma(\omega)F^2/2$. The rate of energy gain is given by

$$R_{\text{gain}} = 2 \, \hbar\omega \int P \, f(E) \, [1 - f(E + \hbar\omega)] \, N(E) \, dE. \qquad (18.82)$$

The factor of 2 is to count both spin directions. The rate of loss of the energy is

$$R_{\text{loss}} = 2 \, \hbar\omega \int P \, f(E + \hbar\omega) \, [1 - f(E)] \, N(E + \hbar\omega) \, dE. \qquad (18.83)$$

Thus, the conductivity is given by

$$\sigma(\omega) = \frac{2\pi e^2 \hbar^3 V}{m^2} \int \frac{[f(E) - f(E + \hbar\omega)] \, |D|^2_{\text{av}} N(E) N(E + \hbar\omega) \, dE}{\hbar\omega}. \qquad (18.84)$$

The term $|D|^2_{\text{av}}$ is $|D|^2$ averaged over all states ψ_E with energy E.

At zero temperature, this becomes

$$\sigma(\omega) = \frac{2\pi e^2 \hbar^3 V}{m^2} \int \frac{|D|^2_{\text{av}} N(E) N(E + \hbar\omega)}{\hbar\omega} \, dE. \qquad (18.85)$$

The dc conductivity is given by taking the limit $\omega \to 0$

$$\sigma_E = \frac{2\pi e^2 \hbar^2 \Omega}{m^2} |D_E|^2_{\text{av}} \{N(E)\}^2 \qquad (18.86)$$

where

$$D_E = \int \psi_{E'}^* \frac{\partial}{\partial x} \psi_E \, d^3x, \text{ at } E' = E. \qquad (18.87)$$

The Kubo formalism reduces to the Boltzmann formalism

$$\sigma = \frac{ne^2 \langle \tau \rangle}{m^*} \tag{18.88}$$

when the mean free path is long. To evaluate the matrix element D, it is useful to consider the volume ℓ^3 over which the wavefunction in the localized state maintains phase coherence. Thus, even though the extended state is not a Bloch state, we argue that in the volume ℓ^3 it can be written as a Bloch state with wavevector k. The coherence is then lost outside the volume ℓ^3. We can then divide the spatial integral over V for D, into volume regions ℓ^3, where the integral is nonzero.

$$D = \left(\frac{V}{\ell^3} \right)^{1/2} \delta \tag{18.89}$$

where

$$\delta = k \int_{\ell^3} \frac{\exp[i(k' - k) \cdot r]}{V} d^3 r \tag{18.90}$$

We may write $|k' - k| = 2k \sin(\theta/2) \approx k\theta$ where θ is the angle between k and k'. The integral is approximately evaluated as

$$\begin{aligned} \delta &= \frac{k\ell^3}{V}, \text{ if } k\ell\theta < 1 \\ &= 0 \quad \text{otherwise.} \end{aligned} \tag{18.91}$$

To obtain $|D_E|^2$, we have to do an averaging over the angle θ

$$\begin{aligned} \langle |D|^2 \rangle &= \frac{V}{\ell^3} \frac{k^2 \ell^6}{V^2} \frac{1}{4\pi} \int_0^\pi \frac{\sin(k\ell\theta/2)}{(k\ell\theta/2)} 2\pi \sin\theta \, d\theta \\ &\approx \frac{\pi\ell}{3V}. \end{aligned} \tag{18.92}$$

We note that ℓ is the mean free path used in the Boltzmann approach, i.e.

$$\begin{aligned} \ell &= v\tau \\ &= \frac{\hbar k}{m^*} \tau. \end{aligned} \tag{18.93}$$

The Kubo formalism provides new results for conductivity only when the mean free path becomes very small. When ℓ approaches a, the atomic spacing, the conductivity that results is called the minimum conductivity. The Kubo formalism is particularly useful since it provides the conductivity values directly from the electronic spectra. Of course, the effect of disorder is already built into the electronic spectra.

The effects of phonon scattering which is not reflected in the electronic spectra directly have to be treated separately. For the extended states the phonon

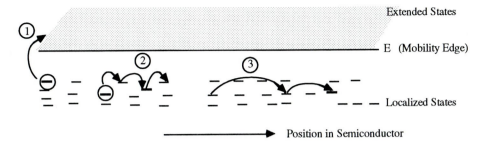

Figure 18.18: Three different mechanisms for transport in the localized states. In case 1, the electron is activated to the states above the mobility edge. In case 2, the electron hops to the nearest localized state while in the case 3, the electron hops to the "optimum" site as explained in the text.

scattering may further reduce the phase coherence length and reduce the conductivity. However, for conductivity in the localized states, phonons actually increase the mobility of the carriers.

The localized states are not connected in real space so that the electron needs to hop from one state to another. The important conduction mechanisms are shown schematically in Figure 18.18. In the first mode of conduction the electrons are excited to the mobility edge by phonons, and the conduction behavior is described by the thermally activated behavior

$$\sigma = \sigma_0 \exp\left[\frac{-(E_c - E_F)}{k_B T}\right] \tag{18.94}$$

where σ_0 is the conductivity at the mobility edge. The conductivity at the mobility edge has been a subject of great interest and is still being examined. Mott has shown that it has a form

$$\sigma_0 = \frac{C e^2}{\hbar a} \tag{18.95}$$

where $C \sim 0.03$ and a is the minimum distance over which phase coherence could occur. This quantity is also called the minimum metallic conductivity. For $a = 3$ Å, the value is $2 \times 10^2 \ \Omega^{-1} \ \text{cm}^{-1}$.

The second process indicated in Figure 18.18 involves thermal activation from one localized state to the nearest state in space, above the Fermi level. This process has been used to explain the impurity conduction in doped semiconductors by Miller and Abrahams. The electron is always assumed to move to the nearest empty localized state. To estimate this conductivity, we assume that the wavefunctions are described by

$$\psi = e^{-\alpha r} \tag{18.96}$$

where α^{-1} is the localization length. The current density is proportional to the overlap between the wavefunctions, the density of states at the Fermi level

$N(E_F)$, the width of the Fermi distribution k_BT, the effective velocity of transport which is chosen as ν_{ph}, the attempt frequency ($\approx$ phonon frequency) times the average spacing between the states R. If ΔE is the average separation between the energies of the two states, and F the applied field, the current density is

$$
\begin{aligned}
J \quad &\sim \quad ek_BT\, N(E_F)\, R\, \nu_{ph}\, \exp(-2\alpha R) \\
&\times \left[\exp\left(\frac{-\Delta E + eFR}{k_BT}\right) - \exp\left(\frac{-\Delta E - eFR}{k_BT}\right)\right] \\
&= \quad 2ek_BT\, N(E_F)\, R\, \nu_{ph}\, \exp\left(-2\alpha R - \frac{\Delta E}{k_BT}\right) \sinh\left(\frac{eFR}{k_BT}\right). \quad (18.97)
\end{aligned}
$$

For small electric fields, the sinh function can be expanded and the conductivity becomes

$$
\begin{aligned}
\sigma \quad &= \quad \frac{J}{F} \\
&= \quad 2e^2 R^2\, \nu_{ph}\, N(E_F)\, \exp\left[-2\alpha R - \frac{\Delta E}{k_BT}\right]. \quad (18.98)
\end{aligned}
$$

An estimate of the energy spacing of the levels is simply obtained from the definition of the density of states, i.e.

$$
\Delta E \approx \frac{1}{N(E_F)R_0^3} \quad (18.99)
$$

where R_0 is the average separation between nearest neighbor states. This kind of nearest neighbor hopping is dominant if nearly all states are strongly localized, e.g., as in impurity states due to dopants.

In most disordered semiconductors, where the disorder is not too strong, one has another important transport process indicated by the third process in Figure 18.18. This process, known as variable range hopping, was introduced by Mott and is a dominant transport mode at low temperatures. At low temperatures, the hop would not occur to the nearest spatial state, but the electron may prefer to go a potentially farther state but one which is closer in energy so that the phonon activation is not required.

In a range R of a given localized state, the density of states per unit energy range near the Fermi level are

$$
\left(\frac{4\pi}{3}\right) R^3 N(E_F).
$$

Thus, for the hopping process involving a distance within R, the average separation of level energies will be

$$
\Delta E = \frac{3}{4\pi R^3\, N(E_F)}. \quad (18.100)
$$

Clearly, the farther the electron hops, the smaller the activation barrier that it needs to overcome. On the other hand, a hop of a distance R will involve an overlap function which falls as $\exp(-2\alpha R)$. Thus, there will be an optimum distance for which the term

$$\exp(-2\alpha R)\exp\left(\frac{-\Delta E}{k_B T}\right)$$

is a maximum. This can easily be seen to occur when

$$\frac{d}{dR}\left[2\alpha R + \frac{3}{4\pi R^3\, N(E)\, k_B T}\right] = 0$$

or

$$R_m = \left[\frac{1}{8\pi N(E)\,\alpha k_B T}\right]^{1/4}. \tag{18.101}$$

Using this value of R_m, we get for the conductivity behavior

$$\sigma = A\exp\left(-\frac{B}{T^{1/4}}\right) \tag{18.102}$$

where

$$B = 2\left(\frac{3}{2\pi}\right)^{1/4}\left(\frac{\alpha^3}{k_B N(E_F)}\right)^{1/4}. \tag{18.103}$$

This variable range hopping temperature behavior has been observed in numerous disordered systems. It is straightforward to show that for 2-dimensional systems the temperature dependence is

$$\sigma = A\exp\left(-\frac{B'}{T^{1/3}}\right). \tag{18.104}$$

Such behavior is observed in silicon MOSFET channels at low temperatures.

We mention that in this chapter we will not discuss some of the remarkable work carried out in the area of transport in disordered structures involving the scaling of macroscopic transport properties with structure dimensions. The usual changes in the conductivity with area and length do not apply to disordered structures once one goes to sub-2-dimensional structures. In fact, the transport in sub-3-D structures in presence of disorder has acquired a new sense of importance due to the significance of mesoscopic structures briefly discussed next.

18.6 MESOSCOPIC STRUCTURES

In the 1980s the ability to fabricate heterostructures of semiconductors has given a tremendous boost to the interest in semiconductor physics. The quantum wells, superlattices, etc., discussed in this book are all the result of great strides in the art and science of epitaxial crystal growth.

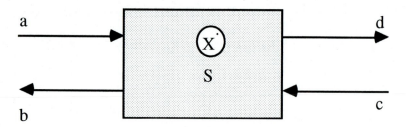

Figure 18.19: A schematic showing the effect of the scattering center S on electron waves a and c incident from the left and right respectively. The waves b and d emerge as a result of reflection and transmission.

Another area where great advances have been made is the area of fine line lithography. With electron beam and X-ray lithography systems it is possible to define lateral structures with resolutions of $\sim 100\text{Å}$–1000Å. This ability, along with the ability to etch away extremely sharp regions of semiconductors, has allowed fabrication of quantum wires and quantum boxes. Devices can be now made for the first time using 2-D or even 1-D systems where separations between contacts is of the order of a few hundred Angstroms. In such structures it is possible at low temperatures that electrons injected into the semiconductor do not lose their phase memory before they reach the other contact. The quantum mechanical coherence of the electrons now dominates the physics of such systems often called mesoscopic systems. Since phase coherence is maintained in transport, the macroscopic averaging procedures we have been using in defining mobility or conductivity does not hold anymore. A dramatic manifestation of the phase coherence is the fluctuation seen in conductivity of mesoscopic structures as a function of magnetic field, electron concentration, etc.

The origin of the fluctuations can be understood on the basis of Landauer formalism which allows one to study transport in terms of the scattering processes directly. For simplicity consider a one-dimensional system with scattering centers. Each of these scatterers is characterized in terms of a transfer matrix which describes what fraction of the incident electron is "reflected" after scattering and what fraction is transmitted. The scatterer is described by the reflection and transmission coefficients shown in Figure 18.19. The reflection and transmission coefficients are R and T for an incident wave from the left or right. To calculate the current flow one needs to identify the relative change in the carrier density on the left and right side of the scatterer. If there is an applied bias δV, the excess carrier density (at low temperatures) is

$$\delta n \approx \frac{dn}{dE}(e\ \delta V). \tag{18.105}$$

The excess carriers on the left over the right side can also be evaluated as the magnitude of the particle currents on the left divided by the velocity minus the magnitude of the particle currents on the right.

$$\begin{aligned} \delta n &= \frac{j_a + j_b}{v} - \frac{j_c + j_d}{v} \\ &= \frac{(j_a - j_c) + (j_b - j_d)}{v}. \end{aligned} \tag{18.106}$$

Now it can be easily seen that

$$(j_b - j_d) = (R - T)(j_a - j_c). \tag{18.107}$$

Thus, since $R + T = 1$

$$\delta n = \frac{2R\,(j_a - j_c)}{v}. \tag{18.108}$$

The electrical current on the left side is

$$\begin{aligned} I_\ell &= eT\,j_a - eT\,j_c \\ &= eT\,(j_a - j_c). \end{aligned} \tag{18.109}$$

These equations then give for the conductance

$$\begin{aligned} G &= \frac{I_\ell}{\delta V} \\ &= \frac{T}{2R}\,e^2\,\frac{dn}{dE}\,\frac{1}{\hbar}\,\frac{\partial E}{\partial k}. \end{aligned} \tag{18.110}$$

Now for a 1-dimensional case

$$\frac{dn}{dk} = \frac{1}{\pi} \tag{18.111}$$

so that (including the spin degeneracy)

$$G = \frac{2e^2}{h}\,\frac{T}{R}. \tag{18.112}$$

Thus, it appears that the fundamental unit of conductance is $2e^2/h$ which will be modified by the values of T/R. In general in the Landauer formalism one has to sum the electron contributions from all different paths the electron could take in going from one contact to another. It may appear that when such an averaging is carried out the conductance fluctuations arising from different paths would average out, especially as the sample size is increased. However, it turns out that there is a remarkable universality in the magnitude of the fluctuations independent of the sample size, dimensionality and extent of disorder, provided the disorder is weak and the temperature is low (a few Kelvin). Such universal conductance fluctuations have been measured in a vast range of experiments involving magnetic field and Fermi level position (voltage).

In Figure 18.20 we show experimental results of Wees, et al., carried out on a GaAs/AlGaAs MODFET at low temperatures. As shown, a pair of contacts

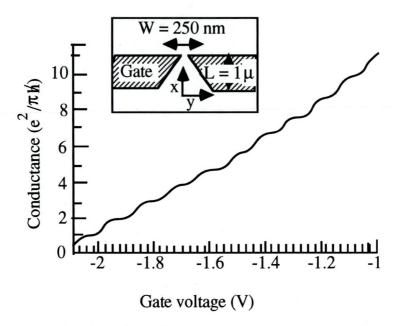

Figure 18.20: Experimental studies on conductance fluctuations arising in a GaAs/AlGaAs channel constricted by the structure shown. The results are for the channel conductance in units of $e^2/\pi\hbar$ ($= 2e^2/h$). (Reproduced with permission, B. J. van Wees, et al., Phys. Rev. Lett., **60**, 848 (1988).)

are used to create a short channel of the high mobility region, and conductance is measured. The gates form a 1-dimensional channel in which the Fermi level and thus the electron wavefunctions can be altered. As can be seen from the Figure 18.20, there are oscillations in the conductance as suggested by the Landauer formalism.

The area of transport in mesoscopic structures is at present in its infancy. However, with increasing capabilities to fabricate these structures, and their obvious applications for low temperature, low voltage devices, interest in them is only going to increase. This, of course, places burden on the electrical engineer to understand the complexities of transport in these structures.

18.7   FOR THE TECHNOLOGIST IN YOU

The issues of defects and disorder are central to any semiconductor technology. One of the key challenges for high temperature electronics based on large band-gap semiconductors is to keep the defect density low. This, along with doping problems, is why microprocessors cannot be mounted near jet engines or dropped in oil wells. However, these challenges are gradually being overcome as is evident in the demonstration of the green laser (CdSe) which until recently was plagued by defects and doping problems.

The area of strained epitaxy is extremely important for many evolving technologies including the possibility of "marrying" different technologies. Figure 18.21 shows some of the motivations and challenges of this technology.

Amorphous semiconductors are usually not used for high performance devices but are extremely useful for technologies where cost or large scale production is critical. Key markets in this context are the solar energy photovoltaics and flat panel displays. The amorphous semiconductor (usually hydrogenated Si) is deposited on large panels (almost like "spray painting!") of glass or similar substrate. These panels could have areas in thousands of square centimeters! The device performance is poor because of localized states and related effects but for technologies where speed is not an issue this does not matter so much.

Mesoscopic devices are still too futuristic, but considering the speed of progress in the field of solid state electronics, in a decade they may have impact on certain niche technologies.

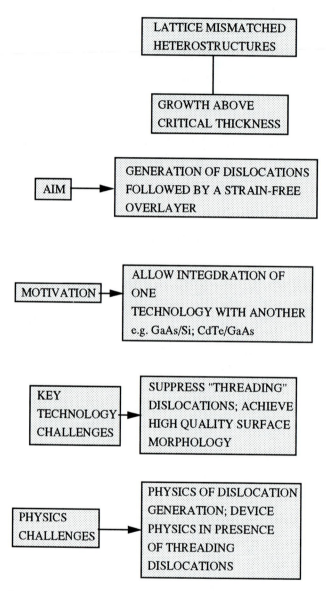

Figure 18.21: Motivations and challenges of the strained layer technology for integrating different material technologies.

18.8 REFERENCES

- **Point Defects in Semiconductors**

    - "Deep Levels in III-V Compound Semiconductors Grown by Molecular Beam Epitaxy," by Bhattacharya, P. K. and S. Dhar, in *Semiconductors and Semimetals* (edited by A. C. Willardson and A. C. Beer, Academic Press, New York, 1988), vol. 26.

    - Economou, E. N., *Green Functions in Quantum Physics* (Springer-Verlag, Berlin, 1979).

    - Foster, G. F. and J. C. Slater, Phys. Rev., **96**, 1208 (1954).

    - Matare, H. F., *Defect Electronics in Semiconductors* (Wiley-Interscience, New York, 1971).

    - Pantelides, S., Rev. Mod. Phys., **50**, 797 (1978).

- **Dislocations and Lattice Mismatched Epitaxy**

    - Amelinckx, S., *Dislocations in Solids* (edited by F. R. N. Nabarro, North- Holland, New York, 1979).

    - Ball, C. A. B. and J. H. van der Merwe, *Dislocations in Solids* (edited by F. R. N. Nabarro, North-Holland, New York, 1983), vol. 5.

    - Matare, H. F., *Defect Electronics in Semiconductors* (Wiley-Interscience, New York, 1971).

    - Mathews, J. W. and A. E. Blakeslee, J. Cryst. Growth, **27**, 118 (1974).

    - Tsao, J. Y., B. W. Dodson, S. T. Picraux, and D. M. Cornelison, Phys. Rev. Lett., **59**, 2455 (1987).

    - van der Merwe, J. H., J. Appl. Phys., **34**, 117 (1963).

    - van der Merwe, J. H., J. Appl. Phys., **34**, 123 (1963).

- **Disordered Semiconductors**

    - Anderson, P. W., Phys. Rev., **109**, 1492 (1958).

    - Cohen, M. H., H. Fritzsche and S. R. Ovshinsky, Phys. Rev. Lett., **22**, 1065 (1977).

    - Halperin, B. I. and M. Lax, Phys. Rev., **153**, 802 (1967).

    - Lifshitz, I. M., Adv. Phys., **13**, 483 (1969).

    - Lloyd, P. and J. Best, J. Phys. C, **8**, 3752 (1975).

    - Mott, N. F. and E. A. Davis, *Electronic Processes in Non-Crystalline Materials* (Clarendon Press, Oxford, 1971).

    - Singh, J. and A. Madhukar, *Band-Tailing in Disordered Systems in Excitations in Disordered Systems* (edited by M. F. Thorpe, Plenum Press, New York, 1982). See other articles in this book, also.

- Thouless, D. J., Phys. Rept., **13C**, 93 (1974).

• **Mesoscopic Structures**

  - Articles in *Nanostructure Physics and Fabrication* (edited by M. A. Redd and W. P. Kirk, Academic Press, New York, 1989).
  - Ferry, D. K., *Semiconductors* (Macmillan, New York, 1991).
  - Landauer, R., Philos. Mag., **21**, 863 (1970).
  - Physics Today, (Dec. 1988). Covers the important aspects of physics in mesoscopic structures.
  - Van Wees, B. J., H. Van Houten, C. W. J. Beenakker, J. L. Williamson, L. P. Kauwenhoven, D. van der Marel, and C. T. Foxon, Phys. Rev. Lett., **60**, 848 (1988).

CHAPTER 19

AND NOW SOMETHING OF REAL CONSEQUENCE: DEVICES

The first eighteen chapters of this text have explored the various physical phenomena that make semiconductors so interesting. While the physics of semiconductors provides an exciting intellectual challenge, the application of the physics in devices provides a deeply satisfying sense. It connects the electrical engineer and the physicist to the rest of humanity and offers them an opportunity to improve the quality of life. The impact of the efforts of such scientists is seen in everyday life. From consumer electronics to defense industries, semiconductors and the devices made from them are transforming the world.

In this chapter we will discuss how physical phenomena translate into effects that can be exploited in devices. Conversely, we will also address the question, "Why don't all interesting effects result in new devices?"

19.1 SOME RECENT TRENDS

In the eighties, as heterostructure technology became accessible to scientists, a tremendous amount of research effort was focussed on the physics and application of heterostructures. Numerous physical effects were proposed and observed. So varied and exciting are these effects, as we have seen in our earlier chapters, that a sense was created that totally "new" devices based on these novel phenomena would displace the conventional devices. To some extent these expectations have been met and technology continues to evolve due to these new materials and structures. However, some expectations proved to be too optimistic and many industries which had positioned themselves to exploit the emerging technologies found themselves readjusting rapidly and often lowering their expectations. While many complex forces guide the success of industries and their products, two problems played an important role. The first was the tremendous versatility of silicon. The stronger the challenge from GaAs, the more Si was able to respond. Not only was the physics of Si (as far as devices are concerned) better than naively expected, its superior processing properties made the compound semiconductor scientists feel like nature was playing favorites. If only Si could be made into lasers!

Optoelectronics and the ever present push to provide devices for select niche applications continues to bring new semiconductor structures into technology. The MODFET, the quantum well laser, the HBT, etc. are already inserted into technology. However, dreams of all optical computers based on nonlinear optics are still dreams. Numerous tunneling related effects in heterostructures and various demonstrations of extremely high transconductances (subject of the cartoon) have not resulted in real devices. It is important for the device scientist to understand some of the basic demands that have to be placed on physical phenomena before a reliable device and a technology based on that device can emerge. While there are no hard and fast guidelines, there are some important requirements which will be explored in the next section. However, it must be remembered that these guidelines are not presented to limit the reader's imagination.

19.2 REQUIREMENTS FOR SUCCESSFUL DEVICES

The earliest electrical measurements were carried out not on semiconductors, but on metals. Ohm's law established the basic response of current in a metal to external fields. Metals are exciting materials to work with. They are pretty, they can be pulled into wires, and they can be formed into any shape. They are great conductors of electricity and heat. They don't smash into pieces if they fall! Semiconductors on the other hand are brittle, difficult to handle, and very difficult to grow with controlled purity. In fact, in the earlier part of this century, semiconductors were considered "impure" materials since their conductivity varied enormously from one sample to another. We now know from our understanding of bandgaps and doping why this can happen.

Why can't we use Ohm's law to design devices using metals? Why is it that in solid state electronics, metals (and insulators) are relegated to the role of "passive" components? Why is all the "decision making" left to semiconductors? To answer these questions we need to consider what devices do and what is needed in a material to perform these functions.

In Table 19.1 we examine the basic functions that solid state devices carry out. Most devices are used for some kind of "information processing." This involves carrying out a variety of functions as shown in Table 19.1. To carry out these functions certain criteria have to be met, as shown in Table 19.2.

THE PURPOSE OF DEVICES $\Rightarrow$ INFORMATION PROCESSING

INFORMATION MANIPULATION	LOGIC UNITS OF COMPUTERS
INFORMATION RETRIEVAL/STORAGE	MEMORIES
INFORMATION ENHANCEMENT	AMPLIFIERS
INFORMATION GENERATION	OSCILLATORS, LASERS
INFORMATION DETECTION	SENSORS, DETECTORS
INFORMATION TRANSFER	CHARGE COUPLED DEVICES

Table 19.1: Some of the many ways devices participate in the overall information processing.

HIGH GAIN	<ul><li>REGENERATION /AMPLIFICATION OF INFORMATION</li><li>LARGE NOISE MARGINS</li><li>LARGE FANOUT $\rightarrow$ SINGLE DEVICE CAN CONTROL MULTIPLE DEVICES</li></ul>
NONLINEAR RESPONSE	<ul><li>EASY TO DISTINGUISH STATES</li><li>LACK OF SENSITIVITY TO INPUT FLUCTUATIONS</li><li>ALLOWS MIXING OF HARMONIC $A\cos\omega_1 t + B\cos\omega_2 t \Rightarrow$ $C\cos(\omega_1 - \omega_2)t + D\cos(\omega_1 + \omega_2)t$</li></ul>
INPUT/OUTPUT ISOLATION	<ul><li>WELL DEFINED LOCAL RESPONSE</li></ul>
TUNABILITY HIGH SPEED LOW POWER CONSUMPTION HIGH POWER OUTPUT HIGH TEMPERATURE OPERATION	<ul><li>CAN ADDRESS SPECIFIC NEEDS</li></ul>

Table 19.2: Requirements for a useful device.

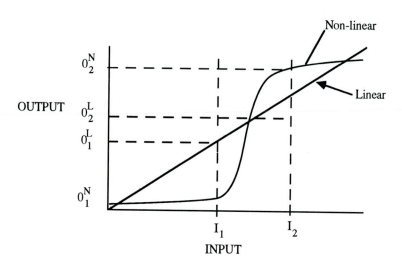

Figure 19.1: Use of a linear and nonlinear response function to distinguish two inputs I_1 and I_2. The nonlinear response function provides a greater distinction in the output.

19.2.1   Nonlinear Response

Whether the function to be accomplished is image enhancement or simple addition of two numbers, the key property the device must possess is the ability to distinguish between two "closely separated" pieces of information. In Figure 19.1, we show the response of two material systems. One has a linear response to an input (e.g. determined by Ohm's law in metals) while the other response is nonlinear (e.g. in a MESFET). As can be seen, in a linear response, the change in input (i.e. in information being fed into the device) produces output states which are much more closely spaced than is the case of a nonlinear response.

Another consequence of a nonlinear response in manifested when two inputs are simultaneously input into the material system. Consider the two inputs to have the form:

$$I_{in} = I_1 \cos \omega_1 t + I_2 \cos \omega_2 t \tag{19.1}$$

and let us assume a simple physical response of the form:

$$O = \alpha I + \beta I^2 \tag{19.2}$$

where α is the linear response coefficient and β is the nonlinear response coefficient. Of course, the real output function may be more complicated. The output of the device to the input of Equation 19.1 is now:

$$\begin{aligned} O &= \alpha \left[I_1 \cos \omega_1 t + I_2 \cos \omega_2 t \right] \\ &+ \beta \left[I_1^2 \cos^2 \omega_1 t + I_2^2 \cos^2 \omega_2 t + 2 I_1 I_2 \cos \omega_1 t \cos \omega_2 t \right] . \end{aligned} \tag{19.3}$$

Noting that,

$$\cos a \cos b = \frac{1}{2} \left[\cos (a + b) + \cos (a - b) \right], \tag{19.4}$$

we have:

$$
\begin{aligned}
O \;=\; & \alpha\left[I_1\cos\omega_1 t + I_2\cos\omega_2 t\right] \\
&+\beta\left[\frac{I_1^2}{2}\left(1+\cos 2\omega_1 t\right) + \frac{I_2^2}{2}\left(1+\cos 2\omega_2 t\right)\right. \\
&\left.+ I_1 I_2\left(\cos\left(\omega_1+\omega_2\right)t + \cos\left(\omega_1-\omega_2\right)t\right)\right].
\end{aligned}
\tag{19.5}
$$

The output now has signals of frequencies not only ω_1 and ω_2, but also $2\omega_1$ and $2\omega_2$ as well as most importantly, $(\omega_1+\omega_2)$ and $(\omega_1-\omega_2)$. Thus, the nonlinearity is able to "mix" the two input signals and provide sum and difference signals. This is extremely useful for communication where a signal to be transmitted (say at audio frequencies) can be "carried" on a carrier frequency and then decoded.

19.2.2 Gain in the Device

An important requirement for a physical phenomenon to translate into a viable device is the presence of gain in the input–output relation. Thus, a small change in the input should produce a large change in the output. In most applications of devices, a "regeneration" of information is required, i.e. the output of a previous step is used to generate another output in successive steps. As seen in the cartoon, even a small loss of "information" at each stage can have a disastrous effect. The ability to introduce gain is one of the most powerful ingredients of most electronic devices as we shall briefly discuss. Lack of gain has also been one of the pitfalls of "all optical" devices that have been demonstrated. Recent work in laser amplifiers may be able to overcome some of these problems.

The ability to provide gain (or amplify the incoming signal) is not only important for signal regeneration, it is also very useful, along with nonlinear effects, in providing large noise tolerances especially in digital technologies. One of the great strengths of digital technologies comes from this "noise immunity" of the processed signal at each step of the processing. Thus, in most processing systems an analog signal is converted to a digital signal (by A/D converters), in spite of the fact that a slight loss of accuracy is suffered in this conversion. However, after this initial loss the digital signal can then be processed by many complex steps and its integrity is maintained by the presence of high gain devices.

Another advantage of a high gain device is that a single output can drive a number of other devices (i.e. have a large "fan-out"). This is an obvious plus, since complex circuitry can be designed based on a large fan-out.

19.2.3 Input–Output Isolation

We have all had the experience when during a conversation, a listener suddenly starts speaking while we are still speaking causing great confusion. The human brain is designed in such a way that it is difficult to shut off our ears and so it is usually not possible to attain input–output isolation during conversation.

A crafty politician is often able to achieve such isolation, speaking with great confidence and vigor while rotten tomatoes are thrown at him!

For devices, the isolation between the input signal and the output signal is essential for most applications. This ensures a well-defined response of the device and the system for a given set of inputs. One of the key attractions of three terminal devices (that are well-designed) is the isolation between the input at the gate (or base in a bipolar device) of a FET and the output at the drain (or the collector). This is often not possible in two terminal devices, causing serious difficulties in technologies that have attempted to use these devices. It may be mentioned that in the sixties, a great deal of work was done to design very clever logic circuitry using the tunnel diode and its negative differential resistance. As we know, the transistor structure, with its greater intrinsic reliability, won out for all such applications.

19.2.4   Tunable Response

One of the driving forces of the modern solid state electronics is tunability of device response. This may involve lasers that can emit in important frequency windows (e.g. green light for displays; 1.55 μm lasers for low loss transmission in fibers, etc.) or resonant tunneling structures which have unusual I–V characteristics. A tunable response, especially if it is achieved while maintaining the other device requirements, is of great importance for the development of technology.

19.2.5   High Speed Operation

The ability to process information at a faster and faster rate is of course the main reason for advances in device technology. Physical phenomena which are "fast" and can be harnessed to produce viable devices, are constantly being researched. However, it must be realized, based on the discussions of this section, that every "femtosecond" phenomenon is not going to lead to a device. Thus, while it may be popular to discuss how a femtosecond laser may be able to transmit all the information in the world's libraries in a second, usually such claims do not survive a closer scrutiny.

The issue of speed is usually a simple one in some technologies, such as microwave technology or optical communication. Here "faster" materials (e.g. Si $\rightarrow$ GaAs $\rightarrow$ InGaAs $\rightarrow$ ...) drive the technology for microwave applications. However, in case of the all purpose computation systems, the speed issue is rather complex and "architecture and layout" play as much if not more of a role in the overall speed of a system. Let us not forget that one of the fastest computers (at least for some operations like recognition, association, etc.), the human brain, has devices that can only switch in tens of milliseconds!

19.2.6   Low Power

In addition to high speed, an important consideration for a physical phenomenon is the power consumed in the process. For many applications, it is the power-delay product that is of most significance. Low power requirements are not only important since less power is demanded from the various sources of power, but less dissipation of power also translates into lower costs for heat sinking and being able to introduce a higher density of devices.

19.2.7   Low Noise

The intrinsic noise produced by a physical phenomena is of great importance in device design. Certain physical phenomena such as impact ionization are intrinsically very "noisy" due to the random nature of charge multiplication. Similarly, many exotic physical phenomena are often seen to be noisy. For example "quantum interference devices" may suffer because of scattering events. "Few electron" devices which may be very low power devices may be extremely noisy due to random statistical fluctuations. Indeed, as device dimensions become smaller and new physical phenomena are introduced into device design, the noise problem is likely to grow in importance.

19.2.8   Special Purpose Demands

A very important consideration in device technology is of course to find physical phenomena which produce devices capable of functioning in domains where current devices cannot operate. For example, Si devices cannot operate above $\sim 150°C$ because of high intrinsic carrier concentrations and related effects. A drive for high bandgap materials is to produce devices which can operate at temperatures where strong needs exist. For example, these devices can be used to monitor functions in engines of machinery or in oil wells, etc. where temperatures are high.

The need for higher density optical memory is driving the search for laser materials which can emit at shorter wavelengths.

Other driving forces for special applications include absorption dips in the dispersion of transmission of waves through the atmosphere. In fact the need for new materials can appear "suddenly," often driven by a specific application. For example, if the optical communication technology switches from glass fibers to plastic fibers, the laser material of choice may have to switch also.

In addition to the requirements discussed for the physical phenomena to produce successful devices, there are important other criteria that have to be met. These are outlined in Tables 19.3 through 19.5. The processing requirements are the main reason for the success of the Si technology. It is also the reason why the "ideal" HBT system GaAs/Ge/GaAs does not work. Ge has the best hole mobility of any semiconductor and is also lattice matched to GaAs. However, the GaAs/Ge system has serious growth problems, due to intermixing and Ge

PROCESSING REQUIREMENTS ON DEVICES
ROBUSTNESS OF THE MATERIAL SYSTEM
AVAILABILITY OF RELIABLE GROWTH TECHNIQUES PRODUCING LOW DEFECT MATERIAL
AVAILABILITY OF RELIABLE DOPING TECHNIQUES
AVAILABILITY OF HIGH QUALITY OHMIC CONTACTS/SCHOTTKY CONTACTS
AVAILABILITY OF HIGH QUALITY PASSIVATION PROCESS
AVAILABILITY OF PRECISE ETCHANTS

Table 19.3: The success of a semiconductor technology depends, to a large extent, on how well the material system is able to withstand the processing steps necessary to fabricate devices and systems.

SYSTEM REQUIREMENTS ON DEVICES/MATERIALS
LARGE SCALE RELIABILITY OF DEVICE REPLICATION
AVAILABILITY OF INTEGRATION STEPS TO HAVE ACTIVE/PASSIVE; ELECTRONIC /OPTOELECTRONIC ELEMENTS ON SAME CHIP
LOW POWER CONSUMPTION OF OPERATING DEVICES
GOOD THERMAL PROPERTIES/AVAILABILITY OF HEAT SINKING

Table 19.4: Eventually, all devices must be inserted into a system and system issues have to be addressed for the device to be useful.

MARKET REQUIREMENTS
HOW DOES THE NEW SYSTEM FIT IN WITH EXISTING TECHNOLOGY?
YIELD, RELIABILITY: IS THE SYSTEM MANUFACTURABLE?
HOW DOES THE PERFORMANCE IMPROVEMENT COMPETE WITH THE INITIAL COST?
DOES THE NEW SYSTEM DO FUNCTIONS WHICH THE OLD SYSTEM CANNOT DO?
DOES THE NEW SYSTEM IMPROVE THE PHYSICAL QUALITY OF LIFE: COMFORT, KNOWLEDGE, SAFETY, RELAXATION?
WILL PEOPLE SOMEWHERE EXCHANGE THEIR MONEY EARNED THROUGH HARD WORK (USUALLY) FOR THE NEW PRODUCT?

Table 19.5: All devices must finally find a market before they can become part of an accepted technology.

acting as a dopant in GaAs. Similarly, processing related problems in the HgCdTe and InSb technology limit the applications of these versatile materials for long wavelength applications.

In addition to processing requirements one has to contend with system requirements where issues of heat sinking, packaging, integration, etc. are as critical as the device performance. Finally, one comes to the market forces and inertia that a new device technology must face. A system that can be inserted into existing technology, with the least amount of perturbation, will have a far greater chance of acceptance. Issues of supply voltages required, input–output pins required, etc., can play an important role in the level of acceptance of the new system. The eventual goal of the new technology is of course to serve a special purpose that is not serviced by existing technology and create an environment where a consumer would want to purchase and use the technology.

As we have seen in this section, the excitement of new physical phenomena has to be tempered with many real life realities to produce acceptable devices. As cautioned earlier, this section is not supposed to dampen the enthusiasm of budding device scientists. We also emphasize that not all the requirements mentioned here need to be satisfied simultaneously.

COMPONENT	KEY FUNCTIONS
OPERATIONAL AMPLIFIERS	• HIGH GAIN DC AMPLIFICATION • PERFORM MATHEMATICAL OPERATIONS (ADD, SUBTRACT, INTEGRATE, ...)
DIFFERENTIAL AMPLIFIERS	• AMPLIFIES THE DIFFERENCE BETWEEN TWO INPUTS
OTHER AMPLIFIERS Video Amplifier Servo Amplifier Sample–Hold Amplifier	• SPECIFIC APPLICATIONS
MEMORY DEVICES	• STORE INFORMATION • READ/WRITE CAPABILITIES
LOGIC FUNCTION HARDWARE FOR ARITHMETIC UNITS	• PERFORM LOGIC FUNCTIONS (AND, NAND, XOR, ...)
COMPARATORS	• COMPARES TWO NUMBERS IN PARALLEL
COUNTERS	• COUNTS INPUT PULSES IN ASCENDING/DESCENDING ORDER
SHIFT REGISTERS	• PERMITS SHIFTING OF DATA TO THE LEFT AND RIGHT
CLOCKS	• MAINTAINS PRECISE TIMING

Table 19.6: Important components of modern electronic and opto-electronic systems.

19.3   A SUMMARY OF SOME IMPORTANT DEVICES

As noted earlier, the intent of this chapter is not to provide an in-depth knowledge of the workings of semiconductors devices—only to provide some of the motivations which drive device research. Some of these motivations have led scientists to new semiconductor materials and their heterostructures. Before summarizing some important devices, let us briefly list, in Table 19.6, some important hardware components which drive the electronic and optoelectronic industry. From the stereo system to the satellite communication systems, these hardware components are chosen by the system designer with fascinating results. The com-

COMPONENT	KEY FUNCTIONS
PARITY CHECKER/GENERATOR	• CHECK ERRORS DURING DATA TRANSMISSION
MULTIPLEXER	• PERMITS MANY DATA SOURCES TO BE CONNECTED TO A SINGLE LINE SEQUENTIALLY
DEMULTIPLEXER	• REVERSE OF ABOVE
ANALOG TO DIGITAL, DIGITAL TO ANALOG CONVERTERS	• ALLOWS ACCURATE PROCESSING OF ANALOG SIGNALS BY DIGITAL ELECTRONICS
DISPLAY COMPONENTS (LEDs, LCDs)	• VISUAL DISPLAY OF INFORMATION
DETECTORS	• DETECT LIGHT BY CONVERTING IT INTO ELECTRICAL SIGNAL
LIGHT SOURCES (LASERS, LEDs)	• GENERATE PHOTONS WITH WELL-DEFINED PROPERTIES
MICROWAVE AMPLIFIERS/TRANSMITTERS	• NUMEROUS APPLICATIONS IN GUIDED AND UNGUIDED ELECTRONIC TRANSMISSION

Table 19.6: (continued)

ponents listed are usually built from the devices to be discussed below along with appropriate resistors, capacitors, etc. Often many electronic devices are needed for a single component. The challenge for the system designer is to choose the "simplest" combination of electronic devices to perform a given function. The ultimate challenge for the device scientist is to design devices that can mimic a component, i.e. perform a complex function. Currently, most devices are unable to do so. However, clever ideas using heterostructures may be able to introduce functional devices. Let us now briefly discuss some devices.

19.3.1 The Field Effect Transistor

The field effect transistor (FET) forms the backbone of the digital and analog microelectronic systems. From consumer electronic goods such as stereo systems and microprocessors on automobiles, to satellite communication systems, the FETs provide a versatile device. This three-terminal device consisting of source and drain ohmic contacts through which current flows and a gate that is isolated from the active channel, can be loosely compared to a water tap. The gate is equivalent to the faucet handle which shuts off the water supply by constricting the flow in the channel.

The most important FET structure is the Si-based Metal-Oxide-Semiconductor FET or MOSFET. One of the reasons for the great success of Si technology is that a high quality oxide (an insulator) can be grown directly on it. This oxide layer, with a bandgap of 9.0 eV, effectively isolates the channel where the charge flows from the gate. A strong bias can then be applied to the gate without drawing any current (remember the input–output isolation discussed in the previous section).

In the MOSFET, the charge in the channel (i.e. at the oxide–semiconductor junction) is not due to any donors, but is produced by "inversion" created by the gate bias. For example, the n-MOS device is produced in p$^-$ Si as shown in Figure 19.2. A sufficient bias on the gate causes an inversion where a high density of electrons are drawn into the active channel that is formed. The variation of the gate bias can change the electron concentration and thus modulate the current flowing through the source and drain.

For semiconductors such as GaAs, InP, InGaAs, etc., there is no oxide (or other simple compound) which could act as an insulator to isolate the gate from the channel. This is a big disadvantage for these materials, since the simple and elegant MOS concept cannot be used. Instead one has to use a Schottky barrier to provide the gate to channel isolation, and the material has to be doped to provide the active charge in the channel. The gate potential modulates the charge in the channel by modulating the depletion width under the gate. This is device is known as a Metal-Semiconductor FET or MESFET and is shown schematically in Figure 19.3.

In the MESFET, the free charge moves through the fixed donor (acceptor) impurities resulting in low mobilities. Also, the device does not work at low temperatures because of the carrier freeze-out effect discussed in Chapter 8. An

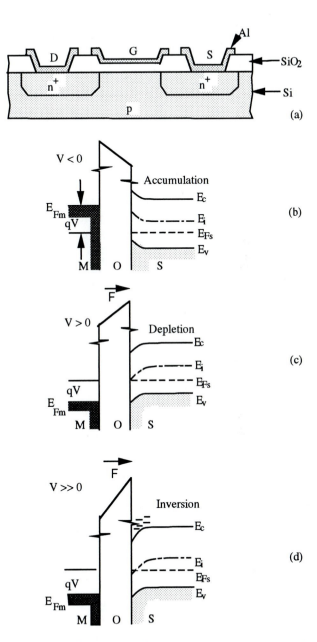

Figure 19.2: (a) A schematic of an n-MOS device. In figures (b), (c), and (d), the effect of the gate potential on the electron and hole density at the interfaces is shown. When the excess electrons are formed under inversion conditions, the device channel is conducting.

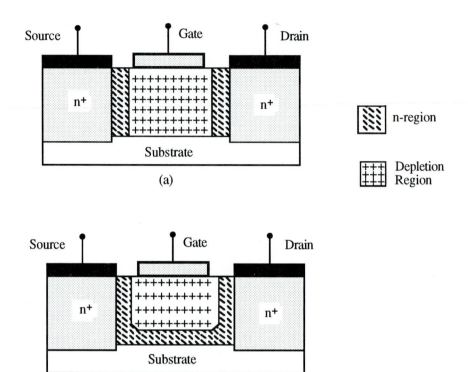

(a)

▨	n-region
⊞	Depletion Region

(b)

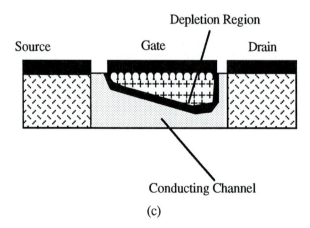

(c)

Figure 19.3: Figures (a) and (b) show schematically how a gate potential can change depletion of the channel to alter the conductivity of the channel. In figure (c), we show schematically the depletion profile with finite source–drain bias.

ingenious way out of both of these problems is provided by the MODFET, using simple heterostructure concepts. In this device, as shown in Figure 19.4, the dopants are placed in a larger bandgap material, which has a positive conduction band offset (for the n-MODFET). The electrons spill into the lower bandgap semiconductor and the resulting charge separation causes band bending according to the Poisson equation, resulting in forming a channel. We discussed in Chapter 14 the scattering processes in a MODFET. The key improvement over the MESFET is the improved mobility and superior low temperature performance due to reduced ionized impurity scattering and lack of carrier freeze-out. In fact, the MODFET has completely taken over all device functions in systems where very high performance is the key requirement. The MESFET, however, still dominates the microwave and digital domain where performance is not yet pushed to the limit.

A number of other field effect transistors have been also suggested and demonstrated. Some of the simpler ones are the Junction Field Effect Transistor (JFET), using a *p-n* junction instead of a Schottky barrier for the control gate and the Heterostructure Insulated Gate Field Effect Transistor (HIGFET), which allows both *n*- and *p*-type devices since it operates like an MOS structure. Some more exotic devices are the real space charge transfer devices, which seek to use the variation in transport properties of different semiconductors in a heterostructure, to modulate current more effectively.

What is the driving force for the FET structures? To answer this question, we must examine a few simple concepts that describe device performance. The FET is a remarkable structure which satisfies most of the criteria for a good device, set out in the previous section. The driving forces for the FET designer come from one of the following general considerations: faster switching time for digital applications; lower power dissipation for digital systems in the switching process; higher frequencies of operation for microwave applications; tolerance to higher power output for microwave applications; and higher temperature performance.

The high power/high temperature operation is mainly tied to the bandgap of the material, although clever device design is important for high power operation. The speed issues (and the high frequency operation issue) are often tied to the transconductance of the device, defined as:

$$g_m = \frac{dI_D}{dV_G} \tag{19.6}$$

i.e., how well the gate controls the source–drain current I_D. High performance FETs have g_m in the range approaching 1000 mS/mm (i.e. a 1 μV swing in the gate bias will produce a 1 mA change in current if the width of the gate is 1 mm). Since the transconductance is mainly determined by the carrier velocity (integrated average over the device field), carrier density, and device design, it is quite straightforward to choose the path to faster devices. However, the technological problems often make this path arduous if not impossible. In Table 19.7 we show some of the directions being pursued for superior FET structures.

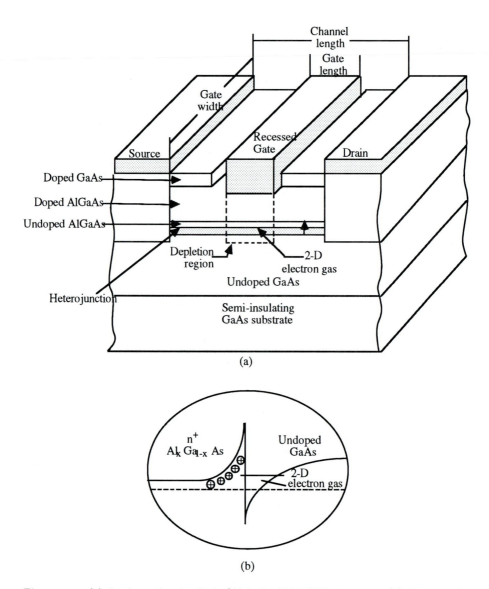

Figure 19.4: (a) A schematic of a GaAs/AlGaAs MODFET structure. (b) The transfer of electrons from the barrier region to the GaAs interface forming a 2-D electron gas.

MESFETs	• NEW FASTER MATERIAL SYSTEMS
	• SUBMICRON GATES
	• IMPROVED OHMIC TECHNOLOGY
	• LARGE BANDGAP SEMICONDUCTORS
MOSFETs	• SMALLER DIMENSIONS
	• USE OF SiGe SYSTEMS
	• SUPERIOR INTERFACE
	• USE OF Si NITRIDE AS INSULATOR
MODFETs	• NEW MATERIAL SYSTEMS
	• SUPERIOR DOPING PROFILES TO INTRODUCE HIGHER SHEET CHARGE
	• HIGHER BAND DISCONTINUITIES
	• PSEUDOMORPHIC STRUCTURES
	• SUBMICRON STRUCTURES
	• IMPROVED CONTACT TECHNOLOGY

Table 19.7: Approaches for improving FET performance.

19.3.2 The Bipolar Device

The bipolar device is another three terminal electronic device which has become a workhorse for important digital and microwave technologies. In many aspects, it shows greater reliability than the FET structures, since many of its properties depend upon intrinsic material parameters, rather than extrinsic properties such as Schottky barrier height, gate to channel separation, and so on. However, it is by no means a simple device to fabricate and optimize, especially in new material systems.

The working concept of the bipolar device is quite simple. Unlike the FET structure, this device uses both electrons and holes. As shown in Figure 19.5 for the *n-p-n* transistor, the electrons are injected from the emitter into the *p*-type base and collected in the *n*-type collector. The biasing of this device is such that the electron injection into the base requires them to go over a potential barrier. Since the injected electrons are essentially thermal, their injection depends exponentially on the barrier they see. This emitter–base barrier can be modulated by the base voltage which then modulates the electron current into the collector. For the device to operate efficiently it is important that the electrons do not recombine with the holes in the base and that the holes are not injected out of the base into the emitter. This latter requirement is the main motivation for using heterojunction bipolar transistors (HBT), since the valence band offset can then effectively confine the holes to the base and allow high levels of base doping.

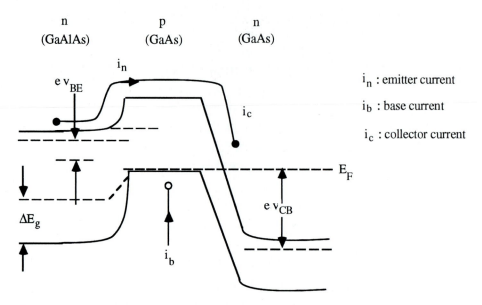

Figure 19.5: A schematic of the n-AlGaAs/p-GaAs/n-GaAs heterojunction bipolar transistor under bias. The emitter–base junction is forward-biased while the base–collector junction is reverse-biased. A small variation in the base potential (say due to injection of base current) can change the injected emitter current in an exponential manner.

Some of the (often conflicting) forces to improve bipolar devices are listed in Table 19.8. Note again that like the FETs, the bipolar device also satisfies the device requirements of the previous section quite well.

19.3.3   Resonant Tunneling Devices

The physics of the resonant tunneling device was discussed in Chapter 14. The resonant tunneling device and its variations have captured the imagination of device designers for almost two decades. The ability to generate negative differential resistance regions and obtain very high switching speeds is a great attraction. The resonant tunneling diode suffers from many serious problems including lack of input–output isolation, poor reliability (only one or two monolayers of barrier or well size fluctuations can greatly alter the operating characteristics), and very low power output. However, it appears that for certain high speed digital operations, the resonant tunneling transistor could be very useful. The transistor is quite difficult to fabricate since the access and control of the "base" or well region is quite a challenge. However, a number of clever schemes have been proposed and demonstrated. The potential of this device remains to be seen.

The driving forces behind resonant tunneling device research include:

1. Use of materials that provide a superior peak to valley ratio for the current

DESIGN CONSIDERATIONS

• LOW BASE RESISTANCE → WIDE BASE & HIGH DOPING
• LOW TRANSIT TIME → NARROW BASE
• HIGH BASE–EMITTER VALENCE BAND OFFSET (for *n-p-n* devices)
• LOW BASE–COLLECTOR CONDUCTION BAND OFFSET (for *n-p-n* devices)
• HIGH QUALITY INTERFACES TO SUPPRESS BASE RECOMBINATION
• SMALL DIMENSIONS
• NEW MATERIAL SYSTEMS (SiGe, InGaAs)

Table 19.8: Driving forces for improved bipolar devices.

by using larger band offsets.

2. Studies of new transistor designs which are easy to fabricate and provide good input–output isolation.

3. Studies of schemes that could allow a larger voltage separation between points where the current reaches its peak and its valley. A larger separation is essential if the device is to yield any useful output power for microwave applications.

19.3.4 Special Microwave Devices

The FET and HBT structures discussed above are widely used for both digital and microwave applications. However, for microwave applications, they require additional elements like inductances, resistors, capacitors, etc. to provide the resonant circuit. However, there are certain devices which utilize instabilities in the device structure to produce charge or current oscillations. These devices depend upon the negative conductance of the structure and include Gunn devices and the IMPATT (and related) devices.

In the Gunn device, one utilizes the fact that in materials like GaAs, InGaAs, etc. there is a region of negative resistance in the velocity–field relationship of the electrons. We discussed the physics behind this phenomenon in Chapter 13, and this is related to the presence of a low effective mass conduction band valley followed by a high effective mass valley. When the electrons start transferring from the low mass valley to the high mass valley at a threshold field E_{th}, the velocity decreases as the field is increased. This leads to a negative resistance region.

A negative conductance can be produced in semiconductor junction structures by using impact ionization and transit time effects. A negative conductance is produced, if for some reason, there is a 180° phase differences between the voltage applied to a structure and the current in the circuit. A number of clever ways have been designed to achieve this and these are manifested in devices such as IMPATTs, TRAPPATs, etc.

The resonant tunneling diode also shows a region of negative resistance as does the tunnel diode which utilizes the band-to-band tunneling. There may be other yet unexplored techniques to produce negative conductance, especially by using heterostructure techniques.

The attraction of being able to design circuits which have negative conductance is that they can be exploited to produce microwave power. The effect can be used to produce microwave amplifiers, oscillators, functional oscillators (generating a variety of waveforms), etc. The frequency of operation of these *diodes* can be much larger than those reached by three terminal transistor structures discussed earlier. However, extra care is to be taken for input–output isolation. The 180° phase difference between the current and voltage is sufficient to provide amplification of signals, much the same way as a properly timed extension of a child on a swing is able to build up a large amplitude. The details of the design of high frequency circuits based on negative conductance are quite intricate and can be found in the references listed at the end of this chapter.

19.3.5   The Semiconductor Laser

The semiconductor laser has rapidly become an integral component of modern day systems, thanks largely to communication networks. Lasers are also used in reading information from compact discs, as well as from bar codes on consumer goods. However, it must be recognized that so far, lasers have not acquired the role that a transistor has in modern products. Even in a communication module, for one laser, there are thousands of electronic devices which are carrying out the actual processing and decision making. The use of lasers in logic or processing information is as yet only in research papers. This is partly due to the fact that the laser does not satisfy many of the criteria outlined in the previous section for successful devices. Thus, it has to rely on electronic devices to make intelligent decisions. So far, the semiconductor laser and other optoelectronic devices are getting their push from beginning to replace electronic systems by more efficient, less power consuming and usually cheaper optoelectronic systems. Of course, the day may come when all optical devices and optical computers do become a reality.

The basic physical processes behind a semiconductor laser were discussed in Chapter 15. The driving forces behind semiconductor lasers include:

1. New materials tuned to specific wavelengths. These special wavelengths may be imposed by considerations such as low loss in fiber transmission or special display requirements such as the need for a green laser.

2. Structures for low threshold lasers. This need drives the research into pseudomorphic lasers and sub-two-dimensional lasers.

3. Higher frequency operation drives the research into new laser design as well as new material systems.

4. "Stable" lasers in which the frequency of the emitted light does not "hop" between different modes and has a small linewidth. Distributed feedback (DFB) lasers and other related approaches are used to achieve mode stability and narrow linewidth.

5. Tunable lasers in which the output frequency can be tuned. This is a challenge and uses of tunable gratings in a distributed Bragg reflector lasers are being explored.

6. Mode locking of laser diodes. This is a very important challenge since each laser diode only provides a few milliwatts of optical power. If an array of diodes are mode locked i.e. are in phase coherence, the output power can be increased to Watts and open new vistas for laser applications.

7. Laser amplifiers. Here the laser cavity is used as an optical amplifier where a light beam triggers spontaneous emission and the laser action precipitates. The cavity is biased just below threshold for such applications.

The applications of lasers will clearly grow as time passes and it may introduce new approaches to current problems. Its ability to carry out operations in free space are always impressive, and the child in us is always fascinated by doors that suddenly open or security systems that recognize us and let us in.

19.3.6 Modulators

Most high speed modulator schemes used at present to alter optical intensity in commercial systems involve use of electronics simply to directly modulate a laser. Nevertheless, semiconductor modulators using excitonic effects in quantum well have been demonstrated and are beginning to make headway into special applications. The need for programmable "transparencies," optical switches, and optical logic is tremendous and the exciton based modulators can fill this need. It must be kept in mind that along with lasers, the modulator performance is extremely sensitive to temperature. While this may not be as important for many laser applications, lack of temperature control can play havoc with modulators. Research in modulators is driven by:

1. Higher speed.

2. High ON/OFF ratio.

3. New physical phenomena which can be implemented more efficiently.

19.3.7   Detectors

The detectors which convert an optical signal to an electrical signal are an integral part of any optoelectronic system. In a sense, this also highlights the dependence of optical systems on electronics at present. With the advent of heterostructures, a number of very clever schemes have been designed to produce high performance detectors. Key issues in detectors are being able to achieve the conflicting properties of high gain, high speed, and low noise. Usually, only detectors are designed for either high speed or high gain.

An area where detector technology is sadly lacking is the area of wavelength selective detection. A highly touted advantage of fiber optic communication is the ability to carry a very high number of channels of information each on a slightly different wavelength. However, because of difficulty in detecting these closely spaced wavelengths by simple detectors, this vast potential is wasted so far.

Integration of optoelectronic devices is an area of intense research at present since it is assumed that just as great strides were made going from discrete devices to integrated circuits (ICs), the same advantage would occur in optoelectronic integrated circuits (OEICs). Serious challenges remain in this area due to the greater sensitivity of optical devices on processing related damage.

In this chapter we have presented a brief overview of some of the important issues in the world of devices. In particular, we have focussed on the use of physical phenomena in devices. Semiconductors and their heterostructures offer us a tremendous variety of physical phenomena to choose from. Many of these phenomena may lead to new and powerful devices for the next generation of electronics and optoelectronics.

(a)

(b)

Figure 19.6: (a) Signal distortion may be a source of fun in the children's game "telephone," but it could be disastrous in modern information processing systems. High gain and tolerance to noise are essential characteristics of devices. (b) Every glitch in an input–output response does not a superior device make. This chapter explores some of the important ingredients for active information processing devices.

19.4   REFERENCES

- **General**

  - Casey, H. C., Jr. and M. B. Panish, *Heterostructure Lasers* (Academic Press, New York, 1978).

  - Keyes, R. W. *The Physics of VLSI Systems* (Addison-Wesley, New York, 1987).

  - Streetman, B. G. *Solid State Electronic Devices* (Prentice-Hall, Englewood Cliffs, 1980).

  - Sze, S. M., *Physics of Semiconductor Devices* (John Wiley and Sons, New York, 1981).

  - Wang, S. *Fundamentals of Semiconductor Theory and Device Physics* (Prentice-Hall, Englewood Cliffs, 1989).

APPENDIX A

THE WAVE PACKET PICTURE

Very often the solution of Schrödinger equation yields eigenstates which represent a pure ideal state which is often not reached in an actual experiment. A case in point are the eigenstates of electrons inside a crystal. We showed in Chapter 4 that the eigenstates are of the spatial form

$$\psi_{\mathbf{k}}(\mathbf{r}) \sim u_{\mathbf{k}}(\mathbf{r})\, e^{i\mathbf{k}\cdot\mathbf{r}} \tag{A.1}$$

where $u_{\mathbf{k}}(\mathbf{r})$ is periodic in the crystal lattice. Thus, the probability of finding the electron is same in all unit cells of the crystal. This is not a useful description of an electron when we wish to describe the transport of an electron. In transport we wish to describe an electron which moves from one point inside the crystal to another. Thus, the wavefunction must be peaked at a particular place in space for such a description. This physical picture is realized by constructing a wavepacket picture. The wavepacket picture is also very useful in developing the correspondence between the classical description of a particle and the quantum mechanical description. The wavepacket picture is also very useful when one examines problems where a pulsed laser excites an electronic state. In this case the electron is not excited in a well-defined k-state (ω-state) but in a wavepacket having a certain spread in energy.

Going back to a one-dimensional plane wave state with a wave vector k_0

$$\psi_{k_0}(x) = e^{ik_0x}, \tag{A.2}$$

we note that if a state was constructed not from a single k_0 component, but from a spread $\pm\Delta k$, then the function

$$F(x, x_0) \;=\; \int_{k_0-\Delta k}^{k_0+\Delta k} dk\; e^{ik(x-x_0)}$$

$$= \frac{2\sin(\Delta k\,(x-x_0))}{(x-x_0)}\,e^{ik_0(x-x_0)} \tag{A.3}$$

is centered around the point x_0 and the probability ($|F|^2$) decays from its maximum value at x_0 to a very small value within a distance $\pi/\Delta k$.

If Δk is small, this new "wavepacket" has essentially the same properties as ψ at k_0, but is localized in space and is thus very useful to describe motion of the particle. A more useful wavepacket is constructed by multiplying the integrand in the wavepacket by a Gaussian weighting factor

$$f(k-k_0) = \exp\left[-\frac{(k-k_0)^2}{2(\Delta k)^2}\right]. \tag{A.4}$$

$$
\begin{aligned}
\psi(x,x_0) &= \int_{-\infty}^{\infty} \exp\left[-\frac{(k-k_0)^2}{2(\Delta k)^2} + ik(x-x_0)\right]\,dk \\
&= \exp\left[ik_0(x-x_0) - \frac{(x-x_0)^2}{2}(\Delta k)^2\right] \\
&\quad \times \int_{-\infty}^{\infty} \exp\left[-\frac{(k-k_0)^2}{2(\Delta k)^2} + i(k-k_0)(x-x_0) + \frac{(x-x_0)^2}{2}(\Delta k)^2\right] \\
&= \sqrt{2\pi\Delta k}\,\exp\left[ik_0(x-x_0) - \frac{1}{2}(x-x_0)^2(\Delta k)^2\right].
\end{aligned} \tag{A.5}
$$

$\psi(x,x_0)$ represents a Gaussian wavepacket in space which decays rapidly away from x_0. We note that when we considered the original state $\exp(ik_0 x)$, the wave was spread infinitely in space, but has a precise k-value. By constructing a wavepacket, we sacrificed its precision in k-space by Δk and gained a precision Δx in real space. In general, the width of the wavepacket in real and k-space can be seen to have the relation

$$\Delta k\,\Delta x \approx 1. \tag{A.6}$$

We can repeat this procedure for a wave of the form

$$\psi \sim e^{i\omega t} \tag{A.7}$$

and also obtain a wavepacket which is localized in time and frequency, the widths again being related by

$$\Delta\omega\,\Delta t \approx 1. \tag{A.8}$$

A.1   MOTION OF A WAVEPACKET

Let us now consider how a wavepacket moves through space and time. For this we need to bring in the time dependence of the wavefunction, i.e., the term $\exp(-iEt/\hbar)$ or $\exp(-i\omega t)$.

$$\psi(x,t) = \int_{-\infty}^{\infty} f(k-k_0)\,\exp\left\{i[k(x-x_0) - \omega t]\right\}\,dk \tag{A.9}$$

If ω has a simple dependence on k

$$\omega = ck, \qquad \text{(A.10)}$$

we can write

$$\psi(x, t) = \int_{-\infty}^{\infty} f(k - k_0) \, \exp\left[ik(x - x_0 - ct)\right] \, dk \qquad \text{(A.11)}$$

which means that the wavepacket simply moves with its center at

$$x - x_0 = ct \qquad \text{(A.12)}$$

and its shape is unchanged with time. If, however, we have a dispersive media and the ω vs. k relation is more complex, we can, in general, write

$$\omega(k) = \omega(k_0) + \left.\frac{\partial \omega}{\partial k}\right|_{k=k_0} \cdot (k - k_0) + \frac{1}{2} \left.\frac{\partial^2 \omega}{\partial k^2}\right|_{k=k_0} (k - k_0)^2 + \cdots. \qquad \text{(A.13)}$$

Setting

$$
\begin{aligned}
\omega(k_0) &= \omega_0 \\
\left.\frac{\partial \omega}{\partial k}\right|_{k=k_0} &= v_g \\
\left.\frac{\partial^2 \omega}{\partial k^2}\right|_{k=k_0} &= \alpha,
\end{aligned}
\qquad \text{(A.14)}
$$

we get

$$
\begin{aligned}
\psi(x, t) &= \exp\left[i(k_0(x - x_0) - \omega_0 t)\right] \int_{-\infty}^{\infty} f(k - k_0) \\
&\quad \times \exp\left[i(k - k_0)(x - x_0 - v_g t) - \frac{i\alpha}{2}(k - k_0)^2 t\right] \, dk. \quad \text{(A.15)}
\end{aligned}
$$

If α were zero, the wavepacket would move with its peak centered at

$$x - x_0 = v_g t \qquad \text{(A.16)}$$

i.e., with a velocity

$$v_g = \left.\frac{\partial \omega}{\partial k}\right|_{k=k_0}. \qquad \text{(A.17)}$$

However, for nonzero α, we show that the shape of the wavepacket also changes. To see this, let us again assume that

$$
\begin{aligned}
f(k - k_0) &= f(k') \\
&= \exp\left(\frac{-k'^2}{2\Delta k^2}\right). \qquad \text{(A.18)}
\end{aligned}
$$

Then

$$\psi(x,t) = \exp\left\{i\left[k_0(x - x_0) - \omega_0 t\right]\right\}$$
$$\times \int_{-\infty}^{\infty} \exp\left[ik'(x - x_0 - v_g t)\right.$$
$$\left. - \frac{k'^2}{2}\left(i\alpha t + \frac{1}{(\Delta k)^2}\right)\right] dk'. \qquad (A.19)$$

To evaluate this integral we complete the square in the integrand by adding and subtracting terms

$$\psi(x,t) = \exp\left\{i\left[k_0(x - x_0) - \omega_0 t\right] - \frac{(x - x_0 - v_g t)^2 (\Delta k)^2}{2\left[1 + i\alpha t(\Delta k)^2\right]}\right\}$$
$$\times \int_{-\infty}^{\infty} \exp\left\{\frac{-1}{2}\left[\frac{1 + i\alpha t\,(\Delta k)^2}{(\Delta k)^2}\right]\right.$$
$$\times \left.\left[k' - i\frac{(x - x_0 - v_g t)\,(\Delta k)^2}{1 + i\alpha t\,(\Delta k)^2}\right]^2\right\} dk'. \qquad (A.20)$$

The integral has a value

$$\sqrt{\frac{2\pi\,(\Delta k)^2}{1 + i\alpha t\,(\Delta k)^2}}.$$

Further multiplying and dividing the right-hand side exponent by $(1 - i\alpha t\,(\Delta k)^2)$ we get

$$\psi(x,t) = \exp\left\{i\left[k_0(x - x_0) - \omega_0 t\right]\right\}\sqrt{\frac{2\pi\,(\Delta k)^2}{1 + i\alpha t\,(\Delta k)^2}}$$
$$\times \exp\left[-\frac{(\Delta k)^2}{2}\frac{(x - x_0 - v_g t)^2}{1 + t^2\,(\Delta k)^4\alpha^2}\right]$$
$$\times \exp\left[\frac{i\alpha t\,(\Delta k)^4}{2}\frac{(x - x_0 - v_g t)^2}{1 + t^2\alpha^2\,(\Delta k)^4}\right]. \qquad (A.21)$$

The probability $|\psi|^2$ has the dependence on space and time given by

$$|\psi(x,t)|^2 = \exp\left[-\frac{(\Delta k)^2\,(x - x_0 - v_g t)^2}{1 + \alpha^2 t^2\,(\Delta k)^4}\right]. \qquad (A.22)$$

This is a Gaussian distribution centered around $x = x_0 + v_g t$ and the mean width in real space is given by

$$\delta x = \frac{1}{\Delta k}\sqrt{1 + \alpha^2 t^2\,(\Delta k)^4}$$

$$= \delta x(t=0) \sqrt{1 + \frac{\alpha^2 t^2}{[\delta x(t=0)]^4}}. \qquad \text{(A.23)}$$

For short times such that

$$\alpha^2 t^2 (\Delta k)^4 \ll 1, \qquad \text{(A.24)}$$

the width does not change appreciably from its starting value, but as time passes, if $\alpha \neq 0$, the wavepacket will start spreading.

In case of particles with mass m (nonzero) the relation between ω and k is

$$\omega = \frac{E}{\hbar}$$
$$= \frac{\hbar k^2}{2m}$$

or

$$\alpha = \frac{\hbar}{m}. \qquad \text{(A.25)}$$

Let us calculate the time it takes a particle of mass 1 gram to double its wavepacket width if it was originally confined to a dimension of 10^{-3} cm. This is given by

$$t = \frac{\sqrt{3}\,[\delta x(t=0)]^2}{\alpha}$$
$$\approx 1.7 \times 10^{21} \text{ s}$$
$$= 5 \times 10^{13} \text{ years!} \qquad \text{(A.26)}$$

which means that, in principle, for such a classical mass, we will never see any broadening. However, for an electron with a mass of $\sim 10^{-27}$ g, this broadening time is quite short (~ 1 ps) if the starting wavepacket is confined over, say, a 100 Å size. The notion of a wavepacket and its width is quite useful in understanding the relationship between the classical or the intuitive picture and the quantum mechanical or wave picture of a particle. For example, in some experiments such as electron diffraction, the electron state is chosen at a very selective k-value (i.e., monoenergetic electron beam) with a narrow spread in k-space and thus a large spread in real space. In such experiments our intuitive particle picture breaks down and the electron behaves as a wave undergoing diffraction and interference effects. A number of devices have been proposed relying on such effects. In most electronic devices, however, the electrons move as if they were particles, i.e., as wavepackets with very narrow spatial extent.

The time evolution of a wavepacket can be studied by a technique described in Goldberg, A., H. M. Schey and J. Schwartz, Amer. J. Phys., **35**, 177 (1967).

APPENDIX
B

ELECTRON
IN A QUANTUM
WELL

With the ability of crystal growers to make semiconductor heterostructures with very narrow dimensions, the simple problem of one-dimensional square well potential, popularly known as the quantum well (shown in Figure B.1), has become very useful. In semiconductor technology a good approximation to such quantum wells are produced when a narrow bandgap material of width $W = 2a$ is sandwiched between a large bandgap material. The simpler form of the quantum well is one where the potential is zero in the well and infinite outside. The equation to solve then is

$$-\frac{\hbar^2}{2m}\frac{d^2\psi}{dx^2} = E\psi \tag{B.1}$$

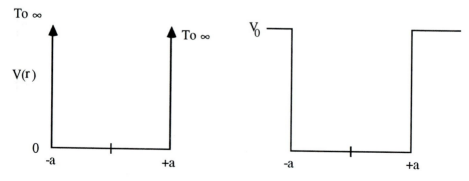

Figure B.1: A quantum well of width $2a$ and barrier infinite barrier height or barrier height V_0.

which has the general solutions

$$\psi(x) = B\cos\frac{n\pi x}{2a}, \; n \text{ is odd}$$

$$= A\sin\frac{n\pi x}{2a}, \; n \text{ is even.} \tag{B.2}$$

The energy is, in general

$$E = \frac{\pi^2\hbar^2 n^2}{8ma^2}. \tag{B.3}$$

Note that the well size is $2a$.

The infinite well problem is often quite accurate for getting the discrete energy states in a quantum well especially for the ground state ($n = 1$) in most semiconductor quantum wells. For more accurate solutions one must often deal with the finite potential step problem. This forces us to examine the region outside the well, where the wavefunction has a finite value. The equation for the barrier region is

$$\frac{-\hbar^2}{2m}\frac{d^2\psi}{dx^2} + V_0\psi = E\psi \text{ for } |x| \geq a \tag{B.4}$$

where V_0 is the potential step.

The solutions inside the well have the form

$$\psi(x) = A\sin(\alpha x) + B\cos(\alpha x)$$

$$\alpha = \sqrt{\frac{2mE}{\hbar^2}}. \tag{B.5}$$

The solution outside the well has the form

$$\psi(x) = C\exp(-\beta x) + D\exp(\beta x)$$

$$\beta = \sqrt{\frac{2m(V_0 - E)}{\hbar^2}}. \tag{B.6}$$

We now impose the boundary conditions that at $x = \pm a$, ψ and $d\psi/dx$ are continuous. This corresponds to saying that the electron probability and the electron current do not suffer a discontinuity at the boundaries. The conditions give

$$A\sin(\alpha a) + B\cos(\alpha a) = C\exp(-\beta a)$$
$$\alpha A\cos(\alpha a) - \alpha B\sin(\alpha a) = -C\beta\exp(-\beta a)$$
$$-A\sin(\alpha a) + B\cos(\alpha a) = D\exp(-\beta a)$$
$$\alpha A\cos(\alpha a) + \alpha B\sin(\alpha a) = \beta D\exp(-\beta a). \tag{B.7}$$

This yields again for nontrivial solutions the results

$$\alpha\tan(\alpha a) = \beta \tag{B.8}$$

and

$$\alpha \cos(\alpha a) = -\beta. \tag{B.9}$$

The energy levels are now obtained by numerically or graphically solving these transcendental equations.

Note that in the case of semiconductors, where the electron may be described as having an effective mass m_w^* in the well and m_b^* in the barrier, it is $(1/m^*)\partial\psi/\partial x$, instead of $\partial\psi/\partial x$, which must be continuous

$$\frac{1}{m_w^*}\frac{\partial\psi_w}{\partial x} = \frac{1}{m_b^*}\frac{\partial\psi_b}{\partial x}. \tag{B.10}$$

THE HARMONIC
OSCILLATOR
PROBLEM

The solution to the harmonic oscillator problem in quantum mechanics provides one of the most widely used results in semiconductor physics. The problems of scattering of electrons by phonons as well as absorption of photons make direct use of our understanding of the harmonic oscillator problem. While the harmonic oscillator problem can be solved by solving the Schrödinger equation directly, for our purpose it is more useful to treat the problem by manipulating the matrix equations. The Hamiltonian for the problem is

$$H = \frac{p^2}{2m} + \frac{1}{2}Kx^2. \tag{C.1}$$

The variables x and p are hermitian matrix operators as they correspond to physical observables. To solve the harmonic oscillator problem we only need to realize that

$$xp - px = i\hbar. \tag{C.2}$$

We will work in the energy representation where H is diagonal and we can write

$$\begin{aligned}
\langle k|H|\ell\rangle &= E_k\langle k|\ell\rangle \\
&= \frac{1}{2m}\langle k|p|j\rangle\langle j|p|\ell\rangle + \frac{1}{2}K\langle k|x|j\rangle\langle j|x|\ell\rangle. \tag{C.3}
\end{aligned}$$

Remember that the states $|k\rangle$ are orthonormal and $\sum |k\rangle\langle k| \equiv |k\rangle\langle k| = 1$. Note that since p and x are hermitian

$$\begin{aligned}
\langle j|p|\ell\rangle &= \langle \ell|p^\dagger|j\rangle^* \\
&= \langle \ell|p|j\rangle^*. \tag{C.4}
\end{aligned}$$

The right-hand side of Equation C.3 is a sum of squares of absolute values and is therefore non-negative. Thus, an energy value E_k can be zero only if the matrix elements $\langle k|p|j \rangle$ and $\langle k|x|j \rangle$ are zero for all j. However, this is not possible due to the uncertainty principle. Thus, the energy eigenvalues must be greater than zero. To find these values we calculate the commutator of x and p with H

$$
\begin{aligned}
xH - Hx &= \frac{i\hbar}{m} p \\
pH - Hp &= -i\hbar K x.
\end{aligned}
\tag{C.5}
$$

The first of these equations can be written as

$$
\begin{aligned}
\langle k|x|j\rangle\langle j|H|\ell\rangle - \langle k|H|j\rangle\langle j|x|\ell\rangle &= (E_\ell - E_k)\langle k|x|\ell\rangle \\
&= \frac{i\hbar}{m}\langle k|p|\ell\rangle.
\end{aligned}
\tag{C.6}
$$

Similarly, the other equation gives

$$
(E_\ell - E_k)\langle k|p|\ell\rangle = -i\hbar K \langle k|x|\ell\rangle
\tag{C.7}
$$

Eliminating $\langle k|x|\ell\rangle$ from these two equations we get

$$
(E_\ell - E_k)^2\langle k|p|\ell\rangle - \frac{\hbar^2 K}{m}\langle k|p|\ell\rangle = 0.
\tag{C.8}
$$

Thus, either $\langle k|p|\ell\rangle = 0$ or

$$
\begin{aligned}
(E_\ell - E_k) &= \pm\hbar\left(\frac{K}{m}\right)^{1/2} \\
&= \pm\hbar\omega_c
\end{aligned}
\tag{C.9}
$$

where ω_c is the classical frequency of the oscillator. If we rule out the conditions $\langle k|p|\ell\rangle = \langle k|x|\ell\rangle = 0$ we note that the energy eigenvalues of the harmonic oscillator differ from each other by $\hbar\omega_c$. We will now show that the eigenvalues for energy have the form $(n+1/2)\hbar\omega_c$. For this we multiply Equation C.6 by $-im\omega_c$ and add it to Equation C.7.

This gives

$$
-im\omega_c(E_\ell - E_k)\langle k|x|\ell\rangle - \hbar\omega_c\langle k|p|\ell\rangle + (E_\ell - E_k)\langle k|p|\ell\rangle + i\hbar K \langle k|x|\ell\rangle = 0. \tag{C.10}
$$

This can be rewritten as

$$
(E_\ell - E_k - \hbar\omega_c)\langle k|(p - im\omega_c x)|\ell\rangle = 0.
\tag{C.11}
$$

Thus, $\langle k|(p - im\omega_c x)|\ell\rangle$ fails to vanish only when $E_\ell - E_k = \hbar\omega_c$. Thus, the effect of operating on a ket $|\ell\rangle$ with the operator $p - im\omega_c x$ is to produce a multiple of the ket $|j\rangle$ which has an energy lower by $\hbar\omega_c$. The procedure can be repeated to show that the operator $p + im\omega_c x$ does the reverse, i.e., when it operates on a ket $|\ell\rangle$, it produces a new state with energy larger by an amount $\hbar\omega_c$.

If the energy lowering operator is repeatedly applied, we will eventually run into difficulty since the energy of the problem is always positive. Thus, there has to be a lowest energy state $|0\rangle$ such that

$$(p - im\omega_c x)|0\rangle = 0. \tag{C.12}$$

To find the lowest eigenvalue of H we operate on Equation C.12 from the left by $(p + im\omega_c x)$.

$$
\begin{aligned}
(p + im\omega_c x)(p - im\omega_c x)|0\rangle &= \left[p^2 + m^2\omega_c^2 x^2 + im\omega_c(xp - px)\right]|0\rangle \\
&= \left[p^2 + m^2\omega_c^2 x^2 - m\hbar\omega_c\right]|0\rangle \\
&= 2m\left[H - \frac{1}{2}\hbar\omega_c\right]|0\rangle \\
&= 0. \tag{C.13}
\end{aligned}
$$

Thus, the eigenvalue corresponding to the $|0\rangle$ or "vacuum" state is $\hbar\omega_c/2$. Application of $(p + im\omega_c x)$ on $|0\rangle$ gives a multiple of the state $|1\rangle$ with energy $3\hbar\omega_c/2$. Continued such application gives the set of energy levels

$$E_n = \left(n + \frac{1}{2}\right)\hbar\omega_c \text{ for } n = 0, 1, 2, \ldots \tag{C.14}$$

with the general state being denoted by $|n\rangle$.

It is useful to put the energy raising and lowering operator in a dimensionless form which we will denote by $a^\dagger$ and a

$$
\begin{aligned}
a^\dagger &= \frac{-i}{\sqrt{2m\hbar\omega_c}}(p + im\omega_c x) \\
a &= \frac{i}{\sqrt{2m\hbar\omega_c}}(p - im\omega_c x). \tag{C.15}
\end{aligned}
$$

It is easy to see that

$$
\begin{aligned}
aa^\dagger &= \frac{H}{\hbar\omega_c} + \frac{1}{2} \\
a^\dagger a &= \frac{H}{\hbar\omega_c} - \frac{1}{2} \tag{C.16}
\end{aligned}
$$

and

$$aa^\dagger - a^\dagger a = 1. \tag{C.17}$$

We may write

$$H = \left(a^\dagger a + \frac{1}{2}\right)\hbar\omega_c. \tag{C.18}$$

The operator $a^\dagger a$ has eigenvalues which are zero and positive integers which represent the number of "quanta" of energy present in a given state.

It is important to note that the results obtained above have only relied upon the commutation principle. No other input was required. The mathematics developed is extremely useful in connection with quantization of the wavefields associated with particles (i.e., treating the wavefields or probability amplitudes as operators—just like we treated x and p as operators). In such a treatment, also, the operators $a^\dagger$ and a appear as combinations of wavefields and have the effect of raising or lowering the number of quanta or particles in a given state. In this context, these operators are called the creation and destruction operators.

This concept is extremely useful in semiconductor physics when we discuss the scattering of electrons from phonons or photons. The phonon field is represented by a particular state where the occupation (number) of phonons of various modes is well-defined. During scattering, the electron absorbs or emits phonons, thus changing the occupation of the final state.

It is useful to find the matrix representation of the operators $a^\dagger$, a (and x and p). We note that the only nonvanishing elements are $\langle n - 1|a|n\rangle$ for the operator a. Similarly, the only nonvanishing element for $a^\dagger$ is $\langle n|a^\dagger|n - 1\rangle$ which is just the complex conjugate of $\langle n - 1|a|n\rangle$. The diagonal element of $a^\dagger a$ is $\langle n|a^\dagger a|n\rangle = \langle n|a^\dagger|n'\rangle\langle n'|a|n\rangle = |\lambda_n|^2 = n$. Thus, apart from a phase factor, which we can choose to be unity

$$\langle n|a^\dagger|n - 1\rangle = \sqrt{n}$$
$$= \langle n - 1|a|n\rangle. \tag{C.19}$$

This gives the matrix elements for the operators $a^\dagger$ and a. The elements for x and p are simple

$$x = \left(\frac{\hbar}{2m\omega_c}\right)^{1/2}(a^\dagger + a)$$
$$p = i\left(\frac{m\hbar\omega_c}{2}\right)^{1/2}(a^\dagger - a). \tag{C.20}$$

APPENDIX D

COMBINATION OF ANGULAR MOMENTUM STATES

In dealing with the bandstructure of semiconductors we find that a very convenient basis to express the central cell periodic part of the wavefunctions is the angular momentum basis. In particular, the atomic physics description sp^3 basis is most useful. These represent the angular momentum states (angular momentum is zero for s function and $\hbar$ for a p function) which are often sufficient to describe the conduction band and valence bands of semiconductors. In particular, the electronic states near the top of the valence band are described by p-type functions. These nonzero angular momentum state electrons generate a magnetic field through which they interact with the spin of the electron. This interaction is called the spin-orbit coupling and is responsible for very important features of the valence bandstructure as discussed in Chapter 5. Because of this interaction, it is appropriate to describe the electronic states not simply by the orbital angular momentum representation but by the total angular momentum basis. The problem of combining angular momentum in quantum mechanics is nontrivial and requires care.

If J_1 and J_2 are two angular momentum operators which commute with each other, we wish to define the eigenfunctions and eigenstates of the total angular momentum operator $J = J_1 + J_2$ in terms of the basis $|j_1, m_1\rangle$ and $|j_2, m_2\rangle$. There are $(2J_1 + 1)$ and $(2J_2 + 1)$ states corresponding to J_1 and J_2 (see Figure D.1). The starting representation will be denoted by $|j_1 m_1 j_2 m_2\rangle$ or $|m_1 m_2\rangle$ for short. We wish to find the expansion coefficients

$$|jm\rangle = \sum a_{m_1 m_2} |m_1 m_2\rangle \tag{D.1}$$

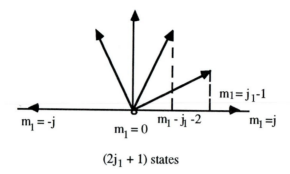

$(2j_1 + 1)$ states

Figure D.1: A schematic representation of the $(2j+1)$ angular momentum states when the total angular momentum is j_1 and the projection ranges from j to $-j$.

where the summation is over the various possible $(2j_1+1)(2j_2+1)$ states which occur in the $|m_1 m_2\rangle$ representation. The coefficients $a_{m_1 m_2}$ are called the Clebsch-Gordan or Wigner coefficients and are sufficiently complex that we will simply catalog them in Figure D.2 for the case of interest in semiconductor physics, viz. $j_1 = 1$; $j_2 = 1/2$. The tabular form allows one to expand either $|jm\rangle$ states in terms of $|m_1 m_2\rangle$ states or vice-versa.

$j_1 = 1 \quad j_2 = \frac{1}{2}:$

		$\frac{3}{2}$	$\frac{3}{2}$	$\frac{1}{2}$	$\frac{3}{2}$	$\frac{1}{2}$	$\frac{3}{2}$
		$\frac{3}{2}$	$\frac{1}{2}$	$\frac{1}{2}$	$-\frac{1}{2}$	$-\frac{1}{2}$	$-\frac{3}{2}$
1	$\frac{1}{2}$	1					
1	$-\frac{1}{2}$		$\sqrt{\frac{1}{3}}$	$\sqrt{\frac{2}{3}}$			
0	$\frac{1}{2}$		$\sqrt{\frac{2}{3}}$	$-\sqrt{\frac{1}{3}}$			
0	$-\frac{1}{2}$				$\sqrt{\frac{2}{3}}$	$\sqrt{\frac{1}{3}}$	
-1	$\frac{1}{2}$				$\sqrt{\frac{1}{3}}$	$-\sqrt{\frac{2}{3}}$	
-1	$-\frac{1}{2}$						1

Figure D.2: Clebsch-Gordan coefficients for $j_1 = 1$; $j_2 = 1/2$.

APPENDIX E

STATIONARY PERTURBATION THEORY

Very few problems in quantum mechanics can be solved exactly and it is extremely important to develop an understanding of important practical problems which cannot be solved exactly. The perturbation (or approximation) methods are, therefore, of critical importance. The exact solutions are also, of course, very important, since they are often used as a starting point or a testing point for the approximate solutions. In this section we will summarize some key results from stationary perturbation theory. Details of the derivation can be found in most quantum mechanics books (e.g., L. I. Schiff, *Quantum Mechanics*, McGraw-Hill, New York, 1968).

Consider a Hamiltonian of the form

$$H = H_0 + H'$$ (E.1)

where the solutions of H_0 are known and are given by

$$H_0 u_k = E_k u_k.$$ (E.2)

We seek the solution of the problem

$$H\psi = E\psi.$$ (E.3)

We are interested in solving for ψ and the eigenvalues of the full Hamiltonian, in terms of the eigenfunctions and eigenvalues of the known Hamiltonian H_0. The eigenfunction ψ and the eigenvalue W are written in terms of a parameter λ

$$
\begin{aligned}
\psi &= \psi_0 + \lambda\psi_1 + \lambda^2\psi_2 + \lambda^3\psi_3 + \cdots \\
W &= W_0 + \lambda W_1 + \lambda^2 W_2 + \lambda^3 W_3 + \cdots
\end{aligned}
$$ (E.4)

where we replace H' by $\lambda H'$ in Equation E.1 and let λ go to zero. Then $\psi_0, \psi_1, \ldots$ and $W_0, W_1, \ldots$ represent the various orders of corrections, due to the perturbation H'. In general, the zero order state ψ_0 could be either nondegenerate or degenerate. The perturbation approach is different for the two cases. We shall discuss the results for both cases.

E.1   NONDEGENERATE CASE

The first order corrections to a state $\psi_0 = u_m$ (or $|m\rangle$ in the Dirac notation) are given by

$$W_1 = \langle m|H'|m\rangle \tag{E.5}$$

which is the expectation value of H' for the unperturbed state $|m\rangle$. The correction to the wavefunction is

$$\psi_1 = \sum_n a_n^{(1)}|n\rangle \tag{E.6}$$

where

$$a_k^{(1)} = \frac{\langle k|H'|m\rangle}{E_m - E_k} \text{ for } k \neq m. \tag{E.7}$$

In second order we have

$$W_2 = \sum_n{}' \frac{|\langle n|H'|n\rangle|^2}{E_m - E_n}. \tag{E.8}$$

The prime denotes $m \neq n$. (H' is assumed to be hermitian.) The second order correction to the wavefunction is given by

$$\psi_2 = \sum_n{}' a_n^{(2)} u_n,$$
$$a_m^{(2)} = 0 \tag{E.9}$$

where

$$a_k^{(2)} = \sum_n{}' \frac{\langle k|H'|n\rangle\langle n|H'|m\rangle}{(E_m - E_k)(E_m - E_n)} - \frac{\langle k|H'|m\rangle\langle m|H'|m\rangle}{(E_m - E_k)^2}. \tag{E.10}$$

To second order we then have for the unperturbed level $|m\rangle$

$$W = E_m + \langle m|H'|m\rangle + \sum_n{}' \frac{|\langle m|H'|n\rangle|^2}{E_m - E_n}$$

$$\psi = u_m + \sum_k{}' u_k \left[\frac{\langle k|H'|m\rangle}{E_m - E_k} \left(1 - \frac{\langle m|H'|m\rangle}{E_m - E_k} \right) \right.$$

$$\left. + \sum_n{}' \frac{\langle k|H'|n\rangle\langle n|H'|m\rangle}{(E_m - E_k)(E_m - E_n)} \right]. \tag{E.11}$$

The wavefunction is *not* normalized now and one must renormalize it.

E.2 DEGENERATE CASE

In the above derivation we have assumed that the initial state $\psi_0 = u_m$ is nondegenerate. Let us now assume that u_m and u_ℓ are degenerate and have the same unperturbed energy. Then the coefficient

$$a_k^{(1)} = \frac{\langle k|H|m\rangle}{E_m - E_k} \tag{E.12}$$

causes difficulty unless $\langle \ell|H'|m\rangle = 0$.

Let us consider the case where $\langle \ell|H'|m\rangle \neq 0$, so that our previous results are not valid. The perturbation is capable of lifting the degeneracy in this case. We assume that H' breaks the degeneracy at some order of perturbation. The two nondegenerate states then approach a certain linear combination of u_m and u_ℓ as the value of $\lambda \to 0$. Let us write

$$\begin{aligned} \psi_0 &= a_m u_m + a_\ell u_\ell \\ W_0 &= E_m \\ &= E_\ell. \end{aligned} \tag{E.13}$$

The first order correction is given by

$$\begin{aligned} W_1 &= \frac{1}{2}\left(\langle m|H'|m\rangle + \langle \ell|H'|\ell\rangle\right) \\ &\pm \frac{1}{2}\left[\left(\langle m|H'|m\rangle - \langle \ell|H'|\ell\rangle\right)^2 + 4|\langle m|H'|\ell\rangle|^2\right]^{1/2}. \end{aligned} \tag{E.14}$$

The two values of W_1 are equal if

$$\langle m|H'|m\rangle = \langle \ell|H'|\ell\rangle$$

and

$$\langle m|H'|\ell\rangle = 0. \tag{E.15}$$

If these are not satisfied, the degeneracy is lifted and the values of a_m and a_ℓ can be obtained.

If the values of W_1 obtained from Equation E.14 are the same, one must go to the second order to see if degeneracy is lifted. The second order correction is given by the eigenvalue equations

$$\left(\sum_n {}' \frac{|\langle m|H'|n\rangle|^2}{E_m - E_n} - W_2\right) a_m + \sum_n {}' \frac{\langle m|H'|n\rangle\langle n|H'|\ell\rangle}{E_m - E_n} a_\ell = 0$$

$$\sum_n {}' \frac{\langle \ell|H'|n\rangle\langle n|H'|m\rangle}{E_m - E_n} a_m + \left(\sum_n {}' \frac{|\langle \ell|H'|n\rangle|^2}{E_m - E_n} - W_2\right) a_\ell = 0. \tag{E.16}$$

The secular equation allows us to then determine W_2. Unless

$$\sum_n{}' \frac{|\langle m|H'|n\rangle|^2}{E_m - E_n} = \sum_n{}' \frac{|\langle \ell|H'|n\rangle|^2}{E_m - E_n} \tag{E.17}$$

and

$$\sum_n{}' \frac{\langle m|H'|n\rangle \langle n|H'|\ell\rangle}{E_m - E_n} = 0, \tag{E.18}$$

the degeneracy is lifted in second order.

A necessary and sufficient condition that degeneracy is removed in any given order is:

1. The diagonal element of H' in the two degenerate states are unequal.

2. Or, the H diagonal matrix element is nonzero in the given order.

APPENDIX
F

EIGENVALUE
METHOD
TO SOLVE
COUPLED
EQUATIONS

A very large class of problems, in classical mechanics and quantum mechanics, can be written in the form of a matrix equation, which can be solved by eigenvalue solvers. Such eigenvalue solvers are generally available at most computer centers. These libraries provide subroutines which can be called to solve the matrix for both eigenvalues and eigenfunctions.

The general equation to be solved is

$$H\Psi = E\Psi \tag{F.1}$$

where H is an $n \times n$ matrix, E is an eigenvalue which can have n values, and Ψ and is an n-dimensional vector. In general, the eigenfunction Ψ can be expanded in terms of an orthonormal basis set $\{\psi_n\}$

$$\Psi = \sum_n a_n \psi_n. \tag{F.2}$$

A particle wavefunction Ψ_i is known when all the a_n's are known for that function. Substituting Equation F.2 in Equation F.1, multiplying successively by

V(x)

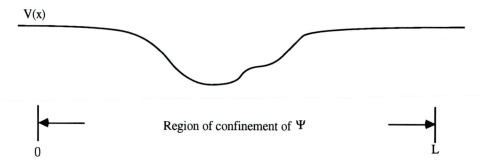

Region of confinement of Ψ

0

L

Figure F.1: A potential profile in which a wavefunction is confined.

$\psi_1^*, \psi_2^*, \cdots, \psi_n^*$ and integrating, we get a set of equations

$$
\begin{bmatrix}
H_{11} - E & H_{12} & H_{13} & \cdots & H_{1n} \\
H_{21} & (H_{22} - E) & H_{23} & \cdots & H_{2n} \\
& & \vdots & & \\
& & \vdots & & \\
H_{n1} & N_{n2} & H_{n3} & \cdots & (H_{nn} - E)
\end{bmatrix}
\begin{bmatrix}
a_1 \psi_1 \\
a_2 \psi_2 \\
\vdots \\
\vdots \\
a_n \psi_n
\end{bmatrix} = 0 \qquad (\text{F.3})
$$

where

$$
H_{mn} = \int \psi_m^* \, H \, \psi_n \, d^3 r. \qquad (\text{F.4})
$$

This is the standard form of the eigenvalue problem. It can be solved analytically if n is small (say less than 4), but, in general, will require numerical techniques.

The general, Schrödinger equation

$$
-\frac{\hbar^2}{2m}\nabla^2\Psi + V\Psi = E\Psi \qquad (\text{F.5})
$$

can be expressed in terms of a matrix equation. This approach is very useful if we are looking for bound or quasi-bound states in a spatially varying potential V. Let us consider the scalar Schrödinger equation (or the single band equation often used to describe electrons in the conduction band). Let us assume that the eigenfunction we are looking for is confined in a region L as shown in Figure F.1. We divide this region into equidistant ℓ mesh points x_i, each separated in real space by a distance Δx. The wavefunction we are looking for is now of the form

$$
\Psi = \sum_n a_n \psi_n \qquad (\text{F.6})
$$

where ψ_n are simply functions at the mesh point which are normalized within the interval centered at x_n and are zero outside that interval.

We can also write the differential equation as a general difference equation

$$-\frac{\hbar^2}{2m}\left[\frac{\Psi(x_i-1)-2\Psi(x_i)+\Psi(x_i+1)}{\Delta x^2}+V\Psi\right]=E\Psi. \qquad (F.7)$$

Once again, substituting for the general wavefunction Equation F.6 and taking an outer product with $\psi_1, \psi_2, \cdots, \psi_\ell$, we get a set of ℓ equations (remember that we are assuming $a_0 = a_{\ell+1} = 0$, i.e., the wavefunction is localized in the space L) which can be written in the matrix form as

$$\begin{bmatrix} A(x_1) & B & 0 & \cdots & 0 & 0 \\ B & A(x_2) & B & \cdots & 0 & 0 \\ 0 & B & A(x_3) & \cdots & 0 & 0 \\ & & & \vdots & & \\ & & & \vdots & & \\ 0 & 0 & 0 & \cdots & B & A(x_\ell) \end{bmatrix} \begin{bmatrix} a_1\,\psi_1 \\ a_2\,\psi_2 \\ a_3\,\psi_3 \\ \vdots \\ \vdots \\ a_\ell\,\psi_\ell \end{bmatrix} = 0 \qquad (F.8)$$

with

$$A(x_i) = \frac{\hbar^2}{m\Delta x^2} + V(x_i) - E$$

$$B = -\frac{\hbar^2}{2m\Delta x^2}.$$

This $\ell \times \ell$ set of equations can again be solved by calling an appropriate subroutine from a computer library to get the eigenvalues E_n and wavefunctions ψ_n. In general we will get ℓ eigenvalues and eigenfunctions. The lowest lying state is the ground state, while the others are excited states. Note that the conditions imposed by us on the wavefunction, viz. the function goes to zero outside our confinement distance L, may not apply to some of the excited states. To check for the accuracy of the condition, one should increase L and see that there is no change in the eigenenergies and eigenfunctions of interest.

APPENDIX G

THE ZEEMAN EFFECT

In Chapter 17, we discussed the effect of a magnetic field on bound state functions (e.g. the relative coordinate exciton problem). The change in the eigenenergies in presence of a magnetic field is called the Zeeman effect. We will evaluate the first order Zeeman effect in this appendix.

A uniform magnetic field may be written in the form (remember $\boldsymbol{B} = \nabla \times \boldsymbol{A}$)

$$\boldsymbol{A} = \frac{1}{2}\boldsymbol{B} \times \boldsymbol{r}. \tag{G.1}$$

The Hamiltonian for the electron in this field is

$$H = \frac{1}{2m}\left(\boldsymbol{p} - \frac{e\boldsymbol{A}}{c}\right)^2 + U(x, y, z) - \frac{e}{mc}\boldsymbol{B} \cdot \boldsymbol{S} \tag{G.2}$$

where the last term is the spin contribution.

In absence of the magnetic field, $H = H_0$, and we may write

$$
\begin{aligned}
H &= H_0 - \frac{e}{mc}\boldsymbol{A} \cdot \boldsymbol{p} + \frac{e^2}{2mc^2}A^2 - \frac{e}{mc}\boldsymbol{B} \cdot \boldsymbol{S} \\
&= H_0 - \frac{e^2}{2mc}\boldsymbol{B} \cdot (\boldsymbol{r} \times \boldsymbol{p}) + \frac{e^2(\boldsymbol{B} \times \boldsymbol{r})^2}{8mc^2} - \frac{e}{mc}\boldsymbol{B} \cdot \boldsymbol{S}. \tag{G.3}
\end{aligned}
$$

Since $(\boldsymbol{r} \times \boldsymbol{p})$ is the orbital angular momentum operator $\boldsymbol{L}$, we have

$$H = H_0 - \frac{\mu_0}{\hbar}(\boldsymbol{L} + 2\boldsymbol{S}) \cdot \boldsymbol{B} + \frac{e^2}{8mc^2}(\boldsymbol{B} \times \boldsymbol{r})^2 \tag{G.4}$$

where

$$
\begin{aligned}
\mu_0 &= \frac{e\hbar}{2mc} \\
&= 0.927 \times 10^{-20} \text{ erg/gauss} \tag{G.5}
\end{aligned}
$$

is called the Bohr magneton. In general m is the reduced mass μ.

We will assume that the magnetic field is not too strong so that the second order term can be ignored. Then, from the first order perturbation theory, the effect of the perturbation on the eigenenergy is simply

$$\Delta E = \frac{\mu_0}{\hbar}\langle L + 2S\rangle \cdot B \tag{G.6}$$

where the average is evaluated for the different states of the unperturbed system.

We write

$$\Delta E = \frac{\mu_0}{\hbar}g\langle J\rangle \cdot B \tag{G.7}$$

where $J = L + S$ is the total angular momentum of the state.

If we choose the magnetic field along z-direction $|\langle J\rangle| = J_z = M$.

$$\Delta E = \frac{\mu_0}{\hbar}gMB. \tag{G.8}$$

Here g is called the Lande factor, and we will now evaluate it by evaluating, $\langle J \cdot (L + 2S)\rangle$ in two different ways

$$
\begin{aligned}
J \cdot (L + 2S) &= J \cdot (J + S) \\
&= J^2 + J \cdot S.
\end{aligned}
\tag{G.9}
$$

Also,

$$
\begin{aligned}
L &= J - S \\
\Rightarrow L^2 &= J^2 + S^2 - 2J \cdot S
\end{aligned}
\tag{G.10}
$$

and

$$J \cdot S = \frac{1}{2}\left[J^2 + S^2 - L^2\right], \tag{G.11}$$

so that

$$
\begin{aligned}
J \cdot (L + 2S) &= \frac{3}{2}J^2 + \frac{1}{2}S^2 - \frac{1}{2}L^2 \\
\langle J \cdot (L + 2S)\rangle &= \frac{1}{2}\left[3\hbar^2 j(j+1) + \hbar^2 s(s+1) - \hbar^2 l(l+1)\right].
\end{aligned}
\tag{G.12}
$$

Also, using the orthonormal basis set of the angular momentum $|\alpha LSJM\rangle$

$$
\begin{aligned}
\langle J \cdot (L + 2S)\rangle &= \sum_{xyz}\sum_{M'}\langle \alpha LSJM|J_i|\alpha LSJM'\rangle \\
&\times \langle \alpha LSJM'|(L_i + 2S_i)|\alpha LSJM\rangle \\
&= g\langle \alpha LSJM|J^2|\alpha LSJM\rangle \\
&= g\hbar^2 j(j+1).
\end{aligned}
\tag{G.13}
$$

Comparing the Equation G.12 and Equation G.13, we get for g

$$g = 1 + \frac{j(j+1) + s(s+1) - l(l+1)}{2j(j+1)}. \tag{G.14}$$

One can see, for example, that

$$
\begin{aligned}
g &= 2 \quad \text{for } 2S_{1/2} \text{ states} \\
&= \frac{2}{3} \quad \text{for } 2P_{1/2} \text{ states} \\
&= \frac{4}{3} \quad \text{for } 2P_{3/2} \text{ states,} \tag{G.15}
\end{aligned}
$$

etc.

By studying the splitting of the eigenenergies with regard to the magnetic field, one can obtain the nature of the state.

APPENDIX H

THE VARIATIONAL METHOD

This method is usually applied to determine the solutions of a problem when there is no closely related problem that is capable of exact solution so that perturbation techniques are not applicable. Very often the variational approach is used for problems which are extremely difficult to solve by any other approach, but one may be able to intuitively "guess" the form of the solution.

According to the variational principle, the true ground state E_0 of a Hamiltonian H, satisfies the inequality

$$E_0 \leq \frac{\int \psi^* H \psi \, dt}{\int \psi^* \psi \, dt}. \tag{H.1}$$

where ψ is any function. The variational method consists of evaluating the integral with a trial function ψ that depends upon a number of parameters. These parameters are varied until the expectation value of the energy is minimum. The variation method can also be applied to obtain the eigenfunctions of the higher excited states if the trial function is orthogonal to the eigenfunctions of the lower states.

Assume that the energy values are arranged in ascending order: E_0, E_1, E_2, ..., E_n. Let us say that we know the eigenfunctions ψ_0, ψ_1, ψ_2, ..., ψ_n somehow. If Ψ is a trial function that is orthogonal to ψ_0, ψ_1, ψ_2, ..., ψ_n, then

$$E_{n+1} \leq \frac{\int \psi^* H \psi \, dz}{\int \psi^* \psi \, dz}. \tag{H.2}$$

It is useful to know that, given a function ϕ, the function $\Phi = \phi - u_i \int u_i^* \phi dz$ is orthogonal to u_i.

The choice of the *form of the eigenfunction* used is quite important in getting accurate values for the eigenenergies. For example, let us consider the ground state of the hydrogen (dopant or exciton) atom problem. Consider the following trial functions

$$\psi_1 = A_1 e^{-(b/a)r}$$

$$\psi_2 = A_2 \frac{1}{b^2 + (r/a)^2}$$

$$\psi_3 = A_3 \frac{r}{a} e^{-(b/a)r} \tag{H.3}$$

where

$$a = \text{Bohr radius}$$

$$= \frac{\hbar^2}{\mu e^2}. \tag{H.4}$$

From normalization conditions we have

$$A_1 = \left(\frac{b^3}{\pi a^3}\right)^{1/2}$$

$$A_2 = \frac{1}{\pi}\left(\frac{b}{a^3}\right)^{1/2}$$

$$A_3 = \left(\frac{b^5}{3\pi a^3}\right)^{1/2}. \tag{H.5}$$

Using the notation

$$\Delta \equiv \nabla^2$$

$$= \frac{1}{r^2}\frac{\partial}{\partial r}\left(r^2 \frac{\partial}{\partial r}\right),$$

in spherical coordinates, we have for ψ_1

$$E_0 = \min \int \psi_1^* \left(-\frac{\hbar^2}{2m}\Delta - \frac{e^2}{r}\right) \psi_1 \, d^3r$$

$$= \min\left\{\frac{2\hbar^2 b^3}{ma^3}\int_0^\infty e^{-(b/a)r} \Delta e^{-(b/a)r} r^2 \, dr\right.$$

$$\left. - \frac{4e^2 b^2}{a^3}\int_0^\infty e^{-2br/a} r \, dr\right\}. \tag{H.6}$$

Now,

$$\int_0^\infty e^{-(b/a)r} \Delta e^{-(b/a)r} r^2 \, dr = -\frac{a}{4b}$$

$$\int_0^\infty e^{-(2b/a)r} r \, dr = \frac{a^2}{4b^2}.$$

Thus,

$$E_0 = \min\left(\frac{\hbar^2 b^2}{2ma^2} - \frac{e^2 b}{a}\right)$$

$$= \frac{-e^2}{2a},$$ \hfill (H.7)

which is the correct result. For the different choices of the trial functions, we get

$$\psi_1 : b = 1 \quad ; \quad E_0 = E_H = \frac{-\mu e^4}{2\hbar^2}$$

$$\psi_2 : b = \frac{\pi}{4} \quad ; \quad E_0 = -0.81 E_H$$

$$\psi_3 : b = \frac{3}{2} \quad ; \quad E_0 = -0.75 E_H.$$

Thus, an incorrect form of the starting trail function can make a significant error in the energy solutions. The error in the wavefunctions is, however, much greater than the error in the energy.

APPENDIX
I

TIME DEPENDENT PERTURBATION THEORY AND THE FERMI GOLDEN RULE

The time dependent perturbation theory has been used extensively in this text to address the problem of scattering of electrons by phonons or photons. The expressions for the scattering rates are given by the Fermi golden rule, derived in this appendix. The form of the scattering rate is also similar to the scattering rate from fixed defects, as given by the Born approximation. The general Hamiltonian of interest is of the form

$$H = H_0 + H^{'} \tag{I.1}$$

where

$$H_0 u_k = E_k u_k \tag{I.2}$$

and E_k, u_k are known. The effect of $H^{'}$ is to cause transitions between the states u_k. The time dependent Schrödinger equation is

$$i\hbar \frac{\partial \psi}{\partial t} = H\psi. \tag{I.3}$$

The approximation will involve expressing ψ as an expansion of the eigenfunctions $u_n \exp(-iE_n t/\hbar)$ of the unperturbed time dependent functions

$$\psi = \sum_n a_n(t) u_n e^{-iE_n t/\hbar} \tag{I.4}$$

Substituting in Equation I.2, using Equation I.1, we get

$$\sum_n i\hbar\, \dot{a}_n(t)\, u_n\, e^{-iE_n t/\hbar} \;+\; \sum_n a_n\, E_n\, u_n\, e^{-iE_n t/\hbar}$$

$$= \sum_n a_n\,(H_0 + H')\, u_n\, e^{-iE_n t/\hbar}. \qquad (I.5)$$

Multiplying by the u_k^* and integrating over space, we get

$$i\hbar\, \dot{a}_k\, e^{-iE_k t/\hbar} = \sum_n a_n\, e^{-iE_n t/\hbar}\, \langle k|H'|n\rangle. \qquad (I.6)$$

Writing

$$\omega_{kn} = \frac{E_k - E_n}{\hbar} \qquad (I.7)$$

$$\dot{a}_k = \frac{1}{i\hbar} \sum_n \langle k|H'|n\rangle\, a_n\, e^{i\omega_{kn} t}. \qquad (I.8)$$

To find the corrections to various orders in H', we can write

$$H' \;\rightarrow\; \lambda H'$$
$$a_n \;=\; a_n^{(0)} + \lambda a_n^{(1)} + \lambda^2 a_n^{(2)} + \cdots. \qquad (I.9)$$

Substituting this expansion in the Equation I.8 and equating the corresponding powers of λ, we get

$$\dot{a}_k^{(0)} \;=\; 0$$
$$\dot{a}_k^{(s+1)} \;=\; \frac{1}{i\hbar} \sum_n \langle k|H'|n\rangle\, a_n^{(s)}\, e^{i\omega_{kn} t}. \qquad (I.10)$$

In principle, these can be integrated to any order to obtain the desired solution. We see that the zeroth order coefficients $a_n^{(0)}$ are constant time and are simply given by the initial conditions of the problem, before the perturbation is applied. We assume that initially only one $a_n^{(0)}$ is finite and all others are zero, i.e., the system is in a single, well-defined state.

$$a_k^{(0)} \;=\; \langle k|m\rangle$$
$$\;=\; \delta_{km}. \qquad (I.11)$$

Integration of the first order term gives

$$a_k^{(1)}(t) = \frac{1}{i\hbar} \int_{-\infty}^{t} \langle k|H'(t')|m\rangle\, e^{i\omega_{km} t'}\, dt'. \qquad (I.12)$$

We choose the constant of integration to be zero since $a_k^{(1)}$ is zero at time $t \rightarrow -\infty$, when the perturbation is not present.

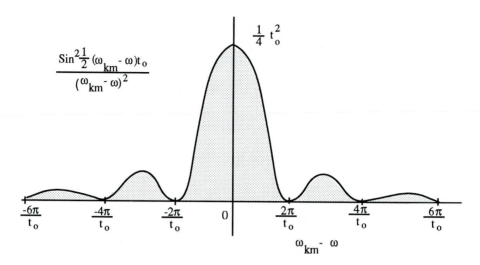

Figure I.1: The ordinate is proportional to the probability of finding the system in a state k after the perturbation has been applied to time t_0.

Consider the case where the perturbation is harmonic, except that it is turned on at $t = 0$ and turned off at $t = t_0$. Let us assume that the time dependence is given by

$$\langle k|H(t')|m\rangle = 2\langle k|H'(0)|m\rangle \sin \omega t'. \tag{I.13}$$

Carrying out the integration until time $t \geq t_0$ in Equation 1.14, we get

$$a_k^{(1)}(t \geq t_0) = -\frac{\langle k|H'(0)|m\rangle}{i\hbar} \left(\frac{\exp[(\omega_{km} + \omega)t_0] - 1}{\omega_{km} + \omega} - \frac{\exp[(\omega_{km} - \omega)t_0] - 1}{\omega_{km} - \omega} \right). \tag{I.14}$$

The structure of this equation says that the amplitude is appreciable, only if the denominator of one or the other term is practically zero. The first term is important if $\omega_{km} \approx -\omega$, or $E_k \approx E_m - \hbar\omega$. The second term is important if $\omega_{km} \approx \omega$ or $E_k \approx E_m + \hbar\omega$.

Thus, the first order effect of a harmonic perturbation is to transfer, or to receive from the system, the quanta of energy $\hbar\omega$. If we focus on a system where $|m\rangle$ is a discrete state, $|k\rangle$ is one of the continuous states, and $E_k > E_m$, so that only the second term is important, the first order probability to find the system in the state k after the perturbation is removed is

$$\left|a_k^{(1)}(t \geq t_0)\right|^2 = 4|\langle k|H'(0)|m\rangle|^2 \frac{\sin^2\left[\frac{1}{2}(\omega_{km} - \omega)t_0\right]}{\hbar^2(\omega_{km} - \omega)^2}. \tag{I.15}$$

The probability function has an oscillating behavior as shown in Figure I.1. The probability is maximum when $\omega_{km} = \omega$, and the peak is proportional to

t_0^2. However, the uncertainty in frequency, $\Delta\omega = \omega_{km} - \omega$, is nonzero for the finite time t_0. This uncertainty is in accordance with the Heisenberg uncertainty principle

$$\Delta\omega \, \Delta t = \Delta\omega \, t_0 \sim 1. \tag{I.16}$$

I.1 TRANSITION PROBABILITY

If there is a spread in the allowed values of $(\omega_{km} - \omega)$, which may occur either because the initial and/or final states of the electron are continuous, or because the perturbation has a spread of frequencies ω, it is possible to define a scattering rate per unit time. The total rate per unit time for scattering into any final state, is given by

$$W_m = \frac{1}{t_0} \sum_{\text{final states}} \left| a_k^{(1)}(t \geq t_0) \right|^2. \tag{I.17}$$

If t_0 is large, the sum over the final states only includes the final states where $\omega_{km} - \hbar\omega = 0$, i.e., energy is conserved in the process.

If we assume that $|\langle k|H'|m\rangle|^2$ does not vary over the (infinitesimally) small spread in final states, we can write

$$x = \frac{1}{2}(\omega_{km} - \omega)t_0 \tag{I.18}$$

and use the integral

$$\int_{-\infty}^{\infty} x^{-2} \sin^2 x \, dx = \pi,$$

to get

$$W_m = \frac{2\pi}{\hbar} \sum_{\text{final states}} \delta\left(\hbar\omega_{km} - \hbar\omega\right) |\langle k|H'|m\rangle|^2. \tag{I.19}$$

This is the Fermi golden rule, which is used widely in our text. It is interesting to note that an identical expression occurs for scattering rate from fixed defects when Born approximation is used for scattering.

In a given scattering problem, one has to pay particular attention to the conditions under which the golden rule has been derived. The more important condition is that the time of interaction of the pertubation be essentially infinite. If the interaction time is finite, the δ-function of the Golden Rule changes over to the broadened function of Figure I.1. Thus, the energy conservation is not strictly satisfied and the final state of the electron is not well-defined. In certain transport problems such as impact-ionization or very high field transport, the time intervals between collision becomes of the order of 0.1 ps and these broadening effects can start to become important. Note that the energy uncertainty for 0.1 ps is about 5 meV.

Related to the Fermi golden rule is the Born approximation, which is used to study scattering from a fixed scattering potential such as an ionized impurity potential or alloy potential. While in this case the Hamiltonian has no time evolution, the problem is treated as a time dependent problem. The full Hamiltonian has the form

$$H = H_0 + V(r) \tag{I.20}$$

where $V(r)$ has no time dependence and the problem of H_0 is known

$$H_0 u_k = E_k u_k. \tag{I.21}$$

Once again, we can assume that the electron is initially in a well-defined eigenstate of H_0. The scattering rate is then calculated by evaluating the probability of finding the electron in a different state, after time t. The first order calculation is similar to the derivation of the Fermi golden rule, except that there is no change of energy due to the time independent pertubation $V(r)$. The transition rate for long time t becomes

$$W_{if} = \frac{2\pi}{\hbar} |V_{if}|^2 \delta(E_f - E_i). \tag{I.22}$$

For the approximation to be valid, t should be large enough and the potential $V(r)$ should be small enough, for the finite order pertubation theory to be valid. From the scattering rate, one can define a differential scattering cross section

$$\frac{d\sigma_{i \to f}}{d\Omega},$$

where $d\sigma$ is the number of particles scattered into the solid angle $(\Omega_f, \Omega_f + d\Omega)$ per unit time, per unit incident flux. Thus, if v_i is the initial electron velocity and n is the electron density

$$d\sigma_{i \to f} = \frac{W_{if}}{n \, v_i} \, d\Omega. \tag{I.23}$$

The total cross section can then be evaluated in the Born approximation. For Born approximation to be valid, one must compare the total cross section calculated by Born approximation, say σ_{tot}^B, to the geometric cross section of the scattering potential. If a is the range of the potential, then the Born approximation can be used, provided that

$$\sigma_{tot}^B \ll 4\pi a^2.$$

The quantity σ_{tot}^B of course depends upon the strength of the potential. It can be shown (see for example *Quantum Mechanics* by A. Messiah, North Holland, 1970, Chapter XIX) that

$$\sigma_{tot}^B / 4\pi a^2 \approx 2\pi \left(\frac{V_0 m^* a^2}{\hbar^2} \right)^2 \quad \text{if } ka \ll 1$$

$$\sigma_{tot}^B / 4\pi a^2 \approx \frac{\pi}{2} \left(\frac{V_0 m^* a}{\hbar^2 k} \right)^2 \quad \text{if } ka \gg 1 \tag{I.24}$$

where V_0 is the average potential in the range a. It is always advisable to check that the Born approximation is valid, before applying it to a new scattering problem.

APPENDIX J

GAUSSIAN AND MKSA UNITS

While there is almost universal agreement on the units of length (centimeter or meter), mass (gram or kilogram), and time (seconds), the situation for electromagnetic quantities is quite nebulous. The most commonly used units are the Gaussian units and the MKSA units. In addition, there are a number of other systems of units (e.g., electrostatic (esu), electromagnetic (emu), Heavyside-Lorentz). The reason for these various choices can be easily seen from the basic law of force between two charges which has the form

$$F_1 = k_1 \frac{q_1 q_2}{r_{12}^2} \tag{J.1}$$

and the current continuity equation

$$\nabla \cdot J + \frac{\partial \rho}{\partial t} = 0. \tag{J.2}$$

The constant k_1 has its units determined by either the choice that the charge units are chosen *independently* or that the charge units are chosen arbitrarily.

The MKSA units are extremely convenient in macroscopic phenomena, especially in engineering phenomena. The Gaussian units are more convenient for microscopic problems involving electrodynamics of individual charges. In our text most of our work is on a microscopic level and the Gaussian units are used. Nevertheless, it is important to study the equations derived in the two systems since the *form* of the equation is different in the two units. This is, of course, a cause of great confusion at times. In this appendix we will write some of the basic equations in the two sets of units, so that the reader is able to judge and compare results in other texts or articles and use the appropriate units. The

Quantity	Gaussian	MKSA
ϵ_0	1	$\dfrac{10^7}{4\pi c^2}$ $(I^2 T^4 M^{-1} L^{-3})$
μ_0	1	$4\pi \times 10^{-7}$ $(MLI^{-2}T^{-2})$
D	$D = F + 4\pi P$	$D = \epsilon_0 F + P$
H	$H = B - 4\pi M$	$H = \dfrac{1}{\mu_0} B - M$
Maxwell's Equations	$\nabla \cdot D = 4\pi\rho$	$\nabla \cdot D = \rho$
	$\nabla \times H = \dfrac{4\pi}{c} J + \dfrac{1}{c}\dfrac{\partial D}{\partial t}$	$\nabla \times H = J + \dfrac{\partial D}{\partial t}$
	$\nabla \times F = -\dfrac{1}{c}\dfrac{\partial B}{\partial t}$	$\nabla \times F = -\dfrac{\partial B}{\partial t}$
	$\nabla \cdot B = 0$	$\nabla \cdot B = 0$
Lorentz Force	$\mathcal{F} = q\left[F + \dfrac{v}{c} \times B\right]$	$\mathcal{F} = q\left[F + v \times B\right]$
Force between two charges	$\mathcal{F} = \dfrac{q_1 q_2}{\epsilon r}$	$\mathcal{F} = \dfrac{q_1 q_2}{4\pi\epsilon_0 \epsilon r}$

Table J.1: A comparison between the units of μ_0, ϵ_0, the relations for D, H, the Maxwell equations, and the Lorentz force form in the Gaussian and MKSA units.

Gaussian units use length, mass, and time as the basic units while the MKSA system uses length, mass, time, and current (Ampere) as the basic units.

In Table J.1 we show the form of various important relations in the Gaussian and MKSA system. Since the form of the equations is quite different in the two systems, it is useful to see how one can convert an equation in one system to the other system. This conversion can be carried out by the use of Table J.2. Finally, we give in Table J.3 the relationship between quantities written in the Gaussian and MKSA units.

Reference: A detailed discussion of the various systems of units used in electromagnetic theory is given by J. D. Jackson, *Classical Electrodynamics*, (John Wiley and Sons, New York, 1975).

Quantity	Gaussian	MKSA
Velocity of light	c	$(\mu_0\epsilon_0)^{-1/2}$
Electric field (potential, voltage)	$\boldsymbol{F}(\Phi, V)$	$\sqrt{4\pi\epsilon_0}\,\boldsymbol{F}(\Phi, V)$
Displacement	$\boldsymbol{D}$	$\sqrt{\frac{4\pi}{\epsilon_0}}\,\boldsymbol{D}$
Charge density (charge, current density, current, polarization)	$\rho(q, \boldsymbol{J}, I, \boldsymbol{P})$	$\frac{1}{\sqrt{4\pi\epsilon_0}}\rho(q, \boldsymbol{J}, I, \boldsymbol{P})$
Magnetic induction	$\boldsymbol{B}$	$\sqrt{\frac{4\pi}{\mu_0}}\,\boldsymbol{B}$
Magnetic field	$\boldsymbol{H}$	$\sqrt{4\pi\mu_0}\,\boldsymbol{H}$
Magnetization	$\boldsymbol{M}$	$\sqrt{\frac{\mu_0}{4\pi}}\,\boldsymbol{M}$
Conductivity	σ	$\frac{\sigma}{4\pi\epsilon_0}$
Dielectric constant	ϵ	$\frac{\epsilon}{\epsilon_0}$
Permeability	μ	$\frac{\mu}{\mu_0}$
Resistance (impedance)	$R(Z)$	$4\pi\epsilon_0 R(Z)$
Inductance	L	$4\pi\epsilon_0 L$
Capacitance	C	$\frac{1}{4\pi\epsilon_0}C$

Table J.2: Conversion table for transforming an equation written in the Gaussian units to MKSA units.

Physical Quantity	Sym.	Rat. MKSA		Gaussian
Length	l	1 meter (m)	10^2	centimeters (cm)
Mass	m	1 kilogram (kg)	10^3	grams (gm)
Time	t	1 second (sec)	1	second (sec)
Frequency	ν	1 hertz (Hz)	1	hertz (Hz)
Force	F	1 newton (N)	10^5	dynes
Work	W	1 joule (J)	10^7	ergs
Energy	U	1 joule (J)	10^7	ergs
Power	P	1 watt (W)	10^7	ergs sec^{-1}
Charge	q	1 coulomb (C)	3×10^9	statcoulombs
Charge density	ρ	1 coul m^{-3}	3×10^3	statcoul cm^{-3}
Current	I	1 ampere (A)	3×10^9	statamp
Current density	J	1 amp m^{-2}	3×10^5	statamp cm^{-2}
Electric field	F	1 volt m^{-1}	$\frac{1}{3} \times 10^{-4}$	statvolt cm^{-1}
Potential	ϕ, V	1 volt (V)	$\frac{1}{300}$	statvolt
Polarization	P	1 coul m^{-2}	3×10^5	dip. mom. cm^{-3}
Displacement	D	1 coul m^{-2}	$12\pi \times 10^5$	statcoul cm^{-2}
Conductivity	σ	1 mho m^{-2}	9×10^9	sec^{-1}
Resistance	R	1 ohm (Ω)	$\frac{1}{9} \times 10^{-11}$	sec^{-1}
Capacitance	C	1 farad (F)	9×10^{11}	sec cm^{-1}
Magnetic flux	ϕ, F	1 weber (Wb)	10^8	maxwells
Magnetic induction	B	1 tesla (T)	10^4	gauss
Magnetic field	H	1 amp-turn m^{-1}	$4\pi \times 10^{-3}$	oersted
Magnetization	M	1 ampere m^{-1}	10^{-3}	mag. mom. cm^{-3}
Inductance	L	1 henry (H)	$\frac{1}{9} \times 10^{-11}$	

Table J.3: Conversion table for the relationship of physical quantities in Gaussian and MKSA units.

NUMERICAL
EVALUATION
OF SOME PHYSICAL
PARAMETERS

In this appendix we will go through a simple exercise of evaluating the numerical values of some of the physical parameters discussed in this text.

K.1   DENSITY OF STATES

The results of density of states are usually expressed in the units of eV^{-1} cm^{-D}, where D is the dimension of the problem. In 3-dimensions the density of states expression (without the spin degeneracy) for a parabolic band is

$$N(E) = \frac{(m^*)^{3/2} E^{1/2}}{\sqrt{2} \, \pi^2 \, \hbar^3}.$$ (K.1)

Expressing m^* in units of free electron mass, energy E in eV, the of density of states is (in units of eV^{-1} cm^{-3})

$$
\begin{aligned}
N(E) &= m^{*3/2} E^{1/2} \frac{(2.7 \times 10^{-41}) \, (1.265 \times 10^{-6}) \, (1.6 \times 10^{-12})}{1.414 \times 9.869 \times 1.16 \times 10^{-81}} \\
&= m^{*3/2} E^{1/2} (3.37 \times 10^{21}) \; eV^{-1} \; cm^{-3}.
\end{aligned}
$$ (K.2)

This is multiplied by 2 if spin degeneracy is to be included.

In 2-dimensions the density of states is

$$N(E) = \frac{m^*}{2\pi\hbar^2}.$$ (K.3)

If m^* is expressed in free electron mass units

$$
\begin{aligned}
N(E) &= m^* \left(\frac{0.9 \times 10^{-27} \times 1.6 \times 10^{-12}}{2 \times 3.1416 \times 1.1 \times 10^{-54}} \right) \\
&= m^* (2.08 \times 10^{14}) \text{ eV}^{-1} \text{ cm}^{-2}.
\end{aligned} \tag{K.4}
$$

Once again, multiply by 2 for spin degeneracy.

In 1-dimension, the density of states is

$$
N(E) = \frac{(m^*)^{1/2} E^{-1/2}}{\sqrt{2}\pi\hbar}. \tag{K.5}
$$

If m^* is in free electron mass units and E is expressed in eV

$$
\begin{aligned}
N(E) &= m^{*1/2} E^{-1/2} \left(\frac{3.0 \times 10^{-14} \times 7.905 \times 10^5 \times 1.5 \times 10^{-12}}{1.414 \times 3.1416 \times 1.05 \times 10^{-27}} \right) \\
&= m^{*1/2} E^{-1/2} (8.13 \times 10^6) \text{ eV}^{-1} \text{ cm}^{-1}.
\end{aligned} \tag{K.6}
$$

Multiply by 2 for inclusion of spin degeneracy.

K.2 MOBILITY

Mobility is usually expressed in the units of cm^2 V^{-1} s^{-1}. The easiest way to obtain the mobility value from a relaxation time value, is to use the MKSA units. However, it is illustrative to use Gaussian units and convert to the results in volts (remember statvolt = 300 volts).

Expressing τ in picoseconds, m^* in free electron mass units

$$
\begin{aligned}
\mu &= \frac{e\tau}{m^*} \\
&= \frac{\tau}{m^*} \left(\frac{4.8 \times 10^{-10} \times 10^{-12}}{0.9 \times 10^{-27} \times 300} \right) \\
&= \frac{\tau}{m^*} (1.778 \times 10^3) \text{ cm}^2 \text{ V}^{-1} \text{ s}^{-1}.
\end{aligned} \tag{K.7}
$$

K.3 CYCLOTRON RESONANCE FREQUENCY

The cyclotron resonance frequency is given by

$$
\omega_c = \frac{eB}{m^*c} \tag{K.8}
$$

in Gaussian units ($= eB/m^*$ in MKSA units).

Expressing m^* in free electron mass units, and the magnetic field in Gauss

$$
\omega_c = \frac{B}{m^*} (1.78 \times 10^7) \text{ s}^{-1}. \tag{K.9}
$$

K.4 BOHR RADIUS AND BINDING ENERGIES OF DOPANTS OR EXCITONS

The Bohr radius is

$$a_b = \frac{\epsilon \hbar^2}{m^* e^2} \tag{K.10}$$

in Gaussian units or $4\pi\epsilon_0\epsilon\hbar^2/m^* e^2$ in MKSA units. If m^* is in units of free electron mass the Bohr radius is

$$a_b = \frac{\epsilon}{m^*}(0.53) \text{ Å}. \tag{K.11}$$

The ground state energy is, similarly

$$E_b = \frac{m^* e^4}{2\epsilon^2 \hbar^2} \tag{K.12}$$

in Gaussian units or $m^* e^4/2(4\pi\epsilon_0\epsilon\hbar)^2$ in MKSA units. Its value in eV is

$$E_b = \frac{m^*}{\epsilon^2}(13.6) \text{ eV}. \tag{K.13}$$

The energy 13.6 eV is equal to 1 Rydberg (Ry).

K.5 EFFECTIVE DENSITY OF STATES AND INTRINSIC CARRIER CONCENTRATION

In undoped semiconductors, the carrier concentrations (n_c, p_v) can be expressed in terms of effective density of states by

$$\begin{aligned}
n_c(T) &= N_c(T)\exp\left(-\frac{(E_c - \mu)}{k_B T}\right) \\
p_v(T) &= P_v(T)\exp\left(-\frac{(\mu - E_v)}{k_B T}\right)
\end{aligned} \tag{K.14}$$

where for Boltzmann statistics, N_c are P_v, known as the bandedge effective density of states, are

$$\begin{aligned}
N_c(T) &= \frac{1}{4}\left(\frac{2m_c^* k_B T}{\pi \hbar^2}\right)^{3/2} \\
P_v(T) &= \frac{1}{4}\left(\frac{2m_v^* k_B T}{\pi \hbar^2}\right)^{3/2}.
\end{aligned} \tag{K.15}$$

Note that N_c and P_v do not have the units of the usual density of states (i.e., $\text{eV}^{-1}\text{ cm}^{-3}$) but of carrier concentration (cm^{-3}).

Expressing m^* in units of free electron mass value, we have

$$N_c(T) = (m_c^*)^{3/2} \left(\frac{T}{300K}\right)^{3/2} (2.5 \times 10^{19}) \text{ cm}^{-3}$$

$$P_v(T) = (m_v^*)^{3/2} \left(\frac{T}{300K}\right)^{3/2} (2.5 \times 10^{19}) \text{ cm}^{-3}. \qquad (K.16)$$

The intrinsic carrier concentration is given by

$$
\begin{aligned}
n_i(T) &= [N_c(T)P_v(T)]^{1/2} \exp\left(-\frac{E_g}{2k_BT}\right) \\
&= (m_c^*)^{3/4}(m_v^*)^{3/4} \left(\frac{T}{300K}\right)^{3/2} \\
&\times \exp\left(-\frac{E_g}{2k_BT}\right) (2.5 \times 10^{19}) \text{ cm}^{-3}.
\end{aligned}
\qquad (K.17)
$$

K.6 ABSORPTION COEFFICIENT AND EMISSION RATE

The band-to-band absorption coefficients in 3-dimensions is given by (for a parabolic joint density of states)

$$\alpha(\hbar\omega) = \frac{4\pi^2 e^2 \hbar}{\eta c m^2 \hbar\omega} |p|^2 a_p N_{cv}(\hbar\omega) \qquad (K.18)$$

where m is the *free electron mass*. The factor a_p is due to the polarization dependence of the matrix elements, as discussed in Chapter 14. The momentum matrix element is usually expressed via

$$E_p = \frac{2p^2}{m} \qquad (K.19)$$

where $E_p \approx 20$ eV for most semiconductors. Thus, the absorption coefficient is

$$
\begin{aligned}
\alpha(\hbar\omega) &= \frac{2\pi^2 e^2 \hbar}{\eta c m} \left(\frac{E_p}{\hbar\omega}\right) a_p N_{cv}(\hbar\omega - E_g) \\
&= a_p \left(\frac{E_p}{\hbar\omega}\right) \left(\frac{N_{cv}(\hbar\omega - E_g)}{\eta}\right) (1.77 \times 10^{-28}) \text{ cm}^{-1} \quad (K.20)
\end{aligned}
$$

where $N_{cv}(\hbar\omega)$ is the joint density of states including spin degeneracy expressed in erg^{-1} cm^{-3}. Let us evaluate the value for GaAs using $a_p = 1/2$. Using $E_p = 23.04$ eV, we get ($E_g = 1.5$ eV)

$$\alpha(\hbar\omega) = 4.37 \times 10^4 \frac{(\hbar\omega - E_g)^{1/2}}{\hbar\omega} \text{ cm}^{-1}. \qquad (K.21)$$

Remember that $(E - \hbar\omega)$ and $\hbar\omega$ are expressed in eV.

Consider now the 2-dimensional expression for the interband absorption coefficients assuming a single pair of conduction and valence subbands

$$\alpha_{2D}(\hbar\omega) = \frac{4\pi^2 e^2 \hbar}{\eta cm^2 \hbar\omega} |p|^2 a_p \frac{N_{2D}}{W} (\hbar\omega - E_g) \tag{K.22}$$

where W is the width of the well. Once again expressing $|p|^2$ in terms of E_p, we get

$$
\begin{aligned}
\alpha(\hbar\omega) &= \frac{2\pi^2 e^2 \hbar}{\eta cm} \left(\frac{E_p}{\hbar\omega}\right) a_p \frac{N_{2D}}{\omega} \\
&= \frac{a_p}{\eta} \left(\frac{E_p}{\hbar\omega}\right) \left(\frac{N_{2D}}{W}\right) \left(1.77 \times 10^{-28}\right) \text{ cm}^{-1}.
\end{aligned} \tag{K.23}
$$

For a 100 Å GaAs well, this turns out to be (using $a_p = 1/2$)

$$\alpha(\hbar\omega) = 7.26 \times 10^3 \text{ cm}^{-1}. \tag{K.24}$$

Note that each pair of allowed subbands will contribute this amount to the absorption coefficient.

K.7 RECOMBINATION TIMES

The recombination rate for an electron at a state k with a hole at state $-k$ is given by (after averaging over polarizations)

$$
\begin{aligned}
W_{em} &= \frac{4}{3} \frac{e^2 \, \eta \, \hbar \, \omega}{m^2 \, c^3 \, \hbar^2} |p|^2 \\
&= \frac{2}{3} \frac{e^2 \, \eta \, \hbar \, \omega \, E_p}{m \, c^3 \, \hbar^2} \\
&= 5.0 \times 10^7 \, [\hbar\omega] \, [E_p]
\end{aligned} \tag{K.25}
$$

where $\hbar\omega$ and E_p are in eV. For example, using $\hbar\omega = 1.5$ eV and $E_p = 23$ eV for GaAs we get

$$W_{em} = 1.725 \times 10^9 \text{ s}^{-1}. \tag{K.26}$$

The recombination time is

$$
\begin{aligned}
\tau_r &= \frac{1}{W_{em}} \\
&= 0.58 \text{ ns.}
\end{aligned} \tag{K.27}
$$

Remember that we have assumed that the electron and hole states are occupied; if they are not, the value of W_{em} could be much lower.

APPENDIX L

SELECTED PROPERTIES OF SEMICONDUCTORS

L.1 TABULATED VALUES

Values are at 300K unless otherwise stated.

Material	Lattice	Lattice Constant 300 K	Linear Expansion Coefficient (K^{-1}) ($\Delta L / L \, \Delta T$)	Density (g cm^{-3})
AlN	WZ	$a = 3.112$ $c = 4.980$	$\alpha_\perp = 5.27 \times 10^{-6}$ $\alpha_\parallel = 4.15 \times 10^{-6}$	3.23
AlAs	ZB	5.661	—	—
AlSb	ZB	6.136	—	4.26
GaN	WZ	$a = 3.160$ $c = 5.13$	$\alpha_\perp = 3.17 \times 10^{-6}$ $\alpha_\parallel = 5.6 \times 10^{-6}$	6.095
GaP	ZB	5.4506	—	4.138
GaAs	ZB	5.6533	6.86×10^{-6}	5.3176
GaSb	ZB	6.096	7.75×10^{-6}	5.6137
Ge	D	5.6461	5.8×10^{-6}	5.3267
InP	ZB	5.8687	4.75×10^{-6}	4.81
InAs	ZB	6.0583	4.52×10^{-6}	5.70
InSb	ZB	6.4794	5.37×10^{-6}	5.775
Si	D	5.4309	2.6×10^{-6}	2.328

Table L.1: Lattice parameters.

Material	Bandgap (eV)	Electron Mass (m_0)	Hole Mass (m_0)	Dielectric Constant	
				ϵ_0	ϵ_∞
AlN	6.2(D)			$C_\parallel$: 5.066	4.10
				$C_\perp$: 6.85	4.95
AlAs	2.14(I)	0.1		10.06	8.16
AlSb	1.63(I)	0.12	$m_{dos} = 0.98$	12.04	10.24
GaN	3.44(D)	0.19	$m_{dos} = 0.60$	$C_\parallel$: 10.4	5.8
				$C_\perp$: 9.5	5.35
GaP	2.268(I)	0.82	$m_{dos} = 0.60$	11.1	9.07
GaAs	1.423(D)	0.067	$m_{lh} = 0.082$	12.91	10.1
			$m_{hh} = 0.45$		
GaSb	0.7(D)	0.042	$m_{dos} = 0.40$	15.69	14.44
Ge	0.66(I)	$m_\ell = 1.64$	$m_{lh} = 0.044$	16.0	
		$m_t = 0.082$	$m_{hh} = 0.28$		
InP	1.35(D)	0.073	$m_{dos} = 0.64$	12.61	9.61
InAs	0.356(D)	0.027	$m_{dos} = 0.4$	15.15	12.25
InSb	0.18(D)	0.13	$m_{dos} = 0.4$	16.8	15.68
Si	1.12(I)	$m_\ell = 0.98$	$m_{lh} = 0.16$	11.9	
		$m_t = 0.19$	$m_{hh} = 0.49$		

Table L.2: Charge carrier parameters.

Material	LO Phonon energy (meV)	μ_e (cm^{2}V^{-1}s^{-1}) $N_D \sim$ (cm^{-3}) (10^{15})	(10^{17})	μ_h (cm^{2}V^{-1}s^{-1}) $N_A \sim$ (cm^{-3}) (10^{15})	(10^{17})
AlN	113	—	—	—	—
AlAs	50.1	—	400	—	—
AlSb	42.1	—	—	450	375
GaN	92.4	—	—	—	—
GaP	50.0	200(2800)	160	150	120
GaAs	35.4	8500(150000)	4800	400(9000)	320
GaSb	—	5000	—	1500	880
Ge	37.0	3900	—	1900	1100
InP	42.8	5000(60000)	3200	180(1000)	150
InAs	29.6	30000(3×10^5)	2000	480	—
InSb	23.7	(4×10^5)	8000	1500(9000)	—
Si	63.0	1500	—	450	350

Table L.3: Transport parameters. Results in parenthesis are for $T = 77$ K.

Material	b (eV)	d (eV)	dE_g/dP $(10^{-12}$ eV cm^2/dyne)	Ξ_u (eV)
Si	−1.5 300K	−3.4 300K	−1.41 300K	9.2 295K
Ge	−2.2 300K	−4.4 300K	5. 300K	15.9 297K
AlSb	−1.35 77K	−4.3 77K	−3.50 77K	6.2 300K
GaP	−1.3 80K	−4.0 80K	−1.11 300K	6.2 80K
GaAs	−2.0 300K	−6.0 300K	11.7 300K	
GaSb	−3.3 77K	−8.35 77K	14. 300K	
InP	−1.55 77K	−4.4 77K	4.7 300K	
InAs			10. 300K	
InSb	−2.05 80K	−5. 80K	16.0 300K	

Table L.4: Strain-related parameters.

L.2 REFERENCES

- Adachi, S., J. Appl. Phys., **58**, R1 (1985).

- Blakemore, J. S., J. Appl. Phys., **53**, R123 (1982).

- Jayaraman,A., B. Kosicki, J. Irvin, Phys. Rev., **171**, 836 (1968).

- *Landolt-Bornstein: Numerical Data and Functional Relationships in Science and Technology*, (edited by O. Madelung, Springer-Verlag, New York, 1982), vol. 17.

- *Landolt-Bornstein: Numerical Data and Functional Relationships in Science and Technology*, (edited by O. Madelung, M. Schulz and H. Weiss, Springer-Verlag, New York, 1987), vol. 22.

- Neuberger, M., *Handbook of Electronic Materials*, (IFI/Plenum, New York, 1971),vol. 2.

- Welber, B., C. Kim, M. Cardona and S. Rodriquez, Sol. St. Comm., **17**, 1021 (1975).

- Wiley, J. D., Sol. St. Comm., **8**, 1865 (1970).

APPENDIX M

EVALUATION OF SCATTERING RATES FOR A MONTE CARLO PROGRAM

The Monte Carlo program for computer simulations of electron transport is one of the most instructive ways to see the combined effect of material properties and scattering processes on device performance. A tremendous insight is gained by developing a computer program and following an electron as it moves in a semiconductor. In this appendix, we evaluate the more important scattering rates that appear in a Monte Carlo program and evaluate them for GaAs.

The bandstructure nonparabolicity parameter α will be widely used and is given here as

$$
\alpha = \frac{1}{E_g}\left(1 - \frac{m^*}{m_0}\right)^2
$$
$$
= 0.576 \text{ eV}^{-1}
$$

in GaAs.

M.1   POLAR L-O PHONON SCATTERING

$$
W = \frac{e^2(m^*)^{1/2}\omega_0}{\sqrt{2}\hbar}\left(\frac{1}{\epsilon_\infty} - \frac{1}{\epsilon_s}\right)\frac{(1 + 2\alpha E_F)}{\gamma^{1/2}(E_i)}F_0(E_i, E_f)\left\{\begin{array}{ll} N & \text{abs.} \\ N+1 & \text{emiss.} \end{array}\right.
$$
$$
= 3.69\left(\frac{\omega_0}{\text{rad/sec}}\right)\left(\frac{m^*}{m_0}\right)^{1/2}\left(\frac{1}{\epsilon_\infty} - \frac{1}{\epsilon_s}\right)
$$

$$\times \ \frac{(1+2\alpha E_f)}{(\gamma(E_i)/\text{eV})^{1/2}} F_0(E_i, E_f) \left\{ \begin{array}{c} N \\ N+1 \end{array} \right\} \ \text{sec}^{-1}$$

with F_0 given in Equation 13.62, $\gamma(E) = E(1 + \alpha E)$ and

$$E_f \ = \ E_i \pm \hbar\omega_0 \left\{ \begin{array}{l} + \text{ for absorption} \\ - \text{ for emission} \end{array} \right.$$

$$N \ = \ \frac{1}{\exp(\hbar\omega_0/k_B T) - 1}.$$

Example: GaAs, $T = 300$ K, Γ valley, L-O phonon absorption, $E_i = 3k_B T/2 = 0.039$ eV.

$$\omega_0 \ = \ 4.5 \times 10^{13} \text{ rad/sec}$$

$$\hbar\omega_0 \ = \ 0.030 \text{ eV}$$

$$E_f \ = \ E_i + \hbar\omega_0 = 0.069 \text{ eV}$$

$$m^* \ = \ 0.067 m_o$$

$$\epsilon_s \ = \ 13.2$$

$$\epsilon_\infty \ = \ 10.9$$

$$N \ = \ \frac{1}{\exp(\hbar\omega_0/k_B T) - 1} = 0.458$$

$$\alpha \ = \ \frac{1}{E_g} \left(1 - \frac{m^*}{m_0} \right)^2 = 0.576 \text{ eV}^{-1}$$

$$\gamma(E_i) \ = \ E_i(1 + \alpha E_i) = 0.040 \text{ eV}$$

$$\gamma(E_f) \ = \ E_f(1 + \alpha E_f) = 0.072 \text{ eV}$$

$$1 + \alpha E_i \ = \ 1.022$$

$$1 + \alpha E_f \ = \ 1.040$$

$$1 + 2\alpha E_i \ = \ 1.045$$

$$1 + 2\alpha E_f \ = \ 1.079$$

$$2\gamma(E_i) \ = \ 0.023$$

$$\alpha\gamma(E_f) \ = \ 0.041$$

$$W \ = \ 3.69 \left(\frac{\omega_0}{\text{rad/sec}} \right) \sqrt{\frac{m^*}{m_0}} \left(\frac{1}{\epsilon_\infty} - \frac{1}{\epsilon_s} \right)$$

$$\times \ \frac{1 + 2\alpha E_f}{\sqrt{\gamma(E_i)/\text{eV}}} F_0(E_i, E_f) N \ \text{sec}^{-1}$$

$$= \ 3.69(4.5 \times 10^{13})\sqrt{0.067} \left(\frac{1}{10.9} - \frac{1}{13.2} \right)$$

$$\times \ \frac{1.079}{\sqrt{0.040}} F_0(E_i, E_f) \ 0.458 \ \text{sec}^{-1}$$

$$= \ 1.70 \times 10^{12} F_0(E_i, E_f) \ \text{sec}^{-1}$$

$$F_0(E_i, E_f) = \frac{1}{C}\left(A\ln\left|\frac{\sqrt{\gamma(E_i)} + \sqrt{\gamma(E_f)}}{\sqrt{\gamma(E_i)} - \sqrt{\gamma(E_f)}}\right| + B\right)$$

$$= \frac{1}{C}\left(A\ln\left|\frac{\sqrt{0.040} + \sqrt{0.072}}{\sqrt{0.040} - \sqrt{0.072}}\right| + B\right)$$

$$= \frac{1.926A + B}{C}$$

$$A = [2(1 + \alpha E_i)(1 + \alpha E_f) + \alpha(\gamma(E_i) + \gamma(E_f))]^2$$

$$= [2(1.022)(1.040) + 0.023 + 0.041] = 4.795$$

$$B = -2\alpha\sqrt{\gamma(E_i)\gamma(E_f)}$$

$$\times \ [4(1 + \alpha E_i)(1 + \alpha E_f) + \alpha(\gamma(E_i) + \gamma(E_f))]$$

$$= -2\sqrt{(0.023)(0.041)}$$

$$\times \ [4(1.022)(1.040) + 0.023 + 0.041] = -0.265$$

$$C = 4(1 + \alpha E_i)(1 + \alpha E_f)(1 + 2\alpha E_i)(1 + 2\alpha E_f)$$

$$= 4(1.022)(1.040)(1.045)(1.079) = 4.794$$

$$F_0(E_i, E_f) = \frac{(1.926)(4.795) + (-0.265)}{4.794} = 1.871$$

$$W = 1.70 \times 10^{12}(1.871) \ \text{sec}^{-1} = 3.18 \times 10^{12} \ \text{sec}^{-1}.$$

M.2   ACOUSTIC PHONON SCATTERING

$$W = \frac{(2m^*)^{3/2}k_B T\, D_{ac}^2}{2\pi\rho\, v_s^2\, \hbar^4}\, \gamma^{1/2}(E)(1 + 2\alpha E)F_a(E)$$

$$= 4.49 \times 10^{21}\frac{\left(\frac{m^*}{m_0}\right)^{3/2}\left(\frac{T}{K}\right)\left(\frac{D_{ac}}{eV}\right)^2}{\left(\frac{\rho}{gm/cm^3}\right)\left(\frac{v_s}{cm/sec}\right)^2}\left(\frac{\gamma(E)}{eV}\right)^{1/2}(1 + 2\alpha E)F_a(E) \ \text{sec}^{-1}$$

with $F_a(E)$ as given in Equation 13.63.

Example: GaAs, $T = 300$K, Γ valley, acoustic phonon scattering,

$$E_i = E_f = \frac{3}{2}k_B T = 0.039 \ \text{eV} = E$$

$$m^* = 0.067m_0$$

$$D_{ac} = 7.8 \ \text{eV}$$

$$\rho = 5.37 \ \text{gm/cm}^3$$

$$v_s = 5.22 \times 10^5 \ \text{cm/sec}$$

$$\alpha = 0.576 \ \text{eV}^{-1}$$

$$\gamma(E) = 0.040 \ \text{eV}$$

$$\alpha E = 0.022$$
$$1 + \alpha E = 1.022$$
$$1 + 2\alpha E = 1.045$$

$$W = 4.49 \times 10^{21} \frac{\left(\frac{m^*}{m_0}\right)^{3/2} \left(\frac{T}{K}\right) \left(\frac{D_{ac}}{eV}\right)^2}{\left(\frac{\rho}{gm/cm^3}\right) \left(\frac{v_s}{cm/sec}\right)^2} \sqrt{\frac{\gamma(E)}{eV}} (1 + 2\alpha E) F_a(E) \; sec^{-1}$$

$$= 4.49 \times 10^{21} \frac{(0.067)^{3/2} (300) (7.8)^2}{(5.37) (5.22 \times 10^5)^2} (0.040)^{1/2} (1.045) F_a(E) \; sec^{-1}$$

$$= 2.03 \times 10^{11} F_a(E) \; sec^{-1}$$

$$F_a(E) = \frac{(1 + \alpha E)^2 + \frac{1}{3}(\alpha E)^2}{(1 + 2\alpha E)^2} = \frac{(1.022)^2 + \frac{1}{3}(0.022)^2}{(1.045)^2} = 0.957$$

$$W = 2.03 \times 10^{11} (0.957) \; sec^{-1} = 1.94 \times 10^{11} \; sec^{-1}.$$

M.3   EQUIVALENT INTERVALLEY SCATTERING

$$W = \frac{(Z_e - 1)(m^*)^{3/2} D_{ij}^2}{\sqrt{2} \pi \rho \, \omega_{ij} \hbar^3} E_f^{1/2} \begin{cases} N & \text{absorption} \\ N+1 & \text{emission} \end{cases}$$

$$= 1.71 \times 10^{10} \frac{(Z_e - 1) \left(\frac{m^*}{m_0}\right)^{3/2} \left(\frac{D_{ij}}{eV \; cm^{-1}}\right)^2}{\left(\frac{\rho}{gm/cm^3}\right) \left(\frac{\omega_{ij}}{rad/sec}\right)} \left(\frac{E_f}{eV}\right)^{1/2}$$

$$\times \begin{cases} N & \text{absorption} \\ N+1 & \text{emission} \end{cases} sec^{-1}.$$

Example: GaAs, $T = 300$ K, L valley, equivalent intervalley scattering by absorption

$$E_i = 0 \text{ eV (at L valley edge; 0.36 eV above } \Gamma \text{ valley edge).}$$
$$Z_e = 4$$
$$m^* = 0.35 m_0$$
$$D_{ij} = 1.0 \times 10^9 \text{ eV cm}^{-1}$$
$$\rho = 5.37 \text{ gm/cm}^{-3}$$
$$\omega_{ij} = 4.56 \times 10^{13} \text{ rad/sec}$$
$$E_f = E_i + \hbar\omega_{ij} = 0.030 \text{ eV}$$
$$N = \frac{1}{\exp(\hbar\omega_{ij}/k_B T) - 1} = 0.457$$

$$W = 1.71 \times 10^{10} \frac{(Z_e - 1)\left(\frac{m^*}{m_0}\right)^{3/2}\left(\frac{D_{ij}}{\text{eV cm}^{-1}}\right)^2}{\left(\frac{\rho}{\text{gm/cm}^3}\right)\left(\frac{\omega_{ij}}{\text{rad/sec}}\right)}\left(\frac{E_f}{\text{eV}}\right)^{1/2} N \text{ sec}^{-1}$$

$$= 1.71 \times 10^{10} \frac{(3)(0.35)(1 \times 10^9)^2}{(5.37)(4.56 \times 10^{13})}(0.030)(0.457) \text{ sec}^{-1}$$

$$= 1.01 \times 10^{12} \text{ sec}^{-1}.$$

M.4 NON-EQUIVALENT INTERVALLEY SCATTERING

$$W = \frac{Z_j (m_j^*)^{3/2}(D_{ij})^2}{\sqrt{2}\pi\rho\,\omega_{ij}\hbar^3}\gamma_j^{1/2}(E_f)\,(1 + 2\alpha_f E_f)\,G_{ij}(E_i, E_f)$$

$$\times \begin{cases} N & \text{absorption} \\ N+1 & \text{emission} \end{cases}$$

$$= 1.71 \times 10^{10} \frac{Z_j \left(\frac{m_j^*}{m_0}\right)^{3/2}\left(\frac{D_{ij}}{\text{eV cm}^{-1}}\right)^2}{\left(\frac{\rho}{\text{gm/cm}^3}\right)\left(\frac{\omega_{ij}}{\text{rad/sec}}\right)}\left(\frac{\gamma_j E_f}{\text{eV}}\right)^{1/2}$$

$$\times \ (1 + 2\alpha_f E_f)\,G_{ij}(E_i, E_f)\begin{cases} N & \text{absorption} \\ N+1 & \text{emission} \end{cases} \text{sec}^{-1}$$

with G_{ij} given in Equation 13.66.

Example: GaAs, $T = 300$ K, Γ valley, non-equivalent intervalley scattering by absorption,

$$
\begin{aligned}
E_i &= E_L - E_\Gamma = 0.36 \text{ eV} = 13.9 k_B T \\
Z_j &= 4 \\
m_j^* &= 0.35 m_0 \\
D_{ij} &= 1.0 \times 10^9 \text{ eV cm}^{-1} \\
\rho &= 5.37 \text{ gm/cm}^3 \\
\omega_{ij} &= 4.56 \times 10^{13} \text{ rad/sec} \\
N &= 0.457 \\
\alpha_i &= 0.576 \text{ eV}^{-1} \ (\Gamma \text{ valley is nonparabolic}) \\
\alpha_f &= 0 \text{ eV}^{-1} \ (L \text{ valley is parabolic}) \\
E_f &= E_i - (E_L - E_\Gamma) + \hbar\omega_{ij} = \hbar\omega_{ij} = 0.030 \text{ eV} \\
\gamma_i(E_f) &= E_f = 0.030 \text{ eV} \\
1 + \alpha_i E_i &= 1.21 \\
1 + \alpha_f E_f &= 1
\end{aligned}
$$

$$1 + 2\alpha_i E_i = 1.41$$
$$1 + 2\alpha_f E_f = 1$$

$$W = 1.71 \times 10^{10} \frac{Z_j \left(\frac{m_j^*}{m_0}\right)^{3/2} \left(\frac{D_{ij}}{\text{eV cm}^{-1}}\right)^2}{\left(\frac{\rho}{\text{gm/cm}^3}\right) \left(\frac{\omega_{ij}}{\text{rad/sec}}\right)} \sqrt{\frac{\gamma_j(E_f)}{\text{eV}}}$$

$$\times (1 + 2\alpha_f E_f) G_{ij}(E_i, E_f) N \text{ sec}^{-1}$$

$$= 1.71 \times 10^{10} \frac{4(0.35)(1 \times 10^9)^2}{(5.37)(4.56 \times 10^{13})} \sqrt{0.030}$$

$$\times (1)(0.457) G_{ij}(E_i, E_f) \text{ sec}^{-1}$$

$$= 7.74 \times 10^{12} G_{ij}(E_i, E_f) \text{ sec}^{-1}$$

$$G_{ij}(E_i, E_f) = \frac{(1 + \alpha_i E_i)(1 + \alpha_f E_f)}{(1 + 2\alpha_i E_i)(1 + 2\alpha_f E_f)}$$

$$= \frac{(1.21)(1)}{(1.41)(1)} = 0.858$$

$$W = 7.74 \times 10^{12}(0.858) \text{ sec}^{-1} = 6.64 \times 10^{12} \text{ sec}^{-1}.$$

M.5 IONIZED IMPURITY SCATTERING

$$W = 4\pi F \left(\frac{2k}{\lambda}\right)^2 \left[\frac{1}{1 + \left(\frac{\lambda}{2k}\right)^2}\right]^2$$

$$F = \frac{1}{\hbar} \left[\frac{Ze^2}{\epsilon_s}\right]^2 \frac{N(E_k)}{32k^4} N_I$$

where the density of states $N(E_k)$ is

$$N(E_k) = \frac{\sqrt{2}(m^*)^{3/2}}{\pi^2 \hbar^3} \gamma^{1/2}(E_k)(1 + 2\alpha E_k)$$

$$F = 6.71 \times 10^{21} \frac{Z^2 \left(\frac{N_I}{\text{cm}^{-3}}\right) \left(\frac{m^*}{m_0}\right)^{3/2}}{\epsilon_s^2 \left(\frac{k}{\text{cm}^{-1}}\right)^4} \sqrt{\frac{\gamma(E_k)}{\text{eV}}} (1 + 2\alpha E_k) \text{ sec}^{-1}.$$

Using

$$\left(\frac{k}{\text{cm}^{-1}}\right)^4 = 6.89 \times 10^{30} \left(\frac{m^*}{m_0}\right)^2 \left(\frac{\gamma(E_k)}{\text{eV}}\right)^2,$$

$$F = 9.74 \times 10^{-10} \frac{Z^2 \left(\frac{N_I}{\text{cm}^{-3}}\right)}{\epsilon_s^2 \sqrt{\frac{m^*}{m_0}}} \frac{1 + 2\alpha E_k}{\left(\frac{\gamma(E_k)}{\text{eV}}\right)^{3/2}} \text{ sec}^{-1}$$

$$\lambda^2 = \frac{(n+p)e^2}{\epsilon_s k_B T}$$

$$= \frac{0.021 \left(\frac{n+p}{cm^{-3}} \right)}{\epsilon_s \left(\frac{T}{K} \right)} \; cm^{-2}.$$

Example: GaAs, $T = 300$ K, Γ valley, ionized impurity scattering

$$E_i = E_f = \frac{3}{2} k_B T = 0.039 \; eV = E_k$$

$$n + p \approx N_I = 1 \times 10^{17} \; cm^{-3}$$

$$Z = 1 \, (\text{singly ionized impurity})$$

$$m^* = 0.067 m_0$$

$$\epsilon_s = 13.2$$

$$\alpha = 0.576 \; eV^{-1}$$

$$\gamma(E_k) = 0.040 \; eV$$

$$1 + 2\alpha E_k = 1.045$$

$$\gamma = \sqrt{\frac{(0.021)(1 \times 10^{17})}{(13.2)(300)}} \; cm^{-1} = 7.28 \times 10^5 \; cm^{-1}$$

$$k = 5.12 \times 10^7 \left(\frac{m^*}{m_0} \right)^{1/2} \left(\frac{\gamma(E_k)}{eV} \right)^{1/2} \; cm^{-1}$$

$$= 2.65 \times 10^6 \; cm^{-1}$$

$$\frac{2k}{\lambda} = 7.29$$

$$W = 4\pi F \left(\frac{2k}{\lambda} \right)^2 \left[\frac{1}{1 + \left(\frac{\lambda}{2k} \right)^2} \right]^2$$

$$F = 9.74 \times 10^{-10} \frac{Z^2 \left(\frac{N_I}{cm^{-3}} \right)}{\epsilon_s^2 \sqrt{\frac{m^*}{m_0}}} \frac{1 + 2\alpha E_k}{\sqrt{\frac{\gamma(E_k)}{eV}}} \; sec^{-1}$$

$$= 9.74 \times 10^{-10} \frac{(1)^2 (1 \times 10^{17})}{(13.2)^2 \sqrt{0.067}} \frac{(1.045)}{(0.040)^{3/2}} \; sec^{-1}$$

$$= 2.82 \times 10^8 \; sec^{-1}$$

$$W = 4\pi (2.82 \times 10^8)(7.29)^2 \left[\frac{1}{1 + \left(\frac{1}{7.29} \right)^2} \right]^2 \; sec^{-1}$$

$$= 1.81 \times 10^{11} \; sec^{-1}.$$

M.6 ALLOY SCATTERING

$$W = \frac{3\pi^3}{8\hbar} V_0 \, U_{\text{all}}^2 \, N(E_k) x (1 - x).$$

For zinc-blende and diamond lattices, $V_0 = a_0^3/4$, where a_0 is the lattice constant (e.g. $a_0 = 5.6533 \times 10^{-8}$ cm for GaAs).

$$N(E_k) = \frac{(m^*)^{3/2}}{\sqrt{2}\pi^2\hbar^3} \gamma^{1/2}(E_k)(1 + 2\alpha E_k)$$

$$W = 1.5 \times 10^{13} \left(\frac{m^*}{m_0}\right)^{3/2} \left(\frac{U_{\text{all}}}{\text{eV}}\right)^2 \left(\frac{a_0}{\text{Å}}\right)^3 x(1-x)$$

$$\times \sqrt{\frac{\gamma(E)}{\text{eV}}} (1 + 2\alpha E) \ \text{sec}^{-1}$$

Example: $Al_{0.1}Ga_{0.9}As$, $T = 300$ K, Γ valley, alloy scattering,

$$E_i = E_f = \frac{3}{2} k_B T = 0.039 \text{ eV}$$
$$m^* = 0.067 m_0$$
$$U_{\text{all}} = 0.2 \text{ eV}$$
$$a_0 = 5.65 \text{ Å}$$
$$x = 0.1$$
$$\gamma(E) = 0.040 \text{ eV}$$
$$1 + 2\alpha E = 1.045$$

$$W = 3.01 \times 10^{13} \left(\frac{m^*}{m_0}\right)^{3/2} \left(\frac{U_{\text{all}}}{\text{eV}}\right)^2 \left(\frac{a_0}{\text{Å}}\right)^3 x(1-x)$$

$$\times \sqrt{\frac{\gamma(E)}{\text{eV}}} (1 + 2\alpha E) \ \text{sec}^{-1}$$

$$= 3.01 \times 10^{13} (0.067)^{3/2} (0.2)^2 (5.65)^3 (0.1)(0.9)\sqrt{0.040}(1.045) \ \text{sec}^{-1}$$

$$= 7.08 \times 10^{10} \ \text{sec}^{-1}$$

WIDE
BANDGAP
SEMICONDUCTORS

There is an increasing interest in semiconductors with bandgaps above 2.0 eV, since these materials offer remarkable optoelectronic devices. At present, the technology for such materials is rather underdeveloped and serious hurdles need to be overcome. Let us examine some of the motivations for large bandgap semiconductor devices.

1. **High Temperature Operation:** High temperature operation of electronic devices is limited by several constraints. An important constraint is the intrinsic carrier concentration of the material. Once the intrinsic concentration, determined by the bandgap and temperature, starts to become comparable to the dopant concentration, the control of the device charge becomes difficult. Additionally, at high temperatures, there could be problems related to the dopant diffusion, contact stability, and, of course, ultimately defect generation and device breakdown. The high bandgap materials not only have low intrinsic concentration at a given temperature, but are also physically "harder" and more robust. The Si-technology is difficult to use reliably above $\sim 130°C$, while GaAs-technology can operate at up to $\sim 200°C$. Since a number of important applications such as microprocessors mounted on engines or used in data processing in oil wells, etc, require higher temperatures, there is need for larger bandgap semiconductors.

2. **Radiation Hardness:** An important source of errors in computational devices (memories, logic gates, etc.) is radiation induced errors. There errors are generated by bursts of charges produced by cosmic rays impinging on the devices, and become especially important for space applications. The

charge burst produced by the cosmic ray (γ-rays) depends upon the bandgap of the semiconductors and can be reduced substantially by increasing the semiconductors bandgap.

3. **High Power Devices:** High power devices are extremely important for microwave applications. The power output depends upon the voltage swing across the device and this is limited by the breakdown voltage of the device. The breakdown voltage increases with material bandgap and thus one expects these materials to provide high power devices.

4. **Short Wavelength Lasers:** Optical memories such as compact discs are limited in their density by the wavelength of the laser diode used to read the information. Currently this wavelength is ~ 0.8 μm and the technology is based on "red" light GaAs lasers. There is a tremendous motivation to use "blue" light or even shorter wavelength light to increase the memory density. These lasers can also operate at higher temperatures as Auger processes would be minimal.

5. **Special Purpose Applications:** A number of special purpose applications can be fulfilled if a wider selection of device response is available. The motivation may come from special "windows" in atmospheric absorption at earth or in outer space. These applications are dependent upon a particular application rather than on a generic technology problem.

While there is a clear need for large bandgap semiconductor technology, there are may hurdles as well. While there is no doubt that with effort these hurdles will be overcome, it is important to examine some of the difficulties.

1. **Crystal Growth:** Two important categories of crystal growth are bulk crystal growth and epitaxial crystal growth. The former produces "boules" of large crystals which are then sliced to form wafers on which devices can be fabricated directly, or which can serve as substrates for epitaxial growth. Large bandgap semiconductors ususally have a very high melting temperature and also require high substrate temperatures for epitaxial growth. Not only is it difficult to reach and control the high temperatures, but also many materials (used in the crystal growth system) can outgas impurities at such high temperatures that can contaminate the crystal. It is thus difficult to obtain large boules or large substrates for crystal growth. Often it may be difficult to obtain substrates more than a few millimeters in contrast to Si technology where substrates as large as 30 cm in diameter can be obtained.

2. **Alternate Substrate Problems:** Since it is usually difficult to obtain high quality substrates which are lattice matched, high bandgap semiconductors are often grown on substrates with which lattice matching is poor. Epitaxy then involves dislocation generation and control. Often it is difficult to grow single crystal films as a result.

3. **Intrinsic Defect Density:** The growth of a defect-free crystal requires one to create a delicate balance between the growth kinetics and growth thermodynamics. The substrate temperature should be high enough to provide enough kinetics so that the atoms are able to reach their equilibrium conditions. On the other hand, the temperature should not be so high that entropy controls the crystal growth. Too low kinetics or too high temperature can both lead to a high defect density. Since intrinsic defects can often cause auto-doping in the crystal as well as trap states, it is essential to understand and control the growth process—a difficult proposition for high temperature growth.

4. **Extrinsic Doping:** Doping of high bandgap materials is also a challenge at present. Some of the difficulty arises from the high intrinsic defect density present, while there are also intrinsic problems of doping "hard" materials.

5. **Processing of Devices:** Due to the strong chemical bonds in large bandgap semiconductors, all the processing steps—etching, contact formation, Schottky formation, etc., are exceptionally difficult.

It is important to realize the difficulties in the path of high bandgap semiconductor technology so that one is aware the to realize the full potential of these semiconductors a great deal of effort has to be made. Let us now examine some of the properties of large gap semiconductors.

1. **Diamond:** This material is not only of interest for its spectacular beauty as a piece of jewelry and its tremendous hardness for use in cutting tools, but it also has a strong potential for electronics. There has been rapid progress in the growth of diamond films using vapor phase epitaxy or ion beam deposition. Simple devices such as p-n junctions have been formed in the material. Diamond is an indirect gap semiconductor with an indirect gap near the X-point of 5.5 eV. The direct bandgap has a value of ~ 7.5 eV. The electron effective mass is $m_\ell^* = 1.4m_0$ and $m_t^* = 0.36m_0$. The hole masses are $m_{hh}^* = 2.18m_0$ and $m_{lh}^* = 0.7m_0$, $m_{dos}^* = 0.75m_0$. The crystal structure is diamond (of course) with a lattice constant of 3.56683 Å (at 300K). The melting point is 3827°C. The dielectric constant is 5.7, while the refractive index is 2.39. Diamond has a very high thermal conductivity of 6-10 W/cm-K, making it an excellent heat sink material. The thermal expansion coefficient is 1.0×10^{-6} K^{-1} at room temperature, which is very small.

2. **Wide Bandgap Nitrides InN, GaN, AlN, BN:** The wide bandgap nitride semiconductors have been of great interest for some time. Their bandgaps and lattice constants are shown in Figures N.1 and N.2. It is interesting to note that the materials could occur in either the zinc-blende or wurtzite form. The wurtzite form is usually the durable one and is formed in most crystal growth studies. However, one prefers a cubic zinc-blende form since it is compatible with GaAs or InP substrates. The properties of

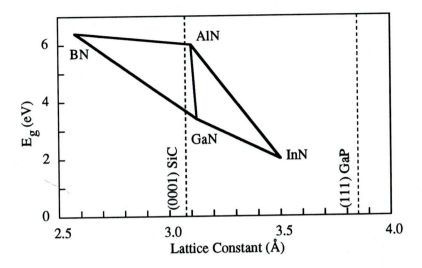

Figure N.1: Lattice constant a of the wurtzite nitrides. $c \approx 1.6a$.

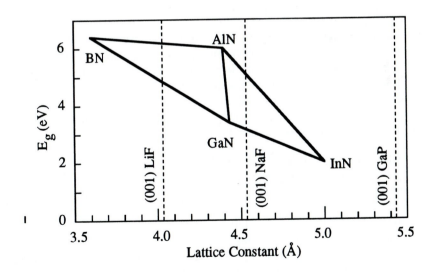

Figure N.2: Lattice constant a of the zinc-blende nitrides.

Property	ZeSe	ZnTe
Density (g/cm^3)	5.28 (at 4K)	5.636 (300K)
Dielectric constant	9.1	7.4
Electron Mass	$0.21m_0$	$0.2m_0$
Hole Mass (m^*_{dos})	$0.6m_0$	$\sim 0.2m_0$
Energy Gap (eV)	2.7 (at 300K)	2.26 (at 300K)
Lattice Constant (Å)	5.6676	6.1037
Refractive Index	2.5	2.72
Mobility (cm^2/V-s)	electron: 500 (300K) hole: 30 (300K)	electron: 340 (300K) hole: 100 (300K)

Table N.1: Properties of ZnTe and ZnSe.

both forms are essentially similar. Possible substrates for the wurtzite form are SiC and GaP while those for the zinc-blende form are LiF, NaF, and GaP. It is not yet entirely clear how growth temperature and the substrate choice influence the polymorph form.

An important problem associated with crystal growth of the nitrides is that there is a high degree of nitrogen vacancies, which appear to act as n-type impurities. This makes it somewhat difficult to obtain reliable p-n junctions. Nevertheless, increased interest in high power devices is expected to allow the technological problems to be solved.

3. **Silicon Carbide:** Silicon carbide is another important semiconductor with a large bandgap, which has been studied for its applications for very high power microwave devices. The bandgap is 2.9 eV at room temperature and the breakdown field is $\sim 2 \times 10^6$ V/cm. The lattice constants of this wurtzite crystal are $a = 3.08$ Å and $c = 15.117$ Å. The thermal expansion coefficient is 2.9×10^{-6} K^{-1}. As with other large bandgap semiconductors there has been marginal success in silicon carbide technology.

4. **Large Bandgap II-VI Semiconductors:** After silicon, the III-V compound semiconductor technology (especially GaAs, AlAs, InP, InAs) is the most advanced. However, with III-V technology, it is difficult to go to high direct bandgap. Thus, it is difficult to fabricate "blue" light lasers which require bandgaps of ~ 2.5 eV. The II-VI semiconductors are able to provide this bandgap range and here received great attention due to the observation of easing in the blue light refine. The motivation comes mainly from optical information processing needs (high density memories for example).

The material of key interest in the II-VI family are the compounds of ZnTe, ZnSe, and ZnS$_x$Se$_{1-x}$. The sulfur is added to ZnSe mainly to provide a good matching to GaAs substrates. Table N.1 provides some of the properties of ZnTe and ZnSe.

Property	SiO$_2$	SI$_3$N$_4$
Breakdown Field (V/cm)	10^7	10^7
Density (g/cm^3)	2.2	3.1
Dielectric Constant (static)	3.9	7.5
Energy Gap (eV)	9.0	~ 5.0
Refractive Index	1.46	2.05
Resistivity (Ω–cm)	10^{14} - 10^{16} (at 300K)	10^{14} (300K)
Thermal Expansion ($^\circ$C^{-1})	5×10^{-7} (at 300K)	

Table N.2: Properties of SiO$_2$ and SI$_3$N$_4$.

5. **Silicon Dioxide (SiO$_2$) and Silicon Nitride(Si$_3$N$_4$):** Silicon dioxide and silicon nitride are not used as active regions of semiconductor devices, but they are extremely important for the semiconductor technology. Silicon dioxide is an essential ingredient of silicon field effect transistors (the metal oxide semiconductor field effect transistor or MOSFET) which dominate the electronics industry. Silicon dioxide is also used as a mask material for a variety of processing steps (e.g. doping by ion-implantation, etching, etc.) as well as a passivation material for many III-V semiconductor devices. Its large bandgap, high breakdown voltage, and low interface state density with Si are of course the main reasons for its tremendous importance in electronics.

Silicon nitride is also a large bandgap material which is widely used for passivating finished devices to protect them from impurities and for tying up dangling surface bonds. It is also an imported material in many processing steps as well. The properties of SiO$_2$ and SI$_3$N$_4$ are shown in Table N.2.

N.1 REFERENCES

- **General**

  - A good source of some material properties of wide gap semiconductors are the appendices in Shur, M., *Physics of Semiconductor Devices*, (Prentice-Hall, Englewood Cliffs, 1990).

- **Diamond**

  - *The Properties of Diamond*, (edited by J. E. Field, Academic Press, London, 1979).
  - Moustakes, T.D., J.P. Dismukes, Ling Ye, K.R. Walton and J.D. Tiedje, in *Proceedings of the 10*th *International Conference on Chemical Vapor Deposition*, edited by G.W. Cullen, (The Electrochemical Society, Manchester, New Hampshire, 1988).

- Pickett, W.D. and M.J. Mehl, in *Micro-Optoelectronics Materials*, edited by C. Kukkonen, (SPIE, Kansas City, 1988).

● **Boron Nitride**

- Mishima, O., J. Tanaka, S. Yamaoka, and O. Fukinaga, Science, **238**, 181 (1987).

- Park, K.T., K. Terakura, and N. Hamada, J. Phys. C, **20**, 1241 (1987).

- Wentzcovitch, R.M., K.J. Chang, and M.L. Cohen, Phys. Rev. B, **34**, 1071 (1986).

● **Other Nitrides**

- Amano, H., K. Hiramatsu, M. Kito, N. Sawaki, and I. Akasaki, J. Cryst. Growth, **93**, 79 (1988): GaN.

- Bloom,S., G. Harbeke, E. Meier, I.B. Ortenburger, Phys. Stat. Sol. B, **66**, 161 (1974): GaN.

- Jenkins, D.W. and J.D. Dow, Phys. Rev. B, **39**, 3317 (1989): InN, $In_x Ga_{1-x}N$ and $In_x Al_{1-x}N$.

- Khan, M.A., R.A. Skogman, R.G. Schulze, and M. Gershonzon, Appl. Phys. Lett., **43**, 492 (1983): $Al_x Ga_{1-x}N$.

- Tansley, T.L. and C.P. Foley, J. Appl. Phys., **59**, 3241 (1986): InN.

● **II-VI Semiconductors for Blue Lasers**

- Bhargava, R.N., J. Cryst. Growth, **86**, 873 (1988).

- Haase, M.A., J. Oui, J.M. DePuydt, and H. Cheng, Appl. Phys. Lett., **59**, 1272 (1991).

- Hagerolt, H., H. Jeon, A. V. Nurmikko, W. Xie, D. C. Grillo, M. Kobayashi, and R.L. Gunshor, Appl. Phys. Lett., **60**, 2825 (1992).

- Reynolds, R.A., J. Vac. Sci. Technol. A, **7**, 269 (1989).

- Suemune, I., H. Masato, K. Nakanishi, K. Yamada, Y. Kan, and M. Yamanishi, J. Cryst. Growth, **101**, 754 (1990).

- Zmudzinski, C.A., Y. Guan, and P.S. Zory, IEEE Photonics Tech. Lett., **2**, 94 (1990).

Index

Absorption coefficient, in indirect semiconductors, 596
Absorption coefficient, relation to absorption rate, 583
Absorption of photons, comparison
between direct and indirect
semiconductors, 598
Acceptor ionization, 269
Acceptor level, 263
strain effects, 277
values in selected semiconduc-
tors, 263
Acoustic phonon, scattering, 411
Acoustic waves, 295
Affinity rule, 193
Aharonov-Bohm effect, 683
Alloy scattering, 369
potentials for selected semicon-
ductors, 373
relaxation time, 372
scattering rate, 453
Alloy, GaAs–AlAs, 187
HgTe–CdTe, 188
InAs–GaAs, 188
phase separated, 181
random, 181
Si–Ge, 189
superlattice, 181
Amorphous silicon, diffraction from,
68
Amphoteric dopants, 265
Angular momentum states, 795
Anharmonic effects, in lattice vibra-
tions, 314
Anti-site defects, as dopants, 280
Anti-Stokes scattering, 317
Atomic levels, for selected elements,
127
Auger processes, 381
Auger rates, 388
Balance equation, 347
approach to high field transport,
471
Ballistic transport, 463
Band, allowed, 105
tailing, 273
Band discontinuities, transitivity of,
194
Band lineups in heterostructures, 192
Bandedge, strain splitting of in SiGe
alloys, 238
Bandgap, 104
narrowing, 273
of selected semiconductors, 186
optical, 273
strain effects, 246
temperature dependence of, 169
Bandstructure, Kohn–Luttinger formalism, 157
$k \cdot p$ method for, 151
Slater–Koster method for, 136
constant energy surfaces for valence bands, 163
constant energy surfaces for valence bands, 164
constant energy surfaces for valence bands, 165
effects on devices, 171
in quantum wells, 194
in superlattices, 201
of AlAs, 168
of GaAs, 166
of Ge, 167
of InAs, 168

843

of Si, 160
of alloys, 179
of electrons in quantum wells, 196
orthogonalized plane wave (OPW) method for, 149
pseudopotential method for, 150
valence band, in quantum wells, 198
valence band, in strained quantum wells, 244
Bandtail states, 743
Basis, 29
Binding, crystal, 286
Bipolar transistor, 775
Bloch function, 127
Bloch oscillations, 539
Bloch state, 93
Bloch theorem, 92
Body centered cubic (bcc) lattice, 37
Bohr magneton, 805
Boltzmann, transport equation, 327
    numerical techniques, 346
Bonds, metallic, 290
Born approximation, 813
    validity of, 814
Boundary conditions, periodic, 15
Bragg's law, 62
Breakdown, in devices, 487
Brillouin zone edge, 107
Bulk modulus, 226
Burger's vector, 729
Carrier, extrinsic, 266
Carrier-carrier scattering, 374
Carrier freeze-out, 267
Carrier multiplication and noise, 487
Cell periodic function, 93
Central cell correction, 263
Central cell symmetry, at bandedges, 231
Charge, effective, 302, 417
Chemical potential, 19, 20
    in intrinsic semiconductors, 256
Clebsch–Gordan coefficients, 142, 796
Coherent regime, 219

Common anion rule, 193
Compensation, 258
Concentration, intrinsic carrier, 254
Conduction bandedge states, 146
Conduction, hopping, 750
Conductivity, 6, 334
Conservation law, for k in collisions, 99
Constant energy surface, for electrons in Si, 161
    for holes in Si, 162
    strain effect in Si valence band, 238
Coupler, directional, 655
Covalent crystal, 290
Creation operator, 794
Critical thickness, 50, 218, 219, 731
    of InGaAs on GaAs, 220
Crystal, binding, 286
    covalent, 290
    inert gas, 287
    ionic, 288
    restoring force, 291
Crystal momentum, $\hbar k$, 97
Crystal orientation during growth, 84
Current, in a filled band, 115
Cyclotron frequency, 672
Cyclotron mass, 673
D-X center, 723
De Haas-Van Alphen effect, 686
Debye, T^3 law, 313
    model, 312
Debye–Scherrer method, 75
Deep levels, in 1-D, 2-D and 3-D systems, 720
    in Si, 722
    theory, 717
Defect, cross section, 724
    Frenkel, 716
    interstitial, 716
    substitutional, 716
Deformation potential theory, 228
Density of phonon modes, 310
Density of states, 16

effect on laser properties, 591
effective, 255
in 2-D systems, 197
in one dimension, 17
in semiconductors, 169
in three dimensions, 16
in two dimensions, 17
valence band, for SiGe alloys, 238
for strained Si, 238
Destruction operator, 794
Detectors, 780
Device components for modern electronics, 768, 769
Devices, gain, 763
high speed operation, 764
input–output isolation, 763
low noise, 765
low power, 765
nonlinear response, 762
requirements for, 760
tunable response, 764
Diamond lattice, 39
Dielectric constant, 567
Dielectric constant, low and high frequency, 302, 417
Dielectric response, 360
Diffraction, finite size effects in, 69
Diffusion coefficient, 351
Dipole matrix element, for selected semiconductors, 580
Directional coupler, 653
Dislocation, 728
electronic effects, 737
Dislocation generation, 219
Disordered semiconductors, 738
optical properties, 744
transport, 745
Distribution function, in presence of electric field, 333
Donor, energy levels, 261
ionization, 268
levels in selected semiconductors, 263
Donor level, Bohr radius, 262

Donor wavefunctions, 262
Dopants, anti-site, 280
Doping, by diffusion, 280
by ion implantation, 280
epitaxially, 280
heavy, 270
modulation, 274
pulse, 280
Double crystal diffraction, 77
Drude model, 2
Drude-Zener theory, 564
Effective charge, 302, 417
Effective mass, 108
equation, 258
equation for donors, 261
in $k \cdot p$ method, 155
strain effects in InGaAs alloys, 238
Eigenvalue method, 801
Einstein model, for lattice vibrations, 314
Elastic constants, 223
Electric fields, built-in, from strained epitaxy, 246
Electro-optic effect, 656
Electron, in a magnetic field, quantum theory, 676
semiclassical dynamics, 670
in a weak periodic potential, 100
in electromagnetic field, 572
Electron-electron interaction, 272
Electron-electron scattering, 379
direct and exchange processes, 377
Electron-hole scattering, 374
Energy, elastic strain, 224
Epitaxy, coherent, 734
incoherent, 734
lattice matched and dislocations, 728
Equation of motion, for electrons in presence of scattering, 8
for k, 98
Ewald construction, 74
Exciton, 617

absorption, strain effects, 645
absorption in quantum wells, 632
absorption spectrum, 622
   in GaAs, 625
   binding energy, 625
   broadening effects, 634
     homogeneous, 636
     inhomogeneous, 634
   dispersion relation, 620
   Frenkel, 618
   in magnetic field, 703
   in quantum wells, 627
   Mott, 618
   quenching, 646
   radiative recombination, 658
   temperature dependence, 660
Excitonic devices, potentials and pitfalls, 661
Extrinsic carriers, 266
Face centered cubic (fcc) lattice, 37
Fermi-Dirac distribution, 19
Field effect transistor, 770
Fermi energy, 19, 20
Fermi golden rule, 324, 813
Form factor, atomic, 72
Freeze-out, carrier, 267
Frenkel defect, 716
Gauge transformations, 559
Gaussian units, 815
   conversion factors, 817
Group velocity, for lattice vibrations, 294
HIGFET, 773
Hall, coefficient, 10
   effect, 9
   factor, 345
   mobility, 342
Harmonic approximation, 291
Harmonic oscillator, in quantum mechanics, 791
Haynes-Shockley experiment, 338
Hexagonal close packed (hcp) structure, 58
HgCdTe, array, 212
Hole, 117

effective mass, 119
   energy, 119
   equation of motion, 119
   momentum, 118
Hopping conductivity, 750
Ideal surfaces, 50
Identical particle scattering, 377
Impact ionization, 381, 475
   impact ionization coefficient, 476
     in selected semiconductors, 479
   in quantum wells, 520
   power output, 392
   threshold, 386, 387
Impurity level, in quantum wells, 276
Impurity level screening, 271
Impurity scattering, 359
Impurity, shallow, in magnetic field, 707
Inert gas, crystal, 287
Insulators, Si_3N_4, 841
   simple description, 115
   SiO_2, 841
Interband transitions, bulk semiconductors, 583
   quantum wells, 581, 583
Interface disorder and bandtail states, 743
Interface roughness, 53
   scattering, 504
Interfaces, 53
Interference, quantum, 541
Interferometer, Mach-Zender, 655
Intervalley scattering, f and g in Si, 407
   in GaAs, 408
Intraband transitions, 599
   in quantum wells, polarization dependence, 600
Intrinsic carrier concentration, in Si, Ge and GaAs, 257
Ionic crystal, 288
   optical mode, 567
Ionization, acceptor, 269
   donor, 268

Ionized impurity scattering, relaxation
        time, 365
    scattering rate, 449
JFET, 773
Kohn–Luttinger Hamiltonian, with
        strain, 237
Koster-Slater model for impurities,
        717
Kramers-Kronig relation, 568
Kronig–Penney model, 203
Kubo formalism for transport, 746
LED, comparison with laser diode,
        605
Landau levels, 680
    density of states, 680
    magneto-optics, 701
Landauer formalism, 752
Lande factor, 805
Laser, 778
    and photonic bandstructure, 607
    cavity loss, 589
    distributed feedback, 609
    material gain, 589
    optical confinement, 589
    quantum well, 586
    recombination time for electron-
        hole pair, 606
    surface emitting, 609
    threshold current, 594
        and strain, 595
Lattice, 29
Lattice constant, of selected semi-
        conductors, 186, 220
Lattice types, in three dimensions,
        34
    in two dimensions, 33
Laue conditions, 64
Laue method, 74
Length, screening, 361
Lennard–Jones potential, 288
Localized states, 739
Lorentz gauge, 560
MESFET, 770
MKSA units, 815
    conversion factors, 817

MODFET, 773
MOSFET, 770
Madelung constant, 289
Magnetic semiconductors, 709
Magnetoresistance, 10
Magnetotransport, semiclassical the-
        ory, 675
Mass action, law of, 256
Material parameters, for transport
        in Si and GaAs, 454, 455
Mathieson's rule, 434
Maxwell equations, 559
Mean free path, 7
Mesoscopic structures, 751
    conductance fluctuations, 754
Metal-organic chemical vapor depo-
        sition (MOCVD), 47
Metallic bonds, 290
Metals, simple description, 115
Microwave devices, 777
Miller indices, 40
Minibands, in superlattices, 206
Minimum conductivity, 748
Mobility, edge, 740
    in GaAs, 369, 436
    in Ge, 369
    in Si, 369, 436
    in a MODFET, 505
    in modulation doped structures,
        368
    in selected semiconductors, 438
    limited by acoustic phonons, 436
    limited by ionized impurities, 366,
        435
    measurement techniques, 338
Modulation doping, 274
Modulators, 779
Molecular beam epitaxy (MBE), 47
Momentum matrix element, 158
Monte Carlo, flowchart, 441
    free flight, 444
    injection of carriers, 443
    scattering times, 444
    transport simulation, 439

Negative resistance, and charge in-
    stabilities, 549
Normal processes, 100
Numerical evaluation, of Bohr radius,
    821
    of absorption coefficient, 822
    of cyclotron resonance frequency,
        820
    of density of states, 819
    of effective density of states, 821
    of mobility, 820
    of physical parameters, 819
    of recombination time, 823
Ohm's law, 5
Optical interband transitions, 578
Optical modulation, strain effects, 657
Optical phonon, scattering, 414
Optical polarization, selection rules,
    578
Optical processes, selection rules, 576
Order parameters, Warren-Cowley,
    369
Overlap function, for holes, 403
Periodicity, in crystals, 28
Perturbation theory, stationary, 797
    time dependent, 810
Phonon, 299
    acoustic scattering, 411
        intravalley, 405
        scattering rate, 457
    confined optical, 319
    conservation laws for scattering,
        300
    dispersion measurement, 315
        by light scattering, 316
        by neutron scattering, 315
    folded, 318
    in heterostructures, 318
    interface, 320
    intervalley scattering rate, 457
    optical, 298
    optical scattering, 414
        intravalley, 406
    polar optical, 301
        interaction with photons, 304

    polar optical scattering, 417
        scattering rate, 451
    quantization of lattice vibration,
        299
    scattering, 397
        in GaAs, 422
        intervalley, 407
        intervalley, 427
        limits on wavevectors, 403
        selection rules, 410
    statistics, 309
Phonon spectrum, of GaAs, 306
    of Ge, 305
    of InAs, 306
    of Si, 305
Photodetectors, noise, 487
Photon, absorption rate, 574
    emission rate, 575
Photonic bandstructure, 607
Piezoelectric coefficient, 247, 251
Piezoelectric effect, 31
Piezoelectric scattering, 425
Plasma frequency, 424, 565
Plasmon, scattering, 424
Point defects in semiconductors, 715
Poisson equation, for a MODFET,
    499
Polar optical phonon, longitudinal and
    transverse, 301
    scattering, 417
Polaron, 429
Potential, screened Coulomb, 362
Powder method, 75
Power–speed issues in devices, 486
Poynting vector, 561
Primitive unit cell, 29
Properties, of selected semiconduc-
    tors, 824
Quantum Hall effect, 695
Quantum confined Stark effect, 637
    logic devices, 662
    modulators, 662
Quantum well, 788
    impurity levels, 276

Quantum wire, transmission electron
    micrograph, 611
RHEED, 81
RHEED oscillations during MBE growth,
    83
Radiative transitions, recombination
    time, 583
Random numbers, to simulate prob-
    ability, 440
Random scatterers, diffraction from,
    66
Real space charge transfer, 518
Reciprocal lattice, 40
    of the bcc lattice, 42
    of the fcc lattice, 44
    of the simple cubic lattice, 42
Recombination, nonradiative, 726
    via deep levels, 723
Reflection High Energy Electron Diffrac-
    tion (RHEED), 81
Reflection coefficient, 564
Refractive index, 562
    modulation of, 653
Relaxation time, 326, 336
    alloy scattering, 372
    approximation, 332
    ionized impurity scattering, 365
    of energy, 327
    of momentum, 327
    temperature dependence, 337
Resonant tunneling, 524
Resonant tunneling current in an RTD,
    529
Resonant tunneling devices, 776
Restoring force, crystal, 291
Rocking curve, 68
Rotating crystal method, 75
Scattering, acoustic phonon, 507
    alloy, 369, 508
    carrier-carrier, 374
    electron-electron, 379
    electron-hole, 374
    f and g in Si, 428
    identical particle, 377
    interface roughness, 504, 509

    intervalley in GaAs, 428
    intervalley phonon, 427
    ionized impurity, 359
    phonon, 397
    piezoelectric, 425
    plasmon, 424
    polar optical phonon, 508
    remote impurity, 506
Scattering factor, 70
    in different lattices, 73
Scattering rate, 324
    acoustic phonon scattering, 457,
        830
    alloy scattering, 453, 835
    angular dependence, 412
    intervalley scattering, 457, 831
    ionized impurity scattering, 449,
        833
    numerical values, 828
    polar L-O phonon scattering, 828
    polar optical phonon scattering,
        451
Scattering time, 4
Schrödinger equation, in k-space, 95
Screened Coulomb potential, 362
Screening, of impurity level, 271
Screening length, 361
    in metals, 367
Self-electro-optic effect device, (SEED),
    643, 664
Semiconductor wafers, 84
Semiconductors, AlN, 838
    BN, 838
    GaN, 838
    II-VI, 840
    InN, 838
    SiC, 840
    diamond, 838
    simple description, 115
    wide bandgap, 836
Shubnikov-De Haas effect, 691
    conductivity, 692
    determination of carrier mass,
        695
SiO_2 lattice, 54

Soret coefficient, 351
Spin–orbit coupling, 140
Spin–orbit splitting, 144
Spontaneous emission rate, 592
Stark effect, quantum confined, 637
Statistics, phonon, 309
Stokes scattering, 317
Strain, Hamiltonian, 236
    effect on acceptor levels, 277
    effect on constant energy surfaces in Si valence band, 238
    elastic, 221
    splitting of bandedge in SiGe alloys, 238
Strain tensor, in epitaxy, 226
Strained epitaxy, lattice symmetry, 230
Strained layers, 48
Sum rules, 571
Superconductor ring, 685
    magnetic flux, 685
Superlattice, 47
Surface reconstruction, 50
Symmetry, inversion, 31
    reflection, 31
    rotation, 31
Temperature, electron, 352
    in transport, 472
Tight binding matrix elements, 131, 139
Tight binding method (TBM), 127
    for the s-band, 131
Time of flight measurement, 341
Transconductance, 773
Transition probability, 813
Transport, averaging procedures, 336
    balance equation approach, 471
    ballistic, 463
    density matrix formalism, 544
    high field in MODFETs, 511
    high field in Si, 462
    in MODFETs, 498
    in quantum wells, 498
    in quantum wires, 517
    in strained structures, 511

    in superlattices, 539
    low field, 434
    of electrons in GaAs and Si, 459
    of holes in Si and Ge, 464
    of holes in SiGe alloys, 516
    quantum, 523
    transient of electrons in GaAs, 461
Transport simulation by Monte Carlo, 439
Trapping, by deep levels, 723
Tunneling, band-to-band, 536
    in GaAs/AlGaAs, 533
    in heterostructures, 530
Umklapp processes, 100
Vacancy, 716
Valence bandedge states, 147
Valence electrons, 3
Variational method, 807
Vector potential, 559
    relation to photon density, 561
Vegard's law, 180
Velocity overshoot, 462
Vertical transitions, 575
Vibration, crystal with diatomic basis, 296
    crystal with monatomic basis, 292
Virtual crystal approximation, 184, 370
Wafer identification, 56
Warren–Cowley order parameters, 182
Wave diffraction, 61
Wavefunctions, at zone edge, 111
Wavepacket, 324
    dispersion of, 785
    motion of, 784
    velocity of, 785
Wavepacket picture, 783
Waves, acoustic, 295
Wigner coefficients, 796
Wigner distribution, for quantum transport, 547
Wigner–Seitz cell, 32

X-ray diffraction, temperature dependent effects, 78
Zeeman effect, 804
Zener-Bloch oscillations, 480
Zinc–blende structure, 39
Zone folding, in superlattices, 207